S. Am   Brazil

GEOGRAPHY.

Sig. Head of Dept. Sr Mary.......

1.74

BRAZIL: *People and Institutions*

T. Lynn Smith

Louisiana State University Press

BATON ROUGE 1972

FOURTH EDITION

BRAZIL

People and Institutions

ISBN 0–8071–0949–5
Library of Congress Catalog Card Number 73–168396
Copyright © 1946, 1954, 1963, 1972 by Louisiana State University Press
All rights reserved
Manufactured in the United States of America
Printed by Kingsport Press, Inc.
Kingsport, Tennessee

Title-page illustration of Sao Paulo, courtesy of
Brazilian Consulate General, New Orleans

To the memory of my father and mother

PREFACE

For proper perspective Latin America should be divided into three rather equal parts. Mexico, Central America, and the Islands constitute one of these, Spanish South America another, and Brazil a third. In writing of Brazil, one treats an area and a population that are as large, and probably as diverse, as those of the remainder of South America. To Portuguese America, one-half of all South America, this book is devoted.

The time has come to bury the stereotype of Latin-American culture that prevails in the popular mind throughout the United States. Analysis will show that most of its principal elements, particularly those having to do with food, dress, and music, apply only to Mexico. Our southern neighbor is sufficiently colorful and interesting to stand on her own. Better acquaintance will reveal equally striking features in many of the other American republics. Brazil, in particular, is so large, so varied, so important economically, and so situated strategically that it deserves a great deal of individual consideration. We in North America should know at least a few elementary facts about her history, geography, and culture. Above all, Brazilians, with their long record of co-operation with the United States, should not continually be bombarded with allusions to their "Spanish language." I would not be misunderstood. This book was not written in order to correct widespread popular misunderstandings. Instead, it takes for granted that the readers already know something about Brazilian history and geography, facts which are readily available in innumerable sources. For those who lack such a background, I suggest *Conquest of Brazil* by Roy Nash, *Brazil: The Infinite Country* by William L. Schurz, and the chapters about Brazil in *Latin America* by Preston E. James. My purpose has been to organize, analyze, and interpret the materials on Brazilian demography and social institutions, a vast field of general interest in which I specialize.

A few comments are necessary about the handling of the Portuguese words and phrases. This has been very difficult because the variations in Brazilian usage are so great. Even the recent attempts at standardization have not been completely successful as yet, and for the present have merely added to the confusion. In references to the titles of books and articles, I have attempted to preserve the original orthography. This leads to the spelling of a word such as *anuário* (*annuario, anuario*) in three ways on the same page. Likewise an author's name sometimes is spelled one way on one of his publications and differently on others. Wherever translations are involved, and where Portuguese expressions are made use of, the third edition of *Pequeno Dicionário Brasileiro da Língua Portuguesa* by Hilde-brando Lima and Gustavo Barroso is relied on. Place names are spelled as they are in the recent publications of the Instituto Nacional de Geografia e Estatística. When Portuguese titles of articles and books are cited, the English rules of capitalization have been fol-lowed. Since the Brazilian practice is not at all consistent, the use of the English system seemed a logical way of resolving the difficulty.

My first visit to South America on a fellowship from the Rosenwald Fund in 1939 gave me a desire to return to Brazil and Peru for addi-tional detailed study. But this book would not have been possible had I not had an opportunity to spend one full year as senior agricultural analyst attached to the American embassy in Rio de Janeiro. Sub-sequent additional assignments to the embassy in 1945, service as a visiting professor at the University of Brazil in 1946, a visit as a fel-low of the John Simon Guggenheim Memorial Foundation in 1951, work as advisor to the National Commission on Agrarian Policy in 1952, and participation as observer for the International Labor Or-ganization in the round tables and field trips organized for the Semi-nar on Rural Welfare Problems in Latin America in 1953, a six-week lecture tour in 1956, and two other subsequent visits enabled me to make the additional observations and secure the more recent data that are utilized in this third edition.

A host of persons have aided in one way or another in the prepara-tion of the three editions of this volume. None of them is responsible in any way for any of the statements or conclusions contained in this book, for those are mine and mine alone. However, I desire to ex-press my appreciation to all. Among those who have been of greatest assistance are various officials of the United States governmental agen-cies, and I owe a particular debt of gratitude to Dr. Carl C. Taylor, formerly chief of the Division of Farm Population and Rural Life of the United States Department of Agriculture; to Jefferson Caffery and Herschel V. Johnson, the American ambassadors in Brazil during much of the time I have spent in that country; Erwin P. Keeler and Guy Bush, the agricultural attachés at the embassy with whom I worked; Kenneth Wernimont, the agricultural commissioner at the embassy in Rio de Janeiro; and Drs. Ross E. Moore and Ralph H. Allee of the Office of Foreign Agricultural Relations of the United States Department of Agriculture.

The list of Brazilian friends and associates who have aided me materially in my studies is a very long one. Among those who must receive specific mention are the following: the late Dr. Arthur Ramos, eminent anthropologist, and his wife and co-worker, Louiza; Dr. A. Carneiro Leão, director, and Professor Hilgard O'Reilly Sternberg, pro-fessor of geography at the Faculdade Nacional de Filosofia of the University of Brazil; José Arthur Rios of Rio de Janeiro, formerly di-rector of the Campanha de Educação Rural; João Cleophas, formerly Minister of Agriculture, and one of the officials of his cabinet, João Gonçalves de Souza, who also served as secretary of the National

Commission on Agrarian Policy; Dr. Giorgio Mortara, eminent demographer, of the Comissão Nacional de Recenseamento; Edmundo Genofre of the Serviço Social da Indústria in Rio de Janeiro; Fernando Mibielli de Carvalho of Rio de Janeiro; Dr. Christovam Leite de Castro, Dr. Virgílio Corrêa Filho, the late Dr. M. A. Teixeira de Freitas, and Percy Lau of the Instituto Brasileiro de Geografia e Estatística; John V. D. Saunders, formerly of Rio de Janeiro and presently a member of the faculty of the University of Florida; the late Dr. F. J. Oliveira Vianna; Carlos Borges Schmidt, J. V. Freitas Marcondes, and T. Suzuki of São Paulo; Professor Thales de Azevedo of the University of Bahia; and Dr. Anísio S. Teixeira of Rio de Janeiro.

The illustrations on pages 13, 15, 17, 18, 19, 20, 21, 23, 326, 373, 375, 377, and 525 were drawn by Percy Lau and are used by permission of the Instituto Brasiliero de Geografia e Estatística, courtesy of Christovam Leite de Castro. The illustrations on pages 205, 215, 216, 235, 237, 239, 240, 334, 335, 383, 384, and 385 are used by permission of the São Paulo Directoria de Publicidade Agrícola, courtesy of Carlos B. Schmidt.

My friends and colleagues at Louisiana State University, Vanderbilt University, and the University of Florida have helped in many ways. The late President W. B. Hatcher and former deans Fred C. Frey and Henry V. Howe of Louisiana State University, along with the late Dr. A. R. Mann and the late Jackson Davis of the General Education Board, did much to make possible the first edition of the book; and thanks are due the deceased president of the University of Florida, Dr. J. Hillis Miller, and Dr. J. Wayne Reitz, who succeeded him as president, along with the late Dr. John M. Maclachlan, head of the department of sociology, Dr. A. Curtis Wilgus, director of the School of Inter-American Studies, Dr. Ralph E. Page, dean of the College of Arts and Sciences, Dr. L. E. Grinter, dean of the Graduate School, and Dean Robert B. Mautz, dean of Academic Affairs, of the same university for the favorable academic environment which makes possible my various publications. Dr. Homer L. Hitt, Dr. E. A. Schuler, and Dr. Vernon J. Parenton, while we were colleagues at Louisiana State University, aided materially by reading and criticizing parts of the original manuscript. Dr. Harry W. Hutchinson of the University of Florida made available important unpublished data from some of his own studies. Invaluable assistance with the tables and charts was given by Louise Kemp, Mrs. Julien R. Tatum, and Mary Ellen Caldwell at Louisiana State University, Mrs. Marylee Vandiver at Vanderbilt University, and Joseph Sardo, Sam Schulman, W. Kennedy Upham, and José Fabio Barbosa da Silva at the University of Florida. Marion Comeaux, Mabel Cleary, and Mrs. Elizabeth Little of Louisiana State University, and Louetta Young and Mrs. Kathleen Hartwell of the University of Florida assisted in typing the manuscripts. The late Dr. Marcus Wilkerson, director of the Louisiana State University Press, earned my sincere thanks for his part in the publication of the first edition of this book. Finally, my wife, Louvina Jackson Smith, and my sons, Jackson Lynn and Richard Lisle, deserve much appreciation for the thousands of things they have done to make this book possible.

T. Lynn Smith

ACKNOWLEDGMENTS TO FOURTH EDITION

THE FIRST SEVEN parts of *Brazil: People and Institutions* published in 1963 remain unchanged. Part Eight comprising Chapters LXXIV–LXXVII contains all new material. I am indebted to a number of people and organizations for assistance in preparing the new chapters. Chief among these are Professor José Arthur Rios of Rio de Janeiro and Professor J. V. Freitas Marcondes of São Paulo. They have aided greatly in keeping me informed about the most significant publications appearing in Brazil and in securing copies for me. Possibly even more important have been their deep insights into the problems of Brazilian society and the many things they have done to help inform me about the same. Dr. Nelson de Barros Camargo of São Paulo was especially helpful in the lengthy discussions we had concerning the process and problems of urbanization in Brazil, and in supplying pertinent data to me. Professor Hilgard O'Reilly Sternberg, eminent Brazilian geographer, presently at the University of California (Berkeley), provided important maps and other essential materials. The officials and staff of the Brazilian Embassy in Washington, D.C., went far beyond the line of duty in securing for me copies of urgently needed maps and documents. My colleagues in the department of sociology, University of Florida, encouraged me in many ways and served as "sounding boards" for many of the ideas I have expressed in this addition. My research assistant, Mr. J. Bruce Minore, a graduate student in sociology at the University of Florida, aided with some of the statistical compilations and computations, and a former assistant, Mr. R. Don Crider, helped with some of the translations. My wife, Louvina Jackson Smith, encouraged me in every way in the pursuit of knowledge about Brazilian society. To all of them I am deeply grateful.

T. Lynn Smith

CONTENTS

Part Eight : Supplement to Fourth Edition

ILLUSTRATIONS

TABLES

FIGURES

PART ONE

Introduction

Introductions are difficult, but anything worth writing deserves to be introduced. This one consists of two short chapters. The first of these is used mainly to state purposes and explain procedures. The second contains a few of the pertinent materials relating to the great cultural and social diversity to be found in Brazil.

CHAPTER I

INTRODUCTION

THIS BOOK is a comprehensive study of Brazil's people and institutions. Ever since 1939 I have been applying the empirical methods developed and used by North American sociologists and demographers in an analysis of Brazil's population and social organization. These pages contain a systematic exposition of the results of that study. It is hoped that such an approach to the Brazilian scene will prove of interest and value to a rather large public. It should provide materials that are useful to all those engaged in the comparative study of populations and institutions; it should supply basic information of great value in giving substance to the more popular accounts of travels; and much of it should prove of interest to the general reader. Perhaps it may also be of assistance to a considerable number of forward-looking Brazilian scholars and officials engaged in bringing Brazil into her rightful position as the leading country of South America and as one of the world's great nations.

The work of gathering the materials for the first edition of this book began during my first visit to Brazil in 1939. That stay of one month only whetted my appetite, and I returned to spend a full year, from February, 1942, to February, 1943. Not less than six months' time was spent in travel throughout the interior. I visited each of the states on at least one occasion and made repeated visits to those most accessible from Rio de Janeiro. The total adds up to some 24,350 miles. Of these about 12,570 were covered by plane, 9,090 by train, 2,220 by car, bus, or truck, and 470 in boats of various kinds. This total does not include rides on horseback and muleback within various communities.

My travels were undertaken with four purposes or objectives uppermost in mind:

(1) I wanted to become intimately familiar with rural Brazil and to learn as much as possible about the farms, neighborhoods, communities, and regions; to know the details of the rural scene and to see the people engaged in their daily activities. Back of this was the desire to be able to formulate significant, tentative hypotheses about the Brazilian system of social organization and the population, hypotheses the establishment or refutation of which would assist in making the principal features of the nation's social organization and demographic situation stand out clearly.

(2) I wanted to visit each of the state capitals, so that I could see and talk with those in charge of the state's educational program, agricultural work, statistical service, and land settlement and colonization activities. This was very important, for Brazil, like the United States, is a federation of states, and it is impossible to secure a large share of the pertinent data that are to be had unless one does go to the capitals of the various states. This is especially true of materials for the divisions of the states, the *municípios*. The immense size and the heterogeneity of most Brazilian states make it necessary to have data for the smaller units and communities if very much real understanding of any phenomenon is to be achieved.

(3) I wanted to meet Brazilian scholars, technicians, and governmental functionaries and to learn of their work and problems. As not all the best or more significant research work in the United States is being done in Washington, so too in Brazil the Federal District by no means has a monopoly on productive scholarship.

(4) As the work progressed, I wanted to be in a position to check provisional hypotheses by additional personal observation.

These travels naturally presented an excellent opportunity for firsthand observation and enabled me to secure access to many materials which are not generally available. Even so, many of the most essential data on some of the more important subjects are simply lacking; hence for the present, many conclusions are more hypothetical than might be wished.

In the pages which follow I have sought to avoid conclusions and generalizations unless they could be checked against objective, quantitative data. Naturally it was possible to formulate some hypotheses on the basis of a general understanding of rural life and peoples; others were suggested by my firsthand observation in Brazil. Conversation with Brazilian scholars gave me many leads. But in all cases, after a tentative hypothesis had been formulated, a diligent search of primary sources such as the census reports, statistical *anuários*, *relatórios* or annual reports of various official agencies, and other reports was made. This was as thorough as time and ability would permit. The pertinent books, articles, and other publications bearing on the question were read. Numerous requests were made to various state and federal agencies for special tabulations of materials in the files, data which so far had not been made public. Because of the courteous co-operation of many officials, these requests yielded valuable results. Finally, much time spent browsing in new and secondhand bookshops brought to light a great deal of useful material for consultation in Brazil and later in the United States. In this connection it should be indicated that in Brazil the bookshop serves much more as a library than it does in the United States; on the other hand, while there are large collections of books in many Brazilian libraries, these serve more as storehouses for books than as centers of research. The system of indexing and cross-referencing is not developed to the point that the library can readily be used for discovering what is known about a given subject. The new municipal library in São Paulo,

however, is building along modern lines, and in the future scholars
will be able to use its facilities to improve greatly the efficiency of
their research activities.

After returning to the United States, I spent three months at the
Library of Congress in Washington, where I was permitted to utilize
fully the excellent holdings of Brazilian materials which that institution possesses. This brought into use a great many important works
which I had not encountered in Brazil and helped to ensure that the
more important works had been consulted.

Subsequent to the preparation of the first edition, I have had the
privilege of returning to Brazil on eight different occasions for additional travel and study. In 1945 an assignment by the United States
Department of State gave me, in the course of three months, the
chance to extend my observations in parts of São Paulo and Central
Goiás and to visit for the first time the São Francisco Valley and
other interior portions of the states of Bahia and Pernambuco. The
following year I spent another three months in Brazil, where I served
briefly as visiting professor at the University of Brazil in Rio de Janeiro. Travels on this occasion included another visit to Corumbá in
Mato Grosso and a trip to see the sugar plantations and the fishing
villages in the vicinity of Campos in the state of Rio de Janeiro.

In 1951, as a fellow of the Guggenheim Foundation, I visited all of
the Latin-American countries in connection with some general demographic studies of Latin America. Three weeks were spent in Brazil,
with visits to the city of Rio de Janeiro, the Paraitinga Valley, and the
capital city in the state of São Paulo, Fortaleza in Ceará, and Belém
in Pará.

In August and September of 1952, at the request of the Brazilian
Minister of Agriculture and under the auspices of the United States
Department of Agriculture, I returned to Rio de Janeiro to advise with
the minister and the members of the National Commission on Agrarian Policy on agrarian reform; and in January and February, 1953,
I returned for another month to participate, as observer for the International Labor Organization, in the Seminar on Rural Welfare Problems in Latin America. In addition to intensive round-table discussions for two weeks at the Rural University, about 35 miles from the
city of Rio de Janeiro, this involved field trips to Campos and the
município of Itaperuna in the state of Rio de Janeiro and to several
parts of the state of São Paulo.

The summer of 1956 I spent lecturing, under the auspices of the
United States Department of State, in Portugal, Brazil, and the Spanish-American countries from Paraguay to Panama. Six weeks of this
time was spent in Brazil, with visits to universities and other cultural
centers in Belém, Fortaleza, Recife, Salvador, Rio de Janeiro, and
São Paulo. On this occasion I also had the opportunity of spending
three days in the cacao zone of Bahia.

A short visit to the city of Rio de Janeiro in 1960 was followed by
another in 1961. On this second occasion, in addition to participating for a full week in a Seminar on Agrarian Reform in Rio de

Janeiro, I also was enabled to visit the new capital, Brasília, and also to spend several days in São Paulo.

Nevertheless, I am far from satisfied with the data. The book should be judged in the light of what it was possible to do, and not by what one might desire to see done. In writing of Brazilian population and institutions, I have not found it possible to outline the subject in a logical manner, and then, with ample data, to prepare an exposition that would treat each subdivision in proper sequence and appropriate detail. Rather the problem has been to assemble as much pertinent data as possible and to do the best job possible with the materials at hand. Even though the phrases "for which data are available," "data are lacking," and "the unsatisfactory nature of the data" occur with monotonous regularity in the pages which follow, they are never inserted unless absolutely essential. The task was made doubly difficult by the lack of comprehensive treatments of the demographic situation and social institutions. Had there been a few general treatises on the family, on the land system, on the vital processes, and on the other subjects to which one could go for a summary of the available data and an indication of the principal sources, the job would have been greatly simplified. As it is, I cannot be sure that I have not missed some important sources.

It should be emphasized, however, that the statistical materials available for use in the preparation of the third edition are far superior to those that could be used in the first and even in the second edition. Modern censuses of population, agriculture, housing, and industry were taken in 1940, 1950, and 1960. These contain invaluable data relative to the population, the family, housing, levels of living, educational institutions, man-land relationships, immigration, and governmental institutions. Even when the revised edition was under preparation, only the preliminary results from the 1940 censuses were available; whereas, for the work on the third edition the present writer has had access to the definitive results of the 1940 and 1950 censuses and to some of the preliminary results of the 1960 enumerations. The major difficulty in this connection is, of course, that the rich storehouses of information now available in these census reports have been subjected to little or no analysis. For the most part the work that needs to be done in order to extract from the masses of raw data information of the kind that can be useful in planning the nation's industrial activities, agricultural programs, educational campaigns, health organizations, and so forth, has been left for the future. For this reason, in making use of the stores of information in these censuses, the present writer has had to depend, for the most part, on his own ingenuity.

Mention should also be made of the considerable number of sociological studies that have been carried out in Brazil since the first edition of this book appeared. As the following pages will show, the present writer is greatly indebted to the scholars, native and foreign, who have made and published these articles, monographs, and books. Certainly many of the principal conclusions presented in this volume are more soundly based and more thoroughly documented as a result of these studies than otherwise could have been the case.

As I began my studies, only gradually did I become aware of the elements in my new cultural environment. Brief experience in southern Brazil during 1939 had given me the impression that rural people and rural life in Brazil were much the same as they are in the United States. Later, as the study progressed, as I visited other and different parts of the immense country, as I observed the growing of new and strange crops, as I spent weeks and months in the back country, and as hundreds of conversations and much reading gave me a better insight into the values and thoughts of Brazil's scholars, very naturally my appraisal of the Brazilian rural scene underwent considerable modification. Slowly I began to appreciate the importance of traditional agricultural practices inherited from the Indians, in which *fire* is the dominant element in the preparation of the soil for planting. I came to see how deeply embedded in the life of the people was this system of agriculture and all of the work habits and consumption practices associated with it—how great was the gap between rural life based on these methods of agriculture and one which utilized the plow, the wheel, and animal traction.

By degrees it also became apparent to me that Brazil's break with Portuguese tradition had been much sharper than that which occurred between the Spanish-American countries and Spain. Brazil's exclusive use of the large estate stood out in contrast to Portugal's widespread system of small farms; Brazil's scattered farmsteads and trade-center towns and villages differed greatly from Portugal's village settlement patterns; the Brazilian diet, deficient in nutritive elements and with its undue dependence on mandioca, beans, and dried fish, or dried meat and sweets, showed few resemblances to the more adequate and better balanced consumption patterns of Portugal.

The study of the demographic data revealed enormous differences between Brazil and the United States, both in the make-up of the population and in the vital processes. The comparative lack of rural-urban migration in Brazil became apparent, and with it the absence there of a whole host of effects which such migration has had on society in our country. However, since the first edition of this book appeared, this situation has changed radically, as is evident by an examination of Chapters IX and XXII.

Little by little I also came to appreciate the importance of the gradual debasing of persons born in the upper classes. I began to see that the high rate of reproduction among the landowning classes, the absence of a system of primogeniture, and the lack of a large-scale development of urban industrial and commercial centers to supply employment for the numerous progeny of the landed aristocracy led to the subdivision of the land, the inability to maintain old standards of luxury, and the gradual leveling of many of the descendants of old families. And all of this took place without the development of a system of family farms in which the use of machinery and manual labor on the part of tne farm operator and his family led to a fairly high level of consumption for the population.

Finally, I became able to appreciate more fully the nature of Brazil's domestic institutions, to comprehend more clearly how the educational institutions performed, to understand local governmental agencies, and to see the numerous evidences of heterogeneity in religious beliefs and practices. In short, one after another I came to a realization of the very fundamental differences between the populations and institutions of Brazil and those in the United States.

Since an attempt is made in this volume to deal with many of the more significant aspects of demography and social organization, it has been necessary to use many technical concepts and terms. Realizing that this book would come into the hands of persons unfamiliar with many of the sociological expressions, I have attempted to clarify or define the technical meaning of many such terms. The constant endeavor, however, has been to make these explanations and definitions as little pedantic as possible.[1]

It also has been judged necessary to adopt, with definitions and explanations, many Brazilian words for which there are no exact English equivalents. Such words as *fazenda, município, caboclo,* and *roça* will be found throughout the book. Many of these are defined in the text or in footnotes, and all of them in the Glossary. It will be evident that the meaning in each case would have been altered had approximate English equivalents such as "plantation," "county," "mixed breed," or "new clearing" been used in their stead.

A word about the quotations is necessary. The pages which follow contain a liberal sprinkling of materials borrowed from other writers. For the most part they are taken from Brazilian works in an attempt to bring at least a few samples of a significant sociological literature within easy reach of students in the United States. In each case I have tried to quote enough to avoid distorting the author's meaning. The English sources quoted are old ones, those generally unavailable in the library. They are books written at a time when the methods of transportation forced the traveler to spend some time in the open country, smaller villages, and cities in order to learn something about the country and the people. This has been changed with the coming of the airplane. Observations made by contemporary travelers are for the most part too superficial to have any real value.

All of the translations of Brazilian materials are my own. In attempting to transfer as accurately as possible the Brazilian writer's thoughts from Portuguese to English, I have endeavored to give as literal a translation as I could without doing an injustice to the Brazilian author because of the stylistic differences between the languages.

The organization of the book is simple and conventional. In addi-

[1] See T. Lynn Smith, *The Sociology of Rural Life* (3d ed.; New York, 1953), for more detailed explanations of these concepts and for an attempt to use them in a systematic analysis of rural life.

tion to the introduction and the conclusion, the treatise consists of five parts subdivided into twenty-one chapters. Following the introduction are seven chapters dealing with the population and demographic features of Portuguese America. A single chapter on standards and levels of living makes up Part Three. The relations of the people to the land, the field of my greatest personal interest, include seven chapters and constitute Part Four. The four chapters of Part Five are used to analyze and describe the principal social institutions in Brazil. Part Six consists of a single chapter on urbanization. In the conclusion I present some of my reflections upon and suggestions relative to the manner in which Brazil's population policies and social institutions might be modified for the purpose of augmenting the welfare and standard of living of the Brazilian people.

Any sociological study of an area, whether it be that of a community, a state, or a nation, almost inevitably must present some facts and conclusions which are not pleasing to those who are dominated by the "chamber of commerce" mentality. There is no reason to suppose that Brazil is an exception to this rule. Furthermore, one who writes of Brazil should remember, or at least console himself with the thought, that it is an agricultural and collecting country living in a family of industrialized nations. There is a tendency nowadays to gauge modern "progress" by industrial advancement. This factor seems to help keep many Brazilian intellectuals constantly on the defensive, oftentimes far more so than would seem to be necessary. Perhaps for this reason some Brazilians may be unduly sensitive to the presentation of facts which show that Brazil, too, has social problems with which it must cope.

Fortunately, my own considered appraisals are somewhat temperate in comparison with those of Brazil's most outstanding scholars who have written on the subject. For example, M. A. Teixeira de Freitas, the leading Brazilian statistician, who also was a notable educator, made an inventory of Brazil's principal social problems. His original work had its impetus in the census of 1920, which he directed in the state of Minas Gerais. However, his observations, reflections, and attempts to formulate clear statements of the major problems did not stop at the limits of Minas Gerais, nor with the termination of the census. They represent the most substantial attempt yet made to appraise the social and economic realities in Brazil. Furthermore,

. . . Minas is so typically Brazilian that the observations apply, with minor variations, to all Brazil. . . . The *Mineiro* population (we could say the Brazilian) is, to the highest degree, dedicated to work, hospitable, of moderate habits, orderly in social conduct, intelligent, honest, thrifty, humble, courageous, sincerely religious, possessed of the most lively sentiments of chivalry and patriotism, without trace of pernicious regionalism, well equilibrated between progressivism and conservatism, and an impassioned champion of liberty.[2]

[2] M. A. Teixeira de Freitas, "Educação Rural," *Revista Nacional de Educação,* Nos. 18–19 (March–April, 1934), 56.

But in spite of all these favorable qualities, "such are the historical contingencies of its distribution over the land, such are the hostilities of the physical environment that it has to face, such are the accumulated errors of administration, that as yet the population has not been able to erect the marvelous political and social structure destined by its innate aptitudes." [3] For these reasons there are serious shortcomings in Brazilian society, social problems in the ordinary usage of the term. To conclude this introductory chapter the twenty-seven "unfavorable realities" given by Teixeira de Freitas are presented. They are as follows:

1. The excessive dispersion of the population, which determines that a large part of the people live in complete social isolation, which is often accompanied by extreme physical and moral degradation.

2. The insufficiency, in some places, of religious participation, facilitating the moral regression provoked by other factors.

3. The lack, sufficiently general, of urban hygiene, and even of domestic and personal hygiene among some social strata.

4. Extreme misery among a part of the agricultural proletariat, subjecting this stratum of the population to the most precarious conditions of diet, dress, and shelter.

5. Frequent appearance of outbreaks of banditry.

6. The widespread abuse of alcohol.

7. The worst sanitary conditions in some zones, resulting from frequent recurrence of one or more of the greater maladies prevailing in the Brazilian interior (syphilis, lung troubles, digestive and intestinal ailments, leprosy, goiter, constipation, malaria and other fevers, grippe, etc.).

8. The exercise with impunity, in all parts, of the pernicious quackery of fetish doctors and charlatans.

9. The lack of medical and pharmaceutic assistance for the great mass of the rural population, and even in numerous centers of relative importance.

10. The injurious development of gambling.

11. Routine in the processes of work.

12. The blind, wasteful, and often unproductive and unnecessary devastation of the forests.

13. Deficient means of communication and transportation.

14. An insufficient number of cities, deserving of the title, as coordinating elements in the social and economic life.

15. Lack of technical and administrative organization in the great majority of agricultural undertakings.

16. Illiteracy among the mass of the rural population and even among a large part of the urban population.

17. Lack of the most rudimentary knowledge of practical life among most social classes.

18. Regression to illiteracy of the ex-students of the primary schools because the backwardness of social life does not provide them an opportunity to utilize the knowledge acquired.

19. Insufficient administrative assistance to the producing classes.

20. The corruptive action of motion pictures without the necessary censorship.

21. Extremely numerous cases in which landed estates are not divided among the heirs, unmarked, and lacking a legal title.

22. Great confusion in weights and measures.

23. The most rudimentary system of institutions of credit.

24. Irrationality in the administrative division of the territory.

[3] *Ibid.*

25. Imperfect and deficient conduct in the administration of the municípios, resulting from the lack of knowledge of the boundaries, from extravagant cases of extraterritoriality of local governmental powers, and from the lack of co-ordination and combination of forces between the various municípios.

26. Lack of harmony and convergence in the undertakings of the various branches of public administration.

27. Deficient selection, discipline, stimulus, and remuneration for the general body of public servants.[4]

The realities with which Teixeira de Freitas was dealing did not originate in the 1920's nor, in many cases, even in the twentieth century; nor have most of them become less acute since he wrote. For the most part they remain to confront those in the second half of the twentieth century who are most concerned with social and economic development and other matters involved in Brazil's struggle to attain a larger share of her potentialities.

[4] *Ibid.*, 56–57.

would understand present-day Brazil must reckon with the multiple
cultural influences from Portugal, an extremely heterogeneous social
heritage from Africa, and the exceedingly important contributions
from the various groups of Indians. Brazilian Indians may not have
been as highly differentiated as those of the United States in language, agricultural practices, methods of transportation, religion,
food habits, and many other phases of human culture, but, on the
other hand, their imprint on Brazilian civilization has been much
greater than the Indian contribution to the pattern of living of the
United States. Africans and African influences were probably much
more varied and certainly have been at work for a much longer time
in Brazil than in the United States. But not only the influences from
Portugal, Africa, and aboriginal America must be taken into account.
There are also the influences of the early Dutch settlers in Pernambuco; the cultural patterns transferred by the Germans into the
southern states of Rio Grande do Sul, Santa Catarina, Paraná, and
São Paulo; Polish systems of living transplanted into Paraná and the
adjacent states; many small editions of Japan set up in São Paulo,
Mato Grosso, and Paraná; the Spanish-American cultural traits and
populations injected into the border areas from the sections adjoining Uruguay, Argentina, Bolivia, and Paraguay, and into those fronting on Colombia and Venezuela. These Spanish-American elements
are especially important in the mate-producing sections of southern
Mato Grosso and in the cattle-growing area of Rio Grande do Sul. In
addition to the numerous cultural islands, the student must also take
into account the cultural luggage sifting into rural Brazil with the
millions of Italian immigrants, and hundreds of thousands of Polish,
Portuguese, Spanish, and German immigrants from twentieth-century
Europe, along with the Asiatic influences brought by some 200,000
Japanese introduced during the last forty years. All these influences
merely add complications to the general pattern of the blanket of
man-made environment or culture which covers the entire nation.
The design of this pattern includes almost every possible combination
and permutation of the original Portuguese, African, and Indian systems of living, together with the multiple less influential social
heritages, as they have been tremendously altered through necessary
adjustments imposed by the hetergeneous natural environment of
Brazil.

A SUPERIMPOSITION OF EPOCHS

But the time element, cultural evolution, and cultural lag are concepts to be reckoned with in properly interpreting the present cultural diversity in Brazil. One would not be far wrong in saying that
Brazil contains representations of all the cultural stages through
which man has passed during the last millenium. A world citizen
feels at home in Rio de Janeiro, São Paulo, and other great metropolitan cities. Areas adjacent to these and other twentieth-century

A Brazilian Type: Rubber Collector of the Amazon Valley

capitals such as Bahia, Pôrto Alegre, Belo Horizonte, Curitiba, and
Recife enjoy all of the cultural accoutrements of civilization. Paved
roads and automobiles, telephones and radios, telegraph lines and
busses provide a system of communication and transportation that
compares favorably with that found anywhere. Newspapers, books,
magazines, and a host of other material and nonmaterial culture
traits are integral parts of the system of living among the farmers

15

situated in close proximity to the metropolitan centers. To a considerable extent these modern cultural appliances and privileges are also enjoyed by the upper classes on the larger fazendas throughout the interior areas, particularly those of São Paulo, Minas Gerais, and parts of the sugar-growing littoral. Yet one does not need to go far from any of the capitals to have firsthand contact with much older material culture and patterns of living.

Thus, very near São Paulo and Rio de Janeiro, as well as throughout the "interior," [2] are found many houses of the wattle-and-daub type—structures lacking glass windows, with a covering of thatch, and a floor formed of the bare earth.[3] As one goes into the interior,

[2] In Brazil "interior" may be used to refer to the parts of a state other than the capital, in addition to its usage as a designation for the central portions of the nation. One can hardly resist smiling at the signs along the Central do Brazil railway in Minas Gerais, the main line between Rio de Janeiro and Belo Horizonte. An arrow pointing in one direction is labeled *"Ao Belo Horizonte"* (To Belo Horizonte) while that pointed towards Brazil's former capital reads *"Ao Interior."*

[3] This house type is to be found throughout all Brazil. Even in Santa Catarina occasional "islands" of dwellings of this caboclo type are seen. There is little doubt that it is of Indian origin, for it is given as Number 6, Plate 26, in J. B. Debret, *Voyage Pittoresque et Historique Au Brésil, 1816–1831* (Paris, 1834), I. By this author this caboclo house was said to *"presente dans la charpente le modèle de toutes les petites maisons faites pour loger les esclaves des cultivateurs brésiliens en géneral"* and to have been common with the Puris, Camacans, and Coroados. *Ibid.*, 41. Various writers have described this house type and commented on its prevalence. John Mawe described the typical house of rural Brazil in unflattering terms: "The farm-houses are miserable hovels of one story, the floor neither paved nor boarded, and the walls and partitions formed of wicker-work plastered with mud, and never under-drawn. For an idea of the kitchen, which ought to be the cleanest and most comfortable part of the dwelling, the reader may figure to himself a filthy room with an uneven muddy floor, interspersed with pools of slop-water, and in different parts fireplaces formed by three round stones to hold the earthen pots that are used for boiling meat. As green wood is the chief fuel, the place is almost always filled with smoke, which finding no chimney, vents itself through the doors and other apertures, and leaves all within as black as soot. I regret to say that the kitchens of many opulent people are in not much better condition." *Travels in the Interior of Brazil* (Philadelphia and Boston, 1816), 81.

Joh. Bapt. von Spix and C. F. Phil. von Martius described the houses in the town of Taubaté, long the chief rival of São Paulo's capital city: "The houses in general are seldom above one story high; the walls are almost in all cases of thin rafters or laths, interwoven with twigs, plastered with loam, and covered with a white clay (*tabatinga*), which is found here and there on the banks of the rivers; the roof is carelessly covered with pantiles or shingles, rarely with maize straw, and the wall has in it one or two wooden latticed windows. The interior corresponds with the light construction and scanty materials. The entrance, which is generally half or entirely closed by a latticed door, leads directly into the largest room in the house, which being without boards, and often with unwhitewashed walls, resembles a barn. This division serves for the habitation of the family. Store-rooms, and in some cases a side-room for guests, occupy the remainder of the front of the building. The back part contains the apartments for the wife and the rest of the family, who, according to the Portuguese fashion, must immediately withdraw on the entrance of strangers. From this we enter the veranda, which generally runs along the whole length of the building, and opens into the court-yard. A similar veranda is sometimes annexed to the front of the house. The kitchen and servants' apartments, generally miserable sheds, lie opposite the house, at the further end of the court. The furniture of these houses is confined to the most necessary articles; often they have no more than a few wooden benches and chairs, a table, a large chest, a bed, consisting of a straw mat, or an ox hide on boards, supported by four pegs (*giráo*). Instead of beds, the Brazilians almost always make use of the woven or braided hammocks (*marqueiras*), the best and most durable of which are manufactured, in the provinces of S. Paulo especially into the more hilly and mountainous portions, roads, trucks, and automobiles give way to foot and saddle paths, saddle horses, pack trains, and ox-drawn carts. Electric- and steam-propelled engines are replaced by water-powered gristmills and saw-mills, of types common in the United States a century or so ago. Other aspects of the cultural landscape belong to what in most parts of the United States is considered a part of the almost forgotten past. As I traveled through the interior of the great state of Minas Gerais I was constantly being turned back in memory to early boyhood days in the Rocky Mountain states of Colorado and New Mexico. But in the interior portions of the northeastern states I found a cultural environment that belonged to a past with which I am acquainted only through reading. In parts of Maranhão, Pará, Amazonas, Goiás, and Mato Grosso, there are vivid reminders that

and Minas, of white or coloured cotton threads. The traveller nowhere meets with any wells, and must therefore be satisfied with rain, spring, or river water, for every purpose. The inhabitants of Taubaté have the appearance of more prosperity and refinement than those of the other small places through which we had before travelled; which is perhaps owing to their more lively intercourse with Rio de Janeiro and S. Paulo. A few vines also are cultivated here, the fruit of which was just ripe, and of an agreeable flavour." *Travels in Brazil, in the Years 1817–1820* (London, 1824), I, 313–14.

A Brazilian Type: Vaqueiro of the Plains of the Rio Branco in the Far North

A Brazilian Type: Negress of Bahia

A Brazilian Type: Leather-clad Vaqueiro of the Northeastern Sertões

neolithic man still is to be reckoned with by rubber gatherers or others who would collect nature's gifts.[4]

Brazilian scholars are well aware of this tremendous cultural diversity existent in their country and many of them have described its essential features. "There is not one Brazil, but many Brazils," frequently says M. B. Lourenço Filho, one of Brazil's outstanding educators.

To a son of the south—used to seeing the constant renovation of life, the feverish activity of progress in cosmopolitan cities, theaters in which are agitated the most contrary interests, moving in waves and cycles towards a

---

[4] Lead for bullets and powder were among the forty-two indispensable items included in the agreement between the Rubber Reserve Company and the Superintendency of Supplies for the Amazon Valley. They received the same consideration as salt, tobacco, cigarette papers, fishhooks, rice, fishing lines, beans, flour, matches, knives, lard, *charque*, lanterns, sugar, kerosene, machetes, and other indispensable items of the rubber gatherer's equipment and supplies. The agreement is published in the *Jornal do Commercio* of Rio de Janeiro, April 14, 1943.

future as yet poorly defined but always tending towards the improvement
of social existence—the first impression when he buries himself in the
Northeast is of going, as in a dream, retreating through time at each step
[taken on his way to the interior]. Life appears to stop and then to begin
a reverse cycle, leaving behind two decades with each day's journey. People, habitations, the appearance of towns and cities, agricultural processes
and means of transportation, ways of dressing and speaking, every manifestation of social, political, esthetic, or religious existence—everything
shows itself out of the dimness of time, or speaks to the soul as the indefinite voices of an ancient past.

Upon viewing the window of a church, of a congregation only slightly
removed from the coast, on a Saint's day at the hour of Mass, framed in a
line of coconut trees or of leafy *mangabeiras,* below whose large and
powdery leaves on rare occasions a Ford introduces the single and scandal-
ous aspect of modern life, one is forced to say: "It was thus in the time of
the Empire." Upon observing, a little beyond, the conditions of rural life in

A Brazilian Type: Gaúcho of Rio Grande do Sul

Catinga

many parts of the *sertão,* where the factor of the "human arm" is so cheap that it comes to be employed as a matter of course in the transportation of burdens and is used as the moving force in small mills for making sugar and mandioca flour, one has to think with me, irresistibly: "It must have been thus in the times of slavery." And later, upon burying himself in the semi-arid vastnesses, where in each one of the poorly arranged villages, a dozen men are engaged in the precarious growing of livestock, cattle or goats, where food that is offered him is on most occasions a plate of dry mandioca flour or a tray of wild fruits, where the sad huts resemble those of Indians, and the rude utensils are reproductions of those of the primitive Tapuyas and retain their original names, one must exclaim with conviction: "It must have been like this in the epoch of the Independence." [5]

As yet, I have not run across the concept of "contemporary ancestors" in Brazilian literature, but a Brazilian historian, Pedro Calmon, expressed much the same fundamental idea:

In the sertão we encounter an archeological picture of our colonial civilization—in race, language, economy, costumes, folk-lore, in mysticism. . . .

[5] M. B. Lourenço Filho, *Joaseiro do Padre Cicero* (2d ed.; São Paulo, 1926), 14–15.

Socially Brazil is not a superimposition of classes but of epochs. It is not divided into layers of human beings but into a juxtaposition of centuries. If near the seacoast, the intensely cultivated regions, there vibrates the same activity as in the countries that are possessed by the machine, in the agricultural band of territory work still has aspects of the eighteenth century, in the pastoral areas society still contains survivals from the seventeenth century, and the sixteenth century survives in the forests of the West, where the drama of collecting the Indians into villages and teaching them the catechism continues to repeat the image of the first day of colonization. As Alberdi observed, "between one man and another there are three centuries of difference." It is for this reason that the history of Brazilian civilization descends indistinctly in time and extends in space, encountering, to the extent that it insinuates itself into the past or invades the sertão, the facts of colonial evolution . . . the typical colonist still is encountered in the northeast of Brazil. He is almost unchanged. In the Empire he considered himself governed by the King of Portugal; in the Republic he considered himself governed by the Emperor of Brazil. He lives in a socially obsolete existence; he vibrates with his old colonial sentiments; he repeats the resistance of fifteen generations of sertanejos. His villages invariably cluster about a square, with a chapel in the center, as were the Indian villages which the Jesuits constructed. The fazendeiro, who is the spiritual chief of the clan, continues to be "major," or "colonel," as were the ancient officials of the ordinances, whose militarily administered government left in small communities pleasant remembrances [saudades] that could not be erased. The priest has powers approximating those of the historic missionaries. Little is done without him, and nothing is done against him. Where there is no priest the role is exercised by the "monk," the ascetic who combines the virtues of the medicine man and of the priest, the re-incarnation of the Indian medicine man [pagé], to whom the families confide cases of conscience and local justice. The mysticism of the sertanejo is intense and complex. He participates in the religious practices of the Portuguese, in the belief of the aborigines, and in some of the fetishism of the African: he necessitates a spiritual chief and considerable manifestations foreign to his cult. This is complicated by the ingenuity of the *Tupis*, thanks to their fear of spirits of the forest and of natural forces—and of the European ancestral worship; the cult is *mamaluco* [mixture of Indian and Portuguese] like the vaqueiro.[6]

DESIGNATIONS FOR THE COUNTRYMAN

A brief discussion of the terms used to designate the country people, with a few comments on their distributions, also helps to bring out the immense cultural diversity encountered in Brazil. Even a cursory examination reveals that the Brazilian species of the Portuguese language is rich in terms used to designate the *homem do campo*, the countryman, or the person who lives outside the towns and cities. For the reason that the overwhelming proportion of Brazil's rural people belong to the laboring class, have enjoyed little or no schooling, and have been limited socially to the narrow vistas of their own small world, these terms seem to reflect even more of the city man's smug sense of superiority than do comparable designations in the United States. Thus, *caboclo, matuto, roceiro*, and *caipira*, the terms most widely used to designate the humble resident

---

[6] Pedro Calmon, *Espirito da Sociedade Colonial* (São Paulo, 1935), 197–99.

of the rural districts, all have depreciative connotations. This is especially true of caipira, probably the term in most general usage, and for which Bernardino José de Souza quotes with approval the following definition by Valdomiro Silveira: "the man or woman who lives outside the village; who lacks instruction or social graces; who does not know how to dress well or to make a good appearance in public." [7] Caboclo, now used almost universally throughout Brazil as synonymous with caipira, also retains its use as the designation (synonymous with *mameluco* and *cariboca*) for the mixed-blood descendants of Indians and whites, a fact suggestive of the importance of the Indian racial strain in the population of Brazil's great interior sections. Probably of even greater importance than the Negroid elements are the strains of Indian blood coursing through the veins of most Brazilians of the lower and middle classes. Matuto, literally a forest dweller, also in almost universal use throughout Brazil as a designation for the countryman of the lower classes, carries much the same connotation as does the expression "backwoodsman" in the United States. Roceiro, literally the seminomadic person who annually selects a site, builds a rude shelter, and makes a roça (the small burned patch in the midst of the forest in which are planted subsistence crops such as corn and beans), by extension also has come to be used as a designation for the man of the small-farming class. On the ra-

[7] *Dicionário da Terra e da Gente do Brasil* (4th ed.; São Paulo, 1939), 82–83.

Jangadas, the Tiny Rafts on which the Fishermen of Northeastern Brazil Put out to Open Sea

dio, in the press, and on the stage, the caipira, the caboclo, the matuto, and the roceiro in caricature are a source of considerable
amusement for the middle and upper classes of Brazilian urban society.

Among terms nearly synonymous with the four given above, but
with a more limited distribution, there is, for example, *babacuara*,
literally knowing nothing, or ignorant, as applied to low-class plantation workers in the sugar-producing sections about Campos in the
state of Rio de Janeiro. In the same area *muxuango*, signifying a
rustic person, is also in rather general use for much the same purpose. The person who travels throughout Brazil may also frequently
hear a member of the more humble class referred to as a *caboré*.
This is the name of a tribe of Indians who formerly lived in what is
now the state of Rio Grande do Norte, and like *cafús* or *cafuso* it is a
designation sometimes applied to the mixed-blood descendants of the
Indian-Negro cross. In the great state of Minas Gerais, most of whose
ten million inhabitants are scattered throughout its immense rural
districts, numerous terms are employed to designate the *homem da
roça* (the man who uses the axe, fire, and the hoe to produce small
subsistence crops on a little patch of ground) and other varieties of
rural people of the lower classes. In addition to being called caipira,
one of these *mineiros* may be designated as *chapadeiro* (plainsman),
bruaqueiro (literally a person who carries produce to market in a
large leather sack or bag), *mandioqueiro* (one who subsists by raising
and eating mandioca or manioc), or *pióca*. If he lives beside one of
the state's numerous streams, "without a master," in a miserable hut
and on a diet of mandioca and fish, he is generally called a *ribeirinho*.

In Brazil's most advanced state of São Paulo the four most generalized terms are all in use. Many of the more regionalized usages also
make their appearance, and in addition at least two terms specific to
the state are found. One of these, *cangussú*, is merely another way
of saying matuto, while *caiçara* is used to differentiate the humble
resident of the coastal lowlands from his fellow caipira on the plateau. Confined largely to certain localities of São Paulo and Minas
Gerais is the use of *mandi* as a synonym for caipira, while throughout Minas Gerais and Goiás *queijeiro* (cheesemaker and eater) is employed in a similar sense, and in Minas Gerais and the state of Rio de
Janeiro *tapiocano* (tapioca maker) is another designation for the caipira.

Along the headwaters of the Rio São Francisco and extending
northward from Minas Gerais into Bahia, *capiau* enjoys widespread
usage as a designation for members of the more humble social
classes of the region, and another synonymous term, *capuava*, has
much the same distribution. Also in these portions of Bahia, which
adjoin the São Francisco, *casacudo*, derived from the coarsely made
costume used by the low-class countryman, is prevalent as a synonym
for caipira or roceiro. Another designation that is widely employed in

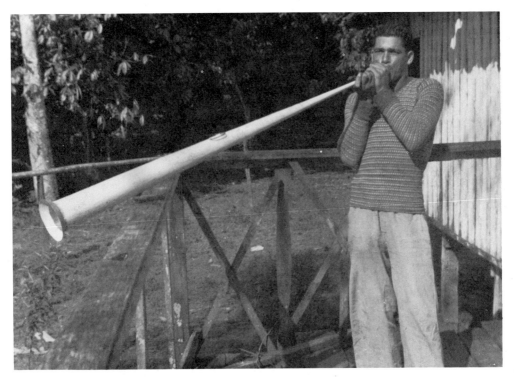

Horn Used for Signaling by Residents of the Amazon Valley. (Courtesy of Hilgard O'Reilly Sternberg.)

Bahia, and which has diffused from there to neighboring states, is *tabaréu*. This almost ranks with caboclo, matuto, roceiro, and caipira, as a designation for the member of the rural Brazilian lower class. Farther to the north, in the interior of Piauí, the widespread use of a dress of leather has led to the employment of *casaca* as a designation for the rural person of low estate. In other parts of the great northeastern interior a person of the same class is referred to as a *corumba* or *curumbú*, but this designation carries the added connotation of one who periodically flees the drought-stricken sertão in search of work in the better-watered coastal sections of the area. Interestingly enough, in the nearby state of Sergipe almost exactly the same shade of meaning is attached to the word *curáu*. Along the Paraíba River in the northeastern state of the same name, the humble Brazilian who lives mainly from fishing is called a *piraquara*.

In the great interior areas of the northeast, where periodic droughts play havoc with the social and economic life of the area, the common folk who care for the herds are usually called sertanejos, a term derived from the common name for the section, sertão, or sparsely populated and, sometimes, semiarid area. Finally, in the extreme south in the cattle-growing state of Rio Grande do Sul, a variety of terms is used to designate the member of the rural working class. In addition to the familiar *peão*, which is applied also to urbanites of the lower class, such expressions as *guasca* and *mambira* enjoy considerable popularity.

The terms given above by no means exhaust the possibilities, but they do indicate the wide variety of designations one meets with when he attempts to discover the names by which the masses of lower-class rural Brazilians are designated. The ones considered do not include such terms as *colono, camarada, empreiteiro,* and *parceiro*, which are specific names for rural workers of particular categories in São Paulo. Colono, in general use also as the name for the smaller farmer of immigrant stock in the southern states, is lacking. Likewise absent is *bahiano*, commonly applied to the cattle-raising people living in the interior of Maranhão and Piauí, and *praiano*, a general designation for the poverty-stricken fisherfolk who live along the coast of southern Brazil. Nor have the designations for members of specific occupational groups been included. These alone would make a long list, merely the beginning of which are terms such as *gaúcho* and *vaqueiro* for cowboy, *garimpeiro* for diamond hunter, *seringueiro* for rubber collector, *machadeiro* for the axeman who fells the forests and also sometimes for the rubber gatherer, *mateiro* for the workman who gathers the branches from the mate forests, and *tropeiro* as the name of the person who conducts one of the nation's thousands of pack mule trains. Finally, *agregado,* a term formerly used to designate one of the fazendeiro's "men" or retainers, in distinction from his slaves, has been omitted. Perhaps this is not entirely justified since today this term is generally applied to the worker who resides on the lands of the fazenda or *engenho*, as distinguished from the camarada, or hired laborer, who does not live on the property. Usually the agregado is permitted to make small plantings of his own, to raise a little poultry or a pig, and to keep a horse or a mule.

WEIGHTS AND MEASURES

Variations in the systems of weights and measures constitute another aspect of the man-made environment, one drawn from the field of nonmaterial culture, that indicates the cultural diversity in Brazil. The rich variety of terms in use and the different values of a given term from one part of the country to another are sometimes confusing even to Brazilians. For others they make necessary great caution in the use of terms for expressing distances, weights, and measures. Otherwise, much confusion is sure to arise. Since, theoretically, and to a considerable extent, practically, the metric system is used in Brazil, the various other Brazilian measures may be equated to the metric units for purposes of this analysis. Consider first some of the linear measures in use.

The largest of these is the *légua* (or league). It is 6,600 meters long, or three *milhas* (miles).[8] This old Portuguese milha of 2,200 meters is equal to about 1.35 English miles. Another very common measure of distance is the braça (arm). The attempt is now under way to standardize this at 2.2 meters, and 1,000 braças has always been considered as equal to one milha and 3,000 as the equivalent of one légua. The braça in turn is equal to 2 *varas* (1.10 meters), the vara to 5 *palmas* (palms) of 23 centimeters each. There is also the *côvado*, corresponding to three palmas. In addition, the *pé* (foot) of 33 centimeters, the *polegada* (inch) of 27 millimeters, or slightly larger than the English inch, and the *linha* (line) 2.3 millimeters are in use. One cannot go far from Brazil's larger centers of population without coming into sections where meters and kilometers are not yet in general use, where the population still thinks and deals in terms of the old braças, milhas, and léguas. If one travels extensively throughout the nation, passing repeatedly from city to sertão, the variations in linear measures are likely to give the impression of a "crazy quilt" pattern.

Measures of area are still more varied. Here one must reckon with the *alqueire*, which itself is not uniform, the *tarefa* (task), likewise of different sizes, and the *quadra* (square), also differing in magnitude from place to place. One variety of alqueire called the *paulista* is used in São Paulo, from which it takes its name, in Paraná, in Santa Catarina, in the northern part of Rio Grande do Sul and the southern part of Mato Grosso. This alqueire paulista designates an area 100 braças long and 50 braças wide, or of 24,200 square meters. Thus, one alqueire of this type contains 2.42 hectares. A second alqueire, the *mineiro*, is in general use in Minas Gerais, from which it takes the name, and also in Espírito Santo, Rio de Janeiro, and Goiás. It is twice as large as the alqueire paulista, being 100 x 100 braças, or containing an area of 48,400 square meters, or 4.84 hectares. As will be noted below, this alqueire mineiro corresponds in size to the quadra that is used in Maranhão and Piauí.

The tarefa is another land measure which, like the alqueire, varies in size. One of the varieties is the *tarefa bahiana*, so called because of its prevalence in the state of Bahia, although it is also used in Ceará, Pernambuco, Goiás, and to some extent in Minas Gerais. This tarefa is 30 x 30 braças, 4,356 square meters or about .44 of a hectare. Farther to the north another tarefa, called the *nordestina* (northeastern), is in general use. This one is only 25 x 25 braças, 3.025 square meters or about .3 of a hectare. This variety of the tarefa is the one most generally used in Alagôas and Sergipe, but it also competes with other measures in Pernambuco, Paraíba, and Ceará. In Rio Grande do Norte an area of this size adds to the variety by going under the name of *mil covas* (1,000 "hills").

Still another tarefa, the *gaúcha*, is found in Brazil's most southerly

---

[8] This must not be taken too literally, for as Sir Richard F. Burton commented, "Koster sensibly divides his leagues into legoas grandes, legoas pequenas, and legoas de nada—of nothing, which may mean four miles." *The Highlands of the Brazil* (London, 1869), I, 156–57.

state. It is only 10 x 20 braças (968 square meters or about one tenth of a hectare), and its use is restricted to the northeastern portion of Rio Grande do Sul. Finally, there is the *tarefa cearense,* named for the state of Ceará. It is an area of 30 x 25 braças, containing 3,630 square meters or about .361 of a hectare.

Much used in Rio Grande do Sul farming districts is the *quadra gaúcha,* literally the "cowboy square." It is an area 60 x 60 braças, or 17,424 square meters, or about 1.74 hectares. In the cattle-growing *fronteira* (frontier) or *campina* (prairie) portions of the same state the *quadra de sesmaria* is in use. It, too, is 60 braças wide but is one légua deep, thus containing 871,200 square meters or 87.12 hectares. One may be sure that in previous times this has been a very indefinite measure of area.

The quadra is a name applied to other areas elsewhere in Brazil. That in use in Maranhão and Piauí has already been described as the equivalent of the alqueire mineiro. There is also the *quadra paraibana,* or of Paraíba. It measures 50 x 50 braças, so that it contains 12,100 square meters or 1.21 hectares.

There may be still other measures in common usage, but these are some most frequently encountered. They also are sufficient to demonstrate that one who is concerned with the land and man's relations to it will encounter plenty of variety as he moves about Brazil.

Measures of weight include a considerable variety of units in addition to grams, kilograms, and so on, of the official system. Although superseded in many places by the metric system, these older measures still continue to be used in the rural districts. The largest of such units is the *tonelada,* the equivalent of 793.24 kilograms. The official *tonelada métrica* of course contains 1,000 kilograms. Next in size is the *quintal,* which contains 58.759 kilograms. Of these, 13.5 are required to make a tonelada. A weight of 100 kilograms is called a *quintal métrico.* The *arroba* is the next of the older measures of weight. Four of them constitute a quintal, so each is the equivalent of 14.69 kilograms. The *arroba métrica* is just slightly larger, or 15 kilograms.

Another old measure was the *arratel,* 32 of them making one arroba, or being equivalent to 459 grams. Today this unit of weight goes under the name *libra.* It is about 5.5 grams lighter than the English pound. This libra in turn is made up of 16 *onças,* so that the onça is equal to 28.69 grams. (Interestingly enough, English writers are prone to translate onça as "ounce" even when the term applies to the South American jaguar.) The eighth part of the onça is called an *oitava,* the equivalent of 3.586 grams. The latter in turn has been considered equal to four *escrópulos,* the escrópulo being used a great deal for weighing the precious stones in which Brazil abounds. Its equivalent in grams is given as 1.195. Next is the *quilate,* also used for weighing precious stones, considered to be one sixth of an escrópulo and as being equal to .199 grams. Exactly .20 grams is called a *quilate métrico.* Finally, there is the *grão,* weighing .049 grams.

The metric system is, of course, generally used in the cities and towns. In the far interior it has hardly penetrated, although it is rapidly diffusing throughout the length and breadth of the land. Until it succeeds in more fully replacing the older units of weight and measurement, the coexistence of the various units will continue to make for cultural diversity in Brazil.

AN EXAMPLE OF RACIAL AND CULTURAL VARIATION

Racial and cultural elements also vary tremendously from one place to another, even within the rather well-defined regions of Brazil. This is brought out clearly for the state of Santa Catarina in a study by Lourival Câmara.[9] Preparatory to a rather detailed analysis of the German, Polish, and Italian colonies, a brief summary was given of the main characteristics of people and society on the seacoast, in the colonial sections which occupy the two principal valleys, and on the mountainous plateaus. The descriptions bring out some of the more striking differences found within a single state, Santa Catarina.

Except for sporadic nuclei, minimum discrepancies, Santa Catarina is composed of three anthropo-geographic zones: that of the oceanside, that of colonization properly so-called (consisting of the valleys of the principal rivers) and that of the *campos* (the prairie-like pasture lands on the high plateau, and mountain tops). Each of these has its norm, its specific type of individual: the praiano [inhabitant of the seacoast], the colono [immigrant small farmer], the *serrano* [mountaineer]. Each of these lives a life divergent from the others and fundamentally different in its composition and spirit.

The praiano is the reincarnation of his Azorian ancestor. "In the midst of incidental variations," says Ribot, "There exists a cell which always remains unattainable, which permits nature to copy itself and imitate itself consistently." The inhabitant of our coasts is essentially the degenerated reproduction of the Azorian who failed on the coast of Santa Catarina in the epic of its settlement. Osvaldo Cabral establishes with exactness the picture of our coastal populations: "They live as their parents lived in times gone by: without stimulation, abandoned, keeping the same primitive organization, gaining for themselves a precarious existence by the day's fishing, by growing small plots of mandioca and by making mandioca flour on a small scale. The inhabitants seem to expect favors and misfortunes from the sky with the fatalism of a Mohammedan, receiving both with the indifference of the conquered."

Degeneracy, in a succession of generations, has affected the morphological (already altered in a large measure because of crossing with Bantu Negroes) and psychological qualities of these populations, of small stature, indolent, resigned, ossified, schizothymic. The degeneracy continues, furthermore, because of the low state of basal metabolism; the diet of these people, monotonous, unbalanced, incomplete, poor in carbohydrates, and highly deficient in vitamins, consists only of fish, mandioca flour, and coffee. Man is a function of his diet, psychologically and morphologically. The result of these periods of undernourishment is inanimation. . . .

Josué de Castro, studying in Brazil the consequences of a monotonous diet, generally having mandioca flour as a basis, as in case of our praiano now under consideration, said that such a diet "made its influence felt in

[9] Lourival Câmara, *Estrangeiros em Santa Catarina* (Florianópolis, 1940).

various ways upon the organic and psychological life of the Brazilian, making him a type of weak and undernourished man, below normal in weight, with a chronic incapacity for working, with an index of longevity fearfully short and above all with an index of infant mortality among the highest in the world." All of these effects are seen in our coastal population, we repeat, originating in their growing subnutrition.

The paternity of the panorama delineated has been attributed to determined characteristics of the soil which magnify the climatic ills, decimating hundreds of lives. But in other countries, thanks to prophylactics and sanitary procedures, the basis of such deterministic theories has been destroyed. Climate does not generate absolutisms. Its influence is relative. . . . The degeneration alluded to did not come from the soil nor from the climate, but from the diet—from the singleness of the diet, precarious, the very poorest, aggravated by alcoholic intoxication.

The colono society is the second type in Santa Catarina. The descendant of the German element, or the Slav, or the Atlanto-Mediterranean, who sought the state in a permanent emigration, located by preference along the rivers Itajaí and Tubarão, disseminating later to the plateau above, in a conquest of perpendicularity. The colono—in pages to come, we will explain in detail his role in the formation of our social organism—constitutes the most exotic, dissonant note in the population of Santa Catarina, ethnically, psychologically, socially.

Economically the colono is a type pattern of monolinear orientation. Anthropologically, however, there is no type: in the colonization zone there is a group of the most varied ethnic stocks, coming from diverse latitudes and with specific characteristics the most divergent. [These colonists are described much more thoroughly in the main body of the publication.]

The third type is the mountaineer, somatic revivification of the *bandeirante*, of the mameluco, whose genetic origin, in its turn, is one of the most complicated: the result of crosses and recrosses of the Portuguese complex, where various bloods are united, with the indigenous Tupí strain. On the ethnological map of the state, the central mountainous region presents the highest proportion of Tupí blood, although these people would be numerically insignificant in the percentage distribution of this stock in Brazil.

Generated by a society composed of another human group and in a habitat different from those which molded the praiano, the serrano has to have, *ipso facto* a different, even an antithetical, psychology. Cattle raising has been the economic base of serrano society, a consequence of the latifundia and of the expansion of the cycle, of which Roberto Simonsen speaks, when herds and herds of cattle went from the campos of the south for consumption in the center.

The environment impressed on the psychological physiognomy of the serrano the sense of extension, of liberty, of grandeur, or richness, of the sense of the infinite.

The Tupí heritage gave to him a profoundness of sentiments, of hate as well as love, the duty of hospitality, and the characteristics of mobility. Heredity impressed on him strongly ambition, authoritarianism, indicative of the Portuguese, tinted by semitism.

The diet of the serrano, predominantly of meat, also served to accentuate his absolutism.[10]

CULTURAL REGIONS

It still is not possible to describe in detail all of the more important regional contrasts in Brazil, to determine accurately the bounda-

[10] *Ibid.*, 11–14.

ries of the principal cultural areas in that great country, nor to supply quantitative data about any of the areas that are delineated with a fair degree of precision. This is all true despite the fact that the delineation and description of the social, cultural, and economic regions of which any nation is made up is a prime objective of many geographers, sociologists, anthropologists, and economists; and it is valid in spite of a considerable number of serious attempts to remedy the deficiency. Indeed the present state of regional delineation of the social, cultural, and economic sections of Brazilian society serves to illustrate the difficulties inherent in such attempts.

For any adequate regional delineation it is necessary: (1) for the areas which are fairly homogeneous with respect to the more important social, cultural, or economic features or characteristics to be bounded as accurately as possible, and (2) for these delineations to be made in terms of the lines which constitute the boundaries of states, provinces, or other major civil divisions of the nation in question. If the first of these is defective, the regions that result lack the homogeneity that is necessary if the statistical data for each of the regions is to be meaningful; and if the regional boundaries do not coincide with state lines, it may be impossible and is certain to be extremely difficult to compute even the most simple totals, indexes, and coefficients for the various regions. In such cases the amount of arithmetic involved may dissuade most investigators from attempting any regional comparisons whatsoever. In combination, these two requirements make extremely difficult the delineation and use of significant regional divisions in Brazil.

The most important regional division of Brazil is, of course, that developed and used by the Instituto Brasileiro de Geografia e Estatística. This national agency, and its branches in all of the states and territories, employs a schema which separates the nation's territory into five great areas, i.e., the North, the Northeast, the East, the South, and the West Central. (See Figure 1.) It possesses the virtue of having regional lines that correspond exactly with state boundaries, and it suffers from the defect that the resulting regions are so heterogeneous that the totals and indexes for the various regions probably conceal social, cultural, and economic differences that are far more significant than those that they reveal. This schema is employed in all, or nearly all, official compilations of statistical materials. It is used in a large share of the tables presented in this volume.

Various other ways of dividing Brazilian territory into significant regions have been presented by serious scholars. Deserving serious consideration is the one developed by Hilgard O'Reilly Sternberg designed to delineate and describe the principal natural regions of Brazil. It is based on the interaction of several physical factors (topography, geognosy, climate, and so forth) and involves the division of Brazil into the following regions: Amazonia, the Northeast, the Middle North (i.e., the intermediate zone between Amazonia and the Northeast), the Central-Western Plateau, the Pantanal, the great Backbone Range, the São Francisco Valley, the Southern Plateau, and the

FIGURE 1. Brazilian states and territories and the major regions in Brazil.

Atlantic Seaboard.[11] Another attempt of considerable importance is that by Preston James, who endeavored to determine and describe the principal cultural regions in Brazil. The divisions employed by him are as follows: the Northeast, the Eastern Littoral, the Southeast, São Paulo, the South, the Sertões, and the North.[12]

Finally, Professor Manuel Diégues Júnior is responsible for the most intensive attempt to delineate and characterize the principal regions in Brazil, and his work deserves serious attention by all who would understand the variations to be found within Brazilian society.[13] Diégues was well aware of the necessity of including more than physical and economic features in any adequate schema for regional delineation. Nevertheless, for the most part the economic factors seem to have been paramount in determining the distinctions between the regions he has differentiated and described. (See Figure 2.)

[11] Hilgard O'Reilly Sternberg, "The Physical Basis of Brazilian Society," in T. Lynn Smith and Alexander Marchant (eds.), Brazil: Portrait of Half a Continent (New York, 1951), 54–85.

[12] Preston E. James, "The Cultural Regions of Brazil," ibid., 86–103.

[13] See Manuel Diégues Júnior, Regiões Culturais do Brasil (Rio de Janeiro, 1960).

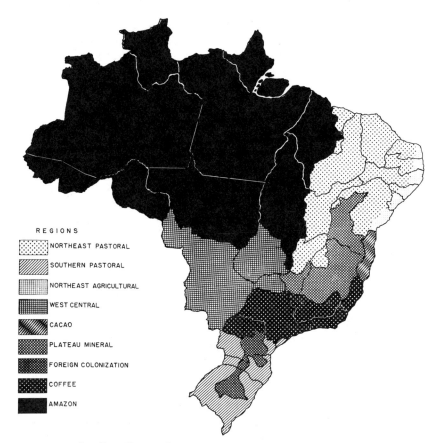

REGIONS

:::: NORTHEAST PASTORAL

/// SOUTHERN PASTORAL

▥ NORTHEAST AGRICULTURAL

▦ WEST CENTRAL

◪ CACAO

▨ PLATEAU MINERAL

▩ FOREIGN COLONIZATION

▨ COFFEE

■ AMAZON

FIGURE 2. Brazilian cultural regions (After Manuel Diégues Júnior, *Regiões Culturais do Brasil*).

Familiarity with his results, however, is highly important. The paragraphs which follow set forth the short descriptions he has given to each of the "cultural regions" he has included and are essentially a close approximation in English of the summary statements he has given in Portuguese.[14] In addition to the nine regions described below, he also took into account a zone of Salt on the northeast coast, the Cacau zone of southern Bahia, and a narrow band of fishing culture which extends all along the coast from Rio Grande do Sul to Maranhão.

1. *Nordeste Agrária* (Northeast Agricultural Coastal Plain). This is characterized ethnically by a high proportion of mulattoes; socially, by the dominant role socially, economically, demographically and politically of the casa grande, symbol of the sugar enhenho; and economically, by the sugar economy, first with the enhenho and now with the usina, primarily responsible for an agrarian society along aristocratic lines and with patriarchial characteristics.

[14] See *ibid.*, 20–22.

NOTRE DAME COLLEGE OF EDUCATION.
MOUNT PLEASANT, LIVERPOOL L3 5SP

2. *Nordeste Mediterraneo Pastoril* (Northeast Pastoral Zone).
This was occupied by expansion from the coastal areas and is an
area in which the society that was formed is typified by (a) the
vaqueiro, with his distinctive dress, one of the three typical costumes
found in Brazil; (b) an intensive crossing of whites and Indians, with
a resulting mameluco type; and (c) the corrals and later the cattle
fazendas which represent the principal social nuclei of the region.

3. *Amazonia.* This region is the dominion of the forest and water
which condition the processes of human occupancy and of regional
life. More than any other region it is one in which the presence of the
Indian is basic, fundamental, and characteristic. Extractive activities, first of drugs and medicines, and now of rubber, timber, and
nuts, indicate the economic stage of the region which has, in the
processing sheds and trading posts, its focal point and most important social center. The mode of life and the gathering of rubber ir-
radiates from it. The water and the forest influence myths and beliefs and, to an equal degree, the sparcity of population.

4. *Mineração no Planalto* (The Mineral Region of the Plateau).
This region was settled as the bandeirantes surged over the Serra do
Mar. It was characterized by the development of mining camps, an
environment of riches, pleasure seeking, and an intense social life.
Mamelucos, mulattoes, Englishmen, Jews—and not merely paulistas
and northeasterners—participated in the formation of its human
type. These created their own cultural conditions which, although
changing with the development of metallurgy, gave form to life in the
region. The habits of life are still based on the traditional ways.

5. *Centro Oeste* (West Central). The occupation of this area began with the brief splendor of the mining period. The decadency of
mining led the region's population to activities such as the collection
of mate, cattle raising, and small farming, although they did not give
up their work of extracting minerals and precious stones. The predominant human element was the Portuguese mixed with the Indian. Today the cultural influences from neighboring portions of
Bolivia and Paraguay are of some importance.

6. *Pastoril do Extremo Sul* (Pastoral Zone of the Extreme South).
This region was settled in the eighteenth century by peoples from
São Paulo, the Province of Rio de Janeiro, and the Northeast. Pastoral
activities were and, in spite of some regional diversification, still remain the basis of its economy. Because of neighboring Spanish-
American societies, Spanish influences give distinctive features to the
region. The *estancia* or cattle ranch is its most expressive and characteristic social unit. It produced the gaúcho type, distinguished by
his distinctive dress; and the horse, closely linked to man, is the
most representative element of regional life.

7. *Colonização Estrangeira* (Region of Foreign Colonization).
This was settled by currents of immigrants, first by Germans and
Italians, followed by Poles, Russians, Arabs, and more recently by
Swabians, Dutch and Japanese, who occupied vacant sections of the
extreme south (Rio Grande do Sul, Santa Catarina, Paraná). It is dis-

tinguished by its non-Portuguese, non-Luso-Brazilian cultural characteristics. It would be possible to distinguish areas of original German settlement from those originally Italian, but it was preferred to handle them as one unit. Cultural assimilation is going on with a change of values and interchange of elements, so as to create in this region a way of life of its own.

8. *Café* (Coffee). This is constituted of the area in which coffee trees promoted human settlement in the nineteenth century. It extended from Rio de Janeiro through the Paraíba Valley into Minas Gerais and São Paulo, from which in our days it has expanded into Paraná. In the middle part of the nineteenth century its phase of splendor was accomplished in two ways: coffee culture based on slave labor (Rio de Janeiro, Minas Gerais, and part of São Paulo), and use of free labor of immigrants (southern Minas Gerais and part of São Paulo). The coffee fazenda is its characteristic nucleus, with social and political influence radiating from it. From it came the notable coffee barons, the holders of high titles, cabinet chiefs, ministers, senators of the Empire. It is in a phase of intense modification because of the introduction of cattle raising in decadent coffee zones and because of industrialization. The latter today is the most significant feature of social and economic development in São Paulo, Guanabara, and Rio de Janeiro, and above all in the Paraíba Valley, which already is known as the "Valley of Smokestacks."

9. *Faixa Industrial* (Industrial Belt). This, which has arisen recently in the zones once occupied by coffee, has been responsible for the social transformations, and not merely the economic ones, which have been taking place. It is constituted by the industrial areas of the states of Rio de Janeiro, Guanabara, São Paulo, and a part of Minas Gerais. From it have spread influences on the social structures of the belt occupied by industrial plants, across the coffee area, and reaching into Minas Gerais, a part of the old mining region.

PART TWO

The People

The study of population is among the most rapidly advancing fields of knowledge. Until recently, when the results of the 1950 Census of the Americas became available, in most comparative studies the data for South American countries have been lacking. This part, consisting of seven chapters, is devoted to the important aspects of Brazilian demography.

CHAPTER III

NUMBER, DISTRIBUTION, AND GROWTH
OF POPULATION

As well as may be determined, in 1960 Brazil's population totaled approximately 70,800,000. This statement is based upon the following facts: a 1960 census was taken as of September 1 of that year; on October 20, 1961, the Serviço Nacional de Recenseamento gave out a press release giving 70,528,681 as the provisional total number of inhabitants enumerated in that census; and a few months later, on January 5, 1962, the *Boletim Informativo* distributed by the Brazilian Embassy in Washington, D. C., contained an item to the effect that the membership of Congress had been established in the manner prescribed by the constitution on the basis of a population of 70,799,422 inhabitants as determined by the latest census. Finally, after the preliminary report for Paraná was released, the total mounted to 70,967,115. Therefore, for a decade to come, the figure of 71,000,000 in 1960 will be the principal "bench mark" in the discussion of the size of Brazil's population.

The most noteworthy thing about this figure is its size. As is well known, most estimates of population tend to exaggerate the number of residents actually present in a city, state, or nation; and the 1960 *Anuário Estatístico do Brasil* carries an estimate of 66,302,271 for the population of Brazil as of July 1, 1960.[1] Therefore, the number enumerated in Brazil's 1960 census comes as a surprise to all who have interested themselves in matters relating to the population of the nation. Not only is it four and one-half millions more than anticipated, but it means that the recorded rate of increase between 1950 and 1960 must be indicated as 3.1 per annum instead of the already exceptionally high figure of 2.7 that had been entering into the calculations. Furthermore, for some years to come there is likely to be debate and disagreement relative to the reasons for the surprise: was there a failure to enumerate two or three million persons in the 1950 census, or is the birth rate actually somewhere between 42 and 46 accompanied by a death rate 31 points lower, or from 10 to 15? Such questions are not likely to be resolved until some time after the age-sex distributions of the 1960 population become available, if they are, even then.

[1] *Anuário Estatístico do Brasil, 1960,* XXI (Rio de Janeiro, 1960), 22.

In 1960 density of population, measured in terms of persons per square kilometer, was 8.3, an increase from 6.2 in 1950. The equivalents in terms of persons per square mile are 21.5 and 16.1, respectively. For purposes of comparison it is also well to have in mind that the number of inhabitants per square mile of territory in the 48 contiguous states of the United States was 20 in 1950 and 22 in 1960. Elsewhere about 1950 the number of people per square kilometer was as follows: Mexico, 13; Argentina, 6; Egypt, 20; Japan, 225; India, 113; the Philippines, 65; France, 76; and the United Kingdom, 207.[2]

Data from the 1950 censuses supplemented by estimates by the present writer indicate that there were in 1950 about 154 million people in the twenty Latin-American Republics and approximately 109 million in the eleven of them that are located in the South American continent. Therefore, Brazil, or Portuguese America, should be thought of as containing fully one-half of the inhabitants of South America, and somewhat more than one-third of the total population of the Latin-American countries. Its population is a little more than double that of Mexico, about three and one-half times that of Argentina, nearly five times that of Colombia, and approximately ten times that of Cuba, Chile, or Venezuela.[3]

DISTRIBUTION

The distribution of Brazil's population among the twenty-one states, five territories, and the Federal District, is indicated in Table I. The largest state in terms of population is São Paulo, which in 1960 had nearly 13 million inhabitants, or 18.3 per cent of all the people in Brazil. Minas Gerais, with almost 10 million, is the second most populous state, followed by Bahia and Rio Grande do Sul. Pernambuco and Paraná rank fifth and sixth, respectively, and the states of Rio de Janeiro, Ceará, and Guanabara are next in order. Amazonas has the fewest inhabitants of any of the Brazilian states, followed by Sergipe; next come Rio Grande do Norte, Espírito Santo, and Piauí in the order named.

In 1950 Brazil's center of population fell in the east south-central part of Minas Gerais, not far from Belo Horizonte, and it probably is located in essentially the same position today. The center of population is, of course, very far from the center of the nation's territory. Since the center of population in the United States is in southeastern Illinois, a comparison of the maps of the two countries will show Brazil's population to be concentrated in the south near the coast, to an even greater extent than our own is in the northeastern part of the country. Furthermore, between 1920 and 1950 the center of Brazil's population moved to the south in a slightly easterly direction, and this trend probably was accentuated between 1950 and 1960. This means that the population has tended to become even more con-

[2] *Demographic Yearbook*, 1951 (New York, 1952), 91–103.
[3] Cf. T. Lynn Smith, *Latin American Population Studies* (Gainesville, 1961), 3.

TABLE I

Number of Inhabitants, Area, Density of Population, and Percentage Distribution of Population in Brazil, by States and Territories, 1960 *

State	Population	Area (square kilometers)	Inhabitants per square kilometer	Per cent of total population
Brazil	70,967,115	8,513,844 †	8.3	100.0
North				
Rondonia ‡	70,783	242,983	0.3	0.1
Acre ‡	160,208	152,589	1.0	0.2
Amazonas	721,215	1,556,988	0.5	1.0
Rio Branco ‡	29,489	230,660	0.1	§
Pará	1,550,935	1,250,003	1.2	2.2
Amapá	68,889	137,303	0.5	0.1
Northeast				
Maranhão	2,492,139	332,174	7.5	3.5
Piauí	1,263,368	251,683	5.0	1.8
Ceará	3,337,856	147,895	22.6	4.7
Rio Grande do Notre	1,157,258	53,069	21.8	1.6
Paraíba	2,018,023	56,556	35.7	2.7
Pernambuco	4,136,900	98,079	42.2	5.8
Alagôas	1,271,062	27,793	45.7	2.0
Fernando de Noronha ‡	1,389	27	51.4	§
East				
Sergipe	760,273	22,027	34.5	1.1
Bahia	5,990,605	563,367	10.6	8.5
Minas Gerais	9,798,880	581,975	16.8	13.8
Serra dos Aimorés ‖	384,297	10,137	37.9	0.5
Espírito Santo	1,188,665	39,577	30.0	1.7
Rio de Janeiro	3,402,728	42,588	70.0	4.8
Guanabara	3,307,163	1,356	4,389.0	4.7
South				
São Paulo	12,974,699	247,222	52.5	18.3
Paraná	4,277,763	200,857	21.3	6.0
Santa Cátarina	2,146,909	94,798	22.6	3.0
Rio Grande do Sul	5,448,823	282,480	19.3	7.7
West Central				
Mato Grosso	910,262	1,261,094	0.7	1.3
Goiás	1,954,862	617,098	3.2	2.7
Distrito Federal	141,742	5,814	24.4	0.2

* Compiled and computed from data on population given in a 1961 release by the Serviço de Recenseamento, Instituto Brasileiro de Geografia e Estatística and data on areas given in the *Anuário Estatístico do Brasil, 1960*, XXI (Rio de Janeiro, 1960), 5.

† Total includes 3,192 square kilometers in an area that is in litigation between the states of Amazonas and Pará, and 2,460 square kilometers in litigation between the states of Piauí and Ceará.

‡ Territory.

§ Less than 0.1 per cent.

‖ Area in dispute between the states of Minas Gerais and Espírito Santo.

centrated in this limited portion of the nation's territory. The growth and development of the cities of Rio de Janeiro, São Paulo, and Pôrto Alegre were of course the principal factors which pulled the center of population to the south. However, such a tendency must be overcome before the much heralded *Marcha para Oeste* can get out of the slogan stage. Moving the nation's capital to Brasília represents a serious attempt to get this process under way.

One need only glance at a map of Brazil showing the distribution of population by municípios (see Figure 3) to see the overwhelming extent to which the population is confined to a narrow band along the seacoast. From the Bragança district of Pará to Rio Grande do Sul there are few areas within two hundred miles of the seacoast which are not rather densely populated. In the same enormous extension of littoral there are only a few places where fingers of dense settlement have been pushed inland for any considerable distance.

The tremendous variations in density of population prevailing throughout Brazil are readily apparent and call for little comment. It is significant, however, that only Amazonas, Pará, Maranhão, Piauí, Mato Grosso, and Goiás have indexes that are below the national average.

The chief exceptions to a concentration of population in coastal areas are the jungles of western Maranhão, the low-lying swamplands that lie between the Serra do Mar and the coast in southern Bahia and the northern portion of Espírito Santo, the lower Ribeira Valley in São Paulo, and the sandy peninsulas which make up most of the coastline of Rio Grande do Sul.

The most significant penetration of dense settlement into the interior is that westward across the state of São Paulo. As will be observed in Figure 3, already the west-central part of this state is one of the most densely populated portions of Brazil. This surge of people to the west continues. It is forming supplementary lines of penetration, imperfectly revealed by the map which has to use municípios as units, along the railroad which crosses southern Mato Grosso, southwest into northern Paraná, and north through the panhandle (Triangulo) of Minas Gerais, and on into central Goiás. One of the most significant features of Brazil's population changes is the rapidity with which the density of population in south-central Goiás is increasing at the present time. The new state capital, Goiânia, founded in 1937 on the crest of the high plains of the region, led all Brazilian cities in rate of growth between 1950 and 1960, a period in which the number of inhabitants in the município in which it is located increased from 53,389 to 153,505, for a gain of 188 per cent. This increase was closely related, of course, to the founding of Brasília, a city which in 1960, only a little more than a year after it became capital, already boasted 89,698 inhabitants, and there were 52,044 more enumerated in the rural portions of the new Federal District.

The second more important penetration of thick settlement into Brazil's hinterland is that which has taken place in Rio Grande do

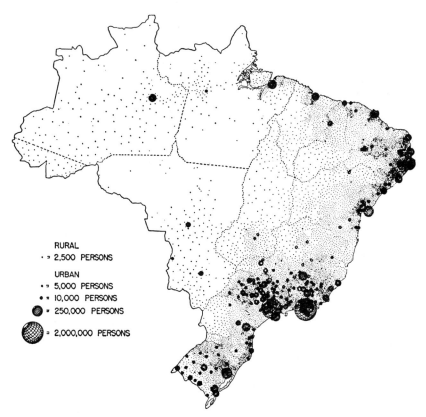

RURAL
• ≥ 2,500 PERSONS

URBAN
• ≥ 5,000 PERSONS
● ≈ 10,000 PERSONS
◉ ≈ 250,000 PERSONS
◍ ≈ 2,000,000 PERSONS

F I G U R E 3 . Distribution of the population in Brazil, 1940, from T. Lynn Smith and Alexander Marchant (eds.), *Brazil: Portrait of Half a Continent* (New York, 1951), 148. Reproduced by permission of the Dryden Press.

Sul. This tide of migration which stemmed from the agricultural colonies north of Pôrto Alegre has already blanketed most of northwestern Rio Grande do Sul with small farms. It is now moving gradually to the south on a broad front.

Several other penetrations of dense settlement into the interior also are reflected on this map. That which has taken place in southeastern Minas Gerais is one of the more important. It is also recent, and as the River Doce Valley is further developed, this area of dense settlement may be expected to increase in size and intensity. In Santa Catarina settlement is pushing up the Tubarão and Itajaí valleys and spilling over onto the highlands. In the east and northeast, too, several rather densely populated sections have been developed at some distance from the coast. Thus the municípios which lie along the railroad from Bahia's capital to Joázeiro on the Rio São Francisco constitute an important penetration of rather dense settlement. Another is found in southern Ceará and western Paraíba. And, finally, it is evident that the density of population already has become rather

43

pronounced along both sides of the Parnaíba River which separates Piauí from Maranhão.

But in Brazil there still remains ample space for millions of additional inhabitants. Most of the country continues to be merely occupied, and not settled. Between the Colombian border and that of Uruguay there are few sections in which thousands of new settlers could not find places for homes and natural resources awaiting their exploitation. To fill its vast empty space, spread a population over the land, and make its vast storehouse of natural resources effective in contributing to man's well being is the tremendous task confronting Brazil.

GROWTH

Before 1890 the counts of Brazil's population left a great deal to be desired. Even the census of 1872, made during the Imperial period, was a short count, especially with respect to the enumeration of young children. Such historical data as are available relative to the early growth of population have been carefully summarized by the nation's foremost population authority, F. J. Oliveira Vianna, in "O Povo Brazileiro e sua Evolução." [4] Table II presents some of the "bench marks" from this compilation, along with the results of the official censuses made in 1872, 1890, 1900, 1920, 1940, 1950, and 1960. These entries are sufficient to trace the principal lines of the

TABLE II

Growth of Population, 1808–1960 *

Year	Population
1808	2,419,406
1823	3,960,866
1830	5,340,000
1854	7,677,800
1872	9,930,478
1890	14,333,915
1900	17,318,556
1920	30,635,605
1940	41,565,083
1950	51,944,397
1960	70,967,185

* Sources: *Recenseamento do Brazil, 1920,* I (Rio de Janeiro, 1922), 403–421; "Censo Demográfico," *VI Recenseamento Geral do Brasil, 1950,* I (Rio de Janeiro, 1956), 1; and *VII Recenseamento Geral do Brasil, 1960* (Rio de Janeiro, 1961).

[4] First published in "Introducção," *Recenseamento do Brazil, 1920,* I (Rio de Janeiro, 1922), it has appeared in separate editions and has also been published in Spanish.

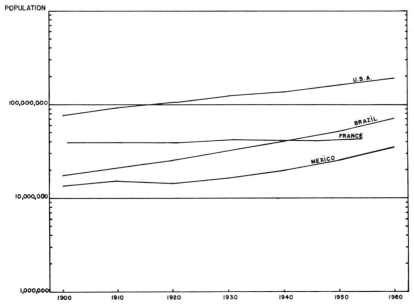

FIGURE 4. The growth of population during the twentieth century in Brazil, the United States, France, and Mexico.

numerical growth of population in Brazil. The manner in which the population of Brazil grew during the twentieth century, along with comparable materials for the United States and a few other selected countries, is portrayed graphically in Figure 4.

During the twentieth century the growth of population in Brazil has been the most rapid of that in any of the larger countries of the world, and this has been especially true since the middle of the century. Between 1900 and 1950 the annual rate of increase averaged about 2.0 per cent, and on the basis of the preliminary data from the 1960 census, a rate of 3.1 per annum seems to have prevailed between 1950 and 1960.

Because of considerable regional differences in the birth and death rates, and especially because of great currents of internal migration, the rate at which the population is increasing varies tremendously from one part of Brazil to another. See Table III and Figures 5, 6, and 7. Table III presents for each of the states and territories information about the absolute and relative increases in population between 1900 and 1950 and between 1950 and 1960. The maps in Figures 5 and 6, respectively, enable one to see at a glance the comparative sizes of the increments and the rates of change in the various states and territories, the first for the decade ending in 1950 and the second for that immediately preceding the 1960 census. Figure 7, in turn, traces the growth of population in each of Brazil's eight most populous states over the entire sixty-year period, 1900 to 1960. In the following brief comment on the changes, attention is given first to those

45

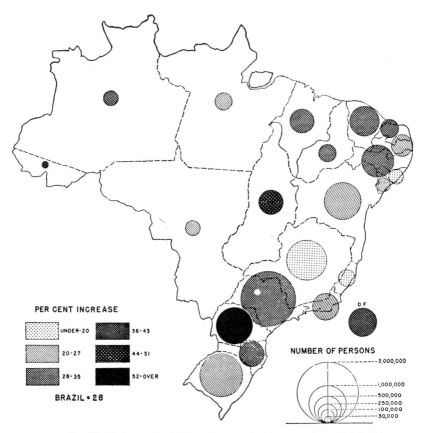

PER CENT INCREASE

UNDER-20		36-43
20-27		44-51
28-35		52-OVER

BRAZIL = 28

D F

NUMBER OF PERSONS

- - - - - - - 2,000,000

- - - - - 1,000,000

- - - - 500,000
- - - 250,000
- - - 100,000
- - - 30,000

FIGURE 5. Absolute and relative changes in the number of inhabitants, 1940 to 1950, by states.

taking place during the first one-half of the twentieth century and then to those between 1950 and 1960.

Great state and regional differences in rates of population growth were the rule in the period 1900 to 1950. Thus, for example, the populations of Alagôas and Sergipe failed to double themselves during the first half of the twentieth century, whereas the number of inhabitants of Paraná was more than six and one-half times greater in 1950 than it had been in 1900. Both Santa Catarina and Goiás had almost five times as many people at the end of the fifty-year period as at the beginning; in the other leading states, Espírito Santo and Mato Grosso, the corresponding ratio is approximately four and one half.

In 1900 Minas Gerais led all the states of Brazil in population, Bahia closely rivaled São Paulo for second position, and Pernambuco was fourth. The differential rates of increase during the half century made considerable changes in these relative positions and also in those of the less populous states. By 1950 São Paulo had by far the greatest number of inhabitants, and the former leader, Minas Gerais,

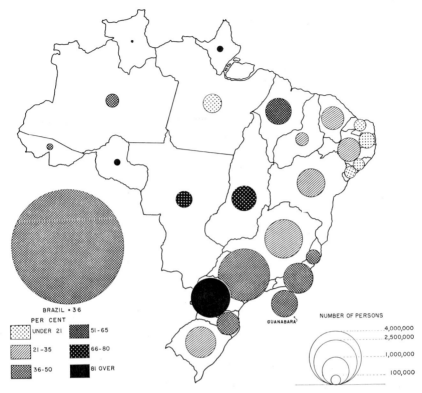

FIGURE 6. Absolute and relative increases in the number of inhabitants, 1950 to 1960, by states and territories.

had been relegated to a poor second. Bahia still held third position, although it was rivaled by Rio Grande do Sul, which had supplanted Pernambuco in fourth place.

The most spectacular rises in rank order were those of Paraná, which moved up from fifteenth position in 1900 to ninth in 1950, Goiás, which rose from eighteenth to thirteenth, and Santa Catarina which ascended from sixteenth to twelfth place. Espírito Santo, Paraíba, Ceará, and the Distrito Federal improved their standings among the states with respect to rank in number of inhabitants. Rio Grande do Norte and Mato Grosso ranked in the same positions, seventeenth and twenty-first, respectively, in both 1900 and 1950. In addition to Minas Gerais and Pernambuco, mentioned before, seven other states were overtaken in the half century and passed by one or more of their sisters in the confederation and, as a result, occupied lower ranks in the population scale in 1950 than they did in 1900. Most drastic were the changes in the cases of Alagôas and Sergipe, which fell from ninth and fifteenth to thirteenth and nineteenth positions, respectively.

The state of São Paulo alone accounted for almost one fifth of the total increase in Brazil's population between 1900 and 1950, although

TABLE III

Growth of Population 1900–1950 and 1950–1960, by States *

State	Increase of population 1900–1950		Increase of population 1950–1960	
	Number	Per cent	Number	Per cent
Brazil	34,413,003	197	19,022,788	37
North				
Rondonia †	—	—	33,848	92
Acre †	22,376	24	45,453	40
Amazonas	282,459	113	207,116	40
Rio Branco †	—	—	11,373	63
Pará	715,394	161	427,662	38
Amapá †	—	—	31,412	84
Northeast				
Maranhão	1,083,940	217	908,891	57
Piauí	711,368	213	217,672	21
Ceará	1,846,323	217	642,406	24
Rio Grande do Norte	693,604	253	189,337	20
Paraíba	1,222,475	249	304,764	18
Pernambuco	2,217,035	188	741,715	22
Alagôas	443,864	68	177,925	16
Fernando de Noronha †	—	—	808	139
East				
Sergipe	288,097	81	115,912	18
Bahia	2,716,619	128	1,156,030	24
Minas Gerais	4,203,357	117	2,081,088	27
Serra dos Aimorés ‡	—	—	224,225	140
Espírito Santo	731,815	349	327,103	38
Rio de Janeiro	1,371,159	148	1,105,534	48
Guanabara	1,566,008	193	929,712	39
South				
São Paulo	6,852,144	300	3,840,276	42
Paraná	1,788,411	547	2,162,216	102
Santa Catarina	1,240,213	387	586,407	38
Rio Grande do Sul	3,015,751	262	1,284,002	31
West Central				
Mato Grosso	440,954	374	388,218	74
Goiás **	959,637	372	881,683	73

* Computed from data in "Censo Demográfico," VI *Recenseamento Geral do Brasil, 1950*, I (Rio de Janeiro, 1956), and a 1961 mimeographed release by the Serviço de Recenseamento, Instituto Brasileiro de Geografia e Estatística.

† Territory. For the purpose of making the computation for the period 1900 to 1950, the 1950 data for Rondonia were included with those for Mato Grosso, the data for Rio Branco with those for Amazonas, and the data for Amapá with those for Pará. The 1900–1950 data for Acre are for the years 1920 to 1950.

‡ Territory in litigation between the states of Minas Gerais and Espírito Santo. For the purpose of making the computation for the period 1900 to 1950, 50 per cent of the 1950 population was allocated to each state.

** 1960 data for the new Federal District are included with those for Goiás.

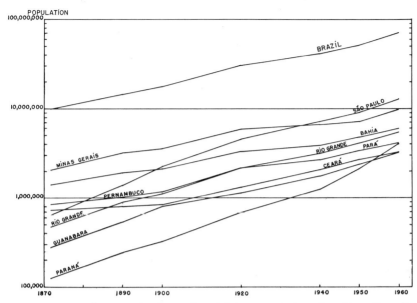

FIGURE 7. The growth of population between 1872 and 1960 in Brazil's most populous states.

her rate of increase for the period (305 per cent) was exceeded by those of five other states. Together the four southern states—São Paulo, Paraná, Santa Catarina, and Rio Grande do Sul—included one third of the total increase in the number of inhabitants in the nation for the period under consideration, although they embrace less than 10 per cent of the nation's area. If the changes in the former Distrito Federal and those in the states of Rio de Janeiro and Espírito Santo are grouped with those for the four southern states, the combined area, less than 11 per cent of the national territory, accounted for almost one-half (48 per cent) of the increase in the Brazilian population. Over the half century under consideration, several of the northeastern states also exhibited rates of population increase considerably above the national average. Those in Rio Grande do Norte and Paraíba were the highest, although the ones for Ceará, Maranhão, and Piauí also were high.

After 1950 the state and regional differentials in rates of growth of the population contrast considerably with those prevailing during the first one-half of the twentieth century. See Table III and Figure 6. It is true that Paraná led all the states in the decade that ended in 1960, just as it did for the half century under consideration. Santa Catarina, however, failed to keep the pace, and Mato Grosso and its close rival, Goiás, became the second and third most rapidly growing states in Brazil. Even their high rates of increase were exceeded by those in the territories of Rondonia and Amapá, and also in the disputed territory of the Serra dos Aimorés. Also in the period 1950 to 1960 great upsurges of population took place in Maran-

49

hão and the state of Rio de Janeiro, in the former because of the heavy influx of squatters from the more arid sections of the Northeast and in the latter because the proximity of available land and the direction and nature of transportation facilities produced a huge mushrooming of population in the suburban portions of the metropolis of Rio de Janeiro which lie just outside the limits of the state of Guanabara.

Alagôas and Sergipe were the states with the lowest rates of population growth between 1950 and 1960, just as they had been during the half century, 1900 to 1950. They were joined in this respect, however, by Paraíba, which previously had ranked much higher; and the rates were comparatively low also in other northeastern states, such as Rio Grande do Norte, Piauí, Pernambuco, and Ceará, although in most other parts of the world increases of above 20 per cent in a single decade would not be considered low.

On the absolute basis, the increase of population between 1950 and 1960 of almost four million in the state of São Paulo deserves special attention. It followed directly upon one of nearly seven million between 1900 and 1950. As a result, that great state's share of the nation's people increased steadily from 13.1 per cent in 1900 to 18.3 per cent in 1960. Next to the large increment in São Paulo, the largest increases during the decade ending in 1960 were in Minas Gerais, Paraná, Rio Grande do Sul, Rio de Janeiro, and Maranhão. Because of these changes between 1950 and 1960, the "march to the south," a trend that was very pronounced during the first half of the twentieth century, went on rapidly. By 1960 the four states of the southern region contained approximately 35 per cent of all the people in Brazil, and if the state of Rio de Janeiro and the city of Rio de Janeiro (or the state of Guanabara) is included with them, the six together accounted for 44 per cent of the population of the entire nation.

CHAPTER IV

RACIAL COMPOSITION

A THOROUGH STUDY of the racial make-up of the Brazilian population and of the manner in which the various elements are distributed among the regions and classes of the country would in itself be a life's work. If the United States is described as a "melting pot," Brazil must be considered a caldron. No other country has had for four hundred years such large numbers of white, red, and black people thrown into so close physical and social contact with one another. To the already extremely heterogeneous population, composed of these three original strains and of which the white Portuguese component was already a composite of many elements, the nineteenth and twentieth centuries brought millions of Europeans, mainly Italians, Germans, Poles, Portuguese, and Spaniards, and the twentieth century has added large contingents of Lebanese and Japanese.

RACIAL ELEMENTS

Nearly all known ethnic stocks have contributed to the present-day racial elements of which Brazil's population is composed. However, until well along in the nineteenth century Portugal's colonial policy was one of severe restriction of immigration, with the result that the bulk of the people in Brazil are descended from the three more important strains: (1) the Portuguese colonists, (2) the native Indians whom the colonists enslaved and by whose women they produced a mixed-blood offspring (the mamelucos), whose exploits as Indian hunters probably have never been equaled, and (3) millions of Negro slaves who were imported from Africa. To these only need be added the elements introduced by immigration of Europeans (especially Italians, Germans, and Poles) during the late nineteenth and early twentieth centuries, and the importation of Japanese since 1908.

If one would know the reasons underlying Brazil's population history, he should first remember that the central theme of the nation's social and economic history is *falta de braços*, which can best be translated as "lack of hands." To secure a cheap supply of agricultural labor has been the dominating motive in Brazil's population policy from the earliest colonial days to the present time. If during early centuries the need of workers on sugar plantations in Bahia, Pernambuco, the lower Paraíba, and other coastal areas dominated the national immigration policy and determined the elements that were added to the population, in later years São Paulo's coffee and cotton fazendas have played a similar role. Therefore, a brief consideration of Brazil's struggle to secure an abundant labor supply for its agriculture is a logical beginning in the analysis of the elements that have entered into its population make-up.

THE LONG-CONTINUED LABOR SHORTAGE

That the shortage of workers, falta de braços, is the central theme of Brazil's social and economic history is well known by all who are acquainted with the nation's history. Thousands of books, pamphlets, and articles have been written about this or that aspect of Brazil's social, economic, agricultural, and industrial problems. They are written in all degrees of quality and in many languages. However, in this immense literature it would be difficult to find a single treatise which does not make reference to the nation's need for more workers. If one travels through Brazil he will hear the same refrain, falta de braços, from Amazonas to Rio Grande do Sul, from Rio Grande do Norte to Mato Grosso. This is not surprising if three important items are kept in mind: (1) that most of Brazil's vast territorial expanse is underpopulated, (2) that much of Brazil is more "occupied" than "settled," and (3) that the dominant position of the huge landed estate in Brazil has determined that the nation's immigration policy should be designed to secure laborers to work on the fazendas rather than independent proprietors to carve new farms out of the wilderness.

That most of Brazil is underpopulated is indicated by the huge distances which, except near the coast, separate the nuclei of population from one another. One sees little to distinguish the vila or povoação in Minas Gerais or Rio de Janeiro from the "town" or "village" in Mato Grosso or Amazonas. But in the former states these small population centers will be encountered every few miles, while in the latter frequently they are separated by hundreds of miles. The underpopulation of the country is also indicated by the fact that its territory, more extensive than the United States minus Alaska, contains only about one third as many inhabitants as our own country. Furthermore, although northeastern Brazil suffers severely from periodic droughts, the proportion of the country where low annual rainfall dictates a sparse population is extremely small in comparison with the huge expanses of our western plains and intermountain regions. Millions of additional Brazilians could grow prosperous in areas which at present seldom or never feel the impress of a human foot, if they were properly equipped with those portions of the man-made environment that would enable them to safeguard health and to magnify the strength of the human arm in its struggle with the jungle.

The emphasis on the need for more workers also grows in part out of the fact that much of Brazil is still more occupied than settled. With minor exceptions, particularly in parts of São Paulo and Rio Grande do Sul, only a narrow stretch of the littoral is really settled. The remainder of the country is more correctly described as merely occupied. This is to say that the greater part of Brazil is cut up into huge estates on which a few cattle are grazed, or a scattered population is engaged in the collection of mate, rubber, rosewood, babassú, carnaúba, Brazil nuts, and hundreds of other forest products, searching for diamonds or other precious stones, washing for gold, or merely in hunting and fishing. The landowner and the handful of people whom he employs to work on his vast acreages, or who are permitted to live there, have occupied the territory, but they have not settled it. When, as is now the situation in western São Paulo, northern Paraná, and northeastern Rio Grande do Sul, hundreds of new farms and thousands of new families are established on acreages that formerly merely provided a meager livelihood for a fazendeiro and a few of his agregados, the significance of this distinction between settlement and mere occupation becomes evident. But even in the 1960's in all the vast expanse of territory between the Colombian frontier and the Uruguayan border there were few sections in which thousands of settlers could not find land and natural resources awaiting exploitation by man. As one studies Brazil's land system, it becomes clear why in Brazilian terminology latifundium means not merely a large landed estate but has the additional significant connotation of large acreages purposely withheld from productive uses.

Finally, it is important to note that in Brazil underpopulation and the demand for more people take the form of a cry for more workers and not, as a rule, for more families to carve homes for themselves out of the wilderness. Very early most of the land passed into the private possession of a limited number of people.[1] From the very

[1] As late as 1821 James Henderson wrote about São Paulo:
"It is a great misfortune to the Brazil, that extensive tracts of land have been granted to donatories, who do not possess the means of cultivating one-hundredth part of it, but hold it on under the expectation that the gradual improvement of the country will render it daily more valuable, and the residence of the court here induces them to adhere more strongly to this impression: if they dispose of any part of it, they generally subject it to a fine, and the consequences attending such a contract will present a decided obstacle to the agricultural improvement of this country, not at all proportioned to its extent or superabundant powers. Individuals who would devote their exertions and property to the culture of the soil, where this mode prevails, must be effectually deterred. The province of St. Paulo, which may be estimated to contain one hundred and twenty thousand square miles, has no land devoluto, or ungranted, although one-thirtieth part of it is not in a state of cultivation." *A History of the Brazil; Comprising Its Geography, Commerce, Colonization, Aboriginal Inhabitants, &c.* (London, 1821), 86–87.
In other places the concentration of land ownership was probably even greater. In Bahia a large share of the land early came into the hands of two families, that of the Senhor da Torre and of Antonio Guedes de Britto. The first possessed "260 leagues of land on the right hand side of the upper São Francisco River and running to the south," and "running on the said river towards the north . . . 80 leagues." The second had "160 leagues . . . from the Morro dos Chapéos to the headwaters of the Rio das Velhas." Gilberto Freyre, *Casa Grande & Senzala* (3d ed.; Rio de Janeiro, 1938), 37.

first Brazil has been a country of large landed estates in which the
overwhelming proportion of the population was engaged in working
the land of others, first as slaves and later as laborers. Therefore,
most of the nation's recent efforts to stimulate immigration, and
particularly the vigorous policy of São Paulo, have been especially designed and administered to attract a supply of agricultural laborers.
It cannot be overemphasized that Brazilian immigration policy has
been dominated by the shortage of workers on its fazendas and not
by the immensity of the sparsely populated portions of the national
territory. It is largely because of this dominance of the large landed
estate that falta de braços has been the dominant note in Brazil's social and economic history.

Highlights in the four-hundred-year-old struggle to supply enough
hands for Brazilian fazendas are (1) the hunting, capture, and enslavement of the native Indian populations, (2) the importation of
millions of Negro slaves from Africa to work the sugar plantations
of the littoral, and (3) São Paulo's long-continued and vigorous efforts to supply its coffee and cotton fazendas with cheap agricultural
labor. Probably the most significant aspects of the latter have been
the importation of more than a million Italians, an immigration
which has contributed to a radical change in the ethnic composition
of São Paulo's population, and the admission of a recorded immigration of some 200,000 Japanese between 1925 and 1940. Together with
their descendants these members of the yellow race now number almost 500,000 persons, or more than 4 per cent of the state's population.

Enslavement of Indians. Brazilian Indians were not pushed westward, or killed, like those of the United States, or gathered together
into missions and taught the elements of Christianity like those in
some parts of Spain's colonies.[2] They were hunted down and enslaved
to provide a supply of laborers for the rapidly expanding sugar
engenhos. These and other large-scale agricultural undertakings set
the pattern and guided the policies in the peopling of Brazil from
colonial times until the present time.

During the entire colonial period Brazil was dominated by the large
sugar plantation—the engenho. According to Oliveira Vianna, Brazil
did not know the small farm until the last century. From the first Brazil was a land of latifundia. "All the long colonial period was a time of
the splendor and glory of the large landed property." [3] To clear and
cultivate the land for these large sugar estates, to wait upon and serve
the members of the land-owning aristocracy, and to perform the other
multifarious tasks of the little world which was the engenho required a large number of workers. Oliveira Vianna cites authorities
who place at two hundred the average number of slaves per Brazilian
sugar plantation.[4] In the formative years these slaves were Indians.

[2] The exceptions are relatively rare instances under the Jesuits.
[3] Oliveira Vianna, "O Povo Brazileiro e sua Evolução," *Recenseamento do Brazil, 1920,* I, 282.
[4] *Ibid.,* 289.

Although the Portuguese possessed African slaves before they began the settlement of Brazil, comparatively few Negroes were introduced into the colony during the first two centuries of its existence. The wars with Holland were largely responsible for this and for forcing the Portuguese in Brazil to look elsewhere for a labor supply. The native Indian population was a logical source. The hunting down and the enslavement of the Indians, again to use the words of Oliveira Vianna, became "a true profession of warlike character, practiced by intrepid *sertanistas* [frontiersmen], who, in the north, as well as in the south, entered the interior at the front of their formidable bands of mamelucos, assaulted the villages of the poorly armed savages, and carried to the latifundia of the coastal areas thousands of Indian slaves." [5]

Of all these early man hunters those of São Paulo gained the greatest notoriety. Paulista bandeirantes ranged far and wide throughout the entire length and breadth of what is present-day Brazil, from the sertões of Ceará on the north to the upper reaches of the Amazon on the west and the plains of Rio Grande do Sul on the south, in search of their human quarry. [6] Not content to confine their enslaving activities to the Indians who remained in their native state, they fell upon and carried into captivity the thousands of red men whom the Jesuit fathers had collected into compact villages and educated far along in the religious and agricultural practices of the whites. [7] The exploits

[5] *Ibid.*, 290.

[6] Cf. Alfred Ellis, Jr., *O Bandeirismo Paulista e o Recúo do Meridiano* (3d ed.; São Paulo, 1938). This, along with the works of other Brazilian scholars, such as those of Afonso de E. Taunay, indicates how these "raids" of the bandeirantes secured for Brazil the vast areas of its territory which lie west of the line which the Pope established to divide the American possessions of Portugal and Spain.

[7] For this phase of their activities consult Thomas J. Page, *La Plata, the Argentine Confederation, and Paraguay* (New York, 1859), 476–83. Page sets at 60,000 the number of Indian slaves sold in the public square in Rio de Janeiro in the years 1628 to 1630, the time of these depredations. See also Oliveira Vianna, "O Povo Brasileiro e sua Evolução," *loc. cit.*, 289–90.

Details of the reduction of these Jesuit missions are given in the following extract from the writings of one of the Jesuit fathers. Even if allowance is made for a large margin of error in the figures, one may be certain that the number of Indians captured and carried to the slave marts for sale was very large. "These rapid progresses in the Christian cause have been miserably retarded by the Mamalukes from Brazil, a bordering country, and principally from St. Paulo. The Mamalukes are a set of people born of Portugueze, Dutch, French, Italians and Germans, and Brazilian women, celebrated for skill in shooting and robbing, ready for any daring enterprize, and thence distinguished by the foreign name of Mamalukes: for it was their constant custom to carry off the Indians, led by the Fathers into the freedom of the children of God, into the hardest slavery. By their incursions, repeated for a number of years, they overthrew the towns of Asumpcion in Yeyuy, of Todos Santos in Caarõ, of the holy Apostles in Caazapaguazù, of St. Christopher on the opposite side of the Ygay, of St. Joachim in the same place, of Santa Barbara, on the western bank of the Paraguay, and of St. Carlos in Caapi. The Guarany inhabitants of these colonies, with the exception of a few who escaped by flight, were led away to Brazil, chained and corded, in herds, like cattle, and there condemned to perpetual labour in the working of sugar, mandioc, cotton, mines, and tobacco. The sucking babes were torn from the bosoms of their mothers, and cruelly dashed upon the ground by the way. All whom disease or age had rendered imbecile were either cut down or shot, as being unequal to the daily march. Others, in sound health, were often thrown by night into trenches prepared for them, lest they should take advantage of the darkness, and flee. Many perished by the way, either from hunger or the hardships of a journey of these bandeirantes from São Paulo constitute as great a chapter in the history of Brazil as those of the Indian fighters and frontiersmen in the annals of the United States.

But the supply of Indians was not sufficient for all purposes; the red men were not tractable workers and were constantly fleeing the plantations; and the wars with Holland finally came to an end. African slaves replaced Indians in agricultural work; and as Indian slavery was gradually abandoned, the red man was used mainly in pastoral areas to look after the corrals and the herds, and as a fighter.[8]

The Magnitude of the "Traffic." Just how many Negroes were imported into Brazil as slaves is a moot question that probably can never be adequately answered. The same applies to the kindred query as to how prolific were the members of the Negro race during the colonial epoch of Brazil. Certain it is that there was no exceedingly large emigration of Negroes from Brazil,[9] but unless it is granted that they failed almost entirely to reproduce [10] or that they

---

protracted for many leagues. In this hunting of the Indians, they sometimes employed open violence, sometimes craft, equally inhuman in both. They generally rushed into the town in a long file, when the people were assembled in the church at divine service, and, blocking up every street and corner, left the wretched inhabitants no way of escape. They frequently disguised themselves as Jesuits, wearing rosaries, crosses and a black gown, and collected companies of Indians in the woods. Many towns that were liable to the treacherous hostilities of the Mamalukes, such as Loretto, St. Ignatius, &c. were removed to safer places, by a journey of many months, and with incredible labour, both of the Fathers and the Indians. Nor did the Mamalukes spare our colonies of the Chiquitos and Moxos, nor others in the hands of the Spaniards, which were administered both by the secular and regular clergy. The Indian towns settled on the banks of the Yeyuy, in Curuquatí, and many others, were entirely destroyed by the Mamalukes. The same fate attended Xerez, Guayra, (Ciudad real,) Villarica, &c. cities of the Spaniards. Who can describe all the devastation committed in Paraguay? Hear what is said on this subject in the collection of *Lettres Curieuses et Edifiantes:*—'It is asserted,' they say, 'that in the space of one hundred and thirty years, two millions of Indians were slain, or carried into capitivity by the Mamalukes of Brazil; and that more than one hundred thousand leagues of country, as far as the river Amazon, was stripped of inhabitants. It appears from authentic letters, (sent by the Catholic King ―――― in the year 1639, 16th Sept.) that in five years three hundred thousand Paraguayrian Indians were carried away into Brazil.' Pedro de Avila, Governour of Buenos-Ayres, declared that Indians were openly sold, in his sight, by the inhabitants of the town of St. Paulo, at Rio Janeiro; and that six hundred thousand Indians were sold, in this town alone, from the year 1628 to the year 1630." Martin Dobrizhoffer, *An Account of the Abipones, An Equestrian People of Paraguay*, trans. (London, 1822), I, 159–62. Robert Southey, *History of Brazil* (London, 1817), II, 309 ff., gives an account that is more charitable to the Paulistas.

[8] The Indian's role of fighter was an important one. "During the 16th and 17th centuries each sugar engenho had to maintain on a war footing its hundreds or at least its tens of men ready to defend the house and the stores accumulated in the warehouses against savages and pirates: these men were almost exclusively Indians or caboclos armed with bows and arrows." Freyre, *Casa Grande & Senzala*, 62.

[9] But there was some. Sir Harry H. Johnston, *The Negro in the New World* (London, 1910), 98, states that 4,000 to 6,000 Negroes from Brazil returned to Africa between 1850 and 1878. See also Donald Pierson, *Negroes in Brazil* (Chicago, 1942), 39, who calls attention to the fact that certain towns on the west coast of Africa may have been named by Negroes who once had lived in Brazil. See also Gilberto Freyre, *Nordeste* (Rio de Janerio, 1937), 130 ff.

[10] Despite the fact that slaves were probably well fed and housed and very well treated generally in Brazil, there seems to have been considerable effort to prevent their reproduction. Note the observations of H. M. Brackenridge, who

died like flies in the new country, one can hardly accept even the more conservative estimates as to the number of slaves that were transported from Africa to Brazil. The necessity of extreme caution in the evaluation of all estimates of the numbers involved in the "traffic" is indicated by the wide discrepancies that appear in the early estimates, those made by people "familiar with the scene," "on the ground," and "in a position to know." Thus the famous Padre José de Anchieta set the population of the Portuguese colony in Brazil as 57,000 in the year 1585. Of this number he said that some 14,000 were African slaves, of whom 10,000 were in Pernambuco, 3,000 in Bahia, and about 100 in Rio de Janeiro. But for the period 1584 to 1590, approximately the same date, Fernão Cardim placed the African

served as secretary to the commission which the United States sent to South America in 1817 to report the situation in the provinces that were revolting from Spain. He stated that the annual importation of slaves into Brazil was about 30,-000, of whom the larger share were males. He also added that it was considered cheaper to import slaves at the prevailing prices of $200 or $300 per head than to rear them. *Voyage to South America* (Baltimore, 1819), I, 167.

In São Paulo: "The black slaves have very few children, which is not entirely explained by the proportion of the female to the male slaves (16:22). One cause may be, that the male slaves, being almost always employed in the labours of agriculture, and tending the cattle, pass the greater part of the year alone in the remote *chacaras* and *fazendas de criar gado*, whereas the female slaves are employed in household services." Von Spix and von Martius, *Travels in Brazil,* II, 11.

A few years later Commander Charles Wilkes of the U. S. Navy stated more positively:

"The slaves do not increase, as procreation is prevented as much as possible. The two sexes are generally locked up at night in separate apartments. The number of slaves imported into Rio and Bahia previous to the prohibition of the slave trade in 1830, was about forty thousand a year for the former, and ten thousand for the latter, as follows:

	Rio	Bahia
1828	41,913	8,860
1829	40,015	12,808
1830 half year	29,777	8,588

"About one-third of these were lost by death, leaving two-thirds as an accession to the labour of the country.

"The number annually imported since 1830, contrary to law, is estimated at seven to ten thousand." *Narrative of the United States Exploring Expedition During the Years 1838, 1839, 1840, 1841, 1842* (New York, 1856), I, 86.

A British writer, Alexander Majorbanks, in the middle of the nineteenth century, also indicated that the Africans in Brazil did not reproduce sufficiently to maintain their numbers:

". . . but who can tell how many slaves it will take to glut the market of Brazil? The half of the population of the continent of Africa would scarcely be sufficient to supply the demand that would spring up under such circumstances. Treated as her slaves are, and as the Brazilians think it their interest to treat them, the time will never come when they will dispense with the necessity of fresh importations from the coast of Africa. But let her be forced to adopt a different line of policy in relation to the treatment of her slaves, and be made to rely upon the natural increase of those already in the country, and the time is not far distant when we may reasonably expect the Brazilians themselves to be utterly opposed to any further accessions to her slaves from the coast of Africa." *Travels in South and North America* (5th ed.; London, 1854), 60. Herbert H. Smith in the 'seventies referred to the practice of locking up Negro men and women in separate quarters at night. *Brazil, the Amazons and the Coast* (New York, 1879), 526.

More recently Calmon generalized: "The Negro, as a rule, did not survive the third generation. Until 1850 the pure blood Negroes were Africans or children of Africans. The number of mulattoes increased as a function of the slave's sociability; that of the Negroes oscillated with the traffic." *Espirito da Sociedade Colonial,* 157.

slave population of Pernambuco at only 2,000 and that of Bahia at 4,000.[11]

The Negroes brought to Brazil included not only representatives of all the various Bantu groups, which also supplied a large share of the slaves for the United States, but also many from the Sudanese groups, including the Minas, Yorbes, Gêges, Haussás, and others from the northern parts of Africa. These peoples in race and culture were considerably different from the Bantus. Many of them through contact with Arabs knew the Arabic language and were of the Mohammedan faith. Negroes of this type were especially important in Bahia,[12] although they could also be found in Rio de Janeiro.[13]

Portuguese Colonists. From the mother country, Portugal, came of course the original white colonists, mostly men. This movement of

[11] Renato Mendonça, *A Influência Africana no Português do Brasil* (São Paulo, 1935), 53.

[12] The last discussion of this subject by Arthur Ramos, Brazil's most noted authority on the Negro, is found in Smith and Marchant (eds.), *Brazil: Portrait of Half a Continent,* Chap. 5. See also Arthur Ramos, *O Negro Brasileiro* (2d ed.; São Paulo, 1940), 22–25; and especially Nina Rodrigues, *Os Africanos no Brasil,* ed. posthumously (São Paulo, 1932). Cf. Oliveira Vianna, "O Povo Brasileiro e sua Evolução," *loc. cit.,* 319.

[13] Of the Minas Negroes in Rio de Janeiro, Wilkes wrote in 1838: "The negroes of Brazil who have been brought from North and South Africa, are divided into two distinct and very dissimilar classes. The natives of that portion of the continent known under the general name of Upper Guinea, include the countries in the interior as far as Timbuctoo and Bornou, being the whole of that region lately explored by the English expeditions. The slaves from this quarter, though of various nations and languages, have yet a general likeness, which stamps them as one race. In Brazil they are known under the name of Minas.

"The Minas slaves are said to be distinguished from others by their bodily and mental qualities. They are generally above middle height, and well formed. The forehead is high, and the cheek-bones prominent; the nose sometimes straight and sometimes depressed; the lips not very thick; teeth small and perpendicularly set; the hair is woolly, and the colour an umber or reddish brown, approaching to black.

"The look and bearing of the Minas blacks are expressive of intelligence and dignity, and they betray little of the levity usually ascribed to the negro race.

"In Brazil they occupy the highest positions that slaves are allowed to attain, being employed as confidential servants, artisans, and small traders. They look down upon, and refuse to have any connexion with, or participation in the employment of the other negroes. Many of them write and read the Arabic, and all can repeat some sentences of it. The greatest number of slaves who purchase their freedom belong to this race.

. . . . . .

"The Minas are held in much fear in Brazil. They are extremely numerous at Bahia, and it is understood, that during a late insurrection, they had fully organized themselves, and were determined to institute a regular system of government. They had gone so far as to circulate writings in Arabic, exhorting their fellows in bondage to make the attempt to recover their liberty." *Narrative of the United States Exploring Expedition,* pp. 54–56.

Wilkes also described the southern, or Bantu, types: "The nations to the south of the equator, have the usual form of the negro, agreeably to our ideas. Those of the slaves at Rio de Janeiro, are, in general, short, badly formed, or clumsy, with narrow foreheads, flat noses, protruding jaws and teeth, and prominent cheek-bones, with the chin sloping backwards. They are indolent, thoughtless, and licentious. They may be seen in the streets at all hours, employed as carriers, earning the stipulated sum for their masters. And when this is gained, they are to be found stretched out on the sidewalk, under the porticoes, or on the steps of churches, enjoying themselves as mere animals, basking in the sun or sleeping in the shade. They are not deficient in intelligence: the defect is less in their intellectual powers than in their character, which appears to want energy." *Ibid.,* 57.

Three Girls from the Same Street, from a Painting by Maria Margarida. (Photo by Arthur Ramos.)

Portuguese to the New World colony, empire, and republic went on incessantly and continues today. This is the migration which furnished the basic white stock for Brazil's upper strata, and it continues to supplement the white blood which in smaller or greater proportion courses through the veins of large percentages of people in the middle and lower classes. It should not be forgotten, however, that in number the colonists were comparatively few and that the present-day importance of their descendants is out of all proportion to the numerical size of the original white population. This point will be developed further in the sections having to do with race mixture and the "bleaching of the population."

Small as was the contingent of Portuguese colonists who came to the New World to establish themselves, a significant percentage of them were of Semitic stock—the "new Christians" (cristãos novos). These former Jews came in relatively large numbers, settled in the small ports along the seacoast where they engaged in trade, skilled labor, and the professions, and became the moneylenders who supplied the capital on loan to the senhores de engenho.[14] From the accounts extant it would seem to be a rare case in which the sugar

[14] Cf. Freyre, Casa Grande & Senzala, 6, 164. See also his Sobrados e Mucambos (São Paulo, 1936), 40 ff.

planter was not heavily indebted to one of these traders and money-lenders—persons engaged in professions the Portuguese disdained.[15]

Other Early White Colonists. In addition to the various elements of white racial stock, including Semites and Moors, who are included among the Portuguese colonists, small groups of French, Dutch, and English early made contributions to the white blood in Brazilian veins. Of most importance among these extraneous elements were the Dutch, whose seventeenth-century occupation of northeastern Brazil has left important racial traces. This is particularly true in Pernambuco. The French, too, attempted to seize various coastal points, notably the bay of Rio de Janeiro; but probably more important still was their long-continued trade in brazilwood. The touch-and-go contacts growing out of this forbidden traffic probably resulted in a considerable infusion of French blood among the Indian peoples inhabiting the coastal areas. Finally, at least a few Englishmen, Italians, and Germans were present among the colonists and contributing their share to the future population of Brazil.[16]

Nineteenth- and Twentieth-Century Immigration. As has been indicated, for the first three centuries of Brazil's existence, the peopling of its vast territory consisted of (1) a small trickle of Portuguese colonists, mostly adventurers seeking a fortune in sugar growing and, later, mining, (2) the numbers added by the hunting down and enslaving of the Indians and through crossbreeding the production of a large mixed white-Indian progeny, and (3) the importation of millions of African slaves, by whose women another large mixed-blood contingent was brought into existence. It is true that French and Dutch also established themselves on the coast and contributed to the racial elements of present-day Brazil. However, in comparison with the Portuguese, the Indian, and the African racial elements, they have been of very minor importance. The introduction of these

---

[15] See Gilberto Freyre, "Some Aspects of the Social Development of Portuguese America," in Charles C. Griffin (ed.), *Concerning Latin American Culture* (New York, 1940), 86. Cf. Rodolfo Garcia, "Os Judeus no Brasil Colonial," in Afrânio Peixoto *et al.*, *Os Judeus na Historia do Brasil* (Rio de Janeiro, 1936), 42–43, who shows that numerically, financially, and professionally the Jews also played a considerable part in the peopling of Brazil's sugar-growing coastal fringe. In spite of the fact that Brazil was by no means too distant for the long arm of the Inquisition, the new Portuguese colonies were for many years a refuge for Jews and "new Christians." Although late in the sixteenth century and early in the seventeenth century representatives of the Bishop and Inquisitor General of Portugal set up tables of the Holy Office in Bahia, Recife, and other population centers, the local ecclesiastics frequently were accused of assisting persons suspected of adhering to the practices of Judaism to evade detection and judgment. A century later, and especially in 1713, the work of the inquisitors sent from Portugal was much more effective. This year saw thirty-two men and forty women condemned in Rio de Janeiro alone. Those sent to Lisbon for judgment included a large number of *senhores de engenho,* and in part the persecutions may have arisen from the motives of jealousy and covetousness. The definitive work on Jews in colonial Brazil and inquisitorial activities in this part of the New World is Arnold Wiznitzer, *Jews in Colonial Brazil* (New York, 1960). See also *Narrativa da Perseguiçaõ de Hippolyto Joseph da Costa Pereira Furtado de Mendonça* (London, 1811).

[16] Cf. Freyre, *Casa Grande & Senzala,* 138–39.

Capitão-do-Mato. (Reproduced from Rugendas, *Voyage Pittoresque dans le Brésil.*)

Teutonic elements represented a departure from the general rule and the attempt to establish small-farming communities.

In the nineteenth century, following the establishment of the empire's capital at Rio de Janeiro and especially after independence, steps were taken to break down the barriers insulating Brazil from the non-Portuguese world. Some of the ports were opened to trade, printing was legalized, scientists and other explorers were admitted, and an attempt was made to induce immigrants other than Portuguese to come to Brazil. The emperor's Teutonic wife probably was largely responsible for the concessions made to German and Swiss immigrants and their introduction and planting in such colonies as

Petrópolis, nestled in the high valleys of the Serra do Mar, where the emperor's summer palace was located.

Following the abolition of slavery late in the nineteenth century the population was swelled and greatly changed in composition by the immigration of over a million Italians, mostly to São Paulo and Rio Grande do Sul; thousands of Polish who settled largely in Paraná; and more thousands of Germans, who concentrated in Santa Catarina, Rio Grande do Sul, São Paulo, and Espírito Santo. Large contingents of Portuguese, Spaniards, and Lebanese also entered Brazil in the late years of the nineteenth century. The Portuguese continued to settle in the cities, especially Rio and São Paulo. The Spaniards went mostly to São Paulo, and many of them located in the newly opened agricultural areas. The Lebanese settled in the city of São Paulo for the most part, although they also spread throughout the small interior trading centers from southern Mato Grosso to the Amazon.

During the twentieth century the immigration of these European elements has continued, although that of the Italians greatly diminished in volume. Otherwise, the introduction of some 200,000 Japanese immigrants, who have already multiplied to about 500,000 persons of the yellow race, is the most significant new factor in the racial composition of Brazil's population. The Europeans and Lebanese who immigrated after 1900 have settled for the most part in the areas previously occupied by their compatriots. The Japanese have located for the most part in São Paulo and the neighboring areas of Paraná, Mato Grosso, and Minas Gerais, although two sizable groups settled on the Amazon. The immigration of these peoples will be treated in detail elsewhere. Here it is sufficient to point out that the introduction of these Europeans and Asiatics, especially in the years since Brazil gained her independence, has done much to change the racial stock of southern Brazil. Today Rio Grande do Sul is largely German and Italian; Santa Catarina, German; and Paraná, Polish, German and Italian. São Paulo, although it contains Brazil's greatest agglomeration of races, runs heavily to Italian. However, the German, Japanese, Lebanese, and Spanish elements are of very considerable size and importance. Portuguese, of course, also are important in Brazil's leading state.

RACE MIXTURE

Not only have the various ethnic strains been present in Brazil, but conditions have been conducive to their mixing and blending. From the very first the relative absence of white women,[17] the inferior

[17] This factor is very important. In the first place, relatively few Portuguese women were among the settlers. In the second place, of the white children born in Brazil a very high percentage took religious orders. Said the Captain General of Minas in 1731, "I suppose every woman in Brazil will be a nun," and eight years later the Count of Galvêas complained that in Bahia, "the heads of families refuse to give their daughters in marriage, placing them in convents," with the

status of the woman in the family, and the superior status of the white master class gave men of the white race almost unhampered access to Indian female slaves. During the first century of Brazilian history there was much more intermixture between the white and the red races than there would have been had more European women been introduced into the colonies, had those who did come wielded a stronger influence over their husbands, had more of the native-born white women married, and had the social positions of the white and the Indian races been more nearly equal. As a result the genes of upper-class white men have not only been passed on to legitimate. offspring who have remained at the top of the social pyramid, but they have contributed greatly to the "bleaching" of the darker populations of the lower social strata.

The rapidity with which this bleaching of the Brazilian population has progressed is startling. This applies equally to the lightening of color derived both from Indian and Negroid ethnic strains. For example, when the Portuguese first established settlements at Bahia they found living there as patriarch of his own village one Corrêa (Indian name Caramurú or "man who makes lightning"), a sailor or possibly a noble, who may have been marooned there by Cabral. For the most part the entire village population consisted of the children and grandchildren of this white chief. Thus, before the Portuguese had a real foothold on the coast, there were already half-breeds and quarter-breeds who were descendants of this prolific progenitor. Even the first priests are said to have followed Corrêa's example,[18] and the flock that of their pastor's, so that by 1550 the already marriageable half-breeds and quarter-breeds were being supplemented by numerous additional offspring of mixed racial stock. As was to be expected, many of the Portuguese colonists chose as wives the half-blood women and produced offspring who were three-quarters white; at the same time the newcomers also contributed through extramarital relations to the rapidly increasing population of half bloods. The process of supplying representatives for all the possible gradations in the color scale went on very rapidly. By 1570 selective mating for color had already produced a native-born elite who were almost entirely white; whereas the matings between persons of various degrees of

result that in 1738 there were only two marriages in the entire city. Calmon, *Espirito da Sociedade Colonial,* 90–95.

[18] Later, after Africans became an important element in the population, many priests left numerous mulatto offspring. This is especially important because the rich inheritances left by their ecclesiastical fathers were the means by which men of the mulatto class came into the possession of wide expanses of lands. Says one of the *Cartas Soteropolitanas* (letters from Bahia) quoted by Calmon: "There are ecclesiastics, and not a few, who in that ancient and bad manner without remembering their estate and character, live thusly in disorder with mulatresses and negresses, by whom they leave at death children as heirs to their property; and by this and similar means there have come into the hands of presumptuous, arrogant, and vagabond mulattoes many of the most valuable properties in Brazil, such as the sugar plantations of this area, which in a short time are destroyed." *Espirito da Sociedade Colonial,* 160. By 1774 mulattoes in Brazil came into the enjoyment of full privileges before the law. *Ibid.,* 162. See also Freyre, *Casa Grande & Senzala,* 323.

mixed blood, plus the numerous illegitimate progeny of the upper-class men, was rapidly diffusing white blood throughout the veins of all classes in the population.[19] Later, with the importation of Negroes from Africa, an exactly comparable pattern of miscegenation took place between upper-class (white or near-white men) and Negro women. Throughout the centuries that have elapsed selective mating of upper-class men with the whitest women has produced a Brazilian elite in whom the traces of Indian or Negro blood are infinitesimal, while their extramarital relations with lower-class women constantly are adding to the proportion of white blood in the veins of the middle-class and lower-class Brazilians.[20]

This indicates that a comparatively few white men contributed far out of all proportion to the present-day ethnic composition of Brazil.[21] In addition to their numerous progeny of legitimate de-

[19] Cf. introductory chapter in Pierre Denis, *Brazil*, trans. bv Bernard Miall (London, 1911), 32–35.

[20] Some of the evidence indicates that upper-class men frequently preferred their dark mistresses to their white wives. Said the French traveler of the early eighteenth century, La Barbinnais, as quoted by Calmon: "To the most beautiful women they prefer the negresses and mulatresses. I know one, a very charming woman from Lisbon, who is married to a Bahiano; however, disorder prevails in their home, because her husband disdains her for the love of a negress who does not merit the attentions of the ugliest negro in all of Guinea." There is also a little rhyme in the folklore of the state of Rio de Janeiro that runs, in a literal translation, as follows:

> "If white women were for sale,
> Either for gold or for silver,
> I should buy one of them
> For a servant for my *mulata*."

Cf. Calmon, *Espirito da Sociedade Colonial*, 161. See also Freyre, *Casa Grande & Senzala*, 9, who quotes the old Brazilian saying about "a white woman for marriage, a mulatress for a mistress, and a negress for work." Cf. Freyre, "Some Aspects of the Social Development of Portuguese America," in Griffin (ed.), *Concerning Latin American Culture*, 83–84.

[21] Says Oliveira Vianna: "In reality during the Colonial epoch the latifundium was the breeding field par excellence. In it the whites—the owners, their relatives, their agregados—exercised a dominating role. They were the sires, the great impregnators of the Indian women, the fiery stallions of the Negro females. Some of them, even among the most noble, left only *'filhos naturaes e pardos'* [illegitimate children and mulattoes] according to the testimony of the Conde da Cunha." *Populações Meridionaes do Brasil* (São Paulo, 1938), 78–79. And again: "The half bloods, are, then, a historical product of the latifundia. To serve as a field for race crossing, a center for integrating the three distinct races, is the second social function of the rural dominion. This function is one of the most important in our history—because in it is the genesis and formation of our nationality." *Ibid.*, 79–80.

Similar is the analysis of Dr. João Pandiá Calogeras: "And the conditions of life on the old fazendas, in which the master possessed unrestricted control of the lives and goods of his slaves and retainers, like the past feudalism, facilitated greatly the production of half bloods, quadroons, and even of children with higher proportions of Aryan blood.

"Among the slaves, appeared a scale of all shades which varied from almost-white, with an almost imperceptible African tint, to the most characteristic Congo." *A Politica Exterior do Imperio* (Rio de Janeiro, 1927), I, 293–94.

To this facility with which a few thousand Portuguese males (*machos*) produced offspring by women of color, Freyre attributes much of tiny Portugal's success as a colonizing nation. Cf. *Casa Grande & Senzala*, 7. Certainly this small country seized and maintained control of huge expanses of the earth's surface at a time when competition with larger countries was keen. Furthermore, the biological and cultural factors involved preserved the colonies for the Portuguese crown, even though it was long subordinated to Spain.

scendants and of the white race, through the keeping of concubines (*mulheres da cama*) and other extramarital relations their genes have been distributed far and wide throughout the masses of the population who have a darker hue. It should not be overlooked that the name *caboclo*, originally applied to the domesticated Indians and later to the white-Indian cross, has now with much reason become a generalized term to denote the Brazilian peasant or rural laborer. As indicated above, from the very first the mixture of the white and red races went on rapidly; but family pride, an endogamous marriage system, and the inheritance of private property preserved a small elite of whites at the very top of the social pyramid. Later, and especially throughout the seventeenth, eighteenth, and nineteenth centuries, the same complex of factors operated in a similar way to make the racial heritage contributed by the comparatively few white people who came during the colonial period almost as important in the make-up of the present-day population as the contribution of great masses of Negro slaves imported from Africa.

It was not long before the numbers of Negroes, Indians, and the crosses and recrosses of the two with the whites were sufficiently numerous that the contact between the various strains did not need the assistance of class differences to ensure a large amount of mingling. However, the fact that the most relentless adepts at the hunting of wild Indians were themselves of mixed Indian and white descent, the mamelucos or sons of white fathers and Indian women, was not a retarding factor in the blending of the races. Nevertheless, in all of the racial mixing it is probable that the crossing involved comparatively little mingling of Indian and Negro ethnic strains, at least until they had both been diluted with those of whites. It is certain that the caboclos or mamelucos, crosses of Indian and white, and the mulattoes or *pardos* greatly outnumbered cafusos, or the offspring of Indian and Negro parents.[22] The factor responsible for the slight degree of Indian-Negro crossing seems to have been the culturally determined division of labor among the Indians which made agriculture a task for women. Because they viewed farming tasks as women's work, Indian men never made tractable slaves on Brazilian engenhos. Later on, the African's docile acceptance of work in agriculture caused the Indian to despise him, thus raising a great social barrier to the mixture of the red and black races.[23]

[22] Oliveira Vianna, *Populações Meridionaes*, 79. Only rarely does one find in the literature descriptions of the cafuso groups. Thus, while von Spix and von Martius, Mawe, Prince Maximilian, Koster, St. Hilaire, Burton, and other early travelers make frequent reference to communities of domesticated Indians and caboclos and of communities composed wholly of Negroes and mulattoes, rarely did they observe settlements of cafusos. When von Spix and von Martius did encounter a group of these people in Taruma in the province of São Paulo, it was the occasion for a detailed description of their features and characteristics. *Travels in Brazil*, I, 323–24.

[23] This interpretation was stressed by Brazil's outstanding historian, Dr. Arthur Cezar Ferreira Reis, in conversations with the author at Belém during December, 1942. However, when von Spix and von Martius visited the *Coroados* of the River Doce in Minas Gerais in 1818 they reported: "The Indian women, we were told, showed more attachment to the negroes than to their own Indian husbands. Run-

Finally, following the abolition of slavery and especially during the last quarter of a century, there has arisen in Brazil what amounts to a veritable cult of racial equality.[24] It numbers among its adherents most of the nation's leading scholars and many of its outstanding political figures. Although not formally organized and possessed of no written creed, two fundamental tenets, both designed to secure racial equality, seem to have general acceptance: (1) under no circumstances should it be admitted that racial discrimination exists in Brazil, and (2) any expression of racial discrimination that may appear always should be attacked as un-Brazilian. Undoubtedly this is effective, if not in securing complete racial equality, at least in preventing many of the grosser features of racial discrimination and in making for a freer legal blending of the races than otherwise could be possible. This, of course, has little effect on the racial composition of the elite class at the top of the social scale, for that matter is cared for by the strong Brazilian institution of the family and its system of consciously selective mating.[25] See Figure 8 for an indica-

---

away negroes, therefore, frequently appear in the woods as the *cicisbei* of the Indian women, and are passionately sought by them. The contrary is the case with the Indian men who consider the negresses as below their dignity and despise them." *Ibid.*, II, 229.

[24] Even this modern attitude has deep roots in the past. Thus long before slavery was abolished in Brazil, visitors were struck by the freedom with which persons of all colors mingled with lack of racial discrimination. For example, Wilkes wrote in 1838: "Every one, on his first landing at Rio, will be struck with the indiscriminate mingling of all classes, in every place, all appearing on terms of the utmost equality;—officers, soldiers, and priests, both black and white, mixing and performing their respective duties, without regard to colour or appearance. The only distinction seems to be that of freedom and slavery. There are many wealthy free blacks, highly respectable, who amalgamate with the white families, and are apparently received on a footing of perfect equality." *Narrative of the United States Exploring Expedition*, II, 45.

[25] Says Manoel de Oliveira Lima, *The Evolution of Brazil Compared with that of Spanish and Anglo-Saxon America* (Palo Alto, 1914), 20: "Indeed, not only has the genealogical tree of many families of distinction been jealously guarded from contact with all strains of inferior blood, but the whites of the colonies maintained and defended their titles and rights to certain posts and functions which had been reserved to them by the laws of their respective mother countries." See also Calmon, *Espirito da Sociedade Colonial*, 158–59. Girls were sent from Portugal, sometimes by the Queen herself, for the explicit purpose of preserving the "social rank and the aristocratic status of the planters." Freyre, "Some Aspects of the Social Development of Portuguese America," in Griffin (ed.), *Concerning Latin American Culture*, 83.

Testimony of others is similar. John Codman, who sometimes was inclined to be severely critical, wrote: "Some years ago, when a census was to be taken, it was proposed to divide the classes of the community, and to enumerate separately the white, black, and mixed. The Brazilians themselves laughed at the imbecile who wasted his ink in the suggestion. 'Mixed!' There is black blood everywhere stirred in; compounded over and over again, like an apothecary's preparation. African blood runs freely through marble halls, as well as in the lowest gutters, and Indian blood swells the general current. There is no distinction between white and black, or any of the intermediate colors, which can act as a bar to social intercourse or political advancement.

"The whole population of Brazil, according to the last census, was 9,083,755, of whom 1,357,416 were slaves; of the remaining 7,726,339, called 'free,' it was wisely determined to make no further classification." *Ten Months in Brazil* (Boston, 1867), 153–54.

As an explanation of the reason for the Portuguese lack of discrimination against peoples of darker color one should keep in mind that Portugal was the last part of the Iberian Peninsula to be occupied by the Moors. For centuries in

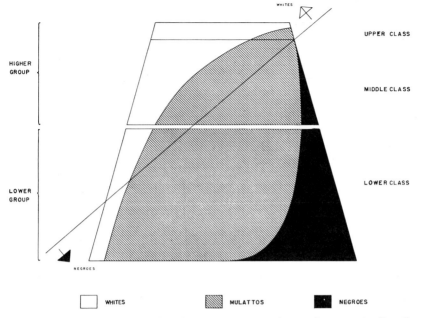

FIGURE 8. The relationship between color and social status in Brazil (After Thales de Azevedo, *Ensaios de Antropologia Social* [Salvador, 1959], 114).

tion of the relationship of color to social status in contemporary Brazil.

Before concluding this discussion of race mixture, a word is necessary about the Japanese population. Although the second and third generations of Brazilian-born Japanese have made their appearance, as yet these Japanese have mixed very little with other Brazilian racial stocks. There has been some crossing through the extra-marital relations of Japanese males. Also, a handful of business and professional Japanese men, who set themselves up in business in São Paulo, have taken Brazilian wives. In this case the men found it more to their taste to cross racial lines in the selection of mates than to marry with their lower-class compatriots. However, this group is of little consequence numerically. The great mass of the Japanese in Brazil came to the country recently as agricultural laborers. For years they were carefully herded around by the various

Portuguese society the darker ethnic elements occupied the higher social positions. Under the circumstances marriage with a person of darker hue generally meant moving up the social scale. This economic factor undoubtedly had much to do with disassociating the combination black and bad or undesirable, which has generally prevailed in the Western world. Probably a great deal of the Brazilian's racial tolerance has stemmed from this factor. Cf. Roy Nash, *The Conquest of Brazil* (New York, 1926), 37; and Freyre, *Casa Grande & Senzala*, 7. The popularity in Portugal of the legends about the "enchanted Mooress" (*moura-encantada*), and especially their settings (*ibid.*, 7–8), also indicates that Portuguese men were by no means immune to the mystical sexual appeals of dark eyes and raven tresses. See also Freyre's contribution in Griffin (ed.), *Concerning Latin American Culture*, 83.

officials of the Imperial Company which introduced, installed, and worked them. Under these conditions they neither had the inclination nor the opportunity to mate with the Brazilians. Except for the insignificant number of offspring from matings between middle-class and upper-class Japanese men and Brazilian women, therefore, mixed-blood descendants of Japanese and Brazilian parents are neither numerous nor legitimate.[26] So little have the Japanese mixed and blended with the other racial groups in São Paulo, it has not been unusual for the Japanese element to be referred to as a "cyst" in the social body.[27]

PRESENT RACIAL MAKE-UP

The task of evaluating the relative importance of the various racial elements in the Brazilian population was greatly facilitated by the 1940 and 1950 censuses of population. This is fortunate, for few subjects have received as much attention from foreigners and Brazilians alike as the absolute and relative importance of the various ethnic and racial strains that have contributed to the population composition as it is today.

For some reason the impression has been widely diffused abroad that the Negroid elements are the principal ones in the Brazilian population. Such a thesis is absolutely untenable. Certainly the Caucasian races have contributed much more heavily than the Negroes to the genes carried by the people of Brazil, and in all probability the members of the black race have contributed no more than have the American Indians.

According to the 1950 census the population of Brazil was constituted racially, or by color, in the following manner:

Color	Number	Per cent
White	32,027,661	61.7
Black	5,692,657	11.0
Yellow	329,082	0.6
Pardo (mixed and Indian)	13,786,742	26.5
Undeclared	108,255	0.2

[26] There are certain studies such as Alfred Ellis, Jr., *Populações Paulistas* (São Paulo, 1934), 178–96, which purport to show that Japanese are assimilating rapidly; the numbers and proportions of mixed Japanese-Brazilian marriages are given as evidence. However, since any child born in Brazil is counted as a Brazilian, all the data really show is that children born in Brazil of Japanese parents have reached a marriageable age. Since Japanese were first imported in 1908, this is not surprising. A much more significant and penetrating study is that by R. Paula Souza, "Contribuição á Etnologia Paulista," *Revista do Arquivo Municipal de São Paulo*, XXXI (1936), 95–105, which takes into account the racial characteristics of the parties contracting marriages. This piece of research revealed that even among Japanese families with children in the University, i.e., those least isolated socially from the Brazilians, no race mixture whatever had taken place. See also Oscar Egidio de Araujo, "Enquistamentos Étnicos," *Revista do Arquivo Municipal de São Paulo*, LXV (1940), 227–46.

[27] Cf. Sud Mennucci, "A Subdivisão do Município de Blumenau," *Geografia*, II, No. 4 (1936), 20.

These figures should be viewed with a considerable degree of caution. To begin with, the category designated as white should be thought of as designating those who are white or whitish. Not a few of them have a considerable admixture of Indian blood in their veins. In addition, Negroid ancestry in a limited degree, although not as prevalent as the Indian, is by no means lacking in many of those classified as whites. The number of those classed as black, or Negro, certainly is the absolute minimum. Any changes in the criteria used would inevitably have the effect of increasing their numbers. The use of the single category of pardos for all those of mixed ancestry, the crosses of whites and Indians as well as those of whites and Negroes, is to be regretted. Furthermore, few of those who use the data will realize that the census has actually included the Indians themselves in the pardo category. It is probable that the white-Indian crosses and the white-Negro blends are present in about the same proportions, but of course, that fact cannot be established with any degree of certainty.

The data for the various states from the 1950 census, along with those from the 1940 enumeration, are presented in Table IV. They call for little comment. Obviously, in Brazil as in the United States, census procedures do not secure accurate anthropological classifications of the population. The apparent changes between 1940 and 1950 must be attributed far more to variations in the criteria actually applied in classifying the population than to any changes in the racial composition of the population. Nevertheless, the fact that the black, or Negro, population decreased in relative importance in most of the states probably is in line with the true developments. On the other hand there was a much greater tendency in 1950 than in 1940 to place the whitish elements in the mixed or pardo category. Those who have been most closely connected with the two censuses report that in some states the 1940 officials in charge were far too zealous in classifying persons in the darkest possible class.

DISTRIBUTION OF THE RACIAL ELEMENTS

Although throughout Brazil white, black, and red racial strains may be found in nearly every conceivable combination,[28] the relative

[28] Even an upper-class Brazilian will make reference to his remote Indian ancestry or feel complimented if another calls him a "caboclo." Similar reference to possible African ancestors is taboo. Says Freyre: "To call some one a 'caboclo' in Brazil almost always is a eulogy of his character or of his capacity for physical and moral resistance. This is in contrast to 'mulatto,' 'negro,' 'muleque,' 'creole,' 'pardo,' 'pardavasco' [brownish], 'sarará,' which in general have a depreciative connotation with respect to the moral, social, or cultural situation of an individual. Many a Brazilian mulatto of high social or political position makes a practice of calling himself 'caboclo': 'we caboclos,' 'if I were not a caboclo.' And Julio Bello informs us that old Sebastião do Rosario, a well-known senhor de engenho in Pernambuco during the 19th Century, a pure Wanderley of means, of the Wanderleys of Serinhaem—a people almost all of ruddy European skin, of blue eyes, of flaxen hair—when in a expansive mood, highly contented, at one of his elaborate dinners, used to speak of himself, falsely, as being a 'caboclo.' Mulatto or touched with negro blood is what no one cares to be when he is in

TABLE IV

Composition of Brazilian Population by Color, 1940 and 1950, by States and Territories *

State	White 1940	White 1950	Black 1940	Black 1950	Yellow 1940	Yellow 1950	Pardo † 1940	Pardo † 1950
Brazil	63.5	61.7	14.6	11.0	0.6	0.6	21.2	26.5
North								
Guaporé ‡	—	28.5	—	8.1	—	0.0	—	63.0
Acre ‡	54.3	30.0	14.2	5.2	0.2	0.0	31.1	64.6
Amazonas	31.3	36.9	7.2	3.4	0.2	0.1	61.1	59.4
Rio Branco ‡	—	41.6	—	5.0	—	0.0	—	53.3
Pará	44.6	29.0	9.5	5.3	0.1	0.1	45.6	65.4
Amapá	—	27.1	—	8.1	—	0.0	—	64.5
Northeast								
Maranhão	46.8	33.7	27.6	15.8	0.0	0.0	25.5	50.3
Piauí	45.2	28.0	31.9	12.9	0.0	0.0	22.6	59.0
Ceará	52.6	43.6	23.3	10.5	0.0	0.0	23.8	45.8
Rio Grande do Norte	43.5	48.8	13.4	9.5	0.0	0.0	43.1	41.6
Paraíba	53.8	67.1	13.7	13.0	0.0	0.0	32.4	19.7
Pernambuco	54.4	49.6	15.5	9.3	0.0	0.0	29.9	40.9
Alagôas	56.7	40.5	13.8	7.4	0.0	0.0	29.3	51.9
East								
Sergipe	46.7	49.7	18.7	14.2	0.0	0.0	34.4	36.0
Bahia	26.7	29.6	20.1	19.2	0.0	0.0	51.1	51.0
Minas Gerais	61.2	58.4	19.3	14.6	0.0	0.0	19.4	26.8
Espírito Santo	61.5	58.6	17.1	11.9	0.0	0.0	21.3	29.4
Rio de Janeiro	59.8	59.8	21.3	17.7	0.0	0.1	18.6	22.1
Distrito Federal	71.1	69.9	11.3	12.3	0.1	0.0	17.3	17.5
South								
São Paulo	84.9	85.7	7.3	8.0	3.0	3.1	4.7	3.2
Paraná	86.6	86.4	4.9	4.4	1.1	1.9	7.4	7.3
Santa Catarina	94.4	94.6	5.2	3.7	0.0	0.0	0.3	1.5
Rio Grande do Sul	88.7	89.1	6.6	5.2	0.0	0.0	4.6	5.4
West Central								
Mato Grosso	50.8	53.3	8.5	9.8	0.7	0.7	39.9	35.9
Goiás	72.1	57.9	16.9	10.1	0.0	0.1	10.8	31.6

* Assembled and computed from data in the "Sinopse do Censo Demográfico: Dados Gerais," *Recenseamento Geral do Brasil, 1940* (Rio de Janeiro, 1947); and "Censo Demográfico," *VI Recenseamento Geral do Brasil, 1950* (Rio de Janeiro, 1956).

† Includes Indians, mulattoes, mestiços, etc.

‡ Territory.

importance of each race varies considerably from one part of the country to another. The 1940 and 1950 census data, as presented in Table IV, also supply the facts necessary for an understanding of these variations.

the *alturas* [higher social levels]. Extremely rare are the exceptions." *Casa Grande & Senzala*, 48. E. Franklin Frazier, after studying fifty families in Bahia, cautiously wrote: "There is reason to believe some of those claiming *caboclo* ancestors preferred the term to mulatto which implied Negro ancestry." "The Negro Family in Bahia, Brazil," *American Sociological Review*, VII (August, 1942), 470.

The white elements predominate to the greatest extent in Santa Catarina, Paraná, Rio Grande do Sul, and São Paulo (probably about in the order named) where the recent immigration from Italy, Poland, and Germany have contributed heavily to the populations of white racial stock. The city of Rio de Janeiro also contains large numbers of whites. Elsewhere throughout Brazil, the white elements are of less relative importance, although they seem to be concentrated in the coastal cities. Then, too, the whiteness of the population is largely dependent upon the social position of the group and to only a limited extent is related to the geographic space it occupies. However, in all parts of Brazil one will find some blond, flaxen-haired, blue-eyed persons, although they do not appear elsewhere with the frequency that they do in the south, particularly in Santa Catarina. In areas where new agricultural settlement is being superimposed upon the old cattle-raising culture, as in western São Paulo, it is interesting to see the intermarriage that occurs between the descendants of the German colonists from the south and the offspring of people of darker hue who have migrated to this promised land from the state of Bahia. This occurs where lower-class whites from the south meet their compatriots of a darker hue from the northeast. The meeting and blending of these two migratory currents is doing much to equalize the color content of Brazil's population, especially throughout the great newly settled areas of western São Paulo and northern Paraná.

Indian elements in the Brazilian population are of greatest relative importance in the Amazon Basin. Here throughout the states of Pará and Amazonas, the territory of Acre, the northern part of Goiás, and the western portion of Maranháo, the Indian strain is predominant in a considerable portion of the population. Oftentimes in these areas people are encountered who show no evidences that either white or Negro blood flows in their veins. Other than in this immense region of sparse population and a collecting economy, Indian racial characteristics are most pronounced in the population of the great interior sertões. This is the heart of Brazil, away from the coast which has felt contact with the rest of the world, in the great open spaces where population is very sparse, where agriculture has hardly spread, and where cattle raising furnishes a meager livelihood for the scattered inhabitants. This area includes most of Mato Grosso, some of the more remote parts of western São Paulo, northern Minas Gerais, the western portions of Bahia, Pernambuco, Paraíba, and Rio Grande do Norte, and the southern two-thirds of the states of Ceará, Piauí, and Maranhão. The population of these parts, the sertanistas, shows evidences of long continued crossing and recrossing. No doubt all three of the principal racial stocks have left their imprint upon nearly every one of the inhabitants in this part of Brazil's vast interior. One great Brazilian scholar, Euclydes da Cunha, has emphasized the importance of the Indian racial heritage, while others, Gilberto Freyre and E. Roquette-Pinto, stress the Negroid contributions to the biological make-up of this population.[29] To choose be-

[29] See Freyre, *Casa Grande & Senzala,* 47–49.

tween the two positions probably is unnecessary. One who visits these portions of Brazil will see many persons with unmistakable Negroid characteristics engaged in the care of herds of cattle, but also he will encounter even more frequently the high cheekbones and especially the heavy straight black hair that is a certain indication of a prevalence of Indian rather than Negroid blood.

Negroid elements, too, are much more prevalent in some regions than in others. Bahia and Negroid characteristics in the population are very closely associated in the Brazilian mind and properly so, since undoubtedly the Negro elements in the population of Bahia are more important than in any other state in the nation. Here too the survival of African cultural traits is easily observed. The dominance of black blood is greatest in the capital city, Salvador, where it seems to have filtered to a limited degree into the veins of the very elite, but Negroid characteristics have penetrated even the remote sertões west of the São Francisco River. About one-fifth of the great contingent of Bahianos who have moved to São Paulo during the last two decades, a very large share of whom came from the sertões of south-central Bahia, were classified as pretos when they passed through the hostel in the city of São Paulo.

Next to Bahia the Negroid elements in the population probably are of greatest relative importance in the state of Rio de Janeiro, whose sugar engenhos were almost as effective in introducing and perpetuating a host of black workers as were those in the sugar-growing recôncavo which surrounds Bahia's capital city. From the state of Rio de Janeiro and from Minas Gerais the granting of freedom to the slaves and the ability to move resulted in a great exodus to the national capital, Rio de Janeiro, so that what is now the state of Guanabara probably contains today about as high a proportion of Negroes, or people of mixed Negroid descent, as is to be found anywhere in Brazil outside of Bahia. In Brazil's former capital the people of darker hue are found to be concentrated in the poorer sections of the city, particularly in the favelas (slums) which overspread the numerous hills that contribute heavily to Rio's superb natural setting. On the other hand, the prevalence of the dark skin and other Negroid characteristics is not as great in Minas Gerais as one might be led to expect from a knowledge of the thousands of slaves who were imported to work the rich mines of the province.

The capital of Maranhão, São Luís, and the coastal areas surrounding it, is probably the section which ranks next in importance of Negroid elements in the population. Sugar and especially cotton plantations were the factors that resulted in the introduction of a large slave contingent to this far northern or equatorial portion of Brazil. Here too, with the freeing of the slaves, there was a strong tendency for the darker racial elements to concentrate in the capital city, a trend similar to that which took place rather generally throughout Brazil. Today, as one witnesses a religious procession in São Luís, after the first few tiers of marchers have passed by, he sees for the most part a seething mass of black humanity. Among hundreds of faces, hardly one in which white features predominate will appear. On the outskirts of the city is the poorer type of dwelling, generally with wattle-and-daub walls, thatched roofs,[30] and dirt floors, from which these darker elements in the population have assembled.

Closely rivaling, or perhaps exceeding, São Luís and its hinterland in the relative importance of Negroid elements in the population are the sugar-growing, coastal sections of Pernambuco, Paraíba, and the neighboring states. Here, too, the engenhos and usinas of the sugar industry have counted on a mass of dark workers. In Recife, also, there is a large Negroid population.

BLEACHING

There can be little doubt that the Brazilian population is steadily becoming whiter in color. As compared with that of 1872 the censuses of 1940 and 1950 show—and correctly so—that the colored strains in the population are of much less importance than they were prior to the freeing of the slaves. It requires no reliance on mystical climatic influences, no belief in somatic changes induced by diet, nor acceptance of the idea that the genes of white people are more potent than those of their colored fellows to account for this tendency. A series of comparatively simple social and demographic factors seem sufficient to explain the change, and they should be given their proper weight before "open sesame" explanations of a highly questionable character are resorted to.

1. Through immigration a net contribution of several million European (white) people have been added to the populations of the city of Rio de Janeiro and of the four southermost states—São Paulo, Paraná, Santa Catarina, and Rio Grande do Sul. Of these, the Italian

---

[30] The darker and lower-class elements live in the suburbs of the city. Rather generally throughout northern Brazil, and even on the outskirts of large cities such as São Luís, the owner of the land permits "squatters" to build a house providing they use thatch for the roof. A more permanent construction with a tile roof, however, may not be built by the squatter.

A young mulatto from southern Piauí, whom I encountered in Teresina, the capital of that state, complained bitterly that the landowners in that section did not comply with this time-honored custom but "kicked out" anyone who tried to build a house on the outskirts of that city. He personally longed for the day when he could go back to his own terra where the donos were more understanding. His statement, however, was probably not a complete description of the prevailing situation, because in the outskirts of Teresina, as in other northern cities, the wattle-and-daub walls, the thatched roofs, and the dirt floors of the huts, and especially the confused, patternless arrangements of the streets and houses seem to indicate an almost complete freedom to build whatever was wanted in the nature of a shelter wherever it was desired to locate a habitation.

In Teresina I made the following entry in my notes: "Cities and towns here (north Brazil) are all of a type and all exactly contrary to the Chicago ecological theories. The center of town is an area of paved streets, electric lights, water, and houses of masonry with tiled roofs. Farther out the facilities give out, but some plastered houses and aligned streets continue. On the edges of town there are no facilities, streets are winding and unaligned, houses are all of thatch or wattle and daub, with thatched roofs. Undoubtedly the center of town is much freer of mosquitoes and, consequently, much less dangerous from the standpoints of malaria and yellow fever."

and Portuguese immigrants formed the largest contingents, although Polish, Spanish, and German elements were also numerous. Minas Gerais and Espírito Santo have also received considerable immigration (white) since the freeing of the slaves.

2. But not all the bleaching of Brazil's population is due to immigration. This lightening of color also goes on in those parts of Brazil which have received few or no immigrants. In Brazil there is little or no tendency towards a differential fertility favorable to the lower, which are also the blacker and redder, classes. Counting only legitimate offspring, the members of the upper classes probably produce as many children on the average as do those of middle-class and lower-class status.

3. Of the offspring produced, the children of the upper classes undoubtedly survive in larger proportions than the children of the lower and more untutored persons in society's lower strata. In other words, it seems also certain that the net reproduction rate increases as one moves up the Brazilian social ladder. This means that the whiter elements make a larger net contribution of legitimate children to the succeeding generation than do their darker fellows.

4. Upper-class (white) men continue to have ready access to women of the lower (darker) class. Thus, in addition to leaving more than their share of legitimate descendants, these men also contribute greatly to the increase, and consequently to the bleaching, of the lower classes. Neither the sex mores of Brazilian society nor the position of women in the upper-class family is sufficient to check the extramarital proclivities of the upper-class men. Even were immigration prohibited entirely, it is likely that Brazil's population would continue to lighten with each succeeding generation.

CHAPTER V

SOME OTHER POPULATION CHARACTERISTICS

Tᴴᴇ ᴘʀᴇᴄᴇᴅɪɴɢ chapter has considered in some detail the racial make-up of the Brazilian population. Other of the most significant characteristics of the population, namely residence, nativity, age, sex, and occupational status are treated in the pages that follow. Still others—marital condition, educational status, and religious affiliations—receive attention in the chapters dealing with domestic institutions, educational institutions, and religious institutions, respectively.

RESIDENCE

Quantitatively and qualitatively, Brazil's population is one of the most rural in the entire world. In fact, despite a recent heavy migration of people to the cities, the percentage of the nation's population living in communities that must be classed as strictly rural is hardly to be equaled in any other large and populous country.[1] On the other hand, the immense extent of the thinly populated country, the great dispersion of its nodules of settlement, the use of scattered farmsteads in arranging the population on the land, the very high proportion of the population that engages directly in agricultural, stock raising, or hunting and fishing activities, and the undeveloped state of the means of communication and transportation are evidences that the degree of rurality is also a very high one. As yet urban influences reach large expanses of the Brazilian countryside only rarely and then in a weakened condition.

The overwhelming importance of the rural environment as a determinant of Brazilian culture and personality has been recognized by the nation's leading thinkers and writers. Says the outstanding Brazilian student of population and cultural history, Oliveira Vianna:

From the first days of our history we have been an agricultural and pastoral people. The commercial spirit of the Portuguese of the period of the Navigators, dominant in their expansion in the Indies, was obscured in the penetration of Brazilian terrain, losing its energy in a short time, and disappearing altogether. The native type early contrasted with the foreigners by its essentially rural configuration, by its fundamental country

[1] See some of the data in Smith, *The Sociology of Rural Life*, 44–49; and in T. Lynn Smith, *Fundamentals of Population Study* (Chicago, 1960), 88–95.

temperament. Urbanism is a modern element in our social evolution. All of our history is that of an agricultural people, is the history of a society of farmers and herdsmen. In the country our race was formed and in it were molded the intimate forces of our civilization. The dynamism of our history in the colonial period came from the countryside. In the country was based the admirable stability of our society in the Imperial period.[2]

More recently José Augusto stated before the Brazilian Congress:

The Brazilian population is the most rural in the world; it is the one which, in relation to its total, presents the largest percentage of country people and furnishes the largest number of agriculturists in every thousand employed persons.[3]

All who visit even a small proportion of the three thousand municípios, more or less, that lie in the country back of Rio de Janeiro, São Paulo, Recife, Pôrto Alegre, and Bahia, must be convinced of Brazil's high degree of rurality. The quantitative aspects of the subject are made abundantly clear by the data gathered in the 1960 census. According to the criteria employed, only 31,990,938, or 45 per cent of the population, was classified as urban; whereas 38,976,247 persons were placed in the rural category. In 1950, however, only 36 per cent was urban. It should be remembered, though, that the Brazilian census classifies as urban the inhabitants of all the seats of the county-like municípios and those in the little clusters of homes which make up the seats of the districts as well. A very large share of this urban population would fall in the rural group if criteria similar to those used by the United States Bureau of the Census were employed.

Because the criteria of urban and rural as used by the Brazilian Census Commission differ from those applied by the United States Census Bureau it is well to examine in some detail the basis that is used for classifying the Brazilian population according to residence. A 1938 decree of the national government, Number 311 of March 2, made each *prefeitura* (office of the prefect or governor of the município) responsible for preparing and depositing with the Regional Directory of Geography a map of its município, prepared in accordance with instructions supplied by the Conselho Nacional de Geografia. This Council, in drawing up instructions for the preparation of these county maps, included the provision that each should be accompanied by a plan of the seat of the município and one of each of the vilas, or district seats, in the município. On these town and village plans the urban and suburban zones of each cidade and vila were to be clearly indicated. The responsibility for making the delineations was placed upon the local governing bodies, but it was stipulated that "the urban and suburban areas of each vila, district seat, together shall include at least thirty dwellings; the urban area of the cidade, seat of the município, shall include a minimum of two

[2] Oliveira Vianna, "O Povo Brasileiro e sua Evolução," *loc. cit.*, 281.
[3] Cf. A. Carneiro Leão, *A Sociedade Rural, seus Problemas e sua Educação* (Rio de Janeiro, 1939), 107.

hundred dwellings." It was provided, however, that existing cidades and vilas should be mapped even though they did not meet the minimum requirements specified. Additional instructions were as follows:

Article 8: The determination of the urban part of the seat, whether of a município or a distrito, shall consist in the clear and simple description of a line, easily identified on the ground, surrounding the center of the greatest concentration of houses, in which, as a general rule, are located the principal public edifices and where the commercial, financial, and social life of the seat is manifested most intensely, and where, in many cases, there is the imposition of special taxes, as for example the urban tenth.

Single Paragraph—The said line of delineation of the urban area shall describe, preferably, a polygon, made of straight lines, which follows closely the periphery of the above-mentioned center of concentration of the houses in the seat.

Article 9: The delineation of the suburban portion of the seats, of municípios or distritos, shall consist in the clear and simple description of a line, also easily recognized on the ground, embracing an area that surrounds, at a variable distance, the urban section, an area into which the expansion of the urban zone is already proceeding or to which, due to its favorable typographic conditions, this expansion is naturally destined. The boundary line of the suburban zone should circumscribe, as rigorously as possible, the area that really corresponds to the present or future expansion of the urban center, it being prohibited to delimit under any pretext whatsoever that may be invoked, even that of regularizing the form, a suburban perimeter which is removed in distance and confrontation, from the area of expansion mentioned above.[4]

These maps of Brazil's municípios have been completed and final copies prepared in Rio de Janeiro, where they form a part of the excellent map collection of the Conselho Nacional de Geografia. In effect, each map divides the territory of its município into one or more urban tracts, one or more suburban zones, and a rural area. In taking the 1940, 1950, and 1960 censuses the populations of the three were classified as urban, suburban, and rural, respectively. Therefore it should be emphasized that the urban population of a Brazilian município consists not only of the people living in the built-up area of the population center which constitutes its seat but includes those living in the cores of the vilas, or small centers which form the seats of the various districts included in the município. Data showing the sizes of the cidades and vilas in 1960 are given in Table v.

This knowledge of the basis of Brazil's residential classification of population makes it evident that an exact comparison with the United States is impossible. It also suggests procedures that might be used as points of departure in improving our own classification; it at least sets a precedent for the abandoning of corporation limits of a town or city as the line separating urban from rural populations.

The 1950 and 1960 data enable us to observe how the large rural population is distributed among the states and territories and to observe the variations from state to state in the absolute and relative

[4] Conselho Nacional de Geografia, *Resolução N. 3, de 29 de Março de 1938* (Rio de Janeiro, 1938), 7–8.

TABLE V

Seats of Municípios and Distritos in Brazil, 1960 *

Number of inhabitants	Seats of municípios		Seats of distritos	
	Number	Per cent	Number	Per cent
Total	2,767	100.0	3,774	100.0
Under 1,001	1,171	42.2	3,132	83.0
1,001–2,000			439	11.7
2,001–5,000	867	31.4	149	4.0
5,001–10,000	358	13.0	20	0.5
10,001–20,000	199	7.2	16	0.4
20,001–50,000	104	3.8	13	0.3
50,001–100,000	37	1.3	5	0.1
100,001–500,000	25	0.9	0	0.0
500,001–over	6	0.2	0	0.0

* Source: "Sinopse Preliminar do Censo Demográfico," *VII Recenseamento Geral do Brasil, 1960* (Rio de Janeiro, 1962), 16–19.

importance of the rural and the urban-suburban populations. See Table vi. The most important fact is, of course, the high degree to which the population in almost all parts of Brazil still falls in the rural category. Thus, in spite of the recent rapid progress of the process of urbanization, which is analyzed in another chapter, the inhabitants of the big majority of all Brazilian states are still predominantly rural. Only in Guanabara, the new name for the central core of the metropolitan community of Rio de Janeiro, in São Paulo, in the state of Rio de Janeiro, and in the territory of Amapá does the urban-suburban population outnumber the rural. On the other hand, as late as 1960 those residing in rural districts constituted more than two-thirds of the total population in Acre, Amazonas, Maranhão, Piauí, Espírito Santo, Santa Catarina, and Goiás, with Ceará and Alagôas failing to qualify for inclusion in this category by less than 1.0 percentage point. At the time of the latest census there were almost six million highly rural people in Minas Gerais, almost five million in São Paulo, nearly four million in Bahia, more than three million in Rio Grande do Sul, approximately three million in Paraná, and well over two million each in Maranhão, Ceará, and Pernambuco.

The growth and development of a few highly urbanized segments of Brazilian society, without a corresponding change in the vast interior, has greatly accentuated rural-urban differences in Brazil. It also helps, by way of contrast, to emphasize the qualitatively high degree of rurality in the bulk of the Brazilian territory. With only about 71,000,000 people (as of 1960) spread throughout its vast area, with relatively few centers ranking as cities, with a high percentage of the population directly engaged in agricultural pursuits and collecting activities, with systems of transportation and communication that remain in a very rudimentary stage, it is readily apparent that

TABLE VI

Absolute and Relative Importance of Rural Population,
by States, 1950 and 1960 *

State	Rural population		Per cent of total population classified as rural	
	1950	1960	1950	1960
Brazil	33,161,506 †	38,977,297 †	64	55
North				
Rondonia ‡	23,119	39,941	63	56
Acre ‡	93,483	126,210	82	79
Amazonas	376,363	481,556	73	67
Rio Branco ‡	12,984	16,772	72	57
Pará	734,262	920,263	65	59
Amapá	23,577	33,499	63	49
Northeast				
Maranhão	1,308,960	2,043,630	83	82
Piauí	875,112	965,216	84	76
Ceará	2,015,846	2,213,027	75	66
Rio Grande do Norte	714,156	722,069	74	62
Paraíba	1,256,543	1,309,972	73	65
Pernambuco	2,227,785	2,280,211	66	55
Alagôas	806,758	842,834	74	66
East				
Sergipe	439,377	464,344	68	61
Bahia	3,584,068	3,906,889	74	65
Minas Gerais	5,397,738	5,858,323	70	60
Espírito Santo	666,627	808,976	77	70
Rio de Janeiro	1,205,835	1,325,507	53	39
Guanabara	74,388	83,755	3	3
South				
São Paulo	4,330,212	4,825,770	47	37
Paraná	1,587,259	2,949,781	75	70
Santa Catarina	1,197,785	1,451,562	77	68
Rio Grande do Sul	2,742,841	3,003,049	66	55
West Central				
Mato Grosso	344,214	546,258	66	60
Goiás	969,254	1,355,458	80	69
Distrito Federal	———	52,044	—	37

* Compiled from a 1961 mimeographed release from the Serviço Nacional de Recenseamento, Instituto Brasileiro de Geografia e Estatística. The figures for 1960 were secured by totaling the enumerators' reports and, consequently, are subject to some rectification.
† Total includes data for Serra dos Aimorés in dispute between states of Minas Gerais and Espírito Santo.
‡ Territory.

the degree of rurality in Brazil is very high. The inhabitant of the average Brazilian town or village is conditioned to a far greater extent by cultural influences originating in the surrounding rural environment and much less by cultural forces emanating from the great urban centers, than the person living in a center of equal size in the

United States, England, Germany, or the other countries of western Europe. It will be many years before good roads, automobiles, electricity, telephones, radios, television sets, newspapers, and many other things that have become necessities in the average rural community in the United States are to be found in any extent in most of the rural districts in Brazil. In the meanwhile, the footpath, trail, or stream; the canoe, pack mule, riding horse, and oxcart; the lamp made at home from an old tin can or candles made from locally produced materials; and communication by word of mouth will remain the basic elements in the Brazilian rural scheme of living. There is no reason to doubt that, although Brazil's cities have moved ahead in the stream of modern progress, her rural districts have continued year after year with little or no visible change. Whereas in the United States the trends during the second quarter of the twentieth century did much to eliminate the differences between the rural and urban patterns of living, in Brazil the same forces have tended to accentuate even more the tremendous differences between the two.

NATIONAL ORIGINS

In 1950 about one inhabitant of Brazil out of every forty-four (2.3 per cent) had been born in a foreign country, mostly in Europe. At that time the corresponding percentage of foreign-born population in the United States was 6.7, indicating that immigration to Brazil had been much less important, even when placed on a relative basis, than that to our country. The nationalities represented among the 1,214,154 foreigners living in Brazil at the time of the 1950 census, and the relative importance of each, are given in Table VII, and a somewhat detailed discussion of the movement of foreigners into the country will be found in a separate chapter on immigration. Here it is important to indicate, however, that the absolute and relative importance of the foreign-born in Brazil's population is on the decline. Between 1940 and 1950 the number fell by almost 200,000 and the proportion from 3.4 to 2.3 per cent; the decrease between 1950 and 1960 probably was even greater.

Distribution. The most obvious fact regarding the distribution of foreigners in Brazil, as revealed by Table VIII, is that more than one-half of them were in São Paulo. The city of Rio de Janeiro and states of Rio Grande do Sul, Paraná, Rio de Janeiro, and Minas Gerais are the other divisions with significantly large foreign populations. However, the number of foreign-born gives a relatively poor index of the importance of foreign nationality, or at least of the foreign language groups. Viewed from this angle, Santa Catarina would probably stand out most strikingly because of the concentration there of people of German language and culture, followed by Rio Grande do Sul, Paraná, São Paulo, the city of Rio de Janeiro, and Espírito Santo, about in the order named. On any basis, eastern and northeastern Brazil must be thought of as the regions in which the original Indian, Ne-

TABLE VII

Nativity of Foreign-born Population, 1940 and 1950 *

Country of origin	Number		Per cent	
	1940	1950	1940	1950
Total	1,425,552	1,214,154	100.0	100.0
Portugal	380,325	310,261	26.7	25.6
Italy	325,305	242,337	22.8	20.0
Spain	160,557	131,608	11.3	10.8
Japan	144,523	129,192	10.2	10.6
Germany	97,105	65,814	6.8	5.4
Poland	47,151	48,806	3.3	4.0
U.S.S.R.	30,413	48,669	2.1	4.0
Syria-Lebanon	51,240	44,718	3.6	3.7
Romania	14,710	17,352	1.0	1.4
Uruguay	24,980	17,023	1.8	1.4
Argentina	17,925	15,492	1.3	1.3
Paraguay	14,660	14,762	1.0	1.2
Austria	22,671	14,634	1.6	1.2
Yugoslavia	9,945	13,216	0.7	1.1
United States and Puerto Rico	4,805	12,381	0.3	1.0
Hungary	13,519	10,483	1.0	0.9
France	8,093	8,604	0.6	0.7
Great Britain	5,844	5,444	0.4	0.4
Bolivia	4,541	5,120	0.3	0.4
Switzerland	4,312	4,484	0.3	0.4
Czechoslovakia	2,061	3,344	0.1	0.3
Holland	2,068	3,153	0.1	0.3
Turkey	3,172	2,726	0.2	0.2
Peru	2,778	2,358	0.2	0.2
Other and unknown	32,849	42,173	2.3	3.5

* Compiled and computed from data in "Censo Demográfico," VI *Recenseamento Geral do Brasil, 1950,* I (Rio de Janeiro, 1956).

gro, and Portuguese strains, which formed the basic elements in the Brazilian racial complex, have been left most to themselves. Very few representatives of foreign nationalities have entered these areas.

Relative Importance. On the basis of immigration statistics, it seems safe to conclude that the foreign nationalities in Brazil now rank as follows in importance: Portuguese and Italians, first and second, followed by Spaniards, Japanese, Germans, Poles, Russians, and Lebanese, in the order named. Except for the Japanese, who immigrated in large numbers only after 1925, the nationalities and the order are practically as they were in 1920.

Concentration in Cities. The tendency of the foreign elements to concentrate in cities is one of the most firmly established principles in the study of peoples and cultures. Therefore, it is of interest to examine the distribution of the foreign portion of the Brazilian population from this point of view. Unfortunately, the direct study of this subject is another investigation handicapped by the failure of the

TABLE VIII

Distribution of the Foreign-born, 1950, by States *

| State | Foreign-born population | | Per cent of Brazil's foreign-born |
	Number	Percentage of total population	
Brazil	1,214,154	2.3	100.0
São Paulo	693,321	7.6	57.1
Distrito Federal	210,454	8.9	17.3
Rio Grande do Sul	78,138	1.9	6.4
Paraná	76,592	3.6	6.3
Rio de Janeiro	38,395	1.7	3.2
Minas Gerais	32,896	0.4	2.7
Mato Grosso	19,753	3.8	1.6
Santa Catarina	19,067	1.2	1.6
Bahia	8,224	0.2	0.7
Pará	8,215	0.7	0.7
Espírito Santo	6,507	0.8	0.6
Pernambuco	5,551	0.2	0.5
Amazonas	5,192	1.0	0.4
Goiás	3,667	0.3	0.3
Ceará	1,206	†	0.1
Maranhão	1,008	0.1	0.1
Paraíba	516	†	0.1
Rio Grande do Norte	453	†	†
Alagôas	421	†	†
Piauí	258	†	†
Sergipe	184	†	†
Territories and Serra dos Aimorés	4,136	1.1	0.3

* Compiled and computed from data in "Censo Demográfico," VI *Recenseamento Geral do Brasil, 1950*, I (Rio de Janeiro, 1956), 71.
† Less than 0.1 per cent

Brazilian census to tabulate separately some of the principal characteristics of the rural and the urban parts of the population. However, the high percentage of foreigners in Rio de Janeiro and some of the other principal cities is easily demonstrated. Thus in 1950 the Distrito Federal, almost the same as the city of Rio de Janeiro proper, with only 4.6 per cent of the nation's inhabitants, had 17.3 per cent of her foreign-born residents. Similarly, the município of São Paulo, almost coextensive with the city of São Paulo, contained in 1950 only 24 per cent of the state's population and 316,589 (or 46 per cent) of the foreign-born segment. Likewise, in Minas Gerais, the município of Belo Horizonte, with 4.6 per cent of the people in Brazil's second most populous state, had 20 per cent of those born in another country, and finally, in the state of Rio de Janeiro, the Baixada da Guanabara (the zone about the Bay), which includes Niterói, Nova Iguaçu, São João de Merití, and numerous other suburbs and satellites of Rio de Janeiro, with 33 per cent of the state's population, had 60 per cent of the foreign-born.

AGE

Characteristics of the Age Profile. Few features of Brazil's population are of greater significance than the manner in which it is distributed according to age. As in other parts of the world in which both the birth rate and the death rate are very high, Brazil's population is highly concentrated in the tender years of life, whereas the percentage of persons at the productive ages of life is somewhat low, and the proportions of those in the advanced ages are very low indeed. See Figure 9. Thus according to data from the 1950 census, the latest available at the time of writing, 41.9 per cent of the population was less than fifteen years of age, a figure much above the corresponding one of 26.9 for the United States the same year. On the other hand, the elderly portion of the population was much less important, rela-

FIGURE 9. A comparison of the age-sex pyramid for Brazil in 1950 with that for the United States in 1850.

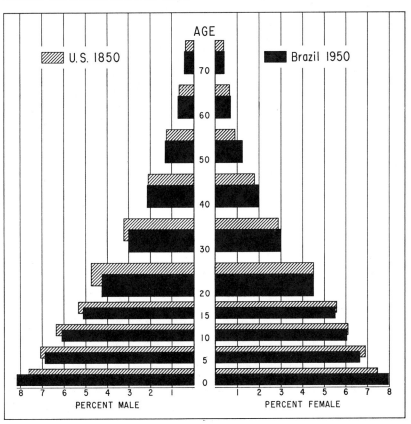

tively, than in countries such as the United States, France, Great Britain, Germany, and Australia, where the rate of reproduction is lower and the length of life considerably longer. To cite the specific data, in 1950 only 2.4 per cent of the Brazilian population was aged 65 years or over, compared with 8.1 per cent in our own country. Since 1950 this percentage in the United States has risen to above 9; whereas it is very doubtful if any significant change has taken place in the proportion of the elderly in the Brazilian population.

If one seeks the age distribution of the population of the United States that corresponds most closely with that of the contemporary Brazilian population, it is necessary to go back to 1850. See Figure 9. During the last century a long-sustained fall in the birth rate, followed by the recovery that set in during the 1930's, has drastically changed the age distribution of those living in the United States, and a similar severe reduction in the rate of reproduction in Brazil is the only factor that can bring about any substantial change in the configuration of the Brazilian age-sex pyramid. Indeed, in spite of dramatic decreases in the death rate, the age distribution of the Brazilian population probably is essentially the same as it was in 1900.

Of particular significance is the ratio of persons in the biologically and economically productive years of life to those who are largely dependent on others for the goods and services they consume. In any

FIGURE 10. Index numbers showing the extent to which the urban, suburban, and rural populations contained more or less than their proportionate shares of each age group in the Brazilian population, 1950.

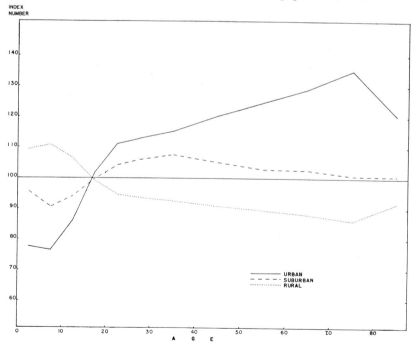

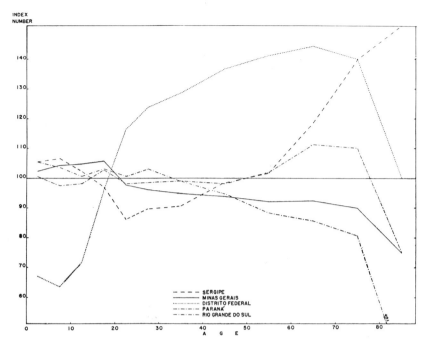

FIGURE 11. Index numbers showing the extent to which Sergipe, Minas Gerais, the Distrito Federal, Paraná, and Rio Grande do Sul contained more or less than their proportionate shares of each age group in the Brazilian population, 1950.

population the ratio of persons between the ages of fifteen and sixty-five to those who are either under fifteen or over sixty-five is a highly significant indicator. On this basis there were in Brazil, in 1950, 80 dependents per 100 producers; in the United States the corresponding ratio was only 54. In other words, the average breadwinner in Brazil has a third more mouths to feed than does his counterpart in the United States.

Rural-Urban Differences. A widely observed demographic tendency is for the young to be concentrated in the rural sections of a country, whereas those in the reproductive ages are found in high proportions in the towns and cities. Brazil is no exception to this rule. See Figure 10. Where cities have been growing with great rapidity in the years just prior to the taking of the census, there also generally is a tendency for the aged to be underrepresented in the urban districts. This, though, definitely is not the case in Brazil.

Other Differences. Because of the heavy flow of population from one part of Brazil to another and because of the general tendency of migration to select persons between the ages of sixteen and thirty, one would expect that the age distributions would vary greatly from one state to another. This expectation is abundantly confirmed by the data. See Figure 11. In making use of this chart one should note the relative scarcity of children in the Distrito Federal (i.e., the city of

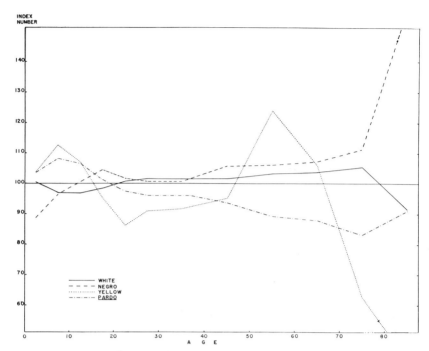

FIGURE 12. Index numbers showing the extent to which the white, Negro, yellow and pardo populations contained more or less than their proportionate shares of each age group in the Brazilian population, 1950.

Rio de Janeiro) and the excessive proportions of the aged in Sergipe, from which such large proportions of the population have migrated. Minas Gerais, the state sending out the largest numbers of migrants —a process that has been going on for decades—contains as a result low proportions of all ages except the very young. Paraná, however, does not contain the concentrations of persons ages twenty-five to fifty that might be expected because of the recent heavy influx of persons, and Rio Grande do Sul has especially low proportions of those above forty, perhaps because of movements from the state prior to 1940.

The differences between the age distributions of the white, Negro, pardo (Indian and mixed), and yellow segments of the population are interesting but not particularly easy to explain. See Figure 12. The yellow or Japanese contingent contains two concentrations of significance: one in the ages fifty to sixty-five, reflecting the heavy immigration immediately before the second world war, and the second, in the ages up to fifteen, representing the offspring of those immigrants. Miscegenation is a possible explanation of the tendency of the Negro population to be concentrated in the ages above forty and that of the pardos to be scarce in all ages above twenty-five. The white population, of course, which represents almost two-thirds of the total, corresponds most closely to the average.

SEX

The population of Brazil is almost exactly equally divided between the sexes, there being in 1950, as reported by the census, 25,885,001 males and 26,059,396 females in the country. This gives a sex ratio of 99.3 males per 100 females. In 1920, however, the corresponding ratio was 101.7, and it was exactly 100 in 1940. Were it not for the fact that Brazil's population has been considerably swollen by immigration from abroad, the sex ratio would be somewhat lower, for among the native-born population in 1950 there were only 98.7 males per 100 females, as compared with sex ratios of 121 and 197 among the persons born in other countries who were classified as foreigners and naturalized Brazilians, respectively. Elsewhere in the Americas some sex ratios revealed by the data of the 1950 censuses are as follows: Costa Rica, 99.7; the Dominican Republic, 100.6; El Salvador, 98.0; Guatemala, 102.3; Mexico, 97.0; Panama, 103.6; Ecuador, 99.7; Paraguay, 96.6; Puerto Rico, 99.5; and the United States, 98.8. In 1947, Argentina had 105.1 males for every 100 females in its population. Thus the sex ratio in Brazil runs slightly higher than that which is general in America. In part this is due to immigration, and in part it may be due to the combined effect of high fertility and high mortality which tends to concentrate the population in the younger ages of life where the proportions of males are high.

The proportions of the sexes vary considerably from one part of Brazil to another. See Table ix. In the first place there is the usual tendency for the males to concentrate in rural districts and the females in towns and cities. Thus in 1950 the sex ratio in the urban population was only 89.8, and that in the suburban population 95.1, compared with one of 104.1 in the rural population. Were it not for the fact that the foreign-born population, with its high proportions of males, is highly concentrated in the cities, these rural-urban differences would be even more pronounced.

The parts of Brazil which are receiving heavy currents of migration from other parts of the country also have had the relative importance of their male populations inflated by that fact; those which are losing heavily by migration are the ones in which females predominate to the greatest extent. For observing this tendency, the materials pertaining to the native population as given in Table ix are especially significant. Acre, Guaporé, Mato Grosso, Amazonas, Amapá, Paraná, São Paulo, and Goiás have received considerable influxes of population from some of the other states; the states in the Northeast, and particularly Sergipe, Alagôas, Bahia, Paraíba, Rio Grande do Norte, and Ceará, in addition to Minas Gerais, have sent forth these currents.

The predominance of females reaches its maximum in the towns and cities of the zones that are giving large numbers of migrants to other sections of the republic; the proportions of males become greatest in the frontier areas into which there is a rush of population.

TABLE IX

Number of Males per 100 Females in Each State, 1950, by Nativity and Residence *

State	Total population	Native-born population	Urban population	Rural population
Brazil	99.3	98.7	89.8	104.1
North				
Guaporé †	130.6	132.5	105.1	147.8
Acre †	120.1	119.8	98.5	125.1
Amazonas	105.3	104.9	88.4	111.3
Rio Branco †	113.8	113.5	107.0	116.2
Pará	100.5	100.1	86.5	106.7
Amapá	110.9	109.9	114.7	112.1
Northeast				
Maranhão	99.6	99.5	83.3	102.7
Piauí	97.9	97.8	78.6	100.8
Ceará	96.2	96.2	79.7	100.5
Rio Grande do Norte	95.9	95.9	82.1	100.3
Paraíba	94.5	94.5	81.8	98.5
Pernambuco	93.9	93.8	81.1	99.0
Alagôas	93.0	92.9	77.2	97.7
East				
Sergipe	90.9	90.9	77.1	96.2
Bahia	94.8	94.7	82.3	98.9
Minas Gerais	98.9	98.7	86.6	103.7
Espírito Santo	102.9	102.7	89.7	106.4
Rio de Janeiro	102.1	101.3	95.4	107.2
Distrito Federal	95.7	92.2	92.3	114.3
South				
São Paulo	103.6	102.5	95.6	111.7
Paraná	106.6	105.9	95.3	109.7
Santa Catarina	102.3	102.0	92.0	105.2
Rio Grande do Sul	99.9	99.4	87.9	104.9
West Central				
Mato Grosso	108.0	107.0	90.7	115.9
Goiás	103.6	103.4	89.9	107.0

* Computed from data in "Censo Demográfico," VI Recenseamento Geral do Brasil, 1950, I (Rio de Janeiro, 1956).
† Territory.

One should note in this connection the very low sex ratios in the urban portions of such states as Piauí, Ceará, Alagôas, and Sergipe, and the very high ones in the rural parts of the Amazon Basin and in the rural districts of the states of São Paulo, Paraná, Goiás, and Mato Grosso.

OCCUPATIONAL STATUS

The occupational statistics are the most unreliable, confusing, and misused portions of the modern census. One seldom can be sure whether an analysis of them has clarified the situation or only added to the existing confusion. Consequently, no detailed discussion of Brazilian occupational statistics is attempted.

There are three points that must be evident to one who studies Brazil, even though he never makes any examination whatsoever of numerical data. These are that (1) the overwhelming proportion of the Brazilian people obtain their livelihood from agricultural and collecting enterprises, (2) the contingents employed in domestic and personal services are exceedingly large in proportion to the population of the nation, and (3) because of the role of the human being as a beast of burden and because such a large share of the things transported are carried on the heads of men and women, or packed on the backs of animals, or hauled in oxcarts, or loaded into small boats, the number of persons engaged in transportation activities is also very large in comparison with the volume transported and the population of the nation.

For those who do make use of the statistical materials relative to the labor force and occupations in Brazil, even more precautions are in order than is generally the case. To begin with, in Brazilian cities it is the general rule for those in moderate and well-to-do economic circumstances to hold more than one job or to exercise more than one profession. As a result the problem of classification is greatly complicated, and neither the Brazilian census nor those of other countries is adequately prepared for the task involved. For example, the 1950 census accounted for only 865,026 persons as having supplementary occupations out of a total of 36,557,900 in the active population aged ten years or over. Moreover, almost one-fourth of these (198,697) had agriculture and pastoral activities given as their secondary activity; 123,254 were classified as having domestic service and other remunerated service activities as their secondary occupations; and considerably more than one-fourth of all (239,068) were grouped in the category that is made up of unpaid domestic workers and persons attending school.

In the second place, of the total active population of thirty-six and one-half millions, 6,308,567, or more than 17 per cent, were children aged ten to fourteen. Inasmuch as most of the tabulations of the occupational data do not include cross-tabulations by age, the inclusion of these children in the totals is a serious complicating factor. It is true that almost 75 per cent of the girls involved are in the category that consists solely of unpaid domestic service workers and those attending school, but of the boys involved 1,108,734 are neither in that category nor in agriculture. Consequently, their inclusion serves to confuse seriously all attempts to secure adequate indicators of the absolute and relative importance of the other principal occupational groupings.

Finally, the inclusion of children attending school and unpaid domestic workers in the active category and the grouping of those engaged in construction, manufacturing and processing into a single category, one which cannot be properly subdivided for most purposes, are other serious deficiencies in the available statistical information relative to the occupations of the Brazilian people.

The most pertinent of the materials on the occupational status of the Brazilian population are summarized in Table x. In the information presented there, all those classified as inactive, those counted as employed solely in unpaid domestic services, those reported as attending school, and the small number of those unclassified or for whom information was lacking were eliminated from the total. This procedure actually reduced the figure from 36,557,990, as given in the census reports, to that of 17,070,688 used in the table. In addition, since it was possible to do so in this particular case, those engaged in construction activities are given separately, as are those engaged in domestic service.

It seems to be worthwhile to comment briefly upon each of the major categories included in this compilation. To begin with, it is important to stress that as late as 1950, 58 per cent of all Brazilian workers were engaged in agricultural, pastoral, and forestry activities. Of those in the general category, those classified as employed in forestry were insignificant in number (only 8,885), and those in stockraising as such were only 358,998, or 3.5 per cent of the group. Even more important are the facts that of the 9,886,934 persons in the general category, 9,337,366 (94.4 per cent) are designated in another tabulation as "laborers and hoe workers" and only 321,814 as those responsible for the management function either as owners, managers, or renters.

The extractive industries include many of the activities for which Brazilians are noted àt home and abroad. Therefore it is interesting to observe that of slightly less than one-half million persons involved, 114,069 were reported as engaged in fishing, 106,362 in the collection and coagulation of rubber, 66,955 in woodcutting and logging, 36,036 in the extraction of metallic and nonmetallic minerals, 35,172 in the search for diamonds and other precious and semiprecious stones, 7,688 in the production of salt, and 1,406 in hunting.

Even with construction taken out of the general category, manufacturing and processing ranks second to agriculture in providing jobs for Brazilian breadwinners. Nevertheless, in 1950 less than one worker in ten was so engaged, although undoubtedly the number and proportion have increased considerably since that time, and they may be expected to rise even more abruptly in the immediate future. The more important components of the category, with the number of workers reported in each, are as follows: textiles, 368,960; food products and stimulants, except edible oils and tobacco, 246,544; metallic and mechanical products, 174,607; processing nonmetallic minerals, 164,902; chemical and pharmaceutical industries, 75,419; and the manufacturing of shoes, 62,218.

Of those in the construction category, the bulk were brick or stone masons and so forth (248,747) or their assistants (118,332).

Wholesale and retail trade ranks fourth, on the basis of the number of workers employed, of all the industrial categories. More than a third (361,300) of all those in the group were occupied in connection with the distribution of food, drink, and stimulants; 158,950 were re-

TABLE X

*Distribution of Economically Active Population 10 Years of Age and over by Industry, 1950, by Sex **

Industry	Both sexes		Males		Females	
	Number	Per cent	Number	Per cent	Number	Per cent
Total	17,070,688	100.0	14,571,810	100.0	2,498,878	100.0
Agriculture, stockraising, and forestry	9,886,934	57.9	9,154,034	62.8	732,900	29.3
Extractive industries	482,972	2.8	454,984	3.1	27,988	1.1
Manufacturing and processing	1,646,561	9.6	1,261,353	8.7	385,208	15.4
Construction	584,644	3.4	580,795	4.0	3,849	0.1
Wholesale and retail trade	958,509	5.6	869,448	6.0	89,061	3.7
Real estate, banking, credit, and insurance	115,488	0.7	102,744	0.7	12,744	0.5
Domestic service	673,558	4.0	46,676	0.3	626,882	25.1
Other services	999,244	5.9	700,153	4.8	299,091	12.0
Transportation, communication, and storage	697,089	4.1	668,267	4.6	28,822	1.2
Liberal professions	78,730	0.5	64,503	0.4	14,227	0.6
Social activities	434,315	2.5	200,689	1.4	233,626	9.3
Public administration, legislation, and justice	260,767	1.5	220,636	1.5	40,131	1.6
National defense and public security	251,877	1.5	247,528	1.7	4,349	0.1

* Compiled and computed from data in "Censo Demográfico," VI Recenseamento Geral do Brasil, 1950, I (Rio de Janeiro, 1956), 34–35.

ported to be occupied in the sale of cloth, wearing apparel, shoes, and related items; and 128,866 were classified as gaining a livelihood in connection with the open markets or as peddlers. As the number of corners occupied by gasoline filling stations multiplies, it is interesting to note that in 1950 only 30,509 workers were reported to be engaged in the sale of fuel and oils.

Real estate, banking, credit, and insurance, although all together in a single general category, supply jobs for less than one per cent of the gainfully employed Brazilians. More than half of these (59,530) were placed in banking alone, and 16,435 were reported to be in activities connected with real estate. In 1950 in all of Brazil only 16,504 persons were reported to be employed in activities connected with insurance of all types. In this connection one easily deduces that a thriving insurance business, such as that of Canada or that of the United States, cannot grow and develop in a country in which inflation is rampant decade after decade. Under such circumstances one of the greatest inducements (perhaps one should say obligations) for the average family to save a substantial part of its income, the building up of huge sums domestically for investment in national projects, and all of the contributions of what may be a nation's greatest business to the growth of the gross national product, all are impossible. Where, as several Brazilian friends have told the present writer, "only a fool would buy life insurance," one of the greatest instruments that may be used for the promotion of social and economic development is almost completely unused.

Four per cent of all Brazilians actively engaged are employed in domestic service. Most of these workers are women. Undoubtedly, though, occupational differentiation has not progressed to the point at which the numerical importance of this category is adequately reflected by the data, a fact that is also of great importance in connection with transportation. This is to say that large numbers of men and women, nominally classified as engaged in agriculture, actually spend much of their time as domestic servants or in carrying, packing, paddling, or hauling products from one place to another.

The "other services" category includes a broad miscellany of activities, of which that connected with making, repairing, and cleaning articles for domestic use accounts for more than two-fifths (415,270) of the total. More than one-half of these (241,410) are women. Second in numerical importance in the general group are the 183,020 persons reported to be occupied in providing meals and lodging for others, and in third place are the 168,004 workers employed to repair and maintain machines and vehicles.

As indicated above, many of the workers who spend substantial amounts of time transporting goods and products do not figure in the formal category of those classified as engaged in transportation, communication, and storage. Indeed, of the 108,127 workers reported in one tabulation to be carters or conductors of pack animals, only 49,461 are accounted for by those in the general occupational category under consideration. Another contingent (39,575), almost as large, is made up of those in agriculture. The larger components of the general group, along with the number of workers reported for each, are as follows: land transportation by means of motor vehicles, 224,961; rail transportation, 196,353; water transportation (sea, river, and lake), 64,668; transportation by means of draft and pack animals, 60,750; port services, 51,376; postal, telegraphic, and radio services, 38,269; urban streetcar services, 21,510; telephone services, 15,253; air transportation, 13,392; and storage, 7,770.

Of the total number reported as engaged in the liberal professions, those engaged in medicine, dentistry, veterinary medicine, and related activities were the most numerous (44,856). In another census table, the number of physicians alone is reported as 22,212 and that of dentists, 18,445. Those reported as engaged in the practice of law and related services are 13,366; and in another table the number of lawyers by profession is given as 15,566.

The category designated as "social activities" in Table x is made up largely of the 214,050 persons reported as engaged in educational activities, of whom 149,088 were attributed to public educational institutions and 64,970 to the private. (In another separate tabulation the number of teachers is given as 169,695). In second place in this general category are the 80,498 workers employed in all activities connected with the disposal of the wastes, cleaning, and supplying of urban centers. Also in this grouping is the conspicuously small number (14,682) of persons reported as occupied in church and church-related activities. (In another table 8,615 men and 5,975 women are reported specifically as being engaged in religious occupations.)

Despite the small sums spent for local governmental services (see Chapter xxi), of the total reported in activities related to public administration, legislative functions, and justice, almost one-third (75,101) were classified as being employed in public administration in the municípios. Public administration at the state level, in turn, accounted for 63,383 of the total, and that at the national level, for 48,617. Activities connected with the administration of justice gave employment to 29,879 persons, and those related to legislative bodies to 3,833.

Finally, the 251,877 persons reported as engaged in activities related to national defense and public security were distributed as follows: the army, 99,137; military police, 44,929; civil police, 35,792; the air force, 32,026; the navy, 31,808; firemen, 3,756; and other, 4,429.

Our knowledge of the fundamental characteristics of the Brazilian labor force is considerably enhanced by an analysis of data gathered in the 1950 census which classify those engaged in each of the broad industrial categories according to their status within the industry. Four classes or categories are employed for this purpose: employer, employee, own account worker, and family worker. These materials are given separately for each of the sexes and are cross-tabulated according to color. Accordingly, the data for males ten years of age and over, further classified according to color, are presented in Table xi.

That those who themselves are performing the management func-

TABLE XI

Brazilian Males 10 Years of Age and over Classified According to Industry and Status, 1950, by Color *

Industry, status, and sex	Total †		Whites		Negroes		Yellow		Pardo ‡	
	Number	Per cent	Number	Per cent	Number	Per cent	Number	Per cent	Number	Per cent
All industries	14,113,044	100.0	8,679,995	100.0	1,631,579	100.0	92,178	100.0	3,683,713	100.0
Employers	607,615	4.3	502,731	5.8	18,337	1.1	10,840	11.8	74,920	2.0
Employees	6,596,093	46.7	4,020,649	46.3	948,774	58.1	21,879	23.7	1,591,187	43.2
Own account workers	4,507,972	32.0	2,687,238	31.0	444,778	27.3	32,149	34.9	1,336,596	36.3
Family workers	2,401,364	17.0	1,469,377	16.9	219,690	13.5	27,310	29.6	681,010	18.5
Agriculture, forestry and fishing	9,144,582	100.0	5,257,543	100.0	1,143,181	100.0	63,613	100.0	2,665,163	100.0
Employers	314,037	3.4	239,223	4.5	13,970	1.2	6,901	10.8	53,543	2.0
Employees	3,154,042	34.5	1,675,638	31.9	552,143	48.3	9,771	15.4	910,596	34.2
Own account workers	3,420,603	37.4	1,966,169	37.4	365,422	32.0	22,436	35.3	1,061,414	39.8
Family workers	2,255,900	24.7	1,376,513	26.2	211,646	18.5	24,505	38.5	639,610	24.0
Extractive industries	454,425	100.0	184,403	100.0	62,971	100.0	467	100.0	205,488	100.0
Employers	8,775	1.9	5,500	3.0	632	1.0	31	6.6	2,600	1.3
Employees	211,473	46.6	99,365	53.9	33,731	53.6	133	28.5	77,733	37.8
Own account workers	182,250	40.1	62,290	33.8	23,535	37.4	188	40.3	95,810	46.6
Family workers	51,927	11.4	17,248	9.3	5,073	8.0	115	24.6	29,345	14.3
Manufacturing, construction, and processing	1,841,115	100.0	1,261,382	100.0	218,953	100.0	5,538	100.0	351,412	100.0
Employers	88,923	4.8	81,858	6.5	1,270	0.6	901	16.3	4,792	1.4
Employees	1,593,516	86.6	1,075,024	85.2	203,198	92.8	3,592	64.8	308,331	87.7
Own account workers	137,009	7.4	87,631	7.0	13,436	6.1	685	12.4	34,955	10.0
Family workers	21,667	1.2	16,869	1.3	1,049	0.5	360	6.5	3,334	0.9
Wholesale and retail trade	868,017	100.0	688,699	100.0	39,672	100.0	9,271	100.0	128,846	100.0
Employers	115,845	13.3	105,165	15.3	1,077	2.7	1,291	13.9	8,166	6.3
Employees	385,904	44.5	304,828	44.3	23,792	60.0	3,147	34.0	53,344	41.4
Own account workers	333,687	38.4	251,539	36.5	14,235	35.9	3,907	42.1	63,471	49.3
Family workers	32,581	3.8	27,167	3.9	568	1.4	926	10.0	3,865	3.0

Industry, status, and sex	Total†		Whites		Negroes		Yellow		Pardo‡	
	Number	Per cent	Number	Per cent	Number	Per cent	Number	Per cent	Number	Per cent
Finance, insurance and real estate	102,653	100.0	93,976	100.0	1,957	100.0	822	100.0	5,761	100.0
Employers	2,748	2.7	2,686	2.9	6	0.3	21	2.6	33	0.6
Employees	87,602	85.3	80,019	85.1	1,777	90.8	551	67.0	5,138	89.2
Own account workers	12,140	11.8	11,125	11.8	171	8.7	247	30.0	579	10.0
Family workers	163	0.2	146	0.2	3	0.2	3	0.4	11	0.2
Services	745,678	100.0	524,978	100.0	64,900	100.0	9,357	100.0	144,739	100.0
Employers	61,031	8.2	53,870	10.2	1,120	1.7	1,526	16.3	4,410	3.0
Employees	407,858	54.7	280,680	53.5	44,495	68.6	3,351	35.8	78,258	54.1
Own account workers	256,411	34.4	175,326	33.4	18,502	28.5	3,228	34.5	58,862	40.7
Family workers	20,378	2.7	15,102	2.9	783	1.2	1,252	13.4	3,209	2.2
Transportation, communications and storage	667,816	100.0	447,799	100.0	77,157	100.0	2,102	100.0	139,197	100.0
Employers	11,058	1.7	9,481	2.1	238	0.3	100	4.8	1,224	0.9
Employees	545,483	81.7	353,709	79.0	69,084	89.5	875	41.6	120,462	86.5
Own account workers	106,393	15.9	80,831	18.0	7,589	9.9	1,049	49.9	16,738	12.0
Family workers	4,882	0.7	3,778	0.9	246	0.3	78	3.7	773	0.6
Liberal professions	64,395	100.0	59,876	100.0	681	100.0	594	100.0	3,174	100.0
Employers	3,894	6.0	3,739	6.2	8	1.2	55	9.2	89	2.8
Employees	12,068	18.7	10,275	17.2	414	60.8	194	32.7	1,161	36.6
Own account workers	47,949	74.5	45,408	75.9	256	37.6	336	56.6	1,889	59.5
Family workers	484	0.8	434	0.7	3	0.4	9	1.5	35	1.1
Social activities	200,445	100.0	146,951	100.0	18,590	100.0	342	100.0	34,158	100.0
Employers	1,084	0.5	1,022	0.7	12	0.1	11	3.2	38	0.1
Employees	182,574	91.1	131,077	89.2	18,152	97.6	211	61.7	32,772	96.0
Own account workers	3,896	1.9	2,986	2.0	181	1.0	62	18.1	661	1.9
Family workers	12,891	6.5	11,866	8.1	245	1.3	58	17.0	687	2.0
Public administration, legislation and justice	220,636	—	171,170	—	14,034	—	90	—	34,945	—
National defense and public security	247,528	—	174,651	—	19,984	—	138	—	52,476	—

* Source of basic data: "Censo Demográfico," VI Recenseamento Geral do Brasil, 1950, I (Rio de Janeiro, 1956), 30, 31.

† Includes those not declared by color.

‡ Includes Indians, mulattoes, mestiços, etc.

tion in connection with their economic activities are relatively few is apparent to all who examine these data. Even in agriculture and the extractive industries, those working under the direction of someone else greatly predominate.

In addition, the facts in Table xi supply additional evidence that socio-economic status and color are closely correlated in Brazil. Within each of the major industrial categories the whites and the Japanese are found in the employer category in much higher proportions, and in the employee group in much lower proportions, than the Negroes. In these respects the *pardos* occupy the intermediate position in occupational status just as they do in color.

CHAPTER VI

FERTILITY

T HE CHILD is the best immigrant," "Brazil is a vast hospital," "the march to the West," "to people is to rule," "our social sertão"— these and the cry that is as old as Brazil, *falta de braços*, have occupied considerable space in Brazilian publications and have been the concern of its thinkers. Facts about fertility and mortality in Brazil are among the most important items of national accounting; for only such information secured on a comprehensive and accurate basis can supply the necessary guidance for programs of immigration, public health, education, agriculture, and industry.

Nevertheless, one who attempts to determine the speed with which the Brazilian population is reproducing, the mortality rates of the population, and the rate of natural increase, or to estimate what the population will be five, ten, or twenty years from now is faced with no easy task. It is not surprising that the Instituto Brasileiro de Geografia e Estatística was off some three and one-half millions, or more than 8 per cent, in its estimates of the population of Brazil preceding the 1940 census. Many improvements, of course, have taken place since then, but even so the available demographic material on Brazil must be used with the greatest skill and caution. Reasonable approximations carefully tested from all possible angles must be relied on.

In demographic study the first task is, of course, to determine the speed with which the population is reproducing—the fertility rate. Then one should attempt to relate this to mortality and migration, to determine natural increase and growth of population; and he should seek to determine the nature and the importance of the factors that are responsible for variations in the rates of reproduction. This chapter is concerned with fertility.

TWO INDEXES OF FERTILITY

In the study of fertility or reproduction there are two principal types of indexes used as yardsticks. One of these is the *birth rate*. Most modern nations have established as one of their specific functions a public recording system which includes periodic reports on the number of births. In Brazil this is called the *registro civil*. Formerly, church records were among the best sources of materials of this type concerning the reproduction of the population. However, church records are of little worth for this purpose where religious heterogeneity is great or where the birth rites are not among the more important of the church ceremonies. Since Latin-American countries, including Brazil, are strongly Catholic and since this church attaches so much importance to the baptism of the infant, its records are of great value in a study of the demography of these American nations.

A second type of approach to the study of fertility or reproduction makes use of data secured by *enumeration*, such data generally being more complete than those secured by the recording method. The enumerations used in this case are those of age and sex secured in a census of the population. By relating the number of young children to the number of women of childbearing ages, a rather highly refined measure of the fertility of population is automatically secured. Usually, children under five are related to the number of women 15 to 44, or 20 to 44, inclusive. During the last three decades this method has been developed and widely applied in the United States, where it has been of material assistance in clearing up many of the more perplexing questions involved in population study.

Nevertheless, measures of the second type, called the *fertility ratio,* must also be used with care on Brazilian data, for several reasons. First, the age distributions used in the census tabulations group all females 40 to 50 in the same category. Therefore, unless one cares to make estimates of the age distribution within this class, which estimates also are time consuming, the females used in the formula must be those aged 15 to 39, or 15 to 49, inclusive. This means either leaving out a good many women who are still in the childbearing ages or including some women who have already passed that state. However, this difficulty is a small one in comparison with the second. The terrific infant and child mortality rates characteristic of some areas and classes in Brazil greatly complicate the use of children under five in the formula. Where infant mortality rates of 300 or more are followed by other heavy decimations during the second, third, fourth, and fifth years of life, one cannot be sure of the relationship between children under five and the number of live births. As a result the fertility ratio loses in value as a measure of the speed of reproduction; especially is it invalidated for comparative purposes, such as a study of the reproduction rate in São Paulo, where the infant and child mortality rates are comparatively low, in relation to that of Piauí or Rio Grande do Norte, where they are excessively high. However, even in this case the fertility ratio is still valuable as a measure of what might be called the "effective fertility," i.e., the reproduction that is not liquidated during the first few years of life.

RATE OF REPRODUCTION

The Registration of Births. In the 1940's it became evident in Brazil that the nation's official birth statistics were woefully deficient, and after the 1939–1940 issue of the *Anuário Estatístico* this official compilation no longer has carried a series giving the reported birth rates. The reason, of course, is that only a part of the births are registered. Materials from the 1960 volume of the *Anuário* illustrate perfectly the state of birth registration in Brazil.

The recording and reporting unit is called a *cartório,* and in the *Anuário Estatístico* cartórios are separated into three categories: those said to supply complete information, those reported to give partial information only, and those reporting no information. The total number of cartórios indicated is 6,531 for 1956, 5,825 for 1957, and 6,501 for 1958. Most of the variation in this reported total is accounted for by the fact that the figure for São Paulo (reported to be 873 for 1956 and also for 1958) is not included in the national total for 1957, and that for Pernambuco (reported at 317 for 1956 and 325 for 1957) does not contribute to the total for 1958. Of the 6,501 cartórios in 1958, 4,310 were reported as having complete records, 1,550 as supplying partial information, and 617 as sending in no information. For the years under consideration the numbers of live births registered are given as 1,326,127 for 1956, 2,035,840 for 1957, and 2,454,682 for 1958. These totals may be compared with an estimate of 2,648,118 live births in 1957 made by the Statistical Laboratory of the Instituto Brasileiro de Geografia e Estatística.

Estimated Birth Rates. Despite the paucity of the data there have been some concerted efforts to determine the approximate level of the birth rate in Brazil. Working with materials on baptisms by the Catholic Church, the present writer some years ago concluded that in 1940 the birth rate must have been at least 40 per 1,000 population. Later Giorgio Mortara, through a study of the 1940 census data and all of the birth records that had been assembled in the various cities and states, concluded that the true birth rate fell somewhere between the limits of 39.5 and 47.8 and that a reasonable figure was 42.3. His calculations indicated that the lowest birth rate was in the Distrito Federal (between 26.5 and 32.0), followed most closely by the state of São Paulo (between 37.8 and 45.7) and Alagôas (between 38.4 and 46.4). The highest rate, according to his computations, was in Santa Catarina (between 45.5 and 55.0), rivaled most closely by Ceará (between 45.4 and 54.8) and Espírito Santo (between 45.2 and 54.5). His minimum estimates were above 40 for all of the states except São Paulo and Alagôas, mentioned above, and Pará (38.6), Pernambuco (38.9), Sergipe (38.9), and Bahia (38.5).[1]

Still more recently members of the staff of the Statistical Laboratory of the Instituto Brasileiro de Geografia e Estatística have prepared estimates of the birth rate in Brazil and in each of the states and territories of which it is composed. These materials are for the year 1957.[2] The rate for Brazil as a whole is given as 43, and indexes varying from 44 to 48 are reported for all major civil divisions ex-

[1] *Estimativas da Taxa de Natalidade para o Brasil, as Unidades da Federação e as Principais Capitais* (Rio de Janeiro, 1948), 11–12.
[2] *Anuário Estatístico, 1960,* XXI, 26.

cept Rio Grande do Sul, São Paulo, and Guanabara, for which the estimated birth rates are 39, 38, and 25, respectively. A birth rate of 43, or even one of 40 is a remarkable figure for a nation to maintain in the middle of the twentieth century. It is matched in very few places in the modern world outside of Latin America.[3]

Fertility Ratios. The conclusion stated above is strongly supported by the data on the rate of reproduction in Brazil as gauged by the fertility ratio, or the number of children under 5 per 100 women in the ages 15 to 49, inclusive. In 1950 this index for Brazil equaled 65, and comparable figures for a few other countries at approximately the same time are as follows: Colombia, 68; Chile, 57; Mexico, 63; Peru, 66; France, 28; Italy, 40; Puerto Rico, 73; and the United States, 42.[4] Furthermore, these fertility ratios support the conclusion, based on the estimated birth rates given above, that the rate of reproduction remains high throughout nearly all parts of Brazil. In fact, except in the old Distrito Federal (i.e., the city of Rio de Janeiro), for which the fertility ratio in 1950 was only 37, and in the state of São Paulo, for which it was 57, there were in every one of the states and territories at least 65 children under 5 per 100 women aged 15–49; in states such as Piauí, Ceará, Santa Catarina, and Mato Grosso this index was above 75.

DIFFERENTIAL FERTILITY

At best, only a few of the more elementary facts about differential fertility in Brazil may be established with the available data. The birth data, as has been seen, are totally inadequate for this and other purposes, and the 1940 population data were not tabulated in a way that permits many of the more significant indexes of fertility to be computed. For example, neither the age distributions of the various color categories nor those of the rural and urban populations were given separately. The 1950 materials, however, are much improved in these respects.

Rural-Urban Differentials. The lower fertility of urban populations in comparison with rural seems to be universal in twentieth century society. One who merely visits Brazilian cities, observes the number of children, sees even the upper-class families with numerous offspring, and visits some of the large apartment houses that are inhabited solely by persons of near kinship may perhaps doubt that Brazil's country people reproduce more rapidly than its city residents. He will have seen many evidences that the urban birth rate is high. Even in a city such as Rio de Janeiro the Catholic baptisms alone are sufficient to make for a birth rate of around 25 per 1,000 population, and Rio de Janeiro is a city of more than three million people. Nevertheless, in the country districts the birth rate is still higher.

To demonstrate this rural-urban differential fertility, the ratios of

---

[3] Cf. **Smith,** *Fundamentals of Population Study,* 290–97.
[4] *Ibid.*

TABLE XII

Fertility Ratios of Urban, Suburban, and Rural Population of Brazil, 1950 *

| State | Number of children under 5 per 100 women 15–49 | | | |
	Total	Urban	Suburban	Rural
Brazil	65	43	59	78
North				
Guaporé †	73	61	77	77
Acre †	90	66	82	96
Amazonas	74	51	59	78
Rio Branco †	84	68	87	90
Pará	67	45	61	76
Amapá †	74	65	74	76
Northeast				
Maranhão	65	46	56	69
Piauí	76	48	63	81
Ceará	77	53	62	85
Rio Grande do Norte	73	52	64	81
Paraíba	70	50	60	78
Pernambuco	65	44	54	75
Alagôas	69	45	52	78
East				
Sergipe	69	48	62	79
Bahia	65	45	57	73
Minas Gerais	68	49	57	75
Espírito Santo	75	50	64	82
Rio de Janeiro	67	53	71	80
Distrito Federal	37	31	55	69
South				
São Paulo	57	39	58	78
Paraná	73	49	63	81
Santa Catarina	81	55	73	88
Rio Grande do Sul	66	41	62	79
West Central				
Mato Grosso	77	55	75	87
Goiás	72	54	63	77

* Compiled and computed from data in the "Censo Demográfico," VI *Recenseamento Geral do Brasil, 1950*, I (Rio de Janeiro, 1956), 66–67. Rate not given for any category in which there were less than 100 women aged 15–49.
† Territory.

children under 5 for each 100 women, ages 15 to 49 inclusive, were calculated for all of the states and territories. See Table XII. These are conclusive and indicate that the tendency observed in other parts of the world is also true in Brazil: urban people multiply much less rapidly than their fellows in the rural districts. These data indicate that the birth rate in the rural parts of Brazil is at least one-third higher than that of its urban districts.

Racial Differentials. On the important subject of racial differentials in the birth rate, it long has been practically impossible to

TABLE XIII

Number of Children Under 5 per 100 Women Aged 15–49, for Each State and Territory, by Color, 1950 *

State	White	Negro	Yellow	Pardo †
Brazil	65	56	80	69
North				
Guaporé ‡	71	52	—	77
Acre ‡	90	59	—	92
Amazonas	75	51	119	74
Rio Branco ‡	82	62	—	86
Pará	67	47	92	69
Amapá	78	43	—	76
Northeast				
Maranhão	69	52	—	66
Piauí	79	61	—	78
Ceará	78	68	—	81
Rio Grande do Norte	75	61	—	74
Paraíba	72	60	—	69
Pernambuco	67	52	—	66
Alagôas	71	51	—	69
East				
Sergipe	75	56	—	67
Bahia	67	54	—	69
Minas Gerais	70	56	82	69
Espírito Santo	77	63	—	76
Rio de Janeiro	66	65	79	71
Distrito Federal	36	34	57	41
South				
São Paulo	57	55	78	66
Paraná	73	65	89	70
Santa Catarina	81	72	—	73
Rio Grande do Sul	67	58	52	64
West Central				
Mato Grosso	78	64	82	78
Goiás	77	53	94	70

* Computations based on data from the "Censo Demográfico," VI *Recenseamento Geral do Brasil, 1950*, VI–XXX (Rio de Janeiro, 1954–1958), Table 5 in each volume. Rate not given for any category in which there were less than 100 women aged 15–49.

† Includes Indians, mulattoes, mestiços, etc.

‡ Territory.

secure any reliable information. Such few facts as have been available have led the writer and others to believe that the white population was reproducing at a rate considerably higher than the colored elements in the population. This is the equivalent of saying that there is in Brazil a positive correlation between social and economic status, on the one hand, and the rapidity of reproduction, on the other.

The 1950 materials already available make it possible to establish definitely the existence of a significant racial differential in the rate of reproduction in Brazil. See Table XIII for fertility ratios calculated from 1950 census materials.[5] In interpreting these ratios, the figures for the states are, of course, much more significant than those for the small populations of the territories. It is not strange that the pardo or brown (Indian and mixed) category frequently shows a higher ratio of children to women than either the white or the black —both whites and Negroes may contribute to its magnitude. Even so, however, in fourteen of the states the ratio for the whites is even higher than that for the pardos. In comparing whites and Negroes, on the other hand, there is only one of the states and territories in which the index for the whites is not significantly higher than the Negroes—the state of Rio de Janeiro. Here the ratios are almost exactly equal. The situation in the area, however, is highly reminiscent of several in the United States in which the concentration of the Negro population in the more rural sections of a state or region has created the delusion that the Negro birth rates were higher than the white. However, when whites and Negroes of equal residential categories have been compared, the asserted racial differential has disappeared. In the state of Rio de Janeiro, likewise, it is likely that the concentration of Negroes in the highly rural sugar-producing section around Campos, and their relative scarcity in the more urban parts of the state, may make their birth rate seem higher in comparison with the white, than would be the case if it were possible to compare rural whites with rural Negroes and urban whites with urban Negroes. As matters stand, though, there is no reason for doubting that the white population of Brazil is multiplying much more rapidly than the colored.

This conclusion is also directly in accord with fertility data secured in the 1950 census by asking each woman how many children she had borne. See Table XVI. Although such materials provide a poor basis for determining the level of the rate of reproduction, there is no obvious reason for believing they are defective for the purpose of comparing the fertility of one color category with that of another.

Finally, the proposition that the rate of reproduction of Brazil's white population is higher than that of her Negroes is directly in line with generalizations based on much earlier materials, and it indicates that the present differences are merely the continuation of differentials that have prevailed for many years. The German geologist W. L. von Eschwege collected vital statistics for the province of Minas Gerais in 1821, long before the abolition of slavery, the destruction of the records, and popular sensitiveness about color or racial classifications. Among the data he assembled are some which, expressed in terms of the conventional birth rates, show the following racial differences among the free population: whites, 40; Indians, 40; mulattoes (free), 37; mulattoes (slave), 38; Negroes (free), 48;

[5] Also consult J. V. D. Saunders, *Differential Fertility in Brazil* (Gainesville, 1958), 37–62; and Giorgio Mortara, "The Brazilian Birth Rate: Its Economic and Social Factors," in Frank Lorimer *et al.*, *Culture and Human Fertility* (Paris, 1954).

TABLE XIV

Number and Proportion of Mothers among Brazilian Women
15 Years of Age and over, 1950, and Average Number of
Children Borne per Mother, by Color *

Color	Number of women	Mothers		Number of live births per mother	Number of still births per mother
		Number	Per cent		
All categories	15,325,852	9,301,578	60.7	3.90	1.57
White	9,504,835	5,822,703	61.3	3.93	1.42
Yellow	84,121	53,250	62.6	4.44	0.76
Black	1,772,599	1,015,348	57.3	3.72	1.83
Pardo †	3,928,799	2,392,658	60.9	3.90	1.85
Undeclared	35,498	17,619	49.6	3.50	1.59

* Source of data: "Censo Demográfico," VI *Recenseamento Geral do Brasil, 1950,*
  I (Rio de Janeiro, 1956), 52–53.
† Includes Indians, mulattoes, mestiços, etc.

Negroes (slave), 29.[6] These rates are all within reasonable expectations. If one makes allowance for the well-known tendency for colored women to secure their freedom in larger proportions than colored men and keeps in mind the fact that the free colored population was relatively small at this time, these data seem to show that the fertility rate increases as we pass from the Negro, to the mulatto, to the white racial categories.

Some of the data presented in the 1890 census of the city of Rio de Janeiro, when analyzed, also have a bearing on the question of differential racial fertility in Brazil. The official who was responsible for the tabulation of the census data for the city introduced a table, not included in the reports for the states, wherein married couples were classified according to the racial affiliations of the man and his wife and this in turn related to the number of children borne and the number still living on the census date. These have been assembled and are presented, along with essential computations, in Table xv.

Observation of these data indicates that, when there was no cross-mating involved, the caboclos were considerably the most fertile group in the population. Whites ranked second, with mestiços third. The Negroes ranked far below the others, having produced only three children per couple compared with four children per caboclo couple. Matings of whites, whether males or females, with persons belonging to the Negro or mulatto stocks produced fewer children than when whites married whites. However, fertility was higher when white men and women crossed with caboclos than when they mated with others of the white race.

Negroes, both men and women, produced fewer children when they mated with whites, and more children when they married caboclos,

[6] Eschwege's data have been quoted by Oliveira Vianna, "O Povo Brazileiro e sua Evolução," *loc. cit.,* 339.

TABLE XV

Fertility in Relation to Race, Rio de Janeiro, 1890 *

Race and sex of parents		Number of married pairs	Number of children	
Males	Females		Total number born	Average number per couple
White	White	31,103	109,784	3.53
Negro	Negro	2,399	7,167	2.99
Caboclo	Cabocla	694	2,747	3.96
Mestiço	Mestiça	4,448	14,703	3.31
White	Negro	334	932	2.79
White	Cabocla	191	719	3.76
White	Mestiça	1,799	5,575	3.10
Negro	White	20	59	2.95
Negro	Cabocla	59	217	3.68
Negro	Mestiça	273	828	3.03
Caboclo	White	96	361	3.76
Caboclo	Negro	54	168	3.11
Caboclo	Mestiça	87	372	4.28
Mestiço	White	368	1,171	3.18
Mestiço	Negro	313	900	2.88
Mestiço	Cabocla	71	211	2.97
Total		42,309	145,914	3.45

* Source: *Recenseamento do Distrito Federal, 1890* (Rio de Janeiro, 1895), 258–59.

than when they selected mates in their own racial group. Negro men and mulatto women produced slightly more children, and Negro women and mulatto men fewer children, than the average for the Negro couples. When caboclos were involved in the cross-matings the average number of children borne fell below that for the caboclo couples, except when a caboclo man mated with a mulatto woman. Such marriages had produced an average of 4.28 children, by far the largest number of any combination. On the other hand, mulatto men and caboclo women proved to be among the least fertile of all possible crosses. Mulatto or mestiço men produced fewer children when mated with whites, Negroes, or caboclos than when united with their own kind. The same was true of mulatto women, except, as indicated above, when they mated with caboclo men, this combination being the most fertile of all.

By combining the data in a manner that assigns the spouses in the mixed marriages to their respective racial groups, along with 50 per cent of the children produced by these mixed marriages, it is possible to determine the net contribution of the reported racial groups to the total number of offspring. When this was done, the average number of children to be attributed to the caboclo couple was 3.88, considerably above the 3.39 per white couple. Mestiços or mulattoes, however, averaged only 3.26; Negro couples fell far below, only 2.98. In no case was the average number of children per couple increased by the inclusion of the data for mixed marriages.

These data are for one city only and are over 70 years old. As time has gone on the caboclo population has tended to lose its identity and fuse more completely with the white group. Mulattoes have continued to attribute their color to Indian ancestry. But prior to 1890 it seems fairly evident that the caboclo and white elements in the population were more fertile than the Negroes. The same differential exists today.

TREND

With the data as they have been and as they are in the 1960's it probably is impossible to determine definitely the nature of the trend, if any, in the birth rate in Brazil. Certainly, though, it remains at a very high level, so that little or no change has taken place in the twentieth century. Members of the staff of the Statistical Laboratory of the Instituto Brasileiro de Geografia e Estatística have made use of census and other data to estimate that crude birth rate decreased slightly but steadily from 46.5 for the period 1872 to 1890, to 46.0 for the decade 1890 to 1900, to 45.0 for the interim between the 1900 and the 1920 censuses, to 44.0 for that between 1920 and 1940, and to 43.5 for the years 1940 to 1950.[7] The ratio of children under 5 per 100 women 15–44, however, is more erratic, being 66.8 for 1920, 68.9 for 1940, and 70.5 for 1950.[8] The fact that the rate of reproduction in the city of Rio de Janeiro (Guanabara) is so much below the national average and that the fertility ratios for the urban districts generally are far below those of the rural suggests that the urbanization and industrialization of Brazil already is beginning to bring about a decrease in the birth rate. This probably will be considerably more pronounced if and when data from the 1960 census make possible another attempt at measurement, and in the decade commencing in 1970 the rate of reproduction may begin to decrease abruptly.

[7] O Brasil em Números, Apéndice do Anuário Estatístico do Brasil, 1960 (Rio de Janeiro, 1960), 13.
[8] Smith, Latin American Population Studies, 51.

CHAPTER VII

MORTALITY

THE REGISTRATION of deaths in Brazil must be greatly improved before it will be possible to determine with any degree of accuracy the death rate, the expectation of life, the relative importance of the various causes of death, the infant mortality rate, and many other essential items of human-resource accounting. Only in the future will it be possible to compute standardized death rates for Brazil, or to construct a reliable life table for the entire country, or to know how mortality varies from state to state, region to region, race to race, or class to class. It will be some time before it is possible to secure the morality data necessary for use in careful year-to-year estimates of the number, composition, and distribution of the labor force. Nevertheless, a start has been made, and Brazil is developing the registration system that may eventually result in adequate mortality statistics.

That the death rate is high is evident from the fragmentary data for the country as a whole and the fairly complete materials available for some of the principal cities. The age-sex pyramid, too, has the configuration typical of a country in which a high mortality rate is found in conjunction with a high birth rate. Just how high the death rate is, however, and how it fluctuates from place to place or year to year it is not yet possible to determine; and the same is true of the extent to which the leading causes of death are being brought under control through the application of modern health and sanitary measures.

In all probability in 1950 the actual death rate in Brazil was somewhere between 18 and 21, and the expectation of life at birth between 40 and 45. This is to say that the number of deaths in the course of a year was between 18 and 21 per 1,000 population and that the average (mean) age at death was between 40 and 45 years. The observations and inferences upon which these conclusions are based may be summarized briefly. Between 1940 and 1950 the rate of population increase, revealed by two excellent censuses, was 2.5 per cent annually. Since immigration was negligible during the decade, this figure is close to the rate of natural increase or to the birth rate minus the death rate. If, as may be entirely possible, the 1950 census enumeration was somewhat more complete than the 1940 count of population, the true rate of natural increase was somewhat less than 2.5 per cent per year; but that factor alone could hardly reduce the figure to less than 2.3 per cent. As indicated in Chapter VI, the birth rate in Brazil is at least 43 per 1,000 population. If the birth rate was 43 and the rate of natural increase was 2.5, then the death rate was 18. If the true rate of natural increase was only 2.3, however, the death rate was 20. Everything considered, it is likely that these figures err in

TABLE XVI

*Estimates of Average Annual Death Rate and Expectation of Life at Birth of the Population Born in Each Brazilian State, 1940–1950 ***

State	Death rate	Expectation of life (years)
Brazil	21	44
North		
Amazonas	23	38
Pará	24	38
Northeast		
Maranhão	22	41
Piauí	21	43
Ceará	20	45
Rio Grande do Norte	21	43
Paraíba	21	42
Pernambuco	21	43
Alagôas	24	39
East		
Sergipe	22	41
Bahia	22	41
Minas Gerais	23	40
Espírito Santo	21	42
Rio de Janeiro	24	38
Distrito Federal	17 †	48 †
South		
São Paulo	15	49
Paraná	22	43
Santa Catarina	16	49
Rio Grande do Sul	13	53
West Central		
Mato Grosso	27	36
Goiás	24	40

* Compiled from data in the *Anuário Estatístico do Brasil, 1960,* XXI (Rio de Janeiro, 1960), 28.
† Estimate is for the resident population.

the direction of being too small, if they err at all, and it probably is reasonable to think of Brazil's death rate at mid-century as being about 20 per 1,000 population.

This conclusion is supported by the extensive computations made, on the basis of age data from the 1940 and 1950 censuses of population, by the staff members of the Statistical Laboratory of the Instituto Brasileiro de Geografia e Estatística. (See Table XVI.) These data, along with those in Table XVII, also provide a basis for noting some of the principal regional variations in mortality rates in Brazil, although it would be unwise to place full confidence in the reliability of the estimates. It is fairly certain, however, that the death rates are lowest, or the expectation of life is highest, in Rio Grande do Sul, São Paulo, Santa Catarina, and the city of Rio de Janeiro; and there likewise is little reason to doubt that health conditions, as reflected

TABLE XVII

Estimated Death Rates in Brazilian Capitals, 1941–1943 and 1956–1958 *

State and capital	Estimated death rates	
	1941–1943	1956–1958
North		
Amazonas, Manaus	19	14
Para, Belém	26	15
Northeast		
Maranhão, São Luís	20	18
Piauí, Teresina	25	22
Ceará, Fortaleza	28	32
Rio Grande do Norte, Natal	33	27
Paraíba, João Pessoa	32	27
Pernambuco, Recife	28	22
Alagôas, Maceió	28	30
East		
Sergipe, Aracaju	23	20
Bahia, Salvador	26	17
Minas Gerais, Belo Horizonte	18	15
Espírito Santo, Vitória	27	21
Rio de Janeiro, Niterói	20	13
Guanabara, Rio de Janeiro	17	12
South		
São Paulo, São Paulo	13	10
Paraná, Curitiba	14	16
Santa Catarina, Florianópolis	23	15
Rio Grande do Sul, Pôrto Alegre	19	14
West Central		
Mato Grosso, Cuiabá	18	19
Goiás, Goiania	35	25

* Compiled and computed from data in *O Brasil em Números, Apéndice do Anuário Estatístico do Brasil, 1960* (Rio de Janeiro, 1960), 13–14.

by indexes of mortality, are poorest in Mato Grosso and the Amazon Basin. However, there may be reason for wondering if the relative positions of Bahia and the state of Rio de Janeiro are correct and if the indexes for the Northeast actually are as favorable as these estimates seem to indicate. Likewise, the rates for some of the cities, and especially those for the years 1956–1958, appear to be questionable. It is highly unlikely, for example, that the death rate in Manaus actually is as low as that in Pôrto Alegre or that the index for Belém really is no higher than the one for Belo Horizonte.

A death rate of 20 or even 18 is high, and an expectation of life at birth of 40 or even 45 is low. Together these indexes emphasize the fact that mortality in Brazil is about double that which would prevail if modern preventive medicine and sanitary measures were applied to the extent that they are in many countries. Germ diseases, killers that might be controlled, still take a frightful toll of life in Brazilian cities, and especially throughout her vast rural territory. Unfortunately, this generalization must rest for the most part upon general and casual observations rather than upon adequate statistical evidence, since comprehensive data on the causes of death in Brazil are conspicuously lacking.

DIFFERENTIAL MORTALITY

Unfortunately too, it is difficult if not impossible to learn anything about how mortality in Brazil varies between city and country, from class to class, and among the races. From general observation one may be inclined to think that mortality in the cities is less than that in the country, especially in those areas where malaria, hookworm, typhoid, dysentery, and other transmissible diseases are most rampant. One may also feel that the upper class must surely outlive the middle and especially the lower social strata. The mere matter of diet suggests this, but here again factual evidence is lacking.

On the whole, a comparison of death rates of the various states (Table xvi) with those in the nation's largest cities, which are their capitals (Table xvii), indicates that the death rates in the urban areas are considerably below those in the rural districts. This corresponds with the impression one receives as he contrasts the rural and the urban modes of life in Brazil. In addition, a fairly well established sociological principle gives reason for supposing, as a working hypothesis, that mortality rates in Brazil's cities are below those in her extensive and remote rural districts. As is indicated below, there has been an abrupt decline in the nation's death rate during the years since the close of the first world war, and it is well known that this was accomplished largely by the application on a large scale of modern scientific knowledge of preventive medicine, sanitation, and related matters. Infectious diseases, once the causes of most deaths, have been controlled to a considerable degree. Therefore it is important to have in mind one of the principles elaborated by Pitirim A. Sorokin. This generalization states that, on the basis of repeated demonstrations, social and cultural changes generally originate in the city and then spread gradually into the surrounding rural areas.[1] Any time that a society is in a period of rapid social change, as presently is the case in Brazil, the new patterns are established in the cities, but the old ways continue to dominate life in the rural districts. Later on we may expect to see throughout rural Brazil ade-

[1] Pitirim A. Sorokin and Carle C. Zimmerman, *Principles of Rural-Urban Sociology* (New York, 1929), 402–407.

quate programs for the control of malaria, measures that will safeguard water and milk supplies, and the use of injections and vaccinations to immunize rural people against dangerous bacteria and viruses to a degree comparable to that already being employed in the urban centers. At the present time, however, the slight extent to which such safeguards to health and life are made use of by the rural population, in comparison with the urban, constitutes a basis for deducing that the death rate of the former must be higher than that of the latter.

Because no general classification of deaths by race or color is available, it is of course impossible to determine the comparative mortality or longevity of the races in Brazil. Such materials as are available on the subject are fragmentary, and few of them are of recent date. For example, there are available for the city of Rio de Janeiro and the state of São Paulo some significant compilations of fertility and mortality data classified according to color. The categories used are white, brown (mulatto), black, and yellow. The data are summarized in Table XVIII.

The striking fact about these data is that in both Rio de Janeiro and São Paulo much higher proportions of the deaths than births were included in the mulatto and the black categories. Similar differences prevailed in Rio de Janeiro in 1920 and 1921, years for which

TABLE XVIII

Births and Deaths in the Distrito Federal and the State of São Paulo, Classified According to Color *

Color	São Paulo (1932–41, incl.)		Distrito Federal (1937)	
	Live births	Deaths	Live births	Deaths
Total number	2,095,404	1,138,599	33,025	27,236
White:				
Number	1,844,600	920,398	25,552	16,242
Per cent	88.1	80.9	77.4	59.7
Brown:				
Number	102,860	106,977	6,006	6,842
Per cent	4.9	9.4	18.2	25.1
Black:				
Number	65,612	86,437	1,451	4,111
Per cent	3.1	7.6	4.4	15.1
Yellow:				
Number	82,332	23,564	16	10
Per cent	3.9	2.1	—	—
Unclassified:				
Number	—	205	—	31
Per cent	—	—	—	.1

* Sources: Data for São Paulo were supplied by the state Departamento de Saude; those for the Distrito Federal were taken from *Anuário Estatístico do Distrito Federal, 1938,* VI (Rio de Janeiro, 1939), 44, 52.

data are also available. Thus, in 1920 white was the classification of 78.7 per cent of the births and only 64.0 per cent of the deaths, brown or mulatto the category of 15.5 per cent of the births and 23.5 per cent of the deaths, and black the class of 4.6 per cent of the births and 12.5 per cent of the deaths. In 1921 white was the category for 80.7 per cent of the births and 63.9 per cent of the deaths, brown for 12.9 per cent of the former and 22.9 per cent of the latter, and black for only 6.4 per cent of the births and 13.2 per cent of the deaths.[2]

How can such differences be explained? Not by a selectivity in rural-urban migration, because the data for São Paulo include the entire state, and the differences prevail to the same extent in the capital and the interior. Conceivably there might be less reluctance in classifying the dead as colored than to so classify newly born infants. But this is extremely hypothetical, and in any case Brazilians are much less sensitive on the score of color than most peoples. Therefore, the most likely hypothesis is that the discrepancies are due to racial differentials in the birth rate, in the death rate, or in both of these vital indexes. Only five of the possible combinations of differential racial birth rates and death rates could have produced the results observed. These are as follows: (1) no significant differential in the fertility of the white and colored population constituents, combined with a much lower mortality among the whites; (2) a distinctly higher fertility and lower mortality among whites than among Negroes and mulattoes; (3) no differential of significance in the mortality of white and colored elements in these populations, combined with a great differential in fertility favorable to the whites; (4) a higher fertility among the colored elements, combined with a differential in mortality so much greater among the colored people than among the whites that it would offset the fertility differential and account for all of the observed differences; and (5) a higher mortality among the whites, combined with such a great differential fertility in their favor that it would offset this mortality differential and still be sufficient to account for all the observed differences. Obviously, the last two are highly improbable. Good scientific procedure would preclude relying on one of them as long as the facts were in agreement with the more simple hypotheses.

The materials in Chapter VI seem to indicate definitely that Brazil's white population has a higher rate of reproduction than her colored. Therefore, the most reasonable hypothesis which fits all the available facts is that there exists in Brazil a differential mortality unfavorable to the Negroes and mulattoes. Mortality increases as social and economic status decreases.

Interestingly enough this hypothesis that the mortality rate tends to increase as the color of the population becomes darker is supported by some early materials. Eschwege assembled data for Minas Gerais, the state in which he was carrying on his geological studies, for the

[2] These percentages were derived from "Cidade do Rio de Janeiro," *Annuario de Estatistica Demographo-Sanitaria, 1920-21* (Rio de Janeiro, 1923), I, 68-69, 81-82, and 136-37.

year 1821. This information was classified according to race; it seems to have revealed differences that have persisted until the present. Expressed in the form of the conventional death rates used today, his data for the year 1821 are as follows: whites, 28; Indians, 37; mulattoes (free), 28; mulattoes (slave), 60; Negroes (free), 54; Negroes (slave), 69.[3]

Keeping in mind the time and the place, these rates are all reasonable. If one remembers that in 1821 the free colored population was small in comparison with the slave, there can be little doubt about tendency of the mortality rates to increase as shades of color get darker. Then, as now, this was equivalent to saying that there was a negative relationship between social and economic status and the death rate.

Some of the data gathered in the 1950 census of population are strictly in accord with the proposition that the death rate of Brazilian Negroes is considerably higher than that of the white population of Brazil. In that enumeration each woman of fifteen years of age and over was asked whether or not she had borne children, and those who reported themselves as mothers were further questioned with respect to the total number of children they had borne and the number of their offspring who were alive at the census date. These data were then cross-tabulated by age and color. Such materials, of course, leave a great deal to be desired, but even so the general results probably are fairly realistic. In any case among all women age fifteen years and over, the percentage of all children borne who were alive at the date of the census varied among the color categories of the mothers as follows: white, 71.3 per cent; yellow, 73.5 per cent; black, 67.0 per cent; and brown (*pardo*), 67.9 per cent. In addition, for all women age fifty or more, the corresponding proportions are as follows: white, 67.0 per cent; yellow, 78.9 per cent; black, 59.6 per cent; and brown, 60.8 per cent.

CAUSES OF DEATH

Although it is impossible to get more adequate statistics on mortality rates so that regional, racial, rural-urban, and other differentials might be explored, it is possible to gain additional facts about mortality in Brazil by examining some of the statistics having to do with causes of death. Unfortunately though, the materials on this subject are mostly those for the cities of Rio de Janeiro and São Paulo, in which major efforts have been made to reduce deaths from infectious and transmissible diseases. As is apparent from the materials on general death rates presented above, the situation in most other parts of Brazil is far less favorable. Even so, as indicated by the data presented in Table XIX, the causes of death that are most easily controlled still take a substantial toll of life in São Paulo and especially in Rio de Janeiro.

[3] Oliveira Vianna, "O Povo Brasileiro e sua Evolução," *loc. cit.*, 339.

TABLE XIX

Selected Causes of Death in the City of Rio de Janeiro and the
Município of São Paulo, 1954–1956 *

Causes of death	Number of deaths per 100,000 population	
	Rio de Janeiro	São Paulo
Diphtheria	2.7	2.2
Dysenteries	5.3	9.8
Ailments of the circulatory system	240.5	203.7
Ailments of the digestive system	171.0	155.5
Ailments of the genital-urinary system	24.5	18.8
Ailments of the respiratory system	84.3	69.2
Typhoid fever	2.8	0.4
Malaria	0.2	0.4
Malignant neoplasms	96.9	111.9
Syphilis	13.9	8.7
Tuberculosis	93.6	36.7

* Compiled and computed from data in Anuário Estatístico do Brasil, 1960,
XXI, 27.

TRENDS

The data on the age distribution of Brazil's population at successive
censuses offer a fairly reliable basis for estimating the trend in the
death rate for the nation's population as a whole. Furthermore, the
extensive arithmetical computations involved in such a task have
been made by the staff of the Statistical Laboratory of the Instituto
Brasileiro de Geografia e Estatística, and the necessary indexes have
been published. Even if liberal allowance is made for possible error
in the rate for any specific intercensal period, the fact that the death
rate has been falling rapidly is hardly to be challenged. The computations to which reference has been made indicate that the death
rate during the period 1872–1890 was thirty, and that thereafter it
fell steadily to twenty-eight for the decade 1891–1900, to twenty-six
for the interim between the 1900 and the 1920 censuses, to twenty-
five for the period 1921–1940, and to twenty in the decade 1941–
1950.[4]

There is evidence in these data that Brazil is making considerable
progress in its war against death and disease. Of this, one sees other
evidences as he visits the various regions of the country. But at all
times one should keep in mind the tremendous task the country is
facing, not alone because of climate and poor dietary habits, but also
because there is little in the way of tradition with which to buttress
health and sanitary measures. Even in Rio de Janeiro health and
sanitary precautions are a relatively late introduction. In 1838, years
after independence and when the city was the seat of the empire and

[4] O Brasil em Números, Apéndice do Anuário Estatístico do Brasil, 1960, 13.

the residence of the thirteen-year-old emperor, commander Wilkes wrote concerning certain sanitary facilities:

Very few of the houses have yards, cellars, or gardens; consequently the dwellers are still greatly incommoded from the want of water-closets, detrimental both to health and comfort, and not only an annoyance and inconvenience to the inhabitants themselves, but is shared by the stranger passing through the streets.[5]

By 1865 the situation in the Federal Capital was on the mend, a North American named Smith had a contract for the construction of sewers, and, according to a qualified observer, Dr. J. McF. Gaston, even more drastic measures were contemplated, so that a privy would be constructed on every man's premises "whether he may desire it or not." [6] The good doctor asserted that "at present it is a common practice for men of all classes to urinate upon the sidewalks in the most fashionable streets of the city, and the stench in passing some of the recesses that are most frequently resorted to is such, that it is a matter of surprise to learn that there is no public ordinance forbidding this offensive nuisance." [7] Were the doctor living today he might find the desired city ordinance on the books, but he would not have to go far from the Avenida Rio Branco to discover that the practice he complained of has not been entirely abandoned.

INFANT MORTALITY

The infant mortality rate is another index that may be used in exploring the subject of mortality in Brazil. It is computed by relating the number of infants who die in the course of their first year to the number of live births during the year.

No age distribution of the general population, a set of population data that is rarely available, is required. This index also is highly significant because the proportion of newly born infants who die is little affected by many of the contagious diseases, not influenced at all by the degenerative ailments, and therefore seems to reflect rather accurately the quality of the general care and feeding that is given to babies by their parents. One may be sure that people who lack the knowledge or the will to care for their infants will, as a rule, not care for themselves. For this reason the infant mortality rate is highly significant as an index for gauging the general health and welfare of a population. In fact, it is probably the best single index that may be had of the general welfare of the people.

But this index must be used with care in Brazil, for the reason that the registry of births is far from complete, probably even more incomplete than the registry of deaths. This was pointed out in the study of fertility. It also is indicated by the data for many interior towns and cities which sometimes report more infant deaths than

---

[5] Wilkes, *Narrative of the United States Exploring Expedition*, I, 46–47.
[6] J. McF. Gaston, *Hunting a Home in Brazil* (Philadelphia, 1867), 15.
[7] *Ibid.*, 16.

live births. For example, the following are some of the 1940 data:
Maria Pereira, Ceará, 82 live births and 111 infant deaths; Areia,
Paraíba, 237 live births and 331 infant deaths; Patos, Paraíba, 237
live births and 543 infant deaths; Caruarú, Pernambuco, 561 live
births and 597 infant deaths; Porto Calvo, Alagôas (in this state 13
out of 31 towns reporting give more infant deaths than live births),
76 live births and 170 infant deaths; and Feira de Santana, Bahia, 70
live births and 159 infant deaths. However, in other states, Espírito
Santo, Minas Gerais, São Paulo, Paraná, Santa Catarina, and Rio
Grande do Sul, the registries of vital statistics show evidences of
much more careful keeping. But, for all of Brazil, only a small part
of the interior reports births and infant deaths, and in many places
for which reports are available, these reports are far from complete.[8]
Furthermore, even the materials for all of the state capitals may not
be entirely reliable. For example, in Table xx are presented the reported infant mortality rates for 1950 and 1956–1958, and also some
estimates for 1950. A comparison of the two 1950 series serves to
highlight the necessity for caution, but all three sets of figures are
useful in helping to emphasize the very high levels of infant mortality that still prevail throughout Brazil.

Beyond all possibility of doubt Brazilian infant mortality rates are
high, and they remain so even when these rates be discounted
liberally to allow for the incomplete coverage of the birth registration.[9] They, too, reflect a general health level that leaves a great deal
to be desired and which indicates that the human resources of the
country are being dissipated by disease, malnutrition, and lack of
medical attention and care. Unfortunately, one cannot place enough
reliance on the materials to justify regional comparisons, but the
fact that the northern and northeastern states generally have high
rates is in agreement with popular opinion among the intellectual
classes of Brazil.

Mortara, by methods too conservative, has estimated the numbers
of live births for the years 1939 to 1941, inclusive, for seven of the
largest cities in Brazil and has also computed the number of infant
deaths in those cities for the corresponding years. Utilizing these
corrected data for the computation of infant mortality rates gives
the following results for the three-year period: Rio de Janeiro (Distrito Federal), 171; São Paulo, 135; Recife, 267; Salvador, 201; Pôrto
Alegre, 187; Belo Horizonte, 158; and Belém, 160.[10]

In his corrected tabulations of live births and infant deaths for the
city of São Paulo and the Distrito Federal, Mortara also classified the
data according to the color categories used in the Brazilian census.
This makes it possible to examine how the infant mortality rate in
Brazil's two great metropolitan centers varies as one passes from the

[8] For the data cited above see *Boletim Mensal do Serviço Federal de Bio-
Estatística*, I, No. 9 (March, 1942).

[9] As birth registration becomes more complete, we may be sure that the infant mortality rate in Brazil will appear to fall.

[10] Cf. Mortara, *Estimativas da Taxa de Natilidade para o Brasil, as Unidades
da Federação e as Principais Capitais*, 39, 43.

TABLE XX

Reported Infant Mortality Rates in Brazilian Capitals, 1950 and 1956–
1958, and Estimated Rates in 1950 *

Capital	Reported infant mortality rates		Estimated infant mortality rates
	1950	1956–1958	1950
North			
Manaus (Amazonas)	171	131	165
Belém (Pará)	105	153	98
Northeast			
São Luís (Maranhão)	166	203	106
Teresina (Piauí)	292	327	92
Fortaleza (Ceará)	353	311	361
Natal (Rio Grande do Norte)	439	431	427
João Pessoa (Paraíba)	186	183	245
Recife (Pernambuco)	230	233	308
Maceió (Alagôas)	225	415	303
East			
Aracaju (Sergipe)	222	390	190
Salvador (Bahia)	221	166	192
Belo Horizonte (Minas Gerais)	104	98	125
Vitória (Espírito Santo)	137	108	142
Niterói (Rio de Janeiro)	111	95	112
Rio de Janeiro (Guanabara)	109	111	112
South			
São Paulo (São Paulo)	90	77	113
Curitiba (Paraná)	104	139	131
Florianópolis (Santa Catarina)	139	122	116
Pôrto Alegre (Rio Grande do Sul)	129	124	136
West Central			
Cuiabá (Mato Grosso)	153	130	57
Goiania (Goiás)	118	139	112

* Reported rates are from *O Brasil em Números, Apéndice do Anuário Estatístico do Brasil, 1960* (Rio de Janeiro, 1960), 16; and the estimates were made by taking the numbers of infant deaths reported and substituting in the standard formula for the number of live births registered in 1950 a number equal to one-fifth of the population of less than five years of age, as enumerated in the 1950 census of population. If it should be that the count of infant deaths is substantially correct, the estimated rates in this table are, of course, considerably too high.

lighter to the darker shades in the population, which is approximately the same as moving from the higher to the lower social and economic strata. Thus in the município of São Paulo the infant mortality rate among the white population for the years 1939–1941 was only 119, and among the Negroes and pardos, or mixed bloods, the rate was 257. Among the Japanese population, however, it was only 61. For the same years in the city of Rio de Janeiro and the other parts of the Federal District the infant mortality rate among white children was only 129, whereas that among the Negroes was 224. However, in the national capital, the pardos showed a rate of 272, far above that of the Negroes.

CHAPTER VIII

IMMIGRATION

I MMIGRATION to Brazil has been confined largely to the period 1887 to 1934. During those years she received a recorded immigration of more than four million persons from other countries. Prior to 1887 the movement into Brazil was a mere trickle, and since 1934 immigration has been restricted by a quota system. The importation of a few thousand colonists prior to and during the first three quarters of the nineteenth century receives detailed consideration in Chapter XVI.

MOTIVATIONS FOR SEEKING IMMIGRANTS

The chief motivating forces in Brazil's promotion of immigration, first as an empire and later as a republic, seem to have been two. One of these was the creation of a small-farming class in the population, a group of farmers engaged in diversified agriculture, to help balance the large scale monoculture carried on in its tremendous agricultural and cattle-growing estates. Quite naturally this motive was strongest during the empire, when slavery still supplied the backbone of the nation's labor force and when diversified agriculture was almost unknown. It also enjoyed a brief reign of popularity in the early years of the republic, when each of the states came into possession of and was confronted with the task of administering the unpatented lands within its borders. This motivation has always been the chief factor in the immigration to Rio Grande do Sul, Santa Catarina, Paraná, and Espírito Santo. It has also been important in the immigration to Minas Gerais. With the granting of freedom to the children of slave mothers in 1871 and the freeing of the slaves themselves in 1888, another motive for promoting immigration came to the fore, the ensuring of what Brazil's upper classes considered an adequate and cheap labor supply to perform the manual work on the coffee, cotton, and sugar plantations of the nation. São Paulo was always the champion in promoting immigration for this purpose. It led the fight to have the Imperial Government subsidize immigration of farm hands, and in anticipation of what was to come, it established the machinery for recruiting a labor supply even before the abolition of the institution of slavery. To the systematic recruiting of agricultural workers by São Paulo and the subsidization of their movement across the ocean, Brazil owes the lion's share of her immigration. The subsidization of immigrants to become farm operators in the colonization projects of federal, state, and private agencies has been important, but it has not brought in a volume of immigrants that compares with those introduced as agricultural laborers.

WHY IMMIGRATION LAGGED

Since Brazil was so late in becoming an important area of absorption for Europe's overcrowded population, although she had long been adopting policies, spreading publicity, and even offering financial subsidies in an attempt to attract immigrants, it is well to pause and ask the reason for this. Why was it that prior to 1887 Brazil, with tremendous spaces to fill, a soil generally reputed to be of unequaled fertility, and an active recruitment program, secured only a handful of immigrants? Others may advance various explanations, but the writer believes that to the defects in her land system Brazil must attribute her failure to become a mecca for the millions who fled from overcrowded nineteenth-century Europe. It matters little that freedom to enter was greatly limited during the first two decades of the century and that more years had to pass before adherence to the Catholic religion was waived as a prerequisite to entrance. During the opening decades of the nineteenth century immigration to the United States also was a mere trickle, while congestion and desire to emigrate were probably almost as great in the Catholic parts of Europe as in the Protestant communities. Had Brazil been as liberal in granting land, had she safeguarded surveys and boundaries, and had she carefully protected property rights to land, she probably would have run a close race with the United States in the volume of immigration. In turn, many of the defects in her land system, and the consequent failure to attract immigrants, must be attributed to the system of large estates and slave labor which prevailed universally throughout the entire empire. Those familiar with the history of immigration to the United States will recall that the same combination of factors effectively deterred the establishment of immigrants in the Southern states, even though hundreds of thousands of them landed there and passed through the region on their way to sections where farming was a family enterprise and where they might reasonably expect to become owners of farms.

Those particular aspects of the Brazilian land system that were deterrents, brakes upon the numerous official and private attempts to attract the surplus population of Europe, may be listed as follows: (1) lack of systematic surveys to establish definitely where property lines lay; (2) faulty or "clouded" land titles that made ownership uncertain and made the settler run the risk of losing all the capital and results of years of work that he had put into the land; (3) the concentration of land ownership in the hands of a few, many of whom withheld it from productive uses, as latifundia, to pass on to their heirs; (4) because a few people held the land and also the political power, the maintenance of slavery, and the smuggling of slaves from Africa; [1] and (5) perhaps most important of all, the failure to provide grants of land to settlers and to abandon the rigid practice, made a law in 1850, that land could be secured once by purchase, or in brief, the failure to develop a Brazilian equivalent of the "homestead law." In the United States "squatting" or the illegal settling on lands quickly gave rise to a legalization and regularization of the process—the moving force in the granting of lands free to actual settlers, which became such a lure for immigrants. In Brazil squatting for the most part has merely resulted in clouded land titles and lawsuits, many of which persist to the present day.

NUMBERS

In order to have a relatively firm basis for beginning the analysis of the data on immigration in Brazil, the year 1874 is selected as a starting point, or more than a decade before the large movement of immigrants into Brazil got under way in 1887. Only a few comments are necessary about the immigration prior to 1874. It was extremely sporadic. It was confined largely to the Portuguese, who had always gravitated to Brazil, settlers introduced in connection with the various colonization projects which are described in another chapter, and workers imported by certain planters who were experimenting with the substitution of free labor for slave. Any data pertaining to the period before 1874 are extremely fragmentary, and there are serious discrepancies between the information provided by various official sources. For example, a publication of the São Paulo Department of Labor states that in the decade 1847 to 1857 "individual initiative alone created in São Paulo more than 60 colonies, in which were located more than 60,000 immigrants, almost all Portuguese." [2] However, on another page, when giving the data on immigration to the state, the same publication shows only 6,303 immigrants to São Paulo during the decade referred to, and of these only 2,515 were classed as Portuguese. (In making these additions both 1847 and 1857 were included to make up for one year omitted in the series.) Still using this long decade, and the data from another official source, the

---

[1] The importation of slaves was prohibited very early. "In reality, however, the traffic was only extinguished on paper, in spite of the treaties of January 22, 1815, of July 28, 1817, and of November 23, 1826, with England, and notwithstanding the vigilance of the British cruisers.

"Useless was the law of November 7, 1831, that declared to be free of all slaves coming from outside who should enter national territory. It was a dead letter during half a century, only coming to be applied by some judges, among them the great Antonio Joaquim de Macedo Soares a little before the extinction of slavery in 1888." Vieira Ferreira, *Azambuja e Urussanga* (Niterói: Diário Oficial, 1939), 36.

[2] Departamento Estadual do Trabalho, *Dados para a Historia da Immigração e da Colonização em São Paulo* (São Paulo, 1916), 7.

total immigration to Brazil was only 71,820, of whom 53,911 were Portuguese.[3]

In the period 1874 to 1957, inclusive, a total of 4,993,565 immigrants is reported as entering Brazil.[4] See Table xxi and Figure 13. This number is equal to about 7.0 per cent of Brazil's population as revealed by the 1960 census. During the same period the records for the United States show an entry of 32,622,063 immigrants, or approximately 18 per cent of the 1960 population.

It is interesting to observe the fluctuations in the movement of the immigrants, to identify the years of the peaks and the depressions, to note how the movement into São Paulo compares with that in the nation as a whole. The graphic presentation of the data in Figure 13 facilitates such observations. Until 1886 immigration to Brazil remained at a comparatively low level, attaining the mark of 30,000 per year only in 1876. However, the yearly level was usually above 20,000. In 1887 the incoming tide began to flow much more rapidly and immigration increased to more than 133,000 in 1888, the year the slaves were freed and the year before the declaration of the republic. These events seem to have brought about a temporary check, but in 1890 the current again began to swell and the immigrant tide reached its all-time high in 1891 when 215,239 (216,760 according to Doria de Vasconcellos) immigrants entered Brazil. After a brief period of recession in 1894, the number of immigrants again reached high levels in 1895, 1896, and 1897, the figure of 164,831 for 1895 being the third highest recorded in Brazil's immigration history. Then a decided slump set in, the number of immigrants dropping to less than 40,000 in 1900 and, following a brief flurry, to 33,000 in 1903. Then a gradual recovery got under way, which by 1913 brought the recorded immigration to above 190,000, the second highest total ever recorded for a single year.

[3] *Boletim Commemorativo da Exposição Nacional de 1908* (Rio de Janeiro, 1908), 83.

[4] This figure is based on the data for the years 1884 to 1957, inclusive, as given by the Departamento Nacional de Imigração and the Instituto Nacional de Imigração e Colonização and published in the *Anuário Estatístico do Brasil, 1958,* XIX (Rio de Janeiro, 1958), 38, and upon data for the years 1874 to 1883, inclusive, compiled by Henrique Doria de Vasconcellos, "Alguns Aspectos da Imigração no Brasil," *Boletim do Serviço de Imigração e Colonização,* No. 3 (March, 1941). The national agencies compiled the data by single years, according to the nationality of the immigrants. Doria de Vasconcellos, formerly director of São Paulo's excellent immigration and colonization service, gives a series for the years 1850 to 1937, showing the total immigration to Brazil and how this stream of immigration divided between São Paulo and the other states in the confederation. There are many differences in the figures from the two sources, possibly because the figures of the national agencies are corrected to eliminate 130,435 returning Brazilian citizens who had been included in the earlier compilations of immigration statistics, although the general outlines of the movement are the same. In the pages that follow the data published by the national agencies are relied on for material relating to the composition of the immigration, while those supplied by Doria de Vasconcellos are utilized for showing the relative importance of the movement into the state of São Paulo. The materials presented on nationality of the immigrants during the decade 1874 to 1883 were secured from the *Boletim Commemorativo da Exposição Nacional de 1908,* 82–84.

TABLE XXI

Annual Immigration to Brazil and to São Paulo, 1874–1957 *

Year	To Brazil	To São Paulo	
	Number	Number	Per cent of total
1874	19,942	120	.6
1875	11,001	3,289	29.9
1876	30,567	1,303	4.3
1877	29,029	2,832	9.8
1878	22,432	1,678	7.5
1879	22,189	953	4.3
1880	29,729	613	2.1
1881	11,054	2,705	24.5
1882	27,197	2,743	10.1
1883	28,662	4,912	17.1
1884	24,890	4,868	20.0
1885	35,440	6,500	18.3
1886	33,486	9,534	28.5
1887	55,963	32,110	57.4
1888	133,253	91,826	68.1
1889	65,946	27,694	42.0
1890	107,474	38,291	35.6
1891	216,760	108,688	50.1
1892	86,203	42,061	48.8
1893	134,805	81,745	60.6
1894	60,984	48,947	80.3
1895	167,618	139,998	83.5
1896	158,132	99,010	62.6
1897	146,362	98,134	67.0
1898	78,109	46,939	60.1
1899	54,629	31,172	57.1
1900	40,300	22,802	56.6
1901	85,306	70,348	82.5
1902	52,204	37,831	72.5
1903	34,062	16,553	48.6
1904	46,164	23,761	51.5
1905	70,295	45,839	65.2
1906	73,672	46,214	62.7
1907	58,552	28,900	49.4
1908	94,695	37,278	39.4
1909	85,410	38,308	44.9
1910	88,564	39,486	44.6
1911	135,967	61,508	45.2
1912	180,182	98,640	54.7
1913	192,683	116,640	60.5
1914	82,572	46,624	56.5

* Sources: Doria de Vasconcellos, "Alguns Aspectos da Imigração no Brasil," *Boletim do Serviço de Imigração e Colonização*, No. 3 (March, 1941), 29–30, 35–36; and for the years 1938 to 1957, *Anuário Estatístico do Brasil*, XI (1950), 55; XIII (1952), 64; XV (1954), 59; XVII (1956), 77; XIX (1958), 39.

TABLE XXI (*Continued*). Annual Immigration to Brazil and to São Paulo *

Year	To Brazil	To São Paulo	
	Number	Number	Per cent of total
1915	32,206	15,614	48.5
1916	34,003	17,011	50.0
1917	31,192	23,407	75.0
1918	20,501	11,447	55.8
1919	37,898	16,205	42.8
1920	71,027	32,028	45.1
1921	60,844	32,678	53.7
1922	66,967	31,281	46.7
1923	86,679	45,240	52.2
1924	98,125	56,085	57.2
1925	84,883	57,429	67.7
1926	121,569	76,796	63.2
1927	101,568	61,607	60.7
1928	82,061	40,847	49.8
1929	100,424	53,262	53.0
1930	74,420	30,924	41.6
1931	24,056	16,216	67.4
1932	34,683	17,420	50.2
1933	48,812	33,680	69.0
1934	50,368	30,757	61.1
1935	35,913	21,131	58.8
1936	?	14,854	?
1937	34,677	12,384	35.7
1938	19,388	?	?
1939	22,668	?	?
1940	18,449	?	?
1941	9,938	?	?
1942	2,425	?	?
1943	1,308	?	?
1944	1,593	?	?
1945	3,168	?	?
1946	13,039	?	?
1947	18,753	?	?
1948	21,568	?	?
1949	23,844	?	?
1950	34,691	?	?
1951	62,568	?	?
1952	84,720	?	?
1953	80,070	?	?
1954	72,248	?	?
1955	55,166	?	?
1956	44,806	?	?
1957	53,613	?	?

* Sources: Doria de Vasconcellos, "Alguns Aspectos da Imigração no Brasil," *Boletim do Serviço de Imigração e Colonização*, No. 3 (March, 1941), 29–30, 35–36; and for the years 1938 to 1957, *Anuário Estatístico do Brasil*, XI (1950), 55; XIII (1952), 64; XV (1954), 59; XVII (1956), 77; XIX (1958), 39.

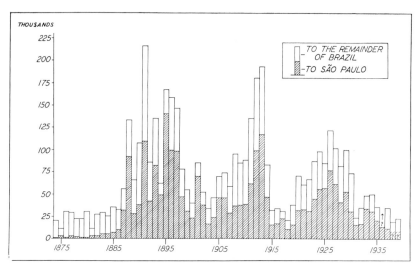

FIGURE 13. Annual immigration to Brazil and to São Paulo, 1874–1939.

The onslaught of World War I naturally brought a decided slump in the number of immigrants disembarking at Brazilian ports, the figure descending to the 30,000 level in 1915 and below 20,000 in 1918. Following the war a considerable recovery was started, but the movement never regained its former vigor. The year 1926 represents the peak for this period: 118,686 immigrants were recorded, the only year after 1913 when immigration to Brazil exceeded 100,000. However, the incoming stream remained near this annual figure until 1929, when it again fell sharply to another low of 37,465 in 1931. A slight recovery, the introduction of the quota system in 1934, and the resumption of immigration levels that approximated those of the 1870's are other features of the 1930's. In 1939 only 22,668 immigrants entered Brazil, a number still further reduced by World War II. In 1946, however, immigration again got under way in considerable volume, and during the 1950's the levels were slightly above those prevailing in the 1920's.

COMPOSITION OF THE STREAM

The compilations made by the Instituto Nacional de Imigração e Colonização for the years 1884 to 1957 provide the details on the nationalities of immigrants to Brazil and the data necessary for judging their relative importance. These materials have been assembled in Table XXII, and percentages have been calculated to show the relative importance of each of the elements. In interpreting these data it should be kept in mind that changes in political units and boundaries between 1884 and 1957 have affected the numbers reported in several important national groups. For example, numerous

Polish immigrants who came before World War I must have been classed as Russians, Austrians, or Germans. Also, it can be proved beyond all doubt that very large numbers of Paraguayans and considerable numbers of Uruguayans, Argentines, Bolivians, Peruvians, Ecuadorians, Colombians, and Venezuelans are not included in the statistics.

These data show Italy and Portugal supplied Brazil with the largest numbers of immigrants, the former leading slightly because of great masses of agricultural laborers who abandoned Italy for Brazil during the closing decades of the nineteenth century. These two countries alone account for nearly two-thirds of the recorded immigration to Brazil during the entire seventy-four-year period. It will come as a surprise to many that Spain ranks third and has contributed more than half a million immigrants to Brazil or almost 14 per cent of the total. Japan, which entered the lists only in 1908 and did not begin her penetration in earnest until about 1925, ranks fourth. Next comes Germany, which lagged during the early decades of the period but greatly stepped up the dispatch of her nationals to Brazil following World War I. No other country except Russia, which ranks sixth, has contributed as many as 100,000, or as much as 2.3 per cent. This high figure needs some explanation for, although there are many thousands of Russians in Brazil, a large part of the immigration classed as Russian is that of the Russian Poles who migrated before World War I. Were it possible to segregate the Poles from the Austrian, German, and Russian contingents and to add the total thus derived to the recorded immigration from Poland, undoubtedly the immigrants from Poland would rank sixth.

It is interesting to observe how the countries making the greatest contributions have varied as time has passed. See Figure 14. In the decade 1874 to 1883, for which a total of 247,888 immigrants was reported, the five leading nationalities were as follows, given in the order of their importance: Italians, Portuguese, Germans, Spaniards, and Russians. Together they accounted for 84.4 per cent of all immigration during the period. Italians constituted slightly more than one-fourth and Portuguese slightly less than one-quarter of all. The other nationalities were far below.

During the following decade immigration was almost four times the previous volume, the total for the ten years equaling 883,668. Of this number Italians alone made up 510,553, far ahead of the 170,621 Portuguese, 103,116 Spaniards, 40,589 Russians, and 22,778 Germans reported for the period. Together, these five nationalities made up 95.9 per cent of all immigrants. The very significant gain in the number of Spanish immigrants should not be obscured by the phenomenal increase of Italian immigration.

In the ten years 1894 to 1903 the total number of immigrants fell slightly to 862,110, but this was the period in which Italian immigration reached its maximum, the total for the decade being 537,784. The number of Portuguese immigrants fell slightly, to 157,542, but as a group they remained in second place. Spaniards were still third,

TABLE XXII

Immigration to Brazil, 1884–1957, Classified According to Country of Origin *

Country of origin	Immigrants	
	Number	Per cent of total
Italy	1,510,078	31.7
Portugal	1,457,617	30.6
Spain	657,744	13.8
Japan	209,184	4.4
Germany	192,574	4.0
Russia	109,889	2.3
Austria	88,789	1.9
Turkey	78,706	1.7
Poland	53,555	1.1
France	41,495	0.9
Romania	40,274	0.8
United States	30,686	0.6
England	28,771	0.6
Lithuania	28,665	0.6
Argentina	25,616	0.5
Yugoslavia	24,109	0.5
Syria	23,113	0.5
Lebanon	14,316	0.3
Hungary	13,218	0.3
The Netherlands	12,989	0.3
Switzerland	12,541	0.3
Uruguay	10,720	0.2
Greece	10,112	0.2
Belgium	7,492	0.2
Czechoslovakia	6,486	0.1
Sweden	5,543	0.1
Denmark	3,388	0.1
Esthonia	2,704	0.1
China	2,485	0.1
Chile	2,306	†
Latvia	2,209	†
Peru	1,325	†
Other Countries	56,414	1.2
Total	4,765,113	100.0

* Sources: *Revista de Imigração e Colonização*, I, No. 4 (October, 1940), 641–42; *Anuário Estatístico do Brasil*, VII (1946), IX (1948), X (1949), XI (1950), XIII (1952), XV (1954), XVII (1956), and XIX (1958). For the years 1952 and 1953 the "other countries" category includes all immigrants except those from Germany, Italy, Japan, Portugal, Russia, and Spain.
† Less than one-tenth of one per cent.

and numbered 102,142, approximately the same as they had during the preceding decade. Russians now disappeared from a place among the leaders, and Austrians were in fourth place, their total being 32,456. German immigration fell precipitously to only 6,698, but so few were the representatives of other nations that the nationality remained in fifth position. Together the five leaders accounted for 97 per cent of all immigration to Brazil during the decade. This indicates that the current of immigration was highly homogeneous from

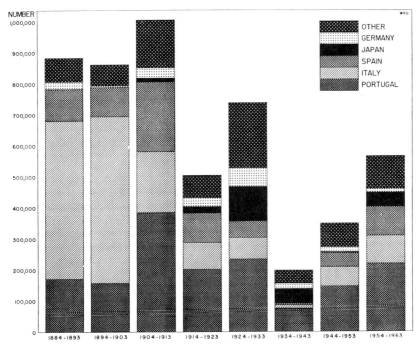

F I G U R E 1 4 . The principal nationalities represented among the immigrants to Brazil, 1884–1963.

the standpoint of nationality. This great concentration in the five leading groups has never been equaled previously or since.

During the period immediately preceding World War I, 1904 to 1913, immigration into Brazil totaled 1,006,617, an all-time high. It also underwent radical changes in composition in comparison with the earlier make-up. The effectiveness of the Italian government's prohibition of migration to São Paulo is indicated by the fact that Italians fell to third place among the immigrants; their total, 196,521, was far below the levels for the preceding decades. Portuguese immigration almost doubled, reaching 384,672, and moved into first place. The Spaniards occupied second position, totaling 224,672, more than double the figure for the preceding decade. Russians, of whom we may be sure a considerable number were Poles, again appeared among the leaders, their total of 48,100 being a little above that of 42,177 for the Turks, who made their debut among the five leading nationalities. The leaders together accounted for 89 per cent of all immigration during the decade.

World War I resulted in a reduction of about 50 per cent in the number of immigrants entering Brazil between 1914 and 1923 in comparison with the preceding ten years, the figure for the decade being only 503,981. Of these, 82.9 per cent was supplied by the five leading nationalities, indicating a continued increase in heterogeneity of the immigrant tide. The Portuguese continued to lead in number, totaling 201,252 and accounting for two-fifths of all the immigrants. The Spanish again occupied second position, and Italians third, 94,779 being the total for the former and 86,320 for the latter. Germans flocked to Brazil in considerable numbers immediately after the war so that their total for the decade rose to 29,339, placing them in fourth position. Austrians, only 6,285 in number, ranked fifth.

In the decade 1924 to 1933 that closed during the depth of the great economic depression, the number of immigrants to Brazil totaled 737,223, about a third higher than during the preceding ten years. The immigrant stream was more heterogeneous in make-up, also; only 71.6 per cent belonged to the five leading nationalities. Portuguese continued to be the most numerous of all nationalities, with 233,650. Japanese suddenly jumped into second place, the first time this Asiatic group appeared among the leaders. There were 110,191 entries of these members of the yellow race recorded during the decade. Italians continued in third position, although their numbers dropped to only 70,177. German immigrants came in greatly increased numbers, totaling 61,728, and this nationality occupied fourth position. On the other hand, the number of Spanish immigrants was almost halved, to only 52,405, and they dropped from their second place position of the previous two decades to fifth place.

In 1934 Brazil began limiting immigration through a system of quotas. Consequently, it is not surprising to find that immigration was considerably reduced from 1934 to 1943, inclusive, in comparison with previous levels, the total for the ten years being 197,238. It also increased slightly in homogeneity. The leading five nationalities included 79.2 per cent of all the immigrants. Portuguese continued to hold the lead, as they had since first they outnumbered the Italians at the close of the nineteenth century. However, their total was only 75,634, not much greater than that, 46,158, of the Japanese, who again were in second place. Germans moved up to third place with a total of 17,862 immigrants, exchanging places with the Italians who numbered 11,432 and now occupied fourth place. For the first time the Spaniards relinquished their place among the leaders. Poles, 10,122 in number, took over fifth position. In the years following World War II the Portuguese, Spaniards, Italians, Germans, and Japanese, in the order named, have constituted the bulk of the immigration to Brazil.

The most prominent features in the composition of Brazilian immigration are these: Italians swarmed into Brazil during the closing decades of the nineteenth century and continued coming in large numbers thereafter. Immigrants from the mother country, Portugal, have always been the most numerous group except during the three decades preceding 1904, when Italian immigration was so high. Immigrants from Spain were very numerous until 1924. Droves of Japanese suddenly began immigrating to Brazil following 1925. So much interest is attached to the immigration of the various nationalities that it is well to give a few of the details concerning the coming of each of the principal groups.

Italians. Italians were entering Brazil in fairly good numbers even before São Paulo got under way with her labor recruitment program. These early comers were placed as colonists in Rio Grande do Sul, Santa Catarina, Paraná, Minas Gerais, and Espírito Santo. However, when São Paulo began seeking in earnest for hands to replace her slaves, the immigration of Italians jumped sharply, the figure rising to 104,353 in 1888. After a recession during the troubled years of 1889 and 1890, and as soon as the republic got under way, the figure shot up to 132,326 for the year 1891. This is the high-water mark in Italian immigration, although after falling to 34,872 in 1894, the number was again up to 104,510 in 1897. After 1902, when the Italian government prohibited the recruiting of immigrants by São Paulo, the annual immigration of Italians to Brazil never again exceeded 20,000 per year except during 1911, 1912, and 1913 when the figures were 22,914, 31,785, and 30,886, respectively.

Portuguese. Year in and year out, members of the Portuguese nationality, immigrants from the mother country, are the ones on whom Brazil may count.[5] Never did the annual tide of Portuguese equal the high marks set by the Italians. The immigration of 76,530 in 1912 and 76,701 in 1913 are the highest figures ever recorded for the entrance of members of this nationality. But from 1908 until

[5] Portuguese immigrants, who were the only Europeans admitted during the colonial period, also kept coming after Brazil had established her independence in the period of the empire. According to one writer, immigration of the Portuguese from the Azores and other islands to Brazil in the middle of the nineteenth century was a form of indentured servitude. Says Codman: "There is something very like a white slave trade going on with the Western Islands, but generally there is nothing objectionable in it. Now and then a Portuguese ship arrives with a company of these islanders. Notice is given in the papers that she is anchored off the Isle of Cobras. The intimation is sufficient. Immediately she is surrounded by boatloads of eager purchasers. The cargo, mostly of young men and girls, is taken on board by the captain, with the understanding that on arrival they shall be temporarily sold for the price of their passages. It is just to these poor people to say that they are generally faithful to their engagements, seldom leaving the masters to whom they are bound until they have earned their freedom. They then commence work upon their own account, and labor with the greatest energy and perseverance to accumulate their little fortunes.

"As might be expected, there occasionally is some immorality in these transactions. But many of the females come over for the express purpose of thus disposing of themselves, having very correct ideas of the morality of the country that gives them so good a chance of success. Many of the more respectable class marry and settle here, but the men generally expect to return. When there are enough of them who are satisfied with the results of their labor, they frequently charter a small brig to take them home. There is something very pleasant in the scenes of these departures." *Ten Months in Brazil,* 135–36.

1929, with rare exceptions other than the war years, 30,000 or more Portuguese immigrants entered Brazil annually. From 1904, when the Portuguese came to outnumber the Italians, until 1957 there were only eight years when they were not the most numerous of all nationality groups included among the immigrants. In 1905, 1906, and 1917 the Portuguese ranked second to the Spaniards; from 1932 to 1935, inclusive, each year the Portuguese were outnumbered by the Japanese; and in 1948 immigrants from Italy once more were more numerous than those from Portugal.

Spaniards. Next to Portugal, Spain has been the most regular contributor of immigrants to Brazil. Never has the immigration for any one year been spectacular, like the pouring in of the Italians, 41,064 in 1913 being the highest figure attained. However, it was above 10,000 each year from 1890 to 1917 with very few exceptions, and most of these were at the time of the Spanish-American War, 1898 and the years that immediately followed. From 1951 to 1957 Spaniards immigrating to Brazil averaged well above 10,000 annually, totaled 17,010 in 1953, and ranked second to the Portuguese except in 1952 when they were slightly outnumbered by Italians.

Japanese. Approximately 200,000 Japanese immigrants have been legally admitted to Brazil since the first contingent of about 800 arrived in 1908. To many it may come as a shock to see that Japan ranks fourth, ahead of Germany, as a contributor of immigrants. Reflecting on the fact that in the fifteen years preceding Pearl Harbor Japan sent as many immigrants to Brazil as did Germany in her whole history will still further stress the significance of this development. Because the movement has been so great, because the Asiatics have proved so resistant to the processes of assimilation and acculturation, and because these Japanese are so different racially and culturally from other immigrants, a short examination of the history of this immigration is advisable.

The provision of hands for São Paulo's agriculture was the motive leading to the introduction of Japanese into Brazil, and it continued to be the motivating force in the admission of Japanese immigrants until 1941. As indicated above, following the abolition of slavery, Paulista fazendas came to depend largely on an Italian labor supply, the state importing between 1887 and 1902 some 800,000 Italian workers,[6] a large share of whom were subsidized either by the state or by the federal government. But many complaints reached Italy regarding the treatment of Italian workers on São Paulo's fazendas, with the result that in 1902 the Italian Government prohibited recruiting and granting of free passage to Italian workers destined for São Paulo. Since this was the only Brazilian state subsidizing the immigration of

[6] Cf. Astrogildo Rodrigues de Mello, "Immigração e Colonização," *Geografia,* I, No. 4 (1935), 29; *Boletim da Directoria de Terras, Colonização e Imigração,* I, No. 1 (October, 1937), 26. The name of the latter publication was changed to the *Boletim do Serviço de Imigração e Colonização,* and data were again given in No. 2 (October, 1940), 145. During this same period São Paulo received some 80,000 Portuguese, 90,000 Spanish, and 18,000 Austrian agricultural laborers, in addition to 25,000 of various other nationalities.

Italian workers, the prohibition greatly reduced the total immigration into Brazil.[7] São Paulo had to seek agricultural workers elsewhere. Japan was one of the sources to which it turned.

After some preliminary negotiations the government of the state of São Paulo in 1907 signed an agreement with the Imperial Japanese Immigration Company for the introduction of 3,000 Japanese immigrants, the state agreeing to pay the expenses of transporting the immigrants from Japan to São Paulo. Under the terms of this contract the first contingent of Japanese immigrants arrived at the port of Santos on June 18, 1908. They were some 800 in number and were destined principally for work in rice farming.[8] A total of 830 Japanese arrived the first year and were sent mostly to locations around Rio Preto in northwestern São Paulo and to the Ribeira Valley near the coast in the southern part of the state.[9] Under the terms of its contract, the company introduced another small number of immigrants in 1909, nearly 1,000 in 1910, and a few more in 1911 to bring the total number up to 1,837. Then in March of 1912 the state government signed a new contract for the importation of Japanese agricultural workers, this time with Ikutaro Acyagui, representative of the Tokyo Syndicate. In the new contract the concessions made by the state were much greater. It granted outright 50,000 hectares of unsettled land lying between the river Ribeira and Cananéia, exempting this land from taxation for five years, and agreed to pay a subsidy of 10 *contos de reis* [10] for each fifty families located on the concession. The syndicate, on the other hand, agreed to introduce and establish on the concession, during a four-year period, a total of 2,000 Japanese families, divide the land into 25-hectare lots, and construct a system that would supply each of the farmsteads with running water.[11] Under this new agreement immigration was rapid, and by the close of 1917 a total of 17,835 Japanese had been transported to Brazil.

Late in 1917 Japanese immigration to Brazil received another great impetus with the organization of the Kaigai Kogyo Kabushiki Kaisha (International Development Company) or K.K.K.K. This company agreed to establish the immigrants either as small holders or as farm laborers on the fazendas of the state. Japanese immigration to Brazil which amounted to only 165 in 1916 increased to 3,899 in 1917 and to 5,599 in 1918. Thus, at the close of the decade the

[7] Rodrigues de Mello, "Immigração e Colonização," *loc. cit.*, 29–30; cf. Ellis, *Populações Paulistas*, 179; Antonio Franceschini, *L'Emigrazione Italiana Nell' America del Sud* (Rome, 1908), 471–73; and Yukio Fujii and T. Lynn Smith, *The Acculturation of Japanese Immigrants in Brazil* (Gainesville, 1959), 3–5.

[8] Rodrigues de Mello, "Immigração e Colonização," *loc. cit.*, 30–31.

[9] Aristoteles de Lima Camara and Arthur Hehl Neiva, "Colonização Nipônica e Germânica no Sul do Brasil," *Revista de Imigração e Colonização*, II, No. 1 (January, 1941), 58. Interestingly enough, the annual report, *Relatorio* (*Serviço de Povoamento em 1908*) (Rio de Janeiro, 1909), contains 208 pages but makes no mention of the Japanese immigration other than to include Japanese in the list of nationalities entering. According to this source, 813 of those arriving in 1908 disembarked at Santos and 17 at Rio de Janeiro.

[10] In 1912 the conto was worth $320.00.

[11] Rodrigues de Mello, "Immigração e Colonização," *loc. cit.*, 31.

movement of Japanese into Brazil was assuming considerable proportions. For the thirteen years 1908 to 1920, inclusive, it totaled 28,661.

An official census taken September 1, 1920, enumerated a total of
27,976 natives of Japan living in Brazil. Taking into account mortality, the presence of diplomatic and consular representatives, and
the fact that a few of the immigrants undoubtedly had returned to
Japan, these two totals seem to be fairly consistent. But it is to be
emphasized that the census of 1920, as well as the subsequent ones,
enumerated as Brazilians the children born in Brazil of Japanese
parentage.

That the bulk of the Japanese immigrants had located in São Paulo
is denoted by the fact that 24,435 of the 27,976, or 87.3 per cent of
all, were residing in the state of São Paulo. The adjacent states of
Minas Gerais and Paraná contained 1,923 and 701, respectively; in
Mato Grosso 514 Japanese were enumerated, in the Federal District
244, and in no other state as many as 100. Furthermore, of the São
Paulo Japanese, only 966 lived in the capital and 606 in Santos.
Most of them were residents of the agricultural sections,[12] such as
municípios lying along the coast below Santos—Iguape with 2,953
and Itahaem with 689 residents born in Japan; Penápolis, Lins, and
Pirajuí, lying across the railroad to Mato Grosso in the western portion of the state and containing 2,614, 1,284, and 1,131 natives of
Japan, respectively; Ribeirão Preto with 1,232 Japanese and its neigh-
bor Araraquara with 908, both situated in north-central São Paulo on
the main route to Goiás; and Rio Preto, in the northwest, containing
725 natives of Japan.

Following 1920 the immigration of Japanese continued at a fairly
low level until 1926. Only 11,963 entered during these five years, and
more than one-half (6,330) arrived in 1925. Then, as may be seen
from the data presented in Table xxiii, the tide of heavy immigration set in, reaching a first peak of 16,648 persons in 1929, and after
a brief recession, an all-time high of 24,494 in 1933. For the entire
period 1929 to 1940 the official data record 157,964 Japanese immigrants to Brazil. If to this number are added the arrivals before
1921, the 1,548 reported for 1941, and approximately 20,000 who
immigrated after World War II, the grand total is 209,184 for the
period since immigration began in 1908. Such are the official data on
Japanese immigration to Brazil.

Some supplementary data for the state of São Paulo, also given in
Table xxiii, serve to show the overwhelming extent to which immigration of Japanese to Brazil has been confined to that state and also
to give some indication as to the net number remaining after departures have been subtracted from arrivals. These data are available only for the years 1926 through 1940, but they are probably
fairly representative of the whole period, since they cover the years
of heavy immigration and a large portion of the immigrants. The ob-

[12] The data for the 1920 census are found in *Recenseamento do Brazil, 1920*,
IV, Pt. 1, pp. 550–877.

TABLE XXIII

*Japanese Immigration to Brazil and to the State of
São Paulo, 1926–1940* *

| Year | Brazil | São Paulo | |
		Total	Net
1926	8,407	7,900	7,393
1927	9,084	9,152	8,516
1928	11,169	11,284	10,303
1929	16,648	16,119	15,335
1930	14,076	13,701	12,880
1931	5,632	5,528	4,692
1932	11,678	11,405	10,941
1933	24,494	24,247	23,384
1934	21,930	22,036	20,660
1935	9,611	10,137	9,052
1936	3,306	5,748	4,490
1937	4,557	4,981	3,630
1938	2,524	2,863	1,752
1939	1,414	1,761	79
1940	1,471	1,300	281
Total	146,001	148,162	133,388

* Sources: Data for Brazil are those of the Departamento Na-
cional de Imigração published in the *Revista de Imigração e
Colonização*, I, No. 4 (October, 1940), 629–34; II, Nos. 2
and 3 (April–June, 1941), 931. Data for São Paulo refer to
Japanese passengers arriving and departing at the port of
Santos and are published by the Secretaria da Agricultura,
Indústria e Comércio of the state in its *Boletim do Serviço
de Imigração e Colonização*, No. 3 (March, 1941), 62, and
No. 4 (December, 1941), 11, 28. Another figure of interest,
as a check upon these data, is that given by Nobutane
Egoshi, Chief Engineer of the Agricultural Section of the
Japanese Consulate in São Paulo. He gives the Japanese immigration to São Paulo through the port of Santos as totaling 115,069 in the years 1908 to 1932, inclusive. Of these,
92 per cent remained. The Brazilian data give a total of only
118,163 Japanese immigrants to Brazil during the corresponding period. Nobutane Egoshi, "O Trabalho e a Producção Agricola do Japonez em São Paulo," *Brazil e Japão,
duas Civilizações que se Completam* (São Paulo, 1934),
59–61.

vious discrepancy in the numbers for some years, with São Paulo
alone reporting more immigrants than the whole of Brazil, is probably due to the difference in the nature of the two series, the one applying to those classed officially as immigrants, and the other to the
arrivals and departures at the port of Santos. That the bulk of the
Japanese immigrants to Brazil, and their offspring as well, has remained in the state of São Paulo is strikingly demonstrated by data
from the 1950 census. Thus of the 329,082 persons classified in the

yellow color category, 276,851 (84.1 per cent) were enumerated in
São Paulo and an additional 39,244 (11.9 per cent) in the adjacent
state of Paraná.

It is also possible to indicate the relative importance of the role
played by the International Settlement Company in the introduction
of the Japanese into São Paulo. Data from official sources supplied to
Brazil's foremost protagonist of Japanese immigration, Professor
Bruno Lobo,[13] indicate that the company transported 100,517 Japanese to Brazil in the years 1908 to 1931. This is sufficient to account
for over 99 per cent of all Japanese immigration during the period.

Germans. The significant feature about German immigration is
not the numbers of persons who left Germany for Brazil, but the extent to which they failed to assimilate with the Brazilian population.
By maintaining their native language and other cultural characteristics, an attachment for the mother country, and a feeling of racial superiority and by reproducing at a very rapid rate, a small number of
immigrants have proved sufficient to blanket much of south Brazil
with people of Teutonic stock and German culture. In fact, it might
be said that Brazil did not need to import large numbers of Germans;
home production of this "commodity" early came to be conducted on
an extensive scale; and the communities of second, third, or fourth
generations constituted cultural islands fully as distinctive as those
of the immigrants themselves. As a matter of fact, as one passes
through parts of Santa Catarina it is the occasional settlement of
caboclos that seems to be a cultural island.

Consider the following description of the early German settlements. When it was written, only a few thousand Germans had entered Rio Grande do Sul. Some of those who came had emigrated to
Argentina, and others had suffered from all the effects of being arranged on opposite sides in a civil war. Nevertheless, in 1871
Michael G. Mulhall, English editor of the Buenos Aires *Standard*,
wrote:

> Imagine to yourself, reader, a country nearly as large as Belgium or
> Holland cut out of these Brazilian forests, where the inhabitants are ex-
> clusively German, and speak no other language; where chapels and schools
> meet you at every opening in the wood; where the mountainsides have been
> in many cases cleared to make room for corn-fields; where women travel
> alone through the forests in perfect security; where agricultural and manu-
> facturing industry flourish undisturbed; where crime is unknown and
> public instruction almost on a level with that of Prussia.[14]

About the same time a governmental inspector who was sent to
look over the situation in Santa Catarina reported the tendency of
the Germans there to preserve their language. Since as late as 1940
German remained the only language intelligible to a large share of
the inhabitants of this community, native and foreign, white and
colored, this report deserves quotation.

[13] Bruno Lobo, *De Japonez a Brasileiro* (Rio de Janeiro, 1932), 179.
[14] Michael G. Mulhall, *Rio Grande do Sul and Its German Colonies* (London,
1873), 105–106.

Among the colonies that I visted, the colony of Blumenau is the one in which the records are organized with most clarity, order and system, of such a type, that they may be given as a model to be followed by the others. . . .

I noted, however, and called it to the attention of the director, as a practice that could not be continued, that the account book is written in German in place of being in Portuguese.

Relative to this Dr. Blumenau gave me unsatisfactory explanations like these: There are entered in this book certain affairs that do not pertain entirely to governmental accounts, this being an account of the mode by which the treasury makes its payments to the directorate, part of the amounts being paid in money and part in drafts in the national treasury; that these drafts are received by their attorney in the capital, Sr. Fernando Hackradt, who, as it is not always possible to cash such drafts promptly without taking a discount so that he could make the remittances to the directorate on time, is under the necessity of receiving from the businessmen of the colony and of the *Vila* of Itajahy the amounts they require, and in exchange giving orders upon the said attorney, who makes the payment due in the capital of the province or in Rio de Janeiro, in accordance with the transaction.

It is true that the system of making payments to the treasury in drafts authorizes indirectly these transactions, that may result in prejudices to the national treasury; it is not less certain, however, that the treasury sometimes proceeds in that manner because it does not always have a cash balance, having only credit. However, I do not see in this a reason that justifies the account books being written in German.[15]

In the years immediately preceding the establishment of the republic, German immigration to Brazil was only about 2,000 per year. It rose sharply to the 5,000 level in 1890 and 1891 but then fell off and was seldom as high as 1,000 until after 1907. In the years before the First World War it again was around 5,000 per year and even reached 8,004 in 1913. Naturally it was very low during the World War I period but rose sharply at the close of the war to 7,915 in 1921 and to 28,168 in 1924. This is the only time German immigrants ever numbered more than 10,000 per year. In 1925 the figure fell back to 7,175, and it never exceeded 5,000 after 1926. Between 1945 and 1957 approximately 20,000 Germans immigrated to Brazil. However, as indicated above, the reproduction in the New World and not the magnitude of the current of immigration from Germany is the significant contribution.

Poles. The bulk of the immigrants contributing to Russia's standing as the sixth most important nationality group probably were Poles. Large numbers of Russians came in 1890, when the 27,125 immigrants of this nationality were second only to the Italians in number, and also in 1891, when the entrance of 11,817 was recorded. Few more came until 1908, when 5,781 new entrants were counted. In 1911 the figure was 14,013. Following the war there was a fairly constant stream of Polish immigrants entering Brazil, the peak year being 1929 when they numbered 9,095. (See also Chapter xvi, "Colonization and Settlement.")

[15] Luiz Manoel de Albuquerque Galvão, *Relatorio sobre as Colonias Blumenau, Itajahy, Principe D. Pedro e D. Francisca* (Rio de Janeiro, 1871), 17–18.

Turks and Syrians. There are present in Brazil, especially in the cities of São Paulo and the towns and cities of Mato Grosso and the Amazon Valley, a considerable number of people from Asia Minor. In Brazil they are known as *Turcos*.[16] For the most part they are found engaging in the trading and merchandising enterprises. According to Bastini the "great" immigration of the Lebanese took place between 1860 and 1870,[17] but the statistical data show that the first Turks, three in number, immigrated to Brazil in 1891. A year later the immigration of 93 Syrians was recorded. After 1895 a considerable flow of Turks began to enter Brazil, a total of 1,823 immigrating in 1899. However, the decade of 1904–1913 was the one in which Brazil received the bulk of her immigrants of this nationality, the peak year being 1913 when the immigration equaled 10,866. The following decade only 19,255 entered, and the next one still fewer (10,277); but some Turks continued to immigrate even after the quota was established in 1934. Nearly all of the Syrians came in the decade 1924–1933, when 14,264 were registered out of a total of 23,113 who have immigrated to Brazil. Of the Lebanese well over one-third of all (5,085) immigrated during the four years 1954 to 1957, inclusive.

FIXATION OF THE IMMIGRANTS

More important than the number of immigrants who arrive is the number of those who stay. Oftentimes there is a large influx of seasonal workers who stay for a few months and then leave. Large numbers of such temporary workers are of less importance in peopling a country than a few who establish themselves permanently. Therefore, it is important to have some index of what the Brazilians call "fixation."

Such an index may be secured by relating the immigration statistics to the census data which classify the foreign-born population according to country of birth. For Brazil such a procedure is most significant for the year 1920, the date of the census most immediately following the heavy immigration. An arbitrary decision must be made as to the years preceding the census for which immigration data will be used in the analysis of the relationship between immigration and the foreign-born populations. A period of 30 years seems to be a reasonable one; Table XXIV was prepared on this basis. This compilation shows the foreign-born population of Brazil in 1920, classified according to national origins, along with the recorded number of immigrants of each nationality entering Brazil from 1890 to 1919,

[16] Says Tanus Jorge Bastini of the Lebanese immigrants: "In spite of the declaration in the passports of the true nationality of their holders, they were called 'Turcos,' since it was Turkey that gave them official permission to travel, and it was the only near eastern nation known in Brazil during the colonial and imperial periods. As a 'Turco' also was known any other person originating in that part of the Orient, be he Egyptian, Persian, Syrian, Palestinian, or Lebanese." *O Libano e os Libanes no Brasil* (Rio de Janeiro, 1943), 123.
[17] *Ibid.,* 124.

TABLE XXIV

*National Origins of Foreign-born Population, 1920, in Relation to Immigration 1890–1919 **

Country of origin	Number of foreign-born persons enumerated in the census	Recorded immigration 1890 to 1919	Number of immigrants per 100 foreign-born population
Total	1,565,961	2,636,187	168
Italy	558,405	1,049,927	188
Portugal	433,577	733,420	169
Spain	219,142	467,548	213
Germany	52,870	56,834	107
Turkey	50,251	54,131	108
Uruguay	33,621	4,223	13
Poland	32,299	1,790	5
Russia	28,941	95,610	330
Japan	27,976	28,293	101
Austria	26,354	67,015	254
Argentina	22,117	8,781	40
Paraguay	17,329	526	3
France	11,894	19,632	165
England	9,637	9,470	98
Peru	7,019	601	9
United States	3,439	6,691	195
Bolivia	2,694	317	12
The Netherlands	1,953	5,061	259
Belgium	1,937	2,672	138
Other Countries	24,506	23,645	96

* Source of basic data: *Recenseamento do Brazil, 1920*, IV (1926), Pt. 1, 312–17; *Revista de Imigração e Colonização*, I, No. 4 (October, 1940), 617–22.

inclusive. For convenience in making comparisons the relationship between the two also is expressed by ratios which show for each nationality the number of immigrants per hundred persons of that nationality enumerated in the census.

There were reported by the 1920 census a total of 1,565,961 foreigners residing in Brazil, and for the preceding thirty-year period a total immigration of 2,636,187 persons was recorded. In other words, 168 immigrants entered the country, in the stated years, for every 100 foreigners residing there in 1920. This might be regarded as an index of "fixation."

Although such a ratio is an extremely crude measure, some of the differences are worthy of discussion, and several unmistakable deficiencies in the immigration statistics are revealed by its use. Italy, Portugal, and Spain were the sources of such a large proportion of Brazil's immigrants that they deserve special attention. That the index is 213 for Spain, 188 for Italy, and only 169 for Portugal may be due to the fact that a larger percentage of the Spanish and Italian immigrants later made their way to Argentina or returned to Europe than did newcomers from the mother country. The low indexes among Germans and Turks indicate two things, that the immigration was recent and that the immigrants remained in Brazil.

Particularly significant are the low indexes for the nationality groups from Brazil's neighbors. The census of 1920 found large contingents of people from Paraguay, Peru, Bolivia, Uruguay, and Argentina living in Brazil, whereas the immigration statistics account for the entrance of only a few persons from those countries. This indicates beyond all possibility of doubt that there has been a large unrecorded immigration from the neighboring countries into Brazil.

The indexes for Poland, Russia, and Austria indicate clearly that many Poles who came to Brazil were entered in the immigration records as Russians or Austrians.

DESTINATION OF THE IMMIGRANTS

That approximately 55 per cent of all persons immigrating to Brazil between 1878 and 1937 located in the single state of São Paulo is indicated by the data presented by Doria de Vasconcellos. See Table XXI and Figure 13. His figures show a total of 4,369,675 immigrants to Brazil during the years 1878 to 1937, inclusive, of whom 2,400,156 went to São Paulo and only 1,969,519 to all other states in the confederation. Furthermore, after 1887 when immigration to São Paulo suddenly shot up to 32,110 in a single year from comparatively low levels, there were very few years in which that state did not take at least 50 per cent of all Brazil's immigrants, and several in which she took more than 65 per cent of the total. The explanation, of course, is the fact that São Paulo early established an excellent immigration service and annually appropriated a considerable sum of money to be used in subsidizing immigration. The state began this subsidization in 1881 and first expended a large sum for this purpose in 1886, when immigration to the state began to mount. The following year it tripled the fund, and immigration to the state increased from 9,534 in 1886 to 32,110 in 1887. From 1897 to 1908 São Paulo's expenses in connection with its immigration program nearly always exceeded those of the federal government for a similar purpose. After expending relatively large amounts on immigrants in 1908 and 1909, the national government abandoned such a policy altogether, but São Paulo continued the practice until 1928 and, after a brief lapse, resumed it again in 1935. For the entire period, 1881 to 1928, the state's expenditures per year on immigration were above 5 per cent of its total budget almost as many times as they were below that proportion. The highest percentages of the state's budget used for subsidization of immigrants were 14.5 in 1895, 10.0 in 1897, 10.8 in 1901, 9.0 in 1905, 8.5 in 1912, 8.2 in 1913, and 7.4 in 1924.[18]

How effective was this subsidization in securing immigrants? Doria

[18] See Doria de Vasconcellos, "Alguns Aspectos da Imigração no Brasil," loc. cit., 6–7, 28–29.

de Vasconcellos, with all the records at his disposal, was able to classify the immigrants to São Paulo during the years 1890 to 1913, inclusive, according to whether they were subsidized or spontaneous. His data count 893,659 subsidized immigrants to the state during that period, or about 62 per cent of all (1,451,047) immigration during the period. There was also a considerable tendency for the volume of immigration to fluctuate in direct proportion to the amounts expended for immigration purposes.[19] The effectiveness of the program is further indicated by data from the census of 1920 showing the distribution of foreigners in the various states. These have been brought together in Table xxv. Observation of this table will indicate that, just as São Paulo received more than half of the immigrants, she also contained in 1920 more than 50 per cent of the foreign-born population of Brazil. Only the population of the capital city of the

TABLE XXV

Numbers and Percentages of Foreign-born Persons in Brazil, 1920, by States *

State	Population in 1920	Number of foreign-born	Per cent foreign-born were of state population	Per cent of nation's foreign-born population
Brazil	30,635,605	1,590,378	5.2	100.0
São Paulo	4,592,188	833,709	18.2	52.4
Distrito Fcdcral	1,157,873	240,392	20.8	15.1
Rio Grande do Sul	2,182,713	154,623	7.1	9.7
Minas Gerais	5,888,174	88,013	1.5	5.5
Paraná	685,711	63,110	9.2	4.0
Rio de Janeiro	1,559,371	53,770	3.5	3.4
Santa Catarina	668,743	32,138	4.8	2.0
Mato Grosso	246,612	25,664	10.4	1.6
Pará	983,507	22,648	2.3	1.4
Espírito Santo	457,328	20,109	4.4	1.3
Amazonas	363,166	17,075	4.7	1.1
Bahia	3,334,465	13,451	0.4	0.9
Pernambuco	2,154,835	12,568	0.6	0.8
Territorio do Acre	92,379	3,571	3.9	0.2
Maranhão	874,337	2,163	0.3	0.1
Goiás	511,919	2,079	0.4	0.1
Ceará	1,319,228	1,534	0.1	0.1
Alagôas	978,748	1,030	0.1	0.1
Paraíba	961,106	850	†	0.1
Rio Grande do Norte	537,135	743	†	0.1
Piauí	609,003	631	†	†
Sergipe	477,064	507	†	†

* Source: *Anuário Estatístico do Brasil*, V (1939/1940), 1302.
† Less than .1 per cent.

[19] *Ibid.*, 21–22.

nation contained a higher percentage of foreigners. Other large contingents of the foreign-born were present in Rio Grande do Sul, Minas Gerais, Paraná, Rio de Janeiro, and Santa Catarina. There were practically no foreigners in the northeastern sections of Brazil.

By 1950 the foreign-born population of Brazil was even more concentrated in São Paulo, the Distrito Federal, and a few other sections of the country. At that time São Paulo alone contained 693,321 persons of foreign birth, 56.6 per cent of the Brazilian total; and there was another 210,454, or 17.2 per cent, in the Distrito Federal. Rio Grande do Sul (78,138), Paraná (76,052), and the state of Rio de Janeiro (38,395), with 6.4, 6.3, and 3.2 per cent, respectively, were the other leaders.

By using data from the census it is possible to determine where the majority of the immigrants of various nationalities entering prior to 1920 had established themselves. Since such a large proportion of all immigrants to Brazil entered the country before 1920, these data are more adequate than might appear at first thought. In any case it is important to know where the earlier immigrants settled.

Of the 558,405 Italians enumerated in the 1920 census, the lion's share, 71.4 per cent, were in São Paulo. Although the important Italian agricultural colonies in Rio Grande do Sul could not have failed to impress one who might have visited the colonial sections of that state following World War I, fewer than 50,000, 8.8 per cent of all, Italian immigrants were enumerated there. Santa Catarina had 7.7 per cent of the total, or 42,943 Italians. The Distrito Federal and Espírito Santo were the units with the other large contingents, 21,929 and 12,553, or 3.9 and 2.3 per cent of all, respectively. However, at this time the *delegado*, who had charge of the census in the latter, reported:

> The existence of so many farms is explained by the fact that the interior of Espírito Santo has been, in a large part, peopled almost exclusively by Italian and German immigration. These elements are so important in certain municípios that the predominant idiom in them is the German or the Italian, there existing thousands of Brazilians who do not understand a single word of the vernacular language.[20]

The Portuguese who have migrated to Brazil have always tended to settle in the cities. There they have become small shopkeepers, taxi drivers, domestic servants, or have engaged in a great many of the other lower-paid jobs. Perhaps this is the reason for their being made the butt of so many Brazilian jokes. In any case it is strictly in line with this observation to note that, of the 433,577 Portuguese living in Brazil in 1920, a total of 172,338 (39.8 per cent) were in the city of Rio de Janeiro. São Paulo had the second largest contingent, numbering 167,198 or 38.6 per cent of the total. Of these, 64,687 were in the capital of the state, and we may be sure a large share of the others were in Santos, Campinas, Ribeirão Preto, and the other smaller cities dotted about the map of São Paulo. The state of Rio de

[20] *Recenseamento do Brazil, 1920,* I, 513.

years of the nineteenth century greatly changed the ethnic composition of that great state. Of considerable concern to the entire nation are the results of the contracts which São Paulo signed in 1908 and again in 1925 with agencies of the Imperial Japanese Government, agreements by which she admitted and paid a considerable share of the cost of transporting some 200,000 Japanese immigrants to the state.

The next fundamental developments in Brazilian immigration policy did not come until after Getúlio Vargas came into power. Earlier, there had been passed in 1921 and 1924, at dates corresponding with important immigration legislation in the United States, two laws designed to establish criteria for the admission of aliens.[21] The most lasting effects of these laws seem to have come from the definition of immigrants as third-class passengers disembarking at Brazilian ports. Out of this came a body of statistics of some interest and debatable value and the identification in the Brazilian mind of "immigrant" with low social and economic status, an association that still prevails. But in 1934 came a much more important development. Then the federal government again assumed a share in the control over immigration policies and procedures and handed down a decree to regulate the conditions under which foreigners might be admitted to Brazil and permitted to remain in the country. Most important of all, a quota system for limiting immigration was placed in effect. The number of foreigners of any one nationality who might enter the nation during any one year was placed at 2 per cent of the immigration from that country during the years 1884 to 1933.[22] This law set the total immigration permitted during any single year at 77,020. As originally drawn, the Portuguese were also given a quota, but a later resolution [23] rescinded this provision. A few years later decree No. 3,010 of August 20, 1938, provided that 80 per cent of the quota of each nationality must be filled by agriculturists or the members of their families. These are the basic items in the policy under which Brazil is now operating.[24]

---

[21] See Péricles de Mello Carvalho, "A Legislação Imigratória do Brasil e sua Evolução," *Revista de Imigração e Colonização*, I, No. 4 (October, 1940), 721.

[22] The decree, No. 406 of May 4, 1938, is published in the *Revista de Imigração e Colonização*, I, No. 1 (January, 1940).

[23] The resolution was adopted April 22, 1939, by the Conselho Nacional de Imigração e Colonização.

[24] For a discussion of some of the legal restrictions on immigrants in Brazil, see J. Fernando Carneiro, *Imigração e Colonização no Brasil* (Rio de Janeiro, 1950), 34–36.

CHAPTER IX

INTERNAL MIGRATION

T HE RURAL Brazilian of the lower classes is notorious for his nomadic or migratory habits, for his lack of permanent attachment to the soil, for his tendency to shift about from place to place. In few nations are such large proportions of the rural people, who in turn are over half of the total population, so constantly on the move. So migratory are the inhabitants of the Amazon that the members of a North American commission became convinced that the rubber gatherers, and especially those from Ceará, are possessed of a "migratory instinct." [1] Unable to find geographical, economic, or religious factors that would account for the residential instability of the workers on the sugar plantations of Pernambuco, Gileno dé Carlí concluded that they, too, were "undoubtedly possessed of migratory instinct. . . . They have regressed to the situation that existed before slavery." However, in this case better housing and schools are said to be modifying the *instincto migratorio*. [2]

The very nature of the processes used in fire agriculture means that millions of Brazilian families must move each year. The same is true of the riverbank agriculture in the Amazon Valley. From north to south, east to west, from extractive industries such as rubber, babassú, and mate, to the highly commercialized agriculture of the coffee and sugar districts, in the immense pastoral sections and in the areas where the garimpeiros camp for a while to search for precious stones, the population is unstable and shifting. As yet, free institutions have not been as successful as slavery and serfdom in attaching the lower-class Brazilian population to the land. It is significant that one of the major objectives of the colonization program is the "fixation" of the rural people.

The residential stability of a considerable share of rural Brazilians is greatly affected by the great *sêcas*, droughts, which periodically scourge the vast northeastern section of the country. As is indicated in other chapters, this area is rather densely populated by a prolific set of inhabitants. But throughout this vast sertão every ten or fifteen years the rains do not come, the streams and water holes dry up, the

---

[1] William L. Schurz, *et al., Rubber Production in the Amazon Valley* (Trade Promotion Series, No. 23 [Washington, D. C., 1925]), 163, 202, 219–21, 271, 273, *passim*.

[2] Gileno dé Carlí, *Aspectos Açucareiros de Pernambuco* (Rio de Janeiro, 1940), 28–29.

vegetation fails, the roças cannot bring forth their corn and mandioca, the livestock die, and the population is forced to flee the
stricken area. These sêcas sent forth large contingents of population
into the Amazon Valley during the closing decades of the last century; in more recent years they have been a strong force motivating
thousands of persons to seek homes in far-off São Paulo; and nearly
every decade they cause hundreds of thousands of persons to flee to
the coastal cities in search of food and water. The migrations induced
by these periodic droughts are among the most significant in Brazil.
It is as though the flight from our own "dust bowl" in a much more
acute form were staged at ten- or twelve-year intervals.

The study of internal migration in Brazil is still in its formative
stages. Therefore, a great deal more investigation and data are
needed before definite classifications of the various types of migration will be possible. For present purposes, however, various kinds of
internal migration may be discussed under the following headings:
(1) rural-urban migration, (2) pushing forward the agricultural frontier, (3) seasonal migration, and (4) flight from the sêcas. Growing
out of the drought-propelled migrations, São Paulo's need for additional hands, and the restriction of immigration, is a significant flow
of population from Minas Gerais, Bahia, and the northeast to São
Paulo. This movement, which is given separate treatment in some detail, has resulted in acute depopulation in some areas, especially
in parts of Bahia. Also included are some materials on other important state-to-state movements.

RURAL-URBAN MIGRATION

Data on rural-urban migration are very few, but the materials at
hand suggest that the migration from Brazil's rural areas to its
towns and cities goes on in about the same manner as it does in other
countries. In recent decades the rapid growth of towns and cities,
notably in São Paulo and other southern states, is ample evidence
that migration from the farms has been of considerable size. According to Brazilians best informed on the subject, the flight to the cities
was especially pronounced when the slaves received their freedom
during the closing years of the nineteenth century. But many of the
elite also took up residence in the cities at that time.[3]

The age and sex distributions in Brazil's cities have a profile and
composition that could only result from a migration which is selective
of young adults, especially those of the female sex. Therefore, since
such selectivity is generally true elsewhere, there is little reason for
doubting that it also prevails in Brazil. However, these age and sex
distributions also seem to indicate that relatively few elderly persons
abandon the city to spend their declining years in the country districts.

[3] Cf. Carneiro Leão, *A Sociedade Rural,* 118–20; and Oliveira Vianna, "O
Povo Brazileiro e sua Evolução," *loc. cit.,* 305–306.

There are available in the various censuses certain data relative to the origins of the population of Rio de Janeiro that contribute to our knowledge of rural-urban migration in Brazil. Thus in 1890 Rio de Janeiro contained 415,559 inhabitants, of whom 29.7 per cent were foreign-born, 44.2 per cent were natives of the Federal District, and 26.1 were migrants from the various Brazilian states. The data on the number of natives of each state who were living in the city of Rio de Janeiro in 1890, along with the sex classification and sex ratio for the migrants from each state, are presented in Table xxvi.

TABLE XXVI

Migrants from Various States Who Were Living in the Federal District, December 1, 1890, Classified According to Sex *

State	Total number	Per cent	Males	Females	Sex ratio
Total	133,765	100.0	68,546	65,220	105
Rio de Janeiro	67,312	50.3	31,559	35,753	88
Bahia	10,300	7.7	5,358	4,942	108
Minas Gerais	9.421	7.0	5,056	4,365	116
Pernambuco	7,023	5.2	4,081	2,942	139
Ceará	6,735	5.0	3,800	2,935	129
São Paulo	6,570	4.9	3,286	3,284	100
Rio Grande do Sul	5,310	4.0	2,827	2,483	114
Maranhão	3,304	2.5	1,884	1,421	133
Paraíba	2,700	2.0	1,825	875	209
Santa Catarina	2,656	2.0	1,265	1,391	91
Alagôas	2,333	1.7	1,471	862	171
Sergipe	2,142	1.6	1,373	769	179
Rio Grande do Norte	2,104	1.6	1,410	694	203
Espírito Santo	1,838	1.4	956	882	108
Pará	1,066	0.8	666	400	167
Paraná	1,021	0.8	539	482	112
Piauí	899	0.7	584	315	185
Mato Grosso	596	0.4	315	281	112
Amazonas	231	0.2	140	91	154
Goiás	204	0.2	151	53	285

* Source: *Recenseamento do Distrito Federal, 1890* (Rio de Janeiro, 1895), xxi.

Observation of these data indicates that one-half of all the migrants to the federal capital had come from the adjoining state of Rio de Janeiro. The second largest number, however, was from Bahia. Nearby Minas Gerais was in the third place, but Pernambuco, even more distant than Bahia, ranked fourth, and Ceará was fifth. This indicates that large contingents of migrants from the east and northeast were flocking to the federal capital during the decades which preceded the abolition of slavery and the establishment of the republic.

The sex composition of the migrant population indicates that the well-known tendency of females to outnumber males among migrants from the rural districts to nearby cities also holds true in Brazil. There were only 88 males per 100 females among the mass of the migrants who moved in from the adjacent areas in the state of Rio de Janeiro. In general, as the distance increased the predominance of males in the migratory current also became progressively larger. However, the male predominance reached its maximum not in those areas most remote from the capital but in the areas at a considerable distance which contributed relatively few persons to the migrant total. Before the railroads were constructed, the migration from Goiás to Rio de Janeiro was a more arduous undertaking than that from a more distant state lying on the coast.

Comparable data for the year 1950 also are available. By this time the population of the metropolis had increased to 2,377,451 inhabitants. The proportion of foreign-born had fallen to 8.9 per cent, the percentage of those native to the city had risen to 51.4, and 39.7 per cent were migrants from elsewhere in Brazil. The data for those born elsewhere in Brazil have been assembled in Table xxvii.

TABLE XXVII

Migrants from Various States and Territories Who Were Living in the Federal District, July 1, 1950, Classified According to Sex *

State	Total number	Per cent	Males	Females	Sex ratio
Brazil	942,812	100.0	442,912	499,900	89
Rio de Janeiro	360,324	38.2	159,948	200,376	80
Minas Gerais	191,917	20.4	83,461	108,456	77
Espírito Santo	55,746	5.9	25,999	29,747	87
São Paulo	46,990	5.0	22,662	24,328	93
Pernambuco	45,157	4.8	24,458	20,699	118
Bahia	44,936	4.8	23,029	21,907	105
Alagôas	27,267	2.9	14,156	13,111	108
Paraíba	23,209	2.5	15,840	7,369	215
Rio Grande do Sul	21,788	2.3	10,413	11,375	92
Sergipe	20,089	2.1	10,283	9,806	105
Ceará	18,061	1.9	10,436	7,625	137
Pará	16,579	1.7	7,849	8,730	90
Rio Grande do Norte	13,468	1.4	7,431	6,037	123
Santa Catarina	9,819	1.0	4,553	5,266	86
Maranhão	8,475	0.9	4,090	4,385	93
Amazonas	6,669	0.7	2,980	3,689	81
Mato Grosso	6,659	0.7	3,019	3,640	83
Paraná	6,258	0.7	2,994	3,264	92
Piauí	3,581	0.4	1,931	1,650	117
Goiás	1,715	0.2	898	817	110
The Territories	1,139	0.1	515	624	83
Unspecified	12,966	1.4	5,967	6,999	85

* Compiled and computed from data in "Distrito Federal: Seleção dos Principais Dados," *VI Recenseamento Geral do Brasil, Censo Demográfico* (Rio de Janeiro, 1951), 10–11.

When compared with 1890 several significant changes may be observed. The state of Rio de Janeiro continued to supply the largest quotas, but the proportion of migrants from this state was reduced significantly. By 1950 Minas Gerais had sent a very large contingent of its natives to the federal capital and ranked second in this respect. Another nearby state, Espírito Santo, was in third position. Migrants from Pernambuco, Bahia, and other eastern and northeastern states were of much less relative importance in the population of the national capital than had been the case thirty years earlier.

The heavy tide of migration from such nearby states as Rio de Janeiro, Minas Gerais, and São Paulo was much more predominantly female than formerly had been the case. Females also outnumbered males among the migrants from Rio Grande do Sul and even among those from far-off Pará, Amazonas, and Maranhão. As a result, the sex ratio among the persons Rio de Janeiro had received from elsewhere in Brazil fell from 105 in 1890 to 89 in 1950. The migrants from the states along the northeastern coast, Paraíba, Alagôas, Pernambuco, and Sergipe continued to include the highest percentages of males.

In the 1940 and the 1950 census reports those born in one state and living in another are also classified according to age as well as by sex. On the basis of these materials one may estimate with some degree of reliability the numbers and proportions of those born outside the Distrito Federal, now the state of Guanabara and almost coterminous with the city of Rio de Janeiro, who moved there in the decade preceding the 1950 census. This may be done as follows: (1) for those of each sex and separately for each age group the number of Brazilians born elsewhere and living in the Distrito Federal in 1940 is reduced in the same proportion that all Brazilians of that age and sex group fell off by 1950 when they made up the next older ten-year age group, as for example the decrease that took place as males aged 20–29 in 1940 came to be those aged 30–39 in 1950; (2) the resulting number is then compared with the figure for the corresponding age group as reported by the 1950 census; and (3) the difference between the two is attributed to migration from elsewhere in Brazil during the decade between the two censuses. Summing the data for the various age groups of both sexes and adding the number of children, ages less-than-ten, reported as having been born outside the Distrito Federal give an estimate of the number of the migrants.

Estimates made in this manner indicate that there were in the Distrito Federal at the time of the 1950 census a total of 392,829 persons, of whom 182,244 were males and 210,585 females, who had been born elsewhere in Brazil and who had migrated to the nation's capital in the period 1940 to 1950. This number is equivalent to 16.5 per cent of the Distrito's population in 1950 and is eloquent testimony of the tremendous influx of population that took place in the years immediately following the second world war. Along with other data these estimates enable us to evaluate the relative importance of the three primary factors which have a direct bearing on the increase of 573,310 in the population of the Distrito Federal between 1940 and 1950. These factors and their comparative importance are: immigration, −3.1 (foreign-born persons were 18,178 fewer in 1950 than in 1940); natural increase, 198,659, or 34.6 per cent; and net migration from other parts of Brazil, 392,829, or 68.5 per cent.

By the same method estimates were made of the numbers of migrants from each of the various states who moved to the Distrito Federal during the decade under consideration. See Table xxviii. From these materials it is evident that heavy influxes, especially of females, came from the nearby states of Rio de Janeiro, Minas Gerais, and Espírito Santo; it also is evident that other large groups

TABLE XXVIII

Estimates of the Numbers of Migrants to the Distrito Federal from the Various Brazilian States, 1940–1950, by Sex

State	Number of migrants			Per cent of the total	Sex ratio
	Male	Female	Total		
Total	182,244	210,585	392,829	100.0	86.5
North					
Acre *	217	338	555	0.2	64.2
Amazonas †	1,025	1,857	2,882	0.7	55.2
Pará ‡	2,529	3,949	6,478	1.7	64.0
Northeast					
Maranhão	1,658	2,221	3,879	1.0	74.7
Piauí	748	845	1,593	0.4	88.5
Ceará	4,759	3,461	8,220	2.1	137.5
Rio Grande do Norte	3,667	3,226	6,893	1.8	113.7
Paraíba	11,139	4,603	15,742	4.0	242.0
Pernambuco	10,380	10,501	20,881	5.3	98.8
Alagôas	5,426	5,783	11,209	2.9	93.8
East					
Sergipe	3,441	3,958	7,399	1.9	86.9
Bahia	10,504	11,558	22,062	5.6	90.9
Minas Gerais	40,892	53,785	94,677	24.1	76.0
Espírito Santo	18,325	20,794	39,119	9.7	88.1
Rio de Janeiro	51,126	65,618	116,744	29.8	77.9
South					
São Paulo	7,557	8,439	15,996	4.1	89.5
Paraná	1,146	1,237	2,383	0.6	92.6
Santa Catarina	2,024	2,188	4,212	1.1	92.5
Rio Grande do Sul	3,933	3,933	7,866	2.0	100.0
West Central					
Mato Grosso §	1,284	1,840	3,124	0.8	69.8
Goiás	464	451	915	0.2	102.9

* Territory.
† Includes Rio Branco.
‡ Includes Amapá.
§ Includes Guaporé.

of migrants had come from northeastern Brazil, and particularly from the states of Pernambuco, Paraíba, Alagôas, Ceará, and Rio Grande do Norte. Furthermore, from three of the northeastern states the migrants included much higher proportions of males than of females, and in the case of Paraíba the newcomers included almost three males for each female. The very low sex ratios among the migrants from the most distant sections of Brazil (Amazonas, Pará, Acre, and Mato Grosso) deserve comment, since they are exactly contradictory to the well-established principle that long-distance migrants run heavily to those of the male sex. Perhaps the explanation lies in the manner in which Brazil's bureaucracy operates. Specifically, it is likely that the younger and less well-established of the nation's public servants are sent to the posts in the remote hinterland and that after a period of service in those outposts many of them succeed in returning to Rio de Janeiro. If so, no doubt many of them acquire wives during their service in the remote interior, so that they are responsible to a considerable degree for the excess, small in number but large in proportion, of females among those born in the states indicated but who live in the Federal District.

Migration to the município of São Paulo during the decade 1940 to 1950 was estimated in a comparable manner. For this great metropolis the calculations indicate that 524,043 of the native-born Brazilians counted by the 1950 census in the city of São Paulo and its immediate environs had migrated to that great center in the decade immediately preceding that census. This figure is the equivalent of 23.8 per cent of the município's inhabitants, and of the total 253,633 were males and 270,410 females. Along with other materials, these computations enable us to account for the increase of 871,835 in the number of inhabitants of Brazil's greatest metropolitan center during the decade 1940 to 1950 as follows: immigration, 19,944 or 2.3 per cent; natural increase, 327,848 or 37.6 per cent; and migration from elsewhere in Brazil, 524,043 or 60.1 per cent. Even though the persons actually migrating to the city of São Paulo, or the city of Rio de Janeiro for that matter, during the period under consideration may have come in some cases from other urban centers, with their places being filled immediately by an influx to those centers of persons from the surrounding rural areas, this figure attests to the dominant role of rural-urban migration in the growth of Brazil's major cities. There is little reason to suppose that it has been of less importance in the growth of such places as Salvador, Recife, Pôrto Alegre, Belo Horizonte, and dozens of other important urban centers.[4]

Factors, Forces, and Media. The factors and forces producing and the media involved in the mass transfers of population from Brazil's rural districts to her cities and towns may be divided logically into two large categories. The first of these consists of the great social and economic changes that have set the stage for the flight from the land

---

[4] For additional significant factors about the migration to the city of São Paulo, see Vicente Unzer de Almeida and Octavio Teixeira Mendes Sobrinho, *Migração Rural-Urbana* (São Paulo, 1951), 63–64, *passim*.

and the consequent mushrooming of urban centers, and the second includes all of the immediate influences or media which act on specific persons to induce them to shift their places of residence from the rural to the urban districts. Each of these is discussed briefly in turn.

Many pages might be filled with an enumeration and discussion of the *broad social and economic changes* which have been taking place in Brazil during the twentieth century and which, in the last analysis, are the forces responsible for the rural exodus currently under way. Such an analysis is far beyond the scope of this chapter, but even so some of these forces or factors should be mentioned. Certainly the list should include: (1) the development of modern means of transportation and communication to link the various parts of the Brazilian half-continent with one another; (2) some progress in the development of what may become a system of universal education within the country; (3) greatly increased contacts between Brazilian society and those in other parts of the western world, and particularly with those societies in which relatively strong middle-class mentality, standards, and values and a high degree of industrialization have been combined to produce exceptionally high standards and levels of living; (4) widespread social and economic ferment among the masses, among the descendants of the humble people who for centuries were completely docile and tractable in the hands of the land-owning, aristocratic elements in Brazilian society; (5) the enactment, particularly in the 1930's, of substantial bodies of social legislation relating to hours of work, security of tenure, minimum wages, paid vacations, sick leaves, severance pay, and so forth, all of which apply mostly in urban employment and thus have helped to broaden the differences between working conditions in the city and the country; (6) the growing conviction on the part of political and financial leaders that industrialization promises the best solution for the multitude of chronic and acute problems which beset Brazil; and (7) some fundamental changes in the nature and functions of Brazilian cities. The last of these is discussed in Chapter XXII, but each of the others is commented on briefly in the paragraphs which follow.

In Brazil, as in most other parts of Latin America, neither the application of steam to propel ships nor its use to move trains of cars over prepared roadbeds revolutionized transportation during the second half of the nineteenth century to the extent that they made for the rapid and relatively cheap movement of persons and things from one place to another in much of Europe, the United States, and Canada. Indeed, even in the second half of the twentieth century most parts of Brazil lack adequate rail facilities. Similarly the telephone and the telegraph did relatively little to modernize communication within Brazil prior to the first world war. But since 1930 and especially since the close of the second world war, the automobile and the motor truck, the airplane, and radio and television have, with startling rapidity, made rapid means of communication and transportation integral portions of interstate and intercommunity relationships in many parts of Brazil. Roads and trails in the interior on which less than two decades ago the present writer spent days and weeks without sighting more than a few score of vehicles now are crowded with trucks, buses, and automobiles moving thousands of persons and many tons of goods from one place to another. In addition, hundreds of new routes, thousands of miles in extension, including links between the populous cities of the South and the Northeast and the Amazon, have been opened to overland traffic. Truck terminals now are prominent features in cities all the way from Belém and Fortaleza, in the North, to Pôrto Alegre and Pelotas, in the South. These expanded and improved facilities for transportation and communication have done much to set the stage for the exodus of people from the rural areas.

In most parts of the Brazilian confederation the condition in which two-thirds or so of the total population, and much higher proportions of the rural population, remain illiterate throughout life is no longer considered as natural, inevitable, or even tolerable. Many of the states already have taken notable strides in the development of a system of primary schools open to all children. (See Chapter xix.) However the schools, and the books, papers, and magazines which they teach people to read, are among the most powerful urbanizing forces that have ever been unleashed in the world. For hundreds of thousands of young Brazilians who have had the privilege of attending school for a few years, the city has become a magnet of irresistible force. As in Canada, the United States, and much of Spanish America, Brazil's effort to develop a system of general education is helping greatly to stimulate the flight of people from the land.

Throughout the entire world the increased contacts of the members of a given society with persons from other parts of the world is one of the features which most distinguish the years since 1940 from all preceding epochs. In few, if any, parts of the globe has this change been more pronounced than in Brazil, and it has involved travel by many thousands of Brazilians to other parts of the earth as well as the influx of those from other countries into all parts of Brazil. Particularly frequent are the contacts of Brazilians with North American and European societies in which middle-class people and industrialization have produced high average levels and standards of living. As a result, almost inevitably the Brazilians who visit such countries do all in their power to speed industrialization and urbanization when they return to their homeland.

The decades in the middle of the twentieth century are ones of great social ferment among the rural masses who for centuries have constituted the bulk of Brazil's population. Once highly docile and tractable, and completely under the control of the large landowners and their representatives, these people are growing increasingly discontented with their lot and with the prospects of life for their children. They are becoming quick to follow any leader who promises an improvement. This social ferment is a powerful influence in bringing Brazil's rural masses to abandon the country and seek a different life in the city.

Following the close of the first world war and the organization of the League of Nations, the various Latin American countries were among the first to enact into law the various models of social legislation that were developed by international agencies. In many ways, particularly during the Vargas regime, Brazil was at the forefront of this movement, although her leaders frequently modified the models to a considerable extent, and they also were prone to look beyond the international agencies for their patterns. In any case the social legislation put into effect during the interim between the two world wars had a substantial effect in bettering the lot of the urban workers, and word of this improvement quickly spread throughout the rural districts. As a result, this factor, too, came to play an important part in the movement of people from the rural to the urban districts.

For many years Brazil has been a highly rural enclave in a world that is governed largely by urban and industrial values. In recent decades particularly, this has led to the conviction on the part of many influential Brazilians that only through urbanization and industrialization can their society hope to solve the host of chronic social and economic problems with which it is afflicted. The day when the senhores de engenho and other rural barons steered the Brazilian ship of state definitely has passed. In turn, the efforts of the new leaders to industrialize Brazil have done much to enlarge the flow of of migrants from the country to the city.

The *immediate influences and media* related to the transfer of residence from rural to urban districts by particular Brazilians are legion. Prominent in this category, however, are the following: (1) word-of-mouth reports and personal letters which some of the migrants give to their friends on the occasion of visits to their home districts or send back to their relatives in the country; (2) the location of almost all secondary schools in towns and cities, a factor which causes many well-to-do landowners to move their families to such urban centers in order that their children may have more than the three years of primary schooling available in their home communities; (3) the advice and counsel of urban-reared or urban-trained schoolteachers to the youth of the neighborhoods in which they are employed; (4) visits by country people to friends and relatives who previously have established themselves in a town or city; and (5) the glowing accounts of city life given by truck drivers, especially in the Northeast, who are engaged in transporting families and their possessions, often as many as fifty persons per truck, on the long, rough, and hot journey to Rio de Janeiro, São Paulo, and other cities in the South. Brief comments on each of these are offered in the following paragraphs.

Among a simple, unsophisticated country folk word-of-mouth reports, during a visit which a migrant pays to his former home, and the letters written personally to relatives and friends in the rural district from which he came are the major determinants in causing João

Castro or Louisa Souza to migrate to an urban center. Information gained in such a manner is that which the rural Brazilian youth feels that he may trust. Such personal reports and advice, plus assistance those who have gone before give to recent arrivals in obtaining jobs and finding places in which to live, probably are the most important factors in the current, heavy rural-urban migration in Brazil.

In most of Brazil's vast interior secondary schools are entirely lacking, and those that may be reached are located in towns and cities most of which are in the coastal areas. Therefore, throughout much of the nation, even a well-to-do landowner must choose early among the following alternatives: (1) allow his children to grow up with no more formal schooling than the three, or at most four, years of elementary training provided in the município in which he lives, (2) send his children to board with friends or relatives in the state capital or other city while they continue their schooling, or (3) move the entire family to one of the important centers of population in which the desired educational facilities are located. Frequently either the second or the third alternative is selected, so that both of them are factors of no slight consequence in Brazilian rural-urban migration.

In Brazil, as elsewhere throughout the world, the school is the most urbanizing force to be found within the rural community. It is practically impossible to secure or prepare teachers who are not dominated by urban values; and this is true even though the teachers themselves may have been reared in the country, and even though, in some instances, those in charge of administering the schools are seeking such teachers. As it is, the extent to which the teacher has an influence on her pupils is a fair index of the degree to which they are motivated to spend the remainder of their lives in urban districts.

Kinship and friendship ties remain close and intimate throughout Brazilian society, and this is changed little by the fact that one or more members of a group has left the rural community and taken up residence in a town or city. The migrant seeks every opportunity for a visit back home, even in cases such as those of the northeasterners living in Rio de Janeiro and São Paulo, where thousands of miles lie between the communities of origin and those of residence. Likewise, the countryfolk make every effort to visit their relatives who have moved to the city. All of this constitutes a potent force in causing some of the rural relatives likewise to change their place of residence from the country to the city or town.

Finally, in some parts of Brazil, and especially in the Northeast, hundreds of proprietors of large trucks are engaged in transporting families and their goods over the long-established migration routes, such as those which lead from Ceará, through the states of Pernambuco, Bahia, and Minas Gerais, and on to Rio de Janeiro and São Paulo. Naturally these entrepreneurs are active in spreading the word in the northeastern states of the opportunities and possibilities for life and work in the great cities to the south. Eventually, of course, they collect a fee for the transportation supplied. As early as 1951, or almost as soon as the last link in the route was traversable by wheeled vehicles, the state of Ceará attempted to combat the exodus to the south by enacting a law making it illegal for a truck to transport passengers across the state line. The net effect of this was, of course, that the migrants had to get off at the state boundary, themselves take a few steps into the adjacent state, and then reboard in order to be on their way several thousands of miles to the south.

Effects of Rural-Urban Migration. Now that the movement of population from the country to the city in Brazil has been considered as a dependent variable or as a result of various factors of Brazilian society, it is important to reverse the equation and to consider some of the effects of this migration on that society. First to be listed in this connection, as it probably also is first in importance, is the fact that the movement of people from rural to urban areas is the principal factor in the remarkable growth of urban centers throughout Brazil. As indicated above, the net migration to Rio de Janeiro and São Paulo from elsewhere in Brazil accounted for more than 68 per cent of the population increase in the former and 60 per cent of that in the latter during the period 1940 to 1950. Even though comparable studies for other cities are lacking, there can be little doubt that the natural increase of population in towns and cities definitely is secondary in importance in the increase of the urban population, and that the primary cause of the mushrooming of urban centers is the movement of people from the country to the city. The third factor that logically needs to be considered in the analysis, namely immigration, is of slight importance for recent decades, although in the past it was of considerable significance in the growth and development of cities such as São Paulo, Rio de Janeiro, and Pôrto Alegre. But by all odds the important cause of the growth of Brazilian cities, large and small, is the urbanward flow of population from the rural districts.

A second highly significant result of the rural-urban migration going on in Brazil is the host of perplexing social, economic, and political problems which it is spawning. Throughout the rural districts the landowners are bemoaning the lack of hands that is produced by the exodus, whereas in the cities problems of housing, sanitation and health, intraurban transportation, riots and other disorders, and pressures on legislative bodies and administrative officials are very much in the news. It could hardly be otherwise, for the migrants to the cities include hundreds of thousands of humble rural folk from the remote sections of the northeast and the states of Bahia and Minas Gerais, as well as large contingents from the states of Rio de Janeiro, Espírito Santo, São Paulo, and the states to the south of the latter. This is to say that high proportions of the newcomers to the cities are from exactly those portions of the Brazilian population that are least prepared educationally, economically, culturally, and politically to confront life in the nation's great metropolitan centers. By the thousands they live in improvised shacks in the teeming *favelas* or slums of these great cities, where daily they carry on their precarious efforts to secure enough food to sustain themselves and the members of their large families. Entirely unequipped by education and experience to resist the suggestions and promises of demagogues of every political hue, they join with the more experienced sectors of the urban proletariat in bitter, destructive outbursts of protest and rioting of every type.[5] Many of Brazil's leaders, and especially those in state and municipal government, think that their problems would be greatly alleviated if the rural-urban migrations could be slowed down or even stopped entirely; with great frequency one hears an expression of the belief that many of the migrants should be returned to the districts in which they originated. Thus in a large measure the tremendous problems with which Brazil presently is confronted are due to the vast movement going on throughout the country of population from the rural districts to the cities. One should not overlook the fact, however, that other equally difficult problems probably would be present if all of the migrants were to remain in the particular rural districts of the republic in which they were born and reared, nor should he forget that a major portion of the nation's territory remains to be settled.

A third important effect of rural-urban migration in Brazil and the backwash to the rural areas of ideas, standards, values, techniques, and other social and cultural phenomena which it engenders is the beginning in eradication of the tremendous rural-urban and regional differences that long have been standard features of Brazilian society. In brief, the stirring of the social and cultural elements produced by rural-urban migration in Brazil is stimulating the process of homogenization of society in that vast half-continent.[6] This is because the migrations and their accompanying social and cultural phenomena are thoroughly mixing the ethnic, social, and cultural elements in the various sections of Brazil which not many years ago were almost hermetically sealed off from one another. For example, the trucking to Rio de Janeiro of hundreds of thousands of persons from the rural sections of Paraíba, Pernambuco, Ceará, Bahia, and other northeastern and eastern states during the years following 1948 had as a side effect the establishment of the *baião* as a rival, or possibly a replacement, for the *samba* as Brazil's most popular form of music and the dance. But the migrants who return to the districts from whence they came, the relatives who visit them in the cities, and the exchange of letters and other messages are powerful factors in the diffusion of food habits, technical skills, ideas, vices,

[5] Cf. Louis J. Lebret, José Arthur Rios, Carlos Alberto de Medina, and Helio Modesto, *Aspectos Humanos da Favela Carioca*, in Suplemento Especial of *O Estado de S. Paulo*, Parts I and II (São Paulo, April 13, 15, 1960); Carolina Maria de Jesus, *Quarto de Despejo* (*Diário de uma Favelada*), (São Paulo, 1960); and T. Lynn Smith, "The Giant Awakes: Brazil," *The Annals of the American Academy of Political and Social Science*, Vol. 334 (March, 1961), 95–102.

[6] For a development of the concept of homogenization of society, a close counterpart of getting all the materials of which milk is composed equally distributed throughout its volume, and an analysis and description of the process in the United States, see T. Lynn Smith, "The Homogenization of Society in the United States," *Mémoire du XIX Congres International de Sociologie*, II (Mexico, 1960), 245–75.

and so forth from the socially and economically advanced sections in southern Brazil to the more tradition-bound areas of the East and Northeast. And so the process of homogenization goes on throughout the length and breadth of Brazil. Local and regional ethnic, social, and cultural differences are being greatly reduced by the movement of people from all parts of the republic into the national and state capitals and other towns and cities, and the subsequent diffusion of social and cultural traits to the rural areas; but within any particular segment of the country, society is becoming more heterogeneous. In addition, the process of social and cultural stirring that is produced by rural-urban migration is itself favorable to the discovery and perfection of new combinations of previously existing traits and complexes, so that the entire process of social and cultural change is greatly facilitated by the migrations taking place.

Finally, the process of rural-urban migration has much to do with the rise in standards and levels of living now going on rapidly throughout Brazil. The wants of the migrants, the goods and services for which they are willing to put forth sustained effort, are tremendously expanded by a few years of residence in urban areas. At the same time, though, the new skills they are acquiring, the social legislation whose benefits they enjoy, and the constant battle of wits in which they must engage contribute greatly to their ability to secure the money needed in order for their plane or level of living to keep pace with their aspirations or standard of living. Much of this flows back into the rural communities from which they came, where it adds to the ferment described above as contributing to the migration and speeds up the process of social change in the rural areas.

PUSHING FORWARD THE AGRICULTURAL FRONTIER

Periodically Brazilians thrust forward with feverish activity at this or that point on the frontier which separates the agricultural sections of the country from the thinly populated districts in which a rudimentary pastoral economy or a primitive collecting mode of existence has undisputed sway. In the 1930's the point of onslaught was the forests of western São Paulo. Rich coffee fazendas came into being in these areas that only a few years previously had been absolutely desolate. A little later the north-central part of Maranhão and the Rio Doce Valley in Minas Gerais felt the swing of the woodman's axe as he opened new clearings in the dense forests. Today the struggle goes on at many places. The agricultural occupation of the most westerly parts of São Paulo, the rapid expansion of a rich coffee district in northern Paraná, the extension of coffee and cotton culture into the southern portion of Mato Grosso, and a great influx of population into central Goiás, into the areas fairly close to Brasília, are the most important recent activities.

Accurate statistics concerning the migrations into these frontier areas are, of course, entirely lacking. One can only make rough estimates by noting the changes in population, counting the numbers who arrive by trains, checking to some extent on the trucks which enter heavily laden with migrants and their household possessions, observing the numerous oxcarts bringing in families from afar, and conversing personally with a few of the newcomers.

In 1945 when the author traveled by train from Araguarí in Minas Gerais to the end of the line at Anápolis, all of the cars of all classes were packed with second-class passengers migrating to Goiás. There was only one train per day, but it seldom carried less than 300 persons. As a result it was very difficult to find lodging in Anápolis, people were sleeping everywhere, and the benches at the station were always full. On the roads and trails there was a constant stream of pedestrians, oxcarts, and not a few trucks. The night I spent at the Colonia Agrícola de Goiás one truck arrived from the Sorocaba district of São Paulo carrying six families and their possessions. They had been on the way six days, stopping to rest only two nights and driving the other four. It was not unusual to see a family making its way to central Goiás with all its worldly possessions, including the old-fashioned spinning wheel, packed into a miniature oxcart drawn by ten or twelve sheep. Carts pulled by from six to sixteen oxen were much more common. Well-informed persons have estimated that the migration into central Goiás alone totals 75,000 per year, but 50,000 may be nearer the correct figure. In several of the years following the close of the second World War the movement into northern Paraná must have been fully as large or even larger.

Among the migrants to Goiás a few are of the small fazendeiro class, men who themselves participate actively in the management of the agricultural operations. Most of them, however, are laborers, persons who either work a few years as peons or who obtain the use of land for a period of three years in return for clearing it. Nearly all have the dream of eventually getting a small tract of their own.

Most of the migrants into Goiás come from the south. From Minas Gerais there is a heavy tide from the areas around Uberaba and Uberlandia in the far western part of that state. At Goiandira, in southern Goiás, these are immersed in a much larger current coming from the older coffee-growing sections, the once heavily forested sections in the eastern part. From northern Minas Gerais, Bahia, and the states of the Northeast, a considerable number of migrants, mostly of the lower class, make their way overland to enter Goiás at Formosa. Even the old residents of the area are impressed by the fortitude and endurance of the migrants from Bahia and the Northeast. It is said to be the rule that a woman migrant who gives birth to a child on the journey stops only one day to rest before continuing the long, wearisome trek on foot.

A few of the migrants come from the North by ascending the Tocantins River. Even some of the rubber workers who were transported to the Amazon from the Northeast during the second World War eventually made their way up the river to Goiás.

The migration is one of families, involving persons of both sexes and all ages. Three generations are included in a very large share of the families entering Goiás. A new fazenda will be opened by a father with the assistance of several of his married sons. The laborers they bring along or send for later also move in family groups. Others of the lower class who hear the good news and set out for Goiás also migrate in families, from babes in arms to grandfathers and grand-mothers. Thus far there has been little tendency for the migrants to return to their old homes.

SEASONAL MIGRATION

The procedure of felling and burning a piece of virgin forest or second growth annually in order to produce a handful of beans, a little mandioca or maize, perhaps a few pecks of rice, and some vegetables does not absolutely necessitate a change of residence each year. In actual practice, however, it results in frequent if not annual moves. The haphazard system of production, which is described as "fire agriculture," [7] makes a very unstable and migratory lot of mil-lions of Brazilians. This phenomenon prevails generally throughout Brazil, except in the southern rice-producing areas, the "colonial" regions of the southern states, and the coffee- and sugar-producing areas. Shortly after the close of the rainy season, the site for next year's roça must be selected. This may be at a considerable distance from the location of the old one. The move must be made early enough that the felled forest will have ample time in which to dry be-fore the first rains come. The months included in the rainy season vary greatly from one of Brazil's regions to another, but in all of them the succession of the wet and dry periods makes for periodic migra-tions on the part of the millions of "intruders" and *moradores* who live in the back country. Most of this movement is without definite direction, does not represent any stage in the movement from coun-try to town, and probably is for short distances in most cases. It can best be described as local milling-around.

Considerable attention has been given to the instability of resi-dence among the members of Brazil's lower rural classes in the chap-ters on fire agriculture and land tenure. To this it is only necessary to add the comments of Oliveira Vianna:

. . . among us the land is still, in the greater part, deserted. On the latifundia the part disposable and to be given out is a vast one. The rural worker who abandons his lot is certain to find another on a neighboring estate. From this comes the facility with which he moves, every time that there comes from the mansion of the fazendeiro a stronger pressure and a closer discipline over his indolence or his arrogance. Such great facility of the lower rural classes to move, to migrate, has led to the amazement of all the foreign observers that have passed through our rural interior. Ferdinand Denis, Eschwege, Saint Hilare, everyone, in unanimity attest to the fact and confess to their surprise and their inquietude before the extraordinary mobility of our plebs.

[7] See Chapter xv.

The facility of migration is one of the greatest factors of disorganiza-
tion of our society.[8]

The migrations of the rubber gatherers deserve analysis at some
length. Observations made while in the Amazon, plus some reading
on the region, formed the basis for the following summary, which is
little altered from my field notes.

Undoubtedly, one of the major obstacles to rubber production in
the Amazon, either as a long-time or a short-time proposition, is the
nomadic nature of the rubber-collecting labor force. As mentioned
above, the nomadic existence led by the rubber gatherers so impressed
the members of the American field party who reported in 1924 [9] that
they endowed the seringueiro with a "migratory instinct." The same
evidences probably could be found for concluding that the more recent arrivals from the Northeast were also possessed of physiological
constitutions which make it necessary for them to keep constantly on
the move. However, it is probably more to the point to analyze the
features of the mode of life followed by these people which result in
a nomadic existence, to detail the elements in their cultural or social
heritage that are largely responsible for the wandering existence
they lead.

In the first place, the material possessions of the Amazonian seringueiro are all such as can easily be transferred from place to place,
or if they must be left behind, they can quickly be replaced in another locality. Consider first the house which is the cultural element
that does most to fix a family in a given location year after year, and
even generation after generation. Sometimes, in the Amazon, the habitation is a houseboat, which may be shifted about at will. Generally,
however, it is a rough shelter of poles and thatch. A few days' or
weeks' labor on the part of the seringueiro and his family is sufficient
to provide a new shelter of the type commonly used. Except in a few
districts in the central portions of the towns and cities, and on a
very limited number of fazendas, the Amazon Valley is completely
lacking in all of the cultural elements whereby one generation contributes to succeeding generations the actual material comforts of a
well-constructed habitation. It cannot be overemphasized that only
the skills involved in the construction of the thatched shelter are
passed on, not the shelter itself. The head of a family may supervise and participate in the construction activities of dozens of dwellings during his own lifetime. The rubber collector's house is little
enough reason for attachment to a given locality.

Nor is the house surrounded with other adjuncts which, because
they represent the expenditure of great amounts of effort and contribute materially to the satisfaction, comfort, and even safety of life,
make a family loath to leave the place in which these aids to satisfac-

[8] Oliveira Vianna, *Populações Meridionaes do Brasil*, 163–64.

[9] Schurz, *et al.*, *Rubber Production in the Amazon Valley*, 163, 202, 219, 221,
271, 273. For a splendid description of the life of contemporary rubber gatherers see Arthur Cezar Ferreira Reis, *O Seringal e O Seringueiro na Amazonia*
(Rio de Janeiro, 1953).

tory living are located for a new place in which they all must be supplied anew. The well, for example, is unknown, drinking water being dipped from the river. Even a cistern for catching a supply of pure rain water for drinking purposes is lacking. Just below Manaus one may observe even upper-class families out on Sunday excursions in their launches, dipping and drinking the river water. Throughout the entire area, neither the well, the cistern, nor devices such as windmills serve as brakes on the migratory proclivities of the population. Yards, fences, outhouses, barns, and all the other features of a permanent country home are lacking in any form requiring material investment of capital or labor. In the Amazon none of these has any great strength as a tie binding a family to a given locality.

Much of the same may be said of the "farm" itself. Most agriculture in the Amazon is of the "riverbank" variety. In this type of agriculture man, or more accurately woman, leans to the utmost on nature. In its simplest form such agriculture differs from a purely collecting economy only in two features: (1) preservation of some seeds for planting, and (2) dropping these seeds and pressing them with the bare foot into the spongy soil left by the receding river. If a few weeds are removed by hand or with the use of a hoe during the growing season, it represents a considerable advance over the minimum essential that is the general practice. In this riverbank type of agriculture it is almost as easy to tramp seeds into the ground in one place as in another. The best locations are those on the inside of a large curve in the river where the slope of the bank is comparatively slight and where the slowness of the current has contributed to the depositing of the finest silt. But there is no advantage to be gained from staying in one locality for two consecutive seasons, since the river does equally well elsewhere in preparing the ground for seeds. Even where fire agriculture is practiced and man uses his axe and the blaze to prepare the ground for the seeds, the plot planted is a different one each year. Since the fields utilized from one season to the next are different ones, they may as well be separated by 100 miles as by the corresponding number of feet. Neither in the Northeast from which a large part of the Amazon's people came, in Maranhão and other states to which people from the same areas have moved, in the Bragança district which supplies food for Belém, nor in the great valley itself does fire agriculture make for a settled mode of existence.

Since work stock, milk cows, and practically all other living things found on the farm are lacking, none of them hinders the seringueiro in his movement from one place to another. In fact, one can well summarize by saying that the material possessions of the Amazonian caboclo are all those which, if they do not actually contribute to nomadism, at least do exceedingly little to hinder such a wandering mode of existence. American farmers have a saying that "three moves are as good as a fire," a meaningful phrase which serves to indicate the impossibility of accumulating material possessions while constantly moving about. In this respect the rural inhabitant of

..e Amazon seems always to be near the position of the North American farmer who has recently been "burned out." But the Amazon caboclo's position is more unsatisfactory because he (1) does not feel the propulsions of a standard of living which takes greater material possessions for granted and (2) lacks the technical skills necessary to obtain more of the material aids to living.

Nor do social institutions of the Amazon region do much to prevent the continuous perambulations of the seringueiro. The rubber gatherer is attached to no specific church congregation. He does not pay taxes in or send his children to an educational institution provided by a particular school district. His recreational activities do not demand a sedentary life. He is an established member of no definite business enterprise. The one institution which does attempt to make him stay put is the *barracão*, the commissary of the *seringalista* for whom he works, who supplies him and to whom he delivers his product. But, as in the plantation sections of the South or the sawmills of the West in the United States, the system of advances, bookkeeping, and payment is fully as likely to create in the seringueiro a desire to leave the locality as to stay. Among the seringueiros themselves, and reaching to far-off Ceará and Paraíba, are passed on stories of cheating on the accounts, unfair weights, corporal punishment, inability to leave because the seringalistas are in collusion and will not allow another's workers to travel in their boats, and even of labor forced at the point of a gun. To the extent that these reports are true, they depict an institutional pattern which generates a desire to flee rather than to remain fixed.

On the other hand, there are a number of elements which actually conduce to a nomadic mode of living. There is, for example, the knowledge the caboclo has of the river, its meanderings, its branches, its habits, and of the things it freely gives to man. He has a culture which enables him to collect almost all the means to live from the forest and the jungle. He has, in his pirogue, a means of transportation. In fact, all his man-made luggage, including his institutions, are those that at least permit, if they do not lead to, a migratory manner of existence. Until the social heritage is changed radically, the inhabitants of the Amazon will continue to move about from place to place. Other attempts to "root" the population will meet with about the same results as the strong efforts of the Serviço de Fomento Agricola of the state of Amazonas. This agency cleared and laid out ten plots of ground, totaling seventeen hectares, on which were established nine families from the Northeast. But "of these lots, only two were effectively occupied, because, of the nine northeastern families which were installed, seven went away in various directions, carrying with them the implements they had received for use in the work." [10]

The seasonal movement of workers from the semiarid, cotton-producing areas of the Northeast to the better-watered sugar cane-

[10] Alvaro Maia, *Exposição ao Exmo. Sr. Dr. Getulio Vargas, Presidente da República* (Manaus, 1942), 67.

growing band along the coast also is an important item in the internal migration in Brazil. This is not to be confused with the flight from the sêcas which periodically scourge the area. Every year during the dry months, in the months between cotton-picking seasons, thousands of men from the sertões and the catinga areas migrate to the coast to work in the cane harvest. Then the sugar section

. . . receives thousands of refugees. The *braço* is cheapened by the excess of workers. They live in thatched sheds, provisional constructions for the accommodation of these men of transitory activity in the littoral. They remain three or four months, until the evening in which, crazy with happiness, they see in the direction of the sertão the distant reflections of the lightning cutting the skies of the sertão. In an instant the *sertanejo* disappears. He has returned to the land which is so ungrateful to him and so harsh.[11]

To those who may wonder why, once employed in the rich, green, coastal area, the refugees so eagerly return to their "native land" in the bleak sertão, the analysis of Limeira Tejo is enlightening. This authority speaks from long residence in the region.

The *retirantes* arrive in the cane fields but their thinking is not detached from their scorched lands. In the lowland they are always restless, always sensing the lack of something, always prepared to begin at any moment the return journey. A notice of rainfall in the thorn bushes is sufficient for them to abandon all and return. They are strongly bound to their world and not even successive climatic calamities have the force to liberate them from it. They are like a scoundrel's women—the more nature castigates them, the more they are dominated by the mysterious attraction of their glebe. Why do they return to the semiarid desert, to a barbaric life, to thc wasted heroics? Why do they abandon the green shelter of the lands where they take refuge? Why do they leave behind streams that always flow, fertile soil, paradise, to return and suffer the punishment of the sun, the misery of the sêca? . . .

The causes are more profound; they are social causes. In the dry country, man is castigated by climatic inclemency, but he has the compensation of immense individual liberty, giving rise to a proud race, to an almost savage independence, undisciplined, without submission to work, without a systematized life. Each man is "master of his nostrils," and, accustomed to broad horizons, for him the world is grand and God is greater. And God is adventure. It is possible to make of his sandals seven league boots, which may be used in the desert, starting from the side on which the sun rises, without ever arriving at the mountains behind which it sets. In this direction the sertanejo may vagabond on a genuine way to the infinite, fleeing from the coercion which comes to him with the police or organized work.

In the lowlands, on the contrary, there develops a repressed type of humanity. Its soul does not expand in that tie which the man of the catinga has with his land. The lowlander never can appreciate a sunrise from the back of a horse, reins loosened, breathing deeply of the free air, arms free in the largeness of all the distant landscape of the setting. The man of the cane fields asserts his personality by turning inward, creating

[11] Dé Carlí, *Aspectos Açucareiros de Pernambuco*, 27. Similar is the movement from the interior to the coast and back in the neighboring states. For Paraíba, see Celso Mariz, *Evolução Econômica de Paraíba* (João Pessôa, 1939), 137.

new emotional worlds, transcendentalized, where he can regain his lost
liberty.

For this reason the lowland is an intolerable world. . . . To return to
the catinga signifies the return to his liberty of movement, signifies the
flight from oppression.

For the people of the catinga, therefore, the stay in the cane fields is a
succession of vexations and humiliations. It [the lowland] is not to be
thanked, as by one who receives hospitality. It is to be cursed, as by one
who suffers a disaster. It is never to be forgotten for its odiousness.[12]

In the mate forests of southern Mato Grosso, Paraná, and Santa
Catarina, the ebb and flow of workers correlates closely with the seasons. In this case many of the workers are from Paraguay, and they
return to their own country at the close of the harvest season. In 1942
it was said that a single mate company in Mato Grosso employed
40,000 Paraguayans. Of these migrants who fail to become "fixed or
assimilated," Nelson Werneck Sodré says:

They do not establish fixed residences because they engage in the collection
of *erva mate,* with short months of harvest and long months of unre-
munerated inactivity, which necessitates a new dislodgement. This shift
usually is back to the Paraguayan interior, where the money they have
acquired has a high value. They return for the new harvest. Thus it continues, permanently "coming and going." A part enters pastoral endeavors
where they constitute the majority of peons on the cattle fazendas and
sitios. But this regime does not permit fixed residences.[13]

The seasons also influence the movements of the seminomads who
care for the cattle in Mato Grosso and other areas of pastoral economy. The author of the most adequate treatment of this society says
that nomadism results from the poverty of the pastoral regime.

The agregados of the fazendas live in place after place on the horizon, now
in the plateaus east of the Serra da Amanabai, now on the plains parallel
to Paraguay, now in the mountains, now on the way north, driving cattle,
rounding up cattle, branding or selling cattle, without habitual residence.
They are a transitory population, primitive, obscure, abandoned.[14]

Residential instability also is very pronounced among the laborers
who perform the manual work on Brazil's great sugar plantations.
Gileno dé Carlí of the National Institute of Alcohol and Sugar, who
knows the situation well and whose studies are among the most objective and comprehensive that have been made in Brazil, has generalized as follows:

The other type of migration is more serious and of greater consequences. Not sufficiently explained is the true cause of this tendency of the
rural worker in the forested zone, the sugar section of Pernambuco, to live
with a small pack on his back, oftentimes carrying children, moving
constantly from engenho to engenho, from one property to another. The
observation of Kunhenn that "prosperous or poor, the nomads are the

[12] Limeira Tejo, *Brejos e Carrascaes do Nordeste* (São Paulo, 1937), 154–56.
[13] Nelson Werneck Sodré, *Oeste* (Rio de Janeiro, 1941), 105–106; see also
Antonieta de Paula Souza, "Impressões de Viagem ao Longo do Rio Paraná,"
Geografia, II, No. 4 (1936), 40–41.
[14] Werneck Sodré, *Oeste,* 85.

slaves of the landscape cannot be applied. Much less do the impulses which dictate this dislocation resemble the causes among other peoples, as for example, those of the steppes, of Uganda, of Algeria. Motivations of a geographical, commercial, or religious order are not in operation. There is, it cannot be doubted, among the laborers of the sugar zone, a migratory instinct, a congenital habit. The father and the grandfather have sought, from one land to another, a better opportunity to feed themselves. Perhaps, however, that liberty which came to him on the 13th of May has stirred in the bosom of the mestiço all of the atavism which slavery repressed . . . this wandering worker, who markets his services to the usinas of Pernambuco, flees from the ruined houses, the difficulties of securing food, pursuing an ideal—perhaps a hallucination—of a Canaan, where, without work, the food will be good and plentiful.[15]

Perhaps if dé Carlí were better acquainted with studies of migration in the southern part of the United States, he would have seen more clearly the influence of certain cultural factors and would have been more cautious in the use of zoological interpretations.

Farther down the coast, in southern Bahia, large numbers of workers come to participate in the harvest of the *cacau* or cocoa. The section about Ilhéus is the part of Brazil most exclusively given over to the production of this crop. It is grown in plots scattered about in the woods, largely cared for by employed administrative overlords called *empreiteiros* or "contractors." The lower the costs per kilo of dried cocoa beans, the larger the profits. A few workers suffice to care for the plantations except during harvest, when large numbers are needed to pick, shell, dry, and process the beans. As is usually the case in crops where the labor requirements are concentrated in a few months of the year, this precipitates a large volume of movement into and out of the area. A very succinct description of this movement is given in one of the reports of the Instituto de Cacáo of Bahia.

The greater part of the workers in the South Cocoa zone are nomads, staying in the zone during the harvest season and returning to the sertão at the end of December or January. There are few fazendas which prefer the permanent, married worker. The workers do not share in the losses or the profits of the fazenda, as is the case in coffee farming, where the "colono" has an interest in the production.[16]

Most of the workers who "rent" themselves to the contractors for the cocoa harvest are from the cotton-growing sections of Sergipe. Formerly, the majority of the workers came from Ceará. But they still come from the sertão.

Cocoa production, like that of sugar, does little to fix the migratory population in the coastal area. More details are given by Pierre Monbeig.

The cocoa, however, does not succeed in fixing the nomads of the high plains; the money earned during the harvest is spent on the return trip to the birthplace and on the celebrations at the year's end, for the journey is made in this season. Afterwards the sertanejo takes again the road to the

[15] Dé Carlí, *Aspectos Açucareiros de Pernambuco,* 28.
[16] Instituto de Cacáo da Bahia, *Relatorio e Annuario de 1932* (Bahia, 1933), 140.

cocoa roças, but he never returns to the one where he worked the preceding year. Later on even he may disappear in the course of the year, attracted to another fazenda by promises of a better salary and still more by the women encountered in the town cabaret on Sundays.[17]

Additional enlightenment concerning internal migration in Brazil may be gained from the following summary statements of the men who reported to the Ministry of Labor concerning the situation of the rural workers.

It is proved that a great mass of rural workers in Brazil move annually, crossing hundreds and thousands of kilometers, using the most varied means of transportation, although there predominates the most natural way of traveling: on foot, over trails that seem incredible because of the distance involved and the nature of the zones through which they pass.

These dispersed masses of workers move across one or more states of the country in search of better wages, of work, of fortune, or of a refuge from the natural scourge, drought. This is what occurs in the Northeast. In this region of the country, a vast zone harassed by maldistribution of the rains, we should localize the principal—if not the only center of dispersion of Brazilian farm hands. It is justified. The drought, devouring everything, even the last leaf, the last drop of water, impels man instinctively to seek better lands where the struggle for life will be more easy and where he will not lack water and the green displayed by forests.[18]

FLIGHT FROM THE SÊCAS

Just when the terrific droughts that periodically scourge the great northeastern section of Brazil first began to drive the sertanejos to the coast in search of water and food is not on record. Probably it began very soon after the Bahianos arrived from the south with their herds of cattle. But there are definite accounts of the great drought in 1710–1711.[19]

Twelve years later, in 1723, began one of the longest on record. It was not over until 1727 after nearly all the cattle had perished and many of the Indians along with them. Lesser droughts occurred in 1736–1737 and again in 1744–1745. In 1777–1778 there was another period of intense suffering, and after the lapse of another twelve years, a drought of between three and four years' duration almost depopulated the province of Ceará and the adjacent portions of the sertão. At this time eyewitness accounts spoke of "habitations where, by the side of putrefying bodies, lay wretches still alive, and covered with blood-sucking bats, which the victims had no strength to drive away." [20] Other less severe sêcas prevailed in 1808–1809 and 1816–

[17] Pierre Monbeig, *Ensaios de Geografia Humana Brasileira* (São Paulo, 1940), 172. See also the novel, *Cacáu*, by Jorge Amado (Rio de Janeiro, 1934).

[18] Evaristo Leitão, Romolo Cavina, and João Soares Palmeira, *O Trabalhador Rural Brasileiro* (Rio de Janeiro, 1937), 16–17.

[19] The fullest account is Rodolpho Theophilo, *Historia da Sêcca do Ceará, 1877–1880* (Rio de Janeiro, 1922).

[20] See the summary of testimony in Smith, *Brazil, the Amazons and the Coast*, 408 ff.

1817. Then in 1824–1825 another terrific drought occurred, and 1844–1845 were dry years. Next came the famous sêca of 1877– 1879. This was the one that propelled the first large body of north-easterners into the Amazon region.

Smith, who visited the section while the distress was at its height, has left a succinct account of what took place. According to him the winters of 1875 and 1876 both were marked by very heavy rains, wet seasons that did much damage to crops and cattle. But by February of 1877 rumors of drought began to circulate in the coastal cities. By the first of March the situation was worse and the bishop ordered prayers in all the churches. Still there were hopes of rains in March and April, but when these months passed, and May also, with no moisture falling in much of the area, it was officially recognized that a drought was on again. There was such want and hunger throughout the sertão that large numbers of the sertanejos flocked into the local towns and cities. Those who possessed livestock slaughtered them in order to secure the hides and tallow. While this lasted there were few deaths from hunger, for the poor were able to beg bits of meat. "But when the herds were gone, the peasants began to starve. From the villages there went up a great cry for food; two hundred thousand people were begging from door to door." [21] When all other resources failed, the country people resorted to the use of all kinds of wild seeds and roots. The most serious difficulties arose from eating the unwholesome seeds of the *mucuman*, which brought on dropsy and death, and the roots of a shrub called *páo de mocó*, whose poisons caused loss of sight. In ordinary times the páo de mocó had other uses. "In the sertoes, for the destruction of ants, they say it is suffi-cient to cover the ant hills with páo de mocó." But "the refugees, desperate from hunger on the long trails of the unfortunate, and not knowing the noxious properties of the tuber, cooked and ate it. A few hours after the ingestion of so toxic a root they were completely blind." [22] Some food was shipped in from the unaffected areas; but as the only way to get it into the interior was on the backs of men, for there were no horses, it was so costly that only the rich could buy. Under these circumstances hunger became so pronounced that many cases of cannibalism were reported. To add to the uncertainty of life, wild robber bands ravaged the countryside, stealing and slaying. Smith, who visited Ceará in 1879, has described in detail the situa-tion at that time. Particularly significant is his relation of the events leading up to the flight of the masses to the coast, from which many of them eventually were dispatched to the Amazon region.

Long, long was the summer of 1877. Drought blazed in the sertão; the birds fell dead from leafless trees; foxes and armadillos died in their holes; insects disappeared. Drought withered the sea-coast woods, dried up the streams, brought thousands of refugees to Fortaleza and the interior towns.[23]

[21] *Ibid.*, 411.
[22] Theophilo, *Historia da Sêcca do Ceará, 1877–1880*, 120.
[23] Smith, *Brazil, the Amazons and the Coast,* 412.

Living in hastily constructed huts and begging daily for food, the refugees were decimated by the thousands. Many starved to death, and lack of food made others a ready prey for epidemics. Fevers came first, then beriberi and smallpox. Probably 50,000 people died the first year of the famine. The only hope was for rains in January.

At the beginning of 1878 the condition of the province was this: the open country was generally abandoned; nearly the whole population was gathered about the villages, and the plains were left, black and desolate. A large proportion of the cattle had perished; the plantations were withered except on a few fertile hill-sides, as at Baturité, where running water still came down from the springs. Between the interior towns and the coast there was a band of almost impassable wilderness, where the ground was utterly dry, where not so much as a blade of green grass appeared, where the river-beds were strips of heated sand and clay, yielding no water, even by the usual method of digging holes to the subsoil. At Icó and Telha, the death-rate, from starvation alone, was more than a score each day. These desolate plains and famishing people were ruled by a weak government; the provincial treasury was almost empty; provisions sent from Rio were locked up in the public store-houses, held back, no one knew why, when the need was most urgent.

January came and crept on, day after day, with clear skies. After awhile there were a few little showers, just moistening the surface, and bringing up stray blades of grass; but the first planting failed utterly.[24]

February, too, passed and still the rains did not come. March also was clear and dry. Government aid nearly ceased, and no food was left for the hopeless sufferers in the villages.

Then, as by one impulse, a wild panic caught them. Four hundred thousand, they deserted the *sertão* and rushed down to the coast. Oh! it was terrible, that mad flight. Over all the roads there came streams of fugitives, men and women and little children, naked, lean, famine-weak, dragging wearily across the plains, staining the rocky mountain-paths with their bleeding feet, begging, praying, at every house for a morsel of food. They were famished when they started. Two, three, four days at a time, they held their way; then the children lagged behind in weakness, calling vainly to their panic-wild fathers; then men and women sank and died on the stones. I have talked with men who came from the interior with the great exodus; they tell stories of suffering to wring one's heart; they tell of skeleton corpses unburied by the road-side, for a hundred thousand dead [some say a hundred and fifty thousand] were left by the way. If you ride today through the *sertão* you will see, in many places a wooden cross by the roadside, marking the spot where some poor wretch expired. So let them rest. Poor peasants they were, ignorant and coarse and filthy; but they are canonized now, with the glory of great suffering.[25]

By April the interior of Ceará was almost deserted. The problem was transported to the coast.

At Fortaleza, nearly a hundred and fifty thousand people were gathered; at Aracaty there were eighty thousand; at Granja and Baturité, lesser armies; all crying for food, crying with the eloquence of starvation, showing their emaciated bodies, weeping, and cursing before the doors of the aid commissioners. Even if supplies had been never so abundant, the com-

[24] *Ibid.*, 413–14.
[25] *Ibid.*, 415–16.

missioners might well have quailed before such a demand. So great was the flood, so sudden in its panic-burst, that all the available supplies were too little. Men who had waited all day to receive a scanty ration, had to turn away, empty-handed. Long processions of mendicants passed through the streets, begging at every door; many were utterly naked; many fell in the streets from weakness. Some who had food given them could not swallow it, so great was their exhaustion, they died even in sight of plenty. More than one body was picked up in the very streets of Fortaleza.

. . . . . .

The merest scraps of food were accepted with tears of gratitude; garbage-piles were searched for melon-rinds and banana-skins. A trader at Baturité told me a refugee asked permission to kill rats in his store, that he might eat them. Dead horses and dogs were devoured; there are dark stories of cannibalism which may be true. God only knows, for little heed was taken to horrors in this time of dismay.

. . . . . .

The entire mortality in Ceará, during 1877 and 1878, was probably not far from 500,000, or more than half the population. Of these, 50,000 died of starvation and disease during the first year; 50,000 during the months of January and February, 1878; during March and April, which included the great exodus, at least 150,000 perished, the most from starvation. Fever and *beri-beri* carried off 100,000, and small-pox 80,000 more; the remaining deaths were from various diseases, the majority more or less directly traceable to starvation and weakness, and unwholesome food.[26]

It was during the height of the terrific *sêca* of 1877–1879 that the flow of migrants from the Northeast to the Amazon began.[27] Crowded as they were into the most cramped, unsanitary, and unprotected refugee camps, dying by the hundreds from starvation and swept off by the thousands from scourges of smallpox and other plagues, it is not surprising that the *flagelados* began thinking of seeking new homes in other sections. Migration as a relief measure also had its appeal to the governing authorities. In June of 1877 "the idea of leaving the province for the fertile and unhealthy lands of Pará and Amazonas commenced to appear among the refugees, principally among the migrants from Uruburetama. Animated by the hope of better fortune, the first refugees, 39 in number, left Ceará on the twentieth of June; they departed for Pará aboard the English steamer, Augustine." The month following, another English vessel carried away 169 more destined for the same port. In the course of the year a total of 4,610 persons sailed from Fortaleza for Belém, many of them having their passage paid by the government of the province of Ceará. From the other smaller points of embarkation went others. However, the Negro slaves of the province were shipped to the south. They were purchased by traveling Italian peddlers at their own price and sent south for resale to the planters of São Paulo, Rio de Janeiro, and other states.[28] For the year 1878 it is estimated that the number of refugees who left Ceará by sea amounted to 54,-

[26] *Ibid.*, 416–21.

[27] Oliveira Vianna, "O Povo Brazileiro e sua Evolução," *loc. cit.*, 306.

[28] Theophilo, *Historia da Sêca do Ceará, 1877–1880*, 99–100, 109, 148, 250, and 361. In 1877 a total of 1,725 slaves left the port of Fortaleza for the south, and the next year the figure increased to 2,909.

875, the larger share of them going to the Amazon. The records of
Fortaleza alone account for the shipment of 15,300 indigents from
that port to Belém.[29]

Fortunately, the great sêca of 1877–1879 has not been repeated,
but there have been numerous serious droughts since this greatest of
them all. The latest are those of 1931–1932 and 1938–1942, and one
which began in 1952 and reached a critical stage in 1953. A president
of the republic estimated that 2,000,000 Brazilians perished as a direct result of the droughts between 1877 and 1919.[30] More recently
the number of fatalities has been less, but still the distress due to
this periodic failure of the rains has been sufficient to send large
numbers of people to the Amazon, before the collapse of the rubber
industry, and to São Paulo in recent years. By the close of the nineteenth century the pattern of migration to the Amazon as a drought-
relief measure was well established in Ceará and the neighboring
states. Encouraged and subsidized, at first by Ceará, from which
many of them came, and later by the governments of Pará, Amazonas, and also by federal agencies, this movement of northeasterners continued well into the twentieth century.

Accurate statistics as to the total movement are, of course, not
available. However, data relative to embarkations on the coastwise
steamers plying north and south give an indication that the movement was always large and that in times of drought it swelled to
great proportions. That there was also an unrecorded overland movement also seems likely. A people who by 1820 were making the overland journey from São Luís to Belém in fourteen days carrying
mails [31] and whose descendants in 1941–1942 walked thousands of
miles on the overland journey to São Paulo surely filtered by land
into the Amazon. Nevertheless, in December, 1942, when four persons completed a forty-day overland hike from Maranhão to Belém it
was a news item of considerable interest to Brazilian papers.

The magnitude of the migratory current that formerly moved into
the Amazon is indicated by some of the available data. A writer who
visited Fortaleza in 1902 sets at 150,000 the number of refugees
fleeing Ceará during the droughts of 1877–1879 and 1888–1889. For
the years 1892 to 1897, inclusive, he cites statistics of the Lloyd
Brasileiro Steamship Company showing that 51,506 persons sailed
north and 9,054 south during the six-year period. In 1900 a new dry
season began and single boats carried away to the north more than
1,000 refugees. During this year 32,062 persons were recorded as
sailing from Fortaleza for Amazonas or Pará either on their own account or with fares paid by one of these state governments. The same
year the migrations of 15,773 persons were subsidized by the federal
government, making a total sea-borne migration to the Amazon Val-

[29] *Ibid.*, 256.
[30] Cf. Cincinato Braga, *Sêccas do Nordeste e Reorganização Economica* (Rio
de Janeiro, 1919), 4.
[31] Cf. Joh. Bapt. von Spix and C. F. Phil. von Martius, *Viagem pelo Brasil*
(Rio de Janeiro, 1938), III, 72–73.

ley of 47,835 during the year.[32] Large contingents from Rio Grande do Norte, Paraíba, and Pernambuco also made their way to the Amazon. They played a very considerable part in the settlement and development of Acre territory.[33]

To summarize briefly: Prior to the collapse of the Brazilian rubber production in the second decade of the twentieth century, a heavy migratory current of population from the northeastern states of Brazil, and especially from Ceará, went into the Amazon Valley. It was these Cearenses who formed a large share of the laborers in the *seringais* of Pará, Amazonas, and Acre. To the Amazon the people of the sertões also looked for a place of refuge from the droughts which devastated their herds and plantings in their areas of permanent residence. In short, prior to the collapse of rubber production in Brazil, the Amazon was the receiving area for much of the surplus population of the Northeast and also the temporary refuge for thousands of families who had to flee from the periodic sêcas which afflict Brazil's great "dust bowl."

The events of the 1920's changed all of this. Economic opportunities in the Amazon for laborers from Ceará and neighboring states dwindled to the vanishing point. Stories drifted back home and were rapidly spread from mouth to mouth of the virtual slavery under which some of the workers were held in the rubber-producing areas. Forced labor, detention at the point of a gun, beatings, falsification of accounts, class struggle, and a host of other injustices came to be associated in the mind of the humble inhabitant of the northeastern sertões with rubber and the Amazon. Naturally the Amazon Valley lost its attraction for him, even as a place of temporary refuge. Population of Amazonas, Acre, and Pará, which had doubled between 1900 and 1920, was stationary during the next twenty years. During the severe droughts of the 1920 to 1940 period, the people from the interior flocked to the coast. Here public and private assistance, plus the use of land on which they could produce food, helped to tide them over the critical years. When lightning flashes signalized the beginning of rains in the interior, many of them flocked back to the sertões.[34] But some found their way into central Maranhão and began devastating the great forests of the area with their system of fire agriculture. Others continued making their way to settle among their friends and relatives in the Bragança district of Pará.

Meanwhile, a small trickle of migration to the south, to São Paulo, also got under way. As favorable notices came back, this current gradually swelled until it became strong enough to replace the immigration which formerly had supplied Brazil's greatest agricultural

[32] Arthur Dias, *The Brazil of Today* (Nivelles, Belgium, 1903?), 249–50.

[33] Cf. Mariz, *Evolução Econômica da Paraíba*, 65–66.

[34] Says a survey of Ceará made in 1922 by the Ministerio da Agricultura, Industria e Commercio: "The exodus of the rural population takes place in times of drought and is directed especially for the State Capital; few remain in the city. "As soon as the first rains fall the refugees return to their old homes and recommence their work in the fields." *Estudo dos Factores da Producção nos Municipios Brasileiros: Quixada* (Rio de Janeiro, 1922), 16.

and industrial state with the hands to carry on its extensive economic activities. Thus, in recent years the migratory stream which formerly fed the extractive enterprises of the Amazon has been routed to São Paulo, where it does much to maintain the supply of coffee and to augment the production of cotton. Because of the importance of this stream of internal migration, it is analyzed in some detail in the following pages.[35]

MIGRATION TO SÃO PAULO

As indicated in Chapter VIII, a very large share of the encouragement for and stimulation of immigration into Brazil has been to augment the supply of agricultural laborers on the fazendas of the state of São Paulo. The need of farm hands for the production of São Paulo's coffee, cotton, and sugar also has been of prime importance in what is now the nation's largest current of internal migration, the movement of people from the states of Bahia, Minas Gerais,[36] Alagôas, Pernambuco, Ceará, and other northeastern states into Brazil's most populous state. Largely because of the importance of these economic motives, and because of the extent to which the migration has been subsidized, guided, and directed, there is available a con-

[35] At this point a few words about attempts during the second world war to secure rubber workers from the Northeast are in order. After December 7, 1941, considerable efforts were made to reopen these old migratory routes in order to obtain a more ample labor force for the rubber program being carried on by the Brazilian and the American governments. All of the old means of transportation, plus the motor vehicle and the airplane, played a part. But it was a tremendous undertaking to secure a labor force large enough to collect, say, an additional 30,000 tons of rubber, even granting that each worker can collect one-half ton per year. First, there was the job of convincing the northeasterners to move to the Amazon instead of going to the promised land, São Paulo, as they had been doing. Second, there were a great many "sieves" between the Northeast and the seringais of the Amazon, so many that the securing of an additional 60,000 rubber workers probably would have meant the transportation of at least 750,000 persons. This "leakage" between the Northeast and the rubber-collecting areas was about as follows: from 30 to 40 per cent of the migrants stopped with the friends and relatives who preceded them to the central portions of Maranhão and the Bragança district of Pará; another 25 or 30 per cent secured employment in Belém, Manaus, and other towns and cities where there was an acute shortage of almost every type of worker; and probably not more than 40 per cent of the original contingent ever got to the seringais. The family of each man included an average of 4 or 5 persons besides himself, very few if any of whom could aid in collecting rubber. In other words, to secure the necessary labor supply for an additional production of 30,000 tons of rubber annually would have meant increasing the population of Amazonas, Pará, and Acre by at least 50 per cent.

[36] Naturally, Minas Gerais has been less content to see its labor supply drawn off to São Paulo than have the states so gravely afflicted by the sêcas. While I was visiting the interior of this great state, I heard numerous complaints about the subsidization of migration to São Paulo. That the complaints were not new is indicated by the following quotation from the results of a survey of the município of Conquista made in 1922 by the Ministerio da Agricultura, Industria e Commercio: "In spite of all there is, however, falta de braços, felt principally at harvest time; mechanical farming, sufficiently diffused, as yet has not solved the problem. Furthermore, there have been *incursions of seducers from the state of São Paulo seeking to round up rural workers. The State Government, as a helpful measure, to restrain the abuse, imposed penalties upon those who sought to obtain workers for another State.*" *Estudo dos Factores da Producção nos Municipios Brasileiros: Conquista, Minas Gerais* (Rio de Janeiro, 1922), 24.

siderable amount of statistical data on the sources and composition of the migratory streams and also on the destination of the newcomers and their pursuits after arrival. The data come from four principal sources: (1) records of third-class disembarkations in the port of Santos, (2) registries of immigrants and internal migrants lodged in the Hospedaria dos Imigrantes in the city of São Paulo, (3) data relative to the persons placed as workers on the state's farms and fazendas by the São Paulo Serviço de Imigração e Colonização, and (4) materials on state-of-birth cross-classified with those on state-of-residence given in the reports of population censuses made in 1940 and 1950. Although it is not always possible to separate the internal migrants from the immigrants, an examination of these data is informative.[37]

Volume of the Movement. One of the more significant bodies of available data is that which gives the number of persons who entered São Paulo and were dispatched to work on the fazendas of the state. This includes, of course, both immigrants and persons from elsewhere in Brazil. But since it covers the period 1900 to 1939, inclusive, it is a good starting place. For these four decades, the records of the state Secretaria de Agricultura, Indústria e Comércio account for a total of 1,307,149 persons, immigrants [38] and migrants from other Brazilian states, who entered São Paulo and were sent for the first time to work on the state's agricultural lands. This agricultural contingent represents 59 per cent of all recorded migration to São Paulo in these years, the total being given as 2,215,639. These data do not, of course, include any who may have migrated to São Paulo's fazendas or sítios without establishing contact with the state's official agencies or passing through the hospedaria maintained by the state Serviço de Imigração e Colonização in the city of São Paulo. This unrecorded movement is believed to be rather large. Also, the data for the year 1934 are entirely lacking; when a reasonable estimate is made to offset this deficiency, the total for the forty-year period is raised to 1,338,349. On the other hand, conversations with persons who have entered Brazil on agricultural visas reveal that a rather careful check is made to reduce to a minimum the number of persons who enter the country as agriculturists only to transfer later into other occupations.[39] The basic data relative to migration in general and the flow of agriculturists into São Paulo during the period 1900 to 1939 are given in Table xxix.

[37] The data are available in the *Boletim do Serviço de Imigração e Colonização.* Four issues of the *Boletim* have appeared: No. 1 in October, 1937; No. 2 in October, 1940; No. 3 in March, 1941; and No. 4 in December, 1941. The first of these appeared when the Serviço was called the Diretoria de Terras, Colonização e Imigração.

[38] Immigrants are by definition third-class passengers, other than Brazilian citizens, disembarking at Santos.

[39] According to Decreto-Lei, No. 406, of May 4, 1938, the quota of immigrants admitted into Brazil from each country must contain 80 per cent agriculturists, and those admitted in this category are prohibited from transferring to another occupation within four years from date of entry. Cf. Doria de Vasconcellos, "Alguns Aspectos da Imigração no Brasil," *loc. cit.*, 24, 27.

From these data one observes three fairly equal periods of rapidly mounting migration to São Paulo's agricultural areas, followed in the first two cases by abrupt interruptions and with the ultimate outcome of the third cycle still to be determined. A heavy flow of agricultural workers to São Paulo's fazendas got under way in the early years of the century and then mounted steadily, with only one slight reverse in 1907, to a peak in 1913. During this year, which immediately preceded the first World War, more than 70,000 persons were dispatched to work on the farms and plantations of the state. (This total does not include those persons placed during the year who had a previous record of placement by official agencies.) This mounting tide of migration to the state was halted abruptly by the first World War, the figure for the year 1915 falling to less than 10,000, hardly one-seventh of the volume attained only two years previously. Following the war another rather steady and consistent rise got under way which crested in the peak years of 1928 and 1929, when the recorded inward movement was 62,346 and 66,961, respectively. But

TABLE XXIX

Migration to São Paulo and Placement of Migrants in Agriculture, 1900–1939 *

Year	Number of migrants	Sent to work in agriculture	
		Number	Per cent
1900	22,802	12,051	53
1901	71,782	14,939	21
1902	40,386	21,409	53
1903	18,161	3,390	19
1904	27,751	11,576	42
1905	47,817	29,185	61
1906	48,429	29,415	61
1907	31,681	20,730	65
1908	40,225	29,095	72
1909	39,674	29,371	74
1910	40,478	32,287	80
1911	64,990	42,527	65
1912	101,947	55,868	55
1913	119,758	70,187	59
1914	48,413	26,505	55
1915	20,937	9,966	48
1916	20,357	11,882	58
1917	26,776	19,908	74
1918 †	15,041	18,251	†
1919	21,812	18,264	84

* Source: *Boletim do Serviço de Imigração e Colonização*, No. 2 (October, 1940), 138, and No. 4 (December, 1941), 130.

† It is not possible to discover the reason for the discrepancy indicated here; it may be due to inclusion of Paulistas among those dispatched to work on farms, or there may be some other type of error in the data.

TABLE XXIX (*Continued*). Migration to São Paulo *

Year	Number of migrants	Sent to work in agriculture	
		Number	Per cent
1920	44,553	29,493	66
1921	39,601	31,513	80
1922	38,635	26,921	70
1923	59,818	37,687	46
1924	68,161	42,068	63
1925	73,335	43,966	60
1926	96,162	40,775	42
1927	92,413	48,166	52
1928	96,278	62,346	65
1929	103,480	66,961	65
1930	39,644	14,954	38
1931	26,390	5,093	19
1932	35,765	13,403	37
1933	64,010	24,295	38
1934	68,581	31,200 ‡	45
1935	71,980	47,127	65
1936	72,497	57,738	80
1937	86,469	69,287	80
1938	56,304	45,033	80
1939	112,346	93,517	83
Total	2,215,639	1,338,349	60

* Source: *Boletim do Serviço de Imigração e Colonização*, No. 2 (October, 1940), 138, and No. 4 (December, 1941), 130.

‡ In the records from which these figures were taken, the data for 1934 are missing. However, the data do indicate that the hospedaria in São Paulo lodged 30,222 Brazilian workers during 1934. *Ibid.*, No. 2, p. 133. For the years 1935 to 1939 inclusive the numbers of Brazilian workers lodged in the hospedaria equaled 97 per cent of the number of workers placed in agriculture. Applying this ratio, it was estimated that 31,200 persons were sent to work in agriculture in 1934.

the following years of world-wide economic depression, coupled with internal political strife in Brazil, brought about another sharp curtailment in the flow of farm laborers to São Paulo's rich coffee lands. In 1931 the total of both internal migrants and immigrants entering agricultural employment in the state of São Paulo equaled only 5,093. But following this brief interlude the opening of vast new cotton lands and the development of new general farming settlements in the western part of the state were accompanied by another rapid upsurge in the curve describing the migration of agricultural workers into São Paulo. By 1937 the recorded number of arrivals who were sent to work on agricultural lands had attained 69,287, and after a slight recession in 1938, it moved to a high of 93,517 in 1939. Supplementary data indicate another sharp break in 1940 with the number dropping to 42,733.[40] Since nearly all migrants who entered the state passed through the Hospedaria de Imigrantes in the capital city, the data of this agency may be used to supplement the figures given. During the year 1941 the inward movement was again cut almost in half, the total number of persons passing through the hospedaria falling to 23,913. The current remained at a fairly low level during the years of the second World War. The numbers of migrants entering São Paulo are recorded as follows: 18,330 in 1942; 23,671 in 1943; 53,186 in 1944; and 24,963 in 1945. Then the figure began to rise rapidly, 42,247 in 1946; 67,131 in 1947; and 72,615 in 1948. With the completion of a road connecting São Paulo and Fortaleza, the number of migrants suddenly shot up to 102,243 in 1949, 100,123 in 1950, and 208,515 in 1951.[41]

Origins of Migrants. Fully as important as the data concerning the volume of migration into the state are those having to do with the origins, make-up, and composition of the population entering agricultural communities of São Paulo. Fortunately, data are available for those migrating between 1935 and 1940 in sufficient detail to enable us to observe the more important facts concerning the sources of the incoming migratory tide.

As given by the official records, a total of 356,147 migrants to the state were sent to work on São Paulo's farms and fazendas during the six years 1935 to 1940, inclusive. Of this total, 326,109, or 92 per cent, were from the other states of Brazil. This leaves only 30,038 as the total contingent supplied to São Paulo's agricultural population by the immigration of this six-year period. In comparison with the movement from elsewhere in Brazil, this immigration is relatively unimportant.

Data are available for the years 1935 to 1940, classifying the Brazilians lodged in the hospedaria at São Paulo, according to the states from which they came. Since the hospedaria lodged most of the persons being sent to work in the state's agriculture, and since practically all those lodged at the hospedaria are sent to the estates and farms, these data give a fairly accurate representation of the origin of the workers who are entering the state's agricultural occupations. For the years 1935 to 1940 the available data have been assembled and are presented in Table xxx and Figure 15.

These materials indicate that almost one-third of a million persons from other Brazilian states were lodged in the hospedaria in São Paulo during the six-year period 1935 to 1940. This total is to be compared with the one which gives 326,109 as the number of mi-

[40] *Boletim do Serviço de Imigração e Colonização*, No. 4 (December, 1941), 39. This sudden decline is due to the slowing up of the movement of people from Bahia and the northeastern states to São Paulo, a movement which involved a total of 100,139 persons in 1939 and only 45,886 in 1940. The drying up of this migration current was in turn due to two factors: (1) rains in the areas from which people were forced to flee by the drought and (2) suspension by the state government of São Paulo of the practice of providing the migrants with free rail passage from Montes Claros or Pirapora to the city of São Paulo. *Ibid.*, 9.
[41] These data are from *Conjuntura Economica*, VI, No. 6 (June, 1952), 41.

grants from elsewhere in Brazil who were sent to work on Paulista fazendas and farms during the same period. The two series are closely comparable, although not identical, since there were some persons dispatched to work in agriculture without being lodged in the hospedaria and also a very small number of persons lodged at the hospedaria who were not subsequently dispatched for agricultural

TABLE XXX

States of Origin of Brazilian Migrants Lodged in the Hospedaria in São Paulo, 1935–1940 *

State	Number	Per cent
Alagôas	26,675	8.0
Amazonas	14	†
Bahia	163,810	49.2
Ceará	5,274	1.6
Distrito Federal	862	0.3
Espírito Santo	3,592	1.1
Goiás	53	†
Maranhão	145	†
Mato Grosso	16	†
Minas Gerais	86,582	26.0
Pará	34	†
Paraíba	611	0.2
Paraná	1,217	0.4
Pernambuco	22,224	6.7
Piauí	2,614	0.8
Rio de Janeiro	8,650	2.6
Rio Grande do Norte	1,281	0.4
Rio Grande do Sul	1,203	0.4
Santa Catarina	1,992	0.6
Sergipe	5,610	1.7
Total	332,459	100.0

* Source: *Boletim do Serviço de Imigração e Colonização,* No. 2 (October, 1940), 32, and No. 4 (December, 1941), 133.
† Less than one-tenth of one per cent.

labor. But for all practical purposes, these data may be utilized to determine essential characteristics of the population migrating from other states for work in agriculture.

The most striking fact about the data is the very large proportion, almost one-half of all the migrants, who came from the state of Bahia. In only six years this one state gave up some 164,000 persons to swell the agricultural population of São Paulo. From Minas Gerais there was also a very heavy movement, the total approaching 90,000 and comprising more than one-fourth of all. Sizable contingents also came from the more distant states of Alagôas and Pernambuco; tiny Sergipe and far-distant Ceará also made significant contribu-

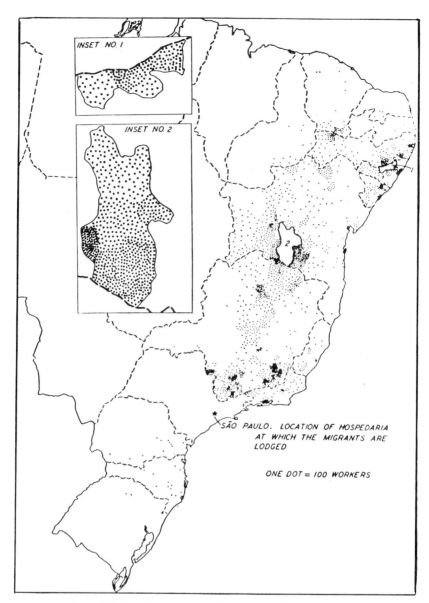

INSET NO. 1

INSET NO. 2

SÃO PAULO. LOCATION OF HOSPEDARIA
AT WHICH THE MIGRANTS ARE
LODGED

ONE DOT = 100 WORKERS

FIGURE 15. Origins of migrants lodged at the hospedaria in São Paulo, 1935–1940.

tions. From the other states of Brazil, only small contingents of migrants were attracted to São Paulo.

Composition of the Migratory Population. It is somewhat difficult to determine the significant characteristics of the Brazilian migrants to São Paulo since most of the tabular material relating to age, sex, family composition, religion, color, and other characteristics does not differentiate Brazilians from immigrants. An exception is the tabulation referring to the migrants lodged in the hospedaria in São

178

Paulo during the year 1940. Fortunately, such a large proportion of all migrants lodged in the hospedaria during the years 1935 to 1939, inclusive, were Brazilians that the data for the whole give a rather accurate description of the Brazilian contingent. With these points in mind, an attempt may be made to indicate some of the principal characteristics of the migrants who are moving into the rural districts of São Paulo from elsewhere in Brazil.

1. *Age.*—The available data make only one subdivision of the migrants according to age, merely separating those aged 12 and over from those under 12 years of age. Even this is not available for 1935. But the four years, 1936 to 1939, inclusive, 63,051 (24 per cent) out of a total of 258,750 persons lodged at the hospedaria were children of less than 12 years of age.[42] In 1940, when the data apply solely to the Brazilians lodged at the hospedaria, children under 12 made up 10,649, or 26 per cent, of all internal migrants lodged at the establishment.[43] Thus, it appears that about one out of four of the persons moving from elsewhere in Brazil to the agricultural districts of São Paulo is a child under twelve years of age. In this respect the internal migration to São Paulo differs sharply from most internal movements of population in the United States, where children seldom figure to any significant extent in the migratory tides.

2. *Sex.*—As should be expected, there is considerable sex selectivity in the migration of persons from Bahia, Minas Gerais, and the northeastern portions of Brazil to the agricultural districts of São Paulo. This migration is long-distant and towards agricultural occupations, both of which are selective of males. This sex selectivity is present to a high degree in the stream of internal migration flowing to São Paulo in spite of two important mitigating circumstances, the great importance of family groups and of children under twelve among the migrants. Among all persons lodged at the hospedaria from 1935 to 1939, inclusive, the sex ratio equaled 198 males per 100 females; among the Brazilians lodged in the establishments in 1940 the sex ratio was 182. Undoubtedly, the presence of immigrants among the persons for 1935 to 1939 is responsible for the difference in these ratios; but even so, the sex ratio among the internal migrants must be at least 180 and is indicative of a high degree of selectivity according to sex.[44]

3. *Family and Other Groupings.*—The extent to which the migratory current of agricultural workers moving from Bahia, Gerais, and northeastern Brazil to São Paulo is composed of family groups is one of the most distinctive features of the movement. In part, this may be owing to the extreme severity of the natural factors propelling the migrants from their homes, but it also is certainly a striking evidence of the strength, unity, and solidarity of the rural Brazilian family, even among the lower classes of society. Observe some of the available data on this point.

[42] *Boletim do Serviço de Imigração e Colonização,* No. 2, p. 134.
[43] *Ibid.,* No. 4, p. 31.
[44] *Ibid.,* No. 2, p. 134, and No. 4, p. 31.

In the five-year period 1935 to 1939, inclusive, a total of 305,595 persons were lodged at the hospedaria in São Paulo.[45] Almost all of these, 292,262, or 96 per cent, were Brazilians. Thus, as indicated above, the data for the whole are relatively applicable to the Brazilian contingent. Of all those lodged at the hospedaria, only 73,940 were persons traveling by themselves, while 231,063, or over 75 per cent, were journeying as members of family groups. During the years under consideration 42,933 families registered at the hospedaria thereby giving an average size family among the migrants of 5.4 persons. Among the families passing through the hospedaria one may observe persons of all ages, from babes in arms to ancients. In this respect the current migrations to São Paulo are more reminiscent of the flight from the "dust bowl" towards the West, or the expulsion of the Mormons from the Middle West, than of any other chapters in the history of migration in the United States. The data for 1940, which separate the Brazilians from the immigrants, indicate that the importance of the family is even greater when it is possible to secure data solely pertaining to Brazilian migrants.[46] In 1940 there were 40,246 Brazilians lodged at the hospedaria out of a total of 40,781, giving a percentage of about 99. The Brazilian migrants were further classified into 7,123 persons traveling alone, and 6,183 families containing 33,123 members. Thus, of all these internal migrants, those traveling in family groups made up 82 per cent, and the average size of family again equaled 5.4 persons.

The migration in family groups is merely one expression of the social solidarity and cohesion among the migrants. Other larger groupings also play an important role during the weeks or months of travel, and even after the migrants reach São Paulo. Statistics on their larger associations are, of course, not to be had, but Humberto Dantas, who has carefully observed all phases of the exodus from Bahia and the northeast, has written as follows:

Whoever travels in the districts through which the migrating streams pass, will encounter large groups of people from the same locality moving southward together.

This traveling in groups gives the migrants a strong feeling of solidarity which contributes to soften the individualist sentiment of the Brazilian country people. They make an interchange of work and help the others when needed; in addition, there is always one who, because of his age or moral influence, assumes leadership and gives orders, his advice being taken with good will.

The feeling of mutual responsibility makes each one throw in his lot with that of the group. They travel like this, united until São Paulo. At the Hospedaria de Imigrantes, it frequently happens that for the advantage of the workers it would be better to send them to different farms, but they prefer to face the incertitude and the risks of not finding work, to separating and breaking the solidarity established by days and days spent together in combating hardships.[47]

[45] *Ibid.*, No. 2, p. 134.
[46] *Ibid.*, No. 4, p. 31.
[47] Humberto Dantas, "Movimentos de Migrações Interna em Direção do Planalto Paulista," *Boletim do Serviço de Imigração e Colonização*, No. 3 (March, 1941), 85.

Upper. Migrants from the Northeast after Their Arrival in São Paulo.
Lower. One of the Coffee Fazendas on which the Migrants Find Work.
(Courtesy of Carlos B. Schmidt.)

181

4. *Color.*—Data are also recorded giving the color of the guests lodged in the hospedaria in São Paulo.[48] As in the United States, so in Brazil, there is considerable tendency to identify white with good and black with evil; for this reason official hints that some of the migrants might have been registered in a class lighter than the one to which they actually belonged probably have some basis. Be that as it may, the data actually recorded are of considerable significance. Subtracting from the total number of persons lodged at the hospedaria in the years 1935 through 1939 the 12,771 foreigners (which may be assumed to include 7,565 persons classed as "yellow," i.e., Japanese) leaves a total of 292,232 Brazilians of whom 182,061 were classed as white, 53,388 as pardo, and 56,783 as black. These data surely do not underestimate the percentage of Negroes and mulattoes among the migrants to São Paulo, but even at this, the proportions (nearly 20 per cent of each) are probably considerably higher than the percentages of these darker strains in the population of Brazil. Certainly they are far in excess of the corresponding percentages in the population of São Paulo. Since the migrants are largely from Bahia and Minas Gerais, where the colored elements in the population are relatively much more significant than they are in São Paulo, this high proportion of Negroes and mulattoes is not strange. But it is important to indicate that this migration is bringing about a more equitable distribution of the various ethnic elements in the population of Brazil among the various states and regions of the federation.

For 1940 the data show an even larger proportion of colored elements in the migratory stream. Thus, of the 40,246 Brazilians lodged at the hospedaria, 17,379 were classed as white, 15,585 as brown or mulatto, 7,281 as black, and one as yellow. The percentages corresponding to these numbers are as follows: white, 43; mulatto, 39; and black or Negro, 18. A changed policy with respect to the immigration of Japanese is responsible for the complete absence of the yellow category in 1940, except for the single Brazilian-born representative of the yellow races.

5. *Literacy.*—For the years 1937, 1939, and 1940 some data are available classifying the Brazilians lodged at the hospedaria in São Paulo according to whether or not they were able to read and write. The data are partially invalidated by the inclusion of young children in the tabulations, but by making allowance for this fact, it is possible to gain some idea of the literacy of migrating groups. The percentages of illiteracy given are as follows: 1937, 76 per cent; 1939, 81 per cent; and 1940, 83 per cent. If all children under twelve were eliminated and the numbers able to read and write taken (a computation that may be made for 1940 in relation to the persons twelve and over) the percentage of illiteracy would be 77. It seems safe to conclude that from seven to eight out of ten of the internal migrants, other than the children under ten, are unable to read or write.[49]

[48] *Boletim do Serviço de Imigração e Colonização*, No. 2, p. 134, and No. 4, p. 31.
[49] *Ibid.*, No. 2, pp. 67, 110, and No. 4, p. 31.

Finally, the materials gathered in the 1950 census of population, wherein the native-born Brazilians were cross-classified according to state-of-birth and state-of-residence, supply much important information relating to the migration to and from São Paulo. (See Table XXXI and Figure 16). These data indicate that in 1950 more than one million persons who had been born in other parts of Brazil were

TABLE XXXI

Exchange of Population Between São Paulo and Other Brazilian States, Based on 1950 Census Data on State of Birth and State of Residence *

State	Number of persons born in designated state and living in São Paulo	Number of persons born in São Paulo and living in designated state	Net migration
Brazil	1,064,005	507,157 †	556,848
North			
Acre ‡	261	33	228
Amazonas §	1,454	126	1,328
Pará ‖	2,611	396	2,215
Northeast			
Maranhão	1,409	115	1,294
Piauí	5,195	146	5,029
Ceará	29,054	650	28,404
Rio Grande do Norte	6,987	274	6,713
Paraíba	10,712	201	10,511
Pernambuco	62,745	1,678	61,067
Alagôas	56,788	542	56,246
East			
Sergipe	25,033	377	24,656
Bahia	189,685	2,130	187,555
Minas Gerais	512,736	45,554	467,182
Espírito Santo	4,569	744	3,825
Rio de Janeiro	56,076	18,685	37,391
Distrito Federal	18,172	46,990	−28,818
South			
Paraná	32,709	352,471	−319,762
Santa Catarina	15,410	2,296	13,114
Rio Grande do Sul	13,743	4,555	9,188
West Central			
Mato Grosso #	13,024	13,964	−940
Goiás	5,632	15,230	−9,598

* Compiled and computed from data in *VI Recenseamento Geral do Brasil, 1950*, I and VI–XXX (Rio de Janeiro, 1954–58).

† Because this total does not include the data for the Island of Fernando de Noronha, the Serra dos Aimorés, persons born aboard ship or abroad, and persons whose state of birth is unknown, it does not agree exactly with the figure given in Table XXXII.

‡ Territory.

§ Includes Rio Branco.

‖ Includes Amapá.

Includes Guaporé or Rondonia.

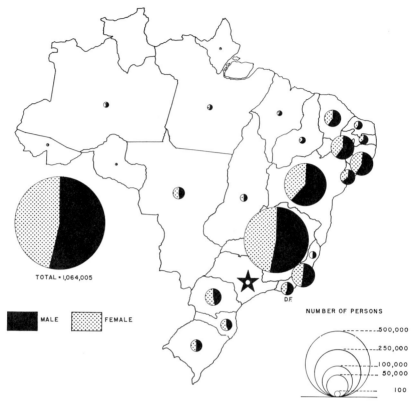

TOTAL = 1,064,005

MALE   FEMALE

NUMBER OF PERSONS

500,000
250,000
100,000
50,000
100

FIGURE 16. Numbers of persons born elsewhere and living in the state of São Paulo in 1950, by state of origin and sex.

living in São Paulo and that slightly more than half a million of those born in São Paulo were living in other parts of the republic. The bulk of the migrants to São Paulo originated in Minas Gerais and Bahia, although substantial contingents had come from the distant sections of the Northeast and especially from the states of Pernambuco, Alagôas, and Ceará.

The figures in Table xxxi also show the extent to which the great "rush" of people to the new coffee districts of northern Paraná involved persons born in São Paulo, most of whom made the move in the decade 1940–1950. Similarly materials in this table make it clear that a substantial movement from São Paulo to Goiás had set in prior to 1950. This migration, which is discussed in more detail below, was increased substantially by the building of Brasília. Indeed it is highly important in connection with the settlement of wide expanses of the rich, new lands which lie to the north of Brazil's new capital city, a development that promises to be one of the more significant features of Brazilian history during the second half of the twentieth century.

184

OTHER INTERSTATE MIGRATIONS

The data supplied by the 1950 census reports in which information on the state of birth of the population is cross-classified with that giving state of residence also make possible significant analyses of the exchanges of population between all of the other states of the Brazilian confederation. Some of these, and particularly the "rush" to the new coffee-producing sections of northern Paraná and the strong currents of migration moving into central Goiás deserve special attention. First of all, though, it is desirable to have an overall view of the exchange of population between the various states. (See Table XXXII and Figure 17.)

At the time of the 1950 census over 5,200,000 Brazilians, or more than 10 per cent of all those born in the country, were living in a state or territory other than the one in which they had been born. Minas Gerais alone had sent well over one and one-third millions of her native sons and daughters to other parts of the republic, São Paulo and Rio de Janeiro each more than half a million, and Bahia and Pernambuco over 430,000 and 310,000, respectively. Due principally to the fact that the old Distrito Federal formed an enclave within its borders, the state of Rio de Janeiro is the one which had sent the largest proportion of its native-born elsewhere (21.1 per cent), with Alagôas, Espírito Santo, Minas Gerais, and Sergipe also ranking high in this respect. All of these except Minas Gerais are small in size; they are shut off from access to unopened lands in the interior; and they contain no cities that are attracting large numbers of migrants from neighboring states. Goiás is at the other end of the scale; less than 4 per cent of those born in that state were reported as living outside its borders in 1950. Goiás is most closely rivaled in this respect by Rio Grande do Sul and Paraná. Were it not for the fact that São Paulo has supplied the lion's share of those who participated in the "rush" to Paraná, it likewise would have shown a very low index on the matter under consideration. Other states in which low proportions of those born in the state have gone elsewhere to live are Mato Grosso, Maranhão, Pará, and Santa Catarina.

The data in Table XXXIII are supplied to supplement those given in Table XXXII and Figure 17, to which reference has just been made. For all cases involving 10,000 or more persons moving in either direction, they show the magnitude of the exchanges between each individual state and every other state in the Brazilian confederation. This information, along with that presented above, enables one to obtain a fair impression about the amount and directions of interstate migration in Brazil.

Because the migration from Minas Gerais is by far the largest in volume of that from any state, it was deemed advisable to analyze that movement in somewhat greater detail. (See Table XXXIV and Figure 18.) It is important to note the extent to which the migrations of those born in Minas Gerais have been confined largely to nearby

State	Population 1950	Number born in the state		Residing in other states	Per cent of those born in state who were living in other states	Number born in & residing in state as percentage of 1950 pop.
		Total	Residing in state of birth			
Brazil	51,944,397	50,727,113	45,462,983	5,206,535	10.3	87.5
Guaporé †	36,935	6,001	5,702	299	5.0	15.4
Acre †	114,755	97,503	84,190	13,313	13.7	73.4
Amazonas	514,099	512,351	458,973	53,378	10.4	89.3
Rio Branco †	18,116	4,135	4,019	116	2.8	22.2
Pará	1,123,273	1,123,972	1,042,540	81,432	7.2	92.8
Amapá †	37,477	7,003	6,886	117	1.7	18.4
Maranhão	1,583,248	1,520,377	1,420,188	100,189	6.6	89.7
Piauí	1,045,696	1,103,534	958,588	144,946	13.1	91.7
Ceará	2,695,450	2,852,855	2,584,369	268,486	9.4	95.9
Rio Grande do Norte	967,921	993,334	889,665	103,669	10.4	91.9
Paraíba	1,713,259	1,858,103	1,611,323	246,780	13.3	94.0
Pernambuco	3,395,185	3,491,249	3,180,111	311,138	8.9	93.7
Alagôas	1,093,137	1,232,802	1,025,552	207,250	16.8	93.8
Fernando de Noronha †	581	86	31	55	64.0	5.3
Sergipe	644,361	715,114	607,635	107,479	15.0	94.3
Bahia	4,834,575	5,112,440	4,682,223	430,217	8.4	96.8
Minas Gerais	7,717,792	8,836,270	7,469,031	1,367,239	15.5	96.8
Serra dos Aimorés	160,072	41,563	41,347	216	0.5	25.8
Espírito Santo	861,562	909,623	761,769	147,854	16.3	88.4
Rio de Janeiro	2,297,194	2,393,863	1,889,733	504,130	21.1	82.3
Distrito Federal	2,377,451	1,365,513	1,223,460	142,053	10.4	51.5
São Paulo	9,134,423	7,867,588	7,360,340	507,248	6.4	80.6
Paraná	2,115,547	1,446,387	1,375,077	71,310	4.9	65.0
Santa Catarina	1,560,502	1,507,119	1,388,371	118,748	7.9	89.0
Rio Grande do Sul	4,164,821	4,245,121	4,039,545	205,576	4.8	97.0
Mato Grosso	522,044	459,676	423,642	36,034	7.8	81.2
Goiás	1,214,921	965,936	928,673	37,263	3.9	76.4

* Source: Compiled and computed from data in "Censo Demográfico," *VI Recenseamento Geral do Brasil, 1950*, I (Rio de Janeiro, 1956), 72–79.

† Territory

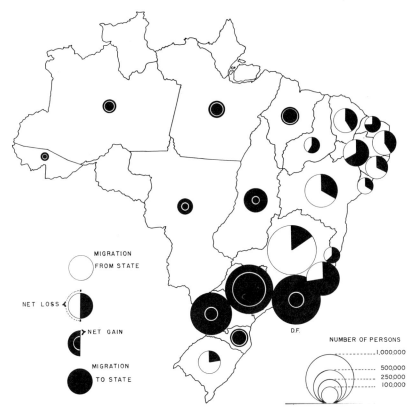

MIGRATION
FROM STATE

NET LOSS

NET GAIN

MIGRATION
TO STATE

D.F.

NUMBER OF PERSONS

1,000,000

500,000
250,000
100,000

FIGURE 17. Numbers of persons enumerated in the 1950 census who had moved to each state and from each state, with net gain or net loss due to migration.

portions of the republic and especially the extent to which they have gone to São Paulo, the Distrito Federal (i.e., the city of Rio de Janeiro), Paraná, the state of Rio de Janeiro, and Goiás. This suggests rather definitely that natives of Minas Gerais have been quick to respond to the economic opportunities in the great cities of Rio de Janeiro and São Paulo, in the new coffee districts of São Paulo and Paraná, and on the new frontier in Goiás. Interestingly enough, Bahia to the north, which shares a long boundary with Minas Gerais, is the only state in Brazil that lost as many as 10,000 persons in an exchange with the latter, as is clear from Table XXXIII. Finally, the migration from Minas Gerais was rather highly selective for males in all important cases except the movement to the city of Rio de Janeiro, in which females predominated to a considerable extent.

It was also thought desirable for two reasons to consider in more detail the movement from Ceará: (1) because of the widespread knowledge that the prolific population of that state sends its progeny to many other parts of Brazil, and (2) because the data in Table XXXIII indicate that it is the only state that has made heavy contri-

TABLE XXXIII

Exchange of Population Between Brazilian States, Based on 1950
Census Data Showing State of Birth and State of Residence *

State A	State B	Number of persons born in State B and living in State A	Number of persons born in State A and living in State B	Net gain or loss to State A by the exchanges
Acre †	Ceará	14,221	848	13,373
	All other	15,198	12,465	2,733
	Total	29,419	13,313	16,106
Amazonas ‡	Ceará	19,575	3,269	16,306
	Pará	12,422	7,072	5,350
	All other	21,441	53,409	−31,968
	Total	53,438	63,750	−10,312
Pará §	Ceará	27,787	2,326	25,461
	Maranhão	13,631	4,927	8,704
	Distrito Federal	716	15,589	−14,873
	Amazonas	7,072	12,422	−5,350
	All other	53,291	46,219	7,072
	Total	102,497	81,483	21,014
Maranhão	Piauí	100,617	17,397	83,220
	Ceará	40,358	2,205	38,153
	Goiás	1,971	47,054	−45,083
	All other	19,023	33,533	−14,510
	Total	161,969	100,189	103,808

State A	State B	Number of persons born in State B and living in State A	Number of persons born in State A and living in State B	Net gain or loss to State A by the exchanges
Piauí	Ceará	50,965	7,126	43,839
	Maranhão	17,379	100,617	−83,238
	Goiás	326	12,125	−11,799
	All other	18,161	25,078	−6,917
	Total	86,831	144,946	−58,115
Ceará	Paraíba	31,031	10,281	20,750
	Pernambuco	26,180	25,701	479
	Rio Grande do Norte	15,980	7,595	8,385
	Alagôas	14,971	2,201	12,770
	Piauí	7,126	50,965	−43,839
	Maranhão	2,205	40,358	−38,153
	Pará	2,326	27,787	−25,461
	São Paulo	650	20,054	−19,404
	Amazonas	3,269	19,575	−16,306
	Distrito Federal	471	18,061	−17,590
	Acre	848	14,221	−13,373
	All other	4,436	31,687	−27,251
	Total	109,493	268,486	−158,993
Rio Grande do Norte	Paraíba	60,654	30,151	30,503
	Ceará	7,595	15,980	−8,385
	Distrito Federal	483	13,648	−13,165
	All other	9,020	43,890	−34,870
	Total	77,752	103,669	−25,917

(Continued, p. 190)

* Compiled and computed from data in VI Recenseamento Geral do Brasil, 1950, I and VI–XXX (Rio de Janeiro, 1954–58).
† Territory.
‡ Includes Rio Branco.
§ Includes Amapá.
‖ Includes Guaporé or Rondonia.

TABLE XXXIII (*Continued*). Exchange of Population Between States *

State A	State B	Number of persons born in State B and living in State A	Number of persons born in State A and living in State B	Net gain or loss to State A by the exchanges
Paraíba	Pernambuco	54,384	89,849	−35,465
	Rio Grande do Norte	30,151	60,654	−30,503
	Ceará	10,281	31,031	−20,750
	Distrito Federal	163	23,209	−23,046
	São Paulo	201	10,712	−10,511
	All other	6,185	31,325	−25,140
	Total	101,365	246,780	−145,415
Pernambuco	Paraíba	89,849	54,384	35,465
	Alagôas	60,387	52,509	7,878
	Ceará	25,701	26,180	−479
	Rio Grande do Norte	10,100	4,464	5,636
	São Paulo	1,678	62,745	−61,067
	Distrito Federal	1,177	45,157	−43,980
	Bahia	6,537	17,734	−11,197
	Rio de Janeiro	1,751	12,166	−10,415
	All other	12,282	35,799	−23,517
	Total	209,462	311,138	−101,676
Alagôas	Pernambuco	52,509	60,387	−7,878
	São Paulo	542	56,788	−56,246
	Distrito Federal	217	27,267	−27,050
	Bahia	1,289	10,708	−9,419
	All other	12,586	52,100	−39,514
	Total	67,143	207,250	−140,107

State A	State B	Number of persons born in State B and living in State A	Number of persons born in State A and living in State B	Net gain or loss to State A by the exchanges
Sergipe	Alagôas	16,379	5,067	11,312
	Bahia	15,202	44,365	−29,163
	São Paulo	377	25,035	−24,658
	Distrito Federal	305	20,089	−19,784
	All other	4,199	12,923	−8,724
	Total	36,462	107,479	−71,017
Bahia	Minas Gerais	44,996	56,649	−11,653
	Sergipe	44,365	15,202	29,163
	Pernambuco	17,374	6,537	10,837
	Alagôas	10,708	1,289	9,419
	São Paulo	2,130	189,685	−187,555
	Distrito Federal	1,200	44,936	−43,736
	Goiás	582	44,277	−43,695
	Mato Grosso	260	18,890	−18,630
	Paraná	175	18,764	−18,589
	All other	22,265	33,988	−11,723
	Total	144,055	430,217	−286,162
Minas Gerais (*see* Table XXXIV)				
Espírito Santo	Minas Gerais	50,911	29,163	21,748
	Rio de Janeiro	28,407	32,054	−3,647
	Distrito Federal	1,357	55,746	−54,389
	All other	12,524	30,891	−18,367
	Total	93,199	147,854	−54,655

* Compiled and computed from data in *VI Recenseamento Geral do Brasil, 1950*, I and VI–XXX (Rio de Janeiro, 1954–58).
† Territory.
‡ Includes Rio Branco.
§ Includes Amapá.
‖ Includes Guaporé or Rondonia.

TABLE XXXIII (*Continued*). Exchange of Population Between States *

State A	State B	Number of persons born in State B and living in State A	Number of persons born in State A and living in State B	Net gain or loss to State A by the exchanges
Rio de Janeiro	Minas Gerais	152,909	36,794	116,115
	Distrito Federal	102,108	360,324	−258,216
	Espírito Santo	32,054	28,407	3,647
	São Paulo	18,685	56,076	−37,391
	Pernambuco	12,156	1,751	10,405
	All other	50,835	20,778	30,057
	Total	368,747	504,130	−135,383
Distrito Federal (*see* Table XXXII)				
São Paulo (*see* Table XXXI)				
Paraná	São Paulo	352,471	32,709	319,762
	Minas Gerais	156,848	1,258	155,590
	Santa Catarina	63,162	24,812	38,350
	Rio Grande do Sul	35,701	3,268	32,433
	All other	55,601	9,263	46,338
	Total	663,783	71,410	592,473
Santa Catarina	Rio Grande do Sul	120,710	26,236	94,474
	Paraná	24,812	63,162	−38,350
	São Paulo	2,296	15,410	−13,114
	All other	5,108	13,940	−8,832
	Total	152,926	118,748	34,178
Rio Grande do Sul	Santa Catarina	26,236	120,710	−94,474
	São Paulo	4,555	13,743	−9,188
	Paraná	3,268	35,701	−32,433
	Distrito Federal	2,047	21,788	−19,741
	All other	10,722	13,634	−2,912
	Total	46,828	205,576	−158,748

State A	State B	Number of persons born in State B and living in State A	Number of persons born in State A and living in State B	Net gain or loss to State A by the exchanges
Mato Grosso ‖	Bahia	19,128	262	18,866
	São Paulo	13,964	13,022	942
	Goiás	11,444	3,735	7,709
	Minas Gerais	11,055	1,142	9,913
	All other	52,161	18,156	34,005
	Total	107,752	36,317	71,435
Goiás	Minas Gerais	150,033	10,537	139,496
	Maranhão	47,054	1,971	45,083
	Bahia	44,277	582	43,695
	São Paulo	15,230	5,632	9,598
	Piauí	12,125	326	11,799
	All other	13,731	18,215	−4,484
	Total	282,450	37,263	245,187

* Compiled and computed from data in *VI Recenseamento Geral do Brasil, 1950*, I and VI–XXX (Rio de Janeiro, 1954–58).

† Territory.
‡ Includes Rio Branco.
§ Includes Amapá.
‖ Includes Guaporé or Rondonia.

TABLE XXXIV

Exchange of Population Between Minas Gerais and Other Brazilian
States, Based on 1950 Census Data on State of Birth and
State of Residence *

State	Number of persons born in designated state and living in Minas Gerais	Number of persons born in Minas Gerais and living in designated state	Net migration
Brazil	210,849	1,275,938 †	−1,065,089
North			
Acre ‡	67	38	29
Amazonas §	350	120	230
Pará ‖	542	296	246
Northeast			
Maranhão	573	97	476
Piauí	866	91	775
Ceará	2,015	274	1,741
Rio Grande do Norte	2,730	199	2,531
Paraíba	1,247	140	1,107
Pernambuco	3,880	687	3,193
Alagôas	1,305	92	1,213
East			
Sergipe	1,267	120	1,147
Bahia	59,649	44,996	14,653
Espírito Santo	29,163	50,911	−21,748
Rio de Janeiro	36,794	152,909	−116,115
Distrito Federal	9,691	191,917	−182,226
South			
São Paulo	45,554	512,736	−467,182
Paraná	1,258	156,848	−155,590
Santa Catarina	544	755	−211
Rio Grande do Sul	1,675	1,624	51
West Central			
Mato Grosso #	1,142	11,055	−9,913
Goiás	10,537	150,033	−139,496

* Compiled and computed from data in VI *Recenseamento Geral do Brasil, 1950,*
I and VI–XXX (Rio de Janeiro, 1954–58).
† Because this total does not include the data for the Island of Fernando de
Noronha, the Serra dos Aimorés, persons born abroad ship or abroad, and
persons whose state of birth is unknown, it does not agree exactly with the
figure given in Table XXXII.
‡ Territory.
§ Includes Rio Branco.
‖ Includes Amapá.
Includes Guaporé or Rondonia.

butions both to the Amazon Basin (Pará, Amazonas, and Acre) and
also to the great commercial and industrial sections of the south (São
Paulo and the city of Rio de Janeiro). Therefore, to facilitate observation of the volume of migration from Ceará Figure 19 was pre-

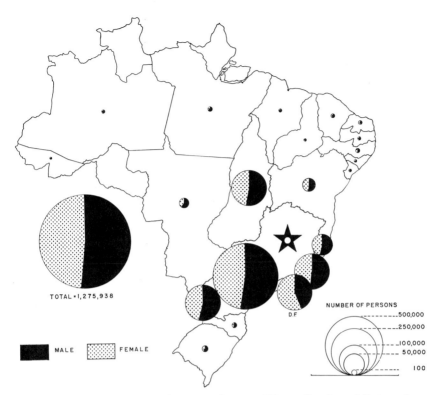

TOTAL = 1,275,938

MALE   FEMALE

NUMBER OF PERSONS
D.F.
- - - - - - - - 500,000
- - - - 250,000
- - - 100,000
- - 50,000
- - - - - 100

FIGURE 18. Numbers of persons born in Minas Gerais and living else-where at the time of the 1950 census, by state of residence and sex.

pared. It confirms the impression so widely held throughout Brazil that natives of this great northeastern state have moved to all parts of the republic. Those born in this drought-stricken part of Brazil were found in substantial numbers by the census of 1950 in neigh-boring sections of the dry northeast (including the city of Recife in Pernambuco), in the heavy rain forests of Maranhão, in both the lower and the upper reaches of the Amazon Basin and in the state of São Paulo and the city of Rio de Janeiro.

The "rush" to northern Paraná that took place during the middle decades of the twentieth century was essentially an extension of the coffee-producing sections of São Paulo, and the Paulistas made up considerably more than one-half of all the migrants involved. On the other hand, comparatively few of those born in Paraná were found living in São Paulo at the time of the 1950 census. Natives of Minas Gerais, Santa Catarina, and Rio Grande do Sul also figured promi-nently among the newcomers who settled in Paraná between 1940 and 1950, but there were relatively few persons from other sections of Brazil involved in this particular movement.

Finally, because of its magnitude, its relation to developments that led to the building of Brazil's new capital (Brasília), and its

portent for the future it seems advisable to give special attention to
the movement of people from Minas Gerais, Bahia, and São Paulo to
the state of Goiás. In 1945, as this migration was swelling to sizable
proportions, the present writer had the opportunity of making personal observations relating to this important new development. The
following paragraphs are based upon field notes made at that time.
Even then, when the decision to build a new capital city was not to
be taken for some years, it was apparent that the central part of
Goiás, the very heart of Brazil, was rapidly becoming the most important area of colonization and settlement in the republic. Already
it was rivaling western São Paulo and northern Paraná as a land of
promise for Brazilians from the overpopulated sections of Minas
Gerais, Bahia, and other states. Probably as many as 50,000 new agriculturists were arriving each year, most of them coming early in
the dry season so that they would have time to fell and burn the new
roças before the rains set in during the month of September. In contrast to the situation in São Paulo, very few of them returned to their
old homes; instead they were sending back the *boas notícias* that attracted thousands more of their relatives and friends to the plateaus
of central Goiás. These thousands of newcomers, working under the

FIGURE 19. Numbers of persons born in Ceará and living elsewhere
at the time of the 1950 census, by state of residence and sex.

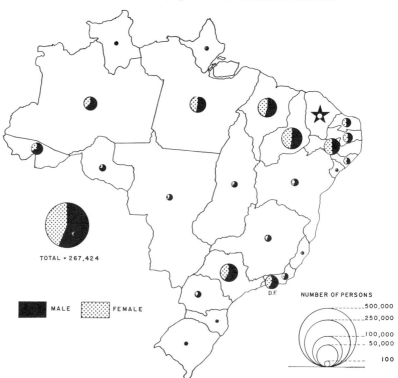

TOTAL = 267,424

MALE   FEMALE

NUMBER OF PERSONS

500,000
250,000
100,000
50,000

100

greatest handicaps in securing materials and supplies and using the primitive aboriginal system of "fire agriculture" to prepare the land for the seed and the sickle to harvest the crop, constituted the chief hope for increasing the production of foodstuffs in central Brazil, a point of vital concern in the 1940's as it continues to be in the 1960's. The new land of Caanan in central Goiás consists of approximately 3,000,000 acres of heavily forested plateau land in a belt which cuts directly across the middle of the state. Roughly it is enclosed by a line running from Formosa to Anápolis, passing westward just north of Goiânia to Rio Verde, thence northwest until it strikes the Araguaia River near Registro. From this point it follows down river to Leopoldina, then turns east and passes through Santa Ana and São José to Cavalcante, and then runs south to Formosa. This area takes in the whole Goiás portion of the divide between the Amazon and the Paraná river systems. Most of it is more than 1,500 feet above sea level, and there are occasional plateaus such as the Chapada dos Veadeiros which are much higher, with altitudes up to nearly 6,000 feet. To the north it is drained by the numerous tributaries of the Araguaia and Tocantins, which disgorge into the Amazon, and to the south (to a much lesser degree) by a few of the upper tributaries of the Paranaiba. The distinction between the seasons is sharp and regular. The dry season begins in April and continues till late September, when light showers may be expected at night. These gradually increase in duration and precipitation, and by December the downpour is extremely heavy. The coldest weather comes in June and July. The soils in the densely wooded sections which are sought by the settlers are of the heavy red type so noted in São Paulo and northern Paraná and are considered to be of the first quality. Interspersed are the *campo* lands, covered only with grass or a thin scrub timber, decidedly inferior, and sought only for grazing purposes.

Rice was the major crop being planted in 1945, although eventually coffee was thought likely to become the chief cash crop. Beans, a little tobacco, sugar cane, mandioca, bananas, papaya, and other fruits also added to the foodstuffs produced in nearly every roça. Near the hut of every family was found a small planting of tree cotton, for these sertanejos still possessed all the skills necessary for the production of their own homespun cotton for clothing and household uses. Pureblood cattle of the Zebu or Brahma breed were increasing rapidly, since many cattlemen from the Triángulo of Minas Gerais had sought out this area for the opening of new cattle fazendas. Fabulous prices were being paid for some of the Zebu bulls.

The system of farming was entirely confined to what is described elsewhere in this book as "fire agriculture." The axe and fire, and not the plow and the harrow, or even the hoe, were the sole agencies used in preparing the soil for the seed. The routine in such a system of farming in central Goiás was about as follows: early in the dry season the *roceiro* with his axe and machete entered the selected tract of virgin forest and "swamped out" the undergrowth and small timber. Then he attacked the larger trees, leaving erect only a few selected varieties of palms. The whole lot then was permitted to dry until the approach of the rainy season, in order that it would burn well and in order, too, that the rains would check the fire before it passed too far beyond the prepared plots. After the general firing the land was further cleaned by assembling the remaining limbs and trunks into large piles and burning them. In these new clearings the seed was dibbled into small openings in the ground prepared with the bare big toe, or with the digging stick, or much more rarely, with the hoe. Except for one or two cleanings given the crop, when the caboclo passed through the roça and cut down the sprouts which had shot up from the stumps and the roots, it received no more attention until harvest. However, it had to be protected from cattle by fencing. If the crop belonged to a caboclo, the fence was of wood, a crude temporary barrier erected from the limbs of the fallen timber saved following the general fire and placed aside during the cleaning; but if it belonged to a fazendeiro, barbed wire frequently was used. When the rice was ripe, it was harvested by hand with the sickle and then threshed there in the roça. Sometimes the worker was aided by animals which treaded out the grain, but frequently the threshing was performed entirely by human effort.

PART THREE

Levels and Standards of Living

Most inquiries and speculations concerning the qualitative aspects of population revolve around questions of levels and standards of living. There are some data showing the amounts of goods and services consumed by parts of the Brazilian population; and there are others which may be used in helping one to appraise the adequacy of their housing. It is possible, also, to learn something about the standards to which the people aspire. These inseparable topics are treated in the single chapter which makes up Part Three.

CHAPTER X

LEVELS AND STANDARDS OF LIVING

B<small>EFORE</small> <small>ATTEMPTING</small> to analyze levels of living in Brazil and the factors responsible for them, it is well to consider briefly the factors most greatly responsible for variations in living levels generally. In the last analysis the level of living of a given people resolves itself into a consideration of three factors: (1) the quantity and quality of the natural resources available for exploitation by man, (2) the output per worker, and (3) the manner of distributing the results of man's efforts among those who share in the productive process. Even the shares the economist attributes to capital, management, and land ultimately find their way to the person or persons performing the managerial function, advancing the capital, or owning the land. The above generalization should not be interpreted as meaning that natural resources by themselves are of any import; for unless man's culture is developed to the stage that society possesses a rich storehouse of knowledge of the ways in which the gifts of nature may be utilized, and unless it contains values and patterns that propel man to labor to satisfy felt needs or to engage in activities that are deemed commendable by the society in which he lives, the presence of certain physical substances may be of no significance.[1] The output per worker of course must also take into account the ratio of workers to dependents in the population or the number of mouths that must be fed by the average person's share of the product. Furthermore, even though a nation may have unlimited natural resources and a sizable output per worker, the level of living may remain very low if the rewards to capital or to management are far out of line with the proportion going to labor. This is most pronounced in a slave society, where labor is at the same time capital and where the share of the products that goes to labor depends on the enlightenment and kindliness of the members of the master class.

In countries like Argentina, the United States, and Brazil, where the pressure of population upon resources is much less than in many other parts of the world, the productivity per worker is largely determined by the extent to which labor is expended in the productive process. Where labor is used lavishly—that is to say, combined with

---

[1] Iron resources, for example, were of no importance to the aboriginal American Indian, whose cultural environment did not include a knowledge of iron and how to get it, although he had many uses for it, such as the making of arrow points. The use of iron for this purpose was one of the first European culture traits borrowed by Brazilian Indians.

relatively small inputs of capital and management—the output per man is much less than is the case where workers make considerable use of tools, machinery, and power. In other words, in the countries mentioned above, production per worker, and particularly per capita agricultural production, becomes chiefly a function of the extent to which the hand of man is strengthened for his struggle with nature. Where, as in huge expanses of Brazilian territory, man's only aid against the jungle is the ax and fire, the output per worker may be so small as to permit only a low level of living. On the other hand, if each worker has an abundance of land, tools, equipment, and power, capital is not being husbanded. Under these circumstances the increased production per person creates a greater product to be divided and permits a higher level of living. When this is the case, the prevailing level of living comes to depend largely on the system of distribution, and the whole axis of human thinking must shift if unemployment, "overproduction," and misery are to be avoided.

The quality of the population has much to do with the relative importance of management in the productive process. If each human being is himself the thinking, deciding, acting agent performing the managerial functions (as is the case in the "colonial" parts of south Brazil and on the typical midwestern farm in the United States), this important factor of production is not relegated to the secondary position it occupies on many large plantations, fazendas, haciendas, and estâncias. Where the worker himself also receives a return for the performance of managerial activities, as well as for his labor, much has been done to ensure a relatively high general level of living. On the other hand, in the types of large-scale agricultural operations mentioned above, the managerial activities of the major domo frequently are merely nominal with the result that the managerial function in the productive process might be said to be carefully husbanded. Under these circumstances both the poor combination of productive factors and the failure of the mass of the workers to receive a return for managerial activities are directly responsible for a comparatively low level of living.

As was also indicated above, where resources are abundant and where the correct combination of productive factors makes the output per worker large, the level of living becomes almost entirely a function of the system of distribution which is employed. However, as already suggested, in the agriculture of the Western Hemisphere under present forms of social and economic organization, the system that makes for the greatest production per capita also does much to ensure that the distribution of income among the agricultural population does not have a depressing effect on the average level of living. (The distribution of incomes between agriculture and other industries is quite another thing.) In the present stage of technical knowledge and its application to agricultural enterprises, the greatest production per farm worker takes place only in the areas where the worth of the human hand is very great. It comes from precisely those areas in which home and formal education train each worker to become his own manager; where in addition to doing the essential labor on the farm, he also is a capitalist, owning the land as well as the tools, machinery, and livestock. It should be repeated for emphasis that, other things being equal, the greatest production per worker probably comes in the family farm system, under those circumstances in which the farmer has sufficient land to occupy himself and the members of his family fully and where he also complements the strength of his arm with tools, equipment, power, and an understanding of the processes of agriculture. Under such a family-sized farm system, where from birth the child is molded in the direction of becoming a self-reliant person capable of exercising the functions of manager and capitalist and also taught the dignity of manual labor, the worth of the average human being is very great—to use a Brazilian word that is too rich in meaning to be restricted to coffee, man has been "valorized." In a society organized on these lines the level of living may come to be very high.

LEVEL OF LIVING

The general level of living of the masses in Brazil is comparatively low. It also seems fairly certain that this low level has been closely associated with a low standard of living or that in the past the masses of lower-class Brazilians have seen very little discrepancy between the amount of goods and services which they actually were privileged to consume and that to which they felt rightfully entitled. This is not to say that *all* Brazilians have a low level and low standard of life. On the contrary, in Brazil there long have been significant elements in both the city and the country that have had as high levels and standards of living as were to be encountered elsewhere in the Western world. Furthermore, as indicated below, in recent decades the standard of living (the aspirations) of Brazil's masses has risen rapidly, far more rapidly than their level of living.

The upper classes of Brazilian society certainly consume as much in the way of material goods and services as their fellows in other countries; they are less specialized, perhaps less competitive, and better equipped educationally, emotionally, and temperamentally for the maximum enjoyment of a luxurious mode of living. Indeed the capacity of Brazil's elite classes to appreciate luxurious living still is perhaps far beyond that of upper-class members in most other societies. Furthermore, it apparently never occurs to a member of this class to question for one moment his inherent right to the enjoyment of these superior elements of living, a certain indication that the standard of living is high.

However, because of the concentration of property and wealth, the relative absence of middle-class groups in many regions, the concentration of the population, both rural and urban, in the unskilled labor categories, the lavish use of labor in the production process, the ease with which a vegetative existence can be carried on, and the lack of social, economic, and climatic propulsions to continuous work activities, the classes which constitute the bulk of Brazil's population live in poverty. In diet, housing, clothing, and all the educational and cultural aspects the level of consumption must be classed as very low. Rather general contentment with their lot or at least a resignation to it, the relative absence of class struggle, little evidence of mental anguish and conflict, a rigid adherence to long-established cultural practices, all are indicative of the fact that the standard of living also is low. For example, until recently the aspiration to land-ownership was a rare phenomenon among Brazil's millions of rural workers. On the other hand, hundreds of thousands of Brazilian caboclos, matutos, and sertanejos would feel deprived of their rights if interfered with in building a hut of wattle and daub, pau-a-pique, or thatch with a thatched roof on the spot of their choosing. They do have standards.

Unfortunately, detailed budgetary studies of levels of living and inquiries designed to determine the standards to which Brazilians aspire are very few, and the results of most of them are of limited value because of the time that has elapsed and the changes that may have taken place since they were made. As a result chief dependence for data about the level of living, its variation from class to class and region to region, and the factors responsible for the observed differences must be secured either from studies tangential to the subject or from mere observation. At best, these make possible only tentative propositions descriptive of the general pattern and not established facts concerning the detailed framework of the level of living.

Perhaps of most assistance in this connection are certain studies of income, expenditures, and diet. These have been carefully examined. Because the diet is so significant in relation to the level of living from the standpoint of cause as well as effect, its nature and adequacy is one of the most important aspects of the study of living levels.

There has been, however, one recent study of the budgets of 103 families, one family out of every five, living on two sugar-cane plantations in the state of São Paulo.[2] Both of these plantations are owned by a corporation, the stock of which is in the hands of the members of one family. A large factory for the manufacture of sugar is located on the central plantation, where the cane from both is processed. Therefore, employees who worked in the mill as well as agricultural laborers working on both plantations were included in the sample. According to their positions in the occupational and technological hierarchy, the 103 families were distributed as follows: 4 families of the "chiefs" or top administrative or technical personnel; 1 family of an administrator (i.e., the man in charge of the second

[2] These data were secured during the months of November and December, 1957, and January and February, 1958, by Dr. Harry W. Hutchinson, subsequently on the faculty of the University of Florida. The work was done as a part of a thorough anthropological study of the plantations involved. The present writer is grateful to Dr. Hutchinson for making these as yet unpublished data available to him.

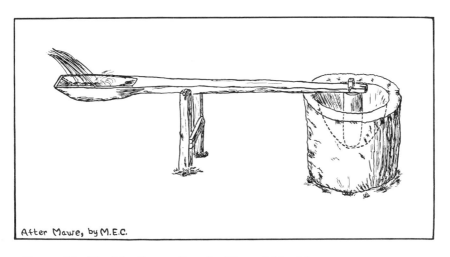

After Mawe, by M.E.C.

Upper. The Monjolo. *Lower.* Exterior View of Monjolo.

plantation); 13 families of foremen; 54 families of industrial workers; and 31 families of agricultural laborers, 19 of them located on
the central plantation and 12 of them on the other one.[3]

Most significant for present purposes are the materials showing
the proportions of the total expenditures that go for food, fuel, clothing, and so forth. See Table xxxv. Comment on this information is
limited to the food item, for the reason that the proportion of a
family's expenditures that goes for food is one of the best indicators
of its level of living. The general rule is, of course, the greater the
proportion going for food, the lower the level of living. When as much

[3] The central plantation involved in Dr. Hutchinson's study was visited by the
present writer on April 10, 1942. Notes taken at that time include the following:
"Monte Alegre is one of two usinas owned by a 'Companhia Brasileira de Usinas
Açucareiras' or by the Morganti brothers. It includes some 2,500 alqueires of the
best terra-roxa in the region. The mill grinds about 150,000 tons of cane annually,
carrying it through all stages. Seventy kilometers of railroad are on the properties;
power is furnished by ten small engines, all of which were constructed on the
place. The machine shops also cast all of the machinery for the mill, even the
vacuum kettles. In addition to the sugar, alcohol is produced, varying from
4,000,000 to 6,000,000 liters per year; the more profitable the sugar the less the
amount of alcohol produced. With the prospects for increased sugar demand
brought on by the war and the probability of no restrictions on production, the
milling facilities are being greatly expanded. The rush is now to complete the
work before the grinding season, due to start in two weeks, or about the twenty-
fifth of April.

"Some 5,800 persons, men, women, and children, live on the fazenda. In the
production of cane the usina furnishes the land to the workers, called colonos.
The colonos receive their pay as a share of the crop, with the price paid for cane
varying according to its sugar content. Each family is supplied quarters for
living, consisting of about three rooms, in houses of brick and tile. The new
houses are of good construction, and the old ones are rapidly being replaced. The
usina has a meat market, macaroni factory, and general store, which sell at
wholesale prices to the workers. Medical attention is available, and a hospital and
a school also are present in the workers' village—all of these supplied by the
usina. An athletic plant with football field, lake for swimming, and other facilities
is located on the grounds, each worker contributing a small amount of his wages
for its upkeep. At the time of our visit the team was practicing in uniform; it
now occupies second place in the local standings, being paced only by the team
from the agricultural college. A recent addition is the church, a duplicate of the
chapel in the Italian community in which the founder of the usina (deceased
seven months) was born. A son now operates the usina. According to his reports,
the establishment of the chapel has reduced the mobility of the operários (skilled
workers) by 40 per cent.

"Each family is given space for a garden and pasture for its mules and is
allowed to plant some food crops among the cane and to keep chickens.

"The layout of the usina is of the village type. The owner's home stands near
the summit of the hill facing nearly due west. It overlooks the mill at a distance of
some 150 yards and is flanked on the left by a guest house and houses for managerial employees and technicians; about 300 yards to the left stands the church,
with houses for workers beyond. On the right are more workers' homes, the
school, and still more distant, beyond the draw and lake, are the football field,
stables, and more homes for workers. The new hospital under construction is to
the right front of the mansion. The mansion itself faces upon a spacious garden.
It has a wide veranda on the front and north, with an arbor on the south extending almost to the guest house. In the garden on the north is a fine tiled swimming
pool, with a corner especially prepared for the children.

"At present the park extending from the owner's home to the mill and including the church is under construction. This, along with the cemetery, is family
property, and does not go with the usina.

"The usina is some eight or ten kilometers from Piracicaba, with a free-
transportation bus running to it three times a day. Carts drawn by mules are
owned by many families."

TABLE XXXV

*Percentages of Expenditures of 103 Families Residing on Two
Sugar-cane Plantations in São Paulo Going for Stated
Purposes, According to Occupational Status of
Heads of Families **

Category of expenditure	Chief	Foreman	Industrial worker	Agricultural laborer Plantation A	Plantation B
Total	100.0	100.0	100.0	100.0	100.0
Hygiene	10.5	4.3	4.4	4.5	4.6
Clothing	15.2	12.0	14.0	14.0	14.4
Combustibles	2.6	3.9	2.9	4.0	3.6
Health	10.4	4.3	6.1	4.8	5.5
Diversions	13.8	8.1	5.5	5.9	4.3
Miscellaneous	12.1	14.4	8.3	0.7	0.3
Food	35.4	53.0	58.8	66.1	67.3

* Data used by the courtesy of Dr. Harry W. Hutchinson.

as two-thirds of a family's budgetary outlay must go merely to care of creature needs of the alimentary type, one may be sure that its level of living is low. This remains the pattern, nevertheless, in the plantation sections of São Paulo, where we may be sure the situation is considerably more favorable than it is in most sections of Brazil. In this respect, though, the workers in the mill are in a much better position.

Among the other studies of family budgets in Brazil are those made some time ago by Josué de Castro. His investigations provide some of the facts that are necessary for a real understanding of consumption practices in Brazil. Highly informing are the results of his study,[4] made in 1934, of 500 laboring-class families, distributed in three districts of Recife, capital of the state of Pernambuco. These 500 families contained a total of 2,585 members, or an average of 5.2 persons per family. Daily earnings of all gainfully employed averaged 3$700 per family, and daily expenditures 3$866.[5] Of the expenditures 71.6 per cent went for food and 18.9 per cent for housing, light, and water. This very high percentage of the income going for food is sufficient to indicate that the level of living was very near the margin of subsistence. An examination of the components of the diet and the number and percentage of the families consuming each of them are given in Table xxxvi. These data, supported by firsthand observation and accounts of others who have studied the level of living in the area, indicate that in the Northeast the working classes,

[4] The study is summarized in Josué de Castro, *A Alimentação Brasileira á Luz da Geografia Humana* (Pôrto Alegre, 1937), 134–39.
[5] At this time in Recife a kilo of *charque* (jerked or dried beef) cost 2$400, a liter of beans $600, a liter of mandioca flour $400, a kilo of sugar 1$200, and a small roll of bread $200. Josué de Castro, *As Condições de Vida das Classes Operarias no Recife* (Rio de Janeiro, 1935), 11. In 1934 the *milreis* (written 1$000) was worth about seven cents.

TABLE XXXVI

Foods Consumed by 500 Families of the Laboring
Class in Recife, Pernambuco, 1934 *

| Foods | Families eating each food | |
	Number	Per cent
Beans	498	100
Flour (corn or mandioca)	500	100
Charque (dried beef)	497	100
Coffee	500	100
Sugar	500	100
Bread	422	84
Fresh meat	163	32
Corn (maize)	124	25
Rice	103	20
Milk	97	19
Milk products	76	15
Green vegetables	91	18
Fruits	78	15
Lard	60	12
Dried fish	20	4
Other foods	84	16

* Source: Josué de Castro, *A Alimentação Brasileira á Luz da Geografia Humana* (Pôrto Alegre, 1937), 137.

even in the cities, spend the lion's share of their earnings on food. Even so, they live almost exclusively on beans, mandioca flour or corn meal, dried meat, coffee which is sweetened with sugar, and in most cases bread. In the rural districts, bread is rarely eaten, but of course, the rural folk are enabled to supplement their diet with berries, roots, and game. Nevertheless, any increase in their earnings would surely result in a larger expenditure for food.[6]

[6] Certain of my firsthand observations tend to confirm, and even generalize, these findings of Josué de Castro. My first opportunity of knowing the diet in Brazil's sertões was during a visit to the Hospedaria dos Imigrantes maintained by the state government in São Paulo. This was during March, 1942. The day of the visit more than one hundred migrants had arrived from the Northeast, although this number was much less than daily arrivals a few months previous. Among the migrants was one family whose members had walked all the way from Ceará to Monte Claros in Minas Gerais; they lacked even the slender resources necessary to pay a second-class fare on the river boats running between Juázeiro and Pirapora. I was at the lodging house at supper time, mingled and talked with the new arrivals, was shown through the kitchen and dining hall, and permitted to sample the food. All the guests were served liberal helpings of charque, mandioca flour, rice, and beans. There was a large tin cup full of milk for each child. The service was cafeteria style, but the rolls of bread were placed at each plate. Little of this was eaten, but the rest of the food was consumed with much gusto. Officials at the lodge explained that they were serving the foods to which the people were accustomed and that the migrants would not enjoy a different diet.

At that time I had certain mental reservations concerning the accuracy of this last statement. These were dispelled in the course of some ten months spent in actual travel throughout Brazil during which all modes of conveyance were used and stops for meals and lodging were made under a wide variety of circum-

On the basis of the data obtained in this investigation, Josué de Castro estimated that the daily consumption per person was 62 grams of proteins, 310 grams of carbohydrates, and 13 grams of fats, quantities which would yield a total of only 1,646 calories. Of mineral salts this average daily consumption of food would include only .4 grams of calcium and .0055 grams of iron.[7] The author concludes that such a diet is deficient in calories, proteins, calcium, and iron and that it is also lacking in vitamins.[8]

These data are for only one class, in one city, in only one of the nation's regions. De Castro also summarized data from studies made in São Paulo which indicate that the dietary practices there, while better than in Recife, also resulted in unsatisfactory nutrition.[9] "It is not possible, from a knowledge of these two regions," he generalizes, "to deduce what are the defects of the diet in the whole of Brazil, but without abuse of logic it is possible to affirm that in all Brazil it is defective." [10]

In 1939 De Castro published a third and enlarged edition of his earlier work, *O Problema da Alimentação no Brasil*.[11] As an appendix to this, he gave the preliminary results of some researches undertaken in 1936 by the Departamento Nacional de Saúde (National Department of Health). Here he summarized data contained in 12,106 budgetary schedules taken from families in the Federal District. Of the families included in the study, 15 per cent lived in the better residential area in Rio de Janeiro; 21 per cent in the more commercial part of the city; 16.5 per cent in the more industrial sections; and 47.5 per cent in the residential areas of the less well-to-do inhabitants. This study has the merit of including all classes in the population, not merely laboring-class families as the one of Recife. Urban, suburban, and a few rural families were all included in the project, although, of course, the data are all for the area in and about Brazil's former federal capital. The 12,106 families included a total of 60,149 members. Classified according to economic status, 23 per cent of the cases fell in the group in which the total earnings of the family

stances. Even ignoring the cases in which only rice, or mandioca, beans, and coffee were available, meals have been taken at dozens of small pensions and hotels. At these, frequently one could eat liberally of meats, including chicken, and, if in the South, of potatoes and even lettuce, tomatoes, and water cress, in addition to the beans. Never did it cease to be an element of surprise to see Brazilian fellow travelers pass by the meat and vegetables, while helping themselves liberally two and even three times to the rice and beans. Still valid seems to be Burton's generalization, "I will observe at once that neither gourmand or gourmet should visit the South American interior, especially the Highlands of the Brazil." *The Highlands of the Brazil*, I, 63.

[7] De Castro, *A Alimentação Brasileira á Luz da Geografia Humana*, 139. The author gives the amounts of these elements that the average diet should contain: 100 grams of proteins, 500 grams of carbohydrates, 36 grams of fats, 1 gram of calcium, 1 gram of phosphorus, and .015 gram of iron. In this standard the total calories would amount to 2,800. *Ibid.*, 147.

[8] Josué de Castro set forth in some detail the foods of each region that might be utilized to attain the desired goal. *Ibid.*, 146–65.

[9] *Ibid.*, 139 ff.

[10] *Ibid.*, 142.

[11] This edition was published in São Paulo, 1939.

were less than 300$ (milreis) per month; 47 per cent in the group earning between 300$ and 500$ monthly; 25 per cent in the class whose members' earnings totaled between 500$ and 1,000$ or more.[12] For the entire group of families taken together, 54 per cent of the income was spent on food, and 25 per cent on housing. The proportion of the family income going for food amounted to 47 per cent in the better residential area, 50 per cent in the industrial zone, 57 per cent in the commercial zone and also 57 per cent in the poorer residential districts.

It is evident that the satisfaction of mere creature needs did not pre-empt such a large share of the family's income in Rio de Janeiro as it did in Recife and that the level of living was higher in the nation's capital than in Pernambuco's metropolis. Nevertheless, by the time food and shelter were provided, even the Carioca family had but a meager sum left to spend on clothing, advancement, and the numerous material and nonmaterial attractions offered by Rio's glittering shops and showplaces.

Josué de Castro's analysis of the dietary situation in these Rio de Janeiro families showed an average consumption of 2,770 calories per person, composed of foods that would yield 116 grams of proteins, 425 grams of carbohydrates, and 88 grams of fat per person. He found that 84 per cent of all families spent part of their earnings for milk, 60 per cent bought eggs, 88 per cent fresh meat, 94 per cent vegetables or greens, and 86 per cent fruits. On the basis of these data it was concluded that there was on the average no deficiency in the total amount of food consumed in Rio de Janeiro, but that proteins and fats might well be reduced in favor of more carbohydrates, minerals, and vitamins. The study concluded with the significant statement that "the dietary regime in Rio de Janeiro may be considered then, incomplete and unbalanced, having a deficiency of essential minerals and vitamins and presenting inadequate proportions of its organic compounds." [13]

These researches reported on in the books of Josué de Castro give some basis for evaluating the level of living and the adequacy of the diet in the larger cities of Brazil. Anything comparable for the rural areas, in which live the overwhelming proportion of the members of Brazil's population, is not available. This does not mean that informed Brazilians do not think of the average rural worker as living on a very low level, underfed, and malnourished. On the contrary, one cannot read far in Brazil's social and economic literature without encountering such statements as the following:

The prosperous, healthy and happy Brazilians who live in the large cities, enjoying the comforts of civilization, should constantly remember the millions of human beings, sons of the same land, their brothers by blood, religion and language, who in the interior of Brazil are dragging out a painful life in sickness, misery and want. And to the ears of those in governmental positions these truths should be cried out insistently,

[12] In 1939 the milreis was worth about five cents.
[13] De Castro, *O Problema da Alimentação no Brasil*, 244.

shouted loudly, repeated time and again, to the end that the custodians of public money should be convinced once and for all that in our country it is an unpardonable crime to build palaces, purchase luxurious automobiles, maintain expensive embassies abroad, and expend public funds on voluptuous and superfluous things, while millions of Brazilians in all our interior zones are imploring instruction, shoes, bread, and medicines.[14]

Another representative writer says:

. . . the Brazilian whom almost all the agents of these colonizing peoples [i. e., the Germans, Italians, and Poles of southern Brazil] vilify in hundreds of documents which they have prepared and we have seized—designating him as a mediocre, useless, lazy, Negro or mulatto—this hero of 400 years, *although generally suffering from worms, undernourishment, lack of productive work,* still carries on the ceaseless struggle and at least has the sacred qualities of perseverance, tenacity, moral resistance, resignation, and an intellectual constitution that is superior, lively and understanding and which [when] well used throws other peoples off their course.[15]

And Josué de Castro, himself, in one of his later works in which he sought to generalize his conclusions for Brazil as a whole, has written:

Insufficient production, deficient distribution, bad dietary habits growing out of a routinized deformation of the healthy nutritive instinct, tabus and dietary restrictions of all types, and, finally, the limited purchasing power of the masses which makes the cost of protective foods prohibitive for their family budgets—all of these economic and social causes, working together in a manner that is most unfavorable to the dietary needs of the collectivity, makes the prevailing type of diet in Brazil one of the most precarious in the world.[16]

In the absence of systematic studies of rural areas, generalizations based upon experience must be relied on. A release from the Information Service of the Brazilian Ministry of Agriculture, February 17, 1942, said:

Strange to say it is the privileged rural man, to whom the soil gives everything, who is the worst nourished.

In the extreme north of Brazil, fish represents the main item in the diet, followed by turtle meat and mandioca. In the northeastern states the diet of the rural man consists mainly of dried meat, mandioca flour or corn meal, goat meat, bananas, coconuts, and other tropical fruits. Droughts reduce the food still more [to certain roots and fruits in the region].

In São Paulo and Minas Gerais, corn meal, beans, beef, pork, rice, and certain vegetables constitute the bulk of the diet.

In the south, the diet consists largely of beef, dried meat, beans, and mandioca. Coffee and mate are almost always used by the rural man.

Thus, we observe the deficiencies of the diets in all of the regions mentioned, in spite of the fact that the rural Brazilian has other foods at hand, which, because he lacks the knowledge of their virtues, he does not use.

[14] João Pinheiro Filho, *Problemas Brasileiros* (Rio de Janeiro, 1938), 208–209.

[15] Hugo Bethlem, *Vale do Itajaí* (Rio de Janeiro, 1939), 15–16. The italics are not in the original.

[16] Josué de Castro, *Geografia da Fome: A Fome no Brasil* (Rio de Janeiro, 1946), 296–97. Cf. *id., The Geography of Hunger* (Boston, 1952), Chap. III.

There are certain fragmentary data which help to give form and substance to such general statements. For example, Gileno dé Carlí, who in 1940 studied the wages paid by eight sugar usinas in Pernambuco, furnishes a detailed list of the purchases made by a field worker who received 2$500 per day. (The wages of field workers varied from 2$000 to 3$500.) This laborer's family consisted of a wife and four children. The 14$900 (roughly 75 cents) earned in a week they spent as follows: for beans, $900; mandioca flour or corn meal, 4$800; charque, 6$000; soap, $500; sugar, 1$200; coffee, $500; tobacco, $400; and rum, $600. After pointing out that the field worker supplemented these purchases made with home-produced foods, the investigator adds: "In spite of all, earning little as he does and prolific as he is, there is always misery in the house of the rural worker." [17] Elsewhere Dé Carlí states his conclusion that the amount of food consumed by the worker's family is strictly dependent on the wages he is paid.

One of the Schmidt studies of São Paulo is informing concerning the more significant elements in the level of living in that state, where in all probability the average is about the highest in Brazil. The introduction to this study by Mario de Sampaio Ferraz, director of the state's Department of Agricultural Publicity, says: "That which is valuable, that which makes for progress, is not the opulence of a dozen or two men, but the average level of the general well-being. . . . That which interests the human community is not the stupendous figures of the potentates, but the good 'average standing' of every one, a significant average per capita production, including in it all sectors of activity." [18] Schmidt, on the basis of intimate acquaintance with the statistical data gathered by the São Paulo Agricultural Service, by far the best in Brazil, and with his insight sharpened and judgment tempered by long excursions through the interior, set himself to analyzing the diet, hygiene, dress, and habitation —the most significant components in the level of living—of the rural inhabitant.

The diet, he says, is responsible for a large share of the misery that exists. "Man feeds himself badly because he earns little. Reduced earnings are the result of weak productive capacity, and this comes from lowered organic resistance. Thus is created a vicious circle, a way out of which needs to be determined, either by the raising of wages, by educating the worker, or by any means whatsoever."

Hygiene also "leaves a great deal to be desired and is another precarious situation in which the rural population lives." The caboclo's close contact with nature gives him great organic resistance, and his ailments are not of alarming gravity. "That which is alarming is the form and the perpetuity of them. Worms, easily eradicated, is the most common of the ailments, and yet they accompany the individual from the early days of infancy to old age."

Poor clothing results in moral and mental depression. It gives one

[17] Dé Carlí, *Aspectos Açucareiros de Pernambuco*, 19–20.
[18] Schmidt, *O Meio Rural*, 3.

a feeling of inferiority even among his equals. "In the regions where the climate is cold," and there are many of them in São Paulo, "much energy is consumed, and stolen from work, in passing the interminable winter nights, awake, huddled about a brazier."

"The house of our rural inhabitant always leaves something to desire in every respect." Commonly, it is poorer than necessitated by the resources of its inhabitants. Schmidt summarizes: "Poorly fed, sick, ragged, and almost without shelter, it is not possible to demand from our country man more than he produces." [19]

Finally, there is the comprehensive material gathered and analyzed in 1938–1939, on which the nation's minimum wage scales were based. Although these data do not give the foods for which expenditures were made, they do include the total per capita monthly expenditures for food and the proportion of all expenses for food. These are the two most significant items in all the long list of data gathered in standard-of-living studies. Fortunately, every state was included in the investigation, and the materials for the state capital were kept separate from those for the other, the "interior" portions of each commonwealth. The scope of the study is indicated by the total of 251,060 persons in the families which resided in the capitals, and 333,278 persons in households of the interior areas. Unfortunately, the data as published have not been accompanied with the essential explanatory material, or tabulated in a manner that would enable them to be of most use. However, it is possible to extract from them some figures which show the average per capita expenditures for food and the percentages of all money spent that went for food. These data are presented in Table xxxvii. The totals showing the numbers of persons included in the families studied are also included. Although it is not specifically stated, we may be fairly certain that the families included are those of the laboring class.

In view of the length of time that has passed since these materials were collected, the present writer will comment very little about them. It does seem necessary, however, to stress that some of the percentages representing the expenditures for food are extremely high. As pointed out above, this indicator is an important one. Therefore, the fact that the families of the laboring class in the capitals of Alagôas, Paraíba, and Sergipe and in the interior portions of Alagôas, Amazonas, Bahia, Maranhão, Paraíba, Pernambuco, Rio Grande do Norte, and Sergipe show recorded expenditures of more than 70 per cent of the entire family budget for food alone must be interpreted to mean that they live very near the level of mere subsistence. In view of what is already known concerning the dietary situations in Rio de Janeiro and Recife, a comparison of the indexes for these two with those for other cities and for the interior sections of the various states leads inevitably to the conclusion that a very large proportion of the Brazilian working class must be seriously undernourished and that the level of living is extremely low. In turn, de-

[19] *Ibid.*, 38–39.

TABLE XXXVII

Per Capita Monthly Expenditures for Food, and Food Costs as a
Percentage of Total Family Expenditures in Capitals and
*Interior Districts, 1940 ***

State	Monthly expenditures per person for food		Food costs as a percentage of total expenditures		Number of persons in families studied	
	Capital	Interior	Capital	Interior	Capital	Interior
Alagôas	33$900	21$300	70.9	87.3	5,694	21,405
Amazonas	35$700	32$300	56.5	84.6	3,409	708
Bahia	24$900	22$600	69.4	73.7	18,296	14,803
Ceará	20$800	17$300	58.9	68.7	7,389	5,642
Espírito Santo	41$000	21$600	68.3	63.2	3,406	16,541
Goiás	34$600	28$400	59.0	55.3	1,257	2,473
Maranhão	25$400	23$800	63.4	77.0	4,011	3,866
Mato Grosso	28$500	29$700	48.7	49.6	391	888
Minas Gerais	28$100	28$300	49.4	58.4	8,968	40,144
Pará	27$300	26$200	67.5	74.7	11,750	1,516
Paraíba	30$200	22$100	80.5	83.8	4,638	18,302
Paraná	43$900	32$300	58.6	61.6	3,354	11,482
Pernambuco	27$100	21$800	68.7	79.3	25,936	24,399
Piauí	31$600	28$200	67.2	69.0	454	1,671
Rio de Janeiro	37$300	29$000	54.8	60.0	6,474	44,906
Rio Grande do Norte	24$600	25$800	52.0	72.2	2,222	12,342
Rio Grande do Sul	47$900	44$600	61.7	69.5	13,280	39,015
Santa Catarina	30$700	32$600	61.8	65.1	2,940	12,203
São Paulo	51$100	41$900	54.9	61.4	65,532	49,648
Sergipe	29$600	18$400	75.8	74.2	2,554	11,325
Distrito Federal	43$500	—	46.5	—	59,285	—

* Source: *Salário Minimo* (Rio de Janeiro, 1940), I, 125–253. In 1940 1$ (one milreis) was worth about five cents.

ficient and poorly balanced diet is certainly reflected in decreased ability and desire to engage in sustained productive activities, a fatalistic acceptance of their lot in life, or a low standard of living. This is a vicious series, similar to that observed in parts of the United States, which only the wisest and most strenuous efforts can break. However, the failure of the data to reveal regional differences, which seem to thrust themselves at the visitor who travels throughout Brazil, probably means that the groups sampled in one part of the country are not strictly comparable with those in another. One cannot go throughout the interior of Brazil without being convinced that the levels and standards of living in the North and Northeast are lower than those in other sections of the country. Also, repeated visits to Brazil's greatest cities since 1939, including a stay in 1946 when serious food riots broke out in Rio de Janeiro, have left the writer with the impression that the situation of the masses is becoming

Caboclos Building Their Home, Ubatuba, São Paulo

progressively worse. Today actual hunger is a factor of prime importance in Brazil's great population centers.

To an increasing degree in recent decades, the censuses of various countries have been providing information about household facilities that could be used in order to secure useful indicators of variations in levels of living within the respective countries. In Brazil the 1950 census of housing gathered important materials showing the numbers of dwellings in each state, and in the urban, suburban, and rural portions of each, which were supplied with running water and electricity and which were equipped with indoor toilets. The counts at that time showed that only 15.6 per cent of the homes in Brazil were supplied with running water, 24.6 per cent served by electricity, and 33.0 per cent equipped with indoor toilets.

Naturally, all of these important features of modern living were much more prevalent in towns and cities than they were in the rural areas. Thus 49.8 per cent of the urban homes had running water, 69.9 per cent were served by electricity, and 78.5 per cent possessed indoor toilets; whereas the corresponding percentages for rural homes were only 1.4, 3.6, and 10.4, respectively. On all three scores the suburban homes were intermediate. Far from reflecting a situation in which the suburbanites enjoy a high and perhaps the highest level of living in the society, such as seems to be the case in the United States, these data indicate that Brazilian suburban homes resemble the rural fully as much as the urban dwellings in Brazil. Thus the proportions of such homes having the conveniences and facilities involved were as follows: running water, 19.8 per cent; electricity, 39.1 per cent; and indoor toilets, 56.2 per cent. This emphasizes a point made elsewhere in this volume to the effect that many of the districts on the peripheries of Brazilian cities are those in which the way of life is most precarious.

In addition to the variations between rural and urban areas with respect to the three indicators under consideration, there also are some very striking regional differences. See Figures 20, 21, and 22. Certainly these data are strictly in line with the proposition that the level of living is highest in the states of Guanabara, São Paulo, Paraná, Santa Catarina, and Rio Grande do Sul and lowest in the northeastern region and the neighboring state of Bahia.

With the data from the 1950 censuses of population and housing it also is possible to calculate ratios between population and rooms within the dwellings and between population and the numbers of bedrooms in use. See Tables xxxviii and xxxix. These materials, and especially the indexes of population to bedrooms, seem to indicate that a large proportion of Brazilian families live in very crowded quarters.

The information gathered in the housing census also included data about the tenure rights of the families to the homes in which they were living. The classification employed, however, included only three categories: ownership, tenancy, and "other." This third class consists largely of the various arrangements under which living quarters are supplied to the many types of agricultural laborers (colonos, agregados, and so forth) as one of the perquisites in connection with their employment.

Caboclo Family and House. This House Type Predominates in the Mountainous Districts between Rio de Janeiro and São Paulo and Is Found throughout Brazil.

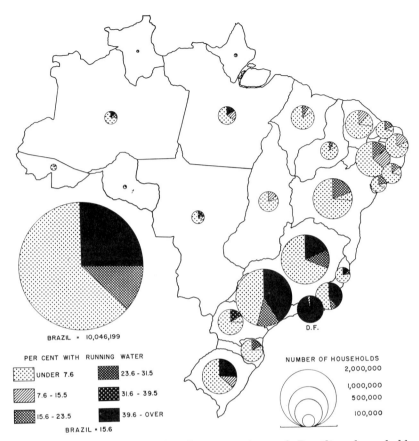

PER CENT WITH RUNNING WATER

UNDER 7.6		23.6 - 31.5	
7.6 - 15.5		31.6 - 39.5	
15.6 - 23.5		39.6 - OVER	

BRAZIL = 15.6

BRAZIL = 10,046,199

NUMBER OF HOUSEHOLDS

2,000,000
1,000,000
500,000
100,000

FIGURE 20. Variations in the proportions of Brazilian households served by running water in the home, 1950, by states and rural-urban residence. (Starting at 12:00 o'clock and reading clockwise, the segments of the circles represent the urban, suburban, and rural categories, respectively.)

Slightly more than one-half (52.1 per cent) of all Brazilian families owned their homes, according to the 1950 enumeration, and another 23.1 per cent were renters. One out of four, though, or 24.8 per cent, were classified in the "other" tenure category, indicating for the most part that they were granted the use of quarters by the proprietors of the same on some basis that did not qualify as a rental contract. Undoubtedly the lion's share of these were employees or other retainers of those owning large landed estates. Ownership and renting were the predominant types of tenure of the householders living in urban and suburban districts, where 44.0 and 51.0 per cent, respectively, were classified as owners, and 50.1 and 40.6 per cent as renters. These proportions reflect, in turn, the prevalence of rental apartments in the major cities and the abundance of homemade shacks on the peripheries of the same.

For Brazil as a whole the proportion of home owners is highest

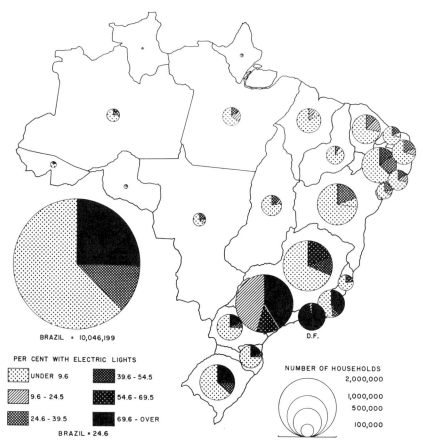

BRAZIL = 10,046,199

PER CENT WITH ELECTRIC LIGHTS

UNDER 9.6   39.6 - 54.5

9.6 - 24.5   54.6 - 69.5

24.6 - 39.5   69.6 - OVER

BRAZIL = 24.6

NUMBER OF HOUSEHOLDS
2,000,000
1,000,000
500,000
100,000

FIGURE 21. Variations in the proportions of Brazilian households served by electricity, 1950, by states and rural-urban residence. (Starting at 12:00 o'clock and reading clockwise, the segments of the circles represent the urban, suburban, and rural categories, respectively.)

(55.6 per cent) in the rural areas, but rental contracts are little used except in the cities and suburban areas. Only 9.0 per cent of the rural families were classified as renters. On the other hand, as is to be expected, the practice of granting the use of living quarters as one of the perquisites in connection with the employment of agricultural laborers, makes for a high proportion of those in the "other" tenure category throughout the rural areas. Thus the proportion of all families in this particular class rises from only 5.9 per cent in urban districts, to 8.4 per cent in suburban sections, to 35.4 per cent in rural areas. Fuller information on the absolute and relative importance of this tenure group in each of the states in the federation is presented in Figure 23. It should be stressed, though, that of the 2,486,448 Brazilian families who occupy their homes under such arrangements, 500,401 were reported for the rural areas of São

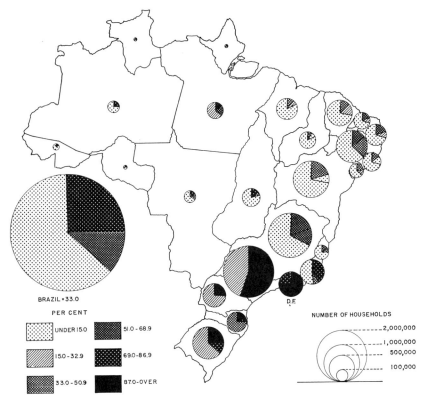

BRAZIL = 33.0

PER CENT

UNDER 15.0		51.0 - 68.9
15.0 - 32.9		69.0 - 86.9
33.0 - 50.9		87.0 - OVER

NUMBER OF HOUSEHOLDS

2,000,000
1,000,000
500,000
100,000

D.F.

FIGURE 22. Variations in the proportions of Brazilian households served by indoor toilets, 1950, by states and rural-urban residence. (Starting at 12:00 o'clock and reading clockwise, the segments of the circles represent the urban, suburban, and rural categories, respectively.)

Paulo, 414,911 for those of Minas Gerais, 188,548 for those of Bahia, and 161,326 for those of Pernambuco.

FACTORS CAUSING VARIATIONS

As suggested above, the study of standards and levels of living in Brazil is still in its infancy. But, although all of the details of the complex of factors that have contributed to the present low level on which the bulk of the Brazilian population is living are not known, still it is possible to indicate in a general way the manner in which some of the more important determinants have worked and continue to operate. Probably the more important factors may be reduced to the three following categories: (1) a very high ratio of dependents to contributors or producers, (2) the very low production per worker, and (3) the lavish use of labor in the production process which results in labor's being entitled to a comparatively small proportion of the

TABLE XXXVIII

*Population Residing in Private Households, Classified According to Number of Rooms in Dwelling, 1950 ***

Number of rooms per dwelling	Number of dwellings	Persons living in dwelling of stated size		
		Number	Per cent	Persons per room
Total	9,943,773	51,065,068	100.0	1.05
1	273,236	755,165	1.5	2.76
2	969,016	3,597,770	7.0	1.86
3	2,033,371	8,890,535	17.4	1.46
4	2,347,783	11,677,083	22.9	1.24
5	1,702,153	9,497,949	18.6	1.12
6	1,156,259	6,971,603	13.7	1.00
7	539,459	3,376,219	6.6	0.89
8	389,400	2,559,026	5.0	0.82
9	203,362	1,366,930	2.7	0.75
10	121,962	843,085	1.6	0.69
11 and over	207,772	1,529,703	3.0	0.56 †

* Compiled and computed from data in "Censo Demográfico," VI *Recenseamento Geral do Brasil, 1950*, I (Rio de Janeiro, 1956), 295.
† Estimated.

TABLE XXXIX

*Population Residing in Private Households, Classified According to Number of Bedrooms per Dwelling, 1950 ***

Number of bedrooms per dwelling	Number of dwellings	Persons living in dwellings		Persons per bedroom
		Number	Per cent	
Total	10,046,199	51,944,397	100.0	2.5
1	3,276,178	11,130,873	21.4	3.4
2	3,944,946	21,032,394	40.5	2.8
3	1,840,743	12,756,526	24.5	2.3
4	615,676	4,875,537	9.4	2.0
5	157,792	1,331,754	2.6	1.7
6	62,289	532,466	1.0	1.4
7	17,697	148,502	0.3	1.2
8	9,797	80,077	0.2	1.0
9	3,346	25,740	0.1	0.9
10	2,002	14,433	†	0.7
11 and over	2,458	16,095	†	0.5

* Compiled and computed from data in "Censo Demográfico," VI *Recenseamento Geral do Brasil, 1950*, I (Rio de Janeiro, 1956), 295.
† Less than 0.1 per cent.

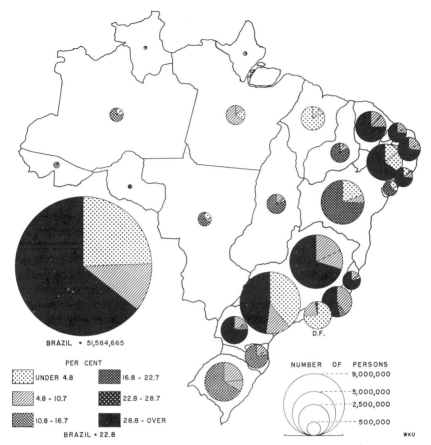

FIGURE 23. Variations in the proportions of Brazilian families whose tenure is neither that of owner nor renter, 1950, by states and rural-urban residence. (Starting at 12:00 o'clock and reading clockwise, the segments of the circles represent the urban, suburban, and rural categories, respectively.)

product and in the necessity of dividing this reduced share among many workers. These will be considered in order.

High Ratio of Dependents to Contributors. There can be no doubt that Brazil's standard of living is adversely affected by the high ratio of dependents to contributors that prevails in the population. In a large measure this is purely demographic, the inevitable result in a country where the birth rate and the death rate are both very high. This can result only in a situation wherein the number of children is exceedingly high in proportion to the persons of working or productive age. This is certain to occur in a country having both a very high birth rate and a high death rate, unless strong immigration is constantly replenishing the people of active working age. The detailed

221

data from which this generalization arises have already been presented in the chapters dealing with composition and the vital processes of the population.

Another factor that serves to increase the number of consumers in relation to the proportion of workers is the high degree of social stratification that prevails in the Brazilian population. The aristocratic tradition by no means came to an end with the abdication of the emperor. It is true that many of the members of the distinguished families who are descended from the barons and counts of the 1880's now perform essential economic functions in Brazilian society, but it is also true that the inheritance of wealth and social position have permitted many members of Brazil's elite class to live a life of ostentation while making no substantial contribution to the national wealth and income. The presence of such "drones" also tends to swell the number of dependents to contributors. Furthermore, because of the generous size of the "helpings" which they receive out of the relatively small national income, the presence of these nonproductive elements in the population has a depressing effect on the general level of living far out of proportion to their numbers.

Low Production per Worker. Another series of factors that determine the relatively low level or standard of living prevailing in Brazil includes all the numerous social, economic, and cultural determinants that make for low productivity per worker.

1. *Concentration of Landownership.*—Because such a large proportion of Brazil's population is rural and therefore dependent on agricultural and collecting enterprises for a livelihood, it seems logical to begin the enumeration of these by mentioning the concentration of landownership and control. As has been indicated in another place, Brazil is the land of large fazendas, a country in which the great bulk of all the people fall in the category of agricultural laborers. In Brazil, as elsewhere, the status of agricultural labor is perhaps the least desirable one in the entire social scale. Probably it is impossible for any system of large agricultural estates to result in a high standard of living for the workers. Certainly it seems beyond all possibility of dispute that the very unsatisfactory standard of Brazil's working masses is directly due to the concentration of landownership and control that has prevailed from the first settlement of the country until the present time. Even though the slave might have fled the fazenda and joined with others in a quilombo (community of fugitive slaves) he still lacked the knowledge and skills essential for independent existence as a farmer. The miserable lot of the swarms of squatters (posseiros) throughout Brazil's vast interior is mute testimony to the validity of this statement.

The reasons for the unfavorable economic and social status of the farm laborer are, in turn, not difficult to discover. Agricultural labor cannot be done in a factory building where the watchful eye of a supervisor can take account of the activities of many workers or on huge assembly lines where the failure to perform specialized tasks in the manner prescribed and time allowed immediately directs the supervisor's attention to the derelict employee. In most agricultural operations a good combination of labor and management is possible only where the two functions are both performed by the same individual. For the most part this is done on the family-operated and family-worked farm. Despite the presence of overseers, major domos, and other bosses of one kind or another, the plantation system is almost sure to result in the sparing use of management and the lavish use of labor in the productive process. This point will receive further attention below.

As has already been indicated, the agricultural laborer loses in two respects when large-scale agricultural operations dictate that he shall perform only the functions of the laborer and not those of the manager. Under these circumstances the head of the rural family is entitled to and receives only the share of the product that belongs to labor. Unlike the operator of a small farm, be he owner or renter, such a worker is not entitled to receive any remuneration for the managerial ability in this line which he might possibly develop. His potentialities as a manager go to waste, and in the deadening process of routine work, experience demonstrates that they also waste away.

There are also many other reasons for the low production per worker. When, as in Brazil, there is concentration of landownership and control and when the bulk of the rural people are found in the farm labor category, there are few stimuli propelling the individual to attempt to climb the social ladder. Social pressures urge resignation to or acceptance of one's lot, rather than continued effort to better one's condition. Social ostracism is likely to result from trying to be better than one's fellows rather than from failing to "keep up with the Joneses." Of such an innovator his Brazilian fellows are likely to say, "He would like to encircle the world with legs that have never encompassed a horse." Since the operation of the agricultural ladder would destroy the Brazilian fazenda system in a single generation, its persistence throughout the centuries is in itself sufficient evidence that the opportunities and propulsions to advance have not been sufficient to stimulate the Brazilian lower classes. The extra effort called forth by such social climbing has not contributed to increase the goods and services that are consumed by the Brazilian population.

Probably the most tragic effect of the concentration of landownership and control prevailing in Brazil is the fact that it perpetuates a rural population that is incapable of exercising economic functions other than those of the laborer. In other countries where the estates are built up through the process of dispossessing small owner-operators and consolidating their former holdings into large plantations, as occurred throughout parts of our own Southland, the process has first produced and then perpetuated such a class. Brazil skipped the first of these stages almost entirely: she obtained the laboring class for her agriculture by enslaving the Indians and importing Negro slaves from Africa. Both of these peoples lacked most of the skills involved in the management of agricultural enterprises, so that the present-day rural Brazilian population could have received very little in management skills from them had the system of slavery never confined them to the sugar engenhos and cattle fazendas. Nor did they receive, as a cultural heritage from those of their white ancestors who mingled their blood with that of the darker slaves, any substantial contributions to help overcome the deficiency. Very few traits of Europe's peasant agriculture were able to sift through Brazil's coastal sugar plantations into the vast interior regions. In summary it should be stated that the net effect of the concentration of landownership and control in Brazil is to lower the level of living of the population. By relegating the bulk of the people to the status of farm labor the system results in a poor combination of labor, capital, and management; it gives to most breadwinners only a share in the product that might go to labor; it fails to use the desire to better one's self as a propulsion to steady, efficient labor and thrift; and it produces generation after generation of people who are lacking in a knowledge of managerial skills and thrifty capitalistic attitudes.

2. *Deficiencies in the Diet.*—Poor diet, one of the leading factors in the poor health situation which is discussed elsewhere in this volume, also renders much of the population incapable of sustained work activities. Loss of efficiency and initiative may be induced by a deficient diet, even though the workers are not reduced to complete disability.

That the Brazilian diet is deficient in essential nutritive elements, often lacking in quantity and almost always in quality, seems to have been established by Brazilian scholars and scientists. Much of their data has been presented above. Here it is important to consider these materials as they relate to the productive capacities of the population. This means a consideration of the adequacy of the diet. Spurred on by the widespread acceptance of the belief that tropical countries, including Brazil, were backward because of climatic influences and because of race mixture, a number of Brazil's leading scientists and scholars have advanced the thesis that in reality the responsible factors are those of diet and disease, especially malaria and hookworm. Says E. Roquette-Pinto: "I continue, however, to preach the same sermon as ever: the evils of race mixture are the evils of hunger and misery." [20] If he, Josué de Castro, and other scholars have not definitely disproved the cases for climatic determinism and physical deterioration of the ethnic stock being brought about by interracial crossing, they have at least thrown a great deal of light upon the dietary problems of Brazil.

One of the best summaries of the situation, and one that makes the necessary allowances for differences between the social classes, is that by Ruy Coutinho. After indicating that hygiene, sanitation, economic situation, and diet (not the lack of Nordic blood) are the basis

[20] Josué de Castro, *Alimentação e Raça* (Rio de Janeiro, 1936), preface.

of the unsatisfactory showing of tropical peoples, he summarizes the dietary situation in Brazil.

If in countries with a high economic and cultural level, such as the United States, England and Canada, there is a large proportion of malnourished people, in countries such as Brazil the proportion must be excessive. In reality, observation reveals how inferior is the nutritional level of the Brazilian. The dietary and hygienic conditions of our poorer classes are miserable, a result of their insufficient wages. They are undernourished—their diet is lacking in quantity and quality.

Their diet is insufficient in calories, with a low percentage of proteins, notably those of class one; deficient in vitamins and mineral salts. These lower classes have as nourishment mandioca flour, dried meat or fish, three poor foods; they are, however, the only ones obtainable with their incomes, although sometimes they are supplemented by beans, already a luxury, and bacon.[21]

The same author also summarizes the dietary position of the middle classes. "Even the Brazilian of the middle class is badly nourished. He uses cereals and sweets in excess, to the exclusion of other dietary elements of greater nutritional value. We do not have the habit of eating salads, and sweets take preference over fruits." [22]

Indeed, according to this authority, not even Brazil's well-to-do classes eat wisely of a well-balanced diet.

In Brazil the wealthy class, although it eats much, does not eat well. Its members do not understand how to nourish themselves. If they do not live on dried meat, dried fish, corn meal or mandioca flour and beans, . . . they eat to excess such foods as *feijoadas* [beans, meats, vegetables, and so on, served over rice], pungent gravies, fatty dishes, conserved meats and vegetables, fine "foie gras" and "leberwurst.". . . In this way the wealthy use an excess of fats and proteins to the neglect of vitamins and mineral salts. These latter elements are furnished almost exclusively by eggs, milk, and fresh fruits and vegetables—foods which enter in relatively small proportions into the diet of the wealthy, who prefer preserves, sweets, and pastries.[23]

Like others who know the situation, Josué de Castro concluded that Brazil's dietary problem is a large one and that malnutrition paralyzes the nation's productive efforts.

What we wish to emphasize is that this diet has a painful weight in the economy of the nation, paralyzing, even stealing, the larger part of its human capital, provoking unobtrusively the major portion of the obstacles which appear to be the work of the climate. The climate would permit, through the richness of the crops that can be grown, by the rational utilization of our natural reserves of nutrition, a diet that is greater and better balanced.[24]

Finally, it is not amiss to ask why the food habits and diets in such a productive land as Brazil are so poor in comparison with those of

---

[21] Ruy Coutinho, *Valor Social da Alimentação* (Rio de Janeiro, 1937), 26–27.

[22] *Ibid.*, 30–31.

[23] *Ibid.*, 35–36. For a discussion of the importance of sugar and preserves in the diet of the Northeast, see Freyre, *Nordeste*, 123 ff.

[24] De Castro, *A Alimentação Brasileira á Luz da Geografia Humana*, 133.

the less favored mother country of Portugal. Climate, of course, may be invoked, or race, but most Brazilian sociologists and anthropologists are not content with such "lazy man's" explanations. They indicate that the Portuguese colonists who settled Brazil failed to retain the food habits and diet which the Portuguese had acquired in their contacts with warm climates and Mohammedan peoples. In Brazil wheat flour was replaced by that made of mandioca,[25] and the cultivation of sugar cane was practiced to the exclusion of all the various fruits and vegetables that formerly occupied such an important part of the diet.

Furthermore, preoccupied with the ambition of gaining quick riches, of making himself master of the land, its gold and its treasures, the colonist, in place of continuing in the new country the routine of customary crops which gave him the materials for a complete diet, threw himself body and soul either into the exclusive cultivation of sugar cane, which made him the rich and respected master of an engenho, or into the search for the hidden veins filled with gold. And master of sugar plantation or miner, the colonist neglected completely his diet, resulting in a great lowering of the dietary level in Brazil.[26]

An interesting detail which helps to illustrate the poverty of agricultural skills and practices resulting from the break with tradition and from the fact that all agricultural knowledge reaching interior Brazil was sifted through the system of monoculture practiced in the coastal areas is given in the following quotation from Mawe:

We left this peaceful abode; and, advancing for six miles through thickets and forests, and over some plain land, we reached a farm called St. Antonio, belonging to a widow named Dona Ana, who is noted through-

[25] Technically, it was only in the North of Brazil that mandioca became the staff of life, for corn meal gained this position in the South. This prevalence of corn meal in the diet of southern Brazil and of mandioca in northern Brazil is of long standing. "The inhabitants of this province [São Paulo] conceive the mandioca flour to be unwholesome, as those of the northern capitanias do maize flour." Von Spix and von Martius, *Travels in Brazil, 1817–1820*, II, 16.

[26] De Castro, *A Alimentação Brasileira á Luz da Geografia Humana*, 127. Read in conjunction with these summary statements of Josué de Castro, the description of diets in Minas Gerais at the opening of the nineteenth century as given by Mawe are interesting.

"The general diet of the country-people in this land of Canaan is somewhat similar to that of the miners in the vicinity of St. Paul's, already described. The master, his steward, and the overseers, sit down to a breakfast of kidney beans of a black colour, boiled, which they mix with the flour of Indian corn, and eat with a little dry pork, fried or boiled. The dinner generally consists, also, of a bit of pork or bacon boiled, the water from which is poured upon a dish of the flour above-mentioned, thus forming a stiff pudding. A large quantity (above half a peck) of this food is poured in a heap on the table, and a great dish of boiled beans is set upon it. Each person helps himself in the readiest way, there being only one knife, which is often dispensed with. A plate or two of colewort on cabbage leaves completes the repast. The food is commonly served up in the earthen vessels used for cooking it; sometimes on pewter dishes. The general beverage is water. At supper nothing is seen but large quantities of boiled greens, with a bit of poor bacon to flavour them. On any festive occasion, or when strangers appear, the dinner or supper is improved by the addition of a stewed fowl. The food prepared for the negroes is Indian corn-flour, mixed with hot water, in which a bit of pork has been boiled. This dish serves both for breakfast and supper. Their dinner consists of beans boiled in the same way." *Travels in the Interior of Brazil*, 203–204; see also *ibid.*, 29, 120–21, and 130.

out the country, for making excellent butter and cheese. The dwelling is of two stories, and neat, but very inconvenient. This good lady gave me a hearty repast, of milk, and we entered into some conversation respecting her dairy, in which I learned that she knew of no other mode of making butter, than that of agitating the cream in a jar or bottle; and her knowledge of cheese-making was equally defective.[27]

Even late in the nineteenth century the traveler who came upon a place where he could obtain milk and butter found it worthy of comment. Thus the Southerners Frank M. McMullen and William Bowen, who submitted a report on the Cananéia area of São Paulo to the Brazilian Minister of Agriculture in 1866, commented as follows:

Following up the valley some two and a half miles, we reached the comfortable dwelling of Mr. Van der Hoff, where we stopped for the night. Mr. Van der Hoff is a Dutchman, and lives in the good old "milk and butter" style, *his* being the only place in Brazil where we found those excellent (not to say luxurious) articles of food, notwithstanding the peculiar adaptation of the country for them in plenty and to spare at all seasons.[28]

That changes have taken place in the last hundred years and that the agricultural practices and diet are better now than they were offer encouragement; for once established, such deficient habits and paucity of agricultural skills are transmitted from one generation to another, as are other parts of the cultural heritage. Frequently, in these parts of man's social environment years may pass with very little change. This is particularly true in an environment that is overwhelmingly rural, as in Brazil. The result is that the Brazilian population of the present day is much more poorly nourished than is necessitated by the agricultural resources and possibilities of the country; but it can only be better nourished if the *wants* and the *agricultural practices* of the people can both be changed.

3. *Poor Health.*—Poor health is another factor which greatly reduces the production per Brazilian worker and contributes to the very low levels of living that prevail throughout most rural sections of the country. Although exaggerated to attract attention, there is at least a grain of truth in the assertion often made by Brazil's leading thinkers that large segments of the rural population are more suitable as clinical materials than as workers.[29] If one keeps in mind the relation of poor health to loss of time and efficiency, a review of the materials on health and mortality of the Brazilian population, discussed in Chapter VII, will help to emphasize this important cause of Brazil's low standard of living. Were the health better, undoubtedly productivity per worker would be much higher. On the other hand, since the bulk of the income is required to maintain the present inadequate diet, poor health follows as a result of present levels of living.

[27] *Ibid.*, 136–37. Later, Mawe had a churn built and gave the lady instructions as to its use. *Ibid.*, 192, 196–97. For comments concerning the lack of, or backward condition of, other agricultural skills, see *ibid.*, 142, 188, 197, and 205.

[28] Ballard S. Dunn, *Brazil, the Home for Southerners* (New York and New Orleans, 1866), 155.

[29] Freyre, *Casa Grande & Senzala*, 34.

As a conclusion to this section relating to the present unsatisfactory dietary and health situations in Brazil, it is fitting to make reference to the excellent analysis made by Gilberto Freyre. This outstanding student of Brazil's cultural evolution speaks with an authority—one based on long years devoted to observation and a careful study of the documentary evidence—that cannot be lightly set aside. In his explanation dietary, health, and sanitary factors loom large. He, too, has little patience with those who attribute the ills of the Brazilian population to racial and climatic factors. Freyre credits the latifundium and slavery with making possible the economic development and the relative political stability of Brazil, which he contrasts with the turbulent situation in neighboring countries.[30] But, at the same time, he maintains that the large estate with its monoculture and slave system "perverted and poisoned the country's springs of nutrition and life." In colonial society the social extremes were better fed than the intermediate strata. "Better fed, we repeat, were the extremes of slave society: the whites of the *casas grandes* and the Negroes of the *senzalas*." For this reason he holds it as natural that the slaves became the progenitors of many of the strongest and healthiest elements in the population, the athletes, the sailors, and some of the agile fighting classes who live outside the law, such as capoeiras and *cabras*. And he also considers diet as the major factor for explaining why the intermediate classes were the ancestors of some of the weakest and most incapable groups in present-day society. Because of their undernourished condition, these "free but miserable" persons were much more susceptible to the ravages of malaria, beriberi, syphilis, and *bouba* (tumor) than either the better-fed slaves or the aristocratic elements in the population. Today he holds that their descendants, "this almost useless population of caboclos and light mulattoes" are "more valuable as clinical material than as an economic force." [31]

When present-day investigators describe the "state of physical misery and unproductive inertia" of these people, lamentations arise because "we are nòt of a pure race and Brazil is not a temperate climate." Freyre has but little sympathy with those who would attribute the inertia or the indolence to racial factors, or to race mixture, and who would eternally damn the Brazilian because he is not of pure racial stock or Brazil because it lies very largely in the torrid zone. Sarcastically he condemns those sociologists who are "more alarmed with the taint of race mixture than with syphilis" or who are "more preoccupied with the effects of the climate than with the social causes that are susceptible to control or rectification." He himself emphasizes the all-important influence of the scarcity of food products brought about by the devotion to monoculture and slavery, the poor chemical composition of the foods that were grown, and above all, that Brazilians, with only a couple of regional exceptions, have been subjected to this diet for three hundred years. Today, even more

[30] *Ibid.*
[31] *Ibid.*

than in colonial times, there are undernourished groups in the population. He quotes the work of Araujo Lima to support the contention that the large proportion of the caboclos of the north, "poetically considered by the artless to be the great reserve of Brazilian vitality," have been reduced to a "state of organic inferiority." Freyre also quotes Araujo Lima to the effect that "the caboclo erases his economic and social value in a deficient diet which, seconded by alcoholism and by the doubly debilitating action of malaria and hookworm, has to be recognized as one of the factors of his physical and intellectual inferiority," and then adds in a footnote that "this observation, relative to the caboclo of the extreme north may be generalized, with one or another regional restriction, to the poor Brazilian in all the other rural zones." [32]

4. *Incentives to Work, Attitudes Towards Labor, and Alternative Opportunities.*—Another factor making for the low productivity per worker, and accordingly for the low levels of living prevailing throughout Brazil, is the general weakness of propulsions to regular work activities. In the states from São Paulo north, and to a certain extent in the southern region, the Brazilian caboclo, or rural worker, lacks a great many of the propulsions to work that are the heritage of his fellows in many other lands. Most obvious of these are the ones associated with the climate, but probably the most significant are those that lie embedded in the social and cultural environment the caboclo has inherited.

a) *The climate.* The extremely mild climate and the rich gifts nature offers merely for the collecting make it possible for many Brazilians in the interior of the country to lead a vegetative existence, to put forth a very minimum of effort. So readily collected or produced are the simple food requirements (except in parts of the northeast), so slight the minimum requirements for clothing, so easily constructed some kind of shelter, so readily furnished with a rough table and a few hammocks, it is possible for life to be maintained in most of Brazil with an output of effort far below that required in more rigorous climes.

Says Burton of the incentives to activity and the type of vegetative life carried on in some of the interior villages:

The life of these country places has a barbarous uniformity. The people say of the country "é muito atrasado," and they show in their proper persons all the reason of the atraso. It is every man's object to do as little as he can, and he limits his utmost industry to the labours of the smallest Fazenda. These idlers rise late and breakfast early, perhaps with a sweet potato and a cup of the inevitable coffee; sometimes there is a table, often a mat is spread upon the floor, but there is always a cloth. It is then time "ku amkía," as the Sawahilis say, to "drop in" upon neighbours, and to slay time with the smallest of small talk. The hot hours are spent in the hammock, swinging, dozing, smoking, and eating melons. Dinner is at 2 P.M., a more substantial matter of fish, or meat, and manioc with vegetables at times, and everywhere, save at Sento Sé, with peppersauce. Coffee and tobacco serve to shorten the long tedious hours, and the evening is devoted

[32] *Ibid.*, 34–35.

to a gentle stroll, or to "tomar a fresca," that is, sitting in a shady spot to windward of the house and receiving visits. Supper ushers in the night-fall, and on every possible occasion the song and drum, the dance and dram are prolonged till near daybreak. Thus they lose energy, they lose memory, they cannot persuade themselves to undertake anything, and all exertion seems absolutely impossible to them. At Sento Sé the citizens languidly talk of a canal which is to be brought from the Rio de São Francisco at the expense of £1680. But no one dreams of doing anything beyond talking. "Government" must do everything for them, they will do nothing for themselves. After a day or two's halt in these hot-beds of indolence, I begin to feel like one of those who are raised here.[33]

Similar statements about one place or another are encountered in most accounts written by those who have traveled through interior Brazil, particularly in the reports of those who passed through the northern portions of the country. Gardner commented about the people living in Alagôas:

The chief productions of the country around Alagôas are sugar, cotton, and a little mandioca. At the time of my visit great complaints were made of the scarcity of the provisions, but it is impossible to feel much commiseration for the starving condition of the poor people, when it is known that it is entirely owing to their own want of industry that sufficient crops of mandioca are not raised, not only for their own consumption, but for exportation to other parts of the country. There is abundance of ground around the city lying waste, which is well adapted for the growth of this plant, and but little labour suffices for its cultivation, but the indolent disposition of the people is such, that, with all the advantages which the country offers, they are contented to obtain just sufficient for immediate use and seldom look forward to the future.[34]

Without overemphasizing the importance of the geographic factors as social determinants, one may safely say that the climate and the natural productions of Brazil are such as to permit man to lead a very unindustrious life. Certainly climate is not the strong force compelling man to sustained labor that it is in many lands.[35]

b) *Cultural factors.* But probably climate is not the most significant influence of Brazilian work habits. In many regions the rural

[33] Burton, *The Highlands of the Brazil*, II, 357.

[34] George Gardner, *Travels in the Interior of Brazil* (2d ed.; London, 1849), 109–10. Similar references are made to the inhabitants of other places along his line of travel through Ceará, Piauí, Goiás, Bahia, and Minas Gerais. Of Riochão in Goiás he wrote: "The inhabitants of this district are so desperately lazy that they scarcely plant sufficient of anything for their own use notwithstanding the unlimited extent of ground that each family possesses." *Ibid.*, 295.

[35] On this point a noted English authority on cotton commented:
"Babassú is not planted or cultivated; the natives steal the fruit from nature. Babassú is a plague in so far as it tends to make people more lazy."
"The wealth of nature has made the Maranhense people idle, and it is to be feared that the recent babassú development will make them almost forget field cultivation."
"The 'babassú' positively makes the people lazy, and were it not for the wealth it brings to the country it should be considered a pest." Arno S. Pearse, *Cotton in North Brazil* (Manchester, 1923), 83, 84, and 121.
When I visited Maranhão in 1942, I learned the significance of the couplet:
Si não fosse babassú
Todo mundo andava nú.
[If it were not for babassú
Everyone would go naked.]

Brazilian of the working class has also inherited a social environment that serves as a brake on the amount of effort expended. The caboclo's house of wattle and daub, pau-a-pique, or thatch, with its rough tile or thatch roof and dirt floor, humble as it is, comes up to standard. To be housed as well as his fellows, he needs but a minimum of household equipment, frequently little more than a few chairs, a rough table, and some hammocks. To provide a house and furnishings that are socially acceptable in the caboclo's environment does not require the years of sustained effort that it does in the family farm sections of São Paulo, Santa Catarina, Paraná, or Rio Grande do Sul.[36]

Probably even more significant than this lack of motivation from material culture is that embedded in the nonmaterial culture of the lower-class rural Brazilians. Particularly pernicious is the socially acquired mindset, or system of attitudes, towards manual work prevalent in the country. In Brazil almost the entire nation has inherited all of the vicious attitudes towards human toil that are the inevitable aftermath of a system of slavery. To work with the hands is considered degrading, is the indelible mark of inferior social position, is a stigma to be avoided as one would shun the plague.[37] Thus, there is a popular saying in Brazil that *trabalho é para cachorro e negro* (manual labor is for the dog and the Negro).[38] The colonist, who may have been a servant in Portugal, upon setting foot in Brazil considered it beneath his dignity, beneath the position of a white man, to labor with his hands. Even the skilled labor of the artisan

[36] Says Pearse of the people of Ceará's sertões: "It almost seems as though the frugality of the people has been so excessive that they have developed few demands for the luxuries of life and consequently they often lack the impetus to work uninterruptedly." *Ibid.*, 28.

Almost one hundred years ago Dunn wrote in a similar vein. It was while he was making the observation that led him to select the area near Cananéia in southeastern São Paulo as the site for his "Lizzieland," that he included the following reflections in one of his reports to the Brazilian Minister of Agriculture: ". . . I have found, by observation, in South America, as in North America, that vicious Europeans, are not improved morally, intellectually, nor industrially by emigration. On the contrary, they easily fall into the indolent habits of the more virtuous and ingenuous natives of the lower classes. The fruitfulness of Brazil is such, that they can subsist almost without exertion; therefore they cease to perform that labor, which necessity, in their native land, rendered compulsory." Other of the data included in Dunn's reports indicate that the lack of natural and cultural propulsions to steady work habits have helped prevent a high standard of living: "Leaving this point early on the morning of the 27th, we reached the mouth of the river in time to ascend the Ribeira one league, where we got lodgings for the night with a colored man, who owns several thousand acres of valuable land, but subsists chiefly upon fish, taken from the Ribeira, and rice raised upon a small field not yet enclosed." *Brazil, the Home for Southerners*, 131–32, 138.

[37] "As the manual labour of gold-washing is performed entirely by slaves, the perverseness of the whites disdains, as dishonourable, every similar employment, even those of agriculture and tending cattle; in consequence there are so many idlers that they are usually distinguished as a separate class, under the name *Vadios*. The traveller, therefore, sees here with the splendour of the greatest opulence, all the images of human misery, poverty, and degradation." Von Spix and von Martius, *Travels in Brazil, 1817–1820*, II, 127. Cf. João Cardoso de Menezes e Souza, *Theses sobre Colonização no Brazil* (Rio de Janeiro, 1875), 175 *passim*.

[38] Pierson, *Negroes in Brazil*, 69.

was thought of as degrading to the white man, i.e., the free man; [39] and labor in farming, which has always been and remains the basis of Brazil's economy, is said to have been considered the most disreputable of all, even more so than the tasks of mining.[40]

It is well known that a comparable attitude towards manual labor still plagues those parts of the United States which knew the slave system and the extreme social stratification that went with it. In Brazil, however, slavery was almost universally practiced, the use of slavery being prohibited only on the lands given by the empire to the states to be used in establishing colonies of small farmers on the land. In effect, this restricted slavery to any considerable extent in only the southern part of the country. Furthermore, in Brazil slavery was not abolished until 1888. Finally, the concentration of land and power, and the resulting social stratification, was even more pronounced than in the southern part of the United States, with the result that the members of the elite class were numerically less important and the laboring classes proportionately more important than in our own country. This quantitative difference also increased the social chasm separating the two layers of society, and at that time Brazil contained almost no small-farming classes, comparable to those of the southern uplands, to fill the gaps between the master and slave classes and to form the nucleus of a middle class. In view of all this, it is not difficult to understand why "the dignity of human labor" should be a concept foreign to most Brazilian thinking.

The hope of improving his economic position, of climbing the agricultural ladder and becoming the operator of his own farm, is a social propulsion that greatly stimulates the agricultural laborers in some countries to regular work activities. Such social climbing is evident in western São Paulo and in portions of the other southern states. However, most Brazilian caboclos, matutos, sertanejos, seringueiros, or other rural workers have no comparable stimulations. Except in restricted areas, particularly in the south, the large estate still reigns supreme throughout Brazil. Its prevalence, as in our own South, is irrefutable proof that the agricultural ladder is not working. Outside the four southernmost states, such division of land as has occurred has been due either to a limited number of governmentally sponsored colonization projects or to the equal inheritance of property among the numerous progeny of the fazendeiros. Until recently the average caboclo probably never entertained for one moment the thought that some day he might operate a small farm of his own. He was mainly concerned with the kind of treatment received from the owner of the land on which he squatted and built his rude shelter and made his roça or on whose fazenda he labored as a colono, agregado, or camarada. As a result, he is sadly unprepared to deal with the blandishments of those who would solve the nation's ills merely by seizing and subdividing the land, and it is easy for demagogues to cause his aspirations and expectations to soar at a

[39] See *ibid.*
[40] Cf. Mawe, *Travels in the Interior of Brazil*, 78.

speed far more rapid than there is any chance, either under a democratic regime or a totalitarian one, that his actual level of living can be increased.

c) *The rudimentary condition of popular education.* Finally, as indicative of the weakness of the motivations to sustained productive effort must be mentioned the rudimentary nature of the school system and the resulting widespread illiteracy among the population. In the last analysis man rises above the level of creature needs only through the acquisition of new wants and the ensuing struggle to obtain the means for satisfying them. If these are not inculcated by the family institution, which itself must possess them before it can hand them down, only the school and other educational institutions, such as the church, can do much to create the new wants and to inculcate the skills which will assist in obtaining their satisfaction. Where one-half of the population never enter a school and where only a very small minority of the population ever acquire more education than an elementary knowledge of the three R's, the motivations to work are correspondingly weakened.

d) *Abundance of alternative opportunities.* Brazil's abundance of unexhausted resources and the wide variety of opportunities for obtaining the necessities of life serve as factors to prevent the stable life and persistent work that is conducive to thrift and saving. The effect of these factors may be vividly emphasized by specific cases. Gold and diamonds are to be found in the stream beds in large portions of Brazil, many of which have been only partially prospected or worked. The finds are sufficient and the lure attractive enough to keep a considerable number of persons always engaged in the search for the precious mineral and stones. The situation reminds one of the "grubstaked" prospectors in the United States' West. Although these garimpeiros ordinarily lead a life of considerable hardship, which year in and year out yields but a meager return, there always exists the chance of quick riches through a lucky find. News of a strike spreads rapidly and results in a rush to the new "diggings." In Goiás and Mato Grosso both diamonds and gold are found in the sands of the rivers which flow through the *seringais* or tracts on which the rubber trees grow. Thus the entrepreneurs engaged in the extraction of raw rubber throughout this area constantly live under the threat that their laborers will suddenly leave in search for gold or diamonds in the vicinity of a new find. Especially persons from Bahia and the Northeast, whence the workers must come, are said to be susceptible to such temptations, since they are said to have a "nose" for diamonds. In any case, the richness of opportunity is a factor which presently endangers the labor supply of this particular enterprise and in the end operates against regular work activities and a high production per worker.

In other parts of Brazil there is a similar situation between the relative opportunities in agriculture and in some of the collective enterprises. For example, the state of Maranhão is largely dependent on locally produced food supplies. It is far from the surplus-food-producing states to the south, and the system of transports is none too adequate, especially to the interior sections of the state which must depend for transportation on small river boats. Although the system of agriculture is that which has been designated "fire agriculture," local farmers ordinarily produce the food for their own use and some to supply the towns and cities as well. But during the second World War, with a sudden demand for babassú and other nuts that are rich in vegetable oils, the population was confronted with an opportunity to benefit by the high prices paid for such products. Since the nuts grow wild in the forests and may be had merely for the collection, there was a sudden rush into this form of activity. Many families did not continue producing food even for their own uses. Certainly they did not fell new trees to make new clearings. The result was a run on existing stocks of food, the soaring of the cost of living, and increased strain on the transportation facilities. In a few months, however, a change in the demand may force the laborer back to agriculture, perhaps after the onslaught of the rainy season has made it too late to fell and burn the forest for that year's roça.

The abundance of alternative opportunities discussed in this section is, of course, limited to the great rural areas of Brazil. The millions of poorly equipped people who have swarmed into the towns and cities since 1945 have not encountered unlimited economic opportunities. Indeed, their unattained aspirations and their increasing exasperations are largely responsible for the explosive situation in contemporary Brazil.

Lavish Use of Labor. All the factors enumerated so far have an important bearing on productivity per worker. But perhaps the most important of all is the manner in which the essential elements of production—land, labor, capital, and management—are combined in the Brazilian productive process. Analysis, study, and reflection will make it more and more apparent that, to a great extent, the comparatively low level of living in Brazil is a function of the extremely lavish use of labor in the productive process. The factors previously analyzed all have an important bearing on existing standards of living, but even with these handicaps the average level of living might be greatly improved if labor were used less lavishly in combination with capital and management. This aspect of the subject is so important that it deserves examination in some detail.

Even the most superficial observer must discern that the Brazilian productive process is one in which the labor element is used lavishly, whereas capital and management play relatively minor roles in most of the various phases of production. This generalization applies in every enterprise from agriculture and the extractive industries, to transportation and domestic and personal services. In all of these the input of human labor is great, and investment of capital in the form of machinery and equipment, or even in the training of labor, is comparatively small. To a certain extent it may also be said that management, too, is carefully husbanded. At least, this is true to the extent that in agriculture, for example, many large-scale undertakings which employ hundreds of families of workers are operated by an entrepreneur who lives away from the land. Because he does not live on the fazenda and since he makes only infrequent trips to oversee the operations, his managerial activities are conducted on a reduced scale, in many cases being merely nominal. Also of dubious quality are the managerial activities of the major domos on many of the estates left in their care. Usually these "bosses" are from the ranks, although in some cases they are trained agronomists or relatives of the owners. Also, the relative lack of a small-farming class contributes to the same reduced use of management in the process of production. On the Brazilian fazenda or usina, the camarada, agregado, colono, or other agricultural worker performs only the labor function. This contrasts sharply with the situation in a family-farm system, such as prevails in parts of Paraná, Santa Catarina, and Rio Grande do Sul, where the worker himself performs as manager and capitalist. Thus, it may fairly be said that the family-farm type of organization contributes to a greater expenditure of management than does the large fazenda that overspreads much of Brazil and is responsible for most of its commercial agricultural production.

Undoubtedly the relatively low wages that prevail, plus the high cost of tools, implements, machines, and other labor-saving devices,

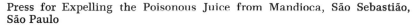

Press for Expelling the Poisonous Juice from Mandioca, São Sebastião, São Paulo

have much to do with the persistence of productive processes in which human labor plays the dominant role. This economic interpretation is probably the most obvious explanation; and were the wages higher, undoubtedly labor would be used less lavishly. Nevertheless, the long continued labor shortage which has followed the abolition of slavery in Brazil has not resulted in the elevation of wages to a degree sufficient to bring about the sparing use of the labor element in production. Therefore, it is at least reasonable to suppose that social patterning and resistance to change have had much to do with the prevailing manner of combining the elements of production in the various enterprises. As a matter of fact, many of the agricultural operations used have been borrowed intact from the Indians. The fire agriculture complex, described in another chapter, was taken over with little change. Even the recent immigrants from Portugal, Italy, and Spain have been habituated mostly to hoe farming and not to machine cultivation. But whatever may be responsible, the fact remains that in the Brazilian productive process large shares of labor are combined with relatively little capital (in form of tools, machines, implements, work stock, and vehicles) and, at least in agriculture where the bulk of Brazil's workers are engaged, with relatively small doses of management.

Because of its overwhelming importance the situation in agriculture deserves analysis in detail. Most of Brazil's commercial crops—coffee, sugar, cotton, rice, and citrus fruits—are the particular ones which call for intensive cultivation. The production of cocoa and mate also demands large inputs of labor. Throughout the entire world these crops, with the possible exception of rice whose production is sometimes highly mechanized, always demand a relatively large amount of human labor. In Brazil this emphasis on handwork is particularly pronounced.

Consider, for example, the production of Brazilian coffee. A great deal of manpower enters into almost every stage of the process of producing this great crop. To begin with, there is the tremendous task of felling and burning the thick tropical forest that covers the land; this is accomplished by the employment of a hand-swung axe, followed by firing the entire lot and then piling and burning the charred tree trunks. Our forefathers had a no more difficult task in carving farms from North American hardwood forests than that facing the Paulista or Paranaense who would open a new coffee fazenda in the dense forests of São Paulo or Paraná. But, with the clearing of the ground, the handwork has merely commenced. Next, for each of the small seedlings, which so far have been propagated and cared for in a covered nursery, a small pit must be dug. Each of these holes must be carefully lined and spaced with relation to every other one, because a coffee fazenda loses much of its value if the trees or bushes are not accurately spaced so that they run in absolutely straight lines when viewed from either direction. Then the small plants must be placed in the holes, the dirt carefully replaced about them, water applied to pack the soil and nurture the roots, and the newly set-out seedlings surrounded with a small fence-like protection of rails two feet square and one foot high. All of these processes require much labor and still more handwork in the years to come. Good coffee culture requires the construction of a small dam or terrace about each plant to help prevent erosion, and this handmade ridge must constantly be renewed. Repeated hoeings are necessary to keep down grass and weeds. The periodic covering of the ground for fertilization and protection of the soil from the tropical sun is essential. Sometimes this is done with straw and grass on which cattle have been bedded, but if the fazendeiro does not keep the cattle necessary to provide the fertilizer, the covering is done with leaves and grass. When the coffee trees come into bearing, all this terracing, hoeing, fertilizing, and covering still must be continued, and in addition, there is much more handwork in harvesting, curing, cleaning, and, if consumed locally, parching the crop. The first of these consists of stripping the berries from the branches and gathering up those that have fallen on the ground. Then the coffee beans are transported to the seat of the fazenda, sometimes washed, and spread on the drying floor to dry. Here they must be given the most careful attention. In order to get the right amount of sun and to avoid exposure to the rain, the valuable beans must alternately be spread out, heaped, and covered many times before they are ready to be passed through machines which remove the hulls and sort the beans according to size. This heaping, covering, respreading, turning, reheaping (all repeated many times) are great consumers of manual

Interior of Caipira's Home, Município of Taubaté, São Paulo

work. In fact, in every one of these processes the employment of human labor bulks large, the use of machinery and equipment relatively small. Where coffee is produced under shade, as in the state of Espírito Santo, the amount of labor required is still further increased.

Consider also the role of labor in the production of sugar. With the possible exception of rice, as it is grown in Rio Grande do Sul, sugar cane is probably the Brazilian crop whose production is most mechanized, that is to say, in which the role of labor is of least importance. But at best the planting of the crop, the repeated hoeings which are necessary in the early stages in order to keep down grass and weeds, and the cutting and loading of the stalks, all are possible only through the expenditures of comparatively large amounts of manual labor. On many Brazilian plantations, especially in the North, all of this is done without the help of animal-drawn implements such as the plow. Where, as in the North, the cane stalks are tied in small bundles and then loaded on pack animals for transportation to the mill, the amount of human labor required reaches astounding proportions.

In cotton, another intensively tilled crop, the situation is similar. Although the agricultural processes used in São Paulo's cotton production are far advanced in comparison with those generally used in growing Brazil's food crops, only a few tools, little mechanized equipment, small amounts of mule or horse (or perhaps ox) power, and relatively large proportions of labor are combined in the productive process. Elsewhere in Brazil cotton farming is almost exclusively handwork. It is well known that in the Cotton Belt of the United States labor is used lavishly in comparison with the other elements of production, but in Brazil the growing of cotton involves far greater expenditures of manual labor. In the Northeast it consumes appalling amounts of human effort.

Even rice, a crop that is highly susceptible to mechanized production, throughout most of Brazil is produced by traditional methods. The large rice plantations in Rio Grande do Sul are an exception to this generalization, some of them utilizing tractors for plowing and harvesting, and generally, machines for threshing. But even here one may see in process plowing in which two or four oxen are combined with three or four men and one plow. Throughout most of Brazil the rice, which is an important half of the daily diet of rice and beans, is planted in small plots (or even dispersed here and there among other crops such as cotton), cut by hand with a knife or sickle, and threshed with the flail or a small hand thresher.

Mention should also be made of the lavish use of labor in Brazil's dairy industry, particularly in Minas Gerais, whose eight million inhabitants produce the great bulk of the cheese and butter that is consumed in Brazil. For the most part, in this state dairying is to be classed as an extensive rather than an intensive enterprise. Many of the cattle which are milked are of the zebu or Brahma types or a cross of native stock with these breeds, although some Holsteins are also to be found. Most of the cows give but a few pints of milk per day.

Upper. Tanks for Fermenting Corn, before It Is Pounded by the Monjolo. *Lower.* Toasting, the Final Step in the Preparation of Farinha de Milho, or Corn Flour.

Old Coffee Fazenda, Paraíba Valley, São Paulo

However, it should be stressed that the labor required in caring for the cattle and in milking is about as great as if the production per cow were much larger. In Minas Gerais, as is also true in the neighboring states of São Paulo and Rio de Janeiro, the practice of mowing the pastures is followed. However, this mowing is done by workers swinging by hand a long-handled cutting knife, a process requiring large amounts of manual labor. The transportation of milk or cheese from the fazendas to the market, creamery, or cheese factory, also calls for utilization of much labor since ordinarily it must be placed in cans and loaded on pack animals. These are then driven to the railroad station or to the village or town trading center. As one travels through Minas Gerais, one cannot fail to be impressed by the troops of pack animals threading along the trails on their way to or from the station or hitched near the depot, always with milk cans swung on either side of the animal. Even the saddle horse is likely to be carrying at least one small milk can in addition to the rider.

One might proceed through the rest of the long list of Brazilian products indicating the lavish manner in which labor is used in the production and marketing processes. In Chapter xv this is done for many of the crops grown for local consumption in connection with the description of fire agriculture. But one might follow through with a description of cocoa production; the gathering and curing of mate; the collection and coagulation of rubber; the gathering, cracking, and transportation of babassú nuts and Brazil nuts; the processing of the fronds of the carnaúba palm to secure the wax; the culture of bananas, pineapples, and citrus fruits. The same lavish use of the human element would be found in all. The significance of these agricultural methods lies in the fact that the squandering of labor results in low productivity per worker. Not enough is produced to permit a high average level of consumption. Widespread poverty and misery must continue to prevail until the human being is "valorized" and labor is used more conservatively in the productive process.

THE WIDENING GAP BETWEEN THE STANDARD OF LIVING AND THE LEVEL OF LIVING

During the last twenty-five years a veritable revolution has taken place in the aspirations or expectations of the masses of the Brazilian population, and to some extent this has been accompanied by increases in the amounts of goods and services actually consumed by the people. However, the rise in aspirations, or the standard of living, has been much more rapid than that in actual consumption practices, the level of living, with the result that the gap between the two has become very much more pronounced. Brazilian families by the hundreds of thousands now aspire to the ownership of a small tract of land, to better dwellings, to greater voices in political affairs, or in short, to a way of life more comparable with that they see enjoyed by the more affluent portions of their own society and that which they are told prevails in some other countries.

This particular social revolution got underway in the southern parts of Brazil, and especially in Rio de Janeiro, long the nation's capital, and in São Paulo. Gradually, however, it has spread throughout all portions of the Brazilian half of the South American continent. Today, in sharp contrast with the past, there are relatively few sections of Brazil in which resignation to their fate appears to be the dominant attitude on the part of the masses of the population.

The preceding paragraphs are intended to indicate that since the early 1930's the masses of Brazil's people have come to believe that they and their children are entitled to far larger incomes; to better food, housing and dress; and to improved educational facilities, health services, and welfare programs. But all of these things are much easier for politicians to promise than for those in office to supply; the aspirations involved are much simpler for agitators to arouse than for statesmen to satisfy; and the individual desires involved are more easily instilled than met.

As a result, the difference between the actual plane on which Brazil's masses presently are living and that at which they now feel entitled to live has increased greatly in the last quarter of a century. Indeed the gap between the standard of living and the level of living, which may be designated as the zone of exasperation, attained critical proportions early in the 1960's.

PART FOUR

Relations of the
People to the Land

*This is one of the most interesting aspects of soci-
ology. It pertains to the institutions governing the
arrangement of the people on the land, the systems
of land division, questions of land tenure, the effects
of holdings of various sizes, systems used in extracting a living from the soil, the strengthening of the
farmer class, and the nature of locality groups. These
are the seven subjects to which the chapters of this
part are devoted.*

CHAPTER XI

SETTLEMENT PATTERNS

T̲HE AGRICULTURAL POPULATION may be arranged on the land in any one of three principal types or patterns of settlement—the village, the line village, and scattered farmsteads. Village settlements are those in which the homes of the cultivators are grouped in a cluster, apart from the land which they work. The distinguishing feature of such an arrangement is that the farmers do not live on the land but must commute daily from the village center to the fields in order to perform the necessary agricultural work. The line village resembles the true village pattern in that the homes of the cultivators are built in rather close proximity to one another. But in the line village each farmer lives on his land and not apart from the fields under his care, as in the true village. In the line-village pattern of settlement farm plots must be longer than they are wide and laid off side by side, all fronting on a common line of departure, such as a road, a stream, or a coast, and all dwellings must be constructed at the same end of the holdings. Finally, when farmers live on the land amid the fields and the farmsteads have not been laid out so as to permit homes to be close to one another, the scattered or isolated farmstead pattern of settlement prevails. Brazil's population has utilized all three of these forms of settlement.

THE VILLAGE

Brazil is almost entirely lacking in village settlements of the small freeholder variety. This species, which was the dominant pattern of settlement in the mother country of Portugal, was not transplanted in the Portuguese settlements in the New World, nor were later attempts to remold established settlements into village patterns successful.[1] Italian, Polish, and German colonists who came during the nineteenth century did not introduce it—their traditional form of settlement—for use in the colonial portions of Brazil. Nor, unless it be in exceptional cases, did the Japanese colonists who have entered Brazil in the twentieth century make use of the village, also their

---

[1] Cf. Carlos Borges Schmidt, "Rural Life in Brazil," in Smith and Marchant (eds.), *Brazil: Portrait of Half a Continent,* 169–71.

traditional settlement pattern, in arranging themselves on the land.[2]

Although the village settlement as represented by the homes of small-farming classes is hardly to be found in Brazil, the village manner of arranging the population on the land is widely used on the large estates that are prominent throughout the Brazilian countryside. For the most part the fazendas and usinas of Brazil utilize this nucleated form of settlement in their "quarters" or "colonies" for the workers who till the crops. This is especially true of the arrangement of homes on the coffee and sugar estates, less true on cotton plantations and on cattle fazendas.

Most coffee fazendas utilize a village arrangement for the homes of the workers and the essential establishments maintained on the fazenda. The point of orientation is the casa grande, or home of the fazendeiro and his family. Usually such a home is well constructed and comfortable, if not elaborate. It is surrounded by well-kept lawns and gardens, which nearly always include a tiled swimming pool. Close by are the washing troughs and drying floors for the coffee, the mill for cleaning and grading the beans, and the barns for the livestock, which usually include some blooded riding and driving horses. Conveniently situated with respect to the "big house" also is the armazém (or commissary), the business offices, and the matadouro (or slaughterhouse where animals for fresh meat are killed). Often a school and a chapel are found in the nucleus of the fazenda, and not infrequently a station on the railroad is also located nearby. But the larger number of houses in the village-like nucleus consists of the cottages of the colonos who perform the manual labor on the fazendas. These cottages may be arranged around a square or oblong, or they may be strung along one side or both sides of a valley, but in any case they do much to give the seat of the fazenda the appearance of a village. If the fazenda is a very large one, there may be more than one of these colonies, together with barns for the livestock. But in any case the form of settlement is clearly of the village type.

Both the old-style sugar plantation and mill, the engenho, and the modern central or usina also utilize the village settlement pattern for arranging the homes of the workers. Freyre's use of *Casa Grande & Senzala* as the title for his classic work on the evolution of the Brazilian family gives this variety of the village form of settlement the place it deserves in the Brazilian social scene. It has performed and continues to perform a significant role in Brazil's rural life. The large sugar estate was for centuries a dominating factor in Brazilian agriculture. Until coffee became of such great importance in the

---

[2] "In Japan the compact nucleus prevails, here dispersed colonization. It is true that the population centers of Jipujura and Registro represent agglomerations—the latter semiurban—but they are to be considered only as the economic complements of an extensive zone that is purely rural." Herbert Baldus and Emílio Willems, "Casas e Túmulos de Japoneses no Vale da Ribeira de Iguape," *Revista do Arquivo Municipal* (São Paulo), LXXVII (1941), 122. Cf. Fujii and Smith, *The Acculturation of Japanese Immigrants in Brazil*, 30–31.

nineteenth century, it held almost undisputed sway in national affairs. As has been indicated, before the process of sugar manufacture advanced to the stage where large modern factories were developed, the cane was ground and the sugar granulated in small mills called engenhos. By extension, this term was applied to the entire estate including the lands, the slave quarters, and the homes of the owner and his retainers. As manufacturing processes improved, the mills were replaced by large factories, or usinas, and the lands were concentrated in the hands of a few large operators. But the entire estate carried the name usina, or factory. It continued the practice of grouping workers' homes in one or more village nuclei. Today in Brazil's sugar areas the large estate is called a usina; in other types of agriculture the corresponding unit is called a fazenda. And as is the case generally throughout the cane-producing areas of the world, including those of the United States, the village form of settlement is used in the arrangement of the population on sugar lands. So large and self-sufficient are the village seats of many Brazilian sugar plantations that they deserve to be classified as genuine communities.

The arrangement of the village center of a Brazilian usina follows no set pattern. In a central location is sure to be the factory proper, closely surrounded by various sheds, machine shops, and other small structures. The casa grande of the owner or manager, usually spacious and often luxurious, is located near the mill but is set amid landscaped grounds and gardens. Nearby there is usually at least one guesthouse. The numerous cottages in which the laborers reside are also in close proximity, giving form and substance to the village center. Usually, the nucleus includes a school and a chapel and sometimes a small hospital. In the north the chapel is likely to be attached to the manor house as one of its most prominent wings. There are one or more commissaries, possibly a small gristmill, and small buildings for the preparation of mandioca and other food stuffs. Stables for the livestock and sheds for farm machinery and equipment are relegated to the outskirts, as is the customary football field and grounds for other sports. As a rule, cattle enterprises are important on each usina, so other stables and sheds may be conveniently spaced here and there on the extensive lands belonging to the usina, near small clusters of workers' cottages. But the seat of the usina, including the sugar factory, the casa grande, the supply depots and commissaries, and the homes of most of the laborers, constitutes a genuine village, from which the bulk of the farming activities are carried on.

Various writers have described the village nature of the old-style engenhos which once dominated the rural scene throughout all the coastal areas of Brazil. For example Southey wrote: "An *Engenho* could not well be conducted unless artificers in every trade necessary for its concerns were attached to the establishment. Every *Engenho* therefore was a community or village in itself, more populous at this time than many of the towns which have been enumerated. About eight square miles were required for the service of an *Engenho,* half in pasture, half in thicket or woodland." [3]

More detailed is the description of the engenho Henry Koster operated at Jaguaribe near Recife:

I had now taken up my abode at the house usually inhabited by the owner or tenant; this was a low, but long mud cottage, covered with tiles, and whitewashed within and without; it had bricked floors, but no ceiling. There were two apartments of tolerable dimensions, several small rooms, and a kitchen. The chief entrance was from a sort of square, formed by the several buildings belonging to the estate. In front was the chapel; to the left was a large dwelling-house unfurnished, and the negro huts, a long row of small habitations, having much the appearance of alms-houses, without the neatness of places of this description in England; to the right was the mill worked by water, and the warehouse or barn in which the sugar undergoes the process of claying; and to the view of these buildings may be added the pens for the cattle, the carts, the heaps of timber, and a small pond through which the water runs to the mill.[4]

Also deserving of quotation is the brief but fairly complete description of the nucleated settlement that forms the central cell of the fazenda given by Sir Richard Burton. Of the Casa Branca estate in Minas Gerais he wrote as follows:

The manor house was in the normal style. fronted by a deep verandah, from which the owner can prospect the distillery, the mill, whose wheel informs us that sugar is the staple growth; and the other offices. At the end of the verandah is the Chapel of Na Sa do Carmo, with her escutcheon of three gilt stars upon a wooden shield painted blue; here there is chaunting on Sunday evenings. The Senzallas or negro quarters are, as usual, ground-floor lodgings within the square, which is generally provided with a tall central wooden cross and a raised stage for drying sugar and maize; the tenements are locked at night, and, in order to prevent disputes, the celibataires are separated from those of the married blacks. These Fazendas are isolated villages on a small scale. They supply the neighbourhood with its simple wants, dry beef, pork, and lard, flour of manioc and maize, sugar and spirits, tobacco and oil; coarse cloth and cotton thread; coffee, and various teas of Caparosa and orange-leaf. They import only iron to be turned into horse-shoes; salt, wine, and beer, cigars, butter, porcelain, drugs, and other "notions." There is generally a smithy, a carpenter's shed, a shoemaker's shop, a piggery, where during the last month the beasts are taken from the foulest food, and an ample poultry yard.[5]

As larger and more modern mills have replaced the primitive machinery of the engenhos, as the usinas have concentrated the sugar lands into even larger holdings, many of these old village clusters have been destroyed. However, the quarters or colonies about the central factories have retained the village form and increased in size. Some of the nuclei of the engenhos also have been retained as colonies. In short, the enlargement of the estates has brought a rearrange-

[3] Southey, *History of Brazil,* II, 674; cf. Oliveira Vianna, "O Povo Brazileiro e sua Evolução," *loc. cit.,* 291.

[4] Henry Koster, *Travels in Brazil* (London, 1816), I, 295.

[5] Burton, *The Highlands of the Brazil,* II, 39.

ment of the nuclei but has not changed the settlement pattern. On some of the estates the homes for workers which have been constructed recently are decidedly more substantial and more desirable as living quarters than the earlier types.

On estates that are given over to cotton production there is also a pronounced tendency for the workers' cottages or huts to be clustered about the home of the proprietor of the fazenda. This is particularly true in the northeastern cotton-growing areas. However, these estates are smaller than those found in the sugar and coffee areas, and the number of workers' families is much smaller. Generally not more than fifteen or twenty cottages will be found in the nucleus of the cotton fazenda. Furthermore, a good share of the cotton is produced on small farms. In São Paulo cotton is frequently grown on the bottom lands belonging to a coffee fazenda. Much of this cotton land has been cleared since about 1935, and interestingly enough, the principle of grouping the workers' homes frequently is abandoned. One sees them scattered over the landscape amid the cotton fields, overshadowed by the standing trunks of trees that have been killed by the fire, in an arrangement reminiscent of cotton areas of the Mississippi Delta that were opened in the 1930's.

Many of the larger cattle fazendas in such states as São Paulo, Minas Gerais, Goiás, and Mato Grosso have small villages or hamlets as headquarters. As one goes overland by truck or train, these seem to be separated by almost interminable distances, especially in Mato Grosso, Goiás, and northern Minas Gerais. During the dry season each of them appears as a small green oasis in the desert of brown grass. From a plane the bird's-eye view shows their arrangement in relation to the trails, the fences, the salting grounds, and the roças and gives a more complete picture of the estates of which they form the central cells.

But cattle raising requires relatively few hands. In the Northeast it is generally entrusted to vaqueiros who care for about five hundred head of cattle each, and in Rio Grande do Sul the proprietors of the estâncias disperse on the plains the barracks for their peons. For these reasons it will be necessary to include a discussion of the cattle fazenda below, when scattered settlement patterns are being considered.

It should be emphasized that the village of freeholders who live in the center and go out daily to till their farm lands is not to be found in Brazil.[6] However, because so much of the populated part of the

---

[6] Perhaps the tendency for nuclei of settlement to come into being near the reservoirs that have been constructed in the Northeast should be mentioned as an exception to this statement. Such a tendency exists, and if property were to become more widely distributed, there might result a genuine village community type of settlement in these locations. In addition, in a few of the colonization projects begun since the close of World War II, the village manner of arranging the population on the land is being used. See Fabio Luz Filho, *Cooperativisimo, Colonização, Credito Agrário* (Rio de Janeiro, 1952), 193–94. Finally, one observer has reported the existence of genuine agricultural village settlements in central Bahia. See Marvin Harris, *Town and Country in Brazil* (New York, 1956), 24–26, 83–90.

country is given over to large coffee and sugar estates, both of which use the village form for arranging the cottages of the workers, nucleated settlement patterns are a prominent feature of the Brazilian landscape. The clustering of workers' homes about that of the proprietor on the larger cotton fazendas of the Northeast and on the largest cattle fazendas of the interior also contributes to the importance in Brazil of this mode of arranging the people on the land.

THE LINE VILLAGE

The line-village form of settlement, intermediate between the village and scattered farmstead types and combining most of the social and economic advantages of both without the most pronounced disadvantages of either, is surprisingly widespread in Brazil. In no other country, unless it be France, has the line village been used to a comparable degree for arranging the population on the land. Furthermore, this is the type of settlement generally used in Brazil's extensive colonization programs, both private and governmental, so that it is rapidly being spread over more and more of the national territory. The line village eventually may be as characteristic of Brazil as scattered farmsteads of the checkerboard style are of the United States.

As yet, I have been unable to discover just what factors led to the adoption of the line-village pattern of settlement in Brazil's early colonization ventures. That the farm tracts were laid out side by side in ribbon-like bands and the houses all built in a line at the front of the holdings is easily proved. The descriptions in the first relatórios state that this was the case; one may see the arrangement preserved in the settlements as they appear today; and one finds that the pattern has become set in the folkways of the people and the policies of the government, so that new settlements or colonies automatically take the line-village arrangement. However, it is important to indicate that the holdings surveyed were never as long and narrow as those frequently laid off in French and Spanish settlements. Rarely in Brazil have the farm plots surveyed been more than ten times as long as they were wide, and generally the disproportion has not been this great.

Because the line village was used in the establishment of the colonies and because these have multiplied so rapidly in the south, a large part of Rio Grande do Sul, Santa Catarina, and Paraná is already covered with settlements arranged in this manner. In addition, there already are extensive settlements of this type in parts of western São Paulo, in Minas Gerais, in Rio de Janeiro, and in Espírito Santo. In recent years state and national colonization projects have begun to spread this type to other sections of the country.

But the line-village arrangement of the population on the land is not confined to the colonial areas of Brazil, and its penetration into other parts of the country did not wait on colonization projects. All along the coast of Brazil from Ceará to Bahia, except where the sand dunes come down to the water's edge, one finds extensive line-village settlements. In some parts of the littoral, especially in Pernambucco, there are thousands of little *sitiozinhos*, each long and narrow, laid off side by side, all fronting on the ocean. These tiny farms are given over, for the most part, to the growing of coconuts. Their inhabitants lead a very simple and unpretentious life, but it would be difficult to discover a more picturesque scene than is presented by the quaint little cottages of thatch, each set amid the palm groves, that are strung along the coast for miles on end. It would also be more difficult to find better examples of small natural groupings of the neighborhood type than are presented in segments of this coastal strip.[7] But at the moment the point to be emphasized is that the use here of the line-village pattern of settlement has contributed considerably to the importance of this mode of arranging the population on the land in Brazil.

Along the São Francisco River in northern Bahia and on some of its small tributaries such as the Salitre, line-village settlements are in evidence. It may be that those in this section have originated spontaneously as an adaptation to the peculiar geographic features of the area and the nature of the economy.[8]

Other extensive line-village settlements are to be found throughout Brazil. For example, as one flies over the middle Amazon region or passes among its labyrinth of channels, frequently he will come upon a settlement, often miles in length, where this pattern of settlement prevails.[9] In the Bragança district east of Belém in Pará are other extensive settlements of this type. Many of them also have developed in the northern states of Maranháo and Piauí. Thus, between Caxias, center of Maranhão's cotton industry, and Teresina, capital of Piauí, one sees densely populated districts in which this pattern of settlement prevails. Just out of Caxias, where the road and the railway both parallel the stream, one observes line villages that are fully as distinctive as those found in the French-speaking portions of Louisiana or those in Quebec. Finally, it should be repeated that, other than France, and possibly Germany, to which this manner of arranging the population on the land diffused from France, Brazil is probably the nation which makes the greatest use of the line-village form of government.

As yet no one has studied the origins of this settlement pattern in Brazil, or at least I have not been able to discover any study of the subject. Possibly it was originated more or less independently under the strong influence of some environmental determinants. Such

---

[7] Cf. *Conceito de Povoado: Contribuição ao seu Estudo* (Recife, 1942), 8–9, for information about some of those settlements where "there is an infinity of little coconut farms, narrow bands of land a few yards wide."

[8] Cf. T. Lynn Smith, "Notes on Population and Social Organization in the Central Portion of the São Francisco Valley," *Inter-American Economic Affairs,* I (December, 1947), 50.

[9] A detailed study of one of these is found in Hilgard O'Reilly Sternberg, *A Água e o Homem na Várzea do Careiro* (Rio de Janeiro, 1956), 131–43.

seems a likely hypothesis in accounting for the extensive settlements along the northeastern coast and in the Amazon region, although more detailed study may show this to be merely a "lazy man's explanation." To south Brazil it may have come with the German settlers, for certainly they used it in their first colonies. But the vigorous complaints of the German colonists at not being settled in villages seems to make this hypothesis untenable.[10] Be that as it may, the line village early formed an indispensable element of official Brazilian colonization projects and has been widely diffused throughout Brazil by these governmental undertakings. Private ventures in the same area, of which there have been many, also made use of this system for arranging the population on the land. As a result, it is now the principal form of settlement used in Rio Grande do Sul, Santa Catarina, and Paraná. It also is much used in São Paulo and Espírito Santo, and in Minas Gerais and other states it also has been introduced on the numerous colonization projects. It is now being widely diffused throughout the North by official colonization ventures.

SCATTERED FARMSTEADS

"In general the colonists lived on their farms [sítios], in the vicinity of the *vila*. To this they only flowed on feast days." In these words Rocha Pombo described the scattered settlement patterns of Paraná,[11] a type of settlement that was and remains of great importance in Brazil.

Great interest should be attached to the widespread use of this type of settlement in Brazil. Like those of the United States, the isolated farmsteads prevailing in Brazil represent a sharp break with tradition, a New World development and one that is very important. All through the valleys of the *Serra do Mar* are scattered in haphazard manner the homes of small farmers, or sitiantes, each located on the land. Sandwiched in between São Paulo's fazendas, and even on the shattered fragments of former fazendas, one also finds numerous homes of persons of the small-farmer class, nearly always widely dispersed over the landscape. These are particularly numerous in the poorer areas of the state where the soils are of second quality or where the terrain is sharply rolling.

Southern Minas Gerais is an immense area of scattered farmsteads.

[10] Cf. Emílio Willems, *Assimilação e Populações Marginais no Brasil* (São Paulo, 1940), 82–83, who quotes the following passage from a publication commemorating the fiftieth anniversary of Brusque, Santa Catarina. "After their strenuous daily work, they could not rest in the accustomed manner of their country of origin. It was not possible to converse in the evening with their neighbors to the right and left. Sunday mornings they did not hear the peal of the bell that should call them to church, in the afternoon they could not stroll through the fields, at night they could not meet with their friends in beer halls to drink beer. Their children were raised without companions, without schooling. They lived in the solitude and desert of a strange country and their eyes saw nothing but the monotonous shade of a virgin forest." See also *ibid.*, 86.

[11] José Francisco da Rocha Pombo, *Historia de Paraná* (São Paulo, 1930), 96. See also Schmidt, *O Meio Rural*.

Here the land has become greatly divided, so that even the remaining fazendas are small. Except for an occasional large estate where the colony for the workers survives, the entire section is now blanketed with the scattered settlement pattern.

The settlement pattern prevailing throughout immense cattle-grazing areas which extend northward from central Minas Gerais to north-central Piauí and Maranhão and westward across Goiás and Mato Grosso is not easy to characterize. A few of the largest fazendas are true villages. Most of the fazendas will have at least a few thatched huts for the workers located near the more substantial dwelling of the proprietor. However, in general, the pattern is that of scattered farmsteads.

The cotton-growing sections of São Paulo, the western parts of Minas Gerais, and those portions of the northeastern states of Brazil which lie next to the cane-growing littoral are also areas in which scattered farm dwellings are predominant. In São Paulo the cabins of the parceiros, who care for the crop, are scattered about in the cotton fields as they are in the southern part of the United States. Elsewhere, the huts of the workers are likely to be found near the proprietor's more pretentious dwelling. However, since the cotton fazendas are small and, since much of the cotton of the Northeast is produced on small farms, there is a considerable dispersion of farm homes in most of the cotton-producing areas.

Finally, it should be indicated that there are many small farmers scattered about on the less desirable lands of the sugar sections, in the little valleys that lead into the São Francisco River, in little pockets amid the line-village settlements of south Brazil, in little "augur holes" in the forests of the North, and in a host of other miscellaneous situations. When these people are actually rooted to the soil, the settlement pattern is generally of the dispersed type.

FINAL PATTERN

One should not close this discussion of the settlement types in Brazil and their distribution without making the point that much of Brazil's settlement pattern is still to be determined. Even today there are large areas of unpatented public lands in the nation. Although there may be some "squatters" or "intruders" living on them, they can hardly be said to have been settled. Which of the patterns will be used when they are settled remains to be seen. Portions now being sold by the government of the state of Mato Grosso in tracts of about five hundred hectares are going into scattered farmsteads. That being used for state and national agricultural colonies is being developed into settlements of the line-village type.

But it is not only on the lands that are in public ownership that settlement patterns are still to be determined. Except on the coast, and in some of the southern states, density of population is comparatively slight even where the land has nearly all been patented. In almost every part of Brazil there is room for many more people, without the necessity of lowering living standards. In fact, a shift from cattle grazing to agriculture might greatly raise the standard of living in other parts of Brazil just as it has in parts of Paraná, Santa Catarina, and Rio Grande do Sul. In any case, just as a Santa Catarina fazenda that formerly provided a scant living for a handful of people is now the site for prosperous line-village settlements, large estates in other parts of Brazil may become the homes of increased numbers of people.

Another reason for asserting that the settlement patterns of Brazil are still to be determined is that the nomadic life associated with the system described as fire agriculture is so significant. At the present time in Brazil's vast interior millions of unattached rural people move about from year to year, destroying large acreages of forest in order to prepare their roças for beans, mandioca, corn, and other crops. Their homes are not fixed for any length of time. If they become attached as agregados on fazendas or are given places in agricultural colonies, they may initiate a considerable change in Brazil's pattern of settlement. But the form of settlement used in their "fixation" may be any one of the three, and if present tendencies persist, those who are incorporated into the labor force of the fazenda will live in village settlements, those placed in the colonies in line villages. However, if through a homestead law they were allowed permanent possession of the public lands on which they had made a roça, large areas in Maranhão, Goiás, and Mato Grosso, and parts of Pará and Amazonas might eventually be covered with scattered farmsteads.

BREAK WITH PORTUGUESE TRADITION

The manner in which the population is arranged on the land, the settlement pattern of Brazil, is another indicator of the sharp break with traditional patterns that was made in the country's colonization. Because small-farming classes were not settled in Brazil, obviously the typical Portuguese village settlement of small freeholders could not be transplanted. Therefore, in contrast to the situation in most of Spanish America where the village pattern of settlement was transplanted from Spain, or the French Colonies where the traditional French patterns became deeply graved, or even Anglo-Saxon America where the first settlements were of the typical English village variety, from the very first stages of colonization there was a break with the traditional Portuguese forms. In Brazil this break with the past and the subsequent evolution of other types was probably even greater than in the United States.

This difference between Brazil and the United States is most pronounced if the former is compared with the northern parts of the latter; less pronounced if the comparison is with our South. In the northern United States, and particularly in New England, the old patterns persisted until well into the nineteenth century. When Timothy Dwight made his famous "travels" throughout New England at the opening of the nineteenth century, the old village settlement patterns were still predominant in the more settled parts of the region; only on the frontier were the scattered farmsteads coming into their own and beginning to form the types of neighborhood and community units that now blanket the United States.[12] Even at the close of the nineteenth century the use of the village settlement pattern for arranging the farm population on the land made some American rural communities so similar to those of Old England that they even compared closely with the Germanic prototypes from which the latter had been derived.[13] In general, in the United States the transition from the European nucleated types of locality groups to the scattered farmsteads, the open country neighborhoods, the village-centered rural communities, and the county units of local government was a gradual process. It came about only after several centuries in the New World had produced a cultural heritage sufficiently modified from that transferred from Europe to enable man to cope with the wilderness, and only then because the force of constituted authority and law had become greatly weakened. For the first hundred years or so in New England the arm of constituted authority was very strong, and the activities of the individual were greatly limited. But by the latter half of the eighteenth century men on the frontier were getting out of hand. Probably the major factor leading to the development of the scattered farmsteads and open country neighborhoods in western New England and in New York was the fact that the hold of the constituted authorities had become weakened to the point that it was possible for the frontier family to move onto a desired tract of land, blaze trees to indicate the boundaries of the territory claimed, and by "squatting" there obtain "tomahawk rights" to the land—rights that were recognized by the mores if not by the law.

In Brazil the break with the past came more immediately. The Portuguese who settled Brazil never attempted to transplant the village communities of small farmers, such as were typical of the old country. Rather, the number of whites moving to the New World was relatively small and consisted of impoverished members of the lower and even upper rungs of the nobility—adventurers seeking to re-establish their fortunes in the colonies. Each of them secured an immense tract of land, the grant of *sesmaria*, and on it established a sugar cane plantation or engenho. Workers to carry on the multifarious activities of the plantation were secured at first by enslaving the Indians and later by importing Negro slaves from Africa. From the first the settlements established in Brazil were quite different from those of Porgugal, for although the latter had a landed nobility, it was for the most part a country cultivated by a peasant class of farm-

---

[12] See Timothy Dwight, *Travels in New-England and New-York* (London, 1823), I, 300–303; III, 167, *passim*.

[13] Cf. Herbert B. Adams, *The Germanic Origin of New England Towns* (Baltimore, 1882).

ers settled on the land in village communities. The Brazilian sugar plantation, although utilizing a village arrangement for its slave quarters, was still only one farm. It had little resemblance to patterns in the mother country. As in the South of the United States, when villages and towns came into being, they were of the trade-center type. If the colonist lacked the means required to equip a sugar engenho and was forced to go inland and establish a cattle *curral* or fazenda, an even greater break with Portuguese tradition resulted. In such cases the equivalent of scattered farmsteads often came into being, if not at first, then later as the land was divided by inheritance. Rocha Pombo, one of Brazil's most distinguished historians, wrote of the colonial period:

It is easy to see that in those times the number of houses constituting the nucleus of a vila was very small. The inhabitants lived widely separated, sometimes in the amplitude of a vast district, on their sítios (name commonly given to the fazendas, pastoral or agricultural); and only on the holidays or Sundays did they congregate at the seat of the vila. Those men that almost always carried on a life of laziness, poorly directing the slaves —upon leaving the sítios for the *freguezia,* already were different men, especially if business was going in a manner that might permit larger aspirations. To the extent that they grew wealthy, they soon had the caprice of building a house in the vila or city, where already they were making more frequent visits.[14]

Also to be remembered in accounting for the break with Portuguese tradition in this and other respects is the absence of European females among the colonists. European women played an insignificant role in the settlement of Brazil. Since it is chiefly women who preserve and diffuse cultural traits, it is possible that Brazil's cultural evolution would have been entirely different had a significant percentage of females been included among the Portuguese who came to Brazil during the colonial period.

[14] José Francisco da Rocha Pombo, *Historia do Brazil* (Rio de Janeiro, n.d.), V, 701.

CHAPTER XII

LAND DIVISION, SURVEYS, AND TITLES

THE MANNER of dividing the land, surveying the boundaries of rural properties, and recording the titles to agricultural holdings are among the most significant aspects of the relationship of men to the land. All three are so closely interrelated that they really constitute a single part of the land system. In the analysis of their situation in any country there are two aspects that should be clearly kept in mind: (1) the extent to which land surveys are definite, determinate, and permanent, and (2) if the farmers reside on their lands, as is generally the case in Brazil and the United States, the extent to which the system in use permits farmhouses to be located near one another, makes for economy in the building, upkeep, and use of roads, electric lines, and other facilities, and allows adaptation of the settlement pattern to the natural environment for maximum adjustment to and benefit from topographical and structural features of the landscape such as slopes, watercourses, soil types, and vegetation.

Unless the surveys are definite, determinate, and built upon permanent bases, a simple system of registering land titles cannot be put into effect. When the surveys are indefinite and indeterminate, disputes over the property lines cannot so easily be settled by the expedient of a resurvey. The passage of time will alter the boundaries of the farms if surface phenomena, such as stones, trees, creek beds, and water divides, are the points of reference used in the surveys. In the perfection of any nation's land system all of these points are cared for in the most satisfactory manner possible if astronomical bases are selected as lines of departure in the making of the surveys and if the dividing lines based on the principal meridians of latitude and longitude are made with strictly parallel lines. These principles have been followed in the system of surveys used in the United States. However, many of the advantages that might come from such a rectangular system have been vitiated in this country by unnecessary rigidity, the prescription that all the parallelograms into which the land was divided should be in the form of squares.

In those portions of the United States surveyed and settled after 1790 the cultural landscape is oriented with respect to parallels of latitude and longitude and is not based on surface features. Along with the obvious influence this system has had on political divisions, roads, lines of trees, and shapes of fields, it has assisted greatly in the perfection of a highly satisfactory method of registering land titles. This situation, found throughout most of the United States, is in sharp contrast to that in the states along the eastern seaboard and in the Old World. Had the surveys permitted choice in the shape of the rectangles, a near perfect system of dividing the land could have resulted. Such a system is more necessary in countries such as the United States and Brazil, where most farmers live on the land, than in Europe and Asia where nucleated settlements predominate.

Man's welfare on the land requires that the system of surveys in use permits him to build his home in fairly close proximity to his neighbors, unless, of course, the village form of settlement is used. He benefits not only by association with his fellows, of extreme importance for children, but also by modern conveniences such as paved roads, telephone lines, electricity, and buses for school children, the costs of which are prohibitive if farm homes are widely dispersed. The checkerboard pattern in use in the United States results in an almost maximum separation of farm homes, density of population and size of farms being what they are. The surveys could have been just as definite, determinate, and permanent as they are, and the dispersal of homes comparatively slight, had the rectangles used in the surveys been considerably longer than they were wide. Even this, however, would not have permitted the adjustment of surveys to topographical features. A nation must choose between (1) orienting its cultural landscape with respect to natural features such as mountains, hills, and rivers, at the cost of land boundaries that are indefinite, indeterminate, and subject to change, and (2) definite, determinate, permanent boundaries which do not permit the fine adjustments of farm boundaries to natural phenomena.

INDETERMINATE LAND SURVEYS

When the North American observer looks at the map of a Brazilian locality he is unconsciously seeking something that is not there. This does not involve a feeling that the map is unreliable or poorly executed, nor does it arise from a lack of detail, because infinite care may have been taken to indicate all small streams, each divide, and every semblance to a hill or mountain. What the observer misses is the man-made additions, the system of co-ordinates that form the warp and woof of our own positional orientation, the systematic division of the territory into ranges, townships, and sections, or in the older areas the pattern of original land grants by means of which the lands were alienated. As a rule, Brazilian maps do give the ranges, but generally these have no functional relation to the man-made features of the landscape such as the roads, the property divisions, the layout of fields, the arrangement of the farm homes, rows of trees, and ditches. Brazilian locality maps are based almost entirely on natural phenomena such as streams, shore lines, and dividing ridges.

If, instead of looking at the map, one travels through the interior, the same fundamental contrast will be exhibited in the arrangement of the cultural landscape. Most Brazilian property lines follow streams or dividing ridges. Roads are not laid out on section lines but are oriented to the topography, a feature generally advantageous. Houses are located without respect to distances west of Greenwich or south of the equator. In short, the cultural landscape of Brazil is adjusted to natural phenomena and not to the man-made degrees of latitude and longitude. Naturally, this contrasts sharply with the geometric arrangement of cultural landscape that is such a prominent feature in the United States.

Land surveys and property descriptions in Brazil, like those of most of Latin America, are based on European models. They are oriented with respect to surface phenomena and delineated along irregular lines. It is, then, practically impossible to give a simple deed that will accurately define the limits of an area, which limits will be the same ten, twenty, or fifty years in the future.

Basing the surveys on surface phenomena inevitably gives rise to the practice of surveying boundaries and describing property limits

River-front Land Division and Line-Village Settlements along One Small Channel of the Amazon River in the State of Amazonas. (Courtesy of Hilgard O'Reilly Sternberg.)

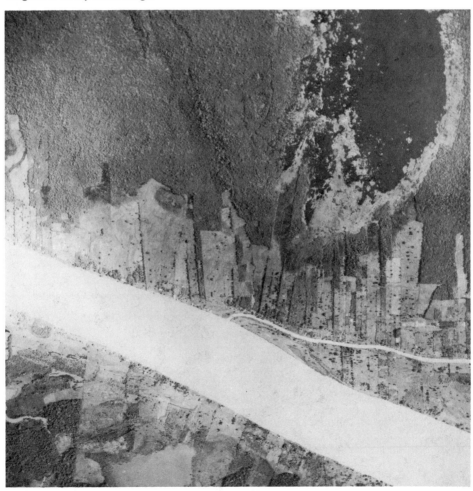

in terms of metes and bounds. Since water courses and dividing ridges follow extremely irregular lines this means that the area in a given piece of land may never be determined with the highest degree of precision; in other words, the surveys are indeterminate. Hence, practically all statements of size in Brazilian property descriptions contain the phrase *mais ou menos* (more or less).[1]

Such a system of surveys is also lacking in permanency because stream beds constantly shift, waterfronts slowly recede or advance, and even the absolute position of a dividing ridge may change significantly in the course of time. Markers may be moved, or knowledge of the exact course followed by previously established property lines may be forgotten or lost with the death of an old settler. All of these circumstances make for lack of permanency in land boundaries and frequently contribute greatly to misunderstandings between the owners of adjacent lands.

On the other hand, as indicated above, such systems of surveying lands permit the greatest adaptation of settlement patterns and farm organization to topography and other features of the natural landscape. In wisely planned settlements or colonies, like many of those to be found in south Brazil, each settler's holding may include a front on the stream, a face on the road, and portions of the various types of soil and land covering that are found in the area. These are of tremendous importance to the people on the land. However, if there is lack of foresight and control, coupled with indiscriminate location and surveys based on metes and bounds, the system greatly facilitates the activities of the monopolist who seeks to secure a right to the springs, water holes, stream fronts, or other limited and essential features of the landscape that give him effective control of an area much larger than the one he owns.

In the early days of Brazil's history land was so plentiful, the estates so large and sparsely populated, and the distance so far from the casa grande of one estate to the seat of a neighboring fazenda or engenho that questions of boundary lines and probably even of titles were of relatively little moment.[2] With the growth of population that

---

[1] A similar situation exists in most sections of Spanish America and in those parts of the United States that were surveyed before the land-minded nation adopted its official system in 1789 in which all surveys were based on the astronomically determined lines of longitude and latitude.

[2] However, the lack of systematic surveys and indeterminate boundaries early led to conflicts. At the opening of the nineteenth century Koster, who himself operated sugar engenhos in Pernambuco, wrote: "Some districts are in a quieter state than others: but very few are totally without disturbance: and there are few plantations in any part of the province, about the boundaries of the lands of which more than one law-suit has not been entered into." *Travels in Brazil*, I, 322.

These law suits were by no means the monopoly of people of means and over-large tracts of land. Koster himself was involved in one such suit during the time he resided on Itamaracá. His neighbors in this instance were "a numerous family of free negroes [who] possessed a small plot covered with coco-trees. These latter people had been much impoverished by the obstinacy of the chief of the family, now deceased, in maintaining a law-suit for many years, about the boundaries of his plot of land. As soon as I took possession, one of his sons wished to commence law proceedings with me, in spite of several awards which had been given against his father." *Ibid.*, II, 29.

situation changed. Even in some of the cattle-growing sections, i.e., those of sparse population, the lack of surveys, proper deeds, and a systematic division of the land were retarding factors. Consider the report of the engineer who surveyed the route for the proposed railway for Bahia's capital across the sertões to the São Francisco River.

It is of vital importance that the proper authorities should provide:
(1) The demarcation of the properties making effective the land law, which has never penetrated into these regions.
(2) The preparation of dams in the most appropriate places, instituting premiums and guarantees to those who might construct them.
When the land law begins to be translated into facts I am certain that there will appear many square leagues of unowned lands which now it is impossible to indicate.
In all of the povoados there are one, two, three and even four square leagues which are said to be patrimonies of the parishes.
There are no traces of the origins of these patrimonies. What can be affirmed however is that in these places one is free to fence the land that he pleases, to plant and to build according to his fancy, to call this his property and to transfer it to others without the consent of the proprietor of the patrimony and without making him the most insignificant payment.[3]

Since 1874, however, there have been great improvements, especially in the southern part of the nation where an agricultural civilization, characterized by a relatively dense population, is rapidly spreading out and overlaying the old pastoral culture. Nevertheless, land troubles continue to bother most of the states. The comments of the state directors or supervisors (*delegados gerais*) of the 1920 census, who were asked to report on the areas of farm properties, constitute a significant body of facts.[4] One of the most comprehensive statements came from Dr. Aurelio de Britto, reporting for the state of Piauí.

In Piauhy the lands are commons, *pro indivisu*. It is customary to speak of a *data de terra* to indicate the area of a sesmaria, whose extension is almost always of three leagues in front by one in depth. Those sesmarias conceded during the colonial regime, although delimited at that time, now generally have the marks obliterated and each one is subdivided into various possessions, in a manner more or less vague and abstract, out of which originate constantly questions among the holders of the various titles, especially in the places most subdivided (which are the areas where are found the carnaúba and coconut palm trees). The proprietors never express the extension of their properties in alqueires, tarefa, or any other agricultural measure; they give the selling price.[5]

Of Ceará, Dr. Hermano Vasconcellos Bittencourt reported: "It appears incredible but the reality is that, excepting the engineers and land surveyors, the majority of those that can read have no idea of

[3] A. M. de Oliveira Bulhões, *Estrada de Ferro da Bahia ao S. Francisco* (Rio de Janeiro, 1874), 54.
[4] "Introducção," *Recenseamento do Brazil, 1920*, I.
[5] *Ibid.*, 504. This practice of giving selling prices, instead of areas, is still followed in the official statistics of Pernambuco, the most advanced of the northeastern states and the only one for which it has been possible to secure figures on the number of rural properties. Cf. the *Anuário Estatístico de Pernambuco*, XI (1942), 180–97.

how to measure an area. Persons who are supposed to be educated know how to estimate an area only when it is a rectangle. . . . Sometimes the owners themselves do not know what they possess." [6]

Dr. Joaquim Pessôa, delegado geral for the census in Paraíba, wrote: "Enormous difficulties were encountered in gathering the agricultural statistics, because the farmers, in addition to being ignorant of their own conditions, avoided giving the information requested, fearing that it was being asked for the purpose of creating new taxes." [7] From Rio Grande do Norte, Dr. Heraclio Villar reported that "not rare is the lack of knowledge of the area of the rural establishments," [8] and the delegado for Pernambuco, Dr. Henrique Barbalho Uchôa Cavalcanti, complained of the "diversity of the methods used in each place for estimating rural areas." [9] Dr. Carlos Cavalcanti de Gusmão who had charge of the census in the state of Alagôas clearly and specifically stated: "Rare, very rare, are the rural properties in Alagôas that are regularly surveyed. Thus the agricultural questionnaires contain entries secured by estimates and calculations, it following also that the heterogeneity of them does not permit the organization of a summary table." [10] From Goiás the delegado also reported that the rural establishments having delimited areas were extremely rare. [11]

These comments are quoted for the more northerly states where the problems introduced by extensive developments of new agricultural zones, on lands previously given over exclusively to grazing, had not been felt to any great extent. In the southern portions of the country the census agents were able to give much more satisfactory answers to this type of question. Nevertheless, even there the questions of indefinite and indeterminate boundaries were then and continue to be acute. [12]

Great headway undoubtedly has been made in systematizing the land surveys, improving the methods of dividing the land, and recording the land titles, particularly in the states from São Paulo south. Gradually these improved systems are eliminating the older, more haphazard methods. As early as 1937 it was possible for one qualified observer to report about São Paulo:

[6] *Recenseamento do Brazil, 1920,* I, 505. This statement has a familiar ring to those acquainted with Koster's comments which were made a hundred years earlier: "The division of property in the Sertam is very undeterminate: and this may be imagined, when I say, that the common mode of defining the size of a *fazenda,* is by computing it as so many leagues; or, as in some cases, by so many hundreds of calves yearly, without any reference to the quantity of the land. Few persons take the trouble of making themselves acquainted with the exact extent of their own property, and perhaps could not discover it if they made the attempt." *Travels in Brazil,* I, 205.

[7] *Recenseamento do Brazil, 1920,* I, 506.

[8] *Ibid.,* 507.

[9] *Ibid.,* 508.

[10] *Ibid.,* 509.

[11] *Ibid.,* 525.

[12] This is even true of such newly opened areas as Acre Territory. For an account of the haphazard surveys, indiscriminate location, squatters' rights in the territory, and the social conflict generated thereby, see Schurz, Hargis, Marbut, and Manifold, *Rubber Production in the Amazon Valley,* 286.

To find small or medium-sized holdings in any considerable numbers, or rather holdings without any fixed boundaries and limited only by the scarcity of the labour available to cultivate them, one must penetrate far inland to the borders of Paraná, where, except at certain spots, there are no properly equipped development schemes, no systematic settlement and no land survey, but only more or less isolated pioneers who carry on at the confines of the civilized zone the out-of-date tradition of the heroic age of immigration and settlement, when the state itself recognized occupation as a valid title to ownership.[13]

In Minas Gerais, too, there early was considerable progress in the improvement of the system of surveying lands and recording the titles to tracts that were alienated. The basic rules in this state are contained in Law No. 4,496 of January 5, 1916, a piece of legislation devoted to regulations pertaining to public lands. Unoccupied lands are defined as those not held privately by a legitimate title or applied to public use by the federal, state, or município governments. Lands occupied by mere possession or by concessions which were not legalized in the manner specified in previous legislation are classed as unoccupied or *terras devolutas*. Titles obtained by sale or donation are legitimate, as are claims to land on which imposts had been paid prior to the regulation of January 30, 1854.

Of the public domain the state proposed to reserve sites for villages and colonies, space for roads, and the woodlands on the upper part of mountain slopes. A service was established for the purpose of surveying, marking, describing, and disposing of state lands. For these purposes Minas Gerais was divided into four districts, each having a commission, composed of an engineer, two surveyors, and a registrar, to carry out the provisions of the law. Each commission apparently was to determine where it would work but was required to give notice at least fifteen days in advance of any proposed surveys. Owners of lands adjoining or included in those to be surveyed were to be invited to exhibit proofs of their titles. If an examination of the documents should not resolve the doubts, the work of measurement was to begin. The law provided for an appeal from the decision of the commission to the courts but indicated that this should not delay the surveys.

It was stated that a detailed map should be made of each tract surveyed, on which was to be indicated the areas to be reserved; the remainder was to be divided into lots varying in size from twenty-five to five hundred hectares, in areas suitable for agriculture; and from fifty hectares to areas capable of grazing four hundred head of cattle, in pastoral sections. It was specified that topographical features and type and quality of the soil should be considered in laying out these lots, the purpose being to form small, independent properties.

Article 25 specified that stone, whenever available, was to be used for the markers at the principal corners; otherwise, hardwood was to be used. Before placing the markers, glass, coal, or other unalterable

[13] Fernand Maurette, *Some Social Aspects of Present and Future Economic Development in Brazil* (Geneva, 1937), 16.

substances were to be placed in the holes to facilitate relocation of the spot if the marker should disappear. The wooden markers should be placed on little mounds of earth, about which small trenches had been dug. The maps were to be oriented according to the true meridian of the place, the magnetic declination being taken into consideration.

In the sale of lands surveyed, Article 32 provided that preference be given to: (1) those who had failed to validate their titles during the periods permitted by the previous laws, (2) squatters who could prove habitual residence and effective cultivation of at least one-fifth of the area, (3) petitioners who had paid for the surveys, (4) owners of adjacent lands who could prove their need and the means to use the area requested, and (5) young graduates of institutions maintained by the state for purposes of agricultural education.[14]

Although notable progress had been made in improving the system of land division, surveys, and titles in south Brazil, over much of the country the system of metes and bounds is still followed. Streams and divides continue to figure prominently in most property descriptions. This is particularly true in the West and in the Amazon Valley. Several property descriptions typical of those used in the sparsely settled pastoral areas of west-central Brazil, appear in the *Diário Oficial* of the state of Mato Grosso for October 6, 1942.

To His Excellency the Secretary General of the State:

Ciriaco Rondon, Brazilian, married, represented by his qualified counsel who formulated this statement and who signs below, desiring to acquire by purchase from the State a piece of unoccupied land, pastures and fields, with 500 (five hundred) hectares, more or less, in the place called "Baia de Santa Terzinha," situated on the right side of the Riozinho; in the município of Herculânea, presents himself very respectfully to request Your Excellency that, following the fulfillment of the legal formalities, you will do him the honor to cede to him by sale the said tract of land, with the following boundaries: on the North, beginning on the bank of the Riozinho at the limit of the lands of Paulino Luiz de Barros, and following this property line to a certain point; on the West and South with unoccupied lands; on the east separated from the Fazenda Cervo by the same Riozinho. The petitioner subjects himself to all the obligations of the law. . . . Cuiabá, August 26, 1942. P. P. Gabriel Neves.

Another tract of five hundred hectares sought by Catulo da Costa Rondon, also located in the município of Herculânea, is described as "beginning at the Corrego Anhumas [a small creek or stream] and extending towards the line of hills, bounded on the North, West, and South by unoccupied lands, and on the East separated from the Fazenda by the same Anhumas creek, Guanandí Bay being situated within the area concerned."

With such indefinite descriptions of lands in the deeds granted by the states, considerable confusion may arise, and there is also a possibility of overlapping claims or "shingle titles" such as characterized the granting of public lands in Kentucky and Tennessee. How-

[14] The law is published in *Relativos aos Serviços de Terras Publicas do Estado de Minas Gerais* (Belo Horizonte, 1925).

ever, some precautions are taken by the various states to prevent this. In some cases the title to a tract of land may be registered only after the owners of the adjoining properties have signified that the dividing limits are accurate. Notice may be given that a certain tract is to be surveyed and that those concerned should look out for their interests. Thus, in the *Diário Oficial* of Mato Grosso for October 7, 1942, appeared five notices regarding lands that had been sold by the state and were to be surveyed and marked. The translation of one of these notices reads:

Notice of Measurements:

The below signed, designated by His Excellency Dr. Secretary General of the State to determine and proceed to the measurement and demarcation of the tract of land called "Sapé," situated in the município of Alto Araguaia, acquired from the State by Sr. Juvenal Alves de Faria, sets the day of November 28 next, at 8 o'clock in the morning for the beginning of the field work and invites all those awaiting and others interested to witness the said services and set forth that which is correct.

The tract being surveyed has the following boundaries: upon the North, commencing at a convenient point on the divide between Jatobá creek and the headwaters of the Sapé, running in a straight line and crossing the bed of the headwaters of the Sapé: on the East by the divide of Engano creek, fronting on the lands belonging to Viriato Bino, for a distance of 2,000 meters; on the South, by a straight line running to a convenient point; on the West, from the latter point through the woods to the point of beginning.

Cuiabá, October 5, 1942
Julio da Costa Marques, Agronomist.

In other cases, notice is given that certain tracts have been applied for, and interested persons are given a certain length of time in which to examine the descriptions and, if they care, to raise objections. Thus in the *Diário Oficial* of the state of Mato Grosso for October 6, 1942, appeared the notice:

Directory of Lands and Public Works
Notice

By order of the Director, I make public, for the information of those interested, during the space of five days from the publication of this notice there will be open to inspection the files of measurements and demarcations of the tracts of land called "São Luiz," "Pedra Furada," "Ribeirãozinho" and "Córrego do Bagre" situated in the municípios of Herculânea (2), Três Lagôas, and in this Capital, purchased from the State, by citizens Joaquim Vincente Ribeiro, Joaquim Crisotomo Furtado, Jovino Pereira de França and Joaquim Pedroso de Barros.

Department of Lands, Cuiabá, October 2, 1942
Carlos Hugueney de Siqueira
Head of the Department

Developments Before 1850. As was inevitable in the occupation of such an immense territory by so few people, the system of dividing Brazil's tremendous acreages grew up in a haphazard fashion.[15]

[15] This is reminiscent in many ways of the parallel developments in North America, where there was little or no system in the surveying, division, and distribution of land until after independence had been attained.

The first legal concessions of land seem to have been made by Martim Affonso de Souza in 1531 and 1532, some on the Island of Guaibe and some in Piratininga (later the city of São Paulo). In 1532, also, the king informed Martim of his decision to form *capitanias* on the coast from Pernambuco to the Rio da Prata, each with an extension of fifty leagues along the coast. Martim himself was to have one hundred leagues, his brother, Pero Lopes, fifty.[16] Since presumably the lines extended westward from the coast, the capitanias created were of very unequal size. The only markers were on the coast.

Also, the fifty-league criterion was not adhered to strictly. In the end Pero Lopes got eighty instead of fifty; João de Barros, one hundred; Duarte Coelho Pereira, sixty; Fernando Alvares de Andrade, seventy-five leagues; on the other hand Antonio Cardoso de Barros got only forty leagues, and Pedro de Góes only thirty.[17] However, this system of capitanias proved quite unsuccessful as an instrument for peopling the new continent, and soon another plan was substituted. The king reassembled the diffused governing powers and placed them in the hands of the *capitão* of Bahia as governor general of all the capitanias. The first governor general, Tome de Souza, carried with him to the New World the elements for greatly altering the land system of the colonies. These elements consisted of ideas for modifying the system of sesmarias, previously adapted to tiny Portugal, which, as used in Brazil, so far had proved inadequate for promoting the settlement of a hemisphere.

In Portugal the sesmarias had been devices for recovering lands from the hands of those who were not making good use of them. The use of these devices in America probably had much to do with retarding the settlement process. Anyway, the early distribution seems to have been very parsimonious. Tome de Souza soon introduced the practice of granting lands for the establishment of sugar engenhos. This meant great liberality in giving away land. Enough lands were given to successful applicants to supply the cane for a mill and to develop an establishment large enough to maintain the towers, fortifications, and private army necessary for defense against the Indians. Hence, it was necessary for those seeking sesmarias to have ample means. Always they tried to demonstrate that they were men of "great possessions and family" or that they possessed numerous cattle and slaves.[18] From this time on, the various incumbents in the office of the governor general granted enormous, ill-defined tracts [19] as sesmarias. In reality, many of them were capitanias, and their

[16] Ruy Cirne Lima, *Terras Devolutas* (Pôrto Alegre, 1935), 30–31.

[17] Augusto Fausto de Souza, *Estudo sobre a Divisão Territorial do Brasil* (Rio de Janeiro, 1878), 35–38. For the estimated areas of these capitanias see Rocha Pombo, *Historia do Brazil*, III, 132.

[18] Oliveira Vianna, "O Povo Brasileiro e sua Evolução," *loc. cit.*, 284.

[19] "The new system of administration produced the necessity of determining better the limits of the different units of government, and abandoning imaginary east-west lines; limits were being modified to the extent that the territory became better known, and advances were made in the conquest of the lands occupied by savage tribes." Fausto de Souza, *Estudo sobre a Divisão Territorial do Brazil*, 41–42.

proprietors in turn parceled them out to others in sesmarias.[20] For example, D. Alvaro da Costa received as a sesmaria all of the land lying between the rivers Paraguassú and Jaguaripe for a depth of ten leagues, a grant the size of a capitania, and indeed it was called the "Capitania de Peroassú." There resulted the complete lack of any system in the division of lands, or, as Cirne Lima has said, one which "abandoned to the colonist himself the selection of his territorial seat," and "the colonial population established itself in our territory in obedience, not to a predetermined plan of geographic distribution, but to the wishes and convenience of the individual." [21] Another Brazilian writer has generalized as follows: "Properties extended themselves along the courses of the rivers. On the Brazilian shores, when colonization commenced, the capitanias only had marks on the coast. The internal limits depended on the ardor, combativeness, and energy of the semiproprietors. In the West there were only fixed limits along the river shore. Inward, if another river was not touched, there was only indetermination." [22]

An Englishman who lived in Brazil in the early years of the nineteenth century, before independence, has supplied some of the details as to techniques used in ensuring boundaries.

Lands are obtained by grant as well as by purchase; and being distributed by the map, instead of survey and measurement, it cannot be wonderful that confusion and contests should arise with respect to their boundaries. To ascertain and establish their claims, many land holders fix around their borders a number of small tenants, called Moradores, who pay a trifling rent, procure their subsistence chiefly by the cultivation of vegetables, and answer the important purpose of Watchmen, preventing the encroachments of neighbouring proprietors and the robbery of the woods. They are generally white people who have families, sometimes a slave or two, and add much to the population of the country; but they love and affect independence, and seldom continue after the limits of an estate are well ascertained, and its remoter parts are brought under cultivation.

The ignorance and listlessness of these people are astonishing. Living almost constantly in the woods, their minds are uncultivated, and become hardly capable of more than one kind of excitement. Accustomed to exercise the violent passions without control, and to slaughter every animal which comes in their way, their fury knows no bounds, and they are ever ready for all that it urges to. Their eyes, incessantly on the watch, become large, distorted, and piercing, even to a frightful degree; and the muscles of their faces assume a concomitant form. Having nothing to lose, easily finding a supply for their wants, and unattached to any particular spot, they leave their abodes without regret, and fix again without any seeming concern but that of avoiding the rivalry and annoyance of a neighbourhood.[23]

Carried forward by such a process of settlement, there can be little doubt that indiscriminate location, haphazard surveys, and little concern with land titles very early laid the basis in much of Brazil

---

[20] Cirne Lima, *Terras Devolutas,* 35.
[21] *Ibid.,* 35–36.
[22] Werneck Sodré, *Oeste,* 119.
[23] John Luccock, *Notes on Rio de Janeiro and the Southern Parts of Brazil* (London, 1820), 293.

for a chaotic condition similar to that which prevailed in Kentucky, Tennessee, and neighboring states. However, because Brazilian holdings were large and because personal adjustments of differences are easier between a few people than among many, less confusion arose than otherwise would have been the case. Brazil seems to have suffered less in the early days from conflicts over "shingle titles" than the United States, in that portion between the Appalachians and the Mississippi. Even so, the conflicting and overlapping claims, generated by the lack of a precise system, undoubtedly have had an adverse effect on the nation's growth and development.

In the latter years of the eighteenth century the granting of sesmarias became much less general and the practice of taking possession of unoccupied lands by the process of "squatting" much more prevalent. Werneck Sodré explains this as being due to "delay and complexity in the acquisition of land titles." However, Brazil, like the United States, had developed a population thoroughly capable of coping with the wilderness, receiving relatively little from the mother country overseas, and quite unwilling to be prevented from occupying desirable sites for fazendas merely because such might not be in accord with old formalities. Werneck Sodré has also pointed out how, as the sesmarias became more rare, there was an increase in the number of those squatters who preferred to seat themselves on the land without formality. They hoped "to obtain, in view of the prevalence of such cases, the benevolence of the organs of public administration, when the case should come to a test." With the cessation of the sesmarias in 1822,[24] this practice became general, and it continued to be so for several decades. It was in an attempt to put an end to this that the emperor promulgated the law of September 18, 1850, which prohibited the acquisition of lands by any means except purchase and threatened removal, loss of benefits, fines, and imprisonment to those who, in the future, illegally occupied public lands. However, the practice of squatting and of claiming ownership through mere possession was then already so old, so firmly established, and so generally practiced that it was impossible suddenly to carry the new provisions into effect without jeopardizing the economic existence of many regions, including the West. Therefore it is not surprising that Article 5 of the law ordered that there should be legitimated lands acquired by first occupation or secured from the first occupant, providing they had been opened to cultivation or actually lived on by the possessor or his representatives.[25] In nearly all cases, however, on both those secured by sesmaria and those obtained by squatting, the property lines, if any, seem to have been traced in terms of streams, divides, and previously established lines. "Wherever possible," one Brazilian writer observes, "natural limits were chosen in the division, such as rivers and brooks, which, be-

[24] A Brazilian friend writing to Burton attributed the exhaustion of much of Brazil's best land to the extralegal system of occupation which followed the cessation of these grants. *The Highlands of the Brazil*, I, 42.

[25] See Werneck Sodré, *Oeste*, 83–84.

sides resolving all doubts as to the boundary lines, serve as natural fences for keeping in the cattle." [26] Despite such a case for metes and bounds, a reliance on these natural features ultimately results in confused and conflicting titles to the land.

Brazil once officially recognized the need to base its land surveys on unalterable astronomical criteria and attempted to introduce rectangular surveys. A preamble to a decree dated December 10, 1796, referred to the necessity of using geometric lines that would fix secure boundaries and be linked unalterably with "trigonometric and astronomic measures" that alone could give the surveys "the necessary stability." [27] Half a century later Article 14 of the important land legislation, Law No. 601 of September 18, 1850, specifically decreed that the surveys should be based on the true meridians and that property dividing lines should cut one another at right angles.[28] The attempt to systematize the land surveys in this manner led to immediate repercussions. A. Francisco de Varnhagen, for example, objected strongly.

> The system of the United States of selling lands in square plots, is, in general, less applicable in Brazil, where, in all the municípios, there exist, irregularly spaced, lands which should be given according to the Brazilian system of water divides, which, moreover, is the most proper for a mountainous country cut by washes and rivers because it is cheaper and more practical; while Meridian lines, or squares, require better engineers, more numerous markings, instruments, etc. Sometimes such a system might have advantages in the great plateaus, as yet absolutely unoccupied; but it is better that the law should not impose it as a principle, with exceptions only when the "local circumstances do not admit it." [29]

Whether objections of this kind were effective or not one cannot be sure, but the intentions of the framers of the law of 1850 were never carried into effect, and the system of metes and bounds based on surface phenomena, continued to be the only system used in the division of Brazilian lands. However, as late as 1895 a law pertaining to public lands signed by the Governor of Rio Grande do Norte included the following provision: "The measurement and division shall be made by lines that run from North to South, in conformity with the true meridian, and by others that cut them at right angles, in a manner that lots or squares are formed of as many hectares as are necessary, truly surveyed, having in view the situation and the end to which they are destined." [30]

Nevertheless, there is little evidence that such legislative provisions ever gained widespread expression in the land system. Irregularly shaped holdings, divided by creeks and ridges, and a cultural landscape oriented to these natural phenomena were bequeathed to

[26] Eugenio Dahne, *Descriptive Memorial of the State of Rio Grande do Sul, Brazil* (Pôrto Alegre, 1904), 24.

[27] Cirne Lima, *Terras Devolutas*, 58.

[28] This law is reproduced in J. O. de Lima Pereira, *Da Propriedade no Brasil* (São Paulo, 1932), 200–206.

[29] Varnhagen is quoted in Cirne Lima, *Terras Devolutas*, 63.

[30] *Terras Públicas* (Natal, 1896), 5.

Brazil by the pattern cut before 1850. An English writer, who studied Brazil intensely for the purpose of determining its possibilities in the production of cotton, generalized: "Land ownership in Brazil is a difficult point; the original titles were made out on the basis of maps, boundaries, etc., but these maps have proved often to be wrong. The country has not yet been thoroughly surveyed and we have found mountain ranges 30 miles from the place indicated by the maps. The courses of rivers are also frequently not properly marked on the maps." [31]

Developments After 1850. The law of 1850 was an attempt to systematize the land system by restricting the activities of squatters. New settlement was to be confined to lands secured by purchase. The law came into being shortly before the tide of immigrant small farmers entering the southern states reached a significant size. Most of its provisions, including the one calling for rectangular surveys, were of little effect.

As late as 1865 some of the North Americans who carefully studied São Paulo and neighboring states as a possible home for emigrants from southern United States described the conditions of land surveys and holdings. "Ask a man 'how much land do you own?' and his usual reply is, 'I do not know exactly, but it is four, six or ten miles long, and from four to six miles broad.' The lands of Brazil, except in rare instances, have not been surveyed, and no one with whom we have conversed on this subject, knows how much land he owns; all guess." [32]

Following the 1860's, however, the developments, stimulated by the problems encountered and the experience gained in the colonies and by reports of what was being done in Argentina, were rather rapid. Thus, in 1871 a representative of the Ministry of Agriculture who presented a report on the condition of the German colonies in Santa Catarina called attention to the necessity for a more systematic registration of land titles.

In the capital there should be a book that would contain the general register of the lands in the province, separated by parishes, as is ordered by Art. 13 of law No. 601 of April 18, 1850. In it should be entered the sales by the State to private individuals, setting forth the manner in which the privately owned lands came into such possession. This book, supplemented by a topographic map of the province, in which could be entered notes concerning surveys made, would give a basis for the inventory of landed properties, a service so necessary for us, and which the Argentine Confederation has so carefully and successfully done, and which has in some way aided the current of immigration that for some years has been establishing itself there.

The register of private lands which has been the responsibility of the priests, will assist in the work of the general land register. . . . It may be

[31] Arno S. Pearse, *Brazilian Cotton* (2d ed.; Manchester, 1923), 86. The Conselho Nacional de Geografia now prepares detailed maps of Brazil that are far superior to anything published in the past. These new maps indicate the degree of reliability that prevails in the delineations for each section of the country. Not infrequently the studies which laid the basis for the new maps indicated radical errors in the older ones.

[32] Dunn, *Brazil, the Home for Southerners,* 232.

that I am in error, but I believe that the work I am doing will be of great utility for the discrimination of the public domain from the private, and for eliminating many misunderstandings between present and future proprietors, preventing many demands, and contributing in this manner for the peace and progress of the province.

In the provinces where colonies exist, it is of great urgency to attend to the necessity of organizing this work. I believe, however, it can only be organized by a permanent commission.[33]

Two years later another report presented to the Minister of Agriculture discussed the same problem.

Even up to this day it has not been possible to establish the general registration of lands; in spite of repeated periods, successively designated for twenty years as the dates for registration, it has not been possible to achieve the result that the law had in view, that is, the competent separation of the public domain from the private.

To expel the intruders and squatters, who took possession of public lands after the regulation of January 30, 1854, would provoke conflicts, destroy agricultural establishments already founded, and, perhaps, nuclei of budding villages. The remedy is to legitimate these possessions, requiring of the possessors the minimum legal price for the lands usurped and to set a new period for the legitimation of the ones prior to the said regulation, dispensing with penalties, whenever possible. . . . The Notice of June 13, 1863, which ordered preference in the purchase of lands be given to the occupants, is a salutary procedure, tending to realize this thinking.[34]

At this time, too, there was aroused some concern about knowledge of the conditions under which land was being held and extent of the unoccupied areas. For example, a map, and accompanying text, of the state of Santa Catarina, published in 1874, estimated the area of the state to be 1,100 square leagues, classified as follows: terras devolutas, 700; occupied lands, 300; and doubtful, 100 square leagues.[35]

There are other evidences of a growing concern for the improvement of the systems of surveying and recording. An official report published in 1875 stated that land surveys were in their beginning and needed to be better regulated. It stated, however, that it would be useless to survey the distant sertões, far from markets and lines of communication. Neither the immigrant nor the Brazilian would establish himself in those vast solitudes, and in a few years all traces of marks would be erased by Brazil's prolific vegetation. It was recommended that the surveys and demarcations made should be close to the centers of population, along the railroads, near the roads, or not far from other lines of communication. In the provinces receiving colonists it would suffice to make the measurements as the newcomers arrived or slightly before. However, the service should be performed with all regularity and in entire accordance with the law of 1850 and by fully qualified surveyors.[36]

[33] Albuquerque Galvão, *Relatorio sobre Blumenau, Itajahy, Principe D. Pedro e D. Francisca*, 22–23.
[34] Cardoso de Menezes e Souza, *Theses sobre Brazil*, 291.
[35] Bernardo Augusto Nacentes de Azambuja, *Descripção Topographica do Mappa da Provincia de Santa Catarina* (Rio de Janeiro, 1874).
[36] Cardoso de Menezes e Souza, *Theses sobre Brazil*, 295–96.

The same report urged the necessity of establishing in Brazil a counterpart of the "homestead" law, a device that might have meant much to Brazil by placing immediately before the eyes of its millions of landless people the goal of landownership. Had Brazil's rural masses been favored with such an opportunity to scale the agricultural ladder, it is highly probable that the pace of agricultural development in that country would have more nearly equaled that of the United States. The author of the report under consideration had written in 1873:

> Brazil, however, is in the primary phase of colonization; its extremely vast territory, which could contain more than 500 million people still includes vast solitudes, unpopulated sertões, that invite human immigration. To foreigners with families who land with capital on our shores and who do not shortly find work with pay to care for their economic necessities, who apply for the purchase of a plot; to the agregados on the fazendas or engenhos; to the mixed bloods—destroyers of the forests—and to all this nomadic and restless population, that idles in the interior; to the persons or companies that propose to found agricultural colonies, orphanages, or homes for the incapacitated there should be conceded as a patrimony, with free title and under careful supervision, unoccupied lands that in a few years would be centers of attraction and birthplaces of cities.[37]

In many parts of the country it is not too late even now to secure some of the gains that could come from the equivalent of a homestead law. In the course of a few decades the incentives for stability of residence and propulsions to steady work habits thus induced in the population probably would far outweigh the small loss of revenue from the sale of lands. Certainly in such an immense country, with so few people and such large percentages of them either held generation after generation in the unenviable status of agricultural laborers on the large estates or leading an unproductive nomadic existence in which they must destroy acres of forest in order to gain a few bushels of corn or mandioca, the experiment is worth trying. As a first step, of course, it would be necessary for the national government to take back the title to the unpatented lands and to consolidate them into a national domain.

CLOUDED TITLES

By 1889 there had already been laid the basis for considerable difficulty and conflict in the southern states to which immigrants had been coming. A consideration of developments there helps to throw the whole problem, and the attempts to cope with it, into bold relief. First, however, a brief summary of the elements in the problem seems to be essential.

As the density of population increases in any country, questions of land surveys, land divisions, and land titles, which previously may

[37] *Ibid.,* 281–82.

have been relatively unimportant, are certain to become of tremendous moment. This is especially likely to be true if (1) the increase in population is due to the introduction of small-farming immigrants into an area previously inhabited by a few large holders and their slaves, or other workers who never aspired to landownership, and (2) the country under consideration has been careless in permitting lands to be alienated without making proper surveys, devising clear deeds, and getting value received for the land. Carelessness in such matters inevitably results in land grabbing, fraud, and the monopolization of the best areas by a few fortune seekers.

As was the case in the United States during the period when lands were abundant, lack of system in surveying and recording titles contributed greatly to land grabbing and frauds in Brazil. "Land sharks" had an unusual opportunity to monopolize valuable lands in south Brazil early in the second half of the nineteenth century. Then, when the persons or companies, who by irregular means had acquired the lands, sold them to immigrants and other settlers, the situation became very complex. Naturally, after what had transpired became known, the state desired to repossess the acres of which it had been defrauded; but to do so, in many cases, would have meant ruin for thousands of the most industrious and productive citizens, farmers who had acted in good faith and built homes, farms, and communities on the land. This problem was particularly acute in the south, where tides of European settlers did much to increase the demand for and enhance the value of terras devolutas, or unpatented land. Much fraud also seems to have taken place during more recent years in parts of the Amazon Valley;[38] in this case, however, the problem was not so greatly complicated by the subsequent establishments of farm communities on the land.

Brazilian writers have done much to assemble the pertinent facts and trace the general lines of development of the situation—a situation more than a little reminiscent of that prevailing in the section between the Appalachians and the Mississippi during the early years of the nineteenth century. The account of the developments in the important state of Rio Grande do Sul are particularly enlightening.[39] Following 1850 large contingents of immigrants began flowing into Rio Grande do Sul. The distribution of land was, of course, under the old federal law of 1850. Land sharks naturally saw an opportunity to make huge fortunes by "grabbing" public lands and parceling them out at substantial prices to the newcomers. Tremendous acreages were patented under titles later held to be invalid. In the year 1881, for example, a total of 1,164 square kilometers of land was granted and the following year the total was almost as great, 1,047. However, during the next two years, because of extra precautions taken by the provincial governor, it is reported that fraud was

[38] See Antonio Borges, *Negociatas Escandalosas* (Rio de Janeiro, 1938).
[39] See Godolphim Torres Ramos, "Terras e Colonização no Rio Grande do Sul," *Revista de Imigração e Colonização*, I, No. 4 (October, 1940), 740–53.

greatly reduced and only 200 square kilometers were alienated. This relative inactivity proved to be temporary, for between September 20, 1885, and November 15, 1889, in this one province, a total of 3,074 square kilometers of the empire's lands passed into private hands.

With the establishment of the republic the public lands came to be the property of the several states. In Rio Grande do Sul this brought about a sharp reduction in the speed with which the public lands were alienated. According to the available data in the three years ending with 1902, only 898 square kilometers of land were patented; and during the five years that followed, the total was only 151 square kilometers.

After the state replaced the nation as possessor of public lands, it also undertook to recover lands that had been secured in a fraudulent manner. A law passed in March, 1897, established a commission charged with the responsibility of determining which lands were held in legitimate possession and which still belonged to the state. The commission began work in the município of Santa Cruz. Apparently it discovered abundant evidences of fraudulent titles. In a little more than a year it had been determined that an area of 193 square kilometers of land should be returned to the state. This was in a single município.

Before revoking title to the land, however, the state found it necessary to take into account other considerations than the mere fact that fraud might have been practiced in connection with the original alienation of the public domain. Thousands of immigrants had purchased in good faith lands from those receiving the original patents. Officials had to recognize that the issue of cloudy land titles could undermine one of the most important agricultural regions in the state and drive its settlers away, perhaps to Argentina.[40] Therefore, the president of the state in a message to the Representative Assembly in 1898 stated:

Under the dictates of natural equity and actuated by motives of manifest public convenience, the government has resolved to cede to the actual occupants these lands liable to the commission, because of unobservance of the conditions expressly essential, judged in accordance with the relative value of the colonial holdings or prices. Proceeding in this manner the government has in view not to aggravate the situation of the small farmers who today hold the said land, through purchases made in good faith from individuals or companies which exploited, in the old regime, these rights of domination from the state, by means of artificial processes to satisfy their insatiable egotistical interests.

[40] There is some evidence that this had already taken place on a considerable scale. The editor of an English language newspaper in Buenos Aires wrote: "Then again the authorities [in Rio Grande do Sul] had not properly measured and marked out the ground, which was considered a trifling matter; but when land subsequently became of value, the number of disputed titles was so confusing that a special commission was at last sent by the Government to restore order and confirm rights, but not before some of the most industrious colonists had thrown up their farms in disgust and removed to the new German colonies that were being formed on the River Plata." Mulhall, *Rio Grande do Sul and Its German Colonies*, 127.

Later, the government of the state found it essential to take additional steps to safeguard the titles of the small farmers. A regulation of July 4, 1900, established that, for possessors of small areas "there will be respected those areas of legitimate possession and of sesmarias and other concessions revalidated in terms of Law 601 . . . as well as lands that are found in private possession by any legitimate title; and on the other hand . . . considered legitimate are possessions established prior to November 15, 1889, that were constituted in good faith and which have been effectively cultivated and habitually lived upon."

Under the terms of this regulation the "area of possession" was to be limited to the "cultivated extension," provided this was not less than 25 hectares of woodlands and 50 hectares of prairie.

Still the titles were not entirely clear and questions concerning them continued to plague the state during the ensuing years. As the small holders multiplied, by natural increase and by further immigration, pressure probably became rather great for removing any clouds that still remained about the titles under which they held the land. A decree of February 10, 1903, reaffirmed that the state still had the right to recover lands that had been secured by fraud, but admitted that the lands were then in the hands of colonos, nationals and immigrants, who had acquired them at relatively high prices, and held that the occupants were entitled to the assistance and protection of the state. Therefore it was resolved that (1) the colonos who had acquired land legitimized in terms of the law of 1850 were relieved of any indemnification to the state, and (2) courts entitled to rescind the sentences would deliver new titles free of charge.

Similar developments took place in other states. Oliveira Vianna discusses the question, with allusions to São Paulo that are obvious. From his comments it is also clear that the latifundium, in the sense of large tracts of land deliberately withheld from productive purposes, might be so much of a problem that even the forging of titles would seem to be the best way of solving it.

Today, in contrast with the past, there are no lands without an owner: either they belong to private individuals, as a heritage from the immeasurable primitive sesmarias, or they are "terras devolutas" and belong, in this case, to the State. These lands, when they do not belong to the State, are preserved virgin and unexplored, but "appropriated" by backward *latifundiarios*, extremely jealous of the greatness of their latifundia, "old guards who hold on to thousands of alqueires in order to draw from them a plate of beans and a handful of grain."

It falls to the "grilleiro" to resolve this difficulty. He is the one who gives to the progressive colonizer, full of ambition and with capital, the right to utilize this unproductive treasury. For this he creates by chicanery and by falsehood, the indispensable property title. "He works the greatest frauds; he falsifies signatures, papers, stamps; falsifies rivers and mountains; falsifies trees and markers; falsifies judges and archive; falsifies the indicator on the scales of Themis; falsifies the sky, the land and the water; falsifies God and the Devil, but he wins. He divides the broad acreages into lots and he sells them to the legions of colonists that follow him as buzzards do the smell of a carcass. Five, ten years later, the flower of the coffee tree whitens the zone and incorporates it into the patrimony of national wealth." [41]

Uncertainties over title to their lands also plagued the colonists in Santa Catarina. Augusto de Carvalho summarizes the accusations of the colonists against the government under three headings: (1) "the refusal to give permanent titles to the property in the colonial tracts granted by the government," (2) "the lack of surveys and demarcation of these tracts," and (3) "the sale of lands that were surrounded by tracts transferred to speculators who had in mind only to resell them at exaggerated prices." [42] And Emílio Willems states that "fraudulent land titles were also frequent in some zones of the South, having been practiced in certain municípios of Santa Catarina as late as 1930." [43]

Finally, the disputes that have arisen with respect to the national government's title to the land on which the new capital (Brasília) has been built call attention dramatically to the all-pervading cloudiness of land titles throughout Brazil. Thus, along with the publicity attending the celebration of the first anniversary of the new capital, one reads in a leading Brazilian daily that "Brasília was constructed on an area that was not expropriated" and that the owners, scattered throughout Brazil, of 40,000 tracts of land in the zone are demanding a payment of 120 billion cruzeiros (about $425,000,000) in payment of their claims! "It is the largest indemnity ever sought in Brazil." [44]

RIVER-FRONT DIVISION IN THE SOUTH

It is necessary to say a few words about the system of dividing lands that has finally been worked out in south Brazil's "colonial" areas.[45] As should be evident from the preceding discussion, this system has been attained at the cost of hard, sometimes bitter, experience. This is only one more reason why south Brazil, and especially the states of Paraná and Santa Catarina, deserve much credit for the systems of land division that have been developed there in the course of a long experience with programs of colonization. Probably the system now in use in Paraná and Santa Catarina represents the highest degree of perfection yet attained in dividing lands. Certainly this is true if importance is attached to the type of division that permits the farmer to reside on the land without sacrificing the social and economic advantages derived from having his home near those

[41] Oliveira Vianna, "O Povo Brazileiro e sua Evolução," loc. cit., 309. The quotations used by this authority are from J. B. Monteiro Lobato, A Onda Verde (São Paulo, 1922), which almost glorifies the "profession" of "grilleiro." See especially pp. 5–37.

[42] Augusto de Carvalho, O Brazil: Colonização e Emigração (2d ed.; Porto, 1876), 204; cf. 205 ff.

[43] Willems, Assimilação e Populações Marginais no Brasil, 82.

[44] Correio da Manhã (Rio de Janeiro), April 23, 1961.

[45] Occupied by colonos or small farmers.

of neighbors and, at the same time, having the boundaries of the farms laid out in a manner best adapted to the topographical features of the area settled.

In the numerous colonies established by federal, state, and private agencies in Brazil, the system of land division most generally used has been a modified version of the river-front type so characteristic of French settlements. In the earlier colonies, such as the German settlement at Blumenau, Santa Catarina, the river was the point of departure, roads followed the streams, and holdings were rectangular in shape, except for the end where each fronted on the stream. In the Santa Catarina colonies these farming plots measured 110 meters (50 braças) in width and 1,100 meters in depth.[46] In those at Moniz in Bahia the lots were 200 by 320 meters.[47] In the colony of Santa Isabel in Espírito Santo they were 200 braças wide and 600 braças deep.[48]

In other colonies still other dimensions were used. However, in all cases the principle of making the width of the holdings considerably less than the length was used. This is the practice that must be followed if line-village settlement patterns are to be used or developed.

From the very first, the systems of land division used in these Brazilian colonies had one distinct advantage over similar systems in use elsewhere. Unlike the practice so generally followed by French and Spanish colonists in dividing their lands, meanders in the streams did not lead to the use of nonparallel lines for bounding the sides of the plots. As a rule in these Brazilian surveys the width of the holding was uniform throughout its length. (See Figure 24.)

The first colonies, however, were marred by one serious defect in their system of land division. The irregular jagged line formed by the rear boundaries of the holdings created great complications for future settlement of the area. It also prevented the fullest adaptation of settlement forms and farm layouts to the topography of the area settled. Since the colonists were hewing homes from a wilderness, perhaps a great deal of importance should not be attached to any disadvantages that accrued to future settlers. Certainly, the early settlers adopted a pattern well fitted to their own needs.

Gradually, as experience was secured, practices were modified and systems of dividing the land were perfected to higher degrees. This important feature in the relationships of man to the land seems to have reached its highest stage of development in the colonization projects of the North Paraná Land Company and in the official colonies established by the state government on the former fazendas of Santa Catarina. Today the procedures used in dividing the land are fairly well defined. When a new settlement project is undertaken, the

[46] Cf. Albuquerque Galvão, *Relatorio sobre Blumenau, Itajahy, Principe D. Pedro e D. Francisca.*

[47] Bernardo Augusto Nascentes de Azambuja, *Relatorio sobre as Colonias ao Sul da Provincia da Bahia* (Rio de Janeiro, 1874), 42.

[48] Joaquim da Silva Rocha, *Historia da Colonisação do Brasil* (Rio de Janeiro, 1918), I, 249.

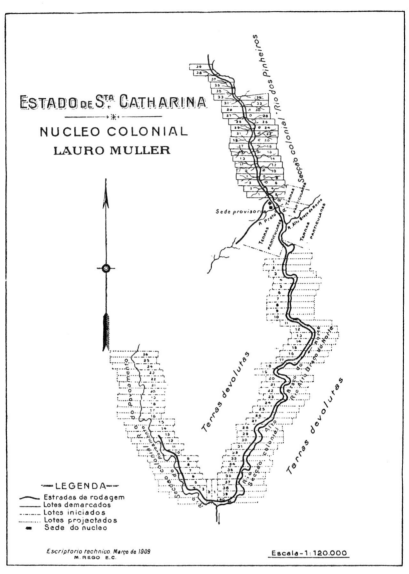

FIGURE 24. Plan of the colony "Lauro Muller," Santa Catarina, founded in 1908, showing the type of surveys used in early colonization projects. (Reproduced from J. F. Gonçalves, Jr., *Relatorio* [Rio de Janeiro, 1909], 123.)

land is first surveyed in order to determine the courses of all streams and to delineate the lines followed by the divides of all the principal watersheds. A detailed map of the area is made on which all of these are plotted. In the North Paraná Land Company's settlements the roads projected for the colony are designed to follow along the ridge of the principal divides; in Santa Catarina they usually follow the

278

stream. But in both states the tract of land cut off for a prospective purchaser or colonist is bounded on the one end by the stream and on the other by the road or dividing ridge. Variations in the size of farms sold or allotted are secured by increasing or decreasing the width of the holding, never by modifying the stream-to-divide principle of determining their length. This system maintains the desirable feature of the long-lot farm, thus allowing the settlers to capitalize on the social and economic advantages of line-village settlement patterns. At the same time it permits a high degree of adaptation to topographical features, both of the farm layout and of the settlement pattern. It gives each settler access to water, to the various kinds of timber, to the lowlands and the uplands. In short, each settler participates in all of the advantages and disadvantages offered by the natural setting.

For typical examples of the system of land division used in these colonies, see Figures 25 and 26. The first of these illustrations shows

FIGURE 25. System of land division used by the North Paraná Land Company. (Courtesy of the Company.)

LEGENDA

ESTRADA DE FERRO
ESTRADA DE RODAGEM
RIO

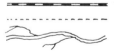

ESCALA 1:100,000

FIGURE 26. The system of land division used by the state of Santa Catarina. (Courtesy of Virgílio Gualberto, Director-Geral of the Departamento Estadual de Estatística.)

280

a section of the new territory which has been opened for colonization by the North Paraná Land Company. The second illustration reproduces a portion of the map of one of the Santa Catarina state government's colonization projects. The latter has added interest because it

FIGURE 27. Map of the lot sold to one of its customers by the North Paraná Land Company. (Courtesy of the Company.)

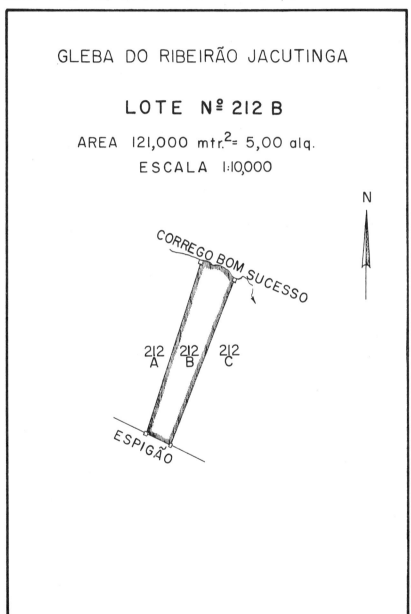

GLEBA DO RIBEIRÃO JACUTINGA

LOTE N⁰ 212 B

AREA 121,000 mtr.² = 5,00 alq.

ESCALA 1:10,000

N

CORREGO BOM SUCESSO

212 A   212 B   212 C

ESPIGÃO

shows the boundaries of fazendas as yet undivided, in addition to the layout of the colonists' sítios. In both, as will be observed, there has been some sacrifice in uniformity of plots and, therefore, in ease of surveying and recording, in favor of greater adaptability to the topography. Both, however, permit the formation of line-village settlement patterns. Both represent very considerable advances in the conscious planning of man's relation to the land so as to secure the most advantageous utilization of natural features of the landscape. Finally, they both represent very material improvements over the systems in use as late as 1908. (See Figure 24.)

The more detailed aspects of the system may be noted by the observation of a single farmstead on one of the projects. In Figure 27 is reproduced the map of a small farm sold to a colonist by the North Paraná Land Company on February 27, 1941. It is located in the Riberão Jacutinga subdivision of the company's project. Along with the map of the plot of land he had purchased, the buyer received a copy of the following description of its boundaries:

Beginning at a hardwood marker which was set on the right bank of the Bom Sucesso Creek and following the border with lot No. 212A in the direction of SW 18 degrees and 31 minutes for a distance of 814 meters to a marker placed on the Bom Sucesso-Jacutinga divide: from there the line follows the said divide in the direction SE 64 degrees and 14 minutes for 126 meters to a marker similar to the others; from this point it follows along the boundary with lot No. 212C in the direction NE 21 degrees and 51 minutes to a marker set in the right bank of Bom Sucesso Creek, and finally it follows up this to the point of departure.

To one interested in the division of farm lands so as to obtain the maximum efficiency in farm organization, in settlement patterns that permit farmers to live on the land without sacrificing all the advantages of near neighbors, and in the adjustment of both farm layouts and settlement patterns to topography, southern Brazil is one of the best possible fields for study. The Brazilians' practices in these respects, based on many years' experience, are deserving of careful study with a view to wide application in other countries. It is to be hoped that the most effective use of this experience will be in Brazil itself. Of course these forms are useful only in carefully planned and supervised or directed settlement. Where occupation of the land is spontaneous, a system such as that described in the concluding chapter of this book is preferable.

CHAPTER XIII

LAND TENURE

$\mathbf{A}$s one reads the very considerable literature dealing with Brazil's social and economic problems, he is impressed by the slight notice given to questions of land tenure. Only recently has this topic received much attention at the hands of Brazilian scholars. Whereas certain phases of this subject, and especially tenancy, long have been placed in the top rank of rural social problems in the United States, before 1950 they went almost without mention in Brazil. This is not because that nation's scholars have been callous to the social problems of agriculture. Both agricultural credit and cooperatives receive specific mention in the constitution; there are numerous books and articles dealing with problems of illiteracy and the rural schools, latifundia and the unfavorable situation of the working masses, poor health, malnutrition, and diet; and there has been extensive discussion of rural poverty, isolation, inadequate systems of transportation and communication, droughts, migration, and almost all the other phases of the rural problem as they are known in the United States. But questions relative to land tenure are only now coming to occupy a place of importance in Brazilian thinking, as a part of a general outcry for "agrarian reform." In the past the press, the magazines, the learned journals, and the classroom rarely if ever have given a place to matters pertaining to the leasing of lands and the relationships between landlord and tenant. Even many of the books on agricultural economics and rural sociology have omitted land tenure from the outline of materials which are presented.[1]

[1] See Carneiro Leão, *A Sociedade Rural;* Hernani de Carvalho, *Sociologia da Vida Rural Brasileira* (Rio de Janeiro, 1951); and Fabio Luz Filho, *Aspectos Agro-Economicos do Rio Grande do Sul* (São Paulo, 1937). See also the significant list of rural social problems given by the outstanding leader in education and statistics, Teixeira de Freitas, "Educação Rural," *loc. cit.,* 54–79. Although the list as given by this authority includes misery of the rural proletariat, routine in the processes of work, lack of technical organization and administration of agricultural enterprises, faulty land titles, confused weights and measures, and a rudimentary system of credit, it makes no mention of tenure problems. Finally, it should be indicated that neither *arrendar* (to rent), *arrendamento* or *arrendação* (rent or renting), *arrendador* (one who rents to another), or *arrendatário* (one who rents from another) appear in the fourth edition of José de Souza, *Dicionário da Terra e da Gente do Brasil.* They are given in Hildebrando Lima and Gustavo Barroso, *Pequeno Dicionário Brasileiro da Língua Portuguesa* (3d ed.; Rio de Janeiro, 1942), but buildings and not lands are used for the purposes of clarifying the nature of the rental contract. However, in some recent works the subject is receiving the attention it deserves. See especially, Manuel Diégues Júnior, "Land Tenure and Use in the Brazilian Plantation System," in Vera Rubin

That Brazilians have paid little attention to matters of land tenure seems to be due entirely to the fact that only in recent years has this aspect of the land problem become acute, and then only in a few parts of Brazil.[2] Although the leasing of lands, especially for grazing purposes, has been known in Brazil since colonial days,[3] as late as 1920 rented farms numbered only 23,371, or constituted but 3.6 per cent of the land in farms. Certainly these data do not indicate a dispossession of farmers from their lands such as has stimulated interest in tenure problems in parts of the United States. Nor do they indicate the confusion of tenancy and share wages which has aroused interest in the farmer in other parts of our nation. However, the small-farming classes of Rio Grande do Sul, Santa Catarina, Paraná, and Espírito Santo already are encountering difficulties in finding sufficient suitable land for their numerous progeny, and the people of São Paulo are becoming cognizant of the fundamental changes that are under way in the land system of their state. As a result the questions of land tenure are attaining considerable significance. The continued subdivision of lands by inheritance in Minas Gerais and other states is bringing a like result. Reduction of the former Northeastern sugar planters and millers to the status of fornecedores, frequently as renters of the lands they once owned, is making tenure problems more acute in the coastal areas of the North and East. Elsewhere in Brazil land questions remain largely those that grow out of huge unused or poorly used estates and large-scale agriculture—the plantation sys-

---

(ed.), *Plantation Systems of the New World* (Washington, 1959), 104–22; Manuel Diégues Júnior, *População e Propriedade da Terra no Brasil* (Washington, 1959), 61–109; Clóvis Caldeira, *Arrendamento e Parceria* (Rio de Janeiro, 1955); João Gonçalves de Souza, "Relações de Homem com a Terra em 4 Comunidades Rurais do Médio São Francisco," *Boletim da Sociedade Brasileira de Geografia*, No. 1 (1950); Serviço de Informação Agrícola, *Reforma Agrária no Mundo e no Brasil* (Rio de Janeiro, 1952); and João Gonçalves de Souza, "Land Tenure Problems in Brazil and Their Solution," in Joseph Ackerman and Marshall Harris (eds.), *Family Farm Policy* (Chicago, 1947), Chap. X. Furthermore in 1953 the Brazilian government, in co-operation with the Food and Agriculture Organization of the United Nations, staged a five-week seminar to study land tenure problems in Latin America.

[2] Nevertheless, early writers, in commenting on leasing arrangements in Brazil, have mentioned that the renting contracts favored the tenants. For example:

"The laws respecting Landlord and Tenant are very much in favor of the latter. If he has built a house, planted fruit-trees, or in any other way benefited an estate, beyond the terms of his contract, he does not on removal lose what he has paid out; appraisers are appointed to ascertain the value of the improvements, and the landlord must pay for them, whether useful to him or not. Indeed they can hardly be considered, in any case, as useless; for, when an estate is sold, these Bemefeitorias, as they are called, are always valued separately, and paid for in addition to the sum agreed upon for the purchase of the land and the woods. The operation of these laws is as beneficial to the public as to the individuals, not only saving them from oppression, but gradually spreading them over the country, when they begin to acquire property. And such a dispersion is by no means uncommon, for landlords here are adverse to wealthy tenants." Luccock, *Notes on Rio de Janeiro, and the Southern Parts of Brazil*, 294–95. Laws of this nature would prevent the genesis of landlord-tenant conflicts in two ways: (1) by safeguarding the interests of the renters, and (2) more important, by preventing the rise of any considerable class of renters.

[3] Cf. Oliveira Vianna, "O Povo Brasileiro e sua Evolução," *loc. cit.*, 284.

tem—rather than the problems of tenure as such.[4] Particularly in the sugar areas a further dispossession of the senhores de engenhos and the continued growth of the larger usinas is to be expected.

Property rights in Brazil adhere closely to the canons of Roman law. Brazilian lands are held under a system of ownership in fee simple similar to our own, except that mineral rights belong to the federal government. The right of eminent domain may be exercised by the state or nation in cases of "public necessity" or "public utility," and these are rather broadly construed. Lands may be expropriated on the grounds of public necessity, if they are needed for the following purposes: (1) the defense of national territory, (2) public security, (3) in times of calamity, for public succor or relief, and (4) public health. Under the category "public utility," lands may be taken for (1) providing locations for populated places and establishments for public assistance, education, and public instruction, (2) the opening, enlargement, or prolongation of streets, parks, canals, railways, or any other public thoroughfares, (3) the construction of works or establishments destined to promote the general welfare or the appearance and hygienic condition of a locality, and (4) the opening and working of mines.[5]

EVOLUTION OF PROPERTY RIGHTS

The evolution of Brazil's body of property rights in land parallels in many respects the development of our our own public land system. But there are some major and highly significant differences. For example, in the United States a very important factor in achieving national unity at the time of the adoption of the Constitution was the relinquishing by the several states of their own rights to the unoccupied western lands. All these lands together were established as the public domain of the federal government, and their sale not only promoted the westward movement of population but also helped to finance the new federal government. In Brazil, on the other hand, the sequence of events was just the opposite. Prior to the establishment of the republic in 1889, the rights to the public land were vested solely in the national government, the empire. With the adoption of the republican constitution, each of the states was, with minor excep-

[4] To one who has long maintained that the social problems of the southern United States are the result of the plantation system and the paucity of farm operators, either owners or renters (tenants), and not to tenancy, Brazil offers an important supporting case. Brazil suffers from all the ills of the plantation system, many of them even more acute than they are in the South, without, however, offering the slightest shred of evidence in support of those who would attribute these evils to tenancy. Brazilians have always placed the blame where it belongs, on the latifundium. Therefore, proposals for agrarian reform properly deal with the maldistribution in the ownership and control of the land, and not with tenure rights and farm tenancy as such.

[5] *Código Civil Brasileiro* (8th ed.; São Paulo, 1942), Arts. 527 and 590; see also Art. 15 of the Constitution of November 10, 1937.

tions, vested with the rights to the public lands lying within its borders. However, this exception should not be given undue importance; in its major outlines Brazil's land system has developed in much the same way as our own.

As in North America the founding nation by right of discovery and conquest assumed the rights to the land in the newly discovered territories. Gradually, throughout the colonial period, property rights in land were transferred from the public power to private hands and passed on from one individual to another. Very early the lands were all given as capitanias to twelve *fidalgos,* or nobles.[6] It might well be said that this divided Portugal's share of the Western Hemisphere into twelve large and almost uninhabited baronies. It was soon discovered, however, that this system did little to promote the settlement of Portuguese America, and so the grants were revoked and the lands again taken by the crown. To replace the capitanias the government of the colonies was placed in the hands of the king's viceroy. Under the direction of this royal representative the settlement of the coastal fringe proceeded rapidly.

During the early period, that of the viceroys, the only manner of granting land by the crown was the giving of large tracts in sesmarias [7] or grants to those who applied for them. Any person trying to qualify for such a grant went to considerable lengths to convince the representative of the crown that he was of "good family," that is, of fidalgo lineage, and that he possessed the means necessary to enable him to open and operate a sugar plantation or engenho. These sesmarias as a rule measured at least two leagues (roughly 7.5 miles) on each side, and some of them were of almost boundless extent. In pastoral regions ten leagues on a side was customary, although there were many larger sesmarias given out. From very early times it was possible for some of the landed potentates to rent lands for cattle raising to their fellows who lacked the lineage or funds necessary to obtain a sesmaria, these rented acreages measuring a minimum

[6] Cf. Fausto de Souza, *Estudo sobre a Divisão Territorial do Brazil,* 34, *passim.*

[7] Sesmaria appears in Portuguese legal codes long before the discovery of America. During the reign of Dom Fernando I was published the *Lei das Sesmarias,* formalizing an old practice of taking from owners any cultivatable lands that they were allowing to go unused. Naturally the concept evolved rapidly when the tiny Kingdom of Portugal attempted the colonization of immense areas of practically unoccupied land in the New World, the Dark Continent, and the Indies. When Martim Afonso de Souza undertook his expedition to Brazil in 1530 he carried with him, among other documents, a royal letter authorizing him to concede in sesmaria lands found that might be utilized. It was under the authority of this royal letter that João Ramalho was given lands on the Isle of Guaibe in 1531 and Braz Cubas in Piratininga on October 10, 1532. Cirne Lima, *Terras Devolutas,* 10, 29–30. When Brazil was divided into capitanias, i.e., between 1532 and 1548, each *capitão* had the right to grant land in sesmaria; after the powers were reassembled in the hands of a governor general, that official alone held the rights of granting sesmarias, although some of those to whom extensive grants were given, in turn, gave them out to others in immense parcels as sesmarias; in fact, the giving of lands in sesmaria was the only legal manner of distributing lands while Brazil was a possession of Portugal. *Ibid.,* 31–32, 33, 51. The regulations abolishing the granting of lands in sesmaria came in 1822. Cf. Werneck Sodré, *Oeste,* 83.

of one league on each side.[8] In addition to the alienation of lands by sesmarias, tracts also passed from public to private ownership through sale, donation, exchange, and the legalization of possessions that had been established.[9]

In Brazil from the very first the transference of rights from public to private hands was rather complete, i.e., vestiges from the feudal land system did not result in the crown's retaining many rights in the land. The collection of the tithe, at first for the church and later for the state, however, was general.[10] The other remnants of feudalism that remained, although numerous, were largely confined to the manner in which the landed proprietor carried on the operation of his vast estate; [11] they did not remain because the public power failed to grant him free and unhampered rights to the land. Once the sesmarias were confirmed by the king, the title was full and complete, and the owner was exempted from any further obligation except the payment of a tenth of the produce to "God, our master." [12] However, the king did reserve the right to establish on the concession towns or villages, when he judged it necessary, and also the right to use the hardwoods growing on the land, especially for the building of vessels.[13] The *donatário* or noble person receiving the original grant enjoyed all the powers and privileges of government, including, besides

[8] Cf. Oliveira Vianna "O Povo Brazileiro e sua Evolução," *loc. cit.*, 284, *passim.* And Freyre, *Casa Grande & Senzala*, 37, gives data for Bahia of holdings measuring 80, 160, and even 260 leagues.

[9] Lima Pereira, *Da Propriedade no Brasil*, 6.

[10] Precautions were taken to ensure that the original concessionaires should not fasten a set of feudal obligations upon the settlers in their colonies. Those receiving donations of capitanias were permitted to cede lands "without fees, nor any obligation, only the tenth of God." But they were prohibited from appropriating the lands for their own use, even in an indirect manner, until they had been used a minimum of eight years by or for those receiving the sesmarias. The prohibitions specified included grants to their own wives, or heirs, and purchase. In other words, the persons to whom the capitanias were given could cede the land to others as sesmarias but could not appropriate it for themselves. Cirne Lima, *Terras Devolutas*, 31–32; cf. Rocha Pombo, *Historia do Brazil*, III, 142–44.

[11] While he was operating a sugar plantation near Recife, Koster often compared his existence with that of a baron of feudal times: "The great power of the planter, not only over his slaves, but his authority over the free persons of lower rank; the respect which is required by these Barons from the free inhabitants of their lands; the assistance which they expect from their tenants in case of insult from a neighbouring equal; the dependence of the peasants, and their wish to be under the peculiar protection of a person of wealth who is capable of relieving them from any oppression, and of speaking in their behalf to the governor, or the chief judge; all these circumstances combined, tend to make the similarity very great." *Travels in Brazil*, I, 297.

[12] Through an interesting development the tithe, once a tribute levied for the support of the church and the clergy, came to be collected to help fill the coffers of the government. Koster called attention to the fact that, in his days, "a tenth is raised in kind upon cattle, poultry, and agriculture, and even upon salt; this in former times appertained, as in other Christian countries, to the clergy." He then explained that during the early days of the colony the priests found it difficult to live on the proceeds from the tithes and petitioned that they be given fixed stipends and that the state take the tithing. Koster also remarked that in the early nineteenth century the clergy were complaining of the bargain made by their predecessors. *Ibid.*, 48.

[13] Lima Pereira, *Da Propriedade no Brasil*, 6.

the right to grant sesmarias, the naming of all officials and a freedom from any superior authority except that of the king. His revenues were derived from a share, one tenth of the tithe.[14]

But there were some significant encumbrances smacking of feudalism which arose within the system of private ownership. One of these interesting and highly significant features of the system of land tenure that developed in Brazil is brought out in the following quotation from an early nineteenth-century writer:

The waste lands I had seen on this and other excursions were satisfactorily accounted for, by the circumstances arising out of an attempt made by a friend of mine to purchase about twenty acres, situated upon the margin of the bay, four miles by water and eight by land from the city. Its cultivation had extended no further than the employment one solitary slave could give it; a few patches of mandioca were visible, and two rows of fruit trees, from the eminence on which a clay tenement stood, formed a pathway towards the bay. Nine hundred milreis (upwards of two hundred pounds) was the sum demanded for the everlasting possession of it, subject to the payment of a fine of five pounds per annum to a lady, whose assent to the transfer was required, and could be immediately obtained. My friend determined to be the purchaser, and called upon the donna, to ascertain under what circumstances the five pounds were to be paid. She had no objections to his becoming the purchaser; but said, she thought the sum demanded was too much, and that she would send in a person to value the *bemfeitoras* [sic], that is, what produce might be upon the ground, if the party wished to sell it. He found, therefore, in place of its being a free purchase, this lady had the full control over the property, in case of the occupier wishing to dispose of it. He would have purchased her five pounds fine; that she would on no account part with, and further stated, that, for every two slaves more that he employed, he must pay five pounds more fine. The present holder was only to work it with two. The object of this would seem to be, that, in the event of its being disposed of, she would not have so many *bemfeitoras* to take. This gentleman would have expended a considerable sum, and have brought the land into a state of fine cultivation, if he could have retained it in his own possession, and that of his successors in perpetuity; but, if circumstances compelled him to part with it, this donna, by the Brazilian laws, would have had the preference; and two people, appointed for the purpose, would have been sent to value the produce standing upon the ground, without regard to improvement of times, or the amelioration of the soil; and, in consequence of this fine, she would have unfairly regained possession of the property for a mere bagatelle. This being the state of the case, my friend immediately declined any further treaty upon the subject. This donna and two sisters, all spinsters, possess a most extensive range of land, the whole under similar circumstances, and nearly in the same condition that it was left by the Indians. The parties occupying it live upon the produce of fruit sold at market, and a little mandioca. Under the present system of landed tenure, it will remain covered with wild grass till doomsday.

It is a great misfortune to the Brazil, that extensive tracts of land have been granted to donatories, who do not possess the means of cultivating one-hundredth part of it, but hold it on under the expectation that the gradual improvement of the country will render it daily more valuable, and the residence of the court here induces them to adhere more strongly to this impression: if they dispose of any part of it, they generally subject it to a fine, and the consequences attending such a contract will present a

[14] Manoel de Oliveira Lima, *Pernambuco, seu Desenvolvimento Historico* (Leipzig, 1895), 10–11.

decided obstacle to the agricultural improvement of this country, not at all proportioned to its extent or superabundant powers. Individuals who would devote their exertions and property to the culture of the soil, where this mode prevails, must be effectually deterred. The province of St. Paulo, which may be estimated to contain one hundred and twenty thousand square miles, has no land devoluto, or ungranted, although one-thirtieth part of it is not in a state of cultivation. Land of course may be bought without a fine, but not generally. I had some conversation with a Portuguese gentleman, whose intention it was to obtain from his Majesty a grant of land to the extent of two or three square leagues, situated upon the northern bank of the river Parahiba; but he could not have placed more than two slaves upon it, and his avowed object was to retain it under the anticipation of futurity producing him an advantage in the sale of it, by portions or otherwise. The King is very liberal in granting land; and would, no doubt, afford encouragement for the agricultural improvement of the country, and even during my short stay at Rio he supplied some individuals with slaves for the purpose of cultivation; but the parsimonious feeling and apathy which prevails will operate against any speedy change or improvement of the system. In the donation of lands, it would be wise to attach a positive obligation to cultivate, or in a certain period either to revert to the crown or be publicly disposed of to those who are competent, and intend to work them; and further, to grant lands only in quantities proportionate to the means the individual receiving them may possess of bringing them into a state of culture; otherwise it would be infinitely better for the lands to remain with the crown, thereby precluding the practice of retailing them out with a fine.[15]

From other sections of Brazil come reports of the entailing of estates, a practice that also seems to have worked against the progress of agriculture. Koster described as follows these arrangements:

There are a few *morgados* or entailed estates in Pernambuco, and I believe in Paraiba likewise: and I have heard that in Bahia there are a great many. There are also *capellados* or chapel lands. These estates cannot be sold; and from this cause are sometimes suffered to decay, or at any rate they yield much less profit to the State than they would under other circumstances. The *capellado* is formed in this manner: the owner bequeaths a certain part of the produce or rent of the estate to some particular church, for the purpose of having masses said for his own soul, or for pious uses of a less selfish nature. On this account the estate cannot, according to law, be sold; so that if the next heir is not rich enough to work the mill himself, he lets it to someone who possesses a sufficient number of negroes. The portion which is due to the favoured church being paid, the owner then remains with the residue of the rent as his share of the profit. Now, lands even with buildings upon them, are let at so low a rate, that after the church is paid, and the tenant has deducted what he has expended in repairing the edifices of the plantation, but a poor pittance remains for the owner. The *engenho* of Catu near to Goiana is placed in these circumstances. The owner lives in the neighbourhood of the Great House or principal residence, and the only advantage which he derives from the possession of this most excellent and extensive estate, is that of residing rent free upon one corner of it, and now and then receiving a trifling sum of money. Whereas if it could be sold, he would immediately receive a sufficient sum to place him in easy circumstances; and the estate would undergo improvement, for the occupier would then have a direct interest in its advancement. I might mention several other plantations which are situated in like manner.[16]

[15] Henderson, *A History of Brazil*, 85–87.
[16] Koster, *Travels in Brazil*, II, 129–30.

During the colonial period there were from time to time established other regulations that somewhat restricted individual property rights in the land and gave more form to public policy. Thus an order of December 27, 1685, established a quit-rent, in addition to the tithe, that had to be paid by the concessionaire. A royal letter of December 7, 1698, limited the extension of sesmarias to three leagues in length by one in breadth, and one of March 3, 1704, required their judicial demarcation. Another of February 23, 1711, provided that the lands should never by any title pass under the "dominion of the Religions," [17] and "where these Orders already possessed estates, they were to pay tenths, like the estates of the laity; and if any lands or houses were bequeathed to them, the bequest was not to take effect without the King's permission." [18] A decree of October 20, 1753, prohibited the confirmation of sesmarias that had not been previously surveyed and marked. The next year a provision of March 11, 1754, reserved space for purposes of public utility on major streams, and a royal letter of March 13, 1797, prohibited the concession of lands fronting on the coast or on the margin of navigable streams.

But most important was the charter of October 5, 1795, which served to systematize the regulations pertaining to the granting and use of lands. Among its provisions were the following: (1) the proprietor receiving a sesmaria was obliged to establish the marks inclosing the grant one year before taking possession of it; (2) there was to be created a registry for the letters which granted and those which confirmed the sesmarias, each in suitable books; and (3) each cidade or vila should receive four square leagues of land located within a radius of six miles of the population center, and the income from this property should be used to defer the expenses of the câmara (local governing body or council) in the particular city or town.[19]

With the separation from Portugal and the establishment of the Empire of Brazil, the granting of sesmarias was discontinued. From this time, 1822, however, dates a thirty-year period of great confusion in land policy and procedure, during which there was a considerable development of unauthorized occupation of vacant lands by squatters.[20] This became so widespread that it gave rise to the next important bench mark in Brazilian tenure legislation. This body of legal provisions concerning the ownership and possession of land in Brazil came in the period of the empire as Law No. 601 of September 18, 1850.[21] This law stipulated that title to unoccupied lands might be acquired only by purchase. All lands were defined as unoccupied (terras devolutas) [22] except those in public use, those held by legitimate title,

[17] Silva Rocha, Historia da Colonisação do Brasil, I, 158.
[18] Southey, History of Brazil, III, 146.
[19] Lima Pereira, Da Propriedade no Brasil, 7–8.
[20] Burton wrote: "A Brazilian friend writes to me—'The iniquitous law of 1823, which put a stop to land concessions, caused substituous occupation to take the place of lawful titles. Thus the best lands were worked out and ruined.'" The Highlands of the Brazil, I, 42.
[21] The law is cited in Lima Pereira, Da Propriedade no Brasil, 200–206.
[22] Literally, terras devolutas at first meant lands that had reverted to the state for failure to comply with the conditions stipulated in the original grant. In gen-

and those to which titles might be confirmed under the provisions of the law entering into force. The liberality of the provisions for confirmation of "squatters' rights" and other extralegal forms of possession may be observed from certain provisions. Article 4 provided that all sesmarias, whether granted by the central or the provincial governments, might be confirmed if the person to whom the grant was made or his representative had lived on the land and cultivated it, although none of the other provisions of the law had been complied with, and Article 5 provided for the confirmation of all claims to land based on first occupancy provided they were cultivated, were beginning to be cultivated, or were the habitual residence of the possessor. The latter also made provisions for the settlement of conflicting claims. Another article, No. 11, stipulated that each possessor must secure a title to the lands claimed, and it also set the fees that should be charged for these services. Article 14 detailed the manner in which lands were to be disposed of in the future, providing specifically that they should first be surveyed, subdivided, marked, and described. Interestingly enough, it stipulated that, local circumstances permitting, the divisions should have as a point of departure the true meridians, that other lines should cut these at right angles, and that the lots should measure five hundred braças (1,111 meters) on each side. It hardly needs mentioning that such a system of surveys never became effective and that dividing ridges and water-courses continued to be followed in the demarcation of Brazilian property limits. (See Chapter xiv.) Article 16 indicated the rights that were withheld from the owner by specifying that he might be required to cede lands for roads or ports; grant right of way to neighbors so that they could have access to highways, population centers, or ports; consent to the drawing off or passage through his property of unused waters; and be subject to laws respecting mines that might be discovered on the land. Article 21 authorized the government to publish a regulamento pertaining to public lands and to establish a department with charge of affairs relating to their surveying, division, sale, distribution, and colonization.

On January 30, 1854, the regulamento referred to above was published as Decreto No. 1,318.[23] Its nine sections and 108 articles specified in detail how the department was to be organized and administered, outlined procedures and responsibilities for the surveying of public land, gave the routine to be followed in the confirmation of land titles, provided for the sale of public lands, specified the categories of land that were to be reserved, established restrictions for unoccupied lands that lay on the nation's boundaries, made the local judges responsible for ensuring that the public lands were not occupied illegally, and provided for a registry of land titles.

With the advent of the republic in 1889 the ownership of public lands which had been vested in the central government passed to

eral practice it later came to mean any unoccupied or unowned lands, or in brief, the public domain. Cf. Ferreira, *Azumbuja e Urussanga*, 13–17.

[23] Cited in Lima Pereira, *Da Propriedade no Brasil*, 206–28.

the states. Even before this, in 1888, as part of the rapid development of state's rights which brought on the republic and also a great decentralization in Brazilian government, Law No. 3,396 of November 24 conceded to the respective provinces the proceeds received from the sale of lands within the province. Funds so derived were to be used by each state in developing its colonization service. Article 64 of the republican constitution specifically provided that the states should possess "the unoccupied lands situated in their respective territories, there falling to the Union only that portion of the territory that may be indispensable for the defense of the frontiers, fortifications, military constructions, and federal railroads."

From the establishment of the republic to date, land laws have fallen within the jurisdiction of the several states, except that the matter of mineral rights and some control of a band along the frontiers have been under federal jurisdiction and administration. Naturally, the provisions in the twenty states have been extremely varied. In many cases the states, in turn, have conceded special privileges to the municípios. For example, the state of São Paulo granted to each município all the unoccupied land lying within a radius of six kilometers from the center of the cental plaza of each center village, town, or city having 1,000 inhabitants or more.[24] São Paulo and Amazonas both gave large grants of land to official land and colonization companies organized by the Imperial Japanese government. These and many other phases of Brazil's land question must enter into the exhaustive study still to be made of Brazil's land system under the republic, which will require the long untiring efforts of a host of scholars. The present writer has cursorily examined the legislation of São Paulo, Minas Gerais, and Rio Grande do Norte. In all of these, provisions were made for determining which lands were legitimately in the hands of private owners and which still legally belonged to the state; procedures were instituted for validation of claims established by occupying, cultivating, and establishing a home on the land or of claims from sesmarias that had never been registered; and a register of deeds was set up. However, no basic changes in the rights to the land seem to have been introduced.

CONTEMPORARY TENURE PATTERNS

The 1940 and 1950 Brazilian censuses of agriculture contain a wealth of information that, if properly and sufficiently analyzed, could supply the answers to most of the tenure problems of the country. In both of these enumerations the materials were so gathered and tabulated in sufficient detail, both with respect to subject matter and geographical divisions, that it is possible to determine the principal features of contemporary Brazilian tenure patterns from the data in the reports. In utilizing this material it is necessary to keep in

[24] *Ibid.,* 13–14.

mind that in 1950 only about 27 per cent of Brazil's area was accounted for by the land in the category called "land in rural establishments." [25]

Unfortunately, in Brazil, as generally is the case in other countries including the United States, it still is impossible to answer accurately some of the most important questions concerning the tenure rights possessed by those who till the soil. Despite their costliness and detail, modern censuses of population and agriculture still do not supply the answers to some basic questions. What is the number and what is the proportion of the nation's families dependent for their livelihood on agriculture (or one of the other principal industries)? What percentage of the nation's farm families are the operators of farms, and what percentage fall into the category of farm laborers? And, of all the families in a given country who are dependent on agriculture, what proportion are the owners of the farms on which they work? Only proximate answers to such questions, based merely upon estimates, can be given for the United States; the same is true for Brazil.

Fortunately, the task of estimating the number of farm families in Brazil is somewhat less involved than it is in the United States, and by ignoring the fact that some rural families engage in little or no agricultural activities one may, with fair ease, get some approximate figures. Thus, from the housing census one may determine the number of rural households or domiciles, which must be approximately the same as the number of families. Relating this to the number of farm owners, as in Table XL, reveals that among each one hundred rural families only twenty-two in 1940 and twenty-five in 1950 could be classified as farm owners. Were rural families who do not live from the soil eliminated, if that were possible, these ratios would be raised slightly. Even so, only about one family in four throughout the vast expanses of rural Brazil owns the land on which it is dependent for a livelihood. The proportion of farm owners reaches its maximum in the states of Rio Grande do Sul and Santa Catarina. (See Figure 28.) It is lowest in the territories of Acre, Guaporé, and Amapá, where the land is monopolized by the owners of a few large estates on which rubber and other forest products are collected, and in Maranhão, where the bulk of the rural families are merely squatting on the land. The low percentages in the states of São Paulo and Rio de Janeiro are highly significant. Even in immense, remote, and sparsely settled Mato Grosso the ordinary family seems to find it difficult to secure land on which to work.

According to the 1950 census there were in all Brazil 2,064,642 rural establishments or farms. Of these only 186,949, or 9.1 per cent, were operated by renters. Certainly those obsessed by the tenancy bugbear could find in these data little basis for raising an alarm.

[25] The basic data on number of farms, land in farms, and tenure are given in "Sinopse do Censo Agrícola, Dados Gerais," *Recenseamento Geral do Brasil, 1940* (Rio de Janeiro, 1948), and "Censo Agrícola," *VI Recenseamento Geral do Brasil, 1950*, II (Rio de Janeiro, 1956).

TABLE XL

Tenure of Farm Operators, 1950, by States *

State	Number of farms	Percentage of farms operated by			
		Owners	Administrators	Renters	Occupants, others, and unknown
Brazil	2,064,642	75.2	5.6	9.1	10.1
North	78,227	65.5	3.5	5.9	25.1
Guaporé †	530	47.9	8.3	6.2	37.6
Acre †	1,701	37.4	6.4	42.1	14.1
Amazonas	15,220	73.2	3.7	6.8	16.3
Rio Branco †	445	59.8	22.7	4.0	13.5
Pará	59,877	64.7	2.8	4.6	27.9
Amapá †	454	42.1	46.9	5.1	5.9
Northeast	543,698	65.6	6.1	13.3	15.0
Maranhão	95,165	26.4	3.0	5.5	65.1
Piauí	34,106	80.6	12.5	4.1	2.8
Ceará	86,690	80.6	11.2	4.9	3.3
Rio Grande do Norte	34,391	76.8	9.9	10.2	3.1
Paraíba	69,117	76.7	6.4	14.6	2.3
Pernambuco	172,268	69.9	3.4	20.6	6.1
Alagôas	51,961	65.8	4.5	24.2	5.5
East	660,732	84.9	6.8	4.1	4.2
Sergipe	42,769	85.5	3.8	7.8	2.9
Bahia	258,043	84.0	7.6	3.2	5.2
Minas Gerais	267,696	87.8	5.7	3.3	3.2
Espírito Santo	46,306	83.5	6.2	2.3	8.0
Rio de Janeiro	40,652	77.8	10.8	8.9	2.5
Distrito Federal	5,266	39.4	14.6	35.1	10.9
South	702,234	76.2	4.3	11.1	8.4
São Paulo	221,611	64.6	7.9	24.0	3.5
Paraná	89,461	76.7	4.9	5.0	13.4
Santa Catarina	104,429	90.4	1.1	3.9	4.6
Rio Grande do Sul	286,733	79.9	2.5	5.6	12.0
West Central	79,751	62.1	6.1	6.4	25.4
Mato Grosso	16,015	72.7	7.8	5.7	13.8
Goiás	63,736	59.4	5.6	6.6	28.4

* Compiled and computed from data in "Censo Agrícola," VI *Recenseamento Geral do Brasil, 1950,* II (Rio de Janeiro, 1956), 28.
† Territory.

Moreover, rented farms were less numerous in 1950 than in 1940, when 221,505 (11.6 per cent of the total) were in that category. However, these tenant-operated farms were somewhat smaller than the average, including only 5.6 per cent of the land in farms; and these embraced on the average lands that were slightly less valuable than other properties, with the result that only 5.2 per cent of farm values were accounted for by those in the rented category. An interesting

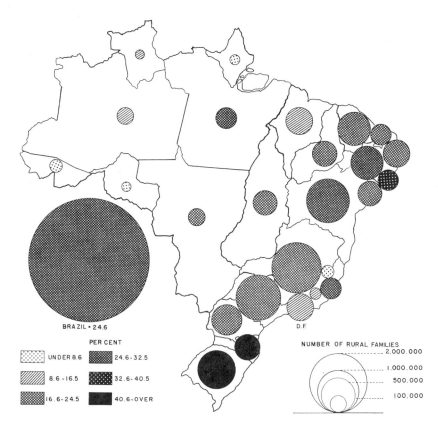

FIGURE 28. Variations in the proportions of farm owners among rural families in Brazil, 1950.

and significant fact is that at mid-century 115,512 (or 5.6 per cent) of Brazil's farms were operated by administrators. Furthermore, that Brazil's larger and more valuable estates were in charge of administrators is indicated by the fact that the rural establishments for which they were responsible contained 23.6 per cent of all farm land and 23.3 per cent of the value of all farm properties in the nation. Owner-operatorship, of the type in which labor is performed by workers who are paid either on a wage or a share basis, is a prominent type of tenure in Brazil, but there are important sections of the country in which the farmers themselves till small farms. In 1950, 1,553,349 Brazilian farms, 75.2 per cent, were operated by their owners. In the establishments of these owner-operators was 66.5 per cent of the farm land, indicating that their farms are considerably smaller than the average, and 68.1 per cent of the farm values. However, the variations from state to state are so great that no conclusions as to the comparative sizes and values of the properties of the various tenure classes should be drawn until the situation in the several states has been observed. To facilitate such observation, Tables XLI and XLII have been prepared. Table XLI shows the percentage of farms with tenant operators and also the percentage of the

TABLE XLI

Relationship of Tenancy to Size of Farm and Value of Farm Land, 1950, by States *

| State | Percentage tenant operated | | |
	Of farms	Of total acreage	Of total land value
Brazil	9.1	5.6	5.2
North			
Guaporé †	6.2	13.9	12.6
Acre †	42.1	36.6	41.1
Amazonas	6.8	27.4	11.0
Rio Branco †	4.0	3.5	3.6
Pará	4.6	6.9	3.5
Amapá †	5.1	1.1	0.5
Northeast			
Maranhão	5.5	1.2	3.9
Piauí	4.1	1.8	2.6
Ceará	4.9	2.1	3.5
Rio Grande do Norte	10.2	3.4	3.8
Paraíba	14.6	3.3	4.5
Pernambuco	20.6	5.0	8.9
Alagôas	24.2	4.7	6.1
East			
Sergipe	7.8	1.4	1.9
Bahia	3.2	0.6	1.2
Minas Gerais	3.3	2.2	3.4
Espírito Santo	2.3	2.0	2.4
Rio de Janeiro	8.9	5.5	5.7
Distrito Federal	35.1	23.0	24.9
South			
São Paulo	24.0	5.2	5.7
Paraná	5.0	2.3	2.6
Santa Catarina	3.9	2.1	2.3
Rio Grande do Sul	5.6	9.6	8.6
West Central			
Mato Grosso	5.7	5.7	3.6
Goiás	6.6	1.3	2.1

* Compiled and computed from data in "Censo Agrícola," *VI Recenseamento Geral do Brasil, 1950,* II (Rio de Janeiro, 1956), Table 22; and *ibid.,* VI–XXX, Table 1.
† Territory.

total land in farms and the total value of the rural properties that are accounted for by farms with tenant operators. Table XLII gives data comparable to those of Table XLI for the farms operated by administrators.

TABLE XLII

*Relationship of Operation by Administrators to Size of Farm and Value of Farm Land, 1950, by States ***

| State | Percentage administrator operated | | |
	Of farms	Of total acreage	Of total land value
Brazil	5.6	23.6	23.3
North			
Guaporé †	8.3	44.4	39.9
Acre †	6.4	25.5	14.2
Amazonas	3.7	12.3	13.0
Rio Branco †	22.7	45.8	24.1
Pará	2.8	40.6	25.5
Amapá †	46.9	69.2	63.9
Northeast			
Maranhão	3.0	27.8	12.8
Piauí	12.5	36.8	23.7
Ceará	11.2	23.8	19.6
Rio Grande do Norte	9.9	30.9	25.5
Paraíba	6.4	22.3	20.7
Pernambuco	3.4	22.6	28.4
Alagôas	4.5	28.5	28.8
East			
Sergipe	3.8	21.8	22.0
Bahia	7.6	27.3	32.9
Minas Gerais	5.7	18.1	14.9
Espírito Santo	6.2	13.1	15.2
Rio de Janeiro	10.8	30.9	32.1
Distrito Federal	14.6	37.0	34.2
South			
São Paulo	7.9	33.4	34.8
Paraná	4.9	26.0	27.9
Santa Catarina	1.1	8.6	4.1
Rio Grande do Sul	2.5	17.7	14.3
West Central			
Mato Grosso	7.8	25.1	22.2
Goiás	5.6	16.1	13.9

* Compiled and computed from data in "Censo Agrícola," VI *Recenseamento Geral do Brasil, 1950,* II (Rio de Janeiro, 1956), Table 22; and *ibid.,* VI–XXX, Table 1.
† Territory.

OTHER TENURE CATEGORIES

The statistical data presented above indicate that farm operators constitute but a small handful of the total rural population of Brazil. The tenure relationships of the masses who are not to be classed as owners, administrators, or renters also must be considered. Many and varied are the possible categories into which rural Brazilians who are not farm operators, or whose tenure is on the borderline between that of farm operator and farm laborer, might be grouped. But the classification into categories, without accompanying description of the relationships between man and land, proprietor and worker, would be of little consequence. Furthermore, a large share of the Brazilian population is to be classed as agricultural laborers or still further down the scale of social evolution. A very large part of all fall in an indeterminate category wherein life varies all the way from that of the unrestrained, nomadic existence of the hunter, fisher, and primitive agriculturist to that of a regular worker on an estate. On the social scale the colono on the São Paulo coffee or sugar plantation would probably rank at the top. Below him are the millions of his fellow countrymen who live on the cattle, sugar, cocoa, and other estates throughout the country, even though technically some of them might be considered tenants or even "farm operators" in the sense that they are responsible only to themselves as to where they "squat" or make a small roça.

The pages that follow set forth briefly the principal varieties of tenure categories, beginning with the most informal, and the processes by which a rather stable class of laborers is secured.

From Squatters to Agregados.   One may well begin the analysis with that numerous group of the lowest social class who inhabit the interior portions of the country, sometimes moving about annually, subject to no one and making their small roças where they please, at other times established as agregados or retainers on the fazenda of some patron. This class is of great importance numerically. Throughout a large part of Brazil land is very cheap and is held in extremely large holdings by proprietors who are primarily interested in keeping enough people about so that they can secure required help. Always there is the falta de braços in Brazil. It is not easy to retain a labor force because population is sparse, it is easy to secure the means for satisfying basic creature wants, and the lower classes lead a nomadic type of existence. Under these circumstances tenure relationships tend to become very informal indeed. Through long practice the rural people (the caboclos, matutos, sertanejos) feel free to "squat" where they please. They may establish their temporary quarters almost anywhere, erecting rough temporary shelters, making small roças [26] from which to harvest a little mandioca or maize, collecting and shelling babassú, preparing carnaúba wax, searching for diamonds, cutting wood, or fishing. If left to themselves this class

[26] Says Emílio Willems: "A certain part of native rural people of a very low economic status is represented by the *intrusos*, that is, intruders who invade large and yet unexplored properties of the state or individual owners, occupy their lands and cultivate the soil in a highly primitive way. When the soil is exhausted or when civilization advances closer, the *intrusos* move on and continue their work in more distant regions." "Some Aspects of Cultural Conflict and Acculturation in Southern Rural Brazil," *Rural Sociology,* VII (December, 1942), 376.

of people will continue to live a nomadic life, gaining a precarious livelihood by hunting, fishing, collecting, and destroying the forests in order to get a little corn or mandioca from the roças they make. Since labor is always the limiting factor in Brazilian production, the landowner may find it to his advantage to allow these rural folk to live on his land; even foreign concerns soon discover that it is a mistake to try to fence them out. Moreover, if the person who owns the land supplies a needed axe, offers a little ammunition now and then, provides necessary medicines, furnishes a few of the minimum essentials for improving the hut, supplies them with some fishing equipment, allows the use of a pack animal, he may in time get them to agree to bring in a pig now and then, or a few chickens, or a portion of the corn crop, a little mandioca, or possibly even to work a day once in a while. In short, he will come to play the same role as the selected leaders who were once sent by the provincial governors to bring under their influence the settlers who had squatted in this valley or along the banks of that stream.[27] By degrees some of these people may come to be part of the fazenda, the owner's agregados,[28] and the others move on. The nature of their tenure is not very clear cut, or rather it does not fall into the categories familiar to students of land tenure in the United States.

The relationship between the proprietor and the agregado, an adjustment between master and man that is so widespread throughout Brazil, is well described in the words of Djacir Menezes, who says of it: "There is an exchange of services, for compensation, in relations which are reminiscent of feudalism: a tribute for activity on the land of the proprietor, as was the case before the consolidation of the capitalistic regime." [29]

Oliveira Vianna gives a detailed description of the agregado's status on the fazenda:

From the class of slaves it is necessary to distinguish that of agregados. They are differentiated from slaves by their ethnic origin, by their social situation, by their economic condition and by their residence apart from the manor house.

They are a kind of free colonos. They differ, however, from colonos proper. The German colono of Santa Catarina is a small proprietor. The Italian colono of the Paulista fazenda is a salaried worker or a share tenant [parceiro]. The Vicentista agregados are neither one nor the other of these. These agregados are moradores or *foreiros* [subjects]. They live outside the limits of the senzalas in rude huts located on small dispersed plots that are scattered about the great house on the hill to which they are oriented and which dominates them. From the fertile land they extract, almost without work, sufficient game, fruits and cereals to live a frugal and

---

[27] Cf. Oliveira Vianna, *Populações Meridionaes do Brasil*, 98, 99–100, 101, 119, and 123.

[28] Says Burton of the situation on the Fazenda Jaguara in Minas Gerais: "Here and there were scattered the huts of 'aggregados,' squatters who are permitted to live up on the Fazenda, but who do not acquire by residence any right to the soil." *The Highlands of the Brazil*, II, 27.

[29] Djacir Menezes, *O Outro Nordeste* (Rio de Janeiro, 1937), 66.

indolent life. They represent a type of small self-sufficing producer vegetating at the side of the large fazendeiro producer.[30]

Other descriptions are in essential agreement. Thus Cardoso de Menezes e Souza first quotes Straten-Ponthoz to the effect that in Brazil "the extension of the old concessions has permitted the proprietors in the interior of the provinces to surround themselves with a population of sharing colonos, or tenants, and renters by various services and occupants by tolerance. There were other bodies of partisans serving in the various truly feudal rivalries and in their resistance to the government." Then he concludes that from this concentration of landownership in a few hands "came the constitution, almost feudal, of the proprietorship of the soil and this band of agregados, that on our rural establishments live in dependency upon, and at the mercy and expense of the fazendeiros, at whose nod they are subservient and bowed, in order not to be ejected from their miserable ranchos [thatched huts] where they live and from the roça or engenho where they work to gain their daily bread." [31] To remedy this situation he strongly recommended the levying of a tax on unused land, citing the experience of various other countries in this respect.[32]

Such informal arrangements, vastly different from the contractual agreements in São Paulo's leading fazendas or in the United States, are typical in large areas of Mato Grosso, Goiás, Bahia, and all of the states to the north of them. One should not make the mistake of thinking that such families of agregados, and even the unattached persons of a comparable social level, are to be found only in the distant interior.

There are just outside the limits of the cities and adjacent to the fazendas many poor families, many people almost proletarietized, who live miserably on the products of hunting and fishing, or from small gardens and groves beside the poor huts of thatch in which they shelter themselves from the inclemencies of the weather. Some work by the day or the task on the clearings of the fazendeiros, being considered as agregados on the agricultural establishments; others idle away in the most degrading laziness playing little guitars and singing *modinhas* [little hits] in the *sambas* and *cateretês*, where, not rarely, disorders break out and bloody tragedies take place, in which these minstrels of the sertão are involved.[33]

It is difficult to find full descriptions of the arrangements between master and man on the various estates that have such informal tenure systems, but here and there some light is thrown on the subject. Of such tenure relationships in Pilão Arcado on the São Francisco River in Bahia, Pearse says:

The principal crops are Carnaúba palm leaves, mandioca and Indian corn. Fishing takes up a lot of the time of the people. There is no share

[30] Oliveira Vianna, *Populacões Meridionaes do Brasil*, 75–76. Rocha Pombo says of the agregado's condition, ". . . it is not known in what it differs from one of the true slaves. He was the serf of the Middle Ages, and perhaps less." *Historia do Brasil*, V, 515.

[31] Cardosa de Menezes e Souza, *Theses sobre Colonização no Brazil*, 309.

[32] *Ibid.*, 309–15; proposed law cited, *ibid.*, Appendix F.

[33] *Ibid.*, 172.

system. Those who rent land do not pay any rental. The landlord is satisfied to have somebody on his land, on whom he may call for help against
payment of a daily wage. The products of such tenants are sold to the
landlord; by these means the landlord probably earns what he loses on the
rent.[34]

In spite of a somewhat strained emphasis on race, the description
by Sir Harry H. Johnston is more adequate. In the following paragraphs he describes the process by which squatters are brought under the dominion of the landowner:

The conditions regarding the acquisition of land (more especially Government land in new districts) require the possession of more or less
ready money. The white man, therefore, acquires the land and surveys it
at his own expense. Before he casts his eye over this likely estate it may
already have been squatted on by negroes, negroids, or "Indians" (these
squatters are called "Moradores" in Brazil), or after the estate had been
acquired and surveyed, the Moradores drift thither and settle on it with or
without permission. But before long they are obliged to come to terms
with the real owner of the estate, who has acquired these rights by a legal
contract. So far from the estate owner desiring to evict the squatter, he is
anxious to come to terms with him, because if he be harsh, the squatter
with his invaluable labour will move off to an unclaimed piece of land or
to a more considerate employer. The unwritten law which all parties believe in and observe is that the Morador shall pay for his rent and other
benefits in labour, and this he is quite ready to do, provided the demands
on his time are not unreasonable. But the estate owner generally keeps a
store, and is in a small way a banker. The result is that the Moradores—
Negro and Indian—are generally more or less in debt to the proprietor
they serve; and the latter, if need be, has recourse to the law to compel
the payment of debt by a reasonable amount of labour. Usually quite patriarchal conditions arise between the white Padrão and the coloured "Camarada." This last receives in theory small monthly wages, which are not
always adequate to the payment of the rent and the purchase of goods; but
then he has a right to share the two principal meals of his Patron, to
whose family he considers he belongs. The Padrão is usually the godfather
—and his wife the godmother—of the Camarada's children. The Padrão
conceives himself obliged by the requirements of good feeling to give occasional entertainments to the tenants with singing, dancing, and fire-
works, usually on saints' days.
Until the negro acquires capital, which he invests in land and in the
development of estates, so long will the white man hold the political and
social ascendancy in Brazil. And it should be noted once again that negro
tenants very much dislike settling down under *negro* landlords (where
there are such). They infinitely prefer to associate themselves with the
development of estates owned by *white men*, or, at any rate, by such persons who endeavour to conceal the slight element of the negro or the
Amerindian in their bodies by behaving with liberality and justice attributed to the white man.[35]

Thus there are millions of Brazilians who fall in the range between
squatters and agregados; and many of the former gradually are being
transformed into the latter. It appears that the agregado who has at-

[34] Pearse, *Brazilian Cotton,* 111.
[35] Johnston, *The Negro in the New World,* 100–101. In connection with the
terminology employed here, note that *camarada* is widely used to refer to a worker
who lives off the estate in distinction to the agregado who lives on the place.

tained the status of a parceiro or *meieiro* is approximating that of the sharecropper in the southern part of the United States. In any case, over much of Brazil tenure questions resolve themselves into considerations of ownership and the rights, duties, privileges, and obligations of the agregado.

Sharecroppers. Although neither the agregado nor camarada could be considered a share hand or a sharecropper, frequently there is an element of share wages in the terms on which one of them is permitted to live on a fazenda and make use of the land. If the owner is absentee, if the proprietor is lax in his supervision, or if what was once a well-managed plantation becomes decadent, a share system is likely to develop. In some cases the former agregado may become so independent that he deserves classification as a renter who secures his land in return for a share of the crop. In any case, in the longer-settled portions of the interior, where sugar or coffee has not developed a rationalized plantation labor system but where density of population is rather high, the tenure system is already in a stage resembling our sharecropping. Thus a share system on half-and-half basis is common in the cotton-producing parts of the Northeast. Arno S. Pearse gives some of the details about this system of *parceria* in the following quotation:

> Mr. Beserra has the usual share-system in vogue on his farm. There are 40 families ("moradores"); each has a small farmstead completely stocked with animals and the lands are properly fenced. The "morador" works in the fields and hands over to Mr. Beserra, the owner, half of the cotton crop in lieu of rent. Each family grows a small quantity of maize, beans, etc., for their own use. Mr. Beserra instructs the "moradores" as to planting, weeding, etc., and his orders must be carried out by the tenant. The other half of the cotton crop the tenant has to sell to the landowner, but he can abide his time for selling.[36]

During the drought of 1942 in these cotton-producing sections of the northeastern sertão a Brazilian government official who visited the area was prompted to write:

> Since the major proportion of the rural population is made up of meieiros [half hands], who are financed by the large proprietors of the rural domains, in accordance with the volume of agricultural production, there occurs, now, as during previous droughts, the suspension of advances in money or in food. The loss of half the harvest, the worst to be expected, will be more prejudicial to the landowner than the inevitable insolvency will be to the meieiro. Without financing, or being furnished with food, the rural worker abandons the house, improvements, and also the cotton trees which may enable him to recover his losses, a few years later, when they begin again to produce normally the "white gold." [37]

In São Paulo cotton production has been highly rationalized, and the Japanese, as renters, have helped introduce a system which en-

[36] Pearse, *Cotton in North Brazil*, 103–104. Cf. Caldeira, *Arrendamento e Parceria, passim,* and Diégues Júnior, *População e Propriedade da Terra no Brasil,* 65–68.

[37] Henrique Doria de Vasconcellos, *Viagem de Inspeção ao Norte* (Rio de Janeiro, 1942), 41.

abled them to get temporary possession of the land for carrying on their soil-mining enterprises, much to the detriment of the land. However, in addition to the genuine renting arrangements in which they are involved, other tenure arrangements of a sharecropping type somewhat closely approximating a system of renting have been evolving. Pearse has described the essential nature of the tenure arrangements prevailing on a cotton plantation near Vila Americana, of São Paulo.

On the estate are 60 families, each of which has three hectares; they work on the share system, keeping the proceeds of two-thirds for themselves and one-third goes to the company. The tenant is debited with two-thirds of the cost of manure; money is advanced for implements, manure, etc. The tenants must conform to the instructions of the manager as regards the cultivation of the plot. The manager has further the call on the tenant when he requires labourers for the land of the company, where he raises special cottons; for this work they get paid a daily wage. A man able to work the disc-cultivator gets five milreis per day.[38]

Today such a system of sharecropping is widespread throughout the cotton-producing portions of the state.

Sharecropping also long has been an important feature of cotton production in the northeastern states, and it also plays an important role in the growing of sugar cane in Pernambuco and the neighboring states. On the old engenhos nearly always there was a miscellaneous lot of fairly independent families allowed to live and work on the place, who turned over to the proprietor a share (usually one-half) of the cane which they grew. Today, some of these remain, either delivering directly to the usinas often a 50 per cent share in addition to a very high interest on advances, or living and working on a share basis under the jurisdiction of one of the owners or tenants who furnishes cane to the central factory.[39]

Thus various kinds of share hands or parceiros make up an important segment of Brazil's rural labor force. According to the 1950 census they totaled 1,245,557, of whom 930,055 were males. Minas Gerais alone accounted for 366,905 of those in this subtenant category, and São Paulo for 234,303. On a relative basis, though, they were most important among the rural workers of the states of Espírito Santo, Rio de Janeiro, and Rio Grande do Norte. See Table XLIII.

Vaqueiros in the Sertão. At best the agregado is a farm laborer. Even though he may eventually become a parceiro, corresponding approximately to a Southern sharecropper, he could hardly be classified as a farm operator. However, there are other types of tenure relationships prevailing in Brazil that do justify classifying as an operator the nonowner who does the work. One of these is found in the cattle-growing sections of the interior, in the sertões. The tenure system in use there is much more formalized than the relationship between the fazendeiro and the agregado, even though it rarely involves

[38] Pearse, *Brazilian Cotton*, 81.
[39] Cf. Gileno dé Carlí, *O Processo Histórico da Usina em Pernambuco* (Rio de Janeiro, 1942), 20–21, *passim*.

TABLE XLIII

Males 15 Years of Age and over Employed in Agriculture, Classified According to Labor Status, 1950, by States *

State	Number	Number of male workers per farm	Per cent working as		
			Farm operators and unpaid members of their families	Hired hands	Share-croppers (*parceiros*)
Brazil	6,688,904	3.2	47.1	40.9	12.0
North	192,158	2.5	60.3	37.2	2.5
Guaporé †	3,918	7.4	16.8	73.8	9.4
Acre †	13,217	7.8	18.2	80.8	1.0
Amazonas	46,473	3.0	51.9	45.7	2.4
Rio Branco †	1,539	3.5	48.0	41.1	10.9
Pará	124,916	2.1	70.0	27.6	2.4
Amapá †	2,095	4.6	26.4	73.2	0.4
Northeast	1,788,948	3.3	45.0	45.0	10.0
Maranhão	198,701	2.1	65.5	31.7	2.8
Piauí	118,867	3.5	44.6	43.7	11.7
Ceará	344,708	4.0	41.4	44.3	14.3
Rio Grande do Norte	159,315	4.6	35.2	38.1	26.7
Paraíba	290,111	4.2	38.7	43.6	17.7
Pernambuco	505,575	2.9	48.0	49.3	2.7
Alagôas	171,671	3.3	39.8	58.4	1.8
East	2,397,845	3.6	41.7	41.2	17.1
Sergipe	98,371	2.3	51.4	43.9	4.7
Bahia	676,076	2.6	57.0	38.5	4.5
Minas Gerais	1,241,108	4.7	33.1	46.0	20.9
Serra dos Aimorés	16,139	3.8	43.8	18.0	38.2
Espírito Santo	153,311	3.5	46.4	19.4	34.2
Rio de Janeiro	199,178	4.9	28.2	44.0	27.8
Distrito Federal	13,662	2.6	52.4	46.9	0.7
South	2,092,929	3.0	53.6	37.5	8.9
São Paulo	1,002,874	4.5	38.2	47.8	14.0
Paraná	299,326	3.4	48.4	46.6	5.0
Santa Catarina	188,688	1.8	83.1	14.4	2.5
Rio Grande do Sul	602,041	2.1	72.7	22.9	4.4
West Central	217,024	2.7	56.4	33.9	9.7
Mato Grosso	51,174	3.2	50.2	46.4	3.4
Goiás	165,850	2.6	58.3	30.0	11.7

* Compiled and computed from data in "Censo Agrícola," VI *Recenseamento Geral do Brasil, 1950*, II (Rio de Janeiro, 1956), 40–42.
† Territory.

a written contract. Euclydes da Cunha in his classic work, *Os Sertões*, has described the system under which the vaqueiro operates.

In contrast with the owner of the estância [in Rio Grande do Sul] the fazendeiro of the sertões lives in the littoral, far from his expanded dominions, which in some cases he has never seen. He has inherited an old historic vice. Like the opulent possessors of sesmarias in colonial times, he enjoys parasitically the return from his unbounded lands. The vaqueiros are his submissive serfs.

Thanks to a contract by which they receive a certain percentage of the product, there they remain, anonymous—being born, living, and dying on the same piece of land—lost in the trails and huts; and throughout a life-time carefully caring for the herds which do not belong to them.

The true owner, absent, knows them to have fidelity without comparison. He does not supervise them. At most he knows only their names.

Dressed in their characteristic garb of leather, the sertanejos raise a hut of upright poles [pau-a-pique] beside the water holes, rapidly as though erecting a tent, and resign themselves to the unprofitable service.

The first thing to do is to learn the abc, and then, all of the exigencies of the art of which they are past masters: to know the *ferros* [brands] of their fazendas and those near by. This is the designation applied to signs of all shapes, or letters, or capricious designs imprinted by hot irons on the flanks of the animals, completed by cutting markings or small angles in the ears. Branded, the animal is guaranteed. He may break through any fence and stray away. He carries the indelible indication that restores him to his original *solta* (unfenced pastures), because the vaqueiro is not content to know the brands of his own fazenda; he learns those of the others. Sometimes, by an extraordinary feat of memory, he comes to know one by one, not only the beasts under his care, but those of the neighbors, including their genealogies and characteristic habits, their names, their ages, etc. Accordingly, when there comes to his place a neigh-bor's animal, whose mark he knows, he promptly restores it. If he does not know the brand he keeps the intruder, treating it as he does the others. But he does not drive it to the annual sale (*feira*), nor use it for any work; he lets it die of old age. It does not belong to him.

If a cow gives birth to a calf, he brands the latter with the same un-known mark, which he reproduces with admirable perfection; and the same is done with all of its descendants. Of each four animals, however, he takes one for himself. It is his pay. He establishes with the unknown patron the same arrangement he has with the other. And he follows strictly, without judges and witnesses, the strange contract which no one wrote or suggested.

Many times it happens that a brand is deciphered only after many years have passed, and the cattleman is happy to receive, in place of the one cow which fled and was forgotten, a small herd produced by her.

This fact may appear fantastic, but it is common in the sertões. It is given as a fascinating feature in the integrity of the countrymen. The great proprietors of lands and herds know it. They all have with the vaqueiro the same contract of sharing, summarized in the single clause that they give to him, as a return for his care of the cattle, one fourth of the products of the fazenda. They know that the percentage will never be violated.

The settling of accounts takes place at the end of the winter and is done, ordinarily, without the party most interested being present. It is dis-pensable formality. The vaqueiro separates, scrupulously, the large por-tion of the increase belonging to the patron (on which are imprinted the brand of the fazenda) from the few, one fourth, which fall to him. On these he places his own private brand; and he keeps them or sells them. Then he writes to the patron, giving him a minute account of the affairs of the sítio, going at length into the slightest details; and he continues un-interruptedly with the work.[40]

---

[40] Euclydes da Cunha, *Os Sertões* (15th ed.; Rio de Janeiro, 1940), 122–24; for an earlier description of the tenure contract of the vaqueiro see Koster, *Travels in Brazil*, I, 199–202.

From other sources one obtains essentially the same picture. Southey gave the following account of the background and development of the system described by Euclydes da Cunha in the quotation which follows:

The lands of Piauhy were given in *sesmarias* of three square leagues: between every two, a league was left common to both for the use of the cattle; but neither owner might build either house or fold upon this intermediate land. This was thought necessary, because of the frequent droughts, and consequent failure of pasturage. The owners also were jealous of neighbours, and liked their state of lonely lordship: they had some reason, considering that there were times when a watering place became of as much value as in Arabia; and that dogs were a nuisance to all cattle, except those which they were trained to guard. But this system tended to keep them in barbarous state of manners. A house was built, usually with a thatched roof, some folds were enclosed, and twelve square miles were then peopled, . . . according to the custom of Piauhy. Ten or twelve men sufficed for managing an estate of this extent. Part of their duty is to destroy the wild cattle and horses, that they may not decoy away the tame, or render them unmanageable. If the owner has no slaves, Mulattos, Mamalucos and free Blacks, who abound in the Sertoens of Seara, Pernambuco, and Bahia, and particularly about the Rio S. Francisco in the higher parts of its course, are eager to obtain employment in these farms. These men, who hate any other labour, are passionately fond of this way of life, which not only gratifies their inclinations, but holds out to them the fairest prospect of attaining to wealth themselves. Every one hopes to become a *Vaqueiro, Creador,* or *Homem de Fazenda,* as the managing herdsman is called, in his turn. These superintendents serve for five years without pay; from that time they are entitled to a fourth of the herd every year. This gives them an interest in its prosperity, and in the course of a few years, some of them establish *Fazendas* of their own.[41]

TENURE CHANGES IN THE SUGAR AREAS

In Pernambuco and other sugar-producing states a rapid change is doing much to add complexity to the tenure systems of Brazil. That time is definitely past when the tenure classes in this sugar-cane area could be clearly divided into the masters, senhores de engenhos, their slaves and agregados, with a few poverty-stricken independent producers of mandioca and other foodstuffs thrown in for good measure. In this section the concentration of land in the properties of the sugar companies has reduced the members of the former aristocracy to the status of renters, tenants on the vast acreages they once owned. It also has replaced many of them with others under a variety of tenure arrangements.

Formerly, it was said of Pernambuco that the greater part of the land was in a few great properties, remains of the undivided sesmarias. The proprietor, or the renter of an engenho, used a small part of it and let the remainder to a multitude of free mulattoes or Negroes, for whom he served as protector, or from "whom he demands absolute obedience and over whom he exerts the most complete des-

[41] Southey, *History of Brazil*, III, 756.

potism." [42] That these free workers had a place on the typical sugar
estate is indicated by Koster: "The lands of sugar plantations are appropriated to five purposes. These are: the woods,—the lands for
planting canes,—those which are cleared for pasturage,—the provision grounds for the negroes,—and the lands which are occupied by
free people." [43] Their tenure is clearly described in the following
paragraph:

An estate contains in general much more land than its owner can
manage or in any way employ, even under the present extravagant system
of changing from one piece of ground to another. I call it extravagant, because it requires so much space for its operations and performs these
with more labour than is necessary. This overplus of land gives room for
the habitations of free people in the lower ranks of life, who live upon the
produce they raise by their own labour. The tenures by which these persons
hold the lands which they occupy, are most insecure, and this insecurity
constitutes one of the great engines of that power which the landholder
enjoys over his tenants. No agreements are drawn out; but the proprietor
of the land verbally permits the peasant who applies to him for a place
of residence, to inhabit a cottage upon his lands, under the condition of
paying him a trifling rent . . . and he is allowed to cultivate as much
ground as he possibly can by himself: but the rent is increased if he calls
in any one to assist him. Sometimes the verbal arrangement which is entered into is, that the tenant shall perform some service in lieu of making
his payment in money. The service required is, for instance, that of going
on errands, or of seeing that the woods are not destroyed by persons who
have not obtained permission from the owner to cut down timber, and
other offices of the same description. [44]

From farther south, in the state of Rio de Janeiro, comes a report
of how a more advanced type of tenant was used to help develop a
sugar plantation, some of these tenants ultimately becoming landowners and the others being reduced to the less advanced status described above. According to John Luccock, the nomadic, ignorant,
and listless moradores, whose chief function was guarding the estate
against infringements from the outside, were

. . . frequently succeeded by a more valuable class of tenants who possess a small capital, which they invest in slaves, cultivate a larger portion
of land, and pay their rent sometimes in money, or by labour, more commonly in produce. If the article raised be sugar-cane . . . half the produce
usually goes to the landlord, for which he not only furnishes the soil, but
crushes the tenant's share of the cane, distils the syrup, or converts it into
sugar. . . . Such a bargain is considered as advantageous to a man, who
possesses land without much capital, because he is hereby enabled to construct Sugar-works adapted to his whole estate, and to keep them more
fully employed. The tenants are bound also to plant a certain quantity of
Cane on additional pieces of ground, and to crush the produce at the Mill
belonging to the estate; and these minor Farms fall successively into the
owner's hand, and add to the value of his property. At the same time, many
of the tenants improve their own condition, become advanced in the
scale of cultivators, and ultimately proprietors of land. [45]

[42] A. P. Figueiredo, writing in *O Progresso* of Recife in 1846, cited in Freyre,
Nordeste, 153.
[43] Koster, *Travels in Brazil*, II, 133.
[44] *Ibid.*, 135–36.
[45] Luccock, *Notes on Rio de Janeiro, and the Southern Parts of Brazil*, 293–94.

In other words, in the sugar areas there were three classes of people on the land: the senhores de engenho, their slaves, and their agregados. Except that slaves became relatively less important and finally disappeared while agregados became more significant, the system seems to have changed little in hundreds of years. However, the introduction of more modern processes and of twentieth-century machinery set in motion some forces that still have not completed the readjustments they were destined to bring about.

Most evident is the fact that the process of land concentration in the sugar-growing littoral of the Northeast has brought into being various types of tenancy on the heavy black soils of that region. The first step, of course, was the reduction of the proprietors of the engenhos to the status of fornecedores of cane for the usinas. This came about because gradually the lands as well as the milling facilities became the property of the sugar company which, having great financial power, followed the policy of "acquiring land for the direct cultivation of cane, liberating it [the usina] from exclusive dependency upon the fornecedores." [46] Naturally, this upset the whole scheme of life of the former landowners. A memorial submitted to the house of deputies of the state of Pernambuco on August 14, 1928, by the Association of Furnishers and Planters of Cane in Pernambuco included the following assertions:

The independent agricultural property, which all peoples aware of its importance seek to safeguard and fortify in their agricultural systems, is disappearing from the State. The soil which grows its most traditional and most prominent crop has become the land of the usinas, which do not care to utilize them directly by themselves and with their own capital, with a progressive technique, with initiative capable of bettering the extremely poor conditions of productivity. Day by day the usinas become larger land capitalists. They expulse the proprietors from their former engenhos and they put in their places temporary renters, who are less apt and less interested than the former owners. [47]

However, the company owning the sugar factory rarely engaged directly in the cultivation of the soil. Instead, it rented lands to small operators in return for 50 per cent of the gross product. In some cases, also, they rented the lands of the former engenho to a fornecedor, who in turn let them out to small farmers for a share rent amounting to 50 per cent of the cane produced. [48] In this way, in addition to the independent farmers who managed to retain their lands, although the mill and their status of senhores de engenho were gone, there came into being several other tenure classes. First of these are the fornecedores who rent their lands from the usinas. These Dé Carlí divides into two classes: the first, called *rendeiros*, are those who pay in cash a sum arrived at on the basis of a stipulated formula. For example, some pay an amount equivalent to 20

[46] *Boletim da União dos Sindicatos Agricolas de Pernambuco*, No. 6 (September, 1910), quoted in Dé Carlí, *O Processo Histórico da Usina em Pernambuco*, 19.

[47] This was cited, *ibid.*, 33–34.

[48] *Ibid.*, 20.

per cent of the value of the first 1,000 tons of cane delivered, 15 per cent of the value of the second 1,000 tons, and 10 per cent of the value of cane supplied in excess of 2,000 tons. Penalties are assessed if the cane is not up to the standard in quality; the renter obligates himself "to keep in good condition the houses on the rented engenho"; and it is specifically stated that if he finds it necessary to erect other houses for his workers, he shall be entitled to no reimbursement for such expense but will be obligated to maintain those in good condition. The second category he calls parceiros. They pay on a share-rent basis, usually giving at least 30 per cent of the harvest, plus fees and interest totaling from 9 to 12 per cent, so that "it was not rare, even in the first quarter of the present century, to find a rent as high as 50 per cent of the gross production." In addition, a penalty might be assessed for *cana branca* or "white cane," because his cane was of the "butter" (*manteiga*) type. With much reason Dé Carlí asks how the usinas can penalize the producer for not producing a better cane, when they themselves do not do so.[49] "Many proprietors rent their lands to their farmers—small agriculturists— for a rent varying between 30 and 50 per cent of the gross production, the farmer receiving financing for his small crop and a base almost always 6$000 per ton," he says again, referring to this class of share renters. "These farmers are the ones responsible for a large share of the harvests of the fornecedores, in whose names the cane is entered at the factory."[50]

Continuing the analysis and description of the classes of fornecedores Dé Carlí quotes with approval the following description presented in 1878 to the Congresso Agrícola in Recife:

Our harvests of sugar are the product of the work of two very distinct classes of agriculturists; the proprietor or renter who plants the cane and manufactures the sugar, and those who live on the farmers' lands, upon condition of dividing with him the sugar produced from the cane which they plant.

This system is general in the Province; it establishes a system of sharing [parceria] *sui generis,* which I have no trepidation in saying, nullifies the labor of the share planter, diminishes the production.

The nonmanufacturing planter follows a precarious life; his work is not remunerative; his feelings are not respected; his interests lie at the mercy of the sugar manufacturer on whose lands he lives. There is not even a written contract to obligate the interested parties; everything is based in the absolute will of the manufacturer. In exchange for a habitation, often the poorest, and a little land given for planting mandioca, *which must be limited and made* on the least productive ground; in exchange for this, the parceiro divides his cane in equal shares; the manufacturer gets all the molasses, all the resulting *cachaça* [rum], all the bagasse, which is excellent fuel for the sugar mill, all the cane tops, succulent food for his cattle. It is a lion's share, gentlemen, the more unjust because all the expenses of planting, cultivation, cutting, arranging [tying up in bundles] and transportation to the mill are cared for exclusively by the half-share farmer.[51]

[49] *Ibid.,* 20–23.
[50] *Ibid.,* 45.
[51] *Ibid.,* 46–47.

According to Dé Carlí, essentially the same tenure relationships still prevail. Data presented by him for the year 1929–1930 led him to believe that these parceiros produced approximately one-half the cane delivered by the fornecedores.[52] More recently Harry Hutchinson has supplied basic facts relative to the transformation taking place in certain portions of the old sugar-cane districts of Bahia's recôncavo. In this section, he reports, there are several large usinas, but that even in these there "is still a maximum of family traditions and paternalism." Indeed, in the particular community upon which his study was focused, the sugar mill itself is owned by a family corporation. By 1951, however, this corporation had bought up six neighboring plantations, but even so at least one-half of the cane processed by the factory came from other "individual, family-owned plantations." [53] Furthermore, in the 1960's these highly commercialized plantations of northeastern Brazil, with their large numbers of wage hands, are the chief targets of the peasant leagues (*ligas campesinas*) in their endeavors to seize the land and divide it among the workers. Thus it is evident that tenure relationships are far different now from those that prevailed when masters and men formed the two widely separated classes in the society that Gilberto Freyre has described so well.

LAND TENURE IN SÃO PAULO

To one acquainted with the history of the land question in the United States it must seem strange that there has been until recently little or no consciousness of a tenant problem in São Paulo. In that state are to be found municípios in which rented rural properties attain 60, 70, 80, and even 90 per cent. There is as yet no carefully devised, systematic set of legal provisions for regulating landlord-tenant relations such as that which keeps tenancy from being a problem in the British Isles, but rather a hit-and-miss system of renting similar to that prevailing in the United States. Why, then, may we ask, was it that, prior to the second world war, there was no burning antagonism between the social classes in agriculture? No widespread agitation for legal and practical reform in the land system? No flood of discussions of the subject in the newspapers, magazines, professional journals, and classroom?

To answer such questions it is necessary to understand the manner in which the system came into being. In part the general analysis given above also applies specifically to the state of São Paulo. As was the case with all Brazil, São Paulo was first cut into large estates which were tilled by slave labor, Indians at first and Negroes later, or devoted to immense pastures for herds of cattle. The system of colonization carried on by the Portuguese did not result in the trans-

---

[52] *Ibid.*, 49.
[53] Harry W. Hutchinson, *Village and Plantation Life in Northeastern Brazil* (Seattle, 1957), 7–8, *passim.*

ference of the small-farming system of northern Portugal, from whence a large portion of the colonists came, nor in the establishment of small-farming communities; it was more on the order of the system of settlement that prevailed in our tidewater South. As a matter of fact, the sugar-cane plantations established along the Brazilian coast by the Portuguese were even larger, more dependent upon slave labor, and probably characterized by a more luxurious life for their owners, than were their feudal counterparts in our own Southland. Even Jefferson Davis and his fellows in the Natchez area probably did not equal these Brazilians in the splendor of their conspicuous consumption. When the Portuguese moved inland and established the small nodules of settlement which secured for Portugal all of the vast territory which constitutes present-day Brazil, they parceled the land into huge tracts. Nor was the land given promiscuously to all who might desire it. In order to secure a grant, or sesmaria, the applicant had to convince the authorities that he came of a good family and that he had plenty of funds for developing the land. Unlike the situation in our own South, there were admitted to Brazil no hundreds of thousands of small farmers, such as the Scotch-Irish and German families who in the United States cut behind the coastal plantations, engaged in cattle raising, spread along the Piedmont, and eventually divided the rolling, hilly, and less desired territory into small farms. The cattle which overspread Brazil were driven forward by persons (mostly Paulistas) seeking locations for more tremendous landholdings and securing them by occupation or by grant from the authorities. There was not even the independent possession and control of small tracts by fugitives from the obligations of the settled communities, comparable to the roles played by indentured servants and fugitive slaves in the settlement of western United States. Many persons did flee to the west and obtain squatter's rights in the land. Such movements were particularly strong when levies of conscripts were being inducted into the army or when the militia was called up for service in war.[54] It also included numerous fugitive slaves. The government recognized that these persons should not be dispossessed at will, but it developed no system comparable to our homestead provisions to legalize their possession. Instead, when the authorities learned that a considerable number of such masterless people had located in a given area, a prominent citizen would be designated to go out, receive a title to the land on which

[54] Cf. von Spix and von Martius, *Travels in Brazil*, I, 319. Enlightenment about the propulsions to such westward movement is given in the observations of a South Carolina doctor who visited the state of São Paulo in October 1865.

"After getting dinner we rode back to survey the village of Jundiahi; and found that it had one rather comely looking church, with two others that presented quite a dilapidated look. There was also a jail, at which a military sentinel was on duty; and it perhaps contained some of the patriotic recruits, who are taken in chains from this section of São Paulo, and thence sent to Rio de Janeiro, for service in the army against the Paraguayans. We have met on the road a number of these fellows handcuffed, and with a chain around their necks, under a mounted guard, who seemed to think that they were doing the country a good service from the large number in charge of a few prisoners." Gaston, *Hunting a Home in Brazil*, 78.

they were settled, establish a new fazenda, and gradually bring them under his influence and control. Thus, frequently, squatting on un-occupied land was not the prelude to the establishment of a small-farming community, but merely one of the steps in the opening of another fazenda.[55] Furthermore, as late as 1809 the legal owner-ship and possession of land was restricted to members of the white race.[56]

São Paulo maintained its fazenda system, largely unaltered by the introduction of the present-day system of renting, until a very recent date. According to the census of 1920 there were in the entire state only 80,921 rural properties (farms), of which nearly one-half (39,190) were less than 41 hectares in area. Including all properties large and small, the average area was 172 hectares; and 85 per cent of all the land in farms was held in tracts of more than 100 hectares in size, the 21 largest averaging almost 50,000 hectares each. At that time there were only 2,354 renters enumerated in the entire state, or only 2.9 per cent of the farm operators. On the other hand, hired ad-ministrators numbered 6,247, or 7.7 per cent, of all operators. In 1920 the renters of São Paulo were operating farms that were below the average for the state in size and value, while administrators were in charge of the operations on the larger estates and more valu-able lands. Thus, the 2.9 per cent of all operators who were renters operated only 2.6 per cent of the land in farms, and this land was valued at only 1.8 per cent of the total for the state; the administra-tors, who constituted 7.7 per cent of the farm operators, were in charge of 29.7 per cent of the land according to area and 36.9 ac-cording to value.[57]

In 1934 the state of São Paulo made a census of agriculture that was, in many ways, one of the best collections of any significant so-cial and economic data ever made in Brazil. The farms were counted, the nationalities of their owners were determined, the crops and livestock inventoried. All of this was tabulated, along with the best information on the population collected up to that time. But no ten-ure classification was introduced into the published counts.[58]

It therefore seems evident that São Paulo's renting system is rela-tively new, and to this in part must be attributed the lack of concern with tenure problems. But there are other factors to be considered as well. Extremely important is the fact that the new system has not grown out of the dispossession of small holders; it did not come about because of former owners' losing control of the land and drop-ping down one rung on the agricultural ladder. Rather, it is merely a new aspect added to the old fazenda system, the long continued con-centration of landownership and control. As has been shown else-where in this volume, following the freeing of the slaves São Paulo

[55] Cf. Oliveira Vianna, *Populações Meridionaes do Brasil*, 98, 99–100, 101, 119, and 123.

[56] *Ibid.*, 128.

[57] "Agricultura," *Recenseamento do Brazil, 1920*, III, Pt. 1, pp. 6–9.

[58] See *Recenseamento Agricola-Zootechnico Realizado em 1934* (São Paulo, 1936).

developed a large program of subsidized immigration to provide a labor supply for its fazendas. At first Italians were the principal immigrants, and according to reports most of them were willing to stay indefinitely on the fazendas, with little concern for improving their status to a position above that of colono, a laborer paid on a piece and a share basis. However, their descendants now own a great many of the largest and most prosperous fazendas in the state. After 1902 Italian emigration to São Paulo was prohibited by the Italian government, and São Paulo had to turn elsewhere for the replenishment of its labor supply. The Spaniards, Germans, Japanese, and other nationalities have been even less content to remain forever in the landless laboring class, and it is undoubtedly this factor that has done much to bring about the changes that have occurred since 1920. To this attitude of the more recent immigrants must be attributed much of the present high development of the renting system of São Paulo.

Thus, the manner in which São Paulo's tenant system has come into being does much to explain the lack of a widespread public consciousness of a land problem and the lack of agitation for land reform. The tenants are newcomers, of foreign stock of extremely heterogeneous origin, without the social and political status possessed by the native-born population; for São Paulo's tenants, renting represents a position on the agricultural ladder that is far above that of agricultural laborer formerly held by themselves or their fathers; the class of renters is not to any significant degree made up of dispossessed farmers, as is the case in our own Midwest; and except for the chosen few in the landowning class who make up society's elite, the foreign elements in the tenant class enjoy a social and economic position considerably above many Brazilian native-born who are confined to the class of agricultural laborers. Thus, on the whole the renting system of São Paulo should be thought of as a step forward in the direction of a system of landownership and control in which the functions of laborer, manager, and capitalist are united in the same person. To such a system of family farms our own Midwest owes its world-recognized agricultural superiority; to it our nation owes the development and maintenance of what is probably the highest average level of rural citizenship that the world has ever known. In this respect São Paulo differs from the "colonial" parts of the more southern states where federal, state, and private colonization projects have established a class of small farmers on the land as owner-operators.

The most negative aspect of São Paulo's recent development of a system of leasing the land is probably the soil-mining practices of the Japanese renters. In the 1930's and 1940's they were able to rent farm lands for the planting of cotton, and it is said they were particularly efficient in extracting everything possible from the land. On this matter the materials and analysis given by Carlos Borges Schmidt are especially valuable. He points out that the interest of the renter is to take from the land the maximum product, in the shortest period, and at the least expense. Then he adds:

This has always been the rule; at the end of the contracted period, the renter returns the land in the condition to which it is reduced after the growing of cotton, whatever this state of affairs may be. No care or precaution is taken to prevent or reduce to a minimum the waste and impoverishment of the soil. The lands which have been rented to the Japanese are a good example of how much the soil can be damaged by being farmed on the basis of an absolutely unilateral interest. Already the conviction is deep rooted that the land which the Japanese has cultivated, as a renter, will produce nothing more, *"nem mesmo capim"* ("not even grass")—say our rural people.[59]

Schmidt also describes the system of sharecropping, parceria, used in the production of supplementary crops in the coffee sections. This parceria is of two types, one in which the landowner participates in the farming operations and one in which he does not. The first prevails in those areas where agriculture is in the most advanced stages, throughout the central part of the state. In this type the owner does the plowing, harrowing, and other operations necessary to prepare the land for the seed and furnishes that as well. In brief, he turns land ready for planting and the seed over to the parceiro. The latter is responsible for the planting, cultivation, and harvesting processes. The product is divided in the field, each party being responsible for the transportation of his share. If insecticides are necessary, the landowner supplies the materials, the parceiro applies them. If fertilizer is used, the cost is usually shared equally by the two parties to the contract. The product is shared equally also as a rule, except in some of the older and more fertile areas, where the preparation of the soil for the seed is relatively easy and no fertilizer required. In such cases the landowner may take only one-third of the crop.

In the older portions of São Paulo, particularly in the mountain sections that encircle the Paraíba Valley, the second type of parceria is found. Here, in return for 20 or 25 per cent of the product, landowners permit the parceiros to make their roças on their holdings. This system differs little, if at all, from that of agregados and moradores on large estates described elsewhere.[60]

[59] See Carlos Borges Schmidt, "Systems of Land Tenure in São Paulo," *Rural Sociology*, VIII (September, 1943), 243–44.

[60] *Ibid.* Extremely interesting is the evolution of parceria in São Paulo. Early in the nineteenth century Paulista fazendeiros were experimenting with substitutes for slave labor. Naturally the legal basis of their operations was in Portuguese law. This defined parceria as "a society which participates in renting. The parceiros are farmers who work under conditions similar to those of renters on plots of ground divided from the great properties." But in São Paulo the land of the fazendas was not divided, the fazendeiros merely divided the labor among the first colonos, and "the parceiro thus remained in the condition of one who had leased his services, subject to the administration of the fazenda and remunerated by the division of the product, which he planted and harvested, and which was later processed [i. e., threshed or husked] by the proprietor." When disputes arose between the imported colonos, or workers, and the fazendeiros, naturally the lawyers found a fertile field for arguments as to whether or not parceria was involved. Finally Sr. José Vergueiro, son of the senator on whose fazenda parceria was first established, substituted a system similar in many ways to that which prevails so widely today. He described it as follows: "The colonos receive the coffee trees they are able to cultivate; they harvest the berries; they receive per

The role of the Japanese immigrants and their descendants is especially important in the changes in land tenure that are taking place in São Paulo and the neighboring states.[61] Fortunately, many of the essential facts about this matter were gathered in the special survey which the Brazilian Japanese made of themselves in 1958 to commemorate the fiftieth anniversary of the arrival of the first Japanese immigrants in Brazil.[62] This comprehensive study secured data concerning 430,101 persons, of whom 138,639 were immigrants born in Japan, 224,186 were of the first generation born in Brazil, 66,914 of

TABLE XLIV

Status of Japanese Immigrants upon Arrival, Cross-Classified with Their Status in 1958

Status in 1958	Status on arrival (1908–1942)					
	Total	Owner-operator	Renter	Share or contract worker	Colonos or camaradas	Nonagricultural
Total						
Number	17,719	1,586	1,345	854	12,983	951
Per cent	100.0	100.0	100.0	100.0	100.0	100.0
Owner-operators						
Number	7,136	825	476	381	5,297	157
Per cent	40.3	52.0	35.4	44.6	40.8	16.5
Renters						
Number	2,740	145	390	116	2,030	59
Per cent	15.4	9.1	29.0	13.6	15.6	6.2
Share or contract workers						
Number	908	36	55	71	724	22
Per cent	5.1	2.3	4.1	8.3	5.6	2.3
Colonos and camaradas						
Number	311	19	19	15	245	13
Per cent	1.8	1.2	1.4	1.8	1.9	1.4
Nonagricultural						
Number	6,624	561	405	271	4,687	700
Per cent	37.4	35.4	30.1	31.7	36.1	73.6

alqueire from 300 to 600 reis; they receive designated lands for their own plantings, lands which are given gratis by some proprietors and for a small rent by others." Finally it appears that in São Paulo "the system of rural economy generally adopted under the name of parceria . . . is nothing if not *metayage* by which the proprietor furnishes land and livestock, the colono furnishes the work and the product is divided in halves." Cardoso de Menezes e Souza, *Theses sobre Colonização no Brazil*, 261–65. The last of the quotations had in turn been quoted from a work by Jules Duval.

61 Cf. Fujii and Smith, *The Acculturation of Japanese Immigrants in Brazil*, 29–31.

62 Through the kindness of the director of the survey, Dr. T. Suzuki, who also is director of the Japanese-Brazilian cultural center in São Paulo, some of the preliminary results of this survey have been made available to the present writer.

the second generation, 242 of the third, and 120 in a small category for which data on place of birth were unavailable. For 17,719 of the adult male immigrants who secured employment immediately, materials were secured which indicated occupation and status within the industry in which they were engaged upon arrival and the same for the year 1958. See Table xliv. Of these immigrants 1,138 entered Brazil prior to 1918, 3,614 arrived between 1918 and 1928, and 12,967 came during the years 1928 to 1942, inclusive.

For present purposes the striking thing that is evident from the materials in Table xliv is the rapidity with which recent immigrants (nearly three-fourths of them arrived in Brazil in the period 1928–

TABLE XLV

Change in Tenure Status of Japanese Immigrants Between Time of Arrival and 1958

| Tenure category | Number and percentages in stated categories | | | |
| | UPON ARRIVAL | | IN 1958 | |
	Number	Per cent	Number	Per cent
Agriculturists who remained				
in agriculture	10,844	100.0	10,844	100.0
Owners	1,025	9.4	6,979	64.4
Renters	940	8.7	2,681	24.7
Share or contract workers	583	5.4	886	8.2
Camaradas and colonos	8,296	76.5	298	2.7
Agriculturists who left				
agriculture	5,924	100.0	5,924	100.0
Owners	561	9.5	—	—
Renters	405	6.8	—	—
Share or contract workers	271	4.6	—	—
Camaradas and colonos	4,687	79.1	—	—
Nonagriculturists who changed				
to agriculture	251	100.0	251	100.0
Owners	—	—	157	62.5
Renters	—	—	59	23.5
Share or contract workers	—	—	22	8.8
Camaradas and colonos	—	—	13	5.2

1942) who arrived as agricultural laborers have moved into the category of farm owners, on the one hand, and into nonagricultural occupations, on the other. Thus upon arrival only 8.9 per cent of the immigrants were classified as farm owners, 7.6 per cent as renters, 4.8 per cent as share or contract workers, 73.3 per cent as camaradas or colonos, and only 5.4 per cent as engaged in nonagricultural pursuits. But by 1958 the situation had changed radically. The survey from which these data are taken revealed that, only fifty years after the first immigrants had arrived, 40 per cent of all were in the farm-owner category and that almost as high a proportion (37.4 per cent) were in nonagricultural pursuits. The very high proportions who worked first as agricultural laborers employed by others (camaradas and colonos) or even on a share or contract basis had dropped to 1.8 and 5.1 per cent, respectively, by 1958.

In order to present more of the significant details with respect to the rapid ascent of the agricultural ladder by the Japanese in São Paulo and the neighboring states and of their shift from agriculture to other industries, Table xlv has been prepared. It presents the data separately for the 10,844 immigrants who began work in agriculture and were still farming in 1958, the 5,924 immigrants who commenced in agriculture and shifted to other pursuits, and the 251 persons born in Japan who did not farm immediately upon arrival but who were engaged in agriculture in 1958. Most significant, of course, are the facts that among the large group who remained in agriculture less than one-tenth were able to commence as farm owners, whereas by 1958 almost two-thirds of all were in that category, and that the proportion of camaradas and colonos had fallen from more than three-fourths to less than 3 per cent of those who gained a livelihood by farming.

Information is also available for the 5,924 Japanese immigrants who began in agriculture and had shifted to nonagricultural activities by 1958. As is evident from Table xlv, most of them once were agricultural laborers. By 1958, however, 21.8 per cent were classified as employers, 62.8 per cent as own-account workers, 1.8 per cent as managers or officials, and only 13.6 per cent as employees.

CHAPTER XIV

THE SIZE OF HOLDINGS

Through a relatively long period spent in the study of rural populations and rural society the writer has become convinced that the size of agricultural holdings, the concentration of landownership, or the distribution of landownership and control is the most important single determinant of the welfare of the people on the land. With a widespread distribution of property ownership and control go (1) the maximum propulsions to steady work and habits of thrift, (2) relatively high average standards of living, (3) minimum class distinctions, the relative absence of caste (inherited social position), and as a result, relatively little class struggle, (4) a fairly high degree of vertical social mobility, (5) comparatively high average intelligence and a minimum range of intelligence, and (6) the most well-rounded personalities in the rural population. In brief, this type of land system produces citizens of an exceedingly high average level. The opposite of this system, the concentration of the land in the hands of a few and the reduction of the masses of the people to the position of landless agricultural laborers, is accompanied by (1) a comparatively low average standard of living, although the elite landowning class may live in a fantastic luxury, (2) great chasms of class distinctions between the favored few of the upper class and the masses who lack rights to the soil, (3) a comparative absence of vertical social mobility so that this chasm is perpetuated by caste barriers even though offspring of the lower classes may in some cases be possessed of rare combinations of biological endowments, (4) a low average intelligence of the population because the high abilities and accomplishments of the few people of the upper class are greatly overweighed by the ignorance and illiteracy of the masses, and (5) a population skilled only in the performance under close supervision of a very limited number of manual tasks and lacking completely training and practice in managerial and entrepreneurial work. Therefore, much significance attaches to the almost universal existence in time and space of the large estate in Brazil. One should try to understand why it is that Brazil, a colony of Portugal, largely a country of small farmers, never knew the family farm for the first three or four hundred years of its history and then received it from other Europeans, not the Portuguese.

INTRODUCTION AND DIFFUSION OF THE LARGE ESTATE

The system of landownership and control established by the Portuguese colonists in Brazil represented a very sharp break with the traditional small-farm agricultural pattern of Portugal. This is only one of the many aspects of rural social organization that underwent radical changes in the colonization of Brazil. Before the establishment of its colonies in America, Portugal had developed the sesmaria as an institution for seizing concentrations of landed property and distributing them among persons who would cultivate the land. In this way it had preserved, for the most part, a system of small farms. From this tradition the land system established in Brazil represented a decided departure. Says Oliveira Vianna relative to the introduction of and role played by the large estate in Brazil:

> In our country . . . agriculture had its beginning in the large estate. The Romans evolved the large property from the small. . . . Other peoples developed in a similar manner. In contrast with this we have been since the beginning a nation of latifundia: among us the history of the small farm can be said to go back only a century. All the long colonial period is one of the splendor and glory of the immense territorial property. In this period it alone appeared and shone; it alone created and dominated; it is the central theme interwoven throughout the entire drama of our history for three hundred fecund and glorious years.[1]

The same writer, after pointing out that the region of northern Portugal from which the colonists came was then, as now, one of small farms, analyzes the reasons for the break with the traditional cultural pattern. He emphasizes the importance of two factors: (1) The colonists were not ordinary citizens (*homens do povo*) but adventurers from the lower and even the upper segments of the nobility who migrated in order to restore depleted fortunes. For the most part plebeians came only in later years, after the discovery of gold and diamonds and the economic development of the country had made a place for small manufacturing and trading enterprises. (2) Lands were granted only to persons who could convince the authorities that they were from "good" families and that they had the slaves, finances, and other requisites to develop sugar plantations and mills.[2] Even those members of the lower classes who reached Brazil and sought lands were careful to represent themselves to the authorities as coming from old established families and possessed of ample means for developing the concession.[3]

But the establishment of a sugar plantation and mill required a considerable amount of capital, and it was not always possible for the impoverished noble or aspiring plebeian to borrow this from the

[1] Oliveira Vianna, "O Povo Brazileiro e sua Evolução," *loc. cit.*, 282.
[2] *Ibid.*, 284–85.
[3] *Ibid.*, 284.

Jewish moneylenders of the coastal towns.[4] But the establishment of a curral for cattle surrounded by vast acreages of pasture lands was much less costly. Hence many who could not obtain the coveted social and economic status of the sugar planter turned their steps inland and carried the pastoral enterprises to the interior—the curral preceded the fazenda and the sugar plantation.[5] Although it took less capital, the development of a curral, later a fazenda, for cattle also served to diffuse the large estate throughout Brazil. Whereas it was considered necessary to have a grant of at least two leagues (some eight miles) square in order to have sufficient land for a sugar plantation, an extension of 10 leagues, or about 40 miles, on each side was the customary size of the sesmaria that was granted for purposes of raising cattle. And even those who were unable to secure concessions of land and rented the areas on which they grazed their cattle leased areas at least one league square.[6]

The diffusion of the large landholding throughout Brazil proceeded very rapidly. Along the entire coastal area the sesmaria was the instrument for the spread of the large estate devoted to sugar production. Few persons of the farmer class gained a foothold there. Nor did small farms develop in the hinterland to constitute a "shelter belt," protecting the plantations from the natives, as was the case in the southern part of the United States. Owing in a large measure to the intrepid Paulistas of the seventeenth century, the menace of Indian attacks from the interior was largely eliminated and the lands themselves appropriated in extremely large tracts for the purposes of cattle raising. Accompanied by their numerous slaves and agregados, these Paulista bandeirantes went on long exploring and Indian-hunting expeditions; but they also drove their herds of cattle before them in a species of "combined operations," and upon this economic base they established nodules of settlement, throughout the entire length and breadth of Brazil. One can hardly overstress the contribution of the small handful of adventurers from São Paulo. They pushed south through what is now Paraná and Santa Catarina to the great plains of Rio Grande do Sul; they spread westward into Mato Grosso and northwest into Goiás; they introduced their particular variety of European civilization, or better, the new American variety, based on pastoral activities, into Minas Gerais, pushed on down the São Francisco through Bahia, and then spread out onto the areas of the great sertão in Pernambuco, Ceará, Piauí, and Maranhão.

Furthermore, they were just as bold in asking for lands in sesmaria as they were in penetrating new areas and enslaving the Indians. As a rule they petitioned for grants of the maximum size, asking them not only for themselves but for all the members of their numerous families. No doubt they felt entitled to the possession of vast expanses of territory by virtue of being the explorers, the first to

---

[4] For a discussion of the role of the Jews as moneylenders in the colonies, see Freyre, *Sobrados e Mucambos*, 39–43, *passim*.
[5] Oliveira Vianna, "O Povo Brasileiro e sua Evolução," *loc. cit.*, 288.
[6] *Ibid.*, 284.

reduce the natives, the founders of the settlements, and the owners of the herds which formed the economic basis of the economy. Oliveira Vianna cites the case of Brito Peixoto, who was not content with a sesmaria for himself, but requested His Majesty the King to grant one to each member of his family.[7] In the mining regions the royal letters confirming the possession of the owners ordered that the lands be distributed to the discoverers and their associates. From the south a governor reported that there were families in possession of 15 and 16 leagues of land, "the fathers have three leagues, and the sons, still living with the father, have secured the remainder."[8]

The valley of the São Francisco River formed a center of dispersion for these Brazilian stockmen and frontiersmen. Here they established strongholds, built up their breeding stock, and then continued their migrations, so that this great valley served as a second point of irradiation in the conquest of Brazil. From here in 1590 Christovão de Barros opened Sergipe for the Portuguese; from here other sertanistas, driving their herds before them and supported by their warriors, made their way along the Rio São Francisco to near the place where Cabrobo, Pernambuco, now stands, and then spread out over the interior parts of Pernambuco, Paraíba, Rio Grande do Norte, Ceará, Piauí, and Maranhão. "For the most part, the villages existing in the high sertões of the northeast, from Bahia to Maranhão, have for this reason their origins in former cattle fazendas," says Oliveira Vianna.[9] Even today, as has been mentioned elsewhere, "Bahiano" is a synonym of "countryman" in the cattle-grazing portions of Maranhão and Piauí.

The manner in which the large concentrations of grazing lands came into private possession, the vicissitudes through which some of the large estates passed, and the central fact that there was no tendency for them to be broken up as one generation succeeded another are brought out in the following quotation:

Domingos Jorge, a Paulista, and Domingos Affonso, from Maffra, in Portugal, were the first persons who began the conquest of this province (Piauí). Towards the year 1674, the latter possessed a fazenda for breeding cattle on the northern side of the river St. Francisco. The great injury which he there sustained from the central Indians, and the desire of augmenting his fortune with similar possessions, urged him to undertake the conquest of the northern country, for which object he assembled all the people he could accumulate, and having passed the serra of Dois Irmaos, (Two Brothers), towards the north, he, fortunately for himself, encountered the Paulista before mentioned, who was in the process of reducing Indians to captivity, and they afforded mutual succour to each other. Having ultimately captured a considerable number, and caused the remainder to retire, the Paulista returned to his country with the greater part of the captive Indians, and the European remained the master of the territory. Other companies made similar entries into this district, the said Affonso

[7] Oliveira Vianna, *Populações Meridionaes do Brasil*, 118.
[8] *Ibid.*, 119.
[9] Oliveira Vianna, "O Povo Brazileiro e sua Evolução, *loc. cit.*, 298.

always remaining supreme captain of the whole, and the vast possessions thus acquired by the entrance of various parties, received the denomination of Certam. It is said that he established above fifty fazendas for the breeding of large cattle, and that he gave away and sold many during his life. It is however certain, that at his death, he left thirty, and appointed the Jesuits of the College of Bahia administrators of them, ordering the revenues of eleven to be appropriated for dowries to young virgins, to the clothing of widows, and to succour other necessities of the poor. With the rest they were to augment the number of fazendas, but it is said that they only established three more. With the extinction of this sect, the whole passed under the administration of the crown, and are preserved in the same state by the inspection of three administrators, each having eleven fazendas in his jurisdiction, with three hundred milreas of salary. They occupy the territory through which the rivers Piauhy and Caninde flow, from the boundary of the province to the north of the capital, in the vicinity of which there are some principal ones. The privilege of forming establishments within their lands is not granted to any one, where the slaves of the fazendas work alone for their subsistence and clothing. The cattle arriving at a certain age are conducted by the purchasers principally to Bahia and its reconcave. Those of the northern district descend to Maranham, others are driven to Pernambuco.[10]

The literature is filled with other references to and descriptions of Brazil's tremendous landed properties. At the opening of the nineteenth century one of these in the province of Paraíba, belonging to the Albuquerque do Maranhão family, was said to extend fourteen leagues along the road leading from Natal to Recife. "Besides this prodigious property the owner possessed estates in the *Sertam*, which were supposed to be from thirty to forty leagues in extent, . . . such leagues as, if measured by time, are each three or four hours' journey." [11]

In the concentration of landownership that prevailed in Brazil, however, there is a distinguishing feature—the role played by the Church was a very modest one. Never did the Church become famous in Brazil, as it has elsewhere, for the control of broad acreages. At most, some of the priests were said to have transferred to mulatto offspring a number of the best engenhos in such provinces as Bahia. In fact, in Brazil the chapel usually seems to have been an adjunct to the engenho or the fazenda, and the priest to have been there at the sufferance of its aristocratic owner. Only the lay brotherhoods were noted for their extensive holdings. The key to this situation, so different from that in Spanish-American countries such as Mexico, is to be found in a royal letter of February 23, 1711, which stipulated that "in the concessions of land in the State of Brazil there shall always be the condition of it never passing by any title to the dominion of Religions." [12]

---

[10] Henderson, *A History of the Brazil*, 425–26. Some fifty years later these fazendas are mentioned as being utilized in an attempt to create a colony for liberated slaves. In 1873 the colony numbered about eight hundred, of whom three hundred were minors and one hundred, invalids. It was established in order to prevent the privation and misery that would result in the formation of criminal bands. Cardoso de Menezes e Souza, *Theses sobre Colonização no Brazil*, 127–31.

[11] Southey, *History of Brazil*, III, 768.

[12] The letter is quoted in Silva Rocha, *Historia da Colonisação do Brasil*, I, 158.

THE SITUATION IN THE NINETEENTH CENTURY

By 1800 Brazil was already cut to the pattern of the large estate.[13] Although there were few landholders, there were not many unclaimed acres. This point needs emphasizing because of the tendency to think of Brazil as a young country. It is not; its cultural patterns are deeply rooted in tradition and in a tradition that grew out of the social relationships of the large landed estate. Brazil's coastal fringe was dotted with sugar plantations, and most of its vast interior was thinly veneered with a pastoral culture long before our thirteen colonies gained their independence. However, this culture merely occupied the country; it did not settle it. And Brazil is still engaged in the process of settling its vast territory.

After the first century or so the settlement process proceeded, and the density of population was increased by the development of new fazendas in established districts, rather than by the occupation of more territory. Early in the nineteenth century, John Mawe described the process of opening a new fazenda in the state of São Paulo.

When he [the farmer] has made choice of a situation, he applies to the governor of the district, who orders the proper officers to mark out the extent required, generally a league, or a league and a half square, sometimes more. The cultivator then purchases as many negroes as he can, and commences his operations by erecting habitations for them and himself, which are generally miserable sheds supported by four posts, and commonly called ranchos. His negroes are then directed to cut down the trees and brushwood growing on the land, to such an extent as he thinks they will be able to manage. This done, they set fire to all they have cut, as it lies on the ground. Much of the success of his harvest depends on this burning. If the whole be reduced to ashes, he expects a great crop; if, through wet weather, the felled trees remain only half burnt, he prognosticates a bad one. When the ground is cleared, the negroes dibble it with their hoes and sow their maize, beans, or other pulse. During the operation they cut down any thing very much in the way, but never think of working the soil. After sowing as much seed as is thought requisite, they prepare other ground for planting cassada, here called mandioca, the root of which is generally eaten as bread by all ranks in Brazil. . . . When enough has been planted for the entire consumption of the farm, the owner, if he is rich enough, prepares means for growing and manufacturing sugar. He first employs a carpenter to cut wood and build a mill with wooden rollers for crushing the canes, by means of water if a stream is at hand, if not, by the help of mules. While some of the negroes are assisting the carpenter, others are employed in preparing ground in the same way as for mandioca. Pieces of cane containing three or four joints, and in length about six inches, cut from the growing stem, are laid in the earth nearly horizontally, and are covered with soil to the depth of about four inches. They shoot up rapidly, and in three months have a bushy appearance not unlike flags; in twelve or fifteen months more they are ready for cutting. In rich virgin soil it is not uncommon to see canes twelve feet high and astonishingly thick.

. . . . . .

In no branch of husbandry are the farmers so defective as in the management of cattle. No artificial grasses are cultivated; no enclosures

[13] Even though a royal letter of June 15, 1711, had forbidden the granting of more than one square league to a person. *Ibid.*

are made; nor is any fodder laid up against the season of scarcity. The cows are never milked regularly; they seem to be considered rather as an incumbrance to a farm than a valuable part of the stock. They constantly require salt, which is given them once in fifteen or twenty days, in small proportions. The dairies, if such they may be called, are managed in so slovenly a manner, that the little butter that is made becomes rancid in a few days, and the cheese is good for nothing.[14]

The concentration of landownership, resulting from the grants of sesmarias, had already reached a high degree in 1822, when Brazil gained her independence. Ruy Cirne Lima states that the results have never been summarized better than by Gonçalves Chaves, who wrote anonymously at the time of the independence:

1. Our population is almost nothing in comparison with the immensity of the territory which we have already occupied for three centuries.
2. The lands are almost all divided and there are few left to distribute, except those subject to invasion by the Indians.
3. The monopolists possess up to 20 leagues of land and rare are the times that they consent for any family to establish itself on any part of their lands, and even when they do consent, it is always temporarily and never by a contract which would permit the family to remain several years.
4. There are many poor families wandering from place to place, following the favor and caprice of landowners and always lacking the means of obtaining some ground on which they could make a permanent establishment.
5. Our agriculture is as backward and unprogressive as is possible among any agricultural people, even the least advanced in civilization.[15]

Similar generalizations about the high concentration of landownership, unused lands, and the consequent loss to the nation are abundant in other writings. In perusing this literature one soon comes to appreciate the special Brazilian flavor given to the term "latifundium," that the principal element in the concept is the withholding from productive uses of extensive tracts of land. An official report to the Minister of Agriculture made in 1873 described the manner of giving lands in sesmaria that once prevailed and then added:

From this amplitude of liberty it resulted that all the lands about the cities and important villages on the coast fell into private ownership, with the result that today it is not possible to find in the populous cities close to the markets and along the great lines of communication a single palm of land that belongs to the state and could be converted into a nucleus of colonization or distributed to immigrants. Since the owners do not possess the necessary means of cultivating such vast extensions of land, much of it remains uncultivated and lacking in villages or houses.

From this concentration of property in the hands of a few comes the abandonment of agriculture in the country districts, the stagnation or lack of development in urban constructions, the poverty and dependency of a large part of the population, who do not find a field for their activity nor means to become proprietors, and finally the difficulties that today sur-

[14] Mawe, *Travels in the Interior of Brazil*, 78–80.
[15] Cirne Lima, *Terras Devolutas*, 43–44.

round the public administration in offering immigrants a commodious and appropriate location.[16]

Gilberto Freyre has done much to delineate social development among the aristocratic families of the Northeast. In his works are presented a wealth of material dealing with the latifundium in Pernambuco. Not of least significance are some extracts from Recife newspapers and periodicals which he has reproduced. Particularly important for those interested in the land system are such articles as one by A. P. Figueiredo published in 1846 in *O Progresso* of Recife.

The major part of the land in our province is divided into great properties, remains of the ancient sesmarias, of which very few have been subdivided. The proprietor or the renter occupies a part of them and abandons, for a small payment, the right to live on and cultivate the other portions to one hundred, two hundred and sometimes to four hundred families of free mulattoes or blacks, of whom he becomes the protector but from whom he demands absolute obedience and over whom he exercises the most complete despotism. From this it results that the guarantees of the law are not for these unfortunates, who compose the greater part of the population of the province, but for the proprietors, of whom three or four, united by the ties of blood, of friendship, or of ambition, are sufficient to annihilate, in a vast expanse of territory, the forces and influence of the government.

It is essential that people of slight means shall be able to obtain lands and cultivate them with the certainty of enjoying the products, conditions which do not exist today, because the senhores de engenhos or fazendas obstinately refuse to sell any portion of their lands, source and guarantee of their feudal power, and because the unfortunate morador who takes the risk of planting remains at the mercy of the proprietor, who may expel him from the land inside of twenty-four hours.[17]

Even more detailed and caustic is another and longer article published by Figueiredo, under the pseudonym Abdalah-el-Kratif, in the *Diario de Pernambuco*, March 24, 1856.

What destiny has the continued increase of population in the interior? Will they come to be employed in agriculture? No; the best elements will leave for Recife to seek their fortune, to solicit a ridiculous employment; the remainder will move to the vilas and other population centers to pass a life of misery, because we have no industry which offers the free worker steady work and regular pay.

This is the source of those masses of men without secure means of subsistence which in certain blocks feed the politics of the parties and in the inferior parts of society practice robbery in all of its varieties.

What is the reason that these grossly dissolute families do not engage in agriculture instead of entering into the precarious careers in public services? Why, instead of leaving to be tailors, masons, and carpenters, do not the sons of families little favored by fortune return to the interior; why also do they not become agriculturists? Why do the inhabitants of the forests not cultivate the soil if they are not forced to do so? Why do their children seek out the vilas? For all of this we do not see more than a single answer, and disgracefully it is fully complete.

In the social state in which we live, the means of subsistence of a father of a family do not increase in proportion to the number of children with

[16] Cardoso de Menezes e Souza, *Theses sobre Colonização no Brazil*, 308–309.
[17] The article was reproduced in Freyre, *Nordeste*, 153–54.

Sugar Plantation in Northeastern Brazil

the result that, in general, the children are poorer than the parents and possess less capital. Now agriculture is encircled by a barrier that makes it inaccessible for the man of modest means; for all those who do not possess a certain number of contos de reis. However, she is the productive function par excellence, the mother (dead soul) of the nations, and it is here that reside the vital interests of our country; but since it is found encircled by a barrier, it is necessary that this barrier fall, cost what it may.

And what is this barrier? The great territorial property. This terrible entity which has ruined and depopulated . . . [illegible] and many other countries.

This region which includes all the littoral of our province and extends to a depth of ten, twelve, and sometimes fifteen or eighteen leagues into the interior, is found divided into engenhos or properties whose dimensions vary from one fourth of a league square to two, three and even four and five leagues square.

Here because cane growing demands a quantity of certain soil which is not found everywhere, it follows that, besides the cane lands, the woods that they must have, and the lands which they require for their oxen and for planting mandioca, indispensable for feeding the slaves, the greater part of the engenhos possess vast extensions of unopened lands, lands that would be eminently suited for small farming, and which, were they cultivated, would be sufficient to furnish an abundance of mandioca flour, beans, and corn to all the population of the province and neighboring provinces, and even for export.

The proprietors refuse to sell these lands and even to rent them. If one possesses thirty or forty contos de reis, then he may buy an engenho; but if you are poor and would like to buy or rent a few acres of land you will not find them.

This is what produces the unproductive population of the cities, the class in search of public employment that increases every day, that makes the crimes against property become more frequent every day, and the country poorer day by day, because of the increased number of consumers while the number of producers remains stationary or at least increases at a slower rate.

But the large proprietors say, we are far from refusing poor people the land they need to cultivate; let them come, and for a modest charge, and sometimes even for nothing, we will give them, not only lands to plant, but wood to build houses. Very well; but this enjoyment only lasts at the pleasure of the large proprietor.

However, whenever they do not please the landowner, because of some small capriciousness, or because they refuse to vote for his candidates, or for failing to comply with an order, they are ejected without recourse. How can these unhappy ones be brought to plant if they are not certain of harvesting? What incentive is there to induce them to improve land of which they may be dispossessed at any moment?

On the lands of the large proprietors, they do not enjoy any political rights, because they have no free opinion; for them the large proprietor is the police, the courts, the administration, in a word, everything; and outside the right and the possibility of leaving him, the condition of these unhappy ones differs in nothing from that of the medieval serfs.[18]

Sugar estates, whether in Pernambuco, Rio de Janeiro, Bahia, or São Paulo, were very much of a kind. It is not necessary to multiply

[18] The *Diario* article account was reproduced *ibid.*, 246–49.

The Old-fashioned Sugar Mill. (Reproduced from Rugendas, *Voyage Pittoresque dans le Brésil.*)

instances to show the concentration of land that prevailed in the areas producing cane. But elsewhere the evidences of concentrated ownership are similar. Cattle estates, fazendas or estâncias, occupied even greater acreages than the sugar engenhos, and, because of the extensive nature of the enterprises, cattle sections were also much more sparsely populated. Nineteenth-century visitors to Rio Grande do Sul even hesitated to report the size of the estâncias they found, for fear their veracity might be challenged. John Luccock, who traveled throughout the province on horseback, wrote: ". . . indeed, the reported extent of farms in this part of the American Continent can scarcely be mentioned with boldness, by one who has himself little doubt of the truth of the accounts. The smallest are stated at four square leagues, or more than twenty thousand acres; the largest are said to reach to a hundred square leagues, or near six hundred thousand acres. To each three square leagues are allotted four to five thousand head of cattle, six men, and a hundred horses." [19]

An official source, dated 1904, says:

These plains are divided up into "Estancias" or "Fazendas," the medium superficial area of an "Estancia" being 1 square League (4356 Hectares or 10,760 Acres), many of them however being 3 to 6 times that size. Wherever possible, natural limits were chosen in the division, such as rivers and brooks, which, besides avoiding all questions and doubts as to the boundary lines, serve as natural fences for keeping in the cattle. Where this has not been possible, strong wire fences serve now almost everywhere the same purpose. Internally the "Estancias," are divided into various enclosures called "Invernadas," to separate the breeding cattle from that to be fattened for sale. The house of the proprietor, more or less modest and simple, according to his means, generally stands on some elevation, near the center, overlooking the surrounding country, and around it are the huts or "ranchos" of the "peons." Agriculture on these estancias is as a rule conducted only to the extent of supplying the wants of the owner and his vassals.[20]

A similar pattern of concentration in landownership prevailed throughout most of the interior of Brazil, including the western portions of Santa Catarina, Paraná, and São Paulo; much of Minas Gerais; Mato Grosso and Goiás; all except the coastal fringes of the states from Bahia to Maranhão; and even the populated portions of the Amazon Valley. (Of course in all of these, collecting and mining activities competed for the available labor, but they did little or nothing to affect the concentration of landownership.) One of the most extreme cases encountered is reported from the state of Paraná by the English engineer Bigg-Wither.

A few more such fazendas as the Forteleza, . . . would turn the whole province of Paraná into a desert. . . .

[19] Luccock, *Notes on Rio de Janeiro, and the Southern Parts of Brazil*, 216.
[20] Dahne, *Descriptive Memorial of the State of Rio Grande do Sul, Brazil*, 24. This publication was organized by "order of the president." It has been thought unnecessary to preserve several obvious typographical errors in the original. Also it should be pointed out that by this time in the "colonial" parts of the state a prosperous class of small farmers was rapidly coming into being.

The whole estate occupies no less than 340 square miles of the zone or belt from whence, as I have shown, all the prosperity of which the province can boast has been primarily derived. Yet its owner will neither use it himself, except to an insignificant extent, nor will he sell any portion of it to others. On both sides, . . . it is flanked by the chief agricultural districts of the province, supporting between them a large population, while itself, it supports just a dozen persons, eight of whom are slaves.[21]

Thomas P. Bigg-Wither, always concerned with the chances of successful English colonization in this part of south Brazil, thought this estate ideally situated for a colony of his compatriots. He believed that the problem of the latifundium in Brazil might be solved by "the imposition of an Imperial landtax, to be levied on all estates whose extents reach above a certain minimum. Such a tax would at once break up all large, idle estates, increase the productive power and consequently the prosperity of the province, and lastly, add a good round sum to the annual revenues of the empire." [22]

Even in Minas Gerais, one of the states in which subdivision of land early made some headway, some estates remained of enormous size. Burton in 1867 described the Fazenda Jaguara and supplied a brief account of how it came into being. "Half a century ago, a certain Colonel Antonio de Abrêu Guimarães amassed a large fortune with 750 slaves, and still more by forgetting to pay the government dues on diamonds exported from Diamantina and other places. He held an enormous property of 36 square leagues (427,504 acres), which was afterwards divided into seven great estates." One of these, the Mello, at the time of Burton's visit was being surveyed for transfer to the emigrants who had left the southern United States following the Civil War. This estate contained sixty-three sesmarias, each of which in this district generally contained one half of a square league.[23]

Fifty years earlier Luccock, through inquiries and observations on the land system of the state, wrote:

These people furnished me with several particulars respecting the state and condition of Minas Geraes. In those parts, they said, which are the most populous, the estates are generally a league broad and as much in depth, or contain sixteen English square miles. On so wide a space there commonly reside no more than about twelve persons, whom alone it supplies with subsistence. They allowed that estates of half a square league, or one-fourth of the former size, are more productive in proportion to their extent, because capital is wanting among the planters to manage more ground, and said that on such estates cattle are kept in larger numbers; but, they added, "with so little land what can we do with our children when they grow up? We shall have no land to spare for them." [24]

Except in the south, where the program of colonization was making real headway, Brazil entered the twentieth century as a nation in which the large estate ruled supreme.

[21] Thomas P. Bigg-Wither, *Pioneering in South Brazil* (London, 1878), II, 243–44.
[22] *Ibid.*, 244.
[23] Burton, *The Highlands of the Brazil*, II, 23–24.
[24] Luccock, *Notes on Rio de Janeiro, and the Southern Parts of Brazil*, 425.

CONTEMPORARY PATTERNS

By far the most comprehensive data concerning the distribution of landownership in Brazil are those secured and tabulated by the 1940 and 1950 censuses. With due allowances for the nature of the trends and the factors responsible for them, the 1950 data shed much light on the land system in Brazil as it is at present. Table XLVI gives for each state and the nation as a whole the acreages of land in farms

TABLE XLVI

Land in Farms, Cropland, and Pastures, 1950, by States *

State	Land in farms (hectares)	Per cent of state's area	Per cent of land in farms classified as	
			Crop-land	Pasture-land
Brazil	232,211,106	27.3	8.2	46.4
North				
Guaporé †	693,775	2.9	0.6	0.4
Acre †	8,897,883	58.3	0.2	1.2
Amazonas	5,592,863	3.6	1.0	1.7
Rio Branco †	595,795	2.6	0.1	85.3
Pará	6,593,399	5.3	2.5	24.2
Amapá †	734,232	5.3	0.1	17.4
Northeast				
Maranhão	9,538,144	28.7	3.4	36.6
Piauí	7,876,552	31.1	2.9	26.7
Ceará	10,200,877	68.4	8.1	23.4
Rio Grande do Norte	3,768,839	71.0	11.8	34.9
Paraíba	3,606,939	63.8	18.3	37.2
Pernambuco	5,022,682	51.2	19.9	20.4
Alagôas	1,482,793	53.4	19.0	20.1
East				
Sergipe	1,111,645	50.5	12.2	36.4
Bahia	15,732,988	27.9	8.7	29.3
Minas Gerais	36,809,466	62.7	8.1	62.4
Espírito Santo	2,700,818	60.5	22.8	22.8
Rio de Janeiro	3,177,395	74.6	18.5	42.3
Distrito Federal	41,331	30.5	52.6	14.2
South				
São Paulo	19,007,582	76.9	22.4	45.5
Paraná	8,032,743	40.0	16.9	28.0
Santa Catarina	5,318,262	56.1	12.6	34.4
Rio Grande do Sul	22,069,375	78.1	11.3	66.2
West Central				
Mato Grosso	29,016,613	23.0	0.5	70.2
Goiás	24,588,115	39.5	1.9	63.4

* Compiled and computed from data in "Censo Agrícola," VI *Recenseamento Geral do Brasil, 1950*, II (Rio de Janeiro, 1956), 122, 123, and *Anuário Estatístico do Brasil, 1959*, XX (Rio de Janeiro, 1960), 5.
† Territory.

and estates, the proportion this is of the total land area, and the proportions of the farm land that are classified as cropland and as pastureland. Table XLVII shows the number of farms, the number of

TABLE XLVII

Number of Persons Employed in Agriculture and Number of Workers per Farm, 1950, by States *

State	Number of farms	Number of persons employed in agriculture	Number of workers per farm
Brazil	2,064,642	10,996,834	5.3
North			
Guaporé †	530	4,678	8.8
Acre †	1,701	15,905	9.4
Amazonas	15,220	80,705	5.3
Rio Branco †	445	2,444	5.5
Pará	59,877	219,985	3.7
Amapá †	454	2,785	6.1
Northeast			
Maranhão	95,165	368,625	3.9
Piauí	34,106	206,307	6.0
Ceará	86,690	498,803	5.8
Rio Grande do Norte	34,391	234,737	6.8
Paraíba	69,117	434,143	6.3
Pernambuco	172,268	879,844	5.1
Alagôas	51,961	274,985	5.3
East			
Sergipe	42,769	154,721	3.6
Bahia	258,043	1,282,771	5.0
Minas Gerais	267,696	1,885,295	7.0
Espírito Santo	46,306	289,630	6.3
Rio de Janeiro	40,652	276,730	6.8
Distrito Federal	5,266	16,541	3.1
South			
São Paulo	221,611	1,531,664	6.9
Paraná	89,461	507,607	5.7
Santa Catarina	104,429	370,912	3.6
Rio Grande do Sul	286,733	1,071,404	3.7
West Central			
Mato Grosso	16,015	86,279	5.4
Goiás	63,736	299,334	4.7

* Compiled and computed from data in "Censo Agrícola," VI *Recenseamento Geral do Brasil, 1950,* II (Rio de Janeiro, 1956), viii–ix.
† Territory.

persons employed in agricultural pursuits, and the number of workers per farm, all three for each of the states and for the nation. Tables XLVIII and XLIX should be analyzed in conjunction with the two that immediately precede. The first of these helps make clear the extent to which the operation of the nation's land is concentrated in a few hands, and the second shows how the degree of this concentration varies from one part of the nation to another.

Observation of Table XLVI indicates that in 1950 only slightly more than one-fourth of Brazil's area was accounted for by the land included in the rural properties enumerated. Even though the census may have missed a considerable number of establishments, there can be little doubt that the greater portion of the nation's land surface still lies without the boundaries of its farms and estates. However, more than one-half of this acreage, or about 313,900,000 hectares

TABLE XLVIII

Percentages of Farm Operators with Farms of Stated Sizes, and Percentages of Land in Farms or Estates of Stated Sizes, in Brazil, 1940 and 1950 *

Size of farm or estate (hectares)	Per cent of operators with farms of stated size		Per cent of land in farms or estates of stated size	
	1940	1950	1940	1950
Under 1	2.1	2.4	†	†
1–4	19.7	19.8	0.6	0.5
5–9	12.6	12.2	0.9	0.8
10–19	16.6	16.7	2.3	2.1
20–49	23.9	23.7	7.2	6.6
50–99	10.8	10.6	7.2	6.6
100–199	6.5	6.4	8.8	7.9
200–499	4.7	4.8	13.9	13.4
500–999	1.6	1.8	10.9	11.3
1,000–2,499	1.0	1.1	14.4	14.4
2,500–4,999	0.3	0.3	9.3	9.7
5,000–9,999	0.1	0.1	7.6	7.3
10,000–99,999	0.1	0.1	13.3	14.2
100,000–over	†	†	3.6	5.2
Total	100.0	100.0	100.0	100.0

* Source of basic data: "Sinopse do Censo Agrícola, Dados Gerais," *Recenseamento Geral do Brasil, 1940* (Rio de Janeiro, 1948), and "Censo Agrícola," VI *Recenseamento Geral do Brasil, 1950,* II (Rio de Janeiro, 1956).
† Less than 0.05 per cent.

out of a total of some 619,150,000, was found in the three states of Amazonas, Pará, and Maranhão, hence, mostly in the Amazon Valley. If the unpatented lands in Mato Grosso, Goiás, and Acre and the other territories were included, this total would be still further swelled. However, in some of the states, and particularly in Rio de Janeiro, São Paulo, Rio Grande do Sul, and Rio Grande do Norte, a relatively high proportion of the total area was included within the rural establishments enumerated in the census.

A study of the data given in Table XLVII indicates that, of the rural properties enumerated in 1950, in total 2,064,642, almost 50 per cent, were in the states of Rio Grande do Sul, Minas Gerais, Bahia, and São Paulo. Rio Grande do Sul alone contained 14 per cent, Minas

TABLE XLIX

*Percentages of Farm Operators with Farms of Stated Sizes, and Percentages of Land in Farms or Estates of Stated Sizes, 1950, by States **

State	Farms of less than 100 hectares		Estates of more than 10,000 hectares	
	Per cent of all farm operators	Per cent of all land in farms	Per cent of all farm operators	Per cent of all land in farms
Brazil	85.4	16.6	0.1	19.4
North				
Guaporé ‡	57.4	1.0	2.8	76.4
Acre ‡	68.4	0.3	11.8	91.8
Amazonas	79.0	3.5	0.4	41.8
Rio Branco ‡	9.0	†	1.1	16.2
Pará	91.7	16.4	0.1	40.5
Amapá ‡	16.1	0.4	0.4	37.1
Northeast				
Maranhão	88.8	5.7	0.1	15.7
Piauí	66.2	8.2	0.2	18.2
Ceará	76.7	18.9	†	5.4
Rio Grande do Norte	81.3	17.1	0.1	14.0
Paraíba	90.9	28.1	†	4.3
Pernambuco	95.1	33.0	†	5.3
Alagôas	95.3	31.4	†	1.0
East				
Sergipe	95.0	39.0	0.0	0.0
Bahia	89.6	27.6	†	10.6
Minas Gerais	75.6	17.0	†	8.6
Espírito Santo	87.6	51.7	0.0	0.0
Rio de Janeiro	85.6	24.4	†	1.7
Distrito Federal	99.2	71.7	0.0	0.0
South				
São Paulo	85.6	24.7	†	5.7
Paraná	85.5	28.9	†	12.8
Santa Catarina	93.0	45.2	†	4.8
Rio Grande do Sul	90.3	28.5	†	3.5
West Central				
Mato Grosso	38.5	0.6	3.7	53.4
Goiás	53.2	5.0	0.2	11.9

* Compiled and computed from data in "Censo Agrícola," VI *Recenseamento Geral do Brasil, 1950*, II (Rio de Janeiro, 1956), 32, 35.
† Less than 0.05 per cent.
‡ Territory.

Gerais 13 per cent, and Bahia 12 per cent. The number of workers per farm, one of the more valuable indicators of the degree of concentration in the ownership and control of the land, is highest in Acre, and Guaporé, followed by Minas Gerais, São Paulo, Rio Grande do Norte, and Rio de Janeiro, in the order named.

Analysis of Table XLVIII brings out some facts of considerable significance about the concentration of control over the land. In this connection it should be recalled that the materials presented in the chapter on land tenure indicated that not more than one out of four of the rural families in Brazil is headed by a person who could be classified as the operator of a farm, even though the squatters who are so numerous in Maranhão and some of the other states are so considered. Even if the comparisons are limited to the minority who are classed as farm operators, however, the data in Table XLVIII indicate that more than one-fifth have for use in their farming operations (as owners, renters, administrators, or merely as squatters) only tracts of land that are less than five hectares (or about thirteen acres) in extent. An additional 52.6 per cent have between five and fifty hectares, and a total of 85.4 per cent have farms that do not exceed one hundred hectares in size. Altogether, this 85.4 per cent of the farmers have the use of only 16.6 per cent of the land. On the other hand, the 0.5 per cent of the operators who have acreages of 2,500 hectares or more together control the use of 36.4 per cent of the land in farms and estates.

The materials in Table XLIX help make it possible to identify the states in which the control of the land is most widely distributed among the rural population and also those in which there is the greatest concentration of such control. In Espírito Santo, Santa Catarina, Sergipe, and Pernambuco, it will be noted, farms of less than one hundred hectares account for the largest proportions of land in farms; and in Acre, Mato Grosso, and Pará the huge landed proper-

A Sítio Belonging to Descendants of Italian Immigrants, Redenção, São Paulo

Small Farm in São Paulo

ties are most numerous. As shown by the 1950 census the landed estates of 100,000 hectares or more numbered 60 and were distributed among the states as follows: Guaporé, 1; Acre, 16; Amazonas, 4; Pará, 6; Amapá, 1; Maranhão, 1; Piauí, 4; Bahia, 3; Minas Gerais, 4; Paraná, 2; Santa Catarina, 1; Mato Grosso, 15; and Goiás, 2.[25] It

[25] The following data from an article in *Estado de São Paulo*, June 12, 1941, are informative concerning this statement and the enormous size of landholdings in Mato Grosso. Unfortunately the data are not confined to the holdings of foreigners, and they are not strictly up to date, some companies having sold and bought lands after the figures were assembled. This article appeared about the time the federal government expropriated the holdings of the Brazilian Land and Cattle Company.

Name of company	Area of holdings in hectares	Municípios in which the lands are located
Brazil Land and Cattle Company	1,858,974	Campo Grande, Cáceres, Corumbá, Paranaíba, Três Lagoas
Brazilian Meat Company	566,010	Aquidauana, Campo Grande, Três Lagoas
Fazendas Francesas	418,808	Corumbá, Miranda
Miranda Estância Company	219,000	Miranda
Agua Limpa Syndicate	549,156	Corumbá
Sud-America Belga S.A.	117,060	Corumbá
Sociedade Anon. Fomento Agrícola	1,001,077	Corumbá
Cia. Mate Laranjeira	345,026	Bela Vista, Dourados, Ponte Porã

should be remembered, however, that these data refer to operation and not to ownership. It is entirely possible that a single owner is proprietor of more than one of the nation's largest latifundia.

The net impressions gained from a study of these data indicate that in 1950 large, sparsely populated Brazil was far from settled, although most of it was occupied. It was still the preserve of the large estate introduced three hundred years previously by the Portuguese. In the sugar sections of the coast large farms in terms of area were also large as indexed by number of workers. In the interior sections devoted to pastoral and collecting pursuits, immense tracts of land, peopled by few inhabitants, made for farms large in terms of area but not so big when measured in terms of average number of workers. Already in 1950 the nation's efforts to develop a small-farming class were bearing fruit in the southern states and in Espírito Santo.

TRENDS

The data assembled in the 1940 and 1950 censuses of agriculture are the only fairly comprehensive and recent materials available for the study of the trend in the size of Brazilian farms. It is to be hoped, though, that eventually enough of the information collected in 1960 will be salvaged and published to enable some additional informative comparisons to be made.

Actually in Brazil as a whole the data in Table XLVIII indicate that very few significant changes are occurring, except that there is a substantial increase in the land in the very largest estates. Between 1940 and 1950 the reported total amount of land in farms increased from slightly less than 198 million hectares to more than 232 hectares. Farms of less than ten hectares, though, comprised exactly the same proportion (34.4 per cent) both in 1940 and in 1950, and the changes in the relative importance of all other size categories below 10,000 hectares also appear to be of slight consequence. Estates of a size between 10,000 and 100,000 hectares, however, included a significantly larger proportion of all land in farms at the close of the decade than they did at the beginning, and the huge holdings of 100,-000 or more hectares increased in number from 37 in 1940 to 60 in 1950. The proportion of Brazil's farm land that was in such estates increased from 3.6 per cent to 5.2 per cent during the same period.

It is difficult, of course, to judge the extent to which these reported changes actually took place and the degree to which they merely reflect variations in the completeness of coverage of the two censuses. In any case the reported numbers of rural establishments of 100,000 or more hectares in size changed as follows between 1940 and 1950: Acre, increased from 8 to 16; Amazonas-Rio Branco, decreased from 6 to 4; Pará-Amapá, remained constant at 7 each census; Bahia, increased from 1 to 3; Paraná, increased from 1 to 2; and Mato Grosso-Guaporé, increased from 12 to 16. In addition, in 1950 Maranhão was reported to have 1 estate of more than 100,000 hectares, Piauí 4, Santa Catarina 1, and Goiás 2, although the 1940 census did not enumerate any places of the size under consideration in any of them. These figures indicate that the huge landed estate is by no means confined to the remote sections of the Amazon Basin.

If all places of 10,000 hectares are taken into consideration, some striking differences in the trends in the various states are thrown into bold relief. Thus one may note increases in number between 1940 and 1950 of from 7 to 69 in Maranhão, from 23 to 58 in Piauí, from 16 to 29 in Ceará, from 13 to 22 in Rio Grande do Norte, from 1 to 13 in Pernambuco, from 14 to 30 in Paraná, and from 393 to 610 in Mato Grosso-Guaporé. These were accompanied, however, by decreases in number from 86 to 62 in Amazonas-Rio Branco, from 5 to 1 in Alagôas, from 69 to 60 in São Paulo, and from 150 to 138 in Goiás.

INHERITANCE AS A FACTOR IN THE SUBDIVISION OF LAND

As has been indicated, the introduction of immigrants and their establishment on the land in small farming communities or colonies is having an important effect in modifying the land system of Brazil. It has increased the number of holdings, decreased the size of farms, and most important of all, has done much to diffuse the system of farming in which a single man (the farm operator) performs the functions of laborer, capitalist, and manager.[26] Another factor that is of considerable influence in increasing the number of holdings and decreasing their average size is that of inheritance. Because it is such an important determinant of changes in the Brazilian land system and because the operation of the system is not checked by other factors as it is in countries such as the United States, Germany, or Great Britain, it is essential to analyze in some detail the manner in which the inheritance of land in Brazil is contributing to the subdivision of landed estates.

First, it must be indicated that in Brazil surely there is no effective differential fertility and mortality that results in a higher net rate of reproduction among the members of the lower classes. Differentials there may be, but if so, it is the average member of the upper classes who leaves a larger number of legitimate descendants than his fellow citizens of the lower social and economic levels. That he also leaves many illegitimate offspring, although frequently asserted, is more difficult to establish. Since the general rate of natural increase is very high in Brazil, this means that the average Brazilian landholder leaves a considerable number of heirs, and frequently these are distributed among two, and even three, succeeding generations—children, grandchildren, and sometimes great-grandchildren. Grandchildren and great-grandchildren usually are a complicating factor only if one of their parents is deceased.

[26] For a discussion of the relation of such a development to the emergence of a genuine middle class, see Smith, *The Sociology of Rural Life*, 386–88.

It must also be pointed out that Brazil resembles the United States in lacking an institution, such as the English system of primogeniture, which keeps the property intact and passes it on to a single heir. In Brazil, as in the United States, each heir is entitled to a share of the land. But Brazil differs from the United States in that it has not undergone an extensive industrialization and urbanization.[27] In the United States, since the passing of the frontier, the cities have absorbed the lion's share of the natural increase of population in the rural areas. Indeed, the farm population of our own country remained almost constant in number from 1900 to 1940 and then fell off sharply and steadily for a quarter of a century. As a rule the heir who remained on the farm, most often the first-born son, bought out the other heirs, kept the farm intact, and in this manner prevented the equal sharing of the heirs in the inheritance from greatly reducing the average size of the farm. Had it not been for this migration from the land, the equal inheritance on the part of all the heirs would have pulverized the already comparatively small landholdings of the United States. In Brazil, on the other hand, where there is no system of primogeniture or rapidly expanding commercial and industrial population, the process of inheritance has brought about a very considerable subdivision of landed estates. Of course, Brazilian landowners were few, estates very large—in many cases unbelievably large—and much division could take place without creating properties that were small.

Throughout Brazil, and especially in Minas Gerais, São Paulo, and Bahia, and the northeastern states, subdivision through inheritance has been going on for some time and has already had noticeable effects. It also bids fair to continue. But it is important to remember that the mere subdivision of a large fazenda among the numerous progeny of a deceased owner does not result automatically in the change from a system of large-scale agricultural exploitation to a well-rounded system of small farming. In the terminology ordinarily used in Brazil, it does not by itself bring about a change from monoculture to polyculture. On the contrary, such a manner of subdivision is likely merely to mean that each heir receives insufficient land to enable him successfully to carry on the type and scale of agricultural enterprises with which he is familiar, to live in the manner that he feels is the right of a member of his family and social class, and in a word, to carry on the type of rural life that he considers to be the mainstay of the nation. Subdivision of land brought about in this manner merely reduces the amount of land available to the farm operator; it does not alter his fundamental values and attitudes, inculcate new habits and skills, develop new motivations, or most of all, make it socially acceptable for the owner and manager of the land also to perform manual agricultural labor. Thus, because inheritance operates upon the land, and not upon the man and the system of social relationships, the reduction in size of holdings through inherit-

[27] Such a process is getting well under way however, especially in São Paulo, the area surrounding the city of Rio de Janeiro, and in Rio Grande do Sul.

ance may merely result in the decadence of the old system. This takes place because the units are no longer economically adjusted to the enterprises attempted and because there may be endless bickerings, misunderstandings, working at cross purposes, and conflicts among the heirs. The net result may be anything but the development of a healthy system of family-sized farms.

The results of subdivision by inheritance were already apparent in 1873 when Wells described the situation on the Fazenda Motta, in the central part of Minas Gerais, near the present location of Belo Horizonte.

F—— had made his own private apartment fairly comfortable; whitewash and a liberal use of broom and water will effect wonders, even in an old abandoned Brazilian fazenda. I learned that there were then so many descendants of the last occupier, each having a greater or lesser share in the estate, that it became impossible for any one or more to utilize this neglected property (even if they possessed individually the capital necessary to work it) without the other shareholders claiming a division of the results of the energy and labours of the more industrious; at present they utilize, to limited extent, the lands, by each one cultivating on a small scale, or a few in combination, large fields of maize, beans, &c. The state of affairs produced by the abandonment of this farm, is primarily caused by the forced distribution of property amongst a numerous family, and then subdivided into smaller interests amongst the descendants of each of the original heirs. It is what can be seen in any day's march in any direction in Minas Gerais, and the curious anomaly is produced of increased poverty following the increased population of a new country.[28]

The longer-settled portions of São Paulo also contain many areas in which the subdivision of lands through inheritance has proceeded to the point that the farm is too small to produce a living for the family which occupies it. For example, in the município of Taubaté this division has developed a situation in which many families have insufficient lands. Some of them may be employed by the prefeitura on road work and other municipal projects, but many of them resort to seasonal work on the citrus-growing properties of the Companhia Brasileira de Frutas in the coastal município of Caraguatatuba, north of Santos. However, it is said that a large proportion of the workers contract malaria during their three or four months' stay in the lowlands and require months to recuperate after their return to the upland valley.

Not always are the lands actually subdivided and each heir given his portion; they may continue as single estates, while the operation of the vital processes and inheritance producers tier after tier of additional *donos* or owners. Thus there are properties lying in southeastern São Paulo whose owners are legion. The purchaser of one of these tracts would have to treat with numerous persons now employed as shopkeepers or governmental employees in the towns and

[28] James W. Wells, *Three Thousand Miles Through Brazil* (Philadelphia, 1886), I, 127; cf. James Wetherell, *Brazil: Stray Notes from Bahia* (Liverpool, 1860), 139–40; and E. D. Brandão, "A Successão da Propriedade Rural," *Ceres* (Rio de Janeiro), VIII, No. 48 (1951), 374–94.

small cities of the area, white-collar workers in São Paulo, and federal functionaries in Rio de Janeiro. In addition, a few of the heirs remain on the land, operating patches of it as best they can under the extreme difficulties created by the impossibility of reaching an understanding with the other heirs and the uncertainty of the future.

Such a condition is by no means new in Brazil. For many years the multiplicity of heirs, no one or small group of whom could undertake improvement of the property without the liability of sharing the benefits with numerous others who had contributed nothing, has plagued other parts of the country. One of the more striking accounts available describes the situation in the great interior portions of Bahia. Here cattle raising long has been unnecessarily precarious because there are not enough small reservoirs or tanks to supply water during the periodic droughts which beset the sertões. The report of the survey for the railroad, which was later built from the capital to Joázeiro, points out clearly how multiplicity of heirs has prevented the necessary construction of these water-storing facilities.

It is very difficult to discriminate the unoccupied lands of the sertão of Bahia because the occupied areas have no determined limits.

In colonial times there were given to some Portuguese fidalgos some grants of tens of leagues square in these parts.

With these titles, which were never established over the land, were effected the first sales of lands on which the first Portuguese established themselves and fazendas for growing animals.

On the death of these proprietors the fazendas came to be divided among the heirs and so on successively until today there exist many properties or possessions of land which count with more than 500 co-owners, having shares represented by insignificant amounts.

All of the co-owners having full right to introduce on the land as many cattle of their own or of their relatives as they please, evident is the disorder resulting from this state of affairs and the considerable barrier to the development and perfection of breeds of animals.

Everyone knows that in the sertão of Bahia the irregularity of the rains constitutes the primary obstacle to the development of these areas and that reservoirs or artificial lakes are the only means of curing the evil. But in the conditions in which presently is found the ownership or occupation of the land it is almost impossible to expect the development of these artificial lakes in the necessary quantities, without the intervention of special legislative dispositions.

Each present co-owner, expecting that the others will make these necessary improvements and that he will enjoy the benefits without assisting in any way for the conservation of the land, appears to be more of a destroyer than proprietor.[29]

In 1945 the author personally participated in a reconnaissance survey of this part of Bahia in connection with proposals for more fully utilizing the power potentials of the Paulo Afonso Falls in the São Francisco River. At that time the failure to subdivide the land legally as one generation of heirs had succeeded another had gone on to the point that virtual communal ownership prevailed in large parts of the region. As indicated elsewhere, the original grants had been large and

[29] Oliveira Bulhões, *Estrada de Ferro da Bahia ao S. Francisco*, 53–54.

ill-defined. In general they fronted on the river, for as many as forty leagues in some cases, and extended back from it indefinitely. As generations came and went the large families of the settlers and the equal division of property rights among the heirs greatly reduced the number of acres claimed by any one person. The land was too low in value, however, to pay for the costs of surveys, records, and physical markings of the property lines, and, as a result, as one generation was added to another each fazenda merely acquired a new tier of owners. Today it is not unusual to find an estate whose ownership is vested in hundreds of persons representing as many as five generations. And even this is not the extreme. In parts of the area the stage has been reached in which definite claims based on occupation extend only to the area immediately surrounding the house and corrals; the rest of the land is regarded as communal property. A native of the area merely selects a location no one else is occupying, or buys the claim of another, and then proceeds to pasture his goats, sheep, and cattle as he pleases.[30]

Although small farms are still a recent development in Brazil, already there are areas in the German, Italian, and Polish settlements in the south where inheritance has brought about excessive subdivision of the land. Unless migration from the farming areas is heavy, such cases will increase rapidly, for these peasant families are large. Already considerable numbers of the young folk are finding their way to the towns and cities, or pushing the agricultural frontier forward in their native states, or moving to northern Paraná and western São Paulo. Willems, who knows some of these German colonies intimately, says:

In the District of Guabiruba, in the Município of Brusque (Santa Catarina), the division of the property has come to the point that the sítios no longer can sustain the large families, making it necessary for the children to seek work in the local factories. The fragmentation of holdings accompanied by erosion and economic, physical and moral impoverishment of the population is slowly but irresistibly proletarianizing hundreds of rural families. And this is taking place in a region with immense reserves of virgin land.[31]

Brazil's high fertility of population and equality of inheritance, unless accompanied by industrialization and migration to the cities, will rapidly increase the number of farms in the country. But unless this is accompanied by widespread education and diffusion of agricultural skills, and in many cases by a willingness of offspring to lower their standards of living to attainable levels, the mere division of the lands will not bring lasting benefits. An encouraging factor is the presence in this country of several millions of native-born Brazilians who have inherited from the peasant backgrounds of their European ancestors the skills, aptitudes, and attitudes of the farming class. Unfortunately, until recently few measures were taken to pre-

[30] See Smith, "Notes on Population and Social Organization in the Central Portion of the São Francisco Valley," *loc. cit.*, 51–52.

[31] Willems, *Assimilação e Populações Marginais no Brasil*, 43.

vent the exploitation of certain of these peasants by schemers in the old countries from which their fathers, grandfathers, or great-grand-fathers came. But the program of Brazilianization now under way, combined with their fullest use in the development of the nation's agricultural possibilities, can result in their full incorporation into the nation to which they owe so much. They and their children are one of the chief hopes for Brazil's development. Their attitudes, skills, and mode of living can help to extend the progress of São Paulo, Paraná, Santa Catarina, and Rio Grande do Sul to other parts of Brazil.

THE CONCENTRATION OF LANDOWNERSHIP
IN THE SUGAR AREAS

In the 1960's problems arising out of the concentration of land ownership and control in the sugar-producing sections of northeast-ern Brazil have attracted worldwide attention. However, even when the first edition of this book was under preparation it was apparent to many that there were few more significant changes under way in Brazil than the trend towards a greater concentration of landowner-ship and control in the sugar-producing sections of the country. This trend is probably characteristic of all the cane-growing areas of the immense country, but it has produced the most acute problems in the Northeast, and particularly in the states of Pernambuco, Alagôas, and Paraíba. The consolidation of agricultural holdings that is under way in the sugar areas is not merely that which takes place through the development of another plantation unit by buying up and placing under a single management a number of small farms, such as oc-curred in Louisiana at the beginning of the nineteenth century. Rather, it is the absorption of already large plantation units, the old engenhos, into the immense holdings of the central sugar companies, the usinas. This has the effect of concentrating the production of cane in the hands of those who also make it into sugar; it is also either eliminating the senhores de engenho, the aristocratic element that has shone so brightly throughout four centuries of Brazilian history, from their ancestral lands or else reducing them to a condi-tion of dependency on the sugar companies. From an elevated posi-tion as the master of broad acreages of sugar lands, the patriarch of a numerous clan of near relatives and hundreds of dependent work-ers, and the proprietor of the old-type mill in which the cane was ground, the monarch of his own little kingdom, the senhor de engenho has been reduced to a mere fornecedor of cane for a central sugar factory. In fact, during the most recent decades he has lost con-trol of the land altogether and now is either permitted to stay merely as a renter or has been forced to abandon the soil altogether. A social system that has endured for hundreds of years is falling apart. With it goes much of which Brazil has been justly proud, as well as some features that few will regret seeing pass. The process deserves a careful study. Only the outlines can be traced in the following paragraphs.

These sugar areas have long been the home of Brazil's most aristocratic families. For more than three hundred years a limited number of them, the class of senhores de engenho, maintained their position at the top of the Brazilian social pyramid. The patriarch of each of these families was supreme in his own little social world, and together they maintained power in the nation. Each of them was an industrialist as well as a planter, grinding his own cane and that of the farmers dependent on him. Without being extremely wealthy, he was among the most distinguished men in the province. "Who," asked Dé Carlí, "amounted to more than a senhor de engenho?" [32] Brazil's distinguished historian, Rocha Pombo, has described the status of these rural aristocrats.

The populations of the colony now [seventeenth century] were divided into masters and serfs, great families and the degraded masses. Treating of the great colonial proprietor, the author of *Cultura e Opulencia do Brazil* wrote: To be senhor de engenho is a title to which many aspire because it carries with it being served, obeyed, and respected by many. And if he should be, what he ought to be, a man of means and authority, it may well be estimated that in Brazil to be a senhor de engenho, is estimated as equal to possessing a title among the fidalgos of the Kingdom. It was still more than this. In general, the senhor de engenho has political importance and is a figure in the government of the land. This is to say that he directs authorities and functionaries. In his fazenda, in the surrounding areas of fields and forests which constitute as it were genuine brims of his patrimony, he orders and rules without opposition. For him, there in his dominions, it may be said there is no law superior to his will. His people, in relation to him, remain in a more humble subordination than that of the most inconsequential subject in relation to his king. Of his people one cares to say only—his slaves; but it includes also the multitude of his dependents—agregados, renters, share farmers, superintendents, clerks, skilled and unskilled workers in the sugar mill.[33]

For more than three centuries, or until the last quarter of the nineteenth century, the pattern of life that had prevailed since the middle of the sixteenth century continued with slight changes in the sugar areas. As indicated in the above quotation, surrounded by his relatives, slaves, and agregados, each senhor de engenho continued to live as the monarch of his own little world. Like his neighbors, who were generally his kinfolk, he paid scant attention to any pressures from the outside. On his own lands with his own slaves and share hands [34] he produced the cane which was transformed to sugar in his own mill. An idea of the social status of the great man who

[32] Dé Carlí, *O Processo Histórico da Usina em Pernambuco*, 5.

[33] Rocha Pombo, *Historia do Brazil*, V, 515–16.

[34] Koster, who for a time at the opening of the nineteenth century operated a sugar engenho at Jaguaribe near Recife, may have been one of the first to use free laborers along with the slaves. He explains that because he lacked enough slaves to perform essential work he "collected free labourers for the purpose; and in a short period between thirty and forty men, some of whom brought their families, moved on to the lands of the plantation: and most of them erected hovels of palm-leaves, in which they dwelt; but a few of them were accommodated with huts of mud. There were Indians, mulattoes, free negroes, and slaves working together; a motley crew." Koster, *Travels in Brazil*, I, 295.

headed such a rural clan can be gleaned from the observations of Koster:

> I frequently visited the plantation of Amparo, which is conducted in the manner which I had attempted at Jaguaribe: but here it was performed with more system. The owner of this place employed constantly great numbers of free workmen, of all casts. But the Indians formed the principal part of them. . . .
>
> One of these Indians was selling crabs at Pasmado, when a purchaser began to pick out those which he preferred; but the Indian stopped him, saying "Don't begin to pick my crabs, for I belong to Amparo." Thus even the crabs which were caught by the dependents of this great man were to be respected.[35]

The extent to which the senhores de engenho as a class controlled the lands of the state and the relations of this aristocratic element to the lower classes in society are both brought out in the quotation from Figueiredo previously presented. Few were the occasions on which their supremacy was even challenged. True, for a time following the removal of the court to Rio de Janeiro, when Portugal was ruled from the New World, the migrant nobles outweighed the Brazilian-born fidalgos in importance. The eclipse was temporary, however, and the landowning class of Brazil soon became dominant at the court and received all the necessary titles. Otherwise they seem to have continued almost without competition. It was only in the second half of the nineteenth century that the position of these ruling classes became insecure and the forces were set in motion which ruined them economically and socially and concentrated their lands in the hands of large companies.

The beginning of the end came late in the nineteenth century, when the slave system was already reeling and when the days of the empire were numbered. At this time many rural senhores became heavily involved with the banks and moneylenders. Then they lost the bases of their power, although for some time they managed to keep up appearances. Social status is seldom threatened until one cannot avoid the *appearance* of poverty. Out of this indebtedness came a time of sharp conflict between the merchant, banking, and professional classes in the towns and the rural aristocrats on the plantations. Power was shifting to the city, but the country did not give up without a struggle, nor was it quickly overcome. To a considerable extent internal family struggle entered into the town-country enmity. Oftentimes one brother who had quarreled with another migrated to the city and went into business or took a degree in law or medicine, frequently abroad; then he became a city resident and carried on the fight from the town. This struggle between the commercial and professional classes in the city and the masters of the land resulted in the downfall of some of these families, but on the whole the family and the system maintained themselves and at least the appearance of their old grandeur. Freyre has analyzed the

---

[35] *Ibid.*, II, 18–19.

decay of the power of the senhores de engenho in face of the growing power of the cities and described the conflict that destroyed the
economic bases of the former aristocracy.

A survival from the seventeenth century was the antagonism between
the activities of the colonial cities and the isolated casas grandes of the
fazendas and engenhos. The power of the cities developed, but the rural
nobility preserved, almost intact, most of its privileges, and principally the
decorative elements of its grandeur, until the end of the nineteenth century. This element, with all of the ritual, all of the social liturgy, is known
to have had an extraordinary capacity to prolong the grandeur of life, or
the appearance of life already wounded to death in its sources.[36]

Although the rise of cities such as Recife and the indebtedness of
the planters brought about a loss in the relative importance of the
senhores de engenho in Brazilian affairs, they nevertheless retained
an important place on the national scene and were dominant in rural
affairs [37] until two other developments began to affect the economic
situation. These were the introduction of the central sugar factory
and the freeing of the slaves. Then the collapse of the old system
and the leveling of the ruling element was sudden and almost complete. During the decades that have elapsed since the new factors
came into action, all but the vestiges of the former grandeur of the
senhores de engenho has disappeared.

The city had gained an important victory in its campaign for reducing the casa grande when its debt collector could invade the
premises of the "great house" with impunity.

The engenhos, holy places where in other days no one came near, except humbly and to request something—to ask asylum, to ask a decision,
to ask for a girl in marriage, to ask a contribution for the celebration at
the church, to ask for a meal, to ask for a cup of water—came to be invaded by these debt collectors, representatives of an arrogant city institution, the Bank, almost as destructive of the prestige of the majesty of the
manor houses as the police were of the Count of Assumar in Minas, or of
the president, Chichorro da Gama, in Pernambuco.[38]

The weak financial position of the planters was made still more
acute when the slaves were freed, without reimbursement, and when
most of the freed Negroes fled the estates for the city.[39] But most important of all was the appearance on the scene, in these decades of
crisis, of the central sugar factory, later called the usina. It is to this
aspect of the subject that the attention of Gileno dé Carlí has been
devoted. For him, the moving force in the debacle was the establishment of the central sugar mill or usina. Perhaps this is merely the
cause of the immediate collapse of a system long losing its vitality

[36] Freyre, *Sobrados e Mucambos*, 36.
[37] As late as 1869 Burton wrote: "In the Northern Provinces of the Empire, the
Fazenda is called Engenho, . . . especially where it is a sugar plantation, and
the owner is Senhor de Engenho, one of the local aristocracy, and not to be con-
founded, unless you want shooting, with the lavrador or farmer." *The Highlands
of the Brazil*, I, 45.
[38] Freyre, *Sobrados e Mucambos*, 49.
[39] Carneiro Leão, *A Sociedade Rural*, 119–20.

in the manner described by Freyre. In any case, the old system disintegrated rapidly with the establishment of new factories.

Interestingly enough, the introduction of the central sugar factory, the step in this process that has ultimately led to the dispossession of many of Brazil's most aristocratic families from their lands, was an attempt to separate the cane-growing agricultural functions in sugar production from those of sugar manufacturing, a goal the very opposite from the actual result.

There had been a crisis in the sugar industry. The government stepped in to aid the sugar planter at a time when Brazil was almost shut out of the international sugar market because of her outmoded system of sugar grinding. The crisis came just on the threshold of the complete abolition of slavery. Under these circumstances it is not strange that the central government had to offer its support to guarantee a return on capital, nor is it unusual that the local governments had to make loans. "All of this prepared a climate for the introduction of new methods of work in Pernambucan fields." [40]

It was the intention at first to make the factory responsible solely for the manufacture of sugar. The first decrees seem to have envisioned substituting modern machinery, with the financial aid of the state and central governments, for the antiquated grinding equipment of the engenhos. At the same time it was the clearly expressed purpose to transform the engenhos into purely agricultural enterprises, each of them continuing the production of cane on the same scale and selling all of it to the central factory. The engaging of sugar companies in the production of cane was contrary to the charters of the first usinas.[41] Under these new arrangements the first four new factories in Pernambuco got under way in 1884, receiving cane from the old engenhos. That year the obsolete grinding machinery of the old mills went unused.[42] But such a division of labor did not last long. The company was not content to confine its activities to the manufacturing process. It was only a few years later, in 1890, that new legislation clearly authorized the usina to own and plant cane lands. Then, with its power to determine the prices to be paid for the cane purchased from the fornecedores, the usinas had the senhores de engenho at their mercy. The reduction and elimination of the old aristocracy was only a matter of time.

Of course there were questions as to the rules to be followed in contests between the usinas for ownership and control of cane lands. For example, there was the matter of zoning. Were the central mills to be left free to compete with one another for cane, to extend their railway lines on a strategic plan that would secure the cane they wanted, cut rivals off from possible supplies, and leave some engenhos isolated, to fall into their hands later like ripe plums?

[40] Dé Carlí, *O Processo Histórico da Usina em Pernambuco*, 5.

[41] For some time before the introduction of the central mill such a division of functions had been urged, but then it was the farmers (lavradores) urging this upon the engenhos. For extracts from an address proposing such a separation made before the Agricultural Congress in Recife, October, 1878, see *ibid.*, 47–48.

[42] *Ibid.*, 6–9.

It is clear that at first a system of zoning was contemplated. In 1890 there was federal legislation to provide that in municípios where factories had been established with governmental assistance, no new factories could receive "equal or greater favors" from the government. The next year the principle of zoning was clearly stated when the government prescribed in connection with a new central mill that "the factory shall be constructed in Sant' Ana do Morro do Chapéu, município of Queluz, and from there as a center will enjoy the privilege of a zone of an area limited by a circumference whose radius is equal to 15 kilometers." [43] However, this provision was also soon suffered to fall into disuse. When it was gone, the rivalry between the usinas had nothing to serve as a check. Dé Carlí is of the opinion that, had the principle of zoning been maintained, much of the conflict that ensued might have been forestalled; the usina would not have been so interested in weakening the proprietor who furnished it with cane, would not have been forced to map out and execute a long campaign, to go to such desperate lengths to see that the lands and woods it needed did not come under the influence of the rails from a rival factory. But the checks were removed, the rivalries grew more intense, "the immediate interest of the usina was that pauperism should strike the furnisher so that he would soon sell his property in order to close the zone." [44] Under these circumstances a bitter struggle ensued between the usinas for the possession of the land. First to be gobbled up were the lands in the engenhos adjacent to the new modern mills. But as soon as the lands of the original furnishers were annexed,

. . . the usinas fell upon the near-by *banguês* [smaller, older and more primitive mills than the engenhos]. One by one they fell. Overcoming the engenho, the railroad came to tie one more property to the growing usina. Then occurred a curious phenomenon: the small usina bought new lands, and, in order not to suffer from indigestion from so much excess land, it enlarged the factory. With the rollers increased in size, they could crush more cane than the lands could produce. There was only one remedy: it was to buy more land in order to care for the needs of the usina. Thus they grew, sacrificing not only the old banguê, incapable of resistance, but bringing families traditionally agriculturists to the supreme sacrifice of transferring the property rights to lands that had been in their hands for more than a century. [45]

Barbosa Lima Sobrinho shows how, with the growth of the usinas and the struggle between them for lands, the senhor de engenho was powerless to resist. He was faced with three alternatives, namely, to sell his land and abandon farming, to become an administrator on an estate, or to become a furnisher of cane. This authority maintains

[43] *Ibid.*, 17. Similar measures were being applied in São Paulo and Minas Gerais.
[44] *Ibid.*, 18.
[45] *Ibid.*, 18–19. For a full description of the banguês and their role in the Brazilian society, see Manuel Diégues Júnior, *O Banguê nas Alagôas* (Rio de Janeiro, 1949).

that the usinas were not interested in the complete elimination of the fornecedor.[46]

Others seem to be of a different opinion. According to documents quoted by Dé Carlí it became the expressed intention of the sugar companies to eliminate entirely the class of owner-operators who produced cane for sale to the mill. When the old João Alfredo property at Goiana was transformed in 1891 into the Companhia Industrial Pernambucana, this company set as its fundamental program "to go forward immediately, carrying on the operation of the Usina Goiana, developing the thought originated by the early company of acquiring lands for the direct cultivation of cane, liberating it from exclusive dependency on the furnishers." Later it was stated by the historian of this usina that "in the course of 17 years, this program has been gradually executed." [47] Only periodic crises in sugar, which prevented the accumulation of enough reserves to make all the desired purchases of land, prevented the complete attainment of this purpose. There was in fact during the early years of the twentieth century an important period in which the process of concentration was practically stopped, when the usina did not cultivate the lands it had attained from the former senhores de engenho with its own labor squads, but let them out to small farmers in return for 50 per cent of the crop; some larger farm operators who leased the lands of the former engenhos likewise used this system, subleasing to small farmers and taking 50 per cent of the cane as rent.[48] But later the process in all its vigor proceeded to complete the reduction of the senhores de engenho, to consolidate the victory of the city and its commercial classes over the old patriarchal rural ruling class.

By 1928 the Association of Furnishers and Planters of Cane in Pernambuco were memorializing the state's House of Deputies for help, "the independent agricultural property is disappearing from the state. The soil which grows its most traditional and most prominent crop has become the land of the usinas." Furthermore it was asserted that these large sugar companies "expulse the former proprietors from their engenhos and put in their places temporary renters" who were said to be less apt and also less interested than the former owners of the land. The association asked the House to authorize the governor of the state to establish a new and more favorable schedule of prices for the cane supplied by the fornecedores.[49] The same year an article published in the *Diario* of Pernambuco warned the government against "this odious thing which is taking place in Pernambuco and probably already in Alagôas: the exodus of the old agriculturists, descendants of the old and traditional masters of the lands, from the profession from which they

[46] Barbosa Lima Sobrinho, *Problemas Econômicos e Sociais da Lavoura Canavieira* (Rio de Janeiro, 1941), 14–15.

[47] Dé Carlí, *O Processo Histórico da Usina em Pernambuco*, 19.

[48] *Ibid.*, 19–20.

[49] *Ibid.*, 33–35.

have lived until now, by the greediness and monopoly of the usinas." [50]

During the 1930's the process of eliminating the proprietor of the land who sells cane to the mill neared its completion. For these final stages the data are more plentiful and more quantitative. The 35 usinas for which Dé Carlí was able to secure records for the 1929–1930 to 1938–1939 period bought cane from 888 furnishers, and in the crop year 1931–1932 the figure rose to 943; but at the close of the decade, 1938–1939, the number had fallen to 798. Average deliveries of cane by these fornecedores had fallen from 1,920 tons per furnisher in 1929–1930 to only 1,483 in 1938–1939; during the drought in 1936–1937 it was only 682. Whereas in 1929–1930 the usinas bought from fornecedores 75.7 per cent of all cane ground in their factories, in 1938–1939 the percentage had fallen to 47.6.[51] The fact that the number of fornecedores fell very little, while the proportion of cane furnished by this group fell so sharply, means that a large share of the former senhores de engenho had lost their lands and even their position in the class of fornecedores, and that their places had been taken by renters operating small acreages.

In the late 1930's what had happened was clear to all. From this time date the novels of Lins do Rego, which describe so well the process of decay and replacement, the decline of the engenho, the rise of the usina.[52] From those years also dates Freyre's introduction to the memoirs of an old senhor de engenho from which the following extract is translated:

> The usina separated the great proprietor not only from the workers—who were a second family of the senhor—but from the landscape and the rivers, formerly so closely linked to the lives of men and today mere sewers into which the factories discharge the hot refuse. It finished the life in the casas grandes; it put an end to the festivals; it extinguished the moral assistance of the chaplains, some of them, it is true, fat and lazy priests, but always serving and helping the people of the engenhos in their needs and sufferings; it developed absenteeism; it substituted for the houses of the engenhos the little palaces of Recife, of Maceió, of Boa Viagem. Out of it came a new form of relations between the patron and the worker; between man and the land. The social distance between them became greater. It became immense.[53]

Perhaps the most expressive summary of this development is to be found in the writings of some of the last survivors of the old pattern of life, of the senhor de engenho who held on while all about him his fellows were going down. From the memoirs of one of these, Julio Bello, the following extracts are translated:

Today how different is the life of the engenho! In less than a quarter of a century, how the life of the country has been transformed! Industrialized

[50] *Ibid.*, 40.
[51] *Ibid.*, 171–73.
[52] Cf. the romances of Lins do Rego dealing with the cycle of sugar. They include *Menino de Engenho, O Moleque Ricardo, Banguê, Doidinho,* and *Usina.*
[53] Gilberto Freyre in his Preface to Julio Bello, *Memorias de um Senhor de Engenho* (Rio de Janeiro, 1938), xi.

lands in the possession of commercial firms in Recife, how it has saddened the earth!

Today when one goes along the magnificent stretch of highway, of such beautiful and marvelous views, that leads from here to Recife and comes to the grounds of Sant' Amaro and of Serinhaem, of the ancient and well-named "beautiful villa of serinhaem," from the height he has in view all of the valley of the river and the engenhos which were the domains of such outstanding families, above all, of the illustrious Wanderleys: those of Rosario, of Canto Escuro, of Coelhos, of Buranhaem, of Palma, of Anjo, of Sibiro, of Trapiche, of Água Fria, and so many others. Where are those Wanderley Chaves, the Lins Wanderleys, the José Netos, the Wanderleys of Coelhos, those of Fontes, those of Peres? All are dispersed. All, almost all, emigrated from the land and the profession of their elders. What remains from those happy beehives full of life and enchantment on the margins and in the vicinity of the great river? The voyager traveling the road for wheeled vehicles for 50 kilometers stops now at one point, then at another, close to the old ruined chapels, near the abandoned ruins of the old type sugar mills, he stops and asks: "who owns this engenho now?" The reply is invariably: "It belongs to the usina."

The usina is great and anonymous—for all it is the commercial firm in Recife. I, in the half fantasy with which ofttimes I consider, thanks to God, the things of life, give body and form to this monster as if it might be a species of Empress Catharine, insatiable conquistador of lands and terrible deporter of colonel Mujiks, senhores de engenho. In my fantasy I consider it as a living person, as a movement of its own in the social drama. For me the usina is not as it is for all Firm A or Firm B. The usina which conquers the lands and scatters and degrades their old masters, is one being. It is not one person or a group of persons who unite together in a commercial body. It is a sentiment. It is monopoly, the force which shuts others out from the lands, almost lacking in tolerance for the distribution, itself only slightly equitable, of the gains from agriculture made by the old class that had cultivated the soil for hundreds of years. It is almost the spirit of avarice.

. . . . . .

In the casas grandes of the old mills, where the old colonels ruled in masterly style during the last century, melancholy and ridiculous carica-tures of them, the administrators, inspectors and supervisors of the usina, vegetate today.[54]

The present size of the holdings in the sugar area of the coastal cane-producing section of Pernambuco has been the subject of re-searches by Gileno dé Carlí of Brazil's Institute of Alcohol and Sugar. Although by necessity this investigator had to rely on esti-mates, he did have the great advantage of ready access to all of the records and of a personal acquaintance with most of the larger es-tablishments. We may be sure that his figures are a close approxima-tion of reality. According to this authority, the sugar cane lands of the state total some 693,149 hectares. Of these, 166,400 hectares re-main in 636 old-style engenhos, making an average of 261 hectares per establishment of this type. Sixty usinas own or control the re-mainder of the sugar lands, the area owned amounting to 395,062 hectares, an average of 6,584 hectares per mill. The remaining acre-age, 131,687 hectares, is in the hands of operators who sell their cane

54 Bello, *Memorias*, 60–61, 191.

to the usinas. Thus, if complete control of the sugar lands of Pernambuco is the goal of the usina, its work would seem to be 57 per cent complete. But in the meantime it dominates 19 per cent more of the cane-producing area, leaving only 24 per cent to the old-type mills. The largest of the usinas is Catende with an area of 27,574 hectares, followed by Cachoeira Lisa with 21,284, and Tiuma with 20,000. Seventeen of the 60 each contain 10,000 hectares or more, the joint holdings of these few mammoths alone accounting for a total of 243,620 hectares or 35 per cent of all the sugar lands in the state.[55] The first central mill was established in 1884. In a little more than half a century the usinas owned or controlled all but 24 per cent of the cane lands. It hardly need be added that the lands of the usinas are the cream of the lot. If the engenhos remaining are a fair sample of those eliminated, which is probably not the case, 2,650 senhores de engenho have been eliminated in the single state of Pernambuco. All through the sugar-producing areas this process has been going on; in Alagôas, Sergipe, and Paraíba the story has been very much the same as in Pernambuco.

EFFECTS OF THE CONCENTRATION OF LANDOWNERSHIP

Brazilian scholars have not failed to recognize the economic and social problems that have risen out of the concentration of landownership and control in the country. In fact, the adverse effects of the latifundium is one point on which Brazilian scholars seem to be in most complete agreement. The following paragraph from the writings of Dr. Oscar Penna Fontenelle, describing the situation of rural workers in the state of Rio de Janeiro, will have a familiar ring to those well acquainted with the heritage of the plantation in the most fertile areas of the southern United States. It was written at a time when questions of obtaining more and better agricultural laborers were of public concern and when the desirability of imitating São Paulo in the introduction of Japanese workers was being debated in the state legislature.

With the present regime [on the fazendas] it is impossible to obtain better colonos than those we have and we are marching towards still worse days. The agricultural worker in the state vegetates in a dismal hut; suffers from malaria and worms; is badly fed and poisons himself with tobacco and cachaça; receives for his work scrip which may only be used at the commissary of the fazenda owner in which he may make purchases; he does not send his children to the school, which, situated as a rule in the urban centers, serves only the children of the fazendeiro families and those of the tradesmen of the locality; in a word, he is a poverty-stricken unfortunate, limited in his knowledge of the world to the surrounding few miles, the area through which he is accustomed to travel in his rounds from one fazenda to another, in following a neighboring fazendeiro who has lured him away from his former location, in order to flee from the compliance with some obligation at a fazenda where he was and which

[55] Dé Carlí, *O Processo Histórico da Usina em Pernambuco*, 56–59.

he was obliged to pay with certain services, or simply through the pleasure of wandering, because there is nothing to attach him to the land he cultivates.[56]

Similar descriptions could easily be secured for other areas; many of them have already found a place at one point or another in this volume. Brazilians clearly recognize that the concentration of land-ownership and the numerical preponderance of the landless class which it brings is largely responsible for the poverty of the country. For a hundred years now they have been struggling to change the system. Among the most adequate analyses available is one by Nelson Werneck Sodré which has reference to the situation in the far West, to Mato Grosso, a sparsely populated land where cattle raising is the basis of livelihood and the estates are of almost unbelievable extent.

In the West inheritance is the only force bringing about a sub-division of properties. But there are frequent cases in which the dispersed portions are regrouped by one heir's acquiring hold-ings of the others and reconstituting the latifundium along the old lines. The laws relating to the sales of land by the state should bring about subdivision of land, but they are frequently evaded. The large proprietors maintain that pastoral enterprises pay only if they have free land.

The concession of immense domains to foreign concerns is a force working against the subdivision of the land. A large part of the west-ern lands belongs to foreigners who are merely holding it, awaiting a favorable opportunity to sell.

Because of these factors small farming exists only in the areas sur-rounding urban nuclei. Here it is carried on mainly by foreigners, particularly the Japanese. The Brazilians are divided into a small handful of proprietors and an overwhelming majority of pauperized laborers who are bound in one way or another to the pastoral re-gime.[57]

According to this same authority entire municípios, although in the West they have extensions comparable with those of states, "have their lands, their possessions, their riches divided, not in a descending scale, but among a half-dozen grand proprietors—and poverty-stricken grand proprietors. They are grand only in the exten-sion of the lands which they possess." The results of this are dis-astrous for the welfare of the region and the nation. Paradoxically, in the West where there seems to be only land, there is no land for distribution. This apparent contradiction is explained by the facts that (1) the pastures are in large and almost inalienable properties, (2) the lands owned by the state are leased to foreign organizations, in concessions, or even sold so as to constitute new latifundia, and

[56] Oscar Penna Fontenelle, *Problemas Economicos do Estado do Rio* (Rio de Janeiro, 1925), 112.
[57] Werneck Sodré, *Oeste*, 128–30.

(3) those that remain are either under water or lacking in water. Werneck Sodré estimates that of 250,000 persons in the southern part of Mato Grosso, only 3,500 are landowners.[58]

The withholding of lands from productive uses by large landholders so that they might have enough to distribute among their numerous heirs is the aspect of this question that has received most attention from Brazilian writers. The absence of a land tax, a reform so strongly urged by João Cardoso de Menezes e Souza,[59] facilitated this "dog in the manger" policy that has been so bitterly attacked by Brazilians and visitors alike. The Brazilian conception of the latifundium, as a large holding of unused lands, undoubtedly had its origin in this practice.

Brazilians have clearly pointed out, in many of the paragraphs quoted in this chapter and others having to do with the relations of people to the land, the human erosion brought about by the concentration of landownership and control. The long-continued fight for the development of a middle class of farmers and the valorization of the Brazilian caboclo also has its base in a correct appraisal of the effects of land concentration in the hands of the few. Finally, the fact is beginning to gain wider recognition that the physical deterioration of the soil, as well as the man, is being brought about rapidly by absenteeism and poor management on estates operated by administrators and by the soil mining practiced on portions of the estates that are let out to renters. To the large estate and the slovenly methods of agriculture perpetuated wherever slave labor was employed, Burton, an observant traveler, attributed the exhaustion of the soil about Entre Rios in the state of Rio de Janeiro. Already in his day (1867) every stream was a "sewer of liquid manure, coursing to the Atlantic, and the superficial soil is that of a brickfield." [60] Later, upon passing through the Parahybuna Valley where the land was divided into farms he said, "Houses and fields became more frequent, and the curse of the great proprietors is no longer upon the land." To this he added the following footnote: "Their effect is that which has been in France, which was in the southern states of the Union, and which is in Great Britain. When will the political economist duly appreciate the benefit derived from the subdivision of land?" [61]

Today, the slaves are gone, but many persons still living were once held in bondage. It would be interesting, however, to have the comments of the same experienced world traveler after he had passed through the newly opened cotton districts of western São Paulo. Here, a few short years of cotton growing, with share hands, by colonos paid a fixed amount for "making the crop" on an alqueire of

---

[58] *Ibid.*, 173–74. For a listing of the areas controlled by large companies, with a map, see pp. 174–76.

[59] Cardoso de Menezes e Souza, *Theses sobre Colonização no Brazil*, 307–15.

[60] Burton, *The Highlands of the Brazil*, I, 42.

[61] *Ibid.*, 47.

land and a fixed amount per arroba for picking it, or by Japanese on rented lands already has wrought havoc with the soil.

The preceding paragraphs summarize a few of the more direct results of Brazil's large size agricultural holdings. Still others, some direct and others more removed, need to be mentioned. The high degree of social stratification prevailing in most of the country, although existing from the very first settlement of Brazil, nevertheless owes its persistence to the continued presence of the large estate. As the small-farm pattern continues to overspread Brazil, this social stratification will become less pronounced, or at least the social pyramid will attain new layers. The social classes will no longer be limited to a handful of the elite at the peak, supported by a great base of agricultural laborers—nearly always the most disadvantaged class in any society—the inevitable result of a society overwhelmingly rural and land possessed by the favored few.

The comparatively low standard of living that prevails throughout most of Brazil also is to be attributed to the concentration of land-ownership and the class system that it has preserved. This matter has already received attention in another chapter; here it is necessary merely to add that the sections where the land has been subdivided are the ones where the levels of living are highest, where general education has made the most headway. It is no accident that public records in the southern states are far superior to those in the other sections of Brazil. The condition of these records is no doubt positively and closely associated with the general level of intelligence of the population. This level in turn has certainly been determined more largely by the degree of concentration of landownership than by any other factor. Brazil's present efforts to develop a much larger class of farm operators is a large stride in the valorization of her people.

Finally, it should be pointed out that in Brazil the large estate, and the slavery that went with it, did not set the sections of the country at one another's throats as in the United States. This deserves a few words of explanation. In contrast with the situation in our own country, in Brazil concentration of landownership and control and the slave system were characteristic of every region in the nation. Whereas in the United States on the eve of the liquidation of slavery the states with few slaves sold Negroes to the states with many, in Brazil the process was reversed and the result was a universalizing of the problem. This has meant that the long list of social problems growing out of the system, and that are still with Brazil, are not mainly confined to certain regions of the country, as is the case in the United States. Brazil as a whole must attempt to cope with them because they are present almost universally, even in São Paulo and Rio Grande do Sul. This makes all Brazilians cognizant of these problems, and all equally sensitive on the subject. The majority of Brazilians cannot pass it off with the superior, holier-than-thou attitude that is the escape mechanism used throughout a large portion of the United States; nor is one section of the country constantly on the defensive because of the institutions its people have inherited from the long past. In Brazil regional differences are not greatly amplified by a social heritage from the time when it was part free and part slave or by the socially inherited bitterness of a war for liberating the slaves and a still more tragic reconstruction period. Whatever the effects of the large estates and slavery may have been, their mark is on national, and not merely on regional, character.

AGRARIAN REFORM

Since the close of World War II talk of agrarian reform has occupied a prominent place in Brazilian newspapers and magazines, on the radio, and in the halls of Congress. Proposals have been many and varied, and it seems fairly certain that legal measures of one kind or another will be forthcoming in the not too distant future. At the core of most of the agitation is the idea of fundamental modification in the size of land holdings in Brazil. More specifically, the general proposal is the elimination or at least reduction of the importance of the latifundia, the large holdings that are deliberately withheld from agricultural production. For the most part the expropriation and subdivision of such large holdings, especially those in areas near the great centers of consumption, are the measures most commonly suggested. In fact they are the only devices many persons, even the leaders of thought and action, have in mind when they speak or write of the *reforma agraria*. Others are advocating vehemently that the sugar plantations and other large estates should be divided among the workers, while still others see the whole problem in much larger perspective and recognize the necessity of dealing in any fundamental reform with man as well as land. They would accompany any distribution of land with fundamental instruction of the Brazilian rural population in methods of farming and other basic aspects of rural living.

Just what lines the agrarian reform will take, it is still too early to predict with any degree of certainty. It probably will be considerably different in the various parts of the nation. São Paulo has led the way by placing a moderate tax on land holdings. Some of the other states no doubt will resort to expropriation of some of the large estates and the distribution of small pieces of them among the rural population. The federal government is likely to place restrictions upon the size of farms and the use of the soil in the areas benefited by its irrigation and drainage projects. It is hardly realistic, though, to expect that certain other fundamental measures will be taken. As yet there is no evidence of any attempt to restrict the sale of public lands to speculators, a practice that is likely to create a dozen new latifundia for every one eliminated. Nor is it likely that a land tax will be utilized as a means of effectively forcing the utilization of the huge unused tracts. For years to come speculators in public lands will likely operate with little or no interference, and land will continue to remain in fact an asylum for capital.[62]

[62] The literature on agrarian reform is voluminous and varied. Among the basic materials that deserve consultation are the following: Serviço de Informação Agrícola, *Reforma Agrária no Mundo e no Brasil*; José Arthur Rios, "Rumos da Reforma Agrária," *Arquivos de Direito Social*, X (1952); Vicente Chermont de Miranda, "A Reforma Agrária e a Experiencia do Estatuto da Lavoura Canavieira," *Revista Forense* (Rio de Janeiro), CXL (1952); Afránio de Carvalho, *Lei Agrária: Anteprojeto* (Rio de Janeiro, 1948); Sociedade Nacional de Agricultura, *Reforma Agrária* (Rio de Janeiro, 1947); J. V. Freitas Marcondes, *Revisão e Reforma Agrária* (São Paulo, 1962); José Arthur Rios (ed.), *Recomendações sobre Reforma Agrária* (Rio de Janeiro, 1961); and T. Lynn Smith, "Agrarian Reform," *Current Social Trends and Problems in Latin America* (Gainesville, 1957), 29–44.

CHAPTER XV

SYSTEMS OF AGRICULTURE

THE SUCCESS or failure of Brazil's bid for a place among the world's great powers probably will be determined largely by the rapidity with which the mass of her agriculturists learn to farm. The crucial factor is the extent to which they quickly learn to substitute efficient and effective means of extracting products from the soil for the inefficient, wasteful, and destructive methods currently being employed. Indeed, the present writer believes that, if the masses of rural Brazil today were employing ways and means of securing food and fiber from the land as effective as those in use as early as 1910 in much of western Europe, Canada and the United States, and Australia and New Zealand, Brazil already would have achieved a high position among the great powers of the world.

NATURE AND IMPORTANCE OF AGRICULTURAL SYSTEMS

The highly integrated social system consisting of ideas, culture traits, skills, techniques, production practices, prejudices, and habits employed by the members of a given society in order to extract a living from the soil is one of the most basic relationships between man and the land. As in the case of the social institutions discussed in the immediately preceding chapters, this portion of the social order also is highly institutionalized. In most parts of the world the customary and accepted methods of preparing the land for the seed, tilling, controlling the weeds, collecting the harvest, caring for livestock, and transporting things on the farm and from farm to market are highly standardized on the local level; and generally the value systems prevailing in the rural community are oriented in ways designed to help preserve existing ways of growing plants and animals. For want of a more satisfactory term this particular part of a general societal and cultural system of a given people is designated as its *system of agriculture.* This term is employed in preference to "agricultural techniques," which probably is the most suitable alternative, in order to stress as forcibly as possible the complexity, the systematic integration, and the organic unity of the specific social system and cultural complex in action to which the designation is applied.

As is implicit from what has been said above, a system of agriculture must be defined broadly enough to include all of the lore, the practical skills, the "know-how," and the scientific knowledge which farm families use in growing crops, securing poultry and livestock products, and in performing the tasks of transportation. Thus the system of agriculture of a primitive agricultural community in a remote section of Brazil may have as its central traits the digging stick manipulated by the women of the tribe and a set of religious and magical beliefs and practices designed to promote fertility and ward off destructive forces or elements; whereas that of a modern farming community, such as exists in parts of São Paulo, may include an integrated combination of tested practices that have come from many parts of the world, well-established scientific principles, and mechanical and engineering knowledge and skills of a high order of perfection.

Historically, the acquisition of the fund of knowledge which makes it possible in the second half of the twentieth century for the farmer in Brazil or any other part of the world to multiply the gifts of nature, to bring forth plant and animal products in abundance, is mankind's greatest accomplishment. Only to the extent that mastery over the natural processes multiplied the amounts of food and fiber that one man could produce have human energies been made available for the other activities that have brought us to the atomic age. From the geographic point of view the present distribution of the various systems of agriculture is probably the most reliable indicator of the underlying causes of the tremendous differences in levels and standards of living of peoples throughout the earth; and politically, socially, and economically one of the principal tasks confronting those united in the Alliance for Progress and similar endeavors throughout the world is to bring the agricultural systems which are still keeping large segments of mankind in an "underdeveloped" stage up nearer the levels already achieved in those nations with the most highly perfected systems of agriculture. Indeed, in the decades that lie ahead efforts to improve existing agricultural systems in many parts of the world are likely to be one of the chief ways of attacking the hunger, poverty, misery, and disease which continue to be the lot of large segments of the human race. In Brazil alone a tremendous task confronts those at home and from abroad who would teach the typical Brazilian countryman to farm and thereby place him in position to leave behind a creature-like existence and move up the socioeconomic scale to a position more commensurate with the needs and aspirations of a human being.

The need for the average Brazilian countryman to learn to farm is patent. After examining mountains of evidence and after repeated visits to many parts of Brazil, from 1939 on, the present writer is convinced that more than one-half of the Brazilians who live directly from the land continue to be dependent on a system of agriculture that is less efficient, more wasteful of human energy, and generally less effective than that practiced by the Egyptians at the dawn of history. Even more important, however, is the fact that the particular system of agriculture in vogue plays a major role in shaping millions of children in the rural sections of Brazil into creatures in which the characteristics of the beast of burden appear to be in the ascendancy over the qualities of the human being. If Brazil is to play her proper role in the second half of the twentieth century, she must develop quickly and put widely into practice a system of agriculture in which the energies of those who work in agriculture are not needlessly and wastefully expended, in which stultifying drudgery is reduced to a minimum, in which men and women cease to be mere beasts of burden, and in which labor in agriculture is productive, humanizing, and socially esteemed. This, in turn, can only come about when there is generally, throughout the entire country, an emphasis on elementary and secondary education and particularly on training in agriculture, mechanical arts, and homemaking that is many times greater than that prevailing in the 1960's. Such an education alone can bring about the changes that are needed, changes that will result in a much more sparing use of labor in the productive process, a far greater use of horses and mules and simple agricultural implements such as the turning plow and the four-wheeled wagon, and most important of all, far more intensive and effective use of managerial skills in the ordinary farm business. The primitive and abhorrently wasteful and destructive system of *derrubadas e queimadas*, referred to below as "fire agriculture," which is still in use throughout most parts of Brazil, and the labor-devouring hoe culture, which is a feature of most of the areas of commercial production, must give way to a system of agriculture in which the manual labor of the ordinary man is used in a much more fruitful combination. In the future the bulk of Brazil's farmers must make use of considerable horsepower and well-designed implements and vehicles as they go about their work of preparing the seedbeds, planting the crops, controlling the weeds, gathering the crops, threshing or otherwise cleaning and processing the products for market, and transporting the produce from the farm to the market place.

The preceding paragraphs are based upon the proposition that there is a close relationship between the agricultural system employed by a given people and its plane or level of living.[1] This important point deserves further elaboration. Whoever travels throughout the world, even in a cursory manner, is almost certain to observe that the levels of living vary tremendously from one area to another. Throughout most of Asia, for example, he surely will note that the lot of the common people is almost inconceivably low. In Europe, on the other hand, levels average much higher, but even there he will quickly learn that per capita consumption of the peoples of northwestern Europe is much higher than that of those who live in the southern and southeastern portions of that continent. In the New World it is apparent to all that the plane of living enjoyed by the

[1] On this point see also the discussion in Chapter X.

masses of the population in the United States and Canada is much above that of the inhabitants of the countries which lie to the south and east of the Rio Grande. Even within a given country tremendous variations are to be found: in the United States there can be no doubt that the average level of living of those who dwell north of the Ohio is considerably higher than that of those who live to the south of that great river; and in Brazil, as is evident from the regional differences discussed in Chapter x, there can be no questioning the fact that the people living in such southern states as Rio Grande do Sul, Santa Catarina, Paraná, and São Paulo have much higher levels of living than those living in the eastern, northeastern, and other sections of the country.

Obviously, because differences in the planes and levels of living of various peoples have been apparent to so many, numerous explanations of such differences have been advanced. By far the most popular of these is, of course, the one which attributes the variations to hereditary or racial factors. According to this line of reasoning, it seems, the level of living enjoyed by a particular people is indicative of its natural ability or inherent biological capacities. Some peoples have high levels of living because they are innately "superior," and the mere fact that others have a very low level of living is all the evidence needed to indicate that they are "inferior" in various respects. Another widely used explanation gives industrialization as the basic factor responsible for differences in levels of living of various peoples: industrialized societies are "advanced" and countries that are not highly industrialized are "backward" or "underdeveloped." Overlooked largely by those promulgating such a thesis is the fact that such differences also were in existence before the industrial revolution. The present writer accepts neither of these explanations, nor others, such as climatic determination, as the important ones, but advances the truly social and cultural proposition that the differences between the basic systems of agriculture used by various peoples are the real key to an understanding of the ways in which the sharply differing planes and levels of living were generated and are perpetuated.

A CLASSIFICATION OF THE SYSTEMS OF AGRICULTURE

Not long ago the authors of the pertinent articles in one of the most widely used reference books in the United States, one prepared with the needs of high school children and their parents chiefly in mind, asserted that the farmer in 1940 could care for 750 acres of land as easily as George Washington's father could cultivate 50 acres. Moreover, the eminent authorities responsible for the materials cited further indicated that the primitive husbandman would have required an equivalent amount of labor merely to cultivate one acre.[2] For present purposes it is unnecessary to know whether or not

[2] *Compton's Pictured Encyclopedia and Fact-Index*, I (Chicago, 1944), 47.

the ratios involved are exactly 50 to 750 and 1 to 750 or to take into account improvements that have been made since 1940. The margin of error could be tremendous, and still the point would be indisputable. During the nineteenth and twentieth centuries improvements in the ways in which man may extract a living from the soil have been tremendous.

There likewise is no need to document in detail the proposition that, historically and geographically, the variations in mankind's systems of agriculture have been very great. It is pertinent to mention, however, that at least five thousand years ago the peoples of Egypt and Mesopotamia already were using systems of tillage vastly superior to those that were being used in much of Brazil and many other parts of the earth during the opening decades of the atomic age. By the time the Sumerians and the Egyptians had perfected writing as a means of communication and record keeping, the accomplishment that marks the beginning of the historical period, they also had developed rather advanced systems of agriculture. In contrast with the situation still existing in many sections of Brazil, they were making abundant use of the plow, wheeled vehicles, draft animals, harnesses and hitching apparatus, and irrigation for the purpose of producing and transporting the food crops on which their civilizations depended. It may be, of course, that the arts and skills involved in agriculture and stockraising never attained any much higher level of perfection until hundreds of years after the discovery of America. Our knowledge of the long painful process by which those early peoples perfected the systems of agriculture which made their high development of civilization possible is extremely fragmentary, in contrast to the recent revolutionary developments in agricultural technology, animal industry, and rural transportation, which are thoroughly documented.

Geographically, too, even in the 1960's, one can easily encounter the most diverse methods of co-operating with nature in the production of food and fiber. These range all the way from the most simple ones, for which fine distinctions are necessary in order to separate them from the mere collecting activities characteristic of a preagricultural stage of existence, to the highly complex mechanized systems of agriculture. Properly classified and arranged, these may even be suggestive of the lines of social and cultural evolution through which mankind increased its control over nature in the ages before recorded history enabled us to be more certain of the sequence of the changes. From this point of view each of the six systems of agriculture enumerated below may be thought of as a stage in the history of civilization, since in the long run the lines of development certainly were from the simple to the more complex. One should not assume on the basis of such materials, however, that any given society must pass through all six such stages in sequential order. The six systems of agriculture as classified and described by the present writer, and which are used in the pages that follow, in an endeavor to analyze one of the most important features of Brazilian society, are as follows: (1) river-bank and stream-bed plantings, (2) fire agriculture, (3) hoe culture, (4) rudimentary plow culture, (5) advanced plow culture, and (6) mechanized farming.

RIVER-BANK AND STREAM-BED PLANTINGS

Before even the simplest system of agriculture can be described and characterized, it is essential to make a clear distinction between agriculture as such and the mere gathering or collecting of nature's gifts which preceded it. Nevertheless, and in spite of the hundreds of thousands of treatises that have been written about agriculture, the early phases of man's agricultural and pastoral activities are not very clear. Is it fair to assume, as most writers on the subject seem to have done, that agriculture commenced with tillage through the use of a digging stick or a crude hoe? "A digging stick was the first hand tool used to scratch the surface of the ground before planting, and a forked stick, held in the ground by the plowman while the oxen dragged it ahead, was the first plow" is the facile way in which all of the basic questions involved are disposed of in the popular and representative source to which reference has been made. But how, where, and when did mankind acquire all of the ideas, knowledge, and skills that these statements take for granted? The saving of seeds, the act of planting them in locations favorable to their growth, the engineering skills involved in the simplest of tillage, the knowledge of how to make and use a crude plow, the domestication of oxen, and the development of apparatus for hitching animals to the plow should hardly be assumed to be spontaneous or instinctive activities of mankind. Certainly much more elementary activities and culture traits than these were involved in the lengthy epoch which marked the transition from a collecting economy to agriculture.

The first farming was, of course, only a slight transition from the collecting activities that preceded it, and this step undoubtedly was taken by various peoples in what is now Brazil quite independently of similar discoveries and developments in Egypt, Asia Minor, and other parts of the world. The early Brazilian woman shares with her sisters in favorable locations elsewhere the honor of being the world's first agriculturist. It is highly probable that she first interfered or co-operated in the processes of nature by thinning out some of the competing plants from among the wild ones from which she had come to expect a gift of seeds, fruits, or tubers. But this practice alone was insufficient to justify designating her share in the process as agriculture. Before she was entitled to be called a farmer, she had to get and apply the idea of taking some of the seeds and depositing them in a spot where they could sprout, take root, and grow. Then and only then did she begin her long career as an agriculturist, and then and only then was the step taken that enabled mankind to develop a social and cultural heritage that would make possible a civilization. The fact that one growing season followed almost immediately upon the other, so that to forgo the consumption of the seeds or tubers was not too great and too long a strain, probably was an important factor in making possible the transition. The soft, mellow loam deposited along its banks by a receding stream probably was the first place women in Brazil, Egypt, and Mesopotamia selected for their first plantings. At least very early they discovered that merely by saving seeds and pressing them into such spongy surfaces with the ball of the foot, they could greatly multiply the gifts of nature. Such activities certainly deserve to be designated as agriculture, but the system of farming involved is the simplest possible. To secure crops in this manner no implements whatsoever, not even a crude digging stick, are necessary.

This system of agriculture, the most elementary possible, is still widely used throughout the Amazon Basin, and a closely related one, in which the seeds are planted in the beds of streams that are dry throughout most of the year, is characteristic of many parts of northeastern Brazil. In these areas alone hundreds of thousands of persons are largely dependent on this simple process for their dietary staples.[3] Briefly, throughout the immense area drained by the Amazon and its numerous tributaries, the rivers rise steadily during one half of the year and fall steadily during the other half. As the streams recede, the inhabitants of the area make their small plantings on the spongy surfaces left by the receding waters. The river alone prepares the seed bed, and if the ball of the foot is not the sole agency used to implant the seeds in the soft earth, a rude digging stick or, in rare instances, a crude hoe is the only implement employed. Only as fairly permanent settlements seek to make use of lands that slope back from the natural levees, as on the *varzea do Careiro* below Manaus [4] and in the area near Santarem which was settled by Confederate exiles from the United States, do more advanced agricultural systems compete with this simple process. In any case the dependence upon such rudimentary ways of producing agricultural products is largely responsible for the basic condition of agricultural activities in a state such as Amazonas, as revealed by

[3] After the present writer had personally observed farming activities of this type during his first visit to the Amazon Basin in 1942, he searched journals of various naturalists who had spent years in the area with the hope of finding the observations that they had made on the subject. This was largely in vain. However, in the writings of Alfred Russel Wallace, *Travels on the Amazon* (London, 1911), 177, there is evidence that the noted elaborator of the theory of evolution was well acquainted with the procedures involved. Thus he relates that in the course of some of the "dull and dreary evenings" he had spent at Javita, a small village near the passage which links the Amazon and the Orinoco river systems, he amused himself and passed the time by describing in blank verse the life of the Indians of the area. The following lines pertain specifically to the system of agriculture in vogue:

> The women dig the manciocca root,
> And with much labour make of it their bread.
> These plant the young shoots in the fertile earth—
> Earth all untill'd, to which the plough, or spade,
> Or rake, or harrow, are alike unknown.

[4] Cf. Sternberg, *A Água e o Homem na Várzea do Careiro, passim.*

the data gathered in the 1950 census of agriculture. (See Tables L and LI.) At that time a total of 15,220 agricultural establishments, or farms, were enumerated in the state, of which 9,612 were devoted exclusively to crops, 1,519 to a combination of crop and livestock enterprises, 775 to stockraising alone, 137 to pastures for fattening livestock, and 2,852 to other undescribed agricultural uses. Together these establishments included 5,592,863 hectares or almost 14 million acres. However, the land reported as actually being utilized was only 146,719 hectares, of which 23,274 were devoted to permanent crops, 29,866 to temporary crops, 56,168 to natural pastures, and 37,411 to permanent pastures. A total agricultural labor force of 80,705 persons (55,516 males and 25,189 females) was reported as working on the farms enumerated, of whom 31,170 were classified as farm operators and the members of their own families and another 1,762 as working on shares. But even midway in the twentieth century the 15,220 farms and 80,705 farm workers in the state taken together had only the following numbers of the fundamental labor-saving vehicles and implements to aid them in their work: 17 oxcarts, 34 other animal-drawn vehicles, 10 tractors, 10 motor trucks and runabouts, 17 disk plows, and 56 turning plows, and this in a state having more than half a million inhabitants spread throughout an area twice the size of Texas.

FIRE AGRICULTURE

In some places at least tillage with the digging stick or the hoe may have developed directly out of the favored situations in which nature's rivers did a thorough job of preparing the seedbeds. It is even possible that the first combinations of agricultural and livestock enterprises were ones in which, as the river's waters receded, oxen were used to tread the broadcast seeds into the muddy surface of the land.[5] But in Brazil and many other parts of the earth another system of agriculture developed long before the digging stick evolved into the hoe.

One can easily demonstrate that soft, pliable surfaces of the soil are left where a fire has encountered, in a dry condition, the results of abundant plant growth. Such a burned-over area in a virgin forest lacks almost entirely the many plants or weeds that might compete with those sown by man or woman. Hence it is merely a short step from the point when human beings depend on nature's rivers to prepare a seedbed to that in which the ax and fire may be employed for the same purpose. Tremendous areas in Brazil and other South American countries, as well as those in Central America, Africa, Asia, and Oceania, are still occupied by peoples

[5] Gaston Maspero, *The Dawn of Civilization, Egypt and Chaldea* (London, 1910), 66, says in the present tense, although referring to ancient practices, "As soon as the water of the Nile retires, the ground is sown without previous preparation, and the grain, falling straight into the mud, grows as vigorously as in the best-ploughed furrows."

who have not passed beyond this elementary, wasteful, and destructive stage of agricultural existence. The words "wasteful" and "destructive" are used advisedly, since the use of this system of agriculture means that annually a section of virgin forest or second growth that has been standing for decades must be destroyed merely in order to produce a few pecks of rice, a bushel of beans, or small amounts of other crops. J. C. Willis' statement that "vast areas of good forest land have been ruined in southern Asia by this destructive practice" [6] is fully supported by the present writer's personal observations throughout large sections of Brazil and other parts of the American tropics. The system involved, the most widespread manner of securing products from the soil in Brazil, was designated by the present writer in the first edition of this volume, as "fire agriculture."

Because of its central position in the pattern of rural living the analysis of this aspect of Brazilian culture does much to bring out the essential aspects of Brazilian rural life; because it is so different from the peasant agriculture of south Brazil's European colonies and São Paulo's rational system of production, a study of this form of agricultural production serves to throw regional cultural differences into bold relief. It is especially worth noting that an official publication of the Brazilian government, prepared in English for distribution in the United States, sets 1939 as the beginning of a period in which "inferiority complexes . . . in Brazil were replaced by a sense of achievement; [and] fire agriculture began to be replaced by the concept of mechanized agriculture." [7]

What is here designated fire agriculture in Brazilian terminology is sometimes obliquely referred to as "empirical methods," although usually it is designated *derruba e queimada* or "felling and burning." [8] This refers to a cluster of agricultural practices in which the land is prepared for planting by clearing the underbrush from a por-

[6] J. C. Willis, *Agriculture in the Tropics* (Cambridge, 1909), 2.

[7] Brazilian Embassy, *Survey of the Brazilian Economy* (Washington, 1959), 1.

[8] In José de Souza, *Dicionário da Terra e da Gente do Brazil, derrubada* is defined as "a general term which denominates the agricultural operation which follows the *broca* or *roçada* or *cabrucar* of the forest, and which consists in felling the large trees with the axe in order to prepare ground for planting. In another sense, it is the wood that has been felled by the axe . . . in order to make use of the land in agriculture." Broca, in turn, is said by the same authority to be "a term used in the north, especially in the northeast, to designate the first operation in the preparation of the soil for planting. It is the act of clearing or cleaning the land of the small timber, undergrowth, brush and vines that grow among the larger trees." The same authority quotes with approval the nine agricultural processes given by Juvenal Galeno: "*Brocar*: to cut the undergrowth with a *foice* [swinging blade]; it is the first task in making the clearing. Second, *derrubar*, to fell the larger trees with an ax. Third: *picar*, to pile the fallen timber to facilitate the firing. Fourth: *queimar* (to burn). Fifth: *encoivarar*, to pile and burn the trunks and limbs that escaped in the general fire. Sixth: *cercar* (to fence). Seventh: *plantar* (to plant). Eighth: *limpar, capinar* (to pull or cut the weeds or saplings). And last: *apanhar, colher* (to harvest)." Much the same order of steps is given in the little classic, *Jéca Tatú e Mané Chique-Chique* by Ildefonso Albano (2d ed.; Rio de Janeiro, n.d.), 11. For a description of similar systems in Asia and a discussion of the relationship of fire agriculture to other ways of extracting a living from the soil, see Smith, *The Sociology of Rural Life*, Chap. XIV.

tion of the forest with the machete, felling most of the larger trees with an ax, permitting the tangled masses of fallen trunks, limbs, branches, twigs, and leaves to dry for a short time, and then firing the entire lot. If the onslaught of the rainy season is predicted correctly, in this process the leaves, the twigs, and the smaller branches are entirely consumed; the larger logs and the stumps merely charred. The burning process leaves the soil extremely pliable, and for a short time the ground is comparatively free of noxious weeds and grasses. In these burned-over patches, amid the standing stumps and between the blackened logs, are planted the seeds that supply the bulk of the food eaten by millions of Brazilian families. By the bulk of Brazil's caboclos, sertanejos, matutos, and other countrymen any other system of preparing the land is either unknown or considered unnecessary. The only implement used in the planting is the hoe or the digging stick, and if there is any further attention given to the growing crop it is merely by use of the hoe or the swinging knife.

After a crop, or at best a few crops, have been taken from a clearing, the incursions of weeds and grasses cause the patch to be abandoned and a new one to be prepared. Second growth is allowed to flourish in the old field and after a few years this *capoeira* attains sufficient size so that the felling, burning, and planting process may be repeated. Whether in the North, as in the state of Maranhão or Ceará, in the West as in Mato Grosso, in long-settled, mountainous parts of the most advanced state of São Paulo, or even in parts of Santa Catarina and Rio Grande do Sul, where peasant immigrants from Europe recently have introduced a well-rounded pattern of small-farming practices, this fire agriculture is to be found. Except in the rice areas of Rio Grande do Sul, the diversified farming sections found elsewhere in the south and São Paulo, and in small zones about the larger centers, it is the system almost exclusively used for producing the foodstuffs with which the nation's people are fed.

This system of fire agriculture is merely one of the complexes, although a central one, in the pattern of living derived from the Indians.[9] Regional differences exist, of course, but many of the essentials in this pattern of life are brought out in the following quotation which details the cultural heritage received from the Indians by the present-day inhabitants of the interior, the vast sertões.

The sertanejo came to live, work, and hunt like the Indian. He simplified the village, making his dwelling of thatch and palms. Inside he places his

[9] The earliest description I have found is in Hans Staden, 1557: "In the places where they intend to plant, they cut down the trees and leave them to dry for one or three months and then set fire to them and burn them. Afterwards they plant the roots between the trunks, from which the roots take sustenance. This root is called mandioca and is a small tree about a fathom high, giving out three kinds of roots." *Hans Staden: The True History of His Captivity* (New York, 1929), 137. Carlos Borges Schmidt, "Rural Life in Brazil," in T. Lynn Smith and Alexander Marchant (eds.), *Brazil: Portrait of Half a Continent* (New York, 1951), Chap. VII, is fundamental for those interested in this and other aspects of Brazil's agricultural pattern.

hammock of cotton twine and stores in a *giráu* [primitive storehouse of sticks elevated off the ground] reserves of food. They consist of dried or jerked meat and his customary war flour, the bread of the aborigines, "principal food of this land," which the near-by *roça* made in the virgin forest or in the second growth gives him with abundance. To obtain that flour he burns and destroys the forests in the surrounding area, in an incessant conquest of new grounds. Where he harvests he never more plants. Primarily a nomad, he advances, devastating [the forests] with his small roça of mandioca: he sacrifices an entire forest. A few handfuls of mandioca flour represent the burning of a majestic forest; a great elaborator of second growth, the sertanejo was, inevitably, a great destroyer of nature which so strongly recompensed him: "the entire system of Brazilian agriculture begins with the destruction of the forests, and where there are no woods there is no culture." The Tupí was like that. The man of the sertão, however, did not imitate him only in his destructive activities. He went to the fields in the same mode, in "the way to the roças," the farmers forming a silent column, with the women in the middle for better defense. With the facility of the Indian he opens the passage way, breaking smaller branches, felling larger trunks. The sertanejos seat themselves, eat, sleep, erect houses of wattle and daub, navigate in dugouts, as did the Indian. The enjoyment of singing to the accompaniment of the *viola,* of the contests between singers as they mutually improvise the elements of the popular account, made of pride and lyricism, is also indigenous.[10]

The acculturation of the Europeans in the New World, the process by which the newcomers adopted the essential elements from the man-made environment of the Indians, has been summarized in a concise form by José Francisco da Rocha Pombo in one of his excellent little books:

The first colonists were adopting the usages and customs of the indigenes: the dietary regime; the processes of work, of farming, of hunting and fishing, and even the rudimentary acts of constructing habitations, the use of domestic objects, the manipulation of implements, etc.

They learned the language of the natives and many even learned the sports and diversions.

What is more extraordinary is that the strangers soon permitted themselves to be influenced by the ideas, the sentiments, and even the vices of the barbarians.

It may be said that, after some years of life in America, the European had more resemblances to the savage than to the civilized man.

There occurred here a cultural regression, a lowering of the level to the primitive sense of life.[11]

Evidences of this fire agriculture may be seen almost everywhere one goes, whether traveling up the Amazon, flying over Bahia, going overland across the Northeast, traveling by truck in Mato Grosso, passing along farm roads in Santa Catarina, or riding on the train near the great industrial plants on the outskirts of São Paulo. It is this system of devastating a forest to gain a few handfuls of mandioca flour that gives the jungle near Belém such a jagged appearance that, when seen from the air, reminds one of a small boy's head after the youngster's first few experiments in cutting his own hair.

[10] Calmon, *Espirito da Sociedade Colonial,* 194–96.
[11] José Francisco da Rocha Pombo, *Historia de São Paulo* (São Paulo, 1925), 62.

But one need not go into the remote parts of Brazil to see this agricultural system in full practice. He who takes the plane from Rio de Janeiro to São Paulo on a spring day (September or October) will see hundreds of smoking patches below, where the burning process is under way, other hundreds of brown patches on which the felled brush is awaiting the fire, and still more hundreds in which a blackened surface gives evidence of a burning process already completed and ground that is ready for the seeds. "Pockmarks" in one of these patches indicate the places where trunks and branches have been piled and fired. Even in those parts of Santa Catarina, Rio Grande do Sul, and Paraná where cultural practices introduced by the German, Italian, and Polish settlers have not penetrated (although the ethnic stock frequently is German) this fire agriculture is the prevailing mode of producing food crops. Needless to say, this system is extremely lavish in its use of labor, as well as wasteful of land, soil, and timber resources. With a minimum employment of modern knowledge and agricultural skills and the most elementary farming tools, such as the plow, the harrow, and the cultivator, the same amount of labor and land would produce many times the present harvest. Certainly the introduction and diffusion of such practices should do much to increase the effective labor force and the level of living in the nation.

A few descriptions of the typical manner in which this fire agriculture is carried on, chosen from the west, the north, and the south of Brazil, serve to make its essential characteristics stand out more clearly.

Agriculture in the State of Matto-Grosso, as in many states of the Brazilian confederation, still continues tied to the routine and to the struggle which come from the employment of the primitive processes.

Until the present, the use and utility of those marvelous agricultural machines which, by multiplying the work of man, facilitate and greatly improve the cultivation of the soil and augment its productivity, are completely ignored in this state.

The ax, the foice, and the hoe are still the sole instruments that are used by the farmers of Matto-Grosso. . . .

Here is the system of culture: As a rule from April to June is spent in cutting the underbrush and felling the trees for a clearing, followed in the month of August by putting the fire which devours everything except the stumps and some of the larger trunks. Farmers say, "He who has a clearing well burned will have a good harvest." In reality soils containing extremely high proportions of humus, perhaps because of the acids which they contain, only produce well when they have been well burned.

There is a significant difference observed in the growth of plants in parts of the clearing well burned over and in those parts in which the burning was not thorough, or where the fire did not pass. In addition to this, well burned-over fields save the farmer much labor and money because they assist him greatly in preparing the ground and decrease the number of weeds, as a consequence of destroying the seeds of the noxious plants; and there is even a decrease in the number of insects due to the action of the fire. So decisive is the influence of fire in the preparation of fields in Matto-Grosso that frequently they are entirely abandoned when out-of-season rains make impossible the firing of them.

When clearing is designated only for the planting of corn and beans, it is customary at felling time to leave the larger trees, these being merely girdled with the machete, about a yard above the ground. . . .

Due to this girdling process the tree dies, the leaves fall and the farmer prevents two things: the shade which is injurious to the plantings and having the field covered with fallen trunks which would result if all the trees were felled. There is also the advantage of keeping for a longer time a supply of wood in the standing trunks than is possible in those that are lying on the ground. Generally also, regardless of what is to be planted, palms such as the *bacaiuveiras, aguasal* and *uacury* [urucarí?] are not felled. The latter, since they give a great deal of shade, are trimmed with an axe, leaving only the growing central portion; but they soon put out beautiful new foliage and assist greatly in keeping the ground fresh and also in the formation and growth of the second growth.

In order to clear and fell one *alqueire* of ground in a day, requires 60 men, more or less.

Following the burning over of the clearing comes the process of breaking off and piling up the limbs and branches that were not consumed by the fire. These are piled in different places throughout the clearing, preferably in those which the fire failed to reach, for burning. But the better sticks are saved for fencing and for wood.

When this operation is completed, the work of fencing follows in order to keep out the cattle, horses, and mules. Then the first September rains are awaited for the planting of the corn.

In the planting of corn, as with all other crops in Matto-Grosso, until the present time only the hoe is used to open hills.[12]

The planting of rice follows a similar routine: "As we have said, rice requires fertile, humid soils, and the ground for its planting should be carefully prepared. Following the burning, it should be thoroughly cleared of limbs and branches, cleaned of weeds and grass and inclosed. The system of planting is the same as that employed for corn and for beans—the routine manner." [13]

Today the diffusion from São Paulo of the plow, and the agricultural techniques associated with it, has considerably modified agricultural practices in southern Mato Grosso. This is especially true in the area around the thriving little city of Campo Grande and near other stations along the railroad (the Noroeste) which links the lower part of the state with São Paulo. However, throughout most of the vast territory within the borders of Mato Grosso fire agriculture continues to hold undisputed sway.

In the region which figures so prominently in the lore of rural Brazil—the sertões of the Northeast—the routine of agricultural practices is cut to the pattern described so well for Mato Grosso. One of the most striking descriptions of farming in this area is that by the Brazilian writer, Gustavo Barroso, also known as "João do Norte." He introduces the subject by referring to the observations made by a French journalist who traveled through Asiatic Turkey and reported that agriculture there was so retarded that only slight use was made

[12] *Album Grafico do Estado de Matto-Grosso* (Hamburg, Germany, 1914), 260–61.
[13] *Ibid.*, 265.

of the plow and that other agricultural implements were unknown. Barroso questions:

> And what would he say if he should go to the sertão of Ceará, where the plow has never been used and the soil has never felt the tooth of the harrow; where wood ashes are the fertilizer, improvidence the base of agriculture, and the generosity of the rainy season the principal reliance; where the only agricultural instrument is the hoe, happily of iron, equal in its rude handle and manipulation to those with which primitive man dug in the hard ground searching for tubers when the river refused fish, the forest game, and stronger tribes had forced him to migrate from the more fertile places? What would he say upon seeing the rustic simplicity of the equipment in the grist mill, its strain of primitive machinery, its backward, confused and disordered ways . . . ? He would say that the cultivation of the soil in the sertão of the North is more rude and primitive than the agriculture of the stony western provinces of Anatolia.[14]

In another chapter the same writer describes the tenacity with which the rural folk of Brazil's Northeast cling to their customary agricultural methods.

> Furthermore he [the sertanejo, or countryman] is a person of routine and does not care for innovations. When one or another departs from the prevailing routine, bad results are soon predicted for the procedure: "He wants to encircle the world with legs that have never encompassed the belly of a horse."
> He plants and harvests in the given way because his father did so; he cares for his cattle in this way because his grandfather did so before him. He scorns farming implements and disdains repeating firearms. During centuries the structure of society in the sertões has not modified a single line in any of its activities, moral, physical, or psychical. The sertanejo is unalterable in his mode of dressing, speaking, planting, caring for cattle, and living.[15]

Going by truck through the Brazilian North and Northeast in December of 1942, I had a good opportunity to observe the countryside, and frequent delays presented many chances to talk with the people of the area. In addition, many facts were secured in conversation with fellow passengers, who varied in number from about thirty to fifty. At this time the drought had been serious for two years, but rains were setting in. The roças were well burned over and ready for planting. The only thing wanting was the rains. Particularly impressive were the fences.

Agricultural specialists describe this fire agriculture similarly. "The cultural processes for all crops may be summarized as felling, burning, etc., and cleaning with the hoe."[16] "Mechanical agriculture is little practiced. Only one agriculturist, in entire contrast with his neighbors, is using some plows in this [sugar cane] culture. Although his methods are deficient and do not conform to the best agronomical standards he has used them with profit. The remainder

[14] Gustavo Barroso, *Terra de Sol* (3d ed.; Rio de Janeiro, 1930), 68–69.

[15] *Ibid.*, 174–75.

[16] Ministerio da Agricultura, Industria e Commercio, *Estudo dos Factores da Producção nos Municípios Brasileiros: Aracajú, Sergipe* (Rio de Janeiro, 1923), 10.

of the cultivation is made according to the old routine. Following the felling and burning the land is planted with the hoe." [17]

Finally, let us turn to the far southern state of Santa Catarina where a large immigration of peasants from Germany, Poland, and Italy has done much to introduce and diffuse the agricultural methods used in Europe. Even in this area, and especially in the stages of sparse settlement which precede compact colonization, there still remain large areas in which fire agriculture is the prevailing mode of farming. A description of farming practices in the município of Rio do Sul, which until 1927 formed part of that little "Germany in Brazil" called Blumenau, reads as follows:

> The most common agricultural process in the município of Rio do Sul is hand labor. Mechanical farming is practiced only in the most extensive river bottoms throughout the various districts. This farming consists of the use of a small plow drawn by animals, the harrow, and the mower.
>
> Artificial fertilization of the land is little practiced. The agriculturist generally farms a part of his land two or three years and then abandons it until it has produced a flourishing second growth, returning only after nature has cared for the fertilization of the soil. In these conditions the colonist does not utilize, out of a tract of 30 hectares, more than 10 in pasture and cultivated fields. In addition to this he always takes care to keep as a wood lot at least one third of the land which he owns.
>
> The farming of the *"posseiro"* [squatter] is different. While the colonist prospers on a tract of 30 hectares, the posseiro requires 200. . . . He never farms two years on the same land, because after the first felling it is necessary to clear the grass and weeds four times between planting and harvest.[18]

Farming in another município of the same state, São Joaquim, a cattle-growing section bordering on the state of Rio Grande do Sul, is described as follows:

> The present farming conditions still do not merit a position of importance [in the description of the município]. Our farming processes are for the time being very primitive. It is true that many farmers and *fazendeiros* already employ the animal-drawn plow. Frankly, other agricultural machinery does not exist. On our extremely uneven lands it is still the machete followed by fire that holds undisputed sway, in a mad fury of destruction which brings deforestation. Behind comes the hoe, slow and expensive, which diminishes the margin of profit and raises the cost of production.[19]

Lying along the mainland, across from and to the north of the island on which stands Florianópolis. the state capital, and on the road to Blumenau and Joinvile, is the município of Biguassú. Here also the old routine agricultural methods hold undisputed sway. The author of the monograph on this município has only the following to say regarding agricultural processes in the section:

[17] Ministerio da Agricultura, Industria e Commercio, *Estudo dos Factores da Producção nos Municípios Brasileiros: Camaragibe, Alagôas* (Rio de Janeiro, 1924), 15. For a more recent description of fire agriculture in this general section of Brazil, see Alfonso Trujillo Ferrari, *Potengi* (São Paulo, 1960), 106–12.

[18] Victor A. Peluso, Jr., *Rio do Sul* (Florianópolis, 1942), 67.

[19] Encdino Baptista Ribeiro, *São Joaquim* (Florianópolis, 1941), 40–41.

The farming process, in almost all parts of the município, is the ancient one: that of burning.

As yet the routine has not been torn away from our people. Still, as with the first colonists, the machete and the axe fell the woods. Following this it is left to dry in order that it may be burned and soon after planted.

When, after some years the soil becomes tired, a new felling and new burning is made in another place. A rickety vegetation, the second growth, takes the place of the former opulent forests.

The worker of Biguassú does not know what fertilizer is.[20]

HOE CULTURE

Once it has been established through trial and error that clean, soft, spongy surfaces are favorable to the growth of seeds, the cultural stage has been set for man to take another basic step in the evolution of his agricultural systems. As a result men and women of many tribes throughout the world hit upon the idea of employing sharp or sharpened sticks for stirring the soil. It is entirely possible that the idea of such tillage grew out of the use of sticks in digging tubers, wild and domesticated, from the earth, but in any case the use of the digging stick is not a complicated development. In most cases merely gripping the wood with the hands was relied on, but in some societies, of which the Indians of highland Peru are an example, the sticks were selected and shaped so that the foot as well as the hand could be used in the application of human energy to the basic tasks of agriculture.

From the digging stick came the hoe, through a development that commonly is regarded as simple and almost inevitable. In this connection, though, one should reflect that apparently none of Brazil's Indians ever independently developed the hoe and that neither did they borrow it from others before the arrival of the white man. Indeed, even in the 1960's the hoe has by no means replaced the ax and fire as the principal aid to rural Brazilians in the production of the food crops upon which they depend for a livelihood. In other parts of the world, however, including Portugal, Brazil's mother country, permanent agriculture with the hoe as the basic implement early was developed, and at the time of the discovery of America much of mankind was using a system of agriculture that best is designated as hoe culture.

The hoe was the principal implement in the system of agriculture used in colonial Brazil to produce the sugar cane on which the opulence of its principal families was founded, and it has remained so to this day in most of the sugar-cane plantations which occupy favored locations on the coastal plain from the state of Rio de Janeiro to Paraíba. Likewise, it has been almost the sole instrument used in caring for the hundreds of millions of coffee trees which have flourished in the states of São Paulo, Minas Gerais, Rio de Janeiro, Espírito Santo, and Paraná during the last 150 years, and it still re-

[20] José M. Born, *Biguassú* (Florianópolis, 1941), 31.

mains as the greatest labor-saving device known to the bulk of Brazil's rural labor force. This is to say that, except in São Paulo, in the production of such commercial crops as cotton, tobacco, pineapples, grapes, and even upland rice, most of the tillage employed is done exclusively with the hoe. In addition it is the implement that most frequently is incorporated into the aboriginal systems of agriculture described above as a first step in strengthening man's hand in the contest with nature. This is especially true in the plantings along the dry beds of streams that are so prevalent throughout the Northeast, but even in the humid coastal sections many rural families are acquiring hoes to assist them, along with the ax and fire, to produce the subsistence crops on which they depend. For example, the author of a social survey of one community in the lower São Francisco Valley reports that "of all the implements used in farming by the inhabitants of the community, the principal one is the hoe, whose use is not limited to agriculture, since it is also employed for the preparation of the mud used in the construction of dwellings and also for shelling coconuts." [21]

[21] Trujillo Ferrari, *Potengi*, 110. Of the role of the hoe in colonial agriculture T. Lycurgo Santos Filho in *Uma Comunidade Rural do Brasil Antigo* (São Paulo, 1956), 308, has the following to say:

For their cultural operations—the felling of the trees and the formation of *roças*—the colonial agriculturists used the axe, billhook, and hoe, that is the agricultural implements brought to Brazil in the sixteenth century by the first settlers, whose use was soon disseminated throughout the entire country. We see in another chapter how intense was the trade of Pinheiro Pinto [master blacksmith and dealer in metal instruments] in axes, billhooks, and hoes. One does not encounter, however, in the manuscript record books of Campo Seco,

Oxen and Oxcart

PERCY LAU

In addition to the introduction of the hoe by the Portuguese for use on the sugar engenhos and its subsequent diffusion to the surrounding areas, two other highly important systems of hoe culture have played and continue to play fundamental roles in Brazil's agricultural production. One of these has flourished in the state of Rio Grande do Sul among the Italian immigrants and their descendants, who have developed the cultivation of tobacco, grapes, and other fruits to a high degree, and the other is that brought by the Japanese immigrants to São Paulo and the neighboring states where their market gardening has come to form a very significant part of Brazil's agricultural economy.

ELEMENTARY PLOW CULTURE

Even before mankind had perfected an alphabet which enabled it to keep written records, the world's agriculturists had developed and diffused widely a rudimentary plow. Probably the first plow was merely a digging stick so shaped or selected that two persons, one pushing and the other pulling, could co-operate in its use, or it may have been a similar adaptation of the hoe. At the dawn of history, though, the crude wooden plow, with a metal point and drawn by oxen, had already come to be employed extensively by agricultural peoples in Egypt, Mesopotamia, and probably other cradles of civilization.[22] This early plow, like its modern counterparts in Spain, Portugal, Spanish America, and many other parts of the world, was highly inefficient. Drawn by the lumbering ox, it merely laboriously rooted the soil instead of lightly cutting and turning it. Nevertheless the fact that animal traction was used to move the instrument was a tremendous gain, indeed a revolutionary achievement, even though several persons were required to manage the oxen and manipulate

---

any reference to the plow, another implement used during the same period in other parts of the country, including the Recôncavo of Bahia. It should be indicated, however, that this author's statements about the use of the plow in and around the Recôncavo of Bahia need to be considered with a degree of caution. Notes entered in his journal by the present writer when visiting this area in August, 1945, include the following:

Before we had been on the road long we passed through Muritiba and then descended rapidly into the valley at São Felix. Here we crossed the bridge at Cachoeira and then ascended to a comparable height on the other side of the valley. All through this area the tobacco, mandioca, beans, peanuts, and a little very poor corn are tilled by a simple hoe culture. The hoe is used to prepare the hills in which the mandioca and tobacco are planted. The former seems to receive little more attention, but the latter is kept clear of weeds. This is the most thorough and the most extensive hoe culture I have seen in Brazil. The era of fire agriculture seems to have passed long ago.

Also, with reference to the lower lands in the Recôncavo itself: "We saw some planting going on. A large plow (the only one seen all day) was being used in the process. It was built largely of wood, and turned the furrow both ways simultaneously. It was carried on a large four-wheeled wooden carriage. Along with this contraption twelve oxen and seven men were involved in the process of plowing."

[22] Cf. E. B. Tylor, "On the Origin of the Plough, and Wheel-Carriage," *Journal of the Anthropological Institute of Great Britain and Ireland*, X (1881), 74–82.

the implement. Awkward oxen, with their jerky movements, have yet to be hitched efficiently to modern turning plows, wheeled vehicles, or harvesting equipment, such as the mowing machine or the grain binder, and their use in combination with the prehistoric variety of rooting plow left even more to be desired.

Rarely, if ever, were horses hitched to the rudimentary plows of the ancient world nor to those of the Iberian Peninsula and other parts of the Roman world from which Brazil received her social and cultural heritage. Indeed, throughout the area blanketed by the Roman Empire the horse enjoyed a privileged position comparable to that of the master whose chariot he drew and with whom frequently he was buried. The thought of hitching that noble steed to a plow or cart and forcing him to participate in menial work connected with agriculture probably would have been abhorrent to the inhabitants of Spain, Portugal, and other heartland sections of the empire.[23]

When Brazil was discovered and colonized, the mother country Portugal, and Spain as well, were dependent on two systems of agriculture: hoe culture, discussed in the preceding section, and an elementary plow culture. The all important features of the latter were three: the old wooden rooting plow, the use of oxen for draft purposes, and the use of the two-wheeled ox cart. Therefore, the Portuguese settlers who took possession of Brazil's coasts were severely

[23] Cf. L. W. Ellis and Edward A. Rumely, *Power and the Plow* (New York, 1911), 25, who indicate that "as late as the tenth century, farmers in England were forbidden, by law, to harness the horse to the plow." Such a law, of course, would never have been promulgated had the old Roman mores with respect to the horse retained their vigor.

Saddle Oxen, Used in the Pantanal of Mato Grosso

limited in the cultural elements related to agriculture that they could carry to the New World. Unlike their English, French, and Dutch counterparts who settled in North America, they were unable to carry along a system of agriculture based upon such all important features as the turning plow, the four-wheeled farm wagon, the horse collar, and the use of horses and mules as draft animals.

But even the elementary plow culture, which had been developed to a high degree in Portugal, was not taken as a functioning system to Brazil. Indeed, it appears that the central trait, the actual wooden plow itself, was eliminated in the process of diffusion and that a mere hoe culture, supplemented to some extent by the use of the ox and the oxcart, was the system of agriculture transplanted to Brazil and maintained almost exclusively, alongside the river-bank plantings and the fire agriculture of the natives, until the establishment of colonies of European farmers late in the nineteenth century.

ADVANCED PLOW CULTURE

Several fundamental conditions had to be met at the same time and place before mankind could advance beyond the stage of elementary plow culture, a rudimentary system of agriculture which, as has just been indicated, was not attained in colonial Brazil. Northwestern Europe was the scene of the commencement of this process, although many of the fundamental improvements were accomplished in the parts of the United States that were dominated by a middle class agricultural society based on the family-sized farm. The first of the basic conditions depended on the use for draft purposes of an animal with a smoother gait than those of the ox and the water buffalo. The horse was, of course, admirably fitted for this role, but in order for him to be given it, his use had to spread into areas in which his function and position were not so firmly fixed by the prevailing class structure. Apparently this condition was fulfilled among the Germanic tribes of northern Europe. In any case this seems to be the section of the world in which horses early came to be used to draw agricultural implements and farm vehicles and in which breeds of horses adapted specifically for draft purposes were developed. Naturally these differed greatly from the horses used by the Romans to draw their war chariots and the Arabian varieties, famed for their speed and riding qualities, developed by the pastoral peoples of western Asia.

The perfection of hitching equipment also was another prerequisite for the development of an advanced plow culture. The old harnesses used by the Egyptians, Greeks, and Romans for the horses which drew their chariots definitely were inadequate. They all made use of the breast strap, and harnessed in that manner, any horse that threw his full weight forward in order to move the load quickly had his wind cut off. Therefore the perfection of the horse collar was of fundamental importance. Unfortunately, though, the history of the development of this basic cultural instrument has not been traced with certainty. Surely its more fundamental improvements took place in northwestern Europe, possibly in connection with the use of horses to draw sleighs and sleds. In any case, the perfection of the horse collar in this area gave the countries of northern Europe, and new countries such as Canada, the United States, Australia, New Zealand, and South Africa which received their basic cultural heritages from them, a tremendous advantage over othere parts of the world in all that has to do with the production and transportation of agricultural commodities.[24]

The invention and perfection of the turning plow is the third indispensable element in the development of any agricultural system superior to that designated above as elementary plow culture. This also took place in northwestern Europe, apparently during Roman times.[25] The attachment of two wheels to the beam did much to ease the work of the plowman. By the fifteenth century this plow had acquired a wooden moldboard, and by the time the United States became an independent nation, the plow had developed to the point in

[24] Charles Parain, "The Evolution of Agricultural Techniques," in J. H. Clapham and Eileen Power (eds.), *The Cambridge Economic History*, I (Cambridge, 1941), 134, indicates that the "stiff collar" may have come from northeast Asia between the fifth and the eighth centuries A.D.

[25] *Ibid.*, 139–41. Pliny knew the wheeled plow and located its origin in the country to the south of the Upper Danube, and Vergil, born in Cisalpine Gaul, also knew such a plow. It is to be stressed, however, that neither they nor any of the other Romans introduced the improved types in the heartland of the Empire and that at the time of Columbus the old Mediterranean *araire*, much like the old Egyptian plow, reigned supreme throughout Spain and Portugal.

Type of Wagon Introduced in South Brazil by Colonists from Poland and the Ukraine

which metal could be used for some of the parts other than the point. Thomas Jefferson was responsible for working out the mathematics of the turning plow, and John Deere in 1837 made the first steel plow from the blade of an old saw. These are only two of the important contributions that came out of a feverish half-century of effort to improve the implements with which the nation's farmers themselves worked the soil. Thereafter progress on all lines of the front were rapid, and by 1910 the stage had been set for the beginning of an epoch of mechanized farming.

Because those owning and managing Brazil's farms themselves did not participate directly in farm work and because even Portugal's elementary plow culture did not diffuse to Brazil, the process of modernizing Brazil's system of agriculture has proved to be very slow. It is true that leading Brazilian thinkers have long recognized the need for improvement in the nation's agricultural practices. For example, in the Constitutional Assembly of 1823 José Bonifacio advocated the widespread use of the plow as a way of solving the nation's labor shortage, pointing out even then that one slave with a plow could do the work of twenty equipped only with hoes.[26] But Brazil's rural people continued in their customary ways, so that a century later the problem and the solution, as described by Bulhões Carvalho, were much the same: "The substitution of present cultural practices by agricultural implements is an essential improvement in a country such as Brazil, where the scarcity of labor constantly becomes more pressing. Only mechanical agriculture, aided by intelligent methods of cultivation, can transform our farming and place it in condition to satisfy the necessities of the nation." [27]

The introduction and diffusion of advanced plow culture in Brazil is due largely to the establishment of colonies of German, Polish, and Italian farmers in southern Brazil during the nineteenth century. To them for the most part Brazil is indebted for such progress as she has made in the use of the turning plow, the four-wheeled farm wagon, and the use of horses as draft animals. Even so, however, the process has been and remains a very slow one, and throughout the bulk of her territory the rural folk still must be taught any agricultural systems that are more efficient than their traditional fire agriculture and hoe culture. Indeed, the situation remains such that there is much point to the observations and recommendations made by North Americans and Europeans during the last century. Fortunately there are many of these, of which the best were made in the years immediately following the Civil War in the United States, at a time when Brazil was receiving careful consideration as a home for those Southerners who desired to emigrate. The representatives of the groups desiring to resettle themselves sent their agents to Brazil to study the country and to seek out the best sites for locations. The

[26] His remarks are quoted in "Agricultura," *Recenseamento do Brazil, 1920,* III, Tomo 3 (Rio de Janeiro, 1927), xv. See also *José Bonifacio* (Pôrto Alegre, 1922).

[27] "Agricultura," *loc. cit.,* v.

descriptions given by these representatives are among the most detailed of the early reports. For example, in November, 1865, the Reverend Ballard S. Dunn, formerly a New Orleans pastor, traveled through parts of Espírito Santo and Rio de Janeiro in search of lands for himself and his Southern friends. During this journey he visited the sugar estate of Colonel João Gomez near Itapemerim in southern Espírito Santo. Although Dunn usually saw the bright side of the picture, possibly from pecuniary motives, in his report to the Brazilian Minister of Agriculture he wrote: "This planter uses no other implement than the broad hoe. As I walked over these favorably situated lands, the thought kept pressing itself upon me, if they produce *such* cane under *such a system,* what would they yield under all the appliances of improved culture?" [28]

Such thoughts also come to the minds of twentieth-century visitors, especially after they become familiar with the Brazilian cultural landscape. Undoubtedly, similar reflections weighed heavily upon R. M. Davis, M.D., who wrote one of the testimonial letters used by Dunn in his appeal to prospective Southern emigrants.

All the productions of the Southern States may be raised here, in as great abundance, with less labor, than in the Southern States at any former period of their history. Corn may be raised in full as great quantity (per acre), and with less labor, and *were the same mode of cultivation*

[28] Dunn, *Brazil,* 107.

Floating Stable for Cows and Floating Island in the State of Amazonas. (Courtesy of Hilgard O'Reilly Sternberg.)

used, I believe that it would be greater than any of the Southern corn-growing regions. Rice grows here most luxuriantly in every portion of this Province, and yields abundant harvests, *even under the rude culture which it receives. With proper cultivation and suitable seed,* the crop would surpass any of the Southern States.

. . . . . .

Tobacco may be raised profitably in all parts of the Province, to compete favorably with any tobacco-growing country. In fact, I do not believe that this plant could be raised in the United States, *if it received no better cultivation than here.*

. . . . . .

I have traveled through different portions of the Province of San Paulo, and have seen all of these crops growing and matured, and have no hesitation in saying, that I do not believe that the United States can compete with this Province in cheapness and quantity, per acre, in any of the articles which I have mentioned, and when our people shall come and settle here, and *use their modes of cultivation,* there is no country that can yield them greater remuneration for their labor.[29]

They come out even more strongly when Dunn comments on sugar and cotton, the predilections of the Southerners, in contrast to coffee, the favorite of the Brazilians in Espírito Santo.

The Dr. [Antonio Olinto Pinto Coelho da Cunha] seemed much amused at our fondness for sugar and cotton culture, and remarked: "A short residence in the country will cause you to transfer your affections to the great staple of Brazil." It is his decided opinion, that the culture of coffee is the most remunerative channel into which labor can be turned. In this I would be obliged to agree with him, if the *mode* of culture is to remain the same. That is, the mountain side shall continue to be scraped by no other implement than the broad hoe; while the level plains lie idle, or are only used as grazing grounds for the surplus stock of the plantation. But let these level lands be torn up by the fertilizing plow; let the numerous old logs and stumps that cumber the ground be removed, so that not a stalk nor a plant shall be missing, and these money yielding mountains will soon find competitors, in all that is useful, in the unpretending plains that now lie, unnoticed and uncared for, at their feet.[30]

Finally, at the end of his journey and during his visit in Campos, Dunn observed the first plow he had seen in Brazil. "While in Campos, we visited the fine sugar estate of Commendador Julião Ribeiro Castéo, a very public spirited gentleman, one mile from the city. This plantation is finely situated, and the most advanced in the mode of culture that I have seen while on this tour. It was here that we met with the first plow. His sugar house, distillery, &c., are very creditable to the establishment." [31] Later in southeastern São Paulo he saw another plow, but his comments indicate that he thought it unlikely to make the favorable impression necessary for promoting its use throughout Brazil: "It was here that I saw a great curiosity in the way of a plow. It is very large, very clumsy, and as nearly as I can judge, after the pattern in use in Europe two centuries ago. This

---

[29] *Ibid.,* 73–74. The italics are not in the original.
[30] *Ibid.,* 113–14.
[31] *Ibid.,* 128. In 1943, also, the sugar plantations about Campos were distinguished by their modern methods of cultivation.

plow has a cast plate nailed to the beam, marked, 'Paris.' I should be sorry to have Brazilians judge the utility of plows, by a trial of this one." [32]

It was in the same part of São Paulo that Dunn observed and described in detail the culture of cotton.

I am sorry to be obliged to note almost a fatal mistake in the planting and management of this cotton. In North America it would prove entirely fatal. First of all, the ground is new. Having been cleared, or rather chopped and burnt off, just previous to planting. No plow has yet been used, either in preparing the soil or cultivating the cotton. But the slaves have taken the cotton seed, just as the North American Indians take corn, and after opening a small orifice in the virgin soil, placed the seed carefully in, and then raked a little soil upon it. When the young plants were up, and the weeds began to grow, they went in with broad hoes, and, scraping *from* the plant, cleared away the weeds. Here the culture ended: so that the cotton stands in the middle of a considerable *depression*, instead of upon an elevation of eight or ten inches above the general level, as its health and maturity require.[33]

Other Americans, Major Robert Merriwether and Dr. H. A. Shaw, who were looking over these lands at the same time and whose reports on São Paulo are included in Dunn's book, described the practice of fire agriculture as follows:

[32] *Ibid.,* 137.
[33] *Ibid.,* 138–39.

The Type of Boat which Plies the Waters of the São Francisco River above Joázeiro. (Photo by the Author.)

The timber is cut down, allowed to lie and dry for two months, commonly, then set on fire. All the timber not consumed by the fire, remains just as the fire left it, till it rots. Then usually with a stick—sharpened at the end, sometimes with a hoe—a hole is made in the ground, the seed, from five to ten grains, put into this hole and covered with the foot, and this is all the cultivation the crops receive.[34]

That the Americans were thoroughly convinced of the superiority of their own farming practices is indicated in a quotation from Dr. J. McF. Gaston of Columbia, South Carolina, who was looking for a home in Brazil in 1865. "The farmer of the United States is needed here to learn the fazundeiro of Brazil the proper use of the plough, and should any considerable number remove to this country, they will effect quite a revolution in agriculture in a few years." [35] That they sought to impress upon the Brazilians the superiority of their methods of agriculture is apparent in one of the reports (that of Frank M. Mullen and William Bowen) submitted to the Minister of Agriculture. "If the state of agriculture among us is at present backward and antiquated, our people are willing and desirous to improve. They say if the improved mode of culture used by the Americans beats theirs, they too will plow their land, and fell their timber with Collins' axes. 'If you prove to us that the valley lands will produce more than the mountain sides, we too will come down and reap the more abundant harvest.' " [36] Judging by the state of Brazilian agricultural practices in 1963, the experiment was not conclusive. This makes it seem probable that the Englishman John Mawe was overoptimistic as

[34] *Ibid.*, 232.

[35] Gaston, *Hunting a Home in Brazil*, 87. Confronted with Brazilian laws forbidding the immigration of Negroes unless they were free born, the doctor wrote: "The negro from the Southern States could give negroes here a practical illustration in the use of the plow, which would be worth more to Brazil than all the treatises on agriculture which are likely to be written for twenty years." *Ibid.*, 227.

[36] Dunn, *Brazil*, 179. A half century earlier on his estate, Mandiocca, near Rio de Janeiro, the Prussian consul general, Langsdorff, had attempted to introduce the plow. An account of the experiment is given by von Spix and von Martius: "During our stay at Mandiocca, our kind host was visited by his neighbours, who regarded with surprise, and not without jealousy, the rapid progress of his establishment. As the first attempt to turn up, with a European plough, the spots which had been cleared by burning the wood, had failed, through the awkwardness of the negroes and for want of oxen trained to work, this gave them sufficient ground to prove the unfitness of European agriculture on the Brazilian soil. Many had not yet seen a plough; some would not allow the justice of the observation, that the soil gained in fertility by being loosened, and by the chemical influence of the atmosphere, because the virgin forests, the surface of which had been the same for thousands of years, afforded the most fertile land; others doubted whether the oxen, which Mr. Von Langsdorff had procured from Minas, possessed strength to bear, even for a few days, the hard labour of ploughing; some again lamented the loss of time of the negroes that must be employed. In truth the use of the plough in these and the more northern districts which cultivate no corn, and have not yet lost their original fertility, appears less to be recommended than in the capitanias of S. Paulo, and Rio Grande do Sul. As the productions of the earth chiefly cultivated here are not sown but planted, and on that account do not require the surface of the ground to be so uniformly prepared, the negro works with the hoe much more effectually and easily than it would be possible for him to do with the plough, the use of which is besides rendered more difficult by the many roots, and the unburnt trunks remaining in the plantations." *Travels in Brazil*, I, 255–56.

to the ease of making social changes when, nearly a century and a half ago, he wrote of experiences in the year 1809:

Being now within the province of Minas Geraes, (a country famed at Rio de Janeiro for its excellent cheese), I expected to see some improvement in the condition of the country—some establishment worthy of being called a farm—some dwelling, constructed not merely for shelter, but for comfort. I hoped to remark among the inhabitants that air of health and animation, which springs from the invigorating occupations, and cheering pursuits of husbandry; but no such pleasing change was perceptible; the same want of exertion prevailed here as in other parts of the country: the people seemed to act as if the tenure by which they held their lands was about to be abolished; all around them had the appearance of *make-shift:* their old houses, fast hastening to decay, bore no marks of repair about them: wherever a bit of garden-ground was inclosed, it appeared over-run with weeds; where coffee-trees, planted in former years, still existed, the present occupiers were too indolent to gather the fruit: no inclosures were made for pasturage; a few goats supplied the little milk that was consumed; and cow's milk was rarely to be procured. On observing these deplorable consequences of the apathy of the inhabitants, I could not but reflect on the advantages which might accrue, from the introduction of the English system of agriculture among them. The example of a single farm, conducted on that system might go far towards rousing the people from their slothful state; and, when they once felt their faculties awakened, they would be ashamed to lounge about as they now do, under an old great coat, for days together, burthens to themselves, and objects of contempt to all strangers who see them.[37]

[37] Mawe, *Travels in the Interior of Brazil*, 159–60. The same writer described the fire agriculture practiced then and now throughout much of this immense state in the following words: "The prevailing method of clearing, and cultivating the land here, is precisely similar to that practiced in the neighborhood of St.

Mule Train Transporting Corn and Beans

Upper. Milk Is Assembled at This Point near Taubaté and then Trucked to São Paulo. *Lower.* Charcoal Is Transported on Pack Animals to This Point near Taubaté and then Trucked to São Paulo.

Much more detailed information concerning Brazil's system of agriculture during our Civil War decade is contained in the following extract from the official report which Dr. Gaston made to the Minister of Agriculture.

The culture of the land in all parts visited is performed with the hoe exclusively, and though improvements of various kinds are observed in

Paul's. After the timber and underwood have been cut down and burnt, (often very imperfectly), the woman negroes dibble the seed; in about six weeks a slight weeding is performed, and then the ground is let alone till harvest. The seedtime begins in October, and lasts to November; the maize is ripe in four or five months. The next year they commonly sow beans on the corn land, which they then let lie, and proceed to clear new ground. It is not common to molest the land from which they have had two crops in succession, before eight or ten years have elapsed." *Ibid.,* 141.

the mechanical department, there seems to be very little disposition to resort to the plow as a more thorough and efficient process of cultivation.

Though a good yield is secured without it, we may calculate that it would be increased at least one half more by the proper use of this important implement of the planter in the United States. Throughout this wealthy province I saw but three persons who used the plow at all and it was limited in their cases to a very narrow sphere, being employed simply to prepare the ground for planting and not used subsequently for the treatment of the growing plant. Could anything I may say induce the adoption of plow-culture for the cotton that is now engaging so much of the attention of planters of this Province, it would serve to enhance greatly the value of this crop, and at the same time lessen the actual amount of labor by those working the lands.

Where the ground is laid out in right lines by the plow, preparatory to planting, it simplifies very much the labor of planting, and the ground being deeply and thoroughly loosened up, gives the young plant a better prospect for taking root in the earth.

I observe but few persons who realize the importance of stirring the soil as a means of promoting the growth of what may be planted, and in most instances cotton and corn are allowed to grow in close juxtaposition as materially to interfere with the supply of nutriment from the soil, and the action of the atmosphere as an invigorating agent.[38]

The state of Brazilian agricultural practices in 1866 is brought out also by this warning to the Americans emigrating to Brazil:

[38] Dunn, *Brazil*, 187–89. (Gaston does not include the report in his own volume.) J. J. Aubertin, Superintendent of the São Paulo Railway Company, who accompanied Gaston, Shaw, and Merriwether through parts of São Paulo, wrote the Baron of Piracicaba: "Your Excellency knows that in all the Province perhaps not a score of men ever saw the plough." J. J. Aubertin, *Eleven Days' Journey in the Province of São Paulo* (London, 1868), 6.

Threshing Beans, Redenção, São Paulo

The Government allows all immigrants to introduce, for their own use, free of duty, all articles of prime necessity, such as tools of all kinds, wagons, gear, machinery, furniture, &c. This should not be forgotten by the emigrant, for in the interior you will find only the hoe, ax, billhook, and bullock cart, and they, except the hoe, of the rudest manufacture. Plows can be had only in the larger towns, and none have been seen by us that are suitable for the ordinary cultivation of the products of this country.[39]

John Codman, an American steamship captain, who in 1866 carried many of the emigrating Southerners from Rio de Janeiro to Cananéia on the coast of São Paulo and back, prophesied that their presence would affect the country.

A number of American immigrants have settled in Campinas, where they have already commenced the cultivation of cotton. More have gone farther south, upon the Iguape and Ribeira Rivers, having there, as a company, purchased a large tract of land, which they intend to plant with sugar-cane. Be these immigrants few or many, their presence will have some influence in developing the resources of the country. They will introduce machinery, and will bring their experience, which is a mighty power as opposed to the old, inherited customs of this slowest of slow nations.[40]

But the considered opinion of John Luccock, an Englishman who knew the country well, was that all attempts to introduce the "English plough" were unavailing. ". . . I have held it myself, and learned from my own brief experience, how utterly impossible it is to teach a black man to manage it; and the Brazilians are almost as dull, and fully as much prejudiced. Should Providence again open to me an opportunity of superintending rural affairs in this country, I would certainly commence with boys." [41]

Such is some of the background. Next let us consider recent statistical data concerning the number and distribution of plows in Brazil. For the years 1920, 1940, and 1950 detailed information is available. In preparing the first edition of this book the present writer hesitated to use the materials for 1920, which were the latest then obtainable, for the reason that they were much out of date and showed a total of only 141,196 plows in all of Brazil. According to the 1920 census only 15 per cent of Brazil's farms possessed that all important implement of tillage. Furthermore, more than one-half of all the plows in the nation, a total of 73,403, were in the single state of Rio Grande do Sul, a section which had received this and other cultural influences from the Old World as the result of a considerable immigration of Germans and other settlers from northwestern Europe. In only five states—Rio Grande do Sul, Santa Catarina, Paraná, São Paulo, and Minas Gerais—was as many as one farm out of ten equipped with a plow. Throughout most of the vast territory of the nation the plow was virtually unknown. To such a great extent were

[39] Dunn, *Brazil*, 239.
[40] Codman, *Ten Months in Brazil*, 131.
[41] Luccock, *Notes on Rio de Janeiro, and the Southern Parts of Brazil*, 297.

Brazil's cultivators dependent on fire agriculture, or at best on hoe culture, for extracting a living from the soil that there was in 1920 an average of forty-four persons engaged in farming pursuits for every plow in the nation.

TABLE L

Distribution of the Plow in 1940 and 1950, by States *

State	Number of plows		Number of persons engaged in agriculture per plow		Percentage of farms with plows
	1940	1950	1940	1950	1950
Brazil †	500,853	714,259	23	15	23.4
North					
Guaporé ‡	§	11	§	425	1.3
Acre ‡	6	33	3,930	482	0.6
Amazonas	36	73	2,386	1,106	0.1
Rio Branco ‡	‖	31	‖	79	5.8
Pará	85	219	2,671	1,004	0.1
Amapá ‡	#	14	#	199	1.1
Northeast					
Maranhão	71	180	4,756	2,048	0.7
Piauí	132	499	1,798	413	1.1
Ceará	725	821	861	608	0.5
Rio Grande do Norte	571	414	401	567	0.8
Paraíba	496	532	950	816	0.4
Pernambuco	3,213	3,902	201	225	1.0
Alagôas	1,007	2,683	228	102	3.9
East					
Sergipe	569	811	220	191	1.1
Bahia	1,645	4,647	706	276	1.3
Minas Gerais	49,373	73,970	34	25	20.9
Espírito Santo	708	1,668	316	174	3.2
Rio de Janeiro	8,248	12,020	48	23	19.2
Distrito Federal	245	258	70	64	4.1
South					
São Paulo	168,073	224,947	10	9	52.7
Paraná	20,498	30,405	11	17	29.9
Santa Catarina	21,431	41,029	14	9	32.9
Rio Grande do Sul	222,657	312,001	4	3	78.9
West Central					
Mato Grosso	719	1,118	105	77	5.2
Goiás	345	1,973	712	152	2.6

* Compiled and computed from data in "Censo Agrícola," VI *Recenseamento Geral do Brasil, 1950,* II (Rio de Janeiro, 1956), 40–42, 46, 126–27.
† The total for Brazil includes the data for the Serra dos Aimorés, territory in dispute between Minas Gerais and Espírito Santo.
‡ Territory.
§ Included in figure for Mato Grosso.
‖ Included in figure for Amazonas.
Included in figure for Pará.

TABLE LI

Number of Oxcarts, Other Animal-drawn Vehicles, and Motor Trucks and Runabouts on Brazilian Farms in 1950, by States *

State	Oxcarts		Other animal-drawn vehicles		Motor trucks and runabouts	
	Number	Number per 100 farms	Number	Number per 100 farms	Number	Number per 100 farms
Brazil	307,290	14.9	404,367	19.6	24,649	1.2
North						
Guaporé †	29	5.5	5	0.9	18	3.4
Acre †	92	5.4	16	0.9	8	0.5
Amazonas	17	1.1	34	0.2	10	0.7
Rio Branco †	370	83.1	13	2.9	7	1.6
Pará	1,057	1.8	320	0.5	73	0.1
Amapá †	5	1.1	4	0.9	6	1.3
Northeast						
Maranhão	3,124	3.3	123	0.1	39	0.1
Piauí	2,201	6.5	114	0.3	47	0.1
Ceará	2,584	3.0	635	7.3	202	0.2
Rio Grande do Norte	1,263	3.7	631	1.8	106	0.3
Paraíba	3,903	5.6	1,565	2.3	253	0.4
Pernambuco	11,805	6.9	2,040	11.8	353	0.2
Alagôas	4,608	8.9	360	0.7	148	0.3
East						
Sergipe	4,408	10.3	1,400	3.3	60	0.1
Bahia	28,560	11.1	796	0.3	320	0.1
Minas Gerais	84,677	31.9	16,972	6.4	3,280	1.2
Espírito Santo	2,699	6.1	403	0.9	383	0.9
Rio de Janeiro	10,641	26.2	4,718	14.1	1,114	2.7
Distrito Federal	115	2.2	650	12.3	158	3.0
South						
São Paulo	16,307	7.4	131,388	59.3	9,292	4.2
Paraná	1,633	1.8	46,435	51.9	2,259	2.5
Santa Catarina	30,495	29.2	36,486	34.9	700	0.7
Rio Grande do Sul	73,942	25.8	152,944	53.3	4,829	1.7
West Central						
Mato Grosso	5,537	34.6	4,210	26.3	519	0.3
Goiás	17,218	27.0	2,105	3.3	465	0.7

* Compiled and computed from data in "Censo Agrícola," VI Recenseamento Geral do Brasil, 1950, II (Rio de Janeiro, 1956), 43.

† Territory.

By 1940 the number of plows enumerated by the census had risen to 500,853. This was one plow for every twenty-three persons employed in agricultural activities. Almost one-fourth, or 23 per cent, of the nation's farms were equipped with a plow. In Rio Grande do Sul 80.6 per cent of all the farms possessed these implements of tillage (compared with only 40.8 per cent in 1920), and the increases were also marked in several other states, from 15.6 to 47.5 per cent in São Paulo, 16.7 to 32.3 per cent in Paraná, and from 16.5 to 26.5 per cent in Santa Catarina. Minas Gerais, too, was characterized by a somewhat greater diffusion of the plow during the twenty-year period, with the number increasing from 17,513 in 1920 to 49,373 in 1940, or with the percentage of farms with plows mounting from 10.2 to 14.3 during the decade. In addition, the states of Mato Grosso, Rio de Janeiro, Sergipe, and Rio Grande do Norte all moved up into the category of those in which at least one farm in ten was equipped with a plow.

During the decade ending in 1950 the number of plows used by Brazil's farmers continued to increase, so that a total of 714,219 was reported by the 1950 census of agriculture. Of these, 54,576 were of the disk variety. This increase was considerably more rapid than that of the labor force engaged in agricultural pursuits, and as a result the number of workers per plow dropped from twenty-three in 1940 to fifteen in 1950 (See Table L). However, the increase in plows was very little faster than that in the number of farms, and even at mid-century more than three-fourths of Brazil's farms were lacking the most important agricultural implement that the ingenuity of man has devised. Along with Rio Grande do Sul, São Paulo continued to be the state in which the plow was in most general use, despite the reliance on hoe culture in the production of coffee, and it is rapidly developing into a state in which advanced plow culture is the prevailing system of agriculture. The plow also has been making its way into Minas Gerais in recent decades, but it still is largely unused in Bahia and all of the states to the north of it. The extreme case is Maranhão where even as late as 1950 there were more than two thousand agricultural workers for every plow in the state. However, ten years earlier the corresponding ratio was 4,756 to 1.

The lack of the plow is accompanied by a scarcity of other essential labor-saving implements and vehicles on the large majority of Brazilian farms. Particularly acute is the lack of the wheel. Even the rude oxcart is rare in most sections of the country, and the four-wheeled farm wagon is found mostly in the four southern states into which it was introduced by immigrant farmers from Germany and Poland. (See Table LI.)

MECHANIZED FARMING

The light, strong, well-balanced, and comparatively large implements characteristic of mechanized farming are unknown throughout most of Brazil. Furthermore, until Brazil's own plants for manufacturing tractors and the complementary implements are greatly expanded, and especially until the nation's production of petroleum and other fuels is greatly increased, it would be folly for her to proceed very far in the mechanization of agriculture. In this connection it is interesting to note that recent agricultural immigrants, such as those in the Dutch colony of Holambra in São Paulo, have found it advisable to rely on horse-drawn equipment for the majority of farm tasks, although they did employ tractors in breaking the ground, removing the stumps, and terracing the fields.[42]

Data from Brazil's census of agriculture indicate clearly that mechanized farming is merely in its beginning stages throughout the agricultural sections of the country's vast territory. Thus, in 1920 the total number of tractors reported on farms was only 1,706, and in 1940, only 3,380. Even in 1950 on all of Brazil's 2,064,642 rural establishments there were only 8,372 tractors. Furthermore, the bulk of the farm tractors reported in 1950 was confined to the states of São Paulo (with 3,819) and Rio Grande do Sul (with 2,245). Minas Gerais, third ranking state in this respect, had only 763 in all of her vast territory, and the state of Rio de Janeiro, next in line, only 457. In all of Pernambuco, with its many sugar-cane plantations, the 1950 census of agriculture accounted for only 142 tractors, and in Bahia there were only 82. It should be noted, however, that since 1950 the development of plants for manufacturing agricultural machines, jeeps, and motor trucks has been rapid and also that the national production of petroleum has been increasing substantially. Perhaps within the next decade or two accomplishments in this aspect of the national economy will permit the development of mechanized farming on a considerable scale.

[42] It is interesting to note that this work has been done on land that long had been devoted to the growing of coffee plants.

CHAPTER XVI

COLONIZATION AND SETTLEMENT

FUTURE HISTORIANS may well decide that the establishment of a class of small farmers in parts of the Brazilian territory was the most important development in the New World during the last half of the nineteenth century. That it was an extremely important development even now is not subject to question. This chapter on colonization and settlement is an attempt to give some of the more salient features of this important series of undertakings. More details will be found in the other chapters in this section devoted to the relations of people to the land.

A few words are necessary concerning the specific connotations of "colonization" and "settlement" as these expressions are used in this chapter. They do not have the meanings usually attached to them in English writings but are intended to denote the more specific concepts prevailing in Portuguese and Spanish America. Thus "colonization" as used here refers not to the establishment of the original settlers in Brazil but to the activity programs or projects by which governmental and private agencies are subdividing large properties; placing families on the farm plots so created; and extending aid, assistance, and supervision in an attempt to establish communities of small farmers on the land. "Settlement" has a similar but broader application. It includes the more independent or spontaneous developments by which the small-farming classes acquire control of the land, the density of population is increased, and large tracts of unused or slightly used lands—the latifundia of the Brazilians—become the seats of numerous firmly established neighborhoods and communities. Together the terms "colonization" and "settlement," used with reference to twentieth-century Brazil, include all the processes by which a class of small farmers is securing possession of the land.

The mounting importance of the small-farming class of population in Brazil can hardly be overemphasized. However difficult it may be, because of the unavailability of the statistical data that one might desire, to measure the progress by which the agricultural civilization based on small farms is pushing forward and submerging the old latifundia and their thinly spread cattle culture, there can be little doubt as to the lasting importance of the movement. The population changes in south Brazil are evidences of what is happening, a trend that may be verified by passing through the interior portions of the country and talking with the inhabitants. From nuclei on the east-central part of the plateau of Paraná, in the valleys of the Itajaí and Tubarão valleys in Santa Catarina, and in the hills that lie to the north of Pôrto Alegre in Rio Grande do Sul, the swarming process is rapidly spreading the small-farming system. Liberalization of the land laws and other factors are having a similar effect in western São Paulo. Northern Paraná is the seat of a remarkable colonization enterprise being carried on by a private company. Along the railroads, too, through all of the states mentioned, and in Mato Grosso, Espírito Santo, and Minas Gerais, significant developments have taken place. Many old-style large estates have been cut to the small-farm pattern. Some of these efforts are the colonization projects of state and federal agencies, others are those of private individuals, but even some of the railroads are attempting to get additional business by subdividing fazendas for sale to small owners. Around the cities, too, the development of the small-farming class is taking place at a rate that would probably have seemed impossible to those who visited Brazil one hundred years ago.

The significance of this development is not to be measured solely in terms of the greatly increased production of foodstuffs and raw materials and the substitution of diversified agriculture for monoculture that it brings about. These are all tremendously important, but probably even more so is the rapidity with which a middle class is being created in Brazilian society. The children from these farm families are leading the industrialization that is progressing on a small scale through the small towns and cities of south Brazil and on a considerable scale in cities like São Paulo and Pôrto Alegre. They have already become a force in business and in government, both state and national. Although the building of a middle class stems largely from the establishment of small-farm society in Brazil, it has already resulted in profound changes in the class structure of even the largest cities.

One of the most significant effects in this more widespread distribution of landownership and control has been a rise in the general level and standard of living in the areas affected by the innovations. A glance at trends in production figures for the various regions in Brazil shows that during the last three decades a static and even decadent situation in much of the north has been accompanied by tremendous expansion along nearly all lines in the south. But this is only one aspect. Educational progress and the determination to build a better Brazil also find their bulwarks in the southern area.

One might multiply the details, but it would all add up to the fact that the development of a class of small farmers, with the consequent rise in the proportion and strength of the middle classes in south Brazil, is one of the more significant forces now pushing Brazil to the front among the nations of the Western Hemisphere. It should be called to mind, however, that the recent political and governmental changes in Brazil have come from the south. Furthermore, these developments represent a change in kind; they are not merely revolutions that substitute one clique of rulers for another of the same type. Municípios are no longer little worlds apart, independent in the ordering of their affairs; the states are no longer feeble confederations of these smaller units; nor does the nation remain an extremely loose union of states similar to our own country under the Articles of Confederation.

By degrees the influence of the central government is making its way into the most remote parts of the national territory. The nation and the states are concerning themselves with the welfare of Brazil's people, even those in the most remote parts of the country. Under the empire, great movements, such as abolition, spread from the north to the south. Since the development of powerful small-farming classes in the south, the tendency is for the important social reforms to move in the opposite direction. One may now meet in interior cities and towns in such states as Piauí or Ceará functionaries sent out by the central government to establish health centers, to assist in the development of safeguards for supplies of drinking water, to help initiate other sanitary measures. He may meet in Goiás or Mato Grosso federal inspectors eying school buildings and curricula in cool appraisal. Since Lampeão was killed in 1938, no new bandit chief powerful enough to defy state and federal law enforcement agencies has arisen. The law is no longer absent from the sertão. And in the Amazon one may see a far-reaching program to bring under control and to the service of man, through the safeguarding of life and health in the region, the unused resources of the great area. Never should it be forgotten, as one reflects on such significant changes, that the moving force, or at least one of the more important of a combination of forces, has been the expansion of small-farming settlements in the south.

Many are the forces that have been in operation, and varied are the ways in which a small-farming class and settlements of small farmers have been developing in Brazil. The more important of these may be summarized under six headings: (1) attempts to establish the aborigines in small-farming communities, (2) colonization, in the sense of establishing planned settlements, (3) the legal restriction of amounts of public lands that might be sold to one person, (4) subdivision of land by inheritance, (5) grants to ex-soldiers of limited tracts of land, and (6) a miscellaneous setup of circumstances and developments that perhaps can best be described as "spontaneous."

CHRISTIANIZING THE INDIANS

From early times attempts to Christianize the Indians by gathering them together into small communities, teaching them more about agricultural processes, and attempting to instill settled habits of living have gone on in Brazil. Perhaps this type of work never attained the significance it did in some of the Spanish-American colonies, notably Paraguay, but it has been of considerable importance. In treating this aspect of the subject it is necessary to go back beyond the nineteenth century, for most of the energetic attempts were made earlier. However, the work with the Indians has been a continuous one and is still going on today. Its story is one of the most interesting in Brazilian history.

In the early days this work with the Indians was undertaken chiefly by the Jesuits. As early as 1570 these clerics had succeeded in obtaining a decree from the Lisbon government prohibiting the enslavement of any Indians except those taken as prisoners of war. This act was generally disregarded for a long time. A few years after it was issued, a considerable part of the settlements in Brazil came under the control of the Dutch. Shortly after the expulsion of the Hollanders in 1661, the attack upon Indian slavery was renewed and with rather marked success. According to João Cardoso de Menezes e Souza, about this time "200,000 Indians who lived in the territory occupied by the planters were established in villages and placed under the direction of the Jesuits." [1]

Robert Southey gives many of the details of this variety of colonization. He cites a second law decreed in 1587 which provided that the Indians who worked for the Portuguese were to be regarded as free laborers and not as slaves, another of 1605 which stated that no Indians should be held as slaves except those taken in hostilities that had been ordered by the king, and one of 1609 which provided that Indians should in no case be held as slaves. The latter was modified two years later to allow for enslavement of captives, after the details had been approved in Lisbon.

This law provided also for the freedom of the reduced Indians: In every one of their villages there was to be placed as Captain for three years, a person of good substance and good extraction, especial care being taken that there should be no Jewish blood in his family. He was authorized to go into the interior, and persuade the natives to return with him, and to live under the protection of the laws: in these expeditions he was instructed to take with him a Jesuit, if there were one who would accompany him, and in default of a Jesuit, a religioner of any other Order, provided he spoke the Tupi tongue. The Indians thus reclaimed were to be settled in villages, consisting of about three hundred houses, at such distance from any *Engenhos*, and woods of the Brazil-tree, that there might be no danger of their injuring them. Lands were to be allotted for their use, and a church built in every village, which should be given to a secular priest conversant in their tongue; if none such were to be found, a Jesuit was then to be preferred, and if there were no subject of the Company, then a regular priest of any other Order might be appointed.[2]

This same author gives an extensive biography of the Jesuit, Vieira, champion of the Indian's cause in Brazil, describes the process of enslaving the Indians in the middle of the seventeenth century, and then sets forth the situation of the Indians who resided in the villages that had been established, as it was in 1653.

[1] Cardoso de Menezes e Souza, *Theses sobre Colonização no Brazil,* 135.
[2] Southey, *History of Brazil,* II, 454.

But in this general system of wickedness, none were more wickedly treated than those who had submitted to the Portugueze, and living apart in villages of their own, were called free Indians, and as such contemplated by the law. These people were in a more cruel state of servitude than those who were actually slaves; the Governor or Capitam Mor for the time being, regarding them as cattle in whose preservation he had no interest, and by whose labour he was to enrich himself as much as possible during the three years for which he held this office. They were chiefly employed in raising and preparing tobacco, which was accounted the severest labour in Brazil: and many resenting the injustice of their treatment more keenly than those who having been originally taken in war, whether justly or unjustly, resigned themselves to its consequences, died of grief and indignation. The men thus employed, were left no time to raise produce for their families, who were left to starve, . . . and the women also taken from their husbands and children, and distributed among such Portugueze as had interest to obtain them from the Governor. Some ruffian of half or whole blood, was placed in the villages of these Indians as Capitam, to be the instrument of this oppression, and oppress the miserable inhabitants himself, . . . and thus the work of depopulation went on. This state was so much worse than actual slavery, that some Indians voluntarily went from their villages to live with the domestic slaves, marry among them, and share their condition, thinking it better to become slaves where some rest was allowed, and some humanity experienced, than to endure this inhuman and unremitting tyranny.[3]

It was against these abuses that Vieira launched himself, first in sermons so powerful that they even had temporary effect on the oppressors, and second by going secretly to Portugal and laying the case before his friend John IV. In 1655 he obtained a decree that placed all the Indian settlements in Maranhão under the Jesuits, made him director of all expeditions to the interior, and authorized him to settle the Indians in the places he judged best.[4] Armed with this decree, he returned to Brazil and again took up the fight which ultimately gave him, and his order, control over the Indian settlements throughout the northern and eastern parts of the Portuguese colonies. However, the struggle to protect these charges was unceasing. There was constant conflict with the planters, a struggle destined to close only when the Jesuit order was expelled from Portuguese America. However, by the time of Vieira's death (1696) according to Southey:

The laws had now done much in favour of the Indians; and more perhaps had been effected in behalf of this long injured people, by introducing in greater number a hardier, and if possible a more injured race, from Africa. Throughout all the old Captaincies, with the single exception of S. Paulo, an Indian was declared free if he demanded his freedom, even though he might have served from his cradle, and his parents before him, provided there was no woolliness in his hair, to indicate a mixture of Negro blood.[5]

Southey also describes the condition of the Jesuit villages in Maranhão and Pará in the middle of the eighteenth century. At that time registers were kept, and all Indians between thirteen and fifty who were capable of service were allotted to the Portuguese settlers for

[3] *Ibid.*, 471–72.
[4] *Ibid.*, 496.
[5] *Ibid.*, III, 33.

six months' service each year. During the other half year they were free to do as they pleased. At the proper time the chief person of the Indian village went with the other Indians to determine which of the village lands should be used that season. That selected was then apportioned among the families in proportion to the number of members in each, but "the Missionaries had great difficulty in inducing them to cultivate their portions, and were sometimes obliged to use compulsory means. When the produce was gathered in, the master of every family was compelled to reserve an ample allowance for the whole household." Indians who had just been brought to the villages were allowed two years for instruction and for preparing their fields, before becoming subject to the compulsory half year of work. The law also allowed the Indians to stipulate that they never "at any time be required to perform personal service, . . . if it was not found possible to persuade them to settle in the *Aldeas* upon any other terms." No Portuguese were permitted to live in the villages or to go there for the purpose of hiring the Indians without special written permission from the governor. However, it was specified that the inhabitants of the surrounding farms were to attend Mass in the villages.[6]

Then came Pombal and his suppression of the Jesuit order. Theoretically the plan seems to have been that the natives were to be immediately incorporated into the Portuguese community. The Indians were declared free; the Jesuits were deprived of their temporal power; the *aldeias* were ordered converted into towns and hamlets; and an elaborate code for governing the conduct of the Indians was promulgated. Among other things it was stipulated that the lands adjacent to the former villages were to be divided among the Indians as their property and that of their heirs.[7] Finally, in 1759 all the Jesuits in Brazil were expelled. "The Indians, . . . [looked] upon their successors as mercenary interlopers," and immediately "insurrections against the system took place; some Indians were cast into prison, others took to the woods; and here also the immediate effect of the sudden and violent change was to thin the *Aldeas,* and corrupt the remaining inhabitants." [8]

Thus came to an end the chief chapter in the attempt to make agriculturists of the native Indians of Brazil. Late in the nineteenth century an official report said of the results of this measure: "It is

---

[6] *Ibid.,* 368–71.

[7] *Ibid.,* 514.

[8] *Ibid.,* 543–44. Just how many villages were affected is not known with exactitude. Southey mentions three score in Maranhão and Pará, seven in Pernambuco, including Paraíba and Ceará, nine in Bahia, five in Rio de Janeiro, and six in São Paulo. *Ibid.,* 515 and 543. However, Dr. Francisco Vicente Vianna states: "In consequence of this order [the Royal Charter of May 8, 1758, ordering the Jesuits back to Portugal] were created the villages of Trancoso, Villa Verde, Olivença, Barcellos, Santarem, Soure, Pombal, Mirandella, Pedra Branca, Abrantes, and some others, all of them quite uninteresting up to the present time." *Memoir of the State of Bahia* (Bahia, 1893), 663. Rocha Pombo says that most of the villages founded by the padres came to be vilas, or towns, and that they were numerous in the south at the end of the nineteenth century. He lists the names of the first ones to be established in São Paulo. *Historia do Brazil,* V, 146.

certain that the extinction of the Company of Jesus was highly prejudicial to the colonization of Brazil and especially to the peopling of the interior regions." Following the expulsion of the Jesuits many of the "Indian villages which the padres of this company had founded and where the savages, already domesticated, engaged in the cultivation of the land, daily calling new families from their tribes to these agricultural nuclei . . . were dispersed and destroyed; there commenced again for these people, who fled from the oppression of the colonists, the vagabond life of the forests with the renewed predominance of ferocious instincts." [9]

But not all the efforts to get the Indians to adopt sedentary habits and live the life of cultivators ended with the Jesuits. One cannot read far in the reports of travelers, after it became possible for a foreigner to visit the interior, without encountering references to villages of Indians or settlements that had their origin in such villages. Of Pernambuco, Southey, following Padre Manoel Ayres de Cazal's *Corografia Brazilica,* after mentioning the last wild Indians in the province, relates that the remnants of the four tribes "were persuaded to settle each in an *Aldea,* and cultivate the ground: nor was any fault imputed to them in their domesticated state, except that, retaining their old passion for the *chace* [*sic*], they could not easily be made to understand, that the sheep and cattle of the neighboring *Fazendas* were not fair game." [10] The same authority refers to six or seven small aldeias, recently established near Ilhéus in Bahia, and mentions "the Indian town of Olivença . . . a large and populous place." [11] In describing Porto Seguro, today part of Espírito Santo, he speaks of Villa Verde "in a fruitful country, inhabited almost entirely by civilized Indians, who exported wood and cotton" and of Belmonte, "formerly an *Aldea* under the missionaries." [12] Thomas P. Bigg-Wither, writing in 1878, stated that there were then "nearly seventy of these Indian colonies scattered about in the various provinces, each being under the directorship of a monk or Frade who is generally of the 'Capuchin' order." [13] Today, North American priests of the same order are directing a considerable number of Indian settlements in Mato Grosso and Paraná.

Ever since the time of the Jesuits most of the attempts at civilizing the Indians have included giving them plots of ground on the outskirts of towns and cities or lands for the establishment of a village and farms. That this was of considerable importance is revealed by the fact that most of the states, following the adoption of the republican constitution which gave the public lands to them, laid claim to the lands once included in these grants to the Indians.[14]

[9] Cardoso de Menezes e Souza, *Theses sobre Colonização no Brazil,* 144.
[10] Southey, *History of Brazil,* III, 788.
[11] *Ibid.,* 805.
[12] *Ibid.,* 809–10.
[13] Bigg-Wither, *Pioneering in South Brazil,* II, 314.
[14] See for example Gregorio Gonçalves de Castro Mascarenhas, *Terras Devolutas e Particulares no Estado de S. Paulo* (2d ed.; São Paulo, 1912), 11, for the articles in the Law of January 5, 1900, claiming for the state the concessions set aside for Indian agriculturists and those included in the extinct Indian villages.

Cardoso de Menezes e Souza in his report on colonization, written in 1873, strongly urged the incorporation of the indigenous population into the effective working force of the nation by converting them into tillers of the soil. He endorsed the technique used in a school for Indian children that Dr. Couto de Magalhães had established on the Araguaia, as a method of attracting the parents. He also described the work being undertaken in the village of Urubá, Pernambuco, where 1,500 Indians had been gathered into a settlement by the Director General of Indians in that province. Finally he urged the necessity of making the forts and military colonies, the posts on the lines of communication, into centers in which Indians would be trained in agriculture and the domestic arts and from which these civilizing influences would radiate into the surrounding sertões.[15]

Brazilians who owned large areas of land sometimes have provided in their wills for a part of their possessions to be used as patrimonies for the Indians of the country. One such case occurred in São Paulo where the Barão de Antonina donated large tracts of land on the borders of São Paulo and Paraná for the use of the Indians. Today this is the site of one of the state's colonial nuclei, it being stated that the Indians had all departed from those lands. The state, in an accord with the heirs of the baron, agreed to cede lands to the Indians in the município of Baurú, where they were living, in exchange for the lands originally left to them. "In this manner the desire of the donor, which was to secure to the Indians the property rights to the land on which they lived, did not fail to be carried out." [16] Even today the work of protecting the Indians from the encroachments of the civilized population, of assisting them in making the transition to a more established, sedentary agricultural life is the concern of an important federal agency. Some of the states also give special attention to the Indians. For example, the Directoria de Terras e Colonização of the state of Rio Grande do Sul has as one of its functions the assistance of the Indian villages and protection of their lands. According to the reports, ten such villages of semicivilized Indians have received attention from the service.[17] The establishment of colonies for military purposes, for posts on telegraph lines and routes of travel, drawing on Indian groups for the settlers and workers, is still not entirely without significance in parts of Brazil.

COLONIZATION

Colonization is by far the most significant of the ways by which a large number of independent, self-reliant, middle-class farm families practicing diversified agriculture have been established in Brazil. It may have contributed the greatest number of small farmers; cer-

[15] Cardosa de Menezes e Souza, *Theses sobre Colonização no Brazil*, 146–59.
[16] "A Colonização Oficial em São Paulo e o Núcleo Colonial 'Barão de Antonina,'" *Boletim do Serviço de Imigração e Colonização*, No. 2 (October, 1940), 11.
[17] Ramos, "Terras e Colonização no Rio Grande do Sul," *loc. cit.*, 749–50.

tainly it has supplied those best equipped materially, physically, and culturally for the multiple tasks involved in the successful operation of genuine farming establishments.

Organized colonization attempts in Brazil got under way early in the nineteenth century, faltered along for some fifty years, spurted ahead as the movement leading to the emancipation of the slaves gained force, got strength from the improved methods that grew out of experience in colonizing activities, received a great impetus when the public lands became state possessions at the time the republic was declared, and came into their own in the first half of the twentieth century. In them Brazil today has a tested and perfected technique for bringing about further radical transformations in her land system and for developing her long-neglected, latent agricultural resources.[18]

First Attempts. Colonization, or the attempt to establish planned settlements of small farmers, was begun in Brazil early in the nineteenth century. The moving spirit seems to have been the prince regent, later Dom João VI, who in 1812 led the founding of a colony of immigrants from the Azores at Santo Agostinho, later Vianna, in the province of Espírito Santo.

It was about this time that von Spix and von Martius sought to look ahead into Brazil's future, predicting the manner in which settlement would proceed, outlining the many difficulties to be faced by the settler, especially the colonist from lower European social classes, and forecasting eventual successes. A significant paragraph from the valuable work of these analysts follows:

But before Brazil shall have attained this period of civilisation, the uncultivated land may yet prove a grave to thousands of adventurers. Attracted by the constant beauty of the climate, the richness and the fertility of the soil, many leave their native land, to seek another home in a foreign atmosphere, and in a quite different climate. However true the suppositions are on which they found the expectations of a happy result of their enthusiastic enterprise, it is far from realizing the hopes of the emigrants, especially those from the north of Europe; and how shall the inhabitant of the temperate zone, suddenly removed as a cultivator of the soil to Rio de Janeiro, or perhaps even to the shores of the Amazons, to a foreign climate, a foreign soil, a new mode of life and subsistence, surrounded by Portuguese, whose language he neither understands, nor easily learns, how shall he be happy and maintain himself in this country? And what in particular must people of the lower classes feel, without general education and aptitude for a new language, mode of life, and climate, when even strangers of superior condition, provided with every means of guarding against inconvenience, alarmed at the disagreeable circumstances attending the climate, complain of the few resources, the poverty and the plagues of the country, of which we have latterly heard so much? If the poor colonist who has come from a northern climate does not meet with a fellow-countryman as his guide, who, acquainted with the mode of life and the cultivation of the soil, kindly assists him in word and deed for the first few years, he is exposed to perish of hunger, even in this rich country,

[18] For a succinct summary of the legal and historical aspects of colonization, see Rios (ed.), *Recomendações sobre Reforma Agrária*, 197–214. See also Fernando Carneiro, *Imigração e Colonização, passim.*

and from the feelings of repentance and longing after home which ensue, becomes a victim to his experiment. He, however, who has happily passed over the first trials, who has secured a settlement in the beautiful country of Brazil, and accustomed himself to the tropical climate, will most willingly acknowledge it for his second home; nay, if he has again visited Europe, he will with increased attachment, wish himself back again; and, notwithstanding the doubts generally entertained of the habitableness of the torrid zone, will celebrate Brazil as the fairest and most glorious country on the surface of the globe.[19]

The second colony seems to have been the settlement in 1818 of some Swiss immigrants at Leopoldina on the banks of the Peruhibe River in the state of Bahia. This colony prospered because, it is said, the newcomers soon acquired slaves, which, however, "gives it no right to be considered an European agricultural establishment." [20]

Also in 1818 two private individuals interested in land speculations secured some ground at Ilhéus in Bahia, where four years later they settled 161 Germans. In the unsettled conditions accompanying the separation from Portugal, most of them were dispersed throughout the country. To a few who remained, Pedro I gave some assistance in settling in a small colony called São Jorge dos Ilhéus, where they engaged in the production of cocoa. They were rapidly assimilated into the Brazilian population.

Nova Friburgo. In the meantime, in 1819 the famous settlement of Swiss at Nova Friburgo, in the high mountain valleys of the province of Rio de Janeiro, was commenced. This originated in an offer of the Swiss canton of Friburg, through Sebastian Nicolas Gachet, to establish a colony of Swiss in Brazil. The proposal was "to recruit and transport to the Port of Rio de Janeiro, 100 families of Swiss colonists, men, women, and children of both sexes, together with their household goods and agricultural instruments, for the price of 100 Spanish pesos per person, excepting children who have not attained the age of three years who will come free of charge." [21] On January 6, 1818, a royal letter accepted this proposition for establishing a colony of "Swiss Roman Catholics in the Kingdom of Brazil" and designated the fazenda of Morro Queimado in the distrito of Cantagallo as the location for the settlement.[22] The terms of the contract entered into for this initial venture are worth consideration. Among the concessions to the colonists were the following: (1) full titles to the land (one of the rare instances in which lands were given freely), (2) the granting of livestock and seeds, (3) exemption from taxation for twelve years, except for the usual levies on merchandise and contracts, and (4) assistance in returning to the fatherland if it were desired. In this case, however, one half of the repatriated colonist's goods were to be left behind for the colony. The colonists in turn were obliged to establish a city and two vilas, and to set aside

[19] Von Spix and von Martius, *Travels in Brazil*, I, 261–62.
[20] Vianna, *Memoir of the State of Bahia*, 200; cf. Silva Rocha, *Historia da Colonisação do Brasil*, I, 136.
[21] This is quoted in *ibid.*, 137.
[22] *Ibid.*, 138.

for each of these population centers sufficient land to care for the necessities of their future administration. Individually they were required to become subjects of the king, to present certificates of good conduct and health, and to prove that they were acquainted with Portuguese law and the contract of colonization. In July, 1819, the first colonists, 1,085 in number, sailed for Brazil.[23] In 1820, by two special decrees the colony was made into a special parish or *freguesia*, at that time a division in the undifferentiated administrative and religious organization of the province; a judge was nominated; and legislative and administrative machinery established in the seat of the colony, Nova Friburgo.[24] In all, about 2,000 of these colonists were established at Nova Friburgo. In the course of time their descendants have been rather completely acculturated and incorporated into the Brazilian population. But in terms of the purpose for which the settlement was established it was a failure; the colony did not serve as a focal point for infecting the empire with small-farming habits and practices. In fact, some of the colonists who could obtain the means to do so hurriedly bought up surrounding lands, purchased slaves, and became planters. This was foreign to the entire philosophy back of their introduction. Nevertheless, some new crops and practices were introduced.[25]

Early German Colonies. Following the establishment of the empire, Dom Pedro I interested himself in the importation of German colonists and turned his attention to Rio Grande do Sul as the place in which to settle them. This was in 1824. São Leopoldo was selected as the site of the colony. The culture contemplated was flax; the holdings were to measure 500 braças; and forests on navigable streams and near the coast were to be reserved.[26] This colony was among the most successful of all the early settlements, serving as a center of attraction for other Germans, including a large number of the soldiers who, after serving in the war against Rosas, settled in São Leopoldo. By 1889, according to Eduardo Prado, this settlement had multiplied from the original 126 to some 40,000 inhabitants.[27] Three years after the founding of this colony, or in 1827, the emperor's Minister of Interior was instrumental in bringing another group of Germans, this time from Bremen. These immigrants were established in an agricultural colony at Rio Negro in Paraná, which then formed part of the province of São Paulo. In the course of a few years some six hundred persons were located in this settlement.[28]

[23] *Ibid.,* 139.

[24] *Ibid.,* 174–76.

[25] Eduardo Prado, "A Imigração no Brasil," *Boletim do Serviço de Imigração e Colonização,* No. 4 (December, 1941), 101.

[26] *Ibid.,* 102.

[27] *Ibid.* The English editor of the *Standard* of Buenos Aires visited São Leopoldo in 1871 and was greatly impressed with the rapid growth and prosperity of the colony. Despite the tribulations of war and disputed land titles, forty-three colonies had already "radiated" from the original. Mulhall, *Rio Grande do Sul and Its German Colonies,* 129.

[28] Departamento Estadual do Trabalho, *Dados para a Historia da Immigração e da Colonização em São Paulo,* 6.

Between 1827 and 1829, despite the trouble in Pernambuco, the emperor founded another colony of Germans in Brazil, this time in the province of São Paulo, at Santo Amaro, very near the capital city. Some four hundred settlers made up this contingent.[29]

In 1829, also, the first German settlement in Santa Catarina was begun at São Pedro de Alcantara, a poor site that was afterwards changed.[30] Later Santa Catarina came to be more completely dominated by the German element than any other state in Brazil.

Opposition to Colonization. In the meantime, in 1828 Bahia again entered the spotlight in colonization matters when 222 Irishmen, formerly soldiers in the employ of the emperor, were established as a colony at Santa Januaria on the Engenho River near the village of Taperoa. The former soldiers seem to have proved unsuccessful as colonists.[31] Other attempts in Bahia about this time appear to have met with little success. One of them is particularly interesting, however, because it was an attempt to introduce "a system of partnership" into the operation of the sugar plantation, the Engenho Novo. About 110 Portuguese settlers were brought in for the purpose, but soon they all left, leaving behind, it is said, their unpaid debts.[32]

In Espírito Santo, a province later to figure greatly in colonization efforts, the first of the agricultural colonies dates from 1830 when four hundred Pomeranians were introduced. They came under the terms of a contract made between a Mr. Henrici and the Imperial Government on November 12, 1829. These first German colonists were established at Borba and set to work on a road leading from Itaciba to Minas Gerais.[33]

After these first few attempts colonization was stifled for a while owing to bitter conflicts and dissensions within the immense, gangling, segmented empire and specifically to a law of September 15, 1830, prohibiting any governmental expense from being incurred in connection with the colonization of foreigners in any of the provinces of the empire.[34] This put a stop to German immigration, the source of these first colonists. This immigration ceased entirely in 1830 and was not resumed until 1838.[35] In 1830 the emperor abdicated in favor of his six-year-old son, who became Pedro II. Even then it was several years before working relationships between the various factions were sufficiently well established for colonization efforts to go forward. Of this period of confusion Lourival Câmara has written, "Antitheses succeeded one another and paradoxes reproduced themselves: pro-immigration propaganda was disseminated in Europe,

[29] *Ibid.*
[30] Oswaldo R. Cabral, *Santa Catharina* (São Paulo, 1937), 116–17.
[31] Vianna, *Memoir of the State of Bahia*, 201.
[32] *Ibid.*, 202.
[33] Antonio Marius, *Minha Terra e Meu Municipio* (Rio de Janeiro, 1920), 23–24.
[34] Lucas Alexandre Boiteux, *Primeira Página da Colonização Italiana em Santa Catarina* (Florianópolis, 1939), 25.
[35] Prado, "A Imigração no Brasil," *Boletim do Serviço Imigração e Colonização,* No. 4, p. 102.

but here in Brazil any expense whatsoever for the colonization of foreigners was prohibited." [36]

Provincial Projects. During this period of turmoil, immigration and colonization both were almost at a complete standstill. The province of Santa Catarina led the way for future developments by removing the colony previously established at São Pedro de Alcantara to a better site at Itajaí, near the mouth of the river of the same name —the first colony in this the most colonized valley in Brazil.

This and other undertakings of the provincial government seem to have amounted to the circumventing of the law of the empire which practically eliminated immigration and colonization. A state law dated May 5, 1835, established two colonies of nationals and strangers at Itajaí. Soon other forms of promoting colonization were developed, the province granting concessions of land to private companies (although theoretically these belonged not to the province but to the empire!) and passing a law, Number 49 of June 15, 1836, that permitted "colonization by business or by company." The law then proceeded to establish all the details of the undertaking, including provisions that the sites might be chosen from any unused or vacant lands, that each single man should receive 200 braças of land, a married man with three children or less, 350 braças, and a married man with more than three children, 450 braças. All holdings were to be 1,000 braças in depth. [37]

With these impulses from provincial sources, immigration again got under way on a reduced scale in 1836, the date of the founding of the first Italian colony, Nova Itália, in Santa Catarina. The colonists for this settlement actually landed in March, 1836, before the adoption of the law mentioned above, and apparently were transported by the firm of Demaria & Schutel. Their number was 186, mostly Italians from Sardinia, of whom 140 were established in the colony. A few Brazilian families also were included among the first settlers of Nova Itália. [38] However, the more significant attempts at colonization had to await the outcome of a policy struggle in Brazilian political circles. [39]

Immigration and Colonization Policy. During Brazil's history as an independent nation there seem to have been two questions uppermost in the minds of the country's directing officials: first, whether or not it was desirable to spend public funds for the purpose of subsidizing immigration, and second, whether efforts in colonization should be directed toward obtaining immigrants of the farmer class and establishing them on the land as farm operators or toward securing agricultural laborers to work for wages or on shares on Brazil's

[36] Câmara, *Estrangeiros em Santa Catarina*, 18.
[37] Boiteux, *Primeira Página da Colonização Italiana em Santa Catarina*, 28.
[38] *Ibid.*, 32–33.
[39] In part the lapse during these years is to be attributed to the fact that many Brazilians "did not feel strongly the necessity . . . of an immigration of free men, when the clandestine traffic in Africans that persisted until the middle of the century, furnished to farming the slave hands that it preferred," Ferreira, *Azambuja e Urussanga*, 36.

large estates. In the decade of indecision and debate following 1830 the decision seems to have been reached on the first question. It was to the empire's interest to encourage immigration. On the second point the provinces disagreed. São Paulo developed a policy of recruiting agricultural laborers; the states to the south of it, and especially Rio Grande do Sul, adopted one of establishing colonists on the land as independent farmers. There was also a third question under discussion at this time—whether immigration and colonization should be promoted by private initiative, of course with the assistance of liberal grants of land to the companies engaging in the formation of the settlements, or conducted by governmental agencies. This was never entirely resolved, and during the last century the federal, state, and local governments and a wide variety of private companies all have made a contribution in the establishment of the small-farming class now so prominent in southern Brazil.

As early as 1840 private initiative was engaged in promoting immigration, although it must be indicated that its major objective seems to have been to secure a labor supply superior to slaves. Senator Vergueiro of São Paulo that year made over the system of operations on his coffee fazenda, paid the transportation expenses of ninety Portuguese families, and established them as half hands on his estate. However, since this sharing, or parceria, as practiced in the New World had quite different aspects from that of Portuguese tradition and law, considerable misunderstandings and difficulties arose. (See the chapter on Land Tenure.) Later the senator brought over eighty German families and set them to work on a similar sharewage arrangement. His example seems to have been widely followed, and it was reported that in the decade 1847 to 1857, "private initiative created in São Paulo more than sixty colonies in which were located more than 60,000 immigrants, almost all Portuguese." [40] Undoubtedly "colonies" as used by the authors of this report refers to the village-like groupings of houses for laborers on the coffee fazendas, for Henrique Doria de Vasconcellos states that only fourteen colonial nuclei were established in São Paulo during the entire period 1850 to 1889. [41]

Pedro II and Efforts at Colonization. Dom Pedro II now came of

[40] Departamento Estadual do Trabalho, *Dados para a Historia da Immigração e da Colonização*, 7; cf. Silva Rocha, *Historia da Colonisação do Brasil*, I, 272–73.

[41] Doria de Vasconcellos, "Alguns Aspectos da Imigração no Brasil," *loc. cit.*, 13. Cf. the *Relatorio da Commissão Encarregada de Examinar as Colonias Martyrios e S. Lourenço* (Rio de Janeiro, 1874), where the nature of these "colonies" of laborers contracted between 1850 and 1890 is clearly brought out. Mulhall stated that São Paulo "counted 40 colonies so far back as 1859, all of which were established by Brazilian planters, except Nova Germania founded by Karl Kruger. . . . Some of these afterwards burst up, the colonists alleging with much truth that they had been grossly deceived, and that their condition was little better than that of the slaves. As the minister of Agriculture says in his report to the legislature, it is culpable to bring out Europeans to work in Brazil unless on their own ground, and the sweat of their toil should never be turned to the advantage of speculators or traffickers in labour. He adds that the conduct of the São Paulo planters not only disgusted the Imperial Government, but damaged so much the name of Brazil abroad that emigration was greatly checked." *Rio Grande do Sul and Its German Colonies*, 191–92.

age and became emperor in his own right. For the next four decades this liberal ruler and statesman had an important part in colonization activities. The years at the middle of the century, when the young emperor was obtaining his maturity and marrying an Austrian princess, were ones during which some of the most noteworthy colonies in Brazil were established. Petropolis, located on grounds that were once part of the emperor's private possessions where his summer palace was located, in the high serras overlooking Rio de Janeiro, dates from 1846. Other German settlements which were established about the same time are Senhora de Piedade in Santa Catarina and Santa Isabel in Espírito Santo, both founded in 1847, and Santa Cruz in Rio Grande do Sul begun in 1849.[42] Santa Isabel, originally a colony of 163 German inhabitants, was "emancipated" in 1866. It was the first colony, in the Brazilian sense of the word, in Espírito Santo, but others were soon founded—Rio Novo in 1854 and Santa Leopoldina in 1857, the latter with Swiss immigrants.[43]

The emperor also promulgated a law in 1848 conceding to each of the provinces of the empire an area of land six leagues square to be used exclusively for colonization. This indicates the growing concern with this phase of the immigration problem. The land selected might be in one block or distributed in several places; it was specifically forbidden that any of it should be cultivated by slaves (to prevent developments such as those in the early colonies in Bahia and at Nova Friburgo in Rio de Janeiro); it was not to be deeded permanently to colonists until they were shown to be effectively cultivating it; and it was to revert to the province if the colonists did not comply with the cultivation requirement within five years.[44]

The year 1850 is to be remembered as the date of one of the most important laws in the history of the Brazilian land system: that which made sale the only legal method of alienating public lands. In 1854 came the regulamento making the new decree effective. That same year the government made it perfectly clear in a relatório that the immigrants were not being introduced to provide labor gangs for the fazendas, by stating that "the government has not assisted the importation of colonists that came to be employed on the fazendas, on parceria, or for wages." [45] Four years later, after a bitter struggle with the fazendeiros who kept insisting that federal and provincial resources should be used to subsidize the importation of agricultural laborers to work on shares or for wages, Minister Teixeira stated the government's position very clearly:

This system [colonial nuclei] in which all are soon called to be proprietors, presents not the single advantage of attracting more quickly and in larger numbers, spontaneous habitants for our soil and cultivators for our fields. Colonial nuclei satisfy necessities of various orders. They are established to overcome deserts, to secure the occupation of lands, to open

[42] Silva Rocha, *Historia da Colonisação do Brasil*, I, 254.
[43] Marius, *Minha Terra e Meu Municipio*, 24–25.
[44] Cardoso de Menezes e Souza, *Theses sobre Colonização no Brazil*, 274.
[45] *Ibid.*, 276; see also 277, 279, and 287.

roads and make secure those that lead to already prosperous centers of population. They are established to open and protect the navigation of rivers, to defend frontiers, to augment the production of supplies that are scarce, and, finally, even to direct the activities of certain classes. Colonization so considered includes various forms and makes use of diverse elements: military colonies and forts, villages of Indians, colonies of nationals, of foreigners imported for the purpose, of spontaneous immigrants, and of foreigners who are already in the country.[46]

Colonization efforts during the decade 1850 to 1860 were limited to the establishment of a few new settlements of Germans in the south. Nine new colonies were founded in Rio Grande do Sul. There were no new colonies in Espírito Santo nor in São Paulo; [47] in Paraná some Germans from Santa Catarina began the first of numerous farm communities near Curitiba.[48] In Santa Catarina was begun what has undoubtedly been the most highly publicized and probably the most important German settlement in all Brazil. This is Blumenau in the Itajaí Valley, up the river from the earlier colony to which the settlers had been transferred from São Pedro de Alcantara. Settlement was begun on September 2, 1850, with 17 immigrants; ten years later the inhabitants already numbered 947.[49] The following year D. Francisca, today Joinville, was established by the Hamburg Colonization Society.[50] Mucury, the first colony in Minas Gerais, begun by a navigation company and afterwards taken over by the Imperial Government, dates from 1852. Colonies were also projected in some of the northern provinces in this decade, with Portuguese or national settlers, but they seem not to have been carried very far. Finally, a large number of colonists were brought over and established as colonos on the coffee fazendas of São Paulo.[51]

The establishment of these colonies of German share hands on Paulista coffee fazendas was a severe setback for the colonization of Germans in south Brazil. The half-share basis gave rise to so many complaints that on November 3, 1859, the famous Heydt rescript was promulgated. This was a Prussian ministerial decree later adopted by other German states, forbidding the emigration of Germans to Brazil. Later, in 1896, it was revoked for Rio Grande do Sul, Santa Catarina, and Paraná.[52] Although the number of Germans entering Brazil was as great during the 1860's as it had been previously, undoubtedly more colonies would have been founded at this time had it not been for the decree and especially the unfavorable publicity accompanying it.

[46] Teixeira is quoted, *ibid.*, 295.

[47] Doria de Vasconcellos, "Alguns Aspectos da Imigração no Brasil," *loc. cit.*, 12–13.

[48] Romário Martins, *Quantos Somos e Quem Somos?* (Curitiba, 1941), 60.

[49] José Ferreira da Silva, *Blumenau* (Florianópolis, 1939), 9–10. Cabral, *Santa Catharina*, 134, gives 1852, the date of the first sale of farm plots, as that of the establishment of the settlement.

[50] Cabral, *Santa Catharina*, 152–53; Mulhall, *Rio Grande do Sul and Its German Colonies*, 189–90.

[51] See the *mappa* in Carvalho, *O Brazil*, Appendix.

[52] Benjamin Franklin Schappelle, *The German Element in Brazil* (Philadelphia, 1917), 16.

The decade 1860 to 1870 was one of various attempts to get settlers, including the one in which a considerable number of Southerners from the United States established new homes in Brazil, particularly in São Paulo and near Santarem in Pará. Coupled with the prohibition of emigration for Brazil in Prussia and other German states, the war with Paraguay brought the establishment of German colonies in Rio Grande do Sul almost to a standstill, but the work of colonizing immigrants from Germany continued in Santa Catarina. The very successful Imperial colonies of Theresopolis, Itajahy-Brusque, Angelina, and Dom Pedro all were begun during this decade. Two new colonies were founded in São Paulo, and further attempts were made in Bahia.

The Critical Years—the 1870's. The 1870's, however, should always be reckoned as the critical years in Brazil's colonization program. This was the time when an accounting had to be made for the haphazard manner in which colonization activities had proceeded, when thorough investigations of the existent colonies were called for in order to satisfy criticisms at home and to combat adverse publicity abroad. Investigations were made, reports were published, many improvements in planning and administration were recommended, and the nation was launched on the program that brought settlers in greatly increased numbers. The investigations included one of relations between fazendeiros and colonos on São Paulo coffee fazendas [53] where the German laborers were raising severe protests, another of the colonies in southern Bahia,[54] and a third investigation of the German settlements in the province of Santa Catarina, including Blumenau and D. Francisca.[55] However, most important of all the studies was one that resulted in the report to the Minister of Agriculture, Commerce, and Public Works, entitled "Theses About Colonization in Brazil," a volume of 429 pages plus Appendixes A to I. This study examined in a systematic manner the deficiencies in Brazil's program of colonization and made recommendations for its improvement. The analysis is very enlightening. After noting that Argentina and the United States were more successful than Brazil in attracting immigrants, it sets forth the defects in Brazilian colonization theory and practice and then proceeds to a detailed analysis of each.

I. The lack of liberty of conscience; the nonexistence of civil marriage as an institution; imperfections of education; ignorance and immorality of the clergy; the ambition of the Brazilian Episcopate for temporal power, transformed into a struggle improperly called—*the religious question.*

II. Lack of educational institutions and principally the absence of agricultural and professional instruction.

III. The small number of institutions of credit, especially of banks designed to aid small farming and industry.

[53] *Relatorio da Commissão Encarregada de Examinar as Colonias Martyrios e S. Lourenço.* Cf. Mulhall, *Rio Grande do Sul and Its German Colonies,* 191–92.
[54] Nascentes de Azambuja, *Relatorio sobre as Colonias ao Sul da Provincia da Bahia.*
[55] Albuquerque Galvão, *Relatorio sobre as Colonias Blumenau, Itajahy, Principe D. Pedro, e D. Francisca.*

IV. Restrictions and hindrances placed upon industrial freedom by legislation and public administration, destroying rather than developing individual initiative.

V. Defects in the law concerning contracting of services and share contracts with foreigners; defects in and failure to execute the public land laws and the lack of land tax upon lands lacking buildings and cultivation.

VI. Lack of transportation systems and ways of communication, that would link the center and the interior of the Empire to consumer and export markets.

VII. The creation of colonies far from markets on sterile, unprepared land, as well as the lack of facilities for receiving immigrants and colonists in the ports of the Empire and for their permanent establishment in the colonies of the State, or on the plots of land that they buy.

VIII. The failure to make Brazil known in the countries from which the emigration which we need proceeds, and to refute, by all the means of a readily understood publicity, and by ready and disinterested pens, the writings by means of which in those states we are depreciated, our errors in relation to the emigrants exaggerated, and hateful calumnies raised against us.[56]

Undoubtedly this study and report had much to do with improvements in Brazil's immigration and colonization policies. Some efforts were made to correct almost every one of the indicated deficiencies. Therefore it is not surprising the migration of colonists from the old sources, Germany and Portugal, was revived. From the recorded immigration [57] of only six Germans in 1870, a mere drop in the bucket compared to 4,037 who came in 1862 or the 3,779 who entered Brazil in 1868, the entrance of new colonists moved back to its old levels. A total of 3,530 Germans immigrated in 1876, and their numbers averaged well over 2,000 per year during the following four years. The entrance of Portuguese also moved up to some 7,000 per year from a previous level of 5,000. Of course the Portuguese always moved readily to Brazil, but they participated to a limited extent in the formation of agricultural colonies. Two other major and several minor currents of migration to Brazil also got under way during this decade. The major streams of immigrants were those from Italy and from the fragments of dismembered Poland. Both of these have had far-reaching consequences in Brazilian colonization efforts. The minor new elements included Volga Germans from Russia, whose colonies were a dismal failure, some English, and a few Swiss, French, Spanish, and Scandinavian colonists.

From this time on, the Italians came in swarms. As early as 1877 the number attained 13,582, a figure above the total annual immigration in any year previous to 1872, except for a short period from 1856 to 1862 when the German and Portuguese immigrants were relatively numerous. Furthermore, during these early years the Italians who came were established on small farms in what have since developed into some of the most prosperous farming communities of

---

[56] Cardoso de Menezes e Souza, *Theses sobre Colonização no Brazil*, 31–32; cf. Carneiro, *Imigração e Colonização no Brasil*, 12–14.

[57] For these immigration data see the *Boletim Commerativo da Exposição Nacional de 1908*, 82–85.

Rio Grande do Sul, Santa Catarina, Paraná, and Espírito Santo.[58] The Italian colonists who came in the closing years of the empire proved one of the most valuable contingents ever added to Brazil's population.

Also extremely important was the influx of Polish farmers that got under way at this time. The immigration of Poles has been almost entirely to the states of Paraná, Santa Catarina, and Rio Grande do Sul and almost exclusively confined to persons who came for the express purpose of securing farms of their own. The "father" of this Polish colonization was Edmund Wos Saporski, who after studying the situation, in an endeavor to help his harassed fellow countrymen, in 1869 presented a plan of colonization to the emperor of Brazil. The first of the Polish peasants arrived in 1869 and were dispatched to the coastal districts of Santa Catarina. But the Poles preferred the cooler climate of the *planalto* and in 1871 moved to Paraná and established their first colony at Pilarzinho near Curitiba. After this the Poles flocked to Paraná and spread out over the state.[59] Later settlers were established in colonies in Rio Grande do Sul and Santa Catarina. In 1937 the Central Union of Poles in Brazil reckoned the numbers of the immigrants and their descendants as 217,000. Polish statistics account for the immigration of 36,159 persons between 1919 and 1935, indicating that the migrants still form a considerable part of the total. Romário Martins calculates the total immigration of Poles and Ukrainians to Paraná as 67,003 for the period of 1871 to 1934, of whom 19,272 were Ukrainians.[60] The Polish data relative to the number of Poles and their descendants in the various states in 1937 are as follows: Paraná, 92,000; Rio Grande do Sul, 83,000; Santa Catarina, 28,000; São Paulo, 12,000; Espírito Santo, 1,500; and other states, 500. In the author's own travels throughout Brazil small groups of Poles were encountered in Minas Gerais and Mato Grosso, probably more than enough to make the five hundred allowed to "other states" in the figures just quoted. The overwhelming proportions of these Polish-Brazilians, 80 per cent according to the Polish data, are in agriculture and on small farms. In the state of Paraná their influence has been tremendous. In Brazil the largest contingents are to be found in the municípios of São Mateus, União da Vitória, Araucária, Campo Largo, and Iratí in Paraná; Erechim, Encruzilhada, and Getúlio Vargas in Rio Grande do Sul; and Canoinhas and Itaiópolis in Santa Catarina. A fitting expression of the debt of gratitude that Brazil owes the Polish colonist for his introduction of European skills, agricultural techniques, and managerial practices is a monument to the Polish sower in Curitiba.

[58] For experiences with some of the first Italian colonists, their lack of experience in coping with the wilderness, the wise administration of a Brazilian leader, and eventual success of the colonists in two Santa Catarina settlements, see Ferreira, *Azambuja e Urussanga*. Considerable data on the Italian and Polish colonies in Paraná will be found in Martins, *Quantos Somos e Quem Somos*.

[59] For much of the data on Polish settlers in Brazil, I am indebted to the Polish Consulate General in Curitiba.

[60] Martins, *Quantos Somos e Quem Somos*, 63–68.

It seems that attempts to establish colonies with other nationality groups never were very successful. North Americans and English colonies never equaled expectations, although the former did contribute materially to agricultural progress in the Campinas section of São Paulo, and Englishmen have directed several very significant colonization enterprises. Nor were the settlements of French of any particular significance.[61] However, all of these attempts were on a comparatively small scale. That of the North Americans could hardly be called colonization in the true Brazilian sense of the word.

There was one other colonization venture, entered into on a comparatively large scale and with high hopes, that seems to have failed most miserably. This was the attempt to transplant the Volga Germans to Paraná. The objective of this endeavor, undertaken in 1878, was to seat 20,000 of these people on the plains of Paraná. Only 3,809 came, most of whom (2,440) were sent to Ponta Grossa, to Palmeira (798), and to Lapa (327). After a few years more than three thousand of them left, going first to Hamburg and later to the state of Nevada. Those who remained in Paraná engaged mostly in transportation, serving a useful function with their teams and wagons. The Brazilian reaction to this attempt is set forth in the relatório of the provincial president of Paraná, Rodrigo Otavio, for 1878, who describes them as "extremely ignorant, fearful, lazy, envious, and, in spite of being extremely religious, lacking in the sense of true charity." Martins quotes the following from the same relatório:

They knew only the culture of wheat; but having to plant corn and beans, they sowed the seeds and afterwards went over the ground with primitive plows, brought from Russia, which were drawn by three pairs of oxen. Confronted with the unsuccessful production they excused themselves and blamed the land. They harvested oranges by cutting down the trees. They burned the fences of their plots and made dikes along the lines, being accustomed to communal landholding, and then complained about the invasions of neighbors' animals in their plantings. They requested and obtained permission to construct their own houses, the government giving them the precious materials and the money that it would have paid to the building contractors—but they burned the planks furnished to them and constructed pits for their dwellings, alleging that in Russia their habitations were of that type. They complained that the lands would not produce without manure and then used this to make fires, although woods in which they could gather firewood were near by, but that required more work.

In general, when they were sick they preferred the priest to the colony doctor, saying that "God is the one who cures and kills." When one of them died while they were traveling (as occurred in São Luiz and in Graciosa) they abandoned the body in the road.[62]

The 1870's also saw other developments of great significance for the colonization of Brazil. The sentiment in favor of the abolition of

[61] The interested reader will find some of the details about these ventures in Bigg-Wither, *Pioneering in South Brazil,* and other data in Martins, *Quantos Somos e Quem Somos.* José Arthur Rios, "Assimilation of Immigrants from the Old South in Brazil," *Social Forces,* XXVI (December, 1947), 145–52, is a highly important sociological study of the North American settlers and their descendants.

[62] Martins, *Quantos Somos e Quem Somos,* 156–57.

slaves reached the point that a law was promulgated (No. 2,040 of September 28, 1871) providing that all children born subsequently were to be free. Naturally, this marked a definite milestone in the abolishment of slave labor on the plantations and set some of the provinces, notably São Paulo, about endeavors that would help to guarantee an ample labor supply for the fazendas. Perhaps this writing on the wall was even the motivation that led to the examination of the existing colonies, an improvement in their administration, and active efforts to combat the very unfavorable publicity that Brazil was receiving in Europe. In any case from 1880 on, the importation of agricultural laborers became the dominant aspect of Brazilian immigration, and the attraction of colonists was relegated to a secondary position. Whereas, in the previous years most of the newcomers came as colonists on terms which assured them of land in a private, provincial, or Imperial colony, in the future the larger proportion of the immigrants were destined to be placed as laborers on the fazendas. In fact, those who came after 1880 were to go, for the most part, to help fill the ever recurring vacancies in the labor force of São Paulo, to help satisfy its long-continued cry of falta de braços. Important contingents of Germans, Italians, and Poles did find their way on to the developing colonial settlements of Rio Grande do Sul, Santa Catarina, Paraná, and Espírito Santo. However, most of the German, Italian, Spanish, and other immigrants who came after this decade went to São Paulo as agricultural laborers. The data on this phase of the movement will be found in the chapter on immigration.

Colonization Since 1880. Colonization efforts in Brazil after 1880 may be summarized under the following five headings: (1) the continued immigration of farmers, (2) the rapid reproduction rates in the old settlements and the "swarming" of the colonies, (3) extensive colonization activities by private agencies, (4) the introduction of Japanese colonists, and (5) the perfection of state and federal colonizing policies and practices. Naturally each of these can be treated only in summary fashion.

1. *Immigration of Farmers.*—After the 1870's the story of colonization attempts ceased to be the history of immigration to Brazil. The importation of agricultural laborers to replace the slave workers became the dominant note in Brazilian policy. Whereas in the first three quarters of the century São Paulo's share of the immigrants was a very modest one, after 1885 she began taking the lion's share of the newcomers and this she continued to do until the outbreak of World War II stopped immigration. Although this movement was overshadowed by the immigration of farm laborers for the fazendas, colonists continued going in considerable numbers to Rio Grande do Sul, Santa Catarina, and Paraná.

For the most part these colonists were Germans, Italians, and Poles, although considerable numbers of Spaniards seem to have used the status of colono on the coffee fazenda as a steppingstone towards ownership of a small farm. In these southern states they added to the strength of the old settlements, joined with those who had been there longer in the "swarming" process by which new settlements were established, furnished a portion of the settlers for privately sponsored colonization projects, and in every way contributed to the prosperity of the region.

2. *The "Swarming" Process.*—As one reads the history of South Brazil he sees ample evidence that new colonies were being established as offshoots of old ones, a process resembling the swarming of a hive of bees. For example, Santa Felicidade in Paraná was an offshoot of Nova Itália; "spontaneous colonists," descendants of the Poles and nationals, are credited with establishing eleven settlements in the município of Lapa, Paraná, one of which (Contenda) is described as "a great farming center" of "around 15,000 inhabitants, all prosperous and proud of their productive lands and of the advanced and industrious community or social order that they constitute"; Santa Barbara, Paraná, is described as consisting of 5,500 plots of 10 alqueires each, "being rapidly occupied by descendants of Italians coming from Rio Grande do Sul"; the município of São Mateus, in addition to large colonies of Ukrainians, Poles, and Russians, also "possesses other spontaneous colonies such as Canoas, Iguaçú, and Taquaral." [63] In Rio Grande do Sul this swarming process began very early. Mulhall, who visited the German settlements in Rio Grande do Sul in 1871, reported that "now every year hundreds of young men leave San Leopoldo for the districts of Triumfo, San Jeronimo, Taquary, Bocca-do-Monte, forming new settlements which radiate in all directions." [64] Later he gave more of the details of the new settlements already established by the sons of the colonists in São Leopoldo who

soon spread themselves and formed the following new settlements, at short distances from San Leopoldo:

Capibary-Schneitz	14	farms, distance	12	miles
Sommer-Schneitz	63	" "	20	"
Picada Demanda	45	" "	20	"
Picada Solitaria	40	" "	30	"
Picada Voluntaria	30	" "	30	"
Morro dos Bois	50	" "	12	"
Costa Cahy	18	" "	25	"
Padre Eterno	200	" "	12	"
Larangeiras	100	" "	20	"
Santa Maria or Bocca do Monte	100	" "	200	"

But even before these were Tomba Grande, New Hamburg, Costa da Serra, Bom Jardin, Dos [sic] Irmaos, Baumschneitz, Campo Bom, Achtundveirzig, Caffee-Schneitz, Picada Hortense, Cuatro [sic] Colonias, and Picada Feliz: these twelve settlements are very prosperous and count no fewer than 23 churches and 46 schools, the latter attended by 1,045 boys and 697 girls: 31 of these schools are maintained by the colonists, and 15 by the State. [65]

[63] *Ibid.*, 148, 149, 156, 162, *passim.*
[64] Mulhall, *Rio Grande do Sul and Its German Colonies*, 125.
[65] *Ibid.*, 132–33.

Some years ago the natural increase of the "colonial" population in the state of Rio Grande do Sul was estimated at 30,000 per year, and with much justification it also was stated that:

This total of 30,000 souls, consisting of the descendants of Luso-Brazilian, Teuto-Brazilian, Italio-Brazilian, and Polish-Brazilian agriculturists, living in the old colonies of the state, is composed of native Brazilians and constitutes the best element that can be used for colonization, whether considered from the ethnic point of view or that of productive capacity. Their location on Brazilian soil, therefore, is a question that interests not only Rio Grande do Sul, but the nation.[66]

In 1940 it was also estimated that there were still 90,000 hectares of state-owned lands that might be used for colonization. However, the largest part of this was "occupied by native *'intrudors'* who have maintained possession with houses and cultivation for many years." [67] The pattern of population distribution is being changed very rapidly by the heavily populated farm settlements that are coming into being in the northwestern parts of the state.

Nearly all immigration to Paraná has been that of small farmers. The list of colonies established includes almost three hundred names, most of which have developed into permanent settlements.[68] In Santa Catarina the German settlers and their descendants forged up the valleys leading into the Itajaí until in 1930 the município of Blumenau was a little "state within a state," dominating state politics. It has since been divided into six municípios.[69] Nowadays one may find numerous descendants from these German, Italian, and Polish colonists in north Paraná in the extensive settlements being established there, in western São Paulo where the state's policy at last is favorable to the establishment of small farmers on the land, and in parts of southern Mato Grosso.

3. *Private Colonization Projects.*—Reference is made frequently in this volume to the activities of private colonization companies. The work of one of the most notable of these, the North Paraná Land Company, an English concern which built the railroad from Ourinhos in São Paulo to the company's seat in Londrina and considerably beyond in the direction of Paraguay, has already received some attention. The company has helped establish many thousands of colonists in the land. It is continuing its colonization activities. But there are many other agencies, including some railroads, engaged in similar projects on a more modest scale.

The activities of one of these companies are related by the International Cotton Mission.

Our main object in visiting Biriguy was to become acquainted with the work of colonization undertaken by the "*Companhia de Terras, Madeiras e Colonisação de São Paulo. . . .*"

[66] Ramos, "Terras e Colonização no Rio Grande do Sul," *loc. cit.*, 753.
[67] *Ibid.*, 750–51.
[68] Cf. Martins, *Quantos Somos e Quem Somos.*
[69] Cf. Mennucci, "A Subdivisão do Município de Blumenau," *loc. cit.*

The Company acquired first some 19,000 "Alqueires" but as the land was taken by settlers, they bought an additional area with the profits. So far, 32,000 "alqueires" (179,200 acres) have been sold and these are under cultivation; the Company has a similar area, in forest land, practically all rich soil, on a high level. Land is sold in lots from 5 to 100 "alqueires" (1 "alqueire"—5.6 acres) the average holding being 15 "alqueires" or 84 acres.

At the time of our visit, 1,763 lots had been sold, but some families have two and three lots. One can say that about 1,700 families have settled on the land since 1912 when the Company started operations. So far, all profits have been used for extension purposes and no dividend has been paid.

The general rule is for the new-comer to pay 30 per cent. of the purchase price of the land in cash and the remainder he pays out of his profits. Practically all have been able to do this within three years.

The land belongs to the settler from the day of the first payment. The company has no right to dictate as to what crops are to be grown or to whom the produce has to be sold. The colonists are entirely free agents.

As everywhere in São Paulo, one meets here too a cosmopolitan crowd; the composition of the colonists as to nationality is as follows:

$$
\begin{array}{lll}
40 \text{ per cent} & \text{Italians} \\
30 \quad " \quad " & \text{Japanese} \\
25 \quad " \quad " & \text{Spaniards}
\end{array}
$$

The rest consists of Germans (three families), Poles, Austrians, French, Americans, Portuguese, and one Brazilian.

The average prices at which land has been sold are:

$$
\begin{array}{lll}
1913\text{--}1917 & 100\$00 & \text{per alqueire (5.6 acres)} \\
1918 & 150\$00 & " \quad " \\
1919 & 200\$00 & " \quad " \\
1922 & 250\$00 & " \quad "
\end{array}
$$

Out of the 1,700 families, only one has given up possession of the land —got the money returned and left. Three other families have left the district, but have let the land to their friends. This is a good sign and speaks well for the management and the fertility of the land.

. . . . . .

The cost of clearing the land, burning down forests, and getting it ready for cultivation is here estimated to be 200 milreis per "alqueire"; this work is generally carried out by natives from the State of Bahia who have specialized in it for many years.

The settlers build their own houses, using the wood of the trees they have felled; there is a saw-mill at the station. Some use nothing but bamboo and clay. The cost of a small dwelling of a primitive kind is 700 milreis.

The method of cultivation is a rough-and-ready one. . . .

. . . . . .

The Company does not buy the produce of the settlers. They sell to small merchants and these again sell to larger merchants in the city.

The railway freight of coffee and cotton from this place to Santos is very high indeed. The freights are a severe handicap and were it not for the enormous fertility of the soil the new settlers would not be able to compete.[70]

The work of private colonization ventures has proceeded to a considerable extent during the years following the second world war, although not on a scale comparable with that in earlier periods. Among the more recent colonies the one established at Holambra, near

[70] Pearse, *Brazilian Cotton,* 85–88.

Campinas in São Paulo, by Dutch settlers deserves special mention.[71] Some information also is available about a very successful colony of five hundred families of Swabians from the lower Danube which was established in five villages at Entre-Rios in the município of Guarapuava in the state of Paraná; a "green belt" settlement of Brazilians and immigrants of various nationalities established in the Paraíba Valley, near Barra Mansa, in the state of Rio de Janeiro; and a less successful colony of northeasterners at Pindorama in the state of Alagôas.[72]

4. *Japanese Colonies.*—Numerous colonies of Japanese have been established in São Paulo since 1908 when the first members of this race were introduced, and a few have been established in recent years in the adjoining states. Undoubtedly the Japanese settlers have contributed to the agricultural production, particularly of cotton and vegetables. They also soon learned the coffee business and secured control of some of the coffee fazendas. Prior to the second World War they rapidly were making themselves masters of the land along all of São Paulo's principal railroads and, in addition, establishing their small truck-farming settlements along most of the railways in Minas Gerais, Paraná, Rio de Janeiro, and Mato Grosso. Brazil is gaining by their presence. The establishment of these Japanese colonies has greatly extended the small-farm system, and it also has done much to promote co-operatives in Brazilian agriculture, particularly in the area about the city of São Paulo.[73]

5. *Improvement of Colonization Policies.*—An official publication which appeared in 1916 gives basic information concerning the colonization projects of the state and federal governments as of the year 1912. A summary of this information shows developments since 1880 and serves as a point of departure for a discussion of subsequent developments. (See Table LII.) In interpreting the data in this table one must keep in mind that the Brazilians "emancipate" a colony as soon as it is running smoothly, so that a great many ventures undertaken after 1880 do not appear in the tabulation.

Finally, it should be pointed out that in the last fifty years or so the state and the federal governments have learned a great deal about colonization methods. They now have the experience, and apparently also the will, to spread a family farm system much more widely in Brazil. Even São Paulo, which for many years was reluctant to adopt legislation favorable to the development of small farming and long held out for the policy of limiting efforts to the importation of farm laborers, now is devoting much more attention to the small-farm-

[71] For details about this settlement, see José Arthur Rios (ed.), *Recomendaçoes sobre Reforma Agrária*, "Anexo I," 301–26.

[72] Cf. Arthur Hehl Neiva, *Algunos Ejemplos de Actividades Colonizadoras Realizadas por Empresas Particulares en el Brasil* (Mimeographed; Montevideo, 1959). This document was prepared for the Second Latin American Seminar on Land Problems conducted by the Food and Agriculture Organization of the United Nations in Montevideo in 1959.

[73] Fujii and Smith, *The Acculturation of Japanese Immigrants in Brazil*, 25–32; and Hiroshi Saito, *O Cooperativismo na Região de Cotia: Estudo de Transplantação Cultural* (São Paulo, 1956).

TABLE LII

Basic Facts about the Government Colonies in 1912 *

Name of colony	Auspices	Year founded	Principal nationalities of settlers	Population in 1912
Minas Gerais				
1. Adalberto Ferraz	State	1899	Italians	100
2. Affonso Penna	State	1899	Spaniards and Italians	175
3. Americo Werneck	State	1898	Italians and Spaniards	292
4. Barão de Ayuruoca	State	1910	Italians, Austrians, and Portuguese	341
5. Bias Fortes	State	1898	Italians	249
6. Carlos Prates	State	1898	Italians	352
7. Conselheiro Joaquim Delfino	State	1912	——	——
8. Constança	State	1910	Italians, Germans, and Portuguese	446
9. Francisco Salles	State	1898	Italians and Spaniards	284
10. Inconfidentes	Federal	1910	Germans, Italians, and Spaniards	939
11. Itajubá	State	1907	Italians, Portuguese, and Russians	220
12. João Pinheiro	Federal	1908	Germans, Italians, and Austrians	552
13. Major Vieira	State	1911	Italians and Portuguese	109
14. Nova Baden	State	1900	Italians and Austrians	387
15. Rio Dôce	State	1911	Italians	71
16. Rodrigo Silva	State	1883	Italians	1,675
17. Santa Maria	State	1910	Italians and Austrians	375
18. Vargem Grande	State	1907	Portuguese and Italians	244
19. Wenceslau Braz	State	1912	Italians	237
Paraná				
20. Apucarana	Federal	1912	Russians	764
21. Cruz Machado	Federal	1910	Russians and Poles	2,686
22. Iraty	Federal	1908	Poles and Russians	2,172
23. Itapará	Federal	1908	Poles	1,455
24. Ivahy	Federal	1907	Austrians, Russians, and Germans	3,535
25. Jesuino Marcondes	Federal	1907	Austrians	351
26. Senador Corrêa	Federal	1907	Poles and Russians	2,172
27. Tayó	Federal	1908	Russians, Austrians, and Germans	362
28. Vera Guarany	Federal	1909	Austrians and Russians	4,219
Rio de Janeiro				
29. Itatiaya	Federal	1903	Portuguese, Germans, and Spaniards	334
30. Visconde de Mauá	Federal	1908	Germans, Austrians, and Russians	492
Santa Catarina				
31. Annitapolis	Federal	1907	Germans and Austrians	1,755
32. Esteves Junior	Federal	1910	——	——
São Paulo				
33. Bandeirantes	Federal	1908	Germans, Portuguese, and Austrians	934
34. Campos Salles	State	1898	Germans, Italians, and Austrians	1,101
35. Conde de Parnahyba	State	1911	Italians, Germans, and Spaniards	809
36. Gavião Peixoto	State	1907	Italians, Spaniards, and Portuguese	1,248
37. Jorge Tibiriçá	State	1905	Italians, Germans, and Russians	1,210
38. Martinho Prado Jr.	State	1911	Spaniards and Italians	134
39. Monção	Federal	1910	Italians, Germans, and Spaniards	957
40. Nova Europa	State	1907	Germans, Russians, and Italians	1,751
41. Nova Odessa	State	1905	Russians and Italians	976
42. Nova Veneza	State	1910	Italians, Russians, and Spaniards	468
43. Pariquera-assú	State	1861	Austrians, Poles, and Germans	2,605
44. Visconde de Indaia-tuba	State	1911	——	——

* Source: *Annuario Estatistico do Brazil,* I (1908–12), 172–81.

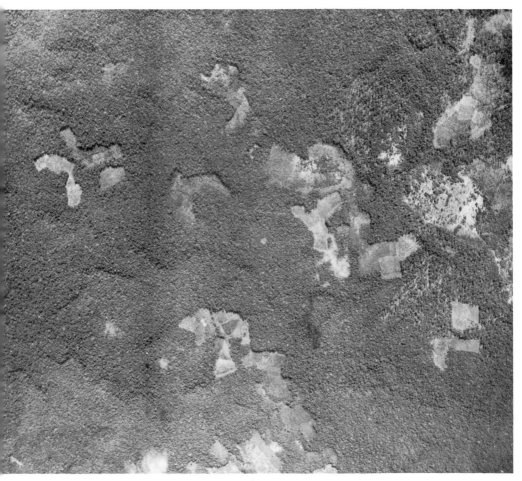

Early Stages in the Settlement of a Portion of the Amazon Jungle. (Courtesy of Hilgard O'Reilly Sternberg.)

ing classes. Especially noticeable is the proffer of assistance toward farm ownership for each worker who has served a minimum of two years as a laborer on one of the state's fazendas. Article 5 of Law No. 7,369 of August 3, 1935, reads as follows: "Only those immigrants who were introduced after this date through the medium of the Department of Agriculture, Industry and Commerce and who have filled regularly the contract of two years, at a minimum, in coffee farming shall enjoy the preferences and privileges conceded by this decree in the concessions of plots in the official colonial nuclei of the state." [74] Even though aid in setting up as a farm operator is made contingent on two years of service as an agricultural laborer, it is significant that such assistance has been offered.

Another piece of publicity circulated by the state for the purpose of

[74] *O Trabalho Agrícola e o Amparo ao Trabalhador* (São Paulo, 1936), 14.

417

attracting workers includes in bold face type the promise: "After working two years in Paulista farming, every worker has the right to buy a plot of ground by paying for it in small monthly installments, over a period of 10 years." [75]

With the establishment of the Estado Novo the federal government immediately began a much more vigorous participation in and control of colonization activities. Since 1890 most of the responsibility for these activities had been in state hands, and the policy followed had been one of extreme *laissez faire*. After 1937 the federal government quickly gathered the reins into its own hands. It had become convinced that the presence of millions of unassimilated colonists and descendants of colonists in the southern states represented a genuine threat to national security. The reason for the difficulties were of course seen in the fact that the immigrants had been permitted to settle in their nationality and foreign-language groups, live unto themselves, have their own press, maintain with state and federal financial assistance their own schools, and in the case of some of the German colonies, follow Evangelical ministers selected in, sent from, and responsible to Berlin. Also there became an increasing uneasiness over the activities of the numerous tourists, professors, and other visitors from Germany who journeyed among the German colonies, participated in the meetings of the settlers, warned of "Yankee Imperialism," constantly reminded the Teuto-Brasileiros of the precious heritage of German blood that flowed through their veins, and influenced them to believe that they were also citizens of the Reich.

Law No. 406 of May 4, 1938, decreed that no colonial nucleus could be constituted of foreigners of a single nationality. Furthermore, it authorized the Conselho Nacional de Imigração e Colonização to prohibit the "concession, transference, or renting of lots to foreigners of a nationality whose concentration or preponderance in a nucleus, center, or colony, now being founded or emancipated, might be injurious to the ethnic or social composition of the Brazilian people." In addition, this law provided that there should be a minimum of 30 per cent Brazilians and a maximum of 25 per cent of any other single nationality group among the settlers in all colonies, whether private or official.[76] This law represented an important progression in Brazilian colonization policy. The attempt to help undo some of the errors of the past was made a few months later when Law No. 1,545 of August 25, 1939, made the use of the Portuguese language mandatory in all schools, closed the foreign-language press, and laid the basis for a strict supervision of political activities in the communities that had developed from the agricultural colonies of south Brazil. These restrictive activities are well known; less has been said about the active manner in which the federal government

[75] *Informações Uteis sobre o Trabalho Agricola no Estado de S. Paulo* (São Paulo, 1935).

[76] Cf. "A Colonização Oficial em São Paulo e o Núcleo Colonial 'Barão de Antonia,' " *loc. cit.*, 15.

has proceeded in the establishment of additional agricultural colonies throughout Brazil.

Just how far the national government has gone in its policy is indicated by the following summary of the more significant provisions of a law regulating national agricultural colonies, approved on February 14, 1941, which remains the basic legislation on the subject.

1. The purpose is clearly stated to be the establishment of Brazilians, of limited resources but possessed of aptitudes for agriculture, as proprietors of farms. In exceptional cases foreigners who have special qualifications will be admitted as settlers.

2. The location for each colony is to be carefully selected with reference to climate, soil, streams, or sites for reservoirs, and possibilities of producing electricity.

3. Lots may range in size from twenty to fifty hectares, 25 per cent of each being preserved in forest. Other forest reserves are to be maintained about the colony.

4. Educational institutions to be established in each colony include facilities for instruction in rural crafts, including work in iron, wood, and leather, in addition to a primary school for all children.

5. Breeding stations for the improvement of livestock are to be established in each colony.

6. The colonists are to be organized into co-operatives for production, marketing, and buying.

7. Lots are to be given free of charge, along with seeds and the

Monjolo and Old Wattle-and-daub Outbuildings on a Recent Arrival's Farm in the Colonia Agrícola de Goiás. (Photo by the Author.)

The Colonia Agrícola de Goiás. *Upper.* The Hospital. *Lower.* A Typical School. (Photos by Herbert K. Ferguson.)

most urgently needed implements. In the beginning the grant is made for use only, but after a trial period full property rights pass to the colonists.

8. Candidates having five or more children and residing in the locality in which the colonies are established are to have preference in the distribution of farming plots. Lots will be given only to those 18 years of age or more, who are not landowners, who have aptitudes for agriculture, and who agree to reside on the concessions. In exceptional cases foreigners possessed of special agricultural knowledge may receive lots. No federal, state, or município employee may receive a concession.

9. Colonists are to receive the following assistance: work at wages or piece work during at least the first year, free medical services and

medicines until the "emancipation" of the colony, loans of agricultural machinery and instruments during the first year, and transportation to the seat of the colony from the station or port.

10. The colonist's plot, crops, vehicles, machinery are to be exempt from state and local taxation until after the colony has been emancipated.

11. Each colonist must clean all drainage channels passing through his land to a width of two meters and maintain the roads that pass through his holding to a width of seven meters.

12. Colonists may be expelled and their rights revoked if it is proved that they failed to cultivate the land during the established period, unless it can be proved that they were hindered by a superior force, if they depreciate the land by destroying the timber without subsequent use of the soil, or if they constitute disturbing elements in the colony.[77]

Aided by this law, those seriously concerned with agricultural development in Brazil are attempting colonization projects in many parts of Brazil. In 1960 thirty-one projects were in operation, including seven in the state of Rio de Janeiro, seven in Bahia, two in Pernambuco, two in Paraná, two in Pará, two in Goiás, and one in each of the following states: São Paulo, Minas Gerais, Amazonas, Rio Grande do Norte, Mato Grosso, Rio Grande do Sul, Maranhão, Piauí, and Ceará. These efforts should help to overcome the feeling in the northern and northeastern states that they have been entirely neglected in colonization matters. Typical of the complaints on this score, formerly very widespread, is a protest contained in an official publication of the state of Alagôas, *Alagôas em 1931*. It is quoted in full because of the light it sheds on the colonization desires in the northern states and the manner in which former national policies have affected these regions:

Unhappily still victorious is the opinion that to the north of the parallel 16° south latitude "there should not be attempted permanent collective establishments of strangers."

This opinion has been one of the reasons why the north lives exclusively from national labor, its lands unpeopled, as good as they may be. Alagôas has suffered the effects of this governmental error. She never had the assistance of foreign hands in the conquest of her lands and in the development of her riches. She has lived to herself, of her own forces, of her own work.

In 1892 immigration for the north was sought. For this end a commission was named of which the president was the major of engineers, Gabino Besouro, governor of Alagôas. This commission studied in detail the various agricultural zones into which the state is divided; the hydrographic system, its conditions of navigability as ways of transportation; the hydrometric condition of the lands watered by the principal water courses, the vegetation which the same produced, and the crops for which they were suited. It made also studies of the orographic system, the geological character of the soil, the classification of agricultural lands,—in short, of

[77] For the text of the law and also that of the decree of December 16, 1943, which regulates agricultural colonies, see Fabio Luz Filho, *Cooperativismo, Colonização, Credito Agrário*, 275–93.

all that was necessary for a complete service of propaganda of immigration and colonization in the state.

The commission charged with this service in Alagôas made excursions in the valley of the Paraíba, in the valley of the Mundaú, to Riacho Dore, to Atalaia, Pilar, and Alagôas, to the valleys of Camaragibe and Jacuípe, to the valley of São Francisco, in a word, it traveled throughout the entire state, publishing fully the results of its observations and scientific studies.

A project of regulations for immigrant colonies in the state was drawn up; a chorographic map of the state was made and a description of Alagôas was published in Portuguese, Italian, and French. Then the commission was dissolved and never more were the governors, federal and state, occupied with the matter.[78]

Of all the colonization projects undertaken by the national government the Colonia Agrícola de Goiás, now the município of Ceres, is by far the most noteworthy. There near the center of the state, not far from the location of Brasília, thousands of families were established on small farms. In 1945 on the occasion of his visit to this colony, the present writer was deeply impressed by this effort to get some of Brazil's vast territory into the hands of the people who till the soil.[79]

SALE RESTRICTIONS ON LAND

Perhaps restriction on the amounts of land sold to one person has not been particularly effective as a method of bringing about the development of a class of small farmers; nevertheless, it was a device that was widely resorted to by the states when the public lands came into their possession following the adoption of the republican constitution. Undoubtedly it has had some effect, particularly in making it more feasible for children and grandchildren of colonists to secure land for carrying on their own farming operations. Usually the procedure was to set legal limits on the amount of terras devolutas that could be purchased by one person.

For example, soon after the immense western state of Mato Grosso received authority over the public domain it took measures designed to help fill, with persons of the small-farming class, its tremendous solitudes. From an official publication, printed in English, one can get an idea of the inducements offered. Among the materials presented is a translation of Law No. 149, of April 14, 1896. In its several articles this law provided that the executive power was authorized to grant lands to Brazilians and foreigners "that may wish to settle in this State as farmers, unappropriated lands in lots of 50 hec-

---

[78] *Alagôas em 1931* (Maceió, 1932), 21.

[79] For more details about the colony, see Conselho de Imigração e Colonização, *Goiás, uma Nova Fronteira Humana* (Rio de Janeiro, 1949), 187–89; and Virginia Prewett, *Beyond the Great Forest* (New York, 1953). Miss Prewett's experiences should be read by all who are interested in Brazil's future. They reveal clearly that the basic "conquest of Brazil" involves a remolding of the institutional patterns and not merely the overcoming of forests and jungles as is so generally, so blithely, and so naïvely assumed.

tares." (It will be kept in mind that prior to the establishment of the republic in 1889, land could be legally obtained only by purchase.) If an applicant had a family he might receive an additional 50 hectares for each four persons. A definitive title was promised after a person had dwelt upon and effectively cultivated the portion allotted to him for one year; if the settler did not comply with requirements after one year the land was to revert to the state and the grantee to have no right to indemnification. Lands were to be surveyed at the cost of the grantees. The previous year another law, that of July 10, 1895, had provided for the granting of land in the band of territory lying within sixty kilometers of the national boundaries. In this area two hundred hectares were to be given when cattle raising was to be the principal enterprise, the petitions were to go to the administrator general of the district, instead of to the governor of the state, and five years were allowed as the period within which the land might be surveyed and marked.[80]

The two summary paragraphs of the small publication indicate the nature of the consideration leading to the adoption of such laws. They read as follows:

The State legislation relating to public lands protects the small farmers, banishing from its territory the *latifundia regime,* limiting the sale of its lands to lots of 3,600 hectares, 900 and 450 hectares, according to their fitness for breeding, for agriculture, or for extractive industries.

This propensity for peopling the land and subdividing it into small properties, the liberal disposition of its political organization and administration, the provision of its laws and their strict observance by those charged with their execution, are means for the development of public credit and of the material prosperity, most indisputably warranted by its natural riches—in the vegetable, mineral and animal kingdoms.

Unfortunately, the situation in the 1960's indicates that these good intentions hardly became solidified into practice. The data given in another chapter indicate that Mato Grosso's lands passed rapidly into the hands of a few large holders, some of whom possessed well over a million hectares each. In 1941 the government expropriated one of those that contained almost two million hectares. Nevertheless, it is interesting to note that it was once contemplated to cut the state's land to the small farm pattern.

São Paulo also placed restrictions on the amounts of state lands that might be purchased by a single buyer. As established by the law of January 5, 1900, of those lands considered suitable for agriculture one person was not to be allowed to purchase more than five hundred hectares; of the prairie land, considered suitable only for grazing, the limit was established at four thousand hectares; and for suburban lands, a restriction of fifty hectares per person was established. The same purchaser might not buy contiguous areas if their totals exceeded these limits.[81]

[80] *Brief Notice on the State of Matto-Grosso* (Rio de Janeiro, 1904), 33–39.
[81] Gonçalves de Castro Mascarenhas, *Terras Devolutas e Particulares no Estado de S. Paulo,* 70.

SUBDIVISION OF LAND BY INHERITANCE

The details of the subdivision of land by inheritance have already been presented. (See Chapter XIV.) Here it is necessary only to emphasize that this type of division of land has resulted in the creation of many thousands of small farms in Brazil. Perhaps it is the factor that is responsible for the development of the majority of all such establishments. However, it is extremely important to bear in mind that farms created by this process do not acquire operators with attitudes and skills equivalent to those transmitted socially in the family farm heritage.

The child in a fazendeiro's family inherits the standard of living of his progenitors, all the mind set as to what the members of his class properly may do, but only a fraction of the land necessary to maintain a level of living that is the equivalent of that standard. Rather than a terrain from which to draw an abundant living, his small fragment of the fazenda may be merely a badge that advertises his poor economic condition, makes it the more impossible to avoid the appearance of poverty. This manner of subdividing lands probably has been one of the most powerful demoralizing forces in operation during the evolution of Brazilian society.

GRANTS TO SOLDIERS

Although the granting of lands to former soldiers was less important in Brazil than in the United States, nevertheless it was one of the elements by which subdivision of land and the development of middle-class farmers were facilitated. Originally, such a reward for voluntary service in the empire's armed forces was decreed a law of January 2, 1865. It would be difficult to determine the extent to which the soldiers took advantage of its provisions or to which they actually established themselves on the lands so granted. However, for years afterwards, it was an item to be reckoned with. When the states got the land following 1889, many of them had to take into account the possibility of having public lands claimed under the provisions of the old law. Thus São Paulo provided that any of the veterans residing in that state, who had not as yet received their allotment, might receive free concessions of twenty hectares of terras devolutas.[82]

OTHER WAYS

The miscellaneous ways in which small farming groups have become established on the land cannot all be identified. One discovers

[82] *Ibid.*, 20–21.

settlements of these sitiantes scattered about throughout Brazil as he travels through the country, but oftentimes the people themselves do not know how the settlements came into being. Some of them have been there for a long time. One does not see much difference, for example, between the small sítios growing coconut trees along the beaches of Pernambuco and Bahia and those described by Koster over 100 years ago.[83]

Also one wonders how the riverbank settlements throughout the Amazon Basin got there, how the people obtained possession of the land, and how long they have been established on it. In the mountainous section between Rio de Janeiro and São Paulo, and elsewhere along the valleys in the tops of the Serra do Mar, he encounters sitiantes who are told by neighboring fazendeiros that they are the owners of the land on which the sitiantes live and that it came into their possession by inheritance. If the title were ever contested one does not know how the case would be determined. At the present time the people themselves do not know how they came to be on the land.

Occasionally, travelers have informed us concerning the motivations for dispersing into the out-of-the-way spots. For example, von Spix and von Martius have described how the desertion of members of the militia during the struggle with the Spanish settlements at the mouth of and to the west of the Paraná had much to do with dispersing population throughout the more remote portions of São Paulo and Minas Gerais.

> The Paulista, it is true, is distinguished above most of the inhabitants of Brazil for obedience to the government; but the greatest dissatisfaction could not fail to be produced by a war, which in the eyes of the multitude was not carried on for urgent reasons, but rather in compliance with the opinions of a few, and to which the farmer, who till then had never been used to war, remained wholly indifferent, till he was roused on finding it required the sacrifice of the lives and domestic happiness of many of his fellow-countrymen. Accordingly a great part of the militia deserted before they marched away, and fled sometimes with their whole families, either into the remote wilderness of the capitania of S. Paulo, or to Minas Geraes, where they settled, and from which province, though demanded back, they were not given up, according to the privileges enjoyed by each capitania.[84]

No doubt some of the small farming settlements in Brazil owe their origins to this type of dispersal. Other foreigners have been privileged to observe the settlement process at work, to catch one of these small farming settlements of the spontaneous variety in the making. Of a particularly well-situated and prosperous one in the state of Paraná, an English writer, Bigg-Wither, has left the following account:

I must introduce the reader to a veritable prairie phenomenon—for so it seemed to me—lying immediately beneath my feet, comprised in a com-

---

[83] Cf. Koster, *Travels in Brazil*, I, 303; and *Conceito de Povoado*, 7–9.
[84] Von Spix and von Martius, *Travels in Brazil*, I, 319.

pact little area of about ten square miles. On this little tract of prairie all the signs of a thriving and well-to-do population were manifested. *Chacaras* and other small houses were thickly sprinkled about it. Gardens and orange orchards, cultivated patches of potatoes and *mandioca,* green paddocks in which mules and cows were grazing, struck the eye, offering altogether a sight so uncommon in the province of Paraná as to excite something more than ordinary surprise and wonderment.

With me was an Englishman, named Mercer, who, though having only lately settled in the district, had prospered so well that he was about to become a son-in-law of one of the wealthiest *fazendeiros* of the neighbourhood. The phenomenon in question Mercer explained to me thus. The *chacaras* and houses had formerly been the habitation of miners. After the abandonment of the mine . . . these men had, contrary to usual experience in Brazil, found it profitable to remain where they were, merely to cultivate the soil, so marvellously fertile was it, as compared with other prairie lands, and moreover, so convenient was its situation with respect to other essential requirements.

This situation, indeed, was perhaps the most important element in insuring the prosperity of this little handful of colonists, for such they really are. Its advantage lay in the fact of its being in close proximity to the Forest, but yet, at the same time, not actually within its borders. Each of these little farmers had his garden and his paddock of twenty or thirty acres on the prairies, close to his house, on which he kept his mules, his cows, and his pigs, while at the same time, within an hour's walk or ride, he had his forest rocas, where he could grow corn and beans, without which his mules would not work, his pigs would not fatten, and he himself could not live. While the prairie enables him to keep his half-dozen mules or so with profit, the forest was the reservoir from whence, by means of his beasts of burden, all his chief necessities of life were drawn. The surplus produce of his rocas he was able in like manner to convey profitably to the neighbouring markets of Ponta Grossa, Castro, and Curitiba, where fair prices were always obtainable.

Here, then, was a case of the vexed problem of colonization in Brazil solved. A class of small proprietors had sprung up, without petting or nursing either by government or by well-meaning enthusiasts such as Dr. Favre [who was responsible for the establishment of the ill-fated French colony at Thereza in the same state], and the evidence of the prosperity to which they had attained was there before our eyes.[85]

The quilombos, or settlements of runaway slaves who established communities in the forests, undoubtedly gave rise to other groups of what are now small-farming families. Despite the vigilance of the *capitães-do-mato* (captains of the forest), a special police, usually composed of mulattoes whose job was to trace down runaways, these Negroes made frequent raids on the fazendas and engenhos, carrying away both booty and female slaves. Sometimes they stole women from the Indians and, on other occasions, affiliated themselves with groups of the natives. The largest and best known of these quilombos was Palmares, or Palm Forests, in Pernambuco, established at the time of the conflict with the Dutch. This Negro settlement became as strong and powerful as a small kingdom and even carried on offensive warfare against the Portuguese.[86] However, there

[85] Bigg-Wither, *Pioneering in South Brazil,* II, 207–209.

[86] Cf. Southey, *History of Brazil,* II, 23, for details; and Edison Carneiro, *O Quilombo dos Palmares, 1630–1695* (São Paulo, 1947).

were numerous others in most of the provinces, "quilombo" surviving today in many place names scattered throughout Brazil's interior. Furthermore, some of these settlements are known to exist to this day in parts of the Amazon [87] and are said to be present in the northern part of Maranhão.

[87] Cf. Ernesto Vinhaes, *Aventuras de um Repórter na Amazônia* (Pôrto Alegre, 1939).

CHAPTER XVII

LOCALITY GROUPS

M AN IN HIS RELATIONSHIPS with his fellows divides the earth's surface into areas of common living, mutual aid, and human association. In addition to the family, which is the smallest group occupying a definite locale, there are always larger areas of association, definite portions of the earth's surface that make up the orbs of larger groups known as neighborhoods and communities. These three are the fundamental cells and tissues out of which the State and the Great Society are composed.

Few aspects of societal structure are worthy of more careful study than the locality groups, particularly the neighborhood and the community. The first of these is the smaller of the two, being the first group of significance beyond the family, an area of face-to-face social relationships, and frequently the circle in which mutual aid prevails. The second, the community, is larger. Its members need not all be in face-to-face contact with one another. Generally it is composed of more than one neighborhood and is large enough that nearly all the needs of its members may be satisfied within its limits. Although any one neighborhood, or any one group of neighborhoods clustered into a community, may be relatively unimportant, in the aggregate they constitute the whole society. It is an aphorism to say that as the family or the village (community or neighborhood) is so will be the society. It is probably even more valid to say that the customs of the community and the neighborhood become the primary determinants of the habits of the individual. For, most important of all, it is on the family, the neighborhood, and the community levels that the individual gets his personality.

These facts make a knowledge of society's natural groupings of considerable moment. There are also other reasons for the study of locality-group structure. As the world moves farther into the phase in which rural affairs are the concern of national and state governments, a knowledge of the natural areas of association becomes of more and more consequence. Neighborhoods and communities cease to be merely local areas of association and become the fundamental social units that may be utilized in the purposeful organization of institutions and agencies. A school system, a health program, social security, a directed agriculture, any activity of the greater society organized on a representative basis draws strength from the natural groupings of society when its areas of activity are delineated in terms of neighborhood and community boundaries. Use in turn serves to invigorate the society's cellular units, so that the neighborhoods and communities thrive, as new functions are added to their roles. For these reasons the general nature of Brazil's neighborhood and community pattern is analyzed here in detail.

OFFICIAL CLASSIFICATION

Brazil is one of the few nations, if not the only one, in the world that has an official definition and classification of its locality groups, although Peru has made considerable progress along these lines. The classification and accompanying definitions are contained in Resolution Number 99 adopted by the Instituto Brasileiro de Geografia e Estatística on July 25, 1941.[1] It seems to have been adopted as a result of a study made in Pernambuco for the purpose of determining the nature of the povoado, or small center of population other than a seat of a *distrito de paz* or the seat of a município. The resolution is as follows:

Be it resolved:
Art. 1.—There is defined as a locality [*localidade*] every place in the national territory where there is a permanent agglomeration of inhabitants.
Art. 2.—The Council establishes, for its use, the following classification and correlated definitions of localities:
Capital, Federal—The locality where the National Government has its seat, with its executive, legislative, and judicial powers.
Capital—A locality where a political unit of the Federation has its seat of government, with the exclusion of the Federal District.
Cidade—The seat of a município, that is a locality having the same name as the município of which it forms a part and where the respective prefeitura [government of the município or county] is situated, excluding municípios containing capitals.
Vila—The seat of a distrito de paz, that is a locality having the same name as the distrito of which it forms a part and where the district authority is situated, excluding the districts containing seats of municípios.
Povoado—A locality which is not the seat of an administrative division, but where there is an agglomeration of residences, generally a religious cohesion about a church or chapel, a commercial function expressed in a fair or a market, and whose inhabitants exercise their economic activities not as a function in the interest of a single proprietor of the soil, but of the group itself.
Propriedade Rural—A locality which is not the seat of an administrative division and where private dominion is manifested exclusively. [This would apply to a village or a hamlet composed of the homes of workers on a fazenda or usina.]
Núcleo—A locality which is not the seat of an administrative division where inhabitants are grouped together under a special regime. [This would apply to various colonies established by federal and state governments.]

[1] Only recently has the term *comunidade* been used in Brazil to apply to a social group living in a specific area. At present, however, its usage is becoming widespread.

Lugarejo or Local—There will be designated in this manner the place, that does not fall in any of the previously mentioned classes, whether it contains inhabitants (when *lugarejo* applies) or not (when *local* is correct), as soon as it possesses a name by which it is known.

Art. 3.—It is the duty of the regional Offices to classify in each type of locality here defined the synonyms in common usage in its territory and to send them to the Central Office inside the space of six months.[2]

It only needs to be pointed out that the differentiation according to single or multiple ownership of the area inhabited by the locality group is quite different from our practice and that more stress is placed on nucleated settlement than has been the case in the United States.

SIMILARITY OF LOCALITY GROUPS IN BRAZIL
AND THE UNITED STATES

Because Brazil, like the United States, has used the single farmstead in arranging its population on the land, its locality-group structure shows little affinity with Old World patterns. For the same reason it does not compare closely with the pattern prevailing in many of the Spanish-speaking countries of America. Upon close observation, both the smaller neighborhood and the larger community of Brazil reveal many characteristics similar to those of the corresponding social groupings in the United States and Canada. In fact, in their essential features all of the locality groupings of Brazil—farms, neighborhoods, communities, and municípios—show more similarities with those of the United States than with those of any other country. Along with our own territorial groupings they bear indelibly the stamp "made in America."

The preceding sentences should not be interpreted to mean that Brazilian neighborhoods and communities and those of the United States are identical. There are differences between North American and Brazilian locality groups, and it is also true that the rural social organization in Brazil has many features in common with that of its Spanish-American neighbors. For example, Brazil, like Mexico, Chile, and Peru, hardly knew the family farm until the nineteenth century; even today Brazil's typical agricultural unit, the fazenda, is large and in itself more closely resembles the Spanish-American hacienda, the Argentine estância, or the Southern plantation, than the Midwestern farm. In Brazil there is a great chasm separating the social classes in agriculture, a degree of social stratification considerably greater than that in the plantation sections of our own South and comparable only with that in Peru, Chile, Argentina, and other of Brazil's neighbors. The Brazilian Indian, like the native of Mexico and Cuba, was reduced to slavery and made to work the estates of his European masters and not killed off or driven away, as were the natives of North America. All these facts have had a bearing on the nature of

[2] For Portuguese text, see *Conceito de Povoado,* Appendix.

locality groups, have brought about differences between the social organization of Brazil and the United States. Nevertheless, in spite of these variances, in Brazil social groupings are more similar to those of the United States and Canada than to those of her Spanish-American neighbors.

As is suggested by these facts, Brazil's locality groupings are more similar to those found in the South than to the ones distributed throughout the other parts of the United States. Like Brazil, our Southland originally was cut to the plantation pattern; it inherited all the multifarious ills that are socially bequeathed by the system of slavery; it continues to this day to be characterized by sharp class and caste distinctions among the rural population, a situation in which a person is born to a certain estate and it is difficult for him to rise above it. In addition to the important factors which have made for general similarity between North American and Brazilian locality-group structures, these elements have served to make Brazil's neighborhoods and communities more like those of the South than those in other parts of our country.

LOCALITY GROUPS IN THE NEW WORLD AND IN THE OLD

In both Brazil and the United States the contemporary rural community is considerably different from European types of agricultural settlements. At the time of the colonization of America the farm in Portugal and England, as well as throughout most of the rest of Europe, consisted of a home and a garden plot located in a small hamlet or village, plus several pieces of arable land scattered about in the fields that surrounded the cluster of homes. Communal rights to the use of pasture and woodlands were also a common feature. In other words, the farm, the smallest locality group, was not a well-differentiated territorial unit but was fused with the neighborhood or the community. It did not stand out as an entity as does the cattle *fazenda* of Minas Gerais or the Iowa farm.

The European neighborhood, on the other hand, was much more clearly distinguishable than its American counterpart. It consisted of a number of families living closely together in a hamlet or small village and surrounded by the farming, pasture, and woodlands which they used. There might, indeed, be difficulty in distinguishing the neighborhood from the rural community which was constituted in the same manner and differed only by being larger and more completely enveloping all the activities of its members. Although it would probably be difficult to classify accurately Portuguese and English locality groups of the sixteenth century into neighborhoods and communities, this does not obscure the essential nature of these social units. In both cases social differentiation had proceeded very little and had not reached the degree in which any considerable number of occupations, other than agriculture, were represented in the hamlet or village; rather, the farming families themselves also performed most of the work that later came to be specialized activities of the butcher, the baker, and the candlestick maker. Both Portugal and England knew the large estate and were burdened with a landed aristocracy, but in spite of this the village and hamlet communities and neighborhoods were inhabited by families who enjoyed a considerable degree of independence and self-direction in the agricultural activities and their social relationships with the others of their class. In many cases they resembled the village community of free cultivators in all respects except that they owed certain obligations and dues to the lord of the manor.

There have been changes of course in the European community and neighborhood, but these have not altered their basic structural features. In most of Europe, although not in England, the rural community still remains a clear-cut, well-defined, closely integrated entity. The village continues to be mainly a residential center for the farm families who till the surrounding lands, nonagricultural occupations being very scantily represented in the small center. The village and its tributary fields are identical with the community.

Observation of the locality-group structure of Brazil and the United States has served to show how great has been the change from such Old World patterns. In these New World countries, nucleated settlement patterns are not the rule; they are to be found only in the workers' quarters on the large estates. The cultivators live scattered about on the land. The farm or fazenda stands by itself as a fundamental unit, clearly distinct, and the families who manage its business and till its lands live amidst the fields or pastures and not in a village or hamlet center.[3] As a result, the Brazilian rural community is not readily visualized and defined; the village is by no means identical with the community; in pre-Galpin days the Brazilian countryman might have been called "the man without a community."

The neighborhood in Brazil and the United States also differs sharply from the type that is predominant in European countries. In both of these New World nations it is not as a rule composed of the families who live together in a nucleated center. Even when this is the case, the tiny village or hamlet is composed of the homes of

[3] As a matter of fact, both in Brazil and the United States the village or town was often an "afterthought"—not, however, when settlement was being pushed by a railroad—or a spontaneous aggregation that arose to care for the multiplying needs of the settlers. This seems to have been even more true in Brazil than in the United States, partially because of the role of the upper classes in colonizing activities. Where the lord of the manor was able to provide on the fazenda itself the church for all classes and the school for children of the upper strata, there was less need for the village. "The rural senhor was at the same time chief of the family and work, head of the government, judge, and chief of police. He was accompanied to his lands, to his latifundium, by the chaplain for the religious cult and the school master for his own children, those of his relatives, and those of his dependents. The villages, towns, and small cities which were founded near the fazendas and engenhos, were at first parasitic upon these rural senhores, remaining frequently subordinate to their prestige and their will. Long is the history of irregularities in the municípios of the matutos and sertanejos whose chiefs were always the tools of the nearest or most powerful rural senhor." Carneiro Leão, *A Sociedade Rural*, 107. However, in many cases the fazenda itself developed into a village, town, and even city.

workers on a plantation or ranch and is not a collection of the dwellings of freeholders who till the surrounding lands. But in general in Brazil, as in the United States, the neighborhood consists of a small number of families who live on adjacent farms, whose members frequently come into face-to-face contact with one another, and who have established a system of mutual aid amongst themselves. Brazilian neighborhoods owe their integration to a wide variety of causes: to the visiting and mutual aid among families who live near one another; to the pooling of efforts in order to secure and maintain a church or a chapel or a school; to a mutual dependence on a landed proprietor, a sugarmill, a cotton gin, a gristmill, a co-operative marketing association, a creamery or cheese factory, a railroad station, or some other economic agency; to the grouping together in close proximity of farm families who are intimately knit together by ties of kinship, national origins and language, and religion; or to the fact that a few families have been thrown into close and constant contact among themselves, and isolated from the larger world, by establishing their residences in a small mountain valley or cove, a fertile and watered area in the midst of a barren region, on a small island, or even on a large fazenda or plantation.

THE COMMUNITY IN BRAZIL AND THE UNITED STATES

Unlike the old village communities of Europe, Asia, and much of Spanish America the rural community in both Brazil and the United States consists of two distinct parts. The first of these is a village or town nucleus whose principal function is not that of providing a location for homes of agriculturists. Rather it serves as a residence for tradesmen, men skilled in the professions, moneylenders, and workmen of all types, and as a center for schools, churches, and recreational institutions. In this village or town center all the social and economic institutions converge. The second indispensable part of the community consists of the farm families who live in the surrounding area, who make the village their trading, ceremonial, and social center, and particularly in the case of Brazil, a location for their "town houses." "Going to town" in Brazil is *ir ao comércio* (go to business). The fact that the primary functions of the village or town are those of trading, manufacturing (mostly small industries), education, government, religion, and recreation and that these are carried on largely as a service for the population living in the area surrounding the center, definitely aligns the Brazilian rural communities with those of the United States and Canada. The same factor also sets them sharply apart from those European, Asiatic, and Spanish-American countries in which the rural village is chiefly a residential center for farm families. Summarizing briefly these points and adding other essential community characteristics it may be said that the modern Brazilian and North American rural community is: (1) a geographic area consisting of a village trade center and some surrounding farms and neighborhoods, (2) an area within which there is a general consciousness on the part of the people of belonging together or at least of identifying themselves with the neighborhoods in which they live, and the larger community within which their farms and their neighborhoods lie and of which they constitute integral parts, and (3) a consensus of opinion among the group of people living in this contiguous area which forms the community's locale that the fortunes of each individual in the locality are closely affected by the welfare of the community as a whole.

Viewed in neighborhood terms, the rural community consists of the village center and the cluster of neighborhoods that are tributary to it. Each of these in turn is made up of a small number of families whose members are in constant, intimate, and face-to-face contact. The community attachments of these neighborhoods may be weak or strong, but the inhabitants of each of them are in more frequent contact with, and have a greater attachment to, the particular service center that forms the community nucleus than to any other service center. The fact that Brazil's rural communities are made up of constellations of neighborhoods also helps make them basically similar to those of the United States.

In Brazil and the southern part of the United States the village-centered rural community envelops large estates—fazendas or plantations—which of themselves may be almost large enough and self-sufficient enough to stand alone as communities. In both countries also it is not unusual to find a family of the landed aristocracy possessed of a "town house" in the community center in addition to the casa grande or "big house" on the land, and dividing its time between the two. In both countries, too, the social horizons and contacts of the landowning aristocracy or elite are far different from those of the laboring classes. Since the attachments of this extremely influential group transcend local neighborhood and community lines in Brazil as in the plantation South, the nature of the rural community is considerably changed from the type prevailing in our own Midwestern and other family farming areas. The landowning aristocracy reaches out and attains attachments and loyalties on a national or even international scale—their lives cannot be contained within the limits of a small piece of rural territory. Deprived of the interest, singleness of purpose, and frequently the residence of its leading elements, many rural communities and neighborhoods atrophy.

There is also a progressive tendency in both Brazil and the United States for the local governmental unit, the município and the county, to function as a larger rural or rurban community. Rather rapidly the county seat in the United States is becoming the economic and social center, as well as the political center, for the numerous smaller towns, villages, and hamlets, the communities and neighborhoods embraced within the county limits. Automobiles and good roads, aided by the elaboration and centralization of governmental function, are rapidly bringing to the fore this revised form of what

Dr. Charles J. Galpin designated the rurban community.[4] Rural Brazil lacks the automobiles and good roads, but in many parts of the country and particularly in São Paulo and Minas Gerais the tendency for the município as a whole to become a rurban community, centered in and about the cidade which constitutes its seat, is even stronger than the corresponding development in the United States. In spite of the lack of cars and roads people do get to the center; it may be on foot, by horseback, or in the numerous jardineiras, but many of them, especially the men, do manage to spend Saturday night and Sunday, or at least Sunday, in town. Where the município is limited in area, as in southern Minas Gerais and São Paulo, this means in the *sede* of the município.

One significant difference between Brazil and the United States, a factor that also is extremely important with respect to town-country unity, is that Brazil does not know the village, town, or city incorporated separately from the surrounding rural area. Even though the lion's share of the tax money may be spent on improvement within the sede of the município, the rural people have a right to consider the public facilities as belonging to them also, and the authorities who spend the money and direct the public services are legally obligated to realize that their responsibility is to the entire município. Consequently, if a small Brazilian city or town becomes an urban "cyst" in the midst of a large rural population, it does so contrary to the spirit of law, and not with its aid and abetment, as frequently is the case in the United States.

There are also several other differences between Brazilian and North American communities that need to be pointed out. First it may be indicated that in Brazil the role of the village as a church and ceremonial center is relatively more important. In the days before administrative and judicial boundaries were carefully delineated, it was customary, in counting the populations of Brazilian centers, to include all persons within the *toque do sino* (sound of the church bell).[5] This seems to be an indication that the community area was then delimited in terms of the service area of the church. In those days the boundaries of communities in the United States were best described by the limits of the "team haul." Today, although the Brazilian village or town may contain a number of churches, they are usually all of the same denomination, Roman Catholic. Furthermore, one of them is the mother church and the others its affiliates. If there are chapels or *oratórios* on the surrounding fazendas, they too are subordinate to and serviced by the mother church or *matriz*. Because of this homogeneity in religious affairs the boundaries of the religious community coincide rather closely with those of the general community.

---

[4] Cf. Charles J. Galpin, *Rural Social Problems* (New York, 1924), 75; Smith, *Current Social Trends and Problems in Latin America*, 7–9; and José Arthur Rios, *A Educação dos Grupos* (Rio de Janeiro, 1954), *passim*.

[5] Cf. Burton, *The Highlands of the Brazil*, I, 81.

A second difference that must be indicated is that ethnic and racial heterogeneity do less to confuse community and neighborhood patterns in Brazil. Within the limits of the same community there are not many places where overlapping neighborhoods of whites and Negroes may be distinguished, as is so generally the case in the southern parts of the United States, i.e., those portions of our country in which Negroes live in open-country areas. Today, as when Koster wrote at the beginning of the nineteenth century, "it is surprising, though extremely pleasing, to see how little difference is made between a white man, a mulatto, and a Creole negro, if all are equally poor and if all have been born free." [6] Where persons of different colors live within the limits of the same community there is no great tendency in most of Brazil for the complexity of the locality-group structure brought about by class and other differences to be further complicated by lines of cleavage that follow color lines. True, class differences are closely correlated with color shades, and any generalization about lack of race discrimination is less valid for São Paulo and the three states south of it than for the other parts of Brazil. Nevertheless, the comparative lack of constellations according to color, combined with the religious homogeneity, make the internal structure of the Brazilian community much less intricate than that of the typical one in the United States.

Finally, there are great differences between the communities of the two countries in the importance of the commercial function and the manner in which it is organized. In the United States trade is the principal function of the village which forms the community's center, whereas in Brazil the religious function may occupy first place. There may be exceptions to this rule, but in general it will probably hold true.

The organization of business in the trading centers of the two countries also is different. In the United States there is little remaining of the old type "market" or "fair," an economic institution which provides that on a designated day of the week a certain village or town is the place to which buyers and sellers from a considerable area will resort for the purchase, sale, and exchange of produce and merchandise. Brazil has retained this ancient institution as a keystone in the business structure of its rural areas. Nearly every village or town has its public market, and many of them have their weekly "fairs" or *feiras*. One may read such descriptions as the following of the commerce carried on in the cotton- and cane-producing município of Quipapa, Pernambuco: "Commerce consists of the local operation of weekly fairs, where the products of the region are sold, others

---

[6] Koster, *Travels in Brazil*, II, 80. However, "conversing on one occasion with a man of colour who was in my service, I asked him if a certain *Capitam-mor* was not a mulatto-man; he answered, 'he was, but is not now.' I begged him to explain, when he added, 'Can a Capitam-mor be a mulatto-man?'" *Ibid.*, 174–76. He also comments as follows about the color of officers in the military: "In the white militia regiments, the officers ought to be by law white men; but in practice they are rather reputed white men, for very little pains are taken to prove that there is no mixture of blood." *Ibid.*, 176.

which come from outside resold, such as dry goods, notions, liquids, utensils, and the goods being displayed in mercantile establishments or in temporary sheds." [7] Or if one reads the descriptions of the povoados themselves he will find that Queimadas in the município of Bom Jardim is chiefly distinguished by the chapel constructed in 1879 and the weekly fair; [8] or that Riberão on the "English" railroad, and near the usinas Riberão and Estrelliana, "has securely established 200 houses, and regularly others are being erected. It is commercial and the location of a weekly fair." [9] On the other hand, Rosarinho in the município of Pau d'Alho, only five kilometers from the seat and having two small chapels and a public school, is extremely poor, and although "founded long ago is without any commercial life and decadent." [10]

These fairs seem to be of least relative importance in the villages and towns of the south, and more important as one moves from Minas Gerais into Bahia, Pernambuco, and the other northeastern states.[11] In a signed article published in the *Correio da Manhã* of Rio de Janeiro, May 26, 1942, Vasconcelos Torres described in some detail this important social institution. He began the article by saying that the "fair is a complement of rural life in the north. It comes once a week and its occurrence is equivalent to a holiday. From all sides arrive persons who have come to secure provisions for the period of a week. They carry baskets and sacks, and oftentimes travel several leagues in order to reach the market place." Some of the fairs have great renown, among them that of Sant' Ana, Cachoeira, and Santo Amaro in Bahia; Propriá, Estância, and Itabaiana in Sergipe. It is popularly believed that goods are cheaper in the fairs. Farinha occupies an important role in the trading; the rural workers will give a kilo of charque for twenty liters of this staff of life. The day is also one of recreation, a popular amusement being that of listening to the folk tales narrated in song by blind singers. Many of the verses are printed in small booklets [12] and sold. After the outbreak of war the fair naturally became a center for fifth columnists. A favorite bit of their propaganda warned the rural people that they might have to leave their homes and go to other countries from which they would never return. This had an adverse effect. "Rural police, which already exist in the state of Rio, would be the proper ones to eliminate these who would disturb the well being of the countryman." [13]

[7] Sebastião de Vasconcellos Galvão, *Diccionario Chorographico, Historico e Estatistico de Pernambuco* (Rio de Janeiro, 1921), III, 4.

[8] *Ibid.*, 2.

[9] *Ibid.*, 495.

[10] *Ibid.*, 507.

[11] For information about the fairs in the various municípios of Bahia, see Vianna, *Memoir of the State of Bahia, passim.*

[12] I made a small collection of those that recount the life of the famous outlaw Lampeão, which seem to be among the most popular. Already this notorious bandit, although dead for only a quarter of a century, is immortalized among the sertanejos as a virtual Robin Hood.

[13] Vasconcelos Torres, "O Trabalhador Rural e a Feira," *Correio da Manhã* (Rio de Janeiro), May 26, 1942. Cf. Trujillo Ferrari, *Potengi*, 148–49.

VILLAGE AND OPEN COUNTRY RELATIONSHIPS

Although one may quickly determine the nature of the Brazilian rural community by traveling and residing in the rural districts of the country, he must search carefully to find descriptions of its essential features. The following interesting description of a village in Minas Gerais on a Sunday morning helps to indicate the role of the village nucleus in the Brazilian village-centered community.

After breakfast we all rode over to the village of Taboleiro Grande, about one mile away, some of our friends intending to put in an appearance at mass. It was a pleasant ride over good roads in pleasant company. The village is very prettily situated on an elevated plain, surrounded by serras, and contains about 600 inhabitants. The houses are detached and form the sides of a square, and the streets leading from it; in the middle of it, is a small, neat, and clean church, amidst a grove of palmetto palm-trees. At one of its corners is a little structure somewhat resembling in form the theater of Punch and Judy, but a closer inspection showed it to be a belfry. Adjoining the church was the canvas booth of a traveling circus, and as the bell of the church ceased its clatter on the termination of mass, the bell of the circus commenced ringing, so that the devout went from the church doors to the neighboring equestrian performance. What a heterogeneous crowd it is that one sees on a Sunday morning in an ordinary thriving Minas village! There are important *fazendeiros* (country squires), white and whitey-brown, on prancing steeds; well-clad farmers, white and brown, also well mounted; *matutors* [sic] and *sertõeneijos* [sic] (labourers from the woodslands and cattle districts), some mounted, some on foot; the wives, daughters, mothers, and sisters accompanying their male relations either on horseback, or pillion-fashion, or on foot. . . .
Amidst the turmoil of noises produced by the hammering of the church bell, the beating of the big drum of the circus, and an occasional bang from a rocket, the proprietor shouted his invitations to "Walk up, gentlemen, walk up, just about to commence," making the scene anything but suggestive of a Sunday morning; the people take their diversions very quietly, even apathetically; those that cannot afford to enter the circus, wander listlessly to and fro, with less animation than afternoon loungers at a seaside esplanade, the females of each family marching solemnly in front of the male friends, the latter jealously watchful of any possible signals of intrigues with the opposite sex. We stand at the door of a large store, and as the crowd pass by, all salute our friends, each according to his kind. . . .
Nearly all the men and women wear boots or shoes, but they look unaccustomed to their use, as they really are, for the walk from home is always performed barefooted, until the village is approached when the shoes are put on, or a treasured fine ribbon is carefully unpacked and fastened to a dress; for it is quite a common sight to see them completing their toilettes by a roadside stream ere entering amidst the "povo." [14]

With minor changes to allow for the presence of an automobile or so in the village and the use of this twentieth-century machine by some of the fazendeiros who live nearby, this description fits the 1960's as well as 1873.
Wells also reported on the change which came over the fazenda

[14] Wells, *Three Thousand Miles Through Brazil*, I, 215–17.

when on Sundays everyone went to spend the day in the village center:

> But on a Sunday all work ceases, there is a general tubbing and cleaning up of a week's dirty faces, the young men appear in clean cotton shirts, trousers, and home-made coats of striped thick cotton, straw hats, and spurs on shoeless feet. It is a sight to see their hair; it is combed and then plastered thick with beef fat, both by the young men, young women, and girls. Old Joaquim also appears smartly dressed, even to long yellow leather boots and silver spurs, and the harness of his horse is studded with silver mountings; the elder ones all mount horses and ride off to mass at the village of Capella Nova. The old blacks saunter about, or sleep, or beg of me a piece of tobacco or a comforting dram of *cachaça,* which is never refused to the poor old souls.
> Whenever I remain at the fazenda on a Sunday old Joaquim hurries back, otherwise he spends his day at the village with his gossips.[15]

Auguste de Saint-Hilaire seems to have been the observant traveler who took most interest in such aspects of community structure. He frequently specified that a good share of the houses in a village or town belonged to fazendeiros who operated agricultural establishments in the surrounding area and visited the little centers only on Sundays and feast days. Thus he says, "The inhabitants of Mogí are, in the majority, agriculturists, who come to the city only on Sundays." [16] After complimenting Franca for the polished manners of its inhabitants he added: "With the exception of a small number of laborers and dealers in foods the remainder were all agriculturists, who, according to the custom, possessed houses in the seat of the *comarca* only in order to pass Sundays in them, houses which, during the other days of the week remained closed, because their respective proprietors reside on their fazendas." [17] The same author made similar observations concerning numerous other villages and towns in the interior of Brazil.

The reports of other observers are in accord. "The city of Itú," wrote Dr. Gaston about Itú, São Paulo, "is made up to a large extent by the residences of parties who own planting interests in the country around, and many of them owning houses here spend most of their time upon their fazendas, so that the population is not usually proportionate to the number of houses." [18] Dr. George Gardner, who traveled extensively through the states of Ceará, Piauí, Goiás, Bahia, and Minas Gerais about 1840, says of Parnagua in Piauí: "The Villa . . . contains in all about a hundred houses, but not more than one-half of them are inhabited, as many belong to fazendeiros who only occupy them during the festival times." [19] And Burton entered the following item about Santa Lucia, Minas Gerais, in his account: "To judge from the streets, prostitution is the most thriving trade; but all

[15] *Ibid.,* 164–65.
[16] Auguste de Saint-Hilaire, *Viagem à Provincia de São Paulo* (São Paulo, 1940), 143.
[17] *Ibid.,* 119.
[18] Gaston, *Hunting a Home in Brazil,* 278.
[19] Gardner, *Travels in the Interior of Brazil,* 220. See also 265, 277, 280, 315.

assured me that it was outdone by Cruvello [Curvello?] a city further north, and ten leagues to the west of the main artery. Both of these are 'church towns,' visited by the planters on Sundays and holidays." [20]

This practice of maintaining a town residence for use on festive occasions is widespread throughout other parts of Brazil also. Of Goiana in Pernambuco, Koster, an Englishman interested in trade and commerce, said: "In the vicinity are many fine sugar plantations. I suppose that some of the best lands in the province are in this neighbourhood. The proprietors of these occasionally reside in the town, and as daily intercourse often creates rivalry among wealthy families, this necessarily increases expenditure, and the town is in consequence much benefited by the augmented consumption of luxuries." [21]

Even Gardner, who rarely gave any details about the ecological arrangement of towns or cities, or the managerial practices followed on the fazendas, commented as follows about a small place in Piauí.

> The Villa de Santa Anna das Merces, or as it is more commonly called Jaicóz, is situated about five leagues to the west of Boa Experança, and contains about seventy or eighty houses built in the form of a large square, but only three sides of it were then completed; in the centre of this square there is a very handsome small church. The outskirts of the town contain many huts belonging to the poorer classes, chiefly constructed of the stems and leaves of the Carnahuba palm, which grows abundantly in the neighbourhood; a few shopkeepers and tradesmen, such as tailors, shoemakers, &., reside constantly in the town, but the greater number of the houses belong to the neighbouring fazendeiros, who only occupy them during the Christmas and other festivals. [22]

Thus not infrequently in Brazil the upper-class family maintains two residences, one in the town—the trading and political center —and another on the estate which lies at some distance. In many cases this has resulted in the wife spending most of her time in the town house, while her husband spent his time on the land. The prevalence of this practice and its effects were commented on by von Spix and von Martius.

> The director of the nearest aldeas of the Coroados does not live in the Presidio de S. João Baptista, though he has a house here, but on his plantation (*rossa*), about a league distant, from which he came on the following day to visit us. This custom of residing for the greater part of the year in a remote country-seat at a distance from the more populous places, prevails throughout Brazil. It has the most injurious consequences on morality and domestic happiness, because the man and wife frequently live separate for months together, which gives occasion to many irregularities. [23]

More recent descriptions of the villages' functions are also to be had, although this aspect in the study of Brazil's natural groupings is still in its infancy. According to Luís Amaral, who has written a three-

[20] Burton, *The Highlands of the Brazil*, II, 10.
[21] Koster, *Travels in Brazil*, I, 67.
[22] Gardner, *Travels in the Interior of Brazil*, 187.
[23] Von Spix and von Martius, *Travels in Brazil*, II, 219.

volume work on the history of Brazilian agriculture, the Brazilian countryman infrequently goes to the town or the city; few are the festive occasions in which he participates in village- or town-centered activities. One of these is the Sunday mass, more or less obligatory, which is also profoundly interesting to him. On Sunday morning he is up early, preparing the animals for the fazendeiros to ride—the laboring classes go on foot. He fortifies himself with a heavy breakfast of fried eggs and corn meal, and also bacon, in addition to the customary coffee with milk. On the way to the center the fazendeiro leads the way, followed by his wife and the other members of his family. They go on horseback. Behind follow the agregados or camaradas and their families, men in front, women following, and children bringing up the rear. The party takes along a host of parcels and packages, containing eggs, fruits, vegetables, fowls, and pigs. Those which belong to the fazendeiro are designed as presents for people living in the center, but mainly for the godmother of the children in the family at whose home they will take lunch and where the fazendeiro's children stay while they are attending school. The packages belonging to the camaradas consist of produce that is being carried in for sale at one of the village stores or in the market place.

Funerals are another occasion on which the country people visit the center. Each person has the sacred duty of attending the last rites for a deceased neighbor. If the one who has passed away belonged to the lower classes, the landowner on whose place he resided is obliged to stand treat to everyone at the *venda* nearest the cemetery. According to Luís Amaral, "the sadness is not soon overcome, this requiring large portions of cachaça. On these occasions even the abstemious partake, because it is a ritual." He also reports that some of the participants are unable to make their way home until the hours by the wayside have enabled them to sleep off the effects of the alcohol. On occasion I have observed the same phenomenon, although Brazil's people are by no means heavy drinkers.

Visits of church dignitaries and the great religious holidays are occasions on which the people from the country may pass several days in the village or town center. These are the times when the fazendeiros open up their town houses for their own use, to assist in sheltering their friends, and also to provide lodging for their most esteemed camaradas.

When there is a marriage of fazendeiros the village or town center again takes on the aspect of a religious holiday. Ostentatious displays of foods and sweets are brought forth, and everyone in the community (village and surrounding area) feels entitled to participate, to betake himself to the house that serves as the headquarters in order "to make an idea of those who do not appear." If one of the families of the fazendeiros concerned does not possess a house in the community center the wedding procession is organized at the home of one of the godmothers. It proceeds from there to the church. The procession is organized as a file of couples, the bride in white and the "little father" (the person who gives away the bride) in black heading the line of marching, followed by the groom and the "little mother"; then come other pairs of adults, and finally the children two by two, boy with boy and girl with girl. On the way to the church the tortuous procession must pass the gantlet of curious eyes and endure the same on the return. A few Sundays later the young couple, this time alone, must go up to the presbytery, where they hear mass and, kneeling side by side, receive the nuptial blessing.

Other than on such occasions the country folk rarely frequent the center. Even then, according to Luís Amaral, they are always in haste to return to the country. A principal motive which he assigns for this feeling is the lack of sanitary facilities in the small centers, and the consequent discomfiture and embarrassment entailed in caring for the physiological necessities of the body. Toilets being absent, men and women alike must resort to the gardens in the back of the houses. But to reach this area of relative seclusion entails passing through the dining room before the eyes of all, going through the patio which always stimulates a great deal of barking by the dogs, and perhaps the disturbance of the guests who have previously made their way to the back of the garden.[24] In the country there is less difficulty and embarrassment involved in attending to nature's needs, and the country folk are relieved to be outside the confines of the village or town. Even now, country folk in the United States are not entirely satisfied with such provisions for their comfort made by the tradesmen in town, although, of course, the modern filling station has done much to alleviate distress. Before the coming of the automobile it was quite a different thing.

Inhabitants of the village also spend part of their time visiting friends and relatives in the fazendas that surround the center. Unless the stay is an extended one, as it frequently is, Sundays are popular occasions for such visits, the townfolk going early to the fazenda and spending the entire day. Visiting back and forth between upper-class families of the towns and the fazendas is still very common. As yet townspeople have not affected "city airs" to any great extent, and so little town-country conflict has arisen on this score.

Village people also go into the open country areas for commercial reasons. The village not only functions as a trade center to which the country people come to buy and sell, but also as the headquarters of numerous peddlers who make regular visits to the surrounding fazendas. In former times especially, the women depended largely on these traveling *mascates* for dress goods, fineries, and other articles of conspicuous consumption. Today nearly every cidade, vila, and even povoado is the home, or at least the headquarters, of some of these hawkers. Koster wrote about this feature of the social organization of the Brazilian rural community: ". . . the place forms a convenient break between Goiana and Rio Grande for the travelling peddlers, a useful, industrious, and, generally honest set of men, as their resting-place and headquarters; from hence they make daily excur-

[24] The materials for the preceding paragraphs were taken from Luís Amaral, *Historia Geral da Agricultura Brasileira* (São Paulo, 1939), I, 39–41.

sions to the plantations, at a little distance, and return here to sleep." [25] Of another village the same author said: "Bom Jardim is a great rendezvous for the hawkers who are proceeding to the Sertam, and for others who merely advance this far." [26] Improved means of communication, since he wrote, have changed the mode of travel in many instances, but in Brazil, as in south Louisiana, the village continues to function as the hub for numerous small trade routes over which movable merchandising units dispense goods throughout the surrounding farms or fazendas.

THE NUMBER OF COMMUNITIES

The number of communities in Brazil is of course not known with any exactitude. Nevertheless these relatively complete social units, more self-sufficient, too, in Brazil than in the United States, certainly are very numerous. Undoubtedly each seat of a município is the nucleus of this type of locality group; together with the families living in its trade, school, and church zones, it is entitled to be classed as a community. In 1950 there were 1,894 of these. A few of them rank as metropolitan communities; others have a small city as a nucleus, i.e., each consists of a small urban center plus the surrounding dependent rural territory. But probably more than one-half of them would in the United States be classed as strictly rural, since the population center itself would have less than 2,500 inhabitants. Thus in 1950 a total of 837 of the cidades had less than 2,000 inhabitants, and an additional 605 of them fell in a population category of 2,000 to 5,000.

In addition to the cidades, many vilas would classify as nuclei of communities, a few as rurban, but most of them strictly rural. There were in 1950 a total of 3,482 vilas in Brazil, including six of more than 20,000 inhabitants. Ten others had populations between 10,000 and 20,000, 28 were in the 5,000 to 10,000 category, and an additional 102 had more than 2,000 but less than 5,000 residents. The bulk of them, however, or a total of 2,920, were less than 1,000 in population, and another 416 fell in the group of from 1,000 to 2,000 inhabitants. Allowing for the fact that a good many small population centers have not yet attained recognition as political centers by being designated as vilas, it is probable that the total number of communities in Brazil is about 6,000. Of the centers which form the nuclei of these communities 2,763 in 1960 were seats of municípios.

THE IMPORTANCE OF THE NEIGHBORHOOD

The role of the neighborhood seems to be a more important one in Brazil than in the United States. In many parts of Brazil rural society is still in the neighborhood stage. This is to say that the areas of ac-

[25] Koster, *Travels in Brazil*, I, 83.
[26] *Ibid.*, 201. See also Freyre, *Sobrados e Mucambos*, 63–64.

quaintance and association are small,[27] and that the person's social relationships are mostly confined to a small circle of families living near one another; that relationships are intimate and enduring; that contacts outside the small intimate circle of acquaintances are of relative unimportance; that many goods, services, and types of association which cannot be provided by or for a small cluster of families must be done without; and that the person and family are closely identified with and bound to the life of the immediate vicinity, and only remotely conscious of and infrequently in contact with the activities of the larger and more complete area of human interaction such as the community. In this respect, the importance of the neighborhood as compared with the community, Brazil also is more like the southern portion of the United States than other parts of our country.

Since neighborhood is a concept applied to all locality groups involving more than a family or two which are not large enough and complete enough to circumscribe the lines of its members, it follows that Brazilian neighborhoods are of varying degrees of size and complexity.[28]

VARIETIES OF NEIGHBORHOODS

Just as for the United States, in this discussion every social group having a territorial basis larger than the family and smaller than the community is called a neighborhood. This concept includes groupings all the way from those in which territorial proximity and face-to-face relationships are the sole integrating factors, to those which provide practically all the essential goods and services and are entitled to be called communities. In the analysis that follows, the attempt is made to allow for this variety. Analysis begins with a discussion of the neighborhood status of the social groupings that are generated on large agricultural holdings—the fazendas; it continues with some reference to the groupings composed of independent family groups and concludes with a short analysis of small population aggregations, where institutions for commerce, education, and religion serve as ties, along with residential propinquity.

Generally speaking, each Brazilian fazenda may be said to constitute a genuine neighborhood, although as is the case with some plantations and ranches in the United States, some of them have enough people and come so near circumscribing the entire life of their inhabitants that they might well be classified as communities. As a rule

[27] As indicated above, this statement is not applicable to members of the upper class, whose contacts frequently extend to the largest metropolitan centers.

[28] For example, one may find the following description of the functions of those in the Pernambuco município of Escada, in the *Annuario do Nordeste para 1937* (Recife, 1937), 353: "The city [Escada] is decadent, because all the life is concentrated in the engenhos and usinas, which form genuine villages with schools, churches, and commerce, in short an intense development, in contrast with the city which decays from day to day, justifying more as time goes on the phrase of the great Tobias Barreto, who lived there many years: 'This is an *Escada* [i.e., a stairway] only for descending.'"

the coffee fazendas and the sugar usinas are the largest and come nearest to supplying all of the services enjoyed by their residents. Some of the largest of these approach the community level on the locality-group scale. The agricultural operations in coffee and sugar are on a relatively intensive basis, the density of population is fairly high, the village pattern of settlement prevails, a chapel and perhaps a school are present on the plantation, and usually the workers are obliged to do most of their purchasing at the management's commissary.[29] Thus, for the laboring classes the coffee fazenda or the sugar usina frequently constitutes a little world; if it did not lack political functions it would rank as a community.

The cattle fazenda, on the other hand, at best ranks as a neighborhood. Frequently, however, it is a closely knit neighborhood, composed of the proprietor and his large family, perhaps a few relatives, and his numerous retainers—agregados and vaqueiros. To the highly integrated small group of persons residing on a cattle fazenda, Brazilian writers, such as Oliveira Vianna, Nelson Werneck Sodré, and A. Carneiro Leão, are prone to apply the name "clan." This practice alone is strong justification for considering the small nodules of settlement which are the cattle fazendas as neighborhoods. These are widely dispersed throughout Brazil's vast interior, and each fazendeiro's home and the six to fifty or even one hundred casebres (huts) clustered about it are the centers from which radiate a network of trails that fade out as one moves away from the small social nucleus at the center. That some of these trails finally attain another fazenda headquarters miles away indicates that these neighborhood groups are not entirely unrelated; and that some of the paths fuse with others on their way to an occasional village or town demonstrates that they are not completely lacking in community attachments.

Similar is the situation on the cattle estâncias of Rio Grande do Sul. One Brazilian has applied the "clan" concept to these locality groups.

In the Rio Grande social fabric the estâncias were always the true cells. The *estanceiros*, their families, and their peons constituted a unity that had something of the Celtic clan and of the patriarchal organization without being identical with either of them.

It had neither the aristocratic aspect of the former, nor the predominant degree of relationship that distinguishes the latter.

The solidarity which was formed within the fazendas, about the chiefs of the same, is explained by the inexistence, after a certain time, of the small property; those that had no land came to live as agregados to the masters of the latifundia. Between the chiefs and employees, by the nature of the friendly ties which united them, are encountered much of the character of patriarchal life, where the patron engages with his subordinates in the work of the community. Because it binds into an equal unity persons who are unrelated by lines of kinship, we see in it something of the organization of the clan, without, however, it presenting a cohesion so great as is noted in the complete type of this collective form.[30]

[29] Cf. Fontenelle, *Problemas Economicos do Estado do Rio*, 112.

[30] Jorge Salis Goulart, *A Formação do Rio Grande do Sul* (2d ed.; Pôrto Alegre, 1933), 28; cf. Oliveira Vianna, "O Povo Brazileiro e sua Evolução," *Recenseamento do Brazil, 1920*, I, 291–92.

Neighborhood groups composed of moradores, sitiantes, and other classes of the povo who have not been brought under the influence and partial control of a fazendeiro and transformed into his camaradas or agregados are of almost endless variety. Sometimes several families of these are clustered together in a mountain cove, strung along a beach under the coconut trees, established in a line on the natural levee of a stream, or grouped about the center of a small clearing in the forest that resembles an auger hole in the tropical jungle. The small valleys of the Serra do Mar from Rio Grande do Sul to Espírito Santo, contain thousands of neighborhoods whose boundaries are set by the mountain walls. Others, similar in form, will be found in the coves that cut into the highlands bordering the São Francisco River in Bahia or almost anywhere in the longer settled and more densely populated areas of mountainous terrain. Those that are established on the seacoast, amid the coconut palms, are most conspicuous north of Rio de Janeiro, and especially on the Atlantic boundaries of Bahia and Pernambuco.[31] Settlements of the neighborhood type are to be found lining many of the natural levees for short distances on the many distributaries of the Amazon, or its tributaries, and also on stretches of the Uruguay, the Paraguay, the Paraná, and their branches. It is in Maranhão, among the multi-spiked forests of the babassú palm, and from the air, that the physical expression of the nut collectors' neighborhood is most clear. There, from six to twenty huts of thatch succeed one another at intervals along a rough trail, in appearance resembling a series of knots on a cord. Each of the "knots" is a small nodule of settlement, a neighborhood, and it has its counterpart in many other forested parts of the nation.

In addition to the thousands of Brazilian neighborhoods on its fazendas and the other thousands of the simplest types in which territorial proximity, face-to-face relations, and frequent kinship are the ties which give cohesion to the group, there remain to be considered the thousands of small population centers, povoações and povoados which also are of the neighborhood species. These range all the way from what would be called hamlets in the United States to villages. They may consist of anything from the smallest congregation of houses about a venda or trading post, to villages that fail to qualify as communities only because they lack the political function. Some of them in fact are larger and more complete as service centers than

---

[31] Of these settlements Koster, who knew them well in the years just preceding Brazil's independence, wrote: ". . . indeed, wherever the surf is not violent the sea-shore is well-peopled, along the whole extent of coast between Olinda and the bar of the river Goiana. In many parts the low straw huts are united, or nearly so, in long rows for half a mile together. White-washed cottages, with tiled roofs, are frequently interspersed; churches and chapels have been built: and few intervals of much extent remain unpeopled. The lands are planted with the coco-trees, which is the most profitable plant of Brazil. . . . These coco groves through which the eye can see for miles, with the hovels composed entirely of the leaves of these trees spread among them, form, in some parts very picturesque views; and if, as frequently occurs, the cottage is situated upon the border of a wood, just where the cocos end, and the dark green foliage of the forest trees is seen behind, then the view is even romantic." *Travels in Brazil*, I, 303–304.

others which have been elevated to the status of a seat of a distrito de paz or vila, or even a seat of a município and therefore a cidade.

Recently there has been an official attempt to analyze and clarify the concept of povoado, followed by the official definition of locality groups of all types. The definitions arrived at have already been given. Here it is important to summarize the significant information pertaining to the structural features of the coastal type of neighborhood as described in the little study.[32] Eight povoados were visited, seven of which are found in the município of Igarassú and one in São Lourenço. The following paragraphs give in a condensed form, with explanations interspersed, a free translation of the more significant parts of this report.

Six of the neighborhoods studied are located on the Isle of Itamaracá.[33] They are strung along the coast in a manner that gives all the families ready access to the coconut groves, to the ocean, and to the pearly beach. The latter functions as a road to link the povoados. Fresh water is abundant on the island in pits, wells, and streams. The inhabitants also know how to cut a coconut tree so that rain water, which runs down the trunk, will be siphoned into their large, narrow-mouthed water jars. Oysters and other shellfish, which thrive in the brackish water, are collected for domestic use and for sale. Some salt is produced by evaporating sea water, and wood is cut for fuel and for construction purposes. Roads are poor, consisting mainly of tracks cut into the sandy soil by the vehicles as they wind along amid the coconut trees. There are on the island only one large bridge, "Getúlio Vargas," two small ones of reinforced concrete, and one of wood, in a ruinous state, which spans the Casado River near Vila Velha. Some 6,000 people live on the island. The little population centers of Vila Velha, São Paulo, and Forno da Cal have very stable populations, while Rio do Ambar, Baixa Verde, and Jaguaribe, which are served by a more passable road, have a seasonal influx of visitors during the summer period.

In each of these settlements the ownership of the land is divided among numerous families. There is said to be an infinity of "small coconut farms" (sitiozinhos) which extend in narrow bands "from the beach to the swamp," "from the beach to the river," or "from the

---

[32] *Conceito de Povoado.*

[33] This island was one of the first places in Brazil to be settled. It was given to Pero Lopez de Souza, who occupied it in 1531. In Koster's day it was the most populous part of Pernambuco, except for the immediate vicinity of Recife. At that time (1814) it contained three sugar plantations "well stocked with Negroes," and also many free persons resided on plantations. In addition there were "other considerable tracts which are subdivided among and owned by a great number of persons of small property. The shores of the island are planted with coco-trees, among which are thickly scattered the straw cottages of fishermen; and oftentimes are to be seen respectable white-washed dwellings which are possessed by persons whose way of life is frugal, and yet easy." By 1814 the island had already lost much of its former importance, its chief center had already lost its rank as a town (vila), and, Koster said, "the only mark which Conception still possesses of its former importance, is the obligation by which the magistrates of Goiana are bound to attend the yearly festival to the Virgin at the parish church." *Travels in Brazil,* II, 7–12.

beach to the woods." If one desires to build a house, "permission is asked of the landowner, to whom no rent is paid, possession of the soil being gained in this way by consent. In some povoados, such as Jaguaribe and Baixa Verde, a fee is paid to the município if the house is covered with a tiled roof."

Coconuts are the principal crop, although some mangoes are grown. When coconuts fall of their own accord they belong to the one who gathers them. In Vila Velha and Jaguaribe some cereals (corn, beans among them) are planted, mostly for home consumption. Livestock raised include a few pigs in Rio do Ambar, some sheep and goats in São Paulo, one or two milch cows in Jaguaribe, and chickens. São Paulo, where the sheep are found, has better pastures and no stock restrictions such as are to be found in Jaguaribe. In São Paulo there are around thirty houses of thatch and a population of about seventy persons.

Merchandising on the island is limited to a few small *bodegas* (canteens) and vendas, the first dealing largely in drinks and the latter in eggs, poultry, shellfish, fish, fruit, grains, and fishing tackle. Products exported from the island include fish, shellfish, fruit, coconuts, coconut palm leaves, which are sent to Recife, wooden spoons made in Jaguaribe, salt, and bricks. Imports are limited to a few items of prime necessity.

Most of the men follow several occupations, because even fishing does not always guarantee security. There are persons who fish and cut coconuts, others who cut and transport logs from the woods, some who extract meat from the coconuts and work in the fields, those who plant grains and cut coconut fronds, men who work at the production of salt and labor in the lime kilns, and those who keep store and make sails for small boats.

The investigators failed to find on the island many popular festival and recreational activities such as *bumbas-meu-boi, maracatús,* and *pastorís.* One carnival club was found in Rio do Ambar.

There were no schools in Vila Velha and São Paulo, and since these settlements were at considerable distance from the others, the children in those places did not learn to read and write.

Most of the inhabitants are Catholics. It is said that there is nearly always a festival at one of the churches, a "bandeira de São João," a novena, or some other religious function. A few Protestant families and some spiritualists are also living on the island.

On the mainland the investigators visited the settlement of Ramalho, where the land all belonged to a Sr. Chacon and the Companhia Paulista. Otherwise it resembled those on the island.

In the município of São Lourenço they visited Itapema, a povoado very different from those on the island. It is located on the lands of the Engenho Refresco, whose proprietor also owns three houses in the small population center. A well-traveled road passes through the locality, where there are 33 houses, all with tiled roofs, and 103 inhabitants. Water is supplied by a little stream, not always running, which passes nearby, and by a well on a neighboring engenho.

Nearly all the families in Itapema live in their own homes, only four or five residing in rented houses. The rent never exceeds ten milreis (fifty cents) per month. Each proprietor pays an annual fee or tax to the landowner (senhor de engenho) of ten milreis and of $930 (a little less than five cents) to the município. Three small bodegas are the only business establishments; however, chickens and eggs are bought and sold, and one peddler, who does business on the neighboring engenhos, resides in the povoado. Itapema exports nothing because the settlement, as distinguished from the engenho on which it is located, has no agriculture, industry, or handicrafts except one seamstress. The men who do not live by trading live by work, "rented work," on the engenhos or in transportation. There are thirteen horses in the povoado which are used to pack fuel from the woods on the engenhos to the sugar factories. There is no church in the locality; the inhabitants must go to mass in nearby Chã de Alegria and Glória do Goitá. There is a school operated by the município in the settlement.

Following their study of these eight little population centers the authors laid down six criteria, in addition to the lack of the political function of seat of município or distrito, as essential in the concept povoado.

1. Permanent population. This distinguishes the locality group in question from the *arraial* or camp.

2. Ownership of land in various hands.

3. Ownership of homes in various hands. On engenhos, usinas, and fazendas they all belong to the owner of the large rural property.

4. The manner of contracting for the houses. In the povoado one makes a contract for the location or use of a house, while on the plantation or in the camp his services are contracted for and he is permitted to use a house.

5. Liberty of work, commerce, industry, art, and profession. The individual is free to do as he will in the povoado. Such is not the case on the fazenda, engenho, or usina.

6. Presence of free internal and external trade or commerce. In each povoado business may be carried on freely, whereas on the engenho, usina, or fazenda it is monopolized by the commissary, is the privilege of one.

Other studies of Brazil's locality-group structure are hard to find. Several of the states have published lists of povoados, showing the manner in which they were connected with the seat of the município where they lie. For example, the state of Alagôas included such a list totaling 230, in a volume compiled for publicity purposes in 1932.[34] There is also an increasing interest in trying to clear up the confusion in regard to place names—a necessity that becomes more acute as the jardineira extends the postal services of the nation. Reminiscent of John H. Kolb's identification of Wisconsin neighborhoods by discovering names the inhabitants called the locality is a

[34] *Alagôas em 1931,* 37–43.

little publication by the Santa Catarina Departamento Estadual de Estatística.[35] In this booklet are listed alphabetically some 3,000 localidades found in the state, in addition to the vilas and the cidades of this commonwealth. A check shows that the sum of the populations of these "localities" is the same as the population of the state, making it evident that every individual lives in a place with a name. Naturally, a considerable number of the localidades are called by the same name, but this publication by placing them according to distrito and município should do much to assist the Instituto Brasileiro de Geografia e Estatística in its efforts to limit the population centers having the same name to one per state. It also suggests the need to learn more about the structure, function, and class of these small locality groups.

Emílio Willems, who is rather intimately acquainted with these Santa Catarina settlements, has described the general characteristics of these small places.

There are also "chapels" with local names, a conglomeration of twenty to thirty houses, more or less, situated about a little church. These little places are active only on Sundays, at the time of religious services and later for the game of football, for the *"domingueiras"* [dances], the horse races, the meeting of a co-operative or agricultural association, for conversations and drinking in the little canteens, for the *kermesses* and the political meetings. During the remainder of the week, the place remains dead, the life of its inhabitants differing in no way from that of the isolated sitiantes in the surrounding area.[36]

A list of povoados is also available for the state of Ceará. I passed through many of these and was able to ascertain that they often have all the physical characteristics of a neighborhood well on its way to becoming a community. Such characteristics include a nucleus of houses, often grouped near a chapel, a small venda or two, and possibly a school. Additional evidence that these povoados of Ceará represent real neighborhoods, many of them developing rapidly into communities, and not merely place names, was secured by checking the list against one giving the locations of Catholic churches and chapels in the state.[37] This comparison indicated that about 65 per cent of the povoados listed are locations for churches or chapels. On the other hand, 95 per cent of the vilas in Ceará contain one or more churches or chapels.

WHY BRAZIL REMAINS IN THE NEIGHBORHOOD STAGE

In Brazil, as in the United States, the trend is towards larger locality groups. The neighborhoods are coming together into larger

---

[35] *Localidades Catarinenses* (Florianópolis, 1940).

[36] Willems, *Assimilação e Populações Marginais no Brasil*, 67.

[37] The names and locations of churches, by município and locality, and the dates on which they were established, is given in Padre João Baptista Lehmann, *Organização Religiosa: Culto Catholico* (Fortaleza, 1942).

unities. This process of community integration in the two countries shows many similarities, although it is by no means complete in either country. In the United States, even in the Midwest, the neighborhoods have not entirely lost their identities in the larger community. Even where the development has proceeded farthest, in Iowa and the surrounding states, the rural areas still are but gradually passing from the neighborhood stage of locality-group structures to one in which the larger community is the fundamental unit. In rural Brazil social evolution is retracing to a considerable extent the same lines in the gradual incorporation of the neighborhoods into the community, but the process is still less far along than in most parts of our country. In other words, the Brazilian rural community today is in an amorphous state reminiscent of that prevailing in midwestern United States until around 1890, and in the South until about the time of World War I. But, whereas in the United States the open country church and the one-room school were the primary elements promoting neighborhood consciousness and loyalty, in Brazil there seem to be other factors which serve to perpetuate the closely knit neighborhood group and to delay its more complete incorporation into a large territorial unit.

Probably the most important of these factors is the system of transportation and communication. In general, Brazil has still to develop road and telephone systems throughout most of its vast interior. Except in selected portions of a few of the southern states, and in the Northeast, where roads have been constructed as drought-relief measures, Brazil's roads are still in the formative stage. The country is not in the horse-and-buggy stage. A country cannot remain where it has never been; this form of transportation was never known in Brazil. Nor was the farm wagon introduced in Brazil, with very minor exceptions, until the German and Polish colonists brought it in the nineteenth century. Since then it has diffused slowly, and even now four-wheeled wagons are never seen except in certain portions of the south and at a few of the army posts. Elsewhere the main reliance for transportation is placed on the oxcart, the pack animal, and the shoulders (or more properly, the head) of man or woman. Brazil does remain in the stage of the oxcart, the saddle horse, the pack mule, and the carregador. On the whole, the oxcart is most prevalent in the south; it gives way to the troops of pack animals as one passes north into Minas Gerais; and this mode of transportation in turn gives first place to the human being in the Northeast. In the Amazon region, of course, small boats are the chief reliance for travel and transportation, and small watercraft are also widely used throughout most of Brazil. Nevertheless, in general throughout the vast interior portions of Brazil the fazenda headquarters is the hub of oxcart and animal trails and footpaths that lead off in all directions.

However, throughout all parts of Brazil many of the fazendeiros possess cars. In São Paulo and parts of Minas Gerais this is rather general.[38] They use them to reach village and town centers where there are other cars, mostly taxis. But there are not many automobiles in Brazil, and it can be said with assurance that the reliance on the oxcart, the saddle horse, the back of the mule, and the head of man for transportation does much to keep Brazil's locality-group structure in the neighborhood stage.[39]

Another factor important in the persistence of the small locality group in Brazil is the kinship basis of many neighborhood groups. In many cases the Brazilian neighborhood is composed of a closely knit group or clan. For example, in many municípios of Minas Gerais an immense area formerly was held by a single owner in one tremendous estate or fazenda. Today, in many cases, this vast terrain has been divided among numerous descendants, whose families maintain a very intimate neighborhood life among themselves. These landowning families also keep the laboring classes rather permanently established on their places. Together they form a closely knit neighborhood, and not infrequently the rural clan will maintain open and long continued conflict with the nearby center.[40] This situation is widely duplicated throughout rural Brazil. Wherever the rural neighborhood is constituted of the territory occupied by a kinship group or clan, it tends to retain a high degree of vitality. In other words neighborhood ties are strong; those of the community, weak.[41]

Another reason why the Brazilian rural community remains in a more amorphous state than that in the United States is the greater retention of essential services within the household and the neighborhood. Household and fazenda enterprises continue to process the

[38] South of Juiz de Fora in Minas Gerais I have even seen trucks picking up milk cans on the road in front of farmers' homes, as is done in the dairying sections of the United States, and the same is taking place on a considerable scale in the Paraitinga Valley and other parts of the São Paulo "milkshed." See Schmidt, "Rural Life in Brazil," Smith and Marchant (eds.), Brazil: Portrait of Half a Continent, 186–87. These cases, however, are by far the exceptions and not the rule.

[39] This statement is based partially on personal observation and partly on the state statistics on automobile registrations.

[40] Cf. Werneck Sodré, Oeste, 164 ff.

[41] Freyre has described the closely knit locality groups once formed by the families of the planter class along the principal streams which wander through the sugar-growing littoral of Pernambuco: "On the Brazilian cultural landscape this varzea [flood plain] was the first to be populated, not by isolated, sporadic mansions, but by a genuine group of them, linked by the water of the river and the blood of the colonists, by means of the marriages with near relatives; later— here, as on the cape of St. Augustine, in the floodplain of the Ipojuca, in that of the Una, in the Reconcavo of Baía, in the Valley of the Parahyba, in Santo Antonio dos Quatro Rios—in the most complete endogamy, cousins marrying cousins, and nieces marrying their uncles. For this intensive endogamy of the whites and near-whites of the mansions of the same varzea, from which resulted the physical type so characteristic of the engenho aristocracy, from which resulted the family types of the northeast, so well defined in their features, in their faults, in their mode of speaking—Paes Barreto, Cavalcanti, Wanderley, Souza Leão—powerful aid was given by the waters of small rivers, making many families one, and of various engenhos a single social and sometimes a single economic, system. Genuine clans developed sometimes on the margins of small rivers, dominated by the patriarch of the largest mansion, more master of the river, of the water and the plain, than the others." Nordeste, 47–48.

great bulk of the products consumed by the people. The gristmill has now largely disappeared from our countryside, but tens of thousands of them continue to grind or pound the corn which occupies such a prominent place in the daily diet of the Brazilian. Thus, for example, as one travels through Minas Gerais he will see every few miles along the stream one of these water-driven devices for grinding corn meal. At each of these the miller grinds the corn of his neighbors, giving back a sack of meal for a sack of corn and keeping the increase for his trouble. Even more widely diffused is the monjolo, another water-driven device for processing corn. This primitive machine, of which there are tens of thousands in daily operation throughout Brazil, pounds or bruises the corn into a meal-like substance. As yet there has been little or no tendency for milling and similar food-processing services to be concentrated in the towns and villages. Likewise, the preparation of mandioca flour, the cleaning of rice, the making of charque (beef cut up, dipped in salt water, and sun dried), and the necessary processing of other food continue to be done for the most part on a household, fazenda, or neighborhood basis. Closely clustered about each of these small rural industrial units is a small number of families living in the immediate vicinity. All of this is favorable to a retention of the neighborhood as the basic locality group. The neighborhood will retain its vitality as long as it retains this economic base.

Similar is the situation in the ginning of cotton, the grinding of sugar cane, the cleaning of coffee, the processing of mate, and the coagulation of rubber. All are done for the most part on the fazenda, or other large rural estate, which in most cases itself constitutes a neighborhood unit. However, in cotton, large firms such as Anderson-Clayton are locating oil mills and gins in commercial and transportation centers. These modern establishments are absorbing the business of smaller processing units and forcing them to shut down. In the sugar areas, too, large usinas are crowding out the thousands of small engenhos and still smaller *engenhocas* which once ground nearly the entire crop.

It would require too much space to give details about all these local industrial units. Only one, the processing of mandioca, is chosen for illustrative purposes. The preparation of mandioca flour is especially significant because of its importance in the Brazilian diet. Mandioca flour for the most part is prepared from the yam-like tubers in small hand-operated factories or mills. Usually one of these consists of a large shed where there is sufficient space for performing the following processes: (1) grating the tubers, (2) pressing the grated mandioca between heavy weights to expel the juice, (3) applying heat to drive off the remaining moisture and leave the resulting flour, or "sawdust." The press and the ovens and pans used in the firing process usually adjoin the shed, but together they all form integral parts of the small factory. Of these the state of Paraíba alone is reported to have some 3,000, making it evident that they are widely distributed throughout the various neighborhood groupings of the state.[42] The state government has made attempts to stimulate the development of larger milling units for this all-important food product. In 1937 it purchased two mills and rented them to two corporations. But until the present the preparation of mandioca flour remains mostly a fazenda and neighborhood industry. From the Amazon to Rio Grande do Sul the small sheds which serve as factories are important neighborhood institutions.

Nor has the transference of various services to the village or town center gone as far in developing interdependence of community parts in Brazil as in the United States. For example, such small business establishments as bakeries, laundries, and meat markets located in the centers receive very little patronage from Brazilian countrymen. In the first place, the rural working classes rarely eat bread, and when they do it is prepared at home. In the village as in the country the *lavadeira* does the washing by hand, at the spring, in the creek, or at the riverside, and spreads the clothes on the grass to dry. Even in the towns and cities there is little refrigeration for meat. Doctors, lawyers, and other professional men are located in many seats of municípios, but in much of Brazil the former are found only in the larger cities. Rural areas are largely lacking in medical services. The curandeiros and other practitioners of dubious quality are as likely to be scattered throughout the open country as resident in the centers. All in all, it is evident that medical and dental services are not as yet attracting rural people periodically to the small centers.

Finally, the relative unimportance of trade itself is a factor tending to keep Brazilian locality groups small. When one gets away from the coffee and sugar estates, he finds relatively little produced for the market. Conversely, few things are purchased. The level of living becomes largely a matter of what is both produced and consumed by the family itself. Sales of produce by many families are restricted largely to those carried in on the way to church, and purchases necessarily are limited to a few indispensables. Competition between trade centers, which does much to expand the horizons of rural folk, remains in a retarded condition. As self-sufficiency decreases, production for market gains in importance; as communication and transportation improve, Brazilian communities will grow and become stronger, her neighborhoods wealthier.

THE CLASS STRUCTURE AND LOCALITY GROUPINGS

In Brazil, as in the plantation South of the United States, there is a great difference in the locality-group attachments of the upper landowning classes and the families who live and work on the estates. The former have contacts with and attachments outside the neighborhood and local community, in the seat of the município, in the larger trade centers of the area to which airplanes make regular

42 Mariz, *Evolução Econômica da Paraíba,* 141.

visits, and in the state capital. The latter are likely to live in a world whose horizon ends with the neighboring fazendas or the nearby village or town. The world of the small-farming classes who are crowded into the mountain coves, badly cut-up areas, or other poor lands is as restricted as that of the workers on the fazendas. The same is true of those assembled in small clearings in the palm forests of the North, strung along the coast amid the coconut groves, or settled along the natural levee of a river.

Probably even more than in our plantation South, the Brazilian landed family is in contact with affairs, not only in the local trade center which it helps to dominate, but in larger trade centers of the area and in the state and national capitals. In former years a great many of them possessed both a town house and a casa grande on the fazenda; and this practice continues even after the automobile has become a possession of many fazendeiros. As indicated above, many such upper-class families spend part of each month, particularly the week ends, in the small city, the seat of the município in which their estates are located. They also make periodic visits to the cities— Rio de Janeiro, São Paulo, Pôrto Alegre, Belo Horizonte, Bahia, Recife. In the case of not a few absentee landlords this process is reversed, and residents of the larger cities spend a little time on their rural estates. Today the airplane makes it possible to reach the larger centers much more quickly. However, the practice of taking along all members of the large families and immense quantities of baggage and extending the stay in the city, makes travel by train and boat both popular and practical among members of the upper classes. I have spent many interesting and profitable hours conversing with fazendeiros who were on their way to or from São Paulo, Rio de Janeiro, Belo Horizonte, Pôrto Alegre, Fortaleza, Recife, Belém, Manaus, and other important Brazilian centers. Not infrequently, such journeys involved several days of travel, including changes from one line to another, or from boat to train. Frequently they necessitated overnight stops at the hotels along the way.

This participation of the Brazilian landed aristocracy in the life of the larger centers has a long history. In colonial Brazil from the very beginning a few persons gained control of vast landed estates, possessions which put them on the way to a practical monopoly of social prestige and political power. This in turn made the members of the rural aristocracy dominating elements in local governmental affairs, even those of towns and cities; and in the nineteenth century, after the monarch established his capital in Rio de Janeiro, enabled the native rural elite to overcome, successively, the imported fidalgos who surrounded the throne during its first years in America and the commercial classes of the cities and towns. Eventually, the landed aristocracy gained undisputed control of national affairs,[43] a position they retain to some extent, although the man of industry and commerce is now to be reckoned with.

[43] Cf. Oliveira Vianna, *Populações Meridionaes do Brasil*, 29–40.

In contrast to the broad radius of social participation characteristic of Brazil's landowning classes is the very narrow horizon of its
numerous caboclos, camaradas, matutos, and colonos. Their area of
social participation is limited mostly to the neighborhood, with occasional visits to the vila or cidade in their home county or município. Then they go mostly on foot or on the back of an animal.
The trail is the principal avenue of communication. Until roads are
improved and the use of rapidly moving vehicles is more general,
Brazil's lower classes must remain shut in their own very small
worlds. Their chief locality group will be the neighborhood.

Thus there has come about a great difference in the locality-group
attachments of the various rural classes. While the slaves and
agregados on the immense rural properties and the sitiantes in the
mountain coves and other more isolated areas remained confined to
their immediate surroundings, the landowning nobility became the
first citizens of the nation. This league between the rural elite and
the metropole was maintained, even after the establishment of the
republic. In many instances it has resulted in absentee landlordism,
the owner of the land rarely or never seeing the locality in which his
domains are found; in others it has resulted in periodic visits to the
estates; and in the remainder it has resulted in continued contact
of upper-class families with the population centers, even though
residence is maintained on the land.

PART FIVE

Social Institutions

Society's principal institutions are those which have been evolved to regulate the domestic, educational, religious, and political aspects of life. One could write a bulky volume about marriage and the family, education and the school, religion and the church, or politics and government. Each of the four is a chapter subject of Part Five.

CHAPTER XVIII

MARRIAGE AND THE FAMILY

VARIOUS PHASES of marital relations and family life are treated elsewhere in this volume. Chapter x is devoted almost entirely to materials that might be given in connection with the family, and Chapters IV, VI, IX, and XV also contain many paragraphs bearing on marriage and the family. But domestic institutions are of primary importance in all societies, and although the data leave a great deal to be desired, it is possible to bring out additional significant points with respect to the Brazilian family.

The large, aristocratic, patriarchal family always has been the most important of Brazil's social institutions. Rarely has this primary kinship group had to play a role secondary to that of the church, as so frequently has been true in Spanish-American countries; nor has its relative importance ever been seriously challenged by the school, as may be the case in a North American community. In colonial times such a large, closely knit group of relatives, acknowledging allegiance to the oldest living male, possessing many slaves, and carrying on the aristocratic tradition at its best, was the chief instrument employed in the occupation of Brazil. This was in sharp contrast to the colonization of Spanish America where the *conquistador* and the priest were largely responsible for establishing the Spaniards as a ruling caste and to the founding of the English colonies in North America where the community and the smaller, more equalitarian family were basic elements. As has been shown so well by Freyre's monumental work, the patriarchal form of social organization early obtained almost unlimited sway in Brazil. For centuries Portuguese America continued to be dominated by a few thousand casas grandes, seats of sugar engenhos and cattle fazendas, each of which was the fortress headquarters of a numerous clan.[1] Even today there remains much of this feudal type of social organization, and this great family is the institution through which the white or near-white upper class maintains its control. Of course this patriarchal family has little in common with the equalitarian family of the United States and western Europe.

---

[1] Freyre, *Casa Grande & Senzala*, 19, 22, 134–35, *passim*. Cf. Nestor Duarte, *A Ordem Privada e a Organização Politica Nacional* (São Paulo, 1939); and Antonio Candido, "The Brazilian Family," in Smith and Marchant (eds.), *Brazil: Portrait of Half a Continent*, Chap. XIII.

Freyre also has indicated that Brazil's patriarchal, aristocratic, and slavocratic family was not merely transplanted from the mother country, but that many of its characteristics and functions were acquired in the New World. This was due in part to a complete change in occupation, for in Portugal a considerable number of colonists who eventually came to head Brazil's rural clans had been neither rich nor agriculturists. Probably the commercial-minded Portuguese would have preferred possessions which had already been more highly developed by the native peoples so that they could have devoted themselves to trading and commercial pursuits. But physical conditions of the land and the cultural attainments of the inhabitants determined otherwise. "Live and absorbent organ of Brazilian social formation, the colonial family united upon a base of rich economic resources and slave labor a variety of social and economic functions." [2]

It is significant that nearly all of the functions of the family came to be performed in a distinctive manner in Brazilian society. Consider first the primary function of the family—the reproduction of the species. As has been brought out in other places, very few of the colonists were women, and mating between the Portuguese men and the Indian women began from the very first. The white men seem to have had few inhibitions about increasing the numbers of their followers and dependents by fathering the children of numerous concubines. On the other hand, the Indian women may have been excessively sensual and strongly attracted by the white men. In any case, they were impelled to give themselves to the whites by the patrilineal nature of native society. Says Capistrano de Abreu, as quoted by Freyre: "The mixture is explained by the ambitions of the Indian women to have children belonging to the superior race, for according to the ideas current among them importance was attached to relationship on the paternal side only." [3] Whatever the causes may have been, the fact is that very early the illegitimate children came to bulk large among the patriarch's retinue of companions and followers. They did their share to contribute to the power and prestige of the master of the big house. To the mores that were set in this colonial epoch must be attributed the fact that illegitimacy still swells the Brazilian population and that very little distinction is made between legitimate and illegitimate children.

The economic functions of the family also underwent elaboration and change. The casa grande became a self-sufficient little world of its own, producing and processing nearly everything used by the patriarch, the great family which he headed, the slaves, and the agregados. Says Oliveira Vianna: "Because of their extreme economic independence, . . . derived from their omniproductive regime, and owing to the extraordinary extension of their economic base, these small rural societies lived almost without relations with their neigh-

[2] Freyre, *Casa Grande & Senzala*, 22.
[3] *Ibid.*, 59.

bors . . . so that they formed truly autonomous nuclei, each having its own economy, its own life, its own organization." [4]

Contributions from the New World were especially great in foods, food habits, and culinary practices. Because of the importance of Indian women in colonial society and because every agricultural effort was devoted to the production of sugar cane and not a food supply, even the master class of Brazilian society soon was eating such foods as corn and mandioca prepared in the Indian way.

The patriarchal, aristocratic, slavocratic family, or clan, also acquired functions rarely thought of in connection with its equalitarian counterpart. Freyre includes political power and control among these. He points out that "the rural family, or better, the latifundium family" early battled and eventually was successful against the attempts of the Jesuits to establish a theocracy, "a holy republic of 'Indians domesticated for Jesus' like those of Paraguay," where the caboclos would obey only the priests and there would be no individuality or autonomy of person or of family." [5] The Jesuits were expulsed and "in Brazil in place of the cathedral or church more powerful than the king himself would be substituted the casa grande of the engenho." [6] Each patriarch maintained his own little army, composed of Indians and mixed bloods, and eventually the casa grande became so powerful that it could defy the state with impunity. Giving shelter and protection to men wanted by the law was a common form of demonstrating this power. "Dom Pedro II," we are told, "attempted to limit the omnipotency of the proprietors of engenhos, frequently the protectors of assassins." [7] The banditry that continues to plague parts of Brazil, especially the northeastern region, probably is intimately associated with political powers possessed by the patriarchs of Brazilian rural clans.

Finally it is important to note the religious function of the great family in Brazil. As suggested above, during early colonial times there was keen rivalry between the landed proprietors and Jesuits for political power. The landowners won, the Jesuits were driven from Brazil, and the casa grande, not the church, became the dominant power in the colony. As a result Catholicism in Brazil became "a religion or cult of the family more than of a cathedral or a church." [8] Against the counsel of the Jesuits, "the other clergymen and even monks, big and fat, accommodated themselves to the functions of chaplains, of teaching padres, of uncles, of godfathers to the children; to a comfortable situation as members of the family, persons of the household, allies and adherents of the great rural proprietors, in the eighteenth century many of them living in the same casas grandes." [9]

[4] Oliveira Vianna, "O Povo Brazileiro e sua Evolução," *loc. cit.*, 291. Cf. Candido, "The Brazilian Family," Smith and Marchant (eds.), *Brazil: Portrait of Half a Continent*, 303–304.

[5] Freyre, *Casa Grande & Senzala*, 22–23.

[6] *Ibid.*, 134.   [8] *Ibid.*, 22.

[7] *Ibid.*   [9] *Ibid.*, 135.

MARRIAGE AND MARITAL STATUS

The registration of marriages in Brazil is hardly more complete than that of births and deaths. As a result, the recent issues of the *Anuário Estatístico* either omit information on this subject altogether or give only total figures for the municípios in which the state capitals are located. Some of the earlier compilations, however, contained enough information so that one could determine a few of

TABLE LIII

*Marriages Reported by Civil and Ecclesiastical Authorities, 1936 **

State	Civil marriages	Church marriages	Ratio of church to civil marriages
Brazil	155,110	236,275	152
Federal District	11,952	7,247	61
Alagôas	1,748	6,102	349
Amazonas	325	1,051	323
Bahia	3,755	25,807	687
Ceará	3,886	8,274	213
Espírito Santo	3,093	2,392	77
Goiás	1,544	4,349	282
Maranhão	1,485	6,986	470
Mato Grosso	816	1,656	203
Minas Gerais	21,668	43,080	199
Pará	2,395	6,646	277
Paraíba	2,467	11,367	461
Paraná	3,556	7,223	203
Pernambuco	5,031	19,266	383
Piauí	1,696	5,917	349
Rio de Janeiro	6,238	7,308	117
Rio Grande do Norte	2,457	6,074	247
Rio Grande do Sul	18,080	15,747	87
Santa Catarina	3,574	7,682	215
São Paulo	58,498	37,524	64
Sergipe	698	3,604	516
Territory of Acre	148	973	657

* Source: *Anuário Estatístico do Brasil*, V (1939/1940), 107–108 and 1166–68.

the more significant patterns, and it is probable that most of these have continued in essentially the same form to the present.

Marital Patterns. In such an analysis, though, it is important to keep in mind that church and state do not recognize one another's marriage ceremonies, so that the Brazilian couple desiring to be married according to church prescriptions and also in a legal manner must have two ceremonies performed. Not all of them do so, and in fact the church marriages in Brazil are very much more numerous than the civil or legal marriages. (See Table LIII.)

The most recent available data reveal that in the year 1936 the number of civil marriages reached its peak, the figure recorded that year being 155,110 compared with 143,534 in 1937, and only 132,404 in 1938. However, in 1936 the number of church marriages was 236,275, of which only 1,236 were performed by Protestant ministers. This total for Protestants is much too low, since data for Rio Grande do Sul, the city of Rio de Janeiro, and Minas Gerais were not included in the tabulation. In spite of such omissions there were 152 ceremonies performed by the church for every 100 legal marriages.

Civil marriages outnumbered church marriages only in the Federal District, Espírito Santo, Rio Grande do Sul, and São Paulo. Large Protestant populations and the greater skepticism of urban populations may be cited as the responsible factors. On the other hand, only a small fraction of the weddings performed by the priests in the eastern and northeastern parts of Brazil have been legalized according to civil law. Bahia, Sergipe, Maranhão, and Paraíba stand out in this respect.

While I was traveling through the northern part of Brazil informants called my attention to some results of the failure of the church and state to recognize each other's marriage ceremonies. It was said that many men are prone to persuade their brides that the church ceremony alone is all that is necessary. This is probably a convincing argument since the women are generally religious. As a result, it was said, some of the men later feel themselves free to set aside their wives on the grounds that they have never been legally married. In a country where divorce is not permitted, such motivations may be much stronger than they would be where it is possible legally to dissolve the marriage bond. In any case, the differences in the number of marriages reported by the church authorities and those registered on the books of the civil authorities give some factual basis for lending credence to the stories of these informants. There is historical evidence, also, which lends validity to such assertions. Of Crato, Ceará, Gardner reported:

Scarcely any of the better class live with their wives: a few years after their marriage, they generally turn them out to live separately, and replace them by young women who are willing to supply their place without being bound by the ties of matrimony. In this manner these people have two houses to keep up: among others who are living in this condition I may mention the Juiz de Direito, the Juiz dos Orfaos, and most of the larger shopkeepers; such a state of immorality is not to be wondered at, when the conduct of the clergy is taken into consideration, the vicar (*vigaro*), who was then an old man between seventy and eighty years of age, is the father of six natural children, one of whom was educated as a priest, afterwards became president of the province, and was then a senator of the Empire, although still retaining his clerical title. During my stay in Crato he arrived there on a visit to his father, bringing with him his mistress, who was his own cousin, and eight children out of ten he had by her, having at the same time five other children by another woman, who died in childbed of the sixth. Besides the vigaro there were three other priests in the town, all of whom have families by women with whom they live openly, one of them being the wife of another person.[10]

An informal marital arrangement highly reminiscent of that prevailing among the Negroes in the southern part of the United States must also be reckoned with in any discussion of marriage in Brazil.[11] An observant visitor reported that "in the rural zones of Sergipe, I found a large number of 'ajuntamentos.'[12] The amasiados [common-law unions] predominate and those truly married are united only by the church."[13] Accurate reports from most other sections of the country would contain similar information, but there has been little systematic examination of the subject. However, in one terse paragraph Sir Harry Johnston has summarized this extralegal system of mating so common among the lower classes of rural Brazil.

The country negroes and many of those who dwell in towns do not trouble themselves very much about contracting a legal marriage. Negro men and women simply live together in what is called locally the companheira system. A woman with or without children simply takes up her abode with a man who pleases her and shares his home as his wife at the pleasure of both parties. Yet these unions are sometimes as permanent as if they were consecrated by the Church or contracted under the law. There is, however, a good deal of unrecognised polygamy, and many negroes are husbands of more than one wife.[14]

Others place less emphasis on the stability of such common-law unions or even on the durability of marriages contracted legally. Amaral did not limit the following generalization to any specific area.

The rural home has no attractions, does not hold the man, who flees and is entangled by perversion. It is more agreeable, or less disagreeable, or more tolerable, to spend the night gambling with friends than in trying to woo sleep in such an environment. As derivatives of gambling come bohemian digressions, unfaithfulness, conjugal discords, the death of affection, flight from the home, where, still the husband reappears from time to time, attracted by homesickness, and where he does the poor wife the disservice of leaving one more child.[15]

An attempt was made in the 1950 census to gather some information having a bearing on this matter. At that time information was gathered and cross-tabulated to show the marital status of all women who reported that they had borne one or more children. See Table LIV. It will be noted that 13 per cent of all unmarried females who

[10] Gardner, Travels in the Interior of Brazil, 141–42.
[11] See Donald Pierson, Cruz das Almas, A Brazilian Village (Washington, 1951), 138–39; and René Ribeiro, "On the Amaziado Relationship and Other Aspects of the Family in Recife (Brazil)," American Sociological Review, X (1945).
[12] The social equivalent of the "tuk up" matings of the southern United States.
[13] Vasconcelos Torres, "Aspectos da Vida Rural Sergipana," Correio da Manhã (Rio de Janeiro), April 17, 1942.
[14] Johnston, The Negro in the New World, 105.
[15] Amaral, Historia Geral da Agricultura Brasileira, I, 37–38.

TABLE LIV

*Number and Proportion of Mothers Among Brazilian Women Aged 15
and Over, 1950, and Average Number of Children Borne per Mother
by Marital Condition* *

Marital condition	Number of women	Mothers		Number of live births reported per mother	Number of still births reported per mother
		Number	Per cent		
Total	15,325,852	9,301,578	60.7	3.90	1.57
Married	8,287,846	7,199,814	86.9	3.96	1.42
Separated and divorced	23,084	18,060	78.2	2.71	1.03
Widowed	1,515,788	1,334,419	88.0	4.31	2.53
Single	5,459,787	726,469	13.3	2.64	1.36

* Source: Compiled and computed from "Censo Demográfico," VI *Recenseamento
Geral do Brasil, 1950,* I (Rio de Janeiro, 1956), 50, 51.

had passed their fifteenth birthdays reported that they were mothers
of one or more children (for an average of 2.6) and that of all mothers,
8 per cent were those indicated as never having been married. It is
unlikely, of course, that these data are very accurate. However, the
mere fact that the queries were made and the results published is
indicative of the relative lack of concern relative to illegitimacy that
has prevailed in Brazil, and the fact that the figures are as low as
they are may foreshadow an important change in the societal values
involved. The latter point receives considerable support from the
manner in which the proportion of unmarried mothers varies from
state to state. See Table LV. Note, especially, the very low proportions
reported in states such as São Paulo and Paraná and the very high
proportions in remote states such as Pará and Maranhão.

Seasonality. It is interesting to note several points relating to the
seasonality of marriage in Brazil. December, not June, is the month
of brides. Of course, December in the southern hemisphere is the
equivalent of June north of the equator.

As is the case with so many subjects, the data on this also are fragmentary. Nevertheless, they probably are sufficient. One series is
available for the city of Recife for the years 1925–1934 and 1935–
1940. In each of these fifteen years the number of marriages in
December was greater than that for any other month, and that
month alone accounted for 14 per cent of all the marriages during
the years specified.[16] The situation is similar in the city of Rio de
Janeiro, for which a short series of data is available. In 1937, 1938,
and 1939, December was much more popular among brides than

[16] The data are given in *Anuário Estatístico do Brasil,* XI (1950), 40; and
Annuario do Nordeste para 1937, p. 298.

TABLE LV

State-to-State Variations in Relative Importance of Unmarried Women Among All Mothers, and Average Number of Children per Unmarried Mother, 1950 *

State	Number of mothers	Unmarried mothers		
		Number	Per cent	Average number of children born alive
Brazil	9,301,578 †	726,469 †	7.8	2.6
North				
Guaporé ‡	5,873	1,106	18.8	2.2
Acre ‡	18,495	1,600	8.6	2.4
Amazonas	89,019	16,646	18.7	2.6
Rio Branco ‡	3,054	352	11.5	1.9
Pará	204,281	52,802	25.8	2.7
Amapá ‡	6,553	1,702	26.0	2.6
Northeast				
Maranhão	292,597	67,342	23.0	2.8
Piauí	180,332	13,990	7.8	2.5
Ceará	441,681	17,378	3.9	2.5
Rio Grande do Norte	172,910	9,624	5.6	2.3
Paraíba	291,005	16,345	5.6	2.4
Pernambuco	604,342	64,862	10.7	2.4
Alagôas	198,292	21,088	10.6	2.5
East				
Sergipe	117,947	21,225	18.0	2.6
Bahia	836,728	159,541	19.1	2.7
Minas Gerais	1,336,802	42,551	3.2	2.4
Espírito Santo	146,910	6,660	4.5	2.8
Rio de Janeiro	419,380	50,530	12.0	3.1
Distrito Federal	478,552	42,664	8.9	2.1
South				
São Paulo	1,739,286	25,931	1.5	2.2
Paraná	375,745	7,607	2.0	2.6
Santa Catarina	272,877	7,892	2.9	2.7
Rio Grande do Sul	746,583	47,157	6.3	2.9
West Central				
Mato Grosso	84,253	12,757	15.1	3.3
Goiás	207,147	16,311	7.9	2.5

* Compiled and computed from data in "Censo Demográfico," *VI Recenseamento Geral do Brasil, 1950*, I (Rio de Janeiro, 1956), 172, 173.
† These totals include the data for the Serra dos Aimorés and the Island of Fernando de Noronha.
‡ Territory.

any other month and accounted for 14.4, 15.2, and 15.9 per cent, respectively, of the marriages during those years.[17] For Curitiba, capital of Paraná, data are available for the years 1940–1941. During this period 14.4 per cent of all marriages were contracted in Decem-

[17] *Anuário Estatístico do Brasil*, V (1939/1940), 124.

ber.[18] São Paulo data are limited to the years 1940 and 1941, but fortunately they are available for the entire state and not merely the capital. This is important because, although December accounted for more than its share of all marriages in the city, in the interior June, July, and September were the months in which the larger numbers of marriages were solemnized. Thus in the capital 11.7 of all marriages in 1940 and 13.0 of all in 1941 took place during December; in the remainder of the state only 8.0 and 8.7 per cent of the marriages in the two years, respectively, were contracted in this month.[19] Also in the extreme south, in Rio Grande do Sul, according to state-wide data which go back as far as 1910, December is not the month of brides. Not once between 1910 and 1937 were December marriages the most numerous; in fact, the month stood far down the list every year in the series. In the statistics for this gaúcho state there is a glaring lack of marriages during August and a relatively large number in the months which immediately precede and follow it. In the twenty-eight years from 1910 through 1937, July's percentage of the year's marriages fell below 13 only in 1923, when it was 12.6, and in 1929, when it was 12.7. Year after year, about 11 per cent of all marriages are contracted during September.

August is shunned by brides and grooms. Here are some of the data: in 1937, only 4.4 per cent of the marriages in Rio Grande do Sul took place in August; in 1936, 4.5 per cent; in 1935, 4.3 per cent; in 1934 and 1933, 3.8 per cent; in 1932, 3.9 per cent; and in 1931, 4.7 per cent. During the twenty-eight-year period only 4.8 per cent of the marriages in the state were solemnized in the month of August.[20] The percentage would be even lower if the figures were as complete for the rural districts as they are for Pôrto Alegre.

This avoidance, which is merely one expression of the Brazilian belief that August is an unlucky month for the initiation of any personal or business venture, is also strong elsewhere in the republic. During the years for which data are available as indicated above, only 2.4 per cent of the marriages in Curitiba, 5.2 per cent in Recife, 4.2 per cent in Rio de Janeiro, 3.4 per cent in the city of São Paulo, and 3.1 per cent in the remainder of the state of São Paulo occurred in August. Thus even fragmentary data are sufficient to prove that in Brazil "the month of December is the one preferred for establishing matrimonial ties, the smallest number falling in August suspected of being unlucky. Thus we see that superstitions leave their impress even upon the most important acts in the lives of the people." [21]

Age. There was a time when Brazilian brides were so young that the system verged on being "child marriage." Freyre says that "the custom for women to marry early, at twelve, thirteen, fourteen years

[18] Data assembled from *Boletim Trimestral de Estatística Demógrafo-Sanitária, Município de Curitiba*, I, II, and III (Curitiba, 1939–41), Nos. 1–12.
[19] The data were assembled from *Resumo do Movimento Demógrafo-Sanitário do Estado de São Paulo* (São Paulo, January-December, 1941).
[20] *Anuário Demográfico do Rio Grande do Sul*, 1938, I (Pôrto Alegre, 1939?), 92.
[21] *Annuario do Nordeste para 1937*, p. 298.

of age, was general in Brazil. With an unmarried daughter of fifteen years in the house, the parents began to be uneasy and to make promises to Santo Antonio or São João. Before twenty years, the girl was an old maid. That which today is green fruit, in those days was feared to be spoiling of ripeness with no one to harvest it in time." [22]

The modal age at marriage continues to be young, but not excessively so, in comparison with that prevailing in Western society generally. From the fragmentary data available it appears that the Brazilian bride is most likely to be about 20 years of age and the groom 24. In Rio Grande do Sul for the 28 years from 1910 through 1937, for which data are available, 47.3 per cent of all brides were less than 21 years of age, the median being 21.4, and the mode probably falling between 19 and 20. Among the grooms the modal age is 24.2, the median, 25.3 years.[23] Data also are available for seven of the capitals in south Brazil for the period from 1908 through 1912. At this time the median ages of the brides were as follows: Belo Horizonte, 20.3; Curitiba, 20.6; Rio de Janeiro, 21.9; Florianópolis, 21.1; Niterói, 21.2; Pôrto Alegre, 23.4; and São Paulo, 20.3. The mode in each case should be about a year or a year and a half less than the median, but it cannot be determined accurately since it is less than 20, and the data for all under 20 years of age was thrown together in the tabulations. In these cities the modal age at marriage for males was 23.3 in Belo Horizonte, 23.1 in Curitiba, 24.2 in Rio de Janeiro, 23.3 in Florianópolis, 23.4 in Niterói, 21.4 in Pôrto Alegre, and 23.0 in São Paulo.[24] Finally, there is information concerning the ages of persons contracting marriage in the Distrito Federal during the years 1937 and 1938. By this time the modal age of brides had risen to 22.2 years, the median age to 23.2. For males the mode was 25.8 and the median 27.7 years.[25] These data for Brazil may be compared with a mode of 22.3, median of 23.3 for brides; and a mode of 23.8 and median of 26.2 for grooms in the 28 states of the United States for which 1940 data are available.[26] More recently, as the comparison in Figure 30 indicates, it seems certain that the age at marriage of women in the United States has dropped considerably below that of women in Brazil.

Marital Status. The data on marital status from the census make it evident that Brazilians do not shun formal marriage ties to the same extent as do Colombians, Peruvians, Venezuelans, and the peoples of some of the other Latin-American countries, but on the other hand, they appear much less likely to contract formal marriage ties than the inhabitants of many of the European countries, Canada, the United States, or Japan. At practically all ages the

[22] Freyre, *Casa Grande & Senzala*, 256.

[23] Data used for the calculations were taken from the *Anuário Demográfico do Rio Grande do Sul*, 1938, I, 88, 90.

[24] Data for the computations are taken from *Annuario Estatistico do Brazil*, I (1908–12), 406–407.

[25] Data for the computations secured from *Anuário Estatístico do Brazil*, IV (1938), 143, and V (1939/1940), 125.

[26] U. S. Bureau of the Census, *Vital Statistics—Special Reports*, XVII, No. 9 (1943), 86, 98.

percentages of Brazilians, males and females alike, who are actually living in a marital state are small in comparison with those of the United States, although they are high in comparison with those of Venezuela. See Figures 29 and 30. Curves showing the proportions of the single population at various ages drop less precipitously in Brazil than in the United States, indicating that Brazilians are somewhat older at the time they leave the single category than are persons in the United States. Brazilian women seem almost twice as likely to live their entire lives without contracting matrimony as are their sisters in our own country. The differences between the sexes may be due in considerable part to the fact that higher death rates in Brazil give previously unmarried men more opportunities for marrying widows than are offered to men in the United States; also immigration, which has been heavier in the United States than in Brazil may help explain the difference.

The curves representing the widowed rise more rapidly in Brazil than in the United States, a fact explained by the higher Brazilian death rates. By the time age sixty-one has been reached, the number of widows in Brazil is equal to the number of married women, whereas a comparable situation does not arise in the population of the United States until age sixty-nine is reached. If a Brazilian woman lives to the age of sixty-four, the chances are equal that she will be a widow; in the United States the corresponding age is seventy-two. The points to stress are that Brazil contains high pro-

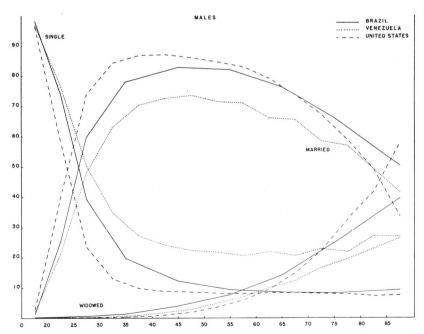

FIGURE 29. Marital status of the male populations of Brazil, the United States, and Venezuela, by age, 1950.

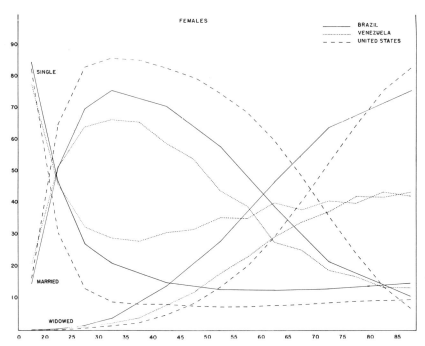

FIGURE 30. Marital status of the female populations of Brazil, the United States, and Venezuela, by age, 1950.

portions of the single and the widowed and relatively low percentages of those who are living in the married condition.

Many important differentials probably exist among the marital status of the various segments of the Brazilian population, but to date this fundamental aspect of the sociological study of Brazilian domestic institutions has received very little study. Moreover, failure to take into account and control properly the all-important age factor negates much of what has been said on the subject, just as the same oversights have destroyed the validity of most of the analysis of the materials on this subject in the United States. In order to illustrate the kinds of differentials that do prevail, Figures 31 and 32 have been prepared. They show, for males and females separately, the great differences between the marital status of white people, pardos (Indian and mixed bloods), and Negroes. These differences should be thought of as being especially important because they probably are very similar to those prevailing between the upper, the middle, and the lower socioeconomic classes.

Especially striking are the differences between the marital conditions of the whites and Negroes, with the pardos occupying consistently a middle position in the range between the two. In comparison with the Negroes, whites (both male and female) marry at a younger age and are far less likely to live out their lives without marrying at all. In addition, at any given age the whites also are much more likely than the Negroes to be living in the married

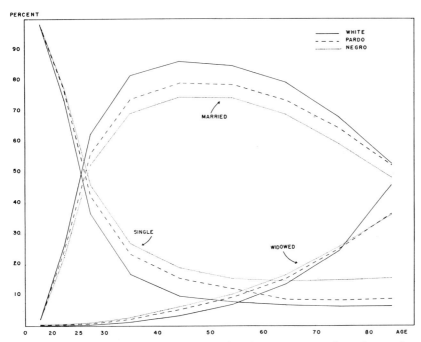

FIGURE 31. Marital status of the male white, Negro, and *pardo* populations of Brazil, by age, 1950.

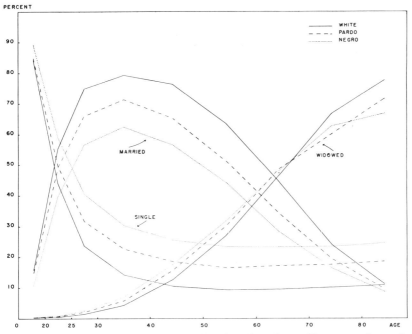

FIGURE 32. Marital status of the female white, Negro, and *pardo* populations of Brazil, by age, 1950.

471

condition; and finally, even though marriage is a prerequisite for widowhood, the former, surely because of their lower mortality rates, are less likely to be widowed than the latter.

SIZE OF THE FAMILY

In Brazil the stereotype of the family has tended to include seven persons, two parents and five children. This contrasts greatly with that of a father, mother, and two children which, especially before the second World War, was so widely used to portray the typical family in the United States. Furthermore, the statistical basis for the Brazilian stereotype has been fully as adequate as that for the one prevailing in the United States. Thus the 1920 census found that the population of 30,625,331 was living in 3,962,585 dwellings, an average of 7.7 persons per household, compared with one of only 4.3 in the United States at the corresponding date.

More recently the data for both countries have become far more adequate and reliable, but the same sort of differences persist, differences which emphasize that the family and household in Brazil continue to be large. Accordingly, some of the more pertinent information has been analyzed and is presented graphically in Figure 33. This illustration, which shows the percentage of each country's population living in families or households of stated sizes, demonstrates that the average Brazilian is a member of a domestic group of six persons, whereas the average person in the United States is a

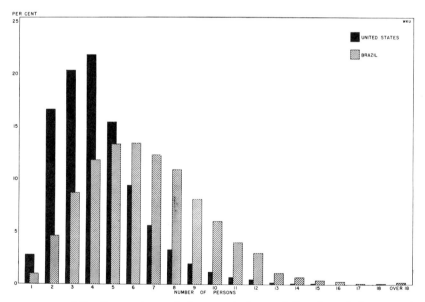

FIGURE 33. Proportions of the populations of Brazil and the United States living in households of stated sizes, 1950.

member of one of only four persons. Furthermore, judging by these 1950 data and on a relative basis, one finds that the Brazilian is much more likely to be a member of a domestic circle of eight persons than the resident of the United States is to be included in one of six; the former is more likely to be included in a household of ten than the latter is to be in one seven. Indeed, although households of ten or more persons have largely disappeared in the United States, considerable numbers of Brazilians still are living in those of eleven, twelve, and even more members.

The basic factor responsible for the large Brazilian family or household is, of course, the large numbers of children borne by Brazilian women. This has been discussed in Chapter VI, but in order to bring the matter into a still bolder relief, Figure 34 has been prepared. This graph shows for Brazil and the United States, respectively, the proportions of the women, aged 50–59 at the time of the census (who consequently may be considered to have completed their child-bearing cycles) who reported that they had given birth to stated numbers of children. Any comment would be largely superfluous: the latest comprehensive statistical data fully support the widely held belief that the Brazilian family and household are large.

There are, of course, considerable variations with respect to the size of the family or household among the various segments into which the population may be divided. The census data, however, do not enable us to determine the nature and magnitude of many of these differences. They do indicate, however, that the tendency for

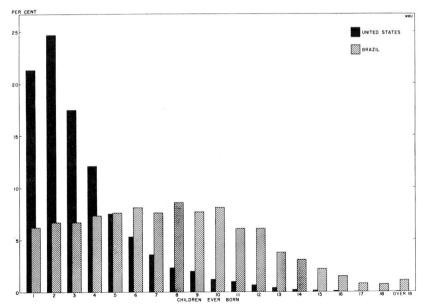

FIGURE 34. Reported numbers of children ever born to women, ages 50–59, in Brazil and in the United States, 1950.

the rural family to be larger than the urban, and the tendency for agriculturists to have larger families than those of persons in other lines of activity prevail in Brazil. See Table LVI. Nevertheless, one should note from observation of these data that the households of those engaged in public administration, in the liberal professions, and in commerce also are significantly above the average in size. Undoubtedly this is a reflection of the fact that the upper-class Brazilian family continues to be large and, in all probability, closely knit as well.

TABLE LVI

Variations in Size of Household by Residence and Occupation of Head of Household, 1950 *

Residence and principal activity of head	Number of households	Persons per household
All residential areas	10,046,199	5.1
Urban areas	2,529,870	4.9
Suburban areas	1,200,498	4.8
Rural areas	6,315,831	5.3
Principal activity of head		
Agriculture, stockraising and forestry	5,405,224	5.5
Extractive industries	283,909	4.7
Manufacturing, construction and processing	1,064,105	4.9
Trade	546,618	5.3
Real estate, banking, credit and insurance	56,205	5.1
Services	468,563	4.6
Transportation, communication and storage	440,201	5.2
Liberal professions	45,917	5.3
Social activities	141,453	5.0
Public administration, legislation and justice	157,689	5.4
National defense and public security	117,175	5.0
Unpaid domestic service or attending school	900,907	4.0
Other activities or unknown	27,694	4.6
Inactive	390,540	4.5

* Compiled and computed from data in "Censo Demográfico," *VI Recenseamento Geral do Brasil, 1950,* I (Rio de Janeiro, 1956), 282–83.

COMPOSITION OF THE DOMESTIC CIRCLE

The materials gathered in the 1950 census also make it possible to determine in a fairly acceptable manner the relative importance of the various elements that go to make up the Brazilian family or household. See Table LVII. Those who head the families, of whom the vast majority are men, make up almost one-fifth of the total, and their wives, along with the husbands of a part of the females who are heads of families, account for an additional 15 per cent. Children living at home with one or with both of their parents constitute more than one-half of all persons living in private households, and

TABLE LVII

Persons Living in Private Households, Classified According to Their Relationship to Head of Household, by Sex, 1950 *

Relationship to head of household	All persons		Males		Females	
	Number	Per cent	Number	Per cent	Number	Per cent
Total	51,584,665	100.0	25,641,719	100.0	25,942,946	100.0
Head	10,046,199	19.5	8,827,218	34.4	1,218,981	4.7
Spouse	7,909,833	15.3	7,025	—	7,902,808	30.4
Child	26,891,483	52.1	13,850,238	54.0	13,041,245	50.3
Grandchild	1,040,949	2.0	526,566	2.1	514,383	2.0
Parent or parent-in-law	712,390	1.4	119,175	0.5	593,215	2.3
Grandparent	24,332	—	3,454	—	20,878	0.1
Other relative	2,417,547	4.7	1,143,006	4.5	1,274,541	4.9
Agregado	970,701	1.9	464,365	1.8	506,336	2.0
Roomer or boarder	854,624	1.7	463,604	1.8	391,020	1.5
Employee	707,931	1.4	232,676	0.9	475,255	1.8
Unknown	8,676	—	4,392	—	4,284	—

* Compiled and computed from data in "Censo Demográfico," *VI Recenseamento Geral do Brasil, 1950,* I (Rio de Janeiro, 1956), 280–81.

grandchildren, parents and grandparents, and other relatives of the heads are also present in considerable numbers (8.1 per cent of all). Servants living in the homes are not particularly numerous, but because of their presence in the households of those of the upper and middle socioeconomic classes, their "visibility" is especially great. The composition of households whose heads are in the ages 30–39 is not particularly different from that of households in general. See Table LVIII. However, as is to be expected, the members of the nuclear family as such are of somewhat greater relative importance in the domestic circles of this particular type than they are in all households. Additional data on how the composition of the household varies with the age of the head are presented in Table LIX, and finally, in order to show the importance of "broken families" of one kind or another, Table LX has been prepared. In interpreting the materials in the latter, one must consider that only half of Brazil's widows (749,533 of a total of 1,496,539) were classified by the 1950 census as being heads of the households in which they resided. This undoubtedly is accounted for by the fact that the Brazilian family still retains to a high degree its function of caring for members, irrespective of age, who are unable to fend for themselves.

The materials in this section and the preceding one are organized from the standpoint of the two-generation or nuclear family. They indicate, however, that a considerable proportion of Brazilians have experience in three-generation households in the course of their formative years, and that much still remains of the old patriarchal

TABLE LVIII

Composition of Brazilian Households that Are Headed by Persons
Aged 30–39, 1950 *

Relationship to head of household	Number of persons	Per cent of total	Number per household
Total	14,899,976	100.0	5.3
Head	2,804,288	18.8	1.0
Spouse	2,426,916	16.3	0.9
Child	8,146,748	54.7	2.9
Grandchild	12,322	0.1	—
Parent or parent-in-law	242,107	1.6	0.1
Grandparent	6,743	—	—
Other relative	613,758	4.1	0.2
Agregado	228,380	1.6	0.1
Roomer or boarder	206,811	1.4	0.1
Employee	206,578	1.4	0.1
Unknown	5,325	—	—

* Compiled and computed from data in "Censo Demográfico," VI *Recenseamento Geral do Brasil, 1950*, I (Rio de Janeiro, 1956), 282–83.

TABLE LIX

Composition of the Brazilian Household in Relation to Age of Head
of Household, 1950 *

Age of head	Number of households	Persons per household			
		Total	Heads, spouses, and own children	Parents, grand-parents, and grand-children	Other relatives
Total	10,046,199	5.1	4.5	0.2	0.2
10–19	91,278	2.8	1.6	0.3	0.7
20–29	2,030,542	3.7	3.1	0.1	0.3
30–39	2,804,288	5.3	4.8	0.1	0.2
40–49	2,335,603	6.2	5.6	0.1	0.2
50–59	1,526,747	5.7	4.9	0.3	0.2
60–69	838,570	4.8	3.8	0.5	0.2
70–79	280,783	4.1	2.9	0.6	0.2
80 and over	87,979	3.5	2.5	0.6	0.2
Unknown	50,409	4.7	4.2	0.2	0.2

* Compiled and computed from data given in "Censo Demográfico," VI *Recenseamento Geral do Brasil, 1950*, I (Rio de Janeiro, 1956).

family. Even in Rio de Janeiro one may find entire apartment houses occupied exclusively by an elderly couple and their descendants. The building may house ten or twelve families of the children and grandchildren. In the rural districts an entire neighborhood will be made up of near relatives. Furthermore, not only is the Brazilian

TABLE LX

Heads of Brazilian Households, Classified According to
Sex and Marital Condition, 1950 *

Sex and marital condition	Number	Per cent
Total	10,046,199	100.0
Single males	965,954	9.6
Single females	282,056	2.8
Married males	7,493,760	74.6
Married females	172,753	1.7
Separated or divorced males	11,987	0.1
Separated or divorced females	9,382	0.1
Widowers	331,560	3.3
Widows	749,533	7.5
Unknown males	23,957	0.2
Unknown females	5,257	0.1

* Compiled and computed from data in "Censo Demográfico," VI *Recenseamento Geral do Brasil, 1950*, I (Rio de Janeiro, 1956).

family of parents and children relatively large, but it remains closely tied into the larger kinship group headed by the patriarch of the clan.

FAMILY FUNCTIONS

In all societies the family is charged with the responsibility for performing certain necessary functions that are carried on not at all or only partially by other social institutions. These functions generally include (1) the reproduction of the race, (2) the care, sustenance, and rearing of children through the dependent ages, (3) the education and training of the young, (4) the induction of the members of the oncoming generation into the great society, and particularly establishment of their status in the various social groups, (5) recreation, (6) mutual aid and protection of members from enemies and dangers of all kinds, and (7) the care of the aged and other incapacitated members and kinfolk. Several observations may be made concerning the manner in which the Brazilian family is carrying on these essential functions.

Reproduction of the Race. The population of Brazil is multiplying at a very rapid rate. (See Chapter VI.) This means that the Brazilian family is performing this primary function in a manner that is equaled in few countries of the world. Nevertheless, the comparatively high rates of illegitimacy demonstrate that the family is not the exclusive agency for reproducing the race that it is in the United States and some other parts of the Western World.

It has been impossible for the present writer to determine the exact status of present-day Brazil with respect to illegitimacy, for

the available data—and they are not at all recent—come only from
Rio Grande do Sul, São Paulo, and the Distrito Federal, the most advanced portions of the nation. Even at that, it may be demonstrated
that a considerable number of all Brazilians are born out of wedlock.
The latest national summary is for the years 1931–1933 only, and
those data are not very satisfactory. Of the 1,808,812 births registered by January 1, 1940, for that four-year period, 193,895 or 10.7
per cent were classed as illegitimate.[27]

Other fragmentary materials are available for a few of the states.
For the state of Rio Grande do Sul data are available for the years
1910 to 1937, inclusive. Total births registered numbered 1,711,416,
of which 173,814, or 10.2 per cent, were recorded as illegitimate.[28]
For São Paulo data are at hand for the years 1930 to 1939, inclusive, and for 1942. In this most advanced of all Brazilian states
the percentages of illegitimacy varied from 5.2 in 1930 to 8.4 in
1942, being 6.5 for the eleven years taken together.[29] In the city of
Rio de Janeiro there were 34,620 births registered during 1940, of
which 4,573, or 13.2 per cent, were classed as illegitimate.[30] Most of
the other states, especially those in the east and the north, do not
include data on legitimacy among the demographic materials published, but Amazonas is an exception. Records completed up to
January 1, 1940, contain this information for 2,108 births registered
during the years 1930 to 1933, inclusive. Of this total, 432, or 20.5
per cent, were illegitimate.[31] Most of these births undoubtedly were
registered in Manaus, the capital. Were the data available for the
outlying areas, the proportion of illegitimacy probably would be
much higher. It would also be high if the record for the states north
of Minas Gerais were accessible. For example, the city of Bahia
contained nearly 300,000 inhabitants in 1920. In 1922 there were
763 marriages recorded in the city and 4,617 births. More than one-
half of the births, 2,432, or 53 per cent, were entered as illegitimate.[32] Prior to 1920 birth registration was confined mostly to a few
of the larger cities in southern Brazil. The first issue of the *Annuario
Estatistico do Brazil*, published in 1916, gave data on births for the
years 1908 to 1912, inclusive, classified according to legitimacy, but
only for the cities of Belo Horizonte, Curitiba, Rio de Janeiro,
Florianópolis, Niterói, Pôrto Alegre, and São Paulo. During the five-
year period the number of births registered in these seven cities
totaled 196,286, a mere fraction of the actual number; of these,
36,395 (18.5 per cent) were classed as illegitimate. In the various
cities percentages of illegitimacy were as follows: Belo Horizonte,

[27] *Anuário Estatístico do Brasil*, V (1939/1940), 121.
[28] *Anuário Demográfico do Rio Grande do Sul*, 1938, I, 80.
[29] The data are found in the *Resumo do Movimento Demógrafo-Sanitário do
Estado de São Paulo*, for the years 1930–42.
[30] *Anuário Estatístico do Distrito Federal, 1941*, IX (Rio de Janeiro, 1942), 43.
[31] *Sinopse Estatística do Estado do Amazonas*, No. 4 (Rio de Janeiro, 1942),
26.
[32] Mario Ferreira Barboza, *Annuario Estatistico da Bahia–1923* (Bahia, 1924),
399.

TABLE LXI

Legitimacy of the Population, 1890, by States *

State	Of legitimate birth	Of illegitimate birth	
		Number	Per cent
Brazil	11,656,431	2,677,484	18.7
Distrito Federal	419,747	102,904	19.7
Alagôas	444,132	67,308	13.2
Amazonas	103,128	44,787	30.3
Bahia	1,431,227	488,575	25.4
Ceará	739,198	66,489	8.3
Espírito Santo	107,164	28,833	21.2
Goiás	184,225	43,347	19.1
Maranhão	252,299	178,555	41.4
Mato Grosso	56,243	36,584	39.4
Minas Gerais	2,703,227	480,872	15.1
Pará	210,343	118,112	36.0
Paraíba	415,224	42,008	9.2
Paraná	210,917	38,574	15.5
Pernambuco	907,086	123,138	11.9
Piauí	216,739	50,870	19.0
Rio Grande do Norte	241,497	26,776	10.0
Rio Grande do Sul	707,160	190,295	21.2
Rio de Janeiro	560,058	316,826	36.1
Santa Catarina	251,474	32,295	11.4
São Paulo	1,240,297	144,456	10.4
Sergipe	255,046	55,880	18.0

* Source: Directoria Geral de Estatistica, *Sexo, Raça e Estado Civil, Nacionali- dade, Filiação, Culto e Analphabetismo da População Recenseada em 31 de Dezembro de 1890* (Rio de Janeiro, 1898), 221.

17.9; Curitiba, 11.1; Rio de Janeiro, 24.6; Florianópolis, 23.4; Ni- terói, 28.9; Pôrto Alegre, 22.4; and São Paulo, 6.9.[33]

Although recent data on illegitimacy are fragmentary, the census of 1890 contained an extraordinary tabulation which classified every- one in Brazil according to whether or not he had been born in wed- lock. (See Table LXI.) It will be observed that nearly one-fifth of all Brazilians at that time were of illegitimate birth and that in the north the proportion was almost two in five. On the other hand Ceará and other parts of the northeast had low proportions of illegitimacy. Probably regional differentials today follow the same general pat- tern that they did in 1890. However, in recent years such agencies as the Serviço Social da Indústria have helped to arrange large cere- monies, civil and religious, in which as many as six hundred couples were married in a single city in the course of one day.

Caring for Children. The high rate of reproduction and the numer- ous children mean that the care, sustenance, and rearing of children consume a comparatively large share of the time and economic re-

[33] *Annuario Estatistico do Brazil,* I (1916), 402–403.

sources of the family; at the same time the high mortality rates, especially through infancy, poor diets, poor housing, and so forth, would seem to indicate that there are many needed improvements to be made in child care. In the lower classes a high proportion of the children are on their own responsibility from a very tender age. However, any very satisfactory information on this subject belongs to the future.

Educating the Young. Because of the lack of schools, the low percentage of children who are privileged to attend, and the shortness of the school period, Brazilian society must depend on the family for educating and training the young to a much greater degree than is general in Western society. Education acquired in this manner— by the boy's working with his father, the girl her mother, in the daily routine of living—is thorough. Rural Brazilians become excellent axmen, mule drivers, boatmen, craftsmen, fishers, hunters, and tillers highly skilled with the hoe. Millions of them are able to live in situations where the average citizen of the United States or Western Europe would perish of hunger and exposure. But education in the family contributes to maintaining the customary routine; it makes for very little change or progress. If the family lacks essential knowledge, habits, and skills, the deficiencies will be perpetuated generation after generation. Therefore, until Brazilian children can acquire a greater share of their mental equipment outside of the home, there is small chance for great progress in agriculture, health and sanitation, transportation, industry, or any other field which the industrial revolution has changed, or for change in rural mores.

Establishing Social Status. There has been little or no study of the subject, and so it is possible only from general observation to conclude that the Brazilian family is highly efficient in determining the position its members are to occupy in the classes and groups of the great society. In fact, since Brazilian society is rather highly stratified, with a strong tendency for social position to be inherited (the caste element) and relatively little vertical and horizontal social mobility, the accident of birth is almost all important as a determinant of which groups a man will belong to and what is to be his position on the social scale. This is not to deny that there is some shifting from one group to another, some rising and sinking, especially in the cities of southern Brazil. But it is intended to point out that the family determines for the great mass of Brazilians the groups to which they are to belong and their position in the class structure.

Recreation. In recreation and all other social affairs the Brazilian family occupies a pre-eminent position. A very large part of all leisure time is spent in the company of the immediate family or near relatives. Even in Rio de Janeiro the married pair of middle- or upper-class status is obligated by the mores to dine at least once a week at the home of the husband's people and once a week with the wife's people. In the interior the visiting back and forth of relatives, both between those who live in the open country and between the farm people and their kinsmen in the towns and villages, is the chief type of social activity.

On occasion one may hear expressions of dissatisfaction by Brazilian leaders in educational and cultural affairs who indicate that family obligations prevent them from mingling socially as much as they would like with those of kindred interests. Moreover, for the visitor from abroad who is not fortunate enough to be "adopted" by one or more Brazilian families, the cohesiveness of the large kinship group may be a barrier that shuts him off from a satisfactory social relationship with his Brazilian fellows. As Hutchinson has emphasized: "The Brazilian social scientist usually has family responsibilities which are augmented by the network of extended family relationships which occupy most of the free time he has. This frequently makes it necessary to confine professional relationships to the working day only." [34]

Mutual Aid and Protection. The highly segmented nature of Brazilian society, a revival of the feudal pattern of social organization, has made it necessary for the family to serve not only as the most important institution of mutual aid but also as the principal agency for providing protection for its members. This is especially true of the upper-class family, the aristocratic possessors of the casa grande and the broad acreages surrounding it. The protecting arm of the patriarch is extended to all the members of his numerous clan; and the neighboring small farmer, along with the workers on the big estate, still finds it necessary to place himself under the protection of the master of the big house. Throughout much of Brazil local history continues to be written largely in terms of the feuds between one of these clans and another, but it is becoming more and more difficult for one clan openly to defy state and national governments.

Caring for the Aged and Infirm. No one seems to have assembled data concerning the extent to which the Brazilian family serves as the social institution for caring for the aged and otherwise incapacitated members of society. However, from general observation it seems to have the principal part in this important social task. As one comes to know the rural communities and neighborhoods it is evident that a considerable number of the families are sheltering one or more grandparents, widowed sisters of the husband or wife, nieces or nephews, or other relatives. Many adopted children find places in Brazilian homes. A study would probably find that the Brazilian family continues to be highly important as an agency to care for the aged, the infirm, and for unmarried female relatives.

POSITION OF WOMEN

Since visitors were first admitted to Brazil early in the 1800's, a large number of them have recorded their impressions. Most of the visitors were from the equalitarian families of Europe and North

[34] Harry W. Hutchinson, *Field Guide to Brazil* (Washington, 1961), 37.

America, so it is small wonder that they were impressed by the status of women in Brazil and commented on the subject. Although the reactions range all the way from extreme amusement to deep disgust, there is no disagreement concerning the factual situation.

The isolation of the woman from nearly all social contacts, especially those with strangers, is the point most frequently made. For example, Burton asserts that "in none but the most civilized families do the mistress and daughters of the house sit down to the table with the stranger; among the less educated the déshabille is too pronounced to admit of reception, without an almost total toilette." [35] Other accounts are in essential agreement. When Koster visited the engenhos of the Northeast he noted the extreme and naïve curiosity of the males, but the women did not appear.[36] And Saint-Hilaire reports that as he worked with the specimens of plants which he had collected "the women, according to habit in Minas [Gerais], push their noses through the door to see what I do. If I turn rapidly, I can catch a glimpse of a bit of the face which protrudes through the door and is hastily withdrawn. What I say here should be repeated on each page of this diary, for this little comedy occurs more or less daily." [37]

Even as late as 1866 a traveler passing through Brazil and stopping overnight at its fazendas, who was permitted to converse with Brazilian women, thought the following incident of sufficient importance that it should be included in his report.

Before leaving Xiririca, there is a circumstance associated with this name that we deem worthy of mention. On our way up, the Sr. Guerra, this gentleman's wife, and a couple of daughters about grown, met us in the parlor, and soon engaged in conversation with us, asking us many questions about the manners and customs of our native country, and expressing a desire to have some American neighbors. We spent a pleasant evening, and, had it not been for the difference in language, might easily have imagined ourselves in an American family. In the morning, at breakfast, we all ate together at the same table. We mention this circumstance because it was the *first* time we had the pleasure of conversing with the Brazilian ladies.[38]

The extreme seclusion of Brazilian women also is recognized by Brazil's best scholars. Rocha Pombo says that in São Paulo "the home was rarely open to strangers" and "the wife left the house only to go to church or for a visit of great importance, always carefully guarded and veiled. . . . The girls almost never left the house." [39] And to the "arabic isolation in which the dames of former times lived, principally in the casas grandes of the engenhos," surrounded almost entirely with female Negro slaves and with their "Mussulmanic submission to their husbands," Freyre attributes the sadistic tendencies

[35] Burton, *The Highlands of the Brazil*, I, 408.
[36] Koster, *Travels in Brazil*, I, 68, 80–81.
[37] Auguste de Saint-Hilaire, *Segunda Viagem do Rio de Janeiro a Minas Gerais e a São Paulo* (1822) (São Paulo, 1932), 112.
[38] Dunn, *Brazil*, 165–66.
[39] Rocha Pombo, *Historia de São Paulo*, 95.

which marred the character of so many of the women. "In the first place, the *senhores* were sadists in relations with their wives." [40]

This suggestion that the wife was the mere creature of her husband-master is amply demonstrated in the pages of Freyre's books. The following quotation illustrates the fact that her vitality and life were rapidly sacrificed in the childbearing process.

> Our patriarchal grandfathers and great grandfathers, almost always great procreators . . . insatiable *machos* securing from marriages with young girls all of a strange sensual savor, rarely had happiness of accompanying the same wife to old age. It was the women, in spite of being younger, who were dying; and the men were marrying the younger sisters or cousins of the first wife. They were almost Bluebeards. Extremely numerous are the cases of the old senhores de engenhos, *capitães-mores,* fazendeiros, barons and viscounts of the time of the empire, married three or four times, and fathers of numerous offspring. This multiplication of the population cost the sacrifice of the women, true martyrs in whom the generative force, consuming first youthfulness, soon would consume life. [41]

Finally, no less flattering estimate of woman's position in the family could be given than the one by Saint-Hilaire. The noted botanist first observed that all the fazendeiros possessed a great many dogs and that, contrary to the practice in Germany and France, the animals were badly treated. Given food only, with never a caress, they were beaten constantly, without the slightest reason for the abuse. "Surrounded by slaves, the Brazilian is accustomed to see only slaves among the beings over whom he has superiority, whether by force or by intelligence. The woman is, frequently, the first slave of the household, the dog is the last." [42]

In a footnote he quotes with approval the Brazilian, Antonio Muniz de Souza, who wrote: "I judge it to be my duty to declare that Brazilian women do not constitute a part of society; except in the large centers of population, they are generally treated as slaves. . . . The common man does not seek a companion; he marries in order to have a slave." [43]

There have been changes in the last hundred years, even in the last twenty. In comparison with colonial times the status of Brazilian women now is relatively good. But, as Nash has pointed out in his discussion of Brazilian domestic relations, ontogeny recapitulates phylogeny. [44]

[40] Freyre, *Casa Grande & Senzala*, 249. For a somewhat contradictory appraisal, however, see Candido, "The Brazilian Family," in Smith and Marchant (eds.), *Brazil: Portrait of Half a Continent*, 295–97.

[41] Freyre, *Casa Grande & Senzala*, 268.

[42] Saint-Hilaire, *Viagem à Provincia de São Paulo*, 137–38.

[43] *Ibid.*, 138.

[44] Nash, *The Conquest of Brazil*, 311.

CHAPTER XIX

EDUCATION AND THE SCHOOL

T HERE IS PROBABLY little chance of being able to find or to present criteria for evaluating the objectives of any educational program that would be generally accepted in either Brazil or the United States. The problem is even greater when a citizen of one of the countries attempts to discover or formulate general bases that would make the educational system of one of the countries more intelligible to persons in another. Nevertheless, the following is an attempt to set forth certain minimum objectives of an educational system, which it is hoped will prove of use in the observation of Brazil's educational system and program. (1) The school should transmit the essential knowledge and develop basic skills which are presumed by modern methods of communication. This means that the three R's (reading, writing, calculation, and speech) must form part of any educational system. On this point there probably is little ground for differences of opinion. The others are not so certain. (2) The school should instill in the student those wants and desires which make for a fuller life and a well-rounded personality which may be realized in the community of which he is a part. This is closely related to the proposition somewhat popular in the United States, that the school should prepare the student for life in the community.[1] In any case, if anything more than mere creature existence is to be achieved, the school must assist the family in instilling new desires and wants in the developing child. If the family is settled into a routine existence, the school must assume an even larger share of the responsibility. But ill fitted is the school which succeeds in transferring to a student only the thought that everything in his local community is of no import, that nothing of value may be achieved there, and that the essence of achievement is to be accomplished only by migrating to another place. Particularly in rural schools there is a likelihood that the substantial elements of rural life and welfare will be depreciated and gaudy aspects of city life held up in glowing colors, with the result that the rural child is stimulated only to leave the rural community for the urban world. (3) In addition to making felt the new wants and desires which stimulate further efforts, the school is obligated to instruct in the skills and techniques with which these new wants and desires may be satisfied. Through this process—education in the

[1] On this point cf. A. Carneiro Leão, *Planejar e Agir* (Rio de Janeiro, 1942), 132–34.

truest sense of the word—a broader base is given to life in the local community. Naturally this involves considerable attention to training in manual skills and aptitudes.

EVOLUTION OF EDUCATIONAL INSTITUTIONS

The development of a system of schools available to the common people and an attempt to give the fundamentals of an education to any considerable part of the population are relatively new in Brazil. Indeed for Brazil to subscribe to Paragraph 7 of Title I of the Charter of Punta del Este is a commitment of the utmost significance, for she has solemnly pledged "to eliminate adult illiteracy and by 1970 to assure, as a minimum, access to six years of primary education for each school-age child in [her one-third of] Latin America; to modernize and expand vocational, secondary and higher educational and training facilities." If those who formulate the plans for the projects undertaken and control the use of the funds raised in Brazil and secured from abroad conscientiously live up to this obligation, Brazil shortly may cease to be merely a "land of the future."

Throughout the long colonial period there was very little instruction of a formal kind. Only toward the end of the eighteenth century were there any important educational improvements, and then they came as a result of new laws issued by Pombal in Portugal. The situation in Bahia, probably fairly representative of the general state of affairs, has been summarized by Francisco Vicente Vianna in his *Memoir of the State of Bahia*.[2] According to this authority, in 1808, when the Prince Regent arrived in Bahia, there were only a very few primary and Latin classes in the province. Any persons seeking a higher education had to go to Portugal for their studies. Instruction was developed to some extent under the governorship of the Count of Arcos, who also was responsible for other improvements in the province. In the capital city of São Salvador the four classes of Latin previously established enjoyed an increased attendance, and a private class was commenced; rhetoric, philosophy, geometry, drawing, and commerce also attracted more students. In 1811 a seminary of theological sciences was established, followed in 1815 by a medical college. About this time private classes in geography, French, English, music, and fencing were instituted by "several gentlemen, influenced by the beneficial direction taken by public instruction."

A few chairs were also established for the teaching of the vernacular language, Latin, geometry, logic, rhetoric, agriculture, and French in some of the villages of what was then a capitania. These

[2] The most complete account of educational developments in Brazil is Fernando de Azevedo, *Brazilian Culture*, translated by William Rex Crawford (New York, 1950). See also, A. Carneiro Leão, "The Evolution of Education in Brazil," in Smith and Marchant (eds.), *Brazil: Portrait of Half a Continent*, Chap. XIV; Manoel Bergstrom Lourenço Filho, "Education," in Lawrence F. Hill (ed.), *Brazil* (Berkeley and Los Angeles, 1947), Chap. IX; and J. Roberto Moreira, *Educação e Desenvolvimento no Brasil* (Rio de Janeiro, 1960), 27–58.

were called the "higher classes"; they numbered forty-three in the province at the time of independence, 1822. There were also a few primary schools.

Following independence, the central government took charge of educational matters in the provinces and undertook to increase the number of primary schools. The constitution of the empire guaranteed free primary instruction to all citizens (Article 179, Paragraph 31) but "at this time . . . there was neither plan nor method of teaching." [3] In this period, that of the empire, the manner of securing the teachers has been described as follows:

As soon as one of them [the chairs] was vacant, the *juiz de fora* . . . issued an edict whereby the chair was put up for competition. The examination of the candidate was trusted to two teachers, who gave him a book, such as, for example, the *elementos de civilidade* (elements of civility), where he was to read a few periods; some common phrases were afterwards dictated to be written by the candidate, who was also obliged to make several addition, subtraction, multiplication and division accounts, and, at length, to answer a few questions on portuguese grammar and christian doctrine. The written proofs were then directed to the archbishop or his substitute, to speak his opinion about the candidates, after which the municipal council appointed the teacher.[4]

In 1836 the responsibility for primary and secondary education in Brazil was transferred to the provinces. At this time a lyceum was established in the state capital and the "higher classes" began to be extinguished. Only twenty-six of them remained in 1838, and by 1860 they were all gone. But the lyceum did not seem to be very successful. Less than ten years after its establishment "it was considered quite useless." [5]

That popular education had made almost no progress up to this time is indicated by data available for 1871. (See Table LXII.) At a time when there were more than 10,000,000 people in Brazil, less than 10,000 were receiving secondary instruction; less than 150,000 were attending elementary schools. There were still nearly 1,700,000 slaves in the empire. In none of the provinces was the showing good, although on a relative basis instruction seems to have been less retarded in the Northeast and North than in the central and southern parts of Brazil.

The rude awakening seems to have commenced when Rui Barbosa and other leading statesmen began to compare the situation in their own country with that in other parts of the Western World. Particularly significant was the report of a commission, headed by Barbosa, presented to the national Senate on September 12, 1882.[6] Much of Barbosa's information was secured at the Philadelphia exposition.

[3] M. P. de Oliveira Santos, "Instrucção Publica," *Diccionario Historico, Geographico e Ethnographico do Brasil* (Rio de Janeiro, 1922), I, 401.

[4] Vianna, *Memoir of the State of Bahia*, 237.

[5] *Ibid.*, 249.

[6] The report was reproduced under the title "A Lição dos Números sôbre a Reforma do Ensino," *Revista Brasileira de Estatística*, II, No. 8 (October–November, 1941), 927–1024.

TABLE LXII

Registration in Schools and Number of Slaves, 1871, by States *

| State | Total enrollment in | | Number of slaves |
	Secondary schools	Primary schools	
Total	9,389	147,621	1,683,864
Amazonas	84	971	1,000
Pará	884	6,569	30,000
Maranhão	850	6,509	80,000
Piauí	41	1,400	20,000
Ceará	309	14,520	20,000
Rio Grande do Norte	117	2,805	20,000
Paraíba	145	3,545	30,000
Pernambuco	1,049	13,443	250,000
Alagôas	285	6,311	50,000
Sergipe	241	4,817	50,000
Bahia	619	13,560	260,000
Espírito Santo	113	1,414	18,772
Rio de Janeiro	604	10,880	300,000
Distrito Federal	3,262	14,426	50,092
São Paulo	42	11,562	80,000
Paraná	138	1,621	10,000
Santa Catarina	—	4,150	15,000
Rio Grande do Sul	144	12,139	80,000
Minas Gerais	314	13,949	300,000
Goiás	99	1,998	15,000
Mato Grosso	49	1,032	4,000

* Source: João Alfredo Corrêa de Oliveira, *Relatorio e Trabalhos Estatisticos* (Rio de Janeiro, 1872).

The facts he assembled led him to say: "The report of our commission cannot fail to leave us grief-stricken for the state of our primary instruction." [7] The commission could discover in all of Brazil for the year 1878 only 5,661 primary schools, with 175,714 students, "one school for 198.6 children of school age" and "one student [enrolled] per 3.57 individuals of school age." [8] Even in the federal capital the showing was more than seven times worse than in the best cities of the United States, and more than 3.4 times worse than in the North American cities whose schools were the most inadequate.[9]

The ferment at this time was soon followed by the abolition of slavery and the establishment of the republic. In 1890 a decree of the provisional government declared primary education to be free, gratuitous, and secular, but the republican constitution made primary education a responsibility of the state governments.[10] Thereafter edu-

[7] *Ibid.*, 927.
[8] *Ibid.*, 939, 941.
[9] *Ibid.*, 949.
[10] Oliveira Santos, "Instrucção Publica," *loc. cit.*, 402–403.

cational advances were slow, but progress did take place. When Getúlio Vargas came to power the central government again began
pushing educational programs. Recent trends are discussed in another section of this chapter.

EDUCATIONAL STATUS

The quality of a population probably is related more closely to its
educational status than to any other determinant. The level of education a people attains is a true indication of the effectiveness of its
educational institutions. Comprehensive recent data on this subject
are available in the results of the 1940 and 1950 censuses. These
sources supply invaluable information for determining the educational situation, for understanding the bases from which the recent
movement for popular education has had to part and the inertia with
which Brazilian educators have had to deal. Of all the materials pertaining to education presented in the census, three series are of prime
importance for present purposes: (1) one showing primary-school
enrollment and attendance in relation to the population of primary-
school age, (2) another having to do with the educational attainments
or status of the population as judged by the ability or inability to read
and write, and (3) still another showing the amount of formal schooling completed.

According to the 1950 data there were in Brazil 11,884,154 children, aged six to fourteen, inclusive. At that time a total of 3,211,708
persons of these ages were receiving instruction of some type, a proportion of 27.0 per cent. This figure was slightly lower for boys (26.4
per cent) than for girls (27.6 per cent). In 1940 the corresponding
indexes for those aged 6–15 were 26.9 per cent for children of both
sexes, 27.5 per cent for boys, and 26.3 per cent for girls. As suggested below, the development of a pattern in which girls have as
great or even greater opportunity as their brothers to secure the rudiments of an education is a social change of prime importance.

Inevitably, with a lag of a few years, the school enrollments are
reflected directly in the educational status of the population. Mere
percentages of the population able to read and write long ago lost
their significance in a society such as that of the British Isles, Scan-
dinavia, Germany, or the United States, where the bulk of the population possesses far more than those elementary skills. But throughout
much of the world, including Brazil, the proportion of literacy or illiteracy is still the most useful indicator for measuring the educational
level of the population, or showing how it varies from place to place
and group to group, and of indicating the nature and direction of the
changes that are taking place. The data from the 1950 census provide a basis for determining some of the more important features of
the educational status of the Brazilian population.

Of most general interest, of course, is an indicator of the general
level of educational attainments, and in this connection the basic fig-

ure is the one indicating that at mid-century almost one-half (48.5 per cent) of the Brazilians who had passed their tenth birthdays were able to read and write. (See Table LXIII.) The proportion of literates, or illiterates, varies greatly with age in a society such as that of Bra-

TABLE LXIII

Percentages of Illiterates among Persons 10 Years of Age and over, 1950, by Age, Sex, and Residence *

Age	Total	Urban	Suburban	Rural
10 and over	51.5	21.3	37.9	67.7
Male	47.3	15.8	32.0	62.9
Female	53.5	26.0	43.4	72.8
10–14	56.3	19.6	35.0	71.2
Male	57.2	19.6	36.3	71.5
Female	55.3	19.5	33.8	70.9
15–19	47.3	15.6	27.4	63.5
Male	47.4	13.5	26.7	63.2
Female	47.2	17.4	28.1	63.8
20–24	45.8	16.0	29.8	62.6
Male	42.5	12.2	25.4	58.5
Female	48.9	19.2	33.7	66.5
25–29	47.9	17.7	33.8	64.9
Male	42.7	12.9	27.3	58.6
Female	52.9	21.9	39.8	71.2
30–39	50.0	20.0	38.6	66.6
Male	42.9	13.8	29.6	58.4
Female	56.4	25.5	47.0	75.2
40–49	53.7	24.7	46.1	70.2
Male	45.2	16.0	35.0	61.0
Female	62.6	32.9	56.9	80.9
50–59	57.5	30.4	53.2	73.1
Male	48.0	19.3	40.5	63.3
Female	67.4	40.6	65.0	84.5
60–69	60.7	35.8	58.1	75.5
Male	52.0	24.4	46.3	66.1
Female	69.5	45.0	68.3	86.5
70–79	64.0	39.9	63.2	78.9
Male	55.5	28.6	51.2	69.3
Female	71.1	47.3	71.7	88.6
80 and over	75.6	52.9	75.6	87.2
Male	68.8	41.3	66.0	79.5
Female	79.9	58.3	80.9	93.0

* Source: "Censo Demográfico," *VI Recenseamento Geral do Brasil, 1950*, I (Rio de Janeiro, 1956), 19.

zil in which considerable headway is being made in the development of a system of schools available to larger and larger segments of the population, and it also differs from the one sex to the other. For both sexes taken together the proportion of illiteracy is lowest in the age group 20–24, and these ages also are the ones in which the index is lowest for males. For females, however, those aged 15–19 have the lowest proportion of illiterates. It is significant, and in accord with the conclusions based on school attendance given above, that in the two lowest five-year age groupings the indexes for females are below those for males. At the older ages, though, the males have substantially higher educational status than the females, due no doubt in large part to the fact that in earlier decades boys were more likely than girls to be given the advantages of formal schooling, but also probably accounted for to some extent by a greater tendency for males than females to learn to read and write after attaining adulthood.

These materials, along with those in a previous paragraph, which indicate that Brazilian girls now are receiving basic instruction in higher proportions than their brothers are highly significant. This is a sharp departure from the practice prevailing until recently, and it reflects the fact that Brazilian social norms are coming to correspond more closely than formerly with those prevailing in other parts of the Western World.

In addition to the variations with age and the differences between the sexes there are several other highly significant differentials in the educational status of various segments of the Brazilian population. One of these is the relatively high educational attainment of the urban population, which prevails among all age groups and for both sexes, in comparison with those of the rural people. As a matter of fact the indexes given in Table LXIII for the entire population aged ten years and over, which indicate that the proportions of illiterates are about three times as high in the rural sections of Brazil as they are in the urban centers, are fairly indicative of the situation.

Also highly significant is the fact that the white and the yellow (Japanese) populations of Brazil are far more likely to learn to read and write than are the Negro, mulatto, Indian, and mestiço populations. (See Figure 35.) Thus in 1950 among those of ten years of age and over only 17 per cent of those classified as yellow and 34 per cent of those in the white category were illiterate, whereas among the Negroes the corresponding percentage was 73 and among the pardos (Indian and mixed peoples) it was 69. Similarly in 1940 the comparable indexes for the various color categories were as follows: yellow, 34 per cent; white, 47 per cent; pardo, 71 per cent; and Negro, 79 per cent.

As might well be anticipated, the educational status of the Brazilian population varies sharply from one part of the country to another. See Table LXIV. If one takes note particularly of the data for 1950, it is clear that literacy reaches its maximum, or illiteracy its minimum, in the old Distrito Federal, now the state of Guanabara. Among the other states, however, Rio Grande do Sul ranked first, barely above São Paulo, in literacy, and then came Santa Catarina, Rio de Janeiro, and Paraná, in the order named. They were followed by Mato Grosso and Pará, two of the largest and most sparsely populated states in Brazil.

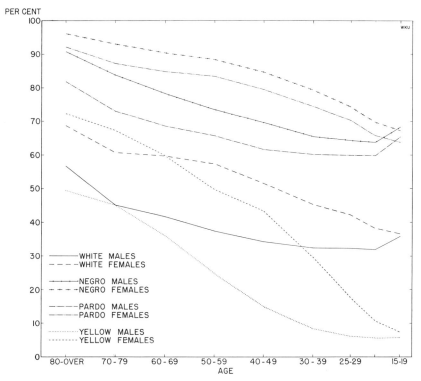

PER CENT

Legend:
——— WHITE MALES
— — — WHITE FEMALES
——•——•—— NEGRO MALES
— • — • — NEGRO FEMALES
— — — PARDO MALES
—•—•—•— PARDO FEMALES
············ YELLOW MALES
············ YELLOW FEMALES

AGE: 80-OVER 70-79 60-69 50-59 40-49 30-39 25-29 15-19

FIGURE 35. The proportions of illiterates in the Brazilian population, by age, sex, and color, 1950.

In 1950 illiteracy was most prevalent in Northeastern Brazil, and especially in the state of Alagôas, with only 24 per cent of its population of ten years of age and over able to read and write. It was closely rivaled for this unenviable position, however, by Maranhão, Piauí, and Paraíba.

The data gathered in the 1950 census which show for all persons ten years of age and over the highest course of training completed also are useful in the analysis of the educational status of the Brazilian population. These data were cross classified by color. See Table LXV. They show clearly that exceedingly low proportions of Brazilians are privileged to acquire a high school or a university education and that this is especially the case for Brazilian Negroes, mulattoes, Indians, and mestiços.

ELEMENTARY EDUCATION

Because the state and the município have a large share of the responsibility for primary education, there is much variation from one part of Brazil to another in the length of the course. In general, primary education continues for three years or grades in rural territory

TABLE LXIV

*Proportion of the Population 10 Years of Age
and over Classified as Able to Read and Write,
by States, 1940 and 1950 ***

State	Percentage able to read and write	
	1940	1950
Brazil	43	48
North		
Guaporé †	—	49
Acre †	40	34
Amazonas	46	43
Rio Branco †	—	45
Pará	53	49
Amapá †	—	44
Northeast		
Maranhão	27	25
Piauí	27	26
Ceará	32	31
Rio Grande do Norte	31	32
Paraíba	26	29
Pernambuco	31	32
Alagôas	23	24
East		
Sergipe	32	34
Bahia	32	32
Minas Gerais	43	44
Espírito Santo	53	47
Rio de Janeiro	54	56
Distrito Federal	87	85
South		
São Paulo	65	65
Paraná	56	53
Santa Catarina	61	64
Rio Grande do Sul	65	66
West Central		
Mato Grosso	51	51
Goiás	32	33

* Computed from data in "Censo Demográfico," VI
Recenseamento Geral do Brasil, 1960, I (Rio de Ja-
neiro, 1956).
† Territory.

and for four years in urban areas. But there are many exceptions. The
latest data the present writer has been able to find on this aspect of
school organization are for 1947 when there still were nineteen
schools in Brazil which offered only one year of elementary school
work. Twelve of these were in Mato Grosso and five of them in Alagôas. Another 1,083 schools offered only two years of training, and
those of this type were most numerous in Maranhão (339), Mato
Grosso (319), Piauí (263), and Rio Grande do Norte (144). Most

TABLE LXV

Brazilians 10 Years of Age and over Classified According to Highest Course of Training Completed, 1950, by Sex and Color *

Sex and Color	NONE		ELEMENTARY SCHOOLING		INTERMEDIATE SCHOOLING		UNIVERSITY	
	Number	Per cent	Number	Per cent	Number	Per cent	Number	Per cent
Total	30,015,311	82.1	5,388,695	14.8	987,148	2.7	158,070	0.4
Males	14,740,639	81.5	2,704,836	15.0	495,910	2.7	144,233	0.8
Females	15,274,672	82.7	2,683,859	14.5	491,238	2.7	13,837	0.1
White	7,800,176	58.2	4,523,535	33.7	928,905	6.9	152,934	1.2
Males	4,292,435	60.0	2,256,632	31.5	463,864	6.5	139,454	2.0
Females	3,507,741	56.1	2,266,903	36.3	465,041	7.4	13,480	0.2
Negro	867,685	78.6	228,890	20.8	6,794	0.6	448	†
Males	494,346	80.2	117,832	19.1	3,929	0.6	409	0.1
Females	373,339	76.6	111,058	22.8	2,865	0.6	39	†
Yellow	100,152	54.3	74,652	40.5	8,744	4.7	924	0.5
Males	56,232	53.9	41,260	39.5	6,016	5.8	867	0.8
Females	43,920	54.8	33,392	41.7	2,728	3.4	57	0.1
Pardo ‡	2,341,930	79.7	551,410	18.8	41,410	1.4	3,568	0.1
Males	1,315,151	81.0	284,247	17.5	21,470	1.3	3,326	0.2
Females	1,026,779	78.2	267,163	20.3	19,940	1.5	242	†

Highest course of training completed

* Source of basic data: "Censo Demográfico," VI Recenseamento Geral do Brasil, 1950, I (Rio de Janeiro, 1956), 20, 24.
† Less than 0.1 per cent.
‡ Includes Indians, mulattoes, mestiços, etc.

numerous of all were the primary schools offering three years of work, numbering 22,526, or more than one-half of the total (43,405) in the entire country. These were the prevailing type in the states of Ceará, Rio Grande do Norte, Alagôas, Minas Gerais, Espírito Santo, Rio de Janeiro, São Paulo, Paraná, Santa Catarina, and Goiás. Schools in which the children were privileged to secure four years of elementary education were more numerous than those of any other type in the territories of Guaporé, Acre, and Rio Branco, and the states of Pará, Piauí, Paraíba, Sergipe, and Rio Grande do Sul. The Distrito Federal, the territory of Amapá, and the states of Amazonas, Pernambuco, and Bahia were attempting to place their elementary schooling on a five-year basis, and substantial numbers of such elementary schools also were found in Ceará, Paraíba, Minas Gerais, Rio de Janeiro, São Paulo, and Paraná. Of all the primary schools in Brazil in 1947 about 0.1 per cent offered only one year of work, 2.5 per cent offered two, 51.8 per cent three, 30.0 per cent four, and 15.6 per cent five years or grades of schooling.[11]

More recently a tabulation has been published showing the enrollment by year of schooling or grade. This provides a basis for inferring that by 1958 there were one or more elementary schools offering five years of work in Rondonia, Amazonas, Rio Grande do Norte, Pernambuco, Bahia, São Paulo, Paraná, and Goiás. However, the total enrollment in the fifth grade was only 45,560, of whom 16,413 were in São Paulo and 12,905 in Bahia. At least a few four-year elementary schools were present in each of the other states and territories, although for the nation as a whole the enrollments by grade indicate that the vast majority of all primary school children in Brazil were in the first and second grades. Thus, out of a total enrollment of 5,775,246, the number in each grade was: first, 3,019,744; second, 1,275,890; third, 896,160; fourth, 537,892; and fifth, 45,560.[12]

Stimulated by the improvements made under the able direction of Carneiro Leão, first in Pernambuco and later in Rio de Janeiro,[13] the larger cities show a growing tendency to increase the duration of primary schooling to five years. But the struggle is not easy. As late as 1921 a legal attempt was made in progressive São Paulo to reduce the primary schools to two grades.[14] Another such attempt is unlikely in that state, although constant pressure from Brasília is necessary to keep some of the others from slipping back still further.

Administratively, the primary schools may be organized and conducted by the government of the nation, the state, or the município, or by private (generally religious) agencies. In the open country the *escola isolada,* the one-teacher, ungraded school, prevails. In the centers of population social organization is generally sufficiently advanced to provide a primary school with two or more teachers. The

[11] Data are from *Anuário Estatístico do Brasil,* XII (1951), 422–23.

[12] *Ibid.,* XIX (1958), 362.

[13] For an account of one of the battles for a better educational system, see Carneiro Leão, *Planejar e Agir.*

[14] Cf. A. Almeida, Jr., *Annuario do Ensino do Estado de São Paulo, 1935–1936* (São Paulo, 1937?), 111–12.

first grading is always by sex, boys together and girls together. If there are sufficient funds, teachers, and students, each sex may be graded by age. In any case the multiple-teacher school is called *grupo escolar.*

Number and Size of Schools. The available data for 1958 give 89,-999 as the number of schools (*unidades escolares*) offering primary work. In these were registered a total of 6,775,791 students, an average of 75 per school. But a large portion of the students did little more than appear at one time or another so that the "effective matriculation" amounted to only 5,801,759, or 64 students per school. Of those whose matriculation was effective, 3,547,509, or 61 per cent, completed the work prescribed for the year and advanced one stage. Over a half million students, 505,864, or 8.7 per cent of the effective registration, graduated from the elementary-school course at the end of the year. This number of graduates considered in conjunction with the total matriculation and the length of the elementary course probably means that at least three out of five children who commence school fall by the way before completing the three- or the four-year course.

The size of the school also is indicated by the number of teachers per unit. There were in 1958 a total of 197,423 teachers instructing in the primary schools, or an average of 2.2 per school. Each teacher had on the average 32 pupils if the total matriculation is considered, or 29 if only the effective registration is taken into account. Together these facts indicate that the schools are small, a very large share being one-teacher units.[15]

Administrative Dependency. Ten per cent of the primary schools are operated by private agencies, most of which are ecclesiastical bodies. (See Table LXVI.) These privately supported schools employ 12.5 per cent of all the primary teachers and enroll 12.2 per cent of the children. They are somewhat larger than the public schools, averaging 93 students as compared with 73, and they have 2.8 teachers per school compared with 2.1 in the public primary schools. Private schools are of greatest relative importance in the city of Rio de Janeiro, and in Rio Grande do Norte, the state of Rio de Janeiro, Pernambuco, Mato Grosso, and Alagôas, where 20 per cent or more of all the children secure a private primary education. On the other hand, private agencies have done very little to provide educational facilities in Acre, Minas Gerais, Espírito Santo, Paraná, and Santa Catarina.

Of the 81,122 publicly supported elementary schools in Brazil in 1958, 36,876 (slightly more than 45 per cent) were financed by the states, 43,926 (54 per cent) by the various municípios, and 320 by the federal government.[16]

The Curriculum. An examination of the detailed program of work specified for the elementary schools greatly assists one in gaining an understanding of Brazilian educational institutions. For this purpose,

[15] Data from *Anuário Estatístico do Brasil*, XXI (1960), 287–91.
[16] *Ibid.*

TABLE LXVI

Relative Importance of Private Elementary Schools, 1958,
by States *

State	Number of schools			Enrollment		
	Total	Private	Per cent private	Total	In private schools	Per cent in private schools
Brazil	89,999	8,877	9.9	6,775,791	827,309	12.2
North						
Rondonia †	52	6	11.5	6,120	1,494	24.4
Acre †	138	11	8.0	10,543	923	8.8
Amazonas	962	80	8.3	46,048	10,396	22.6
Rio Branco †	16	1	6.3	1,957	466	23.8
Pará	2,299	165	7.2	159,520	18,156	11.4
Amapá †	123	11	8.9	9,572	1,456	15.2
Northeast						
Maranhão	1,900	292	15.4	108,953	20,682	19.0
Piauí	1,373	134	9.8	82,583	12,195	14.8
Ceará	5,584	455	8.1	221,781	30,519	13.8
Rio Grande do Norte	2,215	769	34.7	121,456	37,820	31.1
Paraíba	2,590	173	6.7	142,999	14,725	10.3
Pernambuco	6,611	1,317	19.9	346,741	75,422	21.8
Alagôas	1,511	256	16.9	88,378	19,737	22.3
East						
Sergipe	1,102	142	12.9	62,524	9,608	15.4
Bahia	7,265	672	10.7	394,883	50,104	12.7
Minas Gerais	11,303	531	4.7	995,824	59,915	6.0
Espírito Santo	2,714	83	3.1	147,867	4,756	3.2
Rio de Janeiro	3,382	695	20.5	343,431	71,952	21.0
Guanabara	985	657	66.7	308,539	103,498	33.5
South						
São Paulo	13,894	701	5.0	1,586,380	87,119	5.5
Paraná	5,534	174	3.1	367,206	25,101	6.8
Santa Catarina	4,759	89	1.9	298,208	14,093	4.7
Rio Grande do Sul	10,307	1,125	10.9	684,528	107,795	15.7
West Central						
Mato Grosso	1,404	126	9.0	90,504	21,214	23.4
Goiás	1,976	212	10.7	149,296	27,983	18.7

* Compiled and computed from data in *Anuário Estatístico do Brasil, 1960,* XXI (Rio de Janeiro, 1960).
† Territory.

it is convenient to use the plan of study established in 1940 for the rural schools in Paraná, one of the more progressive of the states.[17] This curriculum is less adequate than that of city schools generally but is a considerable improvement over that still used throughout a large portion of the rural territory.

Subjects prescribed for the first year are Portuguese, oral and writ-

[17] Directoria Geral da Educação, *Programa para as Escolas Isoladas: Decreto No. 9592 de 26 de Fevereiro de 1940* (Curitiba, 1940), 5–19.

ten; writing; arithmetic; drawing; geography; Brazilian history;
civic, moral and social education; natural and physical sciences;
hygiene; manual exercises (as paper cutting and making of boxes,
for the boys; sewing and crocheting, for the girls); singing; and
physical education. The work specified for the second year consists
of instruction in Portuguese, oral and written; arithmetic; geometry;
drawing; geography; Brazilian history; civic, moral, and social education; physical, natural, and agricultural sciences; hygiene; manual
exercises; singing; and physical education. During the third year the
children study the same subjects as in the second, except that writing
again has a formal place in the program.[18]

The work to be done in each of the subjects is set forth in the decree establishing the curriculum. For example, it is prescribed that
the first year of arithmetic shall include the following: work in
counting and writing numbers to 1,000; addition, subtraction, division, and multiplication up to 1,000, providing "that in the multiplication and division the multiplier and the divisor shall always be sim-
ple numbers"; learning to find $\frac{1}{2}$, $\frac{1}{4}$, and $\frac{1}{5}$ of any number up to 50;
and learning the first twelve Roman numerals. The second year's
work consists of learning to read and write the numbers to the thousands; studying the tens, hundreds, and thousands; practicing the
four fundamental operations; and learning the Roman numerals to
200. During the third year the program requires the students to make
a complete study of the four fundamental operations, to learn the
rudiments of simple fractions, to study the decimals, to learn the
metric system of weights and measures, to do problems in the deci-
mal metric system, to do practical work in simple proportions, and to
do problems in simple interest.

In the sciences, during the first year, the students are to be taught
the rudiments of the three kingdoms of nature, animal, vegetable,
and mineral, along with the utility of each. The year following, when
agriculture is included, they are to learn the bodies of nature, solids,
liquids, and gases; elementary facts about the human body; the advantages of rational farming in comparison with the old routine, i.e.,
fire agriculture; to know the domestic animals and their uses; and
something about agricultural instruments and how they are used.
Finally, in the third year, it is prescribed that they shall be taught
about the five senses; a little concerning digestion, respiration, and
the circulation of the blood; elementary facts regarding air and water; the preparation and fertilization of the soil; seed selection; the
planting of local crops; and the culture of erva mate, coffee, cotton, rice, wheat, and fruit trees.

Teachers' Responsibilities. The decree also indicates the duties of
the teacher and specifies certain things which he or she must not do.
There are twenty-nine positive requirements as follows: (1) to open
the building at least 15 minutes before time for classes to com-

[18] For a very similar set of requirements, spread over four years and used in
the state of São Paulo, see Almeida, *Annuario do Ensino do Estado de São Paulo,*
1935–1936, 113–23.

mence, (2) to be zealous in cleaning and caring for the classroom and the equipment, (3) to maintain the maximum of order and discipline in the classroom, (4) to take great care in maintaining the record, without erasures, deletions, or additions, (5) to prepare the lessons a day in advance, (6) to set an example in morality, politeness, punctuality, assiduity, and love of work, (7) to appear, if invited, at all school celebrations, civic educational gatherings, even though they occur on holidays, (8) to be present at educational and pedagogical meetings, if invited by the authorities, (9) to assume office during the legal period specified, (10) to notify the students of the opening of school, (11) to commemorate all national holidays and to hold school celebrations on September 21 (Spring Day) and October 12 (Children's Day), (12) to supervise the playground during recess, (13) to fill in all the columns in the register and the roll book, (14) to correct the papers of the students daily, filing them away and returning them to the students at the end of the year, (15) to stay at the school during the official hours, (16) to keep a daily record of the schoolwork, (17) to execute faithfully all of the orders of the school authorities, (18) to wear a duster while classes are in session and see that the students do the same, (19) to make every effort to secure from the students the maximum of assiduity and punctuality, (20) to post school hours in a prominent place and to comply with them faithfully, (21) to treat the students with tenderness, care, and politeness, (22) to compile the tabular report at the end of each month, with data faithfully transcribed from the roll book, to present it for the approval of the inspector of schools, and then to send it to the Director General of Education before the fifth of the month following, (23) to inform the authorities, officially, concerning the performance of teaching duties, the closing and reopening of classes, and the beginning and conclusion of the vacation, (24) in case of resignation or discharge, to make an inventory of school materials and to deliver them, in return for a receipt, to the proper official, (25) to record and send to the Director General of Education the facts concerning all visitors, whether they be school authorities or not, (26) to requisition essential supplies and equipment, (27) to inform the parents or guardians concerning the excessive absences or serious misbehavior of their children, (28) to sing the national hymn at the opening of school and the hymn to the flag at the close, and (29) to inform the Director General of Education of the hours for class work at the beginning of the school year and to refrain from making changes in them unless officially authorized to do so.

The teacher is specifically prohibited from (1) residing more than three kilometers from the school, (2) failing to enter his absences in the monthly report, (3) using his own or the students' time during classes for noneducational activities, (4) omitting parts of the program or altering the order of recitations, (5) changing the distribution of time among the various subjects, (6) permitting outsiders, even members of his own family, in the classroom, excepting visitors and officials, (7) leaving the students by themselves, either in the classroom or at recess, (8) administering physical punishment, (9) securing a substitute during his absences, (10) permitting students to carry books supplied by the state government to their homes, (11) giving students consent to leave the school grounds at recess under the pretext of going home for lunch, (12) permitting the use of the schoolhouse for entertainments or other noneducational purposes, (13) failing to assist the group of examiners, when designated to do so, and (14) sending his students, or appearing with them, in a group at funerals.[19]

SECONDARY EDUCATION

In a modern urban and industrial society the degree of division of labor, specialization, and interdependence prevailing makes it essential that a high proportion of the population has at least a high-school education. It is unlikely that Brazil can be any exception to this rule. Nevertheless, well along in the second half of the twentieth century, she is still in the early stages in the development of any schools beyond the fourth- or fifth-grade level that will be generally accessible to the more capable one-half of her youth. Herein lie the greatest challenges, and also the largest opportunities, in all that has to do with her social and economic development.

Ensino médio, or intermediate education, in Brazil is formal schooling above the three, four, or five years of elementary education and below the university level. It is divided into *ginasial* and *colegial.* The former, that carried on in the *ginasios,* is the lower of the two, corresponding in a general way to instruction in the fifth through the ninth grades in the United States; and the latter, in schools designated as *colegios,* is most comparable with that in high schools (tenth through the twelfth grades) in the United States. For this reason the North American writer who uses the term "college" in any way is almost certain to find that it has been translated by words signifying "high school" if and when his thoughts are published in Portuguese; and a similar confusion prevails in the translation of Brazilian materials into English.

A very small proportion of Brazil's youth is privileged to advance beyond the meager primary educational levels discussed in the preceding section. This is largely because not enough schools have been provided and because those that are functioning are highly concentrated in the state capitals and other cities far remote from the districts in which high proportions of the young people live. Thus for 1960 [20] there were reported for all Brazil a total of only 6,767 secondary schools of all types, of which 3,698 were reported as secondary

[19] *Programa para as Escolas Isoladas: Decreto No. 9592 de 26 de Fevereiro de 1940,* 5–19.

[20] The materials in this and the following paragraphs are from the *Anuário Estatístico do Brasil, 1960,* XXI, 296–99. See also Charles Wagley, "The Brazilian Revolution: Social Changes Since 1930," in Council on Foreign Relations, *Social Change in Latin America Today* (New York, 1960), 177–230.

schools as such, 1,324 as commercial schools, 417 as industrial schools, 94 as agricultural schools, and 1,234 as normal schools (for the training of elementary school teachers). The 3,698 schools in the first category were staffed by a total of 58,296 teachers and had an enrollment of 868,178 students. In 1960, however, the number of persons aged ten to seventeen, inclusive, must have been about thirteen million.

Of the 3,698 basic secondary schools 2,768, or three-fourths, were those of the lower or *ginasio* level and only 930 were *colegios*, with the former accounting for 754,608, or 87 per cent, of the enrollment in both. Of the *ginasios* 1,970 (71 per cent) and of the *colegios* 556 (60 per cent) were private schools.

Even more significant, however, is the fact that both the *ginasios* and the *colegios* are highly concentrated in a few of the most highly urbanized sections of Brazil. Thus, according to the data for 1960, there were 1,359 municípios in Brazil, out of a total of 2,764, in which there were absolutely no schools of any kind except the elementary schools described above. Furthermore, only 275 municípios, one out of ten, contained schools of the *colegio* level, although an additional 950 municípios had *ginasios* within their limits. Even the new Distrito Federal, with Brasília already functioning as the nation's capital, had no school of the higher secondary level in 1960, and the same was true of the territory of Rio Branco. The territories of Acre, Rondonia, and Amapá each had only one município in which a *colegio* was found, and the same was true of the states of Amazonas, Pará, Maranhão, and Sergipe. Two municípios per state was the quota of Piauí and Rio Grande do Norte; three per state of Ceará, Paraíba, and Mato Grosso; and four per state of Pernambuco and Alagôas. Elsewhere high schools were not so rare, but even so in 1960 the number of municípios containing *colegios* and the total number of municípios in the state were as follows: Santa Catarina, 8 and 102; Goiás, 7 and 179; Bahia, 8 and 194; Espírito Santo, 8 and 40; Rio de Janeiro, 17 and 61; Paraná, 20 and 162; Rio Grande do Sul, 26 and 150; Minas Gerais, 52 and 485; and São Paulo, 102 and 504. Such data indicate that the present writer probably was aiming unrealistically high in 1952 when he recommended to Brazil's Commission on Agrarian Policy that the first step in a program of agrarian reform should be the addition to the existing requirements for becoming or remaining a município one that would make it necessary for each such political subdivision to maintain at least one high school with a minimum of five full-time teachers.[21]

HIGHER EDUCATION

Important leaders in educational affairs are doing their utmost to develop facilities for training at the university level of the type required if Brazil is to win a place among the great nations of the world;

[21] The memorandum containing this recommendation has now been published in part. See Rios (ed.), *Recomendações sobre Reforma Agrária*, 177–81.

but their task is not easy and their objectives are not likely to be attained in the near future. Among the host of problems with which they are confronted are the following: (1) the number of universities is only a small fraction of that needed, and there are many important states in which facilities for training at the college or university level are practically nonexistent; (2) large proportions of the university students pursue their studies only on a part-time basis; (3) the great majority of all university professors are on a part-time basis, and most of them exercise one or two other professions other than that connected with the university; (4) until recently there has been very little inclination in university or governmental circles to think of the university as an institution that should serve the needs of the society of which it is a part; (5) the schools of law and medicine traditionally have controlled higher education, and even when other schools are added as part of a university system, the newcomers have difficulty in gaining any position in the structure other than one at the periphery; and (6) the development of facilities for graduate work, those parts of the university which alone can train the tens of thousands of scientists, social scientists, and university teachers whom Brazil must have quickly if she is to attain her goals, has only begun.

For almost a century and a half after Brazil achieved her independence her institutions of higher learning consisted almost exclusively of separate or isolated schools of law, medicine, and theology. Among these the school of medicine at Salvador, Bahia, and the school of law in São Paulo held well-merited positions of esteem. During the twentieth century, however, and especially during the last quarter of a century, there has been a sustained effort to gather together into university systems existing schools and colleges (*faculdades*), along with new ones representing such fields of knowledge as arts and sciences, engineering, economics and business administration, and social work. By 1959 this process had gone on to the extent that there were governmentally supported universities in each of the following states: Pará, Ceará, Rio Grande do Norte, Paraíba, Pernambuco (the Universidade do Recife and the Universidade Rural, consisting of schools of agriculture and veterinary medicine, as well), Bahia, Minas Gerais (the Universidade de Minas Gerais and also a Universidade Rural), Rio de Janeiro (a Universidade Rural only), Guanabara (the Universidade do Brasil and the Universidade do Rio de Janeiro), São Paulo (the Universidade de São Paulo and the Universidade de Campinas), Paraná, and Rio Grande do Sul. Only separate or isolated schools, such as those of nursing, social work, economics, and law in Amazonas, and those of philosophy, economics, law, pharmacy and dentistry, and social work in Santa Catarina, were to be found in the remaining nine states. In addition there were Catholic universities in Pernambuco, Guanabara, São Paulo, and Rio Grande do Sul, and one (Mackenzie University) under Presbyterian auspices in São Paulo.[22]

[22] Cf. Ministério da Educação e Cultura, *Sinopse Estatística do Ensino Superior, 1959* (Rio de Janeiro, 1959), 29–55.

In the twenty-one universities mentioned above, along with all the separate or isolated schools offering higher education of any type, the total enrollment in 1959 amounted to 89,586 of whom 1,983 were classified as graduate students. At the same time the number of faculty members was 19,263. As mentioned above, large proportions of both students and faculty are on a part-time basis, but no comprehensive data about this are available.

The largest numbers of undergraduates were enrolled in law (21,-977), philosophy, arts and sciences (18,453), engineering (10,696), medicine (10,248), economics (7,059), and dentistry (5,217); and the bulk of the graduate students were studying in the fields of law (700), sanitary services, i.e. obstetrical nursing, nutrition, and urban planning (383), philosophy, arts and sciences (305), and hygiene and public health (161).

The number of students completing the requirements for undergraduate degrees is reported at 15,502 for 1958, and the number indicated as having finished a graduate course of study is 483. Of the undergraduates the largest contingents of new degree holders were in philosophy, arts and sciences (4,206), law (3,340), medicine (1,578), dentistry (1,294), and engineering; and of the graduate students the largest numbers of those receiving advanced degrees were in the sanitary services (139), hygiene and public health (90), philosophy, arts and sciences (87), and law (55). Only thirty-two engineers were included in the total of those completing the work for a graduate degree.

Facilities, staff, students enrolled, and graduates are highly concentrated in the states of São Paulo, Guanabara, Rio Grande do Sul, Minas Gerais, and Pernambuco. For example, of the 19,263 faculty members reported, 4,601 were members of the faculties of São Paulo institutions, 3,391 of those in the city of Rio de Janeiro (Guanabara), 2,714 of those in Rio Grande do Sul, 2,201 of those in Minas Gerais, and 1,327 of those in Pernambuco. Likewise, of the 87,603 undergraduate students enrolled, 24,037 were in São Paulo, 18,301 in Guanabara, 8,737 in Rio Grande do Sul, 8,414 in Minas Gerais, and 4,871 in Pernambuco; and of the 1,983 graduate students 853 were in São Paulo, 448 in Guanabara, 261 in Pernambuco, 187 in Minas Gerais, 181 in Bahia, 38 in Ceará, and the remaining 15 in Rio Grande do Sul.[23]

Of the vast amount that has been written about the nature of the Brazilian university, the manner in which it functions in contemporary society, and the ways in which it must be changed if it is to meet the needs of a twentieth-century nation, the works of Dr. Anísio S. Teixeira, director of the Instituto Nacional de Estudos Pedagógicos, occupy an enviable position; and among the most cogent products of his insight and energy is an article comparing the systems of higher education in Brazil and the United States which appeared in a recent

[23] The data in this and the preceding paragraphs were compiled and computed from materials *ibid.*, 10–13. See also Américo Barbosa de Oliveira and José Zacarias Sá Carvalho, *A Formação de Pessoal de Nível Superior e o Desenvolvimento Economico* (Rio de Janeiro, 1960), 28–49, *passim.*

issue of Brazil's leading educational journal.[24] The points elaborated in this article deserve a place in the thinking of all concerned with the development and improvement of universities in Brazil and other Latin-American countries.

Dr. Teixeira first describes the old type of European school and the new type, much more adapted to the needs of the community and the society, which developed in the United States. In particular he contrasts with the institutions in the United States the dual system in Europe, in which there were "primary common schools" for the populace and secondary schools for a small minority who were favored to go on into institutions of higher learning. In the former the schools came to be for *all* the children, did not teach anything special to a *minority*, and were based on the proposition that *talent* was not confined to a few. In the process "*all* human activities became *intellectual* and all *intellectual* activities became *practical:* therefore, the school—whether primary, secondary or higher—also became simultaneously intellectual and practical." In the perfection of her educational institutions "the United States paved the way for the changes which are today taking place all over Europe, and which are bound to take place in all the school systems of the world."

The evolution of Brazilian schools was quite different. "When our independence was proclaimed, our preoccupation was to set up *institutions of higher learning* for the preparation of those in the liberal professions, and one or two separate systems for educating the people, namely, primary instruction and schools of arts and crafts. Everything was based on European standards."

As a result, "until recently, higher learning covered only education for the three major liberal professions, namely, law, medicine and engineering, not to mention theology." Furthermore, the Brazilian institutions were removed from most pressures that might have made them responsive to the broader needs of society. The institution of higher learning in Brazil "may be under the control of law and the government so far as its administrative and financial aspects are concerned, but when it comes to teaching the professors enjoy an impregnable situation. The 'chair' (*cátedra*) is really sovereign and the 'congregation,' i.e., the corps of 'full professors' (*catedráticos*) is the real collective organ of the school. Full professors have life-long jobs and are unremovable; their status is similar to that of justices of the Supreme Court.

"The Brazilian university is a closed world of remote and distant studies, controlled by professors and which, from time to time, is shaken by students' disturbances—with which professors rarely associate—for spasmodic and semi-revolutionary contacts with the nation, the people and the public." [25]

[24] See Anísio S. Teixeira, "Confronto entre a Educação Superior dos Estados Unidos e a do Brasil," *Revista Brasileira de Estudos Pedagógicos*, XXXIII (1960), 63–74. The present writer is grateful to Dr. Teixeira for permission to make use of these materials and for a provisional English translation of the same.

[25] See also especially for comparisons with Spanish-American universities, John P. Harrison, "The Confrontation with the Political University," *The Annals of the American Academy of Political and Social Science*, 334 (1961), 74–83.

A news item [26] relative to the organization and functioning of the new University of Brasília, the establishment of which was authorized in 1961, is indicative of the manner in which Dr. Teixeira and other Brazilian leaders would modify Brazilian institutions of higher learning. Starting with the announcement that the Chamber of Deputies had approved the project for the establishment of a foundation for maintaining the future University of Brasília, this dispatch gave many of the details of the plan.

The plan for the building of this new center of higher learning envisions construction, within a period of ten years, of buildings containing a total of 600,000 square meters of space. The central institutes will occupy an area of 106.000 square meters, the *faculdades* [colleges] 110,000, cultural organs 88,000, and residences for professors, students and functionaries 300,000. . . .

Brazilian universities are mostly an agglomeration of preexisting schools which remain static and self-sufficient. The establishment of the University of Brasília is intended to modify radically this state of things. It is to be made up of three basic and integrated elements: the central institutes, the *faculdades,* and the cultural centers. In the beginning it will have eight central institutes: mathematics, physics, chemistry, geological sciences, biology, human [behavioral?] sciences, and arts and letters, each of them subdivided into departments. The student will enter the university through one of these institutes, in which he will spend two years receiving the scientific and cultural preparation that is indispensable for the subsequent steps. At the end of this period, the student will have two alternatives: to study another two or three years in the same institute, for specialized training in one of its departments, or to enter one of the *faculdades* for professional training covering a period of two or three years.

For example: a student may enter the Institute of Chemistry. Upon terminating his course, he may remain there in order to specialize in research, or he may go on into the *Faculdade* of Engineering, of Pharmacy, or of Technology; another alternative would be for him to go into the *Faculdade* of Education for the purpose of training as a teacher of chemistry. All of these *faculdades* will have post-graduate courses leading to a doctorate.

With such a structure, it will be possible to prevent the onerous multiplication of facilities and personnel. There also are other advantages: the student will have the opportunity of securing a better professional orientation; there will be greater flexibility in technological training; the *faculdades* will be freed from the responsibility of training research workers; and it will be possible to develop a genuine university campus, with an effective interchange between students and professors in the various disciplines.

. . . . . .

The cultural centers will be installed by foreign countries for the teaching of their languages, literature and traditions.

Finally, the present writer can offer several of his own observations relative to Brazilian universities. These are based upon a quarter of a century of contact, more or less intimate, with those universities and their professors. The propositions stated also are fairly applicable to most of the universities in the Spanish-American coun-

[26] In the *Boletim Informativo* published by the Brazilian Embassy, Washington, D. C., September 12, 1961.

tries. It is especially pertinent to comment on the status of the three principal functions of the modern university as these are performed by the Brazilian and other Latin-American institutions, namely the teaching of resident students, research, and extension, or the endeavor to carry the university's benefits beyond the doors of its buildings.

Resident teaching or instruction is inadequately performed. This is largely because most of the teachers are on a part-time basis, but it is also because the offerings are not sufficiently differentiated into the specialized courses that are needed if the student is to be introduced to knowledge as it exists in the second half of the twentieth century. Especially deficient are the offerings in the physical and social sciences. Nevertheless the teaching function is performed far more adequately than the other two.

Research is sadly neglected in most parts of the large majority of Brazilian universities, although there are some highly significant exceptions to the rule. On the whole these institutions are doing relatively little to extend the boundaries of knowledge and to deepen man's knowledge of physical, mental, and social phenomena. In most areas research is still to be institutionalized to any significant degree. Inadequate budgets are partially responsible for this, but again the system of part-time professors is the principal factor. Especially in the social sciences and the humanities, research in the universities in the United States is a "spare time" activity on the part of scholars who actually earn their livings by teaching classes of students. Where, as in Brazil and other Latin-American countries, the teaching is done by part-time instructors who practice two or three other professions, no persistent challenge confronts the university professor to delve into new aspects of his subject, and other obligations would prevent such a use of his time even if the challenge were present.

The extension function is almost completely lacking in the Brazilian university. Almost never does it accept any responsibility for extending the realm of its teaching activities very far beyond the portals of its buildings.

It will be interesting to follow the development of the University of Brasília. This may have profound effects on the future of Brazil's institutions of higher learning. In general, though, the modification of Brazil's university system is not likely to be done easily and quickly. Merely to change the practice of using part-time professors, widely recognized nowadays as essential, is extremely difficult and is unlikely to come about quickly. It is never possible to change the rules of a game, while the game is in progress, without serious disadvantages to those who conscientiously have played according to the old rules. But a large part of social change involves doing exactly this. The consequences are particularly grave when the "game" extends over a lifetime as it does in the profession of university teaching. Well known is the fact that such institutions as the Universidade Rural, in the state of Rio de Janeiro about thirty miles from the city of Rio de Janeiro, and Mexico's national university, have experienced serious difficulties in getting teachers to handle the classes on their campuses. The teacher of geography, of economics, of sociology, to mention only three subjects, who receives most of his income from the practice of medicine, of banking, or law, respectively, simply cannot carry on satisfactorily if his classes are moved to a location at considerable distance from the center of the city; and after fifteen or twenty years of successful work in his particular combination of professions he is unlikely to be enthusiastic about the introduction of a system of full-time professorships. Especially in the medical schools and the law schools, the faculties of which have dominated Brazilian universities in the past, is one unlikely to find even a desire to change the system in vogue. All of these factors are, of course, merely one small aspect of the larger problem involved in such a task as that of moving the nation's capital and the functionaries of the various ministries from Rio de Janeiro to Brasília.

PROSPECTS

The chances are that primary and even secondary education will continue making rapid progress in the larger cities and towns of Brazil. More people will receive the elements of an education. The training is likely to be better and spread over a longer period of time, so that smaller proportions will lapse back into an illiterate state because of failure to use their acquired abilities to read and write. Literacy will improve functionally even more than it will quantitatively. Urban Brazil is bound to meet more fully the educational standards of Western civilization.

In the vast interior the prospects for millions of young Brazilians are not so favorable. An outstanding Brazilian educator, A. Almeida, Jr., of São Paulo, repeated many times the words that are almost as applicable now as they were when he first uttered them: "There are still localities that are not ripe for the school. To ask that the teacher alone, without material or moral assistance, pull the neighborhood to the front, is to ask too much of the poor girl." [27] For the teacher, the majority of rural schools represent the "seven capital sins." Schools cannot go ahead of systems of communications. "Rarely does a school bring a road. Almost always it is the ease of access that makes possible the school." [28] The smaller and more backward the school, the greater the dependence on the teacher. In the more isolated sections even the schoolroom is secured only as a very great favor, at the cost of the girl. All goes well as long as the teacher is *persona grata*, but "there are fazendeiros and farm managers who consider the teacher to be an employee of the fazenda under the orders of the master and subject to the general discipline of the laborers." To dis-

[27] A. Almeida, Jr., "Os Sete Pecados Capitais da Escola Rural," *Revista Brasileira de Estatística*, II, No. 8 (October–December, 1941), 1215.
[28] *Ibid.*

regard this means trouble. On arriving the girl may be transported to the community; on leaving she may have to go afoot, carrying her suitcase. One day she may be seated at the table with the family, and "tomorrow, under the pretext that there is a sick relative, the door is closed in her face." [29] Frequently the girl must find shelter in the house of the caipira, where the "mistress of the house, although an excellent person, cooks the beans badly with no fat; cleanliness is unknown. . . . The teacher is given a room, with the walls full of holes, which is also used for keeping saddles and harness . . . water difficult; lack of sanitary installations." [30]

These are only a few of the obstacles preventing the extension of schools into the remote areas, a task made all the more difficult by the nature of the class system. For a rural schoolteacher to make her home with a middle-class family is one thing, to become the servant of the fazendeiro or exist in the primitive hut of the caipira is quite another. "There are, then, localities immature for the school. Before naming teachers for them, give them roads, sanitation, a dwelling, and a school house. . . . The school plows and sows. Before it, however, should go the ax." [31]

Another of Brazil's leading educators some time ago proposed definite steps for remedying the situation. M. A. Teixeira de Freitas stressed the necessity of changing the settlement pattern of Brazil, of remedying the isolated and illiterate state in which a large portion of the rural population lives. As a technique for accomplishing the dual purpose of bringing the population into closer spatial relationship to one another and for educating them along the most necessary lines he advanced the idea of establishing "colony-schools." [32]

Teixeira de Freitas presented his proposal for the establishment of these nucleated settlements to the nation's educators who assembled in Bahia in November, 1934. He began by pointing out the "notorious fact" that the rural population of Brazil has an "unbelievably low index of social and economic 'worth.'" This he attributed to a threefold incapacity of the Brazilian countryman, who "neither knows how nor is able to care for his health, nor productively orient his work, nor give to his life the values of civilization." For this reason, "our primordial attempts at progress should be in the direction of integrating our nationality by the elevation of the sanitary, economic, and social level of the populations living in the sertões and along the beaches." Before considering how this might be done, the speaker gave an analysis of the reasons for such deficiencies. He contended that there was a "fundamental deficit of 'socialization'" because of dispersion and lack of education. Therefore, he reasoned very logically, it is possible to phrase the problem of Brazil's rural civilization in terms of social gravitation: gravitation on the material level, or the condensa-

[29] *Ibid.*, 1216.
[30] *Ibid.*
[31] *Ibid.*, 1217.
[32] This thesis was presented to the I Congresso de Ensino Regional, held in Bahia during November, 1934. Some of its essentials were also published in Teixeira de Freitas' article, "Educação Rural," *loc. cit.*, 54–80.

tion or aggregation of the demographic mass, and gravitation on the spiritual level, a point of departure for the interlacing of desires, intelligences, and sentiments. "The solution of such a problem, then, is nothing more than to provoke an adequate social centripetency, a centripetency which, harmoniously balancing with an antiurban centrifugation, will give to Brazil in a short time a true agricultural organization differentiated from the metropolitan structure, but firmly articulated with it in the structural equilibrium of a well-equipped social organism."

Many attempts, he stated, had been made to achieve such ends, including "superficial and extensive literacy campaigns; enormous educative effort in the rural schools; generalized sanitary assistance; intensive promotion of rural activities; extending to the maximum the network of communications; the fixation, in colonies, of the dispersed rural inhabitants; and there are other such remedies already thought of and tried." But all of them have been defective in their approach. All have had "a unilateral action. The isolated employment of each of the measures mentioned will always be innocuous, because the weight of the negative factors, left unmodified, always will outweigh the beneficial action of the one that is being modified."

To bring about a convergence of all the forces necessary to change substantially the situation in rural Brazil, this eminent authority proposed that the work of colonization and that of education be undertaken simultaneously and in conjunction with one another. To do this, he proposed the establishment of "colony-schools." These should bring together for a year or so of intensive education and training all of the members of all of the families in an area. They would live in the clean, healthful, and properly constructed homes of the colony-school, in a locality where necessary sanitary and preventive health measures were all taken. Each would have a small plot of ground on which to learn through practice, and each would be supplied the best of instruction and advice on all the technical, industrial, commercial, and administrative problems of the colony. The families themselves would perform most of the activities required to maintain the colony as a healthful place in which to live. The teaching of co-operation and the instruction of the young would be stressed.

Nearby would be selected an area for permanent settlement to which the families could graduate. After completing satisfactorily a period in the colony, each family would be entitled to buy a small tract of ground in the area at a low price and on easy terms. Credit would be furnished, and the agricultural instruction and orientation continued. Great emphasis would be placed on assisting the families in the new settlement to maintain it as a healthful place for living. Schooling for their children would be continued, they would be closely tied into all essential social and economic services, and every effort made to develop a real "social and civic life in the new community."

Since the close of the second World War many Brazilians of considerable mental stature, including many members of the clergy, have been concerned with another attempt to make some headway against the mass of illiteracy and related social problems in the interior of Brazil. They are actively pushing a rural welfare program known as the rural missions. A rural mission consists of a team, including specialists in rural education, medicine, nursing, home economics, social work, geography, and agriculture. One or two other specialists also may be included. It is dispatched by the federal government working in co-operation with the state. The members of the team spend about six weeks in a rural area and may return periodically thereafter. They visit the fazendas offering services, counsel, and demonstrations; they work closely with the teachers in the local schools. If possible they help organize social centers and co-operative associations. Demonstrations in agriculture, pest control, and home economics and the organization of agricultural clubs for boys and homemaking clubs for the girls are fundamental types of activity in their programs. By means of films and demonstrations they attack health and other problems at the adult level of education. In every way they seek to press the battle against ignorance, poverty, disease, lethargy, and the host of problems confronting the people in the remote districts.[33]

It is certain that rural missions are greatly improving the situation in the areas in which they work. Probably they also are helping to create the environment in which rural schools will have better chances of success and to arouse the interest that will lead to the organization of more and better schools. They are not, however, an adequate substitute for the schools that are so desperately needed in many parts of the Brazilian territory. Brazil's great problem—and her great opportunity—still remains the organization of at least one elementary school in every rural community, now called for under the Alliance for Progress, and the establishment of at least one secondary school of the *colegio* level in each unit of national territory that is permitted to enjoy the status of a município.

[33] The literature on the subject already is extensive. Among the most informing titles are Serviço de Informação Agrícola, *Missões Rurais de Educação: A Experiencia de Itaperuna* (Rio de Janeiro, 1952); J. V. Freitas Marcondes, "As Missões Rurais e a Sindicalização Rural," *Arquivos de Direito Social*, X (1952); Escola de Serviço Social do Paraná, "Amparo ao Homem do Campo no Paraná," *Serviço Social*, XII, No. 65 (July-September, 1952); and especially, Rios, *A Educação dos Grupos*. These also show the variety of interests which are promoting rural missions of one type or another.

CHAPTER XX

RELIGIOUS INSTITUTIONS

R OMAN CATHOLICISM WAS the official religion in Brazil while it was a colony and continued to be so all during the period of the empire. Nevertheless, there was a freedom of religion and worship in Brazil that contrasted sharply with the severe restraints imposed in Spanish America.[1] With the declaration of the republic in 1889 and the adoption of the constitution of 1890 there was a separation of church and state and the official establishment of full freedom of religion. Then it was that Brazil came to be juridically secular. The republican constitution of 1891, by its Article 72, provided that "all individuals and religious confessions may exercise their cult publicly and freely, associating together for these purposes and acquiring property in accordance with the dispositions of the common law" (Paragraph 3). It was further provided that no cult nor church should enjoy a subsidy from the government nor have "a relationship of dependency or alliance with the Government of the Union or of the States" (Paragraph 7). Finally it was stipulated that no Brazilian citizen should be deprived of his civil and political rights because of his religious beliefs or functions (Paragraph 28).[2] This freedom of religion was reaffirmed in the constitution of 1937 by Article 122, Section IV, which reads as follows:

All individuals and religious sects may freely and publicly exercise their cult, meet for this purpose and acquire real estate, observing the provisions of common law and the requisites of public and good usage.

And it was perpetuated in the present constitution by Paragraphs 7 and 10 of Article 141.

The liberty of conscience and belief is inviolate and the free exercize of religious cults is assured, except those which are contrary to public order or good usage. Religious associations shall acquire a juridical personality under the civil law.

The cemeteries shall have a secular character and shall be administered by the município. All religious professions are permitted to practice their

[1] Cf. J. Lloyd Mecham, *Church and State in Latin America* (Chapel Hill, 1934), 305 ff. See also D. P. Kidder and J. C. Fletcher, *Brazil and the Brazilians* (Philadelphia, 1857), 143–44.

[2] See the chapter by Dario de Bittencourt, "A Liberdade Religiosa no Brasil: a Macumba e o Batuque em Face da Lei," in *O Negro no Brasil* (Rio de Janeiro, 1940), 169–99. See also Roger Bastide, "Religion and the Church in Brazil," in Smith and Marchant (eds.), *Brazil: Portrait of Half a Continent,* Chap. XV.

rites in them. Religious associations may, in accordance with the law, maintain private cemeteries.

RELIGIOUS AFFILIATIONS

Roman Catholics. According to the 1950 census 93.5 per cent of the Brazilian people are members of the Roman Catholic Church. Most of the differentiation along religious lines has occurred within or been incorporated into the general framework of this universal body. Even the members of the African cults that survive in Bahia, Rio de Janeiro, Pernambuco, and other states are nearly always nominal Catholics. In other sections where the religious syncretism has involved the blending of cultural elements derived from aboriginal In-

TABLE LXVII

Number of Communicants in Protestant Churches in Brazil, by Denominations, May, 1953 *

Denomination	Number of Communicants
Assembly of God (Pentecostal)	200,000
Baptist Convention	109,638
Episcopal Church	7,500
Evangelical Lutheran Church	82,000
Independent Presbyterian Church	17,000
Methodist Church	37,000
Presbyterian Church	67,695
Reformed Christian Church	5,000
Synodical Federation (Lutheran)	500,000
Union of Congregational Churches	13,000
Others	26,500
Total	1,065,333

* For these data the author is indebted to Sr. Rodolfo Anders, general secretary of the Confederação Evangélica do Brasil.

dian sources with Christianity, the process also has gone on within the broad framework of the Catholic faith. However, none of this is revealed by a census of religious affiliations. Nominally, the bulk of the Brazilian population is Catholic. Only highly trained specialists can eventually arrive at an estimate of the relative importance of the groups affiliated with cults originating in Africa or with those of Indian origin.

Protestants. There are, however, several important religious groups in Brazil other than the Roman Catholics. Of these the members of the various Protestant churches are by far the most numerous, a total of 1,741,430, or 3.4 per cent of the population, being enumerated in the 1950 census. A total of 1,065,333 communicants (baptized members) was reported by the Evangelical Confederation of Brazil for May, 1953. The tabulation by the confederation also divides the materials according to denomination, and these are presented in Table LXVII. More recent data indicate that there were

1,766,113 Protestants in Brazil as of December 31, 1957. This figure is 84,917 above that for the corresponding date in 1956, and only 29,577 of the increase is accounted for by the baptism of children.[3]

The 1950 census materials indicate that Rio Grande do Sul is the state with the largest Protestant population, the exact figure reported being 442,242. Next in line were São Paulo and Santa Catarina, with 318,199 and 161,612, respectively. In addition, the following sizable numbers were reported from other parts of the Brazilian confederation: Minas Gerais, 123,358; Rio de Janeiro, 115,672; Paraná, 95,536; Pernambuco, 87,620; the Distrito Federal, 83,940; Espírito Santo, 75,076; and Bahia, 55,791.

Greek Orthodox Catholics. The 1950 census reported 41,156 members of the Greek Orthodox Church in Brazil. Of these more than one-half (25,543) were in the state of São Paulo, and most of the remainder were in Paraná (5,083), Rio Grande do Sul (3,255), and the Federal District (3,321).

Maronites. Although this group is affiliated with the Church of Rome, a married clergy and the use of the Arabic language are significant differentiating features. No recent statistical compilations provide information on the number of persons of this faith in Brazil, but a report published in 1921 supplies the following interesting facts:

The number of persons affiliated with the Maronite rite is calculated at approximately 400,000. Of this total, from 140,000 to 150,000 live in the New World and around 50,000, or one third, reside in Brazil. Their entrance into this country appears to go back to the year 1875, the Maronites having been the first Lebanese to immigrate here.[4]

Jews. Jews long have played an important role in the history of Brazil. As early as 1917 a total of 13 synagogues was listed, three in the city of Rio de Janeiro, two in Belém, and one each in Itacoatiara in Amazonas, Curitiba in Paraná, Passo Fundo, Pôrto Alegre, and Santa Maria in Rio Grande do Sul, and Campinas, Franca, and São Paulo in the state of São Paulo.[5] As of 1912 the numbers of persons affiliated with some of these synagogues were as follows: two in Rio de Janeiro, 155; Belém, 650; Pôrto Alegre, 244; Campinas, 19; Franca, 25; and São Paulo, 100.[6]

The 1950 census supplied by far the most satisfactory data concerning the number and distribution of members. At that time the total number of persons of the Jewish faith reported was 69,957. Of these 26,443 were enumerated in São Paulo and almost as many, 25,222, in the Distrito Federal. But the members of this religious group were widely spread throughout Brazil, with the following states

[3] *Anuário Estatístico do Brasil,* XX (1959), 416.

[4] José Luiz S. de Bulhões Carvalho, *Relatorio* (to the Minister of Agriculture, Industry, and Commerce) (Rio de Janeiro, 1921), 250. See also Bastini, *O Libano e os Libanes no Brasil,* 49–52. According to Bastini the "great emigration" for Brazil occurred in the decade 1860 to 1870.

[5] Bulhões Carvalho, *Relatorio,* 227.

[6] *Annuario Estatistico do Brazil,* III (1927), 3.

having the next largest numbers: Rio Grande do Sul, 8,048; Rio de Janeiro, 2,209; Pernambuco, 1,531; Minas Gerais, 1,528; Paraná, 1,340; Pará, 1,126; and Bahia, 1,076.

Buddhists. The introduction of some 200,000 Japanese into Brazil during the last few decades has also meant the establishment of numerous Buddhist congregations in the country. Some of the immigrants and their children have accepted Christianity, mostly as converts to Roman Catholicism. The great mass of the 450,000 or so Japanese immigrants and their descendants probably maintain their Buddhist faith and form of worship.[7] However, the 1950 census enumerated only 152,572 persons of the Buddhist faith, of whom the lion's share (128,014) were in the state of São Paulo. In addition, in the 1940 census 2,458 Shintoists were counted.

Positivists. More significant in their influence than in their number are the members of the Igreja Positiva Brasileira. Each week the Rio de Janeiro papers carry announcements of the meetings of this society and résumés of the sessions. This offshoot of Comtian philosophy counted in 1912 only 153 members, of whom 90 were men. Probably it does not have many more now, but the group has always included persons who were influential in public and intellectual affairs.

As early as the year 1850, a thesis on statistics introduced Comte's ideas into Brazil. In 1876 the first Positivist society was formed, its principal objectives being the creation of a library and the establishment of courses in science. Prominent among the original members were Dr. Antonio Carlos de Oliveira Guimarães, who took the initiative in the establishment of the society, and Dr. Benjamin Constant. In 1878 the society became the Igreja Positiva do Brazil. The census of 1890 reported a total of 1,327 persons who were affiliated with this church. Of these, 377 were in the Federal District, 321 in São Paulo, 146 in Santa Catarina (mostly in Brusque), 144 in Rio Grande do Sul, and 105 in Minas Gerais.[8] Prior to the end of the year 1912 the group had presented and pushed vigorously 437 projects in connection with state and federal legislation. They fostered such measures as the improvement of relations between Brazil and Argentina, the freeing of the slaves, and the secularization of cemeteries. On the other hand, they opposed compulsory education, obligatory vaccination, anonymity in the press, and Chinese immigration.[9] The 1940 census enumerated only 1,299 Positivists in Brazil, and the 1950 census did not classify them separately.

Other Religious Groups. Negro slaves imported into Brazil included considerable numbers from the more northern parts of Africa who had been reared in the Moslem faith and knew how to read and write

---

[7] For a study of the acculturation process as it is operating among the Japanese and photographs of the symbolism found in Japanese cemeteries, see Baldus and Willems, "Casas e Túmulos de Japoneses no Vale da Ribeira de Iguape," *loc. cit.*, 121–36; see also Fujii and Smith, *The Acculturation of Japanese Immigrants in Brazil*, 43–44.

[8] *Sexo, Raça e Estado Civil, Nacionalidade, Filiação, Culto e Analphabetismo da População Recenseada em 31 al Dezembro de 1890* (Rio de Janeiro, 1898), 297

[9] Cf. *Annuario Estatistico do Brazil*, III, 230–35.

Arabic. This knowledge, incidentally, proved of great assistance to them in the organization of serious slave revolts, especially in Bahia. Undoubtedly there are a few left who still should be counted as Moslems.[10] The 1940 census reported 3,053 Moslems in Brazil, most of whom were in São Paulo (1,393), the Distrito Federal (777), and Mato Grosso (137). These, no doubt, are parts of the significant Arab colonies in those states.

There is also another much more numerous group to be mentioned —the Spiritualists. The rites and ceremonies of this group are closely related culturally and in psychological effects to many of the practices which the Africans brought from the Dark Continent. Consequently Spiritualist centers seem to be particularly attractive to the Negroes, and as one passes through Brazil's towns and cities he finds Spiritualist centers in a surprisingly large number of them. The 1940 census, containing the first statistics about this group that has come to the attention of the writer, reported 463,400 Spiritualists in Brazil, and the 1950 census enumerated 824,553. In 1950 they were most numerous in São Paulo with 242,972 and the Distrito Federal with 123,775, but other large numbers were reported for the following states: Rio Grande do Sul, 115,552; Minas Gerais, 113,920; Rio de Janeiro, 64,501; and Goiás, 44,198. In Bahia, however, a state whose name is closely associated with spiritist practices of the African variety, only 12,458 were enumerated.[11]

THE ROMAN CATHOLIC CHURCH

The Roman Catholic Church in Brazil is organized into 25 ecclesiastical archdioceses presided over by archbishops, 88 tributary dioceses headed by bishops, 30 prelacies nullius, and one abbey nullius. A tabulation for the year 1960 indicated that there were 33 archbishops, 128 bishops, and 10,616 priests in the country, and that 4,116 of the latter were diocesan priests.[12] See Table LXVIII.

The Brazilian Church now supplies three cardinals to the College in Rome. They are from Rio de Janeiro, São Paulo, and Bahia. The primate of Brazil is the cardinal of Bahia, so that in some respects that city and not Rio de Janeiro may be considered as the religious capital of the nation.

There is little point in giving an exhaustive analysis of the Brazilian church, for its organization and function are much the same as that of Catholicism in other countries. A few features, however, seem to call for comment.

[10] The census of 1890 reported 300, of whom 171 were in the Federal District, 48 in São Paulo, and 34 in Pará. None were reported in Bahia! *Sexo, Raça e Estado Civil, Nacionalidade, Filiação, Culto e Analphabetismo, 1890*, 297.

[11] The 1950 census data on religious affiliations presented in this section were compiled and computed from materials in the "Censo Demográfico," VI *Recenseamento Geral do Brasil, 1950*, I (Rio de Janeiro, 1956), 1, 72–73.

[12] Gibbons, Avesing, and Adamek, *Basic Ecclesiastical Statistics for Latin America, 1960*, 6–16, 74.

TABLE LXVIII

Roman Catholic Dioceses, Priests, Parishes, and Churches
in Brazil *

Diocese	Year	Number of priests	Number of parishes	Number of churches
Aparecida †	1959	57	5	49
Lorena	1954	34	—	145
Taubaté	1959	140	32	322
Belém do Pará†	1958	85	41	384
Cametá (P. N.) ‡	1958	14	7	65
Guamá (P. N.)	1955	14	7	190
Macapá (P. N.)	1957	14	4	57
Marajó (P. N.)	1958	8	8	35
Óbidos (P. N.)	1958	10	5	53
Santarém (P. N.)	1956	36	17	136
Ssma Conceição do Araguaia (P. N.)	1954	7	2	15
Xingu	1957	6	4	16
Belo Horizonte †	1958	263	78	635
Aterrado	1957	42	2	35
Divinópolis	1959	52	29	177
Guaxupé	1959	108	55	152
Oliveira	1958	29	19	123
Patos de Minas	1957	33	18	36
Sete Lagôas	1959	24	20	152
Uberaba	1956	81	28	95
Botucatú †	1959	106	35	235
Assis	1959	61	38	142
Lins	1959	82	36	278
Marília	1959	63	45	158
Campinas †	1959	157	49	227
Bragança Paulista	1959	37	17	129
Piracicaba	1958	60	20	55
São Carlos	1959	94	40	210
Cuiabá †	1959	26	11	59
Campo Grande	1959	53	16	85
Corumbá	1959	26	12	54
Dourados	1957	17	9	—
São Luis de Cáceres	1959	7	4	21
Chapada (P. N.)	1959	6	4	12
Diamantino (P. N.)	1959	9	4	4
Guajará-Mirim (P. N.)	1959	6	3	17
Registro do Araguaia (P. N.)	1958	27	9	45
Curitiba †	1959	206	62	573
Campo Mourão	1959	18	15	—
Jacarèzinho	1959	62	29	182
Londrina	1958	63	36	161
Maringá	1959	39	22	170
Palmas	1957	29	14	—
Ponta Grossa	1959	99	27	373
Toledo	1959	21	14	—
Diamantina †	1959	89	57	345
Araçuaí	1959	63	36	334
Governador Valadares	1959	35	18	198
Jánuaria	1959	16	8	96

Table LXVIII (*Continued*). *Roman Catholic Dioceses, Priests, Parishes, and Churches* *

Diocese	Year	Number of priests	Number of parishes	Number of churches
Montes Claros	1958	33	20	250
Paracatú (P. N.) ‡	1958	10	4	21
Florianópolis †	1959	103	28	305
Chapecó	1959	52	25	430
Joinville	1959	125	32	362
Lajes	1959	123	46	815
Tubarão	1959	77	35	262
Fortaleza †	1959	238	71	258
Crato	1959	100	34	320
Limoeiro	1959	33	13	94
Sobral	1956	74	37	230
Goiânia †	1956	103	45	—
Goiás	1958	17	12	55
Jataí	1958	10	4	24
Porto Nacional	1959	13	12	56
Uruaçu	1956	12	7	—
Cristalândia (P. N.)	1959	4	4	6
Formosa (P. N.)	1958	6	5	42
Tocantinópolis (P. N.)	1956	9	6	21
Maceió †	1959	65	31	340
Aracajú	1958	57	47	220
Penedo	1956	38	19	225
Manaus †	1957	78	22	217
Acre e Purús (P. N.)	1957	12	6	30
Alto Solimões (P. N.)	1958	10	5	19
Juruá (P. N.)	1959	15	6	47
Lábrea (P. N.)	1958	6	3	4
Parintins (P. N.)	1958	13	4	35
Pôrto Velho (P. N.)	1958	13	2	37
Rio Branco (P. N.)	1957	—	—	—
Rio Negro (P. N.)	1957	—	—	—
Tefé (P. N.)	1958	14	7	23
Mariana †	1959	306	143	870
Campanha	1959	123	57	288
Caratínga	1959	59	35	296
Juiz de Fora	1959	140	60	306
Leopoldina	1959	67	38	158
Pouso Alegre	1959	100	39	302
Natal †	1959	61	32	257
Caicó	1959	17	10	50
Mossoró	1957	36	16	93
Olinda-Recife †	1955	213	58	281
Afogados da Ingàzeira	1957	22	9	—
Caruarú	1957	21	14	68
Garanhuns	1959	50	22	89
Nazaré	1957	36	22	263
Pesqueira	1956	—	16	—
Petrolina	1957	15	13	72
Paraíba †	1959	76	38	230
Cajàzeiras	1957	43	21	203
Campina Grande	1956	36	25	137
Patos	—	—	—	—

Diocese	Year	Number of priests	Number of parishes	Number of churches
Pôrto Alegre †	1959	464	124	725
Caxias (do Sul)	1959	194	58	704
Passo Fundo	1959	132	43	742
Pelotas	1957	92	26	88
Santa Cruz do Sul	1959	61	38	—
Santa Maria	1959	217	71	1087
Uruguaiana	1959	89	36	409
Vacaria	1959	46	19	313
Riberão Prêto †	1958	150	56	451
Jaboticabal	1959	39	27	99
Rio Prêto	1958	64	61	230
São Luís do Maranhão †	1958	77	44	298
Caxias do Maranhão	1959	194	58	704
Carolina (P. N.) ‡	1959	11	5	—
Pinheiro (P. N.)	1955	15	8	77
Santo Antônio de Balsas (P. N.)	1958	12	6	34
São José do Grajaú (P. N.)	1956	20	8	108
São Paulo †	1959	993	215	231
Santo André	1954	35	17	30
Santos	1959	79	28	161
Sorocaba	1959	97	36	467
São Salvador da Bahia †	1959	222	108	601
Amargosa	1959	26	22	135
Barra do Rio Grande	1959	17	20	154
Bonfim	1959	26	24	121
Caetité	1959	17	24	232
Ilhéus	1957	46	39	148
Rui Barbosa	—	—	—	—
Vitória da Conquista	1958	126	67	905
(São Sebastião do) Rio de Janeiro †	1958	674	121	191
Barra do Piraí	1959	105	49	78
Campos	1958	48	38	285
Neitrói	1959	120	40	301
Petrópolis	1956	89	24	105
Valença	1958	29	20	133
N. Sra. do Monserrate (A. N.) §	1959	60	1	—
Teresina †	1955	26	14	70
Oeiras	1959	8	8	10
Parnaiba	1958	22	14	16
Bom Jesus do Piauí (P. N.)	1958	16	7	59
Vitória (Espírito Santo) †	1959	75	34	400
Cachoeiro de Itapemirim	1957	39	19	305
São Matéus	1959	15	7	270

* Source: William J. Gibbons, Frank B. Avesing, and Raymond Adamek, *Basic Ecclesiastical Statistics for Latin America, 1960* (Maryknoll, N. Y., 1960), 6–16.
† Archdiocese   ‡ Prelacy Nullius   § Abbey Nullius

The Position of the Church. The Church seems never to have gained a control of Brazil that in any way approaches the absolute sway it exercised in Mexico, Peru, and other parts of Spanish America. Over a century ago, Daniel P. Kidder summed up the situation:

On few subjects do Brazilian writers, of all classes, express themselves with greater unanimity of opinion than respecting the state of religion in the country. People and ecclesiastics, officers of state, men of business, and politicians, all agree in representing the condition and prospects of religion as low and unpromising.[13]

Then he presented an interesting documentation for his generalization with a lengthy translation of the report of the Minister of Justice and Ecclesiastical Affairs for 1843 which reads in part:

The state of retrogression into which our clergy are falling is notorious. The necessity of adopting measures to remedy such an evil is also evident. On the 9th of September, 1842, the government addressed inquiries on this subject to the bishop and capitular vicars. Although complete answers have not been received from all of them, yet the following particulars are certified.

The lack of priests who will dedicate themselves to the cure of souls, or who even offer themselves as candidates, is surprising. In the province of Pará there are parishes which, for twelve years and upwards, have had no pastor. The district of the river Negro, containing some fourteen settlements, has but one priest; while that of the river Solimoens is in similar circumstances. In the three comarcas of Belem, the Upper and the Lower Amazon, there are thirty-six vacant parishes. In Maranham twenty-five churches have, at different times, been advertised as open for applications, without securing the offer of a single candidate.

The bishop of S. Paulo affirms the same thing respecting vacant churches in his diocese, and it is no uncommon experience elsewhere. In the diocese of Cuyabá, not a single church is provided with a settled curate, and those priests who officiate as state supplies, treat the bishop's efforts to instruct and improve them with great indifference.

In the bishopric of Rio de Janeiro most of the churches are supplied with pastors, but a great number of them only temporarily. This diocese embraces four provinces, but during nine years past not more than five or six priests have been ordained per year.

It may be observed that the numerical ratio of those priests, who die, or become incompetent through age and infirmity, is two to one of those who receive ordination. Even among those who are ordained, few devote themselves to the pastoral work. They either turn their attention to secular pursuits, as a means of securing greater conveniences, emoluments, and *respect,* or they look out for chaplaincies, and other situations, which offer equal or superior inducements, without subjecting them to the *literary tests,* the trouble and the expense necessary to secure an ecclesiastical benefice.

This is not the place to investigate the causes of such a state of things, but certain it is, that no persons of standing devote their sons to the priesthood. Most of those who seek the sacred office are indigent persons, who, by their poverty, are often prevented from pursuing the requisite studies. Without doubt a principal reason why so few devote themselves to ecclesiastical pursuits is to be found in the small income allowed them. More-

---

[13] Daniel P. Kidder, *Sketches of Residence and Travels in Brazil* (Philadelphia and London, 1845), II, 398.

over, perquisites established as the remuneration of certain clerical serv-ices, have resumed the voluntary character which they had in primitive times, and the priest who attempts to coerce his parishioners into the pay-ment of them almost always renders himself odious, and gets little or nothing for his trouble.[14]

In Portuguese America often the priest was merely one of the de-pendents of the country squire, and the Church an adjunct to the casa grande of the fazenda.[15] This is a far cry from the situation where the sacerdote was absolute master of all that he saw, the Church the repository of all that was of value in the community.

No doubt the complete complex of circumstances that led the Portuguese colonies to diverge so radically from those of Spain in this respect is involved, but one of the most important items seems to be rather self-evident. This has been treated in some detail by Kidder.

The regulations under which the clergy of Brazil are now suffering, were established as far back as 1752. By a royal decree of that date, all the tithes of the Portuguese ultra marine possessions were secularized, being made payable to the state, while the state became responsible for the sup-port of the clergy. The obvious reason for this regulation was the discovery that the state could support the church much cheaper than the church would support itself, while the tithes remained at the disposal of the priest-hood. This was too fine an opportunity for speculation to be neglected by a government crippled and degraded for lack of funds, and, at the same time, having the power to exercise its pleasure.

The arrangement proved no less profitable than convenient; and once being established, could not be changed. The government put the priests on short allowance, and fixed their salaries at fifty, eighty, and one hundred milreis—sums which have been lessening ever since, by a depreciation of the currency. Efforts have been made in Brazil since the era of inde-pendence, to raise the stipend of the clergy, and they have been nominally successful, although the present salary of two hundred milreis, is scarcely more valuable than the sum of one hundred formerly was.[16]

More recently a prominent church writer, Padre Pascoal Lacroix, has defended the thesis that the shortage of secular and regular cler-gymen is Brazil's foremost problem. According to this authority in the 1930's the nation, in order to have one priest for each 1,000 of the faithful, required, instead of the 2,500 priests it had, some 8,000 well-trained and specialized sacerdotes.[17]

The fact that the Brazilian Church lacks the high degree of domination frequently found throughout Spanish America may also be related to the considerable interest it, or an influential part of it, gives to acute problems of the modern day. In any case many of the clergy are urging attention to the problems of the Amazon, the im-provement of the São Francisco Valley, the lessening of obstacles to immigration, rural welfare, agrarian reform, and the acute prob-lems of the urban slums or *favelas*.

[14] *Ibid.*, 399–401.

[15] Cf. Bastide, "Religion and the Church in Brazil," in Smith and Marchant (eds.), *Brazil: Portrait of Half a Continent*, 336.

[16] *Ibid.*, 401; cf. R. Walsh, *Notices of Brazil in 1828 and 1829* (London, 1830), I, 358–60.

[17] Pascoal Lacroix, *O Mais Urgente Problema do Brasil* (Petrópolis, 1936), 59, 71–72.

Holy Days. The large number of religious holidays in Brazil is one feature that impresses all visitors. Even though they may fail to notice it directly, businessmen who employ local labor will call it to their attention. Over one hundred years ago Kidder observed that

> . . . in some particulars the festivals of all the saints are alike. They are universally announced, on the day previous, by a discharge of skyrockets at noon, and by the ringing of bells at evening. During the *festa* also, whether it continue one day or nine, the frequent discharge of rockets is kept up. These missiles are so constructed as to explode high up in the air, with a crackling sound, after which they descend in beautiful curves of white smoke if in the day time, or like meteoric showers if at night. . . .
> Great care is bestowed upon this manner of adorning churches, by day as well as by night. Sometimes regular rows of blazing tapers are so arranged in front of the principal altars, as to present the appearance of semicones and pyramids of light, streaming from the floor to the roof of the edifice. These tapers are all made of wax, imported from the coast of Africa for this express use. . . .
> Sometimes, on the occasion of these festivals, a stage is erected in the church, or in the open air near by, and a species of dramatic representation is enacted for the amusement of the spectators. At other times an auction is held, at which a great variety of objects, that have been provided for the occasion by purchase or gift, are sold to the highest bidder. The auctioneer generally manages to keep the crowd around him in a roar of laughter and, it is presumed, gets paid in proportion to the interest of his entertainment.[18]

He took sufficient interest in this subject to catalogue and describe the religious holidays.

January 6. The Epiphany, "styled the day of Kings."

[18] Kidder, *Sketches of Residence and Travels in Brazil*, I, 145, 146–47.

In Colonial Brazil the Church often Was an Adjunct to the Casa Grande. Home of the Senhor de Engenho da Torre, near Recife. (Reproduced from Henderson, *A History of the Brazil.*)

January 20. San Sebastian's Day. "He is the patron saint of Rio de Janeiro."

The *Intrudo* (Carnival) which

. . . extends through the three days preceding Lent, . . . is generally entered upon by the people with an apparent determination to redeem time for amusement in advance of the long restraint anticipated. It is not with showers of sugar-plums that persons are saluted on the days of the Intrudo, but with showers of oranges and eggs, or rather, of waxen balls made in the shape of oranges and eggs, but filled with water. These articles are prepared in immense quantities before hand, and exposed for sale in the shops and streets. The shell is of sufficient strength to admit of being hurled a considerable distance, but at the moment of collision it flies to pieces, bespattering whatever it hits. Unlike the somewhat similar sport of snow-balling in cold countries, this *jogo* is not confined to boys, or to the streets, but is played in high-life as well as in low, indoors and out. Common consent seems to have given the license of pelting any one and every one at pleasure, whether entering a house to visit, or walking in the streets.

In fact, whoever goes out at all on these days, would do well to expect a ducking, and at least to carry his umbrella; for in the enthusiasm of the game, the waxen balls are frequently soon consumed; then come into play syringes, basins, bowls, and sometimes pails of water, and they are plied without mercy until the parties are thoroughly drenched.[19]

Ash Wednesday:

The first procession which I specially observed, was that of Ash-Wednesday. It was conducted by the third order of Franciscans, from the chapel of the Misericordia, through the principal streets of the city, to the convent of S. Antonio. Not less than from twenty to thirty stands of images were borne along on the shoulders of men. Some of these images were single, others were in groups, intended to illustrate various events of Scriptural history or catholic mythology.[20]

Ember Days: "The procession of *Nosso Senhor dos Passos,* 'our Lord bearing the cross,' occurs on the Ember days." [21]

March 19: "The nineteenth of March is celebrated as the anniversary of St. Joseph, the spouse of the Virgin Mary." [22]

Palm Sunday:

Palm Sunday in Brazil is celebrated with a taste and effect that cannot be surpassed by any artificial ornaments. The Brazilians are never indifferent to the vegetable beauties by which they are surrounded, since they make use of leaves, flowers, and branches of trees, on almost every public occasion; but on this anniversary the display of the real palm branches is not only beautiful, but often grand.[23]

Holy Week:

The days are designated in the calendar, as Wednesday of darkness, Thursday of anguish, Friday of passion, and hallelujah Saturday.

[19] *Ibid.*, 147–48.
[20] *Ibid.*, 148–49.
[21] *Ibid.*, 151.
[22] *Ibid.*
[23] *Ibid.*

Maundy Thursday, as the English render it, is kept from the noon of that day till the following noon. The ringing of bells and the explosion of rockets are now suspended. The light of day is excluded from all the churches; the temples are illuminated within by wax tapers, in the midst of which, on the chief altar of every one, the host is exposed. Two men stand in robes of red or purple silk to watch it. In some churches the effigy of the body of Christ is laid under a small cloister, with one hand exposed, which the crowd kiss; depositing money on a silver dish beside it at the same time. At night the people promenade the streets and visit the churches. This is also an occasion for a general interchange of presents, and is turned greatly to the benefit of the female slaves, who are allowed to prepare and sell confectionery for their own emolument.

Friday continues silent, and a funeral procession, bearing a representation of the body of Christ, is borne through the streets. At night occurs a sermon, and another procession, in which *anjos*, decked out as already described, bear emblematic devices alluding to the crucifixion. One carries the nails, another the hammer, a third the sponge, a fourth the spear, a fifth the ladder, and a sixth the cock that gave the warning to Peter. Hundreds of persons bearing torches at night, as usual in this procession, form certainly a very imposing spectacle.

Hallelujah Saturday is better known as "Judas' day," on account of the numerous forms in which that inglorious patriarch is made to suffer the vengeance of the people. Preparations having been made beforehand, rockets are fired in front of the churches at a particular stage of the morning service. This explosion indicates that the hallelujah is being chanted. The sport now begins forthwith in every part of the town. The effigies of poor Judas become the object of every species of torment. They are hung, strangled, and drowned. In short, the traitor is shown up in fire-works and fantastic figures of every description, in company with dragons, serpents, and the devil and his imps, which pounce upon him. . . .

Lent being over, Easter Sunday is ushered in by the triumphal discharge of rockets in the air, and of artillery from the forts and batteries.[24]

Whitsunday:

On Whitsunday the great feast of the Holy Spirit is celebrated. In preparation for this, begging processions go through the streets, a long while in advance, in order to secure funds. In these expeditions the collectors wear a red scarf (*capa*) over their shoulders: they make quite a display of flags, on which forms of a dove are embroidered, surrounded by a halo or gloria. These are handed in at windows and doors, and waved to individuals to kiss; they are followed by the silver plate or silk bag, which receives the donation that is expected, at least, from all those who kiss the emblem. The public are duly notified of the approach of these august personages, by the music of a band of tatterdemalion negroes, who, with the sound of their instruments, serve the church by day, and the theatre by night.

Collections of this stamp are very frequent in the cities of Brazil, inasmuch as some festa is always in anticipation. Generally a miniature image of the saint, whose honor is contemplated, is handed around with much formality, as the great argument in favor of a donation. The devotees hasten to kiss the image, and sometimes call up their children, and pass it round to the lips of each. These collectors, and a class of females called *beatas,* occasionally become as troublesome as were the common beggars before they were accommodated at the house of correction.

The expeditions assume a very peculiar and grotesque character in remote sections of the empire. The late senator, Cunha Mattos, describes

[24] *Ibid.,* 152–53.

them in the interior, under the name of *fuliões cavalgatas*. He mentions in his Itinerario, having met one between the rivers of S. Francisco and Paranahiba, composed of fifty persons, playing on violins, drums, and other instruments of music, to arouse the liberality, if not the devotion of the people; and also, prepared with leathern sacks and mules, to receive and carry off pigs, hens, and whatever else might be given them.[25]

Corpus Christi: "The procession of *Corpus Christi* is different from most of the others. The only image exposed is that of St. George, who is set down in the calendar as 'defender of the empire.' This is borne on horseback, in a military dress and heavy armor, with men walking on each side to prevent a fall." [26]

St. Anthony, St. John, St. Peter, and The Most Holy Heart of Jesus:

The four great holidays of the month of June are those of the Most Holy Heart of Jesus, of St. Anthony, St. John, and St. Peter. It will be sufficient to say respecting the last three, that these "glorious patriarchs" are considered by their devotees as special patrons of fire and noise. Throughout the live-long days and nights on which their glories are celebrated, there may be heard an incessant explosion of crackers, bombas, rockets, and almost every other invention of pyrotechny; while bonfires blaze in every direction and many persons of the lower classes dance before them till the dawn of the following day. All the Antonios, Joaōs, and Pedros in the community, are on such occasions entitled to salutes for firecrackers, which, inasmuch as their honor is concerned in sustaining the sport, they are not slow to return.[27]

"The principal religious feasts celebrated during the last half of the year, are as follows: —"

July 2d, the Visitation of Nossa Senhora is celebrated by a procession in the morning from the Imperial Chapel to the Misericordia, in which the Camara Municipal makes its appearance. On this day indulgences may be secured in the Carmelite convent, and in the church of S. Francisco de Paula. July 21st is allotted to the Guardian Angel of the Empire; July 25th to St. James, and July 28th to "Santa Anna, Mother of the Mother of God." August 15th, the Assumption of Nossa Senhora; 25th, the Most Holy Heart of Mary. September 8th, the Nativity of Nossa Senhora; 15th, the Most Holy Name of Mary; 22d, Feast of the Grief of Nossa Senhora; 25th, Nossa Senhora das Mercés. October 6th, the Most Holy Rosary of Nossa Senhora, with a procession at night; 9th, the Feast of San Pedro d'Alcantara, principal patron of the empire. November 1st, the Feast of All Saints, with the procession of bones in the Misericordia; 2d, Commemoration of the Dead. December 8th, Feast of Nossa Senhora de Conceiçaō, patronesses of the empire, with indulgence in various churches and convents; 25th the Nativity of Christ.[28]

This list is based upon observations in Rio de Janeiro. Elsewhere, Kidder ran into a large number of local festivities, one of which he described as follows:

25 *Ibid.*, 154–55.
26 *Ibid.*, 155.
27 *Ibid.*, 156.
28 *Ibid.*, 178.

I was informed that the present was the greatest season of religious feasting which occurs at Parahiba during the whole year, the 5th of August being the day of *Nossa Senhora das Neves* the protectress of the town. I inquired who Nossa Senhora das Neves was, but no one could tell me anything more than that she was Nossa Senhora, the same with Nossa Senhora do Conceição, Nossa Senhora do Rozaria, and a score of other names for the Virgin Mary! I doubt whether the mythology of Greece or Rome every became more absurdly confused.

This anniversary, like all other great feast days, was preceded by a *novena*, a service of nine masses performed on as many successive days. Each of these nine evenings had its peculiar entertainment, being allotted to some body of citizens or tradesmen, each of which would, of course, be anxious to rival the other in the pomp and parade of their several performances. I was induced to walk out in the evening to witness what was thought could not fail to be deeply interesting. The Matriz church, at which the fête was held, was situated near by. It stood at one end of an oblong area. Its front was illuminated by candles hung in broken lanterns around the door, and burning before an image in a niche attached to the cupola. Large fires were blazing in different parts of the area. Around them were groups of blacks, eager to fire off volleys of rockets at appropriate parts of the service that was going on within the church. After the novena was finished, all the people sallied out into the campo to witness the fireworks. These commenced about nine o'clock, and continued, I was told, till after midnight.[29]

Currently data for 1957 indicate that more than 37,000 religious processions are organized annually by the Roman Catholic Church in Brazil, more than 10,000 of them in the state of Minas Gerais alone.[30]

The Brotherhoods. Gilberto Freyre has emphasized the importance in Brazil of the religious brotherhoods or *irmandades*. To them he credits much of what was accomplished, work similar to that of governmental and religious authorities in Spanish America. Some of these "third orders" limited their membership to the most aristocratic of the white planters, others received only mulattoes, and some were composed strictly of Negroes. A member of such a religious brotherhood enjoyed a considerable amount of social security, including support in times of sickness and in old age. The irmandade also paid his funeral expenses and provided for masses to be said for the benefit of his departed soul. Since many wealthy men left considerable amounts of economic goods to these associations, some of them were able to establish fine hospitals, orphanages, and retreats for women, and to build beautiful churches.[31]

Shrines and Pilgrimages. Brazil is dotted with shrines, some of them extremely favored, to which the annual quota of pilgrimages reaches astounding proportions. Only one of them, Nossa Senhora de Viagem, east of the bay at Rio de Janeiro, is mentioned in the *Cath-*

[29] *Ibid.*, II, 184–85.

[30] *Anuário Estatístico do Brasil*, XX (1959), 415.

[31] See Charles C. Griffin (ed.), *Concerning Latin American Culture* (New York, 1940), 90–93. Cf. Walsh, *Notices of Brazil*, I, 364–65; Kidder, *Sketches of Residence and Travels in Brazil*, II, 79–80; Kidder and Fletcher, *Brazil and the Brazilians*, 107–108; Thomas Ewbank, *Life in Brazil* (New York, 1856), 136–38; and Harris, *Town and Country in Brazil*, 133, 239–41.

Bom Jesus da Lapa, Bahia

olic Encyclopedia,[32] but several others also have acquired considerable prestige in Brazil. Among the most famous is Nosso Senhora Apparecida, located near Guarantinguetá, São Paulo. Of this von Spix and von Martius entered the following paragraph in their account of their travels.

> The first thing shown us here was the chapel. It was erected about seventy years ago, a long period in this country; it is partly built of stone, and adorned with gilding, bad paintings in fresco, and some in oil. The wonder-working image of the Virgin attracts many pilgrims from the whole province, and from Minas. We met many of these pilgrims when we proceeded on our journey on Christmas-eve.[33]

When the writer passed by on the train in 1942 it was one of the points of interest his companions did not fail to point out.

The famous shrine, the chapel of Bomfim, is located on the crown of a hill about four miles north of Bahia. To it flow pilgrims from all parts, although it appeals particularly to the Negroes. Many are the miracles credited to the patron saint of this shrine, and its hall full of ex-votos is one of the most interesting sights in Bahia. The "washing" of this church on the last Thursday before its great an-

[32] *Catholic Encyclopedia* (New York, 1913).
[33] Von Spix and von Martius, *Travels in Brazil,* I, 306.

nual ceremony was formerly an occasion when African religious dances reached their greatest heights of emotionalism. This particular practice of washing the church was suppressed in 1899.[34]

Another of the most famous shrines of Brazil also is located in the state of Bahia, in the "interior" on the great São Francisco River. This is the holy grotto of Bom Jesús da Lapa. As early as 1868 Sir Richard F. Burton wrote: "This place of pilgrimage has the highest possible reputation; devotees flock to it from all directions, and from great distances, even from Piauhy." [35] Still a third of Brazil's most famous shrines is found in Bahia, in the northern part of the state and not far from Canudos, the New Jerusalem of Antonio Conselheiro. This is Monte Santo. Its principal chapel crowns the highest eminence in the area and is approached by a Via Sacra along which are strung twenty-five little oratories as stations of the cross.

In Holy Week, when from remote villages in the Sertao the Vaqueiros and their families crowd to the holy fair, the scene recalls the Middle Ages. Such orgasms of piety, such wild intensity of faith, are rarely to be seen in a world where the educated turn for their spiritual consolation rather to crystal-gazing or to palmistry than to such vulgar superstitions as satisfy the simple herdsmen of the Sertao.

The scene is marvelous, with its myriad camp fires, its herds of horses grazing loose or picketed, the strange, old-fashioned, medieval types of men. . . . Preacher succeeds preacher, and under the wild eloquence of some illuminated friar, or inspired herdsman, by degrees excitement stirs the multitude into an excess of pious fervor.[36]

In addition to these of nationwide fame, lesser shrines are to be found in many parts of Brazil.[37]

PROTESTANT CHURCHES

Protestantism probably enjoys more freedom and occupies a stronger position in Brazil than anywhere else in Latin America. Its strength seems to be definitely increasing. Whereas the data for 1938 showed only 1,228 Protestant churches in all Brazil,[38] the most recent compilation shows a total of 5,312 churches and 1,955 meeting halls, or 7,267 congregations, in the year 1957.[39] The number of ordained ministers reached a high of 6,135 in 1957.[40] Nevertheless, its relative position is one of comparative unimportance. Except in the colonial sections of Paraná, Santa Catarina, and

[34] Cf. Ramos, O Negro Brasileiro, 152–55; and Pierson, Negroes in Brazil, 366–68.

[35] Burton, The Highlands of the Brazil, II, 290. See also Wells, Three Thousand Miles Through Brazil, II, 37–39; Vera Kelsey, Seven Keys to Brazil (New York and London, 1940), 188–90; and, especially, Cunha, Os Sertões, 220–21.

[36] R. B. Cunningham Graham, A Brazilian Mystic (London, 1920), 45–46.

[37] Cf. Hugh C. Tucker, The Bible in Brazil (New York, 1902), 61, 64–66, 122–23.

[38] Anuário Estatístico do Brasil, IV (1938), 794.

[39] Anuário Estatístico do Brasil, XX (1959), 417.

[40] Ibid.

Rio Grande do Sul, Protestantism is very largely a missionary activity. This, of course, is a far cry from established communities of persons born to the faith. Through their missionary activities the various Protestant churches seem to be making considerable headway in western São Paulo, Minas Gerais, southern Bahia, and Goiás. In Mato Grosso their work compares favorably with that of the Catholic orders, also from the United States, who have established their missions in that great "Wild West." Some of the greatest accomplishments of the Protestants have been in the erection and maintenance of schools and colleges, with such institutions as Bennett College in Rio de Janeiro, the Agricultural College at Lavras in Minas Gerais, and Mackenzie College in São Paulo already having made substantial contributions to Brazil's educational progress.

There has been comparatively little sociological study of Protestants and Protestant activities in Brazil, but a few soundings that have been made have supplied highly informative results. One of these, a detailed study of one Methodist congregation in a small city near Rio de Janeiro, centered attention on the values inherent in one Protestant denomination, the manner in which they were introduced into Brazil, and their positive and negative expressions in the relationships of members of the congregation with one another and with those outside the group. Personal and family prayer, daily reading of the Bible, the singing of hymns, the phenomenon of conversion, evangelization, marriage within the group and virtual limitation of other personal and family relationships to within the group circle, constant participation in services and financial support of the church, and the piety, religious ardor, and transformation of behavior characteristic of a "Christian life" are expected of all. Stress likewise is placed on literacy and education. That conformance with these standards is secured to a high degree is evidenced by the fact that 85 per cent of the marriages are within the group, 74 per cent of the members were classified as "faithful" by their pastor, and 51 per cent either classified as "tithingists" or made regular contributions to the church. On the "thou shalt not" side of the ledger great stress is placed by the group on the avoidance of "worldliness," especially as it is evidenced by the use of alcohol, dancing, gambling, smoking, attending theaters and movies, the cutting of the hair and the use of cosmetics by women, the wearing of "shorts" and other ways of exposing the body, idolatry and witchcraft (the attitude of the Catholics towards the saints being considered as idolatry), profanity, Sabbath-breaking, and premarital and extra-marital sex relations.[41] A second study, involving three communities in various parts of Brazil, indicated that not all Protestant congregations stress proselyting but that "conversion to the new faith constituted a sharp break with traditions both sacred and secular." Religiously the fundamentalism attitudes of the Protestants represent value systems that are in the "sharpest possible contrast with a number of basic values of the

[41] John V. D. Saunders, "Organização Social de uma Congregação Protestante no Estado da Guanabara, Brasil," *Sociologia*, XXII (1960), 415–50.

Brazilian society." But the Protestants also are "more secularized, more literate and have a broader outlook on life than non-Protestants." [42]

OTHER SIGNIFICANT ELEMENTS IN THE RELIGIOUS MOSAIC

Offhand the apparent religious homogeneity among Brazil's population, especially among the majority of its people who reside in rural areas, is likely to make a strong impression on the visitor. That rural Brazil is almost exclusively composed of adherents of the Roman Catholic Church will be accepted as beyond question. Of the relatively few Protestants in the entire nation, the lion's share are concentrated in the larger cities of the republic. Protestant nuclei, as the Presbyterian congregations in such small cities as Lavras in Minas Gerais, or Santa Barbara in São Paulo, and others in Bahia, Mato Grosso, and Pernambuco, are conspicuously rare. New Methodist and Church of God churches in western São Paulo, in the panhandle of Minas Gerais, and in Goiás will be judged correctly as exceptional. Only in the southern states of Paraná, Santa Catarina, and Rio Grande do Sul, where a considerable part of the German immigrants were affiliated with the Lutheran or Evangelican denominations, does any considerable part of the people belong to the Protestant churches.

It is easy for the visitor to attribute important social results to this supposedly high degree of religious homogeneity in the typical rural Brazilian community and município. He is likely to think how different would be the life in each small North American village, town, or community were the people all of one faith, members of one church, believers in a single set of religious ideas and practices. If in no other way than the limitation placed on local discussion, the repercussion might be thought of as immense. With religious differences automatically eliminated as the source of constant and prolonged religious debate, it might well be that politics would remain almost the single source of local controversy.

But the longer such a student remains in Brazil and the more familiar he becomes with religious thinking and practices, the less likely he is to remain convinced of Brazil's religious homogeneity. The conspicuous absence of competing church buildings and the dominating appearance of the Catholic Cathedral near the center of every village or town does not signify complete unity of religious belief and practice. In fact, a thorough knowledge of Catholicism in all its richness of symbolism and belief would give only partial understanding of the religious beliefs, practices, and motivations of Brazil's masses. For, as Ramos has said: "The most advanced forms of religion, even among the most cultured people, do not exist in a pure state. Besides the official religion there are subterranean activities, among the backward strata of society, among the poorer classes, or,

[42] Emílio Willems, "Protestantism as a Factor of Culture Change in Brazil," *Economic Development and Cultural Change,* III (1955), 321–33.

in heterogeneous peoples, among the ethnic groups, that are most backward culturally." [43] While the upper classes and the official religion of a society may have freed themselves to a considerable extent of animistic beliefs and magical practices, such is not the case among the less enlightened masses. "This fundamental form—incarnations of totemic, animistic, and magical beliefs—survives in spite of the most advanced religious and philosophical conceptions of the superior strata of societies." [44] From an intimate firsthand knowledge of great population centers of Rio de Janeiro and Bahia, more than a passing contact with many other parts of the country including his native Alagôas, and an acquaintance with Brazilian scientific literature, this eminent authority could assert, "We [Brazilians] still live under the full domination of a magical world, still impermeable, to a certain extent, to the influxes of a true culture."

Brazil lives impregnated by magic. The medicine man, the fetisheer, has among our populations a prestige considerably greater than the directors of our destinies—it is necessary to have the courage to confess it. Because he is the *image* of the primitive Father, in the silence of the night there are elegant ladies and gentlemen of high rank who go to the *macumbas* to consult the invisible power of Pae Joaquim, Zézinho Curunga or Jubiabá. Padre Cicero of Joazeiro dominates multitudes. Santa Dica is an inspired person [*illuminada*]. And any prophet with cabalistic formulas or medicine man with magical concoctions attracts a large clientele. A specter, the power of mana, dominates the festivals, and this adheres to anything that interlaces the multitudes, hypnotizing them into a single force of fanaticism. The *ebó* [sacrifice] is an institution. The Negro carnival is our great festival. In it dominate the *grude*, the *rôlo*, the *entrudo*, the *vae-quebrar, negrada!* All of this is the erotic force of *Imunu,* or influence of the law of participation, or *Allmacht der Gedanken.* . . . The doctors and learned men who, by the half dozen, exist among us, with trips to Europe and erudite conferences, do not achieve by themselves alone the work of our cultural affirmation. They are individualists and live apart from the masses. It is necessary to penetrate the mass and dissolve the grude, disenchant the force of the law of participation and know the sensual substratum of mana.[45]

Earlier, about the close of the nineteenth century, another great Brazilian scholar, Nina Rodrigues, was emphasizing the same point. His famous volume, long available only in French, opens with the following paragraph:

Only official science, in the superficiality and dogmatism of teaching, could still persist in affirming today that the Bahia population is in its totality one of monotheistic Christians. This affirmation would either have to imply the systematic underevaluation in calculation of two thirds of the Negroes and their crosses who are the great majority of the population, or the ingenuity of common ignorance which submits blindly to an external appearance that the most superficial examination demonstrates to be illusory and deceiving.[46]

[43] Ramos, *O Negro Brasileiro,* 35.
[44] *Ibid.*
[45] *Ibid.,* 406–408; see also 215.
[46] Nina Rodrigues, *O Animismo Fetichista dos Negros Bahianos* (Rio de Janeiro, 1935), 13.

Near the end of the book he again sought to generalize his findings:

> The number of whites, mulattoes, and individuals of all colors and color gradations who, in their afflictions, in their troubles, go to consult the Negro fetisheers, of those who publicly profess the power of talismen and fetishes, of those who, in much larger number, laugh at them in public, but secretly hear them, consult them—this number would be incalculable if it were not more simple to say that in general it is the mass of the population, except for a small minority of superior and enlightened spirits who have a true notion of the exact value of these psychological manifestations. It is that in Brazil the mixture is not only physical and intellectual, it is even emotional, or of the sentiments, equally religious of course.[47]

The relative numerical importance of those who conform closely in religious beliefs and practices to orthodox Catholicism also is recognized by church writers. Thus Padre Pascoal Lacroix, defending his thesis that the lack of sacerdotes is the most urgent problem of Brazil, states that it is "the opinion of many sacerdotes that in our country the general average of true Catholics does not exceed 10 per cent." [48] Assuming as he did that Brazil had a population of fifty million, this would make the total number of genuine Catholics only five million. To be extremely conservative he allowed that it might be fifteen million. Then he inventoried the opposing forces, consisting of "an extremely great number of neo-pagans, . . . Spiritualists there are in every locality, however small it may be, and a very high number in all the cities," Masons, "not a despicable number of Protestants," and the workers in the industrial cities. Together all these, he estimated, might constitute another fifteen million. This left twenty million who are "Catholics in name and by baptism, who do not practice the religion, not from wickedness, but from habit, ignorance and prejudice." [49]

It is, of course, impossible to evaluate reliably the influence among the Brazilian masses of the Catholic and other Christian churches in comparison with fetish cults of African origin and the systems of religious beliefs and practices derived from aboriginal sources. It is undeniable, however, that the medium, the Indian pagé, and the Afro-Brazilian fetisheer all play significant roles in Brazil's religious activities. In fact, as one passes down the social and color scale from the rather pure white population of high estate to the blacks and red men who rank at the bottom of the social ladder, he passes from a population in which Christian monotheism reigns supreme to one in which the fetish cults from Africa and the magico-religious patterns of the aborigines hold almost undisputed sway. In the North, especially the Amazon, it is the Indian medicine man who is most influential; [50] in Pernambuco and south to São Paulo, particularly in Bahia,

[47] *Ibid.*, 186.

[48] Lacroix, *O Mais Urgente Problema do Brasil*, 75.

[49] *Ibid.*, 75. For information on spiritualistic activities in two specific Brazilian communities see Harris, *Town and Country in Brazil*, 208–10, and Hutchinson, *Village and Plantation Life in Northeastern Brazil*, 177–78.

[50] See Charles Wagley, *Amazon Town* (New York, 1953), 224–33. However, the migrations from the Northeast to the Amazon have done much to diffuse African fetish practices into that area. Thus at the time of the Afro-Brazilian

the African influences are most pronounced. Nowhere are either of them entirely absent. But the fact of overwhelming importance is the great extent to which they have blended African with Indian, and the two of them syncretized with spiritualism, and with the orthodox symbolism, beliefs, and practices of Catholicism. As a result, a large share of Brazil's people are conditioned by a religious system which represents a blending of the already heterogeneous European heritage, the rather highly developed religious systems of Africa, and the innumerable traits derived from native sources.

The Gêge-Nagô Cults. The religious complex introduced from Africa which has had by far the greatest influence on New World religious beliefs and practices is the *gêge-nagô* religion brought by the Sudanese groups, or the Yorubas, Gêges, Haussás, and Minas Negroes. Already in Africa this religion represented a blend of the gêge and nagô cults, with the former seeming to dominate.[51] The central core of this religious complex is the grigri or fetish, a "prepared material object." Such a prepared object, a material thing which by the proper ritual procedures has been endowed with mysterious wonder-working or spiritual powers (mana), is not to be confused with the idols. The religious systems of these Sudanese Negroes had a place for such anthropomorphic representations of the saints or *orishas*, but "this conception of the orishas-idols, frankly polytheistic, is beyond the primitive fetishistic idea and proof of contact with other more advanced religions, principally the Catholic, with the entire series of saints in its 'canon.' "[52] In its primitive expressions fetishism is a vast system of cosmopology where each of the orishas is an expression of one of the great forces of nature.

The careful studies of the gêge-nagô cults made in the *macumbas* of Rio de Janeiro and Niterói, the *candomblés* of Bahia, the *xangôs* of Recife, and the *catimbós* of the Northeast by Ramos, Nina Rodrigues, Donald Pierson, Roger Bastide, and numerous other scholars give us most of the details concerning the pantheon, liturgy, and ritual as it exists in present-day Brazil. The same authors also disentangle the original elements from the functional complex and show how the African beliefs and practices have been blended with Indian and influenced by Catholicism.[53]

Congress in Recife in 1934 the most celebrated pagé of the lower Amazon, whose influence extended from Óbidos to Parintins, was a woman from Ceará. She lived in Faro and was consulted by the high society of Pará. "To her house . . . there was a constant pilgrimage of persons who came from the most remote places of the Amazon River and its tributaries. Even persons of the very highest social classes of Belém and Manaus went to consult the oracle. Among them, I saw, one day, the wife of a governor of Amazonas." José Carvalho, *O Matuto Cearense e o Caboclo do Pará* (Belém, 1930), quoted in Gilberto Freyre *et. al.*, *Novos Estudos Afro-Brasileiros* (Rio de Janeiro, 1937), 82.

[51] Cf. A. B. Ellis, *The Yoruba-Speaking Peoples of the Slave Coast of West Africa* (London, 1894), 275 ff.; and P. Baudin, *Fetichism and Fetish Worshipers* (New York, 1885), *passim.*

[52] Ramos, *O Negro Brasileiro*, 38.

[53] Of these accounts, the excellent one by Pierson, *Negroes in Brazil*, 275–317, and that by Ruth Landes, *The City of Women* (New York, 1947), *passim*, are most accessible to North Americans. The paragraphs which follow make most use of the various works by Arthur Ramos, particularly "The Negro in Brazil," in

The pantheon is headed by Oluran who in Yoruba mythology is known as the master of the sky. Although this deity approaches the grade of supreme, he is the object of no special cult; he is represented by no fetish, by no idol; just as an earthly king deals with his subjects only through intermediaries, so this heavenly king enters into contact with men only through secondary divinities called orishas. In Brazil Oluran has been almost entirely forgotten, but the number of orishas is about one hundred.

Brazilian Negroes also have forgotten the gradation of orishas known to the Yorubas. At the head of this list comes Orixalá or Oxalá, a bisexual divinity symbolizing the reproductive energies of nature. Oxalá is represented by means of lemon-green shells set in a circle of lead. His dress and that of the *filhos de santo* (children of the saint) in the *terreiros* or temples devoted to him are entirely of white; to him are sacrificed goats and pigeons. He is honored on Fridays.

Xangô is another of the most powerful divinities and is extremely popular in Brazil. His name is given to a cult in the Northeast. He is the counterpart of Thor, being the god of lightning and thunder. His fetish is a meteoric stone, but this, like the others, is little more than an ornament. In the terreiros this fetish is surrounded by collars of white and red, a lance, and small staff, which are the emblems of Xangô. His feast day is Wednesday and to him are sacrificed roosters and sheep. In the *pegí*, holy of holies in which foods for the gods are kept, those for this diety are *carurú* (a dish of herbs, with fish, shrimp, and oil of a palm) and rice porridge.

The incarnation of evil, Exú, also has his place among the orishas. It is reasoned that it is better to give this devil his dues through sacrifices than to have him constantly interfering in the devotions or counteracting the beneficent activities of the other divinities.[54] The *despacho*, or sacrifice, to appease this malevolent divinity is always the opening activity in any session of worship. Also he is to be reckoned with at all crossroads, being in fact called "the man of the crossroads," and at these spots it is customary to give him offerings of popcorn and flour mixed with a palm oil. The fetish of Exú is a head molded from clay, with eyes and mouth represented by shells,

---

Smith and Marchant (eds.), *Brazil: Portrait of Half a Continent*, Chap. V, *O Negro Brasileiro*, and *Introdução á Anthropologia Brasileira* (Rio de Janeiro, 1943), I. One should also consult Rodrigues, *O Animismo Fetichista dos Negros Bahianos;* Roger Bastide, *O Candomblé da Bahia* (São Paulo, 1961); and René Ribeiro, *Cultos Afrobrasileiros do Recife: um Estudo de Ajustamento Social* (Recife, 1952). One of the best descriptions of all is in the chapter "Macumba" in the novel *Jubiabá* by Jorge Amado (Rio de Janeiro, 1937).

[54] One *pai de santo* defended paying homage to Exú as follows: ". . . they say that in the African *seitas* they practice sorcery by adoring the Devil. This is not true. He who practices sorcery is not the Negro, but is the Portuguese and the Indian. Look: from where comes the Book of the *Feiticeira* or the Book of S. Cipriano? We do not adore the Devil. It is true that we have Exú, who was like an angel that became perverted, just as in the Catholic religion, that represents the same thing as ours for the white. But we do not adore Exú. We seek to satisfy him, to pacify him, in order that he will not come to confuse things, that he will not do ill." Gonçalves Fernandes, *Xangôs do Nordeste* (Rio de Janeiro, 1937), 62–63.

pieces of iron, or other ornaments. To him always is consecrated the first day of a festival and also Mondays. Animals sacrificed to him are the buck goat, the rooster, and the dog. His colors are red and black.

Of all these divinities Ogun is among the most popular. He is the war god. His fetish is a fragment of iron, and he also carries a sword, billhook, lance, shovel, and hoe. His color is yellow, and his preference in sacrifices is the same as those of Xangô, the rooster and the sheep. Tuesday is the day on which he is honored.

There are various orishas of waters, Yemanjá, the Yoruba *mãe d'agua* being among the principal ones, and Oxun another. The fetish of each is a marine stone; they are worshiped on Saturdays. Every year in Bahia there are great votive processions to carry presents to the mãe d'agua. The *pai de santo,* dressed all in white, directs the ceremonies. At the front of the procession twenty or thirty persons carry the white standard of Yemanjá. All the offerings are carried on the heads. They consist of water jars and boxes, highly decorated with ribbons and flowers and filled with fans, powders, soaps, combs, and bottles of perfume—all the things which the goddess requires for her toilet. As they move along, all sing songs of Yemanjá. To a small lake called the Dique on the outskirts of Bahia goes one of the major processions, although others are directed to various other points about the bay which are frequented by this water goddess. Of sixty-six students at the normal school in Bahia who classed themselves as white and who answered Pierson's questionnaire, seven said members of their family gave presents to the mãe d'agua, and nine out of thirty-six pardos answered the same question affirmatively.[55]

Gradually Oxóssi, god of the hunt, has acquired prestige among Brazilian Negroes. His symbol is the drawn bow and arrow, and their representations usually accompany his fetish. Thursdays are consecrated to him; green is his sacred color.

Very closely allied to the worship of Exú is the cult of Ifá. His fetish is the fruit of a certain palm tree. Acts of divining the future are very closely associated with this deity, the process of divination itself being called "to see with Ifá." In making his predictions the sorcerer employs a chain of metal, into which halves of mango nuts are inserted at intervals, called Ifá's necklace, or a handful of fruit from a certain palm tree.

Fearful god of smallpox is Xapanan, also known under many other names. In Bahia he is not disinguished from Exú. To him are sacrificed he-goats and roosters, but he also feeds on corn mixed with a palm oil. His fetish is a broom ornamented with shells. Usually the pegí for this deity is situated outside the ceremonial house, as in Africa, but in other terreiros he is honored with a place among the other orishas. Red and black are his colors, Monday his ceremonial day.

Ibeji, also known as Dois-Dois, and by many other designations,

---

[55] Pierson, *Negroes in Brazil,* 310.

are the twins, so frequently identified by the Negroes as Cosme and Damion where Christian elements are added as items in their superstition and witchcraft. Wednesdays are the days devoted to the Ibeji in the candomblés or macumbas. The carurú is their principal food, but its constitution includes several special ingredients. The meal is carried in small saucers to the saints' room. Since the orishas are interested only in the spirits of the foods and the congregation may consume the substance, the days when Ibeji are honored are ones of much feasting for the children.

This list by no means completes the gêge-nagô pantheon as it exists in Brazil, but most of the principal deities have been included.

Next it is logical to consider the intermediaries between man and the gods, the human beings who are sufficiently prepared that they may come into contact with, manipulate, and even themselves acquire some of the mystical wonder-working mana that is so important in contributing the indispensable attitude of *awe* to religion. The various classes of sacerdotes known in Africa have all been reduced to one type in Brazil. These are known by a variety of terms such as *babalão* in Bahia, *babá* or *baboloxá* in Rio de Janeiro, and *babalorixá* in the Northeast. They also may be designated by the addition of the proper suffix to candomblé or macumba, *candomblezeiro* in Bahia and *macumbeiro* in Rio. When a sacerdote is officiating within the sanctified precincts of the ceremonial houses, he is called *pai de santo* (father of the saint) or *pegi-gan*, which means master of the altar. In Africa women, being of inferior social status, may not receive the priesthood, but in Brazil, many of the sacerdotes are female. The *mãe de santo* (mother of the saint) may direct the ceremonies without making them in any way ineffective.

Throughout many parts of Brazil the religious vocation of the sacerdote has degenerated into a mere matter of dealing in "black magic" or "consulting low spirits." However, where the concentrations of Negro populations are greatest, as in and about Rio de Janeiro, Bahia, and Recife, the pai de santo retains his position as the repository for the secrets of the cult and the director of the ceremonies. His principal function is to prepare the orisha or saint, a performance in which he has the aid of an assistant sacerdote (*achôgun*). The pai de santo possesses the power to "fix" the "saint" in any material object, a fact very important to remember by those who would consider the fetish as an idol. Thus in preparing Xangô, his fetish, a small stone, is put into a small pottery vase and placed in a large basin. About the fetish is laid a preparation of sacred leaves and palm oil. Then the achôgun sacrifices the appropriate animal, either a sheep or a rooster, by spilling its blood over the fetish and the materials about it. The slaughter of each animal follows a prescribed ritual.

After being "prepared" in this manner the fetish or saint is carried to its altar in the terreiro. The vase containing it is set against the wall which forms the back of the altar, amidst the symbols associated with it. In addition, pieces of cloth and paper, necklaces, shells, and so forth, all of the appropriate color are suspended about the room. The water dishes in the ceremonial chambers are constantly re- plenished and the foods either eaten by the priests or thrown out— the Negroes believe that the saints use only the spirit of the food and drink.

Each center of worship has a special inner group of devotees con- secrated to the cult of the orishas. These are called filhos de santo, and may be of either sex, although in Bahia by preference they are females. In them the orishas reveal themselves spontaneously or by provocation. Initiation as a daughter of the saint is a rather involved ceremonial procedure the preliminaries of which include a great deal of bathing in water prepared with aromatic plants, confinement in a small chamber for a number of days, and the preparation of the fe- tish. Then the girl submits to having her hair shaved, which, accord- ing to Ramos, "in the beginning was complete, and today is found limited to the head." [56] She is then washed with a specially prepared infusion of aromatic leaves and drinks some of the concoction. Fi- nally, her head, forehead, and cheeks are painted with dots and circles in designs which are survivals from the facial tattoos used among the African tribes. All of this is designed to help produce the "state of the orisha," or trance, in which her body serves as the medium through which the deity performs.

The daughter of the orisha is now known as Yauô, or "the young- est wife." For a period varying from one month to a year she must remain in the ceremonial house subject to a series of taboos. Among these are the prohibitions against going outside, sexual intercourse, and the use of certain foods. Finally, the day of "giving the name" arrives. On this occasion, after due preparation, the head of the girl is immersed in the blood of the sacrificed animals, and a solemn feast of consecration is celebrated. Then the initiate is called *feita* (made). Now she is prepared to be the instrument which an orisha may use for his manifestations, or as the Brazilian Negroes express it, she is "the horse of the saint."

From now on she belongs to the *mãe de terreiro* in the *seita* where she has been "made" and can return to her parents' house only through a ceremony of "purchase." This may be effected by her husband, members of her family, or other persons previously desig- nated by the girl. In these ceremonies all of the objects which she has used during her novitiate are sold at auction. The purchase over, the filha de santo is accompanied by a great train of people to the house of the buyer, where she is to live from then on. She must, however, continue to fulfill her religious obligations, to obey the orders of the pai or the mãe de santo, and participate in the ceremonies on the days fixed by the cult.[57] The colors worn at these ceremonies depend

[56] Cf. *ibid.*, 287.

[57] Sacred prostitution seems not to be an integral part of the ceremonies of this cult, although in some cases the sacerdotes who operate the xangôs, the can- domblés, or the macumbas may prostitute the filhas de santo of their group. Cf. Fernandes, *Xangôs do Nordeste*, 54–55. The use of the serpent in the ceremonies also has been lost, although once it probably was an integral element in the cere-

on the orisha to whom the girl belongs. When she dies her ceremonial costume and all the other ceremonial paraphernalia she possessed are taken to the sea and dropped in so that the waves may carry them back to Africa.

In addition to the priests, assistant priests, and filhos de santo, each terreiro has its *ogans* or protectors of the temple. These are influential persons who contribute in a financial way, assist in keeping police interference at a minimum, and aid to a limited extent in the ceremonies. Ramos, Pierson, and others were initiated and served in this capacity while making their studies of the candomblés and macumbas.

Periodically the orishas are feted in ceremonies called giving "a meal to the saint." On these occasions the pai and mãe de santo call together all the "children of the orisha," a large crowd gathers, the appropriate animals are sacrificed to the sound of the drum, and then all assemble in the main room of the house of worship. In the center are the sacerdotes nearly surrounded by the filhos de santo, the drummers nearby, the ogans in their places in the armchairs, and the other participants disposed as in the order of their importance. (See Figure 36.) Ceremonies begin with the offering to Exú, made, as are those following, to the roll of the drums. Then at a signal from the musicians the "daughters of the saint" begin the songs and dances of invocation to the orishas, commencing with Exú and continuing through the list. Each divinity is reverenced with the exclamation "Okê!" The drumbeats and songs vary with each orisha, and together they make up a large and varied quantity of music and song.

As the ceremonies progress the emotional pitch of the participants builds higher and higher. In the dances to the orishas there arrives a moment where the orisha "penetrates" the head of one of the "daughters of the saint." When this phenomenon of possession is attained, it is said that the saint has "risen to the head" and attained the state of possession which the Negroes call "falling into the saint." The excitation to this possessed condition is frequent, and after receiving the orisha the daughter of the saint is progressively animated by contorsive movements until at last she falls full length upon the floor. Then she is carried to her small cell where the mãe de santo dresses her with the insignia of the saint to whom she belongs. She now returns to the assembly room and recommences the dance, reverenced by all those present, for they now must bow low or even throw themselves on the floor when the horse of the orisha passes by.

Primitive religion and magic are almost inseparable from music and the dance. Therefore, it is not at all surprising that both of these figure very strongly in the ceremonies of the Afro-Brazilians, particularly in exciting the participants to the pitch in which they fall into the saint or experience the phenomenon of possession. Both the religious and the war dances of the Sudanese and Bantu tribes were

----

monial paraphernalia. It has retained its importance in the equipment of the *curandeiros* or quack doctors who are so numerous throughout the country.

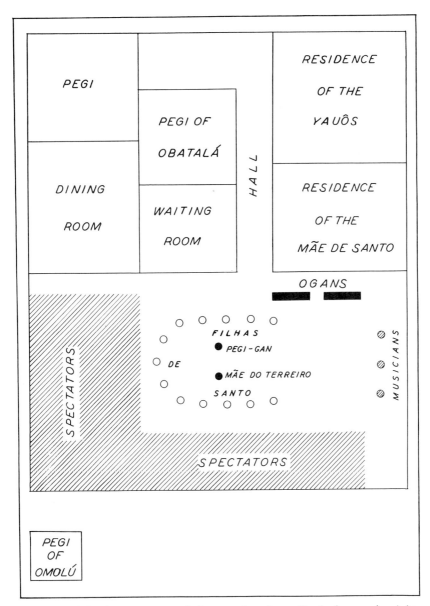

FIGURE 36. Arrangement of the terreiro of a cult of gêge-nagô origin. (After Ramos, *O Negro Brasileiro*.)

carried to Brazil, where they figure strongly in the religious ceremonies, but probably even more important in the common dances of the people.[58] It hardly seems possible that the drum and the dances of

[58] Visitors to Brazil have reported these dances from the most remote sections of the interior. Thus the African dance called the *batuque* was frequently observed by von Spix and von Martius in the course of their travels through the

African origin even remotely approach the importance in any other country that they have in Brazil. Whether one is merely passing along the street, observing children at play in the park on Sunday, or enjoying the tremendous national outburst in the days before Lent, he rarely misses in the Brazilian social scene the evidences of these all-pervasive cultural influences.

Luciano Gallet identified many of the Brazilian dances of African origin, including the *quimbête, sarambéque, sarambú,* and *caxambú* of Minas Gerais; the *sorôngo* of Minas Gerais and Bahia; the fetish dances *alujá* and *jeguedé;* the *cateretê* of Minas Gerais, São Paulo, and Rio de Janeiro; the *samba* found in Bahia, Rio de Janeiro, and Pernambuco; the *candomblé* of Bahia; the *maracatú* of the Northeast; the *jongo, chiba, canna verde* of the state of Rio de Janeiro; the *côco-de-zambê* of Rio Grande do Norte; and the *batuque,* a generalized name for such dances. Ramos accepted the list with some corrections and pointed out that the samba like the batuque is a general term, that the maracatú is confined mostly to Pernambuco, that the cateretê is general throughout the Northeast, that the côco reflects strong Indian cultural influences, and that the chiba and canna verde were merely modified by the Negroes, not original with them. He also cited other dances which belong in the list including the *batucajés* and *batuque do jarê* of Bahia and the *dansas do tambor* of Maranhão.[59]

Ramos, too, was active in the study of the drums of African origin, assembling a fine personal collection of them. At the same time he acquired not a little skill in producing the music of the macumbas and candomblés. It is this authority who stated:

---

central portion of Brazil. From the excellent description which follows, one has no difficulty in recognizing its fundamental similarity to present expressions of the dance to be seen almost everywhere one looks during carnival season, and not at all lacking from the games played by children in Rio's parks on a Sunday. It was in Minas Gerais at the solitary farmhouse called Estiva that these observant Bavarians were stimulated to write as follows:

"The Brazilian is of a lively disposition, and fond of pleasure. Almost everywhere, when we arrived in the evening, we were saluted with the sound of the guitar (*viola*), accompanied by singing or dancing. At Estiva, a solitary farmhouse, with fine extensive campos bounded in the distance by mountains, the inhabitants were dancing the baducca; they scarcely learnt the arrival of foreign travellers when they invited us to be witnesses of their festival. The baducca is danced by one man and one woman, who snapping their fingers with the most extravagant motions and attitudes, dance sometimes towards and sometimes from each other. The principal charm of this dance, in the opinion of the Brazilians, consists in rotations and contortions of the hips, in which they are almost as expert as the East Indian jugglers. It sometimes lasts for several hours together without interruption, alternately accompanied with the monotonous notes of the guitar, or with extempore singing; or popular songs, the words of which are in character with its rudeness; the male dancers are sometimes dressed in women's clothes. Notwithstanding its indecency, this dance is common throughout Brazil, and the property of the lower classes, who cannot be induced, even by ecclesiastical prohibitions, to give it up. It seems to be of Ethiopic origin, and introduced into Brazil by the negro slaves, where, like many of their customs, it has become naturalised." *Travels in Brazil,* II, 114. See also the descriptions of this dance in Mme. Toussaint-Sampson, *A Parisian in Brazil,* trans. by Emma Toussaint (Boston, 1891), 93–95; and Walsh, *Notices of Brazil,* II, 243–44.

[59] Ramos, *O Negro Brasileiro,* 234–36.

In the Afro-Brazilian religious ceremonies the *atabaques* are the essential instruments of the cult. It is they that mark the rhythm of the religious dances (batucajés), and produce the contact with the divinities. . . .

In all of the ceremonies, of initiation, of the preparation of the fetishes, of the feasts destined for the saints, and of the sacrifice of animals, the atabaque is the indispensable element. The rhythm varies for each ceremony, or for each invocation to a specific saint.[60]

In the pure fetish ceremonies only the *atabaques*, one variety of the drum, along with the clapping of hands, is used. For ordinary purposes the more common rhythms suffice, but on occasion, the orisha invoked may be slow in arriving. Then more drastic measures may be necessary. The Brazilian Negroes are prepared for such exigencies with some special beats. They informed Ramos that "there is no saint who resists the beat *adarrum*":

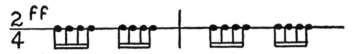

And Ramos testified: "As we had occasion of verifying, Dr. Josannah de Oliveira and I, the possession by 'states of the saint' reaches, with the beat of adarrum, even persons strangers to the cult, onlookers or curiosity seekers, almost always of the feminine sex." [61]

Such music, reinforced by the stimulation of the dance, brings the participants to the very highest levels of emotional excitement. An excellent description of the setting for the dance and the exhibition itself has been given by Nina Rodrigues. This pioneer mentioned the baths, fumigations, "the eating of substances possessed of special virtues," prolonged fastings, sexual abstinence, and various bodily mortifications, all of which play their part in inducing the "state of the saint." Then he asserted:

Of the most powerful in this particular can be considered the influence of the dance. It is necessary to have been a witness of the gestures, of the contortions, of the tumultuous and violent movements to which the Negroes deliver themselves in their sacred dances, for hour after hour, for entire days and nights; it is necessary for you to see them pouring with sweat which their female companions or attendants wipe away from time to time with enormous towels or cloths; it is necessary for you to see them thus with clothing literally running with perspiration, dancing, dancing, still dancing forever, in order to get an idea of what this gruelling exercise may be, to know of its power which, instead of reducing them, incites them more and more. It is a species of mounting fury, of madness, of rabidness whose contortions accompany the varied cadences, always more accentuated, of the batucagé, until the final manifestation of the saint.[62]

The particular days that are devoted to religious ceremonies vary from one terreiro to another and are dependent to a considerable ex-

[60] *Ibid.*, 239–41.
[61] *Ibid.*, 241.
[62] Rodrigues, *O Animismo Fetichista dos Negroes Bahianos*, 110–11; also quoted with slight corrections in Ramos, *O Negro Brasileiro*, 225–26.

tent on the divinity to which the sect or temple is consecrated.
Ramos stated that in the great annual candomblés the orishas are
feted in the following order:

Monday—Exú and Omulú

Tuesday—Nananburucú and Oxumanré

Wednesday—Xangô and Yansan

Thursday—Oxóssi and Ogun

Friday—Oxalá

Saturday—Yemanjá and Oxun

Sunday—All the orishas

But there is nothing absolutely fixed in this order; many orishas may
be honored simultaneously on a single day, or any one of the orishas
may be feted on a day different from the one given above.

Pierson gives the details of one candomblé in Bahia whose pai de
santo is dedicated to Ogun. Its special ceremonial season begins the
second week of September and ends during the first week of December. Throughout this period special ceremonies are held each Sunday, with some of them continuing through Mondays as well. The
first ceremony honors Oxalá, the second Oxagian, and the next
three Ogun; there follow sessions for Xangô, Oxun, Oxóssi, Yemanjá,
and Yansan. The eleventh Sunday and the Monday following are used
to fete Omulú, and the succeeding Sunday and Monday are devoted
to all the mães d'agua. On the thirteenth and final Sunday there is an
elaborate ritual to offer a *feijoada* to Ogun.[63]

The other candomblés or macumbas have their own special ceremonial seasons, and in addition assemblies are held throughout the
year. However, during Lent these African cults suspend their activities.

A word is necessary about the magical practices or despachos,
called *ebó* in Bahia, which are very closely related to this religion.
Ordinarily the vessel involved is a small pottery vase or wooden box,
but paper or cloth will serve. The contents are most frequently a
dead chicken, pigeon, or animal, a piece of cloth, a silver or copper
coin, popcorn, fruits; always they are covered with a palm oil. Only
on very rare occasions is a sheep or a goat sacrificed.

The ebó has various objectives. First there is the necessity of ward-
ing off the malevolent Exú. To do this the despacho may be deposited at the crossroads. A second purpose may be to bring misfortune to a person one dislikes. To accomplish this the ebó should be
deposited in a spot which that person must pass, or better still, in the
doorway of his house. To bring misfortune upon the head of an enemy, one mixes popcorn with flour and palm oil and then tosses a bit
of the preparation in his direction. Another objective of the ebó is
called "a change of the head," i.e., transposing ills from one person
to another. In such a case the magician (*feiticeiro*) prepares the
despacho by fixing in it the tribulations of the persons who desire re-

[63] Pierson, *Negroes in Brazil,* 279–80.

lief. This ebó is then placed in a frequented spot, and the ills will be transferred to the person who touches it.

Mohammedanism. Many of the slaves transported to Brazil previously had been in contact with Arabic culture and the Mohammedan religion. During the early years of the nineteenth century these Negroes, greatly aided by their knowledge of the Arabic tongue and ability to communicate by writing, organized some of the greatest slave revolts that Brazil ever knew. As a result an attempt was made to eliminate them entirely, many being deported. Such influences as they have left have largely been incorporated into the gêge-nagô and Bantu cults, mainly as "lines," or the calling up of spirits within the Bantu ceremonial complex. The particular sacerdotes who are learned in these "lines" are still called *alufá*. The ritual has undergone much syncretism, being combined with Indian as well as other African religious traits.[64]

The Bantu Cults. The many influences which the Negroes of the Bantu groups have had on the language of Brazil are well known, but only recently has their importance as carriers of religious culture come to light. Nina Rodrigues neglected this important aspect of the study to which he gave a large part of his life, and only with the investigations of Ramos and his collaborators was a beginning made in ascertaining survivals of Bantu religious culture in Brazil. The macumbas of Rio de Janeiro and Niterói are those which have yielded the most results in this field.

The great deity of Angola, Zambi or Nzambi, still lives in the macumbas in and about Rio de Janeiro under the names of Zâmbi,[65] Ganga Zumba and Gana Zona. Zambi-ampungu, from the Congo, also is remembered although the name has become so corrupted that it is difficult to recognize. The names of Lemba, Cariapemba, and Calunga are also heard in the macumbas. In fact "the series of the spirits is never ending and a large number came to us, with names modified, transformed, many of them almost impossible of identification." [66]

The Bantus lacked highly developed cults of the fetish gods and animal sacrifices such as those the Sudanese Negroes carried to Brazil. But they brought along a cult of the dead, ancestor worship, household deities, many other friendly and unfriendly supernatural beings, the belief in the transmigration of souls, totemism, and many fetish practices closely allied to spiritualism.

According to Ramos the liturgy of the Bantu cults is closely linked with funeral rites, totemic ceremonies, and magical medicine. The high priest is called *quimbanda* and is a combination of sacerdote, doctor, fortuneteller, and sorcerer. But "among the Afro-Brazilians of

---

[64] Cf. Ramos, "The Negro in Brazil," in Smith and Marchant (eds.), *Brazil: Portrait of Half a Continent*, 136, 141–42; and *id., Introdução á Anthropologia Brasileira*, I, 421–32, and *O Negro Brasileiro*, 75–97.

[65] Not to be confused with the fantastic being called *Zumbi* in Brazil, *Zombie* in Haiti, who is active in the middle of the night.

[66] Ramos, *O Negro Brasileiro*, 112.

Bantu origin, the religious liturgy proper is exceedingly poor and has been almost completely absorbed by that of the gêge-nagô." [67] Thus the quimbanda of Rio de Janeiro has lost much of the prestige of the office. He serves only in the function of head of the macumba, aided by an assistant who is called a *cambône*. Under the influence of the gêge-nagô religion the priest is referred to as pai de santo and the initiates as filhos de santo, although in some macumbas the latter are called "mediums" because of spiritualistic influences. These macumbas of Bantu origin also have functionaries called *sambas* whose duties are to receive the visitors and to care for the women who receive the saint.

In these macumbas of Bantu origin the ritual is simple and very similar to that of the gêge-nagô cults. The terreiros are rudely made and relatively simple in their layout. (See Figure 37.) Each of these temples takes the name of its protecting deity or familiar spirit. The most distinguishing characteristic of Bantu macumbas is the importance of the familiar spirits which incarnate themselves in the quimbanda and who are survivals from the ancestor worship of Angola and the Congo.

There are groups of saints and spirits which come in falanges. These belong to various nations or "lines." The more powerful the sacerdote, the greater the number of "lines" in which he works. Today the rule is . . . syncretism with Spiritualism, Catholicism, and the Negro cults of Sudanese origin. All of the Catholic saints, spirits of the mediums' tables, and Sudanese orishas appear in these "lines" of the terreiros or "centers," of Bantu origin.[68]

As indicated above, there are even "lines" of Mussulman origin, about the only remaining influence of Mohammedanism that can be established definitely.

When all are assembled and disposed as in Figure 37, the *gira* has been formed, and the high priest opens the ceremony by invoking the protecting saint. Then he sings the *ponto* "of the smoker" to purify the temple.[69] There follow pontos to each of the saints or spirits who are to descend from their altars. The cambône leads in the singing, which is accompanied by the clapping of hands and also by music from the various percussion instruments used by the Negroes. The latter include *cuícas* (a small cylindrical instrument), tamborines, *canzás* (of bamboo), and various drums.

Nowadays, the practice of consulting the spirits is common in many of the macumbas. At a certain place in the ceremony the sacerdote "receives" the spirit of an old Negro from the African Coast, generally either Pai Joaquim or Velho Lourenço, who proceeds to give advice.

[67] *Ibid.*, 115.

[68] Ramos, *Introdução á Anthropologia Brasileira*, I, 472–73.

[69] Ponto refers either to a song dedicated to a saint or to the insignia such as the sign of Solomon, the circle, the arrow, and so forth, which are symbolic of the divinities. One who strolls about in the hills where so many of Rio's Negroes live may observe these insignia on the walls of the small cottages which cover the slopes.

Idols and Symbols from the Macumbas, from a Painting by D. Ismailo-vitch. (Photo by Arthur Ramos.)

The "lines" continue far into the night. Rarely does possession become as strong as among the candomblés of Bahia, but in some cases it takes on very violent aspects. The Negroes think that the possessed, speaking in unknown tongue, is talking of "things of the [African] Coast," but their ideas on this subject are very vague.

The ceremony closes as it began with an invocation to the protecting saint. The chorus sings and the quimbanda blesses all with the Catholic invocation, "God be praised," to which the congregation contritely replies, "Let Him be praised forever." [70]

[70] Ramos, *Introdução á Anthropologia Brasileira*, I, 474–75, and *id.*, "The Negro in Brazil," in Smith and Marchant (eds.), *Brazil: Portrait of Half a Continent*, 143–45.

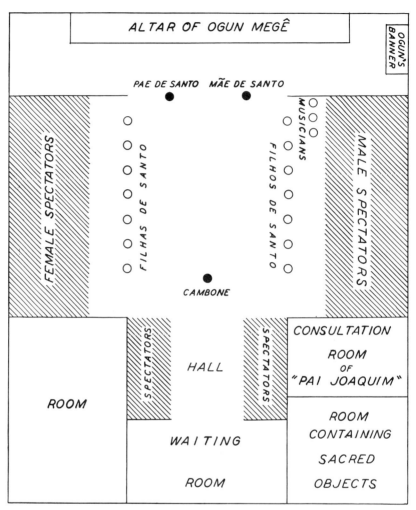

ALTAR OF OGUN MEGÊ

OGUN'S BANNER

PAE DE SANTO MÃE DE SANTO

MUSICIANS

FILHOS DE SANTO

MALE SPECTATORS

FEMALE SPECTATORS

FILHAS DE SANTO

CAMBONE

SPECTATORS

SPECTATORS

HALL

CONSULTATION

ROOM
OF
"PAI JOAQUIM"

ROOM

WAITING

ROOM

ROOM
CONTAINING

SACRED

OBJECTS

FIGURE 37. Arrangement of the terreiro of a cult of Bantu origin. (After Ramos, O Negro Brasileiro.)

Syncretism. In the Brazil of today it is difficult to find examples of the "pure" religious elements, either from African or from indigenous sources. That which prevails is a result of much blending, modification, fusion. The gods of the Africans and the Indians were identified with the saints of the Catholics; the ceremonials of the pagans, sometimes openly, sometimes surreptitiously, were reoriented about the chapel or the cathedral; the Negro found in the symbols of Christianity a wealth of new objects to add to his pegí; and the cultural heritage of the unlettered Brazilian embraced all the elements from all the sources. The identification of São Jorge with Oxóssi, of São Jeronimo with Xangô, of São Roque with Omulú, and the most powerful of all, Senhor do Bomfim (Jesus Christ) with Oxalá are only a

Dancing the Moçambique, Fazenda Santa Maria, Taubaté, São Paulo. (Photo by Carlos B. Schmidt.)

few of the most obvious phases of the cultural blendings. As Ramos has said, "It was impossible to deter the avalanche of syncretism." At first the African cults tended to amalgamate one with the other. Later the process of acculturation widened to the Indian and finally to the religions introduced by the whites—Catholicism and spiritualism. According to this noted authority there is the following ascending order of syncretism.

1. Gêge-Nagô
2. Gêge-Nagô-Mussulman
3. Gêge-Nagô-Bantu
4. Gêge-Nagô-Mussulman-Bantu
5. Gêge-Nagô-Mussulman-Bantu-Caboclo
6. Gêge-Nagô-Mussulman-Bantu-Caboclo-Spiritualist
6. Gêge-Nagô-Mussulman-Bantu-Caboclo-Spiritualist-Catholic [71]

Ramos maintained that it is the last type which prevails among Brazil's backward classes, be they Negro, mixed bloods, or whites. It predominates "in all parts of Brazil, with more intensity in some places than in others, with predominance of one of the forms over the others; here Yoruba, there Bantu, and in other spots, Caboclo-Amerindo." [72] It is only necessary to add that in the last few decades

[71] Ramos, *O Negro Brasileiro,* 168.
[72] *Ibid.,* 169.

various theosophical elements, particularly the visible symbols, seem to be eagerly snatched up and incorporated into the already extremely heterogeneous religious complexes.

SUPERNATURAL BEINGS

In addition to the orthodox mysteries of the Church and to the numerous extraneous elements from African and Indian cultures that the process of syncretism has engrafted onto them, the world of the Brazilian countryman abounds in mysterious occurrences and supernatural beings which have no particular connection with any organized cult. As in other countries, including our own, the city man of middle or upper class status, except for an occasional furtive thought that after all there may be something to them, has relegated all such to the realm of superstition. But to the inhabitants of the forested areas, of the extensive plateaus, of the sertões, these things are a very real part of the environment; these supernatural entities are beings with whom they may be forced to reckon. Since many of these are decidedly dangerous to the individual, they must ever be on guard.

Pé de Garrafa. For example, among the sertanejos who live in southwestern Mato Grosso and derive their livelihood by collecting roots and herbs in the dense forests of the region—the "Green Hell" of popular accounts—there is a widespread belief in a species of mysterious man-like beings called *pé de garrafa* (bottle foot). These beings are shaped like men, except that they have only one leg, which terminates in a rounded hoof whose sole is shaped like the bottom of a bottle—from this comes the name. Their bodies are thickly covered with long, dark, and grizzled hair.

It is at twilight that they practice their witchery upon the poor foresters of the region. At this time the collector of roots and herbs, tired from the long day's work, has already started back along the long trail that leads to the station, with his sack filled with the precious collections. Hearing a strong, clear call resembling that of a fellow worker, he stops and listens. When the cry is repeated, he answers and starts off the trail in the direction whence it came. Arriving in the vicinity he sees nothing, but again comes the call, now from the right, now from the left, leading him first in one direction, then another, in search of the companion. But he sees and meets with no one. Finally on the ground he discovers the fresh, clear imprint, as though made by the pressure of the bottom of a bottle. Here is indisputable evidence of the recent presence of the powerful and monstrous *bicho* which seeks to lure the poor collector of herbs into the confusing depths of the mysterious forests. When confronted by the appalling situation many of the weaker collectors are irreparably lost. Some of the most courageous fighters, those who also possess the best sense of direction, manage to make their way back to the sta-

Setting Off Rockets Is a Feature of Many Religious Celebrations in Rural Brazil. Boa Ventura, Município of Itaperuna, State of Rio de Janeiro. (Photo by the Author.)

tion. There, thoroughly frightened, they relate to their fellows the details of the latest dread occurrence.[73]

Mãe d'Agua. Almost universal among the lower orders of Brazilian society is belief in the mãe d'agua (water mother). This attractive but fatal supernatural being, derived from indigenous folklore and also from African tradition, has more than a little in common with the Lorelei. According to some accounts, on moonlight nights she is to be seen on a leaf of an aquatic plant, singing as she floats along over the smooth surface of a river or a lake. Long, green tresses flowing over shapely shoulders, and tempting, misty eyes attract her victims to their doom, "the easy death of a divine, and ardent, and sensual embrace beneath the cold water." [74] But there are other stories which cast her in roles that are quite different. In Bahia there are widely disseminated accounts of the mãe d'agua whom the poor countryman found stealing corn or beans from his roça. He captured her and finally persuaded her to become his wife. In all cases she

[73] For an excellent description of this phenomenon, see Gabriel Pinto de Arruda, *Um Trecho do Oeste Brasileiro* (Rio de Janeiro, 1938), 14–15. Variations as they appear in Goiás and the Northeast are described in José A. Teixeira, *Folklore Goiano* (São Paulo, 1941), 377–79.

[74] Barroso, *Terra de Sol*, 268.

warns him never to speak disparagingly of the underwater people. For a time following the marriage, the man's affairs prosper miraculously. Soon he has a mansion, numerous servants, large numbers of cattle, and many farms. But after some time has passed, the mãe d'agua ceases to perform her housewifely duties. The children cry for food, and the house is badly disordered, the servants idle away their time for want of direction, while she, dressed in rags, barefooted, and with her hair badly disheveled, spends all day sleeping. Every time the man comes home, the disarranged house, crying children, and demanding servants drive him to desperation. Finally, his nerves can stand no more, and one day he curses the underwater people. For this the mãe d'agua has been waiting. She hastily arises, races out the door, and heads for the water. All the man's efforts to stop her are ineffectual. Furthermore, she is followed by all the children, the servants, the cattle, horses, mules, pigs, chickens, turkeys, and every living thing. Even this is not the end, for the house, the furnishings, the outbuildings, the fences, corrals, even the trees, everything, follow her to the river side and plunge with her into the water. The man lives on alone, poor as at first, but no longer is his roça pillaged by the mãe d'agua.[75]

In the Amazon Region the supernatural being known elsewhere as mãe d'agua is called *yara,* and the former name is applied to the great water spirit who is mother of all the waters and whose exploits rival the powers of the imagination. In addition to these there is the *bôto,* male counterpart of the Lorelei, whose success in attracting women is fully as great as is that of the yara in leading men to their doom.[76]

Lobis Homem. The werewolf is another supernatural being against whom the humble rural Brazilian must be on his guard. A severe anemic condition is an indication that one has been a victim of one of these fiends. Girls must take care that their suitors, however handsome they may be, do not belong to this dread species. Such a husband sooner or later is consumed by an irrepressible desire to drink the blood of his wife. There is one story of a girl who married what she thought was a handsome man, but who in reality was a *lobis homem.* When seized with the desire to drink his wife's blood he tried to create a pretext by forcing her to reveal whom she would have married had he never been born. Always she replied that she would have married only him. Finally, unable to get any other answer he killed her, drank her blood, and went away with all the other devils.[77]

Others. These are only a few of the hundreds of supernatural beings who live in the thoughts of Brazil's rural masses and with whom

[75] See Basílio de Magalhães, O Folclore no Brasil (Rio de Janeiro, 1939), 246–50.
[76] Cf. Raymundo Moraes, Na Planicie Amazonica (5th ed.; São Paulo, 1939), 69–77. See also H. Smith, Brazil, the Amazons and the Coast, 572; and Charles Wagley, "The Folk Culture of the Brazilian Amazon," in Sol Tax (ed.), Acculturation in the Americas, Vol. II of Proceedings of the 29th International Congress of Americanists (Chicago, 1952), 226.
[77] Magalhães, O Folclore no Brasil, 234–35.

they must deal in every day's routine of activities. The headless mule (*mula-sem-cabeça, burra-de-padre,* or *burrinha-de-padre*),[78] the "Negro of the water," the "bicho that eats tongues," the *boitatá* (wandering spirit which sometimes protects the pastures and sometimes destroys them), the *curupira* (a little-known man whose feet are turned backward so that anyone seeing his tracks and trying to run away from him will speed to destruction at his hands),[79] are only a few of the many with whom the rural Brazilian may have to deal. In fact, the peasant's world is thickly populated with these beings who have it within their power to aid and injure man.

Not the least interesting of these is Manoel do Riachão whose satanic activities seem to be concentrated in the northeastern portion of Brazil, from Piauí to Sergipe. Some of the sertanejos are convinced that Manoel is the devil himself, but others think of him as being an iniquitous individual who sold his soul to the Prince of Evil in return for great skill in playing the viola and improvising batuques. Everywhere he is recognized as a bard without rival. However, his passage through any community is marked by sudden and inexplicable calamities. Even though rains have been regular, the small streams dry up, great losses occur among the herds, the crops fail, and even people are attacked by strange and deadly maladies. In spite of his great skills, he can never stop for long in one place. Popular indignation soon arises to the pitch that "the poor *violeiro* is obliged to pack up his viola and seek another place to stay until the time that from new persecutions he recommences his eternal peregrinations. Thus lived Manoel do Riachão, and the places of preference frequented were the taverns, the gambling tables, and principally the batuques, for the pleasure of defeating in verse the most famous singers." [80]

FANATICISM AND SCHISMS

Pedra Bonita. Among the cultural elements inherited from Portugal and introduced in new Brazilian religious complexes is that particular brand of millenarianism known as Sebastianism. These beliefs and the sect of Sebastianists had their origin in events connected with the life of Sebastian, mystic and fanatic King of Portugal (1557–1578). The exalted imagination of this monarch led him to be consumed by an ambition to lead a crusade against the Mohammedans of North Africa. He placed his government in charge of the

[78] So called because the fate of being transformed at death into one of these entities is likely to be the lot of a priest's concubine. *Ibid.,* 74. Cf. Barroso, *Terra de Sol,* 226. All the details of the transformation of a young peasant's bride-to-be into a mula-sem-cabeça, are given in Viriato Padilha, *Os Roceiros* (Rio de Janeiro, 1927), 217–44.

[79] Cf. Wagley, *Amazon Town,* 235–36.

[80] Padilha, *Os Roceiros,* 167–68. As indicated above, the batuque is a dance of African origin. At these gatherings the *desafio* is one of the most popular features of the entertainment. This is a contest in dialogue between two singers, all improvisation, each in turn seeking to answer the opponent's query and then to turn the laugh on his opponent.

Jesuits, refused to marry (although this meant the Portuguese crown would pass to a foreigner), and led two expeditions into Morocco. On the second of these he was killed at the battle of Al Kasr al Kebir. However, many Portuguese refused to accept the fact that he was dead and believed that their "hidden king" was either absent on a pilgrimage or awaiting a second advent on an enchanted island. Sebastianism became a religion.[81] R. Walsh, who supplies the greatest detail on this subject, states that in his day (1828–1829) there was a considerable number of people in Portugal and in Brazil who simply and earnestly believed

> that King Sebastião, who disappeared in Africa, is not dead, but will reappear in his proper person; the Portuguese say at Lisbon, and the Brazilians at Rio de Janeiro, which is a favored city, and originally and properly called after his name. It is generally supposed that the number in Portugal exceeds 1,000 persons, and in Brazil about twice as many more. They have no particular place of meeting, and form no distinct congregation with any peculiar doctrine except this. Their common article of faith is, that Sebastião will certainly appear, and that the event will happen in their own life-time; and they expect him with as much zeal and simplicity as the modern Jews expect the Messiah.[82]

The same authority also indicates that persons of these beliefs were numerous in Minas Gerais and Rio de Janeiro and describes them as similar to English Quakers or Moravians and distinguished for their industry, frugality, simplicity, and benevolence. He mentions the stream of prophecies set forth by one of his acquaintances who saw every event as a sign of the imminent return of the king, provides information about a merchant who disposed of goods to persons who would agree to pay when Sebastião came again, and even presents a copy of a contract for the payment of ten contos in the event the hidden monarch reappeared within ten years.[83] However, Walsh does not speak of the importance of these beliefs in northeastern Brazil, nor does he give any indication that they might soon generate excesses such as those that shortly came to pass.

In 1836 a mestiço by the name of João Santos, or João Antonio, began to disseminate startling notices about Pedra Bonita in central Pernambuco. On this spot stand two tall monoliths, some 100 feet high and of an appearance somewhat resembling dolmens. According to João these stones marked the exact location of an enchanted country in which was hidden untold treasure and which was destined to be the New Jerusalem of King Sebastião. In fact the two stones were the towers of a grand, enchanted temple, already partially visible. Supplied with two common stones of curious shape, João began to wander about in the area asserting that the pebbles had been secured from an enchanted lake. His affirmations produced a strong impression on the humble folk of the sertões, whose cultural heritage contained little to shield them from such

[81] *Encyclopedia Britannica*, 14th edition.
[82] Walsh, *Notices of Brazil*, I, 385–86.
[83] *Ibid.*, 386–87.

ideas and much to lead them to believe the stories. They were already conscious of the brilliant reflections from the pretty stones. They easily accepted the idea of supernatural intervention, and, of course, became very agitated.

In an effort to re-establish calm, the ecclesiastical authorities had João removed to a distant place. But this did not put an end to the beliefs or the agitation. Less than two years passed before another João (Ferreira), brother-in-law of the first, arrived in the locality, gathered about him thirty followers, and took steps to bring about the disenchantment of the kingdom. He remained more than two months, devoting himself to various extreme religious practices, among which sexual promiscuity is reported to have figured prominently. In every way he sought to increase the courage of his followers. He and his intimates orated continuously, ate little but drank much, danced, and in other ways worked themselves into the highest pitches of frenzy, ready for the disenchantment.

In the sermons which João addressed to the multitude that had assembled he made fantastic promises to those who could bring themselves to make the necessary sacrifices. "Negroes and mestiços would become whites, aged persons would be rejuvenated, and poor people would become millionaires, all powerful, immortal." But always the preacher closed by affirming that blood was necessary to effect the disenchantment, blood to bathe the base of the columns and to irrigate the nearby fields!

On May 14, 1838, the "king" announced that the day of sacrifice had come, and numbers of people offered themselves for the supreme ordeal. The first to embrace the stone and offer his head to the two mestiço executioners was the father of the pretended king. An old man carried his two grandchildren 35 feet up the stone and threw them out into space; a widow offered two young sons and was exasperated at not being able to sacrifice two more who were old enough to take to their heels. The king himself offered his wife, spilling her blood by repeated stabs with a knife.

All that day and the two following ones the holocaust continued. By the end of the third day, 30 children, 12 men, 11 women, and 14 dogs had been executed. "The bodies were placed at the base of the rocks in symmetrical groups, in accord with the sex, the age, and the quality of the victims." Still the enchantment prevailed.

On the morning of the seventeenth a brother-in-law of the king and brother of João Santos ascended an improvised throne and declared that one thing was still lacking—the blood of João Ferreira. The king did not come forward, and in spite of the cowardice which he demonstrated the speaker was immediately put to death.

By the eighteenth the remains of the dead were in such a state of putrefaction that the crowd had to retire a short distance. Here they were engaged in the construction of huts when they were attacked by a hastily recruited force from the nearest governmental station. Instead of submitting to the law, the Sebastianists, who had been taught that an attack upon them would be a signal of the restoration of the kingdom, rushed to the combat singing religious songs. In this struggle twenty-two of them, including the king and other leaders, paid with their lives. Others were imprisoned, one for life.

As a sequel the original propagandist, the mestiço João Santos, fled, was arrested, and killed on some pretext by the soldiers who had him in custody.[84]

The New Jerusalem of Antonio Conselheiro. Antonio Maciel, known as the Counselor, is another name to be reckoned with in any attempt to summarize significant religious developments in Brazil. In his background were two generations of feuding between his family, the Macieis, and another powerful Ceará clan, the Araujos. Early in life he was deserted by his wife, assaulted a relative of the seducer who had sheltered the pair, was arrested, escaped, and then dropped from sight for ten years. When he reappeared in the sertões of Bahia he was "an old man of thirty," a self-appointed forerunner to prepare men's souls for the end of the world in 1899.

Like a few other well-known religious leaders of his time, such as Padre Cicero and many lesser ones, Antonio Conselheiro helped himself liberally to the elements in contemporary Brazilian rural religious culture in preparing his own peculiar concoction. The culture traits of the complex known as Sebastianism were very important; significant, too, was the widespread tendency to look on lunacy as supernatural and the mentally deranged as enjoying special privilege in the approach of deity. The Counselor seems to have had as the fundamental tenet in his creed that this is a life of sorrow with the life to come as man's only hope of happiness. After his reappearance, his was an abstemious, stoical, John-the-Baptist type of existence. He lived on alms, spoke little, wore long hair, and in every way conducted himself as a man removed from sin. When he passed, people would remark, "There goes the Counselor." His followers gained no such reputations for restraint.

In a world filled with faith healers and quack doctors of all types, it is not surprising that his ministrations soon gained a reputation for effecting miraculous cures. Apparently he made no effort to attract followers, but disciples flocked around him. He seemed content merely to endure some of the sufferings that had been the lot of Jesus. The government, becoming alarmed at the commotion he was causing among the sertanejos, took him into custody on an old charge. At the time he demonstrated his stoicism by forbidding his followers to oppose the troops sent to arrest him. Nor did he protest

[84] The account followed here is that by Brazil's outstanding scholar Nina Rodrigues in *As Collectividades Anormaes* (Rio de Janeiro, 1939), 135–39. Of other accounts, that of Euclydes da Cunha in *Os Sertões* is most adequate. The Protestant missionary, Daniel P. Kidder, *Sketches of Residence and Travels in Brazil*, II, 148–51, gave details gathered very shortly after the happenings. His account contains the egregious error of identifying the locale as one of two caves, rather than two stone columns. Practically the same account is given in Kidder and Fletcher, *Brazil and the Brazilians*, 520–21. Cunningham Graham seems to have exercised great poetic license without in any way improving the story in *A Brazilian Mystic*, 41–44.

at the cruel beatings to which he was subjected on the way to the capital. The charges, disproved, only gave him the greater prestige of a martyr, upon his release and return to the sertão. By then his person had become highly charged with mana, and even the tree under which he swung his hammock was regarded as sacred.

Now (about 1878) the miracles began to flourish. Now, too, he began to preach reform of the church. It was not long before he realized that he would have to "remove his flock from the world." The rapidly approaching end of the world loomed large in his thoughts and teachings.

The movement built up to its climax and the crisis came with the overthrow of the empire and the establishment of the republic. The emperor he could accept and submit to as enjoying a divine right to rule. But he had no such attitude toward the republic. This time his followers resisted and overcame the troops sent to arrest him. In open revolt he led his people to an old cattle fazenda and began the construction of the New Jerusalem. It was little more than an armed camp surrounded by trenches and earthworks, for the houses were of the crudest construction. But the erection of a pretentious temple was undertaken, with materials brought from throughout the sertão and with labor supplied by the devotees. In the temple the Conselheiro preached his doctrines of salvation through suffering and entrance to the kingdom of heaven through the gateway of Canudos. Here, too, was the headquarters for the vast religious brotherhood, of which he was supreme authority, whose members were known as *jagunços*, a name usually applied to bad men in the sertões.

Four expeditions were sent by the government against Antonio Conselheiro and his rebellious city of the New Jerusalem. It never surrendered, but the fourth expedition completely eliminated the population. After the battle only a child, an old man, and two wounded were left.[85] But Antonio Conselheiro still lives in the memories of the hundreds of thousands of underprivileged people who inhabit Brazil's vast back country.

Padre Cicero and His New Jerusalem. Probably the most noted of schismatic movements in Brazil is the one that was led by Padre Cicero of Juàzeiro. The scene was the Valley of Cariri in southern Ceará, an area earlier known to the history of fanaticism in Brazil because of a severe outbreak in 1850 of penitential scourging among the sect called Serenos.[86] In the early 1870's there came to this valley, to the fazenda Juàzeiro, a newly ordained young priest, Cicero Romão Baptista. Shortly after, the great droughts of 1877–1879 set in. During this time of great tribulation he distinguished himself and earned the deepest gratitude of the sertanejos by having wells dug, shelters constructed, and fields of mandioca planted. With such measures he

[85] Graham, *A Brazilian Mystic, passim;* cf. Kelsey, *Seven Keys to Brazil,* 169–72; and the translation of Euclydes da Cunha, *Os Sertões,* published in 1944 by the University of Chicago Press under the title, *Rebellion in the Backlands.*

[86] Cf. Cunha, *Os Sertões,* 148.

saved the lives of large numbers of refugees. His fame spread throughout the length and breadth of the sertão.

On June 11, 1890, as he was giving Holy Communion to the *beata* [87] Maria de Araujo, she fell to the floor in a terrific nervous state, and a thin stream of blood ran from her mouth. The faithful who were present rushed to her aid. When they saw it was blood issuing from her mouth, the effect was electric. For the actual transformation to occur during the grand and solemn moment when a woman so well known for her devotion and piety was partaking of the sacred host could mean only one thing. It was a miracle! [88] This explanation was not confined to the unlearned sertanejos. A leading sacerdote acclaimed the interruption of natural law.[89] The miracle was repeated on various occasions, and the Bishop of Ceará dispatched a commission of clergymen and medical men from Fortaleza to study the case. After some researches this commission, in its first report, stated that the "case could not have a natural explanation and should be regarded as miraculous." One of the physicians even certified "that the blood into which the host transforms itself cannot be any but the blood of Our Lord Jesus Christ." [90]

But the Bishop refused to accept the conclusions of the commission—they proved too much, they did not satisfy the three criteria of St. Thomas. Again it reported, this time with a complete retraction of its previous findings. Natural explanations sufficient to explain the phenomenon were set forth. This, however, had little effect on the country people. Then some other events followed to confirm their faith. Monseignor Monteiro, a member of the commission and the first to denounce the miracle from the pulpit, went blind and spent his last days in utmost poverty; and misfortunes fell upon other members of the group, including the doctor who attested to the blood of Christ.[91] All of this strengthened Padre Cicero's position with the masses and aided in his transformation into the new messiah.

New miracles were not slow in coming. One day the Padre took in payment for services rendered a young bull calf of mixed zebu breed. Not wishing to have him run with the herd, he placed him in the care of a trusted friend, José Lourenço. The latter was a Negro and a well-known beato.[92] Furthermore, he belonged to the brotherhood of

---

[87] A beata is a woman devoted to religion but not a member of any monastery or community.

[88] See Lourenço Filho, *Joaseiro do Padre Cicero*, 89.

[89] Menezes, *O Outro Nordeste*, 180.

[90] Lourenço Filho, *Joaseiro do Padre Cicero*, 92.

[91] *Ibid.*, 93.

[92] As described by Xavier de Oliveira, *Beatos e Cangaceiros* (Rio de Janeiro, 1920), 39, a beato is "a bachelor, who makes vows of chastity (real or apparent), who has no profession because he has quit work, and who lives through the charity of the kindly and by exploiting the faithful. He passes the day praying in the churches, visiting the sick, at funerals for the dead, in teaching prayers to the credulous, all in accord with the precepts of the catechism! He dresses like a monk: a cassock of cotton dyed black, a cross on the shoulders, a cord of São Francisco tied about the waist, a dozen rosaries, a hundred scapulars of São Bento, some little bags filled with religious papers and powerful prayers, all hanging from the neck, They are, generally, vagabonds, hypocrites, religious fanatics, or bandits."

the Penitentes.[93] One day a friend and companion of this beato vowed he would offer a tender bundle of grass to the Little Father's bull in the event that one of his petitions received the divine favor believed necessary to bring about its fulfillment. The results were favorable and he was under the necessity of keeping the vow. It was a time of drought, but the sertanejo was not dismayed. Knowing of a private meadow at some distance where the grass was always green he went early in the morning when no one was about, helped himself to the grass, and carried his offering to the bull. Apparently the latter was in no mood to eat and turned away from the offering. The cabo-

[93] Among other duties the members of this irmandade have the obligation of dressing as pallbearers and offering prayers for the dead near the cemetery and at the crossroads. Now and then "they carry on strange ceremonies of their cult, in which under the guise of the Catholic liturgy many times are mixed unspeakable crimes." Lourenço Filho, *Joaseiro do Padre Cicero,* 102.

A Beato. (Reproduced from Xavier de Oliveira, *Beatos e Cangaceiros.*)

clo had knelt and begun a prayer appropriate to the occasion, when he was transfixed by a long, sad bellow from the beast. He was able only to cry for mercy and promise not to steal again. For a long time he lay on the ground without power to move. The keeper came on the scene, put these occurrences together with other peculiar actions of the animal, and concluded that it was a genuine miracle. The bull had become a saint; from then on he produced uncounted miracles. The cult of the bull created so many excesses that finally Padre Cicero felt constrained to order the animal slain. José Lourenço and the Penitentes broke out into open revolt at the order, but it was carried out before their eyes in front of the jail into which they had been thrown.[94]

In spite of such divisive events among his followers and discouragement from the higher authorities, Padre Cicero continued to reign as the messiah of the sertões, the absolute monarch of his New Jerusalem. Then came some political events of far-reaching significance. Involved was the overthrow of the clan that had been ruling Ceará for twenty years and a complex question of presidential succession in Rio de Janeiro. But what at first was merely an attempt to use Padre Cicero and his forces as tools for deposing the legal government of Ceará developed into a holy war and the setting up of a state within a state. Soon the state troops were besieging Juàzeiro, resisted bitterly by the Padre's men, probably secretly aided by the federal government, and certainly helped by the sertanejos' belief in new supernatural interventions. The rumor spread that Nossa Senhora de Dores had promised Padre Cicero that the bullets from the muskets of the soldiers, even though they penetrated the bodies of the defenders, would do the sertanejos no harm. "The dead themselves would be resuscitated, after three days, stronger than ever, beside the Little Father in his house at Juàzeiro, or in the mysterious church of the Horto." [95] Aided by such forces, and also by the individual sympathies of the government soldiers, the first expedition (1913) was driven off. A second in 1914 had no better luck, and then Padre Cicero, aided, it is charged, by all the bandits of the sertão including Virgolino Ferreira and Lampeão, took the initiative and marched on the state capital, Fortaleza, his forces sacking such cities as Crato and Barbalha on the way. Federal troops had to intervene on the outskirts of the capital, but the threat was sufficient. The governor stepped out and the Federal Interventor stepped in. Lourenço Filho has reproduced the telegrams of encouragement and felicitation the latter exchanged with Padre Cicero.[96]

Although excommunicated by the Church, Padre Cicero lived out a long life as absolute master of his mecca of the sertões. His man sat as deputy in the Federal Congress. At one time he was claimed to be the most powerful man in Brazil. At his death in 1934 he willed his fortune to the Salesians on condition that they establish a profes-

94 *Ibid.*, 102–105.
95 *Ibid.*, 128.
96 *Ibid.*, 154–55.

of states and territories, highly reminiscent of the United States under the Articles of Confederation. For South America's largest nation the transition from empire to republic had also been the change from a more highly centralized to a loosely federated form of national organization. During the twentieth century in national affairs, the states, or more properly the coalition formed by the two all-powerful states, São Paulo and Minas Gerais, reigned supreme. The other states for the most part submitted to the domination of their two powerful fellows in national affairs, although sometimes the smaller and weaker ones united into blocs to combat the influence of the dominant central powers. The third most populous state, Bahia, the "Virginia of Brazil," seemed content to bask in the memory of a glorious past, which its golden-voiced orators are reported as never having lost an opportunity to extol; but rapidly developing Rio Grande do Sul frequently was found rebelling against the system in vogue and leading insurgent moves of one kind or another. Sometimes support for the Gaúchos was gained from Pernambuco, which had its tradition of greater days when its sugar industry had been more prosperous. However, for the most part in the period between the establishment of the republic in 1889 and the revolution of October, 1930, there seems to have prevailed a neat arrangement whereby São Paulo and Minas Gerais shared the power and rotated the chief political offices among their own citizens. Even the events of 1930 probably never would have arisen had President Washington Luiz from São Paulo been content to select a man from Minas Gerais as his successor instead of trying to pass on the powers to a fellow Paulista.

The powers of the central government were extremely weak, the states and especially the municípios being the seats of the real political power. It is to be emphasized that the município was the primary unit during the colonial period, under the empire, and even in the days of the republic. For centuries national influences penetrated little beyond the federal capital and a few of the more important cities on the littoral. It is not exaggerating to say that prior to 1930 each state was a little world of its own, enjoying most of the privileges of self-government and even raising part of its revenue from levies on interstate commerce.[2]

This separatism on the part of the states had its roots in the weakly federated agglomeration of provinces that was Brazil during the colonial period and even during the empire. Wars of secession were frequent, and states often openly defied the central powers without taking the trouble to declare their independence. In the constitutional assembly that followed the declaration of the republic the advocates of a stronger central government, although they included

[2] However, this statement must not be interpreted to mean that Getúlio Vargas initiated the practice of appointing governors, or *interventors*, for the states. This trait is deeply rooted in Brazilian political culture, having been the general practice during the empire, and frequently resorted to by the presidents who held office between 1889 and 1930. Lowenstein and others are prone to give the impression that Vargas introduced "interventors" into Brazilian government.

some of the most outstanding statesmen of Brazilian history, were not successful. Said Rui Barbosa at a session held December 16, 1890: "The first necessity, the point of departure of all necessities, is ensuring the independent existence of the Federal Union. . . . Those that would make the Union of States instead of dividing the Union into States, transpose the terms of the problem." Still more expressive were the words addressed by Ubaldino do Amaral to the same assembly: "The Brazilian States have had in this case as many defenders as they have representatives. The Union, however, the National Union, our country, appears to have no advocate. . . . For us the Union is the enemy . . . the Union shall be disarmed of all, of power, even of resources to render that assistance that we determine it shall give." [3] The weak form of central government adopted at the beginning of the republic prevailed until 1937 and indeed may be said to have reached its apex under the constitution which was adopted in 1934.

But, as suggested above, the disjointed nature of the Brazilian political structure did not stop with the states. Each of these larger units in turn was an extremely loose confederation of smaller cells, the municípios or counties. Perhaps "agglomeration" is a more suitable word than confederation to describe the situation that existed; each of these units of local government was almost autonomous. Brazil was literally a mosiac of little sovereignties. Like the states, each município also enjoyed the privilege of levying tribute on goods passing across its boundaries; [4] in fact it enjoyed all the privileges,

[3] Amaral is quoted in Carneiro Leão, *A Sociedade Rural*, 163.

[4] The following quotation from an English writer who had lived many years in Brazil serves to bring out the segmented political nature of Brazil in the early twentieth century and illustrates some of the problems inherent in the system:

"All the States of Brazil are now self-governing, that is to say, they have a kind of 'Home Rule,' or, as they themselves call it, 'Autonomia,' and this particular State, i. e., Rio Grande do Sul, only contributes three taxes to the Federal Government, viz., the duties on Imports, Posts and Telegraphs. The remaining branches of administration are strictly internal, i. e., State, or Municipal.

"On the other hand, the Central, or Federal Government, although not intervening in matters of internal administration, is bound to come to the assistance of the State in the event of foreign invasion.

"This 'Autonomia' or right of self-government is granted by the Constitution of the Republic to all the States, and by them, in their turn, to the different Municipalities, and, however wise or just such a measure may appear at first sight, it has brought about some very anomalous conditions, inasmuch as some of the States persist in a course which is clearly a violation of the Constitution, and this is the levying of inter-State duties. In this connection the following incident which arose between the two States of Pernambuco and Rio Grande do Sul will serve as an illustration: —

"Pernambuco, which imports a great deal of produce from Rio Grande do Sul, such as 'jerked' beef, black beans and so on, commenced taxing these commodities whereupon Rio Grande retaliated by taxing alcohol, sugar, etc., entering the State from Pernambuco. This led to an argument between the two States, and finally the matter was carried before the 'Supremo Tribunal' (the High Court of Justice in Brazil), which decided that such taxes were unconstitutional. Nevertheless they continue to be levied in some of the States. A former President, Dr. Rodriguez Alves, tried, in the early part of his term of office, to stop this abuse of power, but failed to achieve his purpose, as the opposition was too strong.

"The various Municipalities in the different States also continue to make certain regulations and to levy taxes as they see fit, the consequence being that, in going from one Municipality to another one does not always know exactly what rights, and powers not specifically reserved to the state or the federal bodies. Perhaps it is not overstating the case to say that a large number of the municípios really enjoyed most of the privileges and powers theoretically reserved to the states and national government so far as these applied to local areas. Influences emanating from state and national capitals reached the municípios in a very emaciated form, if they reached them at all. This is true even today and was much more so thirty years ago. It was in the small miniature world in the interior—the município—that the real power, authority, and responsibility rested. Here they were either exercised or lay dormant. Because Brazil lacked the knowledge or the will to use the general property or land tax as a means of pooling local efforts for the provision of essential services, they generally lay dormant. In 1930 the Brazilian município for the most part still remained the unchallenged domain of the living dono of the founding family. There was no budget worthy of the name, and the people suffered from the lack of educational facilities, health and sanitary services, welfare activities, security of life and property, communication facilities, and the other functions which result from competent local governmental organization.

Finally, it must be indicated that within the local unit the power was either (1) highly concentrated in the hands of the chief or head of the most powerful family or clan, or (2) the bone of contention between two or more rival clans. In the first instance the inhabitants of the local unit might enjoy the benign influences of the feudal stage of existence at its best, or they might be forced to cringe under the tyrannical exercise of almost absolute power over life and death. In the second instance the pages of local history have room for little more than the record of the bitter feuding between rivals for power and authority. But in both cases the bulk of power and the exercise of most governmental power in Brazil centered in the local communities. The real political power lay in the hands of local chieftains who made up the *câmaras* of the municípios. The state and even the nation were merely loosely knit federations of these fundamental political cells.[5]

THE ESTADO NOVO

Since 1937 there has been a great development of centralization in Brazilian government. Nowadays, even in the most remote areas, one can see incipient health services, indications of federal inspection of school programs, and many other evidences of services of the central government. In a large measure this was accomplished dur-

one may be exposed to, in the way of having to pay taxes, as the latter vary considerably in relation to the same article, profession, or business, in different districts." Frank Bennett, *Forty Years in Brazil* (London, 1914), 166–68.

[5] For an excellent case history of governmental and other aspects of life in one small segment of Brazilian territory in the seventeenth, eighteenth, and nineteenth centuries, see Santos Filho, *Uma Comunidade Rural do Brasil Antigo.*

ing the period 1937 to 1945 when Getúlio Vargas ruled by decree in the New State which he had established, but it was even more evident during the administration of Janio Quadros. The obvious change under Vargas was that the President of the Republic named the governor or interventor of each state and that the governor in turn named the prefects of each of the municípios in his state. Naturally this greatly increased the power of the central government. The federal government seemed strong enough to enforce its will upon any single state, although a showdown with more than one powerful state at a time was avoided at all costs. Similarly, within a state it appeared that any one município could be brought to terms by the state governor but that it was considered a serious mistake to antagonize very many of them at the same time.

The degree to which the centralization of government in Brazil was attempted under the Estado Novo is best indicated by a few quotations from the Constitutional Law which was put into effect on November 10, 1937, and from one of the three amending constitutional laws which were promulgated subsequently.

The Nation. Under Article 15 the Nation was given sole jurisdiction:

I—to maintain relations with foreign countries, to appoint the members of the diplomatic and consular corps, to enter into treaties and international conventions;

II—to declare war and to make peace;

III—to decide definitely regarding the limits of the National Territory;

IV—to organize the external defense, the armed forces, the police and the safety of the frontiers;

V—to organize the production of and to supervise the commerce in war material of whatever nature;

VI—to maintain the postal service;

VII—to exploit or to give in concession the telegraph, radio communication and aerial navigation services, including landing facilities, as well as the railway systems which directly link maritime ports with the national frontiers or which cross State limits;

VIII—to create and to maintain Customs Houses and warehouses and to provide for the services of maritime and port police;

IX—to determine the basis and fix the scope of national education, organizing the program which should be followed for the physical, intellectual and moral development of childhood and youth;

X—to take general census of the population;

XI—to grant amnesty.

Article 16 gave the federal government sole authority to legislate on the following matters:

I—the boundaries of the States between themselves, those of the Federal District and those of the National Territory with neighboring Nations;

II—the external defense, including the policing and safety of the frontiers;

III—the naturalization, entry and departure from National Territory, emigration and immigration, passports, expulsion of foreigners from National Territory and the prohibition of remaining or temporarily staying in same, extradition;

IV—the manufacture and commerce of arms, munitions and explosives;

v—the public well-being, order, tranquility and public security, when conditions should require a uniform regulation;

vi—federal finances, matters connected with currency, credit, exchange and banking;

vii—foreign and interstate commerce, exchange and transfer of funds abroad;

viii—monopolies or nationalization of industries;

ix—weights and measures, standard, title and guarantee of precious metals;

x—mail, telegraph and radio-communications;

xi—communications and transportation by rail, by water, by air or highways, whenever they have an international or interstate character;

xii—coastwise transportation of merchandise, which will be permitted only on national ships;

xiii—Customs Houses and warehouses; maritime, ports and river police;

xiv—Federal property, mines and metallurgy, hydraulic power, water rights, forests, hunting and fishing and their exploitation;

xv—unification and standardization of electrical establishments and installations, as well as safety measures to be taken in the electric power industry; regime of high tension lines, when these cross State limits;

xvi—civil, commercial, aerial, labor, penal and judiciary codes;

xvii—insurance regulations and their supervision;

xviii—theatre and cinematograph regulations;

xix—cooperatives and institutions for the keeping and investing of popular saving;

xx—copyright law, the press, the right of association, of meeting, of free circulation; questions of civil status, including civil registration and change of name;

xxi—rights of invention, protection of models, trade marks and other designations of merchandise;

xxii—the judiciary division of the Federal District and of the Territories;

xxiii—electoral matters affecting the Union, the States and the Municipalities;

xxiv—the control of national education;

xxv—amnesty;

xxvi—organization, training, justice and guarantee of the States' police forces and their use as Army reserves;

xxvii—the fundamental rules of defense and protection of public health and particularly of the health of children.

Article 20 granted the Union sole jurisdiction:

i—to decree taxes:

    a) on the importation of merchandise from abroad;

    b) on the consumption of any kind of merchandise;

    c) on income or receipts of whatsoever nature;

    d) on the transfer of funds abroad;

    e) on services executed by its Government, business under its control and its instruments or contracts regulated by Federal Law;

    f) in the territories, over those which are given to the States by the Constitution;

ii—[to] collect, telegraphic and postal taxes and those for other Federal services; for the entry and clearance of ships and airplanes; coastwise trade will be free for domestic merchandise and for foreign merchandise which has already paid export duty.

It was also provided by Article 9:

The Federal Government may intervene in the States, through the nomination, by the President of the Republic, of an interventor, who will assume in the State, those functions which, according to its Constitution, belong to the Executive Power, or those which, in accordance with the necessities and the requirements of each case, are given him by the President of the Republic;

a) to prevent the imminent invasion of the National Territory by a foreign country or of one State by another, as well as to repel both forms of invasion;

b) to re-establish order which has been seriously disturbed in those cases in which the State will not or cannot;

c) to administer the State, when, for any reason whatsoever, any of its powers shall be prevented from functioning;

d) to reorganize the finances of a State which has suspended, for more than two consecutive years, the servicing of its funded debt, or which has failed to liquidate, after more than one year in arrears, the loan contracted with the Union;

e) to assure the execution of the following constitutional principles:

1—republican and representative form of government;

2—presidential government;

3—rights and guarantees assured by the Constitution;

f) to assure the execution of Federal Laws and sentences.

The States. Article 3 of the Constitutional Law asserted: "Brazil is a Federal State, constituted by the indissoluble union of the component States, the Federal District and the Territories. The existing political and territorial divisions are to be maintained." Each state was to organize its own services and pay for them with its resources. Failure to do so for three consecutive years was to result in reduction to the status of a territory (Article 8), which, of course, would have been administered directly by the federal agencies.

Article 23 as amended by Constitutional Law No. 3 of September 18, 1940, provided that the states had exclusive right:

I—to decree taxes on:

a) territorial property, except urban;

b) the transfer of property, in case of death;

c) the transfer of real property "inter vivos," including its incorporation in the capital of a society;

d) sales and consignments effected by merchants and producers, exempting from tax the first operation of the small producer as defined in the State;

e) the export of merchandise of its own production up to a maximum of 10 per centum "ad valorem," all additional taxes being forbidden;

f) industries and professions;

g) acts emanating from their governments and business under their control, or regulated by State law.

II—the collection of taxes on State services.

§ 1 Tax on sales shall be uniform, without distinction of origin, destination, or type of product.

§ 2 The tax on industries and professions shall be assessed by the State, and collected by the State and the Municipality in equal parts.

§ 3 In exceptional cases, and with the consent of the Federal Council, the export tax may be temporarily increased beyond the limit stipulated in letter e of n. I.

§ 4 The tax on the transfer of personal property is for the State in whose territory it is situated, and the transfer, in case of death, of movable property, including securities and credits, is for the State in which the succession is opened. When this has ocurred in another State or abroad, the tax shall be payable to the State in whose territory the inheritance shall have been liquidated or transferred to the heirs.

Through Article 24, "The States may create other forms of taxation. Double taxation is however forbidden, and the tax decreed by the Union will prevail where the jurisdiction is concurrent. It is within the province of the Federal Council, either on its own initiative or at the request of the tax payer, to declare that there is double taxation, and suspend the collection of the State tax."

Local Government. According to Article 26 the municípios:

are to be organized in such a manner as to assure their autonomy in all that concerns their special and peculiar conditions, particularly:
    a) the choice of councillors by direct suffrage of registered voters, according to law;
    b) to decree such taxes and imposts as are permitted by the present Constitution and the Laws of the States;
    c) the organization of public services of local character.

All prefeitos [6] were to be named by the governors of the states (Article 27). In addition to being entitled to one-half the proceeds from state taxes on industries and professions the municípios were authorized by Article 28 to levy:

    i—license taxes;
    ii—tenement tax as well as urban land tax;
    iii—taxes on public amusements;
    iv—taxes on Municipal services.

Under the regulation of the state the municípios of "the same region may join together for the installation, exploitation and administration of common public services. The group thus formed will be considered as a judicial entity, limited to the purposes for which it is organized." (Article 29.)

Obviously the form of government decreed by the Constitutional Law of November 10, 1937, envisioned a highly centralized government for Brazil. To some extent its provisions overcame the inertia of centuries, overpowered the counterinfluences of thousands of cultural lags, and placed Brazil in the way of becoming a nation where all authority and power were seated in and emanated from the Federal District. Even in a decade there was to be seen a sharp departure from the old loosely federated grouping of states and the acute segmentation that made of each município almost an independent little world. Under the terms of this constitution the federal government was supreme, the state a mere subdivision of the nation, and the município, in turn, only an administrative division of the state.

    [6] The prefeito is the administrative officer of the município or county; his office corresponds rather closely with that of the *alcalde* in Spanish-American countries.

THE CONSTITUTION OF 1946

The Estado Novo came to an end abruptly in October, 1945, during the presidential campaign to elect a successor to Vargas, with a revolt by the army. In line with Brazilian law and tradition the chief justice of the supreme court occupied the post of chief executive until the election was held and the returns indicated that Gaspar Eurico Dutra had been elected President. In less than a year a constitutional assembly had completed its work and promulgated on September 18, 1946, the present constitution of the United States of Brazil. Under its terms constitutional government now functions in Brazil, with an elected congress, state officials elected by the people of the various states, and local officials elected by the voters in the municípios. This, of course, is radically different from the practice under the Estado Novo. Nevertheless, the new constitution perpetuates most of the provisions designed to centralize government in Brazil. This is easily seen by comparing the extracts from the former constitution with those of the one presently in force.

Article 5 of the new constitution deals with the powers of the national government, specifying that it is authorized:

I—to maintain relations with foreign states and to enter into treaties and conventions with them;

II—to declare war and make peace;

III—to decree, prolong, and suspend a state of siege;

IV—to organize the armed forces, the security of the frontiers, and external defenses;

V—to permit foreign forces to cross national territory, or, in time of war, to remain within it temporarily;

VI—to authorize the production of and to supervise trade in war materials;

VII—to superintend, throughout all national territory, the services of the maritime, air, and frontier police;

VIII—to coin and emit money and to institute banks of emission;

IX—to supervise the operations of credit, capital, and insurance establishments;

X—to establish the national transportation system;

XI—to maintain the postal service and the national air mail;

XII—to carry on, directly or through authorization or concession, the telegraph service, the radio telephone service, the radio broadcasting service, the interstate and international telephone services, and air and rail services that connect the seaports and the national frontiers or cross the limits of a state;

XIII—to organize a permanent defense against droughts, rural endemic diseases, and floods;

XIV—to concede amnesty;

XV—to legislate concerning:

a) civil, commercial, penal, processual, electoral, aeronautical, and labor law;

b) the general norms of financial law; of insurance and social security; of health protection and defense; and of the penitentiary regime;

c) production and consumption;

d) the policies and bases of national education;

e) public registries and commercial groups;

f) organization, instruction, justice and guarantees of the military police and the general conditions for their utilization by the Federal Government in cases of mobilization or war;

g) expropriation;

h) civil and military requisitioning in time of war;

i) port regulation and coastal trade;

j) interstate traffic;

k) foreign and interstate trade; credit institutions, money exchange, and the sending of exchange out of the country;

l) subsoil riches, mining, metallurgy, waters, electric power, forests, hunting and fishing;

m) the monetary system and measures; the title to and quality of metals;

n) naturalization, admission, extradition, and expulsion of foreigners;

o) emigration and immigration;

p) qualifications for the exercise of the technical-scientific and liberal professions;

q) the use of national emblems;

r) the incorporation of the aborigines into the national community.

Articles 6 and 7 deal with the relationship between the federal government and the governments of the states:

Article 6. The federal right to legislate concerning the matters in Article 5, No. XV, letters b, c, d, f, h, j, l, o and r does not prohibit supplementary or complementary legislation by the states.

Article 7. The Federal Government shall not intervene in the states except in order to:

I—maintain national integrity;

II—repel foreign invasion or the invasion of one state by another;

III—put an end to civil war;

IV—guarantee the free exercise of any of the state powers;

V—assure the execution of a judicial order or decision;

VI—reorganize the finances of the State that, except in cases of superior force, shall suspend, for more than two years consecutively, the servicing of its external funded debt;

VII—insure the observance of the following principles:

a) representative republican forms [of government];

b) independence and harmony of the branches of government;

c) the proper timing of the elective functions, their duration being limited to that of the corresponding federal functions;

d) the prohibition of the re-election of governors and prefects for the immediately subsequent terms;

e) autonomy of the municípios;

f) the rendering of accounts by the administration;

g) guarantees of the Judicial Power.

The powers of the states and the limitations on their authority are specified in Articles 18 and 19, which are as follows:

Article 18. Each State shall be governed by the Constitution and by the laws which it adopts, subject to observance of the principles established in this Constitution.

Paragraph 1. To the States are reserved all of the powers, implicit or explicit, which are not withheld from them by this Constitution.

Paragraph 2. The States shall provide for the necessities of their governments, it being the duty of the Union to lend assistance in case of a public calamity.

Paragraph 3. By agreements with the Union the States may charge federal officials with the execution of state laws and services or of the acts and decisions of their authorities; and, reciprocally, the Union may, in matters in which they are competent, delegate to state officials comparable responsibilities, paying the necessary expenses.

Article 19. It is the right of the States to establish taxes upon:

I—landed property, except urban;

II—the transmission of property *causa mortis;*

III—the transmission of real estate *inter vivos* and its incorporation into the capital of corporations;

IV—the sales and consignments made by merchants and producers, including manufacturers, there being exempt however the first operation of the small producer, as defined by the state law;

V—the exportation to foreign countries of merchandise produced in the State up to a maximum of 5 per cent ad valorem, any additional whatsoever being prohibited;

VI—the activities regulated by state law, those subject to its justice, and the activities in its economy.

Paragraph 1. The land tax shall not apply to farms of less than twenty hectares, when cultivated by a proprietor, alone or with the aid of his family, who owns no other real estate.

Paragraph 2. The imposts upon the transmission of corporal goods (numbers II and III) fall to the State in whose territory they are situated.

Paragraph 3. The impost upon the transmission *causa mortis* of corporal goods, including titles and credits, belong, even when the process was commenced in a foreign country, to the State in whose territory the values of the inheritance were liquidated or transferred to the heirs.

Paragraph 4. The State shall not tax bonds of the public debt emitted by other juridical bodies of internal public right at a rate exceeding that established for its own obligations.

Paragraph 5. The impost upon sales and consignments shall be uniform, without distinction to origin and destiny.

Paragraph 6. In exceptional cases the Federal Senate may authorize the increase, for a specified time, of the tax upon exports to the maximum of 10 per cent ad valorem.

The more basic rights and limitations of the municípios are specified in Articles 23, 28, and 29. These are as follows:

Article 23. The States shall not intervene in the municípios except to regulate their finances when:

I—it is proved there is lack of punctuality in the payment of interest on a loan that is guaranteed by the State;

II—a município fails to meet for two consecutive years the payments upon its bonded debt.

Article 28. The autonomy of the município shall be assured:

I—by the election of the prefect and the *vereadores;*

II—by its own administration of that which concerns its particular interest and especially,

a) the establishment and collection of the taxes it is authorized to levy and the disbursement of its funds;

b) the organization of local public services.

Article 29. In addition to the funds derived from the provisions in paragraphs 2 and 4 of Article 15 [a share of certain taxes collected by the Federal Government and shared with the States and municípios], and of the imports that are in whole or in part transferred to them by the States, the municípios shall have the funds secured by taxes:

I—upon urban real estate;

II—licenses;

III—upon industries and professions;

iv—upon public diversions;
v—upon activities of their economies or matters over which they have
authority.

THE NATURE OF THE MUNICÍPIO

As has been stated, for administrative purposes Brazil is (in 1963)
divided into twenty-one states, five territories, and one Federal District. These large units carry on much the same administrative and
judicial functions in about the same way as the various states in the
United States. But on the local level there are some very significant
differences in the governmental structures of the United States and
Brazil.

The states and territories of Brazil were in 1950 divided into, or
made up of, 1,894 local governmental units known as municípios,
and by January 1, 1960, this number had risen to 2,763. These are
the fundamental cells in the structure of Brazilian local government.
There is a still smaller division, the *distrito de paz,* numbering 5,436
in 1950, but the distrito is merely a nominal unit and lacks real
function and vitality. In 1950 more than one-fourth (551) of all Brazil's municípios were constituted of a single distrito, and another 464
contained only two, although in a few municípios the number of
distritos ran as high as 16. But it should be emphasized that the
município is the significant unit in Brazilian government at the local
level. For this reason it is important to have a concise conception of
its nature and functions.

There is a tendency in hastily prepared reports to translate the
Portuguese word "município" by employing the English "municipality." This practice may serve the purpose in England, but in the
United States it is almost certain to result in misunderstanding, for
the município (other than the single one that constitutes the Federal
District and the city of Brasília) is in no sense an incorporated town
or city. It corresponds more closely to the North American "county"
than to the municipality, and even the county is not an exact counterpart of the município. Like the county each município has two parts,
the sede and some additional territory, usually rural. But unlike the
situation in the United States, the seat of the Brazilian município
(always ranked as a cidade, or city, regardless of the number of inhabitants) never has a corporate existence separate from that of the
município as a whole. In other words, there is no such thing as the
separate incorporation of a Brazilian village, town, or city, a practice
that is almost the rule with county seats in the United States. This
makes a considerable difference between the county and the município and between the town or city and the cidade.

There is also a sharp difference between the subdivisions of the
county and the município, and this likewise contributes to the distinction between the two. The *township, ward, beat,* or other unit into
which our county is divided, differs considerably from the Brazilian
distrito. In Brazil the latter, like the município, always consists of a

sede and a surrounding area. To distinguish the population center which constitutes the seat of a distrito from that which is the central nucleus of a município, the former is called a vila. In the United States the existence of a population center, more or less a commercial rival of the county seat, is by no means a prerequisite for the existence of one of the minor divisions into which the county is subdivided. In Brazil it is, and furthermore the territory embraced in the distrito is recognized as having a fundamental connection with the vila which forms its seat. An interesting feature, which also sheds light on the nature of the organization, is the fact that the cidade which forms the seat of the município also has the same name as the município, and the vila always has the same name as the distrito de paz.

It cannot be overstressed that for Brazilians, and especially for the overwhelming majority of them who live in the interior far from such metropolitan centers as Rio de Janeiro, São Paulo, Recife, and Salvador, the fundamental government unit is the município. As has been indicated this corresponds roughly to the county in the United States in that it is the unit into which the state is subdivided. However, in the Brazil of the past, and it remains true today even after several decades in which centralization has made tremendous strides, the municípios appear to have been the primary units of which the state was merely a loose confederation. In any case it is certain that for the average Brazilian of the lower and middle classes the federal government and even the state government seem very remote indeed. Even in areas within fifty miles of the bustling city of São Paulo, and others less than one hundred miles from the nation's capital, there are hundreds of caboclos who do not know of Getúlio Vargas.[7] In the past about the only contacts between the state and federal governments, on the one hand, and the resident of the rural areas, on the other, were the assessment and collection of taxes, and even these were done through the município. At present a state police system and state-established-and-supported schools do much to make the local people cognizant of their relationship to the larger governmental units, as does also the drafting of young men for military service. But it is still the município to which they must look for most public services and to which they must account for taxes and other obligations to the larger society. The lack of separately incorporated towns and villages and the purely perfunctory functions of the distritos still further serve to accentuate the importance of the município's role.

THE SIZE OF THE MUNICÍPIO

General Considerations. The differences between one município and another in Brazil are so great that averages mean little until the

---

[7] Cf. J. V. Freitas Marcondes and T. Lynn Smith, "The Caipira of the Paraitinga Valley, Brazil," *Social Forces,* XXXI (October, 1952).

range of variation is thoroughly in mind. Therefore, let us begin by examining briefly some of the extremes among the various municípios from the standpoints of area, number of inhabitants, and density of population, which is the relation between area and population. Some Brazilian municípios have areas larger than those of many of the states; and in 1950 the density of population ranged from that in the município of the Federal District (now the state of Guanabara) where there were 2,030 persons per square kilometer to that in the município of Catarimâni, in the territory of Rio Branco, and the município of Aripuanã, Mato Grosso, where there was only one person for each eighty-five and seventy-one square kilometers of territory, respectively. As between various states there are also large differences in the expanse covered by the average município. From these demographic angles, the situation varies all the way from that found in parts of São Paulo and Minas Gerais, where the municípios are small, closely knit town-country communities, to the tremendous, unconnected, and disjointed agglomerations of virtually uninhabited plains and jungles that are included within the limits of single municípios in parts of Mato Grosso, Amazonas, and Pará.

The Number and Distribution of Municípios. In all of Brazil the total number of municípios in 1960 was 2,763, a figure which is considerably more than one-half the number of counties in the United States. At first glance the size of the Brazilian município does not compare closely with that of the county in our country. However, when the immense, thinly populated areas of Mato Grosso and the Amazon Valley are omitted, in size, number of inhabitants, and density, the Brazilian unit much more closely approximates that of the county in the United States. Particularly is this true in the South, in São Paulo, in Minas Gerais, and in the municípios which make up the first few tiers back from the entire length of Brazil's seacoast. However, as is the case with the county, there is great variation in all of these respects between the various states of the union and between the local units within the same state.

Even a little study makes evident the fact that it is very difficult to generalize the rules which have determined the number, distribution, and size of Brazil's municípios. On the whole there seems to be a fairly close association between the number of inhabitants in a state and the number of municípios into which it is divided. However, this relationship is by no means a constant one, and the minimum requirements for the formation of new municípios, as well as the facility with which the process of subdividing existing municípios proceeds, show considerable variation from one state to another. Furthermore, Brazilian statesmen encounter about the same difficulties as do those in the United States when attempts are made to consolidate local governmental units, even in areas that have been suffering from depopulation.

Consider some of the data relative to the distribution of municípios among the states. Brazil's most populous state, São Paulo, was divided, as of 1960, into 504 municípios, 18.2 per cent of all in the nation; and Minas Gerais, with 485 municípios (17.6 per cent of the total), was a close second. Other states with comparatively large numbers of municípios in 1960 are as follows: Bahia, 194; Goiás, 179; Paraná, 162; Rio Grande do Sul, 150; Ceará, 147; and Pernambuco and Santa Catarina, 102 each. On the other end of the scale, there were only forty municípios in Espírito Santo, forty in Amazonas, and fifty-six in Alagôas.

The município of small area is characteristic of the states of Alagôas, Espírito Santo, Paraíba, Pernambuco, Rio Grande do Norte, Rio de Janeiro, São Paulo, and Sergipe. Minas Gerais, although somewhat intermediate because of its extensive pastoral municípios in the northern and western portions of the state, also should probably be placed with this group. Medium-sized municípios are the prevailing

TABLE LXIX

Distribution of Municípios According to Number
of Inhabitants, 1960 *

Number of inhabitants	Number of municípios	Per cent of municípios
Total	2,767	100.0
5,000 or less	279	10.0
5,001–10,000	650	23.5
10,001–20,000	847	30.6
20,001–50,000	782	28.3
50,001–100,000	144	5.2
100,001–500,000	58	2.1
500,001–1,000,000	5	0.2
More than 1,000,000	2	0.1

* Source: "Sinopse Preliminar do Censo Demográfico," VII Recenseamento Geral do Brasil, 1960, 12–13.

type in Bahia, Ceará, Maranhão, Minas Gerais, Paraíba, Paraná, Piauí, Rio Grande do Sul, and Santa Catarina. In this category, too, probably should be placed Goiás, although the northern part of this state extends into the sparsely populated Amazon region where the extensive, gangling, and thinly populated município is the rule. The West and the great Amazon Valley are the areas of the extensive, loosely knit municípios. Here are to be classified the states of Amazonas, Mato Grosso, and Pará, as well as the territories of Acre, Amapá, Rondonia, and Rio Branco.

Number of Inhabitants. The range in the number of inhabitants per município is tremendous. See Table LXIX. A considerable number of them have populations of less then 5,000, and those with less than 25,000 residents are the rule. On the other hand, a few municípios such as those of São Paulo, Rio de Janeiro, Recife, Belo Horizonte, Pôrto Alegre, and Salvador have many hundreds of thousands, and even millions, of people living within their boundaries.

THE EVOLUTION OF THE MUNICÍPIO

The steps by which a population center advances through the various stages essential to becoming the seat of a município have been set forth by Professor Sud Mennucci in connection with his analysis of the breaking up of Blumenau município in the state of Santa Catarina. The division of this município, aimed at reducing the political strength of the German population, finally took place through an act of the Federal Interventor early in 1934. Earlier, on October 10, 1930, the legislative assembly at Florianópolis approved Law No. 1,708 which created the *comarca* of Rio Grande do Sul, formed of the districts of Bela Aliança and Timbó of the município of Blumenau. The law establishing this new judicial district also revoked all the "dispositions to the contrary." Mennucci indicates that this revoked all national tradition and as an explanation set forth the normal process of evolution. A population center begins as a mere *arraial* (a camp or a center at which people gather for festivals); then it develops into a village or police district; next it evolves into the seat of a distrito de paz; finally it is elevated to the category of cidade and made seat of a município, and only then is entitled to be the head or seat of the comarca.[8] The nature of this process is better understood if one becomes familiar with a few case histories.

Palhoça, Santa Catarina. An excellent case illustrating in a general way the evolution of the Brazilian município is that of Palhoça situated on the mainland across from the island on which stands Florianópolis, the capital city of Santa Catarina.[9] The seat of this município had its beginning in 1793. This was during a period of struggle between Spain and Portugal for possession of the lands that now constitute the southernmost states of Brazil. The commanding officer of the Portuguese forces on the island where the present state capital is located desired to ensure his position by providing a possible refuge on the mainland where there would be accumulated a store of corn meal and other essential supplies. For this purpose he ordered a substantial farmer-citizen, who had made clearings and plantings where the cidade of Palhoça now stands, to construct a storehouse or *palhoça* (building covered with thatch) that might serve in case of necessity. Deriving its name in this manner, the future seat of the município lapsed into obscurity for almost a century, remaining merely a small neighborhood where were located a few modest houses.

As was generally the case in Brazil, the next impulse came with the location of a small chapel in 1864. This introduced one of the prime requirements for future growth. About the same time improvements were made in the road or trail leading up the abrupt coastal

[8] "A Subdivisão do Município de Blumenau," *Geografia*, II, No. 4, pp. 11–23.
[9] The data presented in the following paragraphs were drawn from José Lupércio Lopes, *Palhoça* (Florianópolis, 1939), 19 ff.

range to the interior highlands, and the small center gained in economic importance. Only four years later, in 1868, the village had gained sufficient importance that a second chapel was begun—the one that today is the matriz (central church to which a number of surrounding chapels are subordinate) of the parish. The village had then become both a religious and a commercial center.

The other necessary social developments were not long in coming. In 1870 another essential community function was established in the village with the opening of the first school. The addition of the educational function, combined with a further increase of trade and commerce and the adequate provision of religious influences, led to the next essential step—the addition of the political function. In 1872 the vice president of the province handed down a resolution which made the village a police district with a resident subdelegate of police.

In the meanwhile the economic functions of the village were gaining in importance, and in the surrounding area farming and such rural industry as the grinding of meal and the granulation of sugar were gaining in importance on the establishments of the nearby fazendeiros. In 1881 a post office was located in Palhoça, and the same year saw a further development of the educational system with the establishment, in strict accord with the best Brazilian educational patterns, of a school for girls. In this way, step by step, proceeded the development of what was to be the seat of a new município. In the words of Lupércio Lopes it "obtained favors, now from the president of the province, now from the câmara at São José, to which it pertained and whose membership included some persons from Palhoça."

The município next located a paid agent in the village to handle the fiscal affairs of the district and especially to collect imposts. Favored by a smiling providence, agriculture prospered. Commerce and industry developed rapidly, the latter including by 1882 small factories for the extraction of vegetable oils, establishments for the tanning and working of leather, and *charqueadas* (plants in which dried meat or charque is prepared) in addition to the numerous small engenhos engaged in the grinding of meal and making of sugar on the surrounding fazendas. The trading function also flourished. Each Monday a large number of boats overflowing with produce from the neighboring districts arrived at the center. Returning on Tuesdays, they continued throughout the week to transport large quantities of wood, lumber, grain, and other farm products into Palhoça. Much of the building materials merely passed through on the way to large centers of consumption. In the meanwhile a thriving business was developing with the interior settlements in the mountains and on the plateaus. From Palhoça departed each week numerous pack trains carrying salt, kerosene, sugar, and flour to the settlements on the upland interior. To a considerable extent this interior trade developed at the expense of São José, seat of the município to which Palhoça still belonged.

The next important step in the evolution of Palhoça was along religious lines, although under the empire there was no clear demarcation between religious and political structure in Brazil. Complying with petitions that had been received from citizens of the village, the legislative assembly of the province elevated Palhoça to the category of freguesia (parish) through an act passed on November 8, 1882. This procedure, as well as the undifferentiated nature of religious and political authority, is well illustrated by the wording of the act.

Art. 1. The police district of Palhoça is hereby separated from the parish of S. José and constituted a new parish under the protection of Senhor Bom Jesus de Nazaré.

Art. 2. The new parish will have as limits: upon the north, the river Maroim as far as the boundary of the parish of S. Pedro de Alcântara; upon the south, the river Cubatão as far as the limits of the parish of Sto. Amaro do Cubatão; on the east, the Ocean; on the west, the parishes already mentioned.

Art. 3. The chapel under construction in the seat of the same parish shall serve as the Matriz. Given and passed in the Palace of the Governor of the Province Santa Catarina, on the eighth of November of the year eighteen hundred and eighty two. (signed) Antônio Gonçalves Chaves, president of the Province.[10]

The signing of this law was the signal for an enthusiastic celebration in Palhoça, festivities which featured the marching of school children, brilliant lighting of the houses and the streets, a torchlight parade led by the musical society called "Hope and Charity," orations praising the president and the assembly, bonfires, and dances. The celebration continued a second day, which was Sunday, highlighted by a band concert in a stand especially constructed for the purpose.

The new parish did not long delay in the installation of a public cemetery befitting a freguesia. Dry land high on a hill was secured for the purpose and the assistance of the provincial president again enlisted, this functionary decreeing that the lands of the cemetery should be fenced at the expense of the state government. Today the cemetery is divided into three parts—for Protestants, for the general Catholic community, and a third section especially reserved for the Brotherhood of Nossa Senhora do Parto.

In 1886, the same year as the establishment of the cemetery, the police district of Palhoça advanced another step in the political scale and became a distrito de paz, entitled to elect a justice of the peace to function locally in judicial matters. Because of the unstable situation brought about by the freeing of the slaves, the overthrow of the monarchy, and the establishment of the republic, the next few years did not see the carrying out of this provision. But on January 29, 1891, the police district was again (this time by the constituted authorities of the state as part of the republic) raised from a police district to the more advanced justice-of-the-peace district. In its new status the functions of registrar were lodged in local authorities and records of marriages, births, and deaths began to be kept in Palhoça. Formally organized political parties also now came to play an important part in community life.

[10] *Ibid.*, 24–25.

Very shortly afterwards followed the ultimate step attained by the thriving small center, the elevation to the seat of a município; in other words it was officially recognized as the social, political, and economic center or a designated portion of the state of Santa Catarina. In attaining this desired status Palhoça was greatly aided by the resistance offered by its population to the revolutionary forces that attempted to seize control of Brazil in 1893. For a time Santa Catarina was dominated by the rebellious forces, and many of Palhoça's leading citizens were imprisoned. But when the rebellion was put down and government forces once again dominated Santa Catarina, Palhoça received its reward by being elevated to the rank of seat of a new município, one that was constituted out of lands formerly included in the município of São José. The decree which rewarded Palhoça at the same time that it punished São José, not so steadfast in its allegiances, was promulgated on April 24, 1894, and read in part as follows:

Art. 1. The frequesia of Palhoça is hereby separated from the município of São José and raised to the category of vila in order to form, along with the frequesias of Santo Amaro do Cubatão, Enseada de Brito and the districts of Teresópolis, Santa Isabel, Capivarí and Santa Teresa, a município with the denomination of município of Palhoça; having for a seat the vila Maroim and the present boundary of the districts of S. Isabel, with the excolony Angelina; upon the south and the west, the município of S. José.[11]

Since 1894 the position of Palhoça has still further improved. Proper quarters for the various functionaries were provided in a new public building constructed in 1894–95, a building which was inaugurated in August, 1895, with a grand ball. In 1903 a telegraph station was installed in the vila. In 1906 Palhoça added to its distinctions and functions as seat of the município the additional honors of becoming the seat of the comarca.

The territory included in the new comarca comprised the municípios of Palhoça and Garopaba, both of which had previously been included in the comarca whose seat was in São José. The same year was founded a newspaper, *A Voz da Palhoça*. Still another political and governmental function fell to the vila when in 1912 a federal tax-collecting office was established in it. Now, under the provisions of the late decrees, in common with all other seats of municípios, Palhoça ranks as a city.

The manner in which the establishment of the Estado Novo affected Palhoça and other Brazilian municípios may be described in the words of the author of the monograph on this local governmental unit.

At present, by virtue of the provisions of the new Brazilian constitution promulgated by the eminent statesman, his excellency Dr. Getúlio Vargas, on November 10, 1937, all state assemblies as well as municipal councils are dissolved.

[11] *Ibid.*, 29.

The old office of superintendent came to be called *Prefeito Municipal* and is filled only upon nomination by the various Federal Interventors in the States.

The Prefeitos are obligated to present accounts of their acts to an administrative department, composed of capable members nominated by the Federal Interventors.[12]

Pirassununga, São Paulo. Another município that may be chosen to illustrate the evolution of the Brazilian local governmental unit is Pirassununga, lying in the north-central portion of the state of São Paulo. Its chief bid to fame is as the home of Fernando Costa, former Brazilian Secretary of Agriculture and former Federal Interventor in the state of São Paulo. An interesting little monograph has been published which outlines the development of the city and the município [13] and enables us to know of the major features in its evolution.

The city of Pirassununga, seat of the município of the same name, is located some 125 miles north of the capital of the state on the main route to the Triângulo of Minas Gerais and to Goiás. It is rather typical of numerous small industrial and commercial centers scattered throughout the state of São Paulo. Like so many Brazilian place names, Pirassununga is of Indian origin and probably means "where the falling water makes a noise" or else "where the fish make a noise." In either case it has reference to the rapids in the Mogí-Guassú River near the city. The thriving little city is served by the Paulista railroad, by which the distance to São Paulo City is about 150 miles. Today the município has some 27,500 inhabitants, about one-half of whom live in the seat, and occupies an area of 852 square kilometers. Only a little over one hundred years ago, at the time of Saint-Hilaire's travels through this portion of São Paulo, the entire area was settled very thinly by scattered cattle fazendas. At that time the Paulistas occupied a much less prominent place in Brazilian affairs than they do today, and the eminent French scholar seemed always eager to comment on the ignorance and misery of the scattered population he found living in this part of the state. He seemed particularly to enjoy contrasting their poor conditions with the more fortunate lot of their fellows in the state of Minas Gerais.[14] Saint-Hilaire passed through this part of Brazil in 1819 only shortly before the date accepted as the founding of Pirassununga, August 6, 1823. In the absence of precise knowledge relative to the foundation of Pirassununga, August 6, the date of the celebration dedicated to the Senhor Bom Jesus dos Aflitos, patron of the locality, is considered the probable one.

By 1838 there were sufficient inhabitants in the *bairro* (district) of Pirassununga to petition the Bishop of São Paulo for the establishment of a chapel in the settlement. The petition was granted and

[12] *Ibid.*, 133.

[13] *Monografia do Município de Pirassununga* (Rio de Janeiro, 1939). See also Cyro, Jr., *Pirassununga Progride* (São Paulo, 1901), for an account of political struggle which once convulsed this município.

[14] Cf. Saint-Hilaire, *Viagem à Provincia de São Paulo*, 113–14, 116, 124, 130, 131–32, and 138.

the chapel of Senhor Bom Jesus de Pirassununga was "created" by a law of November 21, 1838, signed by Manoel, Bishop of São Paulo. This was the permission for building a chapel and the delineation of the area it should serve. The limits of this religious unit became the first boundaries of what is now the local governmental unit, the município of Pirassununga. (As was generally the case in Brazil until late in the nineteenth century, there was little or no thought of differentiating religious from political boundaries.) The law referred to above described the boundaries of the chapel at Pirassununga as follows:

> Beginning on the rio Mogí-Guassú at the mouth of the Meio creek and ascending this by the principal stream which heads in a portion of the Vila de Constituição, making there a right angle, going to the right through the sertão, dividing with the Chapel of São José where it should be more appropriate and useful to have another chapel to Quilombo creek, descending it dividing with the Freguesia de Araraquara until it empties into the rio Mogí-Guassú, and ascending the latter to the point of beginning.

And it was also specified that the chapel should be built on high ground.

Only four years later, in 1842, the chapel was elevated to the category of freguesia, retaining the former limits.[15] The same year, August 6, when the day of the patron saint was celebrated, the residents of the locality presented lands to constitute a patrimony for the newly established parish.

Either this elevation in the religious scale was equivalent to graduation politically into a município, or the latter was accomplished soon after, for the records begin to contain documents relating to the registry of births and marriages and the pardoning of criminals; and in 1866, when the vila took its next reported step to the judicial category of *têrmo,* the law signed by the governor of São Paulo carried salutations to the president and members of the "Câmara Municipal de Pirassununga." [16] At this time, too, the município, which formed part of the judicial district or comarca of Araraquara, got its first local judge.

The mother church is reported to have been in a deplorable condition at this time, but extensive repairs were commenced in 1870. This same year the parish of Pirassununga was distinguished by being elevated to the category of ecclesiastical comarca. In 1874 another chapel was established in the small center. The railway reached that far west in 1877; the same year a Masonic lodge was established, and Dom Pedro II paid the little city a visit. Two years later (1879) the vila was elevated to the category of cidade.[17]

Outstanding events since the center reached the city stage include the construction of the central park in 1866, the establishment of newspapers in 1887 and 1889, the organization of a unit of the National Guard in 1892, the change to republican forms of government

15 *Monografia do Município de Pirassununga,* 77–78.
16 *Ibid.,* 83.
17 *Ibid.,* 89.

in 1892, the beginning of a new mother church in 1895, the inaugura-
tion of a water system in 1896 and of an electric light system in 1897,
the opening of a hospital in 1902, the completion of a bridge over the
Mogí-Guassú the same year, and, in 1903, the organization of the
municipal band.[18]

PREREQUISITES FOR THE ESTABLISHMENT
OF NEW MUNICÍPIOS

Under what circumstances do new Brazilian municípios come into
being? What are the prerequisites for the establishment of one of
these governmental units? Answers to such questions are of considerable import in understanding the nature of Brazil's local governmental structure and the evolution of its rural governmental institutions. Generally, new municípios come into being by the simple
process of subdivision of an old one. When a vila, seat of one of the
distritos, or a povoção in the município increases to a size and obtains
economic functions as a trade, market, and transportation center to a
point that it rivals the seat, a movement generally is started in local
and state political circles for the creation of a new unit. This is the
process of raising the vila to the category of cidade, which automatically means the creation of a new município out of the new seat and
part of the surrounding area. Before 1939 these division processes
went on in a continuous manner. On January 1 of that year there
were 1,575 municípios functioning in Brazil. This number remained
unchanged for about six years, when, with the end of the Estado
Novo, the process of creating new municípios was resumed with
great fervor.

In the future, changes promise to come in large numbers. However, as in the past, certain rather fixed criteria will probably govern
more or less the dismemberment of old municípios and the establishment of new ones. The word *more* is employed because there is a
certain order embedded in a general idea of the manner in which
local governmental changes should proceed, and in Brazil these have
gained expression in law as well as in practice. *Less* is used because
the endless struggle always going on between parties, factions, and
cliques in any local governmental area (including those of Brazil)
for political advantage, power, or promise may result in favoritism
to certain local areas, districts, or personalities.

What are some of the principal criteria generally used in connection with the establishment of new municípios? The constitution of
1906, the organic law on the subject, prescribed that a new município
must (1) have a minimum of 10,000 inhabitants, (2) be able to raise
twenty contos of taxes for local use, (3) have as its seat a population
center containing at least one thousand "good houses," (4) provide in
the new seat adequate buildings for the local governmental offices, a

[18] *Ibid.*, 90–98.

jail, and at least two schools, one for each sex, (5) be constituted by the elevation of a distrito de paz only upon petition of the inhabitants and after the municípios affected had been given a hearing, and (6) select as the site of the new seat a location that is already possessed of good health conditions or one that may easily be transformed into a healthful locality.[19] However, even in São Paulo as late as 1931 there were more than forty municípios which did not meet these criteria, some of them failing to meet all of the principal ones, the first three listed.[20]

As incorporated into law, the criteria in force vary from state to state, but all insist on a minimum population and a minimum amount of tax receipts. The minimum population established as a prerequisite is set at 40,000 in the state by Rio de Janeiro and at only 10,000 in Paraná and São Paulo. With respect to this particular requirement the statistical section of the São Paulo Instituto de Hygiene, after a study of the situation in that state, recommended as a minimum requirement a population of 12,502 persons of whom at least 3,276 should be residents of the seat. Similar are the variations in the requirement with respect to the minimum amount of tax money collected, Rio de Janeiro establishing the figure of 150 contos ($7,500) per year, São Paulo 100 contos, and Paraná and Paraíba only 50 contos. The São Paulo agency referred to above recommended a minimum of 147 contos.[21] Other states probably vary considerably from these, but all have criteria on the books. In 1952 when he was in Brazil as advisor on agrarian reform the writer recommended that one of the requisites for becoming or remaining a município be the maintenance of at least one secondary school with at least five full-time teachers.

Between 1940 and 1960 a total of 1,003 new municípios were created in Brazil. São Paulo alone created 234 new municípios in that period, and Minas Gerais 196. Goiás and Paraná were the other states in which large numbers of new municípios came into being, the figures being 127 and 113, respectively.

CONSOLIDATION OF MUNICÍPIOS

The various states of the Brazilian confederation face much the same problems growing out of the multiplication of local governmental units, especially municípios, as do the several states in the United States because of the ever-growing number of counties. In Brazil, as in the United States, it has been relatively easy to create new local governmental units but extremely difficult to consolidate

19 Sud Mennucci, *Brasil Desunido* (São Paulo, 1932), 54–55.
20 *Ibid.*, 57.
21 Cf. Orlando M. Carvalho, *Problemas Fundamentaes do Municipio* (São Paulo, 1937), 21–23. Rampant inflation since 1940 has, of course, destroyed the significance of these financial criteria and also has made it difficult to establish new ones that would not be out of date almost as quickly as they were adopted. On this point see Smith "The Giant Awakes: Brazil," *loc. cit.*, 102.

old ones.[22] Even when shifting economies, the exhaustion of natural resources, and the depopulation of some areas leave many municípios with insufficient resources, income, and population to carry on effectively, it is not easy to effect consolidations. This results in an excessive burden, both upon the local citizens and upon the states, for the maintenance and administration of essential services. That there have been numerous attempts to bring about reform indicates that many of Brazil's leaders have correctly analyzed the problem. That these attempts have not brought lasting improvement indicates merely the tenacity with which local governmental units are perpetuated by the "courthouse rings," and the extreme difficulty of getting the general social welfare placed above that of local special interests.

Probably the most important movement for consolidation of municípios in Brazil was that which took place in São Paulo during the early years of the decade 1930 to 1940. Life was given to the movement by a series of newspaper articles written by Professor Mennucci, at that time director of the state press, and published in *O Estado de São Paulo*. These dealt in a straightforward way with the problems of the municípios and their subdivisions, the distritos de paz. These articles pointedly supplied data relative to the population and tax receipts in the various municípios in the state, analyzed the systems of communication between the rural portions of the municípios and the cidades which were their seats, indicated in unmistakable terms that reform was highly necessary, and specified some of the most important abuses that needed correction.[23] So far the story is little more than has happened repeatedly in the United States. But the matter did not end there.

Only a few days after the publication of the last of the articles, January 21, 1931, the Federal Interventor in the state handed down Decree No. 4,846. After recognizing that the existing manner in which the municípios were constituted did not correspond with public necessities and that many municípios did not meet the conditions for separate existence, the decree provided (1) that the secretaria (or department) of the interior should establish a commission of three members for the purpose of reorganizing the administrative division of the state into municípios, (2) that this commission, of which the state director of the *Commissão Geographica e Geologica* was made a member ex officio, should study and make recommendations to the secretary of the interior relative to the reorganization to be effected. In the decree it was stipulated that in the new alignment each município should have a minimum tax income of one hundred contos yielded by an impost of twenty milreis, that the seat of each município should be near enough to the rural territories of the município that it would not work to their advantage to be attached

[22] In neither country has public sentiment arrived at the stage of punishing politicians who lead the way in carving up administrative and judicial areas.

[23] Together with other articles on political and administrative reform these later were published in book form in *Brasil Desunido*, referred to above.

to some other município, that the territory of each município should be all in one piece, and that the debts and contracts of existing municípios should be safeguarded.[24]

The commission, which included Mennucci among its members, reported on September 15, 1931. At this time a detailed analysis was given of the problem and the probable result, if the criteria laid down were applied rigorously. It was recommended that São Paulo move only in concert with the other states of the union and stated frankly that it was impossible to remake the administrative map of the state. Recognized also were the difficulties created and perpetuated by forty years of local political bickering and strife between the municípios and among the various community and neighborhood groups of which they are constituted. The net result in São Paulo was the appointment of another special commission by Decree No. 5,252 of November 5, 1931. Revolutionary years immediately intervened and after this brief flurry of interest, the number of municípios continued to increase to a total of 270 in 1940.

More immediate results came in other states. On June 26, 1931, the Federal Interventor in the northeastern state of Piauí signed Decree No. 1,279, which reduced the number of municípios in that state to twenty-seven by extinguishing nineteen municípios and attaching their territories to the remaining units. Nevertheless, by 1940 all of these extinguished were back on the list, most of them without change of name. Similar was the situation in Bahia, where Decree No. 4,846 signed on January 21, 1932, made a drastic reduction in the number of municípios by the process of consolidatioh. Nevertheless, by 1940 almost without exception the municípios that had been eliminated were again on the list.[25]

RURAL-URBAN CONFLICT WITHIN THE MUNICÍPIO

Since every Brazilian município consists of two parts, the seat and the surrounding territory, the urban and rural portions, a considerable amount of social conflict between the constellation of interests centering in the cidade and those of the people residing in the smaller population centers and on the farms and fazendas of the município is inevitable. As in the United States the village or town forms the line of cleavage between rural and urban societies and is the arena of conflict between city and country. Throughout most of Brazil the advantage in this rural-urban conflict definitely lies with the center. For one thing the concentration of population and the ease of communication contribute to a unity of thought and action on the part of those who live in the seat, whereas the wide dispersal of population, lack of communication between the various rural neighborhoods, and relative scarcity of contact between inhabitants of the rural areas all make joint effort on the part of the agricultural

[24] Mennucci, *Brasil Desunido*, 100–101.
[25] For these decrees and the municípios eliminated, see *ibid.*, 102–108.

classes very difficult. Farmers, cattle growers, miners, fishermen, woodcutters, and other rural groups may resent the spending of tax money for the building of schools, the construction and maintenance of parks, the paving of streets, the supplying of water, lights, and sewage disposal in the cidade, while the rural roads are mere quagmires, streams are unbridged, and rural children are unable to attend a nearby school; but as a general rule, they are able to do very little about remedying the situation. Divided loyalty on the part of many of the wealthiest and most powerful agriculturists makes the advantage of the cidade in município affairs even more pronounced. If the most important fazendeiros do not actually live in the seat and merely commute occasionally to their lands, they at least maintain a "town house" in addition to their country residence. In this manner many of their interests become associated with those of the people in the center. As to the colonos and camaradas who labor on the fazendas, and the sitiantes who till their own small farmsteads in the remote, hilliest, and poorest agricultural lands of the município, what they think, say, or do seldom is of very great import. Thus for the most part the inhabitants of the seat, or cidade, have carte blanche in município affairs.

But there are important exceptions to this rule in Brazil and particularly among the German settlements in Santa Catarina and other southern states. In Santa Catarina the seat of the município is often completely subservient to the farming classes that live in the surrounding areas. In this part of Brazil the farmers live on the land which they own and operate themselves. *Colono,* instead of referring to a farm laborer as in São Paulo, here refers to a small owner-operator, and there are very few farm laborers in the settlements. Thus the rural population is constituted almost entirely of a hard-working, self-sufficient, and homogeneous middle class. Being in the overwhelming majority, they see to it ʰthat the expenditure of public funds does not solely benefit the persons living in the seat of the município. Furthermore, the loyalty and the solidarity of rural folk are more likely attached to such well-known seats of German influence and culture as Blumenau and Joinville rather than to the seats of the municípios in which they reside. Thus in the past it was from Blumenau that they received cultural, political, and religious orientation (the three were not thoroughly differentiated) by means of newspapers (particularly *Der Urwaldsbote* of Blumenau before its publication was prohibited by the Conselho Nacional de Imprensa in September, 1941), visits of German travelers and agents, and the very close attention of the clergy, particularly those of the Evangelical Church. The paper came weekly and furnished the basic orientation in things German. Travelers were numerous. Guided by their fellows from Blumenau, few lost the opportunity to visit the German neighborhoods and agricultural communities. There, in small assemblies called for that purpose, each did his bit to fire these third-, fourth-, fifth-, and sixth-generation Brazilians with pride in their Germanic ethnic origins and contributed his share in helping them understand the wonderful implications of the expression "Auslandsdeutsche."

But the situation in the German colonies is the exception. Elsewhere the advantage is all with the inhabitants of the seat. The best analysis of the situation is that by Nelson Werneck Sodré who has written about Mato Grosso. Here in Brazil's Wild West great rivalry grew up between the urban part of the município and the rural elements. In early times the rural class dominated the câmaras, but with the growth of cities the fazendeiros were repelled to the country, where they remained divorced from the local councils. This greatly restricted the realm of influence of the local government, and in some cases its effectiveness was confined to the urban areas. Says Werneck Sodré:

The plains, large properties, and poverty reduce the municipal organization to a mere conventionality incapable of governing the territory over which it has dominion. The weakening of authority, through these insane anomalies, results in the antagonism between rural and urban, city and country, placing municipal activity in perpetual conflict with human groupings employed in working on the land. . . .

Social instability is sanctioned by this great disparity. On one side the city, on the other the country. On one hand social authority, on the other the rule of the pastoral class. On both sides, poverty.[26]

THE DEBILITY OF LOCAL GOVERNMENT

Gradually in São Paulo and the other southern states governmental activities are becoming sufficiently organized to provide a considerable share of the population with educational and health services, and reasonable security of life and property, and to perform the other governmental functions that are thought essential in modern society. A close scrutiny reveals, however, that most of even local governmental services is being supplied by state agencies. Thus the state is doing more than the municípios in providing schools and in building roads. It is the state police who have rid São Paulo of bandits; state officers at the border take custody of the knives and daggers of pilgrims from Minas Gerais who are going to the shrine of Nossa Senhora Apparecida and give them back when the visitors return. It is the state of São Paulo which is developing an agricultural program that often pioneers for the National Ministry and far outranks any found elsewhere in Latin America. In fact São Paulo is demonstrating what a state may do on the local level, even when it is handicapped by a very rudimentary system of local government.

But the debility of local government is a serious drawback, even in São Paulo, and where state governments are less active it is even more deplorable. It is difficult to see how matters can be remedied to any extent without fundamental changes in thinking that eventually come to be reflected in constitutional changes. Obviously the prohibi-

---

[26] Werneck Sodré, *Oeste*, 165–66.

tion on "double taxation" and the vesting of the right to levy property or land taxes exclusively in the state place the local government in a strait jacket. In an agricultural community, such as is the residence of the majority of Brazil's population, the land seems to be the only economic base that, through taxation, can be used in order to pool individual efforts sufficiently that necessary educational, health, police, welfare, communication, and other essential governmental services may be maintained. Unless local people can use the device of a land tax, or a general property tax, to secure a budget of sufficient size, there seems to be no well-tested technique by which such desirable ends may be achieved. The local government in Brazil long has languished in an anemic condition because the land was in the hands of a few, a small minority who could send their children away to school, maintain private armies to provide their own protection, and supply their own health services. Naturally they would not vote taxes on themselves for the welfare of the community. Now this condition is passing in many parts of the country, and a considerable number of Brazilians feel the necessity of having more and better schools and roads, protection from banditry, and health and sanitary services. They also are beginning to recognize that to finance these benefits each man must contribute not one or two days' effort per year, but the equivalent of weeks', or even a month's, income. Under these new conditions it seems decidedly unwise to deny the people in the local unit of government, the município, the right to levy land or property taxes on themselves and the privilege of using the land tax as a means of pooling their efforts to supply themselves with the services they so badly need. The lack of these services in a world where contacts with other peoples are multiplying rapidly is likely to give Brazilians a decided sense of inferiority.

The very insignificant amount of man's effort that is pooled for the provision of national, state, and local governmental services is inferred from the expenditures of the national, state, and local governments. In 1958 these three levels of government raised a total of 245 million contos in revenues and expended 271 million in the provision of governmental services. At that time the population of the nation was approximately sixty-nine million. In other words, it may be said that national, state, and local governments together spent about $24.00 per inhabitant. This gives a fairly objective basis for estimating the extent to which government has functioned as a means whereby the population pools its efforts in order to provide essential services.

Of the total amount disbursed, the lion's share was spent by the national government. It alone expended 141 million contos or about $13.00 per inhabitant. The states together spent only 104 million contos or some $9.00 per person. Of this sum São Paulo alone paid out 47 million contos, or over two-fifths of the total. The 2,631 municípios expended only 27 million contos or about $2.00 for each man, woman, and child in Brazil. Thus it is evident that the nation, the state, and especially the município get from the ordinary citizen a very small proportion of his total annual effort, and it is little wonder that education, health, and other essential services are poorly supported.

Security of Life and Property. A very significant result of weak local government is the insecurity of life and property that long prevailed in parts of Brazil. As was the situation in the United States when communications and systems of transportation were in a comparable stage of development, there are sporadic outbreaks of banditry in various portions of Brazil. In the Northeast the disease is chronic. Gustavo Barroso said there were states whose "entire sertão is almost solely occupied by *cangaceiros*" and cited the municípios of Teixeira, Alagoa do Monteiro, and Patos in Paraíba as examples.[27] Many of the leaders of such bands attained a notoriety at least approaching those of the James or the Dalton gangs of our own frontier days. Shortly after the writer had passed through the mountainous sections of southern Minas Gerais in April of 1942, the Rio de Janeiro papers carried a dispatch from the small textile center of Juiz de Fora relating the capture and imprisonment of one of these small robber bands. This group of brigands, consisting of some eight or ten men, well mounted and heavily armed with carbines and revolvers, was led by one Mario Alonso, known as "O Lampeão Mineiro" (Lampeão of Minas Gerais). Its field of operations was the mountainous section along the boundary between the states of Rio de Janeiro and Minas Gerais, not very far distant from Brazil's modern and beautiful capital city. At the time of their capture this band had already committed a long list of assaults on the fazendas of the region, their murders alone amounting to several dozen.[28]

It is to the Northeast, however, that one's thoughts most frequently turn when mention is made of banditry or the inability of local and state governments to guarantee security of life and property. The great sertões of this region have spawned a long line of famous desperados and have provided them with an ideal setting in which to carry on their atrocities.[29] Cabeleira, Viriato, Antonio Silvino, Rio Negro, Jesuino Brilhante are only a few of those whose exploits have etched their names in the history and folklore of the region.[30] The

[27] Barroso, *Terra de Sol*, 126.

[28] Cf. *O Globo* of Rio de Janeiro, May 7, 1942.

[29] The literature on this subject is voluminous. An interesting summary statement with some analysis is found in Carneiro Leão, *A Sociedade Rural*, 145–59. More extensive studies are X. Oliveira, *Beatos e Cangaceiros*, and Pedro Baptista, *Cangaceiros do Nordeste* (Paraíba, 1929). Cf. the excellent description in Barroso, *Terra de Sol*, 119–66. The discriminating reader will observe that Antonio Conselheiro, Padre Cicero, and other leaders of schismatic religious movements are not discussed in connection with banditry. There is, however, some justification for including them, as is frequently done by Brazilian writers on the subject.

[30] I have an interesting collection of folk tales concerning the lives and loves of the most noted of the cangaceiros. They are written in verse and are sold for a mere pittance in the markets throughout northern and northeastern Brazil. But more important, they are sung to the accompaniment of the guitar by the blind singers who frequent the market places of these areas. Already Lampeão is taking on many of the characteristics of a Robin Hood. A free translation of some of the titles in the collection are as follows: "Heroic Acts of the Bandit, Antonio Silvino," "Loves and Heroic Deeds of Lampeão," "The Death of Lampeão," "Lampeão,

latest of these bad men to gain national and international notoriety was Virgolino Ferreira, most generally known as Lampeão. For decades he and his band terrorized the states of the Brazilian northeast, and it was not until 1938 that federal troops under the command of Captain João Bezerra, supported by state forces, succeeded in putting an end to the career of Brazil's most famous cangaceiro.[31] The insecurity of life and property which prevailed within the great radius of influence of this famous bandit is well indicated from the following extracts from Carneiro Leão's excellent chapter on "The Natural Conditions and Banditry in the Northeast." Writing in 1938 this eminent Brazilian educator said:

We still remember the accent of conviction with which a *juiz de direito* [judge] of a city in the sertão related to us his encounter with the sinister band.

Traveling one day by car to Recife, accompanied by a lady teacher from his district and a merchant, he was obliged to stop by a signal from Lampeão's men. The happening occurred in a deserted place. Suddenly the travelers saw at a distant hut a group in a suspicious attitude. As they [the judge and his companions] fearfully approached, four men separated themselves from the door of the hut, posted themselves in the road, and covered them with rifles.

The automobile stopped immediately. The men came near. Lampeão did not appear. He contented himself by sending his emissaries. These wanted to know who the travelers were and where they were going.

The judge thought it prudent to conceal his position of authority.

They were two small merchants and a teacher going to Recife, he declared without hesitation.

After getting this information the bandits demanded 200 milreis in money and requested the judge to bring them from Recife some ammunition which they needed.

Arriving at the capital, the judge related the facts to the Governor of the State. The latter said, "What do you intend to do?" The former responded immediately, "To carry out the commission."

And he carried it out; only the band, pursued by the police, had disappeared.

Unfortunate contingency which forces a magistrate to conspire with bandits if he does not care to be at the mercy of an atrocious vengeance!

. . . . . .

The phenomena is very grave. It is not simply a problem of police, as many people imagine, but the result of natural and social conditions in the sertão.

The police could work continuously, the affected states could unite in the prosecution of the struggle, as they have already done, but rid of one bandit, of ten, of a hundred, with Lampeão dead, other bandits will inevitably come forth, another Lampeão is certain to appear.

Cabeleira was followed by Antonio Silvino, and Antonio Silvino by Lampeão and his men, and on all sides of them there always flourished subsidiary groups, of less fame but not less depraved.[32]

His Life, His Crimes, His Death," "Combat and Death of Lampeão," "The *Sertaneja* Story of the Valiant Zé Garcia," "The Story of the Giant Negro, the Most Barbarous Being of Piauí," and "The Valiant Villela."

[31] For an account of the campaign, see Captain João Bezerra, *Como Dei Cabo de Lampeão* (2d ed.; Rio de Janeiro, 1940).

[32] Carneiro Leão, *A Sociedade Rural*, 156–58.

SOCIAL LEGISLATION IN AGRICULTURE

Among the influences emanating from Rio de Janeiro which are having an impact on life in the municípios from one end of Brazil to the other is an important set connected with social legislation. A few comments on this subject are relevant to this discussion of governmental institutions.

As early as 1936 Brazil embarked on a venture in social legislation that continues to occupy an important role in urban affairs and is making its influence felt in the rural districts of the nation. On the fourteenth of January, 1936, President Getúlio Vargas signed Law No. 186 establishing commissions on minimum salaries.[33] Article 1 of this decree provided that "each worker has the right, in payment for service rendered, to a minimum wage sufficient to satisfy, in a specific region of the country at a specific time, his normal necessities for food, shelter, clothing, hygiene, and transportation." Article 2 defined minimum wage as the "minimum remuneration owed to the adult worker for a normal day of service." And Article 3 designated the Comissões de Salario as the agencies for setting the requirements.[34] Although the stimulus for the law probably came from industrial situations, agricultural labor is not excluded from the provisions of the legislation.

In a little more than two years legislation had been prepared establishing minimum wages throughout Brazil, and with the signing of Decreto-Lei No. 399 on April 30, 1938,[35] Brazil had begun an ambitious program relative to minimum wages, hours, and conditions of work. Among other things, however, this legislation had merely provided that "the normal duration of the work day will be regulated, in each case, by the legislation now in force." [36] But there had as yet been no legislation relative to hours and wages in agriculture, and in many areas the rule of work had been from "sun to sun." Consequently, the new legislation brought about considerable perplexity on the part of those rural employers who were inclined to comply with the law. For example, the Societé Sucriere de Rio Branco in the state of Minas Gerais made inquiry to determine what "would be the minimum wage to be paid the agricultural worker for a day of 10 hours?" When this question was passed to the highest authorities in the nation's capital, it was held that although there was no legislation on the subject, eight hours was the universal measure of a normal day of work.[37] Furthermore, it was ruled that the minimum salary in the case in question should be increased in proportion to the excess over eight hours.[38] Still awaited are the effects of this

[33] This and the other legislation on the subject, along with much of the data used in the determination of norms, is published in *Salário Mínimo.*
[34] *Ibid.,* 39.
[35] The text is given *ibid.,* 61–78.
[36] *Ibid.,* 62.
[37] *Ibid.,* 496–97.
[38] *Ibid.,* 498.

official attempt to introduce the eight-hour day in Brazilian agriculture.

The Brazilian legislative power enacted many laws concerning rural unions and rural labor institutes such as minimum wages, labor courts for rural workers, vacations with pay, disability provisions, etc., but even now the rural labor force does not have any rural unions or other organizations which could provide the diffusion of these rights among the rural people. On November 10, 1944, a new Decree, Law Number 7,038, was passed making further provisions regarding the organization of rural unions, but like the previous law it was unfruitful.[39]

[39] J. V. Freitas Marcondes, "A Sociological Study of the First Brazilian Legislation Relating to Rural Labor Unions" (unpublished M.A. thesis, University of Florida, 1953), 88. See the same author's "Social Legislation in Brazil," in Smith and Marchant (eds.), *Brazil: Portrait of Half a Continent,* Chap. XVII; and Fretias Marcondes and Smith, "The Caipira of the Paraitinga Valley, Brazil," *loc. cit.,* 52–53.

PART SIX

Urbanization

After Brazil's existence for centuries as a rural society par excellence her leaders and her people appear to be seeking a solution for many of their chronic ills in urbanization and industrialization. It would appear that hundreds of thousands of those who are fleeing the land and concentrating in towns and cities are paying little heed to their chances for remunerative work and improved living conditions in the urban areas. The single chapter which constitutes Part Six is devoted to some of the more important aspects of the process of urbanization.

CHAPTER XXII

URBANIZATION

DRASTIC CHANGE is the order of the day in Brazil during the 1960's, and the process of urbanization, both as a cause and as an effect, is at the heart of the changes that are taking place. In this chapter attention is directed to several of the more important aspects of this fundamental development.

GROWTH OF CITIES AND TOWNS

In the second half of the twentieth century the pace of urbanization in Brazil is very rapid. Guanabara, the former Distrito Federal, already is almost 100 per cent urban, the center of a great industrial complex, and the central core of a metropolitan community of more than five million inhabitants. In São Paulo, the most populous state in Brazil, almost two-thirds of the population was classified as urban by the 1960 census, and its capital, a metropolis of some four or five million people (depending on how the limits of such are set) is the greatest industrial center in all of Latin America. The state of Rio de Janeiro, into whose area the bulging suburbs of the city of Rio de Janeiro have spread, had two-thirds of her population in the urban category in 1960. But these are only three spectacular examples. Throughout the length and breadth of Brazil people are flocking into the cities in unprecedented numbers and thereby transforming a country which for centuries was exceedingly rural, agricultural, pastoral, and extractive into a nation which probably will be predominantly urban by 1970.

Population Increase in the Municípios Containing State Capitals. One encounters, of course, in Brazil the same sort of difficulties in ascertaining the actual growth of towns and cities that one experiences in other countries. As people flock into the urban centers, the built-up areas of the same spread out over additional territory, and not infrequently one expands into areas that are included in political subdivisions distinct from the one in which the city proper is located. This greatly complicates the matter of measuring and comparing the growth of population in urban centers of various types. For example, as the city of Rio de Janeiro has grown and developed, substantial parts of the people who actually work in and otherwise form part of that metropolis have established their residences across·

the boundary in the state of Rio de Janeiro. As early as 1960 more than one million people classified as urban were living in the densely populated areas adjacent to, but not included within, the limits of the state of Guanabara. Under such circumstances it becomes difficult, if not impossible, to determine the population of the actual city that constitutes the center of this particular large metropolitan community.

In many cases, as cities come to account for the bulk of the population in their respective counties or municípios, in tracing population growth it becomes realistic to take account of the changes in the latter in lieu of trying to account properly for the increases in the constantly changing area of the city itself. In Brazil the data are such that this is the only practicable thing to do if one wants to begin the comparisons with any date prior to 1940. In cases such as that of Cuiabá, Mato Grosso, however, in which the município containing the capital is very large and from which slices of the area it included in 1900 repeatedly have been taken to constitute new municípios, there also are problems in connection with such a procedure. Nevertheless, in beginning this discussion of the growth of towns and cities in Brazil, it seems well to present first of all the materials relevant to the growth of the municípios containing state and territorial capitals during the period 1940 to 1960. In order to do this Table LXX, with data for all such municípios, and Figure 38, to trace graphically the growth and development of Brazil's major cities, have been prepared. In most cases the growth of population in the município is a close approximation to the growth of population in the city involved, although, as indicated above, during recent years the growth of population in Rio de Janeiro has been more rapid than is indicated by the changes in the município that is responsible for its municipal government.

Both the absolute and relative increases of population between 1940 and 1960, in all of the municípios containing capitals, are easily noted from Table LXX. Actual increments of population during the twenty-year period of almost two and one-half millions in the município of São Paulo and of more than a million and one-half in the former Distrito Federal are spectacular to say the least, but the fact that São Paulo and Rio de Janeiro have grown at fantastic rates is well known. On the other hand, probably few people outside of Brazil know that the município of Belo Horizonte grew by almost a half a million during the same period, and they could hardly have expected increases greater than that of 440,000 actually recorded in the município of Recife, of 369,000 in the município of Pôrto Alegre, and of 365,000 in the município of Salvador. Likewise, even though many Brazilians knew that Fortaleza, Curitiba, and Goiânia were developing rapidly, the amounts by which the populations of these municípios have increased from 1940 on probably came as a surprise even to most of them.

On the relative basis, the almost uniformly high rates, especially in the decade 1950–1960, stand out sharply. Only in the municípios containing Manaus, São Luís, Niterói, and Cuiabá did the growth of

TABLE LXX

Growth of Population in Municípios Containing State and Territorial Capitals, 1940–1960 *

Município	Population 1940	Population 1950	Population 1960	Percentage increase 1940–50	Percentage increase 1950–60
North					
Porto Velho (Rondonia)	—	27,244	51,049	—	87
Rio Branco (Acre)	16,038	28,246	47,882	76	70
Manaus (Amazonas)	106,399	139,620	175,343	31	26
Boa Vista (Rio Branco)	—	17,247	26,168	—	52
Belém (Pará)	206,331	254,949	402,170	24	58
Macapá (Amapá)	—	20,594	46,905	—	128
Northeast					
São Luís (Maranhão)	85,583	119,785	159,628	40	33
Teresina (Piauí)	67,641	90,723	144,799	34	60
Fortaleza (Ceará)	180,185	270,169	514,828	50	91
Natal (Rio Grande do Norte)	54,836	103,215	162,537	88	57
João Pessoa (Paraíba)	94,333	119,326	154,950	26	30
Recife (Pernambuco)	348,424	524,682	788,580	51	50
Maceió (Alagôas)	90,253	120,980	170,134	34	41
East					
Aracaju (Sergipe)	59,031	78,364	115,713	33	48
Salvador (Bahia)	290,443	417,235	655,739	44	57
Belo Horizonte (Minas Gerais)	211,377	352,724	680,025	67	93
Vitória (Espírito Santo)	45,212	50,922	85,242	13	67
Niterói (Rio de Janeiro)	142,407	186,309	245,467	31	32
Rio de Janeiro (Guanabara)	1,764,141	2,377,451	3,288,296	34	39
South					
São Paulo (São Paulo)	1,326,261	2,198,096	3,776,581	66	72
Curitiba (Paraná)	140,656	180,575	361,309	28	100
Florianópolis (Santa Catarina)	46,771	67,630	98,520	45	46
Pôrto Alegre (Rio Grande do Sul)	272,232	394,151	641,173	45	63
West Central					
Cuiabá (Mato Grosso)	54,394	56,204	58,192	3	4
Goiânia (Goiás)	48,166	53,389	153,505	11	188
Brasília (Distrito Federal)	—	—	141,742	—	—

* Compiled from a mimeographed release issued in 1961 by the Serviço Nacional de Recenseamento of the Instituto Brasileiro de Geografia e Estatística. The 1960 data were secured by totaling the enumerators' reports and, consequently, are subject to some rectification.

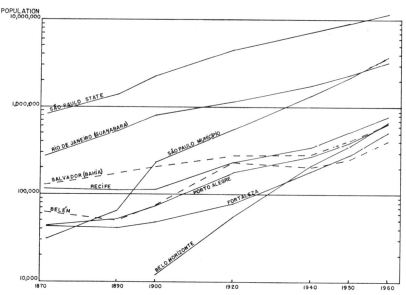

FIGURE 38. The growth of population in selected municípios, 1872 to 1960.

these most urbanized sections of Brazil fail to exceed the very high increase of 36 per cent in Brazil as a whole. Especially noteworthy, however, in terms of the numbers involved as well as the rates, are the changes registered during the twenty-year period in Fortaleza, Belo Horizonte, São Paulo, and Curitiba, along with that in Goiânia for the decade 1950 to 1960.

Rural-Urban Differentials in Population Growth. The adoption of a logical and practicable working definition of "urban" for use in the 1940 and subsequent censuses of population has resulted in the accumulation of several comprehensive bodies of information of great value to those interested in the process of urbanization in Brazil. Materials from the 1940 and 1950 censuses already make possible the definitive study of the growth of towns and cities during the decade ending in 1950, and eventually the tabulation and publication of 1960 census results should supply comparable materials for the period 1950 to 1960.

First concern is, of course, with the over-all changes in the nation as a whole. On this point it is important to note that even during the decade 1940 to 1950 the increment in the urban-suburban population greatly exceeded that in the rural, the former amounting to more than 5,900,000 and the latter to 3,800,000. On the relative basis the percentage increases during the ten years were 46.0 and 16.9 per cent, respectively, and the differential prevailed in all parts of Brazil. See Table LXXI. That the absolute increase of the urban-suburban population actually was 155 per cent of that of the rural is especially noteworthy in view of the fact that in 1940 only 31 per

596

cent of Brazil's population was classified in the urban-suburban category. Between 1950 and 1960 the pace at which the urban-suburban population increased exceeded that of the rural to an even greater degree than it did during the preceding decade. During this ten-year period the absolute increase of the former was 227 per cent that of

TABLE LXXI

Percentage Increases in Urban-Suburban and Rural Populations, 1940–1950, by States *

State	Percentage increase 1940–1950	
	Urban-suburban	Rural
Brazil	46.0	16.9
North		
Acre	50.5	42.4
Amazonas–Rio Branco	36.3	16.8
Pará-Amapá	40.5	15.3
Northeast		
Maranhão	47.8	24.7
Piauí	37.3	26.2
Ceará	43.1	24.7
Rio Grande do Norte	54.5	18.3
Paraíba	46.7	13.1
Pernambuco	48.2	17.2
Alagôas	25.0	11.7
East		
Sergipe	23.3	16.8
Bahia	33.4	20.2
Minas Gerais	37.0	7.0
Espírito Santo	24.2	12.4
Rio de Janeiro	57.4	4.4
Guanabara	51.6	−69.7
South		
São Paulo	51.6	7.9
Paraná	74.8	69.9
Santa Catarina	43.0	29.5
Rio Grande do Sul	37.5	20.0
West Central		
Mato Grosso–Guaporé	48.9	21.0
Goiás	72.9	41.6

* Compiled and computed from data in *VI Recenseamento Geral do Brasil, 1950* (Rio de Janeiro, 1956).

the latter, with actual increments being 13,206,997 and 5,815,791, in the urban-suburban [1] and the rural districts, respectively. On the relative basis the increase of 70 per cent in the urban-suburban population was accompanied by one of only 17 per cent in the rural population.

[1] In the preliminary reports of the 1960 census the distinction between the urban and the suburban population is not made, all being included in the urban category.

Summary information from the 1940 and 1950 censuses also makes it evident that the rapid growth of important towns and cities is characteristic of all parts of Brazil. Thus there were scattered throughout the nation's territory in 1940 a total of 320 places having 5,000 or more inhabitants, and during the decade ending in 1950 the combined population of these towns and cities increased by about 3,844,000. In addition, another 158 centers passed the 5,000 mark between 1940 and 1950, and together these places had a population of almost 1,200,000 by mid-century. Furthermore, the new entrants to the 5,000-over category included representatives from every one of the nation's states and territories (except Fernando de Noronha, for obvious reasons), although the largest numbers quite naturally were in São Paulo (33), Minas Gerais (17), Pernambuco (12), Bahia (12), Rio de Janeiro (12), Paraná (12), Ceará (7), Rio Grande do Sul (7), Maranhão (6), and Santa Catarina (6).

The tendency of the Brazilian population to abandon its centuries-long practice of rural residence for life in towns and cities is best demonstrated, however, by a study of the comparative rates of growth of the rural and urban populations during the decade ending in 1960. During that period, in every state and territory of the Brazilian confederation, the rate of growth of the urban population exceeded that of the rural. See Table LXXII and Figure 39. Indeed, in all except four of these major political units (namely, Rondonia, Acre, Maranhão, and Mato Grosso) the urban population increased at least twice as rapidly as the rural, and in most of them, including all of the most populous ones, percentage increases of less than 15 in the rural populations were accompanied by those of from 44 to 90 in the urban populations. Between 1950 and 1960 no state registered an absolute decrease in rural population to accompany the massing of people into the towns and cities, but in Rio Grande do Norte, Pernambuco, Paraíba, and Alagôas such a development was missed by very slight margins. In all likelihood, between 1960 and 1970 that stage will be attained, and the decade will prove to be one in which not only all of the natural increase of the rural population is drawn away to urban centers, but sizable proportions of the "seed stock" as well. In other words, in many parts of rural Brazil depopulation is imminent.

One may also note from the data in Table LXXII the proportion of the total increase in a state's population that was accounted for by the growth of its urban population. In this connection it is important to recall that in 1950 São Paulo was the only state, and the then Distrito Federal (Guanabara) was the only other major political subdivision in which the urban population exceeded the rural. Because of this fact the increases of the urban population, accounting for over 90 per cent of the total increase in Rio Grande do Norte and Pernambuco, for more than 80 per cent of that in Paraíba, Alagôas, Rio de Janeiro, São Paulo, and Rio Grande do Sul, and for more than 70 per cent of that in Sergipe, Bahia, and Minas Gerais, are eloquent testimony of the fundamental changes that are taking place in Bra-

TABLE LXXII

Growth of Urban-Suburban and Rural Populations, 1950–1960, by States *

State	Increase of urban-suburban population		Increase of rural population		Urban-suburban increase as a percentage of the total increase
	Number	Per cent	Number	Per cent	
Brazil	13,206,997	70	5,815,791	17	69
North					
Rondonia †	17,026	123	16,822	73	50
Acre †	12,726	60	32,727	35	28
Amazonas	101,923	74	105,193	28	49
Rio Branco †	7,585	148	3,788	29	67
Pará	241,661	62	186,001	25	57
Amapá †	21,490	155	9,922	44	68
Northeast					
Maranhão	174,221	64	734,670	56	19
Piauí	127,568	75	90,104	10	59
Ceará	445,225	66	197,181	10	69
Rio Grande do Norte	181,424	71	7,913	1	96
Paraíba	251,335	55	53,429	4	82
Pernambuco	689,289	59	52,426	2	93
Alagôas	141,849	50	36,076	4	80
East					
Sergipe	90,945	44	24,967	6	78
Bahia	833,209	67	322,821	9	72
Minas Gerais	1,620,503	70	460,585	9	78
Serra dos Aimorés	26,804	377	197,421	129	12
Espírito Santo	184,754	95	142,349	21	56
Rio de Janeiro	985,862	90	119,672	10	89
Guanabara	920,345	40	9,367	13	99
South					
São Paulo	3,344,718	70	495,558	11	87
Paraná	799,694	151	1,362,522	86	37
Santa Catarina	332,630	92	253,777	21	57
Rio Grande do Sul	1,023,794	72	260,208	9	85
West Central					
Mato Grosso	186,174	105	202,044	59	48
Goiás ‡	443,435	181	438,248	45	50

* Computed from data in a 1961 mimeographed release by the Serviço de Recenseamento of the Instituto Brasileiro de Geografia e Estatística.
† Territory.
‡ The population of the Distrito Federal for 1960 was included in making the computations for Goiás.

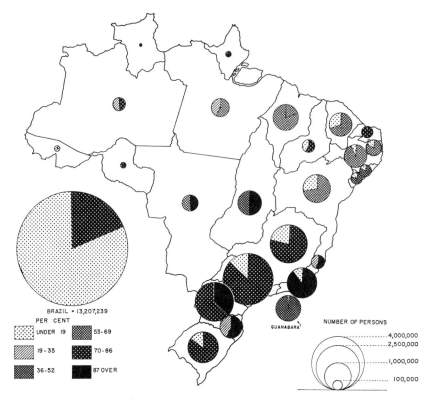

FIGURE 39. Absolute and relative increases in the urban and rural populations, 1950–1960, by states.

zilian society. For better or worse, in the decades immediately ahead, the problems connected with life and labor in urban centers will be the predominant themes of existence throughout the inhabited parts of Brazil.

A few examples, other than the major centers which are the capitals of states and territories, chosen from various sections of Brazil, may serve to emphasize the rapidity with which small cities are developing throughout the settled parts of the country. Thus in Ceará, in the northeastern region, between 1950 and 1960 the population of Crato increased from 15,464 to 27,649, that of famed Juàzeiro do Norte from 41,999 to 53,421, and that of Sobral from 22,628 to 32,281. Even more striking was the mushrooming of a couple of the vilas adjacent to and in reality suburbs of Fortaleza, namely Antonio Bezerra which had only 6,122 inhabitants in 1950 and 19,844 in 1960, and Parangaba which grew from a place of 24,459 to one of 92,534 during the same decade. Also in the Northeast, in Paraíba, Patos doubled population (from 13,889 to 27,275) and Campina Grande passed the 100,000 mark (from 72,464 to 116,226) in the years between the 1950 and the 1960 censuses.

Further south, the state of Espírito Santo is by no means noted for the degree to which it has urbanized. Nevertheless, between 1950 and 1960 the small city of Cachoeiro de Itapemirim developed from a place of 24,021 to one of 39,470 inhabitants, and Calatina grew even more spectacularly, from 6,451 to 26,757. One may also mention, as illustrative of the fact that in Brazil as in the United States satellites and bedroom cities are mushrooming in the vicinity of all the important population centers, that Vila Velha, not far from Vitória, with only 9,701 residents in 1950, boasted a population of 31,027 in 1960.

In the far South the trend was similar. One may note, for example, that in Santa Catarina, between 1950 and 1960, the following increases of population in some of the smaller cities were recorded: Blumenau, from 22,627 to 46,591; Criciúma, from 8,014 to 25,331; Joinville, from 20,951 to 44,255; Itajaí, from 19,797 to 38,889; Lajes, from 14,596 to 35,112; and Tubarão, from 11,740 to 29,615. But even more spectacular were the changes in much more populous Rio Grande do Sul. By 1960 that state alone contained no fewer than fifteen cities with populations of 25,000 or more; and these cities, in turn, had grown as follows between 1950 and 1960: Alegrete, from 19,560 to 33,735; Bagé, from 34,525 to 47,930; Cachoeira do Sul, from 23,270 to 38,611; Canoas, from 19,152 to 95,401; Caxias do Sul, from 31,561 to 60,607; Cruz Alta, from 19,375 to 33,190; Novo Hamburgo, from 19,604 to 25,610; Passo Fundo, from 24,395 to 47,299; Pelotas, from 78,014 to 121,280; Rio Grande, from 63,235 to 83,189; Santa Maria, from 44,949 to 78,682; Santana do Livramento, from 29,099 to 37,666; Santa Angelo, from 13,573 to 25,415; São Leopoldo, from 18,380 to 41,023; and Uruguaiana, from 32,639 to 48,358.

To conclude this section it seems well to mention that by 1960, in addition to Niterói, there were in the state of Rio de Janeiro nineteen places reporting populations of more than 25,000, and that three of these had passed the 100,000 mark. This list included, of course, long-established cities, such as Campos, Novo Friburgo, and Petropolis, with populations of 61,633, 25,458 and 61,001, respectively in 1950, and 90,601, 49,901, and 93,849 in 1960. Likewise, it included Brazil's thriving new steel center, Volta Redonda, with 32,143 inhabitants in 1950 and 83,973 in 1960, and places such as Barra do Piraí and Barra Mansa, situated in close proximity to it. The first of these grew from 20,024 to 29,398 and the second from 20,893 to 47,398, during the decade under consideration. But it also included many of the suburbs of the city of Rio de Janeiro, among which between 1950 and 1960 the growth of Duque de Caxias from a place of 73,527 to one of 173,077, of Mesquita from scratch to 58,835, of Nova Iguaçu from 58,533 to 134,708, and of São João de Meriti from 43,790 to 103,495 were the most spectacular.

"URBANIZATION"

Urbanização, or "urbanization," is widely used in Brazil in a technical sense to denote the planning and construction of the physical features of a city, such as aligned streets, public squares and parks, paved streets and sidewalks, storm sewers and sewer systems, and central water and lighting systems. As a rule in the Brazilian urban center the public improvements involved are concentrated in the central portion of the city, and the surrounding sections may be practically devoid of facilities. Perhaps the difference between the "urbanized" and "nonurbanized" areas, in the Brazilian sense, is best expressed in the following literal translation of the distinction used for census purposes. This states that "an urbanized area is considered as that part of the territory that is served, or is due to be served, by public improvements, as well as that included in the planned zone of expansion, including that along the highways. Considered as a nonurbanized area is that constituted of groups of buildings or dwellings in which there is a predominance of huts or rude dwellings constructed without obedience to any plan, outside the area of aligned streets, without legal rights of occupation [i.e. homes established by squatters], and not served by public utilities."[2] In addition, frequently municipal ordinances require that the houses in the "urbanized" area be built of brick, blocks, or stone and covered with a roof of tiles, and they may also prohibit people who are barefooted, or those conducting oxcarts, from entering the central district. For this reason the degree of *urbanização* in Brazil as a whole, and in the various states and territories of which it is composed, is indicative of the extent to which the process of urbanization has gone forward. Certain data which have been published enable us to take stock of the situation as it was on December 31, 1954.

At that time, to give in literal translation the words of a report from the Conselho Nacional de Estatística on "The Process of *urbanização* and the Deficiency of Public Services or Those of Collective Utility in the Seats of Municípios":

Even leaving out of consideration the small towns and villages (*vilas* and *povacões*), which in general are of less importance demographically, and taking into account only the seats of municípios, there is to be observed an accentuated deficiency of public services and those of collective utility in the interior of the nation. According to data published by the Section of Urbanistic Activities of the former Ministry of Education and Culture, the following was the situation on December 31, 1954: of the 2,399 seats of municípios existing in Brazil, 1,080 had no pavement whatsoever, 1,354 had no system for supplying drinking water, 1,939 lacked systems for disposing of sewage, and 349 were without the benefits of electrical illumination. . . .

Furthermore in some of the capitals the situation was no better: there were no mains for drinking water in Rio Branco, and no sewage system in this same city nor in Boa Vista, Teresina, Maceió, or Cuiabá.[3]

From this report also it is possible to determine the number and proportion of the *cidades*, or seats of municípios, in each of the

[2] Alberto Passos Guimarães, "As Favelas do Distrito Federal," *Revista Brasileira de Estatística*, **XIV**, No. 55 (1953), 259. See also, Lebret, Rios, Medina, and Modesto, *Aspectos Humanos da Favela Carioca*, April 13, 1960, p. 7.

[3] Alceu Vicente W. de Carvalho, *A População Brasileira* (Rio de Janeiro, 1960), 108–110.

TABLE LXXIII

Numbers and Proportions of Cities (Seats of Municípios) Having
Water, Sewer, and Public Lighting Systems, by Regions and States,
1954 *

State	Number of cities	Per cent having		
		Water systems	Sewer systems	Lighting systems
Brazil	2,338	44	19	86
North	122	17	4	80
Rondonia †	2	100	50	100
Acre †	7	0	0	100
Amazonas	25	24	4	96
Rio Branco †	2	50	0	50
Pará	84	12	2	72
Amapá †	4	50	25	100
Northeast	508	21	2	86
Maranhão	87	6	1	71
Piauí	63	8	0	73
Ceará	96	24	2	79
Rio Grande do Norte	65	15	2	97
Paraíba	54	24	4	96
Pernambuco	102	34	1	97
Alagôas	41	37	2	98
East	817	64	32	90
Sergipe	61	9	2	67
Bahia	170	22	7	87
Minas Gerais	485	81	40	93
Espírito Santo	41	73	42	85
Rio de Janeiro	59	95	58	98
Distrito Federal	1	100	100	100
South	766	47	24	86
São Paulo	435	58	34	95
Paraná	150	27	9	63
Santa Catarina	67	24	6	94
Rio Grande do Sul	114	47	17	80
West Central	185	18	1	65
Mato Grosso	59	24	2	68
Goiás	126	15	1	64

* Source: Alceu Vicente W. de Carvalho, *A População Brasileira* (Rio de Janeiro, 1960), 108–109. The data were supplied by the Seção de Atividades Urbanísticas of the Ministério da Educação e Cultura.
† Territory.

states and territories that had installed water mains and sewer systems and were supplied with electricity. See Table LXXIII. Electricity is the one of the three virtually indispensable facilities of the modern urban center that is found in the largest proportion of the villages, towns, and cities that are seats of municípios. Also, probably largely because of the development in recent years of a part of the potential of the Paulo Afonso falls, the northeastern region of Brazil is more on a par with other regions in this respect than it is in the others. However, one certainly must agree with the observation in the report under consideration to the effect that "those who travel through the interior are acquainted with the slight efficiency and the precarious functioning of the electrical installations in a large part of the seats of the municípios." [4] Municipal water systems are present in less than one-half of the administrative centers involved, and sewer systems in less than one out of five of them.

The call for improvements made in this report, or perhaps a broader general awakening to some of the basic prerequisites of life in urban aggregations, apparently has produced some results. Thus, according to data in the 1960 issue of the *Anuário Estatístico*, at the close of 1958 a total of 1,250, or 47 per cent, of the seats of municípios was served by water mains and 884, or 34 per cent, had sewer systems. These proportions are indicative of substantial increases since 1954, particularly with respect to the provisions for disposing of the disagreeable and dangerous wastes that multiply in densely populated areas. Comparable information with respect to lighting systems is lacking, and most of the detail in the more recent statistics pertain solely to the municípios in which state and territorial capitals are located.

The fact that water mains and a sewer system are present in a given city does not, of course, mean that all or even a majority of the homes in that center are served by the same. In this connection a few data may be given for the city of Rio de Janeiro, a great metropolis in which the situation certainly is not less favorable than the average for the urban portions of the nation as a whole. According to the 1960 census there were in the urban and suburban portions of the state of Guanabara 630,390 domiciles, and according to the 1960 issue of the *Anuário Estatístico* there were in the entire state on December 31, 1958, 284,693 water connections. Of the latter 84,168 were gauged by meters and 200,525 were mere *penas d'agua* or simple faucets. This information makes it evident that the majority of the families in Brazil's great former capital get the water they use for household purposes from taps which also supply other dwellings. Similarly the *Anuário Estatístico* for 1960 reports 233,641 buildings in the state as being served by sewer connections on December 31, 1958; and on this basis, even after making a liberal allowance for apartments of various types, one may infer that probably no more than one-half of the dwellings in Rio de Janeiro are equipped with modern, sanitary equipment for disposing of wastes from human bodies and other sources. In this connection one should mention that the 1960 census also reported that 70,353 of the dwellings, the homes of 337,412 people, were in the city's noted *favelas* or slum districts, where by definition almost all the features of *urbanização* are completely lacking.

Many of the implications of the lack of essential facilities were set

[4] *Ibid.*

forth in a comprehensive study of life in the favelas, published in 1960.[5] The perceptive authors of this report indicate that "from the sanitary point of view, the favelas appear to us as suburbs embodied in the heart of the city; and some even resemble certain pieces of the rural zone, in their extremes of under-development, transplanted into the center of the nation's capital." On the basis of their on-the-spot studies, the sociologists in charge of the research concluded that "with rare exceptions, water is the sanitary problem number one of the favelas. Not only water for the bath, a general problem in many middle-class and even upper-class districts of Rio de Janeiro, but water to drink, water for the minimum necessities of the human being. In the favela of Escondidinho, for example, near the Laranjeiras-Rio Comprido tunnel, if the persons who reside on the hill-top wish water to drink, they have to descend a stairway of 352 steps, and then cross a stretch of steep terrain, in order to get it in the Rua Almirante Alexandrino, a kilometer away." From the materials these investigations present about the facilities, or lack of them, for disposing of bodily wastes and garbage, one must conclude that the lack of elementary facilities for these purposes must create a problem only slightly less acute than that of lack of water.[6]

To take stock of the extent to which the urban dwellings in other parts of Brazil are served by the public water and sewer systems is even more difficult and unsatisfactory than it is for the city of Rio de Janeiro. However, a few of the basic facts relative to the situation in such vastly different states as Ceará and Rio Grande do Sul may be presented. The census of 1960 reported 582,739 domiciles in Ceará, of which probably one-third, or about 195,000, must have been in the urban areas. However, the *Anuário Estatístico* for 1960 reported for the entire state, as of December 31, 1958, only 20,433 water connections (12,559 with meters) and 29,487 buildings with facilities for disposing of bodily wastes (22,188 with septic tanks or cesspools and 7,299 with sewer systems). For the city of Fortaleza, which had 355,000 inhabitants in 1960, only 4,500 water connections, 21,973 buildings served by septic tanks or cesspools, and 6,827 sewer connections were reported.

In Rio Grande do Sul there were, according to the 1960 census, a total of 1,026,778 domiciles, of which somewhat more than 40 per cent, or probably about 410,000, were in urban areas. In sharp contrast with the situation in Ceará, however, for 1958 the *Anuário Estatístico* reported 236,666 water connections, of which 116,146 were metered, and 77,919 buildings connected with facilities for disposing of wastes, of which 67,238 were with a sewer system. Of the water connections 65,832 were in Pôrto Alegre, the capital, as were 25,635 of the sewer connections.

These data confirm the impression gained by casual observation that the planning and development of facilities for serving the most pressing needs of densely populated urban districts have progressed

[5] Lebret, Rios, Medina, and Modesto, *Aspectos Humanos da Favela Carioca.*
[6] *Ibid.* 25.

much farther in south Brazil than in other regions such as the Northeast.

THE FUNCTIONS OF BRAZILIAN CITIES

The functions of cities are legion, and to some extent every city in Brazil performs every one of them. Manufacturing and trade, transportation and communication, education and recreation, financial and personal services, administration and protection, construction and maintenance, religious and cultural activities, and residence as such are among the better-known of the categories. It would be possible, however, to extend greatly the list of functions that cities perform for the society of which they are a part. Furthermore, one could subdivide into many varieties each of the classes mentioned without in any way trying to be exhaustive of the possibilities. Familiar and important examples are light and heavy manufacturing; wholesale and retail trade; rail, sea, highway, river, and air transportation; and national, state, and local government and administration. Some of them overlap—for example, educational and cultural activities, or protection and administration. Moreover, the importance of the various categories varies from time to time and place to place. Thus it is certain that the functions of Brazilian cities in the second half of the twentieth century are vastly different from what they were during the colonial period and that at the present time there is a great deal more division of labor and specialization among them than was the case one hundred or even twenty-five years ago. São Paulo has specialized to a considerable extent in the performance of specific functions, Rio de Janeiro in others, Brasília in still others, and the same is true of all the principal cities of the nation.

Cities may be classified into those which specialize in a few basic functions (which may be designated as uni-, bi-, or trifunctional centers) and those which are multifunctional in the true sense of the word. Of course, since all of the functions are necessary in the type of western civilization represented in Brazil, every one of her urban centers performs all of the functions to a limited extent. However, some of her urban centers concentrate largely on two or three of them, whereas others are outstanding with respect to at least half a dozen functions.

That European cities during the medieval period were largely market towns, or market towns and administrative fortresses, is well known. It is possible, however, that a city such as Fortaleza, Recife, or Manaus may be almost as highly specialized in the trading function as were those famous market places of earlier centuries, or as are contemporary Dallas, Salt Lake City, Miami, and Kansas City, Missouri, in the United States.

Fortress cities, that is, strongholds built and maintained for protective purposes or even placed across trade routes so as to facilitate the exacting of tribute, are another well-known feature of the Middle Ages, and the colonial Spanish-American city of Cartegena on the north coast of South America is a more recent example of a city that specialized almost exclusively in the protection function. At present, however, such Brazilian cities as Natal and Florianópolis may claim distinction in this respect, as may San Diego, San Antonio, and Norfolk in the United States.

Manufacturing and industrial centers are a recent development, even more recent in Brazil than in Western Europe and the United States. In earlier days the self-sufficiency of the Brazilian fazenda, the small scale of the transforming operations, and the limited amount of trade made the processing of raw materials largely a rural enterprise. Nowadays, however, São Paulo, some of the suburbs of Rio de Janeiro, and Volta Redonda are about as dependent on industry as are Birmingham in England, its namesake in Alabama, and various other important cities in Europe and the United States.

Spanish-American cities appear to be the ones that during historical times have specialized to the greatest extent in the performance of administrative and other governmental functions. Until very recently Paris, Rome, London, Berlin, and Washington hardly rivaled, in this respect, the degree of specialization of such centers as Lima, Bogotá, Quito, and Santiago; and few if any Brazilian centers, with the possible exception of Rio de Janeiro, deserved inclusion in lists of those specializing in such functions. Nowadays, however, Brasília stands in a class of its own in the degree to which administrative and other governmental functions [7] are its *raison d'être*, and Cuiabá and Goiânia also deserve mention in this respect.

From time immemorial, cities have sprung up at favorable places on the seacoast, where conditions made it necessary and possible to develop port facilities, and inland at a few places in which there was a break in the transportation of goods by land or water. When Brazil's ports were opened to trade early in the nineteenth century, Rio de Janeiro, Salvador (Bahia), and Recife came rapidly to the forefront in this respect, and later such places as Pôrto Alegre, São Luís, and Belém also came to be important as seaports. Early in the second half of the twentieth century the relative importance of transportation as the basis for existence and growth is particularly important for such Brazilian cities as Belém, São Luís, and Vitória.

The preceding paragraphs are designed to suggest that for centuries the functions of Brazilian cities were extremely limited. For the most part they were merely seaports, open only to ships from the mother country, and depots from which mule trains and fleets of canoes departed to carry such items as salt, lead, and gunpowder, and a few textiles, to the mining settlements, agricultural communities, and trading posts in the interior. In the important case of São Paulo, where many exploring parties and slave-making expeditions

---

[7] Even as early as 1961 casual observation seemed to indicate that every important bank in Brazil had established a branch in Brasília in order to be near the seat of governmental financing.

were based, these functions were shared with Santos. Even in this case, though, the principal functions performed by the small city were those of a center of rudimentary transportation services and those of a trading post.[8] Throughout all of the colonial period, and that of the empire as well, manufacturing enterprises in Brazil were conspicuous by their absence, and such transforming activities as were carried on were located for the most part on the fazendas and not in the towns and cities. As José Arthur Rios has stated so well, commenting specifically about Olinda, Bahia, Rio de Janeiro, and São Paulo: "The role of the city was marginal, dependent on the rural environment. Social control was in the hands of the powerful families, owning vast *sesmarias,* lands and slaves, and possessing prestige. The city was only an entrepot where they went to get what they needed, the little that their *engenhos* did not produce. Or it played the role of outlet through which agricultural products went forth. It did not have a nucleus of consumers, an extensive use of money, or a bourgeoisie in the colonial period. Only tardily did these factors arise, and even then their action did not extend itself uniformly to the whole national territory."[9] Rios' generalizations are fully supported by the observations of those who commented at various times about manufacturing, or the lack of it, in the specific Brazilian cities visited by them. For example, Henry Koster, second to none as an observer of and reporter about the Brazilian social scene, who was living in Recife in 1809 and 1810, states that "the only manufactory in Recife of any importance is that of gold and silver trinkets of every description, and of gold lace; but the quantities made of either are only sufficient for the demand of the place. The women employ themselves very generally in making thread lace and in embroidery; but the manufacture of these articles is not sufficiently extensive to allow of exportation."[10] John Mawe, who visited São Paulo in 1807, stated that "here are few manufacturers of any consequence. A little coarse cotton is spun by hand, and woven into cloth, which serves for a variety of wearing apparel, sheets, etc. They make a beautiful kind of net-work for hammocks, which are infringed with lace, and form an elegant piece of furniture, being slung low, so as to answer the purpose of sofas."[11] Furthermore, Mawe's observations are corroborated by the occupational classification of São Paulo's population made for 1818 as set forth in José Jacintho Ribeiro's *Chronologia Paulista.* This is as follows: military service, 566; magistrates, 1; secular clergy, 81; regular clergy, 14; monks and nuns, 56; farmers, 1,640; merchants, 220; skilled workmen, 277; laborers, 98; overseers, 52; carpenters, 18;

---

[8] Cf. Richard M. Morse, *From Community to Metropolis* (Gainesville, 1958), 13–23; and Odilon Nogueira de Matos, "São Paulo no Século XIX," in Arnoldo de Azevedo, *A Cidade de São Paulo* (São Paulo, 1958), II, 61–63.

[9] José Arthur Rios, "The Cities of Brazil," in Smith and Marchant (eds.), *Brazil: Portrait of Half a Continent,* 193–94. Cf. Freyre, *Sobrados e Mucambos, passim.*

[10] Koster, *Travels in Brazil,* I, 50.

[11] Mawe, *Travels in the Interior of Brazil,* 75.

miners, 1; beggars, 152. The total, 3,176, does not include slaves.[12]

In a search for additional understanding of the functions of cities in contemporary Brazil, some analysis was made of the 1950 census data that show, for each município containing a state capital, the industries in which the members of the male labor force were engaged. This information is for all males ten years of age and over, but the persons reported as economically inactive, those engaged solely at unpaid domestic labor, those reported to be attending school, and the small segment for which information was not available were eliminated before the various computations were made. In addition, in an endeavor to limit the analysis as much as possible to the "urban" categories, the numbers classified as engaged in agriculture, stockraising, and forestry, and also those reported as gaining a livelihood from the extractive industries were subtracted from the totals. In municípios such as São Paulo, Recife, Bahia, or Curitiba the elimination of those in agriculture and the extractive industries made relatively little difference, whereas in those such as Manaus or Goiânia such a procedure reduced the total by 25 per cent or more. In the interests of comparability this indicates the absolute necessity of trying to eliminate, in the manner indicated, or in some other way, the portions of the labor force living and working in the rural sections of the municípios containing the state capitals.

For the "urban" male labor force, as defined above, computations were made to show the proportions engaged in each of the remaining industrial categories employed in the Brazilian census reports—namely: manufacturing, processing and construction; wholesale and retail trade; real estate, banking, credit, and insurance; services; transportation, communication, and storage; the liberal professions; public administration, legislation, and justice; and national defense and public security. It was not possible in this case to separate construction from the manufacturing and processing category, nor domestic services from services in general, as was done in the preparation of Table x.

Table LXXIV contains in summary form some of the more significant results of the computations described above. More specifically, it shows for the "urban" male labor force of each of the municípios in which a state capital is located the percentages reported as engaged in manufacturing and construction, commerce, transportation and communication, public administration and so forth, and national defense and public security. This information, in turn, enables one to discern important differences in the relative importance of the various functions performed by Brazil's principal cities. Some comment about the differences is in order.

Manufacturing has formed such an important base for the development of cities in the northeastern part of the United States since 1850 that it is difficult for many people in this country to think of rapid urbanization unaccompanied by substantial industrialization.

---

[12] Reproduced in Morse, *From Community to Metropolis*, 25.

TABLE LXXIV

*Principal Functions of Brazilian Cities as Indicated by Relative Importance of Major Occupational Categories, 1950 ***

City	Percentage of the urban male labor force employed in:				
	Manufacturing and construction	Commerce	Transportation, communication, and storage	Public administration, legislation, and justice	Defense and public security
North					
Manaus	27	22	17	9	5
Belém	23	20	22	4	10
Northeast					
São Luís	28	20	20	6	4
Teresina	29	19	10	8	8
Fortaleza	24	25	14	5	8
Natal	21	17	14	4	23
João Pessoa	26	19	15	9	8
Recife	30	22	13	4	7
Maceió	36	17	14	6	6
East					
Aracaju	30	17	16	7	8
Salvador	28	20	16	5	7
Belo Horizonte	30	16	12	7	7
Vitória	18	20	20	10	7
Niterói	26	15	17	7	11
Rio de Janeiro	23	1C	10	7	10
South					
São Paulo	47	16	8	3	3
Curitiba	37	14	10	5	10
Florianópolis	21	17	14	10	14
Pôrto Alegre	30	20	12	6	9
West Central					
Cuiabá	32	15	10	11	10
Goiânia	30	14	11	11	6

* Computed from data in "Censo Demográfico," VI *Recenseamento Geral do Brasil, 1950*, I (Rio de Janeiro, 1956), 204–51.

As a result, not a few sociologists and economists from the United States are entirely unprepared to deal with the process of urbanization as it is going on in many parts of Brazil, and especially that taking place in the northeastern region. As may be seen from the data in Table LXXIV, the city of São Paulo is in a class of its own in the extent to which manufacturing offers employment to the heads of its families and other male workers. Curitiba ranks second in this respect. Furthermore, in nearly all the other capitals, commerce combined with transportation and communication substantially outranks manufacturing and construction in relative importance, whereas in São Paulo the latter is barely half as important as the former. To a lesser degree, a similar situation prevails in Curitiba.

In Fortaleza commerce exceeds all the other categories in the number of male workers engaged, although Recife and Manaus also are outstanding in this respect. Belém, Niterói, and São Luís are the cities in which transportation and communication ranks high, São Paulo the principal one in which that category ranks low, from the standpoint of the proportions of the male workers engaged in activities so classified.

Because all of the cities involved in the present analysis are capitals, the numbers engaged in public administration, legislative activities, and judicial affairs naturally are of considerable importance on the relative basis. This tendency is especially marked in the smaller cities such as Goiânia, Cuiabá, Florianópolis, and Vitória. In these places most of the other functions are not highly developed, and as a result the personnel employed to man the state governments, those engaged in local government activities, and the federal employees stationed there all taken together amount to at least one worker out of every ten. This is considerably greater than the proportion in Rio de Janeiro, still the national capital in 1950, which is noted throughout Brazil for the large numbers on the federal payroll. In this connection it should be indicated that Rio de Janeiro is probably the most multifunctional city in Brazil. It is important as a manufacturing center, as a great port, as one of the few important centers of rail transportation in the entire country, as a great commercial and financial city, and as a recreational and residential center par excellence.

Natal and Florianópolis are the places in which those employed in the defense of the nation and in activities related to public security loom large on the relative basis. As might be expected, Rio de Janeiro, and Niterói across the bay from it, specialize to a considerable extent in these functions, and employment in these fields also is of more than usual importance on a relative basis in Belém, Curitiba, and Cuiabá. On the other hand, São Paulo is distinguished by the comparatively small number of persons so engaged, as are São Luís and Manaus.

In addition to the categories it was practicable to include in Table LXXIV, the relative importance of the "services" in supplying employment to the members of Brazil's male labor force is of interest to many. In this connection it is unfortunate, of course, that those engaged in domestic service cannot be separated from the others, but even so the data that are available are of considerable significance. As might be expected, the range in proportions of those in the "services" category is very great, with Rio de Janeiro, where 18 per cent of the economically active males were classified in this group, being at one end of the scale, and Teresina, with only 6 per cent so classified, being at the other. Closely rivaling Rio de Janeiro were Goiânia, with 17 per cent, and São Luís, Recife, Salvador, and

Vitória, each with 16 per cent in this category. The second lowest proportion engaged in services was in Aracaju (8 per cent), followed by Fortaleza and Curitiba (10 per cent), Cuiabá (11 per cent), and Manaus and Niterói (12 per cent). In Belo Horizonte 15 per cent were classified in the group under consideration, in São Paulo 14 per cent, and in each of the other capitals (Belém, Maceió, Natal, João Pessoa, Florianópolis, and Pôrto Alegre) 13 per cent. It is entirely possible, of course, that in the cities which rank low in this respect the low degree of social differentiation and specialization is one of the significant factors involved, i.e., that many persons classified in other categories actually spend substantial portions of their time

TABLE LXXV

Relative Importance of the Occupational Categories of the Urban Male Labor Force in the City of São Paulo and the Distrito Federal, 1950 *

Occupational category	Per cent of male labor force	
	São Paulo	Distrito Federal
Manufacturing, processing, and construction	47.3	22.6
Trade and commerce	16.0	15.9
Banking, real estate, credit, and insurance	3.3	4.3
Service activities	14.2	18.0
Transportation, communication, and storage	8.3	10.1
Liberal professions and auxiliary occupations	1.7	2.3
Social activities (teaching, social work, religious activities, etc.)	3.6	9.5
Public administration, legislation, and justice	2.9	6.8
National defense, public security, and related activities	2.7	10.5

* Computed from data in "Censo Demográfico," *VI Recenseamento Geral do Brasil, 1950,* I (Rio de Janeiro, 1956).

doing domestic work or in performing other services. One may also speculate to the effect that the relative scarcity of highly affluent families in Teresina, Aracaju, Fortaleza, Cuiabá, and Curitibá may be involved.

Because of the significant differences in the relative importance of the various urban functions in Rio de Janeiro and São Paulo, as indicated by the materials presented above, it was thought desirable to present the more complete information for the two side by side. See Table LXXV. As is well known, one who visits these two great cities is likely to gain the impression that São Paulo is highly specialized as an industrial and commercial center, whereas Rio de Janeiro appears to function to a large extent as an administrative, defense, cultural, recreational, and residential city. Therefore, it is interesting to note that such observations are supported to a large degree by the occupational data from the 1950 census. São Paulo's large contingent in its manufacturing and construction industries is its chief distinguishing feature. In the relative importance of trade and commerce there is little difference between the two. Rio de Janeiro appears to have functioned somewhat more than São Paulo as a center of transportation and communication, and also as a financial center; in all the others, and especially in activities related to national defense and public security, administration and legislation, and religious and cultural activities, Brazil's former capital has specialized to a much greater extent than the capital of Brazil's largest and most powerful state.

ECOLOGICAL PATTERNS

Relatively little is known about the ecological patterns prevailing in Brazilian cities. The detailed sociological and cartographic studies of specific cities required to secure this type of knowledge are, for the most part, still to be made. It is certain, of course, that in Brazil's towns and cities, as in other parts of the world, various types of social phenomena tend to cluster in specific parts of the urbanized area, and that a truly symbiotic relationship exists between many of the social and cultural elements that are found in a given district. The nature of these clusters and the relationships between the components of which they are made up are, however, still largely unknown.

In all probability the rental value of urban property is fully as important as a factor in bringing about the ecological patterns prevailing in Brazil as it is in the United States. In a very real sense the amount that families can pay for housing serves to sort them into categories and to place those in similar economic circumstances in specific areas of the city. This gives rise to exclusive districts for the wealthy, residential areas occupied almost exclusively by families of middle-class status, working-class sections, slums, and various other types of residential districts. But the arrangement of these areas seems to be vastly different in Brazilian cities from that which is usual in the United States, possibly largely because of differences in intra-urban transportation facilities and differences in the relative importance of the various social classes in the two countries. Thus in the United States, almost without exception, the most exclusive residential districts are in the distant outskirts of a city, and the term suburb usually denotes a better-than-average residential area; whereas in Brazil, as in most other parts of Latin America, the more exclusive residential sections usually are well towards the center of the urbanized area, and the term suburb definitely has depreciative connotations.

Likewise in many cities in the United States, of which Chicago is the much-studied prototype, the cheapest rents, the most undesirable housing and other unsatisfactory living arrangements, the concentrations of antisocial behavior, and so forth are highly concentrated in the disorganized zones immediately surrounding the central business districts. Because of the growth patterns of these cities these areas are in the process of transformation from residential to commercial purposes. But all of this is different in Brazil, where the slums are by no means most common in the hearts of the cities. Instead, the outskirts of each city make up a thick band of rude habitations whose inhabitants are living under the most precarious conditions. These are the densely populated sections which have not yet been "urbanized," i.e., streets have not been aligned, pavement is lacking, there are few if any faucets from which water for drinking and other domestic uses may be secured, and there are not many lines to carry electricity to the huts and alleyways.

Perhaps the Brazilian image of urban ecological patterns is most adequately expressed in the following paragraph which its author used to introduce a fundamental study of the *favelas* of Rio de Janeiro:

In all urban centers there generally are sections which are distinguished from the others by the almost complete lack of public improvements and by the uncomfortable conditions in their dwellings. As a rule, these districts in which the poorest layers of the population live form the periphery of the cities, and they constantly spread to greater distances from the centers of greatest activity, carrying along their human agglomerations, with greater or less mobility, to the degree that the urban expansion becomes more intense. The social groups of high economic levels generally are located in the central districts, or in proximity to them, whereas those lacking resources live on the outskirts.[13]

URBAN SOCIAL PROBLEMS

The flood of migrants from the rural areas into the established towns and cities of Brazil has given rise to a host of serious problems with which Brazilian society is sadly unprepared to deal. The bulk of the newcomers are from the segments of the population who are least prepared culturally, educationally, economically, and politically for life in great metropolitan centers, or even for that in smaller cities. Millions of them are now living in improvised huts and shacks in the favelas which cover the hilltops and hillsides in Rio de Janeiro, in the areas most subject to flooding in São Paulo, on the mud flats daily washed by the tides in Recife, and in the "suburbs" of these and hundreds of other cities and towns. Daily their chief preoccupation is that of getting enough food to sustain themselves and the numerous members of their families. Completely unequipped by education and background to resist the blandishments of demagogues of every political hue, they join the more sophisticated segments of the urban proletariat in bitter and destructive outbursts and rioting of all types.

[13] Guimarães, "As Favelas do Distrito Federal," *loc. cit.*, 250..

But by no means all of the social, political, and economic turmoil now going on throughout Brazilian cities and towns should be attributed to the lack of sophistication and poor adaptation to urban life on the part of the millions of recent arrivals from the rural districts. The newcomers to the cities also include large numbers of persons of middle- and upper-class status, and several million immigrants from Europe and Japan likewise form part of Brazil's urban population. In the last analysis, many of the most serious problems of urban life in Brazil seem to stem from the following factors: (1) rampant inflation; (2) the multiplicity of part-time jobs; (3) inadequate intra-urban and interurban transportation facilities; (4) inadequate services and utilities; (5) the breakdown of the family moorings of many of the newcomers; and (6) the plague of scarcities of all types.[14] Most of these have received attention elsewhere in this volume, and here mention need be made merely of the fact that, taken together, they make life in Brazilian cities a very trying experience for most of those directly involved.

[14] Smith, "The Giant Awakes: Brazil," *loc. cit.*, 97–99, 101–102.

PART SEVEN

Conclusion

CHAPTER XXIII

CONCLUSION

BRAZIL, land of the future? Many have answered this question with an unqualified "yes"; others are not so sure; and some have been impelled to damn all Brazil and everything Brazilian. That Brazil has secured the frontiers to a large share of the world's unsettled and sparsely settled territory, there can be no doubt. Fortunately, for South America and the world, the Portuguese colonies were held together. Innumerable separatist movements were suppressed, so that there has emerged one great nation and not a host of small bickering states. Also beyond question is the fact that there are vast undeveloped resources within the borders of South America's giant. Just what they are is still to be determined. However, even though failure to distinguish between lush vegetation and rich soil has been widespread, one may be sure that there are means of support for millions more people in Brazil. But resources and space, of themselves, do not guarantee that Brazil is on the verge of assuming world or even hemispheric leadership. The cultural heritage, particularly the economic organization, and the efforts made to develop to the fullest the human potentialities are the important points to consider.

Land of the future? Yes, providing Brazilians learn and apply even more of the medical and sanitary techniques which alone can make life healthful in the tropics; providing they make the fullest use of modern technology and cease their fierce destruction of natural resources; providing they borrow or devise a more equitable system for distributing the results of the productive process among capital, management, and labor; and providing they apply much more of what mankind has learned about urban life, so as to reduce the precariousness of life for the millions who now are flocking into her cities and towns. Only a cultural equipment primarily designed to safeguard health, comparable to that employed in the Canal Zone, will make possible the presence of a great population in the Amazon Valley, in the greater portion of unsettled Brazil. If the hand of man is not strengthened for its struggle with nature by the employment of power and labor-saving equipment, the population of Brazil might some day approach that of China or India and without any happier results. If the vicious destruction of the forests is paralleled for other natural resources, many of Brazil's potentialities may be dissipated before there is a chance to use them for human welfare. If the millions of Brazilians who make up the nation's labor force do not receive more of the total national production, preferably in the form of education, sanitation, medical care, and the other services which valorize men, Brazil may continue to be for generation after generation merely a promise for the future, and nothing more.

With the immediate future viewed from the vantage point of recent trends, certain observations and predictions, with a few recommendations, may be made. It seems fairly certain that fire agriculture, the primitive system which wastes Brazil's human, timber, and soil resources, will gradually be eliminated. Slowly but surely it will give way to the more rational, efficient, and less destructive agricultural methods which had their origin in Europe. Brazil will be fortunate if the models followed are those from northern Europe where animal traction, the plow, and the four-wheeled farm wagon are integral parts of the cultural heritage. Except for coffee and a few other crops this heritage need never place a dead weight on the possible level of living by relying on the hoe culture of southern Europe. The Brazilians of Polish and German descent can help greatly to diffuse better farming methods throughout the length and breadth of the republic, to spread the knowledge that will sound the death knell of primitive fire agriculture.

Cultural lag is such a heavy drag, however, that sudden changes should not be expected. Although Saint-Hilaire would never recognize the São Paulo of today as the decadent, poverty-stricken area he encountered a little over a century ago, that state, and its progress, is an exception. The change for the better probably will not be so rapid in most other sections. Nevertheless, the adoption of better agricultural methods will do much to improve the situation throughout the entire nation. Coupled with this, the use of animal traction and the farm wagon can help man and woman rise above their present beast-of-burden status.

Brazil would do well to give considerable attention to its population policy. The cry "falta de braços" is sure to continue, and with it a strong pressure from the landed proprietors for the importation of cheap labor. Immigration per se should not be considered an unmixed blessing. Any immigrant who would be content for long with the status of farm laborer should be shunned as the plague. The large landowners, however, are not likely to be enthusiastic about any other. On the other hand, there will not be many special-interest groups seeking to encourage the immigration of independent farm families or provision of a liberal homestead policy that would enable them quickly to develop farms and become owners of land. However, Brazil probably never again will allow foreign nationality groups to establish their own miniature societies, to seal themselves off hermetically, and form little worlds of their own. This will avoid the one serious disadvantage which has arisen from the importation of German, Italian, and Polish settlers into south Brazil.

The birth rate in Brazil seems likely to remain at a high level for some time to come, at least until 1970. Therefore, even the slight reduction in mortality recently has been reflected in the greater natural increase of the population. The control of the infectious diseases and improved infant, child, and maternal care can save many lives. Fortunately, these are the aspects of the mortality problem that are most susceptible to human control. A possible $1,000,000 spent on a campaign to reduce infant mortality, mainly by educating mothers about the care and feeding of children, probably would increase Brazil's population far more than a similar amount expended for the subsidization of immigration.

Only an increase in longevity, a fall in the birth rate, or both, can greatly reduce the ratio of Brazilians in the dependent ages to those in the productive ages. Therefore, for some time to come the average Brazilian producer will have more mouths to feed than his fellows in North America or Europe. Unless his efforts are correspondingly more productive, the quality of the population will suffer to some extent.

The future of Brazil is dependent on the land system it adopts or fails to adopt more than upon any other factor. That settlement will continue to advance, to project long fingers into the interior, is surely expected. But it will make a difference whether it is merely the haphazard occupation that has gone forward in north and central Brazil, the better-planned colonization such as has been carried on in the South, or a still more rational plan for establishing people on the land. There is no logical reason why Brazil should not make use of the experience that has been gained in the settlement of North America. It still is not too late for Brazil to establish a national land system, but time is running out; and it is not easy for one to be complacent about the manner in which settlement is going on in states such as Maranhão and Goiás.

Brazil's land surveys, titles, and records could be made fully as simple as those in the United States and Canada. Simplification would be highly advantageous and could be accomplished without the necessity of incurring any of the disadvantages inherent in the system of squares which is characteristic of the two North American countries. In fact, the plan the author once recommended for Colombia would fit Brazil just as well. The initial step is a law specifying that future surveys shall all be made in accordance with the new system. The scheme itself provides that the entire country be laid off into square degrees, the divisions which occur by projecting all of the degrees of latitude and longitude across the national territory. Each of these is given a number on the map. The actual survey lines can be run as needed, preferably only a step in advance of actual settlement. This will fit very well into the excellent mapping recently done in Brazil. Each square degree may be divided into squares, sections, lots, and parcels, as in Figure 40. Then to deed fifty hectares it is necessary only to indicate the parcels, lot, section, square, and degree that are involved. For example, if degree No. 75 fell in Amazonas near Manaus, a man's title to a certain fifty hectares might read "parcels a and b of lot B, section 17, square 9, degree 75." Such a system would do much to incorporate Brazil's national slogan "order and progress"

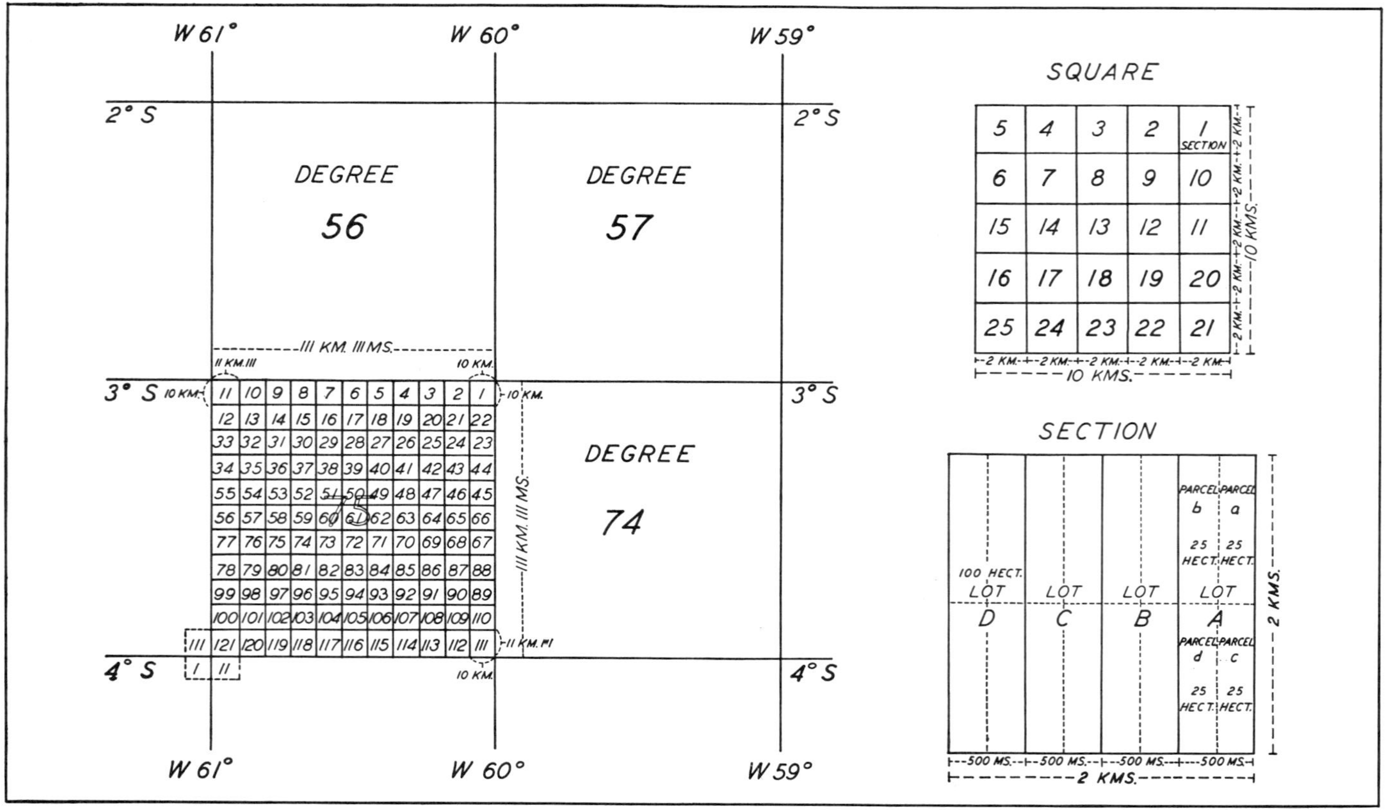

FIGURE 40. System of land surveys recommended for Colombia which also could be used in Brazil.

in her land policy. To make the actual surveys and deed the public lands according to such a plan is less expensive than to do it in the haphazard manner now in use.

In addition to systematic surveys Brazil needs to adopt a homestead law. A wise land policy would encourage actual settlers to occupy and develop unused public lands. By so doing they should become entitled to deeds to land they settle and should not be compelled to pay another price for parts of the public domain. All official efforts should be directed to guiding the settlement in a systematic manner. A considerable amount of public land, as much as one or two sections in every twenty-five, should be reserved as a patrimony for educational purposes. The sections to be reserved should have the same number in every square, and the oncoming generations should never be betrayed by allowing the school lands to be juggled. The amount of land to which one man is entitled should be liberal from the standpoint of the family farm, but small enough to discourage the large landed proprietor. The upper limit might well be around 200 hectares in areas suitable for agriculture, 750 in those adapted only to stock raising. Above all, Brazil should seek to put large acreages of public lands into the hands of those who themselves will till them adequately.

On the lands that have already passed into private ownership it will be more difficult to make the desirable changes. Improvements will be easiest in parts of south Brazil, where the pooling of resources through the property tax and the investment of the funds in education, roads, and sanitation would add greatly to the worth of the average man. Elsewhere the problem of the latifundium is widespread. For dealing with this situation there is nothing so effective as the property tax, especially the graduated property tax. Regardless of the means used, provided they are prudent, the objective should be to get these large, unused tracts into the hands of people who themselves will till the earth. In all of these endeavors Brazil would be wise to utilize the small farmers from the colonial areas of the South to instruct its other millions in European methods of agriculture, in the use of the wheel, the plow, draft animals, and all the other means by which modern agriculture increases production per man.

The renting of lands probably will increase in relative importance. Farm tenancy has already made great headway in São Paulo, and it is likely to come to the fore rapidly elsewhere. On the whole, this practice will come about by farm laborers improving their social status and not because owners slip back into tenancy. However, in Rio Grande do Sul, Santa Catarina, and Paraná there probably will be an increased tendency for owners to drop down one rung on the agricultural ladder, for renting to become more prevalent.

Over most of Brazil holdings will probably be reduced in size. In many places the subdivision of estates by inheritance may bring acute problems such as those already present in parts of São Paulo and Minas Gerais. The subdivision of fazendas brought about by using them for the establishment of colonies of small farmers offers greater promise. But this division of land will not be universal. In the sugar areas the concentration of landownership and control may be expected to continue unabated. Some coffee estates will be split up among several heirs, but it will be some time before they are likely to be greatly subdivided. Cocoa and rubber plantations will continue to be of enormous size. However, many of the huge cattle ranches of Rio Grande do Sul, Mato Grosso, and Goiás are likely to be subdivided into farms.

The standards and levels of living in Brazil will surely improve. This improvement can hardly be done rapidly, but more education, the growth of cities, the improvement of communication and transportation, and the diffusion of new systems of merchandising and display will increase the wants of millions of Brazilians. The nationwide diffusion of knowledge concerning life in south Brazil and in other countries will have the same effect. By degrees the increased wants will lead to more regular work activities, to greater production, and to a higher level of living. Social legislation now being enacted will induce some landed proprietors to improve the living and working conditions of the families on their places. Many others may be shamed into doing the same.

The small município found in São Paulo and Minas Gerais is well on the way to becoming a genuine rurban community. This tendency will be promoted if certain of its functions are strengthened. Most important of all is the establishment of a high school for each little city that forms the seat of a município. Increased local taxation with the proceeds used for the more adequate provision of essential governmental services also would contribute to this end. Brazil's leaders should not endeavor to do everything from Brasília. The município is the logical unit of organization for use in the provision of more adequate protection for life and property, health and welfare services, education, and roads.

Brazil would be wise to double, double again, and then redouble the number of students it is sending to foreign universities. The utmost encouragement and support should be given to those interested in scientific training at the graduate level. The need is not so acute for persons trained abroad in the humanities. With personnel trained abroad, plus those prepared in the national institutions of higher learning, Brazil soon would be able to staff more universities and technical schools. Then it would be equipped to train the teachers for the secondary schools it is opening throughout the length and breadth of the land. Along with this endeavor the program of establishing more public elementary schools and of increasing the length of the elementary course could be pushed ahead even more rapidly than in the last decade. As the teachers receive better training and become more experienced, professional standards will regulate many of the details of school activity which it is now necessary to handle through legislation.

All of this will cost money. Many will ask, some of them with scorn, "Can Brazil afford such improvements?" From the purely economical point of view it is difficult to see how it can afford not to make them. After all, the money necessary is cruzeiros, not dollars or other foreign exchange. One need not be a narrow exponent of the labor theory of value to hold that this means merely putting a larger share of the nation's effort into educational lines. Except for the small amounts necessary to send people abroad for training, money spent on education remains in the country. Resources are not depleted or exported. Brazil can build a great educational system, valorize its people, merely by directing a greater portion of the productive efforts of its population into educational activities. This is exactly what other countries have found it necessary to do. A minimum goal for the next five years might well be the establishment of at least one well-equipped and well-staffed high school in every município. Anything less can hardly be viewed as a realistic approach to the problem; and anything less is hardly in keeping with either the letter or the spirit of the Alliance for Progress.

PART EIGHT

Supplement
to Fourth Edition

BRAZIL

- —··— International boundary
- ··········· Region boundary
- ··········· State or territory boundary
- ⊛ National capital

```
0          300         600
      STATUTE MILES
0      300    600
      KILOMETERS
```

INDEX TO STATES AND TERRITORIES

1. AMAZONAS
2. TERRITÓRIO DO
   RORAIMA
3. PARÁ
4. TERRITÓRIO DO AMAPÁ
5. MARANHÃO
6. PIAUÍ
7. CEARÁ
8. RIO GRANDE DO NORTE
9. PARAÍBA
10. PERNAMBUCO
11. ALAGOAS
12. SERGIPE
13. ACRE
14. TERRITÓRIO DE RONDÔNIA

15. MATO GROSSO
16. GOIÁS
17. BAHIA
18. MINAS GERAIS
19. ESPÍRITO SANTO
20. SÃO PAULO
21. RIO DE JANEIRO
22. GUANABARA
23. PARANÁ
24. SANTA CATARINA
25. RIO GRANDE DO SUL
26. TERRITÓRIO DE
    FERNANDO DE NORONHA
27. DISTRITO FEDERAL

INTRODUCTION

THIS NEW addition to *Brazil: People and Institutions* presents some of the important sociocultural changes in Brazil during the 1960's and the early 1970's. As far as possible my objectives and procedures are essentially the same as those of the earlier editions, namely to apply a genuinely scientific approach in determining and setting forth significant knowledge about Brazilian society. This and all of my studies of societies of the United States, Brazil, Colombia, and elsewhere, represent a lifelong endeavor to participate in building a genuinely scientific sociology that would deserve a place among the natural sciences such as geology, botany, and zoology. From my days as an undergraduate student, when I was associated closely with fellows who since have gained international repute as natural scientists, I have held steadfastly to the idea that the only difference between sociology and the other sciences should be found in the subject matter and not in the objectives and logical methods used. I know from courses I took and from my field and laboratory work that social facts can be more complicated and elusive than those of natural sciences. It is far more difficult to obtain a full objectivity and scientific attitude for instance, in the study of such phenomena as family, church, and social class, than it is in the study of plants, animals, and stones. But these difficulties have never caused me to abandon the attempt, from my graduate student days to the present.

I believe that my ability to avoid many of the fads and fashions in sociology I have seen come and go over the years, has been due to my belief in the methods of the natural scientists, chief among whom in my esteem, were Charles Darwin and Alfred Russell Wallace. My inspiration came largely from their truly scientific procedures: starting with careful observation, description, and classification of rather insignificant bits of nature,[1] and gradually building through pragmatic, inductive patterns of thought to principles and

---

[1] At a time when it is not unusual for careful reports of truly scientific work by some sociologists to be thrust aside disdainfully as "mere description" by many of their colleagues, I myself often turn to Darwin's work as the source of descriptions of enduring value. Thus a few years ago, in connection with some study of the origin and dissemination of the great sociocultural system known as the corn-hog-beef cattle type of farming, I needed accurate information about the types of swine that had been developed in various parts of the world. This I found in Darwin's *The Variation in Plants and Animals under Domestication*. See T. Lynn Smith, "Agricultural-Pastoral Conflict: A Major Obstacle in the Process of Rural Development," *Journal of Inter-American Studies*, XI (January, 1969), 57.

theories of the greatest interest and significance. The fact that these two men, working separately and spending much of their lives in vastly different parts of the world, including Wallace's lengthy sojourn in the Amazon region of Brazil, independently formulated identical theories of the origin of species early impressed me and continues to impress me today as demonstrating conclusively the validity and utility of their methods and procedures. These and other examples of the ways theories and principles are developed in the natural sciences also convinced me that if and when we had any systematic body of verified principles and theories pertaining to society, it would have to be developed in exactly the same empirical, pragmatic, inductive way; it could not be derived through deductive cogitations of social philosophers.

For this reason I consider that the sociological career of my own great teacher and long-time friend Pitirim A. Sorokin reached its apex with the publication of the monumental *A Systematic Source Book in Rural Sociology*,[2] on which Carle C. Zimmerman collaborated, and that his finest sociological work was otherwise best expressed in his *Social Mobility*,[3] and *Principles of Rural-Urban Sociology*.[4] The latter also was done in collaboration with Zimmerman. All of these were published before Sorokin developed his "logico-meaningful method" and produced the great works that have given him deserved renown as a philosopher. I have to confess that I never was able to accompany Sorokin into the realms of his more philosophical intellectual activities, although I always have gained renewed confidence in the course I was trying to follow by reading and rereading the works on which he was engaged during the years I was taking his classes and seminars and serving as his assistant. Thus, for better or worse, I have spent many months in 1970 and 1971 attempting by scientific methods to gain fuller understanding of the structure of Brazilian society, the processes going on in that important part of world society, and especially the sociocultural changes underway and the direction of their trends.

In the first of the four new chapters, the growth of population and other demographic changes in Brazil are presented in relation to the accompanying changes in the various institutions and sociocultural systems that have most to do with the production of food, feed, and fiber. In Chapter XXV, attention is focused upon the process of urbanization and its relation to the drastic changes in social organization and life in Brazil. In Chapter XXVI, I have endeavored to take stock of the changes in the class system in which the lives of all Brazilians are enmeshed. In Chapter XXVII, I attempt to assess the changes in the basic nucleated social institutions —the family and kinship institutions, education and the school, religion and the church, and political and governmental institutions.

[2] Sorokin, Zimmerman, and Galpin, *A Systematic Source Book in Rural Sociology* (Minneapolis, 1930–32).
[3] Sorokin, *Social Mobility* (New York, 1927).
[4] Sorokin and Zimmerman, *Principles of Rural-Urban Sociology* (New York, 1929).

CHAPTER XXIV

POPULATION AND THE FOOD SUPPLY

AS INDICATED in the first three editions of this volume, for well over a century after Brazil gained its independence, the quest for additional inhabitants was one of the great preoccupations of its leaders. Indeed, the plaintive refrain, *falta de braços,* or "lack of arms [hands]," was their theme song. After the close of the second world war, however, and especially during the 1960's, this tune changed; and during the 1970's the demands for population controls are being voiced by more and more of those in positions of responsibility. The time is approaching, if indeed it has not already arrived, in which Brazil will be judged to have "plenty of people," and the concern increasingly will be whether Brazilians in all walks of life are to become a "people of plenty."

The race between population and food supply has figured more and more importantly on the Brazilian scene since 1960. The consideration of population factor is not limited to increases in number of inhabitants, for the problem involves not merely the changing number of people but the unprecedented extent to which Brazilians in all parts of the country have flocked into the burgeoning cities and towns. Moreover, it seems essential to analyze briefly each of the three primary factors that have a bearing on the changes in the number and distribution of the population, namely, the birth rate, the death rate, and net immigration-emigration, as well as those in the more important demographic characteristics of Brazil's people. Similarly, in the discussion of the food supply, attention is focused not merely upon the expanding volume of production of food, feed, and fiber, but upon the changes presently underway in several of the great sociocultural systems that govern man's relationships to the land, including the size of the landed estates and farms, land tenure, the ways of farming, and types of farming. In considering these, it is essential to identify and describe some of the measures presently being used by private individuals and groups and by governmental personnel and agencies as they seek to increase substantially the production for domestic consumption and export.

POPULATION TRENDS

In the paragraphs that follow, consideration is given to four of the large demographic features of Brazilian society, namely, the growth of population, the primary factors involved in population changes, the redistribution of the inhabitants, and changes or the lack of them in some of the more important characteristics of the population. Each of these is treated in turn.

The Growth of Population. The most salient features of the growth of population in Brazil up to 1960 are discussed in Chapter III. From that analysis it is evident that between 1950 and 1960 the rate of growth of population in Brazil, already at the very high level of 2.5 per cent per annum during the 1940's, moved up sharply to an average of 3.1 per cent for the decade. As a result when the census count of the population in 1960 became available, the total amounted to almost 71 million, 5 million more than anticipated by Brazil's official statistical agencies, the experts employed by various international agencies, and demographers generally, including the present writer.

After 1960, as accurately as it was possible to judge until the results of the 1970 census enumeration became available, it was generally thought that the population of Brazil continued to mount at the dizzy pace of about 3 per cent per year, so that by July 1, 1969 the official Brazilian statistical agencies and the Inter-American Statistical Institute estimated the number of inhabitants to be 92,282,000, and the Brazilians projected a population of 95,305,000 for July 1, 1970.[1]

Population forecasting is, of course, a very inexact science, if indeed it is a science at all; and this is especially true in the case of a nation such as Brazil where large but unknown proportions of the births are not registered and in which the definitive results of the various censuses are not published until after a full decade from the time of the enumeration has elapsed. Be that as it may, the preliminary results of the 1970 Brazilian census of population were released while this volume was in press and they showed only 92,300,000 people in the country, a figure substantially below that anticipated. Whether this number is correct can hardly be known for some time even if qualified demographers are inclined to do the essential analysis. Necessarily, this must await the publication of complete results of the census, and in all probability this will not be until long after the materials are of historical interest only. It may be, of course, that the relatively small figure has been caused by a substantially larger underenumeration of the inhabitants in the 1970 census than in the one for 1960. But this is not a very good guess. It is much more likely, as indicated in the following section, that a substantial decrease in the birth rate began during the 1960's, and that Brazil is on the verge of a momentous demographic transition.

If the preliminary results of the 1970 census are not altered

[1] Inter-American Statistical Institute, *América en Cifras, 1970,* "Situación Demográfica: Estado y Movimiento de la Población," Washington, D.C.: Pan American Union, 1970, pp. 3 and 7; and *Anuário Estatístico do Brasil, 1969* (Rio de Janeiro: Fundação IBGE, 1969), 41.

substantially when the final figures on number of inhabitants are published, then for statistical purposes the annual rate of increase of population in the decade ending in 1970 was 2.7 per cent as compared with the 3.1 per cent during the preceding one. Even so, the population of Brazil continues to burgeon, and in about 1972 the country will become a member of the highly restricted 100-million club of nations. Whether it actually will be the fifth (after China, India, the U.S.S.R., and the United States), sixth, seventh, or eighth member of the group is conjectural, for Indonesia, Pakistan and Japan likewise soon will be passing the 100-million mark in population. In any case, with a rate of growth of 2.7 per cent per year, powered by a birth rate that still is high, and one that is offset less each year by a death rate that is being reduced, Brazil seems certain to experience another huge increase in population during the 1970's. Thereafter, as the problems of life in huge urbanized and industrialized areas become more and more acute for the members of the rapidly expanding middle socioeconomic class, as increased educational levels promote higher standards of living for those in the lower and middle classes, and as the consciously designed programs to reduce the birth rate becomes more effective, the rate of growth of population in Brazil will be reduced substantially. In the immediate future, however, the speed with which the population is growing continues to be a formidable competitor in the race with the increase in the food supply.

The Factors in Population Change. As indicated above, the preliminary results of the 1970 census, released in January 1971, indicate a rate of growth of population between 1960 and 1970 of 2.7 per cent per year, about 13 per cent lower than that of 3.1 per cent per annum during the preceding decade. This in turn means either that there was a substantial change in the rate of natural increase (births minus deaths), or in the completeness of the respective enumerations, or in both. Unfortunately, anyone trying to solve the enigma can get little help from the information and analyses available in the demographic and health reports of the various international bodies. The painstaking efforts of the Inter-American Statistical Institute, published late in 1970 by the Organization of American States, which presently is the most up-to-date, reliable, and useful of all the compendia prepared by the international agencies, will now need thorough revision. The figures they give on the population of Brazil, including the estimates for the years 1961 to 1970 and the projections to the year 2,000 are already known to be seriously in error.[2] In the materials supplied by the Pan American Health Organization, the comprehensive report by the Pan American Sanitary Bureau[3] completely avoids the problem. Because the registration of births and deaths is so incomplete, Brazil does not even figure in the comprehensive tables prepared and published

[2] *América en Cifras, 1970, op. cit.*
[3] *Health Conditions in the Americas, 1965–1968* (Washington, D.C.: Pan American Health Organization, September, 1970).

by this agency, although in a few cases some figures for the state of São Paulo are inserted along with appropriate footnotes.

Eventually, when the data on the characteristics of the population gathered in the 1970 census become available, demographers may be able to overcome to some degree the difficulties created by lack of birth and death statistics. If past experience is any guide, however, this will be about 1980; and, as suggested above, by then most of the material will be of historical interest only. For the present any endeavor to determine the absolute and relative importance of the three factors (births, deaths, and migrations) responsible for the changes in the number and distribution of Brazil's population since 1960 are largely conjectural. One thing, though, is sure; *immigration and emigration* had relatively little to do with the rate of Brazil's population increase during the decade ending in 1970, and changes in the importance of these international migrations do not significantly help us to understand the marked decrease in the same. This is easily demonstrated.

During the period 1951–1960, the data in the various issues of the *Anuário Estatístico do Brasil* show admission of 588,039 immigrants. Neglecting, for present purposes, the facts that a few of these died and a few others left the country before the 1960 census was taken, this number amounts to only 3.1 per cent of the increase of population (19,022,718) reported to have occurred between the censuses of 1950 and 1960. Moreover, in relation to an annual rate of 3.1 per cent per year, the average for the decade, it may either be included or omitted without altering the figure, for it would amount to only three one-hundreths of one per cent per year. Even so, immigration between 1951 and 1960 was more than three times as great as that during the decade ending in 1970, which may be estimated at about 175,000 or roughly 0.8 per cent of the increase of population during the latest intercensal period.

Knowledge that immigration was an inconsequential factor in population changes in Brazil 1960–1970 makes it simpler to account for an increase in population of 21,333,000 and a decrease in the annual rate of growth of 0.4 percentage points. They are due solely to the differences between numbers of *births* and *deaths*. There are, of course, numerous values that could be assigned to the birth rate and the death rate to produce a difference between the two of 0.4 per hundred or 4.0 per thousand. For example, if the birth rate were 50 and the death rate 19 for the years 1951 to 1960, then a fall by 1961–1970 to 46 in the former and no change in the latter would produce the reported change in the two; and the same would be true if the rates were 45 and 14 in 1951–1960 and changed to 40 and 13, respectively, for 1961–1970. There is no need to consider seriously the possibility that a reduction of more than 4.0 points in the birth rate was concealed by some rise in the death rate during the period under scrutiny. Such sharp reversals in plummenting death rates rarely, if ever, occur. Moreover, fragments of recent data for some of Brazil's major cities may be compared with the rates given in Table XVII (page 109) of this volume to indicate that the work of reducing the death rate in Brazil continues to make progress. Thus, between 1956–1958 and 1966–1968 the indicated reductions in the death rates of the populations of Brazil's major cities were as follows: Fortaleza, from 32 to 14; Recife, from 22 to 13; Salvador (Bahia), from 17 to 11; Belo Horizonte, from 15 to 12, Rio de Janeiro, from 12 to 10; São Paulo, from 10 to 9; and Pôrto Alegre, from 14 to 10.[4]

Since the detailed information about age, sex, and other characteristics of Brazil's population as they were in 1960 are becoming available only during the 1970's, it has not yet been possible through meticulous analysis of the same to determine the most likely values of the birth rates and death rates during the 1960's. The best guess, however, is that the birth rate was at least 45 per 1,000 population during the period 1951–1960; and this, combined with the annual rate of growth of population of 31 per 1,000, would mean a death rate of only 14. There is small likelihood, indeed, that the death rate during the decade under consideration was any lower than this, and it is more probable that it was nearer 17, a figure that would mean a birth rate of 48. For the period 1961–1970, the death rate may have been reduced to 12, hardly any lower than that; and this, taken in conjunction with a rate of 27 per 1,000 in the population would signify a birth rate of 39. Such conjectures seem to be about the most reliable that can be arrived at, with the data being what they are, and they lead us to conclude that in the decade 1961–1970 in comparison with that 1951–1960: (1) Brazil's birth rate dropped from above 45 to about 40, about 15 per cent; and (2) her death rate was reduced from approximately 15 to 12, about 20 per cent. These guesses, as indicated, are based on the assumption that the total number of inhabitants of Brazil in 1970, given by the preliminary figures from the late enumeration, will not be substantially increased when the final returns are released, and, also, on the assumption that the count of population in 1970 was no less complete than that in 1960.

The conclusion that the birth rate in Brazil has been falling substantially in recent years is not only novel, but, if confirmed by the definitive results of the 1970 census, as the present writer is confident will be the case, signals the onslaught of great demographic change in that immense country. More on this is presented in the section on changes in population characteristics.

Redistribution of the Inhabitants. During the 1960's, while hoping each year for the definitive results of the 1960 census, I continued my efforts to determine and analyze the extent to which a geographical redistribution of Brazil's population was taking place. With the detailed information on the population counts for states and

[4] The data for the most recent years are from the *Anuário Estatístico do Brasil, 1969*, pp. 85–99. In the cases of Salvador and Belo Horizonte, the latest figures are for the years 1965–1967, and in that of Rio de Janeiro the most recent materials are for the years 1960–1962.

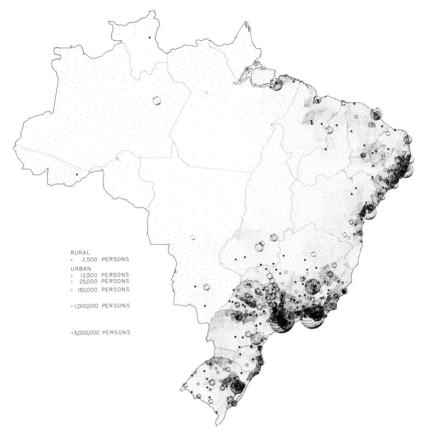

RURAL
= 2,500 PERSONS
URBAN
= 12,500 PERSONS
= 25,000 PERSONS
= 150,000 PERSONS

= 1,000,000 PERSONS

= 3,000,000 PERSONS

F I G U R E 4 1 . Distribution of the Population of Brazil, 1960.

municípios, which became available in 1962 and 1963,[5] it was possible to construct the map used as Figure 41.

Observation of this illustration, which should be compared with Figure 3 showing the distribution in 1940, shows that the most striking feature of the territorial distribution of population in Brazil is its high concentration within a few hundred miles of the immense coast line. From the mouth of the Amazon to the Uruguayan border there are few sparsely populated districts near the seacoast. The great cities are almost all on the coast itself or, as in the case of São Paulo, only a short distance inland; and the narrow coastal band also is where the bulk of the rural population is found. On the other hand, except in the South, where the great colonizing efforts depicted in Chapter XVI took place, very few parts of the interior have been penetrated by substantial numbers of settlers. Exceptions to this rule are the somewhat densely populated zones along the Paranagua River, which forms the boundary between the states of Maranhão and Piauí, the band of thickly inhabited territory ex-

[5] See, for example, Serviço Nacional de Recenseamento, VII Recenseamento Geral do Brasil: 1960 (Rio de Janeiro: Instituto Brasileiro de Geografia e Estatística, 1962). There are separate reports for each of the states and territories.

tending from Paraíba into Ceará, and the areas on both sides of the railway that extends from Salvador to Joàzeiro in the state of Bahia.

Considerable additional study also was made of the role of internal migration in the redistribution of population that took place in Brazil between 1950 and 1960, trends which presumably continued well into the ensuing decade. In many ways the inferences relative to the role of internal migration in recent years are even more significant than the great tendencies treated in Chapter IX.[6]

This is because, between 1950 and 1960, a dramatic exodus got underway throughout Brazil, from the rural districts into urban centers of all sizes, a move that came to overshadow all other aspects of the redistribution of population within the gigantic country. Even if the 1960 materials on state of birth and state of residence were available at this time, the task of separating the internal migration represented by the flow of population into the cities from that going to new agricultural and pastoral areas would still have to be done on the basis of estimates in which the changing numbers of inhabitants represented the primary facts for analysis.

Actually, though, the differentials in the rates of reproduction, except for a significantly lower birth rate in urban districts than in the rural, are not yet sufficiently pronounced to create great margins of error in the estimates; and it is probable that the rate of reproduction for state units is very highly correlated with the rate of natural increase. Therefore, if one takes the rate of population growth between 1950 and 1960, which was a startling 37 per cent, adds a small factor as a margin of safety, and considers that the degree of growth above 40 per cent for the decade is a conservative estimate of the amount of migration, he should not be overstating the matter. In the case of the urban population, any increase of more than 30 per cent for the decade should be a conservative evaluation of the proportion of the growth that is attributable to net migration. Since the foreign-born population actually is falling off, immigration is a negligible factor in the current population changes in Brazil.

If it be considered that the increase of the urban population between 1950 and 1960 is roughly approximated by the part of the reported growth that is in excess of 30 per cent, then the numbers of those who were residing in urban centers in 1960 had been swelled by more than 7,500,000 as a result of the net rural-urban migration since 1950; and even if 37 per cent, the percentage increase of the national population during the period, is taken as the part to be attributed to the natural increase of the urban population, the calculation of the extent to which net migration from rural areas to urban centers during the ten-year intercensal period had increased the urban population enumerated at the end of the decade

---

[6] Some of these materials were presented in a paper entitled "Rural-urban Migration in Brazil," at the Symposium on the Role of Worker Relocation in an Active Manpower Policy, held in Washington, D.C., April 9–11, 1969; and a résumé of the same appears in the *Report* on this symposium published by the International Manpower Institute, U.S. Department of Labor, Washington, D.C., 1969, pp. 63–67.

would still come to a total of more than 6,225,000 persons. Thus, from any objective standpoint, it appears that the wholesale rush of population from the open country to towns and cities between 1950 and 1960 involved at least 1 out of 11 and probably 1 out of every 10 Brazilians who were alive at the time of the 1960 census. Even the least of these ratios is phenomenal; and it is unlikely that the actual amount will ever be gauged with any much greater degree of exactitude. As large as this number and proportion are, they are strictly in accord with expectations of anyone who has observed the mushrooming of existing towns and cities, sudden appearance of great sprawling suburbs in the zones surrounding all the principal metropolitan centers, and the emergence and growth of many additional urban places.

Much of the huge state-to-state migration between 1950 and 1960 is part and parcel of the mass transfer of people from rural to urban residences. In the case of the state of Paraná, though, this is definitely not the case; for in the 102 per cent increase of population in that state during the ten years under consideration, the principal feature was the great rush of people from São Paulo, Minas Gerais, and other nearby states to the newly opened coffee districts in the northwestern part of its territory. For this reason, although Paraná's urban population increased by almost 800,000, or 151 per cent, during the decade, that rapid upsurge accounted for only 37 per cent of the growth of population in the state as a whole. It was accompanied by an expansion of more than 1,360,000, or 86 per cent, in the rural population. Even if a 40 per cent increase in the population is attributed to natural increase, the estimated number of persons living in Paraná in 1960 who had migrated to the state during the 1950's would amount to well over 1,300,000.

Radically different were the developments in São Paulo. There the population rose by some 3,840,000, or 42 per cent, during the decade; but the percentage increase is not much greater than that registered by the nation as a whole, and by any reasonable criterion, relatively little of the growth of population can be attributed to net migration from other parts of Brazil.

Since 1950, much of the growth of metropolitan Rio de Janeiro has taken place in those parts of the city and its suburbs that are located outside the small enclave which once was the Distrito Federal and now is the state of Guanabara. Even so, however, calculations made in the manner described above, with a 30 per cent increase allowed for the natural increase of the population, indicate that there were about 215,000 more people in Guanabara in 1960 than there would have been had there been no interstate migration after 1950. Still more important in this connection, though, is a figure which indicates a net total of 453,000 migrants to the state of Rio de Janeiro, during the years 1950 to 1960. Beyond doubt, the overwhelming proportion of these persons now live in the huge, sprawling, and rapidly industrializing suburbs of the city of Rio de Janeiro.

In addition to the large migrations to Paraná and metropolitan Rio de Janeiro, sizable contingents of interstate migrants also entered central Goiás, north central Maranhão, and southern Mato Grosso during the years 1950 to 1960. The building of Brasília was, of course, an important factor in the movement of people to the plateau sections of Goiás, but the opening during the 1940's of new and rich lands north and west of the new national capital probably exerted an even greater attraction. In any case, my estimates indicate that there were in Goiás at the time of the 1960 census about 400,000 more people than there would have been had there been no interstate migration during the decade under consideration.

The flocking of people from Ceará and other northeastern states into the forested area of north central Maranhão, a large zone on the eastern margins of the Amazon rain forests, for the period 1950 to 1960, involved about 270,000 people.

Finally, a substantial movement of people, largely from São Paulo, westward into the southern parts of the immense state of Mato Grosso took place in the 1950's. My estimates place this at about 180,000 persons.

Fortunately, the recent publication of the population of the Brazilian states and territories as shown by the 1970 census now enables us to get an overall view of the major changes in the distribution occurring during the 1960's. See Table LXXVI.

Changes in the Composition of the Population. Several significant changes in the characteristics or composition of the Brazilian population also have been manifest in the years since 1960. Although few of these have the overall social and economic importance of the changes that will be precipitated in the 1970's by the falling birth rate, it is well to focus attention briefly upon a few of them.

As stressed in Chapter IV, there are few places in the world where the *racial makeup of the population* is more complex than it is in Brazil; also there are few for which the actual importance of the Negro population and its various crosses with other races has been more greatly overemphasized by writers of every genera. We are still awaiting quantitative data more recent than those for 1950 given on page 68 above, but I do not believe that the long-continued trend in the "bleaching" or whitening of the population has yet drawn to a close. However, during the 1970's I expect the fall in the birth rate of middle-class whites to be far more pronounced than that in the rate for the huge and far darker population that makes up the bulk of the lower socioeconomic class. If this proves to be the case, the long trend in the "bleaching" will cease, and, comparable to the reversal during the 1930's in the falling proportion of Negroes in the population of the United States that prevailed from 1790 to 1930,[7] the proportions of Negroes and mulattoes in Brazil will begin to increase.

In order to better see the variation of racial composition from

[7] Cf. T. Lynn Smith and Paul E. Zopf, Jr., *Demography: Principles and Methods* (Philadelphia, 1970), 144.

TABLE LXXVI

Growth of Population, 1960–1970, by States and Territories *

State	Population		Increase 1960–1970	
	1970	1960	Number	Per cent
Brazil	92,237,540	70,967,185	21,270,355	30.0
North				
Rondonia †	95,311	70,783	24,528	34.7
Acre	203,900	160,208	43,692	27.3
Amazonas	714,803	721,215	−6,412	−0.9
Roraima † (Rio				
Branco)	40,855	29,489	11,366	38.5
Pará	1,984,745	1,550,935	433,810	28.0
Amapá †	116,481	68,889	47,592	69.1
Northeast				
Maranhão	2,883,211	2,492,139	391,072	15.7
Piauí	1,735,568	1,263,368	472,200	37.4
Ceará	4,440,286	3,337,856	1,102,430	33.0
Rio Grande do				
Norte	1,603,094	1,157,258	445,836	38.5
Paraíba	2,383,518	2,018,023	365,495	18.1
Pernambuco	5,208,011	4,136,900	1,071,111	25.9
Alagoas	1,606,165	1,271,062	335,103	26.4
Sergipe	900,119	760,273	139,846	18.4
Bahia	7,420,906	5,990,605	1,430,301	23.9
Southeast				
Minas Gerais	11,279,872	9,798,880	1,480,992	28.0
Espírito Santo	1,597,389	1,188,665	408,724	34.4
Rio de Janeiro	4,694,089	3,402,728	1,291,361	38.0
Guanabara	4,296,782	3,307,163	989,619	29.9
São Paulo	17,716,186	12,974,699	4,741,487	36.5
South				
Paraná	6,741,520	4,277,763	2,463,757	57.6
Santa Catarina	2,911,479	2,146,909	764,570	35.6
Rio Grande do Sul	6,652,618	5,448,823	1,203,795	22.1
West Central				
Mato Grosso	1,475,117	910,262	564,855	62.1
Goiás	2,989,414	1,954,862	1,034,552	52.9
Distrito Federal	544,862	141,742	403,120	284.4

* Source: Compiled from data given in the Inter-American Statistical Institute, *Boletin Estadistico*, No. 68, Washington: Organization of American States, February, 1971. The figures are preliminary, they do not include data for the Serra dos Aimorés, and the counts for Maranhão, Mato Grosso, Pará, and Rondonia are indicated as being incomplete. The totals for Brazil include figures of 1,239 in 1970 and 1,389 in 1960 on the Island of Fernando de Noronha, and 384,297 in the Serra dos Aimorés (in litigation between Minas Gerais and Espírito Santo) for 1960. The regional groupings are the ones currently used in Brazil.
† Territory.

one part of Brazil to another, the data in Table IV (page 70 above) were mapped in Figure 42.

Finally, it should be indicated that the great internal migrations in Brazil discussed in the preceding section and in Chapter IX, are

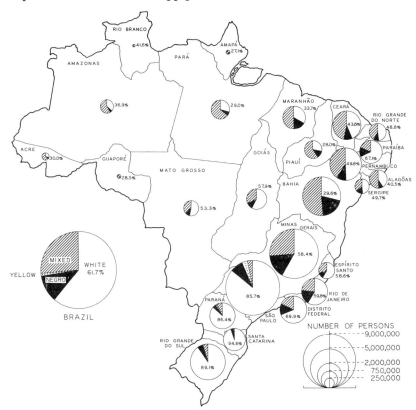

FIGURE 42. Variations in the Racial Composition of the Population, by States, 1950.

bringing about a substantial redistribution of the racial components of Brazil's population, and by so doing, are contributing immensely to the rapid homogenization of Brazilian society. Even without the aid of recent statistical data, one who has made repeated visits to Brazil during the last thirty years can hardly fail to be impressed by this fact. For example, in 1942 when I spent a week or so in and around the beautiful little city of Campinas, São Paulo, I was impressed by the relatively small Negro and mulatto population of the area; whereas, when in 1963 when I spent six weeks there participating in an international course on agrarian reform the large number of blacks and mulattoes present, most of them recent migrants from Bahia and elsewhere to the north and east, was a striking feature of life in the then large and bustling city. More recently, in 1969, I spent a couple of days in Belém where I talked to a few among an obviously recent huge influx of migrants from Pernambuco. I observed far more Negroes and mulattoes than there had been when I had visited Belém and other places in Pará during the 1940's and 1950's.

The *national origins* of Brazil's population have undergone drastic change since 1960, due, of course, to the fact that immigraton has practically ceased and to the fact that the remaining foreign-born population is concentrated in the advanced ages where the mortality rates are high. Unless the admission of immigrants in huge numbers is resumed shortly, which seems highly improbable, Brazil soon will be a country made up almost entirely of people who are native born of native parents.

Between 1960 and 1970 the growth of the *urban* population of Brazil greatly surpassed that of the *rural*, chiefly because of the immense rural exodus discussed in the previous section. As a result, about 1965 Brazil reached the point at which its urban population came to outnumber the rural. Moreover, from the qualitative standpoint the changes in the degree of rurality of the fifty million or so people still residing in rural areas probably is fully as important as the burgeoning numbers of those actually living in urban places. Increasingly the inhabitants of the villages and open country are being influenced by the sociocultural phenomena emanating from the great urban centers, and less exclusively by those influences within their rural environment. It will be some time before good roads, automobiles, electricity, telephones, television sets, and many other culture traits and complexes that long have been among the necessities of rural life in the United States and Canada, are found to any extent in many of Brazil's rural districts. But the change is underway, and on no small scale. For example, in the late 1950's, the radio would have figured in the list just given. But in the 1970's, thanks to the miracle of the transistor, radio sets are present in great numbers of rural homes. Indeed, it is one of the most revolutionary items in contemporary society. In many areas its importance is rivaled by the ubiquitous use of the outboard motor in the propulsion of water craft of various types and sizes. This along with the most feverish program in Brazilian history for construction of roads of all types is revolutionizing transportation. The improvements in communication and transportation, which are discussed in more detail in the chapter on urbanization, are overcoming the cultural lags that long persisted in rural areas, and the changes and quickening pace of the 1960's and 1970's are definitely reducing the tremendous differences between rural and urban life.

THE INCREASE OF THE FOOD SUPPLY

As indicated above, this section was designed to include not merely a discussion of the increase in the supply of food and other agricultural commodities as such, but also to embrace a consideration of the several large and important sociocultural systems that govern man's relationships to the land and therefore are the final determinants of agricultural productivity.

Substantial Increases in the Amounts of Crop and Livestock Products. Actually, during the present century and especially in recent decades, Brazil has taken gigantic strides in the production of the food and fiber relied upon for domestic consumption and for export purposes. It should be recognized, however, that on this subject the statistical data, when they are available at all, are far less satisfactory than those on population trends. In many cases the figures published are hardly more than "educated guesses," and perhaps on some critical matters they are not even that. Nevertheless the volume of crop and livestock products has been expanded tremendously, even more rapidly than the population, so that the per capita production has increased to some extent. For example, from the materials available in various editions of the *Anuário Estatístico do Brasil,* one may observe that the index number showing the relative changes in the volume of agricultural products moved substantially upward from the 100 for 1955, the base year, to 155 for agricultural and 151 for livestock products in 1968. The population grew by about 46 per cent during the comparable period.

It also is important to note that the volume of general agricultural production was held down greatly by the temporary fall (from 239 in 1961 to 102 in 1968) in the index of production of coffee, on which Brazil relies heavily for its foreign exchange, for otherwise the index of physical production would have gone much higher. Thus between 1961 and 1968 the increases in the amounts of various categories of agricultural commodities are reported to be as follows: grains, from 124 to 165; roots and tubers, from 122 to 192; truck crops and vegetables, from 142 to 242; beans and other legumes, from 123 to 178; fruits, from 136 to 195; crops for industrial purposes, from 141 to 172; and other crops, from 186 to 395. Likewise, during the same eight years, the changes in the volume of livestock products is reported to be as follows: general, 121 to 151; cattle, 120 to 143; hogs, sheep, and goats, from 126 to 165; and poultry and eggs, from 126 to 185.[8]

Anyone evaluating these statistical data must keep in mind that the indexes of the volume of physical products are tricky figures. If, for example, a município that had been producing 100 tons of coffee and 100 tons of manioc tubers were to increase its production of the latter to 200 tons, with no variation in the amount of coffee, the change in the index would be from 100 to 150. This is not to assert that any such anomalies actually are present in the cases under consideration. The data required for a full exploration of the subject are not available; and for present purposes it is safe to accept the fact that, despite the recent huge upsurge in Brazil's population, the ratio between the population and the food supply is not worsening. Probably it is improving and to a significant degree.

For many purposes the informed person wants actual figures, and not merely the kinds of relative numbers given in the preceding paragraphs. Accordingly Table LXXVII was prepared to supply figures on the absolute and relative changes in the production of

[8] The data in this paragraph are taken from the 1969 issue of the *Anuário Estatístico do Brasil,* 144, 162.

sixteen of the principal crops and of milk during the period 1960–1970. By any standards these increases represent great achievements, and as indicated below even greater performances reasonably may be expected during the 1970's.

It is interesting to compare the increases in several of these staples with the changes in the production of the same commodities in the United States during the period. This is most readily done by expressing Brazil's production as a percentage of that in the United States. For example in 1960–1961 Brazil's production of rice was reported to be 4,795,000 tons, and this figure rose to 6,652,000 tons in 1968–1969. Comparable amounts in the United States were 2,746,000 tons and 4,777,000 tons, so that Brazilian production expressed as a percentage of that in the United States fell from 194 to 139 during the period under consideration. This is one of the few farm products, however, in which the increase in production in Brazil was less rapid than that in the United States. The corresponding changes in some of the other most important farm products, with the percentage for the year 1960 or 1960–1961 given first are as follows: corn (grain) 8.7 and 10.6; wheat, 1.6 and 2.0; dry beans, 219 and 301; soybeans, 1.4 and 2.2; sweet potatoes, 190 and 340; Irish potatoes, 9.5 and 17.6; cotton lint, 17.3 and 44.2; cotton seed, 19.1 and 49.2; peanuts, 52.4 and 65.4; tobacco 18.3 and 33.2; milk, 9.0 and 12.7; and eggs, 10.1 and 12.5.[9]

Farmers in the United States are justly proud of their remarkable achievements in production; and the data just presented indicates clearly that Brazilian farmers increasingly are helping their own country and the entire world to meet the challenge of the tremendous growth of population. Moreover, Brazil still has far to go before it exhausts the possibilities of applying already tried and tested measures for increasing the production of farms, plantations, and ranches. Improvements in land tenure, adjustments in the sizes of the farms in order to secure far greater inputs of management, the opening of new lands, improvements in the ways of farming, the adoption of more productive types of farming, and the clearing of the titles to hundreds of thousands of her agricultural and pastoral establishments are some of the principal ways by which, during the 1970's, Brazil can greatly increase food, feed, and fiber for domestic consumption and export purposes.

The materials presented in the preceding paragraphs should not be interpreted to mean that the "felt" deprivation in Brazil is on the decrease. In fact, as larger and larger proportions of the population establish their dwellings amid the ferment that is the Brazilian city, as the opportunities for some kind of schooling are extended to greater percentages of the population, and as the members of the lower class and the lower part of the middle class see on every hand displays of the affluence and high levels of con-

---

[9] These indexes were computed from data given in Inter-American Statistical Institute, *América en Cifras, 1970*, "Situación Económica: . . . ," Washington, D.C.: Organization of American States, 1970, pp. 39–93.

TABLE LXXVII

Changes in the Production of Selected
Farm Products in Brazil, 1960–1970 *

Product	Production (1,000 tons)				Change	
	Year	Amount	Year	Amount	Amount	Per cent
Rice (rough)	1960/61	4,795	1968/69	6,652	1,857	39
Corn (shelled)	1960/61	8,672	1968/69	12,814	4,142	48
Wheat	1961	545	1968	856	311	57
Dry beans	1960	1,731	1968	2,420	689	40
Soy beans	1960	206	1968	654	448	217
Sweet potatoes	1960/61	1,283	1968/69	2,120	837	65
Irish potatoes	1960/61	1,113	1968/69	1,606	493	44
Manioc	1960/61	17,613	1968/69	29,203	11,590	66
Oranges	1960	1,910	1968	2,717	807	42
Pineapples	1960	273	1967	337	64	23
Cotton (lint)	1960/61	536	1968/69	718	182	34
Coffee	1960/61	1,797	1968/69	1,311	−486	−27
Sugar cane	1960/61	56,927	1968/69	76,611	19,684	35
Peanuts	1960/61	408	1968/69	754	346	85
Tobacco	1960/61	161	1968/69	258	97	60
Tomatoes	1960/61	397	1968/69	775	378	95
Milk	1960	5,052	1968	7,024	1,972	39

* Source: Compiled and computed from data in Inter-American Statistical Institute, *América en Cifras, 1970,* "Situación Económica:1 . . . ," Washington, D.C.: Organization of American States, 1970, pp. 39–93.

sumption by some of their fellow Brazilians, their wants and aspirations (standard of living) rise sharply. And this can mean nothing more or less than that the "zone of exasperation," or the difference between the plane at which the less priviledged come to feel that they are entitled to live and their actual level of living, continues to become wider and wider.

Fairly secure in the knowledge that Brazil actually is making substantial strides in its efforts to increase the volume of agricultural and pastoral products for domestic consumption, export, and industrial uses, let us next consider some of the factors that are responsible for these gains.

Colonization and Settlement. Although the din of the debates and the plethora of projects for agrarian reform since 1960, which are discussed below, resulted in relatively little colonization in the sense of planned subdivisions into farms of large landed estates, spontaneous movements into and settlement or thicker settlement of many areas have contributed greatly to Brazil's ability to feed her own people and to export farm products to other countries. Moreover in the 1970's, and especially in connection with the building of the Transamazonian Highway and other road projects, the national government once more is engaged in organized colonization projects on a large scale.

An endeavor was made in Chapter XVI to show that since 1920

the rapid expansion of settlement into previously heavily forested areas was by far the most important factor in Brazil's increased production of the means of subsistence and the commodities she has put into the streams of international trade. Of all of this, the phenomenal conquest of a large part of the state of São Paulo for agricultural purposes was by far the most spectacular and important. It is important to keep in mind that during the 1950's and the 1960's, the spread of São Paulo's established system of coffee culture into northern Paraná constitutes one of the outstanding chapters in Brazil's entire agricultural development. In fact, by 1968 Paraná was producing almost half the coffee grown in Brazil, or 1,004,000 tons of the national total of 2,115,000 tons and almost double the 552,000 tons credited to São Paulo.[10] Other outstanding features of the conquest of previously almost unused sections of Brazil during the 1960's are the settlement of large areas of the Rio Doce Valley in Minas Gerais, the opening of the rich new lands in Central Goiás, and the heavy onslaught by migrants from the Northeast (using their primitive and destructive system of fire agriculture) upon the forests of northcentral Maranhão. In both Goiás and Maranhão the expansion of rice culture, accompanied by that of subsistence crops such as beans and manioc, is the principal enterprise of the new settlers. In fact by 1968 Goiás, with an estimated production of 1,250,000 tons of rice (up from 724,000 in 1960), was on the verge of replacing Rio Grande do Sul, with 1,286,000 tons as the largest producer of this great staple in the Brazilian diet; and Maranhão, for which the estimated production in 1960 was only 278,000 tons, had increased its total to 740,000 tons in 1968, when it was exceeded in this basic activity by only Rio Grande do Sul, Goiás, Minas Gerais (1,039,000 tons) and São Paulo (815,000 tons).[11] These data, and others that might be supplied about the great expanded production of the corn, beans, manioc, and other crops on which the settlers depend to feed their own families, should demonstrate conclusively that the spontaneous settlement of virgin lands has contributed substantially to the increased production of food in Brazil.

In the early 1970's Brazil's government again undertook large-scale efforts to colonize extensive areas of the public domain, especially in connection with the construction of the Transamazonian Highway and other roads in the immense, almost uninhabited portions of the national territory. One probably is not far wrong if he thinks that this is intimately related to some of the "spin off" or side effects of the construction during the 1960's of the Belém to Brasília Highway, for much spontaneous settlement radiated from the hundreds of villages and towns that sprang up along the lengthy and badly needed truck route. For example, one analyst, after describing the enormous increases in the production of rice, manioc, beans, and corn in Maranhão since the late 1950's indicates that "the

[10] Data, *ibid.*, 155.

[11] Data, *ibid.*, 151, and *Anuário Estatístico do Brasil, 1962* (Rio de Janeiro: Instituto Brasileiro de Geografia e Estatística, 1962), 57.

tonic that led to this development was the opening of BR-10, Belém-Brasília, at the beginning of this decade. For example, the city of Imperatriz—[in the município] which produces the finest rice in Maranhão—experienced an increase of 67 per cent in recent years, and presently is estimated to have 42,000 inhabitants. . . . The opening of new roads is the most important development. According to a report by the Conselho Nacional de Economia, the increase in the production of babassú and rice is due to the opening of new roads, which permit the establishment of new colonies, and form new fronts of agricultural production." [12]

It also seems certain that the remarkable growth and development of the city and município of Ceres, Goiás, which was started in the 1940's as the Colonia Agrícola de Goías, played a part in convincing Brazil's leaders that it was high time to renew the planned settlement projects in the agricultural development of the nation. In any case, with great fanfare, in 1970 the Brazilian government launched the greatest road-building and colonization program in Brazil's history.

The kick off came on March 18, 1970, when "The President of the Republic announced that actual work on the Highway System for the Colonization and Integration of the Amazon, to be developed by 1974, was to begin immediately, having as its basic component the Belém-Brasília Highway." He then announced:

During the current year the paving of the stretch Anápolis-Jaraguá-Ceres will be completed, and this will be followed by the paving of the stretch from Ceres to Porangatu, already included in the financial negotiations with the World Bank.

Of equal importance with the Belém-Brasília in the opening of the Amazon is the linking of Cuiabá and Pôrto Velho, which also recently has been assured, permitting regularity of transportation by road to the capital of Rondônia, from whence the work will proceed so as to reach this year Rio Branco [Acre] and the Brazilian-Peruvian boundary.

Work also will go ahead in the construction of the road that will link the capital of Amazonas [Manaus] and South-Central Brazil, by way of Pôrto Velho and Cuiabá—with the completion of the stretch from Manaus to Pôrto Velho also planned for this year.

Related projects also are being developed by the Ministry of the Army and the Ministry of Transportation . . . for the completion of the road that will link Manaus with Caracaraí and Boa Vista, and extending to the boundaries with Venezuela and Guiana and of the highway that will connect São Luís and Teresina and Belém, which also is scheduled for completion this year.

Coordinated with the work undertaken in connection with the projects just mentioned, this third government of the Revolution will amplify its contribution by undertaking two new fronts in the building of the basic

[12] Alfredo K. Homma, "O Maranhão Está Chegando," *Correio Agropecuario*, IX (August, 1969), 6. In a report on *Transamazonian Highways*, Montreal, Canada, 1970, p. 22, which Brazil's Ministry of Transportation presented to the VI World Meeting of the International Road Federation, the following changes between 1960 and 1970 in the area traversed by the Belém-Brasília Highway are indicated: population, an increase from 100,000 to 2,000,000 inhabitants; number of cities and villages, an increase from 10 to 120; number of cattle, from negligible to 5,000,000 head; farming, from a little subsistence agriculture to intensive cultures of corn, beans, rice, and cotton.

road system of Amazonia. The first consists of the construction of a highway of penetration along the longitudinal axis of the region, uniting Cuiabá, Cachimbo, Coração de Selva, and Santarém, a port on the Amazon River. This road will function as truly new route for the movement from south to the north, making use of the alternative system of the Cachimbo region. The second will consist of the construction of a pioneer highway uniting the Northeast and Amazonia. Starting with the terminuses of the roads in the Northeast's system, this highway will cross the Belém-Brasília at Marabá on the Tocantins River, and follow across the valleys of the Xingu and Tapajós rivers to Humaitá where it will form a junction with the Pôrto Velho-Manaus highway.

With an extension of 6,750 kilometers [about 4,200 miles], this road, which may be called the Transamazonian, will link the terminal points of navigation on the southern tributaries of the Amazon and will be a clear pathway for the northeasterners in the colonization of the enormous demographic vacuum and the beginning of the utilization of the hitherto inaccessible potentialities of the area.[13]

See Figure 43.

Less than eight months after this momentous announcement, the President, on October 9, 1970, went to Altamira, Pará, where he "watched the felling of a tree of more than fifty meters height, symbolizing the overcoming of one more obstacle in the construction of the road. This solemnity marked the initiation of work on the construction of the Transamazonian Highway."[14] The first work was on the vast portion in the state of Pará. A few months later, on January 11, 1971, "contracts were signed for the construction of the second part of the Transamazonian Highway, between Itaituba and Humaitá, in the state of Amazonas, an extension of 1,000 kilometers."[15]

Some of the details of the grandiose plans for colonization in the monumental endeavors to conquer and settle the Amazon were published in August, 1970.[16] The authorization for the vast undertaking is Decree-Law No. 1,106 which established a Program of National Integration. The territory to be included consists of the areas in which two existing agencies, or the superintendencies for the development of the Northeast and the Amazon, respectively, already were working. In the Northeast the promotion of irrigation projects is the chief type of development envisaged, and in the Amazon road building and colonization are major facets in the program. (In passing I cannot help but express the hope that sooner or later those in charge of SUDENE, the agency for the Northeast, will do what is necessary to promote the growing of alfalfa and its transformation into meat and milk, in that potentially great but constantly bedeviled region.)

[13] Translated from the announcement in the March 18, 1970, issue of the *Boletim Especial* distributed by the Brazilian Embassy, Washington, D.C.

[14] *Ibid.,* October 12, 1970.

[15] *Ibid.,* January 12, 1971.

[16] The fullest account of these that I have been able to obtain is given in *Extensão Rural,* a monthly published by the Associação Brasileira de Crédito e Assistência Rural—ABCAR, in Rio de Janeiro, V (Agosto, 1970), 8–13. The materials in the paragraphs that follow were taken from it.

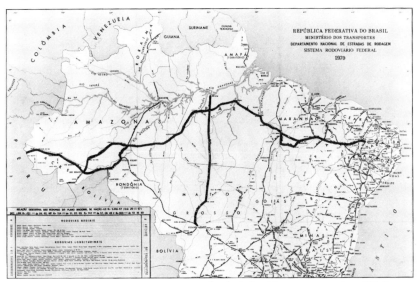

FIGURE 43. Map Showing the Route of the Transamazonian Highway and Other Highways of National Integration. (Courtesy Brazilian Embassy, Washington, D.C.)

The law itself specifies that "there shall be reserved for colonization and agrarian reform the band of territory 10 kilometers deep on each side of the new highway, so that, with the resources of the Program of National Integration, the occupation of the land and the adequate and productive utilization of the same will be accomplished." This same decree assigned the Ministry of Agriculture the responsibility in the Amazon for "colonization and agrarian reform by means of planning and conducting studies and the establishment of projects for the development of agriculture and animal husbandry and the processing of farm products, including the necessary expropriations of land; the selection, training, transportation, and settlement of colonists; the organization of urban and rural communities, and the provision of the basic services required in each."

In his announcement of the plans, the Minister of Agriculture stressed that the new settlements were to be carefully planned and directed and not allowed to develop merely in a spontaneous manner. Specifically, he declared that "the granting of lands—at nominal prices and within the reach of any family—will be carried on as the road is built. Making reference to what occurred in the building of the Belém-Brasília Highway [he stated]: at the conclusion of this project, which lacked the planning of the Transamazonian, there already were 600,000 persons living in reasonably comfortable circumstances on the lands adjacent to it." Finally, he indicated that, to begin with, each family of colonists would receive an allotment of land fronting on the highway for a distance of from 200 to 250 meters and extending to a depth of 10 kilometers. This means that the holdings will vary in size from about 500 to 625 acres. One-half of each allotment is to be maintained in forest.

Inasmuch as the great Amazonian Basin (which includes not only an immense portion of Brazil but huge expanses of territory in Venezuela, Colombia, Ecuador, and Bolivia, as well) forms the one great and potentially fruitful part of the world remaining to experience the impact of twentieth-century sociocultural influences, the present endeavors of the Brazilians are of the utmost interest. Moreover, those who get best acquainted with the immense area are prone to exude the kind of optimism about its possibilities that was exhibited a century ago by some of the world's greatest naturalists who spent many years observing plant and animal life throughout the vast reaches of its virtually unpopulated area. I myself have reacted to many areas in Brazil (and also in Colombia, Peru, and Venezuela) as did Alfred Russell Wallace co-architect with Darwin of the theory of evolution. Consider, for example, his evaluation of the potentialities for colonization of the area along the Rio Negro above Manaus as expressed in the following trenchant paragraphs.

When I consider the excessively small amount of labour required in this country, to convert the virgin forest into green meadows and fertile plantations, I almost long to come over with a half-a-dozen friends, disposed to work, and enjoy the country; and show the inhabitants how soon an earthly paradise might be created, which they had never even conceived capable of existing.

It is a vulgar error, copied and repeated from one book to another, that in the tropics the luxuriance of the vegatation overpowers the efforts of man. Just the reverse is the case: nature and the climate are nowhere so favourable to the labourer, and I fearlessly assert, that here, the "primeval" forest can be converted into rich pasture and meadow land, into cultivated fields, gardens, and orchards, containing every variety of produce, with half the labour, and, what is of more importance, in less than half the time than would be required at home, even though there we had clear, instead of forest ground to commence upon. It is true that ground once rudely cleared, in the manner of the country, by merely cutting down the wood and burning it as it lies, will, if left to itself, in a single year, be covered with a dense shrubby vegetation; but if the ground is cultivated and roughly weeded, the trunks and stumps will have so rotted in two or three years, as to render their complete removal an easy matter, and then a fine crop of grass succeeds; and, with cattle upon it, no more care is required, as no shrubby vegetation again appears. Then, whatever fruit-trees are planted will reach a large size in five or six years, and many of them give fruit in two or three. Coffee and cacao both produce abundantly with the minimum of attention; orange and other fruit-trees never receive any attention, but, if pruned, would no doubt yield fruit of a superior quality, in greater quantity. Pine-apples, melons, and watermelons are planted, and when ripe the fruit is gathered, there being no intermediate process whatever. Indian corn and rice are treated nearly in the same manner. Onions, beans, and many other vegetables, thrive luxuriantly. The ground is never turned up, and manure never applied; if both were done, it is probably that the labour would be richly repaid. Cattle, sheep, goats, and pigs may be kept to any extent; nobody ever gives them anything to eat, and they always do well. Poultry of all kinds thrive. Molasses may be easily made in any quantity, for cane put into the ground grows, and gives no trouble; and I do not see why the domestic process used in the United States for making maple-sugar should not be applied here. Now, I unhesitatingly affirm, that two or three families, containing half-a-dozen working and industrious men and boys, and being able to bring a capital in goods of fifty pounds, might, in three years, find themselves in the possession of all I have mentioned. Supposing them to get used to the mandiocca and Indian-corn bread, they would, with the exception of clothing, have no one necessary or luxury to purchase: they would be abundantly supplied with pork, beef and mutton, poultry, eggs, butter, milk and cheese, coffee and cacao, molasses and sugar delicious fish, turtles' eggs, and a great variety of game, would finish their table with constant variety, while vegetables would not be wanting, and fruits, both cultivatcd and wild, in superfluous abundance, and of a quality that none but the wealthy of our land can afford. Oranges and lemons, figs and grapes, melons and water-melons, jack-fruits, custard-apples, pine-apples, cashews, alligator pears, and mammee apples are some of the commonest, whilst numerous palm and other forest fruits furnish delicious drinks, which everybody soon gets very fond of. Both animal and vegetable oils can be procured in abundance for light and cooking.[17]

It is true that my own view of the potentialities and especially the difficulties is influenced strongly by some knowledge of the experiences of the colonies of Confederate exiles from the United States.[18] It also is tempered by an appreciation of a few of the sociocultural and political obstacles involved. Nevertheless I continue to think that the building of the Transamazonian Highway and the other roads already projected, and the construction of a "bee-line" modern highway to link Villavencio, Colombia, and Caracas, Venezuela, could mean fully as much for the agricultural, industrial, and commercial development of the northern part of South America as the Aswan Dam will for northern Egypt.

Land Surveys and Titles. Little was accomplished in Brazil during the 1960's to improve the nation's chronically chaotic ways of surveying the boundaries of landed properties and recording the titles to the same. The ownership of the public domain remained mostly in the hands of the various states, and little or no thought was given to the institution of a national system of surveys such as the genius of Jefferson bequeathed to the United States and Canada. Speculation in land probably reached new highs, especially in the areas opened by the Belém-Brasília Highway and other roads built largely to penetrate unsettled areas. One report from Maranhão, for example, describing the happenings in the state prior to the opening of the new roads, commented on the work of the *grileiros* in the following words: "The grileiro is generally a man of high social position who has good relationships with the political circles of the State. He 'legalizes' a huge extension of land and establishes dominion over its occupants, obliging them to deliver babassú kernals they have extracted from the little coconuts and agricultural products, principally, rice." [19] The only way the hundreds of thousands of actual

---

[17] Alfred Russell Wallace, *Travels on the Amazon* (London, 1911), 230–32.
[18] Cf. Herbert H. Smith, *Brazil: The Amazons and the Coast* (New York, 1879), 135–76.
[19] Homma, "O Maranhão Está Chegando," 6.

squatters on such lands eventually can obtain clear titles to the lands they must have is through expropriation and subsequently the sale of the land to the settlers. This by no means is always done, although, as mentioned elsewhere in this chapter, the assurance that it will be done in connection with the building of the Transamazonian Highway is highly encouraging.

If various development projects are attempted by privately owned companies, as sometimes is the case, the claims of large numbers of people who eventually will show up to assert that they are the owners of the land involved continues to be a problem of considerable magnitude. The occasional instance in which this problem is resolved is so noteworthy that Brazil's most accomplished geographer, Hilgard O'Reilly Sternberg, presently on the faculty of the University of California (Berkeley), was impelled to laud the work of the North Paraná Land Company, a British firm: "Take, for instance, the matter of clear-cut titles of ownership. A profitable lesson can be learned from what is perhaps the most successful of all large-scale pioneering settlements in Brazil—that carried out by a railroad and colonization company in northwestern Paraná state. In order to guarantee future purchasers clear title to the land, the enterprise bought up all titles presented—even if it meant acquiring the same tract five or six times." [20]

One development in connection with the speculation in Brazilian lands that flourished during the 1960's, and one that helped produce great resentment and even much xenophobia directed against the United States, was the unprecedented degree to which American capital was used for speculative purposes in the purchase of land in Brazil. Eventually, this led to the promulgation of a decree in March, 1969, implementing Ato Complementar No. 45 of that year regulating the acquisition of rural properties. This decree specified that from the date of its issuance, "The ownership of rural property may be acquired only by a Brazilian or a foreigner residing in the country, save in cases of inheritance. Considered to be a resident of the country is the foreigner who establishes proof of permanent establishment in national territory in accord with the legislation currently in force. The acquisition of rural property by a foreigner will require authorization by the Ministry of Agriculture, secured through the Instituto Brasileiro de Reforma Agrária as an intermediary. In the interests of National Security, the Union is authorized to expropriate rural land held by a foreign person, natural or juridical, by means of a decree by the President of the Republic." [21] Lest anyone in the United States think this a sudden development, they should come to know the headlines in the Brazilian papers in early 1969 and the years immediately preceding. They should come to know about such books as *A Amazônia e a Cobiça International* (The Amazon and International Greed) by Arthur Cezar Ferreira

[20] Sternberg, "Brazil: Complex Giant," *Foreign Affairs* (January, 1965), 303–304.

[21] Brazilian Embassy, Washington, D.C., *Boletim Especial*, March 18, 1969.

Reis),[22] noted Brazilian historian and social scientist. See Figure 44. Shortly after the publication of the first edition of this volume in 1960, its author became governor of the state of Amazonas. Prior to that he had served as superintendent of SUDAME, the big governmental agency created to promote the development of the Amazon Valley. But perhaps as significant an item as any connected with the great "scandal" is that published in boldface type under the headline "Pico da Neblina, Shangri-la International" in the *Correio Agro-Pecuario* of São Paulo, from which the following extract is translated:

> If in South Central [Brazil] coffee and cattle are the preoccupations of those in rural areas, on the "New Frontier" of the country the concern is with the land. The Parlimentary Investigation Commission, which studied the sales of land to foreigners, concluded that 80 per cent of them were conducted in an irregular manner and that entire municípios have been sold. They did not fail to note . . . that Neblina Peak, on the Venezuelan border, the highest point in Brazil, ideal site for a publicly owned tourist resort, was subdivided in the exterior.
>
> The sales include more than 20 million hectares, including 8 million in Pará, 5.6 million in Bahia, 2 million in Maracanã, 2 million in Mato Grosso, 1.5 million in Goiás, 800 thousand in Amazonas, and so on. The remote territories of Rondônia, Roraima, and Amapá did not escape. And the subsoil was prospected without legal authorization.
>
> There are 16 groups involved in the deals, most of them made by means of falsified titles, frauds, financial manipulations, the spoilation of the Indians, etc. Shadowy persons bought and sold land, with the documents easily prepared in the land offices. One North American bought the entire município of Ponte Alta, another all of the município of Plaça, both in Pará. Ten per cent of all the land in Bahia was sold. There were buyers (in good faith or bad) in the United States, Haiti, Malasia, India, and China . . . Neblina Peak was becoming a sort of International Shangri-la.[23]

When materials of this kind are featured in the report of a Brazilian congressional committee and disseminated throughout the length and breadth of an entire half continent, not merely by word-of-mouth but by the daily newspapers and even by special displays in farm journals, the populace is bound to be influenced. Undoubtedly, since 1960 these and other stories of the activities of certain U.S. citizens and interests have done much to poison the minds of Brazilians, and to bring many of them to parrot on every occasion the expression "American imperialism" long ago planted by our cold-war adversaries. Stimulated by such activities it is easy for a Brazilian to recall the suggestions made years ago that Puerto Rico's population problem might be solved by resettling many of that island's people in the Amazon Basin; to remember the historical fact that U.S. influence was largely responsible for opening navigation on the Amazon River to the vessels of all nations; and to think again of the ill-fated Hileia Institute for the study and development of the entire Amazon Basin sponsored by UNESCO. It

[22] Reis, *A Amazônia e a Cobiça International* (Rio de Janeiro, 1960, 1965, and 1968).
[23] *Correio Agro-Pecuario,* VIII, 3.

F I G U R E 4 4 . Front cover of the book by Arthur Cezar Ferreira Reis.

also is easy for one pondering such matters to read with great alarm
some of the paragraphs in S. Chandrasekhar's book, *Hungry People
and Empty Lands*, published in London in 1952, and so on. Many
influential Brazilians, including high-ranking military men, have
been convinced that international interests, aided and abetted, if
not actually led by the United States, are plotting the international-
ization of the Amazon.[24]

The flurry of speculation in Brazilian lands by people in the
United States broke loose in the late 1950's, and by 1970 it seemed

[24] See Reis, *op. cit.*, for the picture as seen through the eyes of one exceptionally well-informed and patriotic Brazilian. Especially disturbing is the
thesis, expounded by Chandrasekhar, an expert contracted by UNESCO to direct
an international study of population problems, that in a "desperately overpopulated world" it was criminal to maintain in disuse and practically unpopulated tremendous areas in Argentina, Australia, Brazil, and Canada (pp.
230–31).

to have been controlled by Brazil's government as summarized above.[25] It seems well, however, to include in this section a few of the most salient paragraphs from a mimeographed release issued by the Bureau of International Development of the U.S. Department of Commerce in January, 1968. This is entitled *Information for Prospective Investors in Rural Brazilian Land,* and some of the information it contains is as follows:

Because of widespread interest in purchasing rural land in Brazil, the fraudulent sales brought to the attention of the Department of Commerce, and recent Brazilian Government regulations concerning the sale of land, the following information is presented for the guidance of those interested in land purchase.

The usual way of acquiring Brazilian land is through private land development companies. However, at present, no American firm is properly registered with the competent Brazilian authorities to sell Brazilian subdivided land abroad and therefore cannot convey legal titles.

Experience dictates extreme caution in buying Brazilian land. For example, the same parcel of land has been known to have been sold two or three times by the same company. It is highly advisable to consult an experienced attorney, able to provide precise information on the Brazilian Agrarian Reform Law and the specific land laws and regulations which are continually being issued by Brazilian authorities. Numerous Americans who have failed to take this precaution have been the victims of fraudulent land company schemes. . . .

The procedure for obtaining a clear land title is rigid and complex; if any of the steps are bypassed, the title is likely to be worthless. . . .

Fraudulent Land Sales Common

Land offered for sale by private land development companies is usually located in the interior, especially in the states of Mato Grosso, Goiás, and Amazonas. Various companies, Brazilian and American, offering Brazilian land for sale have misrepresented their offerings with the result that thousands of U.S. investors have lost substantial sums of money. This has usually hit the small investor the hardest. The typical approach is to offer small parcels of land (25, 50, 100 or 500 acres) at prices which are low by our standards. To make the "bargain" more attractive, land companies sometimes include extras, e.g., a cattle management service. Often advertised land is in inaccessible areas, frequently uninhabitable. A high percentage of such land may never be of value or may become valuable only if held in large tracts (thousands of acres) for, perhaps, generations. Furthermore, the official land measurement unit in Brazil is the hectare (2.47 acres) and sales made in acres may be below the minimum (module) size of property permitted to be sold in the area.

As a result of complaints arising from fraudulent claims made by a number of companies, the United States Post Office Department has issued foreign fraud orders against a number of firms. Mail addressed to these firms is not delivered and is returned to the sender stamped "fraudulent." In attempting to circumvent this action, many of these firms operate under several names. The following are some of the names mentioned in foreign fraud orders:

United Farm Cooperatives

United Finance and Production Cooperatives, Inc.

Cooperatives Reunidas de Financas e Producao S.A.

Companhia Pan-Americana de Terras e Desenvolvimento no Brasil

---

[25] Some of the first inquiries for information about buying land in Brazil addressed to the U.S. Department of Agriculture in the late 1940's were referred to me with requests that I assist, if possible, those making the inquiries. For this reason the entire recent episode seems a bit unreal.

United Co-Op
United Farm Co-Op
Commercial United Co-Op Ltda.
COM. U-C LTDA.
Christian de Sepibus. . . .

Stringent New Regulations Imposed

In an attempt to protect buyers from unscrupulous firms which sell non-existent or already-sold land, or land for which title has not been established, the National Agrarian Development Institute (INDA) has issued a regulation requiring that every private firm or individual selling rural land abroad must request registration of the firm and the area for sale at the Institute. In the case of sub-division, at least 30% of the area must be sold to Brazilians. Registered firms or individuals receive a certificate valid for one year, renewable every January. INDA is to police activities of firms which sell rural subdivided lands overseas and to make a survey of all land previously sold. . . .

Unused Land Faces Expropriation, Higher Taxes

In 1964, Brazil promulgated its first major agrarian reform legislation. By this law and subsequent implementing regulations, IBRA is empowered to expropriate rural property with special emphasis on unutilized land. State and municipal governments also have the right to expropriate land. . . .

Clear Land Titles Difficult to Obtain

Real estate laws and practices vary considerably throughout Brazil. Titles to rural lands, even if granted by the states, may be questioned, since several states have granted lands claimed by the Federal Government. In addition, Article 164, paragraph 1, of the Federal Constitution requires prior authorization from the Federal Senate before a state may legally grant a title to public lands in tracts larger than 3,000 hectares (approximately 7,400 acres). As a practical matter, multiple claims, apparently of equal value, to the same land are so frequent that a purchaser of lands in states such as Mato Grosso or Goias often must take possession and actively defend his title if he expects to retain effective control of his property.

No land title insurance is known to be issued in Brazil. Some land companies may issue title warrants, but these would be only as reliable as the company which issues them and then only as long as that company is in existence and capable of guaranteeing the warrants.

Transportation Need Development

A main consideration in buying land in Brazil should be its location and accessibility. Large areas of Brazil are isolated and can only be reached by irregular water transportation or overland by primitive trails. The Brazilian interior has few rail and highway connections, and where connecting roads exist, they are usually dirt roads or trails which may be impassable, especially during the rainy season. Land development company brochures often state that the land they are offering is near a "planned" highway. In such a vast country "near" is a relative term (often 50 miles or more), and these "planned" roads may never get off the drawing board.

Finally, to conclude this discussion of land surveys and titles, it seems necessary to mention that efforts to clear the titles of lands in 50-kilometer zones adjacent to international boundaries is one of the principal tasks undertaken by Brazil's Agrarian Reform Institute. Considerable progress along these lines is being made. For example, information given in the *Boletim Especial* of the Brazilian Embassy in Washington for December 3, 1969, indicated that 44,242 titles to farms already had been cleared.

Land Tenure. Little can be definitely determined about the changes in land tenure since 1960 and any influence this may have had upon the increases in the production of food, feed, and fiber. Between 1950 and 1960 there was an increase in farm tenancy from a reported 9.1 to 17.4 per cent and a slight increase in the proportion of squatters of from 10.1 to 10.7 per cent of the farm operators. These were accompanied by decreases in the proportion of owner-operators from 75.2 to 67.0 per cent, and in that of administrators or managers from 5.6 to 4.9 per cent.[26]

In many ways the most crucial indicators of tenure and tenure changes in Brazil are those showing the proportions of farm laborers among all those taking part in agricultural production. In the United States, really meaningful data on the workers on farms and the classification of these into family workers (farm operators and the members of their families working on the farms) and hired workers, respectively, date from 1909. They are secured and published monthly by the Crop Reporting Board of the United States Department of Agriculture. To date, anything resembling this important series has not been undertaken by the Brazilian statistical agencies, although the excellent organization of the Instituto Brasileiro de Geografia e Estatística is well equipped to do so. The lack of comprehensive materials about the workers on farms makes any statements upon the recent trends in these important features of Brazilian life and labor a matter of conjecture. However, in view of the mass exodus of workers from the rural districts that took place during the 1960's and continues on into the 1970's, and in view of the substantial progress presently being made in the mechanization of agriculture in Brazil, it is likely that a substantial decrease is taking place in the numbers and proportions of farm laborers among those working on Brazilian farms. If this is the case, it represents a substantial improvement in the average tenure status of the Brazilians who are engaged in agricultural activities.

Size of Holdings and Size of Farms. Relatively little that is definite can be established about the changes in the size of the land holdings and the size of farms in Brazil during the 1960's and thereafter. These important features of the overall sociocultural system are ones that require, for worthwhile analysis, the large bodies of well-classified statistical data gathered by a modern census of agriculture. Brazilian procedures in this respect are fairly satisfactory, except for the tremendous lag that takes place between the time the information is gathered and when it becomes available for study. Fortunately we now have some of the more essential tabulations of the data from the 1960 census of agriculture, which enables comparisons to be made with those for 1950; and we also

---

[26] These computations are based upon data in the 1969 issue of the *Anuário Estatístico do Brasil*, 138. To date I have been unable to secure any comparable materials for the various states. It may be that farm tenancy already is reaching the problem stage in some parts of Brazil.

have some of the results of the inventory of land holdings that was made mandatory by *Estatuto da Terra*, or Agrarian Reform Law, of November 30, 1964. As fully as possible the data from this cadastral survey supplied by the Instituto Brasileiro de Reforma Agrária have been made comparable with those from the 1950 and 1960 censuses of agriculture; and all figure in the materials presented in Table LXXVIII.

TABLE LXXVIII

Percentages of Farm Operators with Farms of Stated Sizes, and Percentages of the Land in Farms or Estates of Stated Sizes, in Brazil, 1950, 1960, and 1967 *

Size of farm or estate (hectares)	Per cent of operators with farms of stated sizes			Per cent of land in farms of stated sizes		
	1950	1960	1967	1950	1960	1967
Under 10	34.4	44.8	36.4	1.3	2.4	1.7
10–49	40.3	36.6	41.6	8.7	11.4	10.1
50–99	10.7	8.2	9.4	6.6	7.6	6.9
100–999	13.0	9.4	11.2	32.5	34.4	32.4
1,000–9,999	1.5	1.0	1.3	31.5	28.6	33.1
10,000–over	0.1	†	0.1	19.4	15.6	15.8
Total	100.0	100.0	100.0	100.0	100.0	100.0
Number or area (000's)	2,065	3,338	3,639	232,211	249,862	360,104

* Source of data: Compiled and computed from data in the *Anuário Estatístico do Brasil, 1969*, Rio de Janeiro: Instituto Brasileiro del Geografia e Estatística, 1969, pp. 138–39. The data for 1950 and 1960 are those gathered in the Censo Agropecuário for each of those years. Those for 1967 are from the inventory authorized by the Agrarian Reform Law of 1964 and made by the Instituto Brasileiro de Reforma Agrária. Cf. J. Motta Maia, *Iniciação à Reforma Agrária*, Rio de Janeiro: MABRI Livraria e Editôra, 1969, pp. 167–237 for the text of the law and especially Article 46 of the same which prescribes that an inventory be made.
† Less than 0.1

Little need be added to the facts as shown by this tabulation. Irrespective of what the actual trends may have been, in 1967 the ownership and control of the land still was highly concentrated in the hands of a relatively few large landed proprietors. A mere 1.4 per cent of those who by law were required to supply information about the lands they owned were the possessors of almost one half (48.9 per cent) of all the privately owned land in Brazil. Furthermore, the situation in which a handful of proprietors owned and controlled inordinately high proportions of the land was not limited to the huge, sparsely populated sections of the country, although the inventory revealed twenty-four holdings of more than 100,000 hectares in Mato Grosso, fifteen in Rondonia, six in Goiás, five in Pará, two in Acre, and one in each of the following states: Amazonas, Maranhão, Piauí, São Paulo, and Paraná. In Bahia a mere 0.6 per cent of the proprietors owned 30.9 per cent of the land; and the corresponding proportions (with that of owners given first in each case) for other large and fairly well settled states are as follows: Rio Grande do Sul, 0.6 and 27.4; Ceará, 0.8 and 27.1; São Paulo, 0.9 and 30.6; and Minas Gerais, 1.0 and 28.8. Even in Guanabara, on the outskirts of the city of Rio de Janeiro, 33.6 per cent of the 41,181 hectares of farm land figuring in the cadastral survey, was being held by four owners.

In accordance with the imperatives of the law, and by highly complicated formulas, the Instituto Brasileiro de Reforma Agrária, also classified the landholdings in 1967 into the categories of minifundia, rural *empresas* (farms in which the land is being economically and rationally used in accordance with the economic possibilities of the region and in accordance with norms previously established by the executive power, etc.), and two types of latifundia. On this basis in 1967 75.8 per cent of the landholdings in Brazil were classified as minifundia, 2.4 per cent as empresas, 21.8 per cent as "latifundia por exploração," i.e., latifundia because of the way the land was being used or unused, and only 279 (less than 0.1 per cent) as "latifundia por extensão," or classified as latifundia on the basis of size alone. However, only 12.1 per cent of the area was in minifundia, 4.7 per cent in empresas, 76.7 per cent in inadequately used large properties, and 6.5 per cent in the places that were classified as latifundia on the basis of size alone.

Interestingly enough, none of the states in Brazil, when graded on the basis of the criteria established by the Estatuto da Terra, attained a score of 20 per cent of the land being classified as in empresas, although São Paulo with 19.6 per cent barely missed that distinction. It was most closely followed in this respect by Rio Grande do Sul (13.2 per cent), Espírito Santo (7.8 per cent), and Paraná (7.4 per cent).[27]

CHANGES IN THE WAYS OF FARMING

In 1960, as I prepared the text for the third edition of this book, I expressed the belief that Brazil's future depended largely upon the rapidity with which the masses of its agriculturists could learn and put into practice more effective ways of extracting products from the soil. (See above p. 357.) At that time, after having observed relatively little improvement in the ways of farming throughout large parts of the country over a period of twenty years, it seemed to me that additional decades might pass before significant measures would be taken to replace the antiquated, inefficient, and wasteful practices in vogue with the demonstrably more effective ways of farming used in the more developed countries and in parts of Brazil itself. Happily, it is now possible to state that during the 1960's and

[27] The data in the preceding paragraphs were compiled and computed from information given in the 1969 issue of the *Anuário Estatístico do Brasil*, 138–43.

especially the opening years of the 1970's remarkable progress has been and is being made in the nation's ways of getting products from the soil. Very large increments in the production of food, feed, and fiber, for domestic consumption and for export alike, are resulting from this.

The crux of the matter, of course, is the replacement of the systems denoted as riverbank plantings, "fire agriculture," hoe culture, and rudimentary plow culture (described and discussed in Chapter XV), with the more advanced and productive systems designated as advanced plow culture, and mechanized farming, respectively. Since 1960, important changes have got underway in the education and equipment of the great masses of Brazil's countrymen, so that many who previously relied upon the grossly wasteful, destructive, and inefficient system of *derrubadas e queimadas*, or upon the drudgery of hoe culture have been enabled to employ more advanced ways of farming. Very early in my work in Brazil I became convinced that the use of primitive and antiquated ways of getting products from the soil were responsible for the useless expenditure of the bulk of the energies of millions of rural Brazilians, on the one hand, and the almost wanton destruction of immense expanses of potentially highly valuable forests, on the other. In every way possible I sought to encourage the replacement of fire agriculture by ways of farming that would involve tillage and cultivation, permanent use of the same pieces of land, the application of fertilizers (commercial, barnyard manures, and leguminous plants), and other features of the more efficient methods of gaining a livelihood from the soil. Especially after Brazil's population began increasing at the rate of more than 3 per cent per year, and as the bulk of all Brazilians abandoned the land and took up residence in the burgeoning cities and towns, I came to view better farming procedures as the *sine quo non* of enabling the increase in the food supply to keep pace with the growth of population so as to afford a period of grace in which effective demographic controls could be devised and put into effect.

During the early 1940's many experts of one kind or another were defending the practice of felling and burning. Later on, many others were encountered, some of them engaged on the technical assistance programs. Some are met with even today. Moreover, until recently one had difficulty in finding intensive studies of the ill effects of this devastating way of securing agricultural products, such as those of France's noted agricultural analyst René Dumont has made of the comparable system in tropical Africa. Hence, it seems appropriate to present a few of his data and observations. First he stresses that our world is one in which the demand for cellulose is increasing rapidly and that the supplies available from the forests in the temperate zones are entirely unequal to the need. In view of this it is deplorable that felling and burning the trees on an acre of equatorial forest "involves the waste of enormous quantities of humus, of 600–900 lb. of nitrogen and of 120–400 tons of wood." [28] All of this is over and above the fact that as standards of living rise, "forty-eight days spent in cleaning and burning one acre of forest sill no longer seem worthwhile." [29]

In a great many ways, during the 1960's and with the pace being stepped up in the 1970's, Brazilian farmers are improving the ways in which they go about the work of securing products from the soil. Perhaps the most significant of these, in the long run at least, is the considerable headway being made in the mechanization or motorization of Brazilian agriculture. As late as 1960 there were only 63,493 tractors reported in use on all the farms in Brazil, or one tractor for every 245 persons actively engaged in agricultural production. At that time the bulk of these were on the farms of just two states, 28,101 in São Paulo and 16,675 in Rio Grande do Sul. Minas Gerais, with only 5,024, was third, and Paraná, with 4,996 reported, was fourth. Next came Goiás and Santa Catarina, with 1,299 and 1,049 respectively.[30] Clements, who studied intensively the mechanization of agriculture in Minas Gerais, making use of all the available statistical data and visiting hundreds of farms as he crisscrossed the state, found that the use of the tractor was being disseminated throughout the entire area. For example his tabulations show that in 1940 only 40 per cent of the county-like municípios in Minas Gerais had one or more tractors at work on its farms and ranches; by 1950, the number of municípios had risen to 386 as compared with 288 in 1940, of which only 42 per cent had tractors in use on the farms within their borders. By 1960 the number of municípios had been increased to 483, and the percentage in which tractors were in use had risen to almost 80.[31] His analysis showed that four factors were largely responsible for the adoption and use of the tractor in Minas Gerais or the lack of it as the people of that state went about the work of superimposing an agricultural mode of existence upon the traditional old pastoral culture that had dominated the scene for centuries. These are: (1) proximity to São Paulo, where mechanization began much earlier and had proceeded much farther; (2) proximity to large urban centers and the impact of sociocultural stimuli emanating from them; (3) roads and other improvements in the system of transportation; and (4) the persistence of the attitudes and values that had been generated and perpetuated by a system of large landed estates. The last of these he concluded was particularly strong as a retarding force.[32]

Brazilian industry is now stepping up its production of tractors and their associated implements and machines to provide the equipment so badly needed by the nation's farmers, and this is doing

---

[28] René Dumont, *Types of Rural Economy: Studies in World Agriculture* (London, 1966), 51.

[29] *Ibid.*, 56.

[30] The basic data are from the 1963 issue of the *Anuário Estatístico do Brasil*, 58. They have been assembled and analyzed in Harold M. Clements, Sr., *The Mechanization of Agriculture in Minas Gerais* (Gainesville, 1969), 42, *passim*.

[31] *Ibid.*, 65–67.

[32] *Ibid.*, 74–79.

much to facilitate the improvement in the ways of farming now taking place. The data show a total of 80,000 tractors on the farms in 1969, and the four-year plan for the period 1970–1973 calls for this to be increased by 50 per cent or to 120,000.[33] Moreover the ambitious projects for colonizing the areas on both sides of the Transamazonian Highway and other new "pioneer" roads designed to open new areas are certain to spread the use of the tractor to distant parts of Brazil. Even so, tractors, combines, and other mechanical equipment used on farms are still very expensive in Brazil, and this alone is a great obstacle to the spread of their use. But with the flight of the workers from the land, the modern equipment is becoming more and more essential in the great agricultural states of São Paulo, Rio Grande do Sul, Paraná, and Minas Gerais, especially in wheat culture, rice culture, the production of sugar cane, and of cotton, as these enterprises are conducted in those states. [34] Many of the farms in all of them are making use of the most modern means for tilling the soil.

Brazilian farmers will also improve their methods of getting products from the land by proper use of abundant water supplies for irrigation. Especially in the huge, drought-stricken Northeast, through which the São Francisco River, fed by the heavy rainfall in Minas Gerais and southern Bahia, makes its way to the ocean, great amounts of readily available water some day will enable irrigation to transform completely the productivity of the land. In addition to the abundance of sugar cane, rice, cotton, and corn, eventually to be produced in that area, it is reasonable to expect that irrigation will transform completely the antiquated animal husbandry enterprises thoughout the great *sertão*. And this need not be long in coming about. There is every reason to expect that alfalfa and the sorghums, as well as other forage crops are ideally suited for production in the area. Certainly now that the modernization of agriculture is on the move in Brazil, the efforts required to grow these wonder crops and to turn them into meat and other animal products are going to be made. The production of soy beans already is well established in Rio Grande do Sul, and with the aid of irrigation, the production of these is likely to be extended to the Northeast and other sections. And these are only a few examples of the improvements the development of irrigation will bring to the ways of farming in Brazil. So far, however, as expressed by Brazil's Minister of the Interior in an address on November 3, 1970, to a National Seminar on Irrigation held in Pôrto Alegro, Rio Grande do Sul, "Irrigation is benefiting only 2 per cent of the farm land in Brazil, mostly in the South. In the Northeast, precisely the region that suffers most from the uncertainty of the rainfall, the areas irrigated are insignificant." [35]

[33] Cf. "Ação Programada para o Ingreso no Mundo Desenvolvido," in *Extensão Rural*, V (Outubro, 1970), 8.

[34] Cf. Shackford Pitcher, "Farm Mechanization Comes Slowly to Brazil," *Foreign Agriculture*, V (July 28, 1969), 5–10.

[35] Quoted in the *Boletim Especial* of the Brazilian Embassy, Washington, D.C., November 6, 1970.

Finally, to illustrate the variety of things that can and are being done to improve the ways in which crops and animals are being made to produce more abundantly in Brazil, mention should be made of benefits of modern "genetic tailoring." A striking example is the recent remarkable achievement in the production of seed corn adapted to tropical conditions and consumption by human beings and their animals. As related in the October 26, 1970, issue of the *Alliance for Progress Weekly Newsletter* published by the Pan American Union in Washington, D.C., the essential facts in this case are as follow: Sementes Agroceres, S.A., a Brazilian company engaged in the production of hybrid seed corn, and the largest such company in the world outside the United States, has been associated in research efforts since 1947 with the International Basic Economy Corporation. The latter is a private company organized for profit-making purposes with headquarters in New York City, and devoted to helping initiate and operate corporate ventures that will contribute to the meeting of basic human needs and to the strengthening of the economies of the less-developed countries. In 1963, thirty grains of Opaque-2, a corn developed at Purdue University, were sent to Dr. Gladstone Drummond, chief of research for Agroceres. This corn was characterized by its exceptionally high nutritional value, especially for hogs. Dr. Drummond obtained help from the Federal Agricultural College at Viçosa, Minas Gerais, and in seven years of painstaking work on pollination and other aspects of the problem, obtained a corn greatly superior to other varieties from the nutritional standpoint and adapted to Brazilian soils and climate. In 1970, 200 tons of it were distributed for seed to 600 farmers. In comparison with the best hybrids previously available, which produced about 640 pounds per acre, this new hybrid grown by means of modern techniques of cultivation, but unfertilized, has averaged 1,553 pounds per acre. The spokesmen for International Basic Economy Corporation emphasize that in addition to the measurable ways in which this project has contributed to Brazil's agricultural development, such demonstrations have an immense educational value.

Changes in the Types of Farming. Closely related to the opening and settlement of millions of acres of forested lands to farming and stockraising, discussed in an earlier section, is the superimposition throughout extensive portions of Brazil of farming as such upon the traditional rudimentary pastoral culture that many decades ago spread a thin veneer of civilization over vast areas in the unforested or lightly wooded sections of the country. Here it seems essential to mention the expansion of settlements of farmers in Rio Grande do Sul, Santa Catarina, and Paraná; the great agricultural progress made recently in the Triângulo of western Minas Gerais and several other sections of that immense state; and the less spectacular commencement of the growing of crops in dozens of other areas (such as the establishment of thousands of truck farms in central Goiás by the Japanese) which until recently knew only the rudimentary pastoral activities of the herdsmen. All of this, and the elimination to some extent of monoculture of various types and its replacement with more effective combinations of crop and livestock enterprises, are playing major roles in Brazil's efforts to keep its production of food, feed, and fiber increasing more rapidly than its population.

The term *type of farming* denotes, of course, a given combination of enterprises or the exclusive use of only one enterprise in any agricultural or pastoral entity logically entitled to be classified as a farm. Thus the type of monoculture so roundly denounced by Gilberte Freyre and dozens of other Brazilian thinkers—the sugar *engenho* or *usina*, the coffee fazenda, and even the extensive cattle fazenda—typifies traditional Brazilian types of farming which for the most part involve a single enterprise on a given farm. However plantations on which the production of rice is combined with the growing of beef cattle, or the planting of corn is combined with the farrowing and fattening of hogs (long important in the small farming areas of Rio Grande do Sul), are other distinctive types of farming. By all odds the type of farming that has done most to increase and add to the variety and adequacy of Brazil's food supply is the polyculture, involving the production of fresh vegetables and fruits, which was brought to Brazil by the 200,000 Japanese immigrants who settled in São Paulo and a few other states during the 1930's. During the 1970's there is every reason to suppose that this highly productive type of farming will be extended to many other sections where changing eating habits in rapidly growing cities and towns demand fresh fruits and vegetables.

Perhaps the most significant of all the changes in types of farming now taking place in Brazil, however, is (at long last) a rapid improvement in and expansion of dairy husbandry. To one born and reared in an area where the people knew how to secure dairy products and how to use them effectively for the nourishment of large families, the almost complete lack of milk and milk products in most parts of Brazil was one of the greatest "cultural shocks" experienced when I first began to learn about Brazil and the Brazilians in 1939 and the early 1940's. This was emphasized when in 1942–1943, while my family was living in Rio de Janeiro, milk of some kind was needed for our two small children. We were not even sure that lengthy boiling would make it safe for them to drink in those years. Subsequently, as I delved into the study of the origins and dissemination of this specific sociocultural system, I came to realize that real dairy husbandry was an achievement of peoples of northwestern Europe, and that only those cultures transplanted from that area would know much about the production of milk and milk products and integrate them as fundamental parts of their diets.[36]

[36] The dependence of certain nomadic pastoral people, such as those of North Africa, the Middle East, and the steppes of Russia, upon milk products is no significant exception to this generalization. Such ways as nomadic people have of getting and using milk and cheese neither have nor ever can become an important part of the food supplies for large, modern urban populations. Recently

All during the period 1942–1951 when I travelled extensively throughout Brazil, anything related to dairying was so seldom encountered that I usually made a note of it in my diary, and extracts from that diary constitute large portions of the first two editions of this book, and most of those rare entries [37] concerned developments on ultramodern fazendas, the once-a-year visits during calving time of proprietors to their cattle fazendas, the milking of Zebú or Brahma cows giving about a quart per day, and dairy husbandry in the German settlements in south Brazil. In fact, the more I travelled throughout Brazil the more I became convinced of the validity and importance of Gilberto Freyre's generalization that "However strange it may seem the table of our colonial aristocracy [who resided on great plantations] was lacking in fresh vegetables, fresh meat, and milk. . . ." [38] Moreover, I became thoroughly convinced that the role of milk in Brazilian dietary practice had not changed radically from colonial days to the 1940's.

In the 1940's and more so the 1950's, however, dairy husbandry and the consumption of milk in Brazil began to take on new aspects. One of the important happenings was the initiation of measures by the national and state governments to insure the safety of those drinking milk. In my diary, for example, is an account of a visit in 1942 to a small coffee fazenda near Marília, São Paulo, where "in addition to coffee, some cotton is grown in the lowlands, and there are 20 head of milk cows. Others were sold yesterday. There is a new requirement that all milk must be pasteurized, and the processing plant pays only 2½ cents per liter. This is unsatisfactory so they have sold all the cows except those needed to supply milk for them and their colonos, of whom there are about 20 families." With the publication of the 1952 issue, the *Anuário Estatístico do Brasil* began giving some data on the production of milk in Brazil. The first figures, going back to 1949, are for pasteurized milk, and the totals reported are 149,999 and 161,460, metric tons [39] for 1949 and 1950, respectively. Of the total, about 60 per cent was produced in Minas Gerais and 35 per cent in the state of Rio de Janeiro. São Paulo, third in production, reported only 9,671,000 liters (5.6

---

the insignificant role of milk and milk products in the history of the Iberian Peninsula was dramatically impressed upon me by a reexamination of Gabriel Alonso de Herrera's classic treatise on *Agricultura General*. This monumental work was first published in Madrid in 1513, and my copy is that containing supplements added by the Real Sociedad Económica of Madrid and published there in 1818. The four volumes of the great treatise contain a total of 2,026 pages. Of these less than one page is devoted to milk cows and milk products, and most of that is comment upon some of the cows from the Netherlands and Switzerland that those making the emendation recently had seen in Madrid.

[37] See pp. 57, 67, 70, 73, 84, 93–94, 97, and 99 of the second edition, 1954.

[38] Gilberto Freyre, *The Masters and the Slaves: A Study in the Development of Brazilian Civilization*, trans. Samuel Putnam (New York, 1946), 52. This is one of the two references to milk in the entire volume. The other on p. 46 merely mentions the lack of milk in a list of dietary deficiencies. In the Preface to the English edition, p. xlix, he gives "as the result of monoculture, an irregularity and deficiency in the supply of foodstuffs such as meat, milk, eggs, and vegetables."

[39] A metric ton is equal to 2,204.6 pounds or 1,000 liters.

per cent), and the only other states figuring in the list are Espírito Santo and Santa Catarina.[40] Thereafter, both the production and the data about the same increased rapidly. In 1960 the reported production of pasteurized milk has risen to 363,955 metric tons, or 125 per cent above the 1950 total, and the list of states in which pasteurized milk was produced had been expanded by the addition of Guanabara and Parana. By 1960, moreover, São Paulo rapidly was getting into the picture of milk production. By then it accounted for 13 per cent of the volume of the pasteurized milk; and largely as a result of this, the proportions for Minas Gerais and the state of Rio de Janeiro decreased to 49 and 33 per cent, respectively. By 1960 figures also became available for the production of fresh milk in general, and this amounted to 4,899,816 metric tons. Of this, 33 per cent was attributed to Minas Gerais, 25 per cent to São Paulo, 8 per cent to Rio Grande do Sul, 7 per cent to Goiás, and 6 per cent to the state of Rio de Janeiro.[41]

During the 1960's Brazil took gigantic strides to improve the quality and increase the amounts of milk and milk products available to figure in the diet of its rapidly growing population. By 1970 it ranked among the important milk producing countries of the world, a position which is certain to improve greatly during the 1970's. Indeed, according to a report by the Agricultural Attaché at the American Embassy in Rio de Janeiro, by 1968 milk had come to rank fifth in value among all Brazilian farm products. At this time its estimated value ($536 million) was exceeded only by those of beef ($986 million), coffee ($686 million), corn ($575 million), and rice ($551 million); and it was well ahead of the other five in the list of the ten most important agricultural products, i.e., cotton, (lint and seed combined), sugarcane, pork, bananas, and dry beans, in the order named.[42] This new high rank of milk in the list of Brazil's ten

[40] *Anuário Estatístico do Brasil, 1952*, XIII (Rio de Janeiro: Instituto Brasileiro de Geografia e Estatística, 1953), 202.

It should be indicated that the bulk of the pasteurized milk produced in the state of Rio de Janeiro is consumed in Guanabara, and most of that produced in Minas Gerais goes to the cities of São Paulo and Rio de Janeiro.

[41] The data for 1960 are taken from the *Anuário Estatístico do Brasil, 1962*, XXIII (Rio de Janeiro, 1963), 68, 102.

[42] See John McDonald, "Brazil's Expanding Production and Trade," *Foreign Agriculture*, VII (August 25, 1969), 7–9. Unfortunately neither Brazil nor Argentina, the other Latin American country where dairy husbandry is conducted on a considerable scale, figure in the important periodic compilations of statistical data on milk issued by the U.S. Department of Agriculture's *World Agriculture Production and Trade*. See the issue for July, 1970. There the countries for which data on the production and utilization of milk in 1968 and 1969 are given are seventeen in number, and include the United States and Canada, Australia, and New Zealand, and thirteen European countries. Ranked according to the amount of milk produced, the United States is first, and France is second, followed by West Germany, the United Kingdom, Italy, Canada, the Netherlands, and Australia, in the order named. The amounts for 1968 for the Netherlands and Australia are 16,997 and 15,353 million pounds, respectively. As indicated in Table LXXVII in 1968 the production of milk in Brazil amounted to approximately 7,024,000 metric tons; and if converted to pounds, the total comes to 15,486 million, or slightly above the figure for Australia. Thus, although it is not included in the list of the seventeen principal milk-producing

most valuable farm products came only after the spectacular increase in dairy husbandry that took place in the 1950's was followed by additional great gains in the 1960's. Specifically, the data given in the 1962 and the 1969 issues of the *Anuário Estatístico do Brasil* show that between 1960 and 1968 the production of milk rose by 2,124,633 metric tons (or 45.2 per cent) and that of pasteurized milk by 135,638 metric tons (or 37.3 per cent).

Little if any analysis has been made of the factors that are responsible for the recent rapid expansion of dairy husbandry in Brazil, although from the theoretical as well as the practical standpoints few subjects offer greater challenges or rewards to the serious student of sociocultural change than this sharp break with long-entrenched ways of life. Moreover, at least a few of the more significant of the factors may be identified rather easily. Years ago Carlos Borges Schmidt, one of the most perceptive sociologists who ever lived and worked in Brazil, observed and described in some detail the "invasion" of the mountainous sections of eastern São Paulo by cattlemen from southern Minas Gerais. Consider a few of his portentous statements.

After having been invaded and dominated [for about a century] by the culture of coffee the Paraíba Valley underwent a second invasion. Cattle growers from the state of Minas Gerais established themselves in Cruzeiro and subsequently pushed up the river. In a short time the lands of the Paraíba Valley, previously abandoned, were occupied in a large part by the herds. To penetrate the Paraitinga Valley and that of the Parabuna was only a step.

This stock raising on the extensive scale necessitated great areas of territory. Land was relatively cheap, in comparison with the prices prevailing in the state of Minas Gerais. It cost little for the *mineiro* cattlemen to occupy an ample area of ground. . . . It is not difficult to comprehend the disorder introduced into the agriculture of the region with the entrance of the *mineiros* who acquired the best land. A zone that had been essentially agricultural saw itself day by day being transformed into a pastoral region. The newcomers acquired parts of the old *fazendas* and turned in their cattle. . . .

Throughout the entire valley of the Paraitinga agricultural production fell to the lowest level on record. Until a few years ago São Luís was considered the granary of Taubaté. . . . [Now] the situation is reversed. . . .

As a result the open country is abandoned. The inhabitants of the rural zone move into the small urban center. Finding no employment there, they make their way to the larger cities.[43]

---

countries as carried in one of our most important compendia of world agricultural data, Brazil already actually ranks seventh in milk production among the nations. Moreover, the rapidity with which its production and consumption of milk is increasing, combined with rapid urbanization and the great as yet unused potential, makes it certain that it quickly will move up to fifth place in the ranking, well above the Netherlands, Canada, and Italy. Before 1980 it is almost sure to take the place of the United Kingdom as the fourth largest producer.

[43] Carlos Borges Schmidt, "Rural Life in Brazil," in T. Lynn Smith and Alexander Marchant (eds.), *Brazil: Portrait of Half a Continent* (New York, 1951), 185–86.

Then came the great transformation. As described by Schmidt, who knew the region intimately and spent all the time he could studying the life and labor of its people:

About ten years ago [i.e., about 1940] a small truck, already much used and well-worn, initiated a revolution in the economic system in São Luís. Early each morning this pioneer truck left the city en route to Taubaté, picking up along a route of 50 kilometers all the milk which the cattle growers had brought out to the side of the road.

When cattle raising was established in the region, the cattlemen limited themselves to cattle breeding proper. [They had herds of Zebú or Brahma cattle.] They milked very little, some of them merely enough for domestic needs. Others made a little cheese. . . . Scattered over a relatively large area, lacking easy means of transportation, they had no way of undertaking profitably the production of milk, since this product deteriorated so rapidly. But one cattle grower with greater economic resources resolved to initiate a new enterprise. He made arrangements with the milk cooperative in Taubaté, entered into contracts with various other cattle owners, and assumed the responsibility for the initial expenses.

For a long while that truck left São Luís in the morning and reached Taubaté about noon, when it delivered to the cooperative the milk picked up along the way. At first there was very little—200, later on 500, and then 600 liters of milk over the entire distance.

The milk was sold to the Taubaté cooperative and a certain amount charged to pay the cost of transportation. The remainder which the stockmen came to receive monthly served as a stimulus to give a new orientation to their methods of cattle raising. Instead of being interested merely in cows to raise calves, they came to give some preference to those that would produce some milk as well. As a result the production of milk increased considerably. It was not many years before São Luís had become, in turn, an important milk center. [In 1950 it has] a plant which receives all the milk from those portions of the *município* which are served by roads. From Catuçava, which is 18 kilometers in the direction of Ubatuba, and from Lagoinha, 24 kilometers in the direction of Cunha, two trucks daily collect over 4,000 liters of milk which is made into cheese and butter in the local factory. The livestock industry is expanding and taking in new areas. In place of corn and beans, in place of sugar cane—made into *aguardente* and *rapadura*—in place of tobacco and rice, São Luís has come to produce milk and calves.[44]

Give or take a few years, the change so well described by Schmidt in the Valley of the Paraitinga he knew so well also took place in immense areas of southern and eastern Minas Gerais, much of the state of Rio de Janeiro, parts of Espírito Santo, and eastern São Paulo, all of which presently are in the huge "milk sheds" of Brazil's two immense metropolitan centers.[45]

Once the stage had been set by the push of cattlemen from the north into the old decadent coffee plantation areas of the mountainous areas of heavy rainfall in the southern part of Minas Gerais

[44] *Ibid.*, 186–87.

[45] For many of the details of the social organization and way of life of the people of the Paraitinga Valley as they were at about the time Schmidt called attention to the transformation that was underway, see J. V. Freitas Marcondes and T. Lynn Smith, "The Caipira of the Paraitinga Valley, Brazil," *Social Forces.* XXXI, (October, 1952), 47–53.

and throughout the areas drained by the Paraíba River and its affluents in the state of Rio de Janeiro and eastern São Paulo, progress in the development of dairy husbandry in the zones near the great cities of Rio de Janeiro and São Paulo moved quickly. As already indicated some of the more enterprising herdsmen began taking a quart or so of milk per day from their rangy cattle of Indian origin (Brahma or Zebú breeds) and getting it to the milk-processing plants that sprang up in major towns and cities. As the area urbanized by leaps and bounds, the demand for milk rose dramatically. Thereafter the extent to which Brazilian farm operators adopted and put into practice a few of the other features that characterize modern dairy husbandry (as practiced in countries such as Denmark, the Netherlands, and the Great Lakes region of Canada and the United States) marked the speed with which the production and consumption of milk increased in the most densely populated sections of Brazil. Among these features are: (1) the upgrading of the livestock, substituting cattle selected and bred for their milking qualities for the rangy beef types previously the rule; (2) the improvement of pastures, first by periodic mowing to destroy brush and weeds, and then by seeding more productive grasses and legumes; (3) the combination of some agricultural activities per se, such as the growing of forage crops and feed grains—corn, soybeans, sorghums, even sugar cane—with the strictly animal enterprises that long had been the predilection of those who eventually shifted to dairying; and (4) the mounting educational campaigns designed to change the food habits of adults and to get them to consume more milk.

In the years since 1950 all of these have moved along rapidly. The progress was especially marked during the 1960's. Probably one of the most important factors in the entire change was the transplantation of Brazil of a complete system of modern dairy husbandry by several thousand Dutch farmers, who were resettled in São Paulo and Paraná at the Holambra [46] and other Dutch colonies in those states. But nowadays one can not read far in the pages of Brazilian agricultural periodicals such as the national *Entensão Rural* and the *Correio Agro-Pecuario* of São Paulo, or the Sunday agricultural supplements of the country's great newspapers, without encountering evidences of current substantial endeavors to upgrade the quality of Brazil's dairy cattle. And if one visits the countryside in southern Brazil today, he will be able to see considerable evidence that the efforts are not all in vain. For example, in 1966 Dr. Harold M. Clements, Sr., of the Stephen F. Austin University in Nacogdoches, Texas, travelled extensively throughtout the state of Minas Gerais to collect the materials used in his doctoral dissertation

---

[46] The name comes from the three countries sponsoring and financing the projects, namely Holland, America (the United States), and Brazil. For some of the more significant facts about the history and operations of these dairymen, see C. S. J. Hogenboom, "Plano de Investimento da Holambra" and "O Projeto da Holambra II," in José Arthur Rios, *Recomendações sôbre Reforma Agrária* (Rio de Janeiro, 1961), 301–27.

entitled "A Sociological Study of the Mechanization of Agriculture in Minas Gerais, Brazil." [47] His experiences were in sharp contrast to my own during the early 1940's (when I travelled considerably in the same territory) upon discovering that the butter and cheese I found in the markets of Rio de Janeiro were being made from daily stripping of modicums of milk from hundreds of thousands of Zebú cows that subsisted entirely upon the natural pastures. Clements frequently encountered evidences of improved dairy husbandry. Thus, even though his attention was focused primarily upon another aspect of agriculture, he made reference to milk cows on almost every page of his notes, and in not a few cases the observations pertain to fairly advanced stages of milk production. For example, the notes for his very first day in Minas Gerais, in which he travelled the highway from Rio de Janeiro to Belo Horizonte, contain some highly pertinent entries. Then, almost immediately after crossing into Minas Gerais at Afonso Arinos, he saw evidences of decadent coffee culture and indicated that this entire section of the state once was devoted to coffee production. In 1965, however, "the hillsides were being used largely as pastures for dairy cattle (generally a mixture of Zebú and Holstein); and as we drove along, these were to be seen moving along the steep slopes, making their regular terrace-like trails. At frequent intervals all along the highway we also passed cans of milk at farm entrances and road crossings, awaiting pickup by trucks from plants processing dairy products." [48] Subsequently, as he crisscrossed the state, greatly assisted by the personnel of ACAR, the state's highly effective agricultural extension service, and frequently accompanying them on their visits to the farms, the pages of his journal became replete with observations on dairy husbandry in its various stage of development. Thus on arriving in Ouro Fino, near the border with São Paulo in the southeastern part of Minas Gerais, "we went directly to the local office of ACAR which had been established in 1964. The local supervisor already had 130 *mutuários*, that is, farmers who received both technical and financial assistance (ACAR is interested only in properties from ten to 100 hectares in area, whose operators have legal titles, live on the holdings, and are engaged actively in their operation). . . . We visited first at sítio of 50 hectares whose owner is a mutuário. . . . [He] uses an ox-drawn, wooden plow for preparing the soil; and cultivates and harvests by hand. His herd of 28 milk cows (Zebú with some admixture of Holstein) are fed shredded sugar cane, napier (grass), manioc, and corn. The appearance of most suggests the amount of the rations should be increased. Milk production averages about five liters per cow per day. Milk is poured

[47] Submitted to the graduate school, University of Florida, December, 1966. Subsequently, a part of this study, which omitted, however, the lengthy chapter of quotations from his daily journal which is referred to here, was published under the title, *The Mechanization of Agriculture in Brazil* (Gainesville, Fla., 1969).

[48] Clements, "A Sociological Study of the Mechanization of Agriculture in Minas Gerais, Brazil" (Ph.D. dissertation, University of Florida, 1966), 26–27.

into cans, lashed to the backs of pack mules, and taken to the highway to await the truck from the cooperative." [49]

In the same area, and even more removed from the highway, Dr. Clements visited another place containing 87 hectares and devoted to the production of milk, coffee, and oranges. "It is owned and operated by two brothers who live on the property. Although one is a graduate of an agricultural college, they frequently seek the advice of ACAR technicians. Their herd consists of 85 cows, 30 calves, and several bulls, all *suiços*, or [Brown] Swiss dairy cattle. The milking shed, large enough to accommodate most of the cows, is well constructed with concrete floors and feeding troughs. By reaching over her feeding trough each cow can drink the clear water which constantly runs through another trough parallel to it. Equipment for preparing sugar cane, napier, manioc, and corn is housed in a building on the hillside above. Feed dropped through a chute into carts below can be wheeled along the troughs for easy distribution. Prepared feeding supplements are kept in a storeroom. . . . Milk is taken to the highway in a four-wheel metal trailer hitched to a jeep. Several hillsides are covered with rows of coffee trees, and one with orange trees. Others are in pasture. All feed (with the exception of supplements, such as cotton seed cake) is raised on the farm. The fact that each cow averages eight liters of milk per day is itself indicative of better care and more adequate feeding than on places visited previously." [50]

The same day in the same general locality, Dr. Clements went to see "a caboclo mutuário on his ten-hectare holding. Unlike the others, this man depends entirely upon his dairy enterprise. Despite only two years of schooling, he keeps an accurate account of feeding and milk production. Since his small holding has no level ground, all feed crops must be grown on hillsides so steep that the hoe is about the only feasible implement. Through hard work and thrift (and with the financial and technical assistance of ACAR) he has been able to accumulate within one and one-half years a herd of 42 cows, 15 calves, and one bull. While the animals are of the usual Zebú-Holstein mixture, the latter predominates. . . . With attention and his care about feeding, each of his cows gives from ten to eleven liters of milk per day." [51]

In the same general area the notes of the perceptive observer we are quoting contain entries about "the 1,500-hectare fazenda, owned by a wealthy Brazilian of Italian descent, who lives in the city" which was managed by an administrator. There "as so frequently is the case, activities consist in a large dairy enterprise and the cultivation of coffee and oranges"; and the "even more elaborate dairy operation" on a place of 80 hectares "owned by a person of German extraction who also lives in the city" and which also was "managed by an administrator." On this the cows were "all black and white,

[49] *Ibid.*, 35.
[50] *Ibid.*, 36.
[51] *Ibid.*, 37.

pure-bred Holstein." Then on the same date, "after dark we stopped at a large milk cooperative in São Gonçalo where the milk was "either chilled for immediate shipment to São Paulo or processed as cheese or powdered milk." [52] As he completed his efforts to take stock of the extent of the mechanization of agriculture in the southeastern part of Minas Gerais, on October 28, 1965, Dr. Clements recorded the following general observation in his journal: "It appears that the process of change from the cultivation of coffee to dairy farming (underway since the collapse of the coffee market in the early 1930's) is virtually complete. Almost all farmers have acquired dairy animals and are improving their quality. Even the small operator with his few poor cows is trying to enlarge his tiny herd and secure a bull of improved strain." [53] The entries relating to milk and milk production made in his journal by Dr. Clements as he visited other sections of the huge state of Minas Gerais are less numerous, but in all areas he encountered evidences of the development of dairy husbandry and recorded his observations relating to the same. His cogent materials are of considerable significance to all who seek to understand the important role the development of this highly productive type of farming is playing in the race between the population and the food supply in Brazil.

Dr. Clements' materials pertain only to the milk sheds of Brazil's largest cities, enormous Rio de Janeiro and São Paulo, each now a metropolitan center of well over five million inhabitants and nucleus of a metropolitan community of several million more, and the burgeoning capital of the state of Minas Gerais, Belo Horizonte, where the city proper now contains well over a million inhabitants. It should be stressed, however, that dairy husbandry also is increasing by leaps and bounds in the vicinity of all of Brazil's rapidly increasing assortment of large urban centers. Some of the most adequate of the materials about these developments that have come to my attention are those describing the role of fairly recently established Mennonite colonies in supplying milk for Curitiba, capital of Paraná. In a careful and substantial study, Dr. Reynolds Herbert Minnich has supplied a wealth of detail about the establishment of these colonies, and their system of social organization, including the dairy husbandry which is the type of farming they transplanted from Russia and which forms the economic base of their communities. [54] Dr. Minnich also participated in the very comprehensive study of one of these communities, Witmarsum, made by the specialists in the social sciences of the University of Paraná. This small agricultural community was formed in 1951 about thirty-five miles west of Curitiba in the município of Palmeira. In 1953 it contained 74 families having a total of 378 members. By 1964 the number of families had risen to 129 and the population to 748. Dairying and

[52] Ibid., 39–40.

[53] Ibid., 42.

[54] See Minnich, "A Sociological Study of the Mennonite Immigrant Communities in Paraná, Brazil," submitted to the graduate school, University of Florida, June, 1966, pp. 117–212.

enterprises complementary to it are about the only economic activities carried on by those who make up the colony. In 1953 these Mennonite farmers possessed a total of 450 milk cows and their cooperative sent a total of 261,489 liters of milk to the market in Curitiba. By 1966 the number of milk cows had risen to 1,537, and the amount of milk handled by the cooperative to 3,213,267 liters.[55]

Another excellent source of information about the progress of dairy husbandry in modern Brazil is the *Extensão Rural,* established in 1965 by ABCAR, Brazil's national Agricultural Extension Service. Few of its numbers fail to include at least one account of the increasing supply or improving quality of milk. In the September, 1969, issue, for example, is an illustrated account of ACAR, the rural extension service of Minas Gerais, providing the credit for the purchase of fourteen hundred pure bred dairy cattle by the farmers of that state; in the December issue of the same year a feature story, well illustrated, "Cuiabá Wants More Milk of Good Quality," describes the efforts to improve the milk supply of the capital of Mato Grosso; the number for May, 1970, contains details about the introduction of high-grade Holstein cattle in the município of Botelhos, Minas Gerais, and the tripling of milk production in the same; and that for August, 1970, features the construction of an immense new milk processing plant, the fourth largest in Brazil, underway in the município of São Gonçalo near Niterói, large satellite of the city of Rio de Janeiro and capital of the state of Rio de Janeiro.

As indicated above in one of the quotations from Dr. Clements, Brazil's extension service combines technical assistance and supervised credit and limits credit to farmers on places of somewhat modest proportions. For this reason, the efforts to improve the production of milk on the great fazendas of São Paulo (where the state agricultural extension service has not yet affiliated with the national organization) and the other states figure very little on the pages of *Extensão Rural.* This does not mean, however, that such endeavors are lacking. Moreover, frequently such developments are grandiose. For example, the June 29, 1970, number of *Foreign Agriculture,* published by the Foreign Agricultural Service of the U.S. Department of Agriculture, contains the following item submitted by the U.S. Agricultural Officer at the Consulate General in São Paulo: "On May 11, 1970, 141 head of U.S. dairy breeding cattle were unloaded at Viracopas Airport, São Paulo—the largest shipment of U.S. livestock ever made to Brazil. The Holsteins, 140 heifers aged 9 to 17 months and one bull . . . were purchased by two Brazilian breeders, one of whom is starting an entirely new diary operation with an all-U.S. registered Holstein herd. The cattle were selected during a visit by one of the Brazilian buyers to some 62 farms in six U.S. states."

[55] These data are from Altiva Pilatti Balhana, Brasil Pinheiro Machado, and others, *Campos Gerais: Estruturas Agrárias* (Curitiba, 1968), 89, 93, 114.

These efforts to augment the supply and improve the quality of milk in Brazil are accompanied by rapid changes in the food habits and dietary practices of Brazil's people. Many of these changes are the result of a huge immigration of people from Europe earlier in the century, of the recent mushrooming of the urban populations, of rapidly rising standards and much more slowly rising levels of living, and of the general homogenization of Brazilian society. However, organized educational campaigns, such as "Milk Week," doubtless are having considerable effect. In São Paulo, for example, in 1969 a Milk Educational Campaign organized by the milk producers of that state, with the support of the state governor, received an award as "the best promotional campaign of the year." Some of the details about this effort are supplied by the following translation of a couple of paragraphs from a report in the March 1970 issue of the *Correio Agro-Precuario* of São Paulo:

The milk education program was begun early in 1969. Its principal objective was to combat the prejudices and psychological resistances against milk, such as "milk is a drink for babies," "milk is something extra," and "milk is fattening." The campaign was highly successful. The sale of milk increased. It was common to see men drinking milk in the city's bars. Numerous families began drinking milk with their meals, as a valuable additional nutrient. Organized by the P. A. Nascimento—Acar Propaganda publicity agency, the new phase of the campaign made use of ads in the newspapers, film strips on television, radio announcements, and signs on billboards, in a major attempt to appeal to children, and through them to other consumers, emphasizing the deliciousness and the nutritious and healthful qualities of milk.

The accomplishments to date are only a beginning, but they do represent a substantial start in the production and use of a highly important food. During the 1970's the increased production of milk alone should play a great role in helping the food supply to keep pace with the growth of population and in a substantial improvement in the diet of the Brazilian people. In this connection it should be remembered that only a few parts of Brazil that are best suited for dairying are being used for that purpose; that only a beginning has been made in the improvement of pastures and the growing of forage crops; and that the upgrading of the cows that are milked still has far to go.[56] Moreover, the per capita consumption still is very low; and as late as 1966 pasteurized milk was available in only eight of the states and territories that make up the Brazilian confederation. At that time the cities of Belo Horizonte and Brasília represented the northern and westernmost outposts of this advance in milk processing, which is to say that many of Brazil's greatest cities, including Recife, Salvador, and Fortaleza, lacked such safe-

[56] *Survey of the Brazilian Economy for 1966*, Washington, D.C.: the Brazilian Embassy, December, 1967, p. 95, states that "in some areas of Brazil, it is difficult to establish a clear distinction between beef and dairy cattle; many farmers, as a result of poor milk production, use the same cattle for both purposes. On the other hand, there are no statistics for the numbers of the different breeds of cattle raised in the country as a whole."

guards to their milk supplies. With the headway already accomplished in the densely inhabited parts of southern Brazil, and the increased efforts to expand milk production and develop milk-processing plants included in the four-year development plan, progress to overcome these deficiences seems certain.[57]

Other changes in the types of farming also have contributed substantially to the rise in Brazil's supplies of food, feed, and fiber at a rate even more rapid than that in her population. Ultra modern ways of producing eggs and poultry is one of these, and improvements in the production of corn, beef cattle, and hogs eventually may become another. As yet, however, Brazilian farmers still must learn or be taught the advantages of combining the growing of corn, the farrowing of pigs, and the fattening of beef cattle in a highly symbiotic type of farming. This particular sociocultural system has never contributed to the well-being of the farmers in any part of the world except those in the famous "corn belt" of the United States. There it was discovered about 1820 in Ohio and Kentucky, gradually spread westward throughout the entire area, and persisted as the basis of the unequalled agricultural development of the region until about 1960 when it ultimately gave way to greater specialization by enterprises and to scientifically designed rations for fattening hogs and beef cattle.[58]

Another important development of a type of farming is the substantial increase in wheat production that has been achieved. Unfortunately, wheat culture is largely monoculture, and as conducted does very little to secure an all-important combination of livestock and crop enterprises in the same farm business; but because Brazil's rapidly urbanizing society demands ever larger quantities of wheat (for bread, Italian dishes of many kinds, and so on, in replacement of traditional rice, beans, and manioc, always the staples of the diets in the rural areas) Brazil finds it imperative to expand wheat production as rapidly as possible. In this the country enjoyed striking success during the 1960's. In fact, the 57 per cent increase between 1961 and 1968, presented in Table LXXVII, subsequently has been followed by even greater attainments along this line. Thus, an item in the *Boletim Especial* issued by the Brazilian Embassy in Washington, D.C., dated August 18, 1970, first comments upon the bumper crop being harvested in the município of Santo Angelo in Rio Grande do Sul. In this município, the one that leads Brazil in the production of wheat, the crop for 1970 produced almost one million sacks, a gain of about 50 per cent over that for the preceding year. Moreover, record crops also were reported for other parts of Rio Grande do Sul and Paraná; and the prospects were that in 1970

[57] Some of the highlights of the announced "Metas e Bases para a Ação de Govêrno," including the measures designed to promote dairy husbandry and to enlarge and modernize milk-processing plants are given in "Ação Programada para o Ingreso no Mundo Desenvolvido," 3–13.

[58] On the genesis, spread, and importance of the corn-hog-beef cattle type of farming in the United States, see T. Lynn Smith, "Agricultural-Pastoral Conflict: A Major Obstacle in the Process of Rural Development," 16–43.

Brazil would produce half of the wheat consumed in the country. Inasmuch as annual imports of this basic cereal account for about 11 per cent of the cost of all imports, rivaling petroleum in the amount of foreign exchange required each year, this particular accomplishment is of the utmost significance. Moreover, the thoroughly modern ways of farming presently being applied in wheat culture offer promise that success in wheat production may attend the efforts of progressive farmers in many areas where little or no wheat presently is being grown.[59]

Before terminating this discussion of the changes in types of farming in Brazil and the role these are playing in the rapid increases in production of agricultural commodities, mention should be made of the introduction of a few entirely new crops. This feature of the development process deserves far more study than has been given to it not merely because of what it is adding to the productivity of Brazilian farms, but also for the light it could shed upon the entire process of how sociocultural traits, complexes, and systems get transferred from one place to another.[60] Consider the recent introduction of pepper culture. Brazil is now one of the world's greatest suppliers of the black and white pepper that does so much to add savor to foods consumed by billions of people. The transplantation of the pepper plants themselves and the sociocultural system whereby they are made to produce and their seeds prepared for market was one of the by-products of the admission of Japanese immigrants in the 1930's. It also came about in a chance or accidental way. As detailed by the U.S. Agricultural Attaché in Brazil in a recent article[61] the basic facts are as follows. In 1933 a shipload of Japanese immigrants bound for Belém, Pará, put in at Singapore to bury an elderly passenger who had died. While on shore a representative of the colonization company conducting the migration bought twenty pepper seedlings. Only three of these survived the trip, but by 1970 they had multiplied "2 million times apiece. Here, within the reaches of the Amazon jungle, the initiative and industry of a tiny fraction (1.1 per cent) of Brazil's Japanese colony have made pepper Pará's most valuable agricultural product. In 1968 pepper production there was valued at $4,435,000." Exports began in 1955, after production had been expanded to the point of supplying Brazil's own needs and of leaving an excess to be sold abroad. In 1969 the United States took about one-half of the eight thousand

[59] Data on imports are available annually in the *Anuário Estatístico do Brasil* and in the *Survey of the Brazilian Economy* issued from time to time by the Brazilian Embassy in Washington. For a fuller account of the bumper 1970 harvest and the development of wheat culture in general, see "Trigo," *Extensão Rural*, V (Setembro, 1970), 3–7.

[60] For a brief discussion of some of the issues involved, and especially of the inadequacy of the concept of "diffusion," see the selection entitled "Possibilities and Pitfalls in the Transplantation of Sociocultural Traits, Complexes, and Systems, with Special Reference to Latin America," in T. Lynn Smith, *Studies of Latin American Societies* (New York, 1970), 259–75.

[61] John C. McDonald, "The Story of Pepper Production in Brazil," *Foreign Agriculture*, VIII (February 16, 1970), 9–10.

tons exported, with most of the remainder going to Europe, other Latin American countries, Canada, and Japan.

As a result of the changes since 1960, the types of farming are becoming considerably different from those relied upon by Brazilian farmers and stockmen a few decades ago. Perhaps the most striking change of all is the extent to which farming as such is being superimposed upon the rudimentary pastoral culture which for centuries held undisputed sway over the greater part of the inhabited sections of the country. Substantial headway has been made in dairying, and in the production of such crops as corn, rice, wheat, and even soybeans. Some progess is evident in the growing of improved pastures and forage crops. But much is still to be done, and in the stages of development in which substantial improvements come most easily. Only the barest beginnings have been made in the growing of two of the three "wonder" crops, alfalfa and the sorghums (soybeans is the other), that are responsible for a large share of the phenomenal increases in the production of agricultural commodities in the United States since 1960. However, many areas in Brazil, including portions of the problem-ridden Northeast, probably are eminently suited for the culture of both. Therefore, because of the enthusiasm with which the present generation of Brazilians is pursuing the goals of agricultural development, there is hope that within the next decade or two, alfalfa, soybeans, and milo will form integral parts of types of farming in which livestock and livestock products will contribute far more than ever to the well-being of Brazil's population, even if it continues to increase rapidly.

Agrarian Reform. Despite all the uproar and conflict over agrarian reform that took place in Brazil during the period from about 1958 to 1966, relatively little of the great increase in the production of crops and livestock should be attributed to reforms in ownership and control of the land. It probably would be much more accurate to attribute Brazil's military dictatorship to the tumult over that issue. Indeed, the downfall probably resulted in no small measure from the high emotional pitch generated over reform and the decision of the Goulart government to ignore the experiences of Japan, Taiwan, Italy, Egypt, Venezuela, and various other countries, in accomplishing substantial reforms in relatively peaceful and evolutionary ways, and to seek instead the revolutionary way of Russia, and Cuba, and other countries dominated by Marxist ideologies, confiscating large landed properties and turning them into state farms. However, it probably is idle to speculate about this, for one is never able to "second guess" history.

In the late 1950's and the early 1960's Brazil, in common with other Latin American countries, experienced the greatest outpouring of words on the subject of agrarian reform ever registered with respect to any proposed reform in the entire history of the country. Even the abolition campaign, in the 1880's, because of the underdeveloped stage of communications, was relatively mute in comparison with the explosion of talk and writing about agrarian reform.

In the words of one distinguished Brazilian lawyer and sociologist, J. V. Freitas, Marcondes, "Never was a *reform* so debated, in Brazil or outside of it, as the *agrarian*. At first, the appearance of an article or pamphlet on the subject was a novelty, then the books began to flow, and now [1962] we are in the epoch of indexes and bibliographies of the publications dealing with this controversial subject." [62] José Arthur Rios outlined carefully and dispassionately the development of this important movement in the introduction to the excellent summary of the proceedings of one of the national conferences held in Brazil in 1961 as interest in the subject was building up.[63] This came shortly after President Janio Quadros set up a "work group" to prepare a new land law (*Estatuto da Terra*). After João Goulart succeeded to the presidency, interest in agrarian reform spiraled dramatically, owing in no small part to the radical nature of many of the proposals. This was the period when facts and rumors about the activities of the "Ligas Camponesas," or Peasant Leagues, were at their height and when a large gathering of leftist politicians drew up the "Declaration of Belo Horizonte." [64] Goulart was in attendance at this gathering, and I have found no indication that he opposed in any way or disapproved of the resolution. This is important because the hopes of Brazilian moderates of achieving agrarian reform in a peaceful, evolutionary manner under his regime were rather completely dashed by this resolution and its aftermath. Even more important the resolution as a whole, and espe-

[62] J. V. Freitas Marcondes, "Reforma Agrária à Luz das Ciencias Socias," *Sociología* (São Paulo), XXV (1962), translated in part and used under the title "Salient Features of Agrarian Reform Proposals in Brazil," in T. Lynn Smith (ed.), *Agrarian Reform in Latin America* (New York, 1965), 108–15.

[63] See José Arthur Rios, *Recomendações sôbre Reforma Agrária* (Rio de Janeiro, 1961), xi–xvii. This part of the introduction was translated and published under the title "The Development of Interest in Agrarian Reform in Brazil," in Smith (ed.), *Agrarian Reform in Latin America*, 95–101.

[64] For the founder's account of the nature of these leagues and the Declaration of Belo Horizonte, see, Francisco Julião, *Que São as Ligas Camponeses?* Cadernos do Povo Brazileiro, No. 1 (Rio de Janeiro: Editôra Civilização Brasileira, 1962). The declaration itself in translation is published in Smith (ed.), *Agrarian Reform in Latin America*, 116–22. This small volume by Julião was the first in a widely circulated series of revolutionary political essays. My own copy is number 16,216. Some of the others in the series of which I was able to get copies in Campinas, São Paulo, in 1963 when I was there participating in an International Course on Agrarian Reform organized under the auspices of the Inter-American Institute of Agricultural Sciences, are as follows: Nelson Werneck Sodré, *Quem é O Povo no Brasil?*, No. 2; Theotônio Júnior, *Quais São os Inimigos do Povo?*, No. 6; Bolivar Costa, *Quem Pode Fazer a Revolução no Brasil?*, No. 7; Nestor de Holanda, *Como Seria o Brasil Socialista?*, No. 8; Franklin de Oliveira, *Que é a Revolução Brasileira?*, No. 9; Paulo R. Schilling, *O Que é Reforma Agraria*, No. 10; Maria Augusta Tibiriçá, *Vamos a Nazionalizar a Indústria Farmacêutica?*, No. 11; Helga Hoffmann, *Como Planejar nossa Desenvolvimento?*, No. 14; and various authors, *Violão de Rua: Poemas para a Liberdade*, 2 volumes, extra. The English equivalents of these Portuguese titles, would be approximately as follows: No. 1, *What Are the Peasant Leagues?*; No. 2, *Who Are the Brazilian People?*; No. 6, *Who Are the Enemies of the People?*; No. 7, *Who Can Make a Revolution in Brazil?*; No. 8, *How Will Brazil Be under Socialism?*; *What is the Brazilian Revolution?*; No. 10, *What is Agrarian Reform?*; No. 11, *Shall We Nationalize the Pharmaceutical Industry?*; No. 14, *How Shall We Plan Our Development?*; and extra, *Guitar in the Street: Poems for Liberty.*

cially the provision that lands expropriated for agrarian reform would be paid for with long term, low interest, *nonnegotiable* bonds was viewed as outright confiscation. It thoroughly alarmed the powerful land-owning Brazilian elite and united them in efforts to prevent such measures at all costs.[65] Certainly, dissatisfaction with the government's plans and proposals for agrarian reform was a powerful factor in producing the coalition of widely differing forces that led to the ousting of Goulart.[66]

Thus, as events have transpired, any genuine agrarian reform in Brazil is still a thing of the future. As I have tried to indicate elsewhere,[67] the major alternatives are two: first, the use of the tax upon land and other real property to force the economic utilization of the soil, and to provide the funds for genuine community development (schools, local roads and bridges, health services, protection of life and property, etc.), which if applied in Brazil quickly would be an end to latifundismo; and second, the reform of the Marxist totalitarian type, involving the confiscation of the land, its transformation into huge state farms, and the retention of the workers as mere units of labor that arbitrarily may be dispatched to any point that some bureaucrat thinks their energies may be most efficiently applied in the production process.

Only one serious attempt has been made in Brazil to use the tax on land as a key component in a program of reform. This occurred in São Paulo where the state government levied a very small tax (about one-half of one per cent of the declared value) on the land with the objective of using the proceeds to enable small farmers to acquire ownership and to finance other features of agricultural development. However, the program had barely begun before the Brazilian Senate hastily changed the constitution by revoking right of the state to levy such a tax and transferring it to the municípios.[68]

Nor have the Agrarian Reform agencies established by the Brazil-

---

[65] Cf. Smith, *Agrarian Reform,* 120, for the exact text of this part of the resolution.

[66] The documentation pertaining to the agrarian reform and other aspects of this particular change of government is immense, and represents all shades of opinion. One M.A. thesis in history, "The Brazilian Revolution of 1964," by R. Don Crider, presented at the University of Florida in 1966, contains a bibliography of about 170 titles. One of the most revealing accounts of what actually was transpiring in the peasant leagues and related affairs is the "post mortem" written in exile by one who had spent a life time in organizing the leagues and similar revolutionary activities. See Clodomir Moraes, "Peasant Leagues in Brazil," in Rodolfo Stavenhagen (ed), *Agrarian Problems and Peasant Movements in Latin America* (New York, 1970), 453–501. Another sympathetic view of some of the same activities is that of the brilliant journalist, Antonio Callado, in his *Tempo de Arraes: Padres e Comunistas na Revolução sem Violência* (Rio de Janeiro, 1965).

[67] Consult the following by T. Lynn Smith: "Reforma Agrária," *A Lavoura* LIX (Setembro–Outubro, 1956), 5–20; *Current Social Trends and Problems in Latin America* (Gainesville, Fla., 1957), 29–44; (ed.), *Agrarian Reform in Latin America,* 51–62; *The Process of Rural Development in Latin America* (Gainesville, Fla., 1967), 30–32; *Studies of Latin American Societies,* 311–14, 319–22, 331–38.

[68] For the details of the attempts at agrarian reform in São Paulo see J. V. Freitas Marcondes, *Revisão e Reforma Agrária* (São Paulo, 1962).

ian government since 1964 been able to accomplish very much. As indicated elsewhere in this chapter, the Estatuto da Terra, or basic land law, was developed and put into force, and the cadastral survey of Brazilian privately owned lands prescribed by it has been completed. In addition, substantial work has been done, also mentioned in this chapter, in clearing the titles to lands in the areas near national boundaries, where the federal government is empowered to act. However, over most of Brazil's area, the land system is a matter over which the states, not the national government, have control; and by no means are all of the acute difficulties with land titles limited to the frontier zones. The entire state of Maranhão is a notorious example of clouded land titles, and the difficulties are not limited to it nor to the other locations mentioned in Chapter XII of this volume. Recently, Dr. Harold M. Clements in his study of the mechanization of agriculture in Minas Gerais frequently found areas in which the problem was acute, as indicated by the following and other entries in his field notes: "In this one area [in northeastern Minas Gerais, near Teófilo-Otoni], however, out of 1,034 *proprietários* or landowners, 620 have no legal title to their holdings and, therefore, are not entitled to financial assistance from ACAR. I encountered a similar situation throughout the southern portion of the state." [69]

It should be stressed, in closing this chapter, that the new, great efforts to colonize virgin lands apparently are being guided by the principle of getting the possession and use of these great resources into the hands of actual farmers in amounts suited to the development of genuine family-sized farms. If this principle is adherred to rigidly, and the activities of land speculators are curbed, these activities very well may turn out to be one of the most momentous agrarian reform programs the world has ever known.

[69] Clements, *A Sociological Study*, 53.

CHAPTER XXV

URBANIZATION

During the 1960's Brazil experienced sociocultural changes unparalleled in its entire history, except, perhaps, by those that accompanied the almost simultaneous abolition of slavery and the replacement of the Empire by the Republic (1888–1889). Moreover, few countries in the entire world, if any, have undergone more rapidly a transformation from a nation that for centuries was overwhelmingly rural, pastoral, and agricultural, to one in which the majority of the population live in urban centers and engage in nonagricultural economic activities, than has Brazil. Indeed urbanization both as an effect and as a cause is the central feature of the tremendous metamorphosis of society that has made the Brazil of the 1970's radically different from that of the 1950's. On the one hand the nation is being carried along by a set of forces that are replacing traditional rural forms of social organization and ways of life with urban and industrial activities in the economic, social, educational, and cultural spheres. And on the other the problems of gaining a livelihood, providing a home for a family, rearing and educating children in a large bustling and rapidly changing city is creating hundreds of problems with which the average Brazilian parents are finding it difficult to cope. The impact of influences from all parts of the world, many of which have created considerable chaos in the societies in which they were spawned, often prove incompatible with traditional values and standards; but they have to be confronted day and night. Never has the principle that sociocultural change always involves a change in the rules of the game while a single generation of people are at the societal gaming table been more clearly apparent than is the case in modern Brazil. All of this is producing profound alterations in the personality of the Brazilian, the groups in which he mingles, the class system of which he is a part, the communities and neighborhoods in which he has his being, the social institutions that regularize his behavior, and the values and standards by which he lives. In fact these changes are so many and so profound that I seriously considered paraphrasing Charles Darwin to some extent and entitling the entire new section of this book *Variation of Social Institutions and Sociocultural Systems under Urbanization*. Only the pretentiousness of such a title and the knowledge that many readers would be aggrieved by my inability to do it justice caused me to desist. In this chapter we

attempt to explore a few of the more salient features of the process
of urbanization as it is currently underway in the great Brazilian
half continent.

THE PROGRESS OF URBANIZATION

That the process of urbanization is moving very rapidly in modern Brazil is easily demonstrated. In this section attention is focused
upon two indications of this, namely, the rapid growth of cities and
towns, and the recent changes in the consumption of certain commodities and the use of specific facilities that are essential features
of the building, supplying, and living in modern cities. I also include here a brief discussion of the lag in the provision of certain
essential urban facilities in comparison with the growth of urban
aggregations of population.

The Growth of Cities and Towns. As is shown by the data in
Table LXXII, between 1950 and 1960 Brazil took gigantic strides
towards becoming a nation of predominantly urban people. During
that decade its urban population increased at a rate almost five
times that of the rural. For illustrations of the magnitude of these
differences in two regions see Figures 45, 46 and 47. Moreover well
over half of the growth of the census was due to the migration to an
urban center of people from the farms, for at least one out of every
ten persons enumerated in the cities and towns in 1960 personally
had moved from strictly rural territory since 1950. There was no pause
in the rapid upsurge of the urban population following 1960. Population centers emerged at points where none had been before, villages
grew into towns and towns into cities, many small cities doubled in
population, large cities became much larger, and there seemed to be no
limit to the number of Brazilians who could crowd into gigantic Rio
de Janeiro and São Paulo and the zones immediately surrounding
each of them. Even before the definitive results of the 1970 census
become available one may be fairly certain that the huge movement
of people from the rural to the urban districts continued after 1960,
probably at an average of at least 750,000 per year; and surely the
migration was more than sufficient, when added to the natural increase of population in the urban places themselves, to produce a
situation in the 1970's, in which the urban population considerably
outnumbers the rural and in which the proportion of the former
among all inhabitants continues to mount rapidly.

In order to present some of the most striking facts about the
tremendous growth of Brazil's major cities between 1960 and 1970,
Table LXXIX has been prepared.

The implications of Brazil reaching the mark at which its population is predominantly urban are of the utmost importance. This came
about 1965, or almost exactly fifty years after the United States
passed a similar milestone in its development. In the case of the
United States, that happening probably also marked the point at

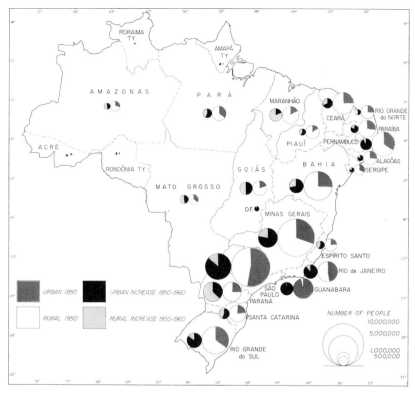

FIGURE 45. The Absolute and Relative Changes in the Populations of Brazil's States and Territories, 1950–1960, by Rural and Urban Residence. (In each state or territory the circle to the reader's right is proportionate to the change in urban population and that to his left to the change in the rural population.)

which the parabola of rural-urban differentiation reached its maximum; and that has been followed by a half century in which rather steadily many of the more pronounced differences between rural and urban people have been obliterated. It is likely that the same pattern is being followed in Brazil. Certainly prior to about 1965 the degree—and it was a high one—to which the inhabitants of Brazil's great cities came to resemble people in the cities of Europe and North America also represented the extent to which they became more different from their fellow Brazilians who lived in the immense and extremely rural sections of the country. But there are some striking differences between Brazil and the United States in respect to the process of rural-urban differentiation, and especially in the facility with which rapid and effective systems of communication and transportation could be brought into play in connection with it. In 1915, when the United States reached the point of becoming predominantly urban, the automobile was just coming into use, and outside the cities most roads were quagmires when it rained.

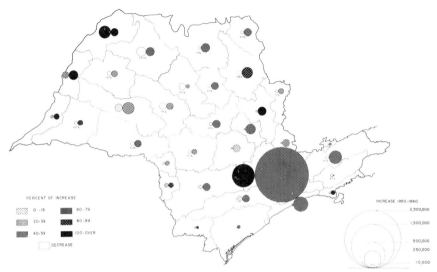

FIGURE 46. The Absolute and Relative Changes in the Populations of the Physiographic Regions of the State of São Paulo, 1950–1960, by Rural and Urban Residence. (In each region the circle to the reader's right is proportionate to the change in urban population and that to his left to the change in the rural population.)

The telephone system was still in its infancy, the radio was yet to come, and at most television was merely a dream of a few visionaries. Airplanes were hardly perfected to the extent that anyone could think of them as forming the backbone of a system for transporting passengers, mail, and great amounts of freight. They played no role in farming and the mobility of farm operators. Yet the development and perfection of all of these, and the building of a huge national system of highways and roads, in which practically every farm and hamlet in the United States is served by an all-weather road, are exactly the things that have reduced the differences that once prevailed in the characteristics and ways of life of rural and urban people.

When Brazil recently reached the stage in its history in which it became predominantly urban, it already was well underway in the construction of a national system of roads and highways. It already was served by a vast system of telephones, a great network of radios, and a substantial chain of television stations. The airplane was playing a tremendous role in its transportation system, both for carrying passengers and for handling freight. The automobile and especially the motor truck were major components of the transportation system. They were being piloted over thousands of miles of prepared roadways; and they also were being driven over many thousands of miles where the roads consisted merely of the ruts formed by the wheels of the vehicles themselves. The transistor radio and the outboard motor used to propel watercraft were playing

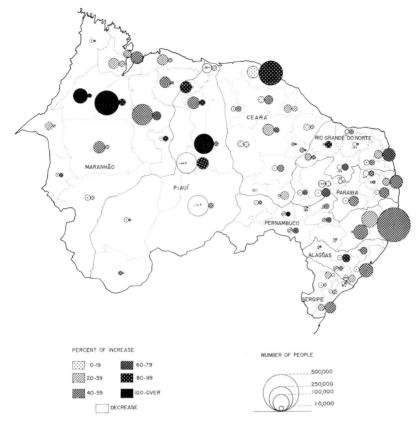

PERCENT OF INCREASE

0-19	60-79
20-39	80-99
40-59	100-OVER
DECREASE	

NUMBER OF PEOPLE

500,000
250,000
100,000
10,000

F I G U R E 4 7 . The Absolute and Relative Changes in the Populations of the Physiographic Regions in Northeastern Brazil, 1950–1960, by Rural and Urban Residence. (In each region the circle to the reader's right is proportionate to the change in the urban population and that to his left to the change in the rural population.)

roles in the system of communication and transportation that never were attained in the United States. Hence it is reasonable to expect that the process of reducing rural-urban differences will move more quickly in Brazil than it did in the United States. In the decades immediately ahead, the newer features of Brazilian society now commonplace in its cities rapidly will be spread to its towns, villages, and farms. In other words the nation is entering a period in which the striking differences now distinguishing the inhabitants of its cities from those in the hinterlands soon will become less and less pronounced.[1]

[1] The principles that the city is the innovator and the country the preserver of national culture traits, and that changes originate in the urban centers and are gradually spread to the rural districts were stated many years ago by P. A. Sorokin and Carle C. Zimmerman. See their *Principles of Rural-Urban Sociology*, 403–17; and T. Lynn Smith, "Sorokin's Rural-Urban Principles," in Philip J. Allen (ed.), *Pitirim A. Sorokin in Review* (Durham, N.C., 1963), 201.

TABLE LXXIX

Growth of Population in Municípios Containing
State and Territorial Capitals, 1960–1970 *

Município and State	Population 1970	Population 1960	Increase Number	Increase Per cent
All capitals	20,157,006	13,235,892	6,921,114	52.3
São Paulo, São Paulo	5,901,533	3,825,351	2,076,182	54.3
Rio de Janeiro, Guanabara	4,296,782	3,307,163	989,619	29.9
Belo Horizonte, Minas Gerais	1,232,708	693,328	539,380	77.8
Recife, Pernambuco	1,078,819	797,234	281,585	35.3
Salvador, Bahia	1,000,647	655,735	344,912	52.6
Pôrto Alegre, Rio Grande do Sul †	885,567	641,173	244,394	38.1
Fortaleza, Ceará	842,231	514,818	327,413	63.6
Belém, Pará †	642,514	402,170	240,344	59.8
Curitiba, Paraná	603,227	361,309	241,918	67.0
Brasília, Distrito Federal	544,862	141,742	403,120	284.4
Goiânia, Goiás	388,926	153,505	235,421	153.4
Niterói, Rio de Janeiro	324,367	245,467	78,900	32.1
Manaus, Amazonas †	303,155	175,343	127,812	72.9
Natal, Rio Grande do Norte	270,124	162,537	107,587	66.2
Maceió, Alagôas	269,415	170,134	99,281	58.4
São Luis, Maranhão †	267,321	159,628	107,693	67.5
Teresina, Piauí	230,168	144,799	85,369	59.0
João Pessoa, Paraíba	221,484	155,117	66,367	42.8
Aracaju, Sergipe	183,333	115,713	67,620	58.4
Florianópolis, Santa Catarina	143,101	98,520	44,581	45.3
Vitória, Espírito Santo	135,570	85,242	50,328	59.0
Cuiabá, Mato Grosso †	103,262	57,860	45,402	78.5
Pôrto Velho, Rondônia †	90,238	51,049	39,189	76.8
Macapá, Amapá †	87,755	46,905	40,850	87.1
Rio Branco, Acre †	72,835	47,882	24,953	52.1
Boa Vista, Roraima †	37,062	26,168	10,894	41.6

* Source: Inter-American Statistical Institute, *Boletin Estadístico*, number 68, Washington, D.C.: Organization of American States, February 1971, p. 6. The data for 1970 are provisional figures. Those for 1960 are the final figures, and are slightly higher than the provisional figures for that year given in Table LXX.

† Data Incomplete.

Other Indicators of the Progress of Urbanization. The rapid increase in the populations of cities and towns is only one of the principal indicators of the progress of urbanization. Other important measures of this fundamental development are changes in the consumption of materials used in construction of homes, streets, highways, and so on; changes in the extent to which the dwellings are equipped with electricity, telephones, running water and other modern facilities; and changes in the essential components of modern systems of communication and transportation. Data showing the increases in some of the more important of the items of this kind, for which information is available, are presented in Table LXXX. Taken together the materials in this tabulation are eloquent in the evidence they present about the rapid pace of urbanization in contemporary Brazil. In some of the facilities, such as telephones and water meters, in many cities the increases would be much greater than they are were it possible for the services to be expanded more rapidly. In Rio de Janeiro, for example, the waiting lists of applicants for telephones and water connections contain hundreds of thousands of names.

More on the Lag in Urbanização in Comparison with Urbanization. As emphasized above (pp. 601–606), for some time Brazilians have been crowding into cities and towns far more rapidly than the local governments have been able to expand the physical facilities (water supplies, sewer systems, lighting systems, etc.) Hence, what is called *urbanização* ("urbanization") in Brazil has lagged greatly in comparison with urbanization in the English meaning of the term. The only items for which statistical data are given in the section entitled "Urbanização" in the 1969 issue of the *Anuário Estatístico do Brasil* for 1969 are those about the public water systems, sewer systems, and garbage collection. The data on the changes in two of these are given in Table LXXX. However, this issue of the great official compilation of statistical data contains important tabulations showing the number and proportion of persons served by public water and sewer systems in the various municípios classified according to the size of the seats of the municípios. Essential figures from these two tables have been assembled in Table LXXXI. They demonstrate conclusively a fact well known from casual observation, namely that essential utilities are lacking for many millions of people who now are crowded together in urban places large and small. Even in the largest cities over one-fourth of the people lack public water supplies, and only slightly more than one-third have homes that are connected with sewer systems. It is important and interesting to note that the best showing of all is made the county-like entities wherein the seats vary between 50,000 and 100,000 inhabitants, especially since most of these municípios are ones in which the populations of surrounding areas contain comparatively high proportions of all the inhabitants of the respective municípios. If the data were given separately for the urban populations, it therefore seems certain that lag in "urbanization" in comparison with urbanization in this category of small cities would be far less than it is in those having over 100,000 residents. This, in turn, suggests that when the finc urban homes of the *fazendeiros* and other affluent people are fairly close to those of the less-favored persons, public water and sewer systems are much more likely to be at the service of all.

José Arthur Rios, able sociologist-lawyer who had the main responsibility for the excellent study of the *favelas* of Rio de Janeiro

TABLE LXXX

Some Indicators of the Progress
*of Urbanization in Brazil, 1960–1968 ***

Items	A. *Consumption of certain commodities*				
	Unit of measurement	Consumption 1960	1968	Increase 1960–1968 Amount	Per cent
Gasoline for automobiles	liters (millions)	4,427	8,219	3,792	86
Diesel oil	" "	2,954	5,513	2,559	87
Fuel for jet engines	" "	31	567	476	523
Electricity	kwh (millions)	18,346	31,399	13,053	71
Cement	metric tons (thousands)	4,447	7,249	2,802	63
Asphalt	" "	232	532	300	129
Rubber	" "	71	127	56	79
Wheat	" "	2,746	3,490	744	27
Coal	" "	2,205	3,970	1,765	80

Items	B. *Selected facilities and vehicles in use*			
	Number 1960	1967	Increase 1960–1967 Number	Per cent
Telephones	1,108,149[1]	1,470,023	361,874	33
Water meters	850,514	1,495,058	644,544	76
Fire hydrants	16,260	30,659	14,399	89
Buildings served by sewers	1,370,152	1,912,306	542,154	40
Passenger vehicles	646,681	1,929,873	1,283,192	198
Automobiles	501,975	1,417,895	915,920	183
Motor trucks (including pickups)	308,329	533,476[2]	225,147	73

* Source: Compiled and computed from data given in the *Anuário Estatístico do Brasil*, 1962, pp. 124, 199–210, and 225–26; and *Anuário Estatístico do Brasil*, 1969, pp. 385, 398–99, 442–56, and 476–78.
(1) Data are for 1961.
(2) This figure includes 129,769 pickup trucks, and the figure for 1960 probably includes an unknown number of the same.

cited above (pp. 604–605), recently did the sociological portions of a comprehensive study of the situation and possibilities for improvement in one of the immense slums in the city of Salvador, Bahia. Some of the results of this detailed survey demonstrate the acuteness of the problem caused by the recent crowding together of millions of Brazilians in great agglomerations in which only the barest beginning has been made in the provision of essential urban services. The district studied is located on the mud flats washed by the incoming tides along the shore of the great bay on which Salvador is situated. It is called Alagados, and the survey showed it to have a population of about 75,000 living in some 15,000 residences. In the words of the excellent monograph itself, "about 8 per cent of the people residing within the urban perimeter of Salvador live in an area called Alagados. This agglomeration of subhabitations represents, along with the most degrading housing and hygienic conditions, an effective potential of human resources made up of a group of the population eagerly desiring to improve their status." [2] Some of the facts brought out by this survey are as follows.

About 10,200 children (14 per cent of the population) are of school age (7 to 17, inclusive), and 17,800 (24 per cent) are younger than that. Of these, 9,578 children were enrolled in forty-six elementary schools. (This seems to demonstrate that once in the city the people are determined to secure some kind of an education for their children). However, only four of these schools were judged to offer any reasonable opportunities for education, "the others being mere residences transformed into schools and lacking the minimum essentials." [3] There are no secondary schools in Alagados.

TABLE LXXXI

Estimates of the Number of People Served by Public Water Systems and Sewers, by Size of the Seats of the Municípios in Which They Reside, 1967 *

Number of inhabitants in the seat of the município	Population	Percentage served by	
		Public water system	Sewers
Total	85,783,003	26.9	13.1
2,000 or less	49,066,558	1.1	0.2
2,001–10,000	7,858,490	35.3	11.4
10,001–20,000	3,478,847	51.5	22.2
20,001–50,000	3,694,745	61.9	31.0
50,001–100,000	3,034,558	73.8	40.5
100,001–over	18,649,805	72.2	38.0

* Source: *Anuário Estatístico do Brasil, 1969*, pp. 476, 478.

Of the 15,000 dwellings, about 11 per cent were connected with the municipal water mains. The remainder of the families had to carry water from twenty-two spigots scattered about the district or from the homes of neighbors. Nearly all the huts were equipped with drums for catching and retaining rain water that falls on the roofs. Electricity was available, at least intermittently, in 5,012 of the homes, and there were 625 private and 6 public telephones in the district of Alagados. No sewer system, except that provided by the periodic ebb and flood of the tide, served the 75,000 residents of the immense slum.[4]

Finally, to terminate this brief discussion of the lag in the provision of essential municipal services in comparison with the rapidity with which Brazilian cities are burgeoning, consider a few of the materials from Rios' excellent survey of Campina Grande, a mushroom-

[2] José Arthur Rios, Wit-Olaf Prochnik, Joel Ghivelder, and others, *Plano de Recuperação dos Alagados: Estudo Preliminar* (Salvador, 1969), 1.
[3] *Ibid.*, 44.
[4] *Ibid.*, 57–62.

ing trade and transportation center in Paraíba. In 1942 this city contained 9,935 dwellings, whereas by 1960, and due largely to the huge influx of people from the great *sertão* of the Northeast, this number had risen to 38,000. In 1960 it had an enumerated population of 126,000. In 1963, though, in this entire city "the proportion of the people who drank uncontaminated water was less than 30 per cent," the "sewer system served less than 20 per cent of the inhabitants," and the infant mortality rate of from 200 to 500 per thousand live births could be explained "by the general nutritional deficiencies and by hygienic deficiencies." [5]

SOME EFFECTS AND CONCOMITANTS OF URBANIZATION

The effects or at least the concomitants of urbanization in Brazil are many and varied. Attention is directed to a few of these in the pages that follow.

Increasing Social Differentiation and the Change in Social Solidarity. Associated with the mushrooming of cities and towns throughout Brazil are substantial changes since 1960 in the size and structure of communities of all kinds and in the nature of social cohesion in social groupings as a whole. These matters sociologists consider of importance, for they seem to determine in a large measure the personality types produced in a given society. Societies in which social differentiation has not proceeded to any great extent, as was the case in most parts of Brazil prior to the twentieth century, are made up of many small, homogeneous, and highly cohesive social groupings. The "experience world" of a given person is limited almost entirely to the small community or neighborhood, that is to the small cluster of families in a small locality, into which he was born. All members of that community are essentially alike with respect to most of the fundamental characteristics and the social bonds which unite individuals into groupings. Occupationally, religiously, educationally, politically, ethically, and morally they are almost as similar as peas in a pod. In addition, centuries of inbreeding frequently developed a physical type that is highly uniform. Age and sex are almost the only bases for any division of social labor, and social cohesion is very strong. The latter comes almost exclusively from the recognition of basic similarities between the members of the small locality group, the type that has given rise to sayings such as "birds of a feather flock together," and "blood is thicker than water." Until recently the comparatively slight development of social differentiation and social solidarity based upon similarities of the people making up each little homogeneous community have been characteristic of the masses of the people in extremely rural Brazil. (The sharp differences between the masses and the members of the small upper class were, of course, indicative of the

[5] José Arthur Rios, *Campins Grande: Um Centro Comercial do Nordeste* (Rio de Janeiro, 1964), 10, 45.

one major cleavage that did exist, but even this does not invalidate the generalization that social differentiation was not highly developed.)

As a community grows, as societal horizons expand, and especially as contacts develop between those living in different locality groups, the process of social differentiation goes on rapidly. Occupational division of labor and specialization are accompanied by similar diversification in religious activities, education, politics, government, and all other parts of the social organization or structure. The mores and other standardized uniformities of behavior cease to command complete acceptance and compliance on the part of those residing in a given locality. Heterogeneity becomes the rule, and the cohesion or solidarity of the particular group and of society as a whole comes to be based in large measure upon the lack of self-sufficiency of any given part and the resulting interdependence which this brings about. Emile Durkheim, whose thinking in this respect I am following, designated this type of solidarity as *organic* because he thought it analogous with the interdependence of parts of a living organism. That based upon similarities he styled as *mechanistic*.

The changes in social differentiation and social solidarity presently taking place in most parts of Brazil resemble those which were going on in the United States about fifty years ago. It is likely, however, that the changes in the Brazilian social body show a greater variation from one part of its extensive territory to another than was true in the United States. This is to say that despite the comparative isolation and lack of contact of those living in such sections of the United States as the Southern Appalachians, the Ozarks, or the swamps of south Louisiana, that country in 1920 was less a superimposition of various epochs than Brazil is in the 1970's. Thus today one may find areas in São Paulo in which social differentiation seems to be keeping pace with that in the United States; but at the same time it is possible for anyone to visit many sections of Brazil in which the social order is only beginning to emerge from the colonial epoch. Lourenco Filho's proposition that one leaves behind a century of time with each day's journey inland from the coast, still has considerable validity.[6] Nevertheless, with the mushrooming of cities and towns, the improvement of transportation facilities, the development and spread of new and revolutionary means of communication, and the increasing spatial mobility of the population, the masses of the people in Brazil no longer are living in almost hermetically sealed-off little neighborhoods and communities. Already enough cities and towns have been built, and each of them has expanded its influence over the farms, hamlets, and villages in the area surrounding it to the extent that it no longer is valid to speak of Brazil as being in the neighborhood stage of social organization. The division of labor between persons, groups, and population centers in

[6] See above, chap. 2, pp. 19–21.

all lines of activity is increasing rapidly. Within each small rural
locality group and urban neighborhood or district social solidarity
of the mechanistic type rapidly is giving way to that based upon
division of social labor, specialization, and the consequent lack of
self-sufficiency of any of the highly integrated parts of the societal
whole; or in the terminology of Charles H. Cooley,[7] the traditionally
all-important Brazilian primary-group relationships are becoming
less important and secondary groupings and special-interest groups
of one kind or another coming to play greater and greater roles.
However, even though each segment of Brazilian society—neighborhood, rural community, village, town, or city—is becoming more
heterogeneous in its makeup, the society as a whole is becoming less
segmented and more of an integrated entity. Its various segments in
different parts of the nation are coming to be more similar in their
internal diversity, or, in brief, as stressed below, the homogenization
of Brazilian society is moving along at a rapid pace. This is to say
that the individual Brazilian is coming to be less completely sub-
merged in and circumscribed by his own small kinship and neighborhood groupings and more a citizen of his município, his state,
and his republic. Although this has not affected greatly the way of
life of the members of the upper classes, it is of far-reaching significance for the humble folk, rural and urban, who make up the majority of the population.

The Widening of the "Zone of Exasperation." As indicated above
(p. 241), by 1960 the rapid rise in expectations, or the standard of
living, accompanied by only modest improvement in the actual
consumption of goods and services, or level of living, had produced
a wide gap, or zone of exasperation, between the two. Since then as
Brazil has come to be predominantly urban, where the contrasts
between the affluent styles of life of some and the straitened circumstances of the many are exhibited on every hand, this big
discrepancy between what the people think they are entitled to enjoy
and what they actually have has become even more pronounced.
Thus, the situation becomes ever more acute even though the rise in
the level of expectations has been accompanied by substantial increases in the amounts of commodities and services they have been
privileged to consume. Nevertheless, the rise in expectations (or
the standard of living) has greatly exceeded that in the actual levels
or planes of living. Thus, in spite of the sizeable advances in actual
accomplishments, by 1970 the difference between the two probably
was much greater than it was in 1960; and one may say that the area
of frustration or the zone of exasperation has increased considerably.

The point to this is that since 1960 the masses of the Brazilian
population have come to believe that they and their children are
entitled to far better real wages, housing, dress, educational opportunities, health services, and so forth, than they have enjoyed in the
past. As a matter of fact, and this is in sharp contrast to the situation

[7] Cooley, *Social Organization* (New York, 1925), 23–26.

prevailing not long ago, by the millions Brazilians now aspire to the ownership of farms, to live in modern houses or apartments, to the personal possession of automobiles and television sets, to voices in political affairs, and to a way of life they see being enjoyed by the more favored portions of Brazilian society, by large numbers of foreigners who live and work in their midst, and by people in some other parts of the world of whom they have heard. But, and this qualification must be underscored, it always is easier for politicians to promise than for statesmen to satisfy, for those willing to promote change to draw up and present 300 projects for agrarian reform than it is to put a few substantial reform measures into practice, for agitators to arouse than for those having the responsibilities of administrative positions to satisfy, for individuals to aspire than for them to attain, or for the standard of living to advance than for the level of living to keep pace with its upward movement. As a result, and this is one of the most important or recent social changes in Brazil in the 1970's, the difference between the actual plane on which Brazil's masses live and that on which they now feel entitled to live is much greater than it was 50, 25 years ago, or even 10 years ago.

Moreover, with much reason one could contend that this spread between aspirations and attainments is a fairly good indicator of the degree of ferment and discontent among the masses with those who direct affairs in their rural and urban communities, in the states, and in the nation; and that it measures fairly well the hostility they feel and frequently express with the managers and white collar employees of the foreign firms doing business in their midst, with the officials and representatives of the countries in which these firms have their home offices, and even with the people in the countries with which, in the past, they have been united in trade, commerce, and even military alliances. Thus, social and economic ferment is the order of the day, and there is little or no effort to distinguish between the elements of the old order which have worked to the advantage of the masses and those which are responsible for the bulk of their ills. The broad zone of exasperation in contemporary Brazil makes rational behavior in local, state, national, and international relationships even more rare than ususally is the case.

The Homogenization of Society. Accompanying the rapid growth of cities and towns, during the 1960's the homogenization of Brazilian society moved along at a rapid rate.[8] This is to say that with the passage of time all of the various components (ethnic or racial, religious, demographic, cultural, economic, social, and so on) of which society is made up are becoming more uniformly distrib-

---

[8] For a development of the concept of homogenization of society and an analysis of the manner and degree in which this is taking place in the United States, see T. Lynn Smith, "The Homogenization of Society in the United States," in *Mémoire du XIX Congres International de Sociologie*, (Mexico, 1960), II, 245–75.

uted throughout the length and breadth of the settled portions of Brazil's immense territory. Indeed the extent to which migration of population from one region to another, the dissemination of cultural traits from one area to another, the transplantation of industrial and other sociocultural systems from south Brazil to other parts of the country, the spread of behavior patterns from the city to the country and from section to section, and so on, rival those presently going on within the United States and Argentina. Probably they considerably outdistance the comparable tendencies in Colombia, Peru, Venezuela, and most of the other countries of Latin America. Societal features long limited to Rio Grande do Sul, to Bahia, to the Northeast, to the great cities such as Rio de Janeiro and São Paulo presently may be observed as integral parts of the way of life of the people in various other parts of the immense nation. Dietary practices, dress, music, the dance, ideologies, machines and implements, agricultural practices, labor organizations, educational content and norms, and social values are only a few of the specific items involved in the momentous redistribution of societal components that is going on. The feverish endeavor to establish universities in all parts of Brazil is one of the most important features of the great process now underway.

All this means, of course, that as one decade succeeds another, the composition of any given territorial segment of Brazilian society of any one city, of any specific community or neighborhood, or of each one of the thousands of small parts of which the national fabric is made up, is becoming much more diverse or heterogeneous. At the same time, however, because of the tendency for all of the components to become more equally distributed throughout the entire body of society, the culture, social organization, and social processes in each of the various subdivisions of Brazilian territory are coming to resemble more closely those which make up the way of life and labor in other sections of the country. Thus the very fact of increasing diversity within any city or município is bringing about more homogeneity on the national scale. As a result, in comparison with the situation fifty or even twenty-five years ago, one who now comes to know any one area in Brazil is far more likely to be acquiring a knowledge of Brazilian society and not merely one of a highly distinctive segment of it.

CHAPTER XXVI

CHANGES IN THE CLASS STRUCTURE

AMONG THE most significant changes in Brazilian society since 1960 are fundamental modifications in social stratification or the class system. Brazilian and other social scientists now have done enough pragmatic work on this subject to enable us to sketch some of the most essential features of this basic transformation. Of primary importance in the substantial change in the traditional two-class system of the rural areas (a small elite and a huge mass of lower-class farm laborers of one kind or another) that has been produced by the mass movement of agricultural workers from the farms to the cities. As in the United States during the same period, this has brought about a huge transfer of "poverty" and all its social, economic, and cultural correlatives from the rural to the urban portion of society; and coupled with the swift rise in the socioeconomic scale by many of the workers that is an inseparable part of the mechanization or motorization of agriculture, this great transfer is profoundly changing the class system in rural Brazil.

Even more important than this, however, are great modifications in the class system that are produced by the rapid urbanization, industrialization, and changing functions of Brazilian cities. Of all these, two developments stand out, namely the rise of a substantial (and largely urban) middle class, and the growing importance of a new upper class. Each of these is discussed briefly in turn.

THE RISE OF A MIDDLE CLASS

Slowly but surely a middle class is arising in many parts of Brazil to help fill the large void that long existed between a small upper class at the top of the social scale and the impoverished, servile or semiservile, uneducated, and underprivileged masses that made up its inordinately large base. It should be stressed, though, that the change is not rapid in most places, is hardly underway in many, and that if Brazil ever is dominated by persons of middle-class status and mentality, this probably will be many decades in the future. The most headway has been made in the small-farming districts of Rio Grande do Sul, Santa Catarina, and Paraná and in all of the larger cities. The immigration during the last quarter of the nineteenth century of a sturdy peasantry who were settled on small farms in South Brazil played a major role in the rise of Brazil's middle class, both in the rural districts, and in the cities to which large numbers of their offspring have migrated. These immigrants were strongly influenced by middle-class standards, and, even though there has been some tendency for their descendants to ape upper-class ways, relatively few of them could attain firm positions in the limited space on the upper rungs of the social ladder. In the middle ranges, though, their rapidly increasing numbers contribute greatly to the growth and development of the intermediate social strata which probably are properly denoted as middle-class people.

The rise of "the new middle class" has been traced in a substantial section of his excellent book by Professor Charles Wagley, noted anthropologist of Columbia University.[1] His analysis and interpretation of this fundamental social change deserves serious consideration. Wagley first points out that since early in the nineteenth century there was in Brazil "a small group of people who might be classified as middle class." These were members of the families of men who had minor positions in government offices or who had other white-collar employment. After 1850, the immigration of Europeans, especially to southern Brazil, "added to the small Brazilian middle class." But Wagley stresses that "until very recently this middle segment has been relatively insignificant in numbers and might even be said to have been actually the lower and poorer fringes of the upper class." I personally have been amazed at the extent to which the Brazilians I know, who appear to live at a middle-class level, actually are the descendants of those who once occupied positions at the very apex of Brazilian society.

Relative to the most recent developments, Wagley emphasizes that all those who have known Brazil well from 1940 on agree "that the middle class has increased many times over and is rapidly expanding." He states that this is reflected in an enormous increase in demand for consumer goods, in the expansion of housing, for those of average incomes, and in the increased demand for public services of all types. "Perhaps the best index of middle-class expansion is the increase in white-collar jobs, for the middle sectors still consider manual labor in any form as a lower-class occupation." A tremendous expansion of civil service positions (federal, state, and at the município level) has opened up many white-collar positions, and such "employment has been perhaps the most single important road to membership in the middle class." In addition as industry and commerce have grown and developed, many new jobs have been created in offices and stores. Likewise, membership in the professions has increased to accompany the tremendous growth of Brazil's population and the increased buying power of the people. There is an urgent need for well-trained people of all kinds. Obviously, "the new middle sector has new demands, and is becoming at least superficially similar to the middle classes of the United States and Europe."[2]

[1] Wagley, An Introduction to Brazil (New York, 1964).
[2] See ibid., 122–27.

THE NEW UPPER CLASS

It should be stressed, however, that the rapid rise of a middle class, especially in the cities in Minas Gerais and to the south of it, is not the only great change that took place in Brazil's class system during the 1960's. Rivaling this in importance is the changing nature of the upper class itself, or perhaps better, the rise of a new upper class to compete with the affluence and influence of the traditional aristocratic families. To a considerable extent the "newly rich" and frequently almost vulgarly ostentatious members of the new "upper crust" have fortunes gained in industry and commerce and not those based upon large landholdings and huge coffee, sugar, and cattle enterprises. Fortunately, attention has been concentrated upon the nature of the new upper class by that pragmatic, perceptive, and industrious Brazilian sociologist, Professor José Arthur Rios. Rios has devoted years of intensive work to the study of his own native city and to analyses of social organization and the process of social change in many other parts of Brazil.[3] Some of his most significant analyses of the changes in Brazil's class structure are given in his excellent study of the city of Campina Grande, an important commercial center in the great drought-stricken, problem-ridden northeastern region of Brazil. At the time of his study in 1964, this important regional hub of trade and commerce contained about 120,000 inhabitants.

Rios opened his section on the class system in this rather large and rapidly growing city by indicating that its social structure still was less complex than those of the state capitals in the northeast, and by indicating that he relied principally upon two criteria in his analysis of the social classes, namely the amount of wealth and its sources and the evidences of prestige and power. It is best, however, to present his analysis through the best translation we have been able to make of his own words. This he begins by commenting upon recent changes:

Twenty years ago there were two classes separated by an enormous distance: the upper class, composed of merchants and/or plantation owners, and the common folk. Between them existed a tenuous middle class composed of bureaucrats, small merchants and members of the several professions. The landowners sought a legal education for their sons with which the latter could enter politics where they defended the privileges of their class. A typical figure of this epoch and of the mentality that had created him was A.F., landowner, lawyer, a politician of local, state, and national dimension, who occupied various posts in the administration and in the legislature. The commercial movement—which had intensified

[3] Among Rios' most important works are "'The Cities of Brazil," in T. Lynn Smith and Alexander Marchant (eds.), *Brazil: Portrait of Half a Continent* (New York, 1951), 188–208; *A Educação dos Grupos* (Rio de Janeiro, 1954); with Louis J. Lebret, Carlos Alberto de Medina and Helio Modesto, "Aspectos Humanos da Favela Carioca," *O Estado de São Paulo: Supplemento Especial,* April 13, 1960; *Campina Grande: Um Centro Comercial do Nordeste.*

early in 1939—left its mark on the administration. The city mayors—some of them attorneys and/or landowners—became merchants and, in this fashion, established a consortium of activities and interests which was to become characteristic of a phase of the city's development. Then, merchants, professionals, landowners, occasionally an industrialist, began alternating in the key posts of the administration in accordance with the traditional lines of the social structure.

In the meantime, the predominance of the traditional families—with one base in land and another in commerce—was giving way to an incursion of great social and ecological significance. This invasion was represented, on the one hand, by newcomers to the area, and, on the other, by a general process of enrichment (produced by the expansion of commerce, of industry, and of the banking business) which is no stranger to the inflationary process in the nation.[4]

Then he continues with an identification of the four major classes revealed by his penetrating study:

Today there are in Campina Grande four great classes, each one subdivided into strata and substrata of lesser importance. The first differentiation, from top to bottom in the social pyramid, was the emergence (alongside the traditional upper-class families) of a "high society" composed of wealthy outsiders. The members of this new upper class are characterized by the same expressions of extroversion and exhibitionism (a phenomenon not confined to Campina Grande but prevalent in other areas as well), and animated by the same tensions and frustrations as those in the "new class" in a number of other cities. The other important differentiation may be observed in the lower strata of the social pyramid and clearly represents a phenomenon of upward mobility and social improvement. This is the formation of an urban middle class with habits, tendencies, and values that still are not firmly established. This stratum is being set apart from the other traditional strata.

These four socio-economic layers, the traditional upper class, the new upper class, the middle class, and the common people, differ in the ease with which they may be characterized. Even the respective "class characteristics" do not follow a definite and consistent pattern, due to the very instability and mobility of the various social strata found in Campina Grande and the fickleness of their interrelationships. Of the four, the one easiest to identify, as a result of the publicity which surrounds its activities and by the self-promotion of its members, is the "high society," the new upper class accounts of whose activities fill the society pages of the newspapers. There is no sharp division between the specific professions carried on by the members of these two upper classes.[5]

Of greatest significance for present purposes, are the characteristics of the new upper class and the ways in which its members are distinguished from the traditional elite.

They are distinguished most, perhaps, by their respective "styles of life." In the case of the traditional upper class, the dominant characteristic is that of aloofness, whereas, for the new upper class, ostentation is conspicuous. It is common to hear that members of the traditional upper class "do not go to parties," or, they "go to the club only during the traditional annual festivals." Members of the new upper class, on the contrary, assiduously attend the celebrations, participate intensely in the life

---

[4] Rios, *Campina Grande*, 39.
[5] *Ibid.*, 39–40.

of the clubs (on whose boards of directors those in this class rotate obligatorily) and through their antics gain publicity in the social columns. The men of traditional upper class are personages of distinction, and the women represent the cream of the high society of the city. Those in this class have sophistication: "It's a family of tradition and fortune," is customarily said of its members. The old upper class also includes members of the professions, who occupy or have occupied public positions in the local or state administrations; who own their own homes and cars; who have country homes or even plantations; who pass their summers in Recife or in South Brazil, and who occupy positions on the boards of directors of the local clubs.

The secondary traits of the traditional upper class are *de rigeur* for the new upper class. Wealth is all important. This class exemplifies the phrase of an informant: "Here, money defines social class. Money establishes the high status of the person even if he happens to be illiterate." From the time a person begins to dress well, to have a bed [the people in this area traditionally have slept in hammocks] and a good house, he becomes a part of "society." Some rich people, who don't make a display of their wealth, go unnoticed. Another informant, defining still better the differences between the two strata, says: "The people who were born with silver spoons in the mouths are more simple. The *nouveau riche* are more ostentatious." Thus, "simplicity" is a feature of inherited wealth. It does not go with rapid enrichment, which, quite to the contrary, must be publicized widely.

In addition to membership in the social clubs, conspicuousness in the festivals, and elaborate participation in "social life," an important symbol of this new upper class is the automobile. The number of new cars promenading slowly through downtown Campina Grande during the afternoons is an impressive sight. For an entire stratum of local society, it is clearly a ritual of urban life. The automobile is a much discussed subject in the city. While, in many cases, this conversation is of a bantering type, it often reflects a current preoccupation and a real theme of life. Many of the cars are of the latest models. All of them taken together do not travel more than five or six thousand miles per year. They are little used simply because there are few places to go. One of their major functions is to lend prestige to members of the working class. "I won't sell my car," said one informant, "however good the price may be, because then I would have to walk. I prefer to remain in debt than to be without my car. People see a professional man driving his car, and they also observe that the car is the only thing he has," said the informant.

The "outsiders," as one would expect in a city of migrants, strangers, and newly rich, have no difficulty in ascending the social scale, from the time they fill the other conditions for entrance into the society. "I am from another place," said one professional man. "I arrived here as a member of the middle class—in social as well as economic terms. I continue as middle class but I am admitted to any place without resistance." This is to say that resistance has not been crystallized and that circulation, in certain areas and within certain limits, is still easy. One's race (or color), at a given point, becomes a limiting factor to social climbing, and tends to outweigh even over one's economic and professional standing.

The new upper class is distinguished in other ways. The ostentatious display of wealth, is intensively practiced in many forms. In addition to the possession of a luxurious car and a palatial home, it also includes the lavish expenditure of money when the individual occupies a position on the board of directors of one of the clubs, without any compensation other than increased social prestige. It includes keeping a mistress: "As they ascend the social ladder, they soon arrange for a mistress in order to lay claim to belonging to 'society.'" Thus, this vain ostentatiousness is reflected in all external conduct, in dress, in conspicuous presence in the cocktail lounges, in the car, and by membership in certain clubs.

Just as the automobile is more a symbol than a means of transportation, so membership in a club is a clear indicator of social climbing and social recognition. Membership just in any club, however, does not confer this status. The clubs of the "society" are the Campinense, Aquático, Médico Campestre, and the Caçadores. The latter, presently, is just in the process of becoming a club for members of the upper class.

The Campinense Club appears to be the most selective. It is the club of tradition, the one frequented by the "best" of society. Its members are admitted to other clubs but the contrary isn't true. "It's a solemn club where all gestures are noticed," that is, where a certain etiquette prevails. The Aqúatico is a new club which is composed of many members of the Campinense, but is presently in a stationary stage; it gives no parties. The Caçadores Club is old, but its dynamism is recent. Presently, it is being promoted by a director who won over some of the people from the Campinense. In this newer phase, there occurred a true phenomenon of invasion and succession in the sociological sense. The founders of the club were hunters; some of them Negroes. With the entrance of the "good people," the oldtimers were retired. Today, it is the second club of Campina Grande.

The social distinctions also extend into the schools. The Colégio da Imaculada and the Colégio das Lurdinas are considered to be upper class. Alfredo Dantas and Pio XI, as well as the Colégio Estadual are more heterogeneous in the sense that they include students of middle-class status.

In the same manner, there is an ecological distribution of the classes throughout the various districts of the city. The more affluent seek to live in the newer suburbs, i.e., Prata, Jardim Lauritzen, and Santo Antônio. "Prata is the best, with good, functional houses, many doctors, 'good people,' and in addition, it's a new suburb." The suburbs are growing and are being divided between the poverty-stricken areas and those with better homes. "Santo Antônio is a good suburb because it is growing. The best street is João da Mata and its cross streets." José Pinheiro is poor as is Liberdade.

While the most-privileged strata cannot be strictly identified with a given profession, there is one professional group, that of the doctors, which deserves special treatment. They have demonstrated an extraordinary ability to rise in Campina Grande society. The medical career is prestigious. It transforms the individual into a "personage." The physicians have formed an elite club, the Médico Campestre, where they associate with the large merchants, the great industrialists, and the attorneys in the "top set." [6]

Rios also gives capsule descriptions of the other social layers in Campina Grande, and the position and role of the new upper class is understood better if these also are taken into consideration.

Beneath these two upper classes which, perhaps, have been most distinguished by a continuous fusion, is a middle class. It is made up of members of the liberal professions, military men, commercial employees, small merchants and small landowners. They also have their clubs, their residential districts and their tensions.

The clubs of the middle class are the "31" and the Gresse. The "31" is one of the oldest. It is rare for members of the Campinense to go there. Its membership is made up largely of landowners, bureaucrats, employees and teachers. The Gresse is a club of sergeants. Until 1960, the club's headquarters were in an old, ugly building in a poor district, and it was frequented by store clerks and women of loose morals. Today, it has a

[6] *Ibid.*, 40–41.

large clubhouse, it is well organized, and even members of the Campinense go to it. The elementary school for children of the middle class is Alfredo Dantas. A great majority of the commercial employees belong to this class, which subsumes those individuals who receive salaries above the minimum wage scale, from office clerks to bureaucrats, but whose pay is less than Cr$50,000. Accountants belong to the middle class. One of the means of access to the middle class is the possession of a university diploma, the bachelor's degree.

Below the middle class are the workers, the industrial wage earners, some commercial employees who earn less than the minimum wage, low-ranking public employees such as the street cleaners and garbage collectors. "But in the lower class, the majority are in industry," which is to say, that most of them are industrial workers. The clubs frequented by those of this lower class, the Paulistano and the Ipiranga. They also have their Samba schools. The Paulistano is one of the oldest of the clubs, and it has the No. 3 football team of the city. Of the 388 members of the Paulistano, 42.5 per cent are commercial workers, 18.8 per cent small merchants, 7.2 per cent industrial workers, and 6 per cent bureaucrats. The remainder is involved in variety of occupations.

The Samba schools are composed of mechanics, skilled workers, and occasionally a few commercial workers. No school has more than 50 members.

Beneath these categories is a social stratum composed of marginals, i.e., the unemployed, handymen, social outcasts of all types who have no class consciousness. Furthermore, class consciousness is rare even among the higher strata. The blue-collar worker, for example, has no perception of class. The persistence of apprenticeship training in industry doesn't permit it. One is the operator of a drill press, another a lathe, yet a third a welding rig, all of which charge for their services—in isolation from one another—in the system of production. Hence, individualism is contrary to the class mentality. In SANBRA, a large enterprise, where the owner is a remote entity, class consciousness does exist. At the other extreme, the employees of the banks evidence a great solidarity and perfect agreement on wage demands.

The commercial employees, who consider themselves as middle class, are accused of indifference and apathy in the area of social struggles. Perhaps the greater social interaction with the business owners, not only at work but socially as well—as the analysis of the membership list of Campinense demonstrates—and the example of many clerks who in the last twenty years have become managers, stockholders and owners of firms, incline the clerks to side with the owners and to avoid taking the part of the wage workers. During the war, sharp transactions elevated many a clerk and manager to the position of owner, and this gives to the store clerk a conviction that some day, by some natural mechanism, he will attain ownership. Thus the commercial employee has an attitude of superiority in relation to the blue-collar worker whose labor is judged to be humiliating (however, the clerk does not deem it humiliating to sweep and mop the floor of the store). He also aspires to become a government bureaucrat, identify himself more with the bureaucracy than with industry, despite the low salary and the effort which it represents for him to have to maintain himself amidst financial difficulties and to dress beyond his means. Because of this the clerks are referred to derogatorily as "tie beggers." In turn, employment in commerce is considered as a promotion by the blue-collar worker. It would appear that commerce is associated with the idea of clean hands, as is bureaucratic work; in other words it is "dignified" in a society which has traditionally marked manual labor with the stigma of slavery. Some bureaucrats are Rotarians and frequent the Campinense Club. The federal jobs, especially, are prestigious. The elective position does not necesarily carry with it social prestige. The city councilman does not have prestige by virtue of his mandate. In the list of local councilmen, those who have access to the upper class have achieved it by means extraneous to their elected offices, i.e., as a result of personal fortune, traditional families, or relations of a particular activity.[7]

Still more recently, Rios has generalized his findings in his studies of the class structure and vertical social mobility in many parts of Brazil. The following translation is a paragraph from that work.

Even today there is a profound difference between the classes that command (*clases dirigentes*) and what is still depreciatively called in certain parts of Brazil "the people" (*o povo*). Brazilian society is still a mandarin society, and the small number of persons in the professional categories which gives them access to the clase dirigente is an excellent indicator of this stratum which is not exactly an aristocracy, nor a plutocracy, but rather an oligarchy having some of the features of both. The difficulties encountered by those of lower social status in the society who attempt to rise to the prestigious positions where decisions are made still are very great. There is a whole set of obstacles to the ascent in the social scale on the part of less-favored persons, obstacles that are not merely economic but those connected with a complex bureaucratic apparatus that permeates every kind of activity in the country from commerce to education.[8]

[7] *Ibid.*, 41.

[8] José Arthur Rios, "Visão Global da Sociedade Brasileira,' in Francisco Leme Lopes (ed.), *Estudos de Problemas Brasileiras* (Rio de Janeiro, 1970), 45.

CHAPTER XXVII

CHANGES IN THE PRINCIPAL
NUCLEATED SOCIAL INSTITUTIONS

AMONG ALL of the great sociocultural changes in Brazil during the last third of the twentieth century those in the basic nucleated social institutions have not lagged. The family and domestic institutions, education and the school, and political institutions and government all have undergone tremendous modifications. Even religion and the church, generally the last parts of society to feel the impact of such forces as urbanization, industrialization, and the general homogenization of society, have changed substantially in response to the stimuli to which they have been subjected since 1960. In this chapter an attempt is made to identify some of the principal changes in these four great portions of the social organization and to indicate some of the factors that are responsible for them.

CHANGES IN THE DOMESTIC INSTITUTIONS

That momentous changes in Brazilian domestic and kinship institutions are accompanying the current rapid upsurge in urbanization and industrialization may almost be taken for granted. Furthermore there is some evidence from serious analytical studies to support such a conclusion, and there is abundant pertinent material bearing on the subject that is merely awaiting the consideration of perceptive students of society. The subject is a massive one, however, with dimensions that approach the maximum. Lineally the traditional, huge domestic unit, so brilliantly analyzed by Gilberto Freyre in his monumental *Casa Grande*, embraced many generations (children, parents, grandparents, great grandparents, and often great great grandparents). With lives inextricably intertwined with these, moreover, were hosts of collateral kinsmen (cousins, aunts, uncles, nephews, and nieces) of many and varied degrees of consanguinity. Furthermore the huge patriarchal kinship group that functioned as the major economic unit in the traditional society, and also as the seat of political and judicial power, involved large numbers of servants and other retainers who did not necessarily have any blood relationship to the head of the clan, although, of course, many of them were his own illegitimate offspring or those of some of his children or grandchildren. Finally the great patriarchal domestic units themselves were interwoven through an elaborate system of tracing descent to some notable ancestor and maintaining a feeling of social solidarity with kith and kin no matter how remote the relationship might be into immense webs or networks. These are what Oliveira Vianna called clans and what today sociologists and anthropologists such as Manuel Diégues Júnior and Charles Wagley prefer to call *parentela*.[1] Still another well-known Brazilian social scientist, Hélio Jaguaribe, characterizes the system as the concentration about a *grand seigneur* of a "following of dependents in a relationship rather like that obtaining between the Roman *paterfamilias* and his circle of *protégés*."[2]

Some of the most significant analysis of recent changes in Brazilian domestic institutions has been done by lawyer-sociologist José Arthur Rios. Particularly significant in this connection is his monographic study of urban life in the interior of the immense, heavily populated, and problem-ridden Northeast, an area that by all odds is the part of Brazil in which traditional ways of life persist in the highest degree. His study of the masses of concrete data gathered in his extensive survey led him to generalize about changes in the family as follows:

> Familial behavior also undergoes changes in accordance with the social stratum. The traditional, patriarchal family continues to be the center of the social life, the basic institution for the raising of children, for social advancement or retrogression. It still controls the activities and work of its members and establishes the standards of behavior. The upper-class families tend to strengthen their positions through marriage. Daughters of merchants marry lawyers and doctors. Industrial, commercial, and financial interests are united in several closely related families whose area of influence is thus extended. . . . In the characterization of the economy, we find the dominant features of the Brazilian and northeastern family. The male is dominant and the female occupies a secondary position in the life of the city and even in the family. All the meeting places, such as bars, cafes, and ice-cream parlors, are for the men. Few women or girls are seen in these places, especially after a certain hour. Referring to a downtown ice-cream parlor, a female informant says: "Girls *can* go there for many people do, but they just don't." The family encloses itself, preserves itself, and isolates itself inside the home. Few families go out visiting; sociability is rare. There are arising, however, some variations which indicate if not a disintegration at least a reaction against the traditional standards.
>
> This rebellion, or crisis, is manifested principally in two areas: (1) in the relations between spouses, and (2) in the relations between father and son. Marriage itself constitutes a serious problem for all social strata by reason of the very composition of the population. There is a close evaluation of the eligible bachelors, such as, "The engineer is a good selection, he is capable." The men enter the matrimonial circle when they are between 25 and 30 years of age. The girls tend to marry at about 20, but they begin thinking of getting married at the age of 12. All this notwith-

---

[1] Cf. Manuel Diégues Júnior, *Regiões Culturais do Brasil* (Rio de Janeiro, 1960), 269–71; Charles Wagley, *An Introduction to Brazil* (New York and London, 1963), 59, 186–204, *et passim*.

[2] "The Dynamics of Brazilian Nationalism," in Claudio Veliz (ed.), *Obstacles to Change in Latin America* (London, Oxford, N.Y., 1969), 177.

standing, many girls do not arrange their own marriages, even among the better families. For this reason, when the boys from the outside arrive, the family circle is tightly drawn.[3]

In other paragraphs Rios described significant features of prevailing sex mores, and gave more details about the disintegration of traditional patterns of family organization and life in Campina Grande:

If we can believe mischievous gossip, concubinage is a common feature of the upper classes. The mistress is a part of the system of ostentation and exhibitionism of that stratum.

In the case of adultery, social sanctions are directed more against the woman than against the man. The mistress enjoys freedom of movement if the man has position, this is to say, money, etc. The unmarried, emancipated girl also suffers under group sanctions, "because one can't accept a girl going out without a chaperon." If the girls drink or smoke in public, it is commented upon. In compensation, there is an over-evaluation of the pure, young maiden, typical of the Brazilian patriarchal society—of which Campina Grande is still an example.

A trace of rebellion against this tradition and of the emancipation of the younger generations from their parents is the type of behavior characterized as "escape," but which has not yet achieved enough continuity and permanence for it to be classed as a custom. This may be a temporary practice but, in any event, it is symptomatic of tension in the family and of a rupture between the generations. "Many youths, both boys and girls, enjoy 'escaping.' Two months ago, these 'escapes' became more frequent. Those involved are couples between 13 and 16 years of age. They flee their homes and go to Recife, João Pessôa, or other Northeastern cities. There they spend a day or night and then return. . . . This is a means of forcing a wedding." Could this be a revival of securing a wife by kidnapping, a custom that still prevails in the Northeast? The secrecy surrounding these cases prevents us from determining adequately the nature of this type of conduct, which is beginning to worry the community. The same is true of the sporadic cases of deviant behavior which are beginning to appear on the part of adolescents "who have money, cars, and are picking up penniless girls, and getting into fights at parties."

The marriage crisis is, however, recognized, and the causes are already being pointed out. According to one informant—a physician of good repute—"the conjugal relations are in terrible shape in all the classes." The man goes out alone to the movies in order to enjoy himself—typical behavior in a patriarchal society. The number of married men maintaining mistresses is—according to several informants—very large. "Each individual who has managed to rise rather high in social scale, in order to announce that he has 'arrived,' soon makes arrangements for a mistress."

Various leaders of the community, who are preoccupied with the problem, consider the principal causes to be: (1) the total ignorance of the objectives of matrimony; (2) lack of knowledge of the conjugal duties ("behaving at home not as a companion but as a master"); (3) the lack of education about sex, so that for girls as well as boys (says one female informant: "Sex education is learned from one's peer group, the sex act is taboo, but stories punctuated by dirty jokes using vulgar language are rife"); and (4) the absence of a religious foundation and of morals in matrimony.[4]

[3] José Arthur Rios, *Campina Grande: Um Centro Comercial do Nordeste*, 41–42.

[4] *Ibid.*, 42.

It should be stressed that Rios' excellent study was made of society in the most conservative part of Brazil where societal changes of all sorts meet the greatest resistances and proceed most slowly. It is probable that, were equally significant studies of family organization and life made in other parts of Brazil, the changes shown to be underway would be fully as great if not greater.

Most obvious of all is the fact that as the traditional sugarcane, coffee, cacao, and other plantations have been organized into corporations, some in which the members of the old elite family hold all the stock and others in which the ownership of the shares is less restricted, the economic basis for the huge old traditional domestic unit has largely disappeared. This is doubly so today because the vast majority of the members of the once powerful rural families now live in cities, and their members engage in a wide variety of economic activities. They visit the plantations in which they own stock rarely if at all. In this connection it is important to note that Gilberto Freyre, in the sequel [5] to his classic study of the great rural, domestic, economic, and political unit (wherein the traditional system was symbolized by "the big house and slave quarters"), described in detail the disintegration of that huge kinship organization when it was transferred to the city and came to be oriented to the "little palaces and the huts" of the transplanted two-class system. Sociocultural values, obligations, privileges, mores, folkways, and the other features of any domestic system "die hard," however, and at first probably only the major economic characteristics were sloughed off as the heads of the large kinship groups transferred their main places of abode from the seats of their baronial estates to elaborate and ostentatious dwellings in the coastal cities. [6]

Even well into the second half of the twentieth century, many

[5] Freyre, *Sobrados e Mucambos* (São Paulo, 1936), trans. Harriet Onis under the title *The Mansions and the Shanties* (New York, 1967).

[6] The intimate, patronal relationships with the workers and various types of retainers on their plantations, naturally, were the first to suffer. Freyre recently summarized the drastic effects of these changes:

> In some areas, such as in the sugar-cane plantation districts, the land serves only to provide what it can for industry, with the most archaic and anti-economic methods of production, by means of a poorly paid agrarian labor force and a rural population held as pariahs by the land-owners. Not a few of these proprietors are absentees from the land which they have long owned and have little contact with their semi-serfs, who live, it is well to repeat, in the condition of pariahs, while the urban workers and also the employees of commercial establishments and banks and the public employees in the cities during recent decades have benefited from the legislation protecting labor and promoting social welfare. It was a situation in which the greater part of the rural population of Brazil was used on the rudest work on plantations and farms, on the estates of men with a mentality quite different from that which years ago characterized the relations between the landowners and their laborers, when the former really were, most of them, a rural gentry: not only proprietors deeply attached to their estates but masters attentive to the needs of their workers in accordance with the patriarchal forms of association.

Translated from Gilberto Freyre: "La lucha no es de clases," in *Life en Español,* 11 May, 1964, pp. 25–26.

of the sociocultural features of the system persist in only slightly weakened form despite the fact that the economic aspects, both those of production and those of consumption, once of primordial importance long since have vanished.

Fortunately, a penetrating, up-to-date analysis of the network of relationships persisting between kinfolk of many degrees of consanguinity has been made by Charles Wagley. This noted social anthropologist enjoyed unique opportunities to observe the system from within, and he has devoted many years of careful study to the subject. His findings, which I shall summarize at length, deserve the most careful consideration. His analysis involves the nomenclature of kinship, however, so before giving Wagley's conclusions respecting Brazil's great *parentela* system, I will consider briefly some of the complexities of Brazilian naming systems.

Brazilian Kinship Nomenclature

Many people, I among them, have almost despaired of ever being able to understand the system by which Brazilian family names are transmitted. Some time ago I personally had the responsibility of translating and editing an excellent chapter in which Antonio Candido, one of Brazil's most able and serious students of the family, undertook to shed light upon this difficult and elusive subject.[7] Candido first indicated that in the traditional upper-class family of Brazil marriage was "considered an act that was too important to be left to the volition of the interested parties," and that human beings "should be mated by the oldest and most experienced, because a good breed crossed with a good breed produces a good breed." Then he proceeded to describe the system in some detail:

> In most cases marriages were contracted in line with a policy designed to strengthen the parental groups. . . . They even preferred unions within the same group—marriages with cousins, nieces, and other relatives—because "from a good stock cannot come a bad thing," and also for the guarantee of preserving status and economic goods in a society filled with mixed breeds and adventurers. Hence, the new famiy was closely linked, because of its origin, to the families of the bride and groom; the fathers-in-law and the mothers-in-law (often brothers and sisters, aunts and uncles, cousins or grandparents) automatically entered into the exercise of a supremacy already outlined or foreseen from the previous relationship. . . .
>
> It is clear that a family formed in this manner was not limited to parents, children, and brothers and sisters; it tended to integrate larger groups, who together constituted the social system par excellence of patriarchal Brazil, one based upon parental solidarity. To defend himself, to prosper, to produce, the individual needed the reciprocal interlocking of related groups. If the father of a family headed one unity composed of children, sons- and daughters-in-law, and grandchildren, the heads of the

---

[7] Antonio Candido, "The Brazilian Family," in Smith and Marchant (eds.), *Brazil: Portrait of Half a Continent*, 291–312.

families were linked to one another as cousins, uncles and nephews, and other relationships of various degrees, forming a powerful system for economic and political domination, and therefore, for the acquisition and maintenance of prestige and status. In addition to marriage—which is one of the principal manifestations and consequences of this type of organization—the study of the nomenclature of kinship and the study of family conflicts give a clear view of the situation.[8]

In order to convey an accurate idea of the complexity of this nomenclature, Candido felt it necessary to stress the ritual involved in the relationships between those who were related by blood and marriage and also those between godparents and their godchildren and the relatives of the same in the great system of *compadrio*. In his own words:

The relationships among relatives were ritualized, as were the other relationships. Cousins of all degrees called one another, Senhor Cousin, Cousin So-and-So, Senhor, or *vossemece;* the most distant or remotely related were called *parente* (relative); aunts and uncles were respectively addressed as Senhor Uncle or Senhora Aunt, and of them also blessings were requested. A basic relationship was that of *compadrio* with or without blood relationship, for it was a kind of superrelationship. The tie which linked godparent and godchild was among the most firm; not only was the godparent obliged to take the place of the father, whenever that might be necessary, but he had to aid his godchild on various occasions and ordinarily to present him with cattle; the godchild, in turn, lent the godfather any help the latter needed, and often took the name of his family.[9]

After giving the reader these essential facts about the traditional Brazilian system of kinship, Candido endeavored to throw some light on the nomenclature of kinship relationships in the following words:

The pattern was made ample and powerful by the fact that in Brazil, as in Portugal, relationship on the maternal side was equally valid and important (as that on the male side). The system of names demonstrates this clearly; daughters by preference took the mother's surname, whereas sons took either that of the father or of the mother. Frequently, they also took the name of one of the grandparents or more remote ancestors, paternal or maternal. Out of this arose the difficulty of determining relationships and affiliations in the old documents. For example [he adds in a footnote], from the marriage, in the seventeenth century, of Tomé de Lara e Almeida with Dona Maria de Almeida Pimental (the pair having one name in common) there were born: Fernando Paes de Barros, Antônio de Almeida Lara, José Pompeu Ordonho, Lucrécia Pedroso de Barros, Maria de Almeida Lara, Sebastiana de Almeida, Branca de Almeida, Inácia de Almeida, Luzia Leme, and Maria de Almeida Lara Pimental." [10]

The author of the lines just quoted might very well have added that others than those attempting to unravel the perplexities involved in the study of old documents find it difficult to determine the degree of relationship between Brazilians he may know or whose names appear with frequency in the newspapers. In fact, unless one is steeped in Brazilian history and genealogy, the degree of freedom

[8] *Ibid.*, 286–98.
[9] *Ibid.*, 298.
[10] *Ibid.*, 298–99.

allowed under the rules Candido cites may make it impossible for one to determine from the names alone whether or not two prominent men, such as two who served as governor of the state of Goiás, are related or not, even though well-informed Brazilians know that they are father and son. Moreover, the practices of referring to well-established Brazilians by their first names, such as Getúlio (Vargas), Adhemar (de Barros), Gilberto (Freyre), and Janio (Quadros), or even by nicknames, such as Jango (João Goulart), further complicates the matter. Indeed, for many, the nomenclature used in connection with Brazil's vast networks of kinship systems is likely to remain largely a mystery.

Brazilian Parentela

Recently anthropologists and sociologists, and especially Charles Wagley, have been analyzing and describing Brazil's "extensive kinship webs," or parentelas, in even clearer ways than those used in the classic works of Oliveira Vianna and Gilberto Freyre. Wagley himself cites Manuel Diégues Júnior [11] as his predecessor in the use of the term "parentela" to denote the huge kinship network embracing "all recognized relatives on both one's mother's and one's father's side, along with the kinsmen of one's own spouse." [12] Moreover, he insists that "it was this *parentela*, and not the nuclear family or even the patriarchial family, that was traditionally the most important single institution in Brazil." [13] Diégues, in turn, introduced the term in his description of the domination since the days of independence of political and administrative affairs in the state of Minas Gerais by a "group of families from which came the governors, cabinet ministers, senators, deputies, and presidents of the Republic." He credits a Professor Horta with previous use of parentela as the designation for one of the huge webs of kinfolk, and maintained that "these families, only a few more than 30 in number, control political affairs, based upon their ownership and control of the land and the patrimonial system of government." [14]

As indicated above, Wagley has done most to develop understanding of Brazil's vast parentela system, to portray its essential features, and to illustrate its importance in the life and labor of a great nation of almost 100,000,000 people. He has emphasized that one of these webs of kinship may include many hundreds of one's contemporaries and additional hundreds of those that have died. The inclusion of remote ancestors is more pronounced in the cases of those who won distinctions of one kind or another. Hence, the "number of people one might consider kin was limited only by genea-

[11] Wagley, *An Introduction to Brazil*, 59.
[12] *Ibid.*, 186.
[13] *Ibid.*, 186.
[14] Diégues, *Regiões Culturais do Brasil*, 269. It seems well to note, however, that the word "parentela" long has figured in dictionaries of the Portuguese language, and that only the stress upon its use is new.

logical memory, willingness to claim kinship with others, and willingness of others to recognize distant kinship bonds." And even in contemporary large urban centers of the parentela of "an upper-class Brazilian" may "include literally hundreds of people." [15]

Wagley also stresses that the parentelas as such are much more extensive than Brazil's huge "ancestor oriented families" which carry the surnames of their original patriarchs; [16] and, as indicated above, an understanding of the system of transmitting names is of crucial importance in relation to the parentela and especially the "ancestor oriented part of it." He contrasts Brazilian kinship nomenclature with the Spanish practice (whereby a child receives the surnames of both parents with that of the father preceding that of the mother), and indicates that, in theory, a Brazilian also received both his father's and his mother's names. Unlike his Spanish and Spanish-American contemporaries, however, the Brazilian's mother's name precedes that of his father. Actually, Wagley indicates the theoretical system was "manipulated to indicate ties with important ancestors and *parentelas*, or simply to honor a particular side of the family or a specific individual." The noted anthropologist generalizes that "if there was any ideal pattern relating to the transmission of names it was that a person should select the names of his parents or grandparents which carried the most prestige." [17] Moreover, Wagley indicates that it was not at all unusual for a Brazilian to adopt as his surname that of any prestigious person he cared to select; and he states agreement with Candido's generalization [18] that traditionally "the name expressed less the tie of filial relationship than participation in a vast kinship system." As a result a few well-known surnames came to stand for large and important parentelas, and in each part of Brazil the interlocking of these huge parentelas and the great ancestor-oriented families produced a "constant recurrence of famous surnames in the upper class." [19]

In addition to persons actually related by blood or marriage, Wagley emphasizes that the traditional parentela also included a wide variety of others, or in Candido's words, "a periphery not always well delineated, made up of the slaves and *agregados*, Indians, Negroes, or mixed bloods, in which were included the concubines of the chief and his illegitimate children" because in many cases the illegitimate offspring of men of good standing were reared by kinsmen of their father and in many cases they were even adopted by a man's legitimate wife who "accepted the children of her husband, especially if they were born before their marriage." [20]

Moreover, the huge families and parentelas were further enlarged by the widespread practice of taking *filhos de criação* or "adopted" children into the family. Many of these, of course, were the illegiti-

[15] Wagley, *An Introduction to Brazil*, 187, 199–200.
[16] *Ibid.*, 188.
[17] *Ibid.*
[18] Candido, "The Brazilian Family," 299.
[19] Wagley, *An Introduction to Brazil*, 189.
[20] *Ibid.*, 189, quoting Candido, *op. cit.*, 294, 299.

mate offspring of kinsmen, but children of persons of the lower classes often were brought into the homes of those of the upper class "partly as servants and partly as members of the family." In many cases the relationship of those of lower-class status with the upper-class family persisted generation after generation, for often the domestics serving one generation were the offspring of servants and retainers, or even slaves in the huge patriarchal families of their parents or grandparents. Understandably, the ties between generation after generation of the elite were especially close with the domestics who had nursed them as children.

Finally, as Wagley with much reason emphasizes, the influence of the parentela was further extended by the way in which it was intertwined with the well-known system of *compadrio* or the all important relationships between godparents and their godchildren. Through this the members of the upper class not only had relationships between themselves and their children and other large ancestor-oriented families and parentelas, but persons of low social status were enabled to link the fortunes of their offspring to those of the powerful members of the upper class.[21]

Among the roles played by the parentela in Brazilian society, Wagley describes their function in establishing the rules for the rearing of children; and in this connection he stresses strongly the extent to which the child's entire experience world was limited to contacts with his kindred. Inevitably, under such circumstances the great bulk of anyone's personality traits are acquired within and from other members of the immense web of kinship within which he is encompassed. Likewise, marriages among those of the Brazilian upper classes traditionally were contracts between members of the same parentela and not infrequently within just one of the large patriarchal families of which it was constituted. Even in those cases in which the adults did not determine who should marry whom, "romantic attachments frequently blossomed between kinsmen." [22]

Traditionally, the ties of kinship under discussion also dominated the various aspects of economic life. Even after the rise of cities and towns one's kinfolk were favored and relied upon in all business and professional activities. And in politics the favoritism and nepotism rife in public affairs is only one side of the shield of a system in which the families who dominate governmental affairs in a given state are dependent upon their kinsmen in various localities. In the communities the politicians have sought the votes of those of middle or lower class status "not so much on the basis of political or public issues as on the basis of personal loyalties to themselves and their families." [23]

---

[21] On this point Wagley, *op. cit.*, 191–92, quotes in translation a highly significant paragraph from Thales de Azevedo's *Povoamento da Cidade do Salvador* (Bahia, 1949).

[22] *Ibid.*, 195.

[23] *Ibid.*, 198. On this point see also José Arthur Rios, "A Família na Organização Social do Brasil," in Francisco Leme Lopes (ed.), *Estudos de Problemas Brasileiros* (Rio de Janeiro, 1970), 82–83.

One is tempted to use the past tense in describing Brazil's vast system of parentelas, especially in view of the drastic changes in Brazilian society presently taking place. Moreover, Wagley states explicitly that "the majority of Brazilians have never had a large *parentela*." [24] Also, he indicates that he consciously dealt with it as "if it were a thing of the past." Nevertheless, he stoutly maintains that "it is my thesis that this institution persists today, as in the past, and that its study is essential to an understanding of modern Brazil." [25] Then in support of this proposition, he supplies cogent reasons for believing that Brazilian parentela remain important in political life and dominate economic affairs. With considerable justification, he maintains that this specific form of familism is a major obstacle to the formation of genuine political parties, that it prevents the creation of a civil service system to replace the traditional nepotism, and that it hinders the establishment of industrial and business enterprises that would involve wide public participation. Even in the urbanized, industrialized society today, Brazilians never forget their far-ranging family connections.[26] Thus, despite the changes in recent years, in the 1970's Brazil's huge networks of kinfolk, both the large extended family and the parentela, continue to play roles that are far more important than those performed by their counterparts in the Spanish American countries or in the United States and Canada, and familism remains an outstanding feature of Brazilian society.

CHANGES IN THE EDUCATIONAL INSTITUTIONS

Some profound changes have been made since 1960 in Brazil's great sociocultural system of education. These include the achievement of the ascendancy by the proponents of new and different ideas about the objectives of the nation's schools and universities, unprecedented efforts to provide some formal education for all of the children, far greater stress on the importance of secondary education, feverish endeavors to establish institutions of higher learning in all parts of Brazil, and the establishment of a national system of agricultural extension designed to instruct Brazilian farmers in modern and effective ways of getting products from the soil. In this section we attempt to present a few of the more important facts about each of these.

Some Basic Changes in Educational Organization. As has been so well demonstrated by Anísio S. Texeira and other leading Brazilian

[24] *Ibid.,* 198. This view can be substantiated on many grounds including the results of some studies of the specific matter. For example Klass A. A. W. Woortmann in "Grupo Doméstico e Parentesco num Vale da Amazonia." *Revista do Museu Paulista,* n. s., XVII (1967), 243, found that in the small city he studied in the Amazon region "the majority of population is unable to trace its genealogy for more than two generations. Even the brothers of their grandfathers generally are unknown. Horizontally the limit is to first cousins, beyond which permanent contacts seldom extend. There exists a sharp differentiation between first cousins and those more remote."

[25] Wagley, *op. cit.,* 199.

[26] *Ibid.,* 200–204.

educators, prior to 1960 Brazilian education was dominated by the philosophy that there should be a dual educational system. Most important was a set of schools of various levels designed to meet the needs of the children from the families of the elite, featuring instruction of a classical type in the humanities, at the lower levels, and training of the select few in law, medicine, and theology, at the highest. Less important was a second type of education limited to a few years of elementary schooling, stressing vocational education, for the children of the masses, and, indeed, often considered as hardly necessary at all for millions of the children in the rural districts and small towns and villages.[27] The entire plan was strictly in accord with Auguste Comte's predilection for a rigidly set, two-class system of social organization, and if not actually inspired in part by his philosophy, certainly was not in conflict with it.[28]

The new ideas of educational organization, as embodied in Lei No. 4,024 of December, 1961, was a decided break with tradition.[29] This law gave the states much more of the responsibility for the organization of secondary schools, greatly reduced the role of the federal government in elementary and secondary school affairs, permitted far more flexibility in the organization of the curricula, and gave the teacher more of the responsibility for the professional aspects of instruction. In brief it greatly reduced the strength of the "strait jacket" in which Brazilian schools and teachers long had been confined.

The Expansion of Educational Facilities. The tremendous expansion in the number of schools of all levels is one of the most notable aspects of sociocultural change in Brazil since 1960. In order to supply definite facts about several of the more important indicators of this, Table LXXXII was prepared. The statistical data it contains reflect the tremendous expansion of educational facilities that took place in Brazil during the 1960's, a process that is continuing with no reduction in speed. Almost 40,000 new elementary schools, most of them in strictly rural areas, alone represents a remarkable break with tradition, and substantial headway in bringing some opportunities for education within the reach of the ordinary Brazilian. To furnish instruction in these elementary schools, the employment of teachers was almost doubled. Over five and one-half million more

[27] For an excellent exposition of the traditional philosophy of educational organization in Brazil, and its effects, see Anísio S. Teixeira, "The Changing Role of Education in Brazilian Society," in John V. D. Saunders (ed.), *Modern Brazil: New Patterns and Development* (Gainesville, Fla., 1971).

[28] An interesting sidelight on this, which I developed to some extent in a still unpublished lecture presented at the União Cultural Brasil-Estados Unidos in São Paulo, November, 1969, is the fact that the two first books published in the United States to employ Comte's neologism *sociology* in their titles both were defenses of slavery and the rigid caste system involved with it. These books are *Treatise on Sociology, Theoretical and Practical* by Henry Hughes, published in Philadelphia in 1854; and *Sociology for the South* by George Fitzhugh, published in Richmond, Virginia, also in 1854. Harriet Martineau's free translation and condensation of Comte's *Cours* was published in London under the title *The Positive Philosophy of Auguste Comte* the year before.

[29] For the English text of this law and an analysis of its specific provisions, see William A. Harrell, *Educational Reform in Brazil: The Law of 1961* (Washington, D.C., 1968).

children were darkening the doors of elementary schoolhouses in 1968 than had been the case in 1960.

Even more striking are the results of the efforts to establish a modern system of secondary education. The number of *ginásios*, roughly the equivalent of the junior high school in the United States, was almost tripled, teachers in them were more than tripled, and enrollments in them multiplied even more rapidly. Accomplishments in establishing the first years of high school instruction, even so, were modest in comparison with those in expanding the opportunities for Brazil's youth to attain instruction in senior high schools. The number of *colégios* shot up by over 700 per cent, the teachers in them by well over 400 per cent, and the young people privileged to attend them by more than 600 per cent. Undoubtedly, this demonstrates the wisdom, embodied in the Educational Reform Law of 1961, of turning major responsibility for secondary education over to the states.[30] From these materials alone it is impossible to determine the extent to which secondary schools of at least the lower level have been established in the most highly rural municípios, but certainly great headway has been made in that respect. Recent issues of the *Anuário Estatístico do Brasil* do not carry a tabulation showing the numbers of municípios having stated types of educational facilities; but the issue for 1960 (p. 296) showed that there then were 2,784 municípios in Brazil, of which a total of 1,358 (49 per cent) provided no secondary schools of any level and only 275 (10 per cent) had colégios located within their borders. The data presented in Table LXXXII make it certain that this condition has been remedied to a considerable degree.

The publicity in newspapers and magazines indicate the endeavor to establish colleges and universities throughout the length and breadth of Brazil to be one of the chief preoccupations of Brazilians at the present time. The fact that enrollment in institutions of higher learning in Brazil in 1968 was three times that for 1960 is eloquent testimony that the quest is not entirely in vain.[31] The 1969 issue of the *Anuário Estatístico do Brasil* (p. 633) lists the names of forty-eight universities functioning in Brazil in 1968, staffed by 35,148 university teachers. According to information supplied to me by Professors Carlos Correia Mascaro and J. V. Freitas Marcondes, in response to a personal request, at least twenty-three of these were established during the 1960's. Furthermore the list does not include a considerable number of flourishing institutions, such as Faculdades Metropolitanas Unidas, recently established by the Methodists in the city of São Paulo, because by Brazilian regulations the designation "Universidade" is reserved for places that have a minimum of five faculdades or colleges.

[30] See *ibid.,* 48.

[31] According to an announcement from the Ministry of Education published in the March 2, 1971, issue of the *Boletim Especial* circulated by the Brazilian Embassy in Washington, D.C., 170,000 new students will be admitted to institutions in 1971, bringing the total enrollment up to about 417,000 another tremendous increase over the 278,295 registered in 1968.

TABLE LXXXII

Indicators of Change in Brazilian Educational Institutions,
1960 to 1968 *

Item	1960	1968	Change Number	Change Per cent
Number of elementary schools	95,938	134,909	38,971	41
In seats of municípios and distritos	26,519	32,310	5,791	22
In rural areas	69,419	102,599	33,180	48
Number of elementary school teachers	225,569	423,145	197,576	88
In seats of municípios and distritos	140,535	272,251	131,716	94
In rural areas	85,034	150,894	65,860	77
Enrollment in elementary schools	6,403,991	11,943,506	5,539,515	87
In seats of municípios and distritos	3,871,945	7,357,570	3,485,625	90
In rural areas	2,532,046	4,585,936	2,053,890	81
Number of ginásios	2,768	7,368	4,600	166
Number of colégios	672	5,433	4,761	708
Number of teachers in ginásios	43,349	132,504	89,155	206
Number of teachers in colégios	14,947	78,634	63,687	426
Enrollment in ginásios	754,608	2,404,614	1,650,006	219
Enrollment in colégios	113,570	801,075	687,505	605
Enrollment in institutions of higher learning	93,202	278,295	185,093	199
Enrollment in graduate courses	2,489	4,358	1,869	75

* Source: Compiled and computed from data in *Anuário Estatístico do Brasil, 1960*, pp. 297–98, 309; *Anuário Estatístico do Brasil, 1962*, pp. 281–83; and *Anuário Estatístico do Brasil, 1969*, pp. 610–26, 644.

The comments made above should not be interpreted to mean that this writer thinks the Brazilians, almost overnight, have overcome most of the difficulties of transforming an antiquated and ineffective educational system into one fully meeting the needs of a modern urban and industrialized society. That is far from the case. Even if adequate funds were available and fine school buildings erected and equipped with every aid to teaching, there still remains the basic problem of staffing the schools with adequately trained teachers. This applies to all levels from the primary grades to the graduate divisions of the universities. In the expansion of the teaching staffs of the elementary and secondary schools and the faculties of the universities, a great deal of improvisation undoubtedly had been necessary. Brazilian normal schools, in general, are little more than senior high schools, and often hardly that. And the facilities for training the highly developed professionals required for the faculties of first-rate universities still remain very slim indeed. Thus Brazil deserves great commendation for the efforts it has made since 1960 to build an educational system befitting a nation of its size and importance; but the nation still has a long, difficult, and expensive road to travel before it has the elementary schools, the high schools, the undergraduate programs and the programs of graduate study in the universities needed in the nuclear age by a great urban, industrial society. The most important thing, though, is that presently Brazil's leaders seem determined to bring about the fundamental transformation needed.

The Development of an Agricultural Extension Service. Even though farmers elsewhere in the world, or even in a country itself, may know and use effective ways of producing food, feed, and fiber, these may prove of little or no benefit to the bulk of the agriculturists in a state or country unless there is a well-organized and well-staffed system of agricultural extension. Except in São Paulo, this was almost completely lacking in Brazil until very recently, and indeed, the development of a nationwide system worthy of the name was an accomplishment made during the 1960's. The story or the origin and spread of the Associação Brasileira de Crédito and Assistência Rural is a remarkable one. From the barest beginnings in 1960, in the 1970's it is hardly equalled elsewhere in Latin America or in any other of the so-called developing countries of the world.

In the late 1940's Dr. John B. Griffing, with years of experience as a Protestant agricultural missionary in China, worked under the auspices of the American International Association in two small rural communities in São Paulo. This organization was created by the Rockefeller brothers in 1946, and Dr. Griffing was the first to undertake extension efforts in Brazil as an employee of the Association. He devised and tested many of the methods of extension that ultimately contributed greatly to Brazil's agricultural development.[32]

---

[32] For some information about Dr. Griffing's pioneering activities, see Martha Dalrymple, *The AIA Story: Two Decades of International Cooperation* (New York, 1968), 33–39.

As indicated by the name itself, however, Brazil's rural extension service combines the provision of credit with educational efforts to promote the use of effective practices. The presence of this feature in the program came largely out of the role Robert W. Hudgens played in the American International Association. Hudgens had gained extensive experience in motivating small farmers to improve their operations as an official in the Farm Security Administration, one of the agencies established in the United States as a part of Franklin D. Roosevelt's "New Deal." In 1948 he studied the situation in Brazil and recommended that an experimental program of supervised agricultural credit be established in Minas Gerais. In September of that year Nelson and David Rockefeller visited Brazil. They wasted no time in reaching an agreement with the Governor of Minas Gerais for a three-year experimental program, and in December, Hudgins signed the formal contract in Belo Horizonte. Walter Crawford, who already had had five years' experience in Latin America, including two years with the International Association in Paraguay, was selected to direct the program. The objective of the new organization called the Associação de Crédito e Assistência Rural (ACAR) stated in the contract is as follows: "Increasing of crop and livestock production and the improvement of economic and social conditions of rural life. This objective will be accomplished through the application of a dual assistance, technical as well as financial. This dual assistance will facilitate the adoption of an adequate credit system for small-crop and livestock producers and a plan of supervision that guarantees the efficient use of credit." [33]

Gradually the program was improved and expanded during the next twenty years, with ever greater responsibility being assumed by the Brazilian members of the organization. Finally in 1968, with the extension service operating nation-wide, the American International Association terminated its work in Brazil. By that time, though, Brazilians working strictly on their own were manning a highly effective program in all parts of the gigantic country.[34] By 1971 state systems affiliated with the Associação Brasileira de Crédito e Assistência Rural (ABCAR) were in operation in every state except São Paulo and Guanabara, and also in the territory of Acre. Their great educational work is proving to be one of the most important forces in the modernization of Brazil.[35]

RELIGIOUS INSTITUTIONS

Comprehensive and reliable information about religious institutions and practices and the changes in them is a rare commodity;

---

[33] *Ibid.*, 41–42.
[34] See *ibid.*, 52–60.
[35] Consult the various issues of *Extensão Rural*, founded by ABCAR in 1966 for accounts of the wide-ranging, both territorially and substantively, educational activities of the important organization.

and this is particularly true for that about Brazilian religious culture in the years since 1960. The great lag in publishing the results of population censuses is part of the problem, although, of course, one could have all of the data on religious affiliations gathered in those enumerations and still lack most of the facts required for adequate study of religious institutions in the society. Nevertheless the fact that the more substantial attempts in sociological study of religion in Brazil made during the 1960's had to use materials from the 1950 census as the latest available is eloquent evidence of the handicap under which they were forced to work.[36] In spite of the handicap, a number of significant developments have been observed and can be presented.

Changes in Roman Catholicism. The Roman Catholic Church retains its position as the ecclesiastical body to which the vast majority of Brazilians profess allegiance, and to which they turn in all the great crises of life. Likewise the number and proportion of serious practicing Catholics hardly can be diminishing, although any real statistical data about this can hardly be found. It is likely, though, that the materials on the numbers of churches, parish priests, baptisms, and marriages presented annually in the *Anuário Estatístico do Brasil* are not greatly in error. These show that between 1960 and 1967, the following changes took place: number of parish churches (*matrizes*), an increase from 4,077 to 4,976, or 22 per cent; number of public chapels, an increase from 26,098 to 32,134, or 23 per cent; number of parish priests, a decrease from 9,033 to 7,982, or a loss of almost 12 per cent; number of baptisms, an increase from 2,790,456 to 3,009,861, or 8 per cent; number of baptisms of those born during the year, an increase from 1,960,739 to 2,052,647, or 5 per cent; and number of marriages performed, an increase from 414,174 to 421,434, or less than 2 per cent. In connection with the very small increase in the number of marriages, it should be recalled that the early 1960's were the years in which "mass marriages" were performed for hundreds of couples who previously had been living together without the benefit of clergy or a civil ceremony. On stated days such couples were assembled, hundreds at a time, at places where priests and civil authorities were provided to perform the ceremonies with dispatch. This factor undoubtedly inflated the figure for 1960 considerably in comparison with the one for 1967, so that the very small increase in religious marriages performed by the priests of the Roman Catholic Church is not as significant as might appear.

The reported increase in the number of parish churches and the

---

[36] Among the most informative studies that have come to the attention of this writer are C. Procópio Ferreira de Carmargo, "Igrejas e Religiões em São Paulo," in J. V. Freitas Marcondes and Osmar Pimental (eds.), *São Paulo: Espírito, Povo, Instituções* (São Paulo, 1968), 365–80; J. Parke Renshaw, "A Sociological Study of Spiritism in Brazil" (Ph.D. dissertation, University of Florida, 1969); and Emilio Willems, *Followers of the New Faith: Culture Change and the Rise of Protestantism in Brazil and Chile* (Nashville, Tenn., 1967). The authors of all of these works were handicapped by the lack of the basic data from the 1960 census of population.

substantial decrease in number of parish priests call for a bit of additional comment. New parishes and parish churches seem mostly to have been a function of the burgeoning urban populations, for the biggest increases were in São Paulo (220), Rio Grande do Sul (186), Paraná (148), and Minas Gerais (109). Moreover, in Guanabara, which is essentially the same as the larger portion of the actual city of Rio de Janeiro, the number of matrizes increased from 121 to 145 during the period under consideration. But the building of new parish churches, or the elevation of other places of worship to the rank of matriz, was not limited to the cities. As the new municípios were created, the consecration of additional parish churches was an indispensable accompaniment of the administrative change.

The substantial reduction in the number of priests reported as serving the parishes is puzzling. Drastic decreases in the numbers reported for some of the states were accompanied by huge increases in others, and it is difficult to correlate these with the changes in the population. The largest reduction indicated is that for São Paulo, where the reports show a decrease from 1,943 priests working in the parishes in 1960 to 1,631 in 1967, or a loss of 312. In Minas Gerais the corresponding change was a decrease of 235; in Rio Grande do Sul, 199; in Ceará, 182; and Pernambuco, 156. On the other hand in Paraná the comparison shows an increase of 187 priests in the parishes, in Goiás one of 60, and in the new Federal District (Brasília), 27. Acre, Amazonas, Roraima, Pará, Maranhão, and Sergipe are the other states and territories in which the data show smaller increases to have taken place. These changes are in accord with an hypothesis that following 1960 the Church began making greater efforts to serve the populations outside the large cities.[37]

The scholars who have devoted most attention to the study of the social aspects of the Roman Catholic Church in Brazil are convinced that some substantial differentiation is taking place within the large mass of adherents to that faith. Some years ago the noted French student of the sociology of religion, Roger Bastide, whose knowledge of Brazilian religious phenomena is second to none, discerned and described the differences between what he denoted as "rural Catholicism and urban Catholicism." His indications of some of the fundamental differences of the first of these are as follows:

Rural Catholicism has remained very nearly the old colonial or imperial Catholicism, not only because the rural groups are essentially more traditional but because the lack of priests prevents a deeper education in the faith. It is more familial and more social, also more tarnished with superstitions. It is a religion that has remained in the *do ut des,* the promise made to a healing saint if he grants such and such a grace, a boon, a good marriage, an abundant harvest. The promise consists, if the saints responds to the prayer, of making a pilgrimage, of begging alms to provide a feast for the saint, or of depositing an ex-voto in such and such a chapel. Hence, there is an abundance of churches to which "miracle rooms" are attached, with legs, hands, or heads in wax or crudely carved in wood by some rural

[37] The statistical data used in this section were compiled and computed from statistics given in the 1962 and 1969 issues of the *Anuário Estatístico do Brasil.*

image maker. But if in spite of everything the grace is not bestowed, then the faithful turns against the saint. He is removed from the familial oratory in order to take him to another house, or is plunged head-down into a well and told that he will remain in that uncomfortable position until he grants the prayer.

But this Catholicism, utilitarian as it is, is sincere. It is like an integrating part of the personality. . . . Brazilian rural Catholicism is turned more to the worship of the saints and the Virgin than of God, and these saints vary according to the regions, as well as according to families. Bom Jesus da Lapa is especially adored in the São Francisco region as is Bom Jesus de Pirapora in the state of São Paulo. The rural families of Minas Gerais maintain the worship of the Holy Cross and plant one before the doors of their dwellings. . . .

Religion cannot live without the rites where souls join. It has been indicated that the distances prevent the priest from officiating in the interior. Thus, in order to survive, this rural Catholicism is obliged to create its own institutions and to invent its own chiefs. Nearly everywhere one finds *resadores,* sometimes an old Negro, sometimes a *Caboclo* or a more or less literate white, who gathers some countrymen around a little private chapel and there recites the litanies and celebrates novenas. Thus, in the absence of the priest, faith, which feels the need of spiritual nourishment, elaborates its own means of conservation. But the layman who celebrates the rites often has only an elementary knowledge of dogma, when he has any at all, and one now understands why superstition can so readily graft itself on the Catholic trunk. The *resador* is not always and necessarily the *benezedor,* he who cures the diseases of beasts as well as of men by making the sign of the cross and mumbling some Latin words— but very often he is.[38]

Quite different are the essential features of what Bastide calls urban Catholicism. These he summarizes as follows:

Urban Catholicism is purer. It rests on a population that is perhaps more restrained but in any case more instructed in its duties. It binds the people together in its brotherhoods, its patronages, its confessional associations. The clergy there is closer to the faithful and thus the control of the Church over its members is stronger in the cities than in the rural zones. It follows the individual from childhood with the catechism to the most advanced age with Catholic Action, in order to educate and support him. The urban clergy is bound to the rest of universal Catholicism by the Catholic hierarchy of which it is a link. Thus it is the bastion of Romanism in Brazil. A complete strategy has been worked out to develop the inclination for communion by organizing paschal days, officers, functionaries, bankers, professors—and, in order to fight immorality, by organizing, for example, retreats during Carnival, Brazil's great pagan feast.

Urban Catholicism is, however, in great contrast to rural Catholicism, for it is necessary to take account of the heterogeneity of the urban population and the diversity of social classes. There is, however, even in the cities and especially in their lowest strata, a popular Catholicism, characterized by miraculous revelations and cures, and despite the orders of an always prudent clergy, by the extraordinary and the supernatural. This leads to the flourishing of more or less heterodox cults, such as that of Antoninho in São Paulo.[39]

[38] Roger Bastide, "Religion and the Church in Brazil," in Smith and Marchant (eds.), *Brazil: Portrait of Half a Continent,* 546–47.
[39] *Ibid.,* 348.

More recently, in an illuminating study of the religious institutions of São Paulo, a noted student of the sociology of religion, Candido Procópio Ferreira de Camargo, built well upon the foundations laid by Bastide. He distinguished between the rural and urban types of "traditional Catholicism" along the same general lines used by the illustrious French scholar; and then went on to identify three varieties of a newer development which he calls "internationalized Catholicism." The three newer types he designates as "traditionalistic," "progressive," and "modernized," respectively. Each consists of those faithful to the Church and general Church doctrine, who give special allegiance to a specific set of religious values and norms of conduct.

Unlike "traditional" Catholicism, the traditionalistic form does not place overwhelming emphasis on the continuity of tradition. Rather, it idealizes and redefines the past, and expresses specifically and purposively the values believed by its adherents to provide the motivations for religious activities. Its values and norms favor the preservation of theological order, and the idealization of the past carries over into the social and economic aspects of life. Its adherents strenuously oppose modern proposals such as agrarian reform.

Those in the faction Camargo calls the progressives consider the values of social justice of primary importance. They try to combine Christian values with concrete beliefs about the needs of Brazilian society that are derived from the social sciences and from populist and leftist political movements. Within this group, the degree of radicalism varies greatly.

The modernized Catholicism described by Camargo is the profession of those who attempt to relate the Catholic doctrine, its values, and norms, to the theories of the behavioral sciences in order to produce a model society that is both Catholic and modern. Its advocates stress especially the need for religious behavior and instruction that is attuned to the needs of the family in a modern urban setting.[40] Obviously, neither Camargo nor anyone else can give any fair estimate of the absolute and relative importance of traditional Catholicism, rural and urban, and the several varieties of international Catholicism as they are in the 1970's in São Paulo and elsewhere in Brazil. Nevertheless, the fact that one of the most accomplished students of the subject attempts such a classification is evidence that considerable differentiation among the general adherents of the Roman Catholic religion is taking place. That such developments extend well into the hierarchy is evidenced by the publicized extent of the differences of thought and action of such high churchmen as Dom Hélder Câmara and his fellow Bishops of the Brazilian Church.[41]

Trends in Protestantism. Religious developments connected with

[40] See Camargo, "Igrejas e Religiões em São Paulo," 370–74.
[41] For a treatment of the activities of this celebrated clergyman, see José de Broucker, *Dom Hélder Câmara: The Violence of a Peacemaker* (Maryknoll, N.Y., 1970).

the importance of those affiliated with the various Protestant religious bodies are among the most striking changes in Brazilian religious life and culture since 1960. We still lack comprehensive data about the numbers of Protestants of various kinds in Brazil, but the fact that they are increasing rapidly can hardly be doubted. As indicated above (p. 512) the compilations of data supplied by the 1959 issue of the *Anuário Estatístico do Brasil* placed the number of Protestants, as of December 31, 1957, at 1,766,113. By the end of 1967 the data published in the 1969 issue of the *Anuário* gave the corresponding figure as 2,738,967, representing an increase of almost a million, or 55 per cent, during the interim. Other indicators of the growing importance of the Protestant groups are even more expressive. If we compare the figures for 1957 and 1967 for some of the other essential features of church organization and activities, the following striking changes are shown: number of churches (buildings), an increase from 5,312 to 12,884, or 143 per cent; number of halls used for religious services, an increase from 1,955 to 10,303, or 427 per cent; number of ministers, an increase from 6,135 to 14,064, or 129 per cent; members admitted during the year, an increase from 238,129 to 522,883, or 120 per cent; members excluded during the year, an increase from 153,212 to 390,882, or 155 per cent; and marriages performed or blessed, an increase from 11,279 to 18,604, or 65 per cent.[42] In 1967 according to the compilation of data we are using, São Paulo was the state containing the largest number of Protestants (623,995), followed by Rio Grande do Sul (509,720), Paraná (267,558), Santa Catarina (246,251), Espírito Santo (111,962), and Guanabara (107,519).

The numbers cited here are large and the increases great. Nevertheless, the membership figures at least probably are substantial understatements. Camargo was convinced that the official data were grossly in error and that even in 1960 there were over three million Protestants in Brazil and 722,000 in São Paulo alone.[43]

The feature of the rise of Protestantism in Brazil in recent years that has commanded most attention, and justly so, is the phenomenal spread of the Pentecostal faith. None of the official statistics give materials for the denominations separately, but both Camargo and Willems who have given competent study to the matter are convinced that the upsurge of Pentecostalism is by far the most important feature of the changes in recent years. The principal denominations involved are the Assemblies of God, the Christian Congregation, the Pentecostal Evangelical Church, and "Brazil for Christ." Camargo estimates that in the 1930's the members of these denominations represented less than 10 per cent of the Protestants in Brazil, and that by the time he wrote (1968), the proportion had risen to 60 per cent. At that time, too, he reports

---

[42] These data have been compiled and computed from materials in the *Anuário Estatístico do Brasil, 1959*, p. 416, and the *Anuário Estatístico do Brasil, 1969*, p. 590.

[43] Camargo, "Igrejas Religiões em São Paulo," 374–75.

that the "Brazil for Christ" organization was constructing in the city of São Paulo "the largest Christian temple in the World" to have a capacity to seat 25,000 persons.[44]

Spiritism or Spiritualism. The data on Spiritism or Spiritualism are such that there is little point in attempting to determine trends in this highly important component of the Brazilian religious spectrum. The figures given in the various editions of the *Anuário Estatístico do Brasil* show an increase of from 680,511 adherents in 1960 to 758,209 in 1967. However, Dr. J. Parke Renshaw who recently made the most comprehensive sociological study ever done of Spiritism in Brazil, concluded that "No one can say with any certainty how many Brazilians are Spiritists; yet, it is generally conceded that their numbers run into the millions and that their influence extends far beyond those included in the formal membership. Conservative estimates indicate that between two and three million persons are members of local centers." [45]

Afro-Brazilian Cults—From the Shadows to the Spotlight. One of the most remarkable changes in Brazilian religious organization and behavior in recent decades has been the extent to which the various Afro-Brazilian religious cults have been enabled to bring their beliefs and ceremonies out of the shadows to which they long were confined, into the glare of the daylight. This seems to be especially true in the cities of Rio de Janeiro and São Paulo, and other highly urbanized areas in southern Brazil. In the years 1942 to 1946, when I spent many interesting hours accompanying Arthur Ramos in his penetrating studies of the African religious heritage in Brazil, one could not even dream of the time when the *macumba* and the *candomblé* would occupy the spotlight before an overflow crowd in Rio de Janeiro's gigantic Maracanã stadium; nor did I think the day would ever come when data on the still furtive practice of *Umbanda* would appear in Brazil's official *Anuário Estatístico.* My recollections of those days are of the great difficulties encountered in attempting to inspire enough confidence in the informants that they would consent to answer questions about their religious beliefs and practices, allow some of their religious songs to be recorded, and so on. Ramos, himself, along with other well-established white men, was serving as an *ogan,* or intermediary with more esteemed portions of society, for one of the cults; and my files include clippings from newspapers, featuring the visit to Rio de Janeiro of a celebrated Pai do Santo from Bahia. For example, on August 7, 1942, *A Noite,* widely circulated evening newspaper, announced above a picture of "The King of the Macumba," João Alves Torres, the arrest of the king and that he was going to be sent back to Bahia immediately. In the *Diario da Noite* of the same date the story, also accompanied with a picture of the *macumbeiro* who had been arrested, played up the fact that he was a teacher of African dances who had trained

---

[44] *Ibid.*, 377. For more of the details about the rise of the Pentecostal movement in Brazil and also in Chile, see Willems, *Followers of the New Faith.*

[45] Renshaw, *Sociological Study of Spiritism,* 110.

some well-known Brazilian ballerinas. In this case the headline, "O 'rei da macumba' veio ao Rio em viagem de recreio," perhaps would be most accurately translated as "The 'King of the Macumba' *Says* He Came to Rio on a Pleasure Trip." In any case, there could have been little doubt in the minds of the readers that he was not welcomed by the authorities in the nation's capital and that he was being sent back to Salvador with dispatch.

Some years later, in 1956, it was my good fortune to be in Salvador on the occasion of the 100th anniversary of the birth of Nina Rodrigues, noted physician who pioneered the study of Afro-Brazilian religious cults in Bahia, and teacher and mentor of Arthur Ramos. At that time by special invitation I attended a gala occasion at the medical school of the University of Bahia in honor of Nina Rodrigues. All of the notables in the city were present, with the exception of the Roman Catholic clergy; and the guests of honor were four noted *mães de santo* bedecked in their best ceremonial attire. This convinced me that things were changing, yet I was somewhat surprised when I read stories in Brazil's great newspapers such as the one featured in the *Journal do Brasil* of Rio de Janeiro for May 13, 1965, well illustrated with photos of prominent orishas, from which the following opening paragraphs are translated:

The Maracanã stadium will be transformed today, beginning at 6:00 P.M. into an immense candomblé terreiro, when to the sound of 500 sacred African drums, the folkloric festival Night of the Macumba will be opened. This is organized by the Spiritist-Umbanda Confederation in commemoration of the abolition of slavery and in honor of the 400th anniversary of the city of Rio de Janeiro.

The ceremonies will be opened with an address by Governor Carlos Lacerda, and presided over by Yialorixá Ilê Afonjá, Dona Maria Bebiana, and great mãe-de-santo of the candomblés of Bahia, who, symbolizing all Negro mothers, will be crowned as Black Mother of the Year.

Finally, the 1969 issue of the *Anuário Estatístico do Brasil* carries statistical data about the *Umbandistas* on a par with the data for the Catholic, Protestant and Spiritist *cultos*. The tabulation indicates a total of 280 buildings dedicated to cult purposes, the use of 1,332 halls for religious meetings of the adherents, and the use of 590 rooms in private homes for religious assemblies of the Umbandistas. They are credited with holding 217,399 worship services during the year, of admitting 101,022 new members and excluding 46,376 former members in 1967, and of having a total membership of 240,088 persons at the end of the year. Rio Grande do Sul, with 59,552 reported members of the cult, São Paulo with 57,663, Guanabara with 45,100, Rio de Janeiro with 29,442, and Minas Gerais with 24,055 are the states in which the bulk of these identified as adherents are located.

These data alone are evidence that only a very small portion of those fully imbued with the Afro-Brazilian religious beliefs are figuring in modern *Umbanda*. Only 332 members are reported for

Bahia, where the actual numbers of those participating in the candomblés must run into the tens if not the hundreds of thousands.

It also should be indicated that the process of syncretism with Spiritism and Catholicism has gone on sufficiently, and the process of giving respectability to Umbanda beliefs and practices have gone on to the extent that it may not be accurate to characterize Umbandistas solely as the members of one of the Afro-Brazilian religious cults. When Ramos was fully conversant with affairs in the macumbas of Rio de Janeiro, in the years immediately before his untimely death in 1950, Umbanda or *Embanda* was the name of the high priest of an African cult of Bantu origin.[46] Since then substantial changes have occurred. Wagley states that the African fetish cults, "once very discrete in Rio de Janeiro," now are found in every part of the city and in the suburbs. He also indicates that the most famous leaders of the cults in Bahia now have residences and "branches" of their temples in the city of Rio de Janeiro. Moreover, "there are innumerable pseudo-African fetish cults in São Paulo, Rio de Janeiro, and other large cities which practice a watered-down version of the traditional ceremonies." [47] But he does not specifically mention that the name Umbanda is given to any of these. Finally, Renshaw, who studied the Umbanda cults intensively, especially in São Paulo, first indicates that the *macumbas* of Rio de Janeiro, *xangós* of Recife, and so on, are popularly referred to as *baxio espíritismo* or *"low spiritism,"* and then adds, "Another cult commonly included in this category is that of *Umbanda,* for under casual observation it appears to be similar to the above-mentioned Afro-Brazilian rites. Nevertheless, Umbanda, referred to as white magic by its sympathizers, claims to be motivated by the virtue of Christian charity and to seek only to help those in need." [48] However, on another page he indicates that the terms "macumba" and "umbanda" are frequently used interchangeably in Rio de Janeiro." [49] Thus, we probably are not greatly in error in thinking that the appearance of statistical data on the Umbandistas in the *Anuário Estatístico* is eloquent evidence of the emergence of certain parts of the Afro-Brazilian religious heritage from the shadows into the light of day.

POLITICAL INSTITUTIONS AND GOVERNMENT

The kaleidoscope of Brazilian political and governmental institutions shifted with unusual rapidity in the years after 1960. It presented many new, unexpected, and fascinating dramas. In fact, the stage settings, the actors and their lines, and the plot of the govern-

[46] See the last treatise Arthur Ramos wrote on the subject, in which there is a summary of his life's work in the study of African religious culture in Brazil, "The Negro in Brazil," in Smith and Marchant, *Brazil: Portrait of Half a Continent,* 145.

[47] Wagley, *An Introduction to Brazil,* 244.

[48] Renshaw, *Sociological Study of Spiritism,* 6.

[49] *Ibid.,* 14.

mental actions shifted so often, so suddenly, and so drastically that it probably would have been almost impossible for anyone, even a specialist working full time on the study of Brazilian political affairs, to have kept fully informed about the happenings. Even then one in the best position to know probably would have had difficulty in separating the trivial from the significant, the picturesque from the essential, the unique from the typical, the enduring from the temporary, and the specimen from the variant. Certainly I make no pretense of the omniscience that would have been required. I am not at all certain that I am able to untangle even a few of the most significant sociological facts (in Sorokin's terminology those that are repeated frequently in time and space) from the insignificant welter of less important phenomena with which they have been intertwined.[50]

Consider briefly the rapidly changing scenes on the stage in which the governmental and political drama was played: *scene 1,* a presidential system in which the executive was popularly elected and enjoyed tremendous power; *scene 2,* a parliamentary regime hastily designed to lessen the power of the chief executive when a vice-president, who, in what amounted to a challenge to fate, had been elected to a second term in that office, succeeded to the presidency; *scene 3,* the revolutionary setting, wherein action on the stage reached a climax, and the power was taken by the top commanders of the military forces; and *scene 4,* a succession of strong presidents installed by the military. All of this in a single decade.

Consider also for a moment some of the colorful "stars" who played before the audience averaging over 80 million Brazilians and occasionally to much of the remainder of the world. Succeeding one another in the spotlight since 1960 were such figures as Juscelino Kubitschek, featured in the act of transferring the capital to Brasília and practically wrecking the financial structure of the economy; Janio Quadros, who rose like a meteor in Brazil's political skies, who gained the presidency with an unparalleled outpouring of popular support, who quickly produced one of the greatest disenchantments with a leader ever to take place in Brazil, and who made the fatal mistake of sending his favorite "resignation" jug to the well once too often and had it accepted; João Goulart, Getúlio Vargas's heir, and his fiery brother-in-law, ally-rival Leonel Brizola, who produced the most massive opposition on the part of the urban middle classes ever experienced in Brazil; the colorful governors of three great states, Adhemar de Barros (São Paulo), Magalhães Pinto (Minas Gerais), and Carlos Lacerda (Guanabara), the most unlikely political bedfellows imaginable, who by combining their forces dominated the scene during the eventful days when Goulart was

---

[50] A useful summary of the happenings in the eventful years from the time Getúlio Vargas appeared on the scene to the collapse of the Goulart regime is to be found in Thomas E. Skidmore, *Politics in Brazil, 1930–1964: An Experiment in Democracy* (London, Oxford and New York, 1967).

being ousted; and the three generals, Castello Branco, Costa e Silva, and Garrastazu Médici, who occupied the presidency in succession under the Revolutionary Government that took power in 1964. This list could be extended indefinitely, for since 1960 Brazil has not lacked colorful and controversial governors in other states, "political" economists in high positions, and lawyer-politicians of various stripes who commanded large followings.

Consider finally portions of the action. Here one seeking to single out the significant changes from the portions of the drama that were merely colorful, fascinating, sometimes amusing, and often misdirected or abortive, faces an unusual challenge. Indeed, it may very well be that the most significant changes, such as the institution and strengthening of more effective measures of taxation, may have gone on mostly without contributing much to the happenings on which most of the publicity was focused. Nevertheless, in passing, mention should be made of a few of the highlights of the action such as: the enthusiastic political campaign in which Janio Quadros won the presidency, and the quick disillusionment that followed; [51] the almost comic opera quality of the act in which Quadros' resignation was submitted and accepted; the suspense, indecision, and tenseness accompanying Vice-President Goulart's return from China, where he was visiting at the time the presidency became vacant, his entrance through Rio Grande do Sul where his support was strongest, and his eventual succession to the presidency under a newly devised parliamentary system; the opening of broad fissures in the military officialdom, and developing insubordination in the army, as exemplified by the "revolt of the sergeants"; the collision course that developed between the Goulart regime and all the less-leftist elements in the country; the "battle of Rio de Janeiro" between the state forces led by Lacerda and the elements loyal to Goulart while the armed forces from Minas Gerais and São Paulo were converging on the de facto seat of federal power; the collapse of the Goulart regime and his flight to Uruguay; and the consolidation of military control, rule by decree, the annulment of the mandates of hundreds of the members of federal and state legislative bodies and other elected officials,[52] and so on. Certainly if one had allowed his attention to be focused primarily upon these interesting happenings on the political scene, he would have had time for little else.

Following these comments upon the scenes, actors, and actions that have commanded the attention of the press, the radio, and television for more than a decade, let us attempt to cite what appear to have been some of the most significant changes in Brazil's political and governmental institutions since 1960. Certainly the installation of a regime in which the strong powers of the executive

[51] On one visit to Brazil, almost without exception the people with whom I talked were supporting his candidacy, and on the next almost to a man they regretted that they had done so. It should be mentioned, of course, that the taxi drivers, barbers, bell boys, waiters, etc., were not the same persons in the two cases.

[52] Skidmore, *Politics in Brazil*, 309–10.

branch of government is directly controlled by the military is one of these. The man to serve as president has been selected by the top officials of the armed forces since 1964, and no promise of a change in that yet is in sight. If anything, the grip of the military on national affairs seems to be tightening. Moreover, the huge fissures that appeared in the leadership of those forces early in the 1960's seem to have been closed definitively, or at least none of them have surfaced to any extent.

The abolition of the various political parties that featured the interim between the end of Vargas' Novo Estado and the fall of Goulart is another of the more significant changes. Actually, many of these parties were little more than the personal followings of powerful politicians. After the military took over, they were reduced to two, one (ARENA) consisting of those supporting the government and the other (MDR) made up of the opposition. If and when new parties are legalized and emerge, they probably will have little in common with those that occupied the headlines between 1945 and 1964.

The ideological conflict continues, with outbursts of violence erupting from time to time. The numbers of political figures, intellectuals, and other opponents living in exile is very large, although, of course there are no reliable figures on the total. Factions of the underground do not hesitate to use terrorist tactics of the most extreme kind, including the kidnapping of ambassadors of Switzerland and the United States. The number of Brazilian planes hijacked to Cuba runs second only to that in the United States. All of this, in turn, brings forth strong countermeasures on the part of the authorities, so that a marked increase of social conflict seems to be one of the clearly distinguishable trends. Charges of the torture of political prisoners are rife in news magazines and newspapers in the United States and elsewhere, and they are hotly denied by the Brazilian government and groups of eminent Brazilians. But the reports will not be stifled. Even famed conservative columnist William F. Buckley, Jr., in a dispatch from Rio de Janeiro [53] sadly reports under the caption "Brazilians Ask: What Does the Disgrace of Torture Gain?"

Have the Brazilians been using torture?
The answer, a businessman told me who is thoroughly apolitical and likes it just fine that way, is—yes. He told me, and others corroborated what he said, about several instances of torture, and not all of them against demonstrable terrorists. . . .
Now there is talk that because General Medici countenances torture in pursuit of conspirators against the safety of the state, and the safety of ambassadors to the state, other government officials—local police chiefs, for instance—are finding themselves attracted to the easy and relatively productive mode of teasing information out of criminal suspects.
The press in Brazil is censored, and discussions of the subject do not take place in the lordly safety of the press, but it is a datum that the Brazilians I spoke to find universally saddening. And, then they ask,—

[53] Published in the Jacksonville, *Florida Times-Union*, February 18, 1971.

why? . . . the dictatorship of General Medici is absolutely secure; the country is going through unparalleled prosperity, the civilized opposition is perfunctory, the terrorist opposition is tiny, and largely neutralized; so that, they ask, why is it accomplishing, to put up against the humiliation and disgrace of it all?

The rise in governmental expenditures that has taken place since 1960 may very well be the most important of all the changes taking place in Brazil's political and governmental institutions in the current period. It is quite unlikely that these will drop back to earlier levels; and highly probable that the increase will continue at a pace greatly exceeding that of the growth of the population. From the data supplied in the 1969 and earlier issues of the *Anúario Estatístico do Brasil* some reasonably accurate approximations, in dollars, to the changes in the budgets of the national government, the totals for the states, and those for the county-like municípios, may be made. These can be summarized as follows. Between 1960 and 1967, the latest year for which details are available at the time of writing, the budget of the federal government rose from about $1,023,000,000 to around $2,155,000,000, or by approximately 110 per cent. On a per capita basis the change was from about $14.50 to $25.00. The greater effort of the national government along developmental lines of various kinds certainly is closely related to this increase in the funds. There also have been some marked changes in the sources from which the federal government derives its revenue. In 1960 about 40 per cent of the total came from taxes on industrial products; and by 1967 this proportion had risen to about 49 per cent. On the other hand, income taxes, which at the beginning of this period accounted for 30 per cent of the tax receipts of the federal government, yielded only 21 per cent at its end. Taxes on imports likewise declined in relative importance, from 11 per cent to about 8 per cent. In addition to the increased revenue from taxes on manufactured products, the big change in source of funds at the disposal of the national government is the addition of taxes on gasoline, and other liquid fuels and oils. These were not in the picture in 1960, but by 1967 they accounted for 15.4 per cent of the funds budgeted by Brazil's national government.

Changes in the sizes of the budgets of the state governments were even larger than those in the federal government. In 1960 the total of the budgets for all of the state governments combined amounted to about $1,086,000,000, or, even more than that of the national government; and by 1967 the corresponding figure had risen to $2,936,000,000, a gain of 170 per cent. Thus, the situation and trend are radically different from those in the United States, where the size of the federal budget is several times the combined total of those of the state governments, and the trend definitely has not been favorable to the states. On the per capita basis the funds in the state budgets rose from about $15.30 in 1960 to $34.15 in 1967. In this connection it should be pointed out, however, that the budget of the state of São Paulo alone accounted for 45 per cent of the total at the end of the period as well as at the beginning. However, the proportions for the other leading states fell somewhat, in the period under consideration, or from 12.5 to 11.5 per cent, 10.6 to 6.9 per cent, and 8.4 to 6.6 per cent, for Guanabara, Rio Grande do Sul, and Minas Gerais, respectively. Changes in the sources of state revenue are difficult to assess in a few sentences, but most of it comes from imposts of one kind or another, of which sales taxes are the most important. Such sales taxes accounted for 63 per cent of state revenues in 1960 and 70 per cent in 1967. In the interim, the states lost, through a hastily devised constitutional amendment, their right to levy a general property tax on the land and other real property. This came about when the government of São Paulo instituted a small land tax (about one-half cent per dollar of assessed valuation) to be used to finance a program of agrarian revision that its governor had developed. As a result of this, such taxes yielded no state revenues in 1967. Actually, this was no very great loss for even in 1960 the general property tax produced less than 1.0 per cent of the revenue for the states.

Finally, all of the municípios in Brazil combined had a budget of only $208,000,000 in 1960, of which the ones in which the state capitals were located accounted for over 41 per cent. Together they all budgeted $629,000,000 in 1967, a gain of over 200 per cent, of which over 41 per cent still was the share of the municípios containing the capitals of the states. On the per capita basis the increase was from about $2.90 to $7.30 per inhabitant. Various stamp taxes, a tax on urban property, licenses for industries and professions, transfers of property, etc., make up the major sources from which the municípios derive their revenue. Even though they now possess the right to levy a general property tax, there is no evidence to show that any pioneering efforts along this line are being made. Therefore, the general debility of local government continues to be about as great as ever. The land tax which might be used as a means of pooling local efforts to supply the funds needed for genuine local *self*-government still is avoided at all costs, and the ownership of land remains an asylum for capital. In spite of all that is said about "community development" no effective way of getting a substantial contribution annually from the members of the community itself has been devised and put into practice. Ineffective purely voluntary efforts must be relied upon to meet the cost of essential community activities, and this simply means that most of them are not provided at all. The day when some relatively small areas, such as the municípios, towns, and villages, can use tax resources in effective programs of community development (for schools, water supplies, sewerage systems, police protection, health services, etc.) still seems to be far in the future.

Glossary

[The definitions and explanations given are those which have a direct relationship to matters treated in the text. Many of the words and phrases have other connotations as well, but no attempt has been made to include them.]

A

achôgun, assistant sacerdote in the Afro-Brazilian cults of gêge-nagô origin.

adarrum, a special beat of the drum used in the Afro-Brazilian cults of gêge-nagô origin; reputed to be particularly effective in inducing the phenomenon of possession.

agregado (aggregado), in colonial times a free man of low social status who placed himself under the protection of the master of the casa grande, thus becoming one of his "men" or retainers; used now in parts of Brazil as a designation for the agricultural laborer who lives on the estate.

agreste, name used in northeastern Brazil to designate the zone which lies between the well-watered coastal plain and the arid sertão. Much of it is rocky and covered by scattered, scrubby timber.

aguasal, a species of palm.

ajuntamento, a common-law marriage. One of the Brazilian equivalents of the "tuk up" matings of Negroes in the southern United States.

alcalde, name generally applied throughout Spanish America to the administrative official who is chief of the government in a município or county.

aldeia (aldea in old writings), a village of domesticated or Christianized Indians.

alqueire, an old measurement of area. The alqueire paulista contains 2.42 hectares; and the alqueire minero is twice as large.

alturas, the higher social levels.

alufá, designation for the sacerdote versed in the religious lore of Mohammedan origin which survives in Afro-Brazilian cults.

alujá, a Brazilian fetish dance of African origin.

amarelo, yellow, used in classifying the population by color.

amasiados, a couple united only by a common-law union.

angú, corn-meal mush. Corn meal in this form is very important in the diet of the lower classes in Minas Gerais and the neighboring states.

anjos, children dressed as angels who participate in religious processions.

anuário (annuario, anuario), yearbook or annual report.

apanhar, to harvest.

armazém, a commissary.

arraial, a camp. Sometimes used to designate a center at which people gather for festivals.

731

arratel, an old weight, the equivalent of 459 grams, still used in Brazil.

arrendação, rent or renting.

arrendador, one who rents to another.

arrendamento, rent or renting.

arrendar, to rent.

arrendatário, one who rents from another.

arroba, an old weight, the equivalent of 14.69 kilograms, still used widely in Brazil. Since the introduction of the metric system a weight of 15 kilograms is called arroba métrica.

atabaque, a variety of drum used in Afro-Brazilian religious ceremonies.

B

babá, one of the names used in Rio de Janeiro to designate a sacerdote of the Afro-Brazilian religious cults.

babacuara, ignorant; used as a designation for the low-class plantation workers in the sugar-producing sections of the state of Rio de Janeiro.

babalão, one of the names used in Bahia to designate a sacerdote of the Afro-Brazilian religious cults.

babalorixá, one of the names used in northeastern Brazil to designate a sacerdote of the Afro-Brazilian religious cults.

babassú (babaçú), a species of palm; very important economically as a source of vegetable oils.

baboloxá, one of the names used in Rio de Janeiro to designate a sacerdote of the Afro-Brazilian religious cults.

bacaiuveira, a species of palm.

Bahiano (feminine, Bahiana), a designation for the native of Bahia.

bairro, a district, or section of a city.

bandeirante, explorer, frontiersman, and hunter of Indians.

banguê, a small sugar mill of the most primitive type.

barracão, the seat of a seringal, i.e., the headquarters of the owner or administrator of lands on which rubber-producing trees are grown, from which supplies are distributed to the workers, and at which the raw rubber is assembled for shipment.

batucajé (batucagé), a Brazilian dance of African origin.

batuque, a Brazilian dance of African origin, and also used as a generalized term for such dances.

batuque do jarê, a Brazilian dance of African origin.

beata, a woman devoted to religion but not a member of any monastery or community.

beato, "a bachelor, who makes vows of chastity (real or apparent), who has no profession because he has quit work, and who lives through the charity of the kindly and by exploiting the faithful."—Xavier de Oliveira.

bemfeitorias, improvements, such as plantings, made on land and valued separately.

beneficiamento, improvement, cleaning, refining, processing, and so forth.

bicho, animal or beast; almost anything from man to supernatural beings may be spoken of as bichos.

bicho de pé, a kind of chigger which burrows under the skin, particularly under the toenails, and deposits its eggs in a neat little sack.

bodega, canteen.

boitatá, a wandering spirit which has the power to protect or destroy pastures.

bôto, a supernatural being, the male counterpart of the Lorelei, that lives in the folklore of the Amazon.

bouba, a tumor produced by a germ very similar to that of syphilis.

braça, an old measure of distance equal to 2.2 meters.

branco, white.

broca, the act of clearing or cleaning the land of the small timber, undergrowth, brush and vines which grow among the larger trees.

brocar, to clear away the undergrowth as a first step in the preparation of a roça.

bruaqueiro, one of the names used in Minas Gerais to designate the rural person of low social status.

bumba-meu-boi, a popular dramatic dance of northeastern Brazil in which the principal participants are the bull, the marine horse, and the doctor.

burra-de-padre (burrinha-de-padre, also), one of the names for the headless mule into which the concubine of a priest is likely to be turned.

C

caboclo (feminine, cabocla), name first applied to domesticated Indians, later used to designate a crossbreed of white-Indian stock, and now generally used to mean any lower-class rural person.

caboré, synonym for cafús, cafuso, indicating a person of mixed Indian and Negro descent, and often used to designate any rural person of low social status.

cabra, designation for the offspring of a mulatto and Negro, i.e., a person of ¾ Negro and ¼ white blood.

cabrucar, to fell large trees with an axe as one step in the preparation of a roça.

cacau (cacaú, cacáo), cocoa.

cachaça, a rum made from the juice of sugar cane.

café, coffee.

cafezinho, a demitasse of strong coffee. Generally the small cup is half filled with sugar before the coffee is poured into it.

cafús (cafuso), a person of mixed Indian and Negro descent.

caiçara, a designation for the lower-class countryman and fisherman used in the coastal districts of São Paulo.

caipira, the man or woman who lives outside the village, who lacks instruction or social graces, who does not dress well or make a good appearance in public. It is the most widely used designation for the lower-class, rural Brazilian.

Calunga, personification of the sea in Bantu religious culture. The name is still to be heard in the macumbas of Rio de Janeiro and also survives as the name of a small doll. (In Africa her fetish was a small wooden figurine.)

câmara, the council or corporation which formerly exercised the legislative function in the government of the município.

camarada, a hired farm laborer who does not reside on the estate.

cambône, assistant sacerdote in the macumbas of Rio de Janeiro.

campina, prairie.

campos, prairie-like pasture lands on the high plateaus and mountain tops.

cana branca, a white sugar cane, generally of inferior quality.

cancha, a race track, and by extension, the place where the erva mate is crushed so that the leaves may be separated from the twigs and branches.

cancheada, erva mate after the leaves, twigs, and branches have been crushed into small particles.

candomblé, the designation used in Bahia for the Afro-Brazilian religious cult of gêge-nagô origin. More specifically it refers to a particular terreiro, sacerdote, and group of worshipers.

candomblezeiro, designation used in Bahia for the sacerdote who operates a terreiro or candomblé of gêge-nagô origin.

cangaceiro, the bad man or bandit of the sertões of the northeast.

cangussú, synonym for caipira or caboclo used in São Paulo.

canna verde, a Brazilian dance of African origin.

canzá, a percussion instrument of bamboo used by Brazilian Negroes in their religious ceremonies.

capiau, synonym for caipira used in Minas Gerais and Bahia.

capinar, to clean the roça by clearing out the weeds and saplings from among the growing plants.

capitania, a designation for the state or province during part of the colonial epoch.

capitão, captain.

capitão-do-mato (plural, capitães-do-mato), official charged with the hunting down and capture of fugitive slaves.

capitão-mor (plural, capitães-mores), commander-in-chief of the military forces in a province during colonial days.

capoeira, the second growth which comes up after a roça has been made in the virgin forest.

capuava, synonym for caipira used in parts of Minas Gerais and Bahia.

caracú, a breed of beef cattle being developed in Brazil.

Cariapemba, an African demon who used to pursue slaves and take possession of their bodies. His name is still mentioned in the macumbas of Rio de Janeiro.

cariboca, synonymous with mameluco as a designation for persons of mixed white and Indian blood.

Carioca, a name applied to the person who lives in Rio de Janeiro, and to the distinctive culture traits of the city.

carnaúba, a species of palm noted for the wax that is produced between its fronds.

cartório, a register in which the vital statistics are recorded.

caruru, a dish prepared with herbs, fish, shrimp, and oil of a palm and served to Xangô in the candomblés of Bahia.

casaca, a designation used in Piauí for the rural person of low estate.

casacudo, Brazilian designation for a rich, important person, but used along the São Francisco River in Bahia to apply to the rural person of low estate.

casa grande, the big house or mansion that forms the seat of a large landed estate.

casebre, a hut of the poorest construction.

cateretê, a Brazilian dance of African origin.

catimbó, name by which the religious cult of African origin is known in northeastern Brazil, i.e., the northeastern equivalent of the macumba of Rio de Janeiro, the candomblé of Bahia, and the Xangô of Recife.

catinga (caatinga), designation for the small, sparse, spiny vegetation which covers the arid sertões of northeastern Brazil.

caxambú, a Brazilian dance of African origin.

Cearense, native of the state of Ceará.

cercar, to fence.

chácara, a small farm near the city and generally used for growing fruits and vegetables.

chapadeiro, plainsman.

charque (xarque), beef that has been cut up, dipped in salt water, and then dried in the sun.

charqueada, a plant in which charque is prepared.

chiba, a Brazilian of African origin.

cidade, city. This rank is given to any population center that has been designated as a seat of a município.

côco-de-zambê, a Brazilian dance of African origin.

colegio, a secondary school offering instruction at a level corresponding roughly to that of the high school (ninth through the twelfth grades) in the United States.

colhêr, to harvest.

colonia, a settlement of small farmers in south Brazil, and the workers' village on the fazenda in central Brazil.

colonial, of or pertaining to the immigrant settlements of small farmers in south Brazil.

colônias agrícolas, colonies of small farmers.

colono, a small farmer in south Brazil; a laborer who obligates himself to work on a one-year contract in the care and obligatory harvest of a certain number of coffee trees or of a certain area of cotton or of other crops such as cane, oranges, rice, and beans in São Paulo.

comarca, a judicial district.

comuna, name used to designate medieval settlements, French administrative units, Jewish quarters in cities, and in Pernambuco, an organized gang in the city.

comunidade (communidade), community. Used generally to refer to community of goods, or community of interests, and rarely to designate a locality group.

conto or conto de reis, 1,000 cruzeiros and equivalent in 1963 to $1.25.

cooperação anual, an agricultural demonstration field established for one year only.

cooperação permanente, an agricultural demonstration field in which work continues longer than one year.

coronel, colonel. A political boss in a município.

corumba (curumba), designation for the rural person of low estate used in parts of the Northeast.

côvado, an old measure of distance equal to three palmas or sixty-six centimeters.

creulo, creole. In some Brazilian communities the term is synonymous with Negro.

Cristã-novo (plural, Christãos-novos), a converted Jew, or new Christian, who came to Brazil in the colonial epoch.

cruzeiro, the new unit of exchange in Brazil. One of them is valued at two cents. One cruzeiro is the equivalent of the old milreis or 1$000.

cuíca, a small cylindrical musical instrument used in Afro-Brazilian religious ceremonies.

curandeiro, an herb doctor.

curáu, designation used in Sergipe for the rural person of low estate who periodically flees before the drought.

curral, corral; formerly used to designate a cattle ranch or fazenda.

curupira, a mythical little man whose feet are turned backward so that anyone seeing his tracks and trying to run away from him will speed to destruction at his hands.

D

dansa do tambor, a Brazilian dance of African origin.

data de terra, the area of a land grant in Piauí.

decreto-lei, law established by executive decree.

delegado geral (plural, delegados gerais), general director or supervisor.

derrubada (derruba), act of felling the trees in the preparation of a roça.

derruba e queimada, felling and burning for the preparation of a roça.

derrubar, to fell the larger trees with an ax in the preparation of a roça.

desafio, a contest in dialogue between two singers, all improvisation, each in turn seeking to answer the opponent's query, and then to turn the laugh on his opponent.

despacho, a designation for the sacrifice in an Afro-Brazilian fetish cult.

distrito de paz, a subdivision of the município, having a vila as its seat. It compares roughly with the township or other minor civil division in the United States.

Dois-Dois, also known as Ibeji, twin deities worshiped in Afro-Brazilian religious cults of gêge-nagô origin and frequently identified with Cosme and Damion.

domingueiras, Sunday dances.

donatario (donatário), recipient of a land grant or sesmaria.

dono de terra, landowner.

E

ebó, the sacrifice or despacho characteristic of Afro-Brazilian fetish cults.

empreiteiro, an administrative overlord; contractor.

encoivarar, to pile and burn the trunks and limbs that escaped in the first burning of the roça.

engenho, an old-fashioned sugar mill; also used to designate the entire sugar plantation.

engenhoca, a very small engenho, used mostly for the manufacture of rapadura.

ensino em geral, a designation for all types of general education collectively.

ensino fundamental: comun, basic education of the ordinary or general type.

entrudo, a carnival.

erva mate (herva-mate or matte), Ilex paraguariensis, from the leaves of which Paraguayan tea is made.

escada, stairway.

escola, school.

escola isolada, a one-teacher, ungraded school characteristic of rural areas.

escrópulo, measure of weight used for weighing precious stones, equivalent to 1.195 grams.

estado novo, the "new state" established by President Getúlio Vargas. It was terminated in 1945.

estância, the common designation for the large cattle ranch in Rio Grande do Sul.

estrangeiro, a foreigner.

Exú, one of the orishas of the Afro-Brazilian religious cults. He is the incarnation of evil.

F

falta de braços, literally the lack of arms, and the equivalent of the English shortage of hands.

farinha de mandioca, mandioca flour.

farinha de milho, flour or meal made of maize.

favelas, the slums which cover some of the hills in Rio de Janeiro.

fazenda, a large estate; the equivalent of *hacienda* in Mexico, Colombia, and Peru.

fazendeiro, the owner-operator of a large landed estate.

fazendola, a small fazenda.

feijoada, a Brazilian dish which includes beans, numerous kinds of meats, served over rice, and liberally sprinkled with mandioca flour.

feira, public market; weekly fair.

feita, the initiate of one of the Afro-Brazilian fetish cults is said to be feita, or made, after she has undergone all of the ceremonial preparation and is ready to become the medium through which the orisha expresses itself.

feiticeiro, sorcerer, conjurer, or magician.

ferros, cattle brands.

festas, holidays or feast days.

fidalgo, a noble.

filha de santo, a female who has undergone long ceremonial preparation and has been consecrated as one of the inner group of devotees in an Afro-Brazilian fetish cult.

filhos de santo, children of the saint or specially prepared devotees of devotees of the orishas in one of the Afro-Brazilian fetish cults.

flagelados (flagellados), refugees fleeing from the great droughts which periodically afflict northeastern Brazil.

foice, billhook, brushhook, or cutting blade attached to a long wooden handle.

foreiro, synonym for morador.

fornecedores, sugar-cane producers who lack milling facilities and must sell their product to a sugar usina.

freguesia, a church parish.

fronteira, frontier.

futebol, football.

G

Gana Zona (also, Ganga Zumba), one of the names by which Zambi or Nzambi, great deity of Angola, is known in the macumbas of Rio de Janeiro.

garimpeiro, one who searches for diamonds, often working in water up to his waist, scooping sand from the bed of a stream into a dugout canoe.

Gaúcho, a native of Rio Grande do Sul.

gêge-nagô, an African religion carried to Brazil by Negroes of Sudanese origin.

ginasio, a school of intermediate level, offering instruction that corresponds roughly with that of the fifth through the eighth grades in the United States.

gira, a circle or the arrangement of the participants in one of the ceremonies of the Afro-Brazilian cults of Bantu origin.

giráu, primitive storehouse made of sticks elevated above the ground.

grão, a weight equivalent to .049 grams.

grau médio, designation for education at the secondary or high-school
level.

grau superior, designation for education at the college or university level.

grude, extremely intimate ties, relation, or understanding between two or
more people.

grupo escolar, a multiple-teacher school.

guasca, designation for countryman used in Rio Grande do Sul.

H

homem da roça, the man who uses the ax, fire, and the hoe to produce
small subsistence crops on a little patch of ground.

homem de cor, colored man.

homem do campo, countryman or person who lives outside the towns and
cities. Usually applied only to persons of low estate.

homens do povo, the common people.

hospedaria, lodginghouse.

I

Ibeji, *see* Dois-Dois.

Ifá, an orisha worshiped in the gêge-nagô cults. He is closely associated
with acts of divination.

igreja, church.

illuminada, a person thought to be inspired.

imunu, contagious magic.

Indio, Indian.

instinto migratório, migratory instinct.

"interior," all of a state lying outside the capital city.

interventor, an official appointed by the president to serve as the governor
of a state.

intrudor (also intruso), one of the names for the rural person of low
estate who squats on the land and makes a roça.

irmandade, a religious brotherhood.

J

jagunços, name applied to the bad men of the sertões and also given to the
members of the religious brotherhood headed by Padre Cicero.

jaraguá, a red-top grass, *Andropogon rufus*.

jardineira, a "pick-up" or truck equipped with seats for passengers and
widely used throughout Brazil's interior—not a bus.

jeguedé, a Brazilian dance of African origin.

jogo, game, pastime, sport.

jongo, a Brazilian dance of African origin.

juiz de direito, a judge of a lower court to which cases are first brought.

juiz de fora, magistrate of colonial days. The name indicates that he came
from outside the community.

juiz municipal, judge having jurisdiction within a município.

L

latifúndio, a latifundium.

lavadeira, washerwoman.

lavrador, farmer.

légua, a league of 6,600 meters.

Lemba, African deity whose name is still to be heard in the macumbas of Rio de Janeiro.

libra, a pound 5.5 grams lighter than the English pound.

liceu, a secondary school.

limpar, to clean a roça by cutting or pulling the weeds and saplings from among the growing plants.

linha, a line; used to designate a sequence of activities in the macumbas and applied also to a row of houses in a line-village settlement.

litoral e mata, designation for the heavily forested coastal zone.

lobis homem, werewolf.

local, a place entirely lacking in inhabitants.

localidade, a locality. Any place in the national territory where there is a permanent agglomeration of inhabitants.

lote colonial, the land allotted to one settler in any agricultural colony.

lugarejo, a place that does not qualify as a núcleo, rural property, or povoado, but which temporarily has inhabitants.

M

machadeiro, an axman who fells the forests; also used to designate a rubber gatherer.

macho, a male famed for his great reproductive capacities.

macumba, name used in Rio de Janeiro to designate an Afro-Brazilian fetish cult. It also applies to a specific terreiro, sacerdote, and group of worshipers.

macumbeiro, one of the designations used for the sacerdote of the Afro-Brazilian cult of Bantu origin.

mãe d'agua, supernatural being who lives in the water. The worship of this goddess is an integral part of many of the fetish cults, especially in Bahia. The belief in such a water spirit is very widespread in Brazil.

mãe de santo (also mãe de terreiro), female sacerdote who operates an Afro-Brazilian fetish cult.

mais ou menos, more or less.

mambira, designation used in Rio Grande do Sul for the rural person of low estate.

mameluco (mamaluco), the half-breed of white and Indian parentage.

mandí, synonym for caipira used in parts of São Paulo and Minas Gerais.

mandioca, the tuber of manioc, *Manihot utilissima*. Made into farinha or flour, this is a basic element in the Brazilian diet.

mandioqueiro, synonym for caipira used in parts of Minas Gerais.

mangabeira, *Hancornia speciosa*.

manteiga, butter.

maracatú, a Brazilian dance of African origin.

marcha para oeste, march to the west. A slogan expressive of Brazil's desire to take more effective possession of her broad unsettled areas.

mascate, an ambulant peddler.

matadouro, local slaughterhouse.

mate, *see* erva mate.

mateiro, the workman who gathers the branches from the erva mate trees.

matriz, mother church; central church to which a number of surrounding chapels are subordinate.

matuto, literally, a forest dweller, and widely used as a synonym for caipira.

meiação, tenure arrangement under which the product is divided equally between the landowner and the worker or tenant.

meieiro, an agricultural laborer who receives one-half of the crop in lieu of wages, or a farm tenant who pays one half of his product as rent.

melhoramentos urbanos, civic improvements such as beautification of public squares or the installation of electric lights, sewer systems, and water works.

mestiço, mixed breed, usually applied to cross of white and Indian.

mil covas, literally, 1,000 hills; name used in Rio Grande do Norte to designate the tarefa of 3,025 square meters.

milha, mile, the equivalent of 2,200 meters.

milreis, unit of value prevailing in Brazil until 1942. One milreis, written 1$000, was then worth five cents. The milreis was replaced by the cruzeiro.

mineiro, native of Minas Gerais.

minha terra, "my land," usually used to refer to one's native state or district, and not to Brazil as a whole.

modinha, a little hit, i.e., a popular song.

moleque (muleque), a small Negro; used to designate any boy who is bad or unruly.

monjolo, a primitive water-driven device for pounding corn or other grain into flour.

morador, a squatter who stops about where he pleases and makes a roça. Eventually some moradores become established agregados and even come to enjoy the status of a share tenant.

moreno, dark.

morgado, an entailed estate that may not be subdivided but must be passed on intact.

moura-encantada, the enchanted Mooress, a mythical being in Portuguese folklore.

mucama, Negro nurse or "mammy."

mucuman, a plant growing in northeastern Brazil said to resemble a sea bean and with seeds that are poisonous to man.

mula-sem-cabeça, a fantastic headless mule, the transformed concubine of a priest.

mulheres da cama, concubines.

município, an administrative subdivision of the state, comparable roughly to the county in the United States. It consists of one cidade and the surrounding territory. It may or may not be subdivided into distritos do paz, each centered about a vila.

muxuango, one of the names applied in the state of Rio de Janeiro to the rural person of low estate.

N

Nananburucú (Anamburucú), Afro-Brazilian orisha worshiped in the gêge-nagô cults. The Negroes of Bahia consider her to be the oldest of the mães d'agua.

negrada, Negro females, collectively.

nordestino, a native of northeastern Brazil.

noroeste, northwest.

Nossa Senhora, Our Lady.

Nossa Senhora das Neves, Our Lady of the Snows.

Nosso Senhor dos Passos, Our Lord bearing the cross.

nota, note.

núcleo, a locality whose inhabitants are grouped together under a special regime but which is not the seat of an administrative division. Agricultural colonies fall in this category.

Nzambi, one of the names of the supreme deity of Angola.

O

ogan, a person of high social status who is initiated into one of the Afro-Brazilian cults and serves as a sponsor for the group in its relation with the outside world.

Ogun, Afro-Brazilian god of war.

oitava, eighth.

okê, an exclamation of reverence used in Afro-Brazilian fetish cults.

Oluran, the master of the sky in Yoruba mythology.

Omulú, one of the orishas honored in Afro-Brazilian fetish cults of gêge-nagô origin.

onça, an old weight equivalent to 28.349 grams; the South American jaguar.

operários, skilled workers.

oratórios, tiny chapels or altars set up on remote fazendas.

orisha, designation used by A. B. Ellis for a divinity of the Yoruban Negroes. The Portuguese equivalent is *orixá*. Each is the expression of one of the great forces of nature.

Orixalá (Oxalá), a bisexual divinity or orisha symbolizing the reproductive energies of nature.

Oxagian, an Afro-Brazilian orisha.

Oxóssi, the orisha who is god of the hunt.

Oxumanré, an Afro-Brazilian orisha.

Oxun, an Afro-Brazilian orisha.

P

padre, priest.

pagé, an Indian medicine man.

pai de santo, sacerdote who operates an Afro-Brazilian fetish cult.

Pai Joaquim, an old Negro from the African coast whose spirit is said to take possession of worshipers in the macumbas of Rio de Janeiro.

palhoça, a building or shed that is covered with a roof of thatch.

palma, a palm; an old measure equivalent to about twenty-three centimeters.

pantanal, a low-lying swamp area.

páo de mocó, a shrub, *Hoffmanuseggia leguminosa,* whose poisonous roots have proved fatal to many of the starving refugees fleeing the sêcas of the Northeast.

paraná, a bayou or distributary of a river.

parceiro, landless agriculturist who plants on shares, similar in many respects to the sharecropper in the southern part of the United States.

pardavasco, a dark mulatto, i.e., more brown than yellow.

pardo, brown, i.e., mulatto. The Brazilian census includes mulattoes, mestiços and also Indians in the pardo category.

pastoril (plural, pastoris), popular open-air, old-fashioned musical comedy.

patrimônio, patrimony; by extension applied in western São Paulo, at least, to designate a small trade center.

pau-a-pique, poles on end, a type of construction used in making the walls of the poorest huts.

Paulista, a native of São Paulo.

pé, foot; an old measure equivalent to about thirty-three centimeters.

peão, peon.

pé de garrafa, bottle foot; one of the malevolent, manlike supernatural beings with whom the rural Brazilian must deal.

pegí, holy of holies of an Afro-Brazilian fetish cult.

pegi-gan, name applied to the sacerdote when he is officiating before the altar in one of the Afro-Brazilian fetish cults.

Pernambucano, a native of Pernambuco.

pescador, fisherman.

picar, to pile the fallen timber in order to facilitate the burning over of a roça.

pilão, mortar and wooden pestle.

pióca, one of the designations for the rural person of low estate.

piraquara, one name for the humble Brazilian who lives mainly from fishing.

planalto, high plain.

plantar, to plant.

polegada, an inch.

ponto, a song dedicated to one of the divinities of an Afro-Brazilian fetish cult.

posseiro, a squatter.

povo, common people.

povoação, a small population center which lacks administrative functions; a village.

povoado, a locality which is not the seat of an administrative division but in which there is an agglomeration of residences, where the inhabitants exercise their economic activities as a function in the interest of the group.

praça, public square or plaza.

praiano, designation for the person of low estate who resides near the seacoast and lives largely by fishing.

prefeito, the administrative officer or mayor of the município.

prefeitura, the headquarters of the prefeito of a município.

preto, black; Negro.

propriedade rural, a rural property; a farm.

Q

quadra, square; an old measure of area. It varies greatly in size: the quadra gaúcha contains 1.74 hectares; the quadra de sesmaria, 87.12 hectares; another used in the states of Maranhão and Piauí contains 4.82 hectares; and a fourth, the quadra paraibana, 1.21 hectares.

queijeiro, literally, cheesemaker and eater; used in parts of Minas Gerais as a designation for the rural person of low estate.

queimar, to burn the fallen timber in the preparation of a roça.

quilate, an old measure of weight equivalent to .199 grams. Since the introduction of the metric system, a weight of .2 grams is known as the quilate métrico.

quilombo, a settlement of fugitive Negro slaves. It survives as a place name in many parts of Brazil.

quimbanda, designation for the chief sacerdote of the macumba in Rio de Janeiro.

quimbête, a Brazilian dance of African origin.

quintal, an old measure equivalent to 58.759 kilograms. Since the introduction of the metric system, a quintal métrico of 100 kilograms also has been used.

R

rancho, a rude hut.

rapadura, a brown sugar from which none of the molasses has been extracted; the equivalent of the Spanish-American *panela.*

recôncavo, designation for the fertile area embracing seventeen municípios which surround the city of Salvador or Bahia.

registro civil, register of births, deaths, and marriages kept by the state.

regulamento, official interpretation of a law in which the details of the manner in which it is to be applied are set forth.

relatório, report.

rendeiro, one who rents land to another.

ribeirinho, designation used in parts of Minas Gerais for the person of low estate who lives along a stream eking out a miserable existence by fishing and growing a little mandioca.

roça, a small burned-over patch of ground in the midst of the forest in which are planted subsistence crops such as corn, beans, and mandioca.

roçada, made into roças.

roceiro, a person who makes a roça, i.e., a countryman who produces a few subsistence crops by employing the primitive system of fire agriculture described in Chapter xv.

rôlo, brawl.

S

sacerdote, a person who performs sacerdotal functions; the term has connotations that are intermediate between those of the words shaman and priest.

samba, a Brazilian dance of African origin; also used to designate a functionary in the macumba who has the duties of receiving the visitors and caring for the women who "receive the spirit."

sapeco, the cancheada of mate after it has been dried over hot coals.

sarambéque, a Brazilian dance of African origin.

sarambú, a Brazilian dance of African origin.

sarará, a light mulatto.

saudades, untranslatable expression, in which pleasant remembrances, homesickness, and deep longing are all involved.

sêca (seca, secca, sêcca), drought.

secretaria, a department in state government. For example, the secretaria da agricultura is the equivalent of department or office of agriculture.

sede, seat. A cidade is the sede of the município.

seita, sect or cult.

senhor de engenho, the aristocratic master of a sugar plantation and the casa grande which forms its nucleus.

Senhor do Bomfim, Jesus Christ.

senzala, slave quarters.

serenos, a penitential sect.

seringal (plural, seringais), an estate, usually large, on which rubber-producing trees are exploited.

seringalista, a businessman who controls the land, owns the commissaries and rubber deposits, and performs the entrepreneurial functions involved in the collection of raw rubber.

seringueiro, the worker who taps the trees and coagulates the raw rubber.

serra, mountain.

Serra do Mar, the coastal range of mountains in southeastern Brazil.

serrano, mountaineer.

sertanejo, the common man who lives in the sertões of northeastern Brazil.

sertanista, the upper-class inhabitant of the sertões of northeastern Brazil; also, a synonym for bandeirante.

sertão (plural, sertões), an isolated, little-known place, distant from population centers and cultivated areas. Sertão bruto refers to a place entirely without inhabitants. The great northeastern interior, a semiarid area, covered with sparse, spiny vegetation, and sparsely populated, is the sertão par excellence.

sesmaria, a grant of land usually large and poorly described, given by the king of Portugal or his representative to a favored person of high social status.

sitiante, a small farmer; the proprietor of a sítio.

sítio, a small farm.

sitiozinho, a very small farm.

sobrado, a house of more than one story in the city; the urban counterpart of the casa grande.

sôlta, an unfenced pasture, especially an area of range land in the sertões of the Northeast.

sorôngo, a Brazilian dance of African origin.

Supremo Tribunal, Supreme Court.

T

tabaréu, one of the most widely used designations for the rural person of low estate. In popularity it ranks with caipira, caboclo, and matuto.

tapiocano, tapioca maker; one of the names used to designate the rural person of low estate.

taquara, a variety of cane used for bedding cattle.

tarefa, task; used widely as a measure of land. Its size varies greatly; the tarefa bahiana contains .44 of a hectare; the tarefa nordestina, .3; the tarefa gaúcha, .1; and the tarefa cearense, .361.

têrmo, a small judicial unit, being a subdivision of the comarca.

terra-roxa, a dark-red soil found in São Paulo and neighboring states and noted for its fertility.

terras devolutas, unpatented or public lands.

terreiro, the temple or church of one of the Afro-Brazilian fetish cults.

tonelada, ton; an old weight equivalent to 793.24 kilograms. Since the introduction of the metric system the tonelada métrica of 1,000 kilograms is also used.

toque do sino, sound of the church bells.

trabalho é para cachorro e negro, manual labor is for the dog and the Negro.

Triângulo, the panhandle of Minas Gerais.

tropeiro, a person who conducts a train of pack mules.

Turcos, designation applied to Syrians, Turks, and other immigrants from Asia Minor.

U

unidade escolar, a designation for the school used for statistical purposes.

urucarí, a variety of palm.

usina, the modern sugar refinery and plantation.

V

vadio, a person without occupation who does no work; a vagabond or vagrant.

vae-quebrar, go to break.

vaqueiro, cowboy.

vara, an old measure equivalent to 1.10 meters.

várzea, the present flood plain of a river.

Velho Lourenço, an old Negro from the African coast whose spirit is said to take possession of worshipers in the macumbas of Rio de Janeiro.

venda, a small store or trading post.

verminose, affected with worms, as for example, suffering from hookworms.

vigário (vigaro), title given to the Catholic priest in some parishes; vicar.

vila, the seat of a distrito de paz.

viola, a musical instrument similar to the violin in shape and to the guitar in tone.

violeiro, one who plays the viola.

X

Xangô, Afro-Brazilian god of lightning and thunder. In Recife his name has been given to the Afro-Brazilian fetish cult.

Xapanan, Afro-Brazilian god of smallpox.

Y

Yansan, one of the orishas honored in Afro-Brazilian fetish cults of gêge-nagô origin.

yara, an Amazonian designation for the water goddess or mãe d'agua.

Yauô, name for the girl who has been initiated into a candomblé in Bahia. She is considered to be the youngest wife of the saint.

Yemanjá, a Yoruba water divinity, or mãe d'agua, who occupies a prominent place among the orishas of the candomblés in Bahia.

Z

Zâmbi, one of the names for the great Angolian deity.

Zambi-ampungu, Congan deity whose name is still heard in the macumbas of Rio de Janeiro.

zona rural, rural territory.

Zumbi, the Brazilian equivalent of the Haitian Zombie; malevolent spirit that roams about at night.

Bibliography

A

Adams, Herbert B. *The Germanic Origin of New England Towns.* Baltimore, 1882.

Alagôas, Serviço de Estatistica do Estado. *Alagôas em 1931.* Maceió, 1932.

Albano, Ildefonso. *Jéca Tatú e Mané Chique-Chique.* 2d ed. Rio de Janeiro, n. d.

Album Grafico do Estado de Matto-Grosso. Hamburg, Germany, 1914.

Albuquerque Galvão, Luiz Manoel de. *Relatorio sobre as Colonias Blumenau, Itajahy, Principe D. Pedro e D. Francisca.* Rio de Janeiro, 1871.

Almeida, A., Jr. *Annuario do Ensino do Estado de São Paulo, 1935–1936.* São Paulo, 1937 (?).

Almeida, A., Jr. "Os Sete Pecados Capitais da Escola Rural," *Revista Brasileira de Estatística,* II, No. 8 (October–December, 1941), 1215–20.

Amado, Jorge. *Cacáu.* 2d ed. Rio de Janeiro, 1934.

Amado, Jorge. *Jubiabá.* Rio de Janeiro, 1937.

Amaral, Luís. *Aspectos Fundamentaes da Vida Rural Brasileira.* São Paulo, 1936.

Amaral, Luís. *Historia Geral da Agricultura Brasileira.* 3 vols. São Paulo, 1939.

Amazonas, Departamento Estadual de Estatística. *Sinopse Estatística do Estado do Amazonas.* Rio de Janeiro, 1942.

Annuario do Nordeste para 1937. Recife, 1937.

Antipoff, Helena. *Encaminhamento dos Alunos que Deixam a Escola Primaria, para Escola de Nivel mais Alto ou para o Trabalho* (mimeographed). Goiânia, 1942.

Araujo, Alceu Maynard. *Documentário Folclórico Paulista.* São Paulo, 1952.

Araujo, Alceu Maynard. "Instrumentos Musicais e Implementos," *Revista do Arquivo Municipal* (São Paulo), CLVII (1954), 150–207.

Aubertin, J. J. *Eleven Days' Journey in the Province of São Paulo.* London, 1868.

Azevedo, Arnoldo de (ed.). *A Cidade de São Paulo.* 4 vols. São Paulo, 1958.

Azevedo, Fernando de. *Brazilian Culture.* Trans. by William Rex Crawford. New York, 1950.

Azevedo, Thales de. *Ensaios de Antropologia Social.* Salvador, 1959.

B

Baldus, Herbert and Willems, Emílio. "Casas e Túmulos de Japoneses no Vale da Ribeira de Iguape," *Revista do Arquivo Municipal* (São Paulo), LXXVII (1941), 121–36.

Baptista, Pedro. *Cangaceiros do Nordeste.* Paraíba, 1929.

Baptista Filho, Olavo. *A Fazenda de Cafe em São Paulo.* Rio de Janeiro, 1952.

Baptista Ribeiro, Enedino. *São Joaquim.* Florianópolis, 1941.

Barbosa, Rui. "A Lição dos Números sôbre a Reforma do Ensino," *Revista Brasileira de Estatística,* II, No. 8 (October–December, 1941), 927–1024.

Barbosa de Oliveira, Américo, and Sá Carvalho, José Zacarias. *A Formação de Pessoal de Nível Superior e o Desenvolvimento Econômico.* Rio de Janeiro, 1960.

Barcellos, Fernanda Augusta Viera Ferreira. *As Favelas: Estudo Sociológico.* Niterói, 1951.

Barroso, Gustavo. *Terra de Sol.* 3d ed. Rio de Janeiro, 1930.

Bastide, Roger. *O Candomblé da Bahia.* São Paulo, 1961.

Bastini, Tanus Jorge. *O Libano e os Libanes no Brasil.* Rio de Janeiro, 1943.

Bastos de Avila, Fernando. *The Economic Impacts of Immigration: The Brazilian Immigration Problem.* The Hague, 1954.

Baudin, P. *Fetichism and Fetish Worshipers.* New York, 1885.

Bello, Julio. *Memorias de um Senhor de Engenho.* Rio de Janeiro, 1938.

Bennett, Frank. *Forty Years in Brazil.* London, 1914.

Bethlem, Hugo. *Vale do Itajaí.* Rio de Janeiro, 1939.

Bezerra, João. *Como Dei Cabo de Lampeão.* 2d ed. Rio de Janeiro, 1940.

Bigg-Wither, Thomas P. *Pioneering in South Brazil.* 2 vols. London, 1878.

Bittencourt, Dario de. "A Liberdade Religiosa no Brasil: a Macumba e o Batuque em Face da Lei," *O Negro no Brasil.* Rio de Janeiro, 1940. Pp. 169–99.

Blair, Thomas Lucien. "Social Structure and Information Exposure in Rural Brazil," *Rural Sociology,* 25 (March, 1960), 65–75.

Boiteux, Lucas Alexandre. *Primeira Página da Colonização Italiana em Santa Catarina.* Florianópolis, 1939.

Borges, Antonio. *Negociatas Escandalosas.* Rio de Janeiro, 1938.

Born, José M. *Biguassú.* Florianópolis, 1941.

Boxer, C. R. *The Dutch in Brazil.* Oxford, 1957.

Brackenridge, H. M. *Voyage to South America.* 2 vols. Baltimore, 1819.

Braga, Cincinato. *Sêccas do Nordeste e Reorganização Economica.* Rio de Janeiro, 1919.

Brandão, E. D. "A Sucessão da Propriedade Rural," *Ceres* (Rio de Janeiro), VIII, No. 48 (1951), 374–94.

Brandão Lopes, Juarez Rubens. "Sistema Industrial e Estratificação Social," *Revista Brasileira de Estudos Políticos,* 10 (1961), 105–29.

Brazil, Agencia de Difusão e Publicidade. *Monografia do Municipio de Pirassununga.* Rio de Janeiro, 1939.

Brazil, Bibliotheca Nacional. *Idea da População da Capitania de Pernambuco e das suas Annexas.* Rio de Janeiro, 1924.

Brazil. *Boletim do Ministério da Agricultura.* Ano XXX, No. 2 (February, 1941).

Brazil. "Cidade do Rio de Janeiro," *Annuario de Estatistica Demographo-Sanitaria, 1920–1921.* Vol. I. Rio de Janeiro, 1923.

Brazil, Commissão Encarregada de Examinar as Colonias Martyrios e S. Lourenço. *Relatorio da Commissão Encarregada de Examinar as Colonias Martyrios e S. Lourenço.* Rio de Janeiro, 1874.

Brazil, Conselho de Imigração e Colonização. *Goiás, uma Nova Fronteira Humana.* Rio de Janeiro, 1949.

Brazil, Conselho de Imigração e Colonização. *Revista de Imigração e Colonização.* Anos I, II, III (1940–42).

Brazil, Conselho Nacional de Estatística. *Anuário Estatístico do Brasil.* Ano IV, 1938, to Ano XXI, 1960. Rio de Janeiro, 1941–60.

Brazil, Conselho Nacional de Estatística. *Estudos sobre a Alfabetização e a Instrução da População do Brasil, conforme as Apurações do Censo Demográfico de 1940.* 2d ed. Rio de Janeiro, 1950.

Brazil, Conselho Nacional de Estatística. *Pesquisas sobre o Desenvolvimento da População do Brasil.* Rio de Janeiro, 1951.

Brazil, Conselho Nacional de Geografia. *Resolução N. 3, de 29 de Março de 1938.* Rio de Janeiro, 1938.

Brazil, Departamento Nacional de Saude. *Boletim Mensal do Serviço Federal de Bio-Estatística.* Ano I (1942).

Brazil, D.I.P. *Constitution of the United States of Brazil with the Constitutional Laws Nos. 1, 2, 3 and 4.* Rio de Janeiro, 1941.

Brazil. *Diário Oficial,* July 24, 1942.

Brazil, Directoria Geral de Estatistica. *Annuario Estatistico do Brazil.* Vols. I, III. Rio de Janeiro, 1916 and 1927.

Brazil, Directoria Geral de Estatistica. *Boletim Commerativo da Exposição Nacional de 1908.* Rio de Janeiro, 1908.

Brazil, Directoria Geral de Estatistica. *Recenseamento do Brazil Realizado em 1 de Septembro de 1920.* Rio de Janeiro, 1922–30.

    Vol. I, "Introducção," 1922.

    "Annexos" to Vol. I, 1922.

    Vol. II, Pt. 1, "População do Rio de Janeiro," 1923.

        Pt. 2, "Agricultura e Industrias: Distrito Federal," 1924.

        Pt. 3, "Estatistica Predial e Domiciliaria da Cidade do Rio de Janeiro," 1925.

    Vol. III, "Agricultura," Pts. 1, 2, and 3; 1923, 1925, and 1927.

    Vol. IV, "População, Pts. 1, 2, 3, 4, 5, and 6; 1926, 1928, 1929, and 1930.

    Vol. V, Pt. 1, "Industria," 1927.

        Pt. 2, "Salarios," 1928.

Brazil, Directoria Geral de Estatistica. *Sexo, Raça e Estado Civil, Nacionalidade, Filiação, Culto e Analphabetismo da População Recenseada em 31 ae Dezembro de 1890.* Rio de Janeiro, 1898.

Brazil, Fundação Getúlio Vargas. *Conjuntura Economica.* Ano VI, No. 6 (June, 1952).

Brazil, Instituto Brasileiro de Geografia e Estatística. "A Educação Brasileira à Luz dos Numeros," *Revista Brasileira de Estatística,* II, No. 8 (October–December, 1941), 1303–68.

Brazil, Instituto Brasileiro de Geografia e Estatística. *Revista Brasileira de Geografia.* Anos I–X (1939–48).

Brazil, Instituto Nacional de Estatistica. *Anuario Estatistico do Brasil.* Ano II, 1936. Rio de Janeiro, 1936.

Brazil, Instituto Nacional de Estatistica. *Anuario Estatistico do Brasil.* Ano III, 1937. Rio de Janeiro, 1937.

Brazil, Ministerio da Agricultura, Industria e Commercio. *Estudo dos Factores da Producção nos Municipios Brasileiros: Aracajú, Sergipe.* Rio de Janeiro, 1923.

Brazil, Ministerio da Agricultura, Industria e Commercio. *Estudo dos Factores da Producção nos Municipios Brasileiros: Camaragibe, Alagôas.* Rio de Janeiro, 1921.

Brazil, Ministerio da Agricultura, Industria e Commercio. *Estudo dos Factores da Producção nos Municipios Brasileiros: Camaragibe, Alagôas.* Rio de Janeiro, 1924.

Brazil, Ministerio da Agricultura, Industria e Commercio. *Estudo dos Factores da Producção nos Municipios Brasileiros: Conquista, Minas Gerais.* Rio de Janeiro, 1922.

Brazil, Ministerio da Agricultura, Industria e Commercio. *Estudo dos*

Factores da Producção nos Municipios Brasileiros: Quixada, Ceará. Rio de Janeiro, 1922.

Brazil, Ministerio da Agricultura, Industria e Commercio. *Estudo dos Factores da Producção nos Municipios Brasileiros: Santa Luzia do Rio das Velhas, Minas Gerais.* Rio de Janeiro, 1921.

Brazil, Ministério da Educação e Cultura. *Sinopse Estatística do Ensino Superior, 1959.* Rio de Janeiro, 1959.

Brazil, Ministério do Trabalho, Industria e Comércio. *Salário Mínimo.* 2 vols. Rio de Janeiro, 1940.

Brazil. *Recenseamento do Brazil, 1872.* (Facts of publication are lacking. It appears to have been pieced together with leaves from the censuses of the provinces.)

Brazil, Serviço de Informação Agrícola. *Missões Rurais de Educação: A Experiencia de Itaperuna.* Rio de Janeiro, 1952.

Brazil, Serviço de Informação Agrícola. *Reforma Agrária no Mundo e no Brasil.* Rio de Janeiro, 1952.

Brazil, Serviço Nacional de Recenseamento. "Censo Demográfico: População e Habitação," *Recenseamento Geral do Brasil, 1940.* Vol. II. Rio de Janeiro, 1950.

Brazil, Serviço Nacional de Recenseamento. *VI Recenseamento Geral do Brasil, 1950.* Vols. I–XXI. Rio de Janeiro, 1954–58.

Brazil, Serviço Nacional de Recenseamento. "Sinopse do Censo Agrícola, Dados Gerais," *Recenseamento Geral do Brasil, 1940.* Rio de Janeiro, 1948.

Brazil, Serviço Nacional de Recenseamento. "Sinopse Preliminar do Censo Demográfico," *VII Recenseamento Geral do Brasil, 1960* (separate reports for each of the states and one for the territories). Rio de Janeiro, 1961.

Brazilian Embassy. *Survey of the Brazilian Economy.* Washington, 1959.

Bulhões Carvalho, José Luiz S. de. *Relatorio* (to the Minister of Agriculture, Commerce and Industry). Rio de Janeiro, 1921.

Burton, Richard F. *The Highlands of the Brazil.* 2 vols. London, 1869.

C

Cabral, Oswaldo R. *Santa Catharina.* São Paulo, 1937.

Caldeira, Clóvis. *Arrendamento e Parceria.* Rio de Janeiro, 1955.

Calmon, Pedro. *Espirito da Sociedade Colonial.* São Paulo, 1935.

Câmara, Lourival. *Estrangeiros em Santa Catarina.* Florianópolis, 1940.

Camargo, José Francisco de. *Exodo Rural no Brasil.* São Paulo, 1957.

Cardoso de Menezes e Souza, João. *Theses sobre Colonização no Brazil.* Rio de Janeiro, 1875.

Carlí, Gileno dé. *Aspectos Açucareiros de Pernambuco.* Rio de Janeiro, 1940.

Carlí, Gileno dé. *O Processo Histórico da Usina em Pernambuco.* Rio de Janeiro, 1942.

Carneiro, Edison. *Candomblés da Bahia.* Salvador, 1948.

Carneiro, Edison. *O Quilombo dos Palmares, 1630–1695.* São Paulo, 1947.

Carneiro, J. Fernando. *Imigração e Colonização no Brasil.* Rio de Janeiro, 1950.

Carneiro Leão, A. *A Sociedade Rural, seus Problemas e sua Educação.* Rio de Janeiro, 1939.

Carneiro Leão, A. *Panorama Sociologique du Brésil.* Paris, 1953.

Carneiro Leão, A. *Planejar e Agir.* Rio de Janeiro, 1942.

Carvalho, Afránio de. *Lei Agrária: Anteprojeto.* Rio de Janeiro, 1948.
Carvalho, Alceu Vicente W. de. *A População Brasileira.* Rio de Janeiro, 1960.
Carvalho, Augusto de. *O Brazil: Colonização e Emigração.* 2d ed. Porto, 1876.
Carvalho, Hernani de. *Sociologia da Vida Rural Brasileira.* Rio de Janeiro, 1951.
Carvalho, Orlando M. *Ensaios de Sociologia Electoral.* Belo Horizonte, 1958.
Carvalho, Orlando M. *Problemas Fundamentaes do Municipio.* São Paulo, 1937.
Carvalho, Péricles de Mello. "A Legislação Imigratória do Brasil e sua Evolução," *Revista de Imigração e Colonização,* I, No. 4 (October, 1940), 719–39.
Castello Branco, João. *Técnicas de Produção.* Rio de Janeiro, 1955.
Castro, Josué de. *A Alimentação Brasileira á Luz da Geografia Humana.* Pôrto Alegre, 1937.
Castro, Josué de. *Alimentação e Raça.* Rio de Janeiro, 1936.
Castro, Josué de. *As Condições de Vida das Classes Operarias no Recife.* Rio de Janeiro, 1935.
Castro, Josué de. *Geografia da Fome: A Fome no Brasil.* Rio de Janeiro, 1946.
Castro, Josué de. *O Problema da Alimentação no Brasil.* São Paulo, 1939.
Castro, Josué de. *The Geography of Hunger.* Boston, 1952.
Catholic Encyclopedia. New York, 1913.
Ceará, Departamento Estadual de Estatística. *Organização Religiosa: Culto Catholico.* Fortaleza, 1942.
Chermont de Miranda, Vicente. "A Reforma Agrária e a Experiencia do Estatuto da Lavoura Canaviera," *Revista Forense* (Rio de Janeiro), CLX (1952).
Cirne Lima, Ruy. *Terras Devolutas.* Pôrto Alegre, 1935.
Código Civil Brasileiro. 8th ed. São Paulo, 1942.
Codman, John. *Ten Months in Brazil.* Boston, 1867.
Compton's Pictured Encyclopedia and Fact-Index. Vol. I. Chicago, 1944.
Corrêa de Oliveira, João Alfredo. *Relatorio e Trabalhos Estatisticos.* Rio de Janeiro, 1872.
Correio da Manhã. Rio de Janeiro, August 8, 1942, and April 23, 1961.
Costa Pinto, L. A. *Migrações Internas no Brasil.* Rio de Janeiro, 1952.
Costa Pinto, L. A. *O Negro no Rio de Janeiro.* São Paulo, 1952.
Coutinho, Ruy. *Valor Social da Alimentação.* Rio de Janeiro, 1937.
Cunha, Euclydes da. *Rebellion in the Backlands.* Trans. by Samuel Putnam. Chicago, 1952.
Cunha, Euclydes da. *Os Sertões.* 15th ed. Rio de Janeiro, 1940.
Curitiba, Departamento de Saude Publica. *Boletim Trimestral de Estatística Demógrafo-Sanitária, Município de Curitiba.* Anos I, II, III. Curitiba, 1939–41.
Cyro, Junior. *Pirassununga Progride.* São Paulo, 1901.

D

Dahne, Eugenio. *Descriptive Memorial of the State of Rio Grande do Sul, Brazil.* Pôrto Alegre, 1904.
Dantas, Humberto. "Movimentos de Migrações Interna em Direção do

Planalto Paulista," *Boletim do Serviço de Imigração e Colonização,* No. 3 (March, 1941), 77–86.

Debret, J. B. *Voyage Pittoresque et Historique Au Brésil, 1816–1831.* Vol. I. Paris, 1835.

Delgado de Carvalho, C. M. *Le Brésil Méridional.* Paris, 1910.

Denis, Pierre. *Brazil.* Trans. by Bernard Miall. London, 1911.

Dias, Arthur. *The Brazil of Today.* Nivelles, Belgium, 1903 (?).

Diégues Júnior, Manuel. *Etnías e Culturas no Brasil.* Rio de Janeiro, 1956.

Diégues Júnior, Manuel. "Land Tenure and Use in the Brazilian Plantation System," in Vera Rubin (ed.), *Plantation Systems of the New World.* Washington, 1959. Pp. 104–22.

Diégues Júnior, Manuel. *O Banguê nas Alagôas.* Rio de Janeiro, 1949.

Diégues Júnior, Manuel. *O Engenho de Açúcar no Nordeste.* Rio de Janeiro, 1952.

Diégues Júnior, Manuel. *População e Açúcar no Nordeste do Brasil.* Rio de Janeiro, 1954.

Diégues Júnior, Manuel. *População e Propriedade da Terra no Brasil.* Washington, 1959.

Diégues Júnior, Manuel. *Regiões Culturais do Brasil.* Rio de Janeiro, 1960.

Distrito Federal, Secretaria do Prefeito, Departamento de Geografia e Estatística. *Anuário Estatístico do Distrito Federal.* Ano VI (1938), Ano IX (1941). Rio de Janeiro, 1939, 1942.

Dobrizhoffer, Martin. *An Account of the Abipones, An Equestrian People of Paraguay.* Trans. by Sara Coleridge. 3 vols. London, 1822.

Doria de Vasconcellos, Henrique (?). "A Colonização Oficial em São Paulo e o Núcleo Colonial 'Barão de Antonina,'" *Boletim do Serviço de Imigração e Colonização,* No. 2 (October, 1940), 9–26.

Doria de Vasconcellos, Henrique. "Alguns Aspectos da Imigração no Brazil," *Boletim do Serviço de Imigração e Colonização,* No. 3 (March, 1941), 5–34.

Doria de Vasconcellos, Henrique. "Viagem de Inspeção ao Norte" (mimeographed). Rio de Janeiro, 1942.

Duarte, Nestor. *A Ordem Privada e a Organização Politica Nacional.* São Paulo, 1939.

Dunn, Ballard S. *Brazil, the Home for Southerners.* New York and New Orleans, 1866.

Dwight, Timothy. *Travels in New-England and New-York.* 4 vols. London, 1823.

E

Egidio de Araujo, Oscar. "Enquistamentos Étnicos," *Revista do Arquivo Municipal de São Paulo,* LXV (1940), 227–46.

Egoshi, Nobutane. "O Trabalho e a Producção Agricola do Japonez em São Paulo," *Brazil e Japão, duas Civilizações que se Completam.* São Paulo, 1934. Pp. 59–73.

Ellis, A. B. *The Yoruba-Speaking Peoples of the Slave Coast of West Africa.* London, 1894.

Ellis, Alfred, Jr. *O Bandeirismo Paulista e o Recúo do Meridiano.* 3d ed. São Paulo, 1938.

Ellis, Alfred, Jr. *Populações Paulistas.* São Paulo, 1934.

Ellis, L. W., and Rumely, Edward A. *Power and the Plow.* New York, 1911.

Ewbank, Thomas. *Life in Brazil.* New York, 1856.

F

Fausto de Souza, Augusto. *Estudo sobre a Divisão Territorial do Brazil.* Rio de Janeiro, 1878.

Fernandes, Floristan. *O Padrão de Trabalho Científico dos Sociólogos Brasileiros.* Belo Horizonte, 1958.

Fernandes, Gonçalves. *Xangôs do Nordeste.* Rio de Janeiro, 1937.

Ferreira Barboza, Mario. *Annuario Estatistico da Bahia—1923.* Bahia, 1924.

Ferreira, Vieira. *Azambuja e Urussanga.* Niterói, 1939.

Ferreira da Silva, José. *Blumenau.* Florianópolis, 1939.

Fontenelle, J. P. *As Doenças Transmissiveis no Rio de Janeiro.* Rio de Janeiro, 1941.

Fontenelle, Oscar Penna. *Problemas Economicos do Estado do Rio.* Rio de Janeiro, 1925.

Fontura, Amaral. *Aspectos da Vida Rural Brasileiro: Seus Problemas e Soluções.* Rio de Janeiro, 1947 (?).

Fourteenth Census of the United States, 1920. Vol. III. Washington, 1922.

Franceschini, Antonio. *L'Emigrazione Italiana Nell'America del Sud.* Rome, 1908.

Frazier, E. Franklin. "The Negro Family in Bahia, Brazil," *American Sociological Review,* III (August, 1942), 465–78.

Freitas Marcondes, J. V. "A Sociological Study of the First Brazilian Legislation Relating to Rural Labor Unions" (unpublished). M.A. thesis, University of Florida, 1953.

Freitas Marcondes, J. V. "As Missões Rurais e a Sindicalização Rural," *Arquivos de Direito Social,* X (1952).

Freitas Marcondes, J. V. "Brasília, the New Capital of Brazil," *Mississippi Quarterly,* XII, No. 4 (1959), 157–67.

Freitas Marcondes, J. V. *Revisão e Reforma Agrária.* São Paulo, 1962.

Freitas Marcondes, J. V., and Smith, T. Lynn. "The Caipira of the Paraitinga Valley, Brazil," *Social Forces,* XXXI (October, 1952).

Freyre, Gilberto. *Casa Grande & Senzala.* 3d ed. Rio de Janeiro, 1938.

Freyre, Gilberto. *Nordeste.* Rio de Janeiro, 1937.

Freyre, Gilberto. *Sobrados e Mucambos.* São Paulo, 1936.

Freyre, Gilberto, *et al. Novos Estudos Afro-Brasileiros.* Rio de Janeiro, 1937.

Fujii, Yukio, and Smith, T. Lynn. *The Acculturation of Japanese Immigrants in Brazil.* Gainesville, 1959.

G

Galpin, Charles J. *Rural Social Problems.* New York, 1924.

Galvão, Helio. *O Mutirão no Nordeste.* Rio de Janeiro, 1959.

Gardner, George. *Travels in the Interior of Brazil.* 2d ed. London, 1849.

Gaston, J. McF. *Hunting a Home in Brazil.* Philadelphia, 1867.

Gibbons, William J., Avesing, Frank B., and Adamek, Raymond. *Basic Ecclesiastical Statistics for Latin America, 1960.* Maryknoll, N. Y., 1960.

Gonçalves, Jr., J. F. *Relatorio (Serviço de Povoamento em 1908).* Rio de Janeiro, 1909.

Gonçalves de Castro Mascarenhas, Gregorio. *Terras Devolutas e Particulares no Estado de S. Paulo.* 2d ed. São Paulo, 1912.

Gonçalves da Rocha, Edgar. "Aspecto Médico-Social da Zona Rural do Distrito Federal," *O Hospital*, XIX, No. 1 (January, 1941), 123–31.

Gonçalves de Souza, João. "Land Tenure Problems in Brazil and Their Solution," Chap. X in Joseph Ackerman and Marshall Harris (eds.), *Family Farm Policy*. Chicago, 1947.

Gonçalves de Souza, João. "Relações do Homem com a Terra em 4 Comunidades Rurais do Médio São Francisco," *Boletim da Sociedade Brasileira de Geografia*, No. 1 (1950).

Goulart, Jorge Salis. *A Formação do Rio Grando do Sul*. 2d ed. Pôrto Alegre, 1933.

Graham, R. B. Cunningham. *A Brazilian Mystic*. London, 1920.

Griffin, Charles C. (ed.). *Concerning Latin American Culture*. New York, 1940.

Guimarães, Alberto Passos. "As Favelas do Distrito Federal," *Revista Brasileira de Estatística*, XIV, No. 55 (1953), 250–78.

H

Harris, Marvin. *Town and Country in Brazil*. New York, 1956.

Harrison, John P. "The Confrontation with the Political University," *The Annals of the American Academy of Political and Social Science*, 334 (1961), 75–83.

Henderson, James. *A History of the Brazil; Comprising Its Geography, Commerce, Colonization, Aboriginal Inhabitants, &c*. London, 1821.

Herrmann, Omer W. *South Brazil: New Land of Cotton*. Washington, 1940.

Hill, Lawrence F. (ed.). *Brazil*. Berkeley and Los Angeles, 1947.

Hunnicut, Benjamin H. *Brazil Looks Forward*. Rio de Janeiro, 1945.

Hutchinson, Harry W. *Field Guide to Brazil*. Washington, 1961.

Hutchinson, Harry W. "The Transformation of Brazilian Plantation Society," *Journal of Inter-American Studies*, III, No. 2 (1961), 201–12.

Hutchinson, Harry W. "Uma Comparação da Estrutura Social da Família no Brasil e nos Estados Unidos," *Arquivos da Universidade da Bahia*. Vol. IV. Salvador, 1959. Pp. 32–45.

Hutchinson, Harry W. *Village and Plantation Life in Northeastern Brazil*. Seattle, 1957.

I

Instituto de Cacáo da Bahia. *Relatorio e Annuario de 1932*. Bahia, 1933.

Instituto Historico e Geographico Brasileiro. *Diccionario Historico, Geographico e Ethnographico do Brasil*. 2 vols. Rio de Janeiro, 1922.

J

James, Preston E. *Latin America*. New York, 1942.

Johnston, Harry H. *The Negro in the New World*. London, 1910.

Jornal do Commercio (Rio de Janeiro), April 14, 1943.

K

Kelsey, Vera. *Seven Keys to Brazil*. New York and London, 1940.

Kidder, Daniel P. *Sketches of Residence and Travels in Brazil*. 2 vols. Philadelphia and London, 1845.

Kidder, D. P., and Fletcher, J. C. *Brazil and the Brazilians.* Philadelphia, 1857.

Koster, Henry. *Travels in Brazil.* 2 vols. London, 1816.

L

Lacroix, Pascoal. *O Mais Urgente Problema do Brasil.* Petropolis, 1936.

Laerne, C. F. Van Delden. *Brazil and Java, Report on Coffee-Culture in America, Asia and Africa.* London, 1885.

Lambert, Jaques. *Le Brésil: Structure Sociale et Institutions Politiques.* Paris, 1953.

Lambert, Jaques. *Os Dois Brasís.* Rio de Janeiro, 1959.

Lamego, Alberto Ribeiro. *O Homem e o Brejo.* Rio de Janeiro, 1945.

Lamego, Alberto Ribeiro. *O Homem e a Guanabara.* Rio de Janeiro, 1948.

Lamego, Alberto Ribeiro. *O Homem e a Restringa.* Rio de Janeiro, 1946.

Landes, Ruth. *The City of Women.* New York, 1947.

League of Nations. *Statistical Year-book of the League of Nations, 1939– 1940.* Geneva, 1940.

Lebret, Louis J., Rios, José Arthur, Medina, Carlos Alberto de, and Modesto, Helio. *Aspectos Humanos da Favela Carioca,* Suplemento Especial of *O Estado de S. Paulo.* São Paulo, April 13, 15, 1960.

Lehmann, Padre João Baptista. *O Brazil Catholico, 1938.* Juiz de Fóra, 1939 (?).

Leitão, Evaristo, Cavina, Romolo, and Soares Palmeira, João. *O Trabalhador Rural Brasileiro.* Rio de Janeiro, 1937.

Lima, Hildebrando and Barroso, Gustavo. *Pequeno Dicionário Brasileiro da Língua Portuguesa.* 3d ed. Rio de Janeiro, 1942.

Lima Camara, Aristoteles de, and Hehl Neiva, Arthur. "Colonizações Nipônica e Germânica no Sul do Brasil," *Revista de Imigração e Colonização,* II, No. 1 (January, 1941), 39–121.

Lima Pereira, J. O. de. *Da Propriedade no Brasil.* São Paulo, 1932.

Lima Sobrinho, Barbosa. *Problemas Econômicos e Socias da Lavoura Canavieira.* Rio de Janeiro, 1941.

Lobo, Bruno. *De Japonez a Brasileiro.* Rio de Janeiro, 1932.

Lopes, José Lupércio. *Palhoça.* Florianópolis, 1939.

Lourenço Filho, M. B. *Joaseiro do Padre Cicero.* 2d ed. São Paulo, 1929 (?).

Lowenstein, Karl. *Brazil Under Vargas.* New York, 1942.

Luccock, John. *Notes on Rio de Janeiro and the Southern Parts of Brazil.* London, 1820.

Luz Filho, Fabio. *Aspectos Agro-Economicos do Rio Grande do Sul.* São Paulo, 1937.

Luz Filho, Fabio. *Cooperativismo, Colonização, Credito Agrário.* Rio de Janeiro, 1952.

M

Macedo, Jozé Norberto. *Fazendas de Gado no Vale do São Francisco.* Rio de Janeiro, 1952.

Magalhães, Basílio de. *O Folclore no Brasil.* Rio de Janeiro, 1939.

Maia, Alvaro. *Exposição ao Exmo. Sr. Dr. Getulio Vargas, Presidente da República.* Manaus, 1942.

Majorbanks, Alexander. *Travels in South and North America.* 5th ed. London, 1854.

Maria de Jesus, Carolina. *Child of the Dark.* New York, 1963.
Maria de Jesus, Carolina. *Quarto de Despejo (Diário de uma Favelada).* São Paulo, 1960.
Marius, Antonio. *Minha Terra e meu Municipio.* Rio de Janeiro, 1920.
Mariz, Celso. *Evolução Econômica da Paraíba.* João Pessôa, 1939.
Martins, Romário. *Quantos Somos e Quem Somos?* Curitiba, 1941.
Martins, Wilson. *Um Brasil Diferente.* São Paulo, 1955.
Maspero, Gaston. *The Dawn of Civilization, Egypt and Chaldea.* London, 1910.
Mato Grosso. *Brief Notice on the State of Matto-Grosso.* Rio de Janeiro, 1920.
Maurette, Fernand. *Some Social Aspects of Present and Future Economic Development in Brazil.* Geneva, 1937.
Mawe, John. *Travels in the Interior of Brazil.* Philadelphia and Boston, 1816.
Mecham, J. Lloyd. *Church and State in Latin America.* Chapel Hill, 1934.
Meijer, Hendrik. *Rural Brazil at the Cross-Roads.* Wageningen, 1951.
Mendonça, Renato. *A Influência Africana no Português do Brasil.* São Paulo, 1935.
Menezes, Djacir. *O Outro Nordeste.* Rio de Janeiro, 1937.
Mennucci, Sud. "A Subdivisão do Município de Blumenau," *Geografia,* II, No. 4 (1936), 11–23.
Mennucci, Sud. *Brasil Desunido.* São Paulo, 1932.
Mibielli de Carvalho, Fernando. "População e Imigração," *Revista Brasileiro de Estatística,* III, No. 9 (January–March, 1942), 111–24.
Minas Gerais. *Relativos aos Serviços de Terras Publicas do Estado de Minas Gerais.* Belo Horizonte, 1925.
Minas Gerais, Serviço de Estatistica Geral. *Album Chorographico Municipal do Estado de Minas Gerais.* Belo Horizonte, 1927.
Monbeig, Pierre. *Ensaios de Geografia Humana Brasileira.* São Paulo, 1940.
Monbeig, Pierre. *La Croissance de la Ville de São Paulo.* Grenoble, 1953.
Monbeig, Pierre. *Pionniers et Planteurs de São Paulo.* Paris, 1952.
Monteiro Lobato, J. B. *A Onda Verde.* São Paulo, 1922.
Moraes, Octavio Alexander de. "Immigration into Brazil, A Statistical Statement and Related Aspects," in Margaret Bates (ed.), *The Migration of Peoples to Latin America.* Washington, 1957. Pp. 49–73.
Moraes, Raymundo. *Na Planicie Amazonica.* 5th ed. São Paulo, 1939.
Moreira, J. Roberto. *Educação e Desenvolvimento no Brasil.* Rio de Janeiro, 1960.
Moreira, J. Roberto. "Rural Education and Socioeconomic Development in Brazil," *Rural Sociology,* 25 (March, 1960), 138–50.
Morse, Richard M. *From Community to Metropolis.* Gainesville, 1958.
Mortara, Giorgio. *Estimativas da Taxa de Natalidade para o Brasil, as Unidades da Federação e as Principais Capitais.* Rio de Janeiro, 1948.
Mortara, Giorgio. "Estudos sôbre a Utilização do Censo Demográfico para a Reconstrução da Estatísticas do Movimento da População do Brasil," *Revista Brasileira de Estatística,* II, No. 6 (April–June, 1941), 267–76.
Mortara, Giorgio. "The Brazilian Birth Rate: Its Economic and Social Factors," in Frank Lorimer, *et al., Culture and Human Fertility.* Paris, 1954. Pp. 405–503.
Mulhall, Michael G. *Rio Grande do Sul and Its German Colonies.* London, 1873.

N

Nacentes de Azambuja, Bernardo Augusto. *Descripção Topographica do Mappa da Provincia de Santa Catarina.* Rio de Janeiro, 1874.

Nacentes de Azambuja, Bernardo Augusto. *Relatorio sobre as Colonias ao Sul da Provincia da Bahia.* Rio de Janeiro, 1874.

Nash, Roy. *The Conquest of Brazil.* New York, 1926.

Nogueira, Oracy. "Skin Color and Social Class," in Vera Rubin (ed.), *Plantation Systems of the New World.* Washington, 1959. Pp. 164–79.

O

O Globo (Rio de Janeiro), May 7, 1942.

Oliveira, Xavier de. *Beatos e Cangaceiros.* Rio de Janeiro, 1920.

Oliveira, Bulhões, A. M. de. *Estrada de Ferro de Bahia ao S. Francisco.* Rio de Janeiro, 1874.

Oliveira Lima, Manoel de. *The Evolution of Brazil Compared with that of Spanish and Anglo-Saxon America.* Palo Alto, 1914.

Oliveira Lima, Manoel de. *Pernambuco, seu Desenvolvimento Historico.* Leipzig, 1895.

Oliveira Santos, M. P. de. "Instrucção Publica," *Diccionario Historico, Geographico e Ethnographico do Brasil.* 2 vols. Rio de Janeiro, 1922.

Oliveira Vianna, F. J. "O Povo Brazileiro e sua Evolução," *Recenseamento do Brazil, 1920.* Vol. I. Rio de Janeiro, 1922.

Oliveira Vianna, F. J. *Populações Meridionaes do Brasil.* 4th ed. São Paulo, 1938.

Osorio de Souza, José, Jr. *A Nossa Organização Agrícola em Face da Evolução Econômica Brasileira.* São Paulo, 1941.

P

Padilha, Viriato. *Os Roceiros.* Rio de Janeiro, 1927.

Page, Thomas J. *La Plata, the Argentine Confederation, and Paraguay.* New York, 1859.

Pandiá Calogeras, João. *A Politica Exterior do Imperio.* 2 vols. Rio de Janeiro, 1927.

Parain, Charles. "The Evolution of Agricultural Techniques," in J. H. Clapham and Eileen Power (eds.), *The Cambridge Economic History.* Vol. I. London, 1941.

Paraná, Directoria Geral da Educação. *Programa para as Escolas Isoladas: Decreto No. 9592 de 26 de Fevereiro de 1940.* Curitiba, 1940.

Paula Souza, Antonieta de. "Impressões de Viagem ao Longo do Rio Paraná," *Geografia,* II, No. 4 (1936), 30–41.

Paula Souza, R. "Contribuição á Etnologia Paulista," *Revista do Arquivo Municipal de São Paulo,* XXXI (1936), 95–105.

Pearse, Arno S. *Brazilian Cotton.* 2d ed. Manchester, 1923.

Pearse, Arno S. *Cotton in North Brazil.* Manchester, 1923.

Peixoto, Afriano, *et al. Os Judeus na Historia do Brasil.* Rio de Janeiro, 1936.

Peluso, Victor A., Jr. *Rio do Sul.* Florianópolis, 1942.

Pereira Furtado de Mendonza, Hippolyto Joseph da Costa. *Narrativa da Perseguição de Hippolyto Joseph da Costa Pereira Furtado de Mendonza.* 2 vols. London, 1811.

Pernambuco, Departamento Estadual de Estatística. *Anuário Estatístico do Pernambuco.* Ano XI. Recife, 1942.

Pernambuco, Departamento Estadual de Estatística. *Conceito de Povoado: Contribuição ao seu Estudo.* Recife, 1942.

Piauí, Departamento Estadual de Estatística. *Sinopse Estatística do Estado de Piauí.* Teresina, 1938.

Pierson, Donald. *Cruz das Almas, A Brazilian Village.* Washington, 1951.

Pierson, Donald. *Negroes in Brazil.* Chicago, 1942.

Pinheiro Filho, João. *Problemas Brasileiros.* Rio de Janeiro, 1938.

Pinto de Arruda, Gabriel. *Um Trecho do Oeste Brasileiro; São Luiz de Caceres, Mato Grosso.* Rio de Janeiro, 1938.

Prado, Eduardo. "A Imigração no Brasil," *Boletim do Serviço de Imigração e Colonização,* No. 4 (December, 1941), 101–16.

Prewett, Virginia. *Beyond the Great Forest.* New York, 1953.

Price, Paul H., and Freitas Marcondes, J. V. "A Demographic Analysis of the Population of the State of São Paulo, Brazil," *Social Forces,* XXVII (1949).

R

Ramos, Arthur. *A Aculturação Negra no Brasil.* São Paulo, 1942.

Ramos, Arthur. *Introdução á Anthropologia Brasileira.* 2 vols. Rio de Janeiro, 1943 and 1947.

Ramos, Arthur. *O Negro Brasileiro.* 2d ed. São Paulo, 1940.

Ramos, Godolphim Torres. "Terras e Colonização no Rio Grande do Sul," *Revista de Imigração e Colonização,* I, No. 4 (October, 1940), 740–55.

Reis, Arthur Cezar Ferreira. *O Seringal e o Seringueiro na Amazonia.* Rio de Janeiro, 1953.

Ribeiro, René. *Cultos Afrobrasileiros do Recife: um Estudo de Ajustamento Social.* Recife, 1952.

Ribeiro, René. "On the Amaziado Relationship and Other Aspects of the Family in Recife (Brazil)," *American Sociological Review,* X (1945).

Ribeiro, René. *Religião e Relações Racias.* Rio de Janeiro, 1956.

Rio Grande do Norte. *Terras Publicas.* Natal, 1896.

Rio Grande do Sul, Departamento Estadual de Estatística. *Anuário Estatístico do Estado.* 3 vols. Pôrto Alegre, 1941.

Rio Grande do Sul, Directoria Geral de Estatística. *Anuário Demográfico do Rio Grande do Sul.* Ano I (1938). Pôrto Alegre, 1939 (?).

Rio Grande do Sul. *José Bonifacio.* Pôrto Alegre, 1922.

Rios, José Arthur. *A Educação dos Grupos.* Rio de Janeiro, 1954.

Rios, José Arthur. "Assimilation of Immigrants from the Old South in Brazil," *Social Forces,* XXVI (December, 1947), 145–52.

Rios, José Arthur (ed.). *Recomendações sobre Reforma Agrária.* Rio de Janeiro, 1961.

Rios, José Arthur. "Rumos da Reforma Agrária," *Arquivos de Direito Social,* X (1952).

Rocha Pombo, José Francisco da. *Historia do Brazil.* 5 vols. Rio de Janeiro, n. d.

Rocha Pombo, José Francisco da. *Historia de Paraná.* São Paulo, 1930.

Rocha Pombo, José Francisco da. *Historia de São Paulo.* São Paulo, 1925.

Rodrigues, Nina. *As Collectividades Anormaes.* Rio de Janeiro, 1939.

Rodrigues, Nina. *O Animismo Fetichista dos Negros Bahianos.* Rio de Janeiro, 1935.

Rodrigues, Nina. *Os Africanos no Brasil.* São Paulo, 1932.

Rodrigues de Mello, Astrogildo. "Immigração e Colonização," *Geografia*, I, No. 4 (1935), 25–49.

Rugendas, Maurice. *Voyage Pittoresque dans le Brésil*. Trans. from German by de Colbery. 3 vols. Paris, 1835.

S

Saint-Hilaire, Auguste de. *Segunda Viagem do Rio de Janeiro a Minas Gerais e a São Paulo (1822)*. São Paulo, 1932.

Saint-Hilaire, Auguste de. *Viagem à Provincia de São Paulo*. São Paulo, 1940.

Saito, Hiroshi. *O Cooperativismo na Região de Cotia: Estudo de Transplantação Cultural*. São Paulo, 1956.

Saito, Hiroshi. *O Japonês no Brasil*. São Paulo, 1961.

Santa Catarina, Departamento Estadual de Estatística. *Localidades Catarinenses*. Florianópolis, 1940.

Santos Filho, T. Lycurgo. *Uma Comunidade Rural do Brasil Antigo*. São Paulo, 1956.

São Paulo. *Boletim da Directoria de Terras, Colonização e Imigração*, No. 1 (October, 1937).

São Paulo. *Boletim do Departamento Estadual de Estatística*, IV, No. 2 (February, 1942).

São Paulo. *Boletim do Serviço de Imigração e Colonização*, No. 2 (October, 1940), No. 3 (March, 1941), and No. 4 (December, 1941). (No. 1 was issued as the *Boletim da Directoria de Terras, Colonização e Imigração*.)

São Paulo, Commissão Central do Recenseamento Demographico, Escolar e Agricola-Zootechnico. *Recenseamento Agricola-Zootechnico Realizado em 1934*. São Paulo, 1936.

São Paulo, Commissão do Recenseamento. *Recenseamento Demographico, Escolar e Agricola-Zootéchnico do Estado de São Paulo*. São Paulo, 1936.

São Paulo, Departamento de Saude. *Resumo do Movimento Demógrafo-Sanitário do Estado de São Paulo por Municípios*. São Paulo, 1930–1942.

São Paulo, Departamento Estadual do Trabalho. *Dados para a Historia da Immigração e da Colonização em São Paulo*. São Paulo, 1916.

São Paulo, Directoria de Terras, Colonização e Immigração. *Informaçoes Uteis Sobre O Trabalho Agricola no Estado de S. Paulo*. São Paulo, 1935.

São Paulo, Directoria de Terras, Colonização e Immigração. *O Trabalho Agrícola e o Amparo ao Trabalhador*. São Paulo, 1936.

Saunders, John V. D. *Differential Fertility in Brazil*. Gainesville, 1958.

Saunders, John V. D. "Organização Social de uma Congregação Protestante no Estado da Guanabara, Brasil," *Sociologia*, XXII (1960), 415–50, and XXIII (1961), 37–66.

Schappelle, Benjamin Franklin. *The German Element in Brazil*. Philadelphia, 1917.

Schmidt, Carlos Borges. *Lavoura Caiçara*. Rio de Janeiro, 1958.

Schmidt, Carlos Borges. *O Meio Rural*. São Paulo, 1958.

Schmidt, Carlos Borges. "Systems of Land Tenure in São Paulo," *Rural Sociology*, VIII (September, 1943), 242–47.

Schurz, William L. *Brazil: The Infinite Country*. New York, 1961.

Schurz, William L., Hargis, O. D., Marbut, C. F., and Manifold, C. B. *Rubber Production in the Amazon Valley*. Washington, 1925.

"Sebastian," *Encyclopaedia Britannica* (14th ed.), XX, 255.

Serviço Social do Paraná. "Amparo ao Homem do Campo no Paraná," *Serviço Social,* XII, No. 65 (July–September, 1952).

Silva Rocha, Joaquim da. *Historia da Colonisação do Brasil.* 2 vols. Rio de Janeiro, 1918 and 1919.

Smith, Herbert H. *Brazil, the Amazons and the Coast.* New York, 1879.

Smith, T. Lynn. "Agricultural Systems and Standards of Living," *Inter-American Economic Affairs,* III (1949), 15–28.

Smith, T. Lynn. *Current Social Trends and Problems in Latin America.* Gainesville, 1957.

Smith, T. Lynn. *Fundamentals of Population Study.* Chicago, 1960.

Smith, T. Lynn. *Latin American Population Studies.* Gainesville, 1961.

Smith, T. Lynn. "Notes on Population and Social Organization in the Central Portion of the São Francisco Valley," *Inter-American Economic Affairs,* I (December, 1947), 45–54.

Smith, T. Lynn. "Sistemas Agrícolas," *Revista Brasileira de Geografia,* IX (1947), 159–84.

Smith, T. Lynn. "The Giant Awakes: Brazil," *The Annals of the American Academy of Political and Social Science,* 334 (March, 1961).

Smith, T. Lynn. "The Homogenization of Society in the United States," *Mémoire du XIX Congres International de Sociologie.* Vol. II. Mexico, 1960. Pp. 245–75.

Smith, T. Lynn. *The Sociology of Rural Life.* 3d ed. New York, 1953.

Smith, T. Lynn, and Marchant, Alexander (eds.). *Brazil: Portrait of Half a Continent.* New York, 1951.

Sociedade Nacional de Agricultura. *Reforma Agrária.* Rio de Janeiro, 1947.

Sorokin, Pitirim A., and Zimmerman, Carle C. *Principles of Rural-Urban Sociology.* New York, 1929.

Southey, Robert. *History of Brazil.* 3 vols. London, 1817.

Souza, Bernardino José de. *Dicionário da Terra e da Gente do Brasil.* 4th ed. São Paulo, 1939.

Staden, Hans. *Hans Staden: The True History of His Captivity.* New York, 1929.

Sternberg, Hilgard O'Reilly. *A Água e o Homem na Várzea do Careiro.* 2 vols. Rio de Janeiro, 1956.

Sternberg, Hilgard O'Reilly. "A Proposito da Colonização Germanica em Terras de Mata da América do Sul," *Revista Brasileira de Geografia,* XIII (1951), 592–612.

Sternberg, Hilgard O'Reilly. "Agriculture and Industry in Brazil," *Geographical Journal,* CXXI, Part 4 (1955), 488–502.

Sternberg, Hilgard O'Reilly. "Aspectos da Sêca de 1951 no Ceará," *Revista Brasileira de Geografia,* XIII (1951), 327–69.

Sternberg, Hilgard O'Reilly. "Floods and Landslides in the Paraíba Valley, December 1948. Influence of Destructive Exploitation of the Land," in *Compte Rendu du XVIᵉ Congrès International de Géographie, Lisbonne, 1949.* Lisbon, 1951.

T

Teixeira, José A. *Folklore Goiano.* São Paulo, 1941.

Teixeira de Freitas, M. A. "Educação Rural," *Revista Nacional de Educação,* Nos. 18–19 (March–April, 1934), 54–79.

Tejo, Limeira. *Brejos e Carrascaes do Nordeste.* São Paulo, 1937.

Theophilo, Rodolpho. *Historia da Sêcca do Ceará, 1877–1880.* Rio de Janeiro, 1922.

Torres, Vasconcelos. "Aspectos da Vida Rural Sergipana," *Correio da Manhã* (Rio de Janeiro), April 17, 1942.

Torres, Vasconcelos. "O Trabalhador Rural e a Feira," *Correio da Manhã* (Rio de Janeiro), May 26, 1942.

Toussaint-Sampson, Mme. *A Parisian in Brazil.* Trans. by Emma Toussaint. Boston, 1891.

Trujillo Ferrari, Alfonso. *Potengi.* São Paulo, 1960.

Tucker, Hugh C. *The Bible in Brazil.* New York, 1902.

Tylor, E. B. "On the Origin of the Plough, and Wheel-Carriage," *Journal of the Anthropological Institute of Great Britain and Ireland,* X (1881), 74–82.

U

United Nations. *Demographic Yearbook, 1951.* New York, 1952.

Unzer de Almeida, Vicente, and Teixeira Mendes Sobrinho, Octavio. *Migração Rural-Urbana.* São Paulo, 1951.

V

Vargas, Getúlio. "Educação," *Revista Brasileira de Estatística,* II, No. 8 (October–December, 1941), 823–28.

Vasconcellos Galvão, Sebastião de. *Diccionario Chorographico, Historico e Estatistico de Pernambuco.* Rio de Janeiro, 1921.

Vianna, Francisco Vicente. *Memoir of the State of Bahia.* Salvador, 1893.

Vinhaes, Ernesto. *Aventuras de um Repórter na Amazônia.* Pôrto Alegre, 1939.

Von Spix, Joh. Bapt., and von Martius, C. F. Phil. *Travels in Brazil, in the Years 1817–1820.* Trans. by H. E. Lloyd. 2 vols. London, 1824.

Von Spix, Joh. Bapt., and von Martius, C. F. Phil. *Viagem pelo Brasil.* 3 vols. Rio de Janeiro, 1938.

W

Wagley, Charles. *Amazon Town.* New York, 1953.

Wagley, Charles (ed.). *Race and Class in Rural Brazil.* Paris, 1952.

Wagley, Charles. "Regionalism and Cultural Unity in Brazil," *Social Forces,* XXVI (1948).

Wagley, Charles. "The Brazilian Revolution: Social Changes since 1930," in Council on Foreign Relations, *Social Change in Latin America Today.* New York, 1960. Pp. 177–230.

Wagley, Charles. "The Folk Culture of the Brazilian Amazon," in Sol Tax (ed.), *Acculturation in the Americas,* Vol. II of *Proceedings of the 29th International Congress of Americanists.* Chicago, 1952. Pp. 224–30.

Wagley, Charles, and Galvão, Eduardo. *The Tenetehara Indians of Brazil.* New York, 1949.

Waibel, Leo. "European Colonization in Southern Brazil," *The Geographical Review,* XL (1950).

Walsh, R. *Notices of Brazil in 1828 and 1829.* 2 vols. London, 1830.

Wells, James W. *Three Thousand Miles Through Brazil.* 2 vols. London, 1886.

Werneck Sodré, Nelson. *Oeste.* Rio de Janeiro, 1941.

Wetherell, James. *Brazil: Stray Notes from Bahia.* Liverpool, 1860.

Wilkes, Charles. *Narrative of the United States Exploring Expedition During the Years 1838, 1839, 1840, 1841, 1842.* Vol. I. New York, 1856.

Willems, Emílio. "Acculturative Aspects of the Feast of the Holy Ghost in Brazil," *American Anthropologist,* LI (1949).

Willems, Emílio. *Aculturação dos Alemães no Brasil.* São Paulo, 1946.

Willems, Emílio. *Assimilação e Populações Marginais no Brasil.* São Paulo, 1940.

Willems, Emílio. *Cunha, Tradição e Transição em uma Cultura Rural do Brasil.* São Paulo, 1948.

Willems, Emílio. "Protestantism as a Factor of Cultural Change in Brazil," *Economic Development and Cultural Change,* III (July, 1955), 321–33.

Willems, Emílio. "Some Aspects of Cultural Conflict and Acculturation in Southern Rural Brazil," *Rural Sociology,* VII (December, 1942), 375–84.

Willis, J. C. *Agriculture in the Tropics.* Cambridge, 1909.

Wiznitzer, Arnold. *Jews in Colonial Brazil.* New York, 1960.

Z

Zarur, Jorge. *A Bacia do Médio São Francisco.* Rio de Janeiro, 1946.

Selected Bibliography
for Supplement

American International Association for Economic and Social Development. *Land Reform and AIA.* New York, 1965.
Associação Brasileira de Crédito e Assistência Rural—ABCAR. *Extensão Rural,* V, No. 56 (1970).

Baklanoff, Eric N. (ed.). *New Perspectives of Brazil.* Nashville, Tenn., 1966.
Balhana, Altiva Pilatti, Brasil Pinheiro Machado, and others. *Campos Gerais: Estruturas Agrárias.* Curitiba, 1968.
Baptista Filho, Olavo. *População e Desenvolvimento.* São Paulo, 1965.
Bombart, Jean-Pierre. "Les Cultes Protestants dans une Favela de Rio de Janeiro," *América Latina,* XII (1969), 137–59.
Brazil, Instituto Brasileiro de Geografia e Estatística. *Anuário Estatístico do Brasil,* Anos XXI–XXX (1961–69). Rio de Janeiro, 1961–69.
Brazil, Ministério de Agricultura. "Ação Programada para o Ingreso no Mundo Desenvolvido," *Extensão Rural,* V, No. 58 (Outubro, 1970), 8.
Brazil, Ministério de Agricultura. "Metas e Bases: Revolução na Agricultura e Abastecimento," *Extensão Rural,* V, No. 58 (Outubro, 1970), 6–12.
Brasil, Serviço Nacional de Recenseamento. *VII Recenseamento Geral do Brasil: 1960,* "Brasil: Sinopse Preliminar do Censo Demográfico." Rio de Janeiro, 1962.
Brazilian Embassy. *Boletim Especial.* Washington, D.C., December 3, 1969; March 18, October 12, and November 6, 1970; and January 12 and March 2, 1971.
Brazilian Embassy. *Survey of the Brazilian Economy, 1966.* Washington, D.C., 1967.
Broucker, José M. de. *Dom Hélder Câmara: The Violence of a Peacemaker.* Maryknoll, N.Y., 1970.

Callado, Antonio. *Tempo de Arraes: Padres e Comunistas na Revolução Sem Violência.* Rio de Janeiro, 1965.
Campelo, Aloísio M. C. (ed.). "Ação Programada para o Ingreso no Mundo Desenvolvido," *Estensão Rural,* Ano V, No. 58 (Outubro, 1970), 3–13.
Candido, Antonio. "The Brazilian Family," in T. Lynn Smith and Alexander Marchant (eds.), *Brazil: Portrait of Half a Continent.* New York, 1951.
Carolina, Maria de Jesus. *Child of the Dark (Quarto de Despejo).* Trans. by David St. Clair. New York, 1962.
Clements, Harold M., Sr. "A Sociological Study of the Mechanization of Agriculture in Minas Gerais, Brazil." Ph.D. dissertation, University of Florida, 1966.
Clements, Harold M., Sr. *The Mechanization of Agriculture in Brazil,* Gainesville, Fla., 1969.
Cooley, Charles H. *Social Organization.* New York, 1925.

Cormier, George H., and Louise Butte. *Labor in Brazil.* Washington, D.C., 1962.

Costa, Bolívar. *Quem Pode Fazer a Revolução no Brasil?* Rio de Janeiro, 1962.

Dalrymple, Martha. *The AIA Story: Two Decades of International Cooperation.* New York, 1968.

Darwin, Charles. *The Variation of Plants and Animals under Domestication.* 2 vols., New York, 1899.

Diégues Júnior, Manuel. "Land Tenure and Use in the Brazilian Plantation System," in Vera Rubin (ed.), *Plantation Systems of the New World.* Washington, D.C., 1959.

Dines, Alberto, Antonio Callado, and others. *Os Ides de Março,* 2nd ed. Rio de Janeiro, 1964.

Dumont, René. *Types of Rural Economy: Studies in World Agriculture.* London, 1966.

Feder, Ernest, and others. *Brazil: Land Tenure Conditions and Socioeconomic Development of the Agricultural Sector.* Washington, D.C., 1966.

Fernandes, Florestan. *The Negro in Brazilian Society.* New York, 1969.

Fernandes, Florestan. *Mudanças Socias no Brasil: Aspectos do Desenvolvimento da Sociedade Brasileira.* São Paulo, 1960.

Fliegel, Frederick C. "Literacy and Exposure to Instrumental Information among Farmers in Southern Brazil," *Rural Sociology,* XXXI, No. 1 (March, 1966), 15–28.

Freitas Marcondes, J. V. "Reforma Agrária à Luz das Ciencias Socias," *Sociologia,* XXIV, No. 4 (1962), 273–90.

Freitas Marcondes, J. V. "Salient Features of Agrarian Reform Proposals in Brazil," in T. Lynn Smith (ed.), *Agrarian Reform in Latin America.* New York, 1965, pp. 106–15.

Freitas Marcondes, J. V., and Oscar Pimentel (eds.). *São Paulo: Espírito, Povo, Instituções.* São Paulo, 1968.

Freyre, Gilberto. *The Mansions and the Shanties (Sobrados e Mucambos).* Trans. by Harriet de Onís. New York, 1963.

Freyre, Gilberto. "La Lucha no es de Clase," *Life en Espanol,* May 11, 1964, pp. 24–27.

Furtado, Celso. "Political Obstacles to the Economic Development of Brazil," in Claudio Velez (ed.), *Obstacles to Change in Latin America.* London, Oxford, and New York, 1969, pp. 145–61.

Galvão, Helio. *Cartas da Praia.* Rio de Janeiro, 1967.

Galvão, Helio. *Novas Cartas da Praia.* Rio de Janeiro, 1968.

Gendell, Murray. "Fertility and Development in Brazil," *Demography,* IV, No. 1 (1967), 143–57.

Havighurst, Robert J., and Aparacida J. Gouvela. *Brazilian Secondary Education and Socio-economic Development,* New York, 1969.

Havighurst, Robert J., and Roberto Moreira. *Society and Education in Brazil.* Pittsburgh, 1965.

Herrera, Gabriel Alonso de. *Agricultura General . . . y Adicionada por la Real Sociedad Económica Matritense.* 4 vols., Madrid, 1818.

Hirschman, Albert C. *Journeys toward Progress: Studies of Economic Policy-Making in Latin America,* New York, 1963.

Hoffman, Helga. *Como Planejar nosso Desenvolvimento,* Cadernos do Povo, No. 14. Rio de Janeiro, 1963.

Holanda, Nestor de. *Como Seria o Brasil Socialista?* Cadernos do Povo No. 8. Rio de Janeiro, 1963.

Homma, Alfredo K. "O Maranhão Está Chegando," Correio *Agro-Pecuario,* Ano IX, No. 154 (Agosto, 1969).

Hopkins, John A. *The Latin American Farmer.* Washington, D.C., 1969.

Horowitz, Irving Louis. *Revolution in Brazil: Politics and Society in a Developing Nation.* New York, 1964.

Inter-American Statistical Institute. *América en Cifras, 1970.* Washington, D.C., 1970.

Inter-American Statistical Institute, *Boletin Estadistico,* No. 68, February, 1971, Washington, D.C.

Inter-American Statistical Institute. *Statistical Compendium of the Americas, 1969.* Washington, D.C., 1969.

Jaguaribe, Hélio, "The Dynamics of Brazilian Nationalism," in Claudio Velez (ed.), *Obstacles to Change in Latin America.* London, Oxford, and New York, 1969, pp. 162–87.

Johnson, Robert W. "Trade Implications of Brazil's Agricultural Frontier," *Foreign Agriculture,* VIII, No. 28 (July 13, 1970), 2–5.

Julião, Francisco. *Que São as Ligas Camponeses?* Cadernos do Povo, No. 1. Rio de Janeiro, 1962.

Jurema, Abelardo. *Sexta-Feira, 13: Os Útimos Dias do Governo João Goulart,* 2nd ed. Rio de Janeiro, 1964.

Kumasaka, Y., and Hiroshi Saito. "Kachigumi: A Collective Delusion Among the Japanese and their Descendants in Brazil," *Canadian Psychiatry Association Journal,* XV (1970), 167–75.

Leeds, Anthony (ed.). *Rio's Favelas.* Austin, Tex., 1970.

Ludwig, Armin K., and Harry W. Taylor. *Brazil's New Agrarian Reform.* New York, 1970.

MacIver, Robert M. *Society: Its Structure and Changes.* New York, 1931.

Maia, J. Motta. *Estatuto da Terra Commentado.* Rio de Janeiro, 1967.

Maia, J. Motta. *Iniciação à Reforma Agrária.* Rio de Janeiro, 1969.

Mayer, John. "The Brazilian Household: Size and Composition." Ph.D. dissertation, University of Florida, 1970.

McDonald, John C. "Brazil's Expanding Production and Trade," *Foreign Agriculture,* VII, No. 34 (August 25, 1969), 7–9.

McDonald, John C. "The Story of Pepper Production in Brazil," *Foreign Agriculture,* VIII, No. 7 (February 16, 1970), 9–10.

Minnich, Reynolds Herbert. "A Sociological Study of the Mennonite Immigrant Communities in Paraná, Brazil." Ph.D. dissertation, University of Florida, 1966.

Miranda, Maria Augusta Tibiriçá. *Vamos Nacionalizar a Indústria Farmacêutica?* Cadernos do Povo, No. 11. Rio de Janeiro, 1963.

Monbeig, Pierre, and François Chevalier (eds.). *Les Problèmes Agraires des Amériques Latines.* Paris, 1967.

Moraes, Clodomir. "Peasant Leagues in Brazil," in Rodolfo Stavenhagen (ed.). *Agrarian Problems and Peasant Movements in Latin America.* New York, 1970, pp. 455–501.

Nasser, David. *A Revolução que se Perdeu a si Mesma; Diário de um Repórter.* Rio de Janeiro, 1965.

Oliveira, Franklin de. *Qué é a Revolução Brasileira?* Rio de Janeiro, 1963.

Pan American Sanitary Bureau. *Health Conditions in the Americas, 1965–1968.* Washington, D.C., 1970.

Pearse, Andrew. "Some Characteristics of Urbanization in the City of Rio de Janeiro," in Philip M. Hauser (ed.). *Urbanization in Latin America.* New York, 1961.

Perlman, Janice E. "Dimensões de Modernidade numa Cidade em Franco Desenvolvimento," *Revista Brasileira de Estudos Políticos,* XXX (January, 1971), 137–78.

Pitcher, Shackford. "Farm Mechanization Comes Slowly in Brazil," *Foreign Agriculture,* VII, No. 30 (July 28, 1969), 5–6.

Poppino, Rollie E. *Brazil, The Land and People.* New York, 1968.

Rabello, Sylvio. *Cana de Açúcar e Região.* Recife, 1969.

Reis, Arthur Cezar Ferreira. *A Amazônia e a Cobiça Internacional,* 3rd ed. Rio de Janeiro, 1968.

Renshaw, J. Parke. "A Sociological Analysis of Spiritism in Brazil." Ph.D. dissertation, University of Florida, 1969.

Ribeiro, Darcy. "Universities and Social Development," in Seymour Martin Lipset and Aldo Solari (eds.), *Elites in Latin America.* New York, 1967, pp. 243–81.

Rios, José Arthur. *Campina Grande: Um Centro Comercial do Nordeste.* Rio de Janeiro, 1964.

Rios, José Arthur. "The Development of Interest in Agrarian Reform in Brazil," in T. Lynn Smith (ed.). *Agrarian Reform in Latin America.* New York, 1965, pp. 95–101.

Rios, José Arthur. "Visão Global da Sociedade Brasileira," "A Familia na Organização Social do Brasil," "O Caráter Brasileiro," "Campo e Cidade," "Religões do Brasil," "O Processo Histórico do Desenvolvimento," "Brasil, Pais Subdesenvolvido?" "A Economia Brasileira: Visão de Conjunto," "Estrutura Agrária e sua Transformação," and "A Educação como Fator de Desenvolvimento," in Francisco Leme Lopes (ed.), *Estudos de Problemas Brasileiras.* Rio de Janeiro, 1970, pp. 43–52, 74–83, 89–105, and 219–69.

Rios, José Arthur, Wit-Olaf Prochnik, Joel Chivelder, and others. *Plano de Recuperação dos Alagados: Estudo Preliminar.* Salvador, 1969.

Rosen, Bernard C., and Manoel T. Berlinck. "Modernization and the Family Structure in the Region of São Paulo, Brazil," *América Latina,* Ano XI, No. 3 (1968).

Saunders, John V. D. (ed.). *Modern Brazil: New Problems and Development.* Gainesville, Fla., 1971.

Schilling, Paulo R. *O Que e Reforma Agrária?* Cadernos do Povo Brasileiro, No. 10, Rio de Janeiro, 1963.

Schmidt, Carlos Borges. "Rural Life in Brazil," in T. Lynn Smith and Alexander Marchant (eds.). *Brazil: Portrait of Half a Continent.* New York, 1951, pp. 165–87.

Silberstein, Paul. "Favela Living; Personal Solutions to Larger Problems," *América Latina,* Ano XII, No. 3 (1969), 183–200.

Skidmore, Thomas E. *Politics in Brazil, 1930–1964: An Experiment in Democracy.* London, Oxford, and New York, 1967.

Smith, T. Lynn. "Agricultural-Pastoral Conflict: A Major Obstacle in the Process of Rural Development," *Journal of Inter-American Studies,* XI, No. 1 (January, 1969), 16–41.

Smith, T. Lynn. "Rural-Urban Migration in Brazil," in International Manpower Institute, *Symposium on the Role of Worker Relocation in an Active Manpower Policy.* Washington, D.C., 1969, pp. 63–67.

Smith, T. Lynn. "Sorokin's Rural-Urban Principles," in Philip J. Allen (ed.), *Pitirim A. Sorokin in Review.* Durham, N.C., 1963, pp. 188–205.

Smith, T. Lynn. *Studies of Latin American Societies.* New York, 1970.

Smith, T. Lynn, and Paul E. Zopf, Jr. *Demography: Principles and Methods.* Philadelphia, 1970.

Sodré, Nelson Werneck. *Quem é of Povo no Brasil?* Cadernos do Povo Brasileiro, No. 2. Rio de Janeiro, 1962.

Staubli, Willy. *Brasília.* New York, 1965.

Sternberg, Hilgard O'Reilly. "Brazil: Complex Giant," *Foreign Affairs,* January, 1965, pp. 297–311.

Sternberg, Hilgard O'Reilly. "A Geographer's View of Race and Class in Latin America," in Magnus Mörner (ed.). *Race and Class in Latin America.* New York, 1970, pp. 279–93.

Sternberg, Hilgard O'Reilly. "Man and Environmental Change in South America," in E. J. Fittkau and others (eds.), *Biogeography and Ecology in South America.* The Hague, 1968, pp. 413–45.

Sternberg, Hilgard O'Reilly. "Le Progrès technique et la décentralisation dans la paysage agraire du Nordeste brésilien," in Pierre Monbeig and François Chevalier (eds.), *Les Problèmes Agraires des Ameriques Latines.* Paris, 1967, pp. 251–75.

Suzuki, Teiiti. *The Japanese Immigrant in Brazil.* 2 vols., Tokyo, 1964 and 1969.

Tamer, Alfredo. *O Mesmo Nordeste.* São Paulo, 1968.

Teixeira, Anisio S. "The Changing Role of Education in Brazilian Society," in John V. D. Saunders (ed.), *Modern Brazil: New Patterns and Development.* Gainesville, Fla., 1971.

Theotônio Júnior. *Quais São os Inimigos do Povo?* Cadernos do Povo Brasileiro, No. 6. Rio de Janeiro, 1962.

Tuinman, A. S. "Dutch Settlement in Brazil," *International Migration,* V, No. 1 (1967), 14–21.

U.S. Department of Agriculture, Foreign Agricultural Service, *World Agricultural Production and Trade: Statistical Report.* Washington, D.C., May, 1970.

Wagley, Charles. *An Introduction to Brazil.* New York, 1963.

Wagley, Charles, and Marvin Harris. "A Typology of Latin American Sub-Cultures," in Richard N. Adams and Dwight B. Heath (eds.), *Contemporary Cultures and Societies in Latin America.* New York, 1965, pp. 42–65.

Wallace, Alfred Russell. *Travels on the Amazon.* London, 1911.

Willems, Emilio. *Followers of the New Faith.* Nashville, Tenn., 1967.

Young, Jordan M. *The Brazilian Revolution of 1930 and Its Aftermath.* New Brunswick, N.J., 1967.

Author Index

Subject Index

Plow culture: advanced, 376–89; elementary, 374–76, 378

Plows, 362, 364, 368, 369, 370, 371, 374, 375, 376, 377–78, 380, 381, 382, 385, 386, 387, 389

Poles, 34, 51, 62, 74, 81, 125, 126, 127, 128, 135, 138, 141–42, 411; colonies of, 13, 29, 245, 378, 408, 409

Polish influences, 14

Political disorders, 155, 214

Pontos, 542

Population: educational status of, 488–91, 492, 493; age composition of, 83–86, 145; center of, 41–42; characteristics of, 7, 50–96; density of, 40, 41, 42, 43–44, 253–54; distribution of, 40–44, 635–39; fixation of, 144; growth of, 39, 42, 44–50, 596–601, 632–35; marital status of, 468–72; national origins of, 80–83, 641–42; occupational status of, 88–96; racial composition of, 51–74, 639–41; religious affiliation of, 511–14; sex composition of, 87–88, 145; size of, 39–40

Population and the food supply, 631–80

Portuguese, 51, 58–60, 62, 74, 81, 120, 121, 125, 126, 127, 128, 129–30, 140–41; colonies of, 120

Portuguese influences, 14

Positivists, 513

Posseiros, 222, 371

Povoações, 52, 446–50

Povoados, 261, 429, 446–50

Praianos, 12, 26, 29

Prefeitos, 565

Presbyterian Church, 511, 528

Priest: role of, 22, 461, 518–19

Primogeniture, 7, 338

Property rights, 285–92; evolution of, 285–92; restriction of individual, 290

Propriedade rural, 429

Protestantism, 448, 511–12, 526–28, 721–23

Public administration, 93, 610, 611, 612

Quack doctors. *See* Curandeiros

Queijeiros, 24

Quilombos, 426–27

Quimbanda, 541–42

Quimbête, 538

Race mixture, 60, 62–68, 224, 228, 460

Races, 51–52

Racial elements, 51–52, 68–69; distribution of, 69–73

Racial equality, 66

Recôncavo, 72, 310, 374, 452

Recreation, 230, 480–81, 521

Reformed Christian Church, 511

Regions, 29, 31–35, 355; delineation of, 31–35

Registration: of births, 98–99, 115–16; of deaths, 100, 115–16

Registro civil, 97

Religion and religious institutions, 10, 22, 72–73, 510–57, 717–25

Religious activities: number engaged in, 93

Rendeiros, 308–10

Retirantes, 163–64, 168–69

Ribeirinhos, 24

River-bank plantings, 362–64

Roças, 8, 197–98, 298, 300, 367, 370

Roceiros, 22–25, 197–98

Rôlo, 529

Roman Catholic Church: position of, 518–19

Roman Catholicism, 510, 511, 514–26, 530, 718–21

Rural missions, 509

Rural population, 75–80, 642; age composition of, 84, 85; fertility of, 100–101; growth of, 596–601; national origins of, 81–83; sex composition of, 87

Rural-urban differences, 78–80, 683–85

Rurban community, 434–35

Russians, 34, 81, 125, 126, 127, 135, 138

Samba, 300, 538

Sanitary facilities, 442

Sanitation, 10, 155, 212

Sarambéque, 538

Sarambú, 538

Schisms, 549–57

School (teachers): responsibilities of, 497–99

Schools, 152, 153, 154, 494–509; administrative dependency of, 494–95, 496; curriculum of, 496–97; enrollment in, 487, 488, 496; number of, 495, 496, 499–500; private, 485, 494, 495, 496; size of, 495

Sebastianism, 549–52

Sêcas, 52, 144–45, 303; flight from, 145, 166–72

Security of life and property, 586–87

Seitas, 535

Semites. *See* Jews

Senhores de engenhos, 59, 153, 306, 308, 343–46, 347–50

Serenos, 553

Seringalistas, 162

Seringueiros, 26, 160–62, 232

Serranos, 29, 30

Sertanejos, 12, 25, 163–64, 165–66, 197, 204, 232, 298, 304–306, 366–67, 370

Sertanistas, 55, 71

Sesmarias, 255, 261, 266–68, 286–87, 288, 290, 291, 292, 306, 319, 320, 321

Settlement patterns, 7, 75, 245–56, 260, 282; line village type of, 245, 250–52, 259, 282; scattered farmstead type of, 7, 245, 249, 252–53,